iRiSH
ALMANAC
AND
YEARBOOK OF FACTS
— 1999 —

C000016134

"Indispensable reference and guidebook.
Perfect resource for facts about Ireland today and in the past."
AMERICAN BOOKSELLER

"A terrific book . . . a must indeed for every home,
school, college, business and library."
GAY BYRNE

"A mine of statistical information about everything . . ."
SUNDAY BUSINESS POST

"Very strongly recommended . . .
the one-look book that you'd fly to first for up-to-date information
about Ireland and as a handy annual archive."
BOOKS IRELAND

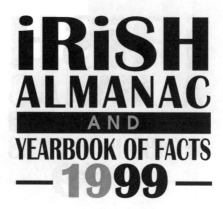

iRiSH ALMANAC AND YEARBOOK OF FACTS — 1999 —

Published by
artcam ireland ltd, inishowen, co. donegal
tel: (077) 68686 *fax:* (077) 68687 *international code:* 00-353-77
e-mail address: editor@artcamil.iol.ie

© Artcam Ireland 1998

executive editor *Pat McArt*

associate editors *Helen Curley and Dónal Campbell*

writers and researchers *Anita Gallagher and Damian Dowds*

design-layout *Dónal Campbell*

printed by *Techman Ireland Ltd.*

ISBN *0 9529596 3 1*

Dedication: Margaret Dowds (1915-1998)

THE **ULTIMATE** ANNUAL IRISH ALMANAC AND BOOK OF FACTS

EDITOR'S FOREWORD

By *Pat McArt*,
Editor Irish Almanac & Yearbook of Facts

An Taoiseach, Bertie Ahern pictured last year with the first copy of 1997 Irish Almanac and Yearbook of Facts. Also pictured is Nobel prize winner, John Hume, and Almanac editor, Pat McArt.

1998 has been a good year for Ireland on both the political and economic fronts but, paradoxically, the bombing at Omagh on August 15th was the most horrific in terms of casualties in the entire thirty years of the "Troubles". Despite that terrible atrocity there is little doubt that the island of Ireland is currently on a peace path.

The paramilitary ceasefires, the signing of the Good Friday Agreement and the closer relationship between Dublin and London have all helped to create the climate where politics, not violence, holds most potency.

In the 1998 edition of *The Irish Almanac and Yearbook of Facts* we examine in considerable detail what has been happening on the island over the past twelve months. It has, indeed, been a remarkable year.

As usual our authoritative facts and statistics have been compiled from primary sources and, we suggest, are simply not available anywhere else. From politics to sport, from profiles of the great Irish writers to the salaries of those elected to the new Assembly in Northern Ireland . . . it's all here.

In addition we have articles from many of the major figures in contemporary Irish life, North and South, outlining their views on what the current state of play is on many of the key issues: Dr. Martin Manseragh, reckoned to be one the most formidable Irish diplomats in recent years, on the road ahead politically; Ronnie Flanagan, the RUC chief, on the role of his force in the new dispensation in the North; outgoing Industrial Development Authority chief executive, Kieran McGowan on his organisation's role in keeping the Celtic Tiger hungry for more; former Minister for Arts, Culture and the Gaeltacht, Michael D. Higgins on Irish culture and its possibilities; RTÉ's political editor, Donal Kelly on Southern perspectives on the North; and Martin Breheny, one of the most respected journalists in the Irish sport, gives his thoughts on Irish sports. And there is much much more.

As usual we extend our thanks to literally hundreds of people who cooperated with us in the compilation of this almanac. Without their generosity of not only their time but also their spirit our task would be impossible.

Pat McArt

Pat McArt
Editor Irish Almanac & Yearbook of Facts

ACKNOWLEDGEMENTS

The Editors and Researchers would like to thank the following people and organisations for their much valued assistance in compiling information for this publication:

Paddy McArt, Burt; Janet Hoy, Joan Cromey, Jim Doran and Clare Alexander, Department of Economic Development, Belfast; Joe Hanrahan, National Treasury Management Agency, Dublin; Central Bank of Ireland, Dublin; An Post, Dublin; Deloitte & Touche Chartered Accountants, Belfast; Chapman Flood Corporate Finance, Dublin; Máire Seo Breathnach, Údarás na Gaeltachta, Galway; Marcella Ring, Office of the Revenue Commissioners, Dublin; Ernst & Young, Dublin; Seamus Hempenstall, Noel Waters, Anthony Hayden and Peter A. Mooney, Department of Justice, Equality and Law Reform, Dublin; B. Counihan, ENFO - The Environmental Information Service, Dublin; Caitrona Halpin, Tree Council of Ireland, Dublin; An Taisce, Dublin; Joe Bourke, Met Éireann, Dublin; Fiona Gormley, Irish Peatland Conservation Council, Dublin; Teagasc - Agriculture and Food Development Authority, Dublin; Livestock & Meat Commission for Northern Ireland, Belfast; Geraldine Morrison and Geraldine McCall, Department of Agriculture for Northern Ireland, Belfast; Michael Murphy, Bord Bia, Dublin; Bord Iascaigh Mhara, Dublin; Kathleen Regan, Department of the Marine and Natural Resources, Dublin; Department of Agriculture, Food and Forestry, Dublin; Coillte Teoranta, Dublin; Stephen O'Rourke, Department of Public Enterprise, Dublin; Bord Gáis Éireann, Cork; Siobhan Browne, Electricity Supply Board, Dublin; Donal Clarke, Bord na Móna, Kildare; Viridian Group Plc., Belfast; Translink, Belfast; Bus Éireann, Dublin; Coras Iompair Éireann, Dublin; Iarnród Éireann, Dublin; Kevin Cahillane, Margaret Killeen and D. Quinn, Department of the Environment, Dublin and Shannon; C. M. Caughey, Driver & Vehicle Licensing Northern Ireland, Coleraine; Aer Rianta, Dublin; Paul King, Roads Services HQ, Belfast; Ewan Alexander and Brian Freich, Department of the Environment for Northern Ireland, Belfast; Irish Trade Board, Dublin; IDA Ireland, Dublin; Colette Mulvany, Department of Social, Community & Family Affairs, Dublin; Labour Relations Commission, Dublin; Catriona O'Donnell, Forfás, Dublin; Northern Ireland Tourist Board, Belfast; Ailbhe O'Kelly, Bord Fáilte Éireann, Dublin; Diarmaid Mac Dáibhéid, Dúchas, The Heritage Service, Dublin; Caroline White, Department of Health & Social Services, Belfast; Gary Lynch, National Roads Authority, Dublin; Kathy Hannon, National Safety Council, Dublin; Dr. Richard Scullion and Grace Kershaw, Central Statistics Unit, Royal Ulster Constabulary HQ, Belfast; Superintendent John T. Farrelly, PRO, Garda Síochána HQ, Dublin; Ruth O'Flaherty, Department of Health and Children, Dublin; Linda Telford, Northern Ireland Court Service, Belfast; Defence Forces Public Relations Section, Dublin; Army Information Services HQ Northern Ireland, Antrim; David Wilson, Northern Ireland Office, Belfast; Office of the Attorney General, Dublin; Elaine Whitehouse, Church of Ireland, Dublin; Rev. E. T. I. Mawhinney, Methodist Church in Ireland, Belfast; Jenny Halliday, Presbyterian Church in Ireland, Belfast; Fr. Brian Glynn, The Office of the Bishop of Raphoe, Letterkenny; Catholic Press and Information Office, Dublin; Karen Finlay, Harrison Cowley, Edinburgh; National Lottery, Dublin; Jacqui Berkeley, Ulster Television Plc., Belfast; Gillian and Karen, TV3, Dublin; Dan McCartney, IRMA, Dublin; Marina McDonnell and Alacoque Kealy, RTÉ Audience Research, Dublin; Neil Russell, Audit Bureau of Circulations (ABC), London; Karen Hall, Market Research Bureau of Ireland Ltd., Dublin; Sinéad Owens, Independent Radio and Television Commission, Dublin; Ann-Marie Lenihan, National Newspapers of Ireland, Dublin; Katriona Burke, Regional Newspapers Advertising Network, Dublin; Ciara Murray, Northern Ireland Post Office Board, Belfast; Pauric O'Raínne, Teilifís na Gaeilge, Galway; Independent Radio Sales, Dublin; Shane Malone and Niall Ó Muilleoir, Fine Gael; Tom Reddy, Fianna Fáil; Tony Heffernan, Democratic Left; Tom Butler, The Labour Party; The Green Party; Anne Moore, United Kingdom Unionist Party; Ann McCann, Northern Ireland Women's Coalition; David Kerr, Ulster Unionist Party, Richard Good, The Alliance Party of Northern Ireland, Conal McDevitt, Social Democratic and Labour Party; Eileen Ward, Progressive Unionist Party; Sinn Féin; Democratic Unionist Party; Office of the Chief Electoral Officer of Northern Ireland; Johanna Finnerty, European Commission Office, Dublin; Sarah Shiel, European Parliament Office, Dublin; Paddy Murphy, Northern Ireland Office; Noreen White, Mary O'Connell, Noreen Keegan, Muiream Ní Murchú, Mary Rodgers and Hazel Murphy; John Keane, North American GAA Board; Tracey Durkin, Canadian GAA board; Marie Scully, Irish Basketball Association; John Wright and Gerry Byrne, Irish Cricket Union; Ita Barry and Patsy McGonagle, BLÉ; Cora Harris, Golfing Union of Ireland; Mary Pat Turvey and Netta Colgan, Irish Ladies Golf Union; Irene Johnston, Irish Ladies Hockey Union; Joan Morgan, Irish Hockey Union; Alex Sinclair, Royal Irish Automobile Club; Paul Byrne and Evan Lyons IRFU; Irish Horse Racing Authority; Irish Turf Club; Harry Havelin, Motorcycle Union of Ireland; Pat Cawley, Connacht IRFU; John Coleman, Munster IRFU; Michael Reid, Ulster IRFU; Pat Geraghty, Leinster IRFU; Brendan McKenna, FAI; William Campbell, IFA; Veronica Byrne and Joan Mulcahy, Irish Amateur Swimming Association; Jan Singleton, Tennis Ireland; Simon Hunter, Northern Ireland Volleyball; Seán Crowley, Irish Amateur Boxing Association; Shelia Wallace, Cumann Camogaíochta na nGael; Norman McCloskey and Billy Stickland, INPHO; Michael Hayes, Dublin; Marshall Gillespie, Portsmouth; Denise McLaughlin, Donegal; Gerard McNamara, Galway; Feargal MacGiolla, Leitrim; Pearse Callaghan, Donegal;

Gerard Callaghan, Donegal; Hugh O'Rorke, Irish Federation of Sea Anglers, Dublin; Brendan Coulter, National Coarse Fishing Federation of Ireland, Cavan; Victor Refausse, Ulster Coarse Fishing Federation, Tyrone; John Feeney, Badminton Union of Ireland, Dublin; Lisa Royal, Northern Ireland Blind Sports, Ann Lyster, Irish BlindSports, Dublin; Belfast; Jack Burke, Bowling League of Ireland, Dublin; June Fincher, Ladies Bowling League of Ireland, Dublin; D. Hunter, Irish Indoor Bowling Association, Belfast; Tara Martin, Equestrian Federation of Ireland, Dublin; Shay McDonald, Irish Amateur Gymnastics Association, Dublin; Jim Graves, Northern Ireland Ice Hockey, Belfast; Bertie Nicholson, Taekwondo Association of Northern Ireland, Lisburn; Rosemary McWhinney, Northern Ireland Netball Association, Belfast; Martin Burke, Olympic Council of Ireland, Dublin; Rebecca Middleton & Sal Shield, British Olympic Association, London; Claire Hunt, Special Olympics Ireland, Dublin; Wendy Henderson, The Sports Council for Northern Ireland, Belfast; Tommy Campbell, PRO, Federation of Irish Cyclists, Dublin; John Keane, Darts; Department of Education, Republic of Ireland; Eddie Mulkeen and Irene Kirwan, Higher Education Authority; Dr Ivor Johnston, Bill Stewart and Nicola Wilson at the Department of Education Northern Ireland (DENI) Statistics and Research Branch; Wendy Montgomery, Dept. of Education Northern Ireland; Gaeilscoileanna; Máire Bean Uí Bhruadair, Iontaobhas ULTACH; Dr Luke Drury; Margaret Crawley, Communications Unit, Department of Education and Science; Peig Uí Dhuibhir, Chomhdháil Náisiúnta; Daithí Ó Dufaigh, Gael Linn; Comhaltas Ceoltóirí Éireann; An Coimisiúin le Ríncí Gaelacha; The Folklore Dept UCD; Irish Traditional Music Archive; Damian Smyth, Public Affairs Officer with the Arts Council of Northern Ireland (ACNI); Jonathan Grimes, Information and Outreach Manager, The Contemporary Music Centre, Ireland; Rowena Neville, IMMA, Dublin; Senior Curator, Ulster Museum; Oliver Dowling, Visual Arts Officer with the Arts Council ROI; Sinéad Mac Aodha, Literature Officer with the Arts Council ROI; Eveline Greif, Administrator RHA Gallagher Gallery; Karen Carleton, PR Officer, Drama League of Ireland; Sharon Sheehan, Dance Administrator, Firkin Crane; Cynthia O'Murchu, Information Co-Ordinator, the Irish Film Board; Luke Dodd, the Irish Film Archive; Joanne Holland, Assistant Information Officer, Northern Ireland Film Commission; Cothú; Music Network; Paddy Murphy, NIO; Dept. of Agriculture NI; Dept. of Economic Development NI; Dept. of Environment Northern Ireland; George Martin, Dept. of Finance and Personnel Northern Ireland; Jennifer Maguire, Information Office, DHSS; Declan Coppinger, Dept. of Agriculture and Food; Dept of Arts, Heritage, Gaeltacht and the Islands; Dept. of Defence; Dept. Environment & Local Government; Dept. of Finance; Monica O'Connor, Dept. of Foreign Affairs; Tadhg O'Leary, Dept. of Health and Children; Dept. of Justice, Equality & Law Reform; Dept. of Marine & Natural Resources; Dept. of Public Enterprise; Dept. of Social, Community and Family Affairs; Evelyn Eager, Dept. of the Taoiseach; Dept of Tourism, Sport & Recreation; Dept. of Enterprise, Trade and Employment; County Secretary's Office, Carlow County Council; Tom Sullivan, Cavan Co. Library; Máirín Hill, Clare Co. Council; Town Clerk's Office, Cork Corporation; Olive Gowen, Cork Co. Council; Marie Deeney, Donegal Co. Council; Mark Teeling, Dublin Corporation; Mary Ruane, Dún Laoghaire-Rathdown Co. Council; Pat Quigley, Fingal Co. Council; Martina Moloney, Galway Corporation; E. Hourigan, Galway Co. Council; Beth Reidy, Kerry Co. Council; Anna Marie Delaney, Kildare Co. Council; A. Waldron, Kilkenny Co. Council; Personnel Dept., Laois Co. Council; County Secretary's Office, Leitrim Co. Council; Bríd Hayes, Limerick Corporation; Eugene Griffin, Limerick Co. Council; County Secretary's Office, Longford Co. Council; County Secretary's Office, Louth Co. Council; County Secretary's Office, Mayo Co. Council; Lisa O'Neill, Marketing Exec. Meath Tourism Ltd; County Secretary's Office, Monaghan Co. Council; County Secretary, Offaly Co. Council; Derry O'Donnell, Roscommon Co. Council; T. Caffrey, Sligo Co. Council; J. Kilgarriff, Administrative Officer, South Co. Council; C. O'Brien, Tipperary (SR) Co. Council; Marion Carey, Tipperary (NR) Co. Council; Town Clerk's Office, Waterford Corporation; N. Williams, Waterford Co. Council; Westmeath County Library; Michael O'Reilly, Wexford Co. Council; Brian Doyle, Wicklow Co. Council; Sandra McKinney, Antrim Borough Council; Ursula Mezza, Ards Borough Council; Wendy Geary, Armagh City & District Council; Ballymena Borough Council; Elizabeth Kinnaird, Ballymoney Borough Council; Nicola Hodge, Banbridge District Council; Press Office, Belfast City Council; Miss A. Beacom, Carrickfergus Borough Council; Castlereagh Borough Council; Coleraine Borough Council; Linda A. McGarvey, Cookstown District Council; Susan Parks, Craigavon Borough Council; Clare Lundy, Derry City Council; Down District Council; Dungannon District Council; Fermanagh District Council; Larne Borough Council; Lisburn Borough Council; Magherafelt District Council; Moyle District Council; Bríd McGill, Newry & Mourne District Council; Newtownabbey Borough Council; North Down Borough Council; Lyn Comac, Omagh District Council; Sandra Pollock, Strabane District Council; Stephen Hannon, Irish Canoe Union; Jane Shorten, Croquet Association of Ireland; John McCullough, Irish Orienteering Assoc.; Michael Hayes, Pitch and Putt Union of Ireland; Peadar Casey, Irish Amateur Rowing Union; Moira MacNamara, Irish Squash; Zoë Lally, Administrator, Irish Surfing Association; Nuala Hubbard, Tug-of-War Assoc.; Michael McAuley, Irish Amateur Wrestling Assoc.; Richard Farrell, Community Games Office; Pauline Murray, Royal Yachting Assoc.; Donal Mulligan; Michael Curley; Fergal Grant; Rosaleen and Jackie Campbell; Colm McKenna; Fr. Kevin O'Doherty; Philip O'Dwyer; Tony, Tommy and Caroline, Octoberstone; Bill Breslin, Wholesale Newspaper Services, Derry; Eamon and Leon Farrell, Photocall; Seán Egan and all at Techman; David McCormack at Pacemaker.

QUICK CONTENTS

Opening Pages ....i-vii (1-2)
Top News Stories 3-4
Quotes of the Year 5-8
Chronology of the Year 9-25
President Mary McAleese's Speech 26-28
Obituaries 29-33
Politics 34-87
   Politics R.O.I. 34-53
   Politics N.I. 54-67
   Public Administration 68-80
   Politics E.U. 81-87
History 88-115
Geography & Environment 116-124
Population 125-134
Counties of Ireland 135-165
Business, Finance & Trade 166-183
Industry, Energy & Transport 184-206

Religion 207-215
Year in Pictures 216-231
Agriculture, Forestry & Fisheries 233-249
Tourism 250-255
Health 256-265
Law & Defence 266-280
Education 281-294
Culture 295-303
Arts 304-339
Entertainment 340-347
Media 348-367
Sport 368-414
Useful Information 415-425
Who Is Who 426-464
Who Was Who 465-485

Index 486-490

SEE DETAILED INDEX PAGE 486-490

FREQUENTLY USED ABBREVIATIONS

approx. approximately
assoc. association
avg. Average
assoc. association
b. born
Brit. Britain
c. circa
Co. Company
d. died
excl. excluding
Fra. France
incl. including
Ire. Ireland
Ita. Italy
Ltd Limited
mth month
no. Number
plc Public Limited Company
rev. revised
v versus

£STG Pound sterling
°C Degrees Centigrade
AIB Allied Irish Banks
ATM Automated Teller Machine
ACNI Arts Council of Northern Ireland
BBC British Broadcasting Corporation
BIK Benefit(s) in Kind
BIM Bord Iascaigh Mhara
BT British Telecom
CIÉ Coras Iompair Éireann
DCU Dublin City University
DENI Department of Education Northern Ireland
DIT Dublin Institute of Technology
DPP Director of Public Prosecutions
EBR Exchequer Borrowing Requirement
EBS Educational Building Society
ESB Electricity Supply Board.
ESRI Economic and Social Research Institute
EC European Community
EEC European Economic Community
EU European Union
GAA Gaelic Athletic Association

FAI Football Association of Ireland
FÁS Foras Áiseanna Saothair
GATT General Agreement on Tariffs and Trade
GDP Gross Domestic Product
GNP Gross National Product
H.E. His / Her Excellency
HEA Higher Education Authority
IBEC Irish Business and Employers' Confederation
IDA Industrial Development Agency
IDB Industrial Development Board
IFA Irish Football Association.
IMMA Irish Museum of Modern Art, Dublin.
IMRO Irish Music Rights Organisation Ltd.
IRMA Irish Recorded Music Association
IRFU Irish Rugby Football Union
IT Institute(s) of Technology
IR£ Irish punt (pound)
LSD Lysergic acid diethylamide
MEP Member of the European Parliament
NATO North Atlantic Treaty Organisation
NCAD National College of Art and Design, Dublin.
NI Northern Ireland
NIB National Irish Bank
NIE Northern Ireland Electricity.
NIFC Northern Ireland Film Commission
NIO Northern Ireland Office
NIHE Northern Ireland Housing Executive
NITB Northern Ireland Tourist Board
NUI National University of Ireland
OECD Organization for Economic Cooperation and Development
OBE Order of the British Empire
PRSI Pay Related Social

Insurance
QUB Queen's University Belfast
RHA Royal Hibernian Academy of Arts.
RIAI Royal Institute of Architects in Ireland RIAI
RIAM Royal Irish Academy of Music
RIR Royal Irish Regiment
ROI Republic of Ireland
RTÉ Radio Telefís Éireann
RUC Royal Ulster Constabulary
SEA Single European Act
TBA To be announced
TEU Treaty on European Union
UCC University College Cork *(NUI, Cork)*
UCD University College Dublin *(NUI, Dublin)*
UCG University College Galway *(NUI, Galway)*
UK United Kingdom
UL University of Limerick
UN United Nations
UNESCO United Nations
US / USA United States of America
UTV Ulster Television
VAT Value Added Tax
VEC Vocational Education Committee
VHI Voluntary Health Insurance
WWI = World War I
WWII = World War II

POLITICAL PARTIES:
Republic of Ireland
C na G Cumann na nGaedheal
C na P Clann na Poblachta
C na T Clann na Talmhan
DL Democratic Left
FF Fianna Fáil
FG Fine Gael
GP Green Party
Ind Independent
Lab Labour Party
NL National Labour
PD Progressive Democrats
SF Sinn Féin

SP Socialist Party
TD Teachta Dála
WP Workers Party

Northern Ireland
All Alliance
DUP Democratic Unionist Party
Ind Independent
MP Member of Parliament
N Nationalist
Northern Ireland
N Nationalist Party
NILP Northern Ireland Labour Party
NIWC Northern Ireland Women's Coalition
Other Lab Other Labour Groupings
Other N Other Nationalist groups
Other U Other Unionist groups
PUP Progressive Unionist Party
SDLP Social and Democratic and Labour Party
SF Sinn Féin
U Unionist/Ulster Unionist Party
UKUP United Kingdom Unionist Party
UUP Ulster Unionist Party
VUPP Vanguard Unionist Progressive Party.

MEASUREMENTS: *See Useful Information chapter* for units and formulae. Metric units are used in most cases throughout this book.
cm centimetre
dwt Deadweight
g grams
ha Hectares
kg Kilogram
kV Kilo volts
kW Kilo watts
l litre
lwt Liveweight
m metre
Mt Million tonnes
MW Mega Watts

ADDITIONAL NOTES

READING THE TABLES: "-" Information less than 0.5 of a unit, **n/a** Information not available.

USE OF SMALL CAPITALS: Events, laws, acts, groups and persons appearing in small capitals in the History Chronology (History chapter), in the Who is Who chapter and in the Who was Who chapter are featured elsewhere in these chapters.

POLITICAL STRUCTURES AND TITLES: References are frequently made to the Dáil (the Irish house of elected representatives), the Seanad which is the Irish Senate and the Taoiseach - the Irish Prime Minister. *See also Politics chapters.*

INTRODUCTION

An Ireland at Peace and Prosperous

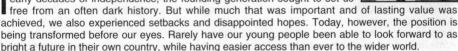

By Dr Martin Mansergh,
Special Advisor to the Taoiseach

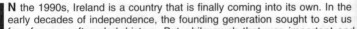

IN the 1990s, Ireland is a country that is finally coming into its own. In the early decades of independence, the founding generation sought to set us free from an often dark history. But while much that was important and of lasting value was achieved, we also experienced setbacks and disappointed hopes. Today, however, the position is being transformed before our eyes. Rarely have our young people been able to look forward to as bright a future in their own country, while having easier access than ever to the wider world.

Over the last ten years or so, we have moved forward decisively on many fronts. Violence, we hope, has finally been brought to an end. The Good Friday Peace Agreement, which has the capacity to resolve peacefully remaining political conflicts in this island, has been negotiated and endorsed by the people North and South, though it awaits full implementation. Our strongly growing economy is providing new and exciting careers for most of our young people as well as for many wishing to return from abroad. We are at last making real inroads into mass unemployment. We are beginning to generate ourselves the resources needed to tackle outstanding deficiencies in infrastructure and social services. We are in a position to do more about social exclusion.

Nevertheless, formidable challenges face us as we approach the new Millennium, if we are to continue to hold our own and still forge ahead. We are in the throes of a rapid catching up process with the average living standards of our European partners, but have still only come about 85% of the way. There is some danger that our speed of progress, combined with misleading nominal statistics, will encourage others to try and place obstacles in our path, before we are able to complete our transition.

The Single Currency begins on 1 January, 1999, when our exchange rate with participating EU countries will be fixed. This should shelter us from some brewing international storms. We do not know what the Euro's relationship with sterling will be, but we have become used to fluctuating within a margin of plus or minus 10%. Whatever the scenario, we seem likely to be entering into an era of low interest rates, by our standards at least. Both as a community and as individuals, that will enable us to do more. Left-leaning European governments will try to fight off the threat of recession in a concerted way.

For us, the period immediately ahead may be more one of consolidation and catching up, as we attend to many of the new pressure points created by the explosive growth of the last few years, as well as more deeply ingrained problems from the past. One of the best ways of relieving pressure is to spread prosperity. A strengthened policy of regional development could see growth spread out from the main centres and benefit the many places that have difficulty reporting any sightings of the Celtic Tiger out in the economic jungle. Measures are in train to increase the supply of housing, which should moderate the increase in cost, but many people will be anxiously calculating what they can afford. Investment over the next few years should create a transport system better able to bear the strain. The most, perhaps, we can hope for is that if we travel at the right time by the most efficient method, we will get to our destination relatively quickly. The availability of choice will be the key factor. Success puts greater pressure on our environment. Yet we have a situation that enables us to create a quality of life in Ireland that needs to be second to none, if we give it the appropriate continuous priority.

People should be able to obtain medical care, when they need it, within a reasonable period. That too will get attention, while the pay and conditions of those who provide nursing care is in the process of being resolved. Education needs strengthening at all levels, so that equality of opportunity becomes a reality, regardless of social or family circumstances, and so that young people are well-equipped to make their way in a rapidly changing world. Those not able to participate in the workforce because of age or disability are entitled to share in the fruits of growth and in better facilities, not just the inflation-proofing of their incomes.

The key to much of our success of the last ten years is social partnership and cohesion, which need to be made deeper and more meaningful all the time. 1999 will be the final year both of the fourth and current national programme, Programme 2000, and of the current round of Structural Funds. It will be the year of Local and European elections, and the Government, led by Taoiseach Bertie Ahern, will be entering its mid-term. Important strategic decisions will require to be taken on where Ireland goes next, relying more on its own resources, but using EU funding still available to tackle the most pressing forms of underdevelopment.

The prerequisite to further dynamic progress is that we keep the economy stable, while strongly growing, in the knowledge that sustained performance over many years is the best indicator of confidence, and the best hope of resolving our many social problems. Inflation must come down in 1999, if we are to hold our present favourable competitive position in EMU. Our American friends, some of whom have invested heavily in this country, see a limitless potential for Ireland, provided we play our cards right and never lose a sense of the precariousness of our achievements by becoming overconfident and careless as we did for instance in the 1970s.

It must be hoped that 1999 will bring in a price recovery and a more favourable year for our stock farmers, who have been under severe pressure since the BSE crisis broke in 1996. As so often in the past, it is necessary to try and stick it out, with appropriate support from Europe and from the community, till better times return, and where possible to diversify family-income dependence. There is a real challenge to convince a younger generation to take on the responsibility of the family farm with a reasonable expectation that they will enjoy an income security from all sources parallel to that of their contemporaries. Much of Ireland's quality and character depends on the countryside, and the EU are right to put an equal emphasis on environment-friendly practices.

People have more and more reason to visit Ireland around the year. People today have a healthy national self-confidence, which is the envy of many others. Apart from our own games which foster a great pride in parish and country, our best performers are capable of excelling almost any sport at international level. Making up for a dearth in the past, there is a steady improvement of community facilities.

1999 will be a year, when a final decision is made on projects for the Millennium, whether they are designated as such or not. I would hope it will be a year, when work will get underway or preparation be far advanced on the National Conference Hall, a National Sports Stadium, a 50-metre swimming pool, a Conservatoire or National Centre for the Performing Arts, and also the LUAS and the port tunnel, as well as many smaller projects which are equally important to their immediate communities.

1999 will be the year when many of the investigations and tribunals will come to the point. They are investigating practices of some years past in relation to planning decisions, political donations and banking practices, where they might involve illegality or ethical breaches or simply have dubious and undesirable implications. Unease must be cleared up, maximum transparency achieved and unmet obligations addressed. The reputations of some prominent public figures and institutions are at stake, but will no doubt be vigorously defended. By establishing what happened and responsibility for it, the purpose would be to establish laws and ethical guidelines, which will try to ensure in the future the highest standards of disinterested public service and commercial practice and to encourage full tax-compliance.

Increasing prosperity and additional resources to tackle crime have contributed to a marked drop in the crime rate, which will hopefully continue. But we have still to get on top of the scourges of drug abuse and underage drinking.

Both market forces and the peace process are drawing both parts of Ireland inexorably closer together. The economic foundations of partition are heavily eroded, though not everyone has yet come to terms with the reality of contemporary Ireland. The logic of North and South working together in many fields, as well as habits of trust and co-operation, will steadily grow and be reflected both in commercial decision-making and institutional structures. 1999 is a year in which we would like to see a universal ceasefire on all sides.

Next to political campaigns of violence, punishment beatings and sectarianism remain ugly manifestations of tensions within and between communities, which we must firmly seek to eliminate. I look forward to seeing a confident and more purposeful Northern Ireland governed in partnership join with the South in creating an island at peace with itself that can create and enjoy widespread prosperity.

TOP NEWS STORIES

OMAGH BOMBING: The worst atrocity in the thirty year history of political disturbance in Northern Ireland occurred on August 15th in Omagh, Co. Tyrone when the so-called "Real IRA" exploded a huge bomb in the town. Twenty eight people died in the immediate aftermath and another man died some weeks later.

The 29 deaths (which included three generations of one family and three children on a day trip from Co. Donegal) and the hundreds of seriously injured led to unprecedented levels of outrage resulting in both the British and Irish governments working in harmony to introduce what Taoiseach, Bertie Ahern, described as "draconian" legislation which was intended to deal with those still engaged in paramilitary violence.

THE PEACE PROCESS: After many highs and lows, including the calling and later breaking of the IRA's historic ceasefire of 1994, the torturous peace process came to a climax on Good Friday (April 10th) when shortly after 5 O'clock Talks chairman, Senator George Mitchell, made the historic announcement that the two governments and the parties engaged in the talks had reached agreement.

The Agreement cleared the way for the establishment of a new 108 seat Assembly in the North and in July 1st. UUP leader, David Trimble and SDLP deputy leader, Seamus Mallon, were elected First Minister and Deputy First Minister respectively. This followed Assembly elections late in June when the UUP won 28 seats to the SDLP's 24 though the latter created a bit of history when it became the first nationalist party to gain more first preference votes than the main unionist party, the UUP.

THE CELTIC TIGER: The Republic of Ireland's remarkable economic upsurge continued unabated in the last twelve months. In February it was confirmed that Ireland had one of the best budgetary figures in the EU during 1997, recording an Exchequer surplus of 0.9 per cent of Gross Domestic Product. By April Ireland was ranked 11th. in a league of the world's twenty most competitive economies, ahead of both Japan and Britain.

In June the Industrial Development Authority announced another year of record breaking progress with 15,000 new jobs created. Just a month later the Revenue Authorities also confirmed that tax receipts reached a record high during 1997 with almost £14bn. of revenue raised, up 15 per cent on 1996. Within a week of the release of these figures, the Department of Finance's economic forecast unit predicted that the economy will grow by 7.5 per cent, 50,000 jobs will be created and unemployment will fall to nine per cent.

A less scientific indicator of the huge growth in the economy was the rise in house prices, one particularly outstanding example being the sale of a Victorian house in Dalkey for £5.9m.

BANK CHARGES: Following allegations in March on RTE the National Irish Bank found itself engulfed in controversy amidst claims that it taken money from customers' accounts without authorisation. The allegations related to events which were said to have occurred in the late 1980's and early 1990's.

Following the allegations the Cabinet met and it was announced that an immediate investigation would be launched. In August , Mr Graham Savage, the Chief Executive of NIB, offered "unreserved apologies" to 370 customers and indicated that the bank would return £131,166 plus interest.

KING RAT KILLED: 1997 in Northern Ireland ended in mayhem in the wake of the murder, on December 27th., in the Maze prison, of leading loyalist, Billy Wright. Known as "King Rat" by both media and security figures Wright, who was the prime mover in the establishment of the Loyalist Volunteer Force, had refused to follow other loyalist groupings and call a ceasefire.

Following his death the LVF went on a killing spree, murdering six Catholics within a month. The killings continued until early March when the deaths of two friends, one a Catholic the other a Protestant, at Poyntzpass, Co. Armagh, caused such outrage and revulsion that the gunmen curtailed their campaign though more killings were to occur before the Peace Agreement was signed. The INLA, which admitted responsibility for the Wright murder, were also involved in a number of other killings during this same period

McALEESE WINS: After one of the most controversial presidential campaigns in recent times former Queen's University Law lecturer, Mary McAleese, the Fianna Fail candidate, was elected in late October to succeed Mrs. Mary Robinson as President of Ireland.

During a very stormy campaign Mrs McAleese was at one stage advised to withdraw from the race by the leader of Northern Ireland's Alliance Party, John Alderdice after newspapers were leaked confidential Department of Foreign Affairs' memos which alleged that she had strong republican sympathies. Mr. Alderdice felt this was sending out the wrong signal to unionists at a sensitive time in the peace process. Mrs. McAleese strongly rejected this interpretation of her views.

The fall-out for the Labour Party was also considerable with the leader, Dick Spring, resigning within a week following the disappointing performance of party candidate, Adi Roche.

The one person who did claim an enhanced reputation was Dana Rosemary Scallon, the former Eurovision Song Contest winner, who came in a creditable third. Her candidature had initially been treated with considerable derision in certain sections of the Irish media establishment.

CLINTON VISIT: While he might have been having plenty of troubles at home, U.S. President Bill Clinton still proved a very popular visitor to Ireland. At the beginning of September Mr. Clinton visited Dublin, where he fielded hostile questions from various members of the international press corps about his relationship with Monica Lewinsky and his own party members' censure of his activities. He also paid a visit to Belfast, Omagh and Armagh and later visited Limerick and Ballybunion where he played a round of golf with former Tanaiste, Dick Spring. The President was widely praised throughout his visit for his role in the peace process.

ROAD DEATHS: Garda Commissioner, Pat Byrne, has advocated that the issues of drink driving and speeding on Irish roads be seriously addressed in the wake of the carnage on Irish roads. Amidst spiralling statistics on deaths and injuries -- 472 deaths in 1997 and 340 up to September 30th this year -- Mr. Byrne said that it might be necessary to review not only the speed limits but also lower considerably the legal alcohol levels. The Irish Road Safety Committee has pointed out on numerous occasions in recent months that an average of nine people are now dying weekly on Irish roads while Galway University Hospital has noted that a majority of its road accident casualties are young males.

DEATHS IN N.I. Apart from the Omagh atrocity, the last twelve months saw quite a lot of violent death in the North. In July the deaths of three young children, Richard, Mark and Jason Quinn, in Ballymoney, Co. Antrim, shocked the entire community when it was learned that they had been murdered by an arsonist who had lobbed a petrol bomb into the family home. The deaths, which occurred during a sustained campaign by Orangemen and various loyalist organisations to ensure that the former got marching down the Garvaghy Road in Portadown after their annual march there had been re-routed by the Parades Commission, soon led to a significant scaling down of the protest, particularly after one of the Orange Order's leaders, the Rev. William Bingham, told his congregation that any march at Garvaghy would be "a hollow victory" particularly as it would be taking place in "the shadows of three little white coffins".

There had been a violent end to 1997 and beginning to 1998 in the wake of the the INLA's murder of Portadown loyalist, Billy Wright.

IRISH RACISM: The flip side of the Celtic Tiger has manifested itself in Ireland, with a growing number of economic refugees, particularly from Eastern Europe, making this country their preferred destination. Their arrival here has prompted racist tensions, particularly in Dublin and other urban areas. The growing resentment of their presence has led to much debate in both the broadcast and printed media with a number of liberal commentators expressing concern at the racist nature of much of the condemnations. It was pointed out that our experience as an emigrant nation should have predisposed us much more favourably to people in similar circumstances.

SPORTING SUCCESS: It was a great year on the international scene for both Ireland's under age soccer players and for our female athletes. In what could be regarded as a major breakthrough for Irish soccer both the U-16 and U-18 teams won the European championships, an unprecedented, and unlikely to be repeated, double. The man behind these superb achievements was Brian Kerr, who managed both teams.

For Ireland's top athlete, Sonia O'Sullivan, it was a year of redemption following her trials at the 1996 Atlanta Olympic games. The Cork runner won two World Cross Country titles in Morocco in March and followed this up with two superb track gold medals in the European Championships in Budapest in August, winning both the 5,000 and 10,000 metres. In September, while representing Europe, she went on to record another 5,000 metres victory in the World Cup in South Africa.

Not to be outdone Cavan girl, Catherine McKiernan, won the prestigious London Marathon while Kilkenny sprinter, Emily Maher (17) became the first Irish athlete to win gold at the World Youth Olympics.

Ireland lost two of its most popular sporting heroes with the retirement of World Middleweight boxing champion, Steve Collins while Paul McGrath, perhaps the national sporting hero of recent years, bowed out of a very distinguished soccer career.

It was, however, a bad year for triple Olympic swimming gold medalist, Michelle deBruin, who was banned for four years by the International Swimming Authority, FINA, amidst allegations of tampering with a drugs test sample, a charge deBruin has vehemently rejected.

TOUR De FRANCE: What has frequently been claimed to be the biggest sporting event in the world, the Tour deFrance began in Ireland this year with huge crowds turning out to not only watch the event live but also on TV screens across the world. Unfortunately the unusual starting place for the tour did not dominate the world's headlines...drug abuse did. Allegations of drug abuse and police raids on various teams eventually led to the cyclists downing bikes in protest in what was, undoubtedly, the most controversial tour in recent times.

THE BEAUTY QUEEN: It was a year of unprecedented success for Irish drama with the highlight being Martin McDonagh's "Beauty Queen of Leenane" winning four Tony Awards, the top award in the American theatre. Garry Hynes made history by being the first woman director to win the top award. In addition, film-maker John Boorman, now based in Ireland, won the "Director's Award" at the 51st. Cannes Film Festival for his film "The General" while Pat O'Connor's film "Dancing at Lughnasa" has garnered much critical acclaim.

"The man on the street finds it very hard to believe that a politician could accept £30,000 in cash without there being any strings attached."

Dick Spring, Labour Party Leader, on Ray Burke, the Minister for Foreign Affairs and calling on his withdrawal from the peace talks of to allow investigations into alleged donations he received in 1989.

"It would appear, to put the most charitable interpretation on it, that Ray Burke was embarrassingly good at political fundraising and at building a large personal political war chest."

Taoiseach Bertie Ahern, following revelations about former Minister of Foreign Affairs Ray Burke.

"There comes a time when even the strongest shoulder bows, when even the stoutest heart falters and when even the best can resist no longer."

Taoiseach Bertie Ahern, on the resignation of Ray Burke.

"Orange Order marches should be treated like those of the Ku Klux Klan and Oswald Mosley's Blackshirts."

Clare Short, Labour MP commenting on the Drumcree crisis during July 1997.

"We're going on a buying trip next Spring. It's a filthy job but someone's got to do it."

George Best, former international soccer player, who is opening a wine importing business.

"Sinn Féin is not going to the negotiating table to strengthen the Union. We are going to smash it."

Martin McGuinness, Sinn Féin's Chief Negotiator on his party's purpose in the peace talks.

"I am very proud to be a Roman Catholic. I am not going to keep my head down. The Penal Days are over."

Dana, singer and Irish Presidential candidate.

"The only solution for dealing with the IRA is to kill 600 people in one night. Let the UN and Bill Clinton and everyone else make a scene and it's over for 20 years."

Alan Clark, Conservative MP, on how the British Government should deal with the IRA.

"I treated Gerry Adams and the members of Sinn Féin in the same way I treat any human being."

Tony Blair, the British Prime Minister, explaining his decision to meet and shake the hand of the Sinn Féin President, Gerry Adams.

"Mr. Blair is significantly placed to be the British Prime Minister who brings about a new history, a new relationship between the peoples of these islands."

Gerry Adams, President of Sinn Féin, following a meeting with the Prime Minister at Downing Street.

"He's not a personal friend. He's not a person I go out with at night. He's not a person I converse with in the normal course of events."

Mary McAleese, presidential candidate, speaking about Gerry Adams, the Sinn Féin President.

"Personally I would probably vote for Mary McAleese if I had a vote."

Gerry Adams, President of Sinn Féin, on the Irish Presidential Contest.

"I would vote for Donald Duck if they opposed Mary McAleese. I think she will make a very dangerous and tribal president."

Eoghan Harris, campaigner for Derek Nally commenting on the Mary McAleese campaign.

"We simply demonstrated to Mr. Andrews that we were not prepared to have him come up and act the macho man and think that we will all bend the knee to him."

Ken Maginnis, Ulster Unionist Party MP, on his party's decision to walk out of the Stormont talks over Articles 2 and 3.

"I say with all humility: could anybody ever imagine me as a macho or as an aggressive person?"

David Andrews, the Minister for Foreign Affairs, following the accusations made by the Ulster Unionist MP, Ken Maginnis.

"Such is the treacherous nature of some in the Joint Secretariat that United Kingdom national security information is now being peddled in the back streets of Dublin and at least four files have been passed direct to the IRA Army Council."

James Molyneaux, former Ulster Unionist Leader, following the leaking of a Department of Foreign Affairs document.

"I owe her lunch and there is nothing I'd like more. I hope at the earliest opportunity to be able to issue that invitation to her. I found her a lovely woman, very hospitable, very warm and very friendly to me."

Mary McAleese, as President-elect, expressing a wish to invite the Queen to Áras an Uachtaráin.

"A great funeral . . ."

Dick Spring TD on his last day in the Dáil, as Labour Leader.

"It was about ethnic cleansing. The fact that the farmers were in the security forces was an easy peg on which to hang the fact that they were targeted."

Arlene Foster, an Enniskillen solicitor, whose father (a farmer and an RUC member) was injured in 1979, claiming the IRA's attack was sectarian.

"This phase of negotiations may fall apart, it may not succeed. And whenever that does happen, then we will simply go back to what we know best."

Francie Molloy, Sinn Féin negotiator, speaking on the Stormont talks at a republican reception in South Armagh.

"I promised Sam I would never embarrass him. I wouldn't want to be carried out of his hotel in a body bag."

Paddy Leahy, a supporter of Euthanasia, explains why a promise not to embarrass the hotel owner, prevents him from ending his own life there.

"I was like a wall beforehand. I was totally paranoid and would never go out without some sort of padding . . . it was a great change from the usual gifts."

A **Dublin lady** explaining why plastic surgery is becoming a popular gift in Ireland.

"It was just like a typical family christmas. No one was talking to anyone."

An anonymous **Unionist**, describing a lunch at the Northern Ireland talks in Stormont.

"When Mo Mowlam was appointed Northern Ireland Secretary, the Maze was already a scandal. She relaxed the discipline still further. This is prison government of the terrorists by the terrorists for the terrorists."

Lord Rees-Mogg, a British political commentator.

"I'm not desperate . . . I'm determined. It takes courage to move things forward."

Mo Mowlam, Northern Ireland Secretary of State, defending her decision to meet loyalist prisoners at the Long Kesh Prison.

"It's her decision and good luck to her."

David Andrews, Minister for Foreign Affairs, on Dr. Mowlam's visit to Long Kesh Prison.

"I was sworn in on July 31 1975. As long as I can ever remember I have been attracted to the UVF. Although it has caused me a lot of heartache and a lot of things have been done that I would struggle with morally, I still believe the the traditional army of Northern Ireland is the UVF."

Billy Wright, leading loyalist in one of his last interviews on his joining the UVF.

"Bobby did not die for cross-border bodies with executive powers, he did not die for nationalists

to be equal British citizens within the Northern Ireland state."

Bernadette Sands-McKevitt, sister of hunger striker Bobby Sands, accusing the peace process as deceptive.

"Isn't it ironic I'm out there with many more people, trying to stop people from different religions shooting each other and others are getting wound up about how they participate in their church services?"

Taoiseach Bertie Ahern, following the controversy over the decision by President Mary McAleese to receive communion in a Church of Ireland Cathedral.

"His own party wouldn't put him up for President. I don't think he represents what Irish-Americans are about. He can lead the parade in Roscommon or Longford if he wants."

Mgr. Tom Leonard, the Chaplain of the New York St. Patrick's Day Parade, who resigned from the committee following the decision to have the former Taoiseach Albert Reynolds as the Parades Grand Marshall.

"It often seemed to find its way back to the IRA."

Ray Seitz, former American Ambassador to London, accusing the White House of leaking British secrets to the IRA.

"I have no evidence in support of Ray Seitz, a person for whom I have the greatest possible respect."

Tom King, Former Northern Ireland Secretary of State, denying Mr. Seitz's claims during his reign at the Northern Ireland Office.

"It is real, it is urgent. For thousands of people, it is literally a life and death issue."

Robin Curry, Friends of the Earth campaigner, on a report which showed the Belfast air to be the filthiest in the UK.

"The historic events of today effectively mean that we can now declare the Widgery Tribunal, its report and conclusions, dead."

John Kelly, the Bloody Sunday Justice Campaign Chairman, wel-

coming the announcement of a new inquiry into the events of January 30, 1972.

"My soldiers behaved according to the very best standards of keeping the peace."

Col. Derek Wilford, the officer who commanded the Parachute Regiment at the time of Bloody Sunday, referring to the massacre.

"The vast majority do not deserve this ridicule."

An **Irish Army spokesman** on the offer by a bookmakers of 10/1 odds on the prospect of Irish soldiers suing for impaired vision due to the glare from their boots and 5/1 odds for sickness arising from travelling to UN duties in Lebanon.

"I'm faced with the kind of bill for soldiers, in terms of compensation for deafness, that hasn't happened in any other country in the world, even those that were at war."

Michael Smith, Minister for Defence, on the controversy over soldiers' claims for deafness.

"I wish to make the point that I was at all times capable of doing the type of work assigned to me and I believe I am capable of continuing to carry those duties at present."

Vincent Crawford, an Army Private from Donegal, after he was granted a temporary High Court Order preventing the Irish Army from discharging him for being overweight.

"I was trying to forget this day."

Pat Kenny on his 50th birthday.

"I have full sympathy for the families of the victims of murder and other crimes, but I do not accept that one death justifies another."

Mary Robinson, the UN High Commissioner for Human Rights, following the execution of Karla Faye Tucker in Texas.

"You are a damned liar."

Ken Maginnis, Ulster Unionist MP, addressing the Northern Ireland Secretary of State Mo Mowlam.

"The Chief Constable has given

me a full briefing on the murders of Mr Campbell and Mr Dougan, along with his assessment that the IRA were involved in these murders. This will now have to be considered very carefully with the Irish government and the other parties in accordance with the proper procedures."

Mo Mowlam, Northern Ireland Secretary of State, reacting to the Chief Constable's comments.

"I'm pissed off."

Gerry Adams, Sinn Féin President, speaking to Today FM's Mark Costigan, when asked about his emotional state following Sinn Féin's suspension from the Multi-Party talks in February.

"Difficult days . . . it is a time for steady nerves."

David Andrews, Minister for Foreign Affairs, commenting on the Stormont talks.

"My first priority is to fix the heater in my car, then to pay the taxman and the Visa bill I ran up researching the book in America."

John Connolly, Irish freelance journalist, who received an advance fee of £350,000 from a London Publishing House for his first novel, *Every Dead Thing*.

"They asked me whether I had any girls in recovery who would like to do some modelling."

Donna O'Connor, Chief Psychologist with the Irish Eating Disorders Association, on advances by a modelling agency.

"These two men . . . in a sense symbolised the future in Northern Ireland and these gunmen, in the evil atrocity they committed, symbolised the past."

Tony Blair, the British Prime Minister, on the Poyntzpass killings.

"I will miss his mischief, generosity and five-a-side skills."

Ardal O'Hanlon, speaking about the sudden death of his *Fr. Ted* co-star Dermot Morgan.

"I have to be honest. I was asked to go for it. I was surprised at the vote on the day."

Albert Reynolds, former

Taoiseach, claiming he was rejected by Fianna Fáil in his bid to become President.

"I would be quite happy to see the Devil's buttermilk banned from society."

Dr Ian Paisley, the DUP Leader, discussing draught Guinness.

"I have never encountered love before - the sort of unconditional love I got in Romania - and maybe I have never given it either. I have never felt fulfilled before but now I really feel there is something I can do to make a difference in that desperate situation."

Daniel O'Donnell, the popular singer, revealing how a visit to a Romanian Orphanage changed his life.

"I'm just going to have to live with it. I don't like it. I don't think it is good government. It's not the sort of behaviour civil servants should indulge in. They clearly have and probably will continue."

Mo Mowlam, Northern Ireland Secretary of State, reacting to the leaking of a Northern Ireland Office document.

"While we only loaded interest to customers who were very demanding, we were certain we were safe in applying the additional interest charges."

An National Irish Bank official, confirming the practice of loading interest onto customers' accounts.

"In a nutshell, the allegations accuse National Irish Bank of theft and fraud."

Michael Noonan, Fine Gael TD.

"And we say to you who have experienced physical or sexual abuse by a Christian Brother, and to you who complained of abuse and were not listened to, we are deeply sorry."

Extracts from the public apology by the Christian Brothers to victims of abuse.

"As well as the weddings, I want other ministers to feel they can use this church for their ceremonies, and it is open to non-Christian faiths as well."

Fr. Pat Buckley, a Catholic

Priest, who has renovated a Church of Ireland church to cater for mixed marriages.

"Fly fishing."

Martin McGuinness, Sinn Féin's Chief Negotiator, when asked what sort of job he would like in the new Northern Ireland Assembly.

"I know that women find it hard to hold their tongues."

Dr Ian Paisley, the DUP Leader, silencing a female reporter who interrupted him during a press conference.

"I'm in charge of this press conference. Shut your mouth."

Dr Ian Paisley, the DUP Leader speaking at a DUP conference to the RTÉ Northern Editor, David Davin-Power.

"I think there has been a massive response from the public. I have never had a reaction like it before, a massive response to the agreement. It is coming from all quarters and it is coming internationally as well."

John Hume, SDLP Leader on public response to the Stormont Agreement.

"I've asked other Olympic winners about it and they've been tested only a fraction of the times that Michelle has."

Eric de Bruin, attacking the International Swimming Body FINA over the treatment of his wife, triple Olympic swimmer Michelle Smith de Bruin.

"They lie out sunning themselves like pedigree dogs while they should be on FÁS employment schemes like everybody else."

John Flannery, a Fine Gael councillor commenting on travellers.

"It's the story of an iconoclast. Cahill invented his own world, his own rules and lived by them. He took on the police, the State and the Church and beat them with his wit and cunning."

John Boorman, film-maker on his film *The General*, about Martin Cahill, a Dublin criminal.

"I'm sure it is the best day of my

life."

Mo Mowlam, Northern Ireland Secretary of State, speaking after the Belfast Agreement was endorsed by 85.46% votes.

"You have done more to damage the Union than the Provos could in 70 years."
A PUP member speaking to Dr Ian Paisley.

"He is monitoring the situation very closely and has contacted Bono, who is very interested in becoming a Celtic shareholder, but to what degree we don't know because nobody knows what Fergus McCann's next move will be."
A friend of Jim Kerr, Simple Minds lead singer, commenting on his interest to take over Glasgow Celtic from Chairman Fergus McCann.

"She is very foolish to do what she is doing. I don't think the people of Northern Ireland will take kindly to it. She has become a parrot."
Dr Ian Paisley, DUP Leader, criticising the Queen for welcoming the Stormont Agreement.

"Haven't the people of Northern Ireland suffered enough?"
John Devlin, in a letter to The Irish Times on recent visits by Elton John and U2 to Belfast.

"A 15-minute walk would be a hollow victory in the shadow of the coffins of three children."
Rev William Bingham, the Co Armagh Orange Order Chaplain.
"This is not protest. This is not principle. This is not statistics. It is three wee boys, Richard Quinn, Jason Quinn and Mark Quinn, burned to death in their beds."
Ronnie Flanagan, RUC Chief Constable speaking after the murder of the three brothers in Ballymoney.

"I want the bastards who did this found, convicted and put behind bars."

Ken Bates, the Chairman of Chelsea Football Club, on offering a £100,000 reward to find the killers of the Quinn brothers.

"Forget Cool Britannia - the action is in Cool Hibernia."
The Financial Times.

"If David Trimble was Pinnochio he would be able to poke my eye out from where he is sitting."
Sammy Wilson, DUP Assembly man, querying the sincerity of David Trimble, the UUP Leader at the first sitting of the Assembly.

"It's good to see Sammy Wilson with his clothes on."
Martin McGuinness, Sinn Féin Assembly member, addressing the DUP's Sammy Wilson at the first sitting of the Assembly. (in reference to the fact that a photograph of Mr. Wilson, naked, was published by a tabloid newspaper).

"Ireland has been a tremendous success for the Tour de France. The crowds lining the streets have been the best we've ever seen at the stages held outside France. They were enthusiastic, warm and friendly."
Jean Marie Leelance, the Tour de France race director, paying tribute to the Irish welcome received during the stages of the Tour.

"There'll never be another Gay Byrne."
Helen Shaw, RTÉ's Head of Radio, following the announcement of Gay Byrne's resignation from radio at Christmas.

"It is difficult to pray. Such events would take tears from a stone."
Fr Joseph Carolan, Buncrana Parish Priest, speaking at the funeral mass for the three Buncrana boys killed in the Omagh bomb.

"For it is indeed as if God turned away at that moment on Saturday in my hometown of Omagh."
Fr Shane Bradley, Buncrana Curate, speaking at the funeral mass for the three Buncrana boys

killed in the Omagh bomb.

"The violence we have seen, must be, for all of us now, a thing of the past, over, done with and gone."
An extract of a statement from Gerry Adams, the Sinn Féin President.

"Those words were music to ears all over the world . . . Thank you, Sir."
President Clinton in Belfast, in response to Gerry Adams' statement.

"There's no President of the USA that has done more for peace in Northern Ireland than you."
Tony Blair, British Prime Minister, addressing President Bill Clinton during his visit to Belfast.

"When I go now to other trouble spots, I point to you as proof that peace is not an idle daydream. For you peace is real . . . ."
President Clinton during his visit to Armagh.

"It's great to be back in Dublin - even though there's a little rain here, it's always bright and sunny for me here."
Bill Clinton, American President, speaking in Dublin.

"Politics is, I often say to my friends, my job and my hobby."
Tánaiste Mary Harney, talking about her life.

"I'm glad that worked out ok."
Taoiseach Bertie Ahern speaking at the Gateway 2000 Computer Company in Dublin during Bill Clintons visit, after using a smart card to sign a communique on electronic commerce.

❐

OCTOBER 1997 - SEPTEMBER 1998

OCTOBER

01: Irish geologists have confirmed that footprints found in rocks on a seashore on Valentia Island in Co. Kerry, are 385 million years old. The footprints have caused a wave of excitement as they are the earliest fossilised footprints of a prehistoric creature ever found in Europe, and possibly in the world. There are about 150 prints made by the same animal, believed to be a tetrapod (a pre-dinosaur creature) at the site.

01: The Revenue Commissioners expect to collect only one-third, £560m, of the £1,690m, owed in outstanding tax arrears. At least £400m was owed by firms which have ceased trading.

01: Derry born writer, Seamus Deane has won *The Irish Times* international fiction prize and Irish fiction prize for his book, *Reading in the Dark*, the first time an author has won in two categories. Other winners of these prestigious prizes were Paul Muldoon for his *New Selected Poems* and Declan Kiberd for his *Inventing Ireland*, which takes a comprehensive look at the factors that explain and explore the development of modern Irish literature.

02: Minister for Finance, Charles McCreevy, has described as "exceptional" the latest figures from the exchequer which indicate for the first nine months of the year Government revenue was more than £1billion ahead of forecasts. The figures are the strongest in 50 years and indicate that almost every sector of the Irish economy is booming. Tax revenue alone was £10,534m, up 14% on the same period last year. Experts estimate that the growth rate is now running at 10 per cent.

03: It has been confirmed that the Taoiseach, Mr. Ahern, has investigated Mr. Ray Burke on three occasions - including once since his appointment as Minister for Foreign Affairs - about the circumstances in which he granted eleven passports to a wealthy Arab banker in return for a promised investment of £20m.

05: Sinn Féin leaders Martin McGuinness and Gerry Adams said they were entering the Stormont talks, due to start in two days time, to "smash the Union" between Northern Ireland and Britain.

06: The novelist, John Banville, has received a prestigious American literary award, the Lannan Award, worth $75,000, for his book, *The Untouchable*.

07: The Minister for Foreign Affairs, Mr. Ray Burke, resigned not only as a member of the cabinet but also as a TD following a prolonged furore regarding his acceptance of an unsolicited political "gift" of £30,000.

07: The long awaited Multi-Party talks to determine the future of Northern Ireland got underway at Stormont today. The Minister for Justice, Equality and Law Reform, Mr. John O'Donoghue, said he represented a party, a government and a nation who have as an ideal the achievement of a united Ireland encompassing "all our people from every political, cultural and religious background."

08: The Taoiseach, Bertie Ahern, has appointed David Andrews as Minister for Foreign Affairs.

10: Broadcaster Vincent Browne apologised to presidential candidate, Dana (Rosemary Scallon), after being accused of verbally bullying her during an interview on Thursday last (October 8). Dana responded by stating that she would not be put off by people who "dressed up" intolerance in the guise of liberalism.

12: The rather lack-lustre Presidential campaign sparked into over-drive after a Department of Foreign Affairs memo was leaked to the media in which it was suggested that Professor Mary McAleese, the Fianna Fail nominee, was sympathetic to Sinn Féin. An angry Mrs. McAleese alleged that the document had been "totally denuded" of the context in which she had been speaking.

13: British Prime Minister, Tony Blair had to be ushered hurriedly out of a Belfast supermarket complex after he was loudly heckled by loyalists. He had annoyed them by earlier shaking hands, away from the cameras, with Gerry Adams, Martin McGuinness and other members of Sinn Féin.

13: Independent presidential candidate, Derek Nally, queried whether Mary McAleese was a "proper person" to be President in the wake of "republican sympathies" allegations made against her.

16: As the controversy surrounding Mary McAleese continues, the Sinn Féin President, Gerry Adams, said that if he had a vote he would give it to her. Professor McAleese, in response to Mr. Adams' comments, said she had "no view one way or the other".

19: Mary McAleese found herself at the centre of further controversy when, in another leaked Department of Foreign Affairs memo, the SDLP's Brid Rodgers was reported to have said Prof. McAleese, along with others, was promoting a new nationalist consensus "which owes more to Sinn Féin than the SDLP". Brid Rodgers described the leaking of the memo as "disgraceful, dishonourable and reckless".

20: Alliance Party leader, Lord Alderdice, called on Mary McAleese to sacrifice her candidacy in the interests of the peace process.

23: According to the Minister for Sport and Tourism, Dr. Jim McDaid, speaking at the launch of the 1998 Tour de France in Paris, said the stages of the race to be run in Ireland would be worth between £20/30m. to the Irish economy.

25: Ulster Unionist Party leader David Trimble told the UUP Annual Conference that his talks team at Stormont would not agree to anything that undermined the rights of the people of Northern Ireland ``still less any Trojan horse that would be a vehicle that will trundle us into a united Ireland." He also stated that their reason for staying in the talks was that nothing could come out of them without unionist party consent.

25: Mr. Michael "Mouse" Kelly and his wife, Ann, from Co. Offaly, celebrated one of the largest ever wins in the National Lotto, winning £4m.

28: Frank McCourt, the Irish born author whose book *Angela's Ashes* has been a sensation in the United States, was awarded an honourary Doctorate of Letters by his home town university, the University of Limerick.

29: In an unusual move, the five main party leaders called for a Yes vote in tomorrow's referendum on cabinet confidentiality. They stated that the main purpose of the referendum was to ensure that no obstacles were placed in the path of courts or tribunals of inquiry. They were, they said, agreed that the public interest would best be served by acceptance of the current proposals.

29: There are now more than 1.3 million people working in the Republic, the highest level recorded in the history of the State. A Labour Force Survey indicated an increase of 41,000 people at work this year when compared to last year -- and a fall of 12,000 in the level of unemployment.

30: The number of people in the Republic who have experienced marital breakdown is now almost 95,000

30: Voting began at 9 a.m. today at polling stations throughout the state to elect a new president of the Irish Republic. Voters were also asked to decide on the issue of cabinet confidentiality.

30: Dublin was almost brought to a standstill by striking taxi-drivers who were angry that their license renewal fee has risen from £7 to £450 since 1992, while the fare rate has only risen by 5p a mile (to 80p) since 1985.

31: Mary McAleese swept to the biggest presidential election win in Irish history. The Fianna Fail candidate won 45.24% of the first preference votes cast, rising to 58.7% on the second count. The Fine Gael candidate, Mary Banotti won 29.3% of the first preference vote to come in second. The other candidates were Dana Rosemary Scallon, who came third with 13.82%; Adi Roche, who was nominated by Labour,

Democratic Left and the Green Party, received 6.96%; and Derek Nally who received 4.69%. The referendum on cabinet confidentiality was passed by a narrow majority.

NOVEMBER

01: More than 500 Irish truck drivers were caught in the blockade of ports, border crossings and fuel depots by French hauliers

03: Principals (who responded to an Association of Secondary Teachers survey) reported rises in student suicides. They noted that of that increase, 80% were boys.

03: *Fortune* magazine, the influential American business/money magazine, judged Dublin as the best European city to do business in.

03: Hundreds of cases were dismissed by District Court judges following a decision in the High Court by Mr. Justice McCracken that a court clerk had been improperly appointed. All 185 of the state's court clerks had to be formally re-appointed later in the day. The State is to appeal the decision to the Supreme Court.

05: The most successful Irish Labour Party leader in modern times, Dick Spring, formally announced his decision to resign as party chief. It is thought the poor showing of his party's presidential election nominee, Adi Roche, was a significant factor in his decision.

05: An inquest into the murder of Dublin master criminal, Martin Cahill, known as "The General" was told that he had been shot dead by "a cool, experienced and dedicated killer."

06: In what is considered the first significant split in republican ranks, at least a dozen senior Sinn Féin members in Co. Louth walked out of a meeting in Dundalk in protest at the party's signing of the Mitchell Principles of non-violence.

06: The Government announced that it is to create a £250m fund to help educational institutions rectify computer, electronics and other skills shortages.

07: Gardaí in Enfield, Co. Meath, seized drugs with a street value of £8 to £9m. It is understood the drugs were destined for the Dublin market.

08: The small village of Turin, near Delvin, Co. Westmeath, was stunned by the double murder of a local couple, Mr. Vincent Cully and his wife, Mary, who were shot dead in their home. A local man was later charged in connection with the incident.

10: Boston Scientific, an American medical instruments manufacturer, has announced plans to establish a factory in Cork employing 1,050 employees and recruiting a further 1,000 workers for its existing plant in Galway. The investment involved is in excess of

£40m. The latest move brings the total employed by the company in Ireland to 3,500.

13: Ruairí Quinn has been elected as the new leader of the Labour Party. He beat his only rival, Brendan Howlin, by 37 votes to 27 in a secret ballot of the 64 member electorate of the parliamentary party and the general council. At his first press conference Mr. Quinn recommended that his party does not rule out a coalition with either Fianna Fail or Fine Gael after the next general election.

15: The SDLP leader, John Hume, told his party's annual conference that he wanted an agreement with unionists. He said any proposed solution to the problems in Northern Ireland would need "their allegiance as well as ours."

16: Three members of the McCauley family died when fire raged through their home in the Rosemount area of Derry. Mr. Jody McCauley (30), his wife Deborah (28) and their son, Ryan (8), died at the scene while two other members, Aaron (10) and Jade (4) were taken to Altnagelvin Hospital, where Aaron died 24 hours later.

17: Gardaí in Dundalk have been unable to locate a man suspected of the rape of a 13-year-old girl who is currently in the care of Eastern Health Board. The girl, who is now pregnant, is understood to want an abortion.

18: It has been confirmed that lawyers for the Eastern Health Board have advised it that as a state agency it could not assist in the procurement of an abortion for the 13-year-old rape victim currently in its care.

18: The Special Criminal Court was told by a Garda that she arrested a Dublin man last April because she believed he had murdered the journalist Veronica Guerin. Patrick Holland (58) is charged with possession of cannabis for supply.

19: In the first High Court civil action alleging sexual harassment, a 22-year-old woman, Ms. Monica Reilly, was awarded £140,000 damages plus legal costs against a former Dublin publican, Mr William Bonny.

23: Paul McGinley and Padraig Harrington won golf's World Cup trophy at the Ocean Course in South Carolina.

25: The Minister for Justice, John O'Donoghue, denied in the Dail that he was to blame for the release of five suspected drug-traffickers arrested by gardaí. The suspects were set free in the District Court when it emerged the judge involved in the case was not among the limited number of judges nominated to grant Garda requests to extend a detention period.

25: The High Court has begun a hearing *in camera* of an appeal by the parents of the 13-year-old rape victim against a Children's Court decision to allow her to travel to England for an abortion.

26: Triple murderer, Brendan O'Donnell, died from heart failure associated with medication he was receiving, an inquest at Dublin City coroner's court has been told.

27: Patrick Holland, suspected by Gardaí of murdering investigative journalist, Veronica Guerin, was convicted by three judges in the Special Criminal Court, of having cannabis with intent to sell or supply.

29: Dr. Desmond Connell, the Catholic Archbishop of Dublin, refused to pay for a Supreme Court appeal by the parents of the 13-year-old girl against a High Court ruling allowing her to travel to England for an abortion. Dr. Connell, who had been asked by the girl's parents to intervene, said that after careful consideration and the taking of legal advice he did not find himself in a position to provide financial assistance.

30: Dubliner, Anthony Beatty (35), was shot dead in a crowded city centre pub when a man wearing a balaclava entered the premises and singled him out. Mr Beatty was shot several times in the chest and collapsed and died at the door of the pub as he tried to make his way out of the premises.

DECEMBER

01: The body of Eileen Costello O'Shaughnessy, a Galway taxi-driver, was found in a field in the townland of Knockdoemore, approximately 100 yards off the main Tuam-Galway road. Gardaí launched an immediate murder inquiry into the circumstances surrounding the death of the mother of two grown-up children.

03: In his first budget as Finance Minister, Charlie McCreevy made it a good day for tax-payers by cutting taxes at most levels. The main features of the budget were: standard income tax rate down 2%, from 26 to 24%; top income tax rate down 2% also, from 48 to 46%; capital gains tax rate halved to 20%; corporation tax reduced to 32%; old age pensions up £5; social welfare payments up £3; cigarettes up 10p for a 20 pack. The most controversial aspect of the budget was a £20m allocation to the GAA.

05: The Loyalist Volunteer Force, possibly aided by other loyalist groupings, is believed to have been behind the murder of Glengormley man, Gerry Devlin, who was shot dead at the St. Enda's GAA club.

07: There was considerable media interest in the decision of the President, Mary McAleese, to break new ecumenical ground when she took Communion during the Eucharist at Christ Church Cathedral in Dublin. Catholic theologians claimed it was not permissible for a Roman Catholic to receive Communion in a Protestant church.

07: In another weekend of carnage on the roads, six people died in four separate accidents.

08: A 35-year-old Galway man, Patrick Gillane, was

found guilty of soliciting two men to murder his wife, Philomena, whose body was found in the boot of her car at Athlone railway station in May 1994. Mrs. Gillane, who was seven months pregnant at the time, had been shot and stabbed.

10: 1,400 jobs are to go in Clonmel following the decision of US computer company, Seagate, to close its plant there. People in the area were said to be "devastated" by the news.

10: According to an *Irish Times*/MRBI poll, 77% of voters believe that abortion should be permitted in the Republic in limited circumstances.

11: Republican leaders bridged a gap of 76 years when a Sinn Féin delegation led by Gerry Adams and Martin McGuinness met with British Prime Minister, Tony Blair, at Downing Street. According to Mr. Adams "it was a good moment in history."

13: There was serious rioting in Derry when trouble flared after an Apprentice Boys march through the city. Business sources were angry not only with the damage done by the rioters but also by the loss of trade on one of the busiest Saturdays of the year. British troops were brought on to the streets for the first time in months to deal with the trouble.

15: Galway man, Patrick Gillane, was jailed for eight years at Dublin's Circuit Criminal Court for soliciting two men to murder his wife whose body was found in the boot of her car in 1994.

18: Dr. Michael Casey, the Central Bank's assistant director general, predicted a growth in Gross National Product of 7.75% next year. He also warned that the country could not indefinitely maintain the current growth rates.

19: In an article in *The Irish Times*, Dr. Desmond Connell, the Catholic Archbishop of Dublin, said the controversy surrounding the decision of President Mary McAleese to take Communion at Dublin's Christ Church Cathedral "had exposed some of the sincerely held differences between Catholics and Church of Ireland members." He also stated that the future of the ecumenical movement was at stake in the pressure to change rules concerning inter-church Communion.

20: Figures released by the Gardaí showed that 700 motorists were arrested on suspicion of drunken driving since the start of this year's pre-Christmas drink-driving campaign. In all 40,000 checkpoints had been mounted by Gardaí. The statistics also showed that 434 people were killed on the Republic's roads by the end of November.

22: As expected, the pre-Christmas rush established a whole host of new records with 760,000 people moving through the Republic's airports and ports on their way home for the holiday period. With the Irish economy on a high, retailers were predicting that this year's over the counter sales would top £600m.

23: The punt fell to its lowest level against sterling for almost a decade when it closed at 86.7p

24: Gale-force winds lashed the country causing widespread disruption to electricity supplies, both North and South. In a tragic accident a 19-year-old Kerry youth, Damien Fogarty, was killed when a wall was blown down on top of him as he walked home.

25: More than a 100,000 homes were left without electricity on Christmas day because of the severe storm damage to power lines. The south of Ireland was worst affected.

27: There was anger, both North and South, about the delays in restoring electricity to homes hit by the Christmas storms. In Kerry, some homes which first lost supply on Christmas eve had still to be connected.

27: One of the North's most notorious paramilitary figures, Billy Wright, was murdered in the Maze Prison by members of the republican grouping, the INLA. Known as "King Rat" by media and security figures, Wright, who was thought to be personally responsible for a number of vicious sectarian murders, had been under death threat from former Loyalist paramilitary colleagues because he refused to abide by the ceasefire called by the Combined Loyalist Military Command. He founded the Loyalist Volunteer Force, which carried on killing Catholics, and which claimed responsibility for killing Co. Tyrone man, Seamus Dillon, within hours of Wright's death in revenge for his murder.

29: Three republicans appeared in court charged with the murder of Billy Wright

30: Portadown came to a complete standstill as Loyalists from across the North came to attend the funeral of Billy Wright. Shops were warned to shut while the media was warned not to take photographs or film those in the cortege.

31: The last person to die in the troubles in Northern Ireland in 1997 was 31-year-old Eddie Traynor who died after loyalists attacked the Clifton Tavern pub in North Belfast. Five others were injured in the attack which took place just hours before the start of the new year. The LVF later claimed responsibility for the attack but republicans cast doubt on their ability to carry out such an operation in that particular area of Belfast.

JANUARY

01: The first baby of the new year was born in Galway, Conor Patrick Quinn being the first person to see life in 1998.

03: The post-Christmas exodus from Ireland was badly disrupted by continuing stormy weather. Flights were delayed and ferry sailings cancelled. Snow made many roads in isolated parts of the country impassable.

05: Forecasts from the Department of Finance indicate that the Republic will be financially in the black for the first time in 30 years. Official returns show receipts in 1997 rose by £1billion more than the Department had estimated.

05: In the wake of the murder of Billy Wright and the revenge murders in various parts of the North the leadership of the Ulster Defence Association in the Maze warned that the Loyalist ceasefire was "extremely fragile".

09: In an unprecedented move for a Northern Secretary of State, Dr. Mo Mowlam held face-to-face talks with UDA prisoners in the Maze. Despite severe criticism from unionist politicians, Dr. Mowlam said she was willing to take the risk of talking to the prisoners if it would aid the Unionist Democratic Party to remain at the table. After the meeting, the prisoners agreed that the UDP should continue in the talks.

10: Terry Enright, a cross-community worker in Belfast, was killed outside a city nightclub. The LVF claimed responsibility for the attack, but David Ervine of the Progressive Unionist Party, who condemned the killing, said the maverick loyalist grouping was not acting alone.

14: In the wake of a growing number of compensation claims from members of the Irish armed forces, a Dublin bookmaker offered odds at 10/1 on the prospect of soldiers suing for impaired vision due to the glare from over-shiny boots.

16: An American expert on child sexual abuse, Dr. Suzanne Sgroi, told the Dublin High Court that the abuse inflicted on Ms. Sophia McColgan (28), a Sligo woman, by her father, Joseph, represented one of the most severe cases of combined mental, physical and sexual abuse, as well as exposure to domestic violence, she had ever encountered. Dr. Sgroi's evidence came on the 10th day of an action brought by Ms. McColgan against the North Western Health Board and Dr. Desmond Moran, both of whom deny negligence and breach of duty. Joseph McColgan is currently serving a 12-year jail sentence after admitting a number of charges.

17: The worsening situation in Northern Ireland showed further deterioration when the LVF murdered a fourth Catholic since the INLA killing of Billy Wright. Fergal McCusker (28) was found shot dead behind a youth club in Maghera, Co. Derry. In a sectarian twist to the murder, it was claimed that those who had carried it out had painted their faces orange.

18: The US Ambassador to Ireland, Jean Kennedy Smith, came under attack from former London-based colleague, Ray Seitz, who branded her "an ardent IRA apologist". Mr. Seitz made his claims in his recently published memoirs. Reacting to the claims, the White House said President Clinton had every confidence in

19: The spiral of violence in the North continued when the INLA shot dead noted loyalist, Jim Guiney (38) in his carpet shop in Dunmurray, outside Belfast. Just hours later loyalists shot dead a 52-year-old Catholic, taxi-driver Larry Brennan.

21: The killings in the North continued unabated when a Catholic, 55-year-old father of three Benedict Hughes was shot dead at his workplace in the Protestant Sandy Row area of Belfast. Hours later Steven Paul was shot at his home in the predominantly Protestant Belvoir Park Estate while John McFarland, a taxi driver for a Catholic-owned firm was shot but not seriously hurt.

21: The IRA has claimed that the recently issued Propositions on Heads of Agreement, issued by the British and Irish governments, is a pro-unionist document which has created a crisis in the peace process. The SDLP rejected claims from Sinn Féin that the document was purely internalist and partitionist.

22: Ronnie Flanagan, the RUC Chief Constable, has accused the UDA of being responsible for three recent murders. His assertions led to calls for the UDP to be expelled from the talks.

22: Chris McMahon, a Catholic, was shot as he left his workplace on the northern outskirts of Belfast.

22: Evidence of Ireland's growing high-tech base was confirmed when Dell Computer announced plans to create 3,000 new jobs in Limerick and Bray, Co. Wicklow, over the next three years in an £180m. expansion plan.

23: Violence continued unabated in the North with the murder of 39-year-old Liam Conway, a Catholic man who was working in a loyalist area. Earlier the Ulster Freedom Fighters announced that it had ceased paramilitary attacks. In their statement, the UFF claimed their spate of murders was "a measured military response" to INLA aggression.

24: Catholic taxi-driver, John McColgan (33), was shot dead after picking up a fare on the Anderson Road, Belfast, bringing to six the number of people killed in Northern ireland in a week.

26: In London, the Ulster Democratic Party (UDP) voluntarily walked out of the multi-party talks rather than face the 'humiliation' of expulsion. Their actions came following the revelation that the UFF had been involved in a number of sectarian murders.

26: The Kerry Group became the biggest speciality ingredients company in Europe after it acquired the food ingredients business, Dalgety plc., at a price of £394 million.

26: David Lawler, a 33-year-old Dubliner, was handed down a life jail sentence when he pleaded guilty to the murder of civil servant Marilyn Rynn.

28: Gerard Doyle, a 5-year-old who suffers from cerebral palsy, was awarded £1.25 million by the High Court after his parents brought a case against the South Eastern Health Board concerning the circumstances surrounding his birth.

28: A woman was killed when a stolen car collided with her car in Milltownpass, Co. Westmeath.

28: The main Irish banks are to be subjected to an inquiry into their non-resident deposit accounts by the Revenue Commissioners. The Central Bank revealed that there was about £3 billion deposited in these accounts.

29: British Prime Minister Tony Blair announced a new inquiry into the events surrounding Bloody Sunday. Relatives announced that they could now consider Lord Widgery's report to be "dead."

29: Former Irish national and Olympic swimming coach, Derry O'Rourke, was sentenced to 12 years' imprisonment by the Dublin Circuit Criminal Court for sexually abusing young girls.

FEBRUARY

01: Almost 40,000 people took part in a march and rally in Derry to mark the 26th anniversary of Bloody Sunday. They were protesting about the shooting dead of 13 civil rights marchers by soldiers from Britain's Parachute Regiment on Sunday, 31st July, 1972.

02: European Cohesion Fund director, Mr. J.F. Verstrynge, has warned that the Commission could force Ireland to introduce water charges. Ireland is currently the only EU country that does not charge for domestic water usage.

03: The Minister for Tourism, Sport and Recreation, Dr. Jim McDaid, ordered that State funding to Irish Amateur Swimming Association be suspended pending the outcome of an inquiry into its handling of the Derry O'Rourke sex-abuse case. The Minister said he wanted assurances that proper procedures were in place to protect members from abuse before he would sanction any funding.

03: The "Celtic Warrior", boxer Steve Collins, has won his High Court battle with former manager, Barry Hearn, who sued the Irish fighter for alleged breach of contract. Mr. Justice O'Sullivan ruled that while there had been an agreement between the two men, Mr. Hearn had been responsible for fundamental breaches of it.

04: Galway taxi-drivers, still deeply concerned about the murder of Eileen Costello-O'Shaughnessy, who was battered to death in December after accepting a fare from a male passenger, have offered a £25,000 reward for information about the killing.

08: In another weekend of carnage on Irish roads six people died between noon on Friday and today (Sunday).

09: A political row has broken out in the North between the Secretary of State, Mo Mowlam, and the UUP's Ken Maginnis. In a letter to the UUP Party leader, David Trimble, Dr. Mowlam demanded an apology from Mr. Maginnis for allegedly calling her "a damned liar" during a talks session. Mr. Maginnis said he had "no intention whatsoever" of apologising. In another row, involving Sinn Féin and the SDLP, the leader of the latter party, John Hume, defended his party colleague, Seamus Mallon, from accusations by republicans that his attitude at the talks was "extremely unhelpful".

10: Direct Action Against Drugs, a cover name for an alleged IRA grouping, claimed responsibility for the killing of Brendan Campbell. Mr. Campbell, an alleged drugs dealer, was shot dead outside a restaurant on the Lisburn Road, Belfast. Sinn Féin's place at the talks was put further in jeopardy after a leading loyalist, Robert Dougan, was shot dead in Dunmurray.

13: One of Ireland's most respected literary figures, the Listowel writer, Bryan McMahon, has died. He was 88. *See Obituaries.*

16: Sinn Féin's Gerry Adams described himself as being "absolutely pissed off" after the Taoiseach, Mr. Ahern, signalled he would support Sinn Féin's expulsion from the talks following a declaration from the British government that it would begin an indictment procedure against republicans, as it concurred with the assessment of the RUC Chief Constable, Ronnie Flanagan, that the Provisional IRA was responsible for two recent murders in Belfast.

16: Tesco Ireland has stated that an advertisement placed by its British parent company pledging not to buy Irish beef for its British stores was a "mistake". The advertisement caused outrage amongst Irish farmers.

17: First-time novelist, John Connolly, has struck a deal with a London publishing company which has paid him an advance fee of £350,000 - believed to be the largest advance fee ever struck by an Irish novelist.

20: Sinn Féin were formally expelled from the talks today by the two governments because of allegations of IRA involvement in recent killings. The deadline for their return has been set for March 9th. An angry Gerry Adams described the expulsion as "disgraceful".

20: £5.3 million worth of "speed" and cocaine was seized by gardaí after a brief car chase on the road between Celbridge and Naas in Co. Kildare. Two men, with Dublin addresses, were arrested. An Anglo-Irish drugs gang was said to be involved, and this seizure is believed to be the third major blow to the gang in recent months.

22: Former Dublin and financier, Patrick Gallagher, claimed in a newspaper today that he gave former Taoiseach, Charles Haughey, £375,000 in 1979.

23: Portadown's town centre was seriously damaged when a huge bomb exploded. It is thought that the explosion is the work of the Continuity IRA.

27: The Republic of Ireland's remarkable economic performance was confirmed with the news that the country had one of the best budgetary figures in the EU for 1997. The Department of Finance figures indicated that Ireland achieved an Exchequer surplus of 0.9 per cent of gross domestic product. The Minister for Finance, Mr. McCreevy described the figures as "a milestone in Ireland's fiscal performance".

28: President Mary McAleese has indicated that she plans to celebrate the two major holidays on the island of Ireland, March 17th and July 12th, with parties at Áras an Uachtarain. It is understood that the proposed celebrations are part of a "bridge building" theme which the President plans to adopt during her term of office

28: At the pinnacle of his success, Irish comedian and actor Dermot Morgan, died unexpectedly at his London home, just a day short of his 46th birthday. His show, *Father Ted*, has recently won most of the top comedy awards for work featured on British television.

MARCH

03: The killing of two friends, one a Protestant, the other a Catholic, in Poyntzpass, Co. Armagh has caused outrage in the North. The two, Damian Traynor (26) and Philip Allen (34), were murdered by two masked gunmen who entered the Railway Bar in the town, ordered the two men, who were having a drink together, to lie on the floor and then shot them. It is believed the LVF was behind the murders.

03: The shock at yesterday's double killing continued to reverberate across the North. In an unprecedented move, UUP leader, David Trimble and SDLP deputy leader, Seamus Mallon, the MP for the area, walked through the village together in a show of unity and condemnation of what had occurred. Church leaders also issued particularly strong condemnations of the violence which has escalated considerably since the shooting dead of Billy Wright.

05: An interim report prepared for the Irish government has indicated that if the 150,000 potential claimants won damages in the hearing impairment claims brought by members of the Defence Forces the total bill for the Exchequer would reach a whopping £5.55 billion.

06: Protestants and Catholics attended both funeral services for the victims of Tuesday night's killings in Poyntzpass. Many political and religious commentators have stated that the killings may have proved a watershed in changing attitudes against violence.

07: A report in *The Irish Times* today confirmed that the Irish nation will be defined in terms of its people, rather than its territory, in the new wording for Article 2 of the Irish Constitution. The new Article 3 will enshrine the principle of consent while "expressing the wish of the majority of the Irish people for a united Ireland". The re-drafting of the Constitution is part of the package to bring about a settlement in the North.

07: There were a lot of angry passengers at Dublin airport today when the airport was closed because of a dispute involving Ryanair baggage handlers escalated. Members of the SIPTU union refused to pass the Ryanair pickets, thereby bringing all activities at the airport to a halt.

08: All Aer Lingus flights were cancelled today because of the Ryanair dispute. However, an agreement for a return to work was reached later in the evening between the company and the union following the intervention of the Taoiseach, Mr. Ahern, and the Tanaiste, Ms. Harney.

09: The British government has decided not to extradite Roisin McAliskey to Germany to face terrorist-related charges. While the nature of the evidence against Ms. McAliskey has always been hotly disputed, it is thought the British government took the decision now to encourage Sinn Féin to re-join the multi-party talks.

09: Despite its other difficulties, Ryanair announced the purchase of 25 new Boeing 737s at a cost of £1.4 billion. The planes will be used for the company's expanding European flight network.

12: The Labour Party has won the by-elections in Limerick East and Dublin North, reducing the government's overall majority to one.

12: The punt has hit its lowest level against sterling for nine years, closing at 81.95p.

12: Former Taoiseach Albert Reynolds has announced that he will not stand for the Dail at the next general election.

13: John O'Mahoney (37), from Tralee, Co. Kerry was sentenced to life imprisonment after being found guilty of the murder of Hannah O'Sullivan (40), also of Tralee. He had killed her in a frenzied knife attack.

14: One of the most respected figures in the Dail and a former Government Minister, Fine Gael's Hugh Coveney, died when, it is believed, he tried to rescue one of his dogs while walking on the cliff top by the coast at Robert's Cove, Cork.

15: David Keys (26), from Banbridge, Co. Down, who had been charged with the murder of two lifelong friends at Poyntzpass, Co. Armagh, was found hanged in his cell at the Maze Prison today. The RUC are treating his death as murder. According to security sources Mr. Keys had been beaten and then hanged from a window to give the impression that he had committed suicide. Three other men have been charged with the Armagh murders.

21/22: It was a great weekend for Ireland's top female athlete, Sonia O'Sullivan, who won gold medals on successive days in the World Cross Country championships, held in Morocco. She won both the long course and the 4,000 metres.

23: After some initial doubts, Sinn Féin rejoined the inter-party talks.

25: National Irish Bank found itself engulfed in controversy when RTÉ revealed that the NIB had taken money from customers' accounts without authorisation in the late 1980s and early 1990s. The seriousness of the allegations were underlined when the Cabinet met to discuss the matter and, following NIB's admission that this had occurred in five branches, announced that it would be fully investigated.

25: After almost two years of inter-party talks in the North, the talks chairman, Senator George Mitchell, gave the parties two weeks to reach an agreement.

26: It has emerged that a senior bank official went to the Gardaí to inform them of allegations that NIB had taken money from clients' accounts without authorisation. The bank indicated it would not oppose a Cabinet petition to the High Court to appoint an inspector under the Companies Act to investigate the allegations.

27: A former RUC man, Cyril Stewart, was shot dead in the centre of Armagh city shortly after he left a local supermarket where he had been shopping with his wife. In his early 50s, Mr. Stewart had left the RUC some months ago because of illness. Mr. Seamus Mallon, MP for Armagh and Newry, described the killing as an act of "absolute savagery".

29: After years of controversy, the Irish Christian Brothers published a formal apology to all those in its care who had been mistreated. It invited all such people to seek help.

31: The RUC found itself in the centre of controversy when a report by the United Nations Commission on Human Rights accused the force of engaging in widespread intimidation of lawyers involved in defending republican and loyalist paramilitaries. It also called for an independent investigation into the murder of Belfast solicitor, Pat Finucane, to determine whether security forces were involved in providing information to his UDA murderers.

APRIL

01: Britain has ruled out any inquiry into the murder of Belfast solicitor, Pat Finucane.

01: Despite three hours of intense negotiations in London, Taoiseach Bertie Ahern failed to reach agreement with British Prime Minister, Tony Blair, on key elements of the Northern settlement. Mr. Ahern said there were " large disagreements which could not be cloaked".

02: A 980lb car bomb was intercepted by the Garda Emergency Response Unit at the Dun Laoghaire ferry terminal. It was thought that the bomb was destined for the Aintree Grand National in England. It is believed dissident republicans were behind the operation.

03: The peace process looked to be back on track again after another intensive round of negotiations in London between the Taoiseach and the Prime Minister. It was their third meeting in three days.

03: A Garda who had won the Scott Medal for bravery was jailed for four and a half years at Dublin Circuit Criminal Court. John O'Neill (34) admitted accepting £16,100 in bribes from two Veronica Guerin murder suspects, Brian Meehan and Paul Ward. The court was told that O'Neill, who neither gambled, drank or smoked, was more than £100,000 in debt because of "desperately bad financial management." Meehan and Ward were fined £45,000 after they pleaded guilty to corruptly giving cash inducements to a Garda.

04: The Tanaiste, Mary Harney, has welcomed the recommendation by the National Minimum Wage Commission that a rate of £4.40 an hour be set. It is proposed that the new rate will come into effect from 1st April, 2000.

04: £2.5 million worth of cannabis resin was seized by Gardaí at Ashbourne, Co. Meath. Three men were arrested in the operation.

05: At a time of great political movement in the North, the Taoiseach, Mr. Ahern suffered a personal loss with the death of his mother, Mrs. Julia Ahern. Mrs Ahern, who was 87, was also the mother of another noted politician, Mr. Noel Ahern, TD for Dublin West.

07: A draft settlement paper was presented by Talks chairman, George Mitchell, to all parties involved. Senator Mitchell appealed that there be no leaking of the document; "Lives and deaths are at stake here", he said.

08: Trevor Deeny, a former UVF prisoner, was shot dead by INLA gunmen in Derry. It was the first political murder in the city for almost four years.

08: The chief risk to the Irish economic miracle could be "overheating", the OECD has warned. It said signs of overheating were already evident; these include labour shortages in a number of skilled professions and trades and a boom in house prices.

09: Amid high drama at Stormont buildings, the Talks deadline passed the designated 12 midnight deadline. There were angry exchanges between loyalists as the Democratic Unionist Party's leader, Dr. Ian Paisley, led a march to the buildings in protest against the talks.

10: After more than a quarter of a century of violence and two years of intensive talks the Northern Ireland Peace Process reached a climax at 5.36 p.m. today when Senator George Mitchell finally made the historic statement: "I am pleased to announce that the two governments and the political parties in Northern Ireland have reached agreement."

The agreement exceeded the Senator's deadline by almost 18 hours, and it was clear that there were still difficulties to be resolved, particularly for the Unionist party. The main points of the Agreement were: A Northern Ireland Assembly with 108 seats, elected by proportional representation; a 12-strong executive committee of ministers to be elected by the Assembly ; the setting up of a North-South ministerial council within one year by the Assembly; the council being accountable to Assembly and Dail; Amendments to Articles 2 and 3, to establish the principle of consent, and the repeal of the (British) Government of Ireland Act; a Council of the Isles with members drawn from assemblies in England, Scotland, Wales, Belfast and Dublin.

11: In a surprisingly heavy "pro" vote, the Northern Ireland Agreement overcame its first popularity test with 55 members of Ulster Unionist Executive voting for it with 23 voting against. It was anticipated that with so many of party's MP's against the Agreement, the vote would have been much closer.

15: The Grand Orange Lodge has decided it could not support the NI Agreement. While not rejecting the Agreement outright the members demanded clarification of a number of issues from British Prime Minister, Tony Blair before it would consider changing its position.

17: Ireland's most popular sportsman of his generation, Paul McGrath, has admitted that his outstanding soccer career is now over. The "Player of the Year" in the 1992 Premier League, McGrath was named in a World Best Eleven after the 1990 World Cup in Italy. He was once again outstanding in the 1994 World Cup in the US, particularly when, despite injury, he played superbly in the match against Italy.

17: Following claims in today's *Irish Independent* that RTÉ journalists, George Lee and Charlie Bird, have been "under surveillance" following their revelations in the National Irish Bank scandal, the Garda Commissioner, Pat Byrne, has appointed a senior garda to investigate the allegations.

18: The ruling council of the Ulster Unionist Party gave the peace agreement another significant boost when delegates backed it by 540 to 210.

19: It was announced that Mr. Peter Sutherland, the former Attorney General, could receive up to £58 million if Goldman Sachs, one of the world's top investment banks, is floated on the stock exchange.

20: The controversial passports-for-sale scheme has been abolished by the government.

21: Adrian Lamph, a 29-year-old Catholic from Portadown, was murdered by the LVF at the council yard where he worked.

21: The Celtic Tiger phenomenon continues. Ireland has been ranked 11th in a league table of the world's 20 most competitive economies, ahead of both Japan and Britain.

21: The Freedom of Information Act, which allows citizens access to personal information held on them at any time by public bodies, came into effect today.

22: Despite denials of direct interference, the Northern Ireland Parades Commission cancelled the publication of a crucial report on contentious parades after the intervention of British Prime Minister, Tony Blair.

24: The growth of asthma in Ireland is causing concern; the Asthma Society claims that more than 225,000 people, half of them children, are affected by the condition.

25: A proposal that MPs elected in the North should be entitled to sit in the Dail is being considered by the Joint Oireachtas Committee on the Constitution. The committee is also considering the possibility of permitting Irish citizens living in the North to vote in presidential elections and referendums.

25: Ciaran Heffron, a 22-year-old student, was murdered by loyalists as he made his way home after a night out with friends in the village of Crumlin, near Belfast. The RUC described the killing as sectarian. There was speculation that the murder was carried out by some of those attending a loyalist rally which had been held earlier in the town.

26: The Taoiseach, Mr. Ahern, told the gathering at the Easter Rising commemoration in Arbour Hill, Dublin, that Britain had been "effectively ruled out of the equation" in regard to the future of Northern Ireland. The principle of consent, he said, was now the guiding factor in any future developments.

26: Gardaí have appealed for witnesses to an horrific rape of an eight-year-old girl in Cork yesterday. A spokesman said it was impossible that passers-by had not seen a man chase the girl in a busy area near the city centre.

26: Cavan's Catherine McKiernan had one of the biggest wins of her outstanding athletic career when she came home first in the London Marathon in a time of 2hrs 26mins and 26 seconds. It's believed her win is worth £100,000.

27: An inquest has found that the late Fine Gael TD, Hugh Coveney, died from drowning and not from injury as a result of a fall from a height, during a walk along a cliff face at Robert's Cove in Cork Harbour last month.

28: It has been confirmed that the former Governor of

Hong Kong, Chris Patten, is to chair the Commission which is to be established to review the role of the RUC. The Ulster Unionist Party had objected to the appointment of an "non British" person to head the commission.

30: Amidst a welter of controversy surrounding the career of Irish swimming star, Michelle de Bruin, the head of the International Olympic Committee's Medical Commission said he had been informed that a urine sample submitted by the swimmer had an alcohol level high enough to be "deadly".

MAY

01: Seamus Heaney has been appointed Saoi of Aosdana, the highest award Ireland can bestow on an artist. The President, Mrs McAleese, described the poet as "the single most important figure in modern Irish literature".

01: Ronan MacLochlainn (28), an IRA dissident, was shot dead when Gardaí foiled a raid by six armed men on a security van in Ashford, Co. Wicklow.

02: There was shock in Limerick after 21-year-old Georgina O'Donnell was murdered in a local nightclub by a man who shot her in the face.

04: Martin McDonagh's *The Beauty Queen of Leenane* received six Tony award nominations in New York, more nominations than any other play nominated.

05: The Cabinet's decision to put part of the Dublin light rail system underground in the city centre has been met with considerable opposition. Opposition parties denounced it as a "shameful surrender to powerful vested interests".

05: One of longest serving group of Irish prisoners in England, the Balcombe Street gang, were transferred to Portlaoise Prison after serving 22 years and five months in English jails.

06: The Sinn Féin leadership has confirmed its support for the Good Friday Agreement, recommending that members in both the North and the South should vote "Yes".

08: The strength of Irish under-age sport was recognised on the international stage when the Irish U-16 soccer team won the European championship.

09: Sinn Féin candidates were cleared to take their places in the proposed new Northern Ireland Assembly after changes were made in the party's constitution at their Ardfheis in Dublin.

12: The deep divisions within unionism since the signing of the Good Friday Agreement have become more pronounced in recent days. The personal antagonism between Dr. Ian Paisley, leader of the DUP and David Trimble, of the UUP, manifested itself once again with the latter accusing the former of "running away again"

after Dr. Paisley pulled out of scheduled TV debate.

15: Despite overtures from British Prime Minister, Mr. Tony Blair and his party leader, David Trimble, Ulster Unionist MP Jeffrey Donaldson confirmed that he will be voting "No" in next Friday's referendum on the Good Friday Agreement. Mr. Donaldson's decision is seen as giving a significant boost to the "No" campaign.

16: There was outrage following the shooting of Larry O'Toole, a prominent member of Sinn Féin, during a First Holy Communion church service for local children in Ballymun, Dublin. His son, Lar, was also shot by the gunman who was chased out of the church and later caught by a number of the pursuers.

16: Three teenage boys were drowned off a beach at Strandhill in Co. Sligo. Bobby Taylor (16), Michael Higgins (17), and Tommy Coyle (18) got into difficulties while wading in the water at the beach which had been declared unsafe by the Irish Water Safety Association. A fourth boy was rescued.

17: Ireland's most popular sportsman of his generation, Paul McGrath, was given an emotional send off when almost 40,000 turned out for his farewell game at Lansdowne Road.

19: In their first public show of unity, SDLP leader, John Hume and UUP leader, David Trimble, met on stage at a U2 concert at Belfast's Waterfront Hall.

21: The Celtic Tiger phenomenon continues to fuel Dublin house prices with a detached five-bedroom house on half an acre of garden in the Dartry area of the city selling for £2.2 million at auction.

22: There was a huge turnout throughout the island of Ireland as the country went to the polls to vote on the Good Friday Agreement and the Ratification of the Amsterdam Treaty (the Republic of Ireland only).

23: When all the votes were counted in yesterday's referendum on the Good Friday Agreement, the results were as follows: Republic of Ireland - Yes (94.39%), No (5.61%), Turnout 56.26%. Northern Ireland - Yes (71.12%), No (28.88%), Turnout (81.10%). Ireland overall - Yes (85.46%), No (14.54%), Turnout (63.70%). in the Republic of Ireland, the Amsterdam Treaty was ratified, with the results as follows: Yes (62%), No (38%).

24: John Boorman won the Best Director award at Cannes for his film on the life of Dublin criminal, Martin Cahill. Accepting his award for *The General* Boorman dedicated his award to "all those people who voted for peace" in the Good Friday Agreement.

25: The Irish Olympic swimmer, Michelle de Bruin, now seems likely to face disciplinary action by the world swimming authority, FINA, following yesterday's confirmation that the second part of a random urine sample she submitted showed signs of tampering.

However, rejecting the FINA allegations, De Bruin's legal advisor, Mr. Peter Lennon, said the entire procedure should be declared null and void as, in his opinion, "this is a negative finding".

25: According to British statistics more than 5,300 women with addresses in the Republic of Ireland had abortions in Britain last year. This is the highest figure on record; in 1987 the figure was 3,673.

26: A German man, Jan Gerrit Jochem Isenborger who shot and injured the Cavan County Sheriff and two bailiffs was given a suspended four-year sentence at Dublin's Circuit Criminal Court. Isenborger shot Mr. Thomas Owens when he went to evict him and his terminally ill mother from the dilapidated house in which they lived at Ballyleenan, Bawnboy, Co. Cavan.

26: The Ulster Unionist party has refused to allow the anti-agreement MP, Jeffrey Donaldson, to stand for election to the new NI Assembly.

28: The Taoiseach, Mr Ahern, gave what most political analysts considered was his "least convincing performance" in the Dail when dealing with allegations which surrounded financial donations made to the former Minister for Foreign Affairs, Ray Burke. Mr. Burke received £30,000 from Rennicks, 50 per cent of which owned by Fitzwilton, the company chaired by Dr. Tony O'Reilly who is also chairman of Independent Newspapers. In his resignation statement some months ago Mr. Burke denied any wrong-doing.

30: The GAA has voted to retain Rule 21 which bans members of the RUC and British security forces from membership of the organisation. The decision was vehemently attacked by unionist politicians in the North.

JUNE

01: Xerox, the giant US multi-national, is to create 2,000 new jobs at its plants in Dublin and Dundalk. This will create a European centre for manufacturing and tele-service facilities.

02: It was learned today Fianna Fail did not inform the Flood Tribunal that Mr. Ray Burke received £30,000 from Rennicks. The Tribunal was told that £10,000 had been passed to the party by Mr. Burke.

03: The Dail voted, on a government proposal, to have the tribunal investigate the revelations relating to Mr. Burke.

08: The complete omission of Irish nominees from the newly established Police Commission in Northern Ireland has caused considerable difficulties between the two governments. A leaked document has indicated that Northern Secretary, Mo. Mowlam personally called the Government, the White House, the SDLP, Sinn Féin and other interested parties to explain her decision and to seek agreement for it.

08: *The Beauty Queen of Leenane* has won four Tony Awards in New York. Garry Hynes made history by becoming the first woman to win the director's award. The other winners were the stars of the play --Anna Manahan, Marie Mullen and Tom Murphy. Ironically, the play's writer, Martin McDonagh, did not win an award.

09: Mr. Ray Burke approved 44 passports for two families under the investment-based naturalisation scheme when he was Minister for Justice from 12th July, 1989 and 11th February, 1992. The information was made available in a written reply in the Dail today following a question by Fine Gael deputy, Mr. Jim O'Keeffe, who added that the information gathered in the Government's own review of the scheme should be handed over to the Flood Tribunal.

10: For the fourth consecutive year, the Industrial Development Authority (IDA) has announced record breaking progress. The Authority's chief executive, Mr. Kieran McGowan, confirmed in his annual report that last year the IDA helped create some 15,000 new jobs – a 10 per cent growth in employment in IDA supported companies – and saw a net growth in its current client companies of almost 10,000 additional new jobs.

10: More than 132,000 students began their Junior and Leaving Cert exams today. The first exam, Ordinary Level English, was described as "straightforward".

11: The latest figures from the Central Statistics Office show Ireland had an inflation rate of 2.7 per cent in May, well above the EU average and the highest rate in this country for three years.

11: The leader of the Labour Party, Ruairí Quinn, was the recipient of the largest amount of money in political donations in 1997. He received more than £27,000. This was for the period between May 15th and the end of the year.

13: The Gardaí staged their second "blue flu" day today by calling in sick, leaving many stations throughout the country operating on skeleton staffs. The Taoiseach, Mr. Ahern, has intervened in the dispute, attempting to set up consultations with the social partners, ICTU and IBEC, in an attempt to find a resolution to the pay demands.

16: Claims that Ireland's economic growth rate for this year could reach 12.5% were given a boost when it was revealed that exports from January to March were up almost 30 per cent on the comparable period last year.

17: The Murphy Report into child sex abuse in Irish swimming has been published. Serious allegations have been made in it against the activities of two former national coaches, George Gibney and Derry O'Rourke. The report basically demanded a radical overhaul of the entire Irish swimming set-up.

18: Following allegations made by unidentified investors on RTÉ, the Fianna Fail TD for Mayo, Ms. Beverly Cooper-Flynn has trenchantly denied she had ever encouraged anyone to invest in a financial product as a means of evading legitimately owed tax to the State. It was claimed that the TD, while she was working for the National Irish Bank, offered the advice to investors that they should put their money in offshore bonds to avoid tax.

19: The former world snooker champion, Belfast's Alex "Hurricane" Higgins, has disclosed that he has throat cancer.

22: Of considerable concern to Irish citizens is a report from the Massachusetts Institute for Resource and Security Studies which states that the high levels of radioactivity at England's Sellafield Nuclear plant were one of the world's "most dangerous concentrations" and that operations should be immediately suspended.

25: Senior Republican sources have confirmed that the IRA is preparing to identify the secret burial sites of about 12 people it abducted and killed between 1972 and 1980. This follows a sustained campaign by relatives of those who disappeared.

25: Hundreds of thousands of voters took to the polls today to elect a new Assembly for Northern Ireland. Opinion polls have suggested that the UUP has recovered some ground in the last few days but that the unionist community remains very divided.

26: The relatively poor early showing of the UUP has resulted in the bitter divisions within the party becoming public. Dissident MP, Jeffrey Donaldson, in a televised debate, accused his party colleague, Ken Maginnis, of "presiding over an electoral disaster" while Mr. Maginnis accused Mr. Donaldson of "gloating over the difficulties that he and others like him" had created for the party. Meanwhile, both nationalist parties, the SDLP and Sinn Féin, had reason to be pleased with very strong first preference showing.

27: As the counting came to a close today following Thursday's Northern Ireland Assembly Elections, the UUP has emerged as the largest party with 28 seats. The SDLP has 24, the DUP 20, Sinn Féin 18, Alliance 6, UK Unionists 5, PUP 2, Women's Coalition 2, Independent Unionist 1, UU 1, and the UUU 1. In a major political breakthrough for the nationalist community, the SDLP emerged as the largest garners of the first preference vote with 22%. They were followed by the UUP on 21.3%, the DUP on 18.1%, Sinn Féin on 17.6%, Alliance on 6.5%, and Others on 14.5%.

27 Two men were killed and another seriously injured when a car ploughed into cyclists who were participating in the Co-operation North Cross-Border maracycle. The vehicle involved did not stop at the scene of the accident.

29: In a surprise development Lord John Alderdice announced his resignation as leader of the Alliance Party.

29: The Parades Commission has announced that it will not permit the Drumcree Orange march along the Garvaghy Road unless there was, what it termed, a "local agreement".

30: More indicators of the Tiger economy . . . A Victorian house in Dalkey, Co. Dublin was sold for £5.9m. The solicitor who bought it on behalf of a client would not confirm the identity of the purchaser though it was later learned that the buyer was a low-profile English based businessman, Terry Coleman, who, according to the *Sunday Times*, was worth £45m.

JULY

01: In another historic first in the North of Ireland, David Trimble was elected First Minister of the new Assembly with the SDLP's Seamus Mallon elected Deputy First Minister.

01: Ms. Beverley Cooper-Flynn has confirmed that she has instigated legal proceedings against both RTÉ and retired Meath farmer, James Howard, after allegations were made that she encouraged the latter to avoid tax by investing his money in off-shore accounts.

02: The economic boom continues unabated with the half yearly figures from the Exchequer indicating that tax revenue forecasts were up by £800m on that predicted at Budget time.

04: With no resolution in sight to the Drumcree crisis there was considerable tension throughout Northern Ireland over the weekend.

08: The situation at Drumcree has deteriorated considerably with sustained attacks on RUC and British army barricades by protesting Orange men.

10: Nine people were arrested in London, Dublin and Dundalk as Gardaí and anti-terrorist police in England swooped on people they alleged were "just minutes away" from launching a bombing campaign in London. It was claimed those arrested were aligned with the 32 County Sovereignty Committee.

10: A middle-aged French woman survived a fall from the highest sea-cliffs in Western-Europe, at Slieve League in Co. Donegal.She was rescued by an Air Corps helicopter after spending six hours on a ledge at the cliffs.

10: Almost 70 people in Donegal have been affected by salmonella poisoning. It was thought that contaminated eggs were responsible for the three outbreaks which have occurred in recent days.

11: After much hype, the Tour de France finally got underway today in Dublin. The prologue was won by the English rider, Chris Boardman. The tour is the biggest ever sporting event staged in Ireland.

12: Events surrounding the crisis at Drumcree took an horrific twist today when three young boys were murdered after their home was petrol bombed in a sectarian attack. Richard (11), Mark (10), and Jason (9) Quinn died in the attack at their home in Ballymoney, Co. Antrim. The boys' mother, Christine, her partner, Raymond Craig, and a family friend, Christina Archibald (18) escaped the blaze. Ms. Quinn's eldest son, Lee (13) was staying with his grandmother when the incident occurred.

12: In the aftermath of the Ballymoney deaths, the Orange Order Deputy Grand Chaplain, the Rev. William Bingham, called for the Drumcree protest to be called off claiming a 15 minute march down the Garvaghy Road would be "a hallow victory" as it would be taking place in the shadows of three little white coffins. His call was echoed by both the NI First Minister, David Trimble, and the Church of Ireland primate, Dr. Robin Eames. Their calls were rejected by the Orangemen.

13: The numbers involved in the Drumcree stand-off have decreased following the almost universal condemnation of the Orange Order's response to the deaths of the Quinn children.

13: An 11-year-old girl was taken to Cork hospital in a critical condition after being struck by a Tour de France cyclist as the race passed through Grange, Co. Waterford.

14: There was a huge turnout in Rasharkin, Co. Antrim, for the funeral of the Quinn children. The three boys were buried in a single grave.

15: Killkenny sprinter Emily Maher (17) became the first Irish athlete to win a World Youth Olympic medal when she came home first in the 100 metres at the finals in Moscow. She later went on to win a second gold.

16: Following serious outbreaks of salmonella in both Donegal and Wicklow, the Department of Agriculture has confirmed that it has traced the source to contaminated eggs originating from a farm in Northern Ireland.

17: After 12 days of often violent protest the Orange Order has conceded that it will not be able to force its way down the Garvaghy Road. Portadown District Master, Harold Gracey, confirmed that only a token presence would be maintained at Drumcree.

22: Former Taoiseach, Charles J. Haughey, received summonses allegedly for obstructing and hindering the work of the McCracken Tribunal.

23: After years of difficulties Aer Lingus announced operating profits of £46.1m.

24: 1997 was a record year for Irish tax revenue earnings. Tax receipts hit new record highs in almost all areas last year with the Revenue Commissioners reporting that almost £14 billion of total revenue was collected. This represents an increase of 15 per cent on the 1996 figure of 12 billion, which was also a record year. The main sources of revenue in 1997 were income tax which raised £5,208 million followed by VAT at £3,707 million.

26: Following Ireland's superb victory over the Italians in the European U-16 soccer championships in Scotland almost three months ago, it was another unbelievable night for under age Irish sport when the Republic's U-18 team beat Germany in the European final in Larnaca, Cyprus. For Brian Kerr, the manager of the side, it was a great double, as he was also in charge of the U-16 side.

27: The Dublin Government is to demand that RTÉ provides a list of its top 20 earners and details of their salaries. The decision was made by the Cabinet after it cleared RTÉ's Annual Report. According to a Government spokesman, the request for information on salaries was consistent with the need for "transparency" in semi-state bodies.

29: The ongoing problem with blood products became evident again today when it was announced that more than 16,000 women may be recalled for hepatitis C testing by the Blood Transfusion Service Board. It is known they received batches of the anti-D blood product believed to be contaminated. It is not known what the health implications are, but it is thought that the risk to the women is "minimal".

29: According to the Department of Finance's annual Economic Review and Outlook the economy will grow by 7.5 per cent this year, 50,000 jobs will be created and unemployment will fall to 9 per cent. The downside is that inflation is expected to rise and that there will be strong demands for substantial increases in wages.

29: Rhonda Paisley, daughter of DUP leader, Dr. Ian Paisley, has been awarded £24,249 by Northern Ireland's Fair Employment Tribunal. It ruled that she had been discriminated against after being turned down for the post of Arts Co-operation Officer. The tribunal ruled that she had been treated "less favourably" than other candidates on the basis of her religious beliefs and political opinions.

30: Former Taoiseach, Charles J. Haughey, appeared in the Dublin District Court on charges that he obstructed the work of the McCracken Tribunal. The DPP's request that Mr. Haughey's trial take place in the Circuit Criminal Court, which has the power to impose much more severe penalties than the District Court, was unopposed.

30: The decision of the President, Mrs. McAleese, not to present the Aga Khan Trophy at the Dublin Horse show caused some eye-brows to be raised. It was the first time a president had not attended in 50 years. The President explained that she would be attending an Irish-language course in Donegal.

01: Thirty-three civilians and two members of the RUC were injured when a 500lb car bomb exploded in Banbridge, Co. Down. Extensive damage was also caused in the explosion which is thought to be the work of a breakaway republican group.

03: In the first break-through of its kind, Nationalists and Loyalists in Derry struck an agreement over the Apprentice Boys march in the city. The agreement came after three days of shuttle negotiations between the parties.

03: In a week which began with 45 Romanian asylum seekers arriving at Rosslare, it was announced today that legislation is to be introduced to stem the flow of illegal immigrants. Truck drivers and freight companies found guilty of bringing in the "illegals" will have their vehicles confiscated and face jail terms of up to five years.

04: Mr. Graham Savage, the National Irish Bank chief executive, offered "unreserved apologies" to 370 customers after two inquiries into allegations of improper interest and fee-loading by the bank. The bank is also to return £131,166 plus interest to the customers.

05: After a prolonged dispute, the Garda Representative Association's membership voted to accept the Government's 9 per cent pay offer.

05: Allied Irish Banks announced pre-tax profits of £401.3 million for the first six months to the end of June.

06: Irish triple winning Olympic gold medallist, Michelle de Bruin, received a four-year ban from FINA, the international swimming authority, after it alleged that one of her dope tests had been tampered with. The swimmer says she will sue FINA for the "blatant attempt" to ruin her career.

07: The 9.1 per cent unemployment rate in the Republic of Ireland is now lower than that of Germany, France or even the EU average. The rate is the lowest in 15 years.

08: Sinn Féin leader, Gerry Adams, told a meeting in West Belfast today that he would not be pressured into uttering the words "the war is over" to satisfy unionists.

08: It has been confirmed that Gay Byrne is to give up his long running show on RTÉ Radio. He will give his last broadcast on Christmas Eve. It was confirmed some days later that he is to host the *Late Late Show* for one more year.

10: Car clamping began in Dublin today. The first vehicle to be clamped was a Nissan Micra in Merrion Square. The fine for "unclamping" is £65.

11: In what has been a remarkable year for him, Ireland's Peter Sutherland is to become co-chairman of one of the world's top three oil companies following the merger of the British company, BP, and American oil giant, Amoco.

12: There were emotional scenes as the bodies of two young Irish men, Shane McGettigan (21), from Drumshambo, Co. Leitrim, and Ronan Stewart (23), from Dundalk, were brought home from the US. The two died when scaffolding they were working on collapsed. Mr. McGettigan was the only son of Charlie McGettigan who won the Eurovision Song Contest for Ireland in 1994 with his son, Rock 'n' Roll Kids.

13: Sinn Féin's National Chairperson, Mitchel McLaughlin, has urged anyone with any information about any of the "missing persons" who disappeared during the course of the Troubles to make that information available.

14: The number of prison suicides in Ireland is causing concern. Statistics quoted in the *Irish Times* confirm that there have been 25 self-inflicted deaths in prisons since 1990, 23 of which were caused by hanging.

15: The single worst atrocity in Northern Ireland's almost 30 year's of trouble occurred today when a bomb exploded at 3.10 p.m. in Omagh, Co. Tyrone. Twenty-eight people, including a woman heavily pregnant with twins, died on the day and another man died three weeks later as as a result of the explosion. Literally hundreds were injured. The dead included three generations of one family, three children from Buncrana, Co. Donegal, who were on a day trip to the town, and a child and an adult from Spain who had been on holiday in Donegal. The carnage was the direct result of a misleading phone warning which led people seeking safety towards the bomb rather than away from it. The code-word used was that of the "Real IRA", a breakaway group from the Provisional IRA who disagree with the political direction being taken by the Sinn Féin leadership.

18: Ireland, North and South, still coming to terms with the magnitude of the Omagh outrage, almost came to a standstill this morning when the first funerals took place. Funerals continued for the rest of the week. *See Obituaries.*

19: The Taoiseach, Mr. Ahern, has announced his intention to introduce tough anti-terrorist measures. The proposals will include seizure of land or other property which has been used for storing weapons or making bombs. In addition, a suspect's right to silence is to be withdrawn. The measures were described by the Taoiseach himself as "draconian".

19: In what is proving to be a vintage year, Sonia O'Sullivan, was in magnificent form when she won the European 10,000 metres championship in Budapest.

21: The INLA, second only to the Provisional IRA in terms of paramilitary strength on the Republican side, announced that it is to go on ceasefire. The Government called on the Continuity IRA to do likewise.

22: The GAA has taken the highly unusual decision of ordering a replay in the All-Ireland hurling semi-final between Clare and Offaly after the match was ended two minutes prematurely by the referee. The Association later announced that it intended to establish a trust fund for the victims of the Omagh bombing and that the proceeds from the replay will be donated to it.

23: Sonia O'Sullivan made it a great week at the European Championship when she won the 5,000 metres.

25: It has been confirmed that both the Dail and the House of Commons are to be recalled next week to enact emergency legislation to deal with those still engaged in paramilitary activities.

27: Ireland's largest clothing manufacturer, Fruit of the Loom, which employs almost 3,500 people in its plants in Donegal and Derry, caused anxiety for its workforce when it announced that it is examining the possibility of moving its T-shirt operations, currently located in Buncrana, Co. Donegal, to Morocco. Two of the company's Irish-based directors have resigned amidst claims that more than 1,000 jobs could be lost.

29: Dublin woman, Elaine Moore, who was arrested on conspiracy charges in London, was freed on bail from Holloway Prison.

29: A crowd of more than 80,000 attended the rockfest at Slane Castle, which was headlined by The Verve.

29: The Hugh Lane Municipal Gallery in Dublin is to be the new home of artist Francis Bacon's studio. The studio was donated by John Edward, the heir of the internationally renowned artist.

30: The Jordan Team - Damon Hill and Ralf Schumacher - managed by Irishman Eddie Jordan, notched up their first Grand Prix win when they came in 1st and 2nd place, respectively, in the Belgian Grand Prix.

30: Dubliner Tommy Tiernan won the Perrier award, the top comedy prize, at this year's Edinburgh Festival.

SEPTEMBER

01: Gerry Adams announced in a statement that violence must now be " thing of the past, over, done with and gone."

01: Northern Ireland First Minister David Trimble has invited Gerry Adams to a round-table meeting.

02: Professor Ernst van de Wetering is to confirm whether the painting owned by the the National Gallery of Ireland - *Head Of An Old Man* - is in fact the work of the great Dutch master, Rembrant. If it is verified as such, it could be worth as much as £20 million.

05: President Clinton left Ireland today after a very successful visit. The President was conferred with the Freedom of Limerick in the morning and concluded his visit to Ireland after playing a round of golf at Ballybunnion in Kerry with, amongst others, former Minister for Foreign Affairs, Dick Spring.

05: It was a good day for the Republic on the soccer front with a surprisingly good result over Croatia, Ireland winning by 2-0 against the team which came third in the World Cup.

07: After weeks of intense pressure in the wake of their disastrous bomb in Omagh, the "Real IRA" announced a "complete cessation" of its campaign of violence. The only republican grouping which has yet to call a ceasefire is the "Continuity IRA".

07: Another Northern Ireland precedent was set today when First Minister, David Trimble met Sinn Féin President, Gerry Adams, during a round table discussion with Northern party leaders.

07: After weeks of intense speculation, the former bishop of Galway, Dr. Eamonn Casey, currently living in England, announced that he would not be seeking any public pastoral ministry in the church in Ireland.

08: On the direct orders of UN High Commissioner for Human Rights, Mary Robinson, the *Irish Times*' Asia correspondent, Conor O'Clery was prevented from accompanying her during her visit to Tibet. Mrs. Robinson claimed that Mr. O'Clery's presence along with that of RTÉ's Charlie Bird, "would send the wrong message."

09: A United Nations report, The Human Development Report 1998, has revealed that the Republic has the highest concentration of poverty outside of the US. In addition, despite the Celtic Tiger phenomenon, the report indicated clearly the wide disparity in the distribution of wealth in the state, including the fact that Irish women are particularly low down the scale in economic terms.

09: The internationally renowned portrait artist, Derek Hill, who has resided in Donegal for many years, has described himself as "delighted" at being awarded honourary Irish citizenship.

10: The first ever "face-to-face" meeting between David Trimble and Gerry Adams took place in private today at Stormont. Both men later described the meeting as cordial and businesslike.

10: With more than 300 people dead on the roads so far this year, Garda Commissioner, Pat Byrne, described what was happening on the roads as "outrageous". He called for an overhaul of the entire legislative process in regard to road traffic management, including the introduction of penalty points for various offences and random breath tests.

11: George Mitchell, a Dublin criminal known as "The Penguin", was jailed in Holland for two and a half years after a Dutch court found him guilty of masterminding a £5 million computer supplies robbery in the Netherlands.

11: The Garda pay dispute is unlikely to be settled amicably as the latest report from the Department of Justice indicates that a third of rank-and-file gardaí took home more pay than their superiors, including those up to the rank of Superintendent.

11: "Going for a pint" took on a whole new meaning for Mr. Yasuyuki Ozeki, a 27-year-old Japanese citizen, who left his hometown of Osaka last April, cycled through China, Siberia, Russia, the Gobi Desert and on to mainland Europe until he reached Guinness headquarters in Dublin today. There he availed of several pints of the blackstuff. Mr Ozeki explained the reason for the 7,500 mile journey: "There is no Guinness in Japan and there is lots of Guinness in Ireland."

11: The first batch of paramilitary prisoners from the North's jails were released today under the terms of the Good Friday Agreement. In total, seven prisoners were released and so began a programme that is expected to take two years to complete.

11: Taoiseach Bertie Ahern has told Chris Patten, chairman of the RUC Review body, that major reform of the force is necessary if the force is to be acceptable to both communities in Northern Ireland. The Taoiseach made his comments during a meeting with Mr. Patten at Government buildings in Dublin.

12: Fears for more than 700 jobs at the Fruit of Loom plants in Donegal grew after a meeting between Tanaiste, Mary Harney, and company chief, Bill Farrelly, failed to agree a way forward.

13: Against all the odds, Offaly claimed this year's All-Ireland hurling title, the first "back door" title winners since the GAA introduced the experimental rules last year. The champions had lost the Leinster title to Kilkenny more than two months ago but were allowed back into the competition at the All-Ireland quarter final stage.

14: The growing carnage on Irish roads continued unabated with the confirmation today that five people, three adults and two children, have died in collision between a school minibus and a lorry at Kilbride in Co. Wicklow.

15: The Minister for Agriculture, Mr. Joe Walsh, was called on to resign by angry farmers who gathered in St. Stephen's Green, in Dublin, to protest at what they described as "an incomes crisis" for Irish farmers. Farming leaders claim unprecedented numbers are leaving the land as more and more find it impossible to make ends meet.

20: Ireland's first commercial television station, TV3, started broadcasting today from its base in Tallaght, Co. Dublin. The Taoiseach, Bertie Ahern, performed the official opening ceremony.

21: The town of Thurles was stunned by the double murder of former Garda Bill Doherty (57) and his wife, Theresa. They had been stabbed to death.

21: Twelve men were detained by Garda and RUC officers investigating the Omagh bombings. Six were arrested in south Armagh, six in north Louth.

22: Martin Doherty (24), of Lelia Street, Limerick, was charged with the murder of his parents, Bill and Theresa Doherty, at their home in Thurles.

22: Against a background of growing tensions in recent days over decommissioning, Unionist leader, David Trimble, who denied he would resign over the issue, supported a call by the Taoiseach, Mr. Ahern, for some movement from the IRA on this issue. Mr. Ahern's call came after a meeting with Mr. Trimble in Dublin.

23: There were sharp exchanges between Mr. Trimble and Sinn Féin President, Gerry Adams, over decommissioning. Mr. Adams, who said IRA decommissioning was not within his party's gift, accused Mr. Trimble of trying to impose conditions, regarding Sinn Féin's entry into the Executive, which were not part of the Good Friday Agreement.

24: The possibility of an Irish serial killer has not been ruled out by Gardaí following the mysterious disappearance of at least seven women over recent years. The Commissioner, Mr. Byrne, has ordered the setting up of a special detective unit to co-ordinate investigations.

25: In a landmark decision, Ennis District Court refused to renew a publican's licence after it ruled he was not a fit person to hold such a licence. The decision was made by Judge Albert O'Dea after he had heard evidence from settled traveller, Mr. David McDonagh, who claimed he was treated "like an animal" in Mr. Jackie Whelan's Railway Bar, Ennis, when he was refused a second drink. Judge O'Dea said he was satisfied that Mr. McDonagh had been refused a drink simply because he was a traveller.

26: Galway footballers were ecstatic following their victory over Kildare in the All-Ireland final at Croke Park. They won by 1-14 to 1-10. It was a bitter blow for Kildare who had not won an All-Ireland in 70 years.

28: A senior Revenue Commission official from Co. Clare, Brendan Murphy, of Parteen, has pleaded guilty at Ennis Circuit Court to conspiring to defraud the Revenue authorities of £3.8 million through false VAT returns.

30: The escalation of the row over decommissioning of paramilitary weapons has, according to both Sinn Féin leader Gerry Adams and Northern Ireland Deputy First

Minister, Seamus Mallon, the potential to wreck the Good Friday Agreement. At the British Labour Party's Annual Conference, both men insisted that IRA decommissioning was not a prerequisite for Sinn Féin's entry onto the Shadow Executive. Mr. Mallon said that while there was nothing in the Agreement to support the Unionist party's stance, there was a need to find a way round their objections. Mr. Adams said IRA decommissioning was not within Sinn Féin's gift.

30: A major row within the Department of Foreign Affairs became public knowledge when it emerged that Minister David Andrews and the department's Secretary General, Padraig MacKernan, had not been on speaking terms for several months. It is understood that the source of tension between the two men was the Minister's decision to issue three written directives to promote his preferred candidates to counsellor and Assistant Secretary posts. According to sources, it was the first time "in living memory" that a minister had taken such a course of action and that such a break in long established practice had caused considerable upset within the Department.

30: Last year was a good year for one prison officer who, according to the Comptroller and Auditor General's Annual report, was the highest overtime earner in the public sector, taking home £38,378 in additional payments. In all almost £100 million was paid in overtime to public servants.

Inauguration Speech of the Eighth President of Ireland, Mary McAleese

November 11, 1997. St Patrick's Hall, Dublin Castle

A uaisle,

L Á STARIÚIL é seo im'shaol féin, i saol mo mhuintire, agus i saol na tíre go léir. Is pribhléid mhór í a bheith tofa mar Uachtarán na hÉireann, le bheith mar ghuth na hÉireann i gcéin is i gcóngair.

This is a historic day in my life, in the life of my family and in the life of the country. It is a wonderful privilege for me to be chosen as Uachtaran na hÉireann, to be a voice for Ireland at home and abroad. I am honoured and humbled to be successor to seven exemplary Presidents. Their differing religious, political, geographical and social origins speak loudly of a Presidency which has always been wide open and all embracing. Among them were Presidents from Connacht, Leinster and Munster to say nothing of America and London. It is my special privilege and delight to be the first President from Ulster.

The span of almost sixty years since the first Presidential Inauguration has seen a nation transformed. This Ireland which stands so confidently on the brink of the 21st century and the third millennium is one our forebearers dreamed of and yearned for: a prospering Ireland, accomplished, educated, dynamic, innovative, compassionate, proud of its people, its language and of its vast heritage; an Ireland at the heart of the European Union, respected by nations and cultures across the world.

The scale of what we have already accomplished in such a short time allows us to embrace the future with well-based confidence and hope. It is the people of Ireland who, in a million big and small ways in quiet acts of hard work, heroism and generosity have built up the fabric of home, community and country on which the remarkable success story of today's Ireland is built.

Over many generations there have been very special sources of inspiration who have nurtured our talent and instilled determination into this country. Many outstanding politicians, public servants, voluntary workers, clergy of all denominations and religions, teachers and particularly parents have, through hard and difficult times, worked and sacrificed so that our children could blossom to their fullest potential. They are entitled to look with satisfaction at what they have achieved. May we never become so cynical that we forget to be grateful. I certainly owe them a deep personal debt and as President I hope to find many opportunities both to repay that debt and to assist in the great work of encouraging our children to believe in themselves and in their country.

Among those who are also owed an enormous debt of thanks are the countless emigrants whose letters home with dollars and pound notes, earned in grinding loneliness thousands of miles from home, bridged the gap between the Ireland they left and the Ireland which greets them today when they return as tourists or return to stay. They are a crucial part of our global Irish family. In every continent they have their love of Ireland, its traditions and its culture deep in their hearts so that wherever we travel in the world there is always a part of Ireland of which we can be proud and which in turn takes pride in us. I hope over the next seven years there will be many opportunities for me to celebrate with them.

At our core we are a sharing people. Selfishness has never been our creed. Commitment to the welfare of each other has fired generations of voluntary organisations and a network of everyday neighbourliness which weaves together the caring fabric of our county. It has sent our missionaries, development workers and peacemakers to the aid of distressed peoples in other parts of the world. It has made us a country of refuge for the hurt and dispossessed of other troubled places. It is the fuel which drives us to tackle the many social problems we face, problems which cynicism and self-doubt can never redress but painstaking commitment can. We know our duty is to spread the benefits of our prosperity to those whose lives are still mired in poverty, unemployment, worry and despair. There can be no rest until the harsh gap between the comfortable and the struggling has been bridged.

The late Cearbhall Ó Dálaigh, Ireland's fifth president and, dare I say it, one of three lawyers to grace the office said at his inauguration in 1974 "Presidents under the Irish Constitution don't have policies. But . . . a President can have a theme." The theme of my Presidency, the Eighth Presidency, is Building Bridges. These bridges require no engineering skills but they will demand patience, imagination and courage for Ireland's pace of change is now bewilderingly fast. We grow more complex by the day. Our dancers, singers, writers, poets, musicians, sportsmen and women, indeed our last President herself, are giants on the world stage. Our technologically skilled young people are in demand everywhere. There is an invigorating sense of purpose about us. There are those who absorb the rush of newness with delight. There are those who are more cautious even fearful. Such tensions are part of our creative genius, they form the energy which gives us our unique identity, our particularity.

I want to point the way to a reconciliation of these many tensions and to see Ireland grow ever more comfortable and at ease with the flowering diversity that is now all around us. To quote a Belfast poet, Louis MacNeice, "a single purpose can be founded on a jumble of opposites." Yet I know to speak of reconciliation is to raise a nervous query in the hearts of some North of the border, in the place of my birth. There is no more appropriate place to address that query than here in Dublin Castle, a place where the complex history of these two neighbouring and now very neighbourly islands has seen many chapters written.

It is fortuitous too that the timing of today's Inauguration coincides with the commemoration of those who died so tragically and historically in two world wars. I think of nationalist and unionist, who fought and died together in those wars, the differences which separated them at home, faded into insignificance as the bond of their common humanity forged friendships as intense as love can make them.

In Ireland, we know only too well the cruelty and capriciousness of violent conflict. Our own history has been hard on lives young and old. Too hard. Hard on those who died and those left behind with only shattered dreams and poignant memories. We hope and pray, indeed we insist, that we have seen the last of the violence. We demand the right to solve our problems by dialogue and the noble pursuit of consensus. We hope to see that consensus pursued without the language of hatred and contempt and we wish all those engaged in that endeavour, well. That it can be done - we know. We need look no further than our own European continent where once bitter enemies now work conscientiously with each other and for each other as friends and partners. The greatest salute to the memory of all our dead and the living whom they loved, would be the achievement of agreement and peace.

I think of the late Gordon Wilson who faced his unbearable sorrow ten years ago at the horror that was Enniskillen. His words of love and forgiveness shocked us as if we were hearing them for the first time, as if they had not been uttered first two thousand years ago. His work and the work of so many peacemakers who have risen above the awesome pain of loss to find a bridge to the other side is work I want to help in every way I can. No side has a monopoly on pain. Each has suffered intensely. I know the distrusts go deep and the challenge is awesome. Across this island, North, South, East and West there are people of such greatness of heart that I know with their help it can be done. I invite them to work in partnership with me to dedicate ourselves to the task of creating a wonderful millennium gift to the Child of Bethlehem whose 2000th birthday we will soon celebrate - the gift of an island where difference is celebrated with joyful curiosity and generous respect and where, in the words of John Hewitt, "each may grasp his neighbour's hand as friend."

There will be those who are wary of such invitations, afraid that they are being invited to the edge of a precipice. To them I have dedicated a poem, written by the English poet, Christopher Logue, himself a veteran of the Second World War. "Come to the edge. We might fall / Come to the edge. It's too high / Come to the edge. And they came / and he pushed, and they flew." No one will be pushing, just gently inviting, but I hope that if ever and whenever you decide to walk over that edge there will be no need to fly, you will find there a firm and steady bridge across which we will walk together both ways.

Ireland sits tantalisingly ready to embrace a golden age of affluence, self-assurance, tolerance and peace. It will be my most profound privilege to be President of this beautiful, intriguing country. May I ask those of faith, whatever that faith may be to pray for me and for our country that we will use these seven years well, to create a future where in the words of William Butler Yeats "Everything we look upon is blest."

Déanamis um todhchaí sin a chruthú le chéile.

OBITUARIES

BALL, Peter (b. England, 1943) sports journalist. Soccer correspondent with *The Sunday Tribune* and Northern Ireland football correspondent for *The Times* at the time of his death. Worked with Eamon Dunphy on the book *Only a Game* and with Graeme Fowler on *Fox on the Run*, which went on to win the Channel 4 Sports Book of the Year in 1988. Died November, 1998.

BALLANTINE, Norman (b. Donegal, 1913) former Northern Ireland journalist. Worked on the *Northern Whig*, the *Belfast Telegraph* and the *Newsletter*, which he worked for up to the late 1980s. Died May, 1998.

BLANCHFLOWER, Jackie (b. Belfast, 1933) former Northern Ireland International and Manchester football player. Brother of Danny, also an Northern Ireland international player. First appeared with Northern Ireland in 1954 and went on to win 12 caps. One of Manchester United's Busby Babes, he survived the Munich air disaster which killed eight of his team mates, but was badly injured and had to retire prematurely from football. Died September, 1998.

BOWLES, Michael (b. Sligo, 1910) musician, writer, former Irish Army captain and university professor. Conducted the No. 1 Army Band, the No. 2 Army Band, Radio Éireann Symphony Orchestra, the New Zealand Symphony Orchestra and the Rhode Island Symphony Orchestra. Edited a US newspaper and wrote for *The Irish Times*. Died April, 1998.

BRADFORD, Roy (b. Belfast, 1921) Unionist politician, Stormont minister, journalist, novelist and television producer. Ulster Unionist Party member for East Belfast

(1973-74), and head of the Department of the Environment (1974). Stormont MP (1965-72). Chairman of the European Movement in Northern Ireland (1977-87). Wrote the novel *The Last Ditch* (1981). Died September, 1998.

BRENNAN, Paudge (b. 1922) former Fianna Fáil TD for Wicklow and parliamentary secretary. First elected to the Dáil in 1954 and served until 1987. Died June, 1998.

BURKE, John Oliver Irish Ambassador to Portugal and former Chief of Protocol. Postings included United Nations in New York, Washington Embassy, Copenhagen Embassy and Consulate General in New York. During his time at the UN, he was chairman of the second committee at the General Assembly of 1991-92. Died November, 1997.

BYRNE, Charlie (b. 1919) comedian and singer. Co-starred with Joe Lynch in the long running radio comedy series *Living with Lynch* in the 1950s, the series later transferred to television in the 1970s. Died March, 1998.

CASSIDY, Lar (b. 1950) Literature Officer of the Arts Council for 17 years and Assistant Registrar of Aosdána. Joined the Arts Council in 1980. Director of Dublin International Writers' Festivals (1988, 1991, 1993) and of the *Ireland and its Diaspora* Festival at the 1996 Frankfurt International Book Festival. Worked to establish the Irish Writers' Centre and many other community arts organisations including Macnas. Died October, 1997.

CONNOLLY, Sybil (b. Wales, 1921) international fashion designer. Returned to Ireland (1941). Joined the Richard Allen fashion shop in Dublin and started

designing her own dresses in 1952. Her designs proved successful both in the US and in Australia. Died May, 1998.

COSTELLO, Dr Joe (b. 1938) former Chairman of the *Connacht Tribune* newspaper company and a consultant anaesthetist practitioner in Galway and former president of the Connacht Branch of the Irish Rugby Football Union. Also played rugby for Galwegians, London Irish, Manitoba in the Canadian League and University College Galway. Died June, 1998.

COVENEY, Hugh (b. Cork, 1935). Fine Gael TD for Cork and former Minister. First elected to the Dáil in Cork South Central in 1981. Minister for Defence and Minister for the Marine (1994-95) when he resigned. Minister of State at the Department of Finance (1995-97). Lord Mayor of Cork (1982-83). Former member of the Higher Education Authority, Cork Harbour Commissioners, Cork-Kerry Tourism, Commissioner of Irish Lights. Captained the Irish Admiral's Cup Sailing Team (1979). Tragically killed, March, 1998.

COWLEY, John (b. Meath, 1923) actor and poet, best known for his role as farmer Tom Riordan in the RTÉ soap opera *The Riordans* (1964-79), which won him the TV Actor of the Year Award in 1967. Founder member of the Irish Council against Blood Sports. Died February, 1998.

CREHAN, Martin 'Junior' (b. Clare, 1907) traditional musician and president of the Willie Clancy Summer School in Miltown Malbay. Died August, 1998.

CROWLEY, Niall (b. Dublin, 1926) accountant and MD of KPMG / Stokes Kennedy Crowley. Also former chairman of Allied Irish Banks (1977-89), chairman of

Irish Life Assurance Company, president of Dublin Chamber of Commerce and president of the Institute of Chartered Accountants in Ireland.Received honorary doctorates from the NUI and the University of Maynooth. Died June, 1998.

CUSACK-SMITH, Mollie (b. Dublin) the first woman hunt-Master of the Galway Blazers, singer, dancer and clothes designer. Founded the Bermingham and North Galway Hunt (later renamed the North Galway Hunt) in 1946, retiring in 1984, but remaining as honorary master until her death. Died February, 1998.

de PAOR, Liam (b. Dublin, 1926) archaeologist, historian and writer. Appointed UNESCO adviser to the government of Nepal on the conservation of national monuments (1960s). Joined the Labour Party in 1965 but left in the early 1970s. Lectured in UCD. Regular contributor to RTÉ and *The Irish Times* with his weekly column *As We Are*. Wrote a number of books including *Early Christian Ireland*. Died August, 1998.

DILLON, Charles former Chairman of ESB (1975-91) and the Nuclear Energy Board. Served on the National Science Council, professor of electrical engineering at UCC from 1959. Died January, 1998.

DITTY, Herbie former Belfast Lord Mayor (1992/93) and Ulster Unionist Councillor for 20 years. Lost his council seat in May 1993. Died July, 1998.

ENRIGHT, Michael (b. Clare, 1952) former Democratic Left Senator and Wexford Councillor. Served in the Seanad (1997). Member of Teastas, the Irish National Certificate Authority. Member of the Executive of Democratic Left. Co-founder of the Wexford and New Ross Centres for the Unemployed. Killed in a car accident. Died October, 1997.

FORDE, Seamus (b. 1921) radio, television, film and theatre actor,

best known for his bass-baritone voice. Founder member of the Radio Éireann Players. Starred in radio productions such as *The Entertainer, Piano in the River* and *King Lear*. His film career includes *Quackser, Fortune* and *Cal*. Died June, 1998.

FOSTER, David (b. 1955) Olympic equestrian. One of Ireland's best-known three-day event riders, he participated in more than 100 three-day events and was the leading rider ten times. Was a member of the Irish Army Equitation School from 1974 and represented Ireland at the 1984, 1988 and 196 Olympic Games. He won the World Military Showjumping Championships (1984) and the International Horse Trials in Punchestown. He was tragically killed in a riding accident, April, 1998.

FRIERS, Rowel (b. Belfast, 1920) cartoonist, illustrator, set designer and member and President (1993-94) of the Royal Ulster Academy. His illustrations featured in many publications, as well as in BBC and UTV television programmes. Awarded an MBE (1977) and an honorary MA by the Open University (1981). Died September, 1998.

GIBBONS, Jim (b. 1924) former Fianna Fáil TD and Minister. Appointed Minister for Agriculture in 1970. Served under three Taoisigh - Éamon de Valera, Sean Lemass and Jack Lynch. Died December, 1997.

JOHNSON PRICE, Cecil Appointed Church of Ireland Archdeacon of Glendalough in 1989. Ordained in 1950. Retired in 1994. Honourary Secretary of the Sunday School Society for Ireland. Died November, 1997.

KELLEHER, Dr Michael (b. Cork, 1937) psychiatrist and campaigner for suicide research. Clinical Director of Our Lady's Hospital and St. Anne's Hospital. Director of the National Suicide Research Foundation. Wrote the book *Suicide and the Irish*. Involved in the setting up of the National Task Force on Suicide in 1996. Died

August, 1998.

LARKIN, James (b. 1939). Independent Fianna Fáil Councillor in Letterkenny and former Senator. Appointed to the Seanad (1982). Died September, 1998.

MacCARTHY, Mick (b. Cork, 1965) Cork senior Gaelic footballer (1987-93), winning All-Ireland medals in 1989, 1990 and captained the side defeated by Derry in the 1993 All-Ireland final. Winner of a Cork County Championship medal with his club, O'Donovan Rossa, in 1992. He also captained them to All-Ireland club championship victory in 1993. Killed tragically in a car accident. Died February, 1998.

MacEOIN, Seán *Lieutenant General* (b. Louth, 1910) former Chief of Staff of the Defence Forces. Joined as a Cadet (1930), appointed Commandant of the Military College (1957), appointed First Commander of the United Nations in the Congo (1961/62), for which he received a commendation from the Secretary General of the UN. Appointed Chief of Staff (1960), retired (1971). Died July, 1998.

McGETTIGAN, Shane (b. 1977) Leitrim senior Gaelic footballer and son of singer Charlie McGettigan. Tragically killed in a construction site accident in Boston. Died August, 1998.

MacMAHON, Bryan (b. Kerry, 1909) writer, poet and playwright, best known for his short stories and member of the Irish Academy of Letters. His plays have been produced by the Abbey. His final collection of short stories *A Final Fling: Conversations Between Men and Women* was published in 1998. Died February, 1998.

MacREDMOND, Ted (b. Limerick, 1933) chairman and chief executive of the Aon MacDonagh Boland Insurance Group. Former Chairman of ICC Bank and member of the Board of Aer Lingus. Established Crotty MacRedmond having working with Norwich Union. Died October, 1997.

MADDEN, Declan (b. 1957) Director of Social Affairs and Specialist Services, Irish Business and Employers Confederation (IBEC). Died December, 1997.

MARSDEN, Derek (b. 1931) former presenter with Ulster's Downtown Radio. Piano player and singer, his talents were spotted at an early age. He toured with James Young and hosted his own chat show on BBC. Died May, 1998.

MARTIN, Liam C. (b. 1934) artist, famous for his scenes of Dublin. Contributed regularly to newspapers and published several books, including *Liam C. Martin's Dublin Sketch Book*, *The World of Brendan Behan* and *Ireland on $5 a Day*. Died May, 1998.

MAYNES, Seaghan (b. Belfast, 1916) journalist. Worked as a war reporter covering the blitz and appointed War Correspondent by Reuters News Agency. Appointed Bureau Correspondent for Reuters in Washington after the war. Died August, 1998.

McCARTHY, Cathal (b. 1912) former archdeacon. Ordained for the ministry in 1937, appointed as Dean, Vice-president and President of Holy Cross College, Clonliffe. Appointed Parish Priest of Holy Name, Beechwood Avenue (1964-83). Died December, 1997.

McQUILLAN, Jack socialist TD. First elected as a TD in Roscommon for Clann na Poblachta (1948), he resigned in support of Noel Browne during the 'Mother and Child' controversy (1951). Served as a TD, both as an independent and member of the NPD which he formed with Noel Browne and Noel Hartnett. Appointed a Senator (1965-69). In 1963, he joined the Labour Party but lost the party whip (1968). Died March, 1998.

MITCHELL, Frank (b. Dublin, 1912) archaeologist, geologist, botanist, ornithologist, geographer, social historian and author. Appointed to TCD as a junior dean in (1945-51) and was a senior lecturer and tutor in TCD (1967-70). Retired (1979) and served as a Pro-Chancellor (1985-88). President of the Royal Irish Academy (1976-79), of the Royal Society of Antiquaries in Ireland and of An Taisce. Received the Cunningham Medal of the Royal Irish Academy in 1989. Wrote his autobiography *The Way That I Followed* in 1990. Died November, 1997.

MORGAN, Dermot (b. Dublin, 1952) comedian and actor. Began to contributing comedy scripts to Mike Murphy's *Live Mike* television show (1979-82) on RTÉ. Best known for his acting in the award-winning Channel 4 comedy programme *Fr. Ted* and for his contribution to the satirical RTÉ radio show *Scrap Saturday*. Winner of a Jacob's Radio Award in 1991 and Ireland's National Entertainer of the Year and a BAFTA Award for Best British TV Comedy in 1996. Died March, 1998.

MURPHY, John (b. Mayo, 1924) playwright, author of *The Country Boy*, a play written for the Abbey Theatre (1959). Died May, 1998.

O'BRIEN, Kate Cruise (b. Dublin, 1948) writer and editor. Daughter of Conor (academic, politician and former newspaper editor). Published her first short story at the age of 22, winning the prestigious Hennessy Literary Award. Won the Rooney Prize for her first book *Gift Horse* in 1979. Worked as editor and publisher with Poolbeg. Died March, 1998.

O'CONNOR, Áine (b. Waterford) film maker, presenter and actor. Most recent works include filming Walter Macken's *Brown Lord of the Mountain* which she was to direct (late 1998). Worked as a production assistant and presenter for RTÉ, left in the early 1980s to act in England. Produced TnaG's first film *Draíocht*, written by and starring Gabriel Byrne (1996). Wrote *Leading Hollywood*, a book on Irish Actors in America, which was later televised in 1996. Died March, 1998.

Ó DOHERTY, Maurice former RTÉ radio and television newsreader. Previously worked with CIÉ at Foynes and with the Meteorological Services Central Analysis and Forecasting Office in Dublin. Joined RTÉ in the early 1960s and started presenting music shows but went on to read the news. Left broadcasting in 1984. President of the Irish Actors Equity (1970s). Died April, 1998.

O'DWYER, Paul (b. Mayo, 1907) leading civil rights lawyer, humanitarian. Emigrated to the US in 1926. A Democrat, was appointed New York Commissioner to the UN. Died June, 1998.

O'RAHILLY, Elgin (b. 1903) revolutionary and sister of Kevin Barry. Played a part in an attempt to rescue her brother from Mountjoy Jail in October 1920. Joined Cumann na mBan, was imprisoned and went on hunger strike for 28 days during the Civil War. Died October, 1997.

O'RIORDAN, Dr. Jack (b. 1915) former national director of the Blood Transfusion Service Board (BTSB). Qualified as a medical practitioner in 1938. Responsible for the BTSB's medical, scientific and administrative functions from 1961 until he retired in 1985. The infection of Anti-D blood product with the hepatitis C virus occured during his tenure as director. Died March, 1998.

O'SULLIVAN, Maureen (b. Roscommon, 1911) film actress and mother of actresses Mia and Tisa Farrow. Appeared in over 60 films, most famously as Jane to Johnny Weissmuller's Tarzan, and starred on television and on Broadway. Other films include *Song O' My Heart* (1930), *David Copperfield* (1935), *Pride and Prejudice* (1940), *All I Desire* (1953), *Never too Late* (1965). Died June, 1998.

PERDUE, Dr Gordon (b. 1910) former Church of Ireland Bishop of Cork, Cloyne and Ross. Ordained in 1933, appointed Archdeacon of Killaloe (1951) and elected Bishop of Killaloe, Kilfenora,

Clonfert and Kilmacduagh (1953 and 1957). Retired in 1978. Died August, 1998.

POWELL, Enoch (b. Birmingham, 1912) former Conservative Minister for Health (1960-63), Ulster Unionist MP for South Down (1974-87) and professor. Infamous for his "rivers of blood" speech on immigrants from the colonies, made in Birmingham, addressing a group of Tory supporters. Died February, 1998.

PRENDERGAST, Michael (b. Kerry). Former Fine Gael Senator (1953-73).

PRINGLE, Mr Justice Denis (b. Dublin, 1902) former High Court Judge, appointed in 1969. President of the Special Criminal Court (1974-76). First Chairman of An Bord Pleanála (1976). Died August, 1998.

RHATIGAN, Lewis (b. Longford, 1918) former managing director of Bord na Móna (1973-83). Joined Bord na Móna (1946) and became closely involved in the development of the ESB's milled peat power stations and briquetting. Died April, 1998.

SHANLEY, Mr Justice Peter (b. Dublin, 1945) High Court Judge. Chairman and vice-chairman of the the the Bar Council. Called to the

Bar in 1968. Appointed Senior Counsel (1982) and to the High Court (1996). Died September, 1998.

SPAIN, Frank (b. 1945) president of the Circuit Court. Called to the Bar in 1968 and the Inner Bar in 1980. Appointed to the Circuit Court in 1987 and became President in 1991. Appointed to the UN Administrative Tribunal in 1993. Died December, 1997.

TAYLOR, Frank (b. 1915) former Fine Gael TD for Clare. Served in the Dáil (1959-81). A prominent member of the IFA, the ICMSA and the Mid-Western Regional Development Organisation. Father of Senator Madeline Taylor-Quinn. Died April, 1998.

VARD, Jack (b. 1926) former wrestler and businessman. A champion wrestler, he won Irish championships and two British Lightweight Titles (1949, 1952). Represented Ireland at the 1952 Olympic Games in Helsinki. A keen chess player, he obtained two draws against the two chess masters Alexhine and Kilkonoski in simultaneous matches. Died April, 1998.

WALSH, Bernie (b. Galway, 1959) stage manager of the Druid Theatre in Galway. Started working with the Druid Theatre in

1983. Died August, 1998.

WALSH, Justice Brian (b. Dublin, 1918) former Supreme Court Judge. Called to the Bar (1941), admitted to the Inner Bar (1954) and appointed High Court Judge (1959-61). Appointed Supreme Court Judge (1961-90). Former member of the European Court of Human Rights in Strasbourg. Leader of the Irish legal team on the Anglo-Irish Law Enforcement Commission in 1974. President of the First Law Reform Commission (1975-85). Retired from the Supreme Court in 1990. Died March, 1998.

WHITTINGTON, Rev Stanley (b. Derry, 1926) former President of the Methodist Church in Ireland (1988-1992), working both in Ireland and Ghana. Died April, 1998.

WRIGHT, Billy (b. England, 1960) Loyalist Paramilitary (known as King Rat). Returned to Northern Ireland (1964). Expelled from the UVF in 1996 and ordered to leave Northern Ireland, he then formed the Loyalist Volunteer Force. Sentenced for eight years in March 1997 for intimidation. Shot dead by an INLA prisoner at the Maze Prison. Died December, 1997.

❐

Listed below are the names of the 29 people who were murdered in the Omagh bombing atrocity which occured on Saturday, August 15, 1998.

BARKER, James (12) Buncrana, Co. Donegal. Schoolboy Moved with family to Donegal from England a year previously. Footballer (player and supporter), cub scout and singer. Killed while on day trip to Omagh.

BLASCO, Fernando (12) Madrid, Spain. Spanish schoolboy on exchange programme with Donegal youngsters. Killed while on day trip to Omagh.

BRESLIN, Geraldine (43) Omagh, Co. Tyrone. Mother of one. Shop assistant in town centre clothes shop.

CARTWRIGHT, Debra Anne (20) Omagh, Co. Tyrone. Town centre

shop assistant.

CONWAY, Gareth (18) Carrickmore, Co. Tyrone. Student, about to enroll at Magee College, gaelic footballer.

DEVINE, Breda (20 months) Donemana, Co. Tyrone. Toddler, killed while in town having shoes fitted for flowergirl duties at uncle's wedding.

DOHERTY, Oran (8) Buncrana, Co. Donegal. Schoolboy. Keen Celtic FC fan. Killed while on day trip to Omagh.

GALLAGHER, Aidan (21) Omagh, Co. Tyrone. Self-employed mechanic.

GIBSON, Esther (36) Beragh, Co. Tyrone. Factory worker and Sunday school teacher. Engaged to be married.

GRIMES, Mary (65) Beragh, Co. Tyrone. Wife, Cork-born mother of 11 and grandmother.

HAWKES, Olive (60) Omagh, Co. Tyrone. Mother of two.

HUGHES, Julie (21) Omagh, Co. Tyrone. Student at Dundee University. Worked in town centre photo shop.

LOGUE, Brenda (17) Omagh, Co. Tyrone. Sixth year student. Played gaelic football for Tyrone ladies.

McCOMBE, Anne (49) Omagh, Co. Tyrone. Mother of two. Worked in town centre clothes shop. Sang in local choir.

McCRORY, Brian (54) Omagh, Co. Tyrone. Father of three. Crane-hire firm owner.

McFARLAND, Samantha (17) Omagh, Co. Tyrone. Student and voluntary worker for Oxfam charity shop. Died with best friend Lorrayne Wilson.

McGRATH, Sean (61) Omagh, Co. Tyrone. Businessman. Died in street he was born in.

McLAUGHLIN, Seán (12) Buncrana, Co. Donegal. Schoolboy. Football fanatic, altar-boy at local church. Killed while on day trip to Omagh.

MARLOW, Jolene (17) Omagh, Co. Tyrone. Student and talented gaelic footballer and camogie player. Member of Amnesty International.

MONAGHAN, Avril (30) Augher, Co. Tyrone. Mother of four. Expecting twins. Died with baby daughter and mother.

MONAGHAN, Maura (18 months) Augher, Co. Tyrone. Toddler, died with her mother and grandmother.

RADFORD, Alan (16) Omagh, Co. Tyrone. High School student.

RAMOS, Rocio Abad (23) Madrid, Spain. Degree student who worked with Spanish exchange students. On her fifth visit to Ireland. Killed while on day trip to Omagh.

RUSHE, Elizabeth (57) Omagh, Co. Tyrone. Mother of three. Businesswoman in Omagh town centre.

SKELTON, Philomena (49) Drumquin, Co. Tyrone. Mother of four. Buying school uniforms in town.

SHORT, Veda (56) Omagh, Co. Tyrone. Grandmother and mother of four. Buyer for town centre clothes shop. Saw her grandchild Lee born the morning she died.

WHITE, Bryan (26) Omagh, Co. Tyrone. Council worker and keen horticulturist. Died with his father Fred.

WHITE, Fred (60) Omagh, Co. Tyrone. Father of two. Worked for local education board. Farmer and horticulturist.

WILSON, Lorraine (15) Omagh, Co. Tyrone. Student and voluntary worker for Oxfam charity shop. Sportswoman who played hockey and went horse-riding.

❑

"In our terrible experience of the last 30 years, Omagh was the worst atrocity of all. Is it too much to ask or too much to hope that it will be the last atrocity of all?"

Bishop Edward Daly

POLITICS

Northern Ireland: a different country ?

By **Dónal Kelly**, RTÉ Political Editor

More than 90% of the Republic's electorate endorsed the Good Friday agreement in a national referendum, but for many outside the border counties, the North is a different country.

AT the end of January, 1972, hundreds of Dubliners took to the streets in a sustained and angry protest over the shooting dead of 13 people in Derry's Bogside, on the now infamous Bloody Sunday. After two days of virtual siege, the British Embassy building on the city's elegant Merrion Square, had been burned to the ground.

Twenty-six years later, nine out of ten people in the Republic voted for the removal of the constitutional claim to Northern Ireland as part of an agreement which effectively underpinned the partition of the country for the foreseeable future. The intervening three decades had seen a huge divergence in the development of society North and South of the border.

As violence drove the Northern communities further apart and the death toll inexorably increased, the people of the Republic were broadening their horizons, enjoying the advantages of membership of the European community and gaining in national self-confidence as their country staked its claim to a place on the world stage. Although the violence in Northern ireland dominated the news media in the South and, increasingly, the seemingly fruitless search for a political solution, ordinary people came to resent the almost daily recitation of bloody deeds and the constant repetition of sterile political slogans. It was said that amongst senior editors in one leading Dublin newspaper, a northern lead story and especially a political one, was more and more regarded as a significant reader turn-off.

This ambivalence among the republic's citizens towards Northern Ireland and its problems, was reflected in the findings of opinion polls - particularly during election campaigns. Repeatedly, the polls showed the North was in the lower half of any list of voters concerns, trailing well behind taxation, jobs, health, crime and social welfare issues. Yes, they favoured Irish unity and they opposed any dilution of the constitutional claim to the north, but they gave a firm thumbs down to any suggestion that they might have to pay more in taxation as a price for the ending of partition.

For many people living outside the Republic's border counties, the North, to all intents and purposes, was a foreign country. Businessmen travelled there in the furtherance of cross-border trade, shoppers sped northwards to Belfast, Newry and Jonesboro for cheap electrical goods and beer. For a time, Gay Byrne's radio show's comparison of prices, North and South, filled more Belfast-bound trains, than the rail companies most expensive advertising campaigns. But the North, for all its superb scenic attractions was not a holiday destination for southerners - not a place they empathised with. The unpredictable and indiscriminate nature of the violence there was obviously a huge deterrent, but there was also a cultural divide.

In his authoritative study of prejudice and tolerance in Ireland, Fr. Michael McGreil, found that over half of those interviewed in the greater Dublin area agreed with the proposition that northerners on all sides tended to be extreme and unreasonable. More pointedly, the respondents also indicated they would be happier to have someone from England, Scotland and Wales marry into their families ahead of a person from Northern Ireland. And more than four out of ten of them agreed that the North and the Republic were separate nations.

Southerners were alienated by the intransigence and tribalism which dominated northern life. The ritual posturing, irredentist sloganeering, fixation with marching and the unyielding prejudice of the hard-liners on either side of the divide were far removed from what the people of the south perceived to be normal political discourse. In a country where there's an intense interest in politics, albeit qualified by a good deal of scepticism and questioning, the failure of the northern parties to escape from the strait-jackets of the past was regarded with disbelief, dismay and despair.

Southerners responded by getting on with their own lives, shutting out the cacophony of immoderate soundbites which punctuated the television and radio news reports from Belfast. They were deeply moved by the human tragedies behind the regular litany of atrocities which marked the passing decades like so many blood-stained milestones. But the politics of the last bomb and bullet only deepened their feelings of helplessness and frustration.

When the bombs went off in Dublin and Monaghan, they experienced for themselves, the devastation and trauma which marked the daily lives of people in the cities and towns of the North. The attacks were a bloody reminder that the south could so easily become embroiled in a wider conflict on the island.

Yet, for many, the north remained a different country.

That, however, was not a thesis the governments of the Republic could accept much as they despaired at times of ever finding a path towards a resolution of the troubles. As Dick Spring's advisor, Fergus Finley, wrote in his book on the Labour Party's involvement in coalition: "The unwritten policy of successive Irish governments was one of containment - whatever happens, don't let it spill down here."

In fact, the Northern problem came to occupy an inordinate amount of government time. In the years before the Celtic Tiger roared, when national finances were severely strained with high taxation and cutbacks the norm, it was costing the Republic millions of pounds annually in extra security along the border. It also impacted severely on tourism revenue and created huge difficulties for agencies responsible for selling Ireland abroad as a base for job-creating industry.

As the bombings and killings continued, with the threat of an island wide conflagration never far away, the search for a Northern settlement became the top policy priority of all Dublin governments. It was a long, frustrating and often unrewarding process which won them few votes. But as the men of violence eventually wearied of the unrelenting warfare and stepped back from the abyss, the British and Irish administrations, and the Northern parties, forged the multi-layered agreement signed in Belfast on Good Friday.

One outcome of the long search for peace, was the enormous improvement in relations between Britain and Ireland. Now there's barely a murmur of protest when members of the British royal family visit the Republic. The Taoiseach, Bertie Ahern, is able to extend an invitation to the Prime Minister to address the Dáil. Tony Blair is only too willing to accept.

Equally, in the North, the once unthinkable is becoming accepted as the norm. The Ulster Unionist leader and North's First Minister, David Trimble, travels south for talks at Government Buildings with Mr. Ahern. Top of the agenda - the structures for the future government of Northern Ireland. But perhaps the biggest indication of how attitudes North and south are changing as the national will for peace takes hold, was the presence of Mr Trimble at the funeral Mass for the three young Buncrana boys killed in the Omagh bombing - that and the applause which greeted him.

Despite the horror of the attack - which triggered a huge outpouring of sympathy south of the border - that moment in the parish church in Cockhill was a potent symbol of the hope that at long last, the black beast of violence may have been vanquished for good.

POLITICS R.O.I.

INTRODUCTION TO THE REPUBLIC OF IRELAND

Explanatory Notes on the President, Parliament and Government

The Republic of Ireland is a parliamentary democracy.

PARLIAMENT: The Oireachtas consists of the President and the Legislature, which has two houses - Dáil Éireann, which is a house of representatives, and Seanad Éireann, which is a senate. The basis of the political system was set out in the Constitution of Ireland, enacted by referendum in July 1937, the power of the Oireachtas is vested in the people.

ELECTIONS: General Elections must be held at least once every five years. The 166 Teachtaí Dála (members of the Dáil) in Dáil Éireann are elected directly by the people by a system of proportional representation and a single transferable vote. Seanad Éireann has 60 Seanadoirí (Senators); 11 are nominated by the Taoiseach, 6 are elected by the graduates of Trinity College Dublin and the National University of Ireland, and the remaining 43 are elected by five panels. The electoral constituency of the Seanad comprises of incoming TDs, the outgoing members of the Seanad, and members of county councils and county borough councils. Eighteen is the age at which a person becomes eligible to vote, and candidates for the Dáil or Seanad must be aged 21 or older, a presidential candidate must be aged over 35.

THE OFFICE OF PRESIDENT OF IRELAND

HEAD OF STATE: The Head of State is the President. Presidential elections are held every seven years, and the President is elected by the direct vote of the people. The current president is Mary McAleese *(pictured right)*.

OFFICE OF PRESIDENT: The office and function of the President of Ireland is dealt with in Articles 12 and 13 of the Constitution. Although the President does not have any executive powers and acts only on the advice and authority of the government, she/he does hold a limited number of functions. All Bills passed by the Oireachtas are promulgated by the President and she/he may, after consultation with the Council of State*, refer any Bill (excluding money bills) to the Supreme Court to attest its constitutionality. The supreme command of the defence forces is vested in the President (subject to the 1954 Defence Act), and she/he receives and accredits ambassadors.

THE PRESIDENT AND THE DÁIL: The President appoints the Taoiseach on the nomination of Dáil Éireann and appoints government ministers on the advice of the Taoiseach. The Taoiseach also advises him/her on accepting the resignations of ministers, and on the summoning and dismissing of the Dáil (the President reserves the right of refusing to dissolve the Dáil but this right has, as yet, never been exercised).

ELECTIONS: The President is elected by the direct vote of the people, and only Irish citizens resident in the 26 counties are entitled to vote in a Presidential election. A Presidential candidate must be an Irish citizen over the age of 35 years. The duration of a term of office is seven years, and a President may serve no more than two terms.

The members of the Council of State are the incumbent Taoiseach, Tánaiste, Ceann Comhairle, Cathaoirleach of the Seanad, Attorney General, President of the High Court and the Chief Justice. Other members are any previous Taoisigh, President, or Chief Justice willing to serve and up to seven nominees of the President.

STATE EMBLEMS OF THE REPUBLIC OF IRELAND

Name of State, National Flag, Emblem, and National Anthem

NAME OF STATE: Article 4 of the 1937 Constitution states 'The name of the State is Éire, or in the English language, *Ireland*'. From independence in 1922 until the enactment of the constitution, the state was known as Saorstat Éireann or the Irish Free State. The Republic of Ireland Act 1948 allowed for the state to be described as the the Republic of Ireland, but Article 4 naming the state as Éire has not been altered.

The name Éire is derived from the name Ériu, a goddess in Irish mythology. Julius Caesar gave Ireland its Latin name when he referred to it as *Hibernia* in the first century B.C., while the ancient Greek cartographer Ptolemy referred to Ireland as *iouernia*.

THE NATIONAL FLAG: Article 7 of the Constitution states 'The national flag is the tricolour of green, white and orange'. The tricolour is rectangular, the width being twice the depth. The colours are of equal size, vertically disposed with the green closest to, and the orange furthest from, the staff. The colours signify the union between older

Gaelic and Anglo-Norman Ireland (green) and the newer Protestant Planter Ireland (orange), while the white, in the words of Thomas Francis Meagher 'signifies a lasting truce between the Orange and the Green'. It was the official flag from independence, and its position was formally enshrined in the Constitution. In 1848 Meagher - a member of Daniel O'Connell's Repeal Association - received the tricolour as a gift from the citizens of France (on whose flag the Irish tricolour is based). Initially a flag of the 'Young Ireland' movement, it came to be identified as the national flag in the aftermath of the 1916 Rising when it was flown from the General Post Office.

THE ARMS OF STATE: The Arms of State have no official statute or regulation, but the President's seal of office has an heraldic harp engraved on it. It is also emblazoned on the President's standard as a gold harp with silver strings on a sky blue background. The harp - modelled on the 14th century Brian Boru harp - is depicted on the coinage and banknotes of the state and is used by all government departments.

THE NATIONAL ANTHEM: The national anthem is Amhrán na bhFiann (The Soldier's Song). Peadar Kearney (1883-1942) wrote the lyrics, and Patrick Heeney (1881-1911) helped him compose the music. The anthem was composed in 1907 and first published in 1912 in the newspaper *Irish Freedom*. It was immediately adopted by the Irish Volunteers and was formally adopted as the national anthem in 1926 replacing 'God Save Ireland'.

REPUBLIC OF IRELAND POLITICAL PARTIES
Main political parties in the Republic of Ireland

FIANNA FÁIL
13 Upper Mount Street, Dublin 2. Tel. (01) 6761551
www.fiannafail.ie

Founded: 1926 by Éamon de Valera. Fianna Fáil (Soldiers of Destiny) comprised of anti-treaty Sinn Féin members. The party did not sit in Dáil Éireann until 1927.
First Leader: Éamon de Valera (1926-59).
Current Party Leader: An Taoiseach Bertie Ahern TD since 1994 *(pictured above)*.
Party Chairman: Dr. Rory O'Hanlon TD.
General Secretary: Martin Macken.
Seats: Dáil Éireann: 76, Seanad Éireann: 30, European Parliament: 7.
European Alliance: Union for Europe
Former Taoisigh: Six - Éamon de Valera (re-elected six times), Seán Lemass (re-elected twice), Jack Lynch (re-elected twice), Charles Haughey (re-elected three times), Albert Reynolds and Bertie Ahern.
In Government: Fianna Fáil was responsible for the drafting of the Constitution in 1937, maintaining Irish neutrality during World War II, the accession of Ireland into the European Economic Community in 1973 and the introduction of major housing developments in the 1960s.
Aims: The aims, as set out in 1926, and still broadly holding today, are to establish an agreed Ireland through inclusive political talks with structures based on partnership and equality throughout the island; to restore and promote the Irish language as a living language of the people; to develop a distinctive national life within the European context, incorporating the diverse traditions of the Irish people; to guarantee religious and civil liberties and eradicate all forms of discrimination; to develop the resources and wealth of Ireland to their full potential through a spirit of enterprise, self-reliance and social partnership; to protect the natural environment and heritage of Ireland; to maintain a balance between town and country and between the regions; to promote the family and a wider sense of social responsibility; and to reform the laws and institutions of state, making

them more humane and caring.
The party aims to maintain Ireland's status as a sovereign nation within the European Union and pledges to retain neutrality but to take part in genuine peace-keeping missions.

FINE GAEL
51 Upper Mount Street, Dublin 2. Tel. (01) 6761573
www.finegael.com

Founded: 1933 by the amalgamation of Cumann na nGaedheal, the Centre Party and the Army Comrades Association (the Blueshirts). Fine Gael translates as 'Tribes of the Irish People'
First Leader: General Éoin O'Duffy (1933-34).
Current Party Leader: John Bruton TD since 1990 *(pictured above)*.
Party Chairman: Phil Hogan TD.
General Secretary: Jim Miley.
Seats: Dáil Éireann: 53, Seanad Éireann: 16, European Parliament: 4.
European Alliance: European People's Party.
Former Taoisigh: Four - John A. Costello (re-elected twice), Liam Cosgrave, Garret FitzGerald (re-elected twice) and John Bruton
In Government: Fine Gael, as major party in coalition governments, was instrumental in the Declaration of the Republic of Ireland in 1949, the signing of the Sunningdale Agreement in 1973, the convening of the New Ireland Forum in 1983 and the signing of the Anglo-Irish Agreement in 1985. The party is committed to constitutional change and has introduced referenda which legalised divorce (1995) and approved the denial of bail to likely re-offenders (1996).
Aims: Fine Gael has a policy of facilitating enterprise through a mixture of state encouragement for private enterprise and direct state involvement. It wants to see decision making devolved to the appropriate level, particularly involving women and young people, and it promotes fairer opportunities in education, an improvement in social welfare provisions and greater tax equity. On Northern Ireland, the party recognises and respects

both the nationalist and unionist traditions and believes inclusive all-party negotiations are the best way to achieve reconciliation.

Fine Gael believes that Ireland's future lies within a safe and prosperous Europe.

THE LABOUR PARTY
17 Ely Place, Dublin 2. Tel. (01) 6612615
www.labour.ie

Founded: 1912 by James Connolly, Jim Larkin and William O'Brien as political wing of Irish Trade Union Congress.
First Leader: Tom Johnston (1922-27).
Current Party Leader: Ruairi Quinn TD since 1997 *(on left)*.
Party Chairman: John O'Brien.
General Secretary: Ray Kavanagh.
Seats: Dáil Éireann: 18, Seanad Éireann: 3, European Parliament: 1.
European Alliance: Party of European Socialists.
Former Taoisigh: None.
In Government: The party has formed part of seven different coalition governments with its leader holding the position of Tánaiste on each occasion. In government, the party's achievements reflect those of their coalition partners. From 1993 until June 1997, when in government, Labour TDs held the important ministerial portfolios of Finance, Foreign Affairs and Education, among others.
Aims: A socialist party, it hopes to use the four main tenets of socialism, namely, freedom, equality, community and democracy, to build a just society. Twelve trade unions are affiliated to the party, representing 50% of all trade union members in the state.

The party's successful campaign on behalf of its nominated candidate, Mary Robinson, in the 1990 presidential campaign remains one of their finest achievements to date.

DEMOCRATIC LEFT
69 Middle Abbey Street Dublin 1. Tel. (01) 8729550
www.connect.ie/users/dl

Founded: March 1992 following a split in the Workers' Party. It is organised in both Northern Ireland and the Republic.
First and Current Party Leader: Proinsias De Rossa TD since 1992 *(pictured left)*.
Party Chairman: Pat Brady.
General Secretary: John Gallagher.
Seats: Dáil Éireann: 4, Seanad Éireann: 0, European Parliament: 0.
Former Taoisigh: None.
In Government: Democratic Left has been in government once, as part of a 'rainbow' coalition with Fine Gael and the Labour Party. Its leader, Proinsias de Rossa, was Minister for Social Welfare in that government.

Aims: The party is a modern, democratic and socialist organisation whose main policy document is 'Strategy 2000', published in 1993. It welcomes moves towards European union along democratic and non-military lines, wants to underline the clear separation of Church and State and is opposed to discrimination on any grounds. The party's belief that the Republic's territorial claim on Northern Ireland should be removed and replaced by an aspiration for the unity of the people of the island and that the future of Northern Ireland must be decided by those who live there has been borne out by the ratification of the 'Good Friday' Agreement.

PROGRESSIVE DEMOCRATS
25 South Frederick Street, Dublin 2 Tel. (01) 6794399
http://ireland.iol.ie/pd/

Founded: 1985 by Des O'Malley, Mary Harney and other former members of Fianna Fáil following a split in that party.
First Leader: Des O'Malley (1985-93).
Current Party Leader: Tánaiste Mary Harney TD since 1993 *(pictured left)*.
Party Chairman: Alderman Declan McDonnell.
National Organiser: Garvan McGinley.
Seats: Dáil Éireann: 4, Seanad Éireann: 4, European Parliament: 0.
Former Taoisigh: None.
In Government: The party is currently in government and was in government once before, in a coalition with Fianna Fáil (1989-92). As junior coalition partners, they played an important part in Ireland's presidency of the EC (July-December 1990) and in securing the ratification of the Maastricht Treaty in 1992.
Aims: The party advocates the lowering of tax rates, the abolition of employees' PRSI, the tightening of bail laws, a new constitution and Bill of Rights for Northern Ireland, increased access to adult education and the creation of more prison places. The party favours further integration with Europe and supports the devolution of some decision making to local level.

THE GREEN PARTY
5A Upper Fownes Street, Dublin 2. Tel. (01) 6790012
http://greenparty.ie.eu.org

Founded: 1981 as the Ecology Party of Ireland, renamed The Green Party in 1986.
Current Co-ordinator: Mary Bowers.
Party Chairman: Functions carried out by a 14 member co-ordinating committee.
General Secretary: Functions carried out by a 14 member co-ordinating committee.
Seats: Dáil Éireann: 2, Seanad Éireann: 0, European Parliament: 2.
European Alliance: Greens.
Former Taoisigh: None.
In Government: The party has never been in government.
Aims: The Green Party supports open government, locally based decision making, the use of renewable

energy sources, recycling, neutral peace keeping in Northern Ireland, workers co-operatives and small businesses, and the wider use of public transport. The party is opposed to the depopulation of rural areas and consequent over-crowding in cities, pollution, the exploitation of animals, the control of industry by large national and multi-national companies, nuclear power and weapons, land and property speculation, the exploitation of the Third World, and both state and paramilitary violence in Northern Ireland.

SINN FÉIN
See entry in Northern Ireland Political Parties.

MINOR POLITICAL PARTIES IN THE REPUBLIC OF IRELAND

Party	Address	Phone
Communist Party of Ireland	James Connolly House, 43 East Essex Street, Temple Bar, D2	01 6711943
Christian Solidarity Party	54a Booterstown Avenue, Blackrock, Co. Dublin	01 2880273
Independent Fianna Fáil	Plunkett O'Boyle Terrace, Letterkenny, Co. Donegal	074 27754
The National Party	16 Revington Park, North Circular Road, Limerick	061 326599
The Natural Law Party	39 Pembroke Lane, Ballsbridge, D4	01 6689773
Muíntír na hÉireann	87 Griffith Avenue, D9	01 2831484
Republican Sinn Féin	Teach Dáithí Ó Conaill, 223 Parnell St, D1	01 8729747
Socialist Party	141 Thomas Street, D8	01 6772592
Socialist Workers' Party	105 O'Hogan Road, Ballyfermot, D10	
The Workers' Party	28 Gardiner Pace, D1	01 8740716

R.O.I. POLITICS - "THE FAMILY TREE"
Origins of the main Irish Political Parties

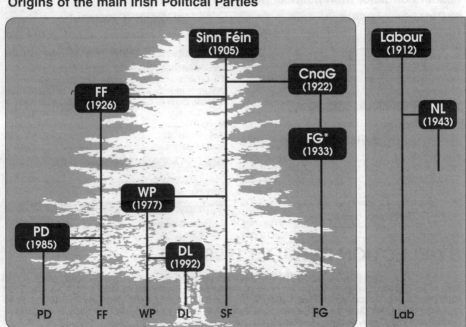

Abbreviations: **(SF)** Sinn Féin; **(FF)** Fianna Fáil; **(PD)** Progressive Democrats; **(WP)** Workers Party; **(DL)** Democratic Left; **(CnaG)** Cumann na nGaedheal; **(FG)** Fine Gael; **(Lab)** Labour; **(NL)** National Labour.
** Fine Gael: Amalgamation of **Cumann na nGaedheal, National Centre Party, Army Comrades Association**.*

REPUBLIC OF IRELAND GOVERNMENT SYSTEM

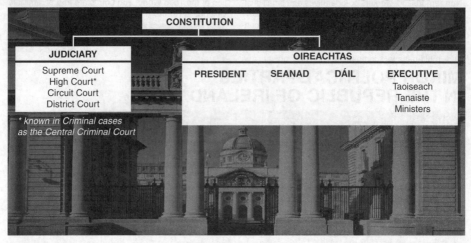

```
                        CONSTITUTION

        JUDICIARY                          OIREACHTAS

     Supreme Court          PRESIDENT    SEANAD    DÁIL    EXECUTIVE
     High Court*                                           Taoiseach
     Circuit Court                                         Tanaiste
     District Court                                        Ministers

   * known in Criminal cases
   as the Central Criminal Court
```

REPUBLIC OF IRELAND POLITICAL PARTY LEADERS
Leaders of major Irish political parties, 1922-1997

FIANNA FÁIL

Éamon de Valera	(1926-59)
Seán Lemass	(1959-66)
Jack Lynch	(1966-79)
Charles J. Haughey	(1979-92)
Albert Reynolds	(1992-94)
Bertie Ahern	(1994-)

CUMANN NA nGAEDHEAL

William T. Cosgrave	(1922-33)

FINE GAEL

Eoin O'Duffy	(1933-34)
William T. Cosgrave	(1935-44)
Richard Mulcahy	(1944-59)
James Dillon	(1959-65)
Liam Cosgrave	(1965-77)
Garret FitzGerald	(1977-87)
Alan Dukes	(1987-90)
John Bruton	(1990-)

CLANN NA POBLACHTA

Seán MacBride	(1946-65)

THE LABOUR PARTY

Tom Johnson	(1922-27)
T.J. O'Connell	(1927-32)
William Norton	(1932-60)
Brendan Corish	(1960-77)
Frank Cluskey	(1977-81)
Michael O'Leary	(1981-82)
Dick Spring	(1982-97)
Ruairí Quinn	(1997-)

PROGRESSIVE DEMOCRATS

Desmond O'Malley	(1985-93)
Mary Harney	(1993-)

DEMOCRATIC LEFT

Proinsias De Rossa	(1992-)

BY-ELECTION RESULTS 1998

DUBLIN NORTH (12 March 1998)

Reason for Election: Resignation of Ray Burke (FF) **Candidates:** 19; **Electorate:** 66,112; **Turnout:** 50.26%; **Total Valid Poll:** 33,046; **Quota:** 16,524. **First Count:** Sean Ryan (Lab) 11,012; Michael Kennedy (FF) 10,334; Philip Jenkinson (FG) 3,185; Clare Daly (SP) 2,692; Paul Martin (GP) 1,092; Paul Donnelly (SF) 1,088; Rena Condrot-Ruigrok (Ind) 780; Ciaran Goulding (Ind) 682; Angela Keaveney (CSP) 565; Finian Fallon (PD) 533; Gertie Shields (Ind) 452; Joe Holohan (DL) 225; Elaine Rooney (Ind) 176; John McDonald (Ind) 107; Alan Nagle (Ind) 44; Peter Farrelly (Ind) 34; Benny Cooney (Ind) 18; Noel P. O'Neill (NLP) 15; Jim Tallon (Ind) 12. **Fourteenth Count:** Sean Ryan (Lab) 16,896; Michael Kennedy (FF) 13,633. **Elected:** Sean Ryan (Lab).

LIMERICK EAST (12 March 1998)

Reason for Election: Death of Jim Kemmy (Lab). **Candidates:** 11; **Electorate:** 78,461; **Turnout:** 54.73%; **Total Valid Poll:** 42,713; **Quota:** 21,352. **First Count:** Jan O'Sullivan (Lab) 10,619; Mary Jackman (FG) 10,445; Sandra Marsh (FF) 10,173; Tim O'Malley (PD) 4,287; John Ryan (DL) 3,868; Jenny Marie Shapland (SF) 909; John Gilligan (Ind) 850; Nora Bennis (NP) 700; Eric Sheppard (GP) 546; Barney Sheehan (Ind) 198; Noel Hannon (Ind) 108. **Fifth Count:** Jan O'Sullivan (Lab) 22,888; Sandra Marsh (FF) 15,188. **Elected:** Jan O'Sullivan.

MEMBERS OF SEANAD ÉIREANN

Cathaoirleach: Brian Mullooly **Leas Chathaoirleach:** Liam T. Cosgrave

Eddie BOHAN	FF	18 Orwell Park, Dublin 6.
Enda BONNER	FF	Gweedore Road, Dungloe, Co. Donegal.
Paddy BURKE	FG	161 Knockaphunta, Westport Road, Castlebar, Co. Mayo.
Ernie CAFFERY	FG	Garden Street, Ballina, Co. Mayo.
Peter CALLANAN	FF	Ballymountain, Innishannon, Co. Cork.
Donie CASSIDY	FF	Church Street, Castlepollard, Co. Westmeath.
Frank CHAMBERS	FF	Main Street, Newport, Co. Mayo.
Paul COGHLAN	FG	95 New Street, Killarney, Co. Kerry.
John CONNOR	FG	Cloonshanville, Frenchpark, Co. Roscommon.
Fintan COOGAN	FG	Menlo Park, Galway.
Liam T. COSGRAVE	FG	Leinster House, Kildare Street, Dublin 2.
Joe COSTELLO	Lab	75 Lr. Sean McDermott Street, Dublin 1.
Margaret COX	FF	7 Fr. Griffin Road, Galway, Co. Galway.
Denis (Dino) CREGAN	FG	7 Elm Grove, Ballinlough, Cork.
John CREGAN	FF	Church Street, Drumcollogher, Co. Limerick.
John DARDIS	PD	Belmont House, Newbridge, Co. Kildare.
Avril DOYLE	FG	Kitestown House, Crossabeg Co. Wexford.
Joe DOYLE	FG	14 Simmonscourt Terrace, Donnybrook, Dublin 4.
Willie FARRELL	FF	5 Mullaghmore Road, Cliffoney, Co. Sligo.
Michael FINNERAN	FF	Feevagh Dysart, Ballinasloe, Co. Roscommon.
Liam FITZGERALD	FF	117 Tonlegee Road, Raheny, Dublin 5.
Tom FITZGERALD	FF	Dingle Heights, Ballinaboola, Dingle, Co. Kerry.
Dermot FITZPATRICK	FF	18 Navan Road, Dublin 7.
Pat GALLAGHER	Lab	8 Hophill Avenue, Tullamore, Co. Offaly.
Jim GIBBONS	PD	St Anne's, Athy Road, Carlow.
Camillus GLYNN	FF	Newbrook Road, Cloonmore, Mullingar, Co. Westmeath.
Des HANAFIN	FF	Parnell Street, Thurles, Co. Tipperary.
Edward HAUGHEY	FF	Ballyedmond Castle, Rostrevor, Co. Down.
Maurice HAYES	Ind	5 Bullseye Park, Downpatrick, BT30 6RX.
Tom HAYES	FG	Cahervillahow, Golden, Cashel, Co. Tipperary.
Mary HENRY	Ind	12 Burlington Road, Dublin 4.
Mary JACKMAN	FG	Newtown, Castletroy, Limerick.
Tony KETT	FF	54 Whitethorn Road, Artane, Dublin 5.
Helen KEOGH	PD	12 Beech Court, Killiney, Co. Dublin.
Dan KIELY	FF	Doonard, Tarbert, Co. Kerry.
Rory KIELY	FF	Cloncrippa, Feenagh, Kilmallock, Co. Limerick
Mick LANIGAN	FF	St Judes, Chapel Avenue, Kilkenny.
Ann LEONARD	FF	Stranagarvagh, Smithboro, Co.Monaghan.
Don LYDON	FF	16 Stillorgan Park Avenue, Stillorgan, Co. Dublin.
Jarlath McDONAGH	FG	Sligo House, Turloughmore, Co. Galway
Paddy McGOWAN	FF	Ballindrait, Lifford, Co. Donegal.
Maurice MANNING	FG	13 Haddington Place, Dublin 4.
Paschal MOONEY	FF	Carrick Road, Drumshanbo, Co. Leitrim.
Pat MOYLAN	FF	Cuba Avenue, Banagher, Co. Offaly.
Brian MULLOOLY	FF	Church Street, Strokestown, Co. Roscommon.
David NORRIS	Ind	18 North Great George's Street, Dublin 1.
Francis O'BRIEN	FF	Corwillian, Latton, Castleblayney, Co. Monaghan.
Denis O'DONOVAN	FF	Montrose House, Slip, Bantry, Co. Cork.
Fergus O'DOWD	FG	24 St. Mary's Villas, Drogheda, Co. Louth.
Kathleen O'MEARA	Lab	Lisheen, Portroe, Nenagh. Co Tipperary.
Labhras Ó MURCHU	FF	An Boithrín Glas, Caiseal Mumhan, Co. Thiobraid Arann.
Joe O'TOOLE	Ind	Kilsallaghan, Co. Dublin.
Ann ORMONDE	FF	2 Arburn Road, Dublin 4.
Máirin QUILL	PD	1 Wellesley Terrace, Wellington Road, Cork.
Fergal QUINN	Ind	Leinster House, Kildare Street, Dublin 2.
Therese RIDGE	FG	4 St. Patrick's Avenue, Clondalkin, Dublin 22.
Shane ROSS	Ind	Leinster House, Kildare Street, Dublin 2.
Brendan RYAN	Ind	Simon Community, Anderson Quay, Cork.
Madeline TAYLOR-QUINN	FG	Frances Street, Kilrush, Co. Clare.
Jim WALSH	FF	Montgarrett Castle, New Ross, Co. Wexford.

GOVERNMENT OF THE REPUBLIC OF IRELAND

Taoiseach Bertie Ahern

Tánaiste, and **Minister for Enterprise, Trade and Employment** Mary Harney

Finance
Charlie McCreevy

Foreign Affairs
David Andrews

Justice, Equality and Law Reform
John O'Donoghue

Education and Science
Mícheál Martin

Health and Children
Brian Cowen

Environment & Local Government
Noel Dempsey

Social, Community & Family Affairs
Dermot Ahern

Public Enterprise
Mary O'Rourke

Agriculture and Food
Joe Walsh

Defence
Michael Smith

Marine and Natural Resources
Michael Woods

Arts, Heritage, Gaeltacht and the Islands
Síle de Valera

Tourism, Sport and Recreation
Jim McDaid

Government Chief Whip and **Minister of State**
Seamus Brennan

Minister of State
Bobby Molloy

Attorney General David Byrne SC

MINISTERS OF STATE

AREAS OF RESPONSIBILITY	MINISTER
Department of the Taoiseach	Seamus Brennan
Defence	Seamus Brennan
To the Government	Bobby Molloy
Environment and Local Government	Bobby Molloy
Education and Science	Noel Treacy
Enterprise, Trade and Employment	Noel Treacy
Agriculture and Food	Noel Davern
Public Enterprise	Joe Jacob
Health and Children	Frank Fahey
Education and Science	Willie O'Dea
Enterprise, Trade and Employment	Tom Kitt
Tourism, Sport and Recreation	Chris Flood
Environment and Local Government	Danny Wallace
Agriculture and Food	Ned O'Keefe
Marine and Natural Resources	Hugh Byrne
Justice, Equality and Law Reform	Mary Wallace
Finance	Martin Cullen
Arts, Heritage, the Gaeltacht and the Islands	Eamon Ó Cuiv
Foreign Affairs	Liz O'Donnell
Health and Children	Tom Moffat

MEMBERS OF THE 28th DÁIL

CEANN COMHAIRLE:
Séamus Pattison

LEAS CEANN COMHAIRLE:
Rory O'Hanlon

Constituency	Name Party	Address	Telephone
Carlow-Kilkenny	Aylward, Liam ....FF	Aghaviller, Hugginstown, Co. Kilkenny	056 68703
	Browne, John ...FG	Ballinacarrig, Carlow	0503 33033
	Hogan, Philip ...FG	25 The Sycamores, Kilkenny	056 61572
	§McGuinness, John....FF	Windsmoor, Brooklawn, Ballyfoyle Road, Kilkenny	056 70672
	Pattison, Seamus .Lab	6 Upper New Street, Kilkenny	056 21295
Cavan-Monaghan	Boylan, Andrew ...FG	11 Rossa Place, Cavan, Co. Cavan	049 31747
	Crawford, Seymour ...FG	Drumkeen, Aghabog, Monaghan	047 54038
	§Ó Caoláin, Caoimhghín...SF	21 Dublin Street, Monaghan	047 82917
	O'Hanlon, Rory ....FF	Mullinary, Carrickmacross, Co. Monaghan	042 61530
	Smith, Brendan ...FF	3 Carrickfern, Keadue, Co. Cavan	049 62366
Clare	Carey, Donal ...FG	3 Thomond Villas, Clarecastle, Ennis, Co. Clare	065 29191
	†Daly, Brendan ...FF	Cooraclare, Kilrush, Co. Clare	065 59040
	De Valera, Sile ...FF	6 Riverdale, Tulla Road, Ennis, Co.Clare	065 21100
	Killeen, Tony ....FF	Kilnaboy, Corofin, Co. Clare	065 41500
Cork East	Ahern, Michael ...FF	'Libermann', Barryscourt, Carrigtwohill, Co. Cork	021 883592
	Bradford, Paul ...FG	Mourne Abbey, Mallow, Co. Cork	022 29375
	O'Keeffe, Ned ...FF	Ballylough, Mitchelstown, Co. Cork	022 25285
	§Stanton, David ...FG	Geragh Cross, Coppingerstown, Midleton, Co. Cork	021 632867
Cork Nth-Central	Allen, Bernard ...FG	7 Mount Prospect, Shanakiel, Cork	021 303068
	Burke, Liam ...FG	The Grove, Douglas Hall, Cork	021 276116
	§Kelleher, Billy ....FF	Ballyphilip, White's Cross, Glanmire, Co. Cork	021 502289
	§O'Flynn, Noel ....FF	Kilnap, Mallow Road, Cork	021 305282
	Wallace, Dan ...FF	13 Killeens Place, Farranree, Cork	021 270214
Cork Nth-West	Creed, Michael ...FG	Codrum, Macroom, Co. Cork	026 41177
	Moynihan, Donal ....FF	Gortnascorty, Ballymakeera, Macroom, Co. Cork	026 45019
	§Moynihan, Michael ....FF	The Square, Kanturk, Co. Cork	029 76200

Cork Sth-Central	§Clune, Deirdre ...FG	Douglas Village East, Douglas, Cork....021 364934
	§Dennehy, John ....FF	Avondale, Westside Estate, Togher, Co. Cork....021 962908
	Martin, Micheál ....FF	'Lios Laoi', 16 Silver Manor, Ballinlough, Cork....021 295218
	O'Keeffe, Batt....FF	8 Westcliffe, Ballincollig, Co. Cork....021 871393
Cork Sth-West	O'Keeffe, Jim ...FG	Old Chapel, Bandon, Co. Cork....023 41399
	Sheehan, P.J. ...FG	Main Street, Goleen, Co. Cork....028 35236
	Walsh, Joe....FF	5 Emmet Square, Clonakilty, Co. Cork....023 33575
Donegal Nth-East	§Blaney, Harry ...Ind	Rossnakill, Co. Donegal ...074 59014
	Keaveney, Cecilia....FF	'Loreto', Moville, Co. Donegal....077 82177
	McDaid, Dr. James....FF	Pearse Road, Letterkenny, Co. Donegal....074 21652
Donegal Sth-West	Coughlan, Mary....FF	Ballybrillighan, Frosses, Mountcharles, Co. Donegal....073 36002
	§Gildea, Thomas ...Ind	Stranaglough, Glenties, Co. Donegal....075 51757
	McGinley, Dinny ...FG	Bunbeg, Letterkenny, Co. Donegal....075 31025
Dublin Central	Ahern, Bertie ...FF	'St. Lukes', 161 Lower Drumcondra Road, D9 ..01 8374129
	Gregory, Tony ...Ind	5 Sackville Gardens, Ballybough, D3....01 6183488
	§McGennis, Marian....FF	44 Bramley Walk, Bramley Woods, D15....01 8212340
	Mitchell, Jim ...FG	4 Rathdown Crescent, Terenure, D6W....01 4904574
Dublin Nth	Owen, Nora ...FG	17 Ard na Mara, Malahide, Co. Dublin....01 8451041
	Ryan, Seán .Lab	1 Burrow Road, Portrane, Co. Dublin....01 6183432
	†Wright, G.V.....FF	58 The Moorings, Malahide, Co. Dublin....01 8452642
	Sargent, Trevor ...GP	37 Tara Cove, Baile Brigín, Co. Átha Cliath....01 8412371
Dublin Nth-Central	Bruton, Richard ...FG	210 Griffith Avenue, Drumcondra, D9....01 8368185
	Callely, Ivor....FF	7 St. Lawrence Road, Clontarf, D3....01 8330350
	Haughey, Seán....FF	Chapelfield Lodge, Baskin Lane, Kinsealy, D17....01 8450111
	McDowell, Derek ..Lab	3 Dunluce Road, Clontarf, D3....01 8336138
Dublin Nth-East	§Brady, Martin....FF	37 Grangemore Drive, Donaghmede, D13....01 8484509
	Broughan, Tommy ..Lab	23 Riverside Road, Coolock, D17....01 8477634
	†Cosgrave, Michael J. ..FG	22 College Street, Baldoyle, D13....01 8322554
	Woods, Dr. Michael ...FF	13 Kilbarrack Grove, Raheny, D5....01 8323357
Dublin Nth-West	Ahern, Noel ...FF	25 Church Avenue, Drumcondra, D9 ..01 8325911
	§Carey, Pat....FF	69 Bourne View, Ashbourne, Co. Meath....01 8644118
	De Rossa, Proinsias....DL	5 Main Street, Finglas, D11....01 6183003
	Shorthall, Róisín ..Lab	12 Iveragh Road, Gaeltacht Park, Whitehall, D9....01 8370563
Dublin Sth	Brennan, Séamus....FF	31 Finsbury Park, Churchtown, D14....01 2957171
	Kitt, Tom....FF	3 Pine Valley Drive, Rathfarnham, D16....01 2982304
	§Mitchell, Olivia ...FG	18 Ballawley Court, Sandyford Road, D16....01 2953033
	O'Donnell, Liz ...PD	23 Temple Gardens, Rathmines, D6....01 4910363
	Shatter, Alan ...FG	57 Delbrook Manor, Dundrum, D16....01 2983045
Dublin Sth-Central	§Ardagh, Seán....FF	168 Walkinstown Road, D12....01 4566389
	Briscoe, Ben....FF	Newtown, Celbridge, Co. Kildare....01 6288426
	Mitchell, Gay ...FG	192 Upper Rathmines Road, D6....01 4903744
	Upton, Pat ..Lab	1 College Drive, Terenure, D6W....01 4909653
Dublin Sth-East	Fitzgerald, Frances ...FG	116 Georgian Village, Castleknock, D15....01 8211796
	§Gormley, John ...GP	71 Stella Gardens, Irishtown, D4....01 6609418
	Quinn, Ruairí ..Lab	23 Strand Road, Sandymount, D4....01 2602852
	Ryan, Eoin ...FF	19 Vavasour Square, Sandymount, D4....01 6600082
Dublin Sth-West	Flood, Chris....FF	22 Birchview Lawn, Kilnamanagh, Tallaght, D24 .01 4518574
	Harney, Mary ...PD	11 Serpentine Terrace, Ballsbridge, D4....01 6793882
	§Hayes, Brian ...FG	27 The Dale, Kingswood Heights, Tallaght, D24....01 4626545
	§Lenihan, Conor....FF	6 Aylmer Road, Newcastle, Co. Dublin....01 4587276
	Rabbitte, Pat....DL	56 Monastery Drive, Clondalkin, D22....01 4593191
Dublin West	Currie, Austin ...FG	'Tullydraw', Ballyowen Lane, Lucan, Co. Dublin....01 6265047
	Lawlor, Liam....FF	Somerton House, Lucan, Co. Dublin....01 6280507
	Lenihan, Brian....FF	'Longwood', Somerton Road, Strawberry Beds, D20....01 8214058
	§Higgins, Joe ...SP	155 Briarwood Close, Mulhuddart, D15....01 8201753
Dún Laoghaire	Andrews, David ...FF	102 Avoca Park, Blackrock, Co. Dublin....01 2835755
	†Barnes, Monica ...FG	5 Arnold Park, Glenageary, Co. Dublin....01 2853751
	Barrett, Seán ...FG	'Avondale', 3 Ballinclea Road, Killiney, Co. Dublin....01 2852077
	Gilmore, Eamon....DL	1 Corbawn Close, Shankill, Co. Dublin....01 2821363
	§Hanafin, Mary....FF	7 Oaklands Drive, Rathgar, D6....01 2836533

Galway East	§Burke, Ulick ...FG	Eagle Hill, Abbey, Loughrea, Co. Galway	....0509 45218
	Connaughton, Paul ...FG	Mount Bellew, Ballinasloe, Co. Galway	...0905 79249
	Kitt, Michael P. ....FF	Castleblakeney, Ballinasloe, Co. Galway	...0905 78147
	Treacy, Noel ...FF	Gurteen, Ballinasloe, Co. Galway	....0905 77094
Galway West	†Fahey, Frank ...FF	4 Carrig Bán, Menlo, Galway	...091 771020
	Higgins, Michael D. ..Lab	Letteragh, Rahoon, Circular Road, Galway	...091 524513
	McCormack, Pádraic ...FG	3 Renmore Park, Galway	...091 753992
	Molloy, Robert ...PD	'St. Mary's', Rockbarton, Salthill, Galway	...091 521765
	Ó Cuív, Eamon ...FF	Corr na Móna, Conamara, Co. na Gaillimhe	...091 562846
Kerry Nth	Deenihan, Jimmy ...FG	Finuge, Lixnaw, Co. Kerry	......068 40235
	Foley, Denis ....FF	St. Joseph's, 2 Staughton's Row, Tralee, Co. Kerry	......066 21174
	Spring, Dick ..Lab	Cloonanorig, Tralee, Co. Kerry	......066 25337
Kerry Sth	§Healy-Rae, Jackie ...Ind	Main Street, Kilgarvan, Co. Kerry	......064 85315
	Moynihan-Cronin, Breeda ..Lab	10 Muckross Grove, Killarney, Co. Kerry	......064 34993
	O'Donoghue, John....FF	Garranearagh, Caherciveen, Co. Kerry	......066 72413
Kildare Nth	Durkan, Bernard J. ...FG	Timard, Maynooth, Co. Kildare	...01 6286063
	McCreevy, Charlie....FF	Hillview House, Kilcullen Road, Naas, Co. Kildare	...045 876816
	Stagg, Emmet ..Lab	736 Lodge Park, Straffan, Co. Kildare	...01 6272149
Kildare Sth	Dukes, Alan M. ...FG	Tranquila, Tullywest, Kildare	...045 521912
	Power, Seán ....FF	Castlekealy, Caragh, Naas, Co. Kildare	...045 432289
	§Wall, Jack ..Lab	Castlemitchell, Athy, Co. Kildare	...0507 31495
Laois-Offaly	Cowen, Brian....FF	Ballard, Tullamore, Co. Offaly	...0506 31365
	†Enright, Tom ...FG	3 John's Mall, Birr, Co. Offaly	...0509 20839
	Flanagan, Charles ...FG	Glenlahen, Stradbally Road, Portlaoise, Co. Laois	...0502 60707
	§Fleming, Seán....FF	'Silveracre', Castletown, Portlaoise, Co. Laois	...0502 32692
	§Moloney, John....FF	27 Patrick Street, Mountmellick, Co. Laois	...0502 24391
Limerick East	Noonan, Michael ...FG	18 Gouldavoher Estate, Fr. Russell Road, Limerick	...061 229350
	O'Dea, Willie....FF	2 Glenview Gardens, Farranshore, Co. Limerick	...061 454488
	O'Malley, Desmond J. ....P.D.	11 Cecil Street, Limerick	...061 419424
	O'Sullivan, Jan ..Lab	7 Lanahone Avenue, Corbally, Limerick	...061 312316
	§Wade, Eddie ....FF	Cahernorry, Drombanna, Co. Limerick	...061 351467
Limerick West	Finucane, Michael ...FG	Ardnacrohy, Newcastle West, Co. Limerick	...069 62742
	§Collins, Michael....FF	Red House Hill, Patrickswell, Co. Limerick	...061 355081
	§Neville, Dan ...FG	Kiltannan, Croagh, Co. Limerick	...061 396351
Longford-Roscommon	†Belton, Louis J ...FG	Kenagh, Co. Longford	....043 22245
	Doherty, Seán ...FF	Cootehall, Boyle, Co. Roscommon	....079 67005
	§Naughten, Denis ...FG	Ardkennan, Drum, Athlone, Co. Roscommon	...0902 37100
	Reynolds, Albert....FF	Church Street, Longford, Co. Longford	...043 45344
Louth	Ahern, Dermot ...FF	The Crescent, Blackrock, Dundalk, Co. Louth	...042 21473
	Bell, Michael ..Lab	122 Newfield Estate, Drogheda, Co. Louth	...041 38573
	Kirk, Séamus ...FF	Rathiddy, Knockbridge, Dundalk, Co. Louth	...042 31032
	McGahon, Brendan ...FG	Annaverna, Ravensdale, Dundalk, Co. Louth	...042 32620
Mayo	§Cooper-Flynn, Beverley....FF	2 Manor Village, Westport Road, Castlebar, Co. Mayo	...094 27035
	Higgins, Jim ...FG	Devlis, Ballyhaunis, Co. Mayo	...0907 31140
	Kenny, Enda ...FG	Tucker Street, Castlebar, Co. Mayo	...094 25600
	Moffatt, Tom ...FF	Ballina House, Castle Road, Ballina, Co. Mayo	...096 71588
	Ring, Michael ...FG	The Paddock, Westport, Co. Mayo	...098 25734
Meath	§Brady, Johnny....FF	Springville, Kilskyre, Kells, Co. Meath	....046 40852
	Bruton, John ...FG	Cornelstown, Dunboyne, Co.Meath	...01 8255573
	Dempsey, Noel....FF	Newtown, Trim, Co. Meath	...046 31146
	†Farrelly, John V. ...FG	Hurdlestown, Kells, Co. Meath	...046 41290
	Wallace, Mary....FF	Ennistown, Fairyhouse Road, Ratoath, Co. Meath	...01 8256259
Sligo-Leitrim	Brennan, Matt....FF	Ragoora, Cloonacool, Tubbercurry, Co. Sligo	...071 85136
	Ellis, John....FF	Fenagh, Ballinamore, Co. Leitrim	...078 44252
	§Perry, John ...FG	Teeling Street, Ballymote, Co. Sligo	...071 83372
	†Reynolds, Gerry ...FG	Tully, Ballinamore, Co. Leitrim	...078 44016
Tipperary Nth	Lowry, Michael Ind	Glenreigh, Holycross, Thurles, Co. Tipperary	...0504 43182
	†O'Kennedy, Michael FF	Gortlandroe, Nenagh, Co. Tipperary	...067 31484
	Smith, Michael FF	Lismackin, Roscrea, Co. Tipperary	...0505 43157
Tipperary Sth	Ahearn, Theresa ...FG	Ballindoney, Grange, Clonmel, Co. Tipperary	..052 38142

Davern, Noel....FF	....Tannersrath, Fethard Road, Clonmel, Co. Tipperary	....052 22991
Ferris, Michael ..Lab	....Rosanna, Tipperary	....062 52265

Waterford	Cullen, Martin....FF	......Abbey House, Abbey Road, Ferrybank, Waterford	....051 851112
	Deasy, Austin ...FG	..................................Kilrush, Dungarvan, Co. Waterford	....058 43003
	Kenneally, Brendan....FF	............38 Viewmount Park, Dunmore Road, Waterford	....051 855964
	O'Shea, Brian ..Lab	................61 Sweetbriar Lawn, Tramore, Co. Waterford	....051 381913
Westmeath	McGrath, Paul ...FG	....................Carna, Irishtown, Mullingar, Co. Westmeath	....044 40746
	Penrose, William ..Lab	......................Ballintue, Ballynacargy, Co. Westmeath	....044 73264
	O'Rourke, Mary ....FF	....................'Aisling', Arcadia, Athlone, Co. Westmeath	....0902 75065
Wexford	Browne, John...FF	..........................Kilcannon, Enniscorthy, Co. Wexford	....054 35046
	Byrne, Hugh....FF	..................Air Hill, Fethard-on-Sea, Co. Wexford	....051 397125
	†D'Arcy, Michael ...FG	............................Annagh, Gorey, Co. Wexford	....055 28177
	Howlin, Brendan ..Lab	..............................Whiterock Hill, Wexford	....053 24036
	Yates, Ivan ...FG	................Blackstoops, Enniscorthy, Co. Wexford	....054 33793
Wicklow	Fox, Mildred ...Ind	..................Lower Calary, Kilmacanogue, Co. Wicklow	....01 2876386
	Jacob, Joe....FF	........................Main Street, Rathdrum, Co. Wicklow	....0404 46528
	McManus, Liz....DL	..........Belton House, Castle Street, Bray, Co. Wicklow	....01 2868407
	Roche, Dick....FF	..2 Herbert Terrace, Herbert Road, Bray, Co. Wicklow	....01 2863211
	Timmins, Billy ...FG	................Shrughaun, Baltinglass, Co. Wicklow	....0508 81655

Key: §= New T.D.; †= Previous member of the Dáil, but not the 27th Dáil.

SEATS HELD BY POLITICAL PARTIES

Party	Dáil Éireann	Seanad Éireann	European Parliament
Fianna Fáil	76	30	7
Fine Gael	53	16	4
Labour	18	3	1
Progressive Democrats	4	4	-
Democratic Left	4	-	-
Green Party	2	-	2
Sinn Féin	1	-	-
Socialist Party	1	-	-
Independents	6	7	1
TOTAL	**166**	**60**	**15**

SALARIES OF ELECTED REPRESENTATIVES

	£		£		£
TD	36,648	Minister	85,512	Leas Ceann Comhairle	58,595
Minister of State	58,595	Ceann Comhairle	85,512	Taoiseach	107,149
Senator	23,190	Tánaiste	92,137		

PRESIDENTIAL ELECTION RESULTS 1997 (October 30)

REGION	Electorate	Total Poll	Turnout %	Spoiled	Valid Poll
Connacht-Ulster	531,286	256,366	48.25	2,133	254,233
Dublin	753,996	328,796	43.61	2,558	326,238
Leinster	631,092	298,518	47.30	2,237	296,281
Munster	771,942	396,008	51.30	2,924	393,084
Overall	2,688,316	1,279,688	47.60	9,852	1,269,836

REGION	Nally 1st Count	Roche 1st Count	Scallon 1st Count	Banotti 1st Count	McAleese 1st Count	Banotti 2nd Count	McAleese 2nd Count
Connacht-Ulster	8,603	10,739	44,937	60,461	129,493	81,841	158,942
%	3.38	4.22	17.68	23.78	50.93	33.99	66.01
Dublin	15,198	21,595	40,283	122,965	126,197	156,860	155,221
%	4.66	6.62	12.35	37.69	38.68	50.26	49.74
Leinster	20,484	18,891	39,877	81,489	135,540	112,396	167,032
%	6.91	6.38	13.46	27.50	45.75	40.22	59.78
Munster	15,244	37,198	50,361	107,087	183,194	146,419	225,064
%	3.88	9.46	12.81	27.24	46.60	39.41	60.59
Overall	59,529	88,423	175,458	372,002	574,424	497,516	706,259
%	4.69	6.96	13.82	29.30	45.24	41.33	58.67

BIOGRAPHIES OF THE PRESIDENTS OF IRELAND

Born: Frenchpark, Co. Roscommon, January 17, 1860.
Party: Non-party.
Elected: Nominated without opposition.
Inaugurated: June 25, 1938, aged 78.
Number of terms: One.
Retired: June 24, 1945.
Died: July 12, 1949, aged 89.
Biographical Details: The son of a Church of Ireland minister, Dr. Hyde was to the forefront of the turn-of-the-century cultural revival, co-founding Conradh na Gaeilge (The Gaelic League) and serving as its first President (1893-1915). Remembered for his play *Casadh an tSúgáin* and his collection of translated poetry *Lovesongs of Connacht*. First Professor of Modern Irish at UCD where he taught from 1909 until 1932; member of Seanad Éireann (1925-38).

SEÁN T. Ó CEALLAIGH (1945-59)

Born: Dublin, August 25, 1882.
Party: Fianna Fáil.
Elected: June 16, 1945.
Inaugurated: June 25, 1945.
Number of terms: Two (re-elected unopposed 1952).
Retired: June 24, 1959.
Died: November 23, 1966, aged 84.
Biographical Details: A veteran of the 1916 Easter Rising, he was a founding member of Sinn Féin (1907) and Fianna Fáil(1926). Elected to the first Dáil in 1918, became its Ceann Comhairle (speaker). Retained his Dáil seat until 1945, serving in a number of ministries including Local Government and Public Health (1932-39) and Finance (1939-45). Also served as vice-president of the Executive Council (1932-37) and Tánaiste (1937-45).

ÉAMON de VALERA (1959-73)

Born: New York, October 14, 1882.
Party: Fianna Fáil.
Elected: June 17, 1959.
Inaugurated: June 25, 1959.
Number of terms: Two, re-elected June 1, 1966.
Retired: June 24, 1973.
Died: August 29, 1975, aged 92.
Biographical Details: The son of an Irish immigrant mother and a Spanish immigrant father he moved to Ireland in 1885. A commandant at Boland's Mills during the 1916 Rising, the British authorities commuted his death sentence because they were unsure of his nationality and wished to avoid alienating the United States by executing one of its citizens. Elected as a Sinn Féin MP for East Clare in 1917 - a seat he held until he became President. Was also elected MP for East Mayo (1918-21); Down (1921-29); and South Down (1933-37), although he never took his seat at Stormont.

President of Sinn Féin (1917-26); President of the Irish Volunteers (1917-22); President of the Irish Republic (1919-20); founder of Fianna Fáil in 1926 and that party's President until 1959; President of the Council of the League of Nations at its 68th and Special Sessions (September and October 1932); and President of the Assembly of the League of Nations in 1938. Founded *The Irish Press* in 1931. In government he was President of the Executive Council (1932-37); Minister for External Affairs (1932-48); Taoiseach (1937-48, 1951-54, and 1957-59) Minister for Local Government (1940); and Minister for Education (1939-40). He also had a significant input in the drafting of the 1937 Constitution of Ireland.
* See Biographies of Taoisigh for further information

ERSKINE CHILDERS (1973-74)

Born: London, December 11, 1905.
Party: Fianna Fáil.
Elected: May 30, 1973.
Inaugurated: June 25, 1973 aged 67.
Number of terms: One.
Died: November 17, 1974, aged 68, while in office.
Biographical Details: His father, Erskine, signatory of the 1921 Anglo-Irish Treaty, was executed by Free State soldiers in 1922. First elected to Dáil Éireann in 1938 he held a number of ministerial portfolios, including Posts and Telegraphs (1951-54 and 1966-69); Lands (1957-59); Transport and Power (1959-69); and Tánaiste (1969-73).

CEARBHALL Ó DÁLAIGH (1974-76)

Born: Bray, Co. Wicklow, February 12, 1911.
Party: Non-party.
Elected: Nominated unopposed following death of Erskine Childers.
Inaugurated: December 19, 1974, aged 63.
Number of terms: One.
Resigned: October 22, 1976.
Died: March 21, 1978, aged 67.
Biographical Details: His tenure was brief; he resigned "to protect the dignity and independence" of the office of President, following comments made by the then Minister for Defence, Patrick Donegan, about his referral of the Criminal Law (Jurisdiction) Bill to the Supreme Court to attest its constitutionality (the bill was found to be constitutional).

Mr. Ó Dálaigh was a barrister by profession and had a distinguished legal career both in Ireland and Europe. Attorney General twice (1946-48 and 1951-53); Chief Justice and President of the Supreme Court (1961-73), having been a Supreme Court Judge from

1953; in 1973 he became a Judge of the Court of Justice of the European Communities and in 1974 became President of the First Chamber of that court.

DR PATRICK HILLERY (1976-1990)

Born: Milltown Malbay, Co. Clare, May 2, 1923.
Party: Fianna Fáil.
Elected: Returned unopposed to the Presidency, following the resignation of Cearbhall Ó Dálaigh.
Inaugurated: December 3, 1976.
Number of terms: Two, re-elected unopposed 1983.
Retired: December 2, 1990.
Biographical Details: TD for Clare (1951-73), he held the following ministerial portfolios: Education (1959-65); Industry and Commerce (1965-66); Labour (1966-69); and Foreign Affairs (1969-73). As Minister for Foreign Affairs, he negotiated Ireland's accession to the European Economic Community in 1973 and became Ireland's first Commissioner to the EEC, serving as vice-president of the Commission with special responsibilities for Social Affairs from 1973 until his elevation to the Irish Presidency in 1976.

MARY ROBINSON (1990-97)

Born: Ballina Co. Mayo, May 21, 1944.
Party: Non-party.
Elected: November 7, 1990.
Inaugurated: December 3, 1990, aged 46.
Number of terms: One.
Resigned: September 12, 1997.
Biographical Details: Mary Robinson was the first woman to hold the office. An emi-

nent barrister, she was the Professor of Constitutional and Criminal Law (1969-75) and lecturer on European Community Law (1975-90) at Trinity College Dublin. Member of Seanad Éireann 1969-89; initially a member of the Labour Party, she resigned from the party in protest at the signing of the Anglo-Irish Agreement in 1985. A series of visits, both domestic and overseas, resulted in a dramatic increase in the profile of the office.

Appointed United Nations commissioner for Human Rights in June 1997, a position she currently holds.

MARY MCALEESE (1997-)

Born: Belfast, 27 June, 1951.
Party: Fianna Fáil.
Elected: October 30, 1997.
Inaugurated: November 11, 1997, aged 46.
Number of terms: Current President.
Biographical Details: Mary McAleese is the first person from north of the border and the youngest person to hold the office of President. A barrister and academic, she was Reid Professor of Criminal Law, Criminology and Penology at Trinity College, Dublin (1975-79 and 1981-87), Director of the Institute of Professional Legal Studies at the Queen's University of Belfast (1987-97) and Pro Vice-Chancellor of the Queen's University of Belfast (1994-97).

TAOISIGH AND TÁNAISTÍ OF IRELAND, 1922-98

Date appointed	Head of Government	Deputy Head of Government	Date appointed
	President of the Executive Council	Vice President of Executive Council	
06.12.1922	William T. Cosgrave (CnaG)	Kevin O'Higgins (CnaG)	26.12.1922
		Ernest Blythe (CnaG)	10.07.1927
09.03.1932	Eamon de Valera (FF)	Seán T. Ó Ceallaigh (FF)	09.03.1932
	Taoiseach	Tánaiste	
29.12.1937	Éamon de Valera (FF)	Seán T. Ó Ceallaigh (FF)	29.12.1937
		Seán Lemass (FF)	14.06.1945
18.02.1948	John A. Costello (FG)	William Norton (Lab)	18.02.1948
13.06.1951	Eamon de Valera (FF)	Seán Lemass (FF)	13.06.1951
02.06.1954	John A. Costello (FG)	William Norton (Lab)	02.06.1954
20.03.1957	Eamon de Valera (FF)	Seán Lemass (FF)	20.03.1957
23.06.1959	Seán Lemass (FF)	Seán MacEntee (FF)	23.06.1959
		Frank Aiken (FF)	21.04.1965
10.11.1966	Jack Lynch (FF)	Frank Aiken (FF)	10.11.1966
		Erskine Childers (FF)	02.07.1969
14.03.1973	Liam Cosgrave (FG)	Brendan Corish (Lab)	14.03.1973
05.07.1977	Jack Lynch (FF)	George Colley (FF)	05.07.1977
11.12.1979	Charles Haughey (FF)	George Colley (FF)	11.12.1979
20.06.1981	Garret FitzGerald (FG)	Michael O'Leary (FG)	20.06.1981

09.03.1982 ....Charles Haughey (FF).......................................Ray McSharry (FF) 09.03.1982
14.12.1982 ....Garret FitzGerald (FG) ....Dick Spring (Lab) 14.12.1982
		Peter Barry (FG) 20.01.1987
10.03.1987 ....Charles Haughey (FF) ....Brian Lenihan (FF) 10.03.1987
		John Wilson (FF) 13.11.1990
11.02.1992 ....Albert Reynolds (FF) ....John Wilson (FF) 11.02.1992
		Dick Spring (Lab) 12.01.1993
		Bertie Ahern (FF) 19.11.1994
15.12.1994 ....John Bruton (FG) ....Dick Spring (Lab) 15.12.1994
26.06.1997 ....Bertie Ahern (FF) ....Mary Harney (PD) 26.06.1997

BIOGRAPHIES OF IRISH TAOISIGH

WILLIAM T. COSGRAVE (1922-32)

Born: Dublin, June 6, 1880.
Parties: Cumann na nGaedheal, leader 1923-33; Fine Gael 1934-44.
President of the Executive Council: 1922-32 (Chairman of the Provisional Government August 25-December 6 1922).
Administration: Single party.
Ministerial Portfolios: Finance (1922-23), Defence (1924) and Justice (1927).
TD: 1917-1944.
Died: November 16, 1965, aged 85.
Biographical Details: A veteran of the 1916 Rising as MP for Clare he was Minister for Local Government in the first Dáil, a position he retained in the Provisional Government until the death of Michael Collins.

His government dealt severely with the anti-treaty IRA and during the bloody civil war ordered the execution of 77 prisoners in response to republican atrocities. The government retained a series of Emergency Powers to maintain law and order after the war ended in April 1923. The government established the Garda Síochana (1923), gained the admittance of the Irish Free State to the League of Nations (1923), initiated the Shannon hydro-electric scheme (1925) and was instrumental at the 1926 Imperial Conference in defining the 'autonomous communities' of the British Empire as 'equal in status' and in no way subordinate to one another which paved the way for constitutional independence from Britain.

ÉAMON de VALERA*

Born: New York, October 14, 1882.
Party: Fianna Fáil, leader 1926-59.
President of the Executive Council: 1932-37.
Taoiseach: Three times (1937-48, 1951-54, and 1957-59).
Administrations: Single party.
Ministerial Portfolios: External Affairs (1932-48), Education (1939-40) and Local Government (1941).
TD: 1917-59.
Died: August 29, 1975, aged 92.
Biographical Details: A commandant in the 1916 Rising, he was the only high ranking male to escape execution. Elected as a Sinn Féin MP in 1917 he was President of the Dáil (1919-22). Withdrew from the Dáil

in 1922 over the signing of the Anglo-Irish Treaty, but abstentionism did not suit him. He was a founding member of Fianna Fáil in May 1926 and, in 1927, he led the new party into the Oireachtas.

In government, he set about deleting all trappings of the Crown from public life, abolishing the Oath of Allegiance in 1933, limiting the powers of the Governor General and eventually abolishing the office. He took advantage of the 1936 abdication crisis to remove all reference to the King from the constitution. The culmination of this policy was the drafting of the Constitution in 1937. The constitution defined the national territory as the whole island of Ireland and provided for the creation of the office of President, the constitution also reflected Catholic teachings of the time. A prolonged and damaging economic war with Britain in the 1930s over the withholding of land annuities stunted economic growth. Despite heavy international pressure (especially from Britain and the US), de Valera steered Ireland on a neutral course during World War II. In 1953 his government passed a Health Act providing free mother-and-child benefits. Elected as President of Ireland on June 17, 1959, he served two full terms. He is the only person to have been both President and Taoiseach.
*See Presidential biographies for further information

JOHN A. COSTELLO

Born: Dublin, June 20, 1891.
Party: Although Taoiseach he never led the Fine Gael Party.
Taoiseach: Twice, 1948-51 and 1954-57.
Administrations: Coalition (Fine Gael/Labour/Clann na Poblachta/Clann na Talmhan and Independents).
Ministerial Portfolios: Health 1951.
TD: 1933-69.
Died: January 5, 1976, aged 84.
Biographical Details: Both of the administrations he headed were multi-party coalitions, and it is a testament to his skills that governments of such disparate parts were cohesive and constructive.

As Attorney General (1926-32), he played an important role in achieving the freedoms implicit in the Anglo-Irish Treaty culminating in the Statute of Westminster (1931). Elected to Dáil Éireann in 1933, he retained his seat until 1969. In 1948 his government passed the Republic of Ireland Act, and Ireland formally left the Commonwealth the following year. It was also during his premiership that the Industrial Development Authority was established (1950), Ireland was admitted to the United Nations Organisation (1955) and tuberculosis was successfully eradicated.

SEÁN LEMASS

Born: Dublin, July 15, 1899.
Party: Fianna Fáil, leader 1959-66.
Taoiseach: Once, 1959-66.
Government: Single party.
Ministerial Portfolios: Industry and Commerce (1932-39, 1941-48, 1951-54, and 1957-59), Supplies (1939-45) and Tánaiste (1945-48, 1951-54, and 1957-59).
TD: 1924-69.
Died: May 11, 1971, aged 71.
Biographical Details: A veteran of the 1916 Rising, the War of Independence and the Civil War, where he fought on the republican side, he was elected to Dáil Éireann in 1924 and was a founding member of Fianna Fáil in 1926. As Minister for Industry and Commerce, he established the national airline, Aer Lingus (1936); Irish Shipping (1941) and the Irish Tourist Board, Bord Fáilte (1952). As Taoiseach he espoused free trade and competitiveness as the way forward for Ireland economically. A free trade agreement with Britain was signed (1966), free secondary school education (announced 1966) and Radio Telefís Éireann made its first broadcast (Dec 31, 1961). Lemass also held two groundbreaking meetings with the Prime Minister of Northern Ireland, Terence O'Neill, in 1965

JACK LYNCH

Born: Cork, August 15, 1917
Party: Fianna Fáil, leader 1966-79
Taoiseach: Twice, 1966-73 and 1977-79
Administration: Single party.
Ministerial Portfolios: Education (1957-59 and 1968), Gaeltacht (1957), Industry and Commerce (1959-65) and Finance (1965-66).
TD: 1948-81
Biographical Details: Lynch's time as Taoiseach was marked by the breakdown of law and order in Northern Ireland. He dismissed ministers Neil Blaney and Charles Haughey for their out spoken statements on the situation; both were later charged and acquitted of supplying arms to republicans in the North. He recalled the Irish ambassador to London in protest at Bloody Sunday in 1972. Lynch presided over Ireland's entry to the European Economic Community in 1973 and, in 1979, negotiated Ireland's entry to the European Monetary System thus ending the one-for-one parity with sterling. In his youth, he won a record six consecutive All-Ireland medals (five hurling and one football) with his native Cork.

LIAM COSGRAVE

Born: Dublin, April 13, 1920.
Party: Fine Gael, leader 1965-77.
Taoiseach: Once, 1973-77.
Administration: Coalition (Fine Gael/Labour).
Ministerial Portfolios: External Affairs (1954-57) and Defence 1976.
TD: 1943-81.
Biographical Details: The son of W.T. Cosgrave, first President of the Executive Council.

His administration struggled with the recession caused by the international oil crisis of the mid-1970s; inflation soared and unemployment rose, but this was a global, and not simply, an Irish phenomenon. He led the Republic's delegation to the tripartite Sunningdale talks in 1973, which established the short-lived Northern Ireland Executive. His government also introduced selective broadcasting censorship in the form of Section 31 of the Broadcasting Act.

CHARLES J. HAUGHEY

Born: Mayo, September 16, 1925.
Party: Fianna Fáil, leader 1979-92.
Taoiseach: Three times (1979-81, 1982 & 1987-92).
Administration: Twice as single party and one coalition (Fianna Fáil/Progressive Democrat 1989-92).
Ministerial Portfolios: Justice 1961-64, Agriculture and Fisheries 1964-66, Finance 1966-70, Health and Social Welfare 1977-79 and Gaeltacht 1987-92.
TD: 1957-92.
Biographical Details: His early administrations struggled in a difficult economic climate. On returning to power in 1987, he saw the referendum on the Single European Act approved, the first Balance of Payments surplus since the 1930s, and inflation and interest rates plummet. In 1989, he became the first Fianna Fáil leader to enter into a coalition when he aligned his party with the Progressive Democrats. Bedevilled by controversy throughout his career (he was charged and acquitted of supplying arms to northern republicans in 1970), he resigned as Taoiseach and leader of Fianna Fáil in February 1992 when allegations about a 1982 phone-tapping scandal re-surfaced. The spectre of scandal returned to haunt Mr. Haughey again in July 1997 when he admitted receiving £1.3 million in donations from Ben Dunne of Dunnes Stores at the payment to politicans tribunal (See Chronology).

DR. GARRET FITZGERALD

Born: Dublin, February 9, 1926.
Party: Fine Gael, leader 1977-87.
Taoiseach: Twice (1981-82 & 1982-87).
Administration: Coalition (Fine Gael/Labour).
Ministerial Portfolios: Foreign Affairs (1973-77).
TD: 1969-92.

Biographical Details: As Taoiseach, his most notable achievements were on Northern Ireland. In 1983 he convened the New Ireland Forum which gave impetus to Anglo-Irish negotiations resulting in the Anglo-Irish Agreement in 1985. The agreement, fiercely opposed by unionists, gave the Irish government a limited input into the government of Northern Ireland via a joint ministerial conference of British and Irish ministers and a permanent secretariat. While in office, Ireland's economic situation improved considerably. Social legislation put to referendum, such as prohibiting the legalisation of abortion, was passed while the proposed legalisation of divorce was defeated.

Since retiring from Dáil Éireann in 1992, he has maintained a high profile through lecturing and writing on Irish politics.

ALBERT REYNOLDS

Born: Roscommon, November 3, 1932.
Party: Fianna Fáil, leader 1992-94.
Taoiseach: Once 1992-94.
Administrations: Coalition (Fianna Fáil/Progressive Democrats February 1992-November 1992 and Fianna Fáil/Labour November 1992-December 1994).
Ministerial Portfolios: Posts and Telegraphs (1979-81), Transport (1979-81), Industry and Energy (1982) and Finance (1988-91).
TD: Since 1977.
Biographical Details: In government, his main concern was Northern Ireland, he was instrumental in the drafting of the Downing Street Declaration in 1993. He held ground-breaking talks with Gerry Adams and John Hume, and broadcasting bans were lifted north and south. It was in this climate that the IRA declared a ceasefire in August 1994 followed two months later by a loyalist paramilitary ceasefire.

A referendum was held on the question of abortion (November 1992), where the right to travel and receive information regarding abortion was approved but the wider availability of abortion was restricted; the Maastricht Treaty was ratified by referendum (June 1992), and over £7 billion in EC structural and cohesion funds were secured during the lifetime of his government.

Mr. Reynolds resigned in November 1994 when the appointment of Harry Whelehan, Attorney General, as President of the High Court proved unacceptable to his coalition partners in Labour.

JOHN BRUTON

Born: Dublin, May 18, 1947.
Party: Fine Gael, leader since 1990.
Taoiseach: Once, 1994-97.
Administration: Coalition (Fine Gael / Labour/ Democratic Left).
Ministerial Portfolios: Finance (1981-82) and (1986-87), Industry and Energy (1982-83), Industry, Trade, Commerce and Tourism (1983-86) and the Public Service (1987).
TD: Since 1969.
Biographical Details: Taoiseach of the three-party 'rainbow' coalition of Fine Gael, Labour and Democratic Left. His was the first government in the history of the state to take office without a general election being held.

The Irish economy grew continuously during his premiership, leaving Ireland well-prepared for European Monetary Union. Referenda were held dealing with the legislation of divorce (1995) and the denial of bail to likely re-offenders (1996). The 'Framework Document' signed by him and former British Prime Minister John Major in February 1995 helped establish multi-party talks on the future of Northern Ireland; yet the I.R.A. ceasefire broke down just over a year later. This resumption of violence and widespread unrest during the marching season placed the peace process under great strain.

BERTIE AHERN

Born: Dublin, September 1951.
Party: Fianna Fáil, leader since 1994.
Taoiseach: Since 1997.
Administration: Coalition (Fianna Fáil/Progressive Democrats).
Ministerial Portfolios: Finance (1991-94), Industry and Commerce (1993) and Labour (1987-91).
TD: Since 1977.
Biographical Details: Mr Ahern and his government developed a distinctly 'hands on' approach to the Peace Process as evidenced by his round the clock efforts in the days leading up to the 'Good Friday' Agreement. The Agreement, and its subsequent ratification by referendum in both Northern Ireland and the Republic can be said to be Mr Ahern's outstanding achievement of his first year in office. Under his leadership the government has managed to sustain and develop the economy which continues to grow apace. In May 1998, his government negotiated the level at which the Punt will enter European Monetary Union on 1st January, 1999. ◫

REFERENDUM RESULTS 1997/98

Referendum on Cabinet Confidentiality 30 October, 1997

Region	Electorate	Total Poll	Spoiled	Turnout	Yes	No
Connacht-Ulster	531,286	253,529	16,343	47.72%	131,542	105,644
%					55.46	44.54
Dublin	753,996	326,381	11,537	43.29%	156,145	158,699
%					49.59	50.41
Leinster	631,092	295,958	15,007	46.90%	150,841	130,110
%					53.69	46.31
Munster	771,942	392,195	23,224	50.81%	194,249	174,722
%					52.65	47.35
Overall	2,688,316	1,268,063	66,111	47.17%	632,777	569,175
					52.65	47.35

Referendum on the Amsterdam Treaty 22 May, 1998

Region	Electorate	Total Poll	Spoiled	Turnout	Yes	No
Connacht-Ulster	542,600	296,809	7,948	54.70%	186,802	102,059
					64.67	35.33
Dublin	765,287	454,314	6,830	59.37%	270,473	177,011
					60.44	39.56
Leinster	650,060	358,983	7,705	55.22%	222,706	128,572
					63.40	36.60
Munster	789,141	433,824	10,745	54.97%	252,651	170,428
					59.72	40.28
Overall	2,747,088	1,543,930	33,228	56.20%	932,632	578,070
					61.74	38.26

Referendum on Northern Ireland Agreement 22 May, 1998

Region	Electorate	Total Poll	Spoiled	Turnout	Yes	No
Connacht-Ulster	542,600	297,156	4,365	54.76%	276,131	16,660
					94.31	5.69
Dublin	765,287	454,771	2,908	59.42%	428,323	23,540
					94.79	5.21
Leinster	650,060	359,265	4,254	55.27%	334,770	20,241
					94.30	5.70
Munster	789,141	434,203	5,537	55.02%	403,359	25,307
					94.10	5.90
Overall	2,747,088	1,545,395	17,064	56.25%	1,442,583	85,748
					94.39	5.61

CONSTITUTIONAL REFERENDA, 1937-98

Date	Issue	Turnout (%)	For (%)	Against (%)	Spoiled (%)
01.07.1937	Endorse new constitution	75.8	56.5	43.5	10.0
17.06.1959	Introduction of plurality voting system (replacing proportional representation)	58.4	48.2	51.8	4.0
16.10.1968	Establishing TD-population ratio	65.8	39.2	60.8	4.3
16.10.1968	Introduction of plurality system (replacing proportional representation)	65.8	39.2	60.8	4.3
10.05.1972	Allow EEC membership	70.9	83.1	16.9	0.8
07.12.1972	Lower voting age to 18	50.7	84.6	15.4	5.2
07.12.1972	Abolish 'special position' of the Catholic church	50.7	84.4	15.6	5.5
05.07.1979	Protect adoption system	28.6	99.0	1.0	2.5
05.07.1979	Allow alteration of university representation in Seanad Éireann	28.6	92.4	7.6	3.9

CONSTITUTIONAL REFERENDA, 1937-98 (continued)

Date	Issue	Turnout (%)	For (%)	Against (%)	Spoiled (%)
07.09.1983	Prohibit legalisation of abortion	53.7	66.9	33.1	0.7
14.06.1984	Extend voting rights to non-citizens	47.5	75.4	24.6	3.5
26.06.1986	Allow legalisation of divorce	60.8	36.5	63.5	0.6
24.05.1987	Allow signing of Single European Act	44.1	69.9	30.1	0.5
18.06.1992	Allow ratification of the Maastricht Treaty on European Union	57.3	69.1	30.9	0.5
25.11.1992	Restrict availability of abortion	68.2	34.6	65.4	4.7
25.11.1992	Right to travel (abortion)	68.2	62.4	37.6	4.3
25.11.1992	Right to information (abortion)	68.2	59.9	40.1	4.3
24.11.1995	Right to divorce	62.2	50.3	49.7	0.3
28.11.1996	Restrictions on right to bail	29.2	74.8	25.2	0.4
30.10.1997	Cabinet Confidentiality	47.2	52.6	47.4	5.2
22.06.1998	Allow ratification of Amsterdam Treaty	56.2	61.7	38.3	2.2
22.06.1998	Northern Ireland Agreement	56.3	94.4	5.6	1.1

POLITICS N.I.

INTRODUCTION TO NORTHERN IRELAND

Explanatory notes on Northern Ireland

Northern Ireland contains the counties of Antrim, Armagh, Derry, Down, Fermanagh and Tyrone. Part of the United Kingdom of Great Britain and Northern Ireland, it was established by the Government of Ireland Act 1920. The Northern Ireland parliament voted to opt out of the Irish Free State in December 1922. From 1921 until 1972 Northern Ireland had its own parliament which dealt with local matters while the Imperial parliament at Westminster dealt with wider matters such as the Crown, taxation and defence.

Following the outbreak of communal violence in 1968, the Stormont Parliament was prorogued in March 1972 to be replaced by direct rule from Westminster, embodied in the powers vested in the Secretary of State. The Northern Ireland Constitution Act 1973 provided for devolved government in the form of a power sharing executive. The executive took office in January with ministers from the UUP, the SDLP and Alliance. It was brought down in May of that year by the Ulster Workers' Council strike. The collapse was followed by the reintroduction of direct rule.

Since May 1974 Northern Ireland has been ruled directly from Westminster under the terms of the Northern Ireland Act 1974 by the Secretary of State for Northern Ireland who is a member of the Westminster cabinet. She/he is responsible for the departments in the Northern Ireland Office and has a team of four junior ministers who head these departments. The departments are Agriculture, Economic Development, Education, Environment, Finance and Personnel and Health and Social Services.

The most recent constitutional initiative, the 'Good Friday' Agreement provides for a 108-member Northern Ireland Assembly. It envisages the creation of an Executive which will assume responsibility for the local government departments within the Northern Ireland Office, although certain powers (such as security, taxation, defence and excise) will remain with the Westminster parliament. Northern Ireland also has 26 district and borough councils which have limited powers of local government.

The Westminster legislature consists of the head of state (i.e. the monarch), and two houses of Parliament: the House of Commons (a house of representatives) and the House of Lords (consisting of members of the Peerage). All bills passed by the houses of parliament must be promulgated by the monarch.

The House of Commons has 659 members of which Northern Ireland returns 18. All MPs are elected by the 'first past the post' system. Northern Ireland also returns three members to the European Parliament.

The House of Lords (as of July 21, 1997) consists of 1,148 eligible hereditary peers, law lords, life peers and Anglican bishops.

HEAD OF STATE

The Head of State is Elizabeth II Alexandra Mary of Windsor. Born London, April 21, 1926, she ascended to the throne on February 6, 1952, and was crowned at Westminster Abbey on June 2, 1953. Married Philip Mountbatten November 20, 1947. They have four children: Charles, Prince of Wales; Anne, the Princess Royal; Andrew, the Duke of York; and Prince Edward. The Queen is represented in Northern Ireland by a Lord Lieutenant in each county or city; they are The Lord O'Neill (Antrim), Colonel E. Wilson (Belfast), The Earl of Caledon (Armagh), W.J. Hall (Down), The Earl of Erne (Fermanagh), Sir Michael McCorkell (Derry), J.T. Eaton (Derry City) and the Duke of Abercorn (Tyrone).

STATE EMBLEMS OF NORTHERN IRELAND

Name of State, National Flag, Emblem, and National Anthem

NAME OF STATE: The name of the state is Northern Ireland, and it is part of the United Kingdom of Great Britain and Northern Ireland. Established by the Government of Ireland Act 1920, it consists of six of the nine counties of the historic province of Ulster.

THE NATIONAL FLAG: The national flag is the union flag. It is a combination of the cross of St. George (a red cross on a white background), the cross of St. Andrew (a diagonal white cross on a blue background) and the cross of St. Patrick (a diagonal red cross on a white background). From partition in 1922 until the imposition of direct rule in 1972 the flag was a six pointed star enclosing a red hand surmounted by a crown at the centre of a red cross on a white background.

THE NATIONAL ANTHEM: The national anthem is 'God Save the Queen'.

NATIONALIST NON-ALLEGIANCE: It is a widely recognised fact that a substantial majority of nationalists do not give their allegiance to the Northern Ireland state. This historical and political reality has been evident in the intermittent civil unrest since the foundation of the Northern state. Since 1969 there has been a serious escalation in this unrest which has resulted in more than 3,000 deaths.

The Northern Ireland 'Good Friday' Agreement has provided for a North/South Ministerial Council which, as well as providing Northern Ireland nationalists with an institutional expression of their Irish identity, will deal with matters which affect the whole of the island of Ireland.

NORTHERN IRELAND POLITICAL PARTIES
Main political parties in Northern Ireland

ULSTER UNIONIST PARTY
3 Glengall Street, Belfast, BT12 5AE
Tel. (01232) 324601.
www.uup.org

Founded: 1905 as Ulster Unionist Council.
First Leader: Edward James Saunderson.
Current Leader: David Trimble MP (on left).
Party President: Josias Cunningham.
General Secretary: Vacant.
Seats: House of Commons: 10, NI Assembly: 28, European Parliament: 1.
European Alliance: European People's Party.
History: Initially opposed to partition, it went on to govern Northern Ireland from 1921 until 1972. Since the introduction of direct rule from Westminster, the party has consistently been the single largest party in Northern Ireland in terms of MPs and councillors and is currently the largest party in the Assembly.

The UUP was divided over the power-sharing arrangement in 1974. The participation of leader Brian Faulkner brought about his resignation and saw the majority of the party enter into a loose pan-unionist coalition with the DUP and the Ulster Vanguard. When this arrangement collapsed in the late 1970s, the UUP plotted a more independent course, refusing to enter into electoral pacts in marginal constituencies. It opposed the 'rolling devolution', suggested by Secretary of State James Prior in 1982, and the Anglo-Irish Agreement in 1985. The opposition to the Agreement saw the revival of tactical cooperation with the DUP in marginal constituencies, and this remained the case in each subsequent Westminster election. A majority of the party, and its 300 member Ulster Unionist Party executive, support the 'Good Friday' Agreement but a number of its MPs made their opposition to it clear and actively opposed it.

Aims: The party has as its aims the maintenance of Northern Ireland under the Crown as an integral part of the United Kingdom; the safeguarding of British citizenship for the people of Northern Ireland; the promotion of a democratic system of local government; and that any change in the constitutional status must be brought about by the consent of a majority within Northern Ireland. The party supports a Bill of Rights and the establishment of a Council of the British Isles to promote and formalise relationships within these islands.

SOCIAL DEMOCRATIC AND LABOUR PARTY
Cranmore House, 611C Lisburn Road,
Belfast BT9 7GT   Tel. (01232) 247700
www.indigo.ie/sdlp

Founded: 1970 amalgamation of Northern Ireland Labour Party, Republican Labour, the Nationalist Party and leading figures from the civil rights movement.

First Leader: Gerry Fitt.
Current Leader: John Hume MP, MEP (on left).
Party Chairman: Johnathon Stephenson.
General Secretary: Gerry Cosgrave.
Seats: House of Commons: 3, NI Assembly 24, European Parliament: 1.
European Alliance: Party of European Socialists
History: The party had representatives on the short-lived Power Sharing executive in 1974 and contributed to the New Ireland Forum in 1983. The party opposed 'rolling devolution' in 1982 but strongly supported the Anglo-Irish Agreement in 1985 and subsequent initiatives such as the Downing Street Declaration and Frameworks Document. The SDLP played a major part in the negotiations leading up to the 'Good Friday' Agreement and is the largest nationalist party in Northern Ireland Assembly.

The party has performed well in all Northern Ireland elections since its inception and has consistently had representatives elected to Westminster and the various Northern Ireland Assemblies and Forums. Since 1979 John Hume, the current party leader, has been a member of the European Parliament.

Aims: A moderate left-of-centre nationalist party, it promotes a united Ireland, freely negotiated and agreed by people both north and south, and contests elections on the following points: the abolition of all forms of discrimination and the promotion of equality among all citizens; the promotion of culture and the arts and the recognition and cherishing of their diversity; the public ownership of all essential services and industries; and the protection of the environment.

SINN FÉIN
51-55 Falls Road, Belfast, BT12 4PD
Tel. (01232) 230261
www.sinnfein.ie

Founded: 1905 (as Sinn Féin League); 1970 as Provisional Sinn Féin.
First Leader: Arthur Griffith; Ruairi Ó Brádaigh (Provisional Sinn Féin).
Current Leader: Gerry Adams MP, since 1983. (on left).
Party Chairman: Mitchell McLaughlin.
General Secretary: Lucilita Bhreatnach.
Seats: House of Commons: 2, NI Assembly: 18, Dáil Éireann: 1, European Parliament: None.
History: Sinn Féin (translated as "We Ourselves") was founded in 1905 as an umbrella group for small nationalist organisations. It won an overwhelming majority in the 1918 general election, and its members constituted themselves as Dáil Éireann. The party was to split in

1922 over the signing of the Anglo-Irish treaty and its republican rump withdrew from the Dáil. Small, abstentionist and ineffective, the party suffered a further split in 1970 when two factions emerged - 'Official' Sinn Féin (later to become the Workers' Party) and 'Provisional' Sinn Féin'.

The party revived its electoral fortunes in the period after the 1981 Hunger Strike, contesting each election in Northern Ireland from 1982 onwards. The party has had members elected to the House of Commons, Dáil Éireann and to most local councils in both Northern Ireland and the Republic. The party's Ard Fheis of May 1998 voted to end the policy of abstentionism with regard to the Northern Ireland Assembly and members duly took up their seats.

Aims: Sinn Féin is a republican party committed to ending the union with Britain and as part of the 'republican movement' has consistently been described, despite vehement denials, as the political wing of the IRA. The party is committed to the establishment of an agreed, inclusive Ireland and believes that a non-sectarian and pluralist society is the way forward. The party was instrumental in brokering the IRA ceasefire of August 1994. Sinn Féin was admitted to the multi-party talks following the restoration of the IRA ceasefire in July 1997 and was involved in the negotiations which culminated in the 'Good Friday' Agreement of April 1998.

DEMOCRATIC UNIONIST PARTY
91 Dundela Avenue, Belfast BT4 3BU
Tel. (01232) 471155
www.dup.org.uk

Founded: 1971 by Rev. Ian Paisley and Desmond Boal.
First and Current Leader: Rev. Ian Paisley *(on left)*.
Party Chairman: James McClure.
General Secretary: Alan Ewart.
Seats: House of Commons: 2, NI Assembly: 20, European Parliament: 1.
European Alliance: Independent.

History: The DUP was founded in 1971 by the leader of the Protestant Unionist Party, Rev. Ian Paisley, and former Ulster Unionist MP, Desmond Boal. Opposed to the 1974 Power Sharing arrangement, it initially secured a vote of around 10%. Its major breakthroughs came in 1979 when it won three Westminster seats and its leader, Rev. Paisley, topped the poll in the European Parliament election. Staunch in its opposition to the Anglo-Irish Agreement in 1985, it at last found common ground with the UUP and all subsequent elections have seen co-operation in a number of marginal constituencies where only one unionist candidate has been nominated. The party opposed initiatives such as the Downing Street Declaration and the Frameworks Document and, after withdrawing from multi-party negotiations in September 1997 when Sinn Féin was admitted, opposed the 'Good Friday' Agreement in coalition with the United Kingdom Unionist Party and anti-Agreement elements within the Ulster Unionist Party.

Aims: The party stands for the union with Britain.

ALLIANCE PARTY OF NORTHERN IRELAND
88 University Street, Belfast, BT7 1HE
Tel. (01232) 324274
www.unite.net/customers/alliance/

Founded: 1970
First Leader: Phelim O'Neill
Current Leader: Sean Neeson.
Party Chairman: Councillor Eileen Bell.
General Secretary: Councillor David Ford
Seats: House of Commons: none, NI Assembly 6, European Parliament: none.

History: Founded in 1970 the party attracted support from disaffected unionists following the O'Neill split and from supporters of the Northern Ireland Labour Party, its members took part in the 1973 Sunningdale conference and went on to take up ministries in the Power Sharing executive in 1974. Strongly in favour of 'rolling devolution' in the 1982 Convention, it lost support when it gave qualified support to the Anglo-Irish Agreement in 1985. The party helped negotiate and then campaigned for a yes vote in the referendum on 'Good Friday' Agreement.

Aims: The party is a moderate unionist party and believes a regional power-sharing government for Northern Ireland is the best method of governance and the best chance for achieving a sustainable and lasting peace. It also advocates a Bill of Rights and a constructive and co-operative North/South relationship. It believes the future of Northern Ireland must be decided by the people of Northern Ireland and through the principle of consent.

PROGRESSIVE UNIONIST PARTY
182 Shankill Road, Belfast, BT13 2BL.
Tel. 01232 326233
www.pup.org

Founded: 1977
First and Current Leader: Hugh Smith OBE *(on left)*.
Party Chairman: William Smyth.
General Secretary: William Mitchell.
Seats: Westminster: None, NI Assembly: 2, European Parliament: None.

History: The Progressive Unionist Party was formed in 1977. It has close links with the Ulster Volunteer Force and played a major part in the negotiating of the Combined Loyalist Military Command ceasefire of October 1994. The party participated in all stages of the negotiations which led to the 'Good Friday' Agreement and campaigned for a yes vote in the referendum which ratified it.

Aims: The party is committed to maintaining the Union with Great Britain and believes that the principle of power sharing with nationalists is the best method for the governance of Northern Ireland. Dedicated to a non-sectarian, pluralist and equitable society, it believes that a written constitution and bill of rights should be implemented to safeguard human rights, minorities and institutions.

NORTHERN IRELAND WOMEN'S COALITION
52 Elmwood Ave., Belfast BT9 6AZ (01232) 660424
www.pitt.edu/~novosel.northern.html

Founded: 1996
The party does not elect a leader or chairperson.
Co-ordinator: Ann McCann
Seats: Westminster: None, NI Assembly: 2, European Parliament: None.
History: Established to raise the profile of women in Northern Irish politics. The party had two delegates at the multi-party talks which culminated in the 'Good Friday' Agreement. Campaigned for a yes vote in the referendum and had two members elected to the Northern Ireland Assembly, Monica McWilliams *(above)* and Jane Morrice.
Aims: The party advocates policy building as opposed to political division and supports the Northern Ireland Assembly as a forum were representatives can solve the community's common problems.

UNITED KINGDOM UNIONIST PARTY
10 Hamilton Road, Bangor, Co. Down BT20 4LE
Tel. 01247 272994
www.ulster.org.uk.ukup

Founded: 1996 **First and Current Leader:** Robert McCartney MP *(on left)*.
Party President: Dr Conor Cruise O'Brien.
General Secretary: Tom Sheridan.
Seats: Westminster: 1, NI Assembly: 5, European Parliament: None.
History: Founded in 1996 and centred around Bob McCartney, the party fared particularly well in the 1998 NI Assembly election. The United Kingdom Unionist Party was not involved in the closing stages of the multi-party negotiations and opposed the 'Good Friday' Agreement
Aims: The party aims to preserve the Union and will form part of the anti Agreement bloc in the Assembly opposing the creation of all Ireland bodies with executive powers, advocate the rule of law and strive to maintain the British identity of the unionist people of Northern Ireland.

Designation within the Northern Ireland Assembly (ie. Nationalist, Unionist, Other)

Ulster Unionist Party.....................................Unionist	Alliance Party of Northern ireland...................Other
Social Democratic and Labour Party ......Nationalist	Progressive Unionist Party ....Unionist
Sinn Féin ....Nationalist	Northern ireland Women's Coalition ....Other
Democratic Unionist Party ....Unionist	United Kingdom Unionist Party ....Unionist

MINOR POLITICAL PARTIES IN NORTHERN IRELAND

CONSERVATIVE PARTY..2 May Ave, Bangor, Co. Down............	01247 469210
GREEN PARTY ....537 Antrim Road, Belfast 15............	01232 776731
LABOUR NORTHERN IRELAND ....54 Wynne Hill, Hill Street, Lurgan, Co. Armagh............	01762 324303
NATURAL LAW PARTY..103 University Street, Belfast 7............	01232 311466
ULSTER DEMOCRATIC PARTY ....36 Castle Street, Lisburn, Co. Antrim............	01846 667056
ULSTER INDEPENDENCE MOVEMENT ....316 Shankill Road, Belfast BT13 1AB............	01232 236815
WORKERS' PARTY ....6 Springfield Road, Belfast 12	01232 328663

NORTHERN IRELAND POLITICAL PARTY LEADERS
Leaders of major Northern Ireland political parties

ULSTER UNIONIST PARTY	
Edward James Saunderson ....(1905-06)
Walter H. Long..(1906-10)
Sir Edward Carson ....(1910-21)
Sir James Craig...(1921-40)
John Miller Andrews ....(1940-43)
Sir Basil Brooke..(1943-63)
Capt. Terence O'Neill....................................(1963-69)
Maj. James Chichester-Clark ....(1969-71)
Brian Faulkner..(1971-74)
Harry West ....(1974-79)
James Molyneaux ....(1979-95)
David Trimble ....(1995-)

DEMOCRATIC UNIONIST PARTY	
Rev. Ian Paisley ....(1971-)

SOCIAL DEMOCRATIC AND LABOUR PARTY	
Gerry Fitt..(1970-79)
John Hume...(1979-)

PROVISIONAL SINN FÉIN	
Ruairí Ó Brádaigh ....(1970-83)
Gerry Adams ....(1983-)

ALLIANCE PARTY	
Phelim O'Neill ....(1972-73)
Oliver Napier ....(1973-84)
John Cushnahan ....(1984-87)
John Alderdice ....(1987-98)
Sean Neeson ....(1998-)

ULSTER DEMOCRATIC PARTY	
John McMichael ....(1981-1987)
Raymond Smallwoods...............................(1987-1994)
Gary McMichael ....(1994-)

PROGRESSIVE UNIONIST PARTY	
Hugh Smyth ....(1977-)

NORTHERN IRELAND
ASSEMBLY ELECTION RESULTS, 25 JUNE, 1998

EAST ANTRIM
Seats: 6; **Candidates:** 16; **Electorate:** 59,313; **Turnout:** 36,103 (60.87%); **Quota:** 5,088; **Elected:** Roy Beggs Jnr (UUP) 5,764 - 1st Ct; Sean Neeson (All) 5,247 - 1st Ct; David Hilditch (DUP) 5,215 - 8th Ct; Ken Robinson (UUP) 6,275 - 12th Ct; Roger Hutchinson (UKUP) 4,220 - 13th Ct; Danny O'Connor (SDLP) 4,191 - 13th Ct.

NORTH ANTRIM
Seats: 6; **Candidates:** 18; **Electorate:** 73,247; **Turnout:** 50,561 (69.02%); **Quota:** 7,100; **Elected:** Rev Ian Paisley (DUP) 10,590 - 1st Ct; Ian Paisley Jnr (DUP) 7,551 - 2nd Ct; Sean Farren (SDLP) 8,300 - 6th Ct; Rev Robert Coulter (UUP) 7,833 - 10th Ct; James Leslie (UUP) 7,580 - 12th Ct; Gardiner Kane (DUP) 5,818 - 12th Ct.

SOUTH ANTRIM
Seats: 6; **Candidates:** 14; **Electorate:** 69,426; **Turnout:** 44,599 (64.24%); **Quota:** 6,285; **Elected:** Jim Wilson (UUP) 6,691 - 1st Ct; Wilson Clyde (DUP) 8,522 - 6th Ct; Norman Boyd (UKUP) 6,381 - 7th Ct; Donovan McClelland (SDLP) 6,384 - 8th Ct; Duncan Shipley-Dalton (UUP) 6,965 - 9th Ct; David Ford (All) 5,655 - 10th Ct.

EAST BELFAST
Seats: 6; **Candidates:** 20; **Electorate:** 60,562; **Turnout:** 40,356 (66.61%); **Quota:** 5,657; **Elected:** Peter Robinson (DUP) 11,219 - 1st Ct; Lord Alderdice (All) 6,144 - 1st Ct; David Ervine (PUP) 5,693 - 7th Ct; Reg Empey (UUP) 6,109 - 12th Ct; Sammy Wilson (DUP) 5,711 - 12th Ct; Ian Adamson (UUP) 5,415 - 15th Ct.

NORTH BELFAST
Seats: 6; **Candidates:** 18; **Electorate:** 62,541; **Turnout:** 42,066 (67.26%); **Quota:** 5,876; **Elected:** Nigel Dodds (DUP) 7,476 - 1st Ct; Alban Maginness (SDLP) 6,196 - 1st Ct; Gerry Kelly (SF) 8,793 - 10th Ct; Billy Hutchinson (PUP) 5,517 - 11th Ct; Fred Cobain (UUP) 5,114 - 11th Ct; William Agnew (UU) 4,971 - 11th Ct.

SOUTH BELFAST
Seats: 6; **Candidates:** 19; **Electorate:** 61,209; **Turnout:** 41,266 (67.42%); **Quota:** 5,818; **Elected:** Michael McGimpsey (UUP) 5,898 - 5th Ct; Alasdair McDonnell (SDLP) 5,963 - 6th Ct; Mark Robinson (DUP) 6,524 - 8th Ct; Esmond Birnie (UUP) 5,881 - 8th Ct; Prof. Monica McWilliams (NIWC) 5,277 - 10th Ct; Carmel Hanna (SDLP) 4,983 - 10th Ct.

WEST BELFAST
Seats: 6; **Candidates:** 15; **Electorate:** 60,699; **Turnout:** 42,754 (70.47%); **Quota:** 5,971; **Elected:** Gerry Adams (SF) 9,078 - 1st Ct; Dr Joe Hendron (SDLP) 6,140 - 1st Ct; Sue Ramsey (SF) 7,371 - 8th Ct; Bairbre DeBrun (SF) 6,994 - 9th Ct; Alex Maskey (SF) 6,328 - 10th Ct; Alex Atwood (SDLP) 5,350 - 10th Ct.

NORTH DOWN
Seats: 6; **Candidates:** 19; **Electorate:** 62,942; **Turnout:** 37,874 (60.17%); **Quota:** 5,331; **Elected:** Robert McCartney (UKUP) 8,188 - 1st Ct; Alan McFarland (UUP) 5,466 - 6th Ct; John Gorman (UUP) 5,346 - 6th Ct; Eileen Bell (All) 5,985 - 9th Ct; Jane Morrice (NIWC) 4,898 - 12th Ct; Peter Weir (UUP) 4,751 - 12th Ct.

SOUTH DOWN
Seats: 6; **Candidates:** 17; **Electorate:** 71,000; **Turnout:** 52,342 (73.72%); **Quota:** 7,337; **Elected:** Eddie McGrady (SDLP) 10,373 - 1st Ct; Mick Murphy (SF) 7,761 - 6th Ct; Dermot Nesbitt (UUP) 7,771 - 8th Ct; Patrick Bradley (SDLP) 7,390 - 10th Ct; Jim Wells (DUP) 8,170 - 11th Ct; Eamon O'Neill (SDLP) 6,163 - 11th Ct.

FERMANAGH & SOUTH TYRONE
Seats: 6; **Candidates:** 14; **Electorate:** 65,383; **Turnout:** 51,923 (79.41%); **Quota:** 7,292; **Elected:** Tommy Gallagher (SDLP) 8,135 - 1st Ct; Sam Foster (UUP) 7,495 - 5th Ct; Gerry McHugh (SF) 9,097 - 7th Ct; Michelle Gildernew (SF) 8,502 - 9th Ct; Maurice Morrow (DUP) 6,627 - 10th Ct; Joan Carson (UUP) 6,582 - 10th Ct.

FOYLE
Seats: 6; **Candidates:** 15; **Electorate:** 68,888; **Turnout:** 49,604 (72%); **Quota:** 6,971; **Elected:** John Hume (SDLP) 12,581 - 1st Ct; Mitchel McLaughlin (SF) 7,043 - 5th Ct; Mark Durkan (SDLP) 6,980 - 6th Ct; John Tierney (SDLP) 7,813 - 7th Ct; Mary Nelis (SF) 7,172 - 8th Ct; William Hay (DUP) 6,322 - 8th Ct.

LAGAN VALLEY
Seats: 6; **Candidates:** 15; **Electorate:** 71,661; **Turnout:** 47,074 (65.69%); **Quota:** 6,645; **Elected:** Seamus Close (All) 6,788 - 1st Ct; Billy Bell (UUP) 6,679 - 5th Ct; Edwin Poots (DUP) 7,642 - 7th Ct; Ivan Davis (UUP) 7,322 - 9th Ct; Patrick Roche (UKUP) 6,859 - 9th Ct; Patricia Lewsley (SDLP) 6,282 - 9th Ct.

EAST LONDONDERRY
Seats: 6; **Candidates:** 14; **Electorate:** 59,370; **Turnout:** 40,167 (67.66%); **Quota:** 5,653; **Elected:** Gregory Campbell (DUP) 6,099 - 1st Ct; David McClarty (UUP) 6,269 - 5th Ct; John Dallat (SDLP) 5,709 - 6th Ct; Arthur Doherty (SDLP) 7,755 - 8th Ct; Pauline Armitage (UUP) 5,379 - 9th Ct; Boyd Douglas (Unionist) 4,260 - 9th Ct.

NEWRY & ARMAGH
Seats: 6; **Candidates:** 14; **Electorate:** 71,553; **Turnout:** 55,293 (77.27%); **Quota:** 7,734; **Elected:** Seamus Mallon (SDLP) 13,582 - 1st Ct; Paul Berry (DUP) 7,900 - 4th Ct; Danny Kennedy (UUP) 10,184 - 6th Ct; Conor Murphy (SF) 7,741 - 8th Ct; Pat McNamee (SF) 7,177 - 8th Ct; John Fee (SDLP) 7,169 - 8th Ct.

STRANGFORD
Seats: 6; **Candidates:** 22; **Electorate:** 70,868; **Turnout:** 43,651 (61.60%); **Quota:** 6,132; **Elected:** Iris Robinson (DUP) 9,479 - 1st Ct; John Taylor (UUP)

9,203 - 1st Ct; Thomas Benson (UUP) 6,327 - 17th Ct; Kieran McCarthy (All) 6,202 - 17th Ct; Jim Shannon (DUP) 5,933 - 18th Ct; Cedric Wilson (UKUP) 4,804 - 18th Ct.

WEST TYRONE
Seats: 6; **Candidates:** 15; **Electorate:** 59,081; **Turnout:** 46,913 (79.4%); **Quota:** 6,565; **Elected:** Oliver Gibson (DUP) 8,015 - 1st Ct; Pat Doherty (SF) 7,027 - 1st Ct; Joe Byrne (SDLP) 6,705 - 4th Ct; Derek Hussey

(UUP) 8,446 - 8th Ct; Eugene McMenamin (SDLP) 6,520 - 9th Ct; Barry McElduff (SF) 5,997 - 9th Ct.

MID ULSTER
Seats: 6; **Candidates:** 13; **Electorate:** 59,991; **Turnout:** 50,622 (84.38%); **Quota:** 7,115; **Elected:** Rev William McCrea (DUP) 10,339 - 1st Ct; Martin McGuinness (SF) 8,703 - 1st Ct; Billy Armstrong (UUP) 7,467 - 6th Ct; Francie Molloy (SF) 7,083 - 6th Ct; Denis Haughey (SDLP) 7,051 - 6th Ct; John Kelly (SF) 5,914 - 6th

Ct.

UPPER BANN
Seats: 6; **Candidates:** 18; **Electorate:** 70,852; **Turnout:** 51,223 (72.29%); **Quota:** 7,200; **Elected:** David Trimble (UUP) 12,338 - 1st Ct; Brid Rodgers (SDLP) 9,260 - 1st Ct; Dara O'Hagan (SF) 7,413 - 10th Ct; Mervyn Carrick (DUP) 8,034 - 13th Ct; Denis Watson (UUU) 7,792 - 14th Ct; George Savage (UUP) 6,527 - 14th Ct.

❐

NORTHERN IRELAND ASSEMBLY MEMBERS

Gerry Adams	SF	
Ian Adamson	UUP	
William Agnew	UU	
Lord Alderdice	All	
Pauline Armitage	UUP	
Billy Armstrong	UUP	
Alex Attwood	SDLP	
Roy Beggs Jnr	UUP	
Billy Bell	UUP	
Eileen Bell	All	
Tom Benson	UUP	
Paul Berry	DUP	
Esmond Birnie	UUP	
Norman Boyd	UKUP	
Patrick Bradley	SDLP	
Joe Byrne	SDLP	
Gregory Campbell	DUP	
Mervyn Carrick	DUP	
Joan Carson	UUP	
Seamus Close	All	
Wilson Clyde	DUP	
Fred Cobain	UUP	
Rev Robert Coulter	UUP	
John Dallat	SDLP	
Ivan Davis	UUP	
Bairbre DeBrun	SF	
Nigel Dodds	DUP	
Arthur Doherty	SDLP	
Pat Doherty	SF	
Boyd Douglas	Ind UUP	
Mark Durkan	SDLP	
Reg Empey	UUP	
David Ervine	PUP	
Sean Farren	SDLP	
John Fee	SDLP	
David Ford	All	

Sam Foster	UUP
Tommy Gallagher	SDLP
Oliver Gibson	DUP
Michelle Gildernew	SF
Sir John Gorman	UUP
Carmel Hanna	SDLP
Denis Haughey	SDLP
William Hay	DUP
Dr Joe Hendron	SDLP
David Hilditch	DUP
John Hume	SDLP
Derek Hussey	UUP
Billy Hutchinson	PUP
Roger Hutchinson	UKUP
Gardiner Kane	DUP
Gerry Kelly	SF
John Kelly	SF
Danny Kennedy	UUP
James Leslie	UUP
Patricia Lewsley	SDLP
Alban Maginness	SDLP
Seamus Mallon	SDLP
Alex Maskey	SF
Kieran McCarthy	All
Robert McCartney	UKUP
David McClarty	UUP
Donovan McCleland	SDLP
Rev William McCrea	DUP
Alasdair McDonnell	SDLP
Barry McElduff	SF
Alan McFarland	UUP
Michael McGimpsey	UUP
Eddie McGrady	SDLP
Martin McGuinness	SF
Gerry McHugh	SF
Mitchel McLaughlin	SF

Eugene McMenamin	SDLP
Pat McNamee	SF
Prof Monica McWilliams	NIWC
Francie Molloy	SF
Jane Morrice	NIWC
Maurice Morrow	DUP
Conor Murphy	SF
Mick Murphy	SF
Sean Neeson	All
Mary Neilis	SF
Dermot Nesbit	UUP
Danny O'Connor	SDLP
Dara O'Hagan	SF
Eamon O'Neill	SDLP
Rev Dr Ian Paisley	DUP
Ian Paisley Jnr	DUP
Edwin Poots	DUP
Sue Ramsey	SF
Iris Robinson	DUP
Ken Robinson	UUP
Mark Robinson	DUP
Peter Robinson	DUP
Patrick Roche	UKUP
Brid Rodgers	SDLP
George Savage	UUP
Jim Shannon	DUP
Duncan Shipley-Dalton	UUP
John Taylor	UUP
John Tierney	SDLP
David Trimble	UUP
Denis Watson	UUUU
Peter Weir	UUP
Jim Wells	DUP
Cedric Wilson	UKUP
Jim Wilson	UUP
Sammy Wilson	DUP

GOVERNMENT OF NORTHERN IRELAND
British Government System

● The Queen is head of state and head of the Anglican Church.

● The House of Commons has 659 members elected on a 'first past the post' basis. Northern Ireland returns 18 members to the House of Commons.

● The Queen appoints the leader of the party who can command a majority in the House of Commons and appoints him/her as Prime Minister. The Prime Minister in turn appoints the members of the cabinet.

● The cabinet acts collectively.

- All acts passed by the Houses of Parliament must be promulgated by the Queen, i.e. given a royal assent.
- As head of the Judiciary, the Lord Chancellor is responsible for the appointment of judges and magistrates. The Lord Chancellor also has a seat in cabinet.
- Britain does not have a written constitution rather a series of documents and legislation which govern the functions of state. These are: common law, legislation (from the Houses of Parliament), conventions, the law and custom of parliament, European Union law and works of authority.

NORTHERN IRELAND GOVERNMENT SYSTEM

The new arrangements for the governance of Northern Ireland can be divided into three interlocking and interdependent strands. In the first strand, executive authority will be vested in up to 12 Ministers who are part of the 108-member Northern Ireland Assembly, allocated in proportion to party strengths. The Assembly will govern the internal affairs of Northern Ireland in areas such as health, education and agriculture, while other areas such as security, taxation and justice will remain the responsibility of the Secretary of State and the Westminster government. Decisions taken by the executive must be ratified by the Assembly by securing the support of majority of both nationalists and unionists.

A North/South ministerial council will be established in the second strand. It will draw members from both the Irish government and the Northern Ireland Executive and will participate in consultation, co-operation and action on matters of mutual interest.

The third strand is a British-Irish Council where representatives are drawn from elected parliaments and assemblies in Northern Ireland, the Republic of Ireland, Scotland, Wales, the Isle of Man, the Channel Islands and the House of Commons. It is envisaged the Council will meet twice yearly to discuss matters of mutual interest.

NORTHERN IRELAND EXECUTIVE 1998 (to be appointed)

First Minister
David Trimble
(UUP)

Deputy
First Minister
Seamus Mallon
(SDLP)

BRITISH GOVERNMENT MINISTERS IN N. IRELAND

SECRETARY OF STATE	
Northern Ireland Office and the Northern Ireland departments ....Dr. Mo Mowlam MP	

Ministers of State	
Political Development, Finance and Personnel, Information and the EU.........Paul Murphy MP	
Security, Economic Development and North/South Co-operation ....Adam Ingram MP	

Parliamentary Under Secretaries of State	
Education, Health and Social Services, Community Relations and Employment Equality ....John McFall MP	
Environment and Agriculture ....Lord Dubs	

Sec. of State
Dr. Mo Mowlam

NORTHERN IRELAND MEMBERS OF PARLIAMENT

Constituency	Name Party	Address	Telephone
Antrim East	Beggs, Roy..UUP	41 Station Road, Larne BT40 3AA	.01574 273258
Antrim North	Paisley, Ian..DUP	17 Cyprus Avenue, Belfast BT5 5NT	.01232 454255
Antrim South	Forsythe, Clifford..UUP	19 Fountain Street, Antrim BT41 4BG	.01849 460776
Belfast East	Robinson, Peter DUP	51 Gransha Rd, Dundonald, Belfast BT16 0HB	.01232 473111
Belfast North	Walker, Cecil..UUP	20 Oldpark Rd, Belfast BT14 6FR	.01232 755996
Belfast South	Smyth, Martin..UUP	117 Cregagh Rd, Belfast BT6 0LA	.01232 457009
Belfast West	Adams, Gerry ...SF	51-55 Falls Rd, Belfast 12	.01232 230261
Fermanagh & Sth Tyrone	Maginnis, Ken..UUP	20 Brooke Street, Dungannon BT71 7AN	.01868 723265

Foyle	Hume, John.SDLP	5 Bayview Terrace, Derry BT48 7EE	.01504 265340
Lagan Valley	Donaldson, Jeffrey..UUP	38 Railway Street, Lisburn BT28 1XP	.01846 668001
Londonderry East	Ross, Willie..UUP	89 Teevan Rd, Turmeel, Dungiven BT47 4SL	.01504 741428
Mid Ulster	McGuinness, Martin ...SF	15 Cable Street, Derry BT48	.01504 361949
Newry & Armagh	Mallon, Seamus.SDLP	15 Cornmarket, Newry BT35 8BG	.01693 67933
North Down	McCartney, Robert UKUP	10 Hamilton Rd, Bangor, Co. Down BT20 4LE	.01247 272994
South Down	McGrady, Eddie.SDLP	Saul Street, Downpatrick BT30 6NQ	.01396 61288
Strangford	Taylor, John..UUP	6 William Street, Newtownards BT23 4AE	.01247 814123
Upper Bann	Trimble, David..UUP	2 Queen Street, Lurgan BT66 8BQ	.01762 328088
West Tyrone	Thompson, Willie..UUP	.156 Donaghanie Rd, Beragh, Omagh BT79 0XE	.01662 758214

CURRENT POSITION OF THE PARTIES

PARTY	EUROPEAN PARLIAMENT	HOUSE OF COMMONS	NORTHERN IRELAND ASSEMBLY
UUP	1	10	28
SDLP	1	3	24
SF	-	2	18
DUP	1	2	20
UKUP	-	1	5
All	-	-	6
NIWC	-	-	2
PUP	-	-	2
Others	-	-	3
TOTAL	3	18	108

NORTHERN IRELAND ASSEMBLY ELECTION RESULTS

The Assembly elections of June 25, 1998, were contested in 18 constituencies by 296 candidates (an average of 16.44 per constituency). It took 195 counts (an average of 10.83 per constituency) to elect the 108 members.

Constituency	Seats	Electorate	Turnout	Turnout %	Spoiled	Valid Poll	Quota
Mid Ulster	6	59,991	50,622	84.38	824	49,798	7,115
West Tyrone	6	59,081	46,913	79.40	962	45,951	6,565
Fermanagh & Sout 1 Tyrone	6	65,383	51,923	79.41	880	51,043	7,292
North Down	6	62,942	37,874	60.17	561	37,313	5,331
Strangford	6	70,868	43,651	61.59	729	42,922	6,132
Foyle	6	68,888	49,604	72.00	810	48,794	6,971
Upper Bann	6	70,852	51,223	72.30	824	50,399	7,200
Lagan Valley	6	71,661	47,074	65.69	564	46,510	6,645
South Down	6	71,000	52,342	73.72	989	51,353	7,337
Newry & Armagh	6	71,553	55,293	77.28	1,157	54,136	7,734
East Antrim	6	59,313	36,103	60.87	493	35,610	5,088
South Antrim	6	69,426	44,599	64.24	608	43,991	6,285
North Antrim	6	73,247	50,561	69.02	864	49,697	7,100
Belfast East	6	60,562	40,356	66.63	763	39,593	5,657
Belfast North	6	62,541	42,066	67.26	941	41,125	5,876
Belfast South	6	61,209	41,266	67.42	542	40,724	5,818
Belfast West	6	60,669	42,754	70.47	960	41,794	5,971
East Derry	6	59,370	40,167	67.66	603	39,564	5,653
Total	108	1,178,556	824,391	69.95	14074	810317	

SALARIES OF ELECTED REPRESENTATIVES

WESTMINSTER	£	NORTHERN IRELAND ASSEMBLY§	£
Member of Parliament	45,066	Assembly Member	29,292
Parliamentary Under Secretary of State*	69,339	Presiding Officer	45,069
Minister of State	77,047	Minister	45,069
Minister (Secretary of State)	106,716	Deputy First Minister	54,876
Prime Minister	147,816	First Minister	60,164

Lord Dubs, as a member of the House of Lords, does not draw an MP's salary.
§ Where an Assembly Member is also an MP or MEP she/he is entitled to one-third of the basic salary.

NORTHERN IRELAND
ASSEMBLY ELECTION RESULTS, OVERALL

Party	Total 1st Preference Votes	% of Total Vote	Seats Won
Ulster Unionist Party	172,225	21.25%	28
Social Democratic and Labour Party	177,963	21.96%	24
Democratic Unionist Party	145,917	18.00%	20
Sinn Féin	142,858	17.63%	18
Alliance Party of Northern Ireland	52,636	6.50%	6
United Kingdom Unionist Party	36,541	4.51%	5
Progressive Unionist Party	20,634	2.55%	2
Northern Ireland's Women's Coalition	13,019	1.61%	2
Ulster Democratic Party	8,651	1.06%	0
Labour	2,729	0.34%	0
Others	37,144	4.59%	3
TOTAL	810,317	100.00%	108

TOP VOTE GETTERS

Name	Party	Constituency	Votes	Multiple of Quota
1. Seamus Mallon	SDLP	Newry & Armagh	13,582	1.76
2. John Hume	SDLP	Foyle	12,581	1.80
3. David Trimble	UUP	Upper Bann	12,338	1.69
4. Peter Robinson	DUP	East Belfast	11,219	1.94
5. Ian Paisley	DUP	North Antrim	10,590	1.47
6. Eddie McGrady	SDLP	South Down	10,373	1.39
7. Willie McCrea	DUP	Mid Ulster	10,339	1.45
8. Iris Robinson	DUP	Strangford	9,479	1.52
9. Brid Rodgers	SDLP	Upper Bann	9,260	1.26
10. John Taylor	UUP	Strangford	9,203	1.48

WOMEN ELECTED TO THE ASSEMBLY

1. Pauline Armitage ....UUP............East Londonderry
2. Eileen Bell ....All......................North Down
3. Joan Carson ....UUP ...Fermanagh & Sth Tyrone
4. Bairbre DeBrun..........SF.................West Belfast
5. Michelle Gildernew ....SF ...Fermanagh & Sth Tyrone
6. Carmel Hanna ......SDLP................South Belfast
7. Patricia Lewsley ....SDLP.....................Lagan Valley
8. Monica McWiliamsNIWC....................South Belfast
9. Jane Morrice.........NIWC.....................North Down
10. Mary Nelis.............SF...............................Foyle
11. Dara O'Hagan.........SF....................Upper Bann
12. Sue Ramsey ....SF..................West Belfast
13. Iris Robinson.........DUP.........................Strangford
14. Brid Rodgers.......SDLP.....................Upper Bann

The 14 female members make up 13%
of the Assembly's total.

ASSEMBLY MEMBERS WHO ARE ALSO MPs

1. ....Gerry Adams ....SF
2. ....John Hume.........................SDLP
3. ....Seamus Mallon.........................SDLP
4. ....Robert McCartney.........................UKUP
5. ....Martin McGuinness ....SF
6. ....Rev Dr Ian Paisley ....DUP
7. ....Peter Robinson ....DUP

8. ....John Taylor ....UUP
9. ....David Trimble ....UUP

Nine Assembly members (8% of total) are also MPs while two, John Hume and Ian Paisley, are also Members of the European Parliament. No MP who stood for election failed to get elected.

HIGHEST & LOWEST

	Highest	Lowes
% Turnout	84.38% (Mid Ulster)	60.17% (North Down)
Quota	7,734 (Newry & Armagh)	5,088 (East Antrim)
Number of Candidates	22 (Strangford)	13 (Mid Ulster)
Candidates-to-Seat Ratio	3.66 (Strangford)	2.17 (Mid Ulster)
Electorate	73,247 (North Antrim)	59,081 (West Tyrone)
Electorate-to-Seat Ratio	12,208 (North Antrim)	9,847 (West Tyrone)

LOWEST VOTE GETTERS

Candidate	Party	Votes	Constituency
1.John Lawrence	Energy106	15	East Belfast
2.David Collins	NLP	22	East Belfast
3.David Evans	NLP	23	Newry & Armagh
4.Sarah Mullins	NLP	27	Strangford
5.George Stidolph	NLP	28	South Antrim
6.Michael Kennedy	NLP	29	West Belfast
7.James McKissock	NLP	32	East Antrim
8.Donn Brennan	NLP	32	Foyle
9.Jack Lyons	NLP	32	Upper Bann
10.Thomas Mullins	NLP	33	South Down

NARROW VICTORIES

Candidate	Party	Lost by	To	Party	Constituency
Jack McKee	DUP	49 votes	Danny O'Connor	SDLP	East Antrim
Steve McBride	All	151 votes	Carmel Hanna	SDLP	South Belfast
Danny McCarthy	SDLP	159 votes	Cedric Wilson	UKUP	Strangford
Martin Morgan	SDLP	289 votes	William Agnew	UU	North Belfast
Alan Graham	DUP	308 votes	Peter Weir	UUP	North Down

N.I. ELECTIONS TO WESTMINSTER, 1922-1997

DATE	NO. OF SEATS	UUP	N	DUP	SDLP	SF	OTHER U	OTHER N	OTHER Lab.	VUPP
15.11.1922	13	11	2	-	-	-	-	-	-	-
06.12.1923	13	11	2	-	-	-	-	-	-	-
29.10.1924	13	13	-	-	-	-	-	-	-	-
30.05.1929	13	11	-	-	-	-	-	2*	-	-
27.10.1931	13	11	2	-	-	-	-	-	-	-
14.11.1935	13	11	-	-	-	-	-	2*	-	-
05.07.1945	13	9	2	-	-	-	1	-	1	-
23.02.1950	12	10	-	-	-	-	-	2*	-	-
25.10.1951	12	9	-	-	-	-	-	2*	1	-
26.05.1955	12	10	-	-	-	2	-	-	-	-
08.10.1959	12	12	-	-	-	-	-	-	-	-
15.10.1964	12	12	-	-	-	-	-	-	-	-
31.03.1966	12	11	-	-	-	-	-	-	1	-
18.06.1970	12	8	-	-	-	-	1	2*	1	-
28.02.1974	12	7	-	1	1	-	-	-	-	3
10.10.1974	12	6	-	1	1	-	-	1*	-	3
03.05.1979	12	5	-	3	1	-	2	1	-	-
09.06.1983	17	11	-	3	1	1	1	-	-	-
11.06.1987	17	9	-	3	3	1	1	-	-	-
09.04.1992	17	9	-	3	4	-	1	-	-	-
01.05.1997	18	10	-	2	3	2	1	-	-	-

* 1929 ....Other N = National League
* 1935 ....Other N = Nationalist Abstentionists
* 1950/51 ....Other N = Anti-Partition League
* 1970 ....Other N = Unity Candidates
* 1974 ....Other N = Independent

ELECTIONS TO PARLIAMENT OF N.I., 1921-73

DATE	NO. OF SEATS	UUP	N	NILP	OTHER N	OTHER U	OTHER Lab	Ind
24.05.1921	52	40	6	-	6	-	-	-
03.04.1925	52	32	10	3	2	4	-	1
22.05.1929	52	37	11	1	-	3	-	-
30.11.1933	52	36	9	2	2	3	-	-
09.02.1938	52	39	8	1	-	3	1	-
14.06.1945	52	33	10	2	-	2	3	2
10.02.1949	52	37	9	-	-	2	2	2
22.10.1953	52	38	7	-	2	1	3	1
20.03.1958	52	37	7	4	1	-	2	1
31.05.1962	52	34	9	4	-	-	3	2
25.11.1965	52	36	9	2	1	-	2	2
24.02.1969	52	36*	6	2	-	3	2	3

* 24 Pro-O'Neill, 10 anti-O'Neill, 2 undeclared

NORTHERN IRELAND SECRETARIES OF STATE

1972-73................William Whitelaw.......Conservative	1984-85.....................Douglas Hurd.......Conservative
1973-74.......................Francis Pym.......Conservative	1985-89............................Tom King.......Conservative
1974-76 ....Merlyn Rees ....Labour	1989-92.....................Peter Brooke.......Conservative
1976-79 ....Roy Mason ....Labour	1992-97 ....Patrick Mayhew.......Conservative
1979-81 ....Humphrey Atkins.......Conservative	1997- ....Dr Mo Mowlam ....Labour
1981-84 ....Jim Prior.......Conservative	

NORTHERN IRELAND PRIME MINISTERS FACT FILE

Name	Party	Born	in	Appointed P.M.	Aged	Died	Aged
Sir James Craig ....UUP		08.01.1871	..Belfast	07.06.1921	50	...24.11.1940	69
John M. Andrews ....UUP		17.07.1871	..Co. Down	25.11.1940	69	...06.08.1956	85
Sir Basil Brooke ....UUP		09.06.1888	..Co. Fermanagh	28.04.1943	54	...18.08.1973	85
Capt. Terence O'Neill ....UUP		10.09.1914	..London	25.03.1963	48	...13.06.1990	75
James Chichester-Clark.......UUP		12.02.1923	..Co. Derry	01.05.1969	46	-	-
Brian Faulkner.......................UUP		18.02.1921	..Co. Down	23.03.1971	50	...03.03.1977	56

BIOGRAPHIES OF NORTHERN IRELAND PRIME MINISTERS

SIR JAMES CRAIG (1921-40)

Born: Belfast, January 8, 1871.
Appointed: First Prime Minister of Northern Ireland on June 7, 1921, a position he held until his death. His tenure as P.M. was contemporaneous with his leadership of the Ulster Unionists.
Died: November 24, 1940.
Biographical Details: A veteran of the Boer War, he was elected to Westminster in 1906 and was vociferous in his opposition to Home Rule. He was an influential member of the Ulster Volunteer Force and was Quarter-Master General of the force (1914-16) - renamed the 36th (Ulster) Division during World War I. Craig used his influence at Westminster to present the unionist case when the Government of Ireland Act 1920 was drafted. The act provided for the partition of Ireland and the creation of the Northern Ireland state.

As P.M. he introduced a Special Powers Act in 1922 (made permanent in 1933), which gave the authorities virtually unlimited powers of arrest and detention. His government abolished proportional representation for local elections in 1922 and for Stormont elections in 1929, and it implemented an extensive system of gerrymandering in nationalist areas, famously commenting in 1934: "We have a Protestant parliament and a Protestant state." He was made Viscount Craigavon on January 20, 1927.

JOHN MILLER ANDREWS (1940-43)

Born: Cumber, Co. Down, July 17, 1871.
Appointed: November 25, 1940, he resigned as P.M. and leader of the Ulster Unionists on April 28, 1943.
Died: August 6, 1956.
Biographical Details: Elected to the House of Commons at Stormont in 1921, he held two ministerial posts prior to his premiership, namely, Minister for Labour (1921-37) and Minister for Finance (1937-40). He resigned from Stormont in 1953. His prominence in the Orange Order was reflected in his holding the position of Grand Master of the Imperial Grand Council of the World (1949-54) and Grand Master in Ireland (1948-54).

SIR BASIL BROOKE (1943-63)

Born: Colebrook, Co. Fermanagh, June 9, 1888.
Appointed: April 28, 1943, he remained in office until his resignation on March 25, 1963. He was also leader of the Ulster Unionists during this period and remained an M.P. until he resigned in 1967.
Died: August 18, 1973.
Biographical Details: He was a prominent figure in the Ulster Volunteer Force. He saw front line action during World War I and was decorated for his bravery. A unionist M.P. from 1929, he was Minister for Agriculture (1933-41) and Minister for Commerce and Production (1941-45). As P.M. he introduced social welfare legislation to harmonise Northern Ireland standards with those in Britain, and the important Education Act of 1947, which provided free secondary schooling for all. His government dealt ruthlessly with the I.R.A. border campaign of 1956-62, enacting tough security legislation. He refused to have any official contacts with Roman Catholics or trade unionists during his time in office. He was elevated to the peerage as Viscount Brookeborough on July 4, 1952.

TERENCE O'NEILL (1963-69)

Born: London, September 10, 1914.
Appointed: March 25, 1963, but resigned on April 28, 1969, when tensions within his party made his position untenable.
Died: June 13, 1990, aged 75.
Biographical Details: He saw action throughout World War II as a captain in the Irish Guards. Elected to Stormont in 1946, he was Minister for Finance (1956-63). As P.M. he advocated closer ties with the Republic, and in 1965 met with Taoiseach Seán Lemass in Belfast, the first meeting of its kind, followed by a meeting in Dublin. O'Neill also attempted to introduce measures granting civil rights to the minority Catholic popu-

lation, and his premiership was marked by the rise of the civil rights movement. Such concessions resulted in fierce opposition from both within his party and the unionist community at large. The resignation of senior ministers from his government precipitated his resignation, but ultimately, his failing was that he had raised the expectations of the Catholic community and was unable to deliver the necessary reforms. He was elevated to the peerage as Lord O'Neill of the Maine in January 1970.

JAMES CHICHESTER-CLARK (1969-71)

Born: Castledawson, Co. Derry, February 12, 1923.
Appointed: May 1, 1969, he resigned from the post March 20, 1971. Leader of the Ulster Unionist Party during that period.
Biographical Details: Elected to the Northern Ireland House of Commons in 1960, he was the Minister for Agriculture from 1967 until April of 1969 when he resigned over O'Neill's reforms. In August 1969 he requested that Whitehall send British troops to help quell the civil unrest endemic from July 1969. His request was granted, and British troops duly arrived on August 15. The B-Specials were disbanded in April of 1970, and this, coupled with the transferral of the control of security matters to the army, led to his resignation in March 1971.

He was made a life peer taking the title Lord Moyola in June 1971.

BRIAN FAULKNER (1971-72)

Born: Helen's Bay, Co. Down, February 18, 1921.
Appointed: March 23, 1971, and was the last man to hold the post. His tenure ended with the introduction of Direct Rule from London on March 24, 1972. He was leader of the Ulster Unionist Party from March 1971 until January 1974.
Died: Killed in a riding accident on March 3, 1977.
Biographical Details: First elected to the Northern Ireland House of Commons in 1949, he held a number of ministerial portfolios, including Home Affairs (1959-63), Commerce (1963-69) and Development (1969-71). In 1969 he resigned from government on the grounds that Terence O'Neill, the then Prime Minister, was introducing too many reforms at too great a pace.

As P.M., Faulkner presided over two events which signalled the end of the Northern Ireland Parliament, namely, the the introduction of internment without trial on August 9, 1971, which was directed almost exclusively at nationalists and 'Bloody Sunday' on January 30, 1972, where 13 civilians on a civil rights march were shot dead by British paratroopers in Derry (one man later died from his injuries). These events changed both world and British government opinion and precipitated Direct Rule.

In January 1974, he became the Chief Minister in the short lived 'Power Sharing' Executive, which was brought down less than five months later by the Ulster Workers' Council strike. He retired from politics in August 1976 and was elevated to the peerage in January 1977. ◻

CHANGING STATE OF THE PARTIES, 1977-98 (%)

ELECTION	UUP	SDLP	DUP	SF	All	Others
1977 Local	29.6	20.6	12.7	-	14.4	22.7
1979 Gen	36.6	18.3	10.2	-	11.8	23.1
1979 Euro	21.9	24.6	29.8	-	6.8	16.9
1981 Local	26.5	17.5	26.6	-	8.9	20.5
1982 Asm	29.7	18.8	23.0	10.1	9.3	9.1
1983 Gen	34.0	17.9	20.0	13.4	8.0	6.7
1984 Euro	21.5	22.1	33.6	13.3	5.0	4.5
1985 Local	29.5	17.8	24.3	11.8	7.1	9.5
1987 Gen	37.8	21.1	11.7	11.4	10.0	8.0
1989 Local	31.3	21.0	17.7	11.2	6.9	11.9
1989 Euro	22.2	25.5	29.9	9.1	5.2	8.1
1992 Gen	34.5	23.5	13.1	10.0	8.7	10.2
1993 Local	29.4	22.0	17.3	12.4	7.6	11.3
1994 Euro	23.8	28.9	29.2	9.9	4.1	4.1
1996 Forum	24.2	21.4	18.8	15.5	6.5	13.6
1997 Gen	32.7	24.1	13.6	16.1	8.0	5.5
1997 Local	27.8	20.7	15.6	16.9	6.6	12.4
1998 Asm	21.3	22.0	18.0	17.7	6.6	14.4

Asm ....Northern Ireland Assembly Election   **Gen**......General Election   **Local** ....District Council Election
Forum..Northern Ireland Forum Election   **Euro** ....European Parliament Election

CONSTITUTIONAL REFERENDA

Date	Issue	Turnout %	For %	Against %
March 8, 1973	....Northern Ireland remaining within the United Kingdom	59	98.9	1.1
June 5, 1975	........United Kingdom remaining within the EEC	47	52.1	47.9
May 22, 1998	.......'Good Friday' Agreement	81.1	71.1	28.9

THE HISTORY OF THE PEACE PROCESS

WHEN John White, of the Progressive Unionist Party, publicly paid a warm tribute to an Taoiseach, Bertie Ahern, on Good Friday, April 10th, it was, for many, a defining moment in the entire peace process. Symbolically, it was the breaking of the last taboo.

The sight of a hardline former loyalist paramilitary paying tribute to an Irish Taoiseach suggested that the peace process had broken down not only old suspicions and hostilities between the two parts of the island but also eased much of the old enmity between political leaders who hold diametrically opposed views on the future governance of this island.

When the Northern "troubles" broke out in the late 1960s, there were no mechanisms in place to resolve what were very serious communal difficulties.

After Bloody Sunday in Derry (1972), Dublin called home its ambassador in London. The burning of the British Embassy in Dublin around the same time further strained relationships. And the alleged involvement of the British Intelligence Services in the bombings in Dublin and Monaghan (1974) heralded the era of what was later to be known as 'megaphone' diplomacy.

It wasn't until the early 1980s that the two governments began to co-operate more closely in an effort to find a widely acceptable political solution.

Here are some of the key signposts along the way:

ANGLO-IRISH INTERGOVERNMENTAL COUNCIL: Following a meeting in Dublin in 1980 between An Taoiseach, Charles Haughey, and British Prime Minister, Margaret Thatcher, the Council was set up to provide a formal framework within which relationships between the two countries could be explored. The work of the council laid the groundwork for the Anglo-Irish Agreement.

ANGLO-IRISH AGREEMENT: Signed in November 1985, the Anglo-Irish Agreement was received with great hostility by unionists in the North. In the agreement (signed by Mrs. Thatcher and Garret FitzGerald, the then Taoiseach), an Intergovernmental Conference was established, chaired jointly by a representative of each Government and served by a permanent Joint Secretariat based at Maryfield, just outside of Belfast.

The unionist hostility was premised on the fact that the Agreement enabled the Irish Government to put forward views and proposals on many aspects of Northern Ireland affairs. The agreement brought co-operation between the two countries to unprecedented levels.

ROUND-TABLE TALKS: In an effort to get things moving in the North, the two Governments convened round table talks during 1991/1992, involving the main constitutional parties in the North. These were based on the three-strand approach long promulgat-

ed by SDLP leader, John Hume. The strands were: 1) Relationships within Northern Ireland; 2) Relationships within the island of Ireland; 3) Relationship between Ireland and Britain.

No overall agreement was reached.

JOINT DECLARATION: A Joint Declaration was issued by An Taoiseach, Albert Reynolds, and British Prime Minister, John Major, on December 15, 1993. The Declaration set out the basic principles which, it was felt, would be required to underpin any political settlement. At the core of this document were the principles of self-determination and consent. One of the key phrases contained in the document was that the British Government had "no selfish strategic or economic interest in Northern Ireland". In regard to the principle of consent, the British also affirmed that they would uphold the democratic wish of a greater number of the people in the North on the issue of whether they would prefer to support the Union or a sovereign united Ireland.

The Irish Government stated ". . . the democratic right of self-determination by the people of Ireland, as a whole, must be achieved and exercised with and subject to the agreement and consent of the majority of the people of Northern Ireland."

Of particular importance was the offer in the Declaration to those engaged in paramilitary violence that if they established a commitment to exclusively peaceful means and were willing to abide by the democratic process they would be free to participate fully, in the due course, in the dialogue between the two governments. This, along with SDLP leader John Hume's extensive talks with Sinn Féin President, Gerry Adams, sowed the seeds for the IRA ceasefire.

IRA CEASFIRE: After 25 years of a sustained campaign, the IRA announced, on August 31, 1994 a "complete cessation of military operations". The Combined Loyalist Military Command announced a similar cessation on October 13, 1994. Both Governments moved swiftly to engage Sinn Féin, and the two loyalist parties, the Progressive Unionist Party (PUP) and the Ulster Democratic Party (UDP), in political dialogue.

FRAMEWORK DOCUMENT: Officially titled "A New Framework for Agreement", the Framework Document basically sought to apply the principles enunciated in the Joint Declaration. It envisaged balanced constitutional change on both sides and new political structures covering all three relationships. It also committed the Governments to comprehensive negotiations with the Northern Ireland parties and that any agreement resulting from those negotiations be put to the people, North and South, for democratic ratification.

INTERNATIONAL BODY: The entire process stalled during 1995 because unionists refused to engage in talks with Sinn Féin without IRA decommissioning. In an attempt to move things forward, the Governments established an International body under the chairmanship of US Senator George Mitchell to provide an independent assessment of how best to handle the decommissioning issue.

In its report in January, 1996, the International Body recommended that all parties participating in negotiations should commit themselves to six principles of democracy and non-violence. It also suggested that the parties might consider a proposal whereby decommissioning might occur during negotiations.

IRA CEASFIRE ENDS: Amidst a welter of recriminations, much of it directed against An Taoiseach, John Bruton, the IRA ceasefire ended on February 9, 1996, with a huge explosion at Canary Wharf in London. Republicans claimed that they had delivered on their side of the bargain – by delivering a ceasefire – but once that had been achieved, the two Governments had stalled the entire process.

MULTI-PARTY TALKS: After much delay, nine parties assembled in June 1996 for multi-party talks involving the two governments. Sinn Féin was excluded in the absence of an IRA ceasefire. The talks were chaired by Senator Mitchell who was assisted by former Finnish Prime Minister, Harri Holkeri and former Canadian General, John de Chastelain. Progress at the talks was painfully slow, much time being devoted to procedural detail.

IRA RENEW CEASEFIRE: On Friday, July 20, 1997, the IRA announced a renewal of its ceasefire thus clearing the way for Sinn Féin's entry into the talks on September 9. In protest at the Sinn Féin entry, two unionist parties, the DUP and the UKUP, then left the talks. The largest unionist party, the UUP, under the leadership of David Trimble, decided to stay.

SUBSTANTIVE NEGOTIATIONS BEGIN: More than three years after the IRA first called its ceasefire, substantive negotiations finally got underway on September 24, 1997. The three-strand agenda on relationships within these islands provided the basis for the negotiations.

PROPOSITIONS ON HEADS OF AGREEMENT: On January 12, 1998, the Governments published a series of proposals/suggestions which they hoped would focus the negotiations. Sinn Féin reacted angrily to these "Heads of Agreement" claiming they were more kindly disposed to the unionist position. Against this background, Senator Mitchell imposed a deadline of April 9 for the ending of negotiations.

THE GOOD FRIDAY AGREEMENT: On Friday, April 10 (Good Friday), one day after the agreed deadline, the Northern Ireland parties agreed a comprehensive political settlement. The two Governments immediately signed a new British-Irish Agreement committing themselves to give effect to the provisions of this multi-party agreement. The main points agreed were the setting up of a new Assembly in the North, a North-South Ministerial Council, the establishment of a British-Irish Council and a British-Irish inter-governmental Conference which is to be set up to promote bilateral co-operation at all levels in matters of mutual interest.

AGREEMENT REFERENDA: On May 22, 1998, referenda were held in both parts of the island to ratify the Agreement. In the North, 71.1% supported it while in the South, 94.4% voted to allow the Government to become party to the Agreement. The combined 'Yes' vote on the island of Ireland was 85%. The referendum in the Republic allows for the change of the Irish Constitution; the Irish nation will be defined in terms of its people, rather than its territory, in the new wording for Article 2 of the Irish Constitution. The new Article 3 will enshrine the principle of consent while "expressing the wish of the majority of the Irish people for a united Ireland". The British government will repeal, through legislation, the 1920 Government of Ireland Act.

ASSEMBLY ELECTIONS: On June 25, 1998, elections took place to elect members to the new Assembly. For the first time in a Northern election, a nationalist party, the SDLP, received the largest share of first preference votes cast. Eventually, under the PR system, the Ulster Unionist Party emerged as the largest party,

ASSEMBLY MEETS: At the inaugural meeting of the new Assembly on July 1st, 1998, UUP leader, David Trimble, was elected Northern Ireland's First Minister while the SDLP's Seamus Mallon was elected Deputy First Minister. On September 7, an unprecedented meeting took place - First Minister, David Trimble met Sinn Féin President, Gerry Adams, during a round table discussion with Northern party leaders.

PUBLIC ADMINISTRATION

ROI: GOVERNMENT DEPARTMENTS

DEPARTMENT OF AGRICULTURE AND FOOD
Kildare Street, Dublin 2.
Tel. *(01) 6072000.*
e-mail: *infodaff@indigo.ie **Web site:** www.irlgov.ie*

Minister: Joe Walsh TD.
Ministers of State: Noel Davern TD, Ned O'Keefe TD.
Secretary General: John Malone.
Description: The department's functions are to promote and develop the agri-food sectors, maximise their contribution to the national and rural economy, maintain the maximum number of viable farms in Ireland, discharge legal and administrative functions as required under Irish and EU law, ensure food safety and protect general consumer welfare, safeguard the environment and to support rural development and maintain high standards of animal and plant health/welfare.
State Bodies / Agencies: Teagasc, An Bord Glas, An Bord Bia, the Irish Horseracing Authority, the Irish National Stud Company Limited, the National Milk Agency, Bord na gCon.

DEPARTMENT OF ARTS, HERITAGE, GAELTACHT & THE ISLANDS
'Dun Aimhirgin', 43-49 Mespil Road, Dublin 4.
Tel. *(01) 6670788.*
e-mail: *webmaster@ealga.irgov.ie*
Web site: *www.irlgov.ie/ealga/*

Minister: Síle de Valera TD.
Minister of State: Eamon Ó Cuiv TD.
Secretary General: Tadhg Ó hEaláithe.
Description: In order to enrich the quality of life and sense of identity of the Irish people and preserve their inheritance for present and future generations, the department aims to foster and promote our culture and heritage, specifically the Irish language. In particular, the department is responsible for the cultural, social and economic welfare of the Gaeltacht; encourages the preservation and extension of use of the Irish language; supports and develops cultural institutions responsible for heritage and contemporary arts; and formulates and implements national policy relating to arts and culture, broadcasting and the audiovisual Industry and heritage.

State Bodies / Agencies: National Gallery of Ireland, National Library of Ireland, National Museum of Ireland, National Archives An Chomhairle Ealaíon / The Arts Council, National Theatre Society, Irish Museum of Modern Art, National Concert Hall, Chester Beatty Library, an Chomhairle Oidhreachta / The Heritage Council, Bord Scannán na hÉireann / The Irish Film Board, Irish Manuscripts Commission, Radio Telefís Éireann, Independent Radio and Television Commission, Broadcasting Complaints Commission, Údarás na Gaeltachta, Bord na Gaeilge, Bord na Leabhar Gaeilge.

DEPARTMENT OF DEFENCE
Infirmary Road, Dublin 9.
Tel. *(01) 8042000*
e-mail: *defence@iol.ie**Web site:** www.irlgov.ie/defence*

Minister: Mr. Michael Smith TD.
Minister of State: Seamus Brennan TD.
Secretary General: David O'Callaghan.
Description: The department is responsible for the administration, training, organisation, maintenance, equipment, management, discipline, regulation and control of the military defence forces. The department must ensure that it provides value-for-money military services which meet the needs of the government and the public and encompass an effective civil defence capability.
State Bodies / Agencies: Coiste an Asgard, the Irish Red Cross Society, the Army Pensions Board.

DEPARTMENT OF EDUCATION AND SCIENCE
Marlborough Street, Dublin 1.
Tel. *(01) 8734700.*
e-mail: *webmaster@educ.irlgov.ie*
Web site: *www.irlgov.ie/educ/*

Minister: Mícheál Martin TD.
Ministers of State: Willie O'Dea TD, Noel Treacy TD.
Secretary General: Mr. John Dennehy.
Description: The department manages public, private, post-primary, and special education and subsidises third level institutions in the Republic of Ireland. It is responsible for formulating and implementing national policies in relation to education. It is also responsible for several national youth agencies.
State Bodies / Agencies: Advisory Council for English Language Schools, Dublin Institute for Advanced Studies - Council, Dublin Institute for Advanced Studies - School of Celtic Studies, Dublin Institute for Advanced Studies - School of Cosmic Physics, Dublin Institute for Advanced Studies - School of Theoretical Physics, Gaisce, the Higher Education Authority (HEA), Institiúd Teangeolaíochta Éireann, LEARGAS, National Centre for Guidance in Education, National Council for Curriculum and Assessment, National Council for Educational Awards, National Council for Vocational Awards, Secondary Teachers Registration Council, Teastas - the Irish National Certification Authority.

DEPARTMENT OF ENTERPRISE, TRADE AND EMPLOYMENT
Kildare Street, Dublin 2.
Tel. *(01) 6614444.*
e-mail: *webmaster@entemp.irlgov.ie*
Web site: *www.irlgov.ie/entemp/*

Minister: Mary Harney TD.
Minister of State: Tom Kitt TD.

Secretary General: Paul Haran.
Description: The department aims to promote employment by encouraging enterprise, ensuring competitiveness, securing an educated and skilled workforce, tackling exclusion from the labour market, promoting a fair employment environment and implementing an effective business system.
State Bodies / Agencies: Forfás, Enterprise Ireland (formerly Forbairt, an Bord Trachtala and relevant elements of the business service functions of FÁS), IDA Ireland, Shannon Free Airport Development Co. Ltd., the Health and Safety Authority, Nitrigin Éireann Teo., the Labour Court, the Labour Relations Commission (incl. the Rights Commissioner), the Employer-Labour Conference, the Employment Appeals Tribunal, the Competition Authority, the County Enterprise Boards, the Office of the Director of Consumer Affairs, the Registrar of Friendly Societies, the Patents Office.

DEPARTMENT OF ENVIRONMENT AND LOCAL GOVERNMENT
Custom House, Dublin 1.
Tel. (01) 6793377.
e-mail: secretary_general@environ.irlgov.ie
Web site: www.ienviron.ie/

Minister: Noel Dempsey TD.
Minister of State: Danny Wallace TD.
Secretary General: Jimmy Farrelly.
Description: The department is responsible for environmental programmes and other services associated with the local government system. It aims to ensure, in partnership with local authorities and its own agencies, that Ireland has a high quality environment where infrastructure and amenities meet economic, social and environmental needs and where development is properly planned and sustainable.
State Bodies / Agencies: An Bord Pleanála, an Comhairle Leabharlanna (The Library Council), Dublin Docklands Development Authority, the Environmental Information Service (ENFO), the Environmental Protection Agency (EPA), the Fire Services Council, the Housing Finance Agency Plc., the Local Government Computer Services Board, the Local Government Management Services Board, the National Building Agency Ltd., the National Roads Authority, the National Safety Council, the Rent Tribunal, Temple Bar Properties Ltd., Temple Bar Renewal Ltd., the Medical Bureau of Road Safety, Dublin Transportation Office.

DEPARTMENT OF FINANCE
Government Buildings, Upper Merrion Street, Dublin 2.
Tel. (01) 6767571.
e-mail: webmaster@finance.irlgov.ie
Web site: www.irlgov.ie/finance/

Minister: Charlie McCreevy TD.
Minister of State: Martin Cullen TD.
Secretary General: Patrick H Mullarkey.
Description: The department is responsible for the administration and business generally of the public finance of Ireland, including the collection and expenditure of the revenues of Ireland from whatever source arising. Additional functions are to promote and co-ordi-

nate economic and social planning (including sectoral and regional planning), identify development policies, review the methods adopted by departments of state to implement such policies and generally advise the government on economic and social planning matters. The work of the Department of Finance is distributed between six Divisions: the Budget and Economic, Public Expenditure, Personnel and Remuneration, Finance Division, Corporate Services and Organisation, Management and Training Divisions. The department is responsible for public expenditure, taxation, the budget, economic policy and managing the public service.
State Bodies / Agencies: ACC Bank, the Central Bank of Ireland, the Civil Service Commission, the Economic and Social Research Institute, ICC Bank, the Institute of Public Administration, the National Lottery, the National Treasury Management Agency, the Office of Public Works, the Office of the Ombudsman, the Office of the Revenue Commissioners, the Ordnance Survey, the State Laboratory, the Trustee Savings Bank, the Valuation Office.

DEPARTMENT OF FOREIGN AFFAIRS
Iveagh House, St Stephen's Green, Dublin 2.
Tel. (01) 4780822.
e-mail: library1@iveagh.irlgov.ie
Web site: www.irlgov.ie/iveagh/

Minister: David Andrews TD.
Minister of State: Liz O'Donnell TD.
Secretary General: Pádraic MacKernan.
Description: The department aims to promote and protect the interests of Ireland and its citizens abroad and to pursue peace, partnership and reconciliation on the island of Ireland. Its responsibilities include monitoring developments and advising the Government in relation to Northern Ireland, co-ordinating Irish policies in the context of membership of the European Union and developing European integration, managing Irish Aid (the Government's development co-operation programme), assisting the promotion of Ireland's external trade and economic interests, negotiating and ratifying international treaties and conventions, granting passports and visas.
Divisions: Administration and Consular Division, Anglo-Irish Division, Protocol and Cultural Division, Political, Economic Division, Development Cooperation Division, Legal Division, Inspectorate Division.

DEPARTMENT OF HEALTH AND CHILDREN
Hawkins House, Hawkins Street, Dublin 2.
Tel. (01) 6714711.
e-mail: queries@health.irlgov.ie
Web site: www.doh.ie

Minister: Brian Cowen TD.
Ministers of State: Frank Fahey TD, Dr. Tom Moffatt TD.
Secretary General: Jerry O'Dwyer.
Description: The department has overall responsibility for the administration and controlling of health services throughout the country. It also formulates and implements policy on the provision of these services.
State Bodies / Agencies: Beaumont Hospital Board, Blood Transfusion Service Board, Board for the

Employment of the Blind, Board of the Adelaide and Meath Hospital Dublin incorporating the National Children's Hospital, an Bord Altranais (Nursing Board), Bord na Radharcmhastóirí (Opticians Board), an Bord Uchtala (Adoption Board), Comhairle na Nimheanna, Comhairle na n-Ospideal, Dental Council (An Comhairle Fiacloireachta), Drug Treatment Centre Board, Dublin Dental Hospital Board, Food Safety Authority of Ireland, General Medical Services (Payments) Board, Health Research Board (An Bord Taighde Slainte), Health Service Employers Agency, Hospital Bodies Administrative Bureau, Hospitals Trust Board, Irish Medicines Board (Bord Leigheasra na h-Eireann), Leopardstown Park Hospital Board, Medical Council, National Ambulance Advisory Council, National Cancer Registry Board, National Council on Ageing and Older People (National Council for the Elderly), National Rehabilitation Board, Office for Health Management, Postgraduate Medical and Dental Board, St. James's Hospital Board, St. Luke's and St. Anne's Hospital Board, Tallaght Hospital Board, Voluntary Health Insurance Board, Women's Health Council.

DEPARTMENT OF JUSTICE, EQUALITY AND LAW REFORM
72-76 St. Stephen's Green, Dublin 2.
Tel. *(01) 6028202.*
e-mail: *pagemaster@justice.irlgov.ie*
Web site: *www.irlgov.ie/justice/*

Minister: John O'Donoghue TD.
Minister of State: Mary Wallace TD.
Secretary General: Tim Dalton.
Description: The department manages the courts, prisons and police force in keeping with law and order. It is also responsible for terminating inequality for all social groups that face discrimination in any form. It oversees citizenship matters, EU matters, the courts, the Garda Síochána, immigration, prisons and the probation and welfare service.
State Bodies / Agencies: The Charitable Donations & Bequests for Ireland, the Criminal Injuries Compensation Tribunal, Censorship of Publications, the Data Protection Commissioner, the Forensic Science Laboratory, the Garda Síochána Complaints Board, the Irish Film Censor's Office, the Land Registry, the Probation and Welfare Service, the Registry of Deeds and the State Pathologist.

DEPARTMENT OF THE MARINE AND NATURAL RESOURCES
Leeson Lane, Dublin 2.
Tel. *(01) 6199200.*
e-mail: *contact@marine.irlgov.ie*
Web site: *www.irlgov.ie/marine/*

Minister: Michael Woods TD.
Minister of State: Hugh Byrne TD.
Secretary General: Tom Carroll.
Description: The department supports the availability of efficient, competitive sea transport and port services; the long-term contribution of the fisheries sectors to the national economy; the sustainable management and development of the marine coastal zone for economic,

tourism and leisure purposes; the exploration of minerals and hydrocarbons and their development for the optimum benefit to the Irish economy within the highest safety and environmental protection standards; and the development of the marine and natural resources sectors through effective research and technology development. It is also responsible for the prevention, as far as possible, of loss of life at sea through high safety standards and effective emergency response services and for the preservation and protection of the quality of the marine environment.
State Bodies / Agencies: Bord Iascaigh Mhara, Central Fisheries Board, Coillte Teoranta, the Regional Fisheries Boards (Eastern, Northern, North Western, Shannon, Southern, South Western, Western), Marine Institute, Arramara Teoranta, Salmon Research Agency, Foyle Fisheries Commission, Port Companies (Dublin, Dun Laoghaire, Port of Cork, Shannon Estuary, Drogheda, Galway, Foynes, New Ross), Harbour Authorities under the Harbours Acts 1946-76 (Annagassan, Arklow, Ballyshannon, Baltimore/Skibbereen, Bantry, Buncrana, Dingle, Dundalk, UDC - Kilrush, Kinsale, River Moy/Ballina, Sligo, Tralee and Fenit, Waterford, Westport, Wexford, Wicklow, UDC - Youghal).

DEPARTMENT OF PUBLIC ENTERPRISE
44 Kildare Street, Dublin 2.
Tel. *(01) 6707444.*
e-mail:*webmaster@tec.irlgov.ie*
Web site: *www.irlgov.ie/tec/*

Minister: Mary O'Rourke TD.
Minister of State: Joe Jacob TD.
Secretary General: John Loughrey.
Description: The department develops and implements national policies in relation to aviation and airports; rail and road transport; telecommunications; postal, radio and meteorological services; the supply and use of energy; and the exploration and extraction of minerals and petroleum. It is also responsible for investigating hazards to health from ionising radiation and radioactive contamination of the environment.
State Bodies / Agencies: Aer Lingus, Aer Rianta, an Post, Bord Gais Éireann, Bord na Mona, Córas Iompair Éireann, the Electricity Supply Board, the Irish National Petroleum Corporation, the Irish Aviation Authority, Met Éireann, the Radiological Protection Institute of Ireland, Telecom Éireann.

DEPARTMENT OF SOCIAL, COMMUNITY AND FAMILY AFFAIRS
Aras Mhic Dhiarmada, Store Street, Dublin 1.
Tel. *(01) 8748444.*
e-mail: *webweaver@welfare.eirmail400.ie*
Web site: *www.dscfa.ie*

Minister: Dermot Ahern TD.
Secretary General: Edmond Sullivan TD.
Description: The department formulates policies relating to the social security system within the country and is responsible for the administration of this system. It deals with the provision of social welfare services, pensions, child benefits, social welfare appeals, disability

and injury benefits, unemployment schemes and employment support services.
State Bodies / Agencies: The Social Welfare Appeals Office.

DEPARTMENT OF THE TAOISEACH
Government Buildings, Upper Merrion St, Dublin 2.
***Tel.** (01) 6624888.*
***e-mail:** webmaster@taoiseach.irlgov.ie*
***Web site:** www.irlgov.ie/taoiseach/*

Taoiseach: Bertie Ahern TD.
Minister of State: Seamus Brennan TD.
Secretary General: Patrick Teahon.
Description: The department is responsible for communication between government departments and the President, for the National Economic and Social Council and for Government Information Services. The Taoiseach carries out functions under the Constitution and under statute, including the administration of public services, the co-ordination of local policies and the administration of the collection, compilation, abstraction and publication of statistics. The department also takes responsibility for a number of programmes, including the co-ordination of local development policy, support at central government level for development of the West and the Strategic Management Initiative in the public service.
State Bodies / Agencies: The National Economic and Social Council, the Government Information Services,

the Central Statistics Office, the Law Reform Commission.

DEPARTMENT OF TOURISM, SPORT AND RECREATION
Kildare Street, Dublin 2.
***Tel.** (01) 6621444.*
***e-mail:** dtsrweb@entemp.irlgov.ie*
***Web site:** www.irlgov.ie/dtt*

Minister: Dr. Jim McDaid TD.
Minister of State: Chris Flood TD (for Local Development and with Special responsibility for the National Drugs Strategy).
Secretary General: Margaret Hayes.
Description: The department aims to contribute to Ireland's economic and social progress by developing a sustainable tourism sector that promotes high standards in marketing, service quality and product development; an active culture in sport and recreation; and a better partnership approach to local development with an emphasis on enhancing the quality of life in communities with high levels of social deprivation. The day-to-day implementation of these policies has been devolved to the four bodies listed below.
State Bodies / Agencies: Bord Fáilte Éireann (the Irish Tourist Board), Shannon Development, CERT (the State Tourism Training Agency), the Irish Sports Council.

❐

N. IRELAND: GOVERNMENT DEPARTMENTS

DEPARTMENT OF AGRICULTURE FOR NORTHERN IRELAND (DANI)
Dundonald House, Upper Newtownards Road, Belfast BT4 3SB.
***Tel.** (01232) 520100.*
***Web site:** www.nics.gov.uk/danihome.htm*

Minister: Lord Dubs (Parliamentary Under Secretary of State)
Secretary: Peter Small.
Description: The department is responsible for encouraging sustainable economic growth and the development of the countryside in Northern Ireland by promoting the competitive development of the agri-food, fishing and forestry sectors of the economy; by being both proactive and responsive to the needs of consumers with regard to food; and by being responsible for the welfare of animals and the conservation of the environment. In addition, it aims to strengthen the economy and social infrastructure of disadvantaged rural areas.

State Bodies / Agencies: the Agricultural Research Institute of Northern Ireland; the Agricultural Wages Board for Northern Ireland; the Fisheries Conservancy Board for Northern Ireland; the Forest Service; the Foyle Fisheries Commission; the Livestock and Meat Commission for Northern Ireland; the Northern Ireland Fishery Harbour Authority; the Pig Production Development Committee.

DEPARTMENT OF ECONOMIC DEVELOPMENT (DED)
Netherleigh, Massey Avenue, Belfast.BT4 2JP.
***Tel.** (01232) 529900.*
***Web site:** www.nics.gov.uk/denihome.htm*

Minister: Adam Ingram MP (Minister of State).
Secretary: Gerry Loughran.
Description: The department is responsible for providing an optimum framework for strengthening economic development in Northern Ireland. Its aims are the promotion of economic growth, leading to increased employment in Northern Ireland; the achievement of a fair and flexible labour market; the targeting of programmes at regions of social and economic deprivation and at the needs of the long-term unemployed; and the administration of the DED's financial and human resources. The DED is organised on a model that is similar to a holding company with specific operation subsidiary businesses or bodies.
State Bodies / Agencies: The Industrial Development Board (IDB), the Training and Employment Agency (T&EA), the Industrial Research and Technology Unit (IRTU). *DED-sponsored non-departmental bodies:* the Local Enterprise Development Unit, the Commission for Racial Equality, the Northern Ireland Tourist Board, the Labour Relations Agency, the Fair Employment Commission, the Equal Opportunities Commission, the General Consumer Council, the Health & Safety Agency.

**DEPARTMENT OF EDUCATION
FOR NORTHERN IRELAND (DENI)**
*Rathgael House, Balloo Road, Bangor,
Co. Down, BT19 7PR.*
Tel. (01247) 279279.
Web site: www.nics.gov.uk/deni.htm

Minister: John McFall MP (Parliamentary Under Secretary of State).
Secretary: Nigel Hamilton.
Description: The department plays a strategic role in developing and implementing education policies and it is concerned with the whole range of education, from nursery education through to further and higher education, as well as sport and recreation, youth services, the arts and culture (including libraries) and the development of community relations within and between schools. The department administers the Teachers' Superannuation Scheme and pays teachers' salaries on behalf of the Education and Library boards (Belfast, South Eastern, North Eastern, Southern and Western), the Council for Catholic Maintained Schools, some Voluntary Grammar and Grant-Maintained Schools.
State Bodies / Agencies: Arts Council of Northern Ireland; Council for Catholic Maintained Schools; National Museums and Galleries of Northern Ireland; Northern Ireland Council for the Curriculum, Examinations and Assessment; Northern Ireland Higher Education Council; Northern Ireland Museums Council; Sports Council for Northern Ireland; Five Education and Library Boards; Staff Commission for Education and Library Boards; Youth Council for Northern Ireland.

**DEPARTMENT OF ENVIRONMENT
FOR NORTHERN IRELAND (DOE)**
*Clarence Court, 10-18 Adelaide Street,
Belfast BT2 3NR.*
Tel. (01232) 540540.
Web site: www.doeni.gov.uk/index.htm

Minister: Lord Dubs (Parliamentary Under Secretary of State)
Secretary: Ronnie Spence.
Description: The department is responsible for a wide range of services which affect the daily lives of everyone in Northern Ireland, including planning, roads, water and works services, housing and transport policies and fire services. It also administers specific controls over local government and manages certain lands and properties, urban regeneration, country parks, nature reserves, areas of outstanding natural beauty, environmental protection, the registration of titles of land and deeds and the listing and preservation of historic buildings, ancient monuments and archaeological surveys.
State Bodies / Agencies: the Central Policy and Management Unit; the Construction Service; the Driver and Vehicle Licensing Agency; the Environment and Heritage Service; the Land Registers of Northern Ireland; the Urban Regeneration Division; the Ordinance Survey Agency; the Planning Service; the Public Record Office for Northern Ireland; the Rate Collection Agency; the Roads Service; the Water Service.

Minister: Paul Murphy MP (Minister of State).
Secretary: Pat Carvill.
Description: The department supervises and controls the expenditure of the Northern Ireland departments and liaises with Her Majesty's Treasury and the Northern Ireland Office on a number of financial and socio-economic areas. It also develops and administers the equal opportunities policy for the civil service in Northern Ireland and is responsible for personnel, pay, pensions, conditions of service and the coordination of pay policies in the civil service.
State Bodies / Agencies: the Law Reform Advisory Committee for Northern Ireland, the Northern Ireland Economic Council, the Statute Law Committee for Northern Ireland, the Valuation and Lands Agency, the Government Purchasing Agency, the Northern Ireland Statistics and Research Agency, the Business Development Service.

Minister: John McFall MP (Parliamentary Under Secretary of State).
Secretary: Clive Gowdy.
Description: The department aims to maintain and improve the health and social well-being of the people of Northern Ireland by formulating policies and strategies, providing health and personal social services and securing the planning and delivery of these services through the Health and Social Services Boards, the Health Trusts and general practitioners. The department is also responsible for child support, social security and a wide range of social legislation, in addition to providing financial support for those who are retired, sick, disabled, unemployed or in need through the Social Security Agency.
State Bodies / Agencies: the Child Support Agency; Central Services Agency; Northern Ireland Blood Transfusion Service Agency; the Health Estates; Health Promotion Agency; NI Regional Medical Physics Agency; NI Guardian Ad litem Service Agency; the Mental Health Commission for Northern Ireland; the National Board for Nursing, Midwifery and Health Visiting for Northern Ireland; the Northern Ireland Council for Post-Graduate Medical and Dental Education; the Social Security Agency.

LOCAL ADMINISTRATION IN IRELAND
City and County/District and Borough Councils

REPUBLIC OF IRELAND
General Council of County Councils,
3 Greenmount House,
Harold's Cross Road, Dublin 6W.
Tel: (01) 4548700

CARLOW COUNTY COUNCIL
County Offices, Carlow.
Tel: (0503) 31126. Fax: (0503) 41503.

County Manager: Jim Kearney (Deputy).
Chairperson: Jim Townsend.
Councillors: (21 - 9 FF, 7 FG, 4 Lab., 1PD) Declan Alcock, John Browne, Nicholas Carpenter, Michael Deering, Michael Doyle, Fred Hunter, Des Hurley, Arthur Kennedy, Mary Kinsella, Walter Lacey, Arthur McDonald, Mary McDonald, John McNally, Michael Meaney, Jimmy Murnane, Enda Nolan, M.J. Nolan, Pat O'Toole, John Pender, James Townsend, Brendan Walsh.
Council Meeting Dates: 1st Monday each month.

CAVAN COUNTY COUNCIL
Courthouse, Cavan.
Tel: (049) 31799. Fax: (049) 61565.

County Manager: Brian Johnston.
Chairperson: Clifford Kelly.
Councillors: (25 - 11 FF, 9 FG, 5 Ind) Daniel Brady, Patrick J. Conaty Jnr., Eddie Feeley, Francie Fitzsimons, Michael Giles, Clifford Kelly, Gerry Murray, Michael Smith, Sean Smith, T.P. Smith, Anthony P. Vesey, Andrew Boylan, Dessie Boylan, Aidan Boyle, Mary Maguire, Philip Miney, Joe O'Reilly, Andy O'Brien, Paddy O'Reilly, Paddy O'Reilly, May Coleman, Matthew Fitzpatrick, Seamus Harten, Dolores Smith, Winston Turner.
Council Meeting Dates: 2nd Monday each month.

CLARE COUNTY COUNCIL
New Road, Ennis, Co. Clare.
Tel: (065) 21616 Fax: (065) 28233.
e-mail: clarecoco.ie

County Manager: William Maloney.
Chairperson: P.J. Kelly.
Councillors: (32 - 19 FF, 6 FG, 5 Ind, 1 PD, 1 Lab) Michael Begley, James Breen, Tom Burke, Bill Chambers, Peter Considine, Flan Garvey, Raymond Greene, Bernard Hanrahan, Michael Hillery, Seán Hillery, Patrick Keane, Michael Kelly, P.J. Kelly, Richard Nagle, Pat McMahon, Jimmy Nagle, Joe O'Gorman, Tom Prendeville, Colm Wiley, Paul Bugler, Cissie Keane, Tony McMahon, Anna Mulqueen, Sonny Scanlan, Madeline Taylor-Quinn, Martin Lafferty, Thomas Brennan, P.J. Burke, Christy Curtin, Brigid Makowski, Patricia McCarthy, Mary Mannion.
Council Meeting Dates: 2nd Monday each month.

CORK COUNTY COUNCIL
County Hall, Cork.
Tel: (021) 276891. Fax: (021) 276321.
e-mail: ccc ajc@iol.ie Web site: corkcoco.com/

County Manager: Noel Dillon.
Chairperson: Kevin Murphy.
Councillors: (47 - 19 FF, 19 FG, 3 Ind, 1 PD, 4 Lab, 1 DL) Maurice Ahern, Vivian Callaghan, Peter Callanan, Barry Cogan, Alan Coleman, Daniel Fleming, Patrick Carey Joyce, Laurence Kelly, Annette McNamara, Donal Moynihan, John B. Murphy, Denis O'Donovan, Batt O'Keeffe, Kevin O'Keeffe, Tom O'Neill, Ted O'Riordan, Jack Roche, Donal F. O'Rourke, Donnchadh O'Sullivan, Matt Ahern, Billy Biggane, Paul Bradford, Braham Brennan, Sylvester Cotter, Michael Creed, Frank Crowley, Michael Harrington, Michael Hegarty, Eddie Lucey, Frank Metcalfe, Gerard Murphy, Kevin Murphy, Aileen D. Pyne, Conor O'Callaghan, Tadg O'Donovan, Jim O'Sullivan, Thomas Ryan, P.J. Sheehan, Michael J. Calnan, Paula Desmond, John Mulvihill, Sheila O'Sullivan, Noel Collins, Paddy Hegarty, Michael Pat Murphy, Derry Canty, Joe Sherlock.
Council Meeting Dates: 2nd, 4th Monday each month.

CORK CORPORATION
City Hall, Cork.
Tel: (021) 966222. Fax: (021) 314238.

City Manager: Jack Higgins.
Mayor: Joe O'Flynn.
Councillors: (31 - 9 FF, 6 FG, 2 Ind, 3 PD, 6 Lab, 2 DL, 1 GP, 1WP) Tim Brosnan, Donal Counihan, John Dennehy, Tim Falvey, Sean Martin, David McCarthy, Tom O'Driscoll, Noel O'Flynn, Damien Wallace, Colm Burke, Liam Burke, Tom Considine, James Corr, Denis Cregan, P.J. Hourican, Michael Ahern, John Murray, Frank Nash, Joe O'Callaghan, Joe O'Flynn, Frank Wallace, Brian Bermingham, Maírín Quill, Pearse Wyse, Pat Murray, Con O'Leary, John Kelleher, Kathleen Lynch, Dan Boyle, Jimmy Homan, Ted McCarthy.
Council Meeting Dates: 2nd and 4th Monday each month.

DONEGAL COUNTY COUNCIL
County House, Lifford, Co. Donegal.
Tel: (074) 72222 Fax: (074) 41205.
e-mail: donegalcoco.ie

County Manager: Michael McLoone.
Chairperson: Danny Harkin.
Councillors: (29 - 11 FF, 9 FG, 5 Ind, 1 DPP, 1 SF, 1 Lab, 1DL) Francis Brennan, Hugh Conaghan, Mary Coughlan, Cecilia Keaveney, Peter Kennedy, James McBrearty, Seán McEniff, Noel McGinley, Bernard McGlinchey, Denis McGonagle, Patrick McGowan, Charlie Bennett, Maureen Doohan, Colm Gallagher, Seamus Gill, Paddy Harte, Joachim Loughrey, Bernard

McGuinness, Frank O'Kelly, J.J. Reid, Harry Blaney, Fred Coll, Danny Harkin, Padraig Kelly, Anne O'Donnell, Jim Devenney, Jim Ferry, Seán Maloney, Seamus Rodgers.
Council Meeting Dates: Last Monday each month.

DUBLIN CORPORATION
Civic Offices, Wood Quay, Dublin 8.
Tel: (01) 6796111. Fax: (01) 6792226.
e-mail: dublinc@iol.ie

City Manager: John Fitzgerald.
Mayor: Senator Joe Doyle.
Councillors: (52 - 20 FF, 6 FG, 6 Ind, 1 PD, 10 Lab, 4 GP, 2 WP, 1 DL, 1 SF) Noel Ahern, Michael Barrett, Olga Bennett, Martin Brady, Ben Briscoe, Ivor Callely, Pat Carey, Michael Donnelly, Patrick J. Farry, Liam Fitzgerald, Dr. Dermot Fitzpatrick, Ita Green, Sean Haughey, Tony Kett, Mary Mooney, Michael Mulcahy, Eoin Ryan, John Stafford, Thomas Stafford, Tony Taaffe, Paddy Bourke, Tommy Broughan, Joe Connolly, Joe Costello, Mary Freehill, Sean Kenny, Dermot Lacey, Derek McDowell, Eamon O'Brien, Roisin Shortall, Brendan Brady, Joe Doyle, Cathy Fay, Mary Flaherty, John Kearney, Ruairi McGinley, Donna Cooney, Ciarán Cuffe, John Gormley, Claire Wheeler, Michael Conaghan, Tony Gregory, Vincent Jackson, Carmencita Hederman, Sean D. Dublin Bay Loftus, Brendan Lynch, Linda Kavanagh, Lucia O'Neill, Eric Byrne, Christy Burke, Alan Robinson, Anthony Creevey.
Council Meeting Dates: 1st Monday each month.

DÚN LAOGHAIRE-RATHDOWN
County Hall, Dún Laoghaire, Co. Dublin.
Tel: (01) 2054700. Fax: (01) 2806969.
e-mail: dlrcoco.ie Web site: www.dlrococo.ie

County Manager: Derek Brady.
Chairperson: Richard Conroy.
Councillors: (28 - 7 FF, 7 FG, 5 Lab, 3 DL, 2 GP, 2 PD, 2 Ind) David Boylan, Larry Butler, Betty Coffey, Richard Conroy, Don Lydon, Tony Fox, Trevor Matthews, Liam T. Cosgrave, William Dockrell, Mary Elliott, Patrick Hand, Donal Lowry, Donal Marren, Olivia Mitchell, Jane Dillon-Byrne, Eithne Fitzgerald, Fearghal O'Boyle, Sean Mistéil, Frank Smyth, Helen Keogh, Larry Lohan, Bernadette Connolly, Larry Gordon, Patrick Fitzgerald, Eamon Gilmore, Denis O'Callaghan, Richard Greene, Paddy Madigan.
Council Meeting Dates: 2nd Monday each month.

FINGAL COUNTY COUNCIL
PO Box 174, 46-49 Upper O'Connell Street, Dublin 1.
Tel: (01) 8727777. Fax: (01) 8725782.

County Manager: William Soffe.
Chairperson: Cathal Boland.
Councillors: (24 - 9 FF, 6 FG, 5 Lab, 2 GP, 1 Ind, 1 PD) Liam Creavan, Christopher C. Gallagher, Sean Gilbride, Joe Higgins, Michael Kennedy, Dermot Murray, Marian McGennis, G.V. Wright, Ned Ryan, Cathal Boland, Michael J. Cosgrave, Anne Devitt, Philip Jenkinson, Joan Maher, Tom Morrissey, Peter Coyle, Ken Farrell, Tom Kelleher, Michael O'Donovan, Sean Ryan,

Therese Fingleton, David Healy, Sean Lyons, Sheila Terry.
Council Meeting Dates: 2nd Monday each month.

GALWAY COUNTY COUNCIL
PO Box 27, Liosbán Retail Centre,
Tuam Road, Galway.
Tel: (091) 509000 Fax: (091) 509010
e-mail: galwaycoco.ie

County Manager: Donal O'Donoghue.
Chairperson: Joe Brennan.
Councillors: (30 - 13 FF, 10 FG, 3 Ind, 4 PD) Joe Callanan, Joe Brennan, Michael Finnerty, Michael Mullins, Pat O'Sullivan, John M. Mannion, Connie Ni Fhatharta, Michael O'Neill, Peadar O'Tuathail, Joseph Conneely, Seamus Gavin, Pádraic McCormack, Jarlath McDonagh, Paddy McHugh, Séan Ó'Neachtain, Evelyn Varley, Willie Burke, Toddie Byrne, Michael Cunningham, Michael Fahy, Matt Loughnane, Jimmy McClearn, Michael Regan, Joe Burke, Paul Connaughton, Patrick Finnegan, Tom Hussey, Kathleen Quinn, Michael Ryan, Tiarnan Walsh.
Council Meeting Dates: 4th Monday, 2nd Friday each month.

GALWAY CORPORATION
City Hall, College Road, Galway.
Tel: (091) 568151. Fax: (091) 567493
e-mail: tclerk@galwaycorp.ie

City Manager: Joe Gavin.
Mayoress: Angela Lynch-Lupton.
Councillors: (15 - 4 FF, 4 FG, 2 Lab, 1 Ind, 4 PD) Margaret Cox, Michael Leahy, Henry O'Connor, Michael Ó hUiginn, Fintan Coogan, Angela Lynch-Lupton, Padraic McCormack, John Mulholland, Martin Connolly, Donal Lyons, Declan McDonnell, Bridie O'Flaherty, Tom Costello, James Mullarkey, Paddy Lally.
Council Meeting Dates: 1st and 3rd Monday each month.

KERRY COUNTY COUNCIL
County Buildings, Tralee, Co. Kerry.
Tel: (066) 7121111. Fax: (066) 7121169

County Manager: Noel Brassil.
Chairperson: Martin Nolan.
Councillors: (27 - 11 FF, 7 FG, 4 Lab, 5 Ind/NP) Noel Brassil, Michael Cahill, Ted Fitzgerald, Tom Fleming, Denis Foley, Dan Kiely, Tom McEllistrim, Paul O'Donoghue, Brian O'Leary, Michael O'Shea, Ned O'Sullivan, Dan Barry, Bernie Behan, Tim Buckley, Paul Coghlan, Michael Connor-Scarteen, Danny Kissane, Bobby O'Connell, John Commane, Pat Leahy, Breda Moyhnihan-Cronin, Maeve Spring, James Courtney, P. J. Cronin, Tommy Foley, Jackie Healy-Rae, Breandán MacGearailt.
Council Meeting Dates: 3rd Monday each month.

KILDARE COUNTY COUNCIL
St. Mary's, Naas, Co. Kildare.
Tel: (045) 873800 Fax: (045) 876875.
e-mail: secretar@kildarecoco.ie

County Manager: Niall Bradley.
Chairperson: Jim Reilly.
Councillors: (25 - 8 FF, 7 FG, 3 Lab, 2 PD, 1 GP, 1 Ind, 1 DL, 1 SF) Gerry Brady, Liam Doyle, Martin Miley, Seán Ó'Fearghail, Jimmy O'Loughlin, John O'Neill, Paddy Power, P.J. Sheridan, Mary French, Senan Griffin, Rainsford Hendy, Michael McWey, Michael Nolan, Jim Reilly, Seán Reilly, Jim Keane, John McGinley, Colm Purcell, Timmy Conway, John Dardis, Sean English, Patsy Lawlor, Catherine Murphy, Paddy Wright, Francis Browne.
Council Meeting Dates: 4th Monday each month.

KILKENNY COUNTY COUNCIL
County Hall, John Street, Kilkenny
Tel: (056) 52699. Fax: (056) 63384
e-mail: secretar@kilkennycoco.ie

County Manager: P.J. Donnelly.
Chairperson: Phil Hogan.
Councillors: (26 - 12 FF, 10 FG, 4 Lab) Robert Aylward, Ann Blackmore, James J. Brett, Dick Dunphy, Michael Fenlon, Kevin Fennelly, Martin Fitzpatrick, Michael Lanigan, John J. McGuinness, Michael J. McGuinness, Patrick Millea, Brigid Murphy, John Brennan, Andy Cotterell, Kieran Crotty, Dick Dowling, Philip Hogan, William Ireland, Mary Hilda Kavanagh, John Maher, Tom Maher, Margaret Tynan, Dick Brennan, Michael O'Brien, Joe Coady, Joe Walsh.
Council Meeting Dates: 3rd Monday each month (except August).

LAOIS COUNTY COUNCIL
County Hall, Portlaoise, Co. Laois.
Tel: (0502) 22044. Fax: (0502) 22313.
e-mail: secretar@laoiscoco.ie

County Manager: Michael Malone.
Chairperson: Kieran Phelan.
Councillors: (23 - 12 FF, 8 FG, 1 Lab, 1 Ind, 1 PD) Raymond Cribbin, Joseph Digan, Joseph Dunne, Thomas Jacob, Jeremiah Lodge, Seamus McDonald, John Moloney, Teresa Mulhare, Fintan Phelan, Kieran Phelan, Eamonn Rafter, Mary Wheatley, William Aird, James Daly, James Deegan, Charles Flanagan, Thomas Keenan, Michael Lalor, John Moran, Martin Phelan, Larry Kavanagh, Cathy Honan, James Kelly.
Council Meeting Dates: Last Monday each month.

LEITRIM COUNTY COUNCIL
Governor House, Carrick-on-Shannon, Co. Leitrim.
Tel: (078) 20005. Fax: (078) 21023.

County Manager: Patrick Fahey.
Chairperson: Thomas F. McCartin.
Councillors: (22 - 9 FF, 9 FG, 3 Ind, 1 SF) Mary Bohan, John Ellis, Tony Ferguson, Aodh Flynn, Michael Guckian, Farrell McElgunn, Seán McGowan, Paschal C. Mooney, Jim Joe Shortt, Damian Brennan, Charlie Cullen, Thomas P. Faughnan, Thomas F. McCartin, Siobhán McGloin, Jim McPadden, John McTernan, Thomas Mulligan, Gerard Reynolds, Gerry Dolan, Pauline McKeon, Liam McGirl, Larry McGowan.
Council Meeting Dates: 1st Monday each month.

LIMERICK COUNTY COUNCIL
County Buildings, 79-84 O'Connell Steet, Limerick.
Tel: (061) 318477. Fax: (061) 318478.
e-mail: secretar@limerickcoco.ie

County Manager: Roibeard O'Ceallaigh.
Chairperson: Mary Jackman.
Councillors: (28 - 13 FF, 10 FG, 4 PD, 1 Lab) Maureen Barrett, Michael Barry, Michael Brennan, John Clifford, Michael J. Collins, John Cregan, Noel Gleeson, John Griffin, Michael Healy, Mary Jackman, Michael O'Kelly, William Sampson, Kevin Sheahan, Eddie Wade, Seán Broderick, Matt Callaghan, Michael Finucane, James Houlihan, Mary Jackman, Jim McCarthy, David Naughton, Dan Neville, Michael Whelan, Peader Clohessy, Eddie Creighton, John Finucane, Tim O'Malley, Mary Kelly.
Council Meeting Dates: 4th Friday each month.

LIMERICK CORPORATION
City Hall, Limerick.
Tel: (061) 415799. Fax: (061) 418342.
e-mail: manager@limerickcorp.ie

City Manager: Conn Murray.
Mayor: Joe Harrington.
Councillors: (17 - 1 FF, 4 FG, 5 Lab, 3 PD, 2 Ind, 1DL) Jack Bourke, Bobby Byrne, Tim Ledden, Patrick Kennedy, Gus O'Driscoll, Seán Griffin, Frank Leddin, Judy O'Donoghue, Frank Prendergast, Jan O'Sullivan, Kieran O'Hanlon, John Quinn, Dick Sadlier, John Gilligan, Joe Harrington, John Ryan, Seamus Houlihan.
Council Meeting Dates: 2nd Monday each month (except August).

LONGFORD COUNTY COUNCIL
Longford.
Tel: (043) 46231. Fax: (043) 41233.

County Manager: Michael Killeen.
Chairperson: Bernard Steele.
Councillors: (21 - 9 FF, 7 FG, 5 Ind) Jimmy Coyle, Mickey Doherty, Paddy Farrell, Fintan Flood, Peter Kelly, Brian Lynch, Luie McEntire, Michael Nevin, Barney Steele, James Bannon, Louis J. Belton, Gerry Brady, Seamus Finnan, Adrian Farrell, Victor Kiernan, Maura Kilbride-Harkin, Philo Kelly, Seán Lynch, Peter Murphy, John Nolan, Mae Sexton.
Council Meeting Dates: 3rd Monday each month (except August).

LOUTH COUNTY COUNCIL
County Offices, Dundalk, Co. Louth.
Tel: (042) 35457. Fax: (042) 35449.

County Manager: John Quinlivan.
Chairperson: Micheál O'Donnell.
Councillors: (22 - 9 FF, 9 FG, 3 Ind, 1 SF) Declan Breathnach, Frank Godfrey, Seamus Keelan, Noel Lennon, Nicholas McCabe, Jacqui McConville, Jimmy Mulroy, Tommy Murphy, Maria O'Brien-Campbell, Micheál O'Donnell, Tommy Reilly, Peter Savage, Terry Brennan, Jim Lennon, Bernard Markey, Conor McGahon, Fergus O'Dowd, Oliver Tully, Betty Bell,

Michael Bell, Helen Bellew, Martin Bellew, Hugh Conlon, Jim Cousins, Seán Kenna, Finian McCoy.
Council Meeting Dates: 3rd Monday every month.

MAYO COUNTY COUNCIL
Áras an Chontae, Castlebar, Co. Mayo.
Tel: *(094) 24444.* **Fax:** *(094) 23937.*
e-mail: *secretar@mayocc.ie*

County Manager: D. Mahon.
Chairperson: Al McDonnell.
Councillors: (31 - 15 FF, 13 FG, 2 Ind, 1 Lab) Geraldine Bourke, Frank Chambers, Brian Golden, Jack Heneghan, Seamus Hughes, Jimmy Maloney, Al McDonnell, Pat McHugh, Stephen Molloy, P.J. Morley, Paddy Oliver, Martin J. O'Toole, Annie May Reape, Tim Quinn, Beverley Cooper-Flynn, Michael Burke, Patrick Burke, Ernie Caffrey, John Noel Carey, John Devaney, John Flannery, Pat Higgins, Henry Kenny, Pat Kilbane, Jim Mannion, Seán McEvoy, Michael Ring, Eddie Staunton, Paraic Cosgrove, Richard Finn, Johnny Mee.
Council Meeting Dates: 2nd Monday each month (except August).

MEATH COUNTY COUNCIL
County Hall, Railway Street, Navan, Co. Meath.
Tel: *(046) 21581.* **Fax:** *(046) 21463.*

County Manager: Joe Horan.
Chairperson: Hugh Gough.
Councillors: (29 - 13 FF, 9 FG, 4 Lab, 2 Ind, 1 DL) John Brady, Garbriel Cribbin, Patrick Fitzsimons, Hugh Gough, Owen Heaney, Patricia Hegarty, Colm Hilliard, Michael Lynch, Seamus Murray, Sebastian Rooney, Conor Tormey, Mary Wallace, Jimmy Weldon, William Carey, John Fanning, John V. Farrelly, Noel Foley, Gerry Gibney, Tom Kelly, Shaun Lynch, Patsy O'Neill, Mary Sylver, Brendan Clusker, Jimmy Cudden, Brian Fitzgerald, Philip Lowe, Jack Fitzsimons, Gerry Marry, Christy Gorman.
Council Meeting Dates: 1st Monday each month.

MONAGHAN COUNTY COUNCIL
County Offices, Monaghan.
Tel: *(047) 30500.* **Fax:** *(047) 82739.*

County Manager: Joe Gavin.
Chairperson: Willie McKenna.
Councillors: (20 - 8 FF, 7 FG, 3 Ind, 2 SF) Brendan Hughes, Olivia Keenan, Jimmy Leonard, Willie McKenna, Pádraig McNally, Francis O'Brien, Rosaleen O'Hanlon, Patsy Treanor, Arthur Carville, John F. Conlan, Bill Cotter, Seymour Crawford, Patrick Jones, Stephen McAree, Hugh McElvaney, Noel Maxwell, Peter Murphy, Walter Pringle, Brian McKenna, Caoimhghin Ó Caoláin.
Council Meeting Dates: 1st Monday each month.

OFFALY COUNTY COUNCIL
Courthouse, Tullamore, Co. Offaly.
Tel: *(0506) 46800.* **Fax:** *(0506) 46868.*
e-mail: *secretar@offalycoco.ie*

County Manager: Niall Sweeney.

Chairperson: John Flanagan.
Councillors: (21 - 10 FF, 6 FG, 3 Ind, 1 Lab, 1 PD) Noel Bourke, Barry Cowen, Eamon Dooley, Joseph Dooley, Thomas Feighery, John Flanagan, Séamus Loughnane, Patrick J. Moylan, Miriam O'Callaghan, Francis Weir, Percy Clendennen, Bernard Corcoran, Thomas Enright, Michael Fox, Constance Hanniffy, Thomas McKeigue, John Butterfield, Thomas Dolan, James Flanagan, Patrick Gallagher, Brigid Emerson.
Council Meeting Dates: 3rd Monday each month (except August).

ROSCOMMON COUNTY COUNCIL
Courthouse, Roscommon.
Tel: *(0903) 37100* **Fax:** *(0903) 37108.*
e-mail: *secretar@roscommoncoco.ie*

County Manager: Eddie Sheehy.
Chairperson: Michael Scally.
Councillors: (26 - 10 FF, 11 FG, 5 Ind) Des Bruen, Tom Crosby, Patrick Dooney, Michael Finneran, Paul Lynch, Seán McQuaid, Paul Morris, Brian Mullooly, Eugene Murphy, Colm O'Donnell, Seán Beirne, Thomas Callaghan, Domnick Connolly, John Connor, Gerard Donnelly, Kitty Duignan, Charlie Hopkins, Patrick Moore, Michael McGreal, Denis Naughten, Michael Scally, Paul Beirne, Danny Burke, Tom Foxe, Patrick Moylan, Eithne Quinn.
Council Meeting Dates: 4th Monday each month.

SLIGO COUNTY COUNCIL
Riverside, Sligo.
Tel: *(071) 56666.* **Fax:** *(071) 41119.*
e-mail: *sligococo.ie*

County Manager: Leo Conlon.
Chairperson: Padraig Branley.
Councillors: (25 - 12 FF, 10 FG, 1 Lab, 2 Ind) Matthew Brennan, Aidan A. Colleary, Leo Conlon, Michael 'Boxer' Conlon, Patrick Conway, Jimmy Devins, Willie Farrell, Gerry Healy, Seán McManus, Syl Mulligan, Eamon Scanlon, John Sherlock, Mary Barrett, P. J. Cawley, Paul Conmy, Ita Fox, Peter Henry, Tommy Lavin, Joe Leonard, Jim McGarry, Tony McLoughlin, Gerry Murray, Declan Bree, Michael Carroll, Margaret Gormley.
Council Meeting Dates: 1st Monday each month.

SOUTH DUBLIN
PO Box 4122, Town Centre, Tallaght, Dublin 24.
Tel: *(01) 4149000.* **Fax:** *(01) 4149111.*
e-mail: *secretariatdept@sdublincoco.ie*

County Manager: Frank Kavanagh
Chairperson: Mick Billane.
Councillors: (25 - 7 FF, 6 FG, 3 Lab, 2 Ind, 4 PD, 2 DL, 1 GP) Sean Ardagh, Finbar Hanrahan, Margaret Farrell, John Hannon, Colm McGrath, Charles O'Connor, Ann Ormonde, Peter Brady, Brian Hayes, Stanley Laing, Mary Muldoon, Therese Ridge, Alan Shatter, Ned Gibbons, Pat Upton, Eamon Walsh, Gus O'Connell, John O'Halloran, Cait Keane, Joe Neville, Catherine Quinn, Colm Tyndall, Máire Hennessy, Don Tipping, Máire Mullarney.

Council Meeting Dates: 2nd Monday each month (except August).

TIPPERARY (NORTH RIDING) COUNTY COUNCIL
Courthouse, Nenagh, Co. Tipperary.
Tel: *(067) 31771.* **Fax:** *(067) 33134.*
e-mail: *secretary@northtippcoco.ie*

County Manager: John McGinley.
Chairperson: Michael Hough.
Councillors: (21 - 11 FF, 7 FG, 1 Ind, 2 Lab) Jim Casey, John Egan, John Hanafin, Tom Harrington, Michael Hough, Tony McKenna, Seán Mulrooney, Harry Ryan, Mattie Ryan, John Sheehy, Dan Smith, Noel Coonan, Gerard Darcy, Willie Kennedy, Philip Lowry, Mae Quinn, Denis Ryan, Tom Ryan, Martin Kennedy, John Ryan, Joseph O'Connor.
Council Meeting Dates: 3rd Monday each month.

TIPPERARY (SOUTH RIDING) COUNTY COUNCIL
Áras an Chontae, Emmet Street,
Clonmel, Co. Tipperary
Tel: *(052) 25399.* **Fax:** *(052) 24355.*
e-mail: *secretare@southtippcoco.ie*

County Manager: Edmund Gleeson.
Chairperson: Brendan Griffin.
Councillors: (26 - 10 FF, 9 FG, 4 Lab, 3 Ind) Tom Ambrose, Michael Anglim, Denis Bourke, Seán Byrne, Con Donovan, Bridie Hammersley, Michael Maguire, Seán McCarthy, Susan Meagher, Pat Norris, Theresa Ahearn, Jack Crowe, Tom Hayes, Jimmy Hogan, John Holohan, Michael Fitzgerald, Brendan Griffin, Seán Sampson, Tom Wood, Ted Boyle, Seamus Healy, Christy Kinahan, Edmond Brennan, Michael Ferris, Denis Landy, Seán Lyons.
Council Meeting Dates: 1st Monday each month.

WATERFORD COUNTY COUNCIL
Árus Brúgha, Dungarvan, Co. Waterford.
Tel: (058) 42822. Fax: (058) 42911.

County Manager: Donal Connolly.
Chairperson: Nora Flynn.
Councillors: (23 - 10 FF, 9 FG, 3 Lab, 1 DL) Thomas Cunningham, Dan Cowman, Jackie Fahey, Austin Flynn, Patrick Kenneally, Pat Leahy, Geoffrey Power, Kieran O'Ryan, James Quirke, Ollie Wilkinson, John Carey, Con Casey, Oliver Coffey, Patrick Coffey, Nora Flynn, William McDonnell, Garry O'Halloran, Richard Power, Michael Queally, Lar Hart, Billy Kyne, Patrick O'Callaghan, Fiachra O'Ceilleachair.
Council Meeting Dates: 2nd Monday each month.

WATERFORD CITY
City Hall, Waterford.
Tel: *(051) 873501.* **Fax:** *(051) 879124.*

City Manager: Edward J. Breen.
Mayor: Brian Swift.
Councillors: (15 - 4 FF, 3 FG, 3 Lab, 2 Ind, 2 WP, 1 DL) Patrick Hayes, David Walsh, Hilary Quinland, Patrick Power, Labhrás Ó Dóir, David Daniels, Liam Curham, Brian Swift, Stephen Rogers, Thomas Cunningham,

Sean Roche, Patrick Gallagher, Martin O'Regan, Thomas Browne, Maurice Cummins.
Council Meeting Dates: 2nd Monday each month.

WESTMEATH COUNTY COUNCIL
Mullingar, Co. Westmeath.
Tel: (044) 40861. Fax: (044) 42330.

County Manager: Ciaran McGrath (acting).
Chairperson: Kieran Molloy.
Councillors: (22 - 11 FF, 6 FG, 4 Lab, 1 Ind) Thomas Bourke, Donie Cassidy, P.J. Coghill, Tom Cowley, Camillus Glynn, Kieran Molloy, Egbert Moran, Patrick O'Shaughnessy, Michael Ryan, Ciaran Temple, Thomas Wright, Joseph Flanagan, J.H. Keegan, Frank McDermott, Brendan McFadden, Paul McGrath, Joe Whelan, Des Coleman, Michael Dollard, Mark Nugent, Willie Penrose, Stephen Price.
Council Meeting Dates: 4th Monday each month.

WEXFORD COUNTY COUNCIL
County Hall, Spawell Road, Wexford.
Tel: *(053) 42211.* **Fax:** *(053) 43406.*
e-mail: *postmaster@wexfordcoco.ie*

County Manager: Seamus Dooley.
Chairperson: Leo Carthy.
Councillors: (20 - 8 FF, 7 FG, 1 Lab, 4 Ind) Lorcan Allen, John T. Browne, Gus Byrne, Seamus Whelan, John A. Browne, Jimmy Curtis, Michelle Sinnott, Jim Walsh, Deirdre Bolger, Jack Bolger, Pat Codd, Michael D'Arcy, James Gahan, Rory Murphy, Laurence O'Brien, Leo Carthy, John O'Flaherty, Seán Doyle, Padge Reck, Thomas Carr.
Council Meeting Dates: 2nd Monday each month.

WICKLOW COUNTY COUNCIL
Aras an Chontae, Wicklow.
Tel: (0404) 20100 Fax: (0404) 67792.
e-mail: wicklowcoco.ie

County Manager: Blaise Treacy.
Chairperson: Liam Kavanagh.
Councillors: (24 - 8 FF, 4 FG, 5 Lab, 5 Ind, 1 GP, 1 DL) Joe Behan, Pat Doyle, Noel Jacob, Pat Doran, Michael Lawlor, J. William O'Connell, Dick Roche, Pat Vance, Vincent Blake, Thomas Honan, Shane Ross, Godfrey Timmins, Mildred Fox, George Jones, Vincent McElheron, James Ruttle, John Byrne, Thomas Cullen, Susan Philips, Liam Kavanagh, James O'Shaughnessy, Kevin Ryan, Colm Kirwan, Alex Perkins.
Council Meeting Dates: 1st, 2nd Monday each month.

NORTHERN IRELAND

ANTRIM BOROUGH
The Steeple, Antrim BT41 1BJ.
Tel: *(01849) 463113.* **Fax:** *(01849) 464469.*
e-mail: *contact@antrim.gov.uk*

Chief Executive: S.J. Magee.
Chairperson: F.R.H. Marks.
Councillors: (19 - 9 UUP, 4 SDLP, 3 DUP, 2 All, 1 SF)

Council Meeting Dates: 2nd Tuesday each month.

ARDS BOROUGH
2 Church Street, Newtownards, Co. Down BT23 4AP.
Tel: *(01247) 824000.* **Fax:** *(01247) 819628.*
e-mail: ards@ards-council.gov.uk

Chief Executive: David J. Fallows
Chairperson: George Ennis.
Councillors: (23 - 10 UUP, 5 DUP, 5 All, 2 Ind, 1 SDLP) Tom Benson, Paul Carson, Margaret Craig, Ronnie Ferguson, Tom Hamilton, Robert Gibson, David McNarry, John Shields, David Smyth, Jeffrey Magill, George Ennis, Robin Drysdale, Hamilton Gregory, David Gilmore, Jim Shannon, Wilbert Magill, Bobby McBride, Kathleen Coulter, Jim McBriar, Kieran McCarthy, Alan McDowell, Linda Cleland, Danny McCarthy.
Council Meeting Dates: Last Wednesday each month.

ARMAGH CITY AND DISTRICT
Council Offices, The Palace Demesne, Armagh BT60 4EL.
Tel: *(01861) 529600.* **Fax:** *(01861) 529601.*

Chief Executive: Desmond R. Mitchell
Mayor: Robert Turner
Council Meeting Dates: Last Monday each month.

BALLYMENA BOROUGH
Ardeevin, 80 Galgorm Road, Ballymena, Co. Antrim BT42 1AA.
Tel: *(01266) 660300.*

Chief Executive: Mervyn Rankin
Chairperson: James Currie
Council Meeting Dates: 1st Monday each month.

BALLYMONEY BOROUGH
Riada House, 14 Charles Street, Ballymoney, Co. Antrim BT53 6DZ.
Tel: *(012656) 62280.* **Fax:** *(012656) 65150.*
e-mail: ballmoneybc@psilink.co.uk

Chief Executive: John P. Dempsey.
Chairperson: Frank A. Campbell.
Councillors: (15 - 6 DUP, 4 UUP, 3 SDLP, 2 Ind) Frank A. Campbell, William J. Logan, Harry P. Connolly, Robert McComb, Joseph A. Gaston, Samuel McConaghie, Cecil J. Cousley, Robert T. Halliday, William T. Kennedy, Malachy McCamphill, Francis J. McCluskey, Thomas W. McKeown, John Watt, Bill Williamson, Robert Wilson.
Council Meeting Dates: 1st and 3rd Monday each month.

BANBRIDGE DISTRICT
Civic Building, Downshire Road, Banbridge BT32 3JY.
Tel: *(018206) 62991.* **Fax:** *(018206) 62595.*
e-mail: info@banbridgedc.gov.uk

Chief Executive: Robert Gilmore.
Chairperson: Seamus Doyle.
Councillors: (16 - 9 UUP, 3 DUP, 2 SDLP, 2 Ind) Joan

Baird, Derick Bell, William Bell, Mel Byrne, Violet Cromie, Tom Gribben, John Hanna, David Heron, John Ingram, William Martin, Malachy McCartan, William McCracken, Catherine McDermott, Wilfred McFadden, Cyril Vage, Paul Walsh.
Council Meeting Dates: 1st Monday each month.

BELFAST CITY
City Hall, Belfast, Co. Antrim BT1 5GS.
Tel: *(01232) 320202.* **Fax:** *(01232) 438075*

Chief Executive: Brian Hanna.
Mayor: David Alderdice.
Councillors: (51 - 13 UUP, 13 SF, 7 SDLP, 7 DUP, 6 All, 3 PUP, 1 Ind, 1 UDP) Margaret Crooks, Thomas A. Ekin, Carmel Hanna, Catherine Molloy, Harry Smith, Bob Stoker, David Browne, Tom Campbell, Nigel Dodds, Danny Lavery, Nelson McCausland, Alban Maginness, Fred Cobain, Frank McCoubrey, Christopher McGimpsey, Eric Smyth, Hugh Smyth, Jim Clarke, Seán Hayes, Steve McBride, Alasdair McDonnell, Michael McGimpsey, Tom Hartley, Francis McCann, Seán McKnight, Marie Moore, Margaret Walsh, Mick Conlon, Billy Hutchinson, Bobby Lavery, Gerard Brophy, Máirtín Morgan, Fred Proctor, Margaret Clarke, Robert Cleland, Reg Empey, David Ervine, Mervyn Jones, Sammy Wilson, Alex Attwood, Michael Browne, Gerard O'Neill, Chrissie McAuley, Alex Maskey, Ian Adamson, David Alderdice, Wallace Browne, Alan Crowe, Danny Dow, Robin Newton, Jim Rodgers,
Council Meeting Dates: 1st day of the month (but not on Fridays, week-ends or bank holidays).

CARRICKFERGUS BOROUGH
Town Hall, Carrickfergus, Co. Antrim BT38 7DL.
Tel: *(01960) 351604.* **Fax:** *(01960) 366676.*
e-mail: info@carrickfergus.org
Web Site: *www.carrickfergus.org*

Chief Executive: Raymond Boyd.
Mayor: Mrs. B.J. Crampsey.
Councillors: (17 - 5 UUP, 5 All, 4 Ind, 3 DUP) S. Neeson, W.S. Hamilton, D.W. Hilditch, S.Y. McCamley, N. Wady, C.J. Brown, W. Ashe, R.F. Cavan, B.J. Crampsey, S. Crowe, E. Ferguson, S.C. Dickson, M.M. Beattie, T. Creighton, C. Johnston, N. McIlwrath, J.C. Reid.
Council Meeting Dates: 1st Monday each month.

CASTLEREAGH BOROUGH
368 Cregagh Road, Belfast, Co. Antrim BT6 9EZ.
Tel: *(01232) 799021.* **Fax:** *(01232) 704158.*

Chief Executive: Adrian Donaldson.
Mayor: Jack Beattie.
Council Meeting Dates: 4th Thursday each month.

COLERAINE BOROUGH
Cloonavain, 41 Portstewart Road, Coleraine, Co. Derry BT52 1EY.
Tel: *(01265) 52181.* **Fax:** *(01265) 53489.*

Chief Executive: H.W.T. Moore
Mayor: James McClure

Council Meeting Dates: 4th Tuesday each month.

COOKSTOWN DISTRICT
Council Offices, Burn Road, Cookstown,
Co. Tyrone BT80 8DT.
Tel: *(016487) 62205.*
Fax: *(016487) 64360.*
e-mail: *chiefexecutive@cookstown.gov.uk*

Chief Executive: Mr. M.J. McGuckian
Chairperson: Pearce McAleer.
Councillors: (16 - 5 SF, 4 UUP, 4 SDLP, 2 Ind, 1 DUP) Finbar Conway, Samuel Glasgow, James McGarvey, John F. MacNamee, Samuel R. Parke, Mary J. Baker, Sean Campbell, Thomas W. Greer, Patrick P. McAleer, Anne McCrea, Patsy McGlone, Sean Begley, Denis Haughey, William J. Larmour, Trevor J. Wilson.
Council Meeting Dates: 2nd Tuesday each month.

CRAIGAVON BOROUGH
Civic Centre, Lakeview Road, Craigavon,
Co. Armagh BT64 1AL.
Tel: *(01762) 341199.* ***Fax:*** *(01762) 312444.*
e-mail: *info@craigavon.gov.uk*

Chief Executive: Trevor E. Reaney.
Chairperson: Mervyn Carrick.
Councillors: (26 - 11 UUP, 7 SDLP, 3 DUP, 2 SF, 2 Ind, 1 All) Patricia Mallon, Francie Murray, Mark Neale, John O'Dowd, George Savage, Kenneth Twyble, Meta Crozier, John Duffy, Ignatius Fox, John Hagan, Arnold Hatch, Breandan MacCionnaith, Mary McAlinden, Kieran McGeown, Sean McKavanagh, Mary McNally, Mervyn Carrick, Dolores Kelly, Samuel Gardiner, James McCammick, Joseph Trueman, Ruth Allen, William Allen, Jonathan Bell, Sydney Cairns, Frederick Crowe.
Council Meeting Dates: 1st and 3rd Monday each month.

DERRY CITY
98 Strand Road, Derry BT48 7NN.
Tel: *(01504) 365151.* ***Fax:*** *(01504) 264858.*
e-mail: *derrycc@derrycity.gov.uk*

Chief Executive: John Keanie.
Mayor: Joe Miller.
Councillors: (30 - 14 SDLP, 8 SF, 4 DUP, 3 UUP, 1 Ind) J. Miller, L. Fleming, G.L. Campbell, R. Dallas, A. Davidson, J.R. Guy, E. Hamilton, W. Hay, P. Anderson, Martin Bradley, Mary Bradley, J. Clifford, A. Courtney, C. Crumley, J.M. Durkan, S. Gallagher, M. Garfield, T. Hassan, M. Hutcheon, P. Kelly, J. Kerr, K. McCloskey, J.M. McLaughlin, S. McNickle, M. Nelis, W. O'Connell, G. Ó hEára, G.V. Peoples, P. Ramsey, J. Tierney.
Council Meeting Dates: 4th Tuesday each month.

DOWN DISTRICT
24 Strangford Road, Downpatrick,
Co. Down BT30 6SR.
Tel: *(01396) 610800.* ***Tel:*** *(01396) 610801.*

Chief Executive: Owen P. O'Connor
Chairperson: Jack McIlheron.
Council Meeting Dates: 3rd Monday each month.

DUNGANNON DISTRICT
Council Offices, Circular Road, Dungannon,
Co. Tyrone BT71 6DT.
Tel: *(01868) 720300.* ***Fax:*** *(01868) 720333.*
e-mail: *central@dungannon.gov.uk*

Chief Executive: Mr. W. Beattie
Chairperson: James Canning
Councillors: (22 - 8 UUP, 5 SF, 4 SDLP, 3 DUP, 1 Ind, 1 DL) S.F. Flanagan, A. McGonnell, W.J. McIlwrath, N.R.D. Mulligan, R.L. Mulligan, N. Badger, J. Canning, J.I. Cavanagh, B. Doris, M. Gillespie, F. Molloy, D.J. Brady, P. Daly, J. Ewing, J. Hamilton, D.C.G. Irwin, M.J. Carson, G.C. Cullen, V. Currie, V. Kelly, M. Morrow, J. Reilly.
Council Meeting Dates: 2nd Monday each month.

FERMANAGH DISTRICT
Town Hall, Enniskillen, Co. Fermanagh BT74 7BA.
Tel: *(01365) 325050.* ***Fax:*** *(01365) 322024.*

Chief Executive: Mrs. Aideen McGinley.
Chairperson: Patrick McCaffrey.
Councillors: (21 - 9 UUP, 5 SF, 4 SDLP, 2 DUP, 1 Ind) H. Andrews, G. Cassidy, J. Dodds, W. Elliott, R. Ferguson, E. Flanagan, S. Foster, G. Gallagher, T. Gallagher, Basil Johnston, Bert Johnston, B. Kerr, R. Lynch, B. McCaffrey, C. McClaughry, G. McHugh, T. McPhillips, F. McQuillan, R. Martin, D. Nixon, C. Noble.
Council Meeting Dates: 1st Monday each month.

LARNE BOROUGH
Smiley Buildings, Victoria Road, Larne,
Co. Antrim BT40 1RU.
Tel: *(01574) 272313.* ***Fax:*** *(01574) 260660.*

Chief Executive: Colm McGarry.
Chairperson: Joan Drummond.
Council Meeting Dates: 1st Monday each month.

LIMAVADY BOROUGH
7 Connell Street, Limavady, Co. Derry BT49 0HA.
Tel: *(015047) 22226.* ***Fax:*** *(015047) 22010.*

Chief Executive: John Stevenson.
Mayor: Stanley Gault.
Council Meeting Dates: 4th Wednesday each month.

LISBURN BOROUGH
The Square, Hillsborough, Co. Down BT26 6AH.
Tel: *(01846) 682477.*

Chief Executive: Norman Davidson.
Chairperson: Peter O'Hagan.
Council Meeting Dates: 4th Tuesday each month.

MAGHERAFELT DISTRICT
50 Ballyronan Road, Magherafelt,
Co. Derry BT45 6EN.
Tel: *(01648) 32151.* ***Fax:*** *(01648) 31240.*

Chief Executive: John McLaughlin.
Chairperson: Robert Montgomery.
Council Meeting Dates: 2nd Tuesday each month.

MOYLE DISTRICT
Sheskburn House, 7 Mary Street, Ballycastle,
Co. Antrim BT54 6QH.
Tel: *(012657) 62225.* ***Fax:*** *(012657) 62515.*

Chief Executive: Richard G. Lewis
Chairperson: Helen Harding
Council Meeting Dates: 2nd, 4th Monday each month.

NEWRY AND MOURNE DISTRICT
Council Offices, O'Hagan House, Monaghan Row,
Newry, Co. Down BT35 8DJ.
Tel: *(01693) 65411.* ***Fax:*** *(01693) 65313.*

Chief Executive: Kevin O'Neill
Chairperson: Brendan Curran.
Council Meeting Dates: 1st Monday each month.

NEWTOWNABBEY BOROUGH
1 The Square, Ballyclare, Co. Antrim BT39 9BA.
Tel: *(01960) 352681.* ***Fax:*** *(01960) 340417.*

Chief Executive: Norman Dunn.
Chairperson: E.J. Crilly.
Council Meeting Dates: 4th Monday each month.

NORTH DOWN BOROUGH
Town Hall, The Castle, Bangor, Co. Down BT20 4BT.
Tel: *(01247) 270371.* ***Fax:*** *(01247) 271370.*

Chief Executive: Adrian McDowell.
Chairperson: Marsden Fitzsimmons.
Council Meeting Dates: 4th Tuesday each month.

OMAGH DISTRICT
The Grange, Mountjoy Road, Omagh,
Co. Tyrone BT79 7BL.
Tel: *(01662) 245321.* ***Fax:*** *(01662) 252380.*

Chief Executive: John P. McKinney
Chairperson: Sean Clark.
Councillors: (21 - 7 SF, 6 SDLP, 3 UUP, 3 DUP, 1 Lab, 1 All) Thomas Buchanan, Patrick McDonnell, A. Crawford McFarland, Kevin McGrade, Liam McQuaid, Cathal Quinn, George Rainey, Drew Baxter, Terence Brogan, Joe Byrne, Sean Clarke, Michael McAnespie, Patsy McMahon, Seamus Shields, Vincent Campbell, Oliver Gibson, Ann Margaret Gormley, Francis Mackey, Patrick McGowan, Reuben McKelvey, John McLaughlin.
Council Meeting Dates: 1st Tuesday each month.

STRABANE DISTRICT
47 Derry Road, Strabane, Co. Tyrone BT82 8DY.
Tel: *(01504) 382204.* ***Fax:*** *(01504) 382264.*
e-mail: *strabanedc@nics.gov.uk*

Chief Executive: Victor R. Eakin
Chairperson: I.C. Barr.
Councillors: (16 - 5 SDLP, 4 SF, 3 DUP, 3 UUP, 1 Ind) Mrs. A. Bell, D.A. Bresland, M.J. Conway, J. Donnell, J.A. Emery, D.R. Hussey, T. Kerrigan, T. McBride, C.H. McHugh, E.A. McMenamin, J. McNulty, T. Murtagh, J.J. O'Kane, E. Turner.
Council Meeting Dates: 2nd, 4th Tuesday each month.

EUROPEAN UNION

HISTORY OF THE EUROPEAN UNION

ORIGINS The E.U. originated in the period immediately after World War II largely as a result of one man's vision of how to reconcile the inevitable revival of the then ravaged German economy and nation with the fears of her neighbours of future attempts at domination. Jean Monnet, a French economic expert, who, in 1950, was the originator of what became known as the Schuman Plan (a scheme to pool French and German coal and steel production - the two essential elements for war at that time). He was the visionary who sought to unify Europe politically, socially and economically.

Since neither France nor Germany felt secure unless they controlled all the coal and steel resources available, and consequently all territory containing them, Monnet's proposal was to place the whole of German and French production under an international authority. Membership of this authority was to be open to other European countries, and this authority was to have as its purpose the unification of the conditions of production, leading to a gradual extension of effective co-operation in other areas.

E.C.S.C. TREATY Monnet's solution contained sufficient political symbolism to attract political and popular support and had a technical content sufficiently detailed to address the the difficulties of translating a complex scheme into a practical reality. Thus, after an international conference, the Treaty on the European Coal and Steel Community (E.C.S.C.) was signed in Paris in April, 1951, between France, Germany, the Benelux countries and Italy.

The E.C.S.C. Treaty provided for the creation of four institutions:

- **The High Authority**: A body which was politically independent of any member country and given the role of interpreting the treaty and ensuring its implementation. (It is comparable to the current E.U. commission.)
- **The Council of Ministers:** An institution comprised of ministers from member countries whose role as elected representatives was to control the powers of the Higher Authority. (The council's control is comparable to that of the current Council of Ministers in today's E.U. commission.)
- **The Common Assembly:** A parliamentary-type body created to provide democratic input into the community's actions. (It is comparable to the current E.U. parliament.)
- **The Court of Justice:** A court designed to settle conflicts or arguments between member states. (It is comparable to the current European Court of Justice.)

The aim of the E.C.S.C. was not, according to Monnet, to replace the responsibilities of the existing steel companies with that of the Higher Authority, but rather to create the conditions of true competition in a vast market where producers, workers and consumers would all gain. The continuation of these aims can be seen in later E.E.C. (European Economic Community) and E.U.

policies and treaties.

Winston Churchill, in a speech in Zurich in 1946, called for "a kind of United States of Europe," and Monnet stated frequently that he had no doubt that the process of the E.E.C. development would lead eventually to a United States of Europe. He also argued that it was impossible to say if such a Europe would be a federation or confederation or a combination of the two, as the entire project was without precedent.

IRELAND, BRITAIN AND THE EEC Ireland and Britain did not join the E.U. at its initial stages but for very different reasons. Ireland had an agriculturally based economy at the time (no coal or steel) and was so economically integrated with Britain that it was not feasible for it to consider joining any European grouping without Britain.

Britain was in a different position from that of the rest of Europe after World War II. Its economic infrastructure, although damaged, was still largely intact (the decline of this infrastructure made Britain structurally uncompetitive in future years). It was still politically committed to its empire, it had not been invaded and British political debate in post-war era focused more on the future balance of public and private industry than on economic reconstruction or on the country's strategic political future.

Mr. Churchill stated in his Zurich speech that the first step towards European union must be a partnership between France and Germany. He later added that if France and Germany could be woven "so closely together economically, socially and morally as to prevent the occasion of new quarrels, and make old antagonisms die in the realisation of mutual prosperity and interdependence, Europe would rise again." Mr. Churchill also believed that the integration of Europe would best be achieved without British involvement at this time.

Critically, in the then prevailing atmosphere of uncertainty, there was a consensus in Britain that it should not commit itself to Europe to such an extent that it lost its independent viability. If Europe collapsed economically or militarily, Britain must retain the ability to survive and continue to develop its American and Commonwealth connections.

Britain has maintained this policy and, until recent times, the Republic of Ireland had little or no option but to follow a similar path. The break with punt-pound parity was one of Ireland's first real signs of economic independence, and Ireland's commitment to join a single European currency regardless of British intentions has been its most recent show of autonomy.

EUROPEAN ECONOMIC COMMUNITY (EEC) Monnet went on to become the architect of the European Economic Community. His aim was to substitute the arbitration of differences by force with rules of conduct between nations and to substitute attempts to negotiate individual reciprocal advantages with the pursuit of a common objective in the common interest.

In seeking to build a Europe-wide democratic union, one of Monnet's guiding principles was that at birth all men are the same, but as they grow they do so within a system of rules, which determines their later behaviour and under which they seek to maintain the privileges they have gained, often by a policy of domination.

On the basis of Monnet's principles and taking the view that the benefits of integration, as opposed to just co-operation, would outweigh what appeared to some to be some loss of sovereignty, the six members of the E.C.S.C. signed the Treaties of Rome in 1957 to found the E.E.C. and Euratom. These treaties were Monnet's basis for a framework for the people of Europe's future. On January 1, 1973, the Republic of Ireland, Northern Ireland (via Britain's accession) and Denmark joined these founding six members. ❑

EUROPEAN COMMUNITY DEVELOPMENTS: A CHRONOLOGY

1951 Treaty of Paris to found the E.C.S.C. (the European Coal and Steel Community). The signatories were France, Germany, Belgium, Luxembourg, Italy and the Netherlands.

1957 Treaty of Rome to found the E.E.C. (the European Economic Community) and Euroatom. Once again the signatories were France, Germany, Belgium, Luxembourg, Italy and the Netherlands.

1961 The first accession application by Ireland, Britain and Denmark. Vetoed by France.

1965 A merger of European institutions is created by the treaties of Paris and Rome.

1967 The second accession application by Ireland, Britain and Denmark. Vetoed by France.

1968 The phased abolition of tariffs between existing members is completed, and a customs union is finalised.

1970 The opening of negotiations on accession with Ireland, Britain, Denmark and Norway.

1973 Ireland, Britain and Denmark become the first post-foundation members of the E.E.C.

1979 First direct elections to the European Parliament.

1979 The European Monetary system is established.

1981 Greece joins the E.E.C.

1986 Spain and Portugal join the E.E.C.

1986 An intergovernmental conference closes with a revised treaty, resulting in the Single European Act. The act increases majority voting, provides direction for creating a single market and lays the legal basis for the practice of political co-operation.

1987 The Single European Act (S.E.A.) is ratified by referenda by the Republic of Ireland and by the British parliament.

1989 A political declaration of the Social Chapter by 11 of the 12 E.C. states. Britain opts out of the declaration, and its provisions do not apply in Northern Ireland.

1989 The Committee of E.C. Central Banks proposes a three-stage path towards a single European currency.

1990 Two parallel conferences open to consider the questions of both European Monetary Union (E.M.U.) and political union.

1991 The above conferences result in completion of the Maastricht Treaty (the T.E.U. creates a legal framework for the creation of a single currency - the E.M.U. - with a British opt-out provision). Members commit themselves to an even closer union, increased powers for the European Parliament and the European Court, and a Common Foreign and Security Policy is established.

1993 The Single Internal Market, brought about by Single European Act is almost complete, abolishing most border controls. Maastricht comes into effect after referendum difficulties in Denmark. The E.C. subsequently becomes the E.U.

1995 Austria, Finland and Sweden join the E.U.

1996 The Dublin E.U. Summit finalises plans for E.M.U. by confirming the starting date for the new currency and by displaying for the first time the new European Bank Notes.

1997 The Amsterdam Summit. Resulted in the E.U.'s latest treaty. Ireland ratified the treaty by referendum on May 22, 1998.

1998 Ireland confirmed as founding member of EMU.

EUROPEAN UNION INSTITUTIONS

The four major institutional pillars of the E.U. are the European Commission, the European Council Of Ministers, the European Parliament and the European Court of Justice

The European Commission is the executive organ of the community which ensures that the community's rules and the provisions of treaties are implemented and observed correctly. It puts forward policy proposals and executes the decisions taken by the Council of Ministers. The Republic of Ireland has one commissioner, while Northern Ireland is included in the allocation of two commissioners to Britain. Commissioners are each allocated an individual portfolio and are required to act in the general interests of the community, not as national representatives.

The European Council of Ministers is the executive or decision-making body of the E.U.. It is the principal meeting place of the members' national governments and is the only institution in which members represent each country in direct negotiations between member states. The council is normally convened in the country that holds the presidency of the E.U., which rotates between the member countries every six months.

The European Parliament provides for the democratic input of the people of Europe in the E.U. Its members are elected from member states every five years and sit in the parliament according to political affiliations rather than nationalities - for example, the European Peoples group, the Socialist Group, the Rainbow Group, etc. The parliament has acquired increased powers in recent years and can propose its own legislation. Its opinion must now be sought on important legislative proposals or else they will be rendered invalid.

Prior to 1987, any legislation coming before the parliament was subject to a consultative procedure. The Single European Act created two new procedures - the co-operation procedure and the assent procedure - while the Treaty on European Union introduced the co-decision procedure.

Each of the above procedures applies to different types of legislation. The co-operation procedure requires the co-operation of the European Parliament to avoid delaying legislation. The European Parliament can veto legislation put before it only under the co-decision procedure.

The European Court of Justice interprets E.U. law and ensures its application throughout the E.U. It has a wide-ranging role, being required by various treaty articles to act as an international court, an administrative court, a civil court, an industrial tribunal and a transnational constitutional court. Where there is conflict between European law and the domestic laws of member countries, European law prevails and domestic parliaments must amend their laws to take into account the opinions of the European court.

EUROPEAN ACTS

THE SINGLE EUROPEAN ACT 1987
The four main aims of the act are:
A Common External Tariff;
Free Movement of Goods, Services, Persons and Capital;
Competition rather than co-operation between companies within the E.U. and
Approximation of regulations, rather than common or new regulations.

THE EUROPEAN SOCIAL CHAPTER
This is a political declaration by most members of the E.U., including Ireland, but was opted out of by Britain (and therefore Northern Ireland). It provides workers with the right to improved living and working conditions;
Freedom of movement (the right to work anywhere in the E.U.) and equal tax treatment;
The right to exercise an occupation or trade anywhere in the E.U.;
Social protection by host states of E.U. citizens in gainful employment;
Basic daily and weekly rest periods;
A maximum 48-hour working week;
Maximum night work of 8 hours in 24;
Four weeks' holidays per annum;
Rest periods at work (minimum standards);
Fair wages;
Freedom of association (the right to join or not to join a trade union);
The right to vocational training throughout a person's working life;
Equal pay for work of equal value;
Workers' rights to information at their place of work, as well as participation in the decision-making process, and protection at the workplace from any dangers; and
Rights for pregnant women (time off, protection in the workplace etc.).

THE AMSTERDAM TREATY
The Treaty provides for the following:

New powers to co-ordinate member states' drive for jobs;
The enshrining of sustainable development as a core environmental value;
Enhanced E.U. powers in public health, consumer rights and social exclusion;
Enhanced equality provisions;
The end of the British opt-out on social policy;
The right to correspond with E.U. institutions in Irish;
A treaty right of access to official documents;
A commitment by the 13 continental members to open their internal borders by 2004;
Opt-outs for Ireland and Britain allowing them to retain control of their borders;
Enhanced co-operation in the fight against crime and new powers for Europol;
The potential involvement of the E.U. in peacekeeping and humanitarian military missions;
No merger with the Western European Union and a dilution of the Maastricht aspiration to an eventual common defence;
A new foreign and security analysis and planning unit for Brussels;
A new foreign policy supremo and reorganisation of the E.U.'s diplomatic troika;
Postponement of much institutional reform;
No change in the entitlement of member states to a commissioner;
A pledge that large states will get a re-weighting of votes in their favour;
Marginal extension of majority voting;
Extra powers for the Commission President to share in picking his team and then reshuffling it;
Extension of M.E.P.s' powers to approve legislation; and
'Flexibility' provisions to allow groups of states to collaborate on projects that do not have unanimous support.

The treaty was signed by E.U. Foreign Ministers in October, 1997. Ireland ratified the treaty by referendum on May 22, 1998.

ECONOMIC AND MONETARY UNION
Chronology and Timetable

STAGE ONE: January 1, 1990 - December 31, 1993
01.01.93............Single European Market comes into operation.
01.11.93............Maastricht Treaty on European Union comes into force.

European Monetary Institute established. Member states agree to work towards economic convergence.

15.12.95............Name of the single currency, 'euro', adopted at Madrid European Council meeting.

15.12.95............Timetable for introduction of the euro decided.

14.12.96............Design of euro banknotes unveiled at Dublin European Council meeting.

16.06.97............Design of euro coins revealed at Amsterdam European Council meeting.

17.06.97............Legal framework for using the euro agreed at Amsterdam European Council meeting.

02.05.98   Member States which fulfil the economic criteria set by the Maastricht Treaty join the 'first wave' of EMU. The states are: Austria, Belgium, Finland, France, Germany, Holland, Ireland, Italy, Luxembourg, Portugal and Spain.

01.07.98............European Central Bank comes into existence.

STAGE THREE: January 1, 1999 - December 31, 2001

01.01.99   Economic and Monetary union commences in the eleven member states; Euro formally comes into existence; European Central Bank takes control of European monetary policy; currencies of eleven member states irrevocably locked together, national currencies will become de facto denominations of the euro; rate at which euro will trade against other currencies set; paper trans actions in euros to be used increasingly by business.

01.01.2002........Euro banknotes and coins come into circulation alongside national currencies.

01.07.2002........National currencies to be withdrawn from circulation by this date.

CRITERIA FOR ADMITTANCE INTO EMU

● Public finance. Public debt must be less than 60% GDP, and Public deficit must be less than 3% GDP.

● Inflation must be less than 1.5% above the rates in the three Member States with the lowest rates.

● The national currency must have remained within the fluctuation bands of the European Monetary System for the preceding two years.

● Medium and long term interest rates must be less than 2% above the interest rates in the three Member States with the lowest inflation.

VALUE OF IRISH POUND FROM JANUARY 1999.

The following is the exchange rate at which the Punt will trade vis-a-vis other currencies in the euro bloc. The value of the euro will be set near the end of 1998.

Austrian Schilling	17.47	German Deutschmark	2.483
Belgian Franc	51.22	Italian Lira	2,459
Dutch Guilder	2.798	Portuguese Escudo	254.6
Finnish Markka	7.550	Spanish Peseta	211.3
French Franc	8.329		

REPUBLIC OF IRELAND M.E.P.S *(by political allegiance)*

The European Parliament has 626 members. The Republic of Ireland Members of the European Parliament are as follows:

FIANNA FÁIL/ UNION FOR EUROPE

Niall ANDREWS (Dublin), 43 Molesworth St., Dublin 2. Tel: (01) 6794368.

Gerard COLLINS (Munster), The Hill, Abbeyfeale, Co. Limerick. Tel: (01) 6620068.

Brian CROWLEY (Munster), 39 Sunday's Road, Cork. Tel: (021) 394598.

Jim FITZSIMMONS (Leinster), 43 Molesworth St., Dublin 2. Tel: (01) 6719189.

Pat 'the Cope' GALLAGHER (Connacht-Ulster), Dungloe, Co.Donegal. Tel: (075) 21276.

Liam HYLAND (Leinster), Fearagh, Ballacolla, Portlaoise, Co. Laois. Tel: (0502) 34051.

Mark KILLILEA (Connacht-Ulster), Caherhugh House, Belclare, Tuam, Co. Galway. Tel: (093) 55414.

FINE GAEL/ EUROPEAN PEOPLE'S PARTY

Mary BANOTTI (Dublin), 43 Molesworth St., Dublin 2. Tel: (01) 6625100.

Alan GILLIS (Leinster), Ballyhook House, Grangew Con, Co. Wicklow. Tel: (0508) 81229.

Joe McCARTAN (Connacht-Ulster), Mullyaster, Newtowngore, Carrick-on-Shannon, Co. Leitrim. Tel: (049) 33395.

John CUSHNAHAN (Munster), Bedford House, Bedford Row, Limerick. Tel: (061) 418289.

GREEN PARTY/ GREENS

Nuala AHERN (Leinster), 5 Oaklands, Greystones, Co. Wicklow. Tel: (01) 2876574.

Patricia McKENNA (Dublin), 43 Molesworth St., Dublin 2. Tel: (01) 6616833.

LABOUR PARTY
PARTY OF EUROPEAN SOCIALISTS

Bernie MALONE (Dublin), 43 Molesworth St., Dublin 2. Tel: (01) 6765988.

INDEPENDENT/ GROUP OF THE EUROPEAN
LIBERAL AND REFORMIST PARTY

Pat COX (Munster), 21 Cook Street, Cork. Tel: (021) 278488.

NORTHERN IRELAND M.E.P.S *(by political allegiance)*

Ian PAISLEY M.P. (DUP/Independent) 17 Cyprus Avenue, Belfast BT5 5NT. Tel. (01232) 454255.
John HUME M.P. (SDLP/Party of European Socialists) 5 Bayview Terrace, Derry. Tel. (01504) 265340.

Jim NICHOLSON (UUP/European's People Party) 3 Glengall Street, Belfast BT12 5AE. Tel. (01232) 439431.

EUROPEAN REFERENDA RESULTS IN IRELAND

Due to the Republic of Ireland's Constitution, most European treaties are required to be ratified by a referendum. Britain does not have a written constitution, treaties such as the Amsterdam Treaty need only to be ratified by a parliamentary majority.

NORTHERN IRELAND RESULTS

DATE	ISSUE	TURNOUT (%)	FOR (%)	AGAINST (%)
June 5, 1975	United Kingdom remaining within the E.E.C.	47	52.1	47.9

REPUBLIC OF IRELAND RESULTS

DATE	ISSUE	TURNOUT (%)	FOR (%)	AGAINST (%)
May 10, 1972	Allow E.E.C. membership	70.9	83.1	16.9
May 26, 1987	Allow signing of Single European Act	43.9	69.9	30.1
June 18, 1992	Ratification of Maastricht Treaty	57.3	69.1	30.9
May 22, 1998	Ratification of Amsterdam Treaty*	56.2	61.7	38.3

* For detailed results on Amsterdam Treaty referendum see Politics Chapter.

MEP AND EUROPEAN COMMISSIONERS SALARIES

M.E.P.s are paid a salary equivalent to that of their locally elected representatives.
European Commissioners are paid in Belgian Francs. Their salaries are adjusted annually in line with inflation.

	BFr	IR£	STG£
M.E.P.	-	36,648	45,066
Commissioner*	7,413,066	144,111	129,058
Vice-President of the Commission	8,236,740	160,123	143,397
President of the Commission	9,093,361	176,776	158,311

*Calculated using the exchange rate as of October 22, 1998. IR£ = 51.44 BFr, STG£ = 57.44 BFr.

MEMBERS OF THE EUROPEAN COMMISSION

Name	Nationality	Responsibilities
Jacques Santer	Luxembourg	President. Secretariat-General, Legal Service, Security Office, Monetary Matters*,Forward Studies Unit, Inspectorate-General, Common Foreign and Security Policy and Human Rights*, Institutional Matters and Intergovernmental Conference, Joint Interpreting and Conference Service.
Sir Leon Brittan	British	Vice President. External relations with North America, Australia, New Zealand, Japan, China, Korea, Macao and Taiwan. Common Commercial Policy, Relations with OECD and WTO.
Manuel Marín	Spanish	Vice President. External relations with southern Mediterranean, the Middle East, the Near East, Latin America, Asia (excluding Japan, China, Korea, Macao and Taiwan) including development aid.
Martin Bangemann	German	Industrial Affairs, Information and Telecommunications technologies.
Karel Van Miert	Belgian	Competition
Hans Van Den Broek	Dutch	External relations with countries of Central and Eastern Europe, the former Soviet Union, Mongolia, Turkey, Cyprus, Malta and other European countries. Common Foreign and Security Policy and Human Rights*, External Diplomatic Missions
João de Deus Pinheiro	Portuguese	External relations with South Africa, African, Caribbean and Pacific countries including development aid, Lomé Convention.
Pádraig Flynn	Irish	Employment and Social Affairs, Relations with Economic and Social Committee
Marcelino Oreja	Spanish	Relations with European Parliament, Relations with Member States, Culture
Anita Gradin	Swedish	Immigration, Justice and Home Affairs, Relations with the Ombudsman, Financial Control, Fraud Prevention
Édith Cresson	French	Science, Research and Development, Joint Research Centre, Human Resources, Education, Training and Youth.

Ritt Bjerregaard ....Danish ....Environment, Nuclear Safety
Monika Wulf-Mathies.......German ....Regional Policies, Cohesion Fund*,
Relations with Committee of the Regions.
Neil Kinnock ....British ....Transport (including trans-European networks)
Mario Monti ....Italian ....Internal Market, Customs, Taxation,
Financial Services and Financial Integration.
Franz Fischler..................Austrian ....Agriculture and Rural Development
Emma Bonino..................Italian ....Fisheries, Consumer Policy, European Community Humanitarian Office
Yves-Thibault de Silguy ..French ....Economic and Financial Affairs, Monetary Matters*,
Credit and investments, Statistical Office.
Erkki Liikanen..................Finnish ....Budget, Personnel and Administration,
Translation and in-house computer services
Christos Papoutsis ....Greek...Energy and Euratom Supply Agency,
Small and Medium-sized enterprises, Tourism.
*Denotes shared responsibility.

FORMER IRISH COMMISSIONERS TO THE EUROPEAN COMMISSION

Name	Term of Office	Responsibilities
Patrick J. Hillery	1973-76	Social Affairs
Richard Burke	1977-80	Transport, Taxation, Consumer Protection, Relations with European Parliament, Education, Science and Research
Michael O'Kennedy	1981-82	Presidents Delegate, Personnel and Administration, Statistical Office, Publications Office
Richard Burke	1982-84	Personnel and Administration, Joint Interpreting and Conference Services, Statistical Office, Publications Office
Peter Sutherland	1985-88	Competition, Social Affairs, Education and Training. From 1986: Competition and Relations with the European Parliament
Ray MacSharry	1989-93	Agriculture and Rural Development
Pádraig Flynn	1993-	Social Affairs and Employment, Internal and Judicial Affairs Questions linked to Immigration, Relations with Economic and Social Committee.

EUROPEAN PARLIAMENT ELECTION RESULTS

1994 Election. Constituency-by-constituency results.

CONNACHT-ULSTER
Seats: 3; **Candidates:** 9; **Electorate:** 496,352; **Turnout:** 47.87%; **Total Valid Poll:** 232,630; **Quota:** 58,158. **First Count:** Pat 'The Cope' Gallagher (FF) 53,171; Mark Killilea (FF) 45,638; Joe McCartin (FG) 38,039; Jim Higgins (FG) 30,947; Bobby Molloy (PD) 21,219; Ann Gallagher (Lab) 19,826; Pat Doherty (SF) 13,939; Richard Douthwaite (GP) 8,628; Mary Lacey (NLP) 1,223. **Elected:** Pat 'The Cope' Gallagher (FF) 59,372 - 4th Ct; Mark Killilea (FF) 59,773 - 5th Ct; Joe McCartin (FG) 49,371 - 5th Ct.

DUBLIN
Seats: 4; **Candidates:** 15; **Electorate:** 755,486; **Turnout:** 37.16%; **Total Valid Poll:** 277,844; **Quota:** 55,569. **First Count:** Patricia McKenna (GP) 40,388; Mary Banotti (FG) 38,053; Niall Andrews (FF) 36,877; Jim Mitchell (FG) 28,116; Pat Rabbitte (DL) 24,133; Bernie Malone (Lab) 22,419; Orla Guerin (Lab) 16,674;

Tómas MacGiolla (WP) 15,830; John Stafford (FF) 12,811; Éamonn Murphy (Ind) 9,296; Olive Braiden (FF) 8,237; Stephen O'Byrnes (PD) 8,212; Larry O'Toole (SF) 8,190; Paddy Madigan (Ind) 6,903; John Burns (NLP) 1,705. **Elected:** Patricia McKenna (GP) 57,749 - 10th Ct; Niall Andrews (FF) 56,904 - 10th Ct; Mary Banotti (FG) 53,897 - 12th Ct; Bernie Malone (Lab) 47,696 - 12th Ct.

LEINSTER
Seats: 4; **Candidates:** 12; **Electorate:** 624,561; **Turnout:** 43.08%; **Total Valid Poll:** 262,445; **Quota:** 52,490. **First Count:** Liam Hyland (FF) 46,448; Alan Gillis (FG) 42,826; Jim Fitzsimons (FF) 41,375; Nuala Ahern (GP) 30,997; Monica Barnes (FG) 29,958; Michael Bell (Lab) 22,987; Séamus Pattison (Lab) 17,580; John Dardis (PD) 12,591; Jack Fitzsimons (Ind) 6,752; Lucilita Bhreathnach (SF) 6,523; Peter Sweetman (Ind) 3,228; Thomas Mullins (NLP) 1,180. **Elected:** Liam Hyland (FF) 54,161 -

7th Ct; Alan Gillis (FG) 50,896 - 7th Ct; Jim Fitzsimons (FF) 50,263 - 7th Ct; Nuala Ahern (GP) 45,821 - 7th Ct.

MUNSTER
Seats: 4; **Candidates:** 16; **Electorate:** 755,176; **Turnout:** 48.98%; **Total Valid Poll:** 364,571; **Quota:** 72,915. **First Count:** Brian Crowley (FF) 84,463; Gerry Collins (FF) 49,677; John Cushnahan (FG) 36,906; Des O'Malley (PD) 31,674; Tom Raftery (FG) 31,250; Pat Cox (Ind) 27,920; Jim Kemmy (Lab) 25,486; Paddy Lane (FF) 19,369; Nora Bennis (Ind) 18,424; Kathleen Lynch (DL) 15,573; Dan Boyle (GP) 10,033; Martin O'Regan (WP) 6,270; Kieran McCarthy (SF) 5,171; Stewart Luck (NLP) 890; Conor Moloney (Ind) 858; Denis Riordan (Ind) 607. **Elected:** Brian Crowley (FF) 84,463 - 1st Ct; Gerry Collins (FF) 75,527 - 9th Ct; John Cushnahan (FG) 72,018 - 12th Ct; Pat Cox (Ind) 52,495 - 12th Ct.

NORTHERN IRELAND
Seats: 3; **Candidates:** 17;

Electorate: 1,150,304; **Turnout:** 48.67%; **Total Valid Poll:** 559,867; **Result:** Rev Ian Paisley (DUP) 163,246; John Hume (SDLP) 161,992; Jim Nicholson (UUP) 133,459; Mary Clarke-Glass (All) 23,157; Tom Hartley (SF) 21,273; Dodie McGuinness (SF) 17,195; Francie Molloy (SF) 16,747; Rev Hugh Ross (Ulster Ind) 7,858; Myrtle Boal (Con) 5,583; John Lowry (WP) 2,543; Niall Cusack (Ind Lab) 2,464; Jim Anderson (NLP) 1,418; June Campion (Peace) 1,088; David Kerr (Ind for Ulster) 571; Robert Mooney (NI Con) 400; Suzanna Thompson (NLP) 454; Michael Kennedy (NLP) 419. **Elected:** Rev Ian Paisley (DUP), John Hume (SDLP) and Jim Nicholson (UUP).

❑

REPUBLIC OF IRELAND RESULTS, 1979-94

Year	Total No. of seats	Turnout %	F.F.	F.G.	LAB.	W.P.	P.D.	GREEN	OTHERS
1979	15	63.6	5	4	4	-	-	-	2
1984	15	47.6	8	6	-	-	-	-	1
1989	15	68.3	6	4	1	1	1	-	2
1994	15	44.0	7	4	1	-	-	2	1

NORTHERN IRELAND RESULTS, 1979-94

YEAR	TOTAL SEATS	S.D.L.P.	U.U.P.	D.U.P.
1979	3	1	1	1
1984	3	1	1	1
1989	3	1	1	1
1994	3	1	1	1

HISTORY

The Good Friday Agreement: Sunningdale for Unionists

By **Dr. Emmet O Connor**, *University of Ulster.*

After the Sunningdale Agreement (1973), the Anglo-Irish Agreement (1985), and the Framework Document (1995), the Good Friday Agreement is the fourth inter-governmental compact on Northern Ireland's constitution since the beginning of the recent troubles, and in many ways the most remarkable.

Sunningdale marked a formal end to the Anglo-Irish 'cold war' on the North, in which both states had sat 'back to back', each asserting a traditional claim of sovereignty over the region, the Irish vainly pleading their case to anyone willing to listen, and the British denying that Northern Ireland was anyone else's business. The Agreement stood on three points: the principle of consent, ie. Northern Ireland to stay in the UK as long as a majority of its people so wished; cross-community 'power-sharing' government; and North-South co-operation, or the 'Irish dimension' as it was called at the time. Although destroyed by loyalist opposition in 1974, the Sunningdale tripos remained for constitutional nationalists the only possible basis of a fair settlement. And by the 1990s, this view was becoming accepted by the Ulster Unionist Party (UUP) and Sinn Fein as well. Indeed, Seamus Mallon was to describe the negotiations leading to the Good Friday Agreement as 'Sunningdale for slow-learners'.

One reason for the moderation of UUP attitudes was a shift of emphasis in nationalist demands. Primarily, Sunningdale was an attempt to make Northern Ireland work, albeit with a strong 'Irish dimension'. The Anglo-Irish Agreement however, did not involve the Northern Ireland parties, concluded that regional government was not an option in the foreseeable future, and sought to reduce nationalist 'alienation', especially support for the IRA, through promoting links with the Republic. Of all the Anglo-Irish compacts, this was by far the most sympathetic to nationalists, and rooted in a nationalist analysis of the problem. The Framework Document, an inter-governmental agenda for multi-party talks in the peace process, proposed powerful cross-border structures, and seemed to confirm that nationalists now prized all-Ireland institutions before 'power-sharing' government within the North.

In the light of this trajectory, the Good Friday Agreement came as a surprise. Reversing trends of the past two decades, the Agreement prioritized reform and cross-community co-operation within Northern Ireland at the expense of cross-border structures. The Agreement has three aspects: security, 'parity of esteem', and the constitution. The first provides for the release of paramilitary prisoners and decommissioning within two years. The second is the most pro-nationalist element, and promises, in strong but unspecific language, to promote equality in employment, reform policing, and grant greater recognition to the Irish language. In its constitutional aspect, the deal is pro-Unionist. For example, Sunningdale, the last comparable attempt at a settlement, gave nationalists 'power-sharing' and extensive cross-border co-operation, in exchange for devolution and the principle of consent. In the Good Friday Agreement, nationalists secured 'power-sharing' and very restricted cross-border co-operation, and conceded devolution, the principle of consent, the end of the Republic's claim to Northern Ireland, the replacement of the Anglo-Irish Agreement with a more pro-Unionist British-Irish Agreement, and the establishment of a British Isles council, which will bring the Republic back into a British Isles context for the first time since the end of Imperial Dominion status in 1937.

Why the shift in emphasis from all-Ireland structures to reform within Northern Ireland? Why did Bertie Ahern, John Hume, and Gerry Adams accept less favourable terms than those secured by Liam Cosgrave and, *inter alia,* Conor Cruise O'Brien in 1973? And why did nationalists acclaim the deal with much greater enthusiasm than they had greeted previous accords?

In the first instance, for all their political rhetoric, nationalists had done little in practice to advance the cross-border co-operation allowed for in the Anglo-Irish Agreement. Mentally, they had become contextualized by the state they wanted to eliminate. 'Making the border invisible' did not therefore seem to be a way of ending violence or resolving the conflict; a settlement between the parties in Northern Ireland had to be found.

The peace process powerfully reinforced this conviction. The process was initiated as a strategy for constitutional change. To republicans, 'peace' was cant for an acceptable deal. The IRA would call a ceasefire, and in return Sinn Fein would join a formidable nationalist coalition which, with White House support, would be able to compel the British to concede constitutional concessions, with or without Unionist assent. However, as the process unfolded, it was transformed by the White House into a quest for peace through inclusivity and agreement. So powerful was the American intervention, and the desire for peace, that what began in bargaining mode ended in reconciliation mode, and nationalists hailed the Good Friday accord with near euphoria. Agreement was victory. Even Sinn Fein was swept along in the emotive tide, and quickly completed some extraordinary *voltes face.* At the outset, Unionists had feared that they would have to pay the political price of peace. Ironically, the nationalists ended up footing the constitutional bill. This was seen at its most bizarre in the presentation of the amendment to Articles 2 and 3 as a vote for peace. In other words, the Republic dropped its claim to the North to get a permanent IRA ceasefire!

Finally, the Good Friday Agreement was determined by the limits to which the Unionists, and more especially the British government, were prepared to go. The 1990s has seen an extensive erosion of sympathy with Irish unity among the British political elite. Those who framed the Government of Ireland Act (1920) and the Anglo-Irish Treaty (1921) believed that partition would be temporary. In the 1970s and 1980s, British governments represented themselves as 'honest brokers' on the Northern question, neutral between the warring factions. In the 1990s however, the Scottish question, among numerous other pressures on Britain's creaking constitution, has made Unionism a cause in British politics for the first time since 1921. John Major and Tony Blair have come out firmly in favour of the Union, and Blair aims to strengthen pro-Union feeling in Northern Ireland by making the region more inclusive, secular, and pluralist, friendly towards the Republic, but a cherished and unequivocal part of the UK. Thus Blair supported UUP objections to strong or political cross-border structures, while pressing David Trimble to accept reform within Northern Ireland. And it is difficult to believe that Blair could induce Trimble to approve a power-sharing system that would include Sinn Fein, but could not persuade him to endorse stronger North-South links. Significantly, Unionist opposition to the Agreement focused on the security aspect, the implications for policing, and Sinn Fein's inclusion in the new Assembly executive, rather than on the cross-border dimension.

In the past, Unionists complained that the Irish government openly favoured a united Ireland, while the British government was neutral on the future of Northern Ireland. Today, the position is virtually reversed. Britain is pro-Union, while Dublin is committed to a treaty which makes Northern Ireland an undisputed part of the UK. The Good Friday Agreement asks a lot of Unionists in requiring them to work with Sinn Fein members of the Assembly executive. But on the constitution it gives them a better deal than they could have hoped for. The Framework Document has been gutted. The Anglo-Irish Agreement is scrapped. The principles behind Sunningdale have been vindicated, but this time it's Sunningdale for Unionists.

The author is a lecturer in History and Politics at the University of Ulster.

CHRONOLOGY OF IRISH HISTORY 2500 BC - 1997

Events, laws, acts and persons appearing in small capitals in the chronology are featured elsewhere in the Irish Almanac.

BC

2500 BC Radiocarbon dating for the building of Newgrange (Co. Meath).

680 BC Radiocarbon dating for first inhabited enclosure at Navan Fort (Co. Armagh).

51 BC Julius Caesar refers to Ireland as *Hibernia* in written text.

1-1000 AD

130-80 Detailed map of Ireland appears in Ptolemy's 'Geography'.

297 Irish raids on Roman Britain begin, continue until middle of fifth century.

367 Irish, Picts and Saxons stage major raid on Britain.

431 Arrival of the first bishop in Ireland, PALLADIUS, sent by Pope Celestine.

432 ST. PATRICK'S mission begins.

493 Traditional date of Patrick's death (March 17).

546 Derry founded by ST. COLUMCILLE.

563 Monastery at Iona founded by St. Columcille.

575 Convention at Druim Cett (Co.Derry). Poets threatened with exile by kings, and alliances between kings forged.

670-90 Hagiographical writings on St. Patrick, combining the lives of several missionaries especially Palladius, into one legend. Part of an attempt to establish Armagh's primacy in the Irish Church.

740 Compilation of the law text *Senchas Már.*

750-800 Book of Kells illuminated.

795 First Viking raids on Ireland.

841 Vikings establish settlements at Dublin and Louth.

876 Beginning of 'Forty Years Peace' - a respite from Viking attacks.

914 Viking fleet arrives in Waterford, marking the beginning of a second wave of Viking attacks.

922 Foundation of Viking settlement at Limerick.

995 First mint established by the Vikings in Dublin.

1001-1299 A.D.

1005 BRIAN BORU (high-king 1002-1014) visits Armagh and confirms its primacy in the Church.

1014 Battle of Clontarf. Brian Boru defeats the Vikings decisively but is killed himself.

1028-36 Christchurch Cathedral, Dublin, built.

1095 First Crusade proclaimed by Pope Urban II. Irish join in great numbers.

1124 Round tower at Clonmacnoise completed.

1142 First Cistercian monastery in Ireland founded at Mellifont.

1152 Synod of Kells-Mellifont establishes diocesan organisation of Church, with four dioceses - Armagh, Dublin, Cashel and Tuam. Armagh enjoys the primacy.

1169 Normans arrive in Ireland at invitation of exiled Leinster king, DIARMAIT MAC MURCHADA (Dermot MacMurrough).

1169-c.1300 Normans conquer much of Leinster, north and east Ulster, Munster and parts of Connacht.

1171 (May) RICHARD DE CLARE (STRONGBOW) succeeds Diarmait Mac Murchada as king of Leinster.

1171 (October) Henry II, king of England, lands at Waterford.

1175 Treaty of Windsor: High-king Ruairdhí Ua Conchobair (Rory O'Connor) recognises Henry II as his overlord, while Henry recognises Ua Conchobair as high-king of unconquered parts of Ireland.

1177 Prince John (son of Henry II) appointed lord of Ireland. Becomes king of England 1199.

1204 Normans start building Dublin Castle.

1216 (October) John, king of England, dies. Succeeded by Henry III as king and lord of Ireland.

1216 (November) Magna Carta issued for Ireland.

1254 Henry's son Edward is styled 'Lord of Ireland'.

1272 Henry III dies, succeeded by Edward I.

THE 1300s

1301- 5 Irish soldiers fight with Edward I in Scotland. Scots, led by William Wallace, defeated 1305.

1307 Edward I dies, succeeded by Edward II.

1315 Edward Bruce (crowned king of Scotland 1306) arrives in Ulster. Crowned king of Ireland in 1316 but never reigned. Killed 1318 at Battle of Faughart.

1327 Edward II abdicates, his queen rules until their son Edward III comes of age in 1330.

1348 First record of Black Death in Ireland. Occurrences at Howth and Drogheda.

1366 Parliament at Kilkenny. STATUTE OF KILKENNY enacted, designed to prohibit assimilation of Anglo-Irish and Gaelic Irish.

1377 Edward III dies, succeeded by Richard II.

1395 Richard II defeats Leinster Irish in battle. Most Irish kings and rebel Normans submit to him.

1399 Richard II deposed, Henry IV crowned king of England, also Lord of Ireland.

THE 1400s

1413 Henry IV succeeded by Henry V.

1422 Henry V succeeded by Henry VI.

1460 Irish parliament declares that only acts passed by it are binding on the country.

1461 Edward IV assumes English Crown and with it the lordship of Ireland.

1470 Henry VI reinstalled to the English Crown.

1471 Edward IV restored to the throne.

1479 Gearóid Mór Fitzgerald, the eighth earl of Kildare, appointed Lord Deputy (king's representative in Ireland).

1483 (April) Edward V, son of Edward IV succeeds to throne on his father's death.

1483 (June) Edward V deposed, replaced by Richard III.

1485 Henry Tudor kills Richard III at Battle of Bosworth and becomes king as Henry VII.

1487 First recorded use of a firearm in Ireland.

1494 Edward Poynings appointed Lord Deputy. POYNINGS' LAW enacted by parliament at Drogheda. All legislation passed by subsequent Irish parliaments to be approved by the king. Act not amended until 1782.

1495 Parliament makes reference to the English Pale in Ireland in a statute.

1496 Earl of Kildare reappointed Lord Deputy.

THE 1500s

1504 Battle of Knockdoe - Clanricard and O'Brien

defeated by forces of the Pale, the Lord Deputy and O'Donnell, king of Tír Conaill. Estimates suggest 2,000 are killed.

1509 Death of Henry VII. Accession of his son Henry VIII.

1513 Gearóid Óg Fitzgerald, ninth earl of Kildare, appointed Lord Deputy following the death of his father.

1534 (June) THOMAS FITZGERALD (SILKEN THOMAS) son of Gearóid Óg rebels against English rule. Surrenders August 1535 and imprisoned. Executed February 1537.

1534 Gearóid Óg dies in Tower of London.

1536 Reformation parliament, held in Dublin, recognises Henry VIII as temporal head of the Church in Ireland.

1537 Act of Irish parliament provides for suppression of monasteries throughout the country.

1541 Act of Irish parliament recognises Henry VIII as king of Ireland. The English king had hitherto been styled 'lord of Ireland'.

1541 First instance of the system of 'surrender and regrant' where Irish lords recognised the king as sovereign, revoked their Gaelic title, assumed an English title and gained a royal grant of their lands.

1547 Accession of Edward VI following death of his father, Henry VIII.

1549 Act of Uniformity orders the use of the Book of Common Prayer in England and Ireland.

1553 Mary I accedes to the throne on the death of Edward VI. Pace of Reformation halted.

1557 Plantation of Laois and Offaly begins.

1558 Death of Mary I. Accession of the virgin queen, Elizabeth I. Reformation gains new impetus.

1562 Shane O'Neill, earl of Tyrone in rebellion. Submits to Lord Deputy in 1563 but continues warring with local lords until his death in 1567.

1570 Elizabeth I excommunicated by the Pope.

1568-74 Desmond Rebellion in Munster.

1579-83 Further rebellion in Munster. Earl of Desmond killed in 1583.

1582 Pope Gregory XIII reforms calendar - 4/10/1582 to be followed by 15/10/1582 - and year to commence on January 1. Britain and Ireland do not adopt Gregorian calendar until 1782.

1583 HUGH O'NEILL takes the Gaelic title of The O'Neill. Conferred with English title of Earl of Tyrone in 1587.

1587 First grant of land in the plantation of Munster.

1588 Spanish Armada founders off Irish coast, 25 ships wrecked, survivors aided in Connacht and Ulster but put to death elsewhere.

1592 Trinity College Dublin established.

1595-1603 Nine Years War - Rebellion of Hugh O'Neill, earl of Tyrone, and Red Hugh O'Donnell who enlist Spanish support (troops land at Kinsale in 1601).

THE 1600s

1601 Battle of Kinsale - Forces of O'Neill and O'Donnell heavily defeated by Lord Deputy Mountjoy.

1603 (March) Accession of James I (James VI of Scotland), first of Stuart line, following the death of Elizabeth I.

1603 (March) Treaty of Mellifont. O'Neill submits to Mountjoy and pledges loyalty to the Crown.

1607 'Flight of Earls'. Earls of Tyrone and Tirconnell leave Ireland, sailing from Lough Swilly. Their lands are forfeited to the Crown.

1608 Cahir O'Doherty, the last Irish chieftain in rebellion, sacks Derry. Killed in Donegal, the rebellion collapses and O'Doherty's lands are forfeited to the Crown.

1609 Beginning of the plantation of Ulster in counties Donegal, Derry, Tyrone, Armagh, Cavan and Fermanagh.

1625 Death of James I, accession of Charles I.

1632 Compilation of the ANNALS OF THE FOUR MASTERS, a significant historical work, begins and is completed 1636.

1641 A rising, ostensibly in support of Charles I, begins in Ulster and spreads southwards. Thousands of Protestants reported massacred.

1649 (January) Execution of Charles I. England a republic until 1660.

1649 (August) Oliver Cromwell lands in Ireland. Massacre of Catholics in Drogheda and Wexford.

1653 Acts providing for the transplanting of Catholic Irish to Connacht and Ulster Presbyterians to Munster. Their lands are subsequently taken by Cromwellian soldiers and English settlers.

1660 Charles II proclaimed king in Dublin following restoration of the monarchy.

1673 Non-Anglicans excluded from public office by Test Act.

1685 Accession of James II on the death of Charles II.

1689 (February) William and Mary crowned as joint monarchs.

1688 James II flees to France from England

1689 (April) Siege of Derry. Jacobites (followers of James II) lay siege to the city until July when sea-borne supplies arrive.

1690 William defeats James at river Boyne (July 1); James departs for France (July 4); unsuccessful siege at Limerick by Williamite forces (August 9 - 30).

1691 Jacobites defeated at Battle of Aughrim (July 12).

1691 Siege of Limerick (August 25 - September 24) followed by a truce allowing the signing of the TREATY OF LIMERICK (October 3), which guaranteed Catholic rights of worship and free passage of Jacobite soldiers to France.

1691 (December) First of the PENAL LAWS passed, Catholics excluded from parliament and public office by means of oath of supremacy.

1692-1703 Williamites begin confiscation of land from those who supported James.

1694 Death of Mary II.

THE 1700s

1702 William III dies and is succeeded by Queen Anne.

1714 Queen Anne dies without an heir, succeeded by George I, first of the Hanoverian line.

1718 Significant numbers of Ulster Scots (largely Presbyterian) begin emigration to North America.

1719 Toleration Act passed for dissenting protestants. Legal toleration of their religion.

1720 Declatory Act - British parliament affirms its right to legislate for Ireland.

1727 George I succeeded by George II.

1737 First edition of *The Belfast Newsletter*.

1740-1 Severe famine in Ireland; several hundred thousand die.

1745 The Rotunda Maternity Hospital is founded in Dublin.

1745 (May) Battle of Fontenoy (part of the War of

Austrian Succession) at which Irish troops, known as the Wild Geese, distinguished themselves.

1752 George II brings Britain and Ireland into line with Europe by adopting Gregorian Calenader - 2/9/1752 followed by 14/9/1752.

1756 Work begins on construction of Grand Canal.

1760 (March) CATHOLIC COMMITTEE founded in Dublin to lobby for removal of penal laws.

1760 (October) George III becomes king on death of his grandfather George II.

1778 VOLUNTEER MOVEMENT founded in Belfast.

1782 Ireland attains legislative independence. Declaratory Act 1720 repealed, and Poynings' Law 1494 amended.

1783 Bank of Ireland begins trading.

1791 Society of UNITED IRISHMEN founded in Belfast.

1793 CATHOLIC RELIEF ACT - Catholics given rights to vote, to third level education and to hold all but the highest offices of state.

1795 (September) ORANGE ORDER founded in Armagh.

1795 (October) Roman Catholic seminary opens at Maynooth.

1797 (July) Fourteen are killed in violence at an Orange parade in Stewartstown, Co. Tyrone.

1798 (May) United Irishmen rebellion begins. Fighting confined to Leinster and Ulster. Government forces defeat the rebels.

1798 (August) French troops land in Mayo in support of the rebellion. Surrender on September 8.

1798 (November) THEOBALD WOLFE TONE, leader of United Irishmen, arrested at Buncrana. Convicted of treason by court martial and sentenced to death. Commits suicide before sentence can be carried out.

THE 1800s

1800 ACT OF UNION passed to provide for legislative and political union between Great Britain and Ireland.

1801 Union of Great Britain and Ireland commences.

1803 Rebellion in Dublin led by ROBERT EMMET. Emmet hanged for treason September 20.

1813 Four men are killed following violence at an Orange parade in Belfast.

1814 APPRENTICE BOYS OF DERRY formed.

1820 Death of George III, accession of George IV.

1822 Act of parliament provides for an all-Ireland police force.

1823 CATHOLIC ASSOCIATION founded in Dublin to lobby for Catholic Emancipation.

1825 Unlawful Societies (Ireland) Act passed, Catholic Association dissolves, as does the Grand Lodge of the Orange Order (not reconstituted until 1828). The law is ignored by Orange lodges who continue to parade.

1828 DANIEL O'CONNELL elected to House of Commons but unable to take his seat because he is Roman Catholic.

1829 (April) CATHOLIC EMANCIPATION granted. Roman Catholics permitted to enter parliament and hold the high offices of state.

1829 Sixteen die in violence accompanying Orange marches during the summer.

1830 Death of George IV, accession of William IV.

1831 (June) 'Tithe war' begins. Recurring outbreaks of violence caused by the collection of Anglican tithes from members of all religious denominations.

1831 (November) Scheme for nationwide primary schooling initiated - the first in the world.

1832 Party Procession Act passed curtailing marches.

1834 First railway line in Ireland comes into operation.

1836 (April) Grand Lodge of the Orange Order dissolves to avoid suppression.

1836 (May) IRISH CONSTABULARY formed (earned prefix 'Royal' in 1867).

1837 Queen Victoria accedes to the throne on death of William IV.

1838 TOTAL ABSTINENCE MOVEMENT founded in Cork by Fr. Theobald Matthew and William Martin.

1839 (January 6) 'Night of the Big Wind,' storms cause widespread damage.

1840 Daniel O'Connell forms LOYAL NATIONAL REPEAL ASSOCIATION to lobby for the repeal of the Union between Ireland and Great Britain.

1841 Census. Population of Ireland - 8,175,124.

1841 First edition of *The Cork Examiner.*

1843 Daniel O'Connell organises 'Monster meetings' in support of Repeal throughout the country; the biggest is at Tara (an estimated 750,000 attend).

1845 (June) Party Processions Act lapses, Orange Order reformed.

1845 (July) Queen's Colleges Act provide for the establishment of new third level colleges.

1845 (September) First report of potato blight. Beginning of the Famine. Crop decimated in 1846. 1847 (Black '47) is worst year. Blight and famine continue until 1850. In excess of one million die and more than one million emigrate.

1848 YOUNG IRELAND rebellion in Munster easily put down. Leaders transported.

1849 Opening of Queen's Colleges at Belfast, Cork and Galway.

1850 (March) Party Processions Act renewed, police empowered to seize weapons and emblems.

1850 (August) IRISH TENANT LEAGUE formed to lobby for rights of tenant farmers.

1851 Census. Population of Ireland 6,552,385.

1854 Catholic University of Ireland (now University College Dublin) opens.

1855 First edition of *The Irish News.*

1858 IRISH REPUBLICAN BROTHERHOOD founded in Dublin. A sister movement, the FENIAN BROTHERHOOD founded in New York 1859.

1859 First edition of *The Irish Times.*

1861 Census. Population of Ireland - 5,798,967.

1867 (February/March) Fenian rising in Munster easily suppressed.

1867 (July) Orange procession against Party Processions Act leads to a reduction in its powers. Marches now permitted in non-contentious areas. Party Processions Act formally repealed 1872.

1869 IRISH CHURCH ACT provides for disestablishment of Church of Ireland.

1870 (August) Gladstone's first LAND ACT.

1871 Census. Population of Ireland - 5,412,377.

1872 Ballot Act. Secret voting introduced.

1873 (May) ISAAC BUTT forms the HOME RULE LEAGUE, precursor of IRISH PARLIAMENTARY PARTY.

1877 CHARLES STEWART PARNELL becomes leader of Home Rule Confederation of Great Britain (elected chairman of Irish Parliamentary Party 1880).

1879 IRISH NATIONAL LAND LEAGUE formed in Dublin to

agitate for land reform. Proscribed 1882.

1879-82 'The Land War'. Huge increase in rural crime. Directed almost exclusively at landlords and their agents.

1880 'Boycotting' of land agent CHARLES CUNNINGHAM BOYCOTT in Mayo.

1881 (April) Census. Population of Ireland 5,174,836.

1881 (August) Gladstone's second LAND ACT.

1882 Murders of the Chief Secretary and his Under Secretary (the principal government officials in Ireland) in the Phoenix Park by the INVINCIBLES.

1884 GAELIC ATHLETIC ASSOCIATION founded in Thurles.

1885 (May) IRISH LOYAL AND PATRIOTIC UNION formed to oppose Home Rule and maintain the union.

1885 (August) ASHBOURNE ACT provides government loans to tenant farmers for land purchase.

1886 First HOME RULE BILL defeated in House of Commons. Fifty people lose their lives in sectarian rioting in Belfast.

1888 (November) Borough of Belfast created a city by charter.

1888 Pioneer and Total Abstinence Association founded by James Cullen SJ.

1890 Parnell ousted from leadership of Irish Parliamentary Party. He is cited as co-respondent in the William O'Shea divorce petition. Unacceptable to Liberal Party and Catholic hierarchy, causes split in party.

1891 (March) Anti-Parnellite Irish National Federation founded.

1891 (April) Census. Population of Ireland - 4,704,750.

1891 (August) BALFOUR ACT. Extends tenant purchase scheme and establishes Congested Districts Board.

1891 First edition of the *Evening Herald*.

1892 (June) Ulster Convention at Belfast. Delegates vote to oppose workings of a Home Rule parliament.

1892 (June) Primary school education made compulsory.

1893 (July) CONRADH NA GAEILIGE (the Gaelic League) formed.

1893 (September) HOME RULE BILL passed in the House of Commons but defeated in House of Lords.

1894 (April) IRISH AGRICULTURAL ORGANISATION SOCIETY founded.

1894 (April) Trade Union Congress held for first time.

1898 Local Government (Ireland) Act. Establishes county and district councils.

1899 (May) IRISH LITERARY THEATRE founded in Dublin.

1899 (October) Beginning of the Boer War.

1900 - 1909

1900 Irish Parliamentary Party reunites with JOHN REDMOND as leader.

1901 (January) Queen Victoria dies. Accession of Edward VII.

1901 (March) Census. Population of Ireland - 4,458,775.

1903 (March) St. Patrick's Day, March 17, declared a bank holiday.

1903 (June) Independent Orange Order founded in Belfast.

1903 (August) WYNDHAM ACT. Culmination of the series of land acts dating back to 1870.

1905 (March) ULSTER UNIONIST COUNCIL formed to oppose Home Rule.

1905 First edition of the *Irish Independent*.

1907 (April) SINN FÉIN LEAGUE founded (adopts name Sinn Féin 1908).

1907 (July) Irish Crown jewels stolen. They have never been recovered.

1908 (August) IRISH UNIVERSITIES ACT, instituting the National University of Ireland (NUI).

1908 (December) IRISH TRANSPORT AND GENERAL WORKERS' UNION (ITGWU) founded in Dublin.

1910 - 1919

1913 Irish becomes a compulsory subject for matriculation in NUI.

1910 Death of Edward VII, accession of George V.

1911 (April) *Titanic* launched in Belfast.

1911 (April) Census. Population of Ireland - 4,390,219.

1911 (August) Parliament Act abolishes veto powers of House of Lords.

1912 (April) *Titanic* sinks on her maiden voyage.

1912 (June) Labour Party founded at Clonmel, Co. Tipperary.

1912 (September) ULSTER SOLEMN LEAGUE AND COVENANT signed by 218,000 men pledging to use all necessary means to oppose Home Rule.

1913 (January) ULSTER VOLUNTEER FORCE founded in Belfast.

1913 (August) Beginning of the Dublin 'Lock-Out', where Dublin Employers' Federation shuts out members of ITGWU from their places of employment. Continues until January 1914.

1913 (November) IRISH CITIZENS ARMY founded in Dublin to protect the locked-out workers.

1913 (November) IRISH VOLUNTEERS founded in Dublin as a response to formation of UVF.

1914 (March) Curragh Incident - British officers serving at the Curragh indicate that they will not aid the imposition of Home Rule in Ulster.

1914 (April) Gunrunning by Ulster Volunteers at Larne passes off without incident.

1914 (July) Four civilians killed by troops when Irish Volunteers engage in gunrunning at Howth.

1914 (August 4) Britain declares war on Germany. The 36th Ulster Division is established, drawing on UVF membership.

1914 (September) HOME RULE BILL passed but suspended because of World War I.

1914 (September) Split in Irish Volunteers. Majority answer John Redmond's call to join the war. Remainder become National Volunteers under leadership of ÉOIN MAC NEILL.

1915 IRB reorganised and Military Council formed. Plans for an Irish rebellion at advanced stage.

1916 (April) Easter Rising in Dublin. Independent Irish Republic proclaimed. Rebellion suppressed within five days; over 3,000 injured and 450 killed.

1916 (May) Fifteen of the leaders of the Rising executed, including the seven signatories of the proclamation - THOMAS J. CLARKE, SEÁN MACDIARMADA, THOMAS MACDONAGH, PADRAIG PEARSE, EAMONN CEANNT, JAMES CONNOLLY and JOSEPH PLUNKETT.

1916 (July) Battle of the Somme begins (continues until November), the 36th Ulster Division decimated.

1916 (August) SIR ROGER CASEMENT hanged for his part in the Easter Rising.

1918 (November 11) Armistice day. End of World War I.

1918 (November) Universal Suffrage granted. Women win right to vote and right to sit in parliament.

1918 (December) Final all-Ireland general election to Westminster parliament. Seats: SF: 73, OUP: 25, Nat: 6, Ind: 1.

1919 (January 21) Sinn Féin MPs, in keeping with their declared policy of abstention, do not take their seats at Westminster and meet as Dáil Éireann at the Mansion House in Dublin.

1919 (January 21) First engagement of War of Independence; two policemen killed in Tipperary.

1919 (June) First non-stop transatlantic flight completed when Alcock and Brown land in Galway.

1919 (October) Irish Volunteers swear allegiance to the Irish Republic becoming the IRISH REPUBLICAN ARMY.

THE 1920s

1920 (January) First British soldiers are recruited by RIC, commonly termed the BLACK AND TANS. AUXILIARIES recruited from July onwards.

1920 (March) Lord Mayor of Cork, Tomás Mac Curtáin, shot dead by crown forces outside his home in Cork.

1920 (November) 'Bloody Sunday'. Fourteen British secret agents assassinated by IRA in Dublin. Black and Tans retaliate by shooting into a crowd watching a Gaelic football match at Croke Park, killing 12.

1920 (December) Black and Tans and Auxiliaries destroy centre of Cork city.

1920 (December) GOVERNMENT OF IRELAND ACT - Provides for the partition of Ireland and two Home Rule parliaments, one in Dublin, one in Belfast.

1921 (May) General election to Northern Ireland (NI) parliament. Seats: OUP: 40, Nat: 6, SF: 6.

1921 (May) One hundred and twenty-four Sinn Féin and four independent MPs are returned unopposed to the Parliament of Southern Ireland.

1921 (May) Custom House in Dublin is destroyed by IRA.

1921 (June) NI parliament opened by George V.

1921 (June) Parliament of southern Ireland meets in Dublin. Only the four independent MPs turn up; the 124 Sinn Féin MPs refuse to accept its legitimacy and do not take their seats.

1921 (July) Truce agreed between IRA and British army.

1921 (July) Fifteen Catholics killed and 68 seriously injured in one day when members of Orange Order, aided by police officers attack Catholic areas in Belfast.

1921 (August) Sinn Féin MPs elected to the parliament of southern Ireland meet in the Mansion House as the second Dáil.

1921 (December) ANGLO-IRISH TREATY signed in London establishing the Irish Free State (IFS).

1922 (January) Anglo-Irish Treaty approved by Dáil Éireann by 64 votes to 57. Split in Sinn Féin; those in opposition to the Treaty walk out. MICHAEL COLLINS becomes the chairman of the Provisional Government.

1922 (May) Royal Ulster Constabulary established.

1922 (May) IRA declared an illegal organisation in NI.

1922 (June) General election in IFS. Seats: Pro-treaty SF: 58, anti-treaty SF: 36, Lab: 17, Farmers' Party 7, others 10. Pro-treaty Sinn Féin form the government.

1922 (June) Civil War breaks out in IFS.

1922 (August) Chairman of Provisional Government and Commander in Chief of the Free State forces, Michael Collins, assassinated in Cork.

1922 (October) Dáil Éireann ratifies the CONSTITUTION OF THE IFS (approved by British parliament in December).

1922 (November) Provisional Government orders the first of 77 executions of anti-treaty prisoners.

1922 (November) NI elections to Westminster. Seats: OUP: 11, Nat: 2.

1922 (December) Executive Council of the IFS takes office with W.T. COSGRAVE as President.

1922 (December) NI parliament opts out of the IFS.

1923 (March) CUMANN NA NGAEDHEAL founded from pro-treaty Sinn Féin.

1923 (May) Civil war ends.

1923 (August) Garda Síochána established by act of Free State Dáil.

1923 (August) General election in Free State. Seats: Cumann na nGaedheal 63, SF 44, Lab. 14, Farmers' Party 15, others 17. Cumann na nGaedheal form the government.

1923 (September) IFS becomes member of the League of Nations.

1923 (November) W.B. YEATS receives Nobel Prize for literature.

1923 (December) NI elections to Westminster. Seats: OUP 11, Nat. 2.

1924 (March) Mutiny in IFS army.

1924 (September) BBC starts radio broadcasts from Belfast as 2BE.

1924 (October) NI elections to Westminster. OUP win all 13 seats.

1925 (April) General election to NI parliament. Seats: OUP 32, Nat. 10, other U. 4, other Lab. 3, other Nat. 2, Ind. 1.

1925 (July) Shannon hydro-electric scheme approved by Dáil.

1925 (December) Governments of Britain, NI and IFS agree to rescind powers of the Boundary Commission.

1926 (January) 2RN, the forerunner of RTE commences radio broadcasts.

1926 (April) Census. Population of NI - 1,256,561. Population of IFS - 2,971,992.

1926 (May) FIANNA FÁIL founded by ÉAMON DE VALERA.

1926 (November) GEORGE BERNARD SHAW receives Nobel Prize for literature.

1927 (June) General election in Free State. Seats: Cumann na nGaedheal 47, FF 44, Lab. 22, Farmers' Party 11, National League 8, SF 5, others 16. Cumann na nGaedheal remain in office.

1927 (July) KEVIN O'HIGGINS, Minister for Justice in the IFS, assassinated.

1927 (August) Éamon de Valera and Fianna Fáil take Oath of Allegiance and take their seats in Dáil Éireann.

1927 (September) Cumann na nGaedheal 62, FF 57, Lab 13, Farmers' Party 6, others 15. Cumann na nGaedheal retain office.

1929 (April) Proportional Representation abolished in NI parliamentary elections.

1929 (May) General election to NI parliament. Seats: OUP 38, Nat.11, other U. 3.

1929 (May) NI elections to Westminster. Seats: OUP 11, Nat. 2.

1929 (July) CENSORSHIP OF PUBLICATIONS ACT in IFS

establishes a board with wide-ranging powers of censorship.

1929 (October) Shannon hydro-electric scheme comes into operation.

THE 1930s

1931 (September) First edition of the *Irish Press*.

1931 (October) IRA declared an illegal organisation in IFS.

1931 (October) NI elections to Westminster. Seats: OUP 11, Nat. 2.

1931 (December) STATUTE OF WESTMINSTER passed by British parliament. Gives Dominion parliaments equal status with Imperial parliament at Westminster.

1932 (February) Quasi-fascist ARMY COMRADES ASSOCIATION - BLUESHIRTS - founded.

1932 (February) General election in Free State. Seats: FF 72, Cumann na nGaedheal 57, Lab. 7, Farmers' Party 4, others 13. Fianna Fáil form the new government.

1932 (June) Payment of land annuities to Britain withheld. Beginning of economic war between Ireland and Britain.

1933 (January) General election in Free State. Seats: FF 77, Cumann na nGaedheal 48, Lab. 8, National Centre Party 11, others 9. Fianna Fáil remain in office.

1933 (May) Oath of Allegiance removed from constitution of IFS.

1933 (September) FINE GAEL formed by amalgamation of Cumann na nGaedheal, Centre Party and National Guard (Blueshirts). ÉOIN O'DUFFY first leader.

1933 (November) General election to NI parliament. Seats: OUP 36, Nat. 9, other U. 3, other Nat. 2, other Lab. 2.

1935 (July) Nine are killed and 2,241 Catholics across NI are intimidated out of their homes in riots accompanying 12th of July parades by the Orange Order.

1935 (November) NI elections to Westminster. Seats OUP 11, Nat. 2.

1936 (January) Death of George V, accession of Edward VIII.

1936 (April) Census in IFS. Population - 2,968,420.

1936 (May) Senate of IFS abolished by Dáil.

1936 (August) Aer Lingus established as national airline of the IFS.

1936 (November) Irish brigade, under leadership of Éoin O'Duffy, join General Franco's fascists in Spanish Civil War.

1936 (December) Abdication of Edward VIII.

1936 (December) EXTERNAL RELATIONS ACT passed by Dáil during abdication crisis in Britain. It removes all reference to the Crown from the constitution.

1936 (December) CONNOLLY COLUMN, under leadership of FRANK RYAN, join socialists in Spanish Civil War.

1937 (February) Spanish Civil War (Non-intervention) Act forbids involvement of Free State citizens in the war.

1937 (February) Census in NI Population - 1,279,745.

1937 (July 1) CONSTITUTION OF ÉIRE is ratified by referendum and comes into effect December 29. General election in Free State. Seats: FF 69, FG 48, Lab. 13, others 8. Fianna Fáil retain office.

1938 (February) General election to NI parliament. Seats: OUP 39, Nat. 8, other U. 3, other Lab. 2.

1938 (April) Economic War with Britain ends, and Britain transfers the 'treaty ports' to Éire.

1938 (June) General election in Éire. Seats: FF 77, FG 45, Lab. 9, others 7. Fianna Fáil remain in government.

1938 (June) DOUGLAS HYDE inaugurated as the first President of Ireland.

1939 (September 2) De Valera announces Éire will remain neutral during World War II. Britain declares war on Germany (September 3).

THE 1940s

1941 (April/May) German air-raids on Belfast kill almost 1,000.

1941 (May) Germans bomb North Strand in Dublin, killing 34.

1942 American troops arrive in NI.

1943 General election in Éire. Seats: FF 67, FG 32, Lab 17, CLANN NA TALMHAN 14, others 8. Fianna Fáil form the government.

1944 (May) General election in Éire. Seats: FF 76, FG 30, Clann na Talmhan 11, Lab. 8, others 13. Fianna Fáil remain in office.

1944 (December) Coras Iompair Éireann established as national transport company.

1945 (May 8) War ends in Europe (Ends in Pacific on August 14).

1945 (June) General election to NI parliament. Seats: OUP 33, Nat.10, other Lab. 4, other U. 2, other Nat. 1.

1945 (June) SEÁN T. Ó CEALLAIGH inaugurated as President.

1945 (July) N.I. elections to Westminster. Seats: OUP 9, Nat. 2, others 2.

1946 (May) Census in Éire. Population - 2,955,107.

1946 (June) Bórd na Móna established.

1947 EDUCATION ACT in NI provides free secondary school education for all.

1948 (February) General Election in Éire. Seats: FF 68, FG 31, Lab. 14, CLANN NA POBLACHTA 10, Clann na Talmhan 7, others 17. Inter-party government formed by Fine Gael, Labour, Clann na Poblachta, Clann na Talmhan and independents.

1948 (December) REPUBLIC OF IRELAND ACT passed by Dáil. Republic declared on April 18, 1949, accompanied by a formal withdrawal from the British Commonwealth.

1949 (February) General election to N.I. parliament. Seats: OUP 37, Nat. 9, other U. 2, Ind. 2, other Nat.1, other Lab. 1.

1949 (February) Government announces it cannot join North Atlantic Treaty Organisation because of Britain's sovereignty in NI.

1949 (May) Council of Europe established. Ireland and Britain amongst founding members.

1949 (June) IRELAND ACT passed at Westminster recognising Ireland's withdrawal from the Commonwealth and reaffirming the constitutional position of NI.

THE 1950s

1950 NI elections to Westminster. Seats: OUP 10, Nat. 2.

1951 (April) Census. Republic of Ireland (RoI) population - 2,960,593. NI population - 1,370,921.

1951 (April) Opposition to the Mother-and-Child Scheme from the Roman Catholic hierarchy results in resignation of Minister for Health and collapse of the government.

1951 (May) General election in RoI. Seats: FF 69, FG

40, Lab. 16, Clann na Talmhan 6, Clann na Poblachta 2, others 14. Fianna Fáil form a minority government.
1951 (October) NI elections to Westminster. Seats: OUP 9, Nat. 2, others 1.
1951 (November) E.T.S. WALTON awarded Nobel Prize for Physics.
1952 (February) Death of George VI, accession of Elizabeth II.
1952 (July) Bord Fáilte, Irish tourist board, established by Act of Dáil Éireann.
1953 (January) Car ferry between Stranraer and Larne sinks with loss of 130 lives.
1953 (May) BBC begins television transmissions from Belfast.
1953 (October) General election to NI parliament. Seats: OUP 38, Nat. 7, other Lab. 3, other Nat. 2, other U. 1, Ind. 1.
1954 (April) Flags and Emblems (Display) Act in NI makes it an offence to interfere with the Union Jack and empowers police to remove flags or emblems likely to incite trouble.
1954 (May) General election in RoI. Seats: FF 65, FG 50, Lab. 19, Clann na Talmhan 5, Clann na Poblachta 3, others 5. Inter-party government formed by Fine Gael, Labour, Clann na Talmhan and Clann na Poblachta.
1955 (May) NI elections to Westminster. Seats: OUP 10, SF 2.
1955 (July) Led by BRIAN FAULKNER, MP, and protected by 300 RUC officers, 12,000 Orangemen march along a contentious route at Annalong, Co. Down.
1955 (December) RoI admitted to United Nations Organisation.
1956 (April) Census in RoI. Population - 2,898,264.
1956 (December) Beginning of IRA border campaign (ends February 1962).
1957 General election in RoI. Seats: FF 78, FG 40, Lab. 12, Clann na Poblachta 5, Clann na Talmhan 3, others 9. Fianna Fáil form the government.
1958 General election to NI parliament. Seats: OUP 37, Nat. 7, other Lab. 6, other Nat. 1, Ind. 1.
1959 (June) Éamon de Valera elected President; proposal to abolish proportional representation in Republic defeated by referendum.
1959 (October) NI elections to Westminster. Seats: OUP 12.
1959 (October) First broadcast by Ulster Television.

THE 1960s

1960 (November) Nine Irish soldiers killed while serving as UN peacekeepers in Belgian Congo.
1961 (April) Census. RoI population - 2,818,341. NI population - 1,425,042.
1961 (October) General election in RoI. Seats: FF 70, FG 47, Lab. 16, Clann na Talmhan 2, Clann na Poblachta 1, others 8. Fianna Fáil remain in office.
1961 (December 31) Inaugural television broadcast of Radio Telefís Éireann.
1962 (May) General election to NI parliament. Seats: OUP 35, Nat. 9, other Lab. 7,others 1.
1962 (July) M1 between Belfast and Lisburn - the first motorway in NI - opens.
1963 (June) President of the United States, John Fitzgerald Kennedy, pays official visit to Ireland.
1964 NI elections to Westminster. Seats: OUP 12.

1965 (January) Taoiseach SEÁN LEMASS and Prime Minister TERENCE O'NEILL meet in Belfast followed by a meeting in Dublin in February.
1965 (April) General election in RoI. Seats: FF 72, F.G. 47, Lab. 22, Clann na Poblachta 1, others 2. Fianna Fáil form government.
1965 (June) New Towns Act in NI provides for establishment of Craigavon.
1965 (November) General election in NI. Seats: OUP 36, Nat. 9, other Lab. 4, others 3.
1966 (March) Nelson's pillar in Dublin is blown up.
1966 (March) NI elections to Westminster. Seats: OUP 11, Republican Lab. 1.
1966 (April) Census. RoI population - 2,884,002.
1966 (June) Éamon de Valera re-elected President.
1966 (October) Census in NI. Population - 1,484,775.
1967 (January) NI CIVIL RIGHTS ASSOCIATION (NICRA) formed.
1968 (August) Higher Education Authority established in Republic.
1968 (August) NICRA holds its first demonstration.
1968 (October) Proposal to abolish proportional representation defeated by referendum in RoI.
1969 (January) Civil rights march attacked by loyalists at Burntollet, Co. Derry.
1969 (February) General election in NI. Seats: OUP 39, Nat. 6, other Lab. 4, others 3.
1969 (June) General election in RoI. Seats: FF 75, FG 50, Lab. 18, others 1. Fianna Fáil remain in government.
1969 (August) British troops move into NI, following sustained clashes between Bogside residents and the 'B' SPECIALS in Derry sparked off by the annual Apprentice Boys march.
1969 (October) SAMUEL BECKETT awarded Nobel Prize for literature.
1969 (December) Act of NI parliament establishes Ulster Defence Regiment (UDR).

THE 1970s

1970 (January) Split in Sinn Féin between abstentionists (PROVISIONAL SINN FÉIN) and non-abstentionists (OFFICIAL SINN FÉIN). IRA splits along same lines.
1970 (April) 'B' Specials disbanded.
1970 (April) ALLIANCE PARTY OF NI founded.
1970 (May) Irish Government ministers CHARLES HAUGHEY and NEIL BLANEY charged with procuring arms for the IRA, Blaney's charges are dropped; Haughey is acquitted.
1970 (June) NI elections to Westminster. Seats: OUP 8, others 4.
1970 (August) SOCIAL DEMOCRATIC AND LABOUR PARTY founded.
1971 (February) Decimal currency introduced in both NI and the RoI. Pre-decimal 240 pence pound replaced with 100 pence pound.
1971 (April) Census. RoI population - 2,978,248. NI population - 1,536,065.
1971 (August) Internment without trial reintroduced in NI. Measures aimed at nationalist community in particular. Continues until December 1975. All parades and marches are banned for six months.
1971 (September) DEMOCRATIC UNIONIST PARTY founded by IAN PAISLEY.
1971 (September) Protestant paramilitary organisation,

the ULSTER DEFENCE ASSOCIATION (UDA) formed.

1972 (January) 'Bloody Sunday' - 13 civilians on civil rights march in Derry shot dead by British army paratroopers. One man later dies from his injuries.

1972 (February) British embassy in Dublin is attacked and burned following 'Bloody Sunday'.

1972 (March) NI parliament prorogued and direct rule from Westminster introduced.

1972 (May) RoI's proposed entry to European Economic Community (EEC) approved by referendum.

1972 (December) Referendum in the RoI lowers the voting age to 18 and removes the special position of the Roman Catholic church from the constitution.

1973 (January) RoI joins European Economic Community along with Britain and Denmark.

1973 (February) General election in RoI. Seats: FF 69, FG 54, Lab. 19, others 2. Fine Gael and Labour form coalition government.

1973 (March) Referendum in NI on remaining within United Kingdom: 98.9% in favour, 1.1% against (nationalists boycott poll).

1973 (May) ERSKINE CHILDERS elected President; inaugurated June 25.

1973 (June) Elections to NI Assembly. Seats: OUP 23, SDLP 19, Alliance 8, DUP 8, VANGUARD UNIONIST PROGRESSIVE PARTY 7, others 13.

1973 (July) NORTHERN IRELAND CONSTITUTION ACT. NI parliament abolished and provision made for a 12-member executive.

1973 (December) Tripartite Conference results in SUNNINGDALE AGREEMENT. Power-sharing executive for NI agreed upon.

1974 (January) Power-sharing executive takes office.

1974 (February) NI elections to Westminster. Seats: OUP 7, DUP 1, SDLP 1, VUPP 1.

1974 (May) ULSTER WORKERS' COUNCIL declares general strike in opposition to power-sharing executive. Executive falls after two weeks.

1974 (October) SEÁN MACBRIDE shares Nobel Peace Prize.

1974 (October) NI elections to Westminster. Seats: OUP 6, DUP 1, SDLP 1, VUPP 1, others 1.

1974 (December) CEARBHALL Ó DÁLAIGH inaugurated as President following death of Erskine Childers.

1975 (May) Election to N.I. Convention. Seats: OUP 19, SDLP 17, VUPP 14, DUP 12, Alliance 8, others 8.

1976 (March) Special category status for persons convicted of paramilitary offences phased out, followed by Republican protests in Long Kesh.

1976 (July) British ambassador to the Republic killed in I.R.A. bomb attack in Dublin.

1976 (August) Peace People founded.

1976 (November) Betty Williams and Mairead Corrigan, founding members of the Peace People awarded Nobel Peace Prize.

1976 (December) DR. PATRICK HILLERY inaugurated as President following resignation of Cearbhall Ó Dálaigh.

1977 (June) General election in RoI. Seats: FF 84, FG 43, Lab. 17, others 4. Fianna Fáil return to government.

1978 (November) Second national television channel established by RTÉ.

1979 (January) Oil tanker explodes at Whiddy Island oil terminal Cork, killing 50.

1979 (March) Ireland joins European Monetary System, ending parity between Punt and Sterling.

1979 (April) Census in Republic. Population - 3,368,405.

1979 (May) General election in NI. Seats: UUP 5, DUP 3, SDLP 1, others 3.

1979 (June) Elections to European parliament. Seats in RoI: FF 5, FG 4, Lab. 4, others 2. Seats in NI: SDLP 1, UUP 1, DUP 1.

1979 (August) Earl Mountbatten is killed by IRA bomb explosion on his boat off the Co. Sligo coast. Three others including two teenagers also die. Eighteen British soldiers are killed in an explosion in Co. Down on same day.

1979 (September/October) Pope John Paul II visits Ireland, celebrating public mass at Knock, Drogheda and Dublin and a private mass at Maynooth.

THE 1980s

1980 (April) Two Irish soldiers serving as UN peacekeepers shot dead in Lebanon.

1981 (February) Forty-eight die as fire sweeps through Stardust Ballroom in Artane, Dublin. Over 160 injured.

1981 (March) Republican hunger strike to regain special category status, led by BOBBY SANDS, begins in Long Kesh.

1981 (April) Imprisoned hunger striker Bobby Sands elected to House of Commons in Fermanagh & South Tyrone by-election. He and nine other prisoners die during the hunger strike before it is called off in October. Sixty-four die in accompanying disturbances throughout NI.

1981 (April) Census. RoI population - 3,443,405. NI population - 1,481,959.

1981 (June) General Election in RoI. Seats: FF 78, FG 65, Lab. 15, WORKERS' PARTY 1, others 7 (including two hunger strikers). Fine Gael and Labour form coalition government.

1981 (August) Death of hunger striker Kieran Doherty TD.

1982 (February) General election in RoI. Seats: FF 81, FG 63, Lab. 15, WP 3, others 3. Fianna Fáil form minority government.

1982 (October) General election to NI. Assembly. Seats: UUP 26, DUP 21, SDLP 14, Alliance 10, SF 5. Assembly dissolved July 1986.

1982 (November) General election in RoI. Seats: FF 75, FG 70, Lab. 16, WP 2, others 3. Fine Gael and Labour form coalition government.

1982 (December) Seventeen killed in INLA bombing of a disco in Co. Derry.

1983 (May) New Ireland Forum meets for first time.

1983 (June) NI elections to Westminster. Seats: UUP 11, DUP 3, SDLP 1, SF 1, others 1.

1983 (August) Twenty-two republicans convicted on the word of supergrass Christopher Black (18 have their convictions quashed within three years).

1983 (September) Thirty-nine IRA inmates escape from Long Kesh - 20 are almost immediately recaptured.

1984 (May) Report of the New Ireland Forum published.

1984 (June) Ronald Regan, President of the United States, pays official visit to Ireland.

1984 (June) Elections to European parliament. Seats in Republic: FF 8, FG 6, others 1. Seats in NI: SDLP 1, UUP 1, DUP 1.

1984 (October) IRA bomb the Brighton hotel where the Conservative Party conference is being held. Five are killed and many members of the British cabinet narrowly escape serious injury or death.

1985 (June) Air India jet crashes off Co. Kerry coast with loss of 329 lives.

1985 (October) First commercial flight from Knock airport.

1985 (November) ANGLO-IRISH AGREEMENT signed by British and Irish governments. Setting up British/Irish governmental conference.

1985 (December) PROGRESSIVE DEMOCRATS founded.

1986 (January) Fifteen by-elections in NI caused by simultaneous resignation of all unionist MPs in protest at the Anglo-Irish Agreement. Seats:OUP 10, DUP 3, SDLP 1, others 1.

1986 (June) Referendum in RoI rejects legalisation of divorce.

1986 (April) Census in RoI. Population 3,540,643.

1987 (January) Government reveals that one-third of the country's haemophiliacs contracted HIV through the transfusion of contaminated blood.

1987 (February) General election in RoI. Seats: FF 81, FG 51, PD 14, Lab. 12, WP 4, others 4. Fianna Fáil form minority government.

1987 (March) National Lottery launched in the RoI.

1987 (May) Eight members of the IRA and one passer-by killed in a British army ambush at Loughgall, Co. Armagh.

1987 (May) Referendum in RoI ratifies SINGLE EUROPEAN ACT.

1987 (June) NI elections to Westminster. Seats: UUP 9, DUP 3, SDLP 3, SF 1, others 1.

1987 (November) IRA bomb kills eleven civilians at Remembrance Day service in Enniskillen.

1988 Dublin celebrates its Millennium Year.

1988 (March) Week of unrest in NI following killing of three IRA members in Gibraltar by SAS. Three mourners killed at their funerals by loyalist gunman. Two soldiers killed at subsequent funerals.

1988 (August) Eight British soldiers killed in an IRA explosion near Ballygawley, Co. Tyrone.

1988 (October) British government introduces a broadcasting ban, based on the Republic's Section 31, on direct statements by paramilitary organisations.

1989 (January) Forty-five die in British Midland air crash on London-Belfast route.

1989 (February) Belfast lawyer Pat Finucane shot dead by the UFF amid claims of security force collusion.

1989 (March) Three Irish soldiers serving with the UN in Lebanon killed by a landmine.

1989 (May) Church of Ireland General Synod votes in favour of the ordination of women.

1989 (June) General election in RoI. Seats: FF 77, FG 55, Lab. 15, WP 7, PD 6, others 6. Government formed by Fianna Fáil/Progressive Democrat coalition.

1989 (June) Elections to European Parliament. Seats in RoI: FF 6, FG 4, Lab. 1, WP 1, PD 1, others 2. Seats in NI: UUP 1, SDLP 1, DUP 1.

1989 (September) Ten British army bandsmen are killed by an IRA bomb explosion at their headquarters in Deal.

1989 (October) 'Guildford Four,' imprisoned in October 1975, have their convictions quashed and are released.

THE 1990s

1990 (January) Beginning of the six-month Irish presidency of the European Community.

1990 (April) Minor earthquake (5.2 on the Richter scale) felt along the east coast of Ireland.

1990 (May) Report of the Stevens inquiry finds evidence of collusion between the UDR and loyalist paramilitaries.

1990 (June) First punt pound coins minted.

1990 (August) Brian Keenan, Irish hostage in the Lebanon, released after four-and-a-half years in captivity.

1990 (November) MARY ROBINSON becomes the first woman to be elected President.

1991 Dublin is the European City of Culture for the year.

1991 (January) Fourteen are killed during violent storms in the first weekend of the new year.

1991 (March) The 'Birmingham Six', convicted of the 1974 Birmingham pub bombings which killed 18, have their convictions quashed and are released having spent more than 16 years in prison.

1991 (April) Census. RoI population - 3,525,719. NI population - 1,577,836.

1991 (April) Talks begin in NI under the chairmanship of Sir Ninian Stephens (they break down in July).

1991 (October) Tribunal of Inquiry into the Irish beef industry begins.

1992 (January) Eight workmen die when their van is blown up by an IRA bomb at Teebane crossroads, Co. Tyrone.

1992 (February) Five men are shot dead in a betting shop on Belfast's Ormeau Road by the UDA. Four IRA members are killed by the British army following an attack on Cookstown RUC station.

1992 (February) The Supreme Court overturns the Attorney General's injunction against a 14 year-old girl, preventing her travelling to Britain to procure an abortion in what became known as the 'X-Case'.

1992 (April) NI elections to Westminster. Seats: UUP 9, SDLP 4, DUP 3, others 1.

1992 (May) Bishop Eamon Casey resigns as Bishop of Galway following revelations that he had an 18-year-old son in the United States and had used diocesan funds to pay maintenance.

1992 (July) Three of the 'UDR Four' are released when the NI Court of Appeal finds their convictions unsafe.

1992 (June) MAASTRICHT TREATY ON EUROPEAN UNION ratified by referendum in RoI.

1992 (October) President Robinson becomes the first head of state to visit hunger stricken Somalia.

1992 (November) General election in RoI. Seats: FF 68, FG 45, Lab. 33, PD 10, DEMOCRATIC LEFT 4, others 6. Coalition government formed by Fianna Fáil and Labour.

1992 (November) Referendum on abortion in RoI. Right to travel and right to information passed. Availability of abortion (the 'substantive issue') rejected.

1993 (January) Single European market comes into effect.

1993 (March) IRA bomb in Warrington kills two children and provokes widespread and sustained public outcry.

1993 (July) Tribunal of Inquiry into the beef industry comes to an end having met for 226 days.

1993 (October) IRA bomb explodes prematurely on Belfast's Shankill road killing ten including the bomber; loyalist gunmen retaliate one week later by killing seven at a pub in Greysteel, Co. Derry.

1994 (January) Irish government revokes the Section 31 broadcasting ban.

1994 (June) Elections to European Parliament. Seats in RoI: FF 7, FG 4, GREEN PARTY 2, Lab. 1, Ind. 1. Seats in NI: UUP 1, SDLP 1, DUP 1.

1994 (June) Six Catholics killed by the UVF in a Co. Down pub while watching the Republic of Ireland v. Italy World Cup soccer match.

1994 (August) IRA ceasefire begins. Loyalist paramilitary ceasefire begins in October. British government lifts broadcasting ban.

1994 (November) Fianna Fáil/Labour coalition collapses, replaced by Fine Gael/Labour/Democratic Left 'rainbow' coalition.

1995 (February) Taoiseach John Bruton and British Prime Minister John Major launch the FRAMEWORK DOCUMENT.

1995 (May) *The Irish Press* newspaper goes out of business with the loss of 600 jobs.

1995 (October) Derry poet SEAMUS HEANEY awarded the Nobel Prize for Literature.

1995 (November) Referendum on legalisation of divorce in the Republic - 50.3% in favour, 49.7% against.

1995 (November) President Clinton visits Ireland receiving a rapturous welcome in Belfast, Derry and Dublin. Addresses a full sitting of both houses of the Oireachtas.

1996 (February) IRA ceasefire ends with bombing of London's Docklands.

1996 (April) Census in RoI. Population 3,621,035.

1996 (May) Elections to NI Forum. Seats: UUP 30, DUP 24, SDLP 21, SF 17, Alliance 7, other U. 7, other Lab. 2, others 2.

1996 (June) Multi-party talks under the chairmanship of George Mitchell get under way at Stormont. Sinn Féin refused entry because of the absence of an IRA ceasefire.

1996 (June) Investigative journalist Veronica Guerin shot dead outside Dublin in an apparent 'contract killing'.

1996 (July) Ireland assumes a six-month presidency of the European Union.

1996 (July) NI experiences its worst rioting in 15 years following the decision of the RUC to ban an Orange Order march along the nationalist Garvaghy Road and the subsequent reversal of that decision.

1996 (July) Swimmer Michelle Smith becomes Ireland's most successful Olympian winning three gold medals and one bronze medal at the Olympic Games in Atlanta Georgia.

1996 (November) Referendum in RoI on the denial of bail to likely reoffenders - 74.8% in favour, 25.2% against.

1997 (May) NI elections to Westminster. Seats: U.U.P. 10, SDLP 3, SF 2, DUP 2, others 1.

1997 (June) The SDLP's Alban Maginness was installed as Belfast's first ever nationalist Lord Mayor

1997 (June) General Election in Republic. Seats: FF 77, FG 54, Lab. 17, PD 4, WP 4, GP 2, SF 1, SP 1, others 6. Fianna Fáil and Progressive Democrats form coalition government.

1997 (July) NI witnessed a five days of sustained rioting following the RUC's decision to force an Orange Order march along the nationalist Garvaghy Road

1997 (July) The IRA restored their August 1994 ceasefire.

1997 (September) Sinn Féin are admitted to multi-party talks at Stormont, substantive negotiations in the three stranded process began in October.

1997 (October) MARY MCALEESE is elected President (the first person from north of the border to hold the office). Inaugurated November 11th. Referendum on cabinet confidentiality passed.

HISTORICAL MOVEMENTS AND ORGANISATIONS

ABBEY THEATRE

Founded: Dublin 1904.
Founders: William Butler Yeats, Lady Gregory and Edward Martyn.
Profile: The national theatre of Ireland, it was established to produce plays written by Irish playwrights and dealing with Irish themes. Staged works by Yeats, Synge and O'Casey. Has received government funding since 1924. Went into artistic decline from early 1930s until late 1960s.

AMNESTY ASSOCIATION

Founded: 1868.
Founder: John Nolan.
Profile: Campaigned for the release of Fenians imprisoned after the 1867 rebellion, who were being held under harsh conditions in British jails. Prominent figures for whom amnesties were secured were O'Donovan Rossa and John O'Leary. The organisation lapsed in the 1870s and 1880s but was reformed in the early 1890s to campaign for the release of remaining Fenian prisoners. Dynamite expert Thomas J. Clarke was the last of the Fenian prisoners to be released in September 1898, and the association was wound up.

ANCIENT ORDER OF HIBERNIANS

Founded: 1641 (reformed United States 1836).
Profile: Traditionally associated with nationalism and the defence of the Catholic faith. Marches continue to be held annually on the Feast of the Assumption, 15th August.

APPRENTICE BOYS

Founded: Derry, 1814.
Profile: A political Protestant society, it commemorates the Siege of Derry (April-July 1689). Takes its name from the 13 apprentices who shut the city's gates to Catholic troops. The organisation was affiliated to the Ulster Unionist Council from 1911 until the mid 1970s. Continues to hold marches throughout Northern Ireland with its main demonstration on the Saturday closest to August 12.

AUXILIARIES (THE)

Founded: July 1920 (first recruits enlisted).
Profile: A force similar to the Black and Tans, its mem-

bers were drawn from demobilised officers of the British army. The force was even less under the control of the RIC than the Black and Tans. The Auxiliaries demise accompanied that of the RIC.

BLACK AND TANS

Founded: January 1920 (first recruits enlisted)
Profile: Formed to supplement the RIC, it recruited demobilised British soldiers to maintain operational strength, following widespread resignations and dismissals from the RIC. The name derived from the force's mufti uniform which consisted of both army and police issue.

The Black and Tans were given a free hand in their fight against the IRA and acted with extreme lawlessness. The fierceness of their reputation was based on their attacks on innocent civilians and major atrocities such as the burning of Cork City and Balbriggan, Co. Dublin, and Bloody Sunday at Croke Park in November 1921, when they shot into the crowd and killed eleven spectators and one player. Their demise accompanied that of the RIC.

BLUESHIRTS

Founded: February 1932.
Profile: A political movement, with Edmund Cronin as its first leader, it was formally known as the Army Comrades Association. Consisting mainly of veterans of the Free State army, the association adopted a distinctive uniform of a blue shirt and black beret (hence the name). Former Garda Commissioner Eoin O'Duffy was elected as leader in July 1933 and changed the name of the movement to the National Guard. It was an anti-communist, quasi-fascist organisation and drew inspiration from Mussolini and his Blackshirt movement.

In October 1933, it merged with Cumann na nGaedheal and the National Centre Party to form Fine Gael with O'Duffy as its first president. It declined in the years 1934-36, but in November 1936, O'Duffy, with the blessing of members of the Catholic hierarchy, raised an 'Irish Brigade' to fight with Franco in the Spanish Civil War. They returned in June 1937.

BROY HARRIERS

Formed: 1933.
Founder: Eamon Broy (Garda Commissioner).
Profile: An armed auxiliary police force whose membership was largely drawn from former members of the anti-Treaty IRA. The group was formed in reaction to the alarm caused in government and throughout the state with the formation of the Blueshirts. It was disbanded in 1935 when the Blueshirts had dissipated.

CATHOLIC ASSOCIATION

Founded: May 1823.
Founders: Daniel O'Connell and Richard Lalor Shiel.
Profile: A nationwide movement, it agitated for Catholic Emancipation. It collected a 'Catholic Rent' which mobilised Catholic society as never before. In 1826, it succeeded in having four pro-emancipation MPs elected. O'Connell's victory in the 1828 Clare by-election forced the British government to grant Catholic Emancipation on April 13, 1829, but the Act disenfranchised many Catholic voters. Disbanded February 12, 1829.

CATHOLIC COMMITTEE

Founded: March 1760.
Founders: Dr. John Curry, Charles O'Connor and Thomas Wyse.
Profile: Organised the small urban Catholic middle-class and lobbied government for a relaxation of the Penal Laws. Met with considerable success in early 1790s, culminating in a Catholic Relief Act in 1793, which repealed many of the Penal Laws. Suppressed 1811.

CLAN NA GAEL

Founded: June 1867 in New York.
Founder: Jerome Collins.
Profile: A secret organisation, it recognised the Supreme Council of the Irish Republican Brotherhood as the legitimate government of Ireland. The Clan supported Parnell and Davitt's 'New Departure' in the 1880s. The movement played an active role in plans for the 1916 Rising, especially in procuring German aid. It survived the aftermath of the Rising but became embroiled in bitter personal disputes between its leading members. Divided over the Civil War, the organisation petered out in the early 1940s.

CLANN NA TALMHAN

Founded: Galway, 1938.
Founder: Michael Donnellan.
Profile: A political party representing the small western farmer, it contested the general election of 1943 and won 14 seats. At each subsequent election, the number of seats it won decreased; by 1961, its representation was reduced to just two TDs. Part of the Inter-Party coalition governments of 1948-51 and 1954-57, its leader Joseph Blowick was twice Minister for Lands. The party did not contest the 1965 general election.

CLANN NA POBLACHTA

Founded: July 1946.
Founder: Sean MacBride (former IRA Chief-of-Staff).
Profile: A republican party, it formed part of the Inter-Party coalition of 1948-51 and held two central ministerial portfolios: MacBride at Foreign Affairs and Dr. Noel Browne at the Department of Health. The controversy engendered by Dr. Browne's 'Mother and Child' scheme brought about the fall of the government in May 1951 and split the party. It was never again to be a political force and did not fulfil its promise of providing a viable republican alternative to Fianna Fáil. Winning only one seat in both the 1961 and 1965 general elections, it formally dissolved in 1965.

COMDHÁIL NÁISIÚNTA NA GAEILGE (NATIONAL CONGRESS OF THE IRISH LANGUAGE)

Founded: October 1943.
Profile: A co-ordinating body for Irish language organisations, including Conradh na Gaeilge.

CONGESTED DISTRICTS BOARD

Established: August 1891 by the 'Balfour' Land Act
Profile: A government appointed board of commissioners whose function was to give aid to designated congested areas (in the province of Connacht and in the counties of Clare, Cork, Donegal, Limerick and Kerry). Funded by income from the sale of church land accruing from the 1869 Irish Church Act, it made grants avail-

able to improve the infrastructure, to modernise methods of farming and to aid indigenous industries, such as fishing and the blossoming cottage industries.

The Board was empowered to purchase estates and distribute the land to small farmers, often involving relocation. Dissolved in 1923 by the Free State government, its functions were transferred to the Land Commission.

CONGRESS OF IRISH UNIONS

Formed: April 1945.
Founder: William O'Brien.
Profile: A breakaway from the Irish Trades Union Congress and the Labour Party, because of "communist tendencies within the ITUC." In February 1959, it reunited with the ITUC to form the Irish Congress of Trade Unions.

CONNOLLY COLUMN

Formed: December 1936.
Founder: Frank Ryan.
Profile: The column was a group of republican volunteers who joined the Abraham Lincoln Battalion in the 15th International Brigade and fought with the socialists against Franco in the Spanish Civil War (1936-39).

CUMANN NA nGAEDHEAL

Founded: September 1900.
Founders: Arthur Griffith and William Rooney.
Profile: An umbrella group for small anti-English organisations. The organisation called on the IPP to abstain from Westminster in 1902 and organised protests against the visit of Edward III in July 1903. It became part of Sinn Féin in 1907. It had no link to the political party of the same name founded by W.T. Cosgrave in 1923.

CUMANN NA nGAEDHEAL

Founded: March 1923.
Leader: W.T. Cosgrave (its first and only leader).
Profile: Consisting of the pro-Treaty wing of Sinn Féin, Cumann na nGaedheal formed every government from the Provisional Government in 1922 until 1932 due to the republican policy of abstentionism.

The party played an important role in the formation and consolidation of the fledgling Free State, ruthlessly pursuing the anti-treaty IRA, executing 77 republicans during the Civil War and crushing the real threat that the IRA posed. The party also provided for the establishment of the Garda Síochána, the Electricity Supply Board, the Shannon hydro-electric scheme and the Agricultural Credit Corporation.

In the field of foreign affairs, the party set about pursuing the freedoms implicit in the Treaty. Its members were prominent at Commonwealth conferences in exploring these freedoms. Their greatest success came in 1931 with the Statute of Westminster, which put the parliaments of the Dominions (including Ireland) on an equal footing with the Imperial Parliament at Westminster.

The party lost power in 1932, and less than a year later it merged with the Blueshirts and the National Centre Party to form Fine Gael.

DEFENDERS

Founded: Armagh, July 1784.
Profile: A nationalist secret society found largely in Ulster, absorbed into the United Irishmen in the 1790s.

DEMOCRATIC UNIONIST PARTY

Founded: 1971 *(See Politics Chapter)*.

FARMERS' PARTY

Formed: 1922.
Profile: The party contested Dáil elections between 1922 and 1932, winning eleven seats in its first election in 1922, its best return came in 1923 when it secured 15 seats. Support was drawn from more affluent farmers, and the party generally supported the Cumann na nGaedheal government. Following a disastrous election in 1932 when it won only four seats, its members went on to found the National Centre Party.

FENIAN BROTHERHOOD

Founded: April 1859 in New York.
Founder: John O'Mahony.
Profile: An American auxiliary of the IRB, its name came to be used when describing both groups. Chiefly concerned with the procurement of weapons for the IRB, it staged an abortive attack at New Brunswick in Canada in 1866. Formally merged with the IRB in 1916.

FIANNA FÁIL

Founded: 1926 (*See Politics Chapter*)

FINE GAEL

Founded: 1933 (*See Politics Chapter*)

GAELIC ATHLETIC ASSOCIATION (GAA)

Founded: November 1, 1884 in Thurles, Co. Tipperary.
Founders: Michael Cusack and Maurice Davin, under the patronage of the Archbishop of Cashel, Dr. T.W. Croke.
Profile: Gaelic games had been slipping into decline because of disorganisation and apathy. The GAA hoped to preserve and cultivate Irish pastimes such as gaelic football and hurling. Initially the GAA's main efforts were concentrated in athletics but Gaelic Games quickly became its main focus. Unashamedly nationalist in outlook, it prohibited members from playing foreign games (such as rugby, hockey and soccer) until 1971 and continues to exclude members of the security forces in Northern Ireland from membership.

The association spread gradually until it established itself in every parish in the country providing Gaelic pastimes to vast numbers of people and becoming the largest organisation (sporting or otherwise) in the country, a distinction it retains. A voluntary and completely amateur organisation (save for a handful of administrators) its major games attract crowds in excess of 65,000.

GAELIC LEAGUE (THE) - CONRADH NA GAEILGE

Founded: July 1893.
Founders: Dr. Douglas Hyde, Eoin MacNeill and Fr. Eugene O'Growney.
Profile: The League sought to preserve the Irish language as a spoken language and de-Anglicize Ireland. Successes included the recognition of St. Patrick's Day as a national holiday (1903) and the inclusion of Irish as a matriculation subject in the NUI (1908).

The League sent teachers (or timirí) around the country to set up classes and had up to 600 branches countrywide by 1908. Infiltrated by the IRB in 1915, Douglas Hyde resigned as president because of the increasingly political role it was fulfilling. Following the formation of the Free State in 1922, it lobbied successfully for Irish to be made a compulsory subject in both primary and secondary schools. The League remains one of the largest Irish language organisations in the country.

HOME RULE LEAGUE

Founded: November 1873 in Dublin.
Founder: Isaac Butt.
Profile: With the objective of self-government for Ireland, it was a precursor to the Irish Parliamentary Party. It won 60 seats in the 1874 general election.

INDEPENDENT IRISH PARTY

Founded: September 1852 in Dublin.
Profile: An amalgamation of the Irish Tenant League, the Irish Brigade and 41 liberal MPs who were sympathetic to the plight of the tenant farmers. It demanded land reform, the repeal of the Ecclesiastical Titles Act and the disestablishment of the Church of Ireland. Beset by splits and defections, it petered out by the mid 1850s.

INVINCIBLES

Founded: 1881.
Profile: An extremist group which broke away from the IRB. In May 1882, it assassinated the Chief Secretary and the Under Secretary (the top government officials in Ireland) in what became known as the Phoenix Park Murders. Its leaders were tried in May 1883, convicted of the murders and hanged.

IRISH AGRICULTURAL ORGANISATION SOCIETY

Founded: April 1894.
Founders: Sir Horace Plunkett and Fr. Thomas Finlay
Profile: Established to co-ordinate the activities of the nationwide Co-operative Movement (established in 1890). It allowed dairy producing farmers to collectively sell their produce, it provided credit to farmers and purchased agricultural goods in bulk to sell to its members.

IRISH CITIZEN ARMY

Founded: November 1913 in Dublin.
Founders: James Connolly and James Larkin.
Profile: Formed to protect workers from police attacks during the 1913 Dublin Lock-Out. Following the Lock-Out, Connolly turned his attention to the creation of a workers' republic. His intention to stage a Citizen Army rebellion caused alarm within the IRB, and their leaders informed him of plans for the Easter 1916 rebellion. Connolly pledged his army's support for the Rising and when it came, the Citizen's Army fought with distinction. It also fought in the War of Independence and on the anti-treaty side in the Civil War. Disbanded in 1923 after the Civil War ended.

IRISH CONFEDERATION

Founded: January 13, 1847, in Dublin by Young Irelanders who had seceded from the Loyal National Repeal Association.
Profile: A militant nationalist organisation, it promoted an independent, self-sufficient Ireland and linked self-determination to the land question. 1848 saw revolutions throughout Europe, and inspired by this, the Confederation drafted plans for an Irish rebellion. By July, the government had suspended *habeas corpus* and proscribed the Confederation. In July, it staged a poorly planned and ill-timed rebellion which was easily defeated. The movement, having lost its leaders through arrest and transportation, collapsed.

IRISH LITERARY THEATRE

Founded: May 1899 in Dublin.
Founder: William Butler Yeats.
Profile: A literary society dedicated to the promotion of Irish culture and customs through the production of plays written and set in Ireland. The first society to stage a play in the Irish language (Douglas Hyde's *Casadh an tSúgáin*). Dissolved in 1904 and was absorbed into the Abbey Theatre.

IRISH LOYAL AND PATRIOTIC UNION

Founded: May 1885.
Profile: A political association of unionist landlords, businessmen and scholars opposed to Home Rule. Contested the 1885 general election but won little support. Superseded in 1891 by the Irish Unionist Alliance.

IRISH NATIONAL LAND LEAGUE

Founded: October 1879 in Dublin.
Founders: Charles Stewart Parnell and Michael Davitt.
Profile: The League aimed to protect tenant rights through the securing of the 'three Fs' and sought the complete abolition of landlordism. Ostensibly a moral force organisation which developed and utilised the tactic of 'boycotting', it enjoyed the support of the Fenians, Clann na Gael and the IRB. The appeal of the League was wide and all classes of society, encompassing all religions, were members. The Land Act of August 1881 was a major success, but it was accompanied by a Coercion Act which banned the League. The League was reformed by Parnell in October 1882 under the name of the National League where the emphasis was on Home Rule rather than land reform.

IRISH NATIONAL LIBERATION ARMY

Formed: Dublin, 1975.
Profile: A splinter republican group responsible for some of the most ruthless attacks in Northern Ireland during the 'troubles'. Initially, it drew members from those disenchanted with the 'Official' IRA. It later attracted members from the fringes of the 'Provisionals'. The INLA has been plagued by feuds since the late 1980s, resulting in the deaths of many of its members. The organisation called a ceasefire in August 1998, in the aftermath of the Omagh bombing.

IRISH PARLIAMENTARY PARTY (IPP)

Formed: 1882, it evolved from the Home Rule League.
Profile: With the securing of Home Rule as its primary objective, it gained widespread support through its action and leadership on the land question, the single biggest issue of the day. Ineffective under the leadership of Isaac Butt, save for its filibustering obstruction of business at Westminster, it met with huge success especially with regard to the land question under the leadership of Charles Stewart Parnell (elected chairman May 1880).

The party became the model for modern political parties in that it developed an extensive grass roots constituency organisation, established a party whip and had its members take a party pledge to vote *en bloc*. These innovations and the skill of its leadership helped achieve significant land reform and brought Home Rule to the top of political agenda at Westminster. Despite its success, the party, under pressure from Gladstone's Liberal Party and the Catholic hierarchy in Ireland, split in 1890 following revelations about Parnell's adulterous affair with Katharine O'Shea.

Reunited under the leadership of John Redmond in 1900, it went on to secure the passage of the third Home Rule Bill in 1914, the implementation of which was suspended until after World War I. The 1916 Rising and executions, along with British government attempts to introduce conscription in 1918, precipitated a huge swell in support for Sinn Féin at the expense of the IPP. Their representation at Westminster fell from 70 MPs in 1910 to 6 in 1918. Sinn Féin replaced the party as the major party within nationalism. The Northern rump of the party reconstituted itself as the Nationalist Party of Northern Ireland in 1921, but southern members joined Cumann na nGaedheal after 1923.

IRISH REPUBLICAN ARMY (IRA)

Founded: January 1919 (The oath to the Republic taken by the Volunteers in can be seen as the starting point of the IRA).

Profile: It successfully adopted and developed guerrilla warfare during the War of Independence and created such a state of disorder that the British authorities sued for a truce. The Anglo-Irish Treaty was not accepted by the IRA, and a split ensued along pro- and anti-Treaty lines. There followed a bloody and bitter civil war where erstwhile comrades fought one another; those who supported the Treaty became the army of the Free State, and the republicans became known as the 'Irregulars'. Defeat for the Irregulars followed, and a truce was called in May 1923. The IRA formally withdrew from Sinn Féin in November 1925. The organisation was proscribed in Northern Ireland in 1922 and in the Free State in 1931

The IRA staged an offensive in England (January 1939-March 1940) which resulted in further anti-republican legislation being passed in both jurisdictions in Ireland. It was relatively inactive from then until the period 1956-62 when it engaged in a 'Border Campaign'. The advent of the Civil Rights movements in the late 1960s saw an increasingly political and non-militaristic IRA emerge particularly in the south. The arrival of British troops in Northern Ireland in August 1969 precipitated a decisive split between the Marxist, southern-based leadership, whose commitment to physical force was on the wane, and northern members, who were less concerned with ideology now that British troops were once again in Ireland. The movement split in December 1969 into 'Provisional' (largely northern-based) and 'Official' (largely southern-based) wings. *(See also Official IRA and Provisional IRA)*

IRISH REPUBLICAN BROTHERHOOD (IRB)

Founded: 17 March, 1858 in Dublin.
Founder: James Stephens.
Profile: A secret, republican, oath-bound society its 1867 rebellion was easily put down. It survived this setback and later in the century infiltrated nationalist movements such as the Gaelic Athletic Association, the Gaelic League and the Land League. Reorganised in 1904, it infiltrated the Irish Volunteers and with the out-

break of World War One, its military council began planning the Easter 1916 rebellion. Following the Rising it was again reorganised (all of its leaders had been executed) and exerted much influence between 1916 and 1919. Its influence declined during the War of Independence, and a split occurred during the Civil War. The movement disbanded in 1924.

IRISH SOCIALIST REPUBLICAN PARTY

Founded: May 1896 in Dublin.
Founder: James Connolly.
Profile: A small socialist nationalist party, it was reorganised and renamed the Socialist Party of Ireland in 1903. In 1921 the Socialist Party was reorganised as the Communist Party of Ireland.

IRISH SOCIETY

Profile: The Society of London companies entrusted with the strategic plantation of Derry. It fortified the towns of Derry and Coleraine, established other small towns and villages and brought English settlers. Some of the companies sold their holdings in the early 18th century while the remainder sold theirs in the late 19th century. In 1952 the Foyle Fisheries was sold by the Society.

IRISH TENANT LEAGUE

Founded: August 1850 in Dublin.
Founders: Charles Gavan Duffy and Frederick Lucas.
Profile: Drawing its membership from larger tenant farmers, it aimed to secure the 'three Fs' - fair rent, fixity of tenure and free sale. Following the 1852 general election, it combined with the Irish Brigade to form the Independent Irish Parliamentary Party which had the allegiance of about 40 MPs. The League collapsed in 1855 when Lucas died and Duffy emigrated.

IRISH TRANSPORT AND GENERAL WORKERS' UNION

Founded January 1909 in Dublin.
Founder: James Larkin.
Profile: Formed as a breakaway from the British National Union of Dock Labourers, it survived the disastrous Dublin Lock-Out. Increasing in size throughout the revolutionary period, internal bickering, power struggles and splits tore at the union from 1923 until 1959. Formally joined the Irish Congress of Trade Unions in 1959.

IRISH UNIONIST ALLIANCE

Founded: 1891.
Profile: The successor to the Irish Loyal and Patriotic Union - its membership comprised mainly southern unionists opposed to Home Rule. Despite its rather small membership, the alliance exerted considerable influence at Westminster and in the House of Lords in particular. Rendered obsolete by the passing of the Home Rule Bill in 1914.

IRISH VOLUNTEERS

Founded: November 1913 in Dublin.
Founders: Éoin MacNeill and Bulmer Hobson.
Profile: Formed as a response to the formation of the UVF, the Volunteers secured arms in a gun-running episode at Howth on July 26, 1914. Membership had reached around 180,000 at the outbreak of World War I when, in September 1914, leader of the Irish

Parliamentary Party, John Redmond, called on the Volunteers to join "in defence of right, of freedom and religion in this war." Over 170,000 did, renaming themselves the National Volunteers. Approximately 11,000 remained with the Irish Volunteers.

Many of the senior posts of the Irish Volunteers were occupied by members of the IRB's Supreme Council, and the Volunteers fought in the 1916 Rising. Reorganised in 1917, the Volunteers became a powerful and increasingly belligerent force. When the first Dáil met in 1919, the Volunteers took an oath to the Republic and fought in the War of Independence as the Irish Republican Army.

IRREGULARS

Profile: The name given to the anti-Treaty IRA which fought the Free State army during the Civil War (June 1922-April 1923). Led by Liam Lynch, his death in April 1923 was swiftly followed by a truce.

LABOUR PARTY (THE)

Founded: 1912 *(See Politics Chapter)*

LADIES LAND LEAGUE

Founded: October 1880 in New York.
Founder: Fanny Parnell (established in Ireland in January 1881 by her sister Anna, both women were sisters of Charles Stewart Parnell).
Profile: The League stepped into the breach when the Land League was banned in 1881 and was vociferous in the campaign against landlordism. The first Irish political movement organised by women, it met with opposition from elements within the Catholic Church and the Irish Parliamentary Party who found their radicalism unacceptable. When Charles Stewart Parnell was released from prison in May 1882, he cut their funding and in August 1882 suppressed the movement entirely.

LAND LEAGUE OF MAYO

Founded: August 1879 in Westport, Co. Mayo
Founder: Michael Davitt.
Aims: Securing the 'three Fs' of fair rent, fixity of tenure and free sale.
Profile: Precursor of the Irish National Land League.

LOYAL NATIONAL REPEAL ASSOCIATION

Founded: April 1840.
Founder: Daniel O'Connell.
Profile: The Association aimed to secure repeal of the Act of Union and create an Irish legislature subservient to Westminster. Organised along the same lines as the Catholic Association, it used mass agitation and organised 'monster meetings'. Its finest year was 1843 with over 750,000 attending a monster meeting at Tara. The onset of famine in 1845, tensions between O'Connell and the 'Young Irelanders', which came to a head in 1846, and O'Connell's death in 1847 led to the movement fading out without realising its objective.

NATIONAL COUNCIL

Founded: June 1903.
Founder: Arthur Griffith.
Profile: Formed to oppose the 1903 visit of Edward III, its members included senior figures from Cumann na nGaedheal. Became part of Sinn Féin in 1908.

NATIONAL LEAGUE

Founded: October 17, 1882, in Dublin.

Founder: Charles Stewart Parnell.
Profile: It replaced the proscribed Land League, securing Home Rule was its primary objective with land reform of lesser importance. It also served as the 'grass roots' organisation of the Irish Parliamentary Party. The movement provided finance and delegates for the IPP and had the support of the majority of the Catholic clergy. The League, split along the same lines as the IPP in 1890, faded into oblivion and was replaced by the United Irish League in 1900, when the IPP was reunited.

NORTHERN IRELAND CIVIL RIGHTS ASSOCIATION

Founded: Belfast, February 1967.
Profile: Aimed to secure the introduction of universal suffrage; an end to gerrymandering; the disbanding of the 'B' SPECIALS; the repeal of the Special Powers Act; and the fair allocation of public housing. The Association was organised along the same lines as the British National Council for Civil Liberties. The main weapon employed by the association was protest marches, the first of which was held in Dungannon in August 1968. Marches were organised throughout the late 1960s and early 1970s and often led to clashes with the RUC. The association's influence declined from the mid 1970s.

'OFFICIAL' IRISH REPUBLICAN ARMY

Profile: Formed following the split in the IRA in late 1969. It was allied to 'Official' Sinn Féin and was more Marxist than its 'provisional' counterpart. A feud ensued between the two wings of the IRA with casualties on both sides. The official IRA has ceased to operate since it called a ceasefire on May 29, 1972, but strongly contested allegations have persisted that the group continued to exist and carried out robberies and assassinations well into the 1980s.

'OFFICIAL' SINN FÉIN

Formed: January 1970.
Profile: Formed following a split with what became known as 'Provisional' Sinn Féin, the party was led by Tomás MacGiolla and applied a socialist analysis to the conflict in the North. The party was organised throughout the 32 counties and, in 1977, changed its name to Sinn Féin The Workers' Party. Since 1982 the party has been known as The Workers' Party.

ORANGE ORDER

Founded: Armagh, September 1795 after serious disturbances between Catholics and Protestants at the Diamond in Loughgall.
Profile: The Order came into existence as a Protestant response to the relaxation of the anti-Catholic penal laws at the end of the 18th century. It comprised Protestant males who pledged their allegiance to the Crown (as long as it remained Protestant) and their Protestant faith. The Order commemorates the Battle of the Boyne (1690) and the Battle of the Somme (1916) with marches each summer. The main marches are held at different county centres throughout Northern Ireland on July 12.

The Order has played a significant role in Irish politics; it was prominent in the formation of the Ulster Unionist Council in 1905, it organised the Solemn League and Covenant in 1912 and harnessed Protestant opposition to Home Rule. With its membership concentrated in Northern Ireland, it played a central role in the formation of the Northern Ireland state - each of Northern Ireland's six Prime Ministers were Orangemen. In recent years, restrictions have been placed on where it can march.

PEEP O' DAY BOYS

Founded: July 1784 in Armagh.
Profile: A Protestant secret society founded after a sectarian clash with the Defenders. Precursor of Orange Order.

PEOPLE'S DEMOCRACY

Founded: Belfast, October 1968.
Founders: Michael Farrell and Bernadette Devlin.
Profile: A socialist organisation, it demanded an end to discrimination against Catholics in Northern Ireland, one man-one vote and the revoking of the Special Powers Act. The group was involved in one of the bloodiest encounters of the Civil Rights era when unarmed marchers were attacked by baton-wielding loyalists at Burntollet on January 4th, 1969. Some of its leaders were interned in August 1971, and with the increasing violence of the 'troubles', it became less significant.

PHOENIX SOCIETY

Founded: 1856, in Skibbereen, Co. Cork.
Founder: Jeremiah O'Donovan (O'Donovan Rossa).
Profile: Outwardly, it had the appearance of a debating society, but it was, in reality, a revolutionary society and precursor to the Irish Republican Brotherhood into which it was subsumed in 1859.

'PROVISIONAL' IRISH REPUBLICAN ARMY

Profile: Formed following a split in the IRA in late 1969. The split was led by the IRA's northern command who felt that the ideological swing to the left by the southern-based leadership was detrimental to the movement as a whole. With the traditional enemy, in the form of the British army, on the streets of Northern Ireland, the 'Provisionals' felt that it was time to leave politics behind and respond in a military fashion. From 1969 until 1994 they waged a relentless war against the British Army and RUC and also attacked civilians. The ruling Army Council declared a ceasefire in August 1994, which ended in February 1996 but was restored in July 1997 and is currently *(at time of going to print)* holding.

ROYAL IRISH CONSTABULARY (RIC)

Formed: 1836 as Irish Constabulary, earned prefix 'Royal' after suppressing the 1867 Fenian Rising.
Profile: A quasi-military national police force, it was hugely unpopular due to its role in enforcing evictions and quelling the agrarian violence endemic in the late 19th century. Its members suffered terribly during the War of Independence; many resigned out of fear or disapproval of the tactics of the Black and Tans, and many more were dismissed because of their nationalist sympathies. Disbanded in 1922 following the Anglo-Irish Treaty, its northern members were absorbed into the Royal Ulster Constabulary by an Act of the Northern Ireland Parliament in May 1922.

SINN FÉIN

Founded: 1905 *(See Politics Chapter)*.

SOCIAL DEMOCRATIC AND LABOUR PARTY:

Founded: 1970 *(See Politics Chapter)*

TOTAL ABSTINENCE MOVEMENT

Founded: 1838.
Founders: Fr. Theobald Matthew and William Martin.
Profile: With the aim of promoting abstinence from alcohol in Ireland, it reputedly recorded 5 million pledges in Ireland. Revenue from alcohol dropped from £1.4 million in 1839 to £350,000 in 1844.

ULSTER DEFENCE ASSOCIATION

Founded: September 1971.
Profile: Established to co-ordinate the loyalist vigilante groups endemic in the early 1970s. A working class loyalist paramilitary organisation, it was heavily involved in the Ulster Workers' Council strike which toppled the Power Sharing Executive in 1974. Through its terrorist wing - the Ulster Freedom Fighters - it killed many civilians; the killings continued until 1994. Part of the Combined Loyalist Military Command, it declared a ceasefire in October 1994.

ULSTER DEFENCE REGIMENT (UDR)

Established: December 1969 (by Act of Parliament).
Profile: A largely part-time force under the command of the British Army. Many of its members were drawn from the disbanded 'B' Specials, and its original aim of recruiting from both communities was never realised (only 3% of the force were Catholic). The UDR was used as a back up for RUC patrols. Its members were targeted both on and off duty by the IRA and INLA, and 197 members were killed from its inception until it was disbanded in 1992. The Regiment was amalgamated with the Royal Irish Rangers in 1992 to form the Royal Irish Regiment.

ULSTER SPECIAL CONSTABULARY

Formed: 1922.
Profile: An auxiliary part-time police force established to supplement the Royal Ulster Constabulary and defend the newly founded Northern Ireland from IRA attack. Membership of the force was exclusively Protestant. There were three grades - A, B and C. The 'A' and 'C' specials were used only in the 1920s, while the 'B' specials went on to gain notoriety, especially in the late 1960s when they attacked civil rights marches. The force was disbanded in April 1970, and many of its members joined the newly established Ulster Defence Regiment.

ULSTER UNIONIST COUNCIL

Founded: March 3, 1905 in Belfast.
Profile: A political organisation founded at a conference of Ulster unionist MPs, its members were drawn from the Orange Order, the Apprentice Boys of Derry, unionist associations, MPs and peers.

The Solemn League and Covenant in 1912, the formation of the Ulster Volunteer Force in 1913 and the Larne gun-running in 1914 were all organised under its auspices. In 1913 it appointed a Provisional Government for Ulster to take effect should Home Rule become law. The Council initially opposed partition but went on to play a significant role in the formation of Northern Ireland. Its political arm, the Ulster Unionist Party governed Northern Ireland from 1921 until 1972. The council remains in place today as an executive for

the Ulster Unionist Party.
(For Ulster Unionist Party see Politics Chapter)

ULSTER VOLUNTEER FORCE (UVF)

Founded: January 1913.

Profile: Formed to oppose the implementation of Home Rule by military force if necessary, James Craig and Sir Edward Carson were prominent members of its leadership. Guns were procured and landed at Larne in April 1914. The outbreak of World War I and the suspension of Home Rule resulted in the UVF becoming the 36th (Ulster) Division of the British Army. The division was all but wiped out in the Battle of the Somme (July-November 1916). Following partition the force was disbanded and its members recruited by the RUC.

The UVF was re-established in 1966 by Gusty Spence, amongst others. It immediately declared war on the IRA but was banned by Prime Minister Terence O'Neill in June of that year. It called a cease-fire in October 1994 under the auspices of the Combined Loyalist Military Command.

ULSTER WORKERS' COUNCIL

Formed: 1974.

Profile: Formed to oppose the Sunningdale Agreement and the imposition of Direct Rule. It organised the loyalist strike of May 14-29, 1974 (enforced by loyalist paramilitaries). The cutting off of electricity supplies ensured the success of the strike, and the executive fell on May 28. Prominent members of the UWC co-ordinating committee were the leaders of the main unionist parties, including Harry West (UUP), Rev. Ian Paisley (DUP) and William Craig (VUPP). The UDA, the UVF and other loyalist paramilitary groups also had members on the co-ordinating committee.

The committee organised an abortive loyalist strike in May 1977 which failed to get unanimous unionist support. The council was reorganised in 1981.

UNITED IRISHMEN

Founded: October 1791 in Belfast.

Founders: Thomas Russell, Theobald Wolfe Tone and James Napper Tandy.

Profile: A revolutionary oath-bound secret society. Inspired by the American and French revolutions, it aimed to secure an Irish republic and attracted radical Presbyterians in the north and an almost equal mix of Catholics and Protestants in the Dublin area. Procured French aid for its rising in 1798, which tragically turned into a sectarian massacre in Wexford and which the government put down with great force. The rising's leaders were executed and the movement crushed.

UNITED ULSTER UNIONIST COUNCIL

Formed: January 1974.

Profile: A coalition of unionist interests formed to oppose the Sunningdale Agreement ranging from the Ulster Unionist Party, the Democratic Unionist Party to the Vanguard Unionist Progressive Party. The Council opposed all aspects of the Sunningdale Agreement, and the Council of Ireland proposals in particular. It called for the removal of the power-sharing executive and co-operated fully with, and gave support to, the Ulster Workers' Council (UWC) strike in May 1974 which paralysed Northern Ireland and brought down the power-sharing executive.

It suffered a split in 1975 when the VUPP suggested some form of coalition that would include the SDLP. The Council collapsed when paramilitary groups were admitted and when prominent MPs, John Dunlop and Rev. Ian Paisley, supported the abortive 1977 loyalist strike which the UUP opposed.

VANGUARD UNIONIST PROGRESSIVE PARTY

Founded: March 1973.

Founder: William Craig.

Profile: A unionist political party whose roots were in the Ulster Vanguard, with the majority of its members drawn from the ranks of the UUP. The party contested the 1973 Northern Ireland Assembly election, winning seven seats, and it won three Westminster seats in two general elections in 1974. Opposed to Direct Rule, the Sunningdale Agreement and the power sharing executive, it became part of the United Ulster Unionist Council and was prominent in the Ulster Workers' Council strike in 1974. A split occured in 1977 when its leader suggested some form of voluntary coalition with the SDLP. In 1978, it ceased to function as a party. Current Ulster Unionist Party leader, David Trimble, was a prominent member and was deputy leader of the party (1977-78).

VOLUNTEER MOVEMENT (THE)

Founded: March 1778.

Profile: Armed corps established to help defend Ireland against French or Spanish invasion. Lobbied for free trade, legislative independence and relaxation of the Penal Laws. Suppressed March 1793.

WHITEBOYS

Emerged: Munster October 1761.

Profile: Generic term for different Catholic secret societies. Engaged in violent disturbances related to resentment at taxes and changes from arable to dairy farming as well as to sectarianism.

WILD GEESE

Profile: The name given to the 14,000 Irish Jacobite soldiers (commanded by Patrick Sarsfield), who left Ireland after the Treaty of Limerick (October 1691) and distinguished themselves on European battlefields in the 18th century. The Wild Geese also refers to other Irish soldiers who fought in continental Europe throughout the 18th century. The most celebrated action of the Wild Geese occurred at the Battle of Fontenoy in 1745.

YOUNG IRELANDERS

Profile: The name given to the adherents of the nationalism expounded by Thomas Davis, Charles Gavan Duffy and John Blake Dillon in their newspaper - *The Nation* (first published in October 1842). Not content with repeal, they wanted to achieve an independent Ireland and were prepared to use physical force. This propensity towards physical force led to their break with the Repeal movement in 1846 when O'Connell sought a pledge stipulating that force could never be justified.

SIGNIFICANT DOCUMENTS IN IRISH HISTORY

STATUTE OF KILKENNY

Enacted: 1366 by the Irish Parliament at Kilkenny.
A series of apartheid-type laws forbidding English settlers assimilating with native Gaelic Irish and adopting their culture. Gaelic laws, customs and language were banned among the settlers, as was marriage between the 'races'. The laws were ultimately ineffective and were revoked in 1537.

POYNINGS' LAW

Enacted: December 1, 1494 (named after the Lord Deputy, Sir Edward Poynings).
• Forbade the Irish parliament to convene without the King's prior permission.
• All intended legislation had to be approved by him. The law was almost completely repealed in 1782, the only part of it which remained was the Crown's right to veto a bill.

THE ANNALS OF THE FOUR MASTERS

Compiled: Between 1632 and 1636.
The Annals are a history of Ireland compiled in book form by religious scribes (completed by Michael O'Clery and others on August 10, 1636) in Donegal Town.

TREATY OF LIMERICK

Signed: October 3, 1691,
Signatories: Patrick Sarsfield and the Williamite General Ginkel.
• Irish soldiers allowed to join other Jacobites in France.
• Roman Catholics to be allowed rights of worship, to retain their property and to practice their professions.
The articles dealing with religious freedoms for Catholics were not honoured by the British parliament which, within two months, put in place an anti-Catholic Oath of Supremacy and, in the years 1695-1709, enacted a comprehensive series of penal laws.

PENAL LAWS (1695-1709)

The collective name for a series of laws designed to secure the privileged position of members of the Church of Ireland, the established Church. The laws were aimed at eradicating the Roman Catholic religion in the country and showed little tolerance towards Presbyterianism.
Included were restrictions on rights to education, the bearing of arms, the purchase of land, taking a seat in parliament and holding any government office. The Roman Catholic clergy, including virtually all of the hierarchy, was banished in 1697 (although some priests were permitted to stay) and the ordination of new priests was forbidden.
A Toleration Act for Protestant Dissenters was passed in 1719, while Catholics had to wait until late in the century for many of their restrictions to be formally repealed and until 1829 before they were eligible to sit in parliament or hold high public office.

CATHOLIC RELIEF ACTS (1774-93)

Enacted: April 9, 1793.
A series of acts which repealed the penal laws.
• Catholics permitted to purchase and own land.
• Catholics permitted to practice law.
• Catholics permitted to hold selected public and military positions.
• Parliamentary franchise extended to Catholics.
• Official bar on Catholics receiving university degrees removed.

ACT OF UNION

Enacted: July 2, 1800 (effective January 1, 1801).
• Legislatures of Great Britain and Ireland joined.
• Irish Parliament abolished.
• One hundred Irish MPs, 28 Lords and 4 bishops to sit in the Houses of Parliament at Westminster.
• Church of Ireland amalgamated with Church of England.
The act was superseded by the Government of Ireland Act, 1920, and the Anglo-Irish Treaty of 1921.

ROMAN CATHOLIC RELIEF ACT

Enacted: April 13, 1829.
• Oaths of Allegiance, Supremacy and Abjuration replaced, enabling Roman Catholics to sit in the Houses of Parliament; belong to any corporation; and hold the higher offices of State.

IRISH CHURCH ACT

Enacted: July 26, 1869 (effective January 1, 1871).
• Churches of England and Ireland separated.
• Church of Ireland disestablished (i.e. the dissolution of the legal union of Church and State).
• Property of the Church of Ireland confiscated.
• Grants to Maynooth College and the Presbyterian Church discontinued (although compensation paid).
• Ecclesiastical Courts disbanded.
• Tithes due to Church of Ireland by all denominations abolished
• Provision made for tenants residing on Church of Ireland lands to purchase their holdings.

LAND ACTS

Landlord and Tenant (Ireland) Act (Gladstone)
Enacted: August 1, 1870.
• Attempted (but failed) to legalise the 'Ulster Custom' of not evicting tenants who had paid their rent in full and allowing tenants to sub-let their holdings.
• Landlords required to pay compensation for any improvements made by a tenant to his holding.
• The 'Bright Clause' provided tenants with a government loan of 66% of the cost of their holdings to enable them to buy their farms.
Land Law (Ireland) Act (Gladstone)
Enacted: August 22, 1881.
• The 'Three Fs' (Fair rents, Fixity of tenure and Free Sale) were incorporated in statute.
• **Fair rents:** To be decided by arbitration at a Land Commission hearing.
• **Fixity of tenure:** Tenants who had their rent fully paid could not be evicted. A Land Court was established to arbitrate in tenant-landlord disputes.
• **Free sale:** Payment for any improvements made would be ensured by the Land Court.
• A land purchase scheme was put in place providing a 75% loan to tenants wishing to purchase their holdings.
Purchase of Land (Ireland) Act (Ashbourne)
Enacted: August 14, 1885.

• £5 million made available to tenants to purchase their holdings. Grants were made available for 100% of the value of the holding.
In 1888, money available was increased to £10 million.
Purchase of Land (Ireland) Act (Balfour)
Enacted: August 5, 1891.
• £33 million made available to tenants to purchase their holdings.
• A Congested Districts Board established to administer aid to designated congested areas.
Irish Land Act (Wyndham)
Enacted: August 14, 1903.
• £83 million made available to tenants to buy out their lands. Landlords got a bonus if they sold their entire estate.

HOME RULE BILLS

1886 • Two-tier Irish legislature with limited powers.
• Ireland would not be represented at the Imperial Parliament at Westminster.
• Lord Lieutenant to remain as representative of the Crown in Ireland and gave royal assent to Bills.
• Revenue would come from taxes collected in Ireland (excluding customs and excise tariffs) and a portion of Imperial taxes.
• Control of the Royal Irish Constabulary (RIC) to remain with the Imperial Parliament.
Bill defeated June 8, 1886 in House of Commons by 341 votes to 311.
1893: As 1886 except it proposed to send Irish MPs to Westminster.
Bill defeated September 9, 1893, in House of Lords by 419 votes to 41.
1914: Introduced in the House of Commons in 1912 it was defeated in the Lords, whose veto had been reduced to two years by the 1911 Parliament Act. The Bill was signed into law by the King on September 18, 1914, but its implementation was suspended, with the agreement of the Ulster Unionists and Irish Parliamentary Party, for the duration of World War One.
• Two-tier Irish legislature to be established.
• Ireland to send 42 MPs to the House of Commons.
• Revenue to come from taxes collected within Ireland and custom and excise tariffs.
• Control of the RIC to remain with the Imperial Parliament but would revert to the Irish parliament after six years.

IRISH UNIVERSITIES ACT

Enacted: British parliament August 1, 1908
• Royal University abolished.
• Established two new bodies, the National University of Ireland (consisting of University Colleges Cork, Dublin and Galway and other smaller colleges) and the Queen's University of Belfast.
• The governing body of the National University, although officially non-denominational, had a significant number of Roman Catholic bishops.

ULSTER'S SOLEMN LEAGUE AND COVENANT

Signed: 28 September, 1912 (218,000 male signatories).
• A pledge to oppose Home Rule by 'using all means which may be found necessary' and, in the event of a Home Rule parliament being foisted on Ireland, to refuse to recognise its authority.

PROCLAMATION OF THE IRISH REPUBLIC

Issued: April 24, 1916 (beginning of the Easter Rising).
Signatories: (On behalf of the Provisional Government) Thomas Clarke, Seán MacDiarmada, Thomas MacDonagh, Padraig Pearse, Eamonn Ceannt, James Connolly and Joseph Plunkett. All seven were executed within three weeks.
• Asserted the right of the people of Ireland to the ownership of a sovereign and independent republic.
• Proclaimed the Irish Republic as a 'Sovereign Independent State'.
• Guaranteed religious and civil liberty, equal rights and equal opportunities to all its citizens.
• Resolved to pursue the 'happiness and prosperity of the whole nation and of all its parts' and to cherish all of the children of the nation equally.
• Established a Provisional Government until such time as a permanent national government could be elected by universal suffrage.

GOVERNMENT OF IRELAND ACT

Enacted: December 23, 1920.
• Home Rule Act of 1914 repealed.
• Proposed to establish two Home Rule parliaments - one in Belfast to legislate for the counties of Antrim, Armagh, Derry, Down, Fermanagh and Tyrone - and one in Dublin to legislate for the other 26 counties.
• Control of finance and defence would be retained by Westminster.
• A Council of Ireland, comprising MPs from both Irish parliaments to deal with matters of mutual interest proposed. The council would have limited powers and would pave the way for an end to partition if both parliaments assented to it.
The act was superseded in the Free State by the Anglo-Irish Treaty of 1921 and in Northern Ireland by the Northern Ireland Constitution Act and the Northern Ireland Assembly Act, both of which were passed by the British parliament in 1973.

THE ANGLO-IRISH TREATY

Signed: December 6, 1921.
Irish Signatories: Arthur Griffith, Michael Collins, Robert Barton, Edmund Duggan and George Gavan O'Duffy.
British Signatories: David Lloyd George, Austen Chamberlain, Lord Birkenhead, Winston Churchill, L. Worthington-Evans, Hamar Greenwood and Gordon Hewart.
Ratified: British parliament December 5, 1921.
Ratified: Dáil Éireann - January 7, 1922, by 64 votes to 57.
• Established the Irish Free State (IFS) as a nation of the British Empire with Dominion status, i.e. same as status of Canada, Australia etc.
• Established a new Irish parliament, Dáil Éireann.
• Crown to be represented by a Governor General.
• All members of the IFS Parliament required to swear an Oath of Allegiance to the IFS Constitution, the Crown and the British Empire.
• IFS to assume a portion of United Kingdom's war debt.
• The British military to retain control of the coastal defence of the IFS and the ports of Berehaven, Queenstown, Belfast Lough and Lough Swilly.

- Size of the Irish army limited.
- Northern Ireland had choice of opting out of the IFS within one month of the Treaty being signed.
- In the event of Northern Ireland opting out of the IFS, a three-person Boundary Commission was to be established. The remit of the Commission was to determine the border, in accordance with the wishes of the inhabitants, as far as those wishes were compatible with economic and geographic conditions.
- Religious discrimination expressly forbidden in both jurisdictions.

CIVIL AUTHORITIES (SPECIAL POWERS) ACT (NORTHERN IRELAND)

Enacted: Northern Ireland parliament on April 7, 1922.

Delegated a series of wide-ranging powers to the Minister for Home Affairs permitting him to take any steps necessary to preserve the peace. These powers included:
- Arrest without warrant.
- Internment without trial.
- Flogging.
- Execution.
- Banning of organisations or publications.

Initially, it was renewed every year, but in 1928 it was renewed for five years and in 1933 it was made permanent. Rescinded in 1972.

CONSTITUTION OF THE IRISH FREE STATE

Ratified by: Dáil Éireann October 25, 1922.
Ratified by: British parliament December 5, 1922.
- Irish Free State declared a co-equal member of the British Commonwealth of Nations.
- The legislature of the new state established (the King, the Senate and the Dáil).
- The Irish language recognised as the national language with official recognition of status of the English language.
- *Habeas corpus* ensured.
- Freedom to practice religion and the free expression of opinion assured
- All citizens entitled to free elementary education.
- The Oath of Allegiance, as agreed in the Treaty, included.
- Articles relating to eligibility to vote and run for public office also included.

Superseded by the 1937 Constitution.

CENSORSHIP OF PUBLICATIONS ACT

Enacted: Dáil Éireann July 1929.
- Established a censorship board of five members empowered to censor or ban publications, the main targets being obscenity and information about birth control. The nature of the act resulted in thousands of books, including many by Ireland's most eminent authors, being banned.

No adequate avenue for appeal was provided until the act was amended in 1967.

STATUTE OF WESTMINSTER

Enacted: British parliament December 11, 1931.
- Conferred equal status on the parliaments of the British Dominions (including Ireland) with the Imperial parliament at Westminster.
- Dominion parliaments empowered to pass any law and amend or repeal any existing or future law enacted by Westminster.
- Dominion parliaments not obliged to implement any British act with which they did not agree.

EXTERNAL RELATIONS ACT

Enacted: Dáil Éireann, December 12, 1936 (during the abdication crisis of Edward VIII).
- Crown recognised only for purposes of external association (i.e. accreditation of diplomats and international agreements).
- The Constitution Amendment (No. 27) Bill, passed on December 11, deleted all reference to the crown from the Irish Free State Constitution.

The Act made the Free State a republic in all but name.

CONSTITUTION OF IRELAND

Ratified: By referendum on July 1, 1937. *See Law and Defence chapter.*

EDUCATION ACT

Enacted: Northern Ireland parliament - 27 November, 1947.
- Grants towards the building and extension of schools provided.
- Financial assistance provided to any student, irrespective of denomination or economic background, to attend university having attained the required educational standards.
- Universal secondary schooling established.

REPUBLIC OF IRELAND ACT

Enacted: Dáil Éireann - December 21, 1948 (effective from April 18, 1949)
- 1936 External Relations Act repealed.
- The 26 counties of Éire declared a Republic.
- Republic of Ireland leaves British Commonwealth of Nations.

IRELAND ACT

Enacted: British parliament June 2, 1949.
- Recognised the Republic of Ireland's withdrawal from the British Commonwealth.
- Affirmed the position of Northern Ireland within the United Kingdom and stated that no change could be effected on its status without the consent of the Northern Ireland parliament.
- Irish citizens would not be considered as aliens in Britain.
- Free travel area between the Britain and Ireland enshrined.

EUROPEAN MONETARY SYSTEM

Established: March 13, 1979.

By entering the European Monetary System the Republic of Ireland ended one-for-one parity between the Irish and British currencies which had existed since independence.

Explanatory Notes:
Prior to January 1801, all Acts referred to were Acts of the Irish parliament (with all, excluding the Statute of Kilkenny, subject to Poynings' Law). From 1801 until 1921 all Acts referred to were Acts of the British parliament. Acts referred to from 1922 onwards are clearly distinguished as Acts of Dáil Éireann, the Northern Ireland parliament or the British parliament, as appropriate. ❐

SIGNIFICANT DOCUMENTS IN RECENT TIMES

NORTHERN IRELAND ASSEMBLY ACT

Passed by the British parliament May 3, 1973. It proposed:

• A 78-member Assembly elected from the 12 Westminster constituencies by proportional representation. The Assembly would also have law making powers.

NORTHERN IRELAND CONSTITUTION ACT

Passed by the British parliament (July 18, 1973), it superseded the Government of Ireland Act. In it:

• The Northern Ireland Parliament was abolished.

• The Office of Governor was abolished.

• Basic legislation for a system of devolved government, complementary to the Northern Ireland Assembly Act, was laid out including provision for the creation of a 12-member Executive with limited functions.

• The constitutional status of Northern Ireland within the United Kingdom was guaranteed and would not change save for a majority indicating the desire to do so in a border poll.

• In the absence of a devolved administration taking office, provision is made for the functions to be carried out by a Secretary of State and team of junior ministers.

SUNNINGDALE AGREEMENT

Signed December 9, 1973, by Taoiseach Liam Cosgrave, British Prime Minister Edward Heath and leaders of the UUP, SDLP and Alliance parties. Its main points were:

• The Irish government accepted there would be no change in the constitutional status of Northern Ireland without the consent of a majority of people living there.

• The British government affirmed Northern Ireland's position within the United Kingdom but stated that if a majority demonstrated indicated a desire to join a united Ireland they would legislate for that.

• A Council of Ireland, consisting of seven ministers from both Northern Ireland and the Republic, was to be established to deal with matters of mutual concern.

• On law and order, proposals relating to extradition, the establishing of a common law enforcement area and policing were made.

PREVENTION OF TERRORISM (TEMPORARY PROVISIONS) ACT

Passed by the British Parliament November 29, 1974, it provided for:

• Exclusion orders banning individuals suspected of terrorism from Northern Ireland, Britain or the United Kingdom as a whole.

• Extended detention for terrorist suspects. Police may detain suspects for 48 hours without charge and for a further five days subject to approval from the Home Secretary or the Secretary of State for Northern Ireland.

• The banning of certain organisations.

• In 1988 remission for those convicted of terrorist offences was reduced from 50 to 33 per cent.

REPORT OF THE NEW IRELAND FORUM

Published May 2, 1984, it was the report of the Forum (convened May 1983) which took submissions from Fianna Fáil, Fine Gael, Labour, the SDLP, the Roman Catholic Church and other smaller (and invariably nationalist) organisations on a potential Northern Ireland settlement. Its main findings were:

• All parties favoured a unitary 32-county state.

• Joint authority in Northern Ireland could be exercised by the British and Irish governments or federal arrangements could be put in place.

• All parties pledged to remain open to other views which could contribute to political development.

The Report was rejected by unionists, Sinn Féin and British Prime Minister Margaret Thatcher.

THE ANGLO-IRISH AGREEMENT

Signed November 15, 1985, by Taoiseach Garret FitzGerald and British Prime Minister Margaret Thatcher. Its main points were:

• Both governments affirmed that change in the status of Northern Ireland could only come about through the consent of a majority of the people of Northern Ireland. While recognising that such a majority did not exist, the governments declared that they would legislate for a change in Northern Ireland's status should a majority wish to establish a united Ireland.

• An Intergovernmental Conference was established to deal with political, security and legal matters and promote cross-border co-operation.

• The possibility of establishing an Anglo-Irish Parliamentary body was left for decision of the respective parliaments.

DOWNING STREET DECLARATION

Signed December 15, 1993, by Taoiseach Albert Reynolds and British Prime Minister John Major. Its main provisions were as follows:

• The British government affirmed that it was for the people of Ireland alone, and the two parts respectively, to exercise their right of self-determination, and it stated it had no 'selfish strategic or economic interest in Northern Ireland'.

• The Irish government accepted that Irish self-determination must be achieved and exercised with the consent and agreement of a majority of people in Northern Ireland.

• The Irish government pledged that in the case of a balanced constitutional accommodation it would put forward and support changes to the Irish Constitution which would reflect the principle of consent.

• Both governments confirmed that democratically mandated parties who demonstrated a commitment to exclusively peaceful methods would be free to participate fully in the democratic process.

• The Irish government announced its intention to establish a Forum for Peace and Reconciliation.

FRAMEWORKS DOCUMENT

Signed by Taoiseach John Bruton and British Prime Minister John Major on February 22, 1995, it set out what both governments saw as the possible format of the talks process. The guiding principles as set out in paragraph ten were:

• The principle of self-determination must be in keeping with the principle of consent.

• Agreement must be pursued and achieved through exclusively democratic and peaceful methods.

• Any new political arrangements must afford parity of

esteem to both traditions.

The document also set out three interlocking strands as a basis for areas of negotiation, these were:

• **Structures within Northern Ireland.** Locally elected representatives would exercise "shared administrative and legislative control over agreed matters."

• **North/South Institutions.** These institutions would be consultative, harmonising and executive. A parliamentary forum drawing members from a Northern Assembly and the Dáil would also be established.

• **East/West Structures.** A new agreement between the sovereign governments "reflecting the totality of relationships between the two islands" supported by a permanent secretariat.

The document concludes with the governments agreeing that the matters raised should be examined in negotiations between democratically mandated parties committed to peaceful means and that the outcome to these negotiations should be submitted for ratification through referenda, north and south.

THE 'MITCHELL' REPORT

Published January 22nd, 1996, it is the report of the International Body on the Decommissioning of Illegal Arms. The body was chaired by US Senator George Mitchell and included former Finnish Prime Minister Harri Holkeri and Canadian General John de Chastelain.

• The six 'Mitchell principles' of democracy to which all parties at the multi party talks had to 'affirm their total and absolute commitment' were:

(1) to use democratic and exclusively peaceful means to resolve political issues;

(2) to the total disarmament of paramilitary weapons;

(3) to agree that disarmament must be independently verifiable;

(4) to renounce the use of force by themselves or by other organisations;

(5) to accept the outcome of negotiations no matter how repugnant it may be and to use only democratic methods to alter the outcome;

(6) to call an end to "punishment" killings and beatings.

• The report recommended that the decommissioning of illegally held paramilitary weapons should take place during multi-party talks as a tangible confidence building measure.

• The report also recommended the holding of elections as a further confidence-building measure.

THE 'NORTH' REPORT

Published in 1997, it is the report of the Independent Review of Parades and Marches under the chairmanship of Dr Peter North with members Father Oliver Crilly and the Reverend John Dunlop. Recommendations include:

• the establishing of a five-person Independent Parades Commission, appointed by the Northern Ireland Secretary of State.

• responsibility for decisions on contentious parades should lie with the Commission rather than with the RUC.

THE GOOD FRIDAY AGREEMENT

The Settlement was signed on Good Friday, 10 April, 1998 by Taoiseach Bertie Ahern, Prime Minister Tony Blair and the participants at the multi-party talks name-ly the Alliance Party, the Labour Party, the Northern Ireland's Women Coalition, the Progressive Unionist Party, the Social Democratic and Labour Party, Sinn Féin, the Ulster Democratic Party and the Ulster Unionist Party. *(Both Sinn Féin and the Ulster Unionist Party submitted the Agreement to their parties for ratification.)*

Constitutional Issues

• The British government will repeal, through legislation, the 1920 Government of Ireland Act.

• The Secretary of State for Northern Ireland may order a poll on the status of Northern Ireland on the question of remaining within the United Kingdom or unification with the Republic. Such polls must be held at least seven years apart.

• The Irish government will submit Articles two and three of Bunreacht na hÉireann for amendment by referendum.

Strand One

• Northern Ireland Assembly to be established with 108 seats, six members will be returned by proportional representation from the 18 Westminster constituencies.

• Assembly to elect a 12-member executive committee of ministers. The ministerial committee will be headed by a First Minister and Deputy First Minister, ministerial posts will be allocated in proportion to party strength.

Strand Two

• A North/South Ministerial Council to be established within one year, consisting of ministers from the Dáil and the Assembly. Its remit will be to consider matters of mutual interest through consultation, co-operation and action. The Council will be accountable to the Assembly and the Oireachtas.

Strand Three

• A British-Irish Council, supported by a permanent secretariat, is to be established, drawing members from the Assembly, the Dáil, the House of Commons, the Isle of Man, the Channel Islands and the new Assemblies in Scotland and Wales.

British-Irish Intergovernmental Conference

• A new British-Irish Agreement will establish a new Conference to replace that set up by the Anglo-Irish Agreement in 1985.

Rights, Safeguards and Equality of Opportunity

• The European Convention on Human Rights will be incorporated into Northern Ireland law.

• A Human Rights Commission and a statutory Equality Commission will be established in Northern Ireland.

• The Irish government will establish a Human Rights Commission. A joint North-South committee of these Commissions will also be established.

• The British government will take resolute action to promote the Irish language.

Decommissioning

• Participants will use their influence to achieve decommissioning of all illegally held arms in the possession of paramilitary groups within two years of the May referenda in the context of an overall settlement.

Security, Policing, Justice and Prisoners

• The British government will seek to normalise security in Northern Ireland through reducing the numbers and role of security forces, removing security installations and ending emergency powers.

• The Irish government will initiate a review of the

Offences Against the State Acts with a view to reforming and dispensing with certain provisions.
• An independent commission will make recommendations on the future of policing in Northern Ireland by May of 1999.
• A review of criminal justice will be undertaken by the British government.

• The British and Irish governments will legislate for the accelerated release of paramilitary prisoners whose organisations are observing a ceasefire.

On May 22nd the Settlement was ratified by referendum in both Northern Ireland and the Republic of Ireland. ❐

HISTORICAL ANNIVERSARIES

25 Years Ago (1974)

01 Jan. Beginning of office of the Northern Ireland Power Sharing Executive. The executive was toppled by the Ulster Workers' Council strike which paralysed Northern Ireland and Unionist members resigned in May.
29 May The Northern Ireland Assembly was prorogued and Direct Rule reintroduced.
17 May Car bombings in Dublin and Monaghan claimed 31 lives - 25 people were killed in three explosions in Dublin, while 6 were killed in a single explosion in Monaghan. The perpetrators have never been apprehended.
10 Oct. United Nations Commissioner in Namibia, Seán MacBride, was awarded a half-share of the Nobel Peace Prize.
19 Dec. Cearbhall Ó Dálaigh was inaugurated as the fifth President of Ireland.

Died
20 Mar. Poet Austin Clarke.
17 Nov. President Erskine Childers - the only president of Ireland to die in office.

50 Years Ago (1949)

18 Apr. Republic of Ireland formally declared and the Republic leaves the British Commonwealth.
10 Jul. End of an era in Dublin when the last tram to run returned to its garage.

Died
12 Jul. Gaelic scholar and former President of Ireland, Douglas Hyde.

75 Years Ago (1924)

March Mutiny in Irish Free State army. The mutiny was led by IRA veterans who opposed the large scale demobilisation of the army and who wanted to see what efforts the national government was making in realising the Republic.
11 Jul. Anglo-Irish Treaty registered with the League of Nations as an international agreement.
02-17 Aug. Tailteann Games, a type of Celtic Olympics, staged in Croke Park.
15 Sep. 2BE, the BBC's first radio station in Ireland starts broadcasting from Belfast.
19 Dec. Last edition of the influential nationalist newspaper, *The Freeman's Journal*, issued.

Died
19 Nov. Roman Catholic Primate of All-Ireland, Michael Cardinal Logue.

100 Years Ago (1899)

08 May Irish Literary Theatre staged its first play, *The Countess Cathleen* by W.B. Yeats.
11 Oct. Outbreak of the Boer War in South Africa, an Irish Brigade, led by Major John MacBride fight alongside the Boers against the British.

Died
18 Oct. Irish language educator, Fr Eugene O'Growney.

150 Years Ago (1849)

1849: The last year of the Great Famine. The potato, staple diet of up to 3 million Irish people, failed throughout the country from 1845 to 1848, the direct effects of which were felt for the last time in 1849. However, famine did occur on a localised basis for a number of years after 1849.
Oct. Queen's Colleges at Belfast, Cork and Galway opened their doors to students.

Died
20 Jun. Poet James Clarence Mangan.
27 Dec. Writer and agrarian activist James Fintan Lalor.
22 May Novelist Maria Edgeworth.

GOVERNORS GENERAL OF THE IRISH FREE STATE

Name	Born	Appointed	Retired	Died
Timothy Healy	17.05.1855	1922	1928	26.03.1931
James MacNeill	29.03.1869	1928	01.11.1932	12.12.1938
Domhnall Ua Buachalla*	1865	1932	08.06.1937	30.10.1963

The office of Governor General was provided for by Article 3 of the 1921 Anglo-Irish Treaty. Its function was to represent the Crown in the Free State, the office was formally abolished by the 1937 Executive Powers (Consequential Provisions) Act.

*Ua Buachalla was merely a figurehead, his only function was to sign bills presented by the government. He did not reside in the official residence and was referred to as 'Seanascal' (translation: high steward) rather than Governor General.

GOVERNORS OF NORTHERN IRELAND (1922-73)

Governors of Northern Ireland Statistics

Name	Born	Appointed	Aged	No. of Terms
Duke of Abercorn	1869	06.12.1922	53	4
Vice-Admiral Earl Granville*	1880	07.09.1945	65	2
Lord Wakehurst*	1895	01.12.1952	57	2
Lord Erskine of Rerrick*	1893	01.12.1964	71	1
Lord Grey of Naunton	1910	03.12.1968	58	1

*resigned from the office.

The governor was the monarch's representative in Northern Ireland and was appointed by the monarch for a six year term. He summoned, prorogued and dissolved the Northern Ireland parliament in the monarch's name, read the monarch's speech at the beginning of a new parliamentary session and gave or withheld the Royal Assent to bills passed by both Houses. The post was abolished on July 18, 1973, by the Northern Ireland Constitution Act.

FAMOUS SPEECHES

President Éamon De Valera's speech to a joint sitting of the Dáil and Seanad in the Round Room of the Mansion House on January 21, 1969. The speech was delivered on the 50th anniversary of the first meeting of Dáil Éireann, January 21, 1919, also held in the Round Room of the Mansion House.

Ceann Comhairle: Address on the occasion of the fiftieth commemoration of the convening of the first Dáil Éireann, 21 January 1919 - His Excellency the President of Ireland.

The President (Éamon de Valera): Ceann Comhairle, a Chathaoirleach an tSeanaid, Members of the Dáil and Seanad:

ALL of you must be delighted as you recall what happened here fifty years ago when the representatives of the Irish people gathered at this spot and Dáil Éireann was founded and it was announced to the world that we were an independent nation.

In memory, thanksgiving, and in honour of all those people who toiled and suffered every hardship, even death, so that a day such as today could happen I ask you now to stand and join me in a minute's silence in memory of those heroes of Easter Week . . . may they all be in heaven.

(The Members Stood)

People who were alive at that time will recall that the Great War ended in November 1918, and the following month, December, we had a General Election. Sinn Féin used that election to show the world that the people of Ireland desired to be free and independent. During the war, American and British leaders declared that it was to protect and preserve the rights of small nations that the war was being fought. The result of this election left no doubt as to to the desires of the people of Ireland - that they wished to be free, independent and that they wanted a republican government.

Of the people who came together then, six are still alive, six members of the Dáil; and there's another six alive who were absent on the day. After the election an invitation was sent to the elected members. Two-thirds of them were from Sinn Féin. Members associated with Sinn Féin came here, those able to come, those who were free. A lot of them, the majority of them, could not attend, they were in prison in England, banished, or engaged in some other work for the nation.

In charge of those who did attend was Cathal Brugha, and after Fr. Flanagan had said the prayer, Cathal Brugha rose and, speaking in Irish, read the Declaration of Independence. Some others read it in French and English. He made it known to the whole world that it was our desire to be free, independent and that we'd have a republican system of government.

Of those who were alive, there's six of them, as I said, alive and I salute them, and the people here who were absent as they were in prison or as was said at the time, imprisoned by foreigners, I salute them also. A special congratulation goes to the Dáil member Seán Mac an tSaoi, as he was a member at that first time, and thanks be to God, is still alive and still a member of the Dáil today. And Dr. Ó Riain who was present here fifty years ago, he is still a member of the Oireachtas as a senator; I salute him as well. May they live long.

At that time many members of Sinn Féin were members of the Volunteers also, and even though they were two distinct organisations, Sinn Féin and the Volunteers, they worked in such close proximity that a person would be forgiven if he were to think of them as one organisation. They were full of zeal and when they came together their intention was to fulfil the desires of the people as quickly as possible.

Not only did they release a statement, as I said, that we wanted to be free and independent, but also they were sending a message out to all the free nations of the world asking them for recognition for the Republic. Also read out was a programme of Sinn Féin's social and economic aims. That day's work was well and truly finished.

Now you are the Irish people's representatives - the two Houses, the Dáil and the Seanad: our people have placed their trust in you. It's a great weight on you to fulfil all that's desired and needed. The people of Ireland have placed their trust in you. You are the guides of our people. You are trusted and your responsibility is great. I am sure that you will not disappoint them.

There are people who, at present, would be critical of the ideas and aims of the nationalism as expressed by our leaders fifty years ago, claiming that they are old fashioned and out of date. There's a lot of talk at present about internationalism and therefore that it's the small nation's destiny to be cast aside, suppressed, or absorbed by the superpowers.

That is not my opinion at all. We should be more confident that this nation will survive than our forefathers were fifty years ago. The leaders of Easter Week believed that the Rising would ensure the survival of this nation. That much is to be understand from Seán Mac Diarmada's last letter sent from Kilmainham the day before his execution.

We should, as I have said already, have more confidence, like then, that this nation will survive. We are not reckoned as a province now but as a nation. We are taking our place amongst the nations and working with them to promote the welfare of the human race.

I do not believe that there are many who believe that we should set aside our nationalism. In my opinion they are wrong. Old nations will not lose their characteristics and cultures; they will not set them aside. They could, and they are, entering partnerships with each other to promote their joint welfare. That, in my opinion, is the most direct and beneficial way forward for the human race. That is the best way, in my opinion, and is how it's going to be. We are, at any rate, resolved in our minds that we will not fail our predecessors in keeping this ancient Gaelic nation alive.

Now I pray, as you all prayed when you began this work, that the Holy Spirit will guide you and all of us in our work, and I pray God's blessing on all your actions.

GEOGRAPHY & ENVIRONMENT

The Climate of Ireland: Yesterday, Today and Tomorrow

*By **Brendan McWilliams**, Met Éireann Meteorologist*

SOME centuries ago, a visitor to our island compared our climate to his native Britain: "There is little difference," he said, "other than that more rain falls, as the country is more mountainous and exposed full to the westerly wind, which blowing from the Atlantic Ocean prevails during the greater part of the year. This moisture, as it has enriched the country with large and frequent rivers, and spread out a number of fair and magnificent lakes, has on the other hand encumbered the island with an uncommon multitude of bogs and morasses."

If one subscribes to this despondent school, one can at least console oneself by recalling that there have been times when things have been considerably worse. Climates change over the centuries, and even more so over millennia, and the average temperature of our island has risen and fallen at various periods in our history to give us at times, weather patterns very different from those familiar to us now.

Fifteen thousand years ago, for example, we were in the throes of the last Ice Age. Glaciers extended over much of North America, as well as Scandinavia, Britain, Denmark and, of course, Ireland. When this Ice Age ended about 10,000 years ago, it was followed by a sudden warming, and by 5000 BC the average temperature in these parts was about 2°C above its present value; as the great accumulation of ice over northern Europe gradually melted, the level of the sea rose by 50 metres to give to our island a shape not too dissimilar from that defined by its present coastline.

There was a short, sharp shock about 3,000 years ago. A change to much colder conditions took place over a relatively short period around 1000 BC, and the drop in average temperature was accompanied by a general increase in storminess and rainfall. But this deterioration lasted for a mere millennium; by the early centuries AD, the climate had recovered and was not significantly different from that we know today. This trend for warmer weather continued through the Dark and Middle Ages and by the time of the Viking settlements, the average temperature over Ireland had again increased to about 1°C above present-day values. Our forefathers and their uninvited guests enjoyed conditions unusually congenial for this island, and across the channel the Normans, newly-arrived in the south of England, drank wine from English vineyards.

This climatic golden age, alas, was brief, and during the next few centuries conditions once again became colder and often wetter, and the period from about 1450 to 1850 is remembered as the "Little Ice Age", reaching its peak in the freezing decade of the 1690s. The summers were short, the winters long and severe, and average temperatures were a degree or more lower than before or since. The winter scenes with copious amount of snow depicted by contemporary artists contrast sharply with even the worst conditions familiar to us now.

As the middle of the 19th century approached, however, there occurred yet another change in thermal direction on our island: from 1850 onwards, to the middle of the present century, the average temperature over Ireland gradually increased, the total rise over the period amounting to about half of a degree Celsius. Since the late 1940s, and continuing to the end of the 1970s, the average has shown a small but persistent tendency to fall, and this systematic cooling has been followed during the 1980s and early 1990s by a certain ambivalence of trend - something of an anomaly in a period when the rest of the world has been inclined to panic about global warming.

Nowadays we live on an island whose temperature averaged over the year is in the region of 10°C. The prevailing westerly winds that blow from the Atlantic take their temperature from the warm waters of the North Atlantic Drift that bathes our coast. They mollify the heat of summer - but even more importantly, they temper the severity of winter. The average temperature ranges from about 5 degrees in the coldest month, January, to the pleasant warmth of July and August when we enjoy an average of near 16 degrees. The national average rainfall is about 1,100 millimetres, and varies from about 3,000 mm per annum in some mountainous areas of the west to 800 mm or thereabouts in the vicinity of Dublin. The sun shines unobscured by cloud for some 1700 hours per year in the extreme southeast in the vicinity of Carnsore Point in Co. Wexford - although it must be said that the national mean is somewhat lower - more like 1300 hours or thereabouts.

Such is the climate of our island as we approach the beginning of a new millennium - but what does that millennium have in store for us? As everybody knows by now, there are fears that the increasing amounts of carbon dioxide and other greenhouse gases in the atmosphere may cause the planet's average temperature to rise.

The best models available today predict that if nothing is done to reduce greenhouse gas emissions, the average temperature of the world will rise by about 2°C between now and the end of the next century. What the local effects of such a change might be at any particular spot, however, are uncertain; some places might experience warming significantly in excess of the average, while others might well remain unchanged - or might even become colder at certain times of year.

In general, in the middle latitudes, wetter winters and drier summers are predicted as the likely norm. It is also probable, we are told, that the frequency and intensity of extreme weather events like storms and hurricanes may change - but nobody knows quite how. Neither do we know for sure whether or not greenhouse warming could trigger significant changes in ocean circulation - like, for example, a weakening of the Gulf Stream that keeps Ireland and the rest of western Europe relatively warm in wintertime.

It is difficult, therefore, to anticipate what lies in store for us. It is tempting, of course, to embrace the most benign scenario - that the anticipated increase in global temperature might apply directly here in Ireland, with the pleasant consequence that we would acquire a climate with many of the characteristics of that are enjoyed in the South of France at present. If that were to happen, then for us global warming has distinct advantages.

If, for example, the average temperature of Ireland were to increase by a degree or two, the national yield of grass would increase by about a fifth, with significant benefits for the economy. The variety of crops available would also greatly widen, with maize, flax and sunflower becoming much more viable in the new environment. Gooseberries and raspberries might be successfully harvested in our western counties, and it is even possible that vine-growing might become a viable occupation in the east and southeast.

But such unsullied optimism is likely to be over-optimistic. The truth is, as so often the case in matters of the future, that we simply do not know. Those of us lucky enough to live long enough to observe any changes that may come, will simply have to wait and see.

FACTFILE - AT A GLANCE

TOTAL AREA	32,593 sq. miles
Area: Republic of Ireland	27,137 sq. miles
Area: Northern Ireland	5,456 sq. miles
Total Land Area	31,557 sq. miles
Land Area: Republic of Ireland	26,401 sq. miles
Land Area: Northern Ireland	5,156 sq. miles
Total Water Area	1,036 sq. miles
Water Area: Republic of Ireland	736 sq. miles
Water Area: Northern Ireland	300 sq. miles
TOTAL COASTLINE	1,970 miles
Coastline: Republic of Ireland	1,737 miles
Coastline: Northern Ireland	232 miles
Greatest Length (north to south)	302 miles
Greatest Width (east to west)	171 miles
Highest Point	Carrantuohill, Co. Kerry (3,414 ft)
Lowest Point	No point below sea level
Largest Island	Achill Island, Mayo (36,248 acres)
Longest River	The Shannon (224 miles)
Largest Lake	Lough Neagh (149.61 sq. miles)
Highest Waterfall	Powerscourt, Co. Wicklow (350 ft)
Highest Cliff	Croaghan, Achill Island, Mayo (2,192 ft)
Longest Stalactite	Pollan Ionain, Co. Clare (20ft 4 in.)
Highest Temperature Recorded	Kilkenny Castle - 26/06/1887 (92°F/33.3°C)
Lowest Temperature Recorded	Omagh, Co. Tyrone - 23/01/1881 (2.92°F/-19.4°C)
Heaviest Rainfall	Orra Beg, Antrim - 01/08/1980 (3.82 inches in 45 min)
Driest Year Recorded	1887
Longest Drought Recorded	Limerick (03/04/1938-10/05/1938, 37 days)
Heaviest Snowfall	January 1917
Highest Windspeed	Kilkeel, Co. Down - Jan. 1974 (108 knots)
Northernmost Point	Malin Head, Co. Donegal
Northernmost Town	Carndonagh, Co. Donegal
Northernmost Village	Malin, Co. Donegal
Southernmost Point	Mizen Head, Co. Cork
Southernmost Town	Skibbereen, Co. Cork
Southernmost Village	Baltimore, Co. Cork
Easternmost Point	Wicklow Head, Co. Wicklow
Easternmost Town	Wicklow Town, Co. Wicklow
Westernmost Point	Dunmore Head (Slea Head), Co. Kerry
Westernmost Town	Dingle, Co. Kerry
Westernmost Village	Ballyferriter, Co. Kerry
Largest County	Cork (2,878 sq. miles)
Smallest County	Louth (318 sq. miles)
Biggest Dam	Poulaphuca Reservoir, Co. Wicklow
Tallest Building	County Hall, Cork
Tallest Structure	ESB Chimneys, Co. Clare (738 ft)
Longest Bridge Span	Barrow Railway Bridge
Largest Island	Achill Island, Mayo (36,248 acres)
POPULATION: IRELAND	5,198,800
Population: Republic of Ireland (1996)	3,621,035
Population: Northern Ireland (1991)	1,577,836

THE ISLAND OF IRELAND - LOCATION

Location of the island of Ireland: In the Atlantic Ocean to the west of Great Britain and the extreme north-west of the continent of Europe. The Irish Sea separates Ireland from the island of Britain, the distances between the two islands ranging from 11 to 120 miles apart at the closest and farthest points, respectively.

Latitude and Longitude: Between 51.5° and 55.5° north, 5.5° and 10.5° west.

Elevation: Generally less than 150m above sea level, although nearly 5% of the island's total area is between 300 and 600m above sea level (ensuring sparse plant life in these areas).

THE ISLAND OF IRELAND - GEOLOGY

Geological Description: The island can be described as a large central plateau, ringed almost entirely by coastal highlands which vary considerably in geological structure. In the south, the mountain ridges consist of old red sandstone separated by deep limestone river valleys. To the west and north-west the mountains of Donegal, Mayo and Galway are mostly granite, as are those in counties Down and Wicklow, while the north-east of the island is predominantly covered by a basalt plateau. The central plain is largely covered with glacial deposits of sand and clay and contains numerous areas of bog, the most notable of these being the Bog of Allen, as well as being interspersed with lakes.

Geological History: Geologists state that the Irish terrain, marked by ice-smoothed rock, mountain lakes, glacial valleys and deposits of sand, gravel and clay, points to at least two great glaciations of the island. They also state that Ireland was separated from mainland Europe following the last Ice Age.

THE ISLAND OF IRELAND - CLIMATE

General Description: Ireland's climate is influenced by the warm waters of the Gulf Stream, resulting in a temperate climate. The relatively small size of the island and the prevailing south-west winds ensure a uniform temperature over the whole country and minimal change in temperature variation between summer and winter.

Winter: Irish winters are generally mild, while the summers are generally cool. The coldest months of the year are usually January and February, with temperatures averaging between 4°C and 7°C. Snow does fall from time to time but is short-lived and slight, generally lasting for only a few days at a time. The minimum length of day occurs in late December, with around 7 to 7.5 hours of daylight.

Summer: May and June are the sunniest months, averaging 5 - 7 hours of sunshine per day. July and August are the warmest summer months, averaging between 14°C and 16°C. The maximum length of day occurs in late June and ranges between 16.5 and 17.5 hours between sunrise and sunset.

Rainfall: Rain is carried in from the Atlantic by prevailing westerly winds and is well-distributed all over the island. However, the west has a greater annual rainfall than the east due to its proximity to the Atlantic Ocean and its being much more mountainous. In low lying areas, the average annual rainfall is between 800 and 1,200mm (31" to 47"), and in mountainous areas as much as 2,000mm (79") rainfall per annum is not unusual.

REPUBLIC OF IRELAND: AREA BY PROVINCE & PERSONS PER SQUARE KILOMETRE, 1991 &1996

Description	Connacht	Leinster	Munster	Ulster*	Total
1991 Census:					
Total Population	423,031	1,860,949	1,009,533	232,206	3,525,719
Total Area (hectares)	1,771,342	1,979,432	2,468,874	808,862	7,028,510
Persons per sq. kilometre	25	95	42	29	51
1996 Census:					
Total Population	433,231	1,924,702	1,033,903	234,251	3,626,087
Total Area (hectares)	1,771,056	1,980,066	2,467,410	808,776	7,027,308
Persons per sq. kilometre	24	97	42	29	52

* part of

IRELAND: WORLD TIME DIFFERENCES

Hours Plus or Minus GMT - The 0 degree meridian has been established as the reference line for setting time. This line runs through Greenwich in London and is known as Greenwich Mean Time (GMT). Because of Ireland's proximity to London, it shares the same time zone as Britain. The times listed below should be added to / subtracted from the standard time in Ireland to ascertain various world time differences in relation to Ireland.

Accra (Ghana)	00.00	**Liverpool** (England)	00.00
Adelaide (Australia)	+09.30	**London** (England)	00.00
Amsterdam (Netherlands)	+01.00	**Los Angeles** (United States)	-08.00
Athens (Greece)	+02.00	**Madrid** (Spain)	+01.00
Baghdad (Iraq)	+03.00	**Manchester** (England)	00.00
Bangkok (Thailand)	+07.00	**Melbourne** (Australia)	+10.00
Beijing (Peking)	+08.00	**Mexico City** (Mexico)	-06.00
Berlin (Germany)	+01.00	**Montevideo** (Uruguay)	-03.00
Brussels (Belgium)	+01.00	**Montreal** (Canada)	-05.00
Buenos Aires (Argentina)	-03.00	**Moscow** (Russia)	+03.00
Cairo (Egypt)	+02.00	**Nairobi** (Kenya)	+03.00
Calgary (Canada)	-07.00	**New Delhi** (India)	+05.30
Cape Town (South Africa)	+02.00	**New York** (United States)	-05.00
Cardiff (Wales)	00.00	**Oslo** (Norway)	+01.00
Chicago (United States)	-06.00	**Paris** (France)	+01.00
Christchurch (New Zealand)	+12.00	**Perth** (Western Australia)	+08.00
Colombo (Sri Lanka)	+05.30	**Reykjavik** (Iceland)	00.00
Copenhagen (Denmark)	+01.00	**Rio de Janeiro** (Brazil)	-03.00
Detroit (United States)	-05.00	**Rome** (Italy)	+01.00
Durban (South Africa)	+02.00	**San Francisco** (United States)	-08.00
Glasgow (Scotland)	00.00	**Seoul** (Korea)	+09.00
Gibraltar (Spain)	+01.00	**Singapore** (Malaysia)	+08.00
Halifax (Canada)	-04.00	**Stockholm** (Sweden)	+01.00
Helsinki (Finland)	+02.00	**Sydney** (Australia)	+10.00
Hong Kong (China)	+08.00	**Tehran** (Iran)	+03.30
Honolulu (Hawaii)	-10.00	**Tokyo** (Japan)	+09.00
Houston (United States)	-06.00	**Toronto** (Canada)	-05.00
Istanbul (Turkey)	+02.00	**Valletta** (Malta)	+01.00
Jakarta (Indonesia)	+07.00	**Vancouver** (Canada)	-08.00
Johannesburg (South Africa)	+02.00	**Vienna** (Australia)	+01.00
Karachi (Pakistan)	+05.00	**Warsaw** (Poland)	+01.00
Lagos (Nigeria)	+01.00	**Wellington** (New Zealand)	+12.00
Lima (Peru)	-05.00	**Winnipeg** (Canada)	-06.00
Lisbon (Portugal)	00.00	**Zurich** (Switzerland)	+01.00

METEOROLOGICAL STATIONS

METEOROLOGICAL OFFICE STATIONS
Belfast Climate Office, 32 College Street, Belfast BT1 1BQ. Tel: (01232) 328457.

Two synoptic stations are maintained under the auspices of the Meteorological Office in Northern Ireland: The Principle Meteorological Office, Belfast International Airport, Belfast BT29 4AB. Tel: (01849) 422804. The Meteorological Office, Hillsborough, Maze, Lisburn, Co. Antrim BT27 5RF. Tel: (01846) 682416.

MET ÉIREANN STATIONS
Met Éireann, Glasnevin Hill, Dublin 9. Tel: (01) 8064200.

The Irish Meteorological Service has 13 synoptic stations throughout the Republic of Ireland, manned on a 24-hour basis, the main function of which is to maintain a continuous watch on the weather and to make detailed reports every hour on the hour. These reports provide the basis for all advice and information supplied to the general public regarding the 'weather forecast' and to the various specialised sectors. In addition, there are also Automatic Weather Stations throughout Ireland.

Station	County	Est.	Station	County	Est.
Valentia Observatory	Kerry	†1866	Clones	Monaghan	1950
Birr	Offaly	†1872	Belmullet	Mayo	1956
Malin Head	Donegal	1885	Rosslare	Wexford	1956
Shannon Airport	Clare	1945	Kilkenny	Kilkenny	1957
Dublin Airport	Dublin	1939	Cork Airport	Cork	1961
Mullingar	Westmeath	1943	Knock Airport	Mayo	1996
Casement Aerodrome	Dublin	*1964			

* Met Éireann staff took over; † already in existence

REPUBLIC OF IRELAND: METEOROLOGY STATISTICS

Station	Average Daily Temperatures (°C) 1995	1996	1997	Total Rainfall (mm) 1995	1996	1997	Average Daily Sunshine (hrs) 1995	1996	1997
Belmullet (Mayo)	10.7	10.0	11.1	1,203.2	1,136.0	1,265.9	3.49	3.81	3.32
Birr (Offaly)	10.4	9.3	10.5	828.6	837.7	943.3	3.62	3.21	3.21
Valentia Observatory (Kerry)	11.5	10.5	11.7	1,540.7	1,567.7	1,393.7	3.66	3.58	3.42
Casement Aerodrome (Dublin)	10.3	9.3	10.4	691.9	748.8	647.9	4.17	3.71	3.60
Claremorris (Mayo)	10.0	8.7	-	1,107.9	995.7	-	3.79	-	-
Clones (Monaghan)	10.1	9.1	10.4	962.9	929.5	881.2	4.02	3.39	3.14
Cork Airport (Cork)	10.7	9.6	10.7	1,254.1	1,433.5	1,269.2	4.32	4.06	3.79
Dublin Airport (Dublin)	10.1	9.1	10.1	711.2	787.3	725.9	4.41	3.71	3.77
Kilkenny (Kilkenny)	10.7	9.5	10.7	822.5	951.6	932.6	4.15	3.67	3.58
Malin Head (Donegal)	10.1	9.6	10.4	1,176.3	926.6	999.7	3.74	3.75	3.71
Mullingar (Westmeath)	9.9	9.0	10.2	894.4	870.6	938.6	4.16	3.50	3.48
Rosslare (Wexford)	11.2	10.3	11.4	801.6	961.7	1,012.2	4.63	4.47	4.21
Shannon Airport (Clare)	11.4	10.5	11.7	1,031.7	886.0	1,026.9	3.86	3.59	3.29

IRELAND AREA COMPARISON TABLE

The total land area of the island of Ireland is 32,595 sq. miles. The comparison table below shows the country's size in relation to the land area of selected countries throughout the world, indicating the number of times greater (+) or smaller (-) or approximately the same size (=) in relation to the size of Ireland. *(All figures are approximations)*

Country	Area (sq. miles)	Greater/Smaller	Country	Area (sq. miles)	Greater/Smaller
Argentina	1,073,518	+33	Monaco	0.75	-32,594
Australia	2,966,200	+91	Netherlands	16,033	-2
Austria	32,378	=	New Zealand	104,454	+3
Brazil	3,286,500	+101	Norway	125,050	+4
Canada	3,849,674	+118	Pakistan	339,697	+10
China	3,696,100	+113	Peru	496,225	+15
Greenland	840,000	+26	Philippines	115,860	+4
Egypt	385,229	+12	Poland	120,728	+4
Ethiopia	437,794	+13	Portugal	35,574	=
France	210,026	+6	Saudi Arabia	865,000	+27
Germany	137,823	+4	South Africa	472,281	+14
India	1,222,243	+37	Spain	194,898	+6
Iraq	167,975	+5	Sweden	173,732	+5
Indonesia	741,052	+23	Switzerland	15,940	-2
Iran	632,457	+19	Syria	71,498	+2
Israel	7,992	-4	Thailand	198,115	+6
Italy	116,334	+4	U.K.	94,251	+3
Japan	145,850	+4	U.S.A.	3,679,192	+113
Kenya	224,961	+7	Venezuela	352,144	+11
Libya	678,400	+21	Vietnam	127,246	+4
Luxembourg	999	-33	Zimbabwe	150,872	+5
Mexico	756,066	+23			

NORTHERN IRELAND: CHEMICAL QUALITY OF RIVER WATER, 1990-96

Quality (in kilometres)	1990-92	1991-93	1992-94	1993-95	1994-96
Bad	6.2	12.0	12.0	-	21.4
Poor	106.8	81.3	180.0	283.8	266.2
Fair	143.5	194.4	307.7	328.9	387.8
Fairly Good	766.9	767.5	757.5	688.4	633.8
Good	781.7	987.3	956.8	910.7	871.4
Very Good	164.8	215.6	138.6	140.8	177.6

BIRDS OF IRELAND*

Accentors - *Prunellidae* (Dunnock).

Auks - *Alcidae* (Razorbill, Guillemot, Black Guillemot, Puffin).

Barn Owls - *Tytonidae* (Barn Owl).

Buntings - *Emberizidae* (Corn Bunting, Yellowhammer, Reed Bunting, Snow Bunting).

Cormorants - *Phalacrocoracidae* (Cormorant, Shag)

Crows - *Corvidae* (Raven, Hooded Crow, Rook, Jackdaw, Magpie, Jay, Chough).

Cuckoos - *Cuculidae* (Cuckoo).

Dippers - *Cinclidae* (Dipper).

Divers - *Gavidae* (Great Northern Diver, Red-throated Diver).

Ducks, Geese & Swans - *Anatidae* (Mallard, Teal, Gadwall, Wigeon, Pintail, Shoveler, Scaup, Tufted Duck, Pochard, Goldeneye, Long-tailed Duck, Common Scoter, Eider, Red-breasted Merganser, Shelduck, Greylag Goose, White-fronted Goose, Brent Goose, Barnacle Goose, Mute Swan,Whooper Swan, Bewick's Swan).

Falcons - *Falconidae* (Peregrine, Merlin, Kestrel).

Finches - *Fringillidae* (Greenfinch, Goldfinch, Siskin, Linnet, Twite, Redpoll, Bullfinch, Chaffinch, Brambling).

Gannets - *Sulidae* (Gannet).

Grebes - *Podicipitidae* (Great Crested Grebe, Little Grebe)

Grouse - *Tetraonidae* (Red Grouse).

Gulls & Terns - *Laridae* (Great Black-backed Gull, Lesser Black-backed Gull, Herring Gull, Common Gull, Black-headed Gull, Kittiwake, Common Tern, Arctic Tern, Roseate Tern, Little Tern, Sandwich Tern).

Hawks, Harriers etc. - *Accipitridae* (Sparrowhawk, Hen Harrier).

Herons - *Ardeidae* (Grey Heron).

Kingfishers - *Alcedinidae* (Kingfisher).

Larks - *Alaudidae* (Skylark).

Nightjars - *Caprimulgidae* (Nightjar).

Owls - *Strigidae* (Long-eared Owl, Short-eared Owl).

Oystercatchers - *Haematopodidae* (Oystercatcher).

Partridges & Pheasants - *Phasianidae* (Partridge, Pheasant).

Petrels & Shearwaters - *Procellariidae* (Fulmar, Manx Shearwater).

Phalaropes - *Phalaropidae* (Grey Phalarope, Red-necked Phalaropidae).

Pigeons & Doves - *Columbidae* (Stock Dove, Rock Dove, Wood Pigeon, Turtle Dove, Collared Dove).

Pipits & Wagtails - *Motacillidae* (Meadow Pipit, Rock Pipit, Pied Wagtail, Grey Wagtail).

Plovers - *Charadriidae* (Lapwing, Ringed Plover, Grey Plover, Golden Plover, Turnstone).

Rails, Crakes & Coots - *Rallidae* (Water Rail, Corncrake, Moorhen, Coot).

Skuas - *Stercorariidae* (Great Skua, Pomarine Skua, Arctic Skua).

Snipe, Curlews etc. - *Scolopacidae* (Snipe,Woodcock,Curlew,Whimbrel,Black-tailed Godwit, Bar-tailed Godwit, Common Sandpiper, Redshank, Spotted Redshank, Greenshank, Knot, Purple Sandpiper, Little Stint, Dunlin, Curlew Sandpiper, Sanderling, Ruff).

Sparrows - *Ploceidae* (House Sparrow, Tree Sparrow)

Starlings - *Sturnidae* (Starling).

Storm Petrels - *Hydrobatidae* (Storm Petrel).

Swallows & Martins - *Hirunundinidae* (Swallow, House Martin, Sand Martin).

Swifts - *Apodidae* (Swift).

Thrushes, Warblers, etc. - *Muscicapidae* (Mistle Thrush, Fieldfare, Song Thrush, Redwing, Ring Ouzel, Blackbird, Wheatear, Stonechat, Whinchat, Robin, Grasshopper Warbler, Sedge Warbler, Blackcap, Garden Warbler, Whitethroat, Willow Warbler, Chiffchaff, Goldcrest, Spotted Flycatcher).

Tits - *Paridae* (Great Tit, Blue Tit, Coal Tit, Long-tailed Tit).

Treecreepers - *Certthiidae* (Treecreeper).

Wrens - *Troglodytidae* (Wren).

*Includes birds resident and living in Ireland and also occassional and visiting birds.

COMMON TREES OF IRELAND

Tree cover in Ireland is approximately 8% compared to the EU which has an average of 31%. Earliest recordings of tree plantings in Ireland date back to 1344. The tallest tree in Ireland is planted at Curraghmore Estate, Co. Waterford (Sitka Spruce, 170 ft tall). The oldest tree in Ireland is planted at the National Botanic Gardens, Dublin (Cedar of Lebanon, dating back to 1750). The life-span of a conifer is 40 to 60 years, while a broadleaf can reach 200 years before it is matured. The list below includes some of the most common trees planted in Ireland.

Species	Name	Irish	Origin
Broadleaves:	Alder	Fearnog	Ireland
	Ash	Fuinseog	Ireland
	Beech	Faibhile	Southern England & Europe
	Birch	Beith	Ireland
	Lime	Teile	England & Europe
	Oak	Dair	Ireland
	Poplar	Poibleóg	Britain, Europe & North America
	Sycamore	Seiceamar	Central Europe
	Wild Cherry	Silín	Ireland
	Hazel	-	Ireland

Continued from previous page

Species	Name	Irish	Origin
	Spanish Chestnut	-	Europe
Conifers:	Douglas Fir	Giúis Dhúchlais	Western North America
	Larch	Learóg	Central Europe & Honshu Island
	Lodgepole Pine	Péine Chontortach	Western North America
	Norway Spruce	Sprús Lochlannach	Europe
	Scots Pine	Péine Albanach	Ireland
	Sitka Spruce	Sprús Sitceach	Western North America
	Western Hemlock	Himlice Iartharach	Western North America
	Western Red Cedar	Céadar Crón Iartharach	Western North America

IRISH MAMMALS:

Mammal	Family	Irish Name	Latin Name
American Mink	Mustelidae	Minc Mheiriceánach	Mustela vision
Badger	Mustelidae	Broc	Meles meles
Bank Vole	Muridae	Vól Bruaigh	Clethrionomys glareolus
Bats: Daubenton's Bat	Vespertilionidae	Ialtóg Dhaubenton	Myotis daubentoni
Whiskered Bat	Vespertilionidae	Ialtóg Ghiobach	Myotis mystaciuus
Natterer's Bat	Vespertilionidae	Ialtóg Natterer	Myotis nattereri
Leisler's Bat	Vespertilionidae	Ialtóg Leisler	
Pipistrelle	Vespertilionidae	Ialtóg Fheaserach	Pipistrellus pipistrellus
Long-Eared Bat	Vespertilionidae	Ialtóg Chluasach	Plecotus auritus
Lesser Horseshoe Bat	Rhinolophidae	Ialtóg	Rhinolophus hipposideros
Deer: Red Deer	Cervidae	Fia Rua	Cervus elaphus
Fallow Deer	Cervidae	Fia Buí	Dama dama
Japanese Sika Deer	Cervidae	Fia Seapánach	Cervus nippon
Feral Goat	Bovidae	Gabhar Fia	Capra hircus
Field Mouse	Muridae	Luch Fhéir	Apodemus sylvaticus
Fox	Canidea	Sionnach / Madra Rua	Vulpes vulpes
Hare: Irish or Blue Hare	Lagomorpha	Giorria Éireannach	Lepus timudus hibernica
Brown Hare	Lagomorpha	Giorria	Lepus capensis
Hedgehog	Erinaceidae	Gráinneog	Erinaceus europaeus
Irish Stoat	Mustelidae	Easóg	Mustela erminea hibernica
Otter	Mustelidae	Dobharchú	Lutra lutra
Pine Marten	Mustelidae	Cat Crainn	Martes martes
Pygmy Shrew	Soricidae	Dallóg Fhraoigh	Sorex minutus
Rabbit	Lagomorpha	Coinín	Oryctolagus cuniculus
Rat: Brown Rat	Muridae	an Francach Donn	Rattus norvegicus
Black Rat	Muridae	an Francach Dubh	Rattus rattus
Squirrel: Grey Squirrel	Sciuridae	Iora Glas	Sciurus carolinensis
Red Squirrel	Sciuridae	Iora Rua	Sciurus vulgaris

IRELAND'S ENDANGERED SPECIES

Species	Irish Name	Latin Name
Birds:		
Corncrake	Traonach	Crex crex
Barn Owl		Tyto alba
Roseate Tern		Sterna dougalli
Canadian Brent Goose	Cadhan	Branta bernicla
Little Tern	Geabhróg bhídeach	Sterna albifrons
Red-Throated Divers	Lóma rua	Gavia stellata
Mammals:		
Whiskered Bat	Ialtóg Ghiobach	Myotis mystaciuus
Hedgehog	Gráinneog	Erinaceus europaeus
Pine Marten	Cat Crainn	Martes martes
Irish Hare	Giorria Éireannach	Lepus timudus hibernicus
Badger	Broc	Meles meles
Otter	Dobharchú	Lutra lutra

MAP OF IMPORTANT SITES:
REPUBLIC OF IRELAND & NORTHERN IRELAND

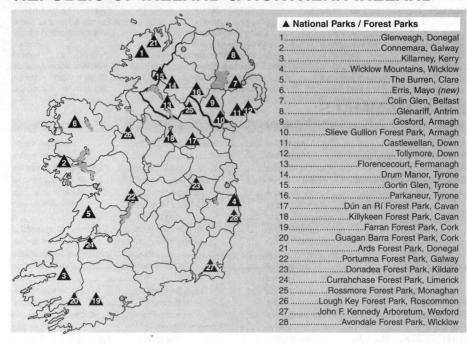

▲ National Parks / Forest Parks

1. ....Glenveagh, Donegal
2. ....Connemara, Galway
3. ....Killarney, Kerry
4. ....Wicklow Mountains, Wicklow
5. ....The Burren, Clare
6. ....Erris, Mayo *(new)*
7. ....Colin Glen, Belfast
8. ....Glenariff, Antrim
9. ....Gosford, Armagh
10. ....Slieve Gullion Forest Park, Armagh
11. ....Castlewellan, Down
12. ....Tollymore, Down
13. ....Florencecourt, Fermanagh
14. ....Drum Manor, Tyrone
15. ....Gortin Glen, Tyrone
16. ....Parkaneur, Tyrone
17. ....Dún an Rí Forest Park, Cavan
18. ....Killykeen Forest Park, Cavan
19. ....Farran Forest Park, Cork
20. ....Guagan Barra Forest Park, Cork
21. ....Ards Forest Park, Donegal
22. ....Portumna Forest Park, Galway
23. ....Donadea Forest Park, Kildare
24. ....Currahchase Forest Park, Limerick
25. ....Rossmore Forest Park, Monaghan
26. ...Lough Key Forest Park, Roscommon
27. ....John F. Kennedy Arboretum, Wexford
28. ....Avondale Forest Park, Wicklow

■ Wetlands

1. ....Lough Foyle, Derry
2. ....Strangford Lough, Down
3. ....Loughs Neagh and Beg, Antrim
4. ....Dundalk Bay, Louth
5. ....North Bull, Dublin
6. ......Wexford Harbour and Slobs, Wexford
7. ....Dungarvan Harbour, Waterford
8. ....Ballymacoda, Cork
9. ....Cork Harbour, Cork
10. ....Shannon Estuary, Limerick/Clare
11. ....Little Brosna, Offaly/Tipperary
12. ....Sloblands, Burt, Donegal

● Nature Reserves

1. ....Coole, Gort, Galway
2. ....Dromore Wood, Ruan, Ennis, Clare
3. ......Doneraile Wildlife Park, Doneraile, Cork
4. ....Wexford Wildfowl Reserve, Wexford
5. ......Rathlin West Seabird Viewpoint, Antrim
6. ...Murlough National, near Dundrum, Down

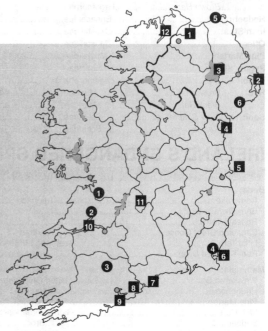

MAP OF IRELAND

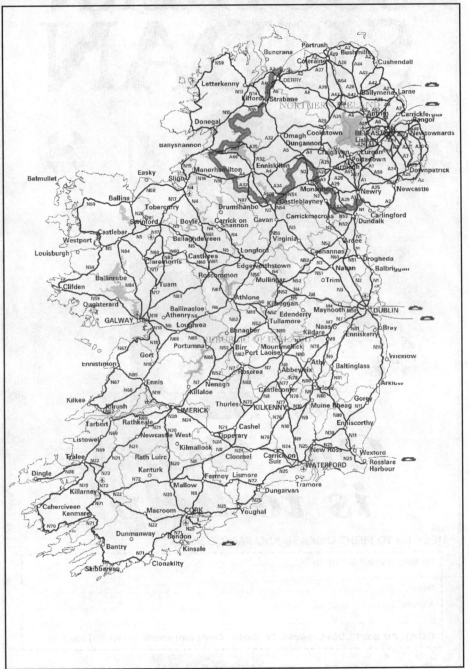

SOUTHERN SUDAN

Our GOAL is to help!

HELP US TO FIGHT DISEASE AND FAMINE

I enclose cheque/P.O./cash for £ _____

Name: ....

Address ....

....

GOAL P.O. Box 19, Dún Laoghaire, Co. Dublin. Credit card donations - Tel: (01) 280 9779

POPULATION

The Ireland of Today

*By **Pat McArt**, Executive Editor Irish Almanac*

Most people over the age of thirty-five in today's Ireland are, to put it simply, bewildered by what's currently happening. Those brought up in an the 1960's and '70's – those years of budget deficits, mass emigration, strong rural traditions, low expectations, limited job opportunities and a strong attachment to "the mother church" – are now living in the era of the Celtic Tiger and all has changed, changed utterly.

More than anything else it is the rapidity and the scale of the change that has jolted the equilibrium. The romantic image of an idyllic rural landscape hardly matches the reality of a country which is second only to the U.S. in the exportation of computer software, where a third of population now lives in and around Dublin, where the targets for Dublin traffic set for the year 2011 will be reached ten years early and where the traffic at both Dublin airport and Dublin docks has almost doubled in the last five years.

And, in the personal wealth stakes, who could ever have envisaged a house in Co. Dublin being bought for £5.9m.

But it is not just a Dublin phenomenon. West coast towns like Galway, Sligo and Letterkenny, hardly to the fore economically in years gone by, are now booming. House and land prices there, while cheap compared to much of the East coast, are rising rapidly.

From a situation some years ago of mass emigration we have now arrived at a situation of net immigration. Anyone with a worthwhile skill or trade is encouraged to come back home.

Indeed, the return of the economic emigrant is a challenge for not only Irish society but also for the Irish psyche.

Traditionally, even culturally, we were a nation whose most adventurous young people left and the chasm that that emigration caused created the conditions for a conservative country where social change was slow. Old ways were revered and those who dared to be different, be it in a religious, business or even sexual sense, risked public ostracism.

But those days are largely gone. Economic performance is, perhaps, the main dynamic of that change.

During the first nine months of this year Irish Exchequer Revenues exceeded spending by £1.3bn. and for the full year the Government now expects an £800m. surplus.

This followed on from the remarkable performance in 1997 when a total of £14bn. in tax revenue was collected. This was an increase of 15 per cent on 1996 which was, in turn, a record year. Tax revenue for the first nine months of this year is £11.8bn.

The vastly improved financial situation is mirrored in the employment sector. The jobless rate has fallen to a new low of 8.8%, the lowest figure since the modern method of computing began in 1983. The long term unemployed are now reckoned to be less than 100,000.

The IDA's chief executive, Mr. Kieran McGowan confirmed that his Authority was involved in the creation of 15,000 new jobs in 1997 and this year has also seen significant job opportunities provided, again mostly in the computer software sector.

But there is little doubt that not all boats are rising with the tide.

A recent report from the Eastern Health Board has claimed that children as young as eight are opting out of school and home life because of the abject poverty in which their families live. Indeed the same report points out that 15% of boys think that life is not worth living.

It is also a matter of record that deaths by suicide are increasing every year.

The problem in Ireland is that we have a young population, one of the youngest in Europe. In the Republic, for instance, more than 130,000 sat their Leaving Certificate back in June. The pressure to succeed is growing stronger as are the number of points needed to get into the university course of one's choice.

It is unlikely that the competition will ease any as most schools, particularly in the urban areas, are busting at the seams with ever growing numbers of children. The demand for facilities, for equipment, for teachers will create their own pressures on the system in the years ahead.

While the numbers attending church services still remains high there is little doubt that there is almost an a la carte approach to much of the churches' teachings.

Many Catholics, the main religion of the vast majority on the island of Ireland, now differ from church teaching on such areas as divorce, cohabiting, sex before marriage, confession, contraception, etc.

According to British statistics more than 5,300 women with addresses in the Irish Republic had abortions in Britain last year. It is generally accepted that the true figure is much higher, many women opting to give a convenience address rather than their real one.

The power of the church has also waned with considerable speed in recent years and, while it is hardly a direct consequence, it would seem the religious life no longer holds the attraction for Irish boys and girls that it once did.

The decline in the numbers going forward for the religious life has also resulted in a major change in another sphere of Irish life, education.

Since the foundation of the State most schools, both primary and secondary, were run by the church. As we approach the millennium the vast majority of schools are now run by lay people.

Indeed, what was unthinkable some years ago has now happened - some parishes no longer have their own Catholic priests. From a time when Irish clergy in huge numbers went forth across the world to spread the Good News this is a remarkable turnaround.

The newly created wealth has also resulted in a whole plethora of other problems, some of which were hardly even envisaged.

The treatment of asylum seekers, mostly from the former Eastern bloc countries, has given rise to serious concerns about civil rights and the latent racism in Irish society.

Drugs are now commonplace. Earlier this year Gardaí and Customs officials intercepted a drugs haul in the South-East which they reckoned had a street value in excess of £100m. It was destined for the Dublin market.

The consumption of alcohol has reached almost epidemic proportions

Wealth has also created a car owning class, namely almost the entire population. Traffic chaos has meant pandemonium on Irish roads and allied with high speed, better roads, high performance vehicles it has resulted in an horrific increase in the numbers killed.

The East coast has been particularly badly hit by car chaos and while the Government is investigating a number of wide-ranging public transport initiatives it will be several years before any meaningful improvement will occur.

Overall, the acid test in the years ahead will be how Irish society adapts and deals with this unprecedented level of change. The challenge will truly be to hold on to the best of the old while embracing the new.

In contrast, Northern Ireland has been dominated by the momentous events on the political front. There have been many historic firsts this year ... The Good Friday Agreement, a remarkable endorsement of the Agreement by a substantial section of the Northern Ireland population, the election of David Trimble and Seamus Mallon to the top posts in the Executive, Trimble's ground breaking meeting with Gerry Adams, of Sinn Féin, Sinn Féin first meeting with a British Prime Minister etc.

And, unfortunately, there were the tragedies: numerous paramilitary murders in the early part of year, the Quinn children burned to death in a sectarian attack at their home in Ballymoney in July, and the atrocity at Omagh in August which left 29 people dead. It was the worst single incident of the entire Troubles.

But now there is optimism that the corner has been turned, that two communities sickened by violence are willing to work together for the betterment of all. The ceasefires of all the main paramilitary parties has increased confidence that a lasting peace can be achieved.

The fact that Northern Ireland comes under the Governance of Westminster leaves it little autonomy to steer its own economic course. But this should change significantly if the Assembly gets up and running and executive powers are devolved to its ministers.

The lack of local accountability has, most definitely, stilted the growth of the Northern Irish economy. Local initiatives, particularly in areas like agriculture, could have easily improved the lot of many people but being tied to London left little room for manoeuvre.

The Assembly, with a budget expected to be in the region of £6/8bn., should make a significant contribution to the region.

Northern Ireland society has undergone so much political change in recent years that social change has almost gone unobserved. The 900,000 Protestant / Unionists and 600,000 Catholic / Nationalists have become island communities with little or no interaction between them. The abnormal nature of this kind of society has made significant trends difficult to detect. The catch all terms "Protestant" /"Catholic" has obscured much and explained little. What is really happening should become clearer with "normalisation.

NORTHERN IRELAND & REPUBLIC OF IRELAND: DEMOGRAPHIC STATISTICS, 1991 AND 1996

Category	Northern Ireland - 1991 (000s)	Rep. of Ireland - 1996 (000s)
Population	1,577.8	3,626.1
Aged 0-14	385.4	859.4
Aged 15-24	253.7	632.9
Aged 25-44	432.9	1,016.1
Aged 45-64	306.9	703.8
Aged 65+	199.1	413.9
Births	26.2	249.5
Deaths	15.1	157.4
Marriages	9.2	82.8
Marital Status:		
Single	773.7	1,997.3
Married	661.1	1,444.4
Widowed	96.7	184.4
Numbers in Full-time Education (1995/96)	457.5	962.3
Primary School Pupils	197.3	485.9
Secondary School Pupils	155.0	373.7
Third Level Pupils (incl. FE Colleges)	105.1	102.7
Unemployment	98.2	191.0

REPUBLIC OF IRELAND: CENSUS STATISTICS
OVERVIEW IRISH CENSUS INFORMATION, 1891-1996

Year	Total Persons	Births Registered	Deaths Registered	Marriages Registered	Natural Increase	Change in Population	Est. net Migration	Intercensal Period
1891	3,468,694	835,072	639,073	145,976	195,999	-401,326	-597,325	1881-91
1901	3,221,823	737,934	588,391	148,134	149,543	-246,871	-396,414	1891-01
1911	3,139,688	713,709	534,305	153,674	179,404	-82,135	-261,539	1901-11
1926	2,971,992	968,742	731,409	230,525	237,333	-167696	-405,029	1911-26
1936	2,968,420	583,502	420,323	136,699	163,179	-3,572	-166,751	1926-36
1946	2,955,107	602,095	428,297	159,426	173,798	-13,313	-187,111	1936-46
1951	2,960,593	329,270	201,295	80,868	127,975	+5,486	-122,489	1946-51
1956	2,898,264	312,517	178,083	79,541	134,434	-62,329	-196,763	1951-56
1961	2,818,341	302,816	170,736	76,669	132,080	-79,923	-212,003	1956-61
1966	2,884,002	312,709	166,443	80,754	146,266	+65,661	-80,605	1961-66
1971	2,978,248	312,796	164,644	95,662	148,152	+94,246	-53,906	1966-71
1979	3,368,217	548,413	267,378	171,705	281,035	+389,969	+108,934	1971-79
1981	3,443,405	146,224	65,991	42,728	80,233	+75,188	-5,045	1979-81
1986	3,540,643	333,457	164,336	95,648	169,121	+97,238	-71,883	1981-86
1991	3,525,719	277,546	158,300	91,141	119,246	-14,924	-134,170	1986-91
1996	3,626,087	249,455	157,389	82,804	92,066	+100,368	+8,302	1991-96

REPUBLIC OF IRELAND & NORTHERN IRELAND:
MARRIAGES, BIRTHS & DEATHS, 1994-96

Category	Republic of Ireland			Northern Ireland		
	1994	1995	1996	1994	1995	1996
Marriages	16,297	15,623	16,255	8,683	8,576	8,297
Births: Total	47,928	48,530	50,390	24,289	23,860	24,582
Female	23,184	23,498	24,149	11,824	11,475	12,105
Male	24,744	25,032	26,241	12,465	12,385	12,477
Deaths: Total	30,876	31,645	31,514	15,114	15,310	15,218
Female	14,590	14,882	15,002	7,752	7,828	7,800
Male	16,286	16,763	16,512	7,362	7,482	7,418

NORTHERN IRELAND: CENSUS STATISTICS
OVERVIEW OF CENSUS INFORMATION, 1891-1991

Year	Total Persons	Births Registered	Deaths Registered	Natural Increase	Change in Population	Est. net Migration	Intercensal Period
1891	1,236,056	312,249	240,339	71,910	+68,760	140,670	1881-91
1901	1,236,952	314,795	246,161	68,634	+896	67,738	1891-01
1911	1,250,531	309,502	230,506	78,996	+13,579	65,417	1901-11
1926	1,256,561	431,148	317,545	113,603	+6,030	107,573	1911-26
1937	1,279,745	280,641	199,806	80,835	+23,184	57,651	1926-37
1951	1,370,921	402,187	243,744	158,443	+91,176	67,267	1937-51
1961	1,425,042	298,808	152,459	146,349	+54,121	92,228	1951-61
1966	1,484,775	182,489	85,055	97,434	+59,733	37,701	1961-66
1971	1,536,065	148,706	72,578	76,128	+51,290	24,838	1966-71
1981*	1,532,196	274,786	167,232	107,554	-3,869	111,423	1971-81
1991	1,577,836	273,227	158,167	115,060	+45,640	69,420	1981-91

Estimated - due to protests over the Hunger Strikes, many households were not included in the 1981 Census; the population effect was estimated at 44,500. This effect must be taken into account with regard to all Northern Ireland population tables.

REPUBLIC OF IRELAND & NORTHERN IRELAND:
POPULATION BY AGE-GROUP, 1971-96

Age Group (years)	Republic of Ireland Persons (000's)				Northern Ireland Persons (000's)		
	1971	1981	1991	1996	1971	1981	1991
0-4	315.6	353.0	273.7	250.4	156.2	130.8	128.3
5-9	316.9	349.5	318.5	282.9	157.1	134.3	129.2
10-14	298.6	341.2	348.3	326.1	143.6	148.8	127.9
15-19	267.7	326.4	335.0	339.5	126.3	144.5	127.6
20-24	215.3	276.1	266.6	293.4	114.9	122.3	126.1
25-29	173.0	246.1	246.3	259.0	101.9	100.0	122.2
30-34	151.4	232.0	249.0	260.9	86.7	98.7	113.5
35-39	149.1	193.8	237.9	255.7	82.4	92.5	99.3
40-44	152.7	165.9	225.7	240.4	84.3	81.2	97.9
45-49	160.1	151.9	187.8	225.4	86.1	76.1	89.9
50-54	159.1	149.7	156.8	186.6	80.1	76.0	76.6
55-59	154.8	149.6	142.5	153.8	78.5	75.1	71.1
60-64	134.1	139.3	134.6	137.9	72.0	68.0	69.3
65-69	111.8	133.9	130.8	126.8	60.2	63.4	65.0
70+	218.1	235.0	272.1	287.1	105.8	120.5	134.1
TOTAL:	2,978.2	3,443.4	3,525.7	3,626.0	1,536.1	1,532.2	1,578.0

NORTHERN IRELAND:
POPULATION BY COUNCIL AREA, 1981-91

District Council Area	1981 Persons	1991 Persons	Change '81-'91 Actual	%
Antrim	45,029	44,322	-707	-1.6
Ards	57,088	64,026	6,938	11.4
Armagh	49,237	51,331	2,094	4.2
Ballymena	54,829	56,032	1,203	2.1
Ballymoney	22,952	23,984	1,032	4.3
Banbridge	30,118	33,102	2,984	9.4
Belfast	314,360	283,746	-30,614	-10.2
Carrickfergus	28,633	32,439	3,806	12.4
Castlereagh	60,802	60,649	-153	-0.3
Coleraine	46,752	51,062	4,310	8.8
Cookstown	28,265	30,808	2,543	8.6
Craigavon	73,281	74,494	1,213	1.6
Derry	89,126	94,918	5,792	6.2
Down	53,208	57,511	4,303	7.8

Continued from previous page

District Council Area	1981 Persons	1991 Persons	Change '81-'91 Actual	%
Dungannon	43,895	45,322	1,427	3.1
Fermanagh	51,609	54,062	2,453	4.6
Larne	29,084	29,181	97	0.3
Limavady	26,972	29,201	2,229	7.9
Lisburn	84,022	99,162	15,140	16.5
Magherafelt	32,503	35,874	3,371	9.9
Moyle	14,400	14,617	217	1.4
Newry and Mourne	76,596	82,288	5,692	7.1
Newtownabbey	72,266	73,832	1,566	2.1
North Down	66,283	70,308	4,025	5.9
Omagh	44,300	45,343	1,043	2.3
Strabane	36,289	35,668	-621	-1.7
TOTAL:	**1,531,899**	**1,573,282**	**41,383**	**2.7**

REPUBLIC OF IRELAND:
OVERVIEW RELIGIOUS DENOMINATIONS, 1881-1991

Year	Catholic	Church of Ireland	Presby-terian	Methodist	Jewish	Other	No Religion	Not Stated
1881	3,465,332	317,576	56,498	17,660	394	-	12,560	-
1891	3,099,003	286,804	51,469	18,513	1,506	-	11,399	-
1901	2,878,271	264,264	46,714	17,872	3,006	-	11,696	-
1911	2,812,509	249,535	45,486	16,440	3,805	-	11,913	-
1926	2,751,269	164,215	32,429	10,663	3,686	-	9,730	-
1936	2,773,920	145,030	28,067	9,649	3,749	-	8,005	-
1946	2,786,033	124,829	23,870	8,355	3,907	-	8,113	-
1961	2,673,473	104,016	18,953	6,676	3,255	5,236	1,107	5,625
1971	2,795,666	97,739	16,052	5,646	2,633	6,248	7,616	46,648
1981	3,204,476	95,366	14,255	5,790	2,127	10,843	39,572	70,976
1991	3,228,327	82,840	13,199	5,037	1,581	45,090	66,270	83,375

NORTHERN IRELAND: OVERVIEW OF RELIGIOUS
DENOMINATIONS, 1961-91

Year	Cath.	Presb.	COI	Meth.	Breth.	Baptist	Cong.	Unitn.	Other	None	Not Stated
1961	497,547	413,113	344,800	71,865	16,847	13,765	9,838	5,613	23,236	-	28,418
1971	477,919	405,719	334,318	71,235	16,480	16,563	10,072	3,975	40,848	-	142,511
1981	414,532	339,818	281,472	58,731	12,158	16,375	8,265	3,373	72,651	-	274,584
1991	605,639	336,891	279,280	59,517	12,446	19,484	8,176	3,213	79,129	59,234	114,827

REPUBLIC OF IRELAND:
POPULATION BY PROVINCE AND COUNTY, 1991

Province & County	Total Persons	RC	COI	Prot.	Presb.	Meth.	Jewish	Other	No Religion	Not Stated
Total:	3,525,719	3,228,327	82,840	6,347	13,199	5,037	1,581	38,743	66,270	83,375
Connacht:	423,031	397,848	5,321	516	333	286	21	3,208	5,392	10,106
Galway	180,364	168,640	1,358	228	81	76	16	1,772	3,191	5,002
Leitrim	25,301	23,682	721	41	17	61	-	80	217	482
Mayo	110,713	105,839	817	116	101	27	2	601	929	2,281
Roscommon	51,897	50,204	358	28	13	21	2	221	333	717
Sligo	54,756	49,483	2,067	103	121	101	1	534	722	1,624
Leinster:	1,860,949	1,685,334	50,912	3,391	3,799	2,815	1,439	24,829	43,843	44,587
Carlow	40,942	37,767	1,747	42	15	25	5	262	343	736

Continued from previous page

Province & County	Total Persons	RC	COI	Prot.	Presb.	Meth.	Jewish	Other	No Religion	Not Stated
Dublin	1,025,304	911,454	26,169	2,157	2,716	1,895	1,383	17,571	33,269	28,690
Kildare	122,656	113,828	2,923	147	153	102	9	1,212	1,859	2,423
Kilkenny	73,635	68,699	1,586	74	143	56	2	559	822	1,694
Laois	52,314	48,461	2,417	41	38	94	1	312	256	694
Longford	30,296	28,645	705	24	46	37	-	161	163	515
Louth	90,724	85,770	939	49	137	20	5	907	974	1,923
Meath	105,370	98,766	1,926	133	142	42	2	797	1,236	2,326
Offaly	58,494	55,172	1,604	52	39	142	1	279	323	882
Westmeath	61,880	58,508	1,059	80	32	38	-	401	528	1,234
Wexford	102,069	94,832	3,287	169	81	77	8	554	1,052	2,009
Wicklow	97,265	83,432	6,550	423	257	287	23	1,814	3,018	1,461
Munster:	1,009,533	941,675	15,758	1,385	548	1,185	111	9,192	15,402	24,277
Clare	90,918	84,847	699	72	55	43	12	861	1,778	2,551
Cork	410,369	379,011	8,864	792	240	690	57	4,291	7,567	8,857
Kerry	121,894	114,253	1,415	173	46	34	17	920	1,696	3,340
Limerick	161,956	152,364	1,409	158	86	210	15	1,365	2,084	4,265
Tipperary	132,772	125,607	2,132	101	52	147	1	885	1,074	2,773
Waterford	91,624	85,593	1,239	89	69	61	9	870	1,203	2,491
Ulster:(part of)	232,206	203,470	10,849	1,055	8,519	751	10	1,514	1,633	4,405
Cavan	52,796	46,703	3,622	160	710	94	1	240	291	975
Donegal	128,117	111,427	5,602	555	5,412	603	8	866	1,029	2,615
Monaghan	51,293	45,340	1,625	340	2,397	54	1	408	313	815

NORTHERN IRELAND:
POPULATION BY DISTRICT COUNCIL AREA, 1991

Council Area	Total Persons	RC	Presb.	COI	Meth.	Other	None	Not Stated
TOTAL:	1,577,836	605,639	336,891	279,280	59,517	122,448	59,234	114,827
Antrim	44,516	14,117	13,614	6,384	786	3,600	2,025	3,990
Ards	64,764	7,341	25,219	12,137	3,386	7,069	3,904	5,708
Armagh	51,817	23,518	8,627	10,604	1,236	3,964	825	3,043
Ballymena	56,641	10,392	26,067	6,869	1,442	6,115	1,845	3,911
Ballymoney	24,198	7,311	9,411	3,151	123	2,184	524	1,494
Banbridge	33,482	9,256	9,608	6,362	624	3,977	929	2,726
Belfast	279,237	108,954	47,743	50,242	14,667	20,113	14,756	22,762
Carrickfergus	32,750	2,269	10,166	7,698	3,162	4,390	2,476	2,589
Castlereagh	60,799	5,743	17,445	14,638	5,323	8,481	3,797	5,372
Coleraine	50,438	11,323	15,946	12,550	784	4,214	2,104	3,517
Cookstown	31,082	16,522	4,779	5,288	331	2,131	382	1,649
Craigavon	74,986	30,060	7,718	18,666	3,904	7,190	1,955	5,493
Derry	95,371	66,260	10,539	8,503	853	2,629	1,353	5,234
Down	58,008	32,507	9,025	6,183	559	3,454	1,658	4,622
Dungannon	45,428	25,299	5,822	8,245	912	2,416	384	2,350
Fermanagh	54,033	29,657	1,549	14,283	2,724	2,534	745	2,541
Larne	29,419	6,510	11,136	4,083	1,107	2,771	1,291	2,521
Limavady	29,567	15,281	5,683	4,699	203	1,035	512	2,154
Lisburn	99,458	26,786	20,980	26,286	4,095	9,154	4,780	7,377
Magherafelt	36,293	21,377	5,466	4,372	165	2,632	313	1,968
Moyle	14,789	7,723	2,766	2,587	29	452	254	978
Newry & Mourne	82,943	59,555	8,890	3,861	314	3,376	947	6,000
Newtownabbey	74,035	9,635	23,610	14,976	6,437	8,125	4,476	6,776
North Down	71,832	6,435	23,658	16,591	5,077	7,500	6,140	6,431
Omagh	45,809	29,469	5,141	5,766	785	1,910	570	2,168
Strabane	36,141	22,339	6,283	4,256	489	1,032	289	1,453

REPUBLIC OF IRELAND & NORTHERN IRELAND: OCCUPATIONS BY INDUSTRIAL GROUP, 1991

Industrial Group (000s)	Republic of Ireland Persons	Male	Female	Northern Ireland Persons	Male	Female
Agriculture, Forestry, Fishing	158,208	142,255	15,953	23,962	22,274	1,688
Building & Construction	76,625	72,687	3,938	41,079	38,489	2,590
Banking/Business Services	235,300	137,433	97,867	40,075	21,200	18,875
Electrical & Electronic Engineering	-	-	-	32,929	26,451	6,478
Energy & Water Supplies	11,948	10,269	1,679	7,180	6,120	1,060
Manufacturing Industries	218,725	152,609	66,116	60,174	33,992	26,182
Mining (quarrying & ores)	6,015	5,568	447	9,147	7,566	1,581
Personal Services	71,161	25,927	45,234	109,550	56,755	52,795
Professional Services	196,903	71,317	125,586	131,987	37,109	94,878
Public Administration and Defence	75,541	52,158	23,383	66,875	42,587	24,288
Transport & Communications	69,397	55,422	13,975	24,484	19,604	4,880
Other Services	29,257	18,303	10,954	27,508	17,253	10,255
TOTAL:	**1,149,080**	**743,948**	**405,132**	**574,950**	**329,400**	**245,550**

REPUBLIC OF IRELAND & NORTHERN IRELAND: SELECTED OCCUPATION STATISTICS, 1991

Occupation	Republic of Ireland Persons	Males	Females	Northern Ireland Persons	Males	Females
Accountancy	11,634	6,842	4,792	-	-	-
Advertising	1,723	946	777	-	-	-
Aircraft Manufacture	1,545	1,348	197	-	-	-
Banking & Finance	28,747	12,517	16,230	8,897	3,497	5,400
Cinemas & Film Studios	1,601	808	793	-	-	-
Dentistry	2,060	879	1,181	-	-	-
Education	75,114	29,094	46,020	45,667	14,935	30,732
Electricity	10,326	8,920	1,406	-	-	-
Fishing	2,895	2,669	226	973	942	31
Footwear & Clothing	13,688	3,997	9,691	15,175	2,801	12,374
Forestry	2,298	2,222	76	438	397	41
Garda Síochána	10,851	10,146	705	-	-	-
Hairdressing & Beauticians	9,946	1,387	8,559	-	-	-
Health Board Hospitals	30,209	6,415	23,794	-	-	-
Hotels & Catering	35,098	13,149	21,949	17,872	6,859	11,013
Insurance	15,150	8,521	6,629	4,206	2,379	1,827
Paper, Printing & Publishing	19,397	13,276	6,121	6,198	4,026	2,172
Plumbing & Domestic Heating	4,557	4,414	143	-	-	-
Postal & Communications	21,438	16,401	5,037	8,612	6,426	2,186
Rail Transport	5,625	5,036	589	794	715	79
Religion	8,484	5,053	3,431	-	-	-
Research & Development	-	-	-	767	514	253
Textiles	-	-	-	8,684	4,953	3,731
Turf Production	2,756	2,586	170	-	-	-
Water Supply	292	257	35	1,295	1,236	59

REPUBLIC OF IRELAND: INTERNATIONAL COMPARISONS OF POPULATION DENSITY, 1997

Country	No. of People per km²	Country	No. of People per km²
Belgium	333	Netherlands	379
Germany	230	Norway	14
IRELAND	53	Switzerland	172
Italy	191	United Kingdom	244

REPUBLIC OF IRELAND & NORTHERN IRELAND: POPULATION OF MAIN IRISH CITIES AND TOWNS

Republic of Ireland (1996 Census)			Northern Ireland (1991 Census)		
City/Town	County	Population	City/Town	County	Population
Greater Dublin Area	Dublin	953,000	Belfast	Antrim	279,237
Cork	Cork	180,000	Derry	Derry	72,334
Limerick	Limerick	79,000	Newtownabbey	Antrim	57,103
Galway	Galway	57,000	Bangor	Down	52,437
Waterford	Waterford	44,000	Lisburn	Antrim	42,110
Dundalk	Louth	30,000	Ballymena	Antrim	28,717
Bray	Wicklow	28,000	Newtownards	Down	24,301
Drogheda	Louth	25,000	Newry	Down	22,975
Swords	Dublin	22,000	Carrickfergus	Antrim	22,885
Tralee	Kerry	20,000	Lurgan	Armagh	21,905
Kilkenny	Kilkenny	19,000	Portadown	Armagh	21,299
Sligo	Sligo	19,000	Antrim	Antrim	20,878
Ennis	Clare	18,000	Coleraine	Derry	20,721
Clonmel	Tipperary	16,000	Larne	Antrim	17,575
Wexford	Wexford	16,000	Omagh	Tyrone	17,280
Athlone	Westmeath	16,000	Armagh	Armagh	14,640
Carlow	Carlow	15,000	Banbridge	Down	12,529
Naas	Kildare	14,000	Strabane	Tyrone	11,981
Malahide	Dublin	14,000	Enniskillen	Fermanagh	11,436
Leixlip	Kildare	13,000	Limavady	Derry	10,764
Newbridge	Kildare	13,000	Cookstown	Tyrone	10,472
			Downpatrick	Down	10,257

REPUBLIC OF IRELAND & NORTHERN IRELAND: POPULATION AT EACH CENSUS, 1901-96

	Republic of Ireland			Northern Ireland		
Year	Total	Males	Females	Total	Males	Females
1901	3,221,823	1,610,085	1,611,738	1,236,952	589,955	646,997
1911	3,139,688	1,589,509	1,550,179	1,250,531	602,539	647,992
1926	2,971,992	1,506,889	1,465,103	1,256,561	608,088	648,473
1936	2,968,420	1,520,454	1,447,966	-	-	-
1937	-	-	-	1,279,745	623,154	656,591
1946	2,955,107	1,494,877	1,460,230	-	-	-
1951	2,960,593	1,506,597	1,453,996	1,370,921	667,819	703,102
1961	2,818,341	1,416,549	1,401,792	1,425,042	694,224	730,818
1966	-	-	-	1,484,775	723,884	760,891
1971	2,978,248	1,495,760	1,482,488	1,536,065	754,676	781,389
1981	3,443,405	1,729,354	1,714,051	1,532,196	749,480	782,716
1991	3,525,719	1,753,418	1,772,301	1,577,836	769,071	808,765
1996	3,626,087	1,800,232	1,825,855	-	-	-

R. of IRELAND: POP. BY COUNTRY OF BIRTH, 1996

Country	Connacht	Leinster	Munster	Ulster*	Total
Canada	257	1,908	629	107	2,901
England and Wales	21,135	67,849	42,457	7,889	139,330
France	445	2,146	931	71	3,593
Germany	1,065	2,846	2,182	250	6,343
Italy	136	1,353	325	30	1,844
Netherlands	294	1,150	1,004	42	2,490
Northern Ireland	2,939	22,590	4,279	9,759	39,567
Republic of Ireland	393,939	1,784,070	959,178	207,732	3,344,919
Scotland	1,190	4,786	1,514	4,261	11,751
Spain	136	1,611	345	12	2,104
USA	2,919	7,248	4,531	921	15,619
Other EU	204	1,946	633	75	2,858

Continued from previous page

Country	Connacht	Leinster	Munster	Ulster*	Total
Other European Countries	298	2,436	802	69	3,605
Other Countries	1,570	13,552	4,006	491	19,619
TOTAL:	**426,527**	**1,915,491**	**1,022,816**	**231,709**	**3,596,543**

* part of

N. IRELAND: POP. BY COUNTRY OF BIRTH, 1991

District Council	Northern Ireland	Britain	Republic of Ireland	Commonwealth Countries	Other Countries*	Not Stated	Total
Antrim	39,885	3,101	671	342	346	171	44,516
Ards	60,365	2,668	884	377	317	153	64,764
Armagh	47,877	1,587	1,708	189	174	282	51,817
Ballymena	53,468	1,864	567	287	267	188	56,641
Ballymoney	23,158	598	198	88	44	112	24,198
Banbridge	31,840	904	404	116	107	111	33,482
Belfast	259,214	9,316	4,962	1,916	1,818	2,011	279,237
Carrickfergus	30,152	1,746	388	208	215	41	32,750
Castlereagh	56,496	2,383	992	391	366	171	60,799
Coleraine	46,281	2,420	920	339	330	148	50,438
Cookstown	29,709	728	329	80	98	138	31,082
Craigavon	70,180	2,513	1,168	352	369	404	74,986
Derry	85,044	3,954	4,633	407	462	871	95,371
Down	53,084	3,023	957	315	370	259	58,008
Dungannon	42,714	1,129	1,028	123	136	298	45,428
Fermanagh	48,167	1,807	3,426	125	221	287	54,033
Larne	27,560	1,245	302	133	127	52	29,419
Limavady	26,360	2,211	452	140	263	141	29,567
Lisburn	89,656	6,122	1,748	679	947	306	99,458
Magherafelt	34,804	712	365	116	92	204	36,293
Moyle	13,829	563	227	56	59	55	14,789
Newry & Mourne	75,200	3,125	3,356	263	356	643	82,943
Newtownabbey	69,474	2,756	754	465	388	198	74,035
North Down	63,399	5,132	1,758	678	709	156	71,832
Omagh	41,883	2,049	1,162	162	233	320	45,809
Strabane	32,710	1,078	2,021	80	58	194	36,141
TOTAL:	**1,452,509**	**64,734**	**35,380**	**8,427**	**8,872**	**7,914**	**1,577,836**

* including at sea

REPUBLIC OF IRELAND: DIVORCE STATISTICS*

Circuit Court Office	Applications Received	Numbers Granted
Carlow	18	9
Carrick-on-Shannon	3	2
Castlebar	35	14
Cavan	17	-
Clonmel	22	15
Cork	136	57
Dublin	563	196
Dundalk	30	14
Ennis	31	13
Galway	43	14
Kilkenny	25	5
Letterkenny	17	6
Limerick	66	7
Longford	6	3
Monaghan	10	2
Mullingar	23	3
Naas	36	7
Portlaoise	6	2
Roscommon	6	3
Sligo	11	7
Tralee	40	10
Trim	29	38
Tullamore	9	3
Waterford	29	-
Wexford	32	20
Wicklow	35	10
Total Circuit:	**1,278**	**430**
High Court:	**17**	**5**
TOTAL:	**1,295**	**435**

*as of 20th April, 1998

N. IRELAND: DIVORCE STATISTICS, 1995-97

Grounds	High Court			County Court			Total		
	1995	1996	1997	1995	1996	1997	1995	1996	1997
Adultery	115	113	118	67	63	67	182	176	185
Behaviour	300	301	311	152	175	218	452	476	529
Desertion	5	7	7	7	6	8	12	13	15
Separation *(2 years & consent)*	556	484	502	627	586	632	1,183	1,070	1,134
Separation *(5 years)*	326	326	283	355	332	348	681	658	631
Other Grounds	24	18	27	1	8	11	25	26	38
TOTAL:	**1,326**	**1,249**	**1,248**	**1,209**	**1,170**	**1,284**	**2,535**	**2,419**	**2,532**

COUNTIES OF IRELAND

COUNTY ANTRIM (Province: Ulster)

LOCATION: County Antrim is set in the north-east corner of Ireland. The county could be described as a basaltic tableland. Its most remarkable feature is the Giant's Causeway, found on the north-western part of the county and designated a World Heritage Site. The causeway is made up of approximately 40,000, mostly hexagonal, basaltic columns that are packed tightly together. The columns were formed from the cooling of lava from volcanic eruptions, and solidified lava can be seen in the cliffs, 90 feet thick in places. Ancient Irish legends attributed the geological phenomenon to the giant Finn MacCool, who fell in love with a lady giant in Scotland and built the causeway for her, so that she could cross the sea to visit him. Further east along the coast can be found the Glens of Antrim; nine green river valleys which are bisected by rivers and waterfalls and full of wild flowers and birds. Their occupants are mostly descended from old Irish and Hebridean Scots, and the Glens were one of the last places in Northern Ireland where Gaelic was spoken.

HISTORY: The Antrim coast is where Ireland's first inhabitants - nomadic boatmen from Scotland - landed circa 7000 BC. The early Christians and the Vikings were also drawn to Antrim's coast. The Normans conquered the county and began building castles; John de Courcy built a huge castle in 1180 at Carrickfergus, and Richard de Burgh, the Earl of Ulster, first built Dunluce Castle, a fortification that clings on to the sea cliffs on the north. Edward Bruce, King of Scotland, landed in Larne in 1315 and besieged Carrickfergus Castle for more than a year. This established a pattern for the castle and town of Carrickfergus for the next several centuries (primarily due to the site's strategic importance at the entrance of Belfast Lough). The MacDonnells had possession of Dunluce Castle and its surrounding lands in the late 15th century, while the rest of the Armagh region was ruled over by the MacQuillans, the O'Neills and the Hebridean Scots of the Glens, indicating that Antrim was unofficially planted by the Scots long before the formal plantation of the other counties in Ulster in 1610. The Bushmill Whiskey Distillery, which is still in operation, was established at Bushmills in 1608, making it the world's oldest legal distillery. Antrim was one of the few counties in Ireland to be directly affected by the Industrial Revolution. It, along with Armagh and Monaghan, was a county of domestic linen production and consequently, was heavily populated, particularly in southern Antrim. This led to tension over occupation of land, dislocation and ultimately, the growth of Belfast as a major industrial centre with a large Protestant working class.

ORIGIN OF COUNTY NAME: Derived from the Irish 'Aontroim', meaning solitary farm.

LAND AREA: 1,093 sq. miles (County's rank in size in the island of Ireland: 9).

LARGEST CITY: Belfast.

MAIN TOWNS: Antrim, Ballymena, Ballycastle, Belfast, Carrickfergus, Larne, Lisburn, Newtownabbey.

CENSUS DETAILS: 562,216 *(estimated)*.

NUMBER OF SCHOOLS: 198 primary schools, 43 secondary schools, 4 institutes of further and higher education, 1 university.

LOCAL ADMINISTRATION: *See Public Administration Chapter.*

LOCAL RADIO STATIONS & NEWSPAPERS: *See Media Chapter.*

THEATRES & ART GALLERIES: *See Arts Chapter.*

TOP 12 TOURIST ATTRACTIONS *(by visitor numbers):* Giant's Causeway Visitor Centre (378,481 - a world Heritage Site), Carnfunnock Country Park (127,326 - contains a maze and walled garden), Old Bushmills Distillery (105,502 - world's oldest whiskey distillery), Fantasy Island, Portrush (100,000), Dunluce Centre (75,000 - gives the myths and legends of the North Antrim coast), Glenariff Forest Park (74,800 - glen walk with three waterfalls), Waterworld in Portrush (72,604), Carrick-a-rede Rope Bridge (64,077 - the famous landmark bridge linking the mainland to a rocky outcrop), Carrickfergus Castle (58,417 - initially built in 1180 by John de Courcy), Portrush Countryside Centre (45,000), Antrim Castle Gardens (38,690 - restored 17th century garden in Anglo-Dutch style), Irish Linen Centre (25,538 - recreates Ulster's Linen industry heritage with weaving workshop and looms).

FAMOUS NATIVES OF THE PAST: John Ballance (New Zealand Prime Minister 1891-1893, died 1893), Sam

Hanna Bell (writer/radio producer, born Scotland, died 1990); Sir John Biggart (pathologist / created Northern Ireland blood transfusion service, died 1973), Ernest Blythe (politician/theatre promoter, died 1975); Alexander Brown (founder of oldest investment bank in US; died 1834); Fred Daly (golfer, died 1990); Arthur Dobbs (Governor of North Carolina 1753/ Surveyor General of Ireland, born 1689); Francis Fowke (designed Belfast's Royal Albert Hall/Dublin's National Gallery, died 1865); Sir Joseph Larmour (mathematician/physicist, died 1941); Captain Terence O'Neill (politician, born London, died 1990); Archibald Hamilton Rowan (United Irishman/revolutionary, died 1834); Dean Jonathan Swift (author of *Gulliver's Travels*, has links with the county).

BELFAST CITY

LOCATION: Belfast is located in County Antrim and is the capital of Northern Ireland. It is set on the River Lagan and ringed by high hills. Belfast has an industrial tradition that dates back to the beginning of the industrial revolution, with industries such as linen manufacturing, rope making and ship building directly affecting the city's growth. It now accommodates some of Northern Ireland's leading employers and is a major education and retailing centre for the region. One-third of Northern Ireland's population lives here. Buildings of note in the city include Queen's University, the Linen Hall Library, the Botanic Gardens, the Grand Opera House and the new Waterfront Hall.

HISTORY: The area was first settled circa 1177 around an ancient fort. Its growth as a city stems from the 17th century with the arrival of English settlers and Huguenot refugees who developed linen weaving in the area. It was one of the few areas in Ireland to be directly affected by the Industrial Revolution due to its linen producing capacity, and consequently, it grew as a major industrial centre with a large Protestant working class. In the 1790s, it was plunged into the throes of agitation for Irish Independence when the Society of United Irishmen was founded by a native son - Henry Joy McCracken. However, by the end of the 19th century, the city was strongly unionist to the extent that the emerging Protestant proletariat gained economic and social ascendancy. In 1888, the borough was established as a city by charter. From this time onwards, the city became the centre of opposition to Home Rule in Ireland. After the partition of Ireland in 1920, Belfast was established as the capital of the self-governing British province of Northern Ireland, a form of governance that continued until the imposition of direct rule from London in 1972. The city was bombed during World War II and over 1,000 of its citizens lost their lives. The strife of the troubles from the 1960s onwards also served to badly scar the city, both physically and economically.

ORIGIN OF CITY NAME: Derived from the Irish 'Beal Feiriste', meaning the mouth of the Farset, a river flowing through Belfast.

LAND AREA: 25 sq. miles.

CENSUS DETAILS: 297,300.

NUMBER OF SCHOOLS: 113 primary schools, 46 secondary schools, 2 institutes of further and higher education, 3 universities, 2 teacher training colleges.

LOCAL ADMINISTRATION: *See Public Administration Chapter.*

LOCAL RADIO STATIONS & NEWSPAPERS: *See Media Chapter.*

THEATRES & ART GALLERIES: *See Arts Chapter.*

TOP 15 TOURIST ATTRACTIONS*(by visitor numbers):* Botanic Gardens (680,000 - noted for its rose gardens and herbaceous borders), Cave Hill Country Park (390,000 - as well as being the site of Neolithic caves and geological features, the United Irishmen planned 1798 Rebellion here), Belvoir Forest Park (360,000), Ulster Museum (328,823 - contains Irish antiquities, an art gallery and natural science collection), Sir Thomas & Lady Dixon Park (300,000 - the international rose trials are held in this park), Belfast Zoo (206,362 - contains a wide variety of species and includes an underwater viewing area), Malone House & Barnett Demesne (60,000 - an early 19th century house in parkland), Streamvale Open Dairy Farm (50,000), Colin Glen Forest Park (37,000 - a 200-acre park at the foot of the Black Mountain), Linenhall Library (35,000), Queen's Visitor Centre (25,500), Belfast City Hall (24,500 - completed in 1906), St Anne's Cathedral (18,800), Lagan Lookout Centre (12,412 - explains the River Lagan's weir, as well as the river's industrial and folk heritage), Craftworks Gallery (6,500).

15 MOST FAMOUS NATIVES OF THE PAST: George Birmingham (novelist, died 1950), Danny Blanchflower (international footballer/manager, died 1993), Sir James Craig (Prime Minister of Northern Ireland 1921-40, died 1940), John Dunlop (produced first pneumatic tyre, born Scotland, died 1921), Benjamin Glazer (first Irish Oscar winner 1927-28, died 1956), Edward Harland (established Harland & Wolff shipyard 1862, born Yorkshire, died 1895), Paul Henry (oil painter, died 1958), John Hewitt (poet/art critic, died 1987), Chaim Herzog (President of Israel 1983-93), Sir John Lavery (artist, died 1941), C.S. Lewis (novelist/academic/theologian, died 1963), Henry Joy McCracken (founding member of United Irishmen, died 1798), Siobhán McKenna (actress, wife of Denis O'Dea who died 1978, died 1986), Louis MacNeice (poet/dramatist/broadcaster, died 1963), Betty Sinclair (trade unionist/communist, died 1981).

COUNTY ARMAGH (Province: Ulster)

LOCATION: Set in the north-east of Ireland, Armagh is an inland county, although it is almost surrounded by water - with the River Blackwater in the west, the River Bann in the east and Lough Neagh, Ireland's largest lake, in the north. Armagh's rolling hilly terrain is due to its being part of Ireland's drumlin belt. South Armagh is home to the Ring of Gullion, with its varied mountainous topography. The gentle landscape of the north-east of the county is ideal for fruit growing, which has led Armagh to be called the Orchard County. Records reveal that apples have been grown in Armagh for more than 3,000 years. St. Patrick himself reputedly planted an apple tree at Ceangoba, an ancient settlement east of Armagh city. The Bramley apple has proven to be the easiest species to grow in the northern climate, and an orchard trust has been established by local growers to keep alive traditional orchards and old apple varieties that are currently under threat from the cheaper, more standard varieties.

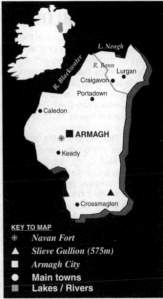

KEY TO MAP
* ✳   *Navan Fort*
* ▲   *Slieve Gullion (575m)*
* ■   *Armagh City*
* ●   Main towns
* ■   Lakes / Rivers

HISTORY: Armagh, particularly the city of Armagh, holds an important place in Irish history. Navan Fort or 'Emain Macha', two miles west of the city, was home to the kings of Ulster. Although traces of man at the site date back to 5500 BC, it is thought that Navan Fort was at its height from 700 BC. It is the focal point of the Ulster cycle in early Irish literature. This literature recounts Celtic rituals and the history of CúChulainn and the Táin. Although tradition has it that Armagh became the centre of Irish Christianity during the fifth century with the arrival of St. Patrick, in reality a collection of hagiographic writings on St. Patrick, compiled between A.D. 670 and 690, attempted to bring the primacy of the Irish church to Armagh. This attempt proved successful, and Armagh's primacy within the Irish Church was officially confirmed in 1005 by Brian Boru, the high king at that time. Armagh still retains its place as ecclesiastical capital of Ireland. During medieval times, Armagh was ruled over by the O'Neills, but was planted in 1610 along with other counties in Ulster. In 1646, Owen Roe O'Neill rose up against the settlers at the Battle of Benburb. In the centuries that followed, bloody conflicts continued between the native Irish and the Protestant settlers. The Orange Order was founded in Armagh in 1795 and united disparate Protestant groups. During the 18th century, Richard Robinson, the Church of Ireland Primate, used a large portion of his personal wealth to convert Armagh into a city of Georgian splendour, rivalling that of Dublin, and many of the city of Armagh's public buildings date to this time, including Armagh Observatory (which contains the Robinson Dome with its 10-inch telescope).

ORIGIN OF COUNTY NAME: Derived from the Irish 'Ard Macha', meaning Macha's Height and referring to the legendary queen Macha who reputedly built a fortress on top of a hill around the mid-first millennium BC.

LAND AREA: 484 sq. miles (County's rank in size in the island of Ireland: 29).

LARGEST TOWN: Armagh.

MAIN TOWNS: Portadown, Lurgan and Keady.

CENSUS DETAILS: 141,585 *(estimated).*

NUMBER OF SCHOOLS: 89 primary schools, 22 secondary schools, 2 institutes of further and higher education, 1 university.

LOCAL ADMINISTRATION: *See Public Administration Chapter.*

LOCAL RADIO STATIONS & NEWSPAPERS: *See Media Chapter.*

THEATRES & ART GALLERIES: *See Arts Chapter.*

TOP 12 TOURIST ATTRACTIONS*(by visitor numbers):* Oxford Island National Nature Reserve (155,000 - situated on Lough Neagh), Gosford Forest Park (123,700 - has associations with Dean Swift), Peatlands Country Park (90,000 - peatlands with small loughs and outdoor exhibits on peat ecology), Tannaghmore Gardens/Farm/Museum (77,000 - rose gardens, rare breeds farm and agricultural museum), St Patrick's Trian (48,327 - tells the Armagh story and an adaptation of *Gulliver's Travels*), Armagh Planetarium (47,300 - astronomical instruments and allows visitors to explore the universe with computers), Lough Neagh Discovery Centre (45,200 - wildlife, management and history of Lough Neagh), Navan Centre (40,028 - interpretive centre near the famous Navan hill fort dating back 5,000 years, home to the kings of Ulster and legends), Armagh's Palace Stables Heritage Centre (31,009 - restored Georgian stable block featuring a day in the life of the Palace), The Argory (21,176 - house dating back to 1824 overlooking the River Blackwater, has an acetylene gas lighting system), St Patrick's Cathedral (16,200 - the city's Anglican cathedral - a church has stood on this site for 1,500 years, although it has been destroyed and rebuilt over 17 times), Armagh County Museum (7,632).

FAMOUS NATIVES OF THE PAST: Frank Aiken (politician/revolutionary, died 1983), Edward Bunting (musician, died 1843), Donn Byrne (novelist reared in Armagh, died 1928), Thomas Cooley (architect, died 1784), Greer Garson (best actress Oscar winner 1942, born 1908), St. Malachy (church reformer/scholar, died 1148), Sir Robert McCarrison (medical scientist, died 1960), Tomás Ó Fiaich (Archbishop of Armagh/Primate of All Ireland, died 1990), E.J. Opik (astronomer, born Estonia, died 1985), St. Patrick (Ireland's patron saint, died 490), George Farquhar Patterson (historian/antiquarian/curator/creator of Armagh County Museum, born Canada, died 1971), George Russell (author/co-op movement promoter/economist/mystic, died 1935).

COUNTY CARLOW (Province: Leinster)

LOCATION: An inland county in the south-east of the country, Carlow is the second smallest county in Ireland and is one of the few inland counties that does not constitute part of the central plain. Carlow is bounded in the east by the granite walls of the Blackstairs Mountains and is split in three by the great rivers of the Barrow and the Slaney as they travel southwards. The Castlecomer Plateau, which Carlow shares with County Kilkenny, contains coal shale - a geological feature that has given Carlow an industrial tradition, unusual in Ireland.

HISTORY: The county's fertile land has been prized for centuries, and this factor, along with Carlow's strategic position between Kilkenny and the east coast, has contributed to the county's violent history. During early Christian times, Carlow's rich river valleys were the sites for many monastic settlements, most of which were destroyed by the Vikings. In the 14th century, Art MacMurrough Kavanagh of Borris became king of Leinster and a thorn in the side of the English armies. His attacks on the Pale were so frequent that Richard II was himself compelled to confront the chieftain with an estimated 10,000 strong expeditionary force. However, Art Oge, as he was known, inflicted defeat upon defeat on the king, giving Richard's enemies the chance to usurp the English throne. Carlow remained a stronghold of Gaelic power until after the Cromwellian plantation of the 1650s. County Carlow and County Wexford were the sites of most of the fiercest fighting in the 1798 rebellion, and more than 600 rebels were slaughtered in the county. A monument now commemorates them at Graiguecullen.

ORIGIN OF COUNTY NAME: Derived from the Irish 'Ceatharlach', meaning quadruple lake.

LAND AREA: 346 sq. miles (County's rank in size in the island of Ireland: 31).

COUNTY CAPITAL: Carlow.

MAIN TOWNS: Borris, Muinebeag, Tullow.

CENSUS DETAILS: Total population - 41,616 - a 1.6% increase since 1991.

NUMBER OF SCHOOLS: 43 primary schools, 11 secondary schools, 1 institute of technology.

LOCAL ADMINISTRATION: *See Public Administration Chapter.*

LOCAL RADIO STATIONS & NEWSPAPERS: *See Media Chapter.*

THEATRES & ART GALLERIES: *See Arts Chapter.*

TOP 12 TOURIST ATTRACTIONS: Altamount Gardens,Tullow; the Barrow Way, a tow path walk; Black Castle, one of the Ireland's earliest Norman Castles; Borris Castle, residence of the ancient rulers of Leinster; Brownshill Dolmen, believed to be the largest in Europe; Carlow Museum; the Celtic Cross, a memorial of 1798 massacre in Carlow Town; Eagle Hill, where views take in most of the county, Hacketstown; St. Lazerian's Cathedral, one of Leinster's foremost monastic houses; 'Old Derry' House and the site of the first monastery founded by St. Diarmuid, Killeshin; Royal Oak village and the Stone Fort of Rathgall, where ancient kings are believed to be buried; St Moling's Mill, a blessed well and bath house, and St Mullin's Abbey.

FAMOUS NATIVES OF THE PAST: Peter Fenlon Collier (founded first subscription publishing enterprise, emigrated to U.S. 1866; died 1909), William Dargan (constructed the first Irish railway; died 1867), Michael Farrell (physician/marathon novelist; died 1962), Samuel Haughton (scientist/mathematician/doctor, calculated drop needed for instant death by hanging; died 1897), Art Mac Murrough Kavanagh (Art Oge, King of Leinster; 14th century), Patrick Francis Moran (Australia's first Cardinal; died 1911), John Tyndall (scientist, discovered why sky is blue 1859; died 1893).

COUNTY CAVAN (Province: Ulster)

LOCATION: Cavan, the most southerly of the nine Ulster Counties, is divided into the eastern highlands, the Erne valley and the mountainous region of west Cavan. An inland county, it is bounded by six other counties. Cavan plays host to two great river systems: the Shannon, the longest river in Ireland, which rises from the Shannon Pot on the southern slopes of the Cuilcagh Mountain near Glangevlin, and the River Erne, which rises east of Lough Gowna and contains Ireland's largest heronry, based in Upper Lough Erne.

HISTORY: In the tenth century, the county formed the greater part of the ancient kingdom of Breifne (together with west Leitrim) ruled over by the Clan Uí Raghallaigh, with the O'Reillys in East Breifne and the O'Rourkes in West Breifne. In 1584, East Breifne was formed into the present county of Cavan and added to Ulster. A favourite legend is that the ancient town of Cavan lies beneath the waters of the Green Lake. Cavan was assimilated into the province of Ulster in the 17th century and subsequently settled by the English and Scottish. It was one of the three Ulster counties to be incorporated into the Irish Free State in 1921.

ORIGIN OF COUNTY NAME: Derived from the Irish 'Cabhánn', a hollow.

LAND AREA: 730 sq. miles (County's rank in size in the island of Ireland: 19).

COUNTY CAPITAL: Cavan Town.

MAIN TOWNS: Cavan, Cootehill, Bailieboro, Kingscourt, Belturbet.

CENSUS DETAILS: Total population - 52,944 - a 0.3% increase since 1991.

NUMBER OF SCHOOLS: 81 primary schools, 10 secondary schools, 1 third-level institute, 1 college of theology & philosophy.

LOCAL ADMINISTRATION: See Public Administration Chapter.

LOCAL RADIO STATIONS & NEWSPAPERS: See Media Chapter.

THEATRES & ART GALLERIES: See Arts Chapter.

TOP 12 TOURIST ATTRACTIONS: The Black Pig's Dyke (an ancient frontier fortification at Dowra), County Cavan Heritage and Genealogical Research Centre, Cavan County Museum, Cavan Crystal Factory (Ireland's second oldest glass making factory), Clough Oughter Castle, Dún a Rí Forest Park, 'Finn McCool's Fingers' (bronze age stones at Shantemon), the GAA Gallery, Killykeen Forest Park, The 'Pighouse' Folk Museum, the Shannon Pot (the source of the River Shannon), St Killian's Heritage Centre at Mullagh (has links with Wurtzburg, Germany, through St Killian).

12 MOST FAMOUS NATIVES OF THE PAST: Dr. William Bedell (first translator of Bible into Irish, died 1642), Richard Coote (Governor of New York, Massachusetts and New Hampshire, died 1701), Marcus Daly 'The Copper King' (owned mines in US, died 1900), Matthew Gibney (Bishop of Perth, Australia, died 1925), Bunda Hunt (writer; circa 1880), Sheridan Le Fanu (gothic novelist/newspaper proprietor, died 1873), John C. McQuaid (Roman Catholic Archbishop of Dublin, died 1973), Francis O'Reilly (Brother Potamian, made first medical test of the X-ray in Ireland, died 1917), John K. O'Reilly (nationalist, died 1926), Richard Brinsley Sheridan (writer/politician, died 1816), Rev. Thomas Sheridan Jr. (lexicographer/theatrical impressario/writer, died 1788), Francis Sheehy-Skeffington (socialist/writer; died 1916).

KEY TO MAP
* Source of River Shannon
▲ Cuilcagh Mtn. (667 m)
■ Cavan
● Main towns
■ Lakes / Rivers

COUNTY CLARE (Province: Munster)

LOCATION: Clare is situated on the west coast of the country and could be referred to as a peninsula; it is joined on its north-east border to Galway and bounded by Lough Derg in the east, the biggest of the River Shannon's lakes; by the Shannon estuary in the south; by the Atlantic Ocean in the west and by Galway Bay in the northwest. The county has a diverse topography, which includes the bare karst landscape of the Burren National Park, the Cliffs of Moher and the beaches of the Atlantic Coast.

HISTORY: Evidence of human habitation in Clare dates back to the Stone Age. There are around 120 dolmens and wedge tombs in the Burren National Park, the most famous being Poulnabrone Dolmen. Brian Boru, the high king of Ireland, who defeated the Vikings, had overlordship of Clare. The Normans failed to secure a permanent hold in the county, and the English did not appear in Clare until Murrough O'Brien was made Earl of Thomond in 1541. A subsequent 17th-century earl supported King Charles but reluctantly allowed Cromwell's forces to garrison at Bunratty Castle. The wars of this period ravaged the county, leaving it ruined by famine and depopulation. Although the native people were oppressed by the Penal Laws of the 18th century, they led the way towards civil and religious liberty. It was they who returned Daniel O'Connell as a Member of Parliament, which led to Catholic Emancipation in 1829, earning Clare the title of the Banner County.

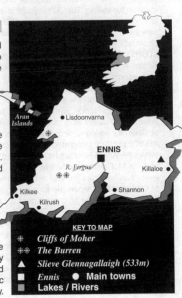

KEY TO MAP
* Cliffs of Moher
** The Burren
▲ Slieve Glennagallaigh (533m)
■ Ennis ● Main towns
■ Lakes / Rivers

However, the county fared badly during the Great Famine, and its population fell from 286,000 in 1841 to half this number in 1871.

ORIGIN OF COUNTY NAME: Derived from the Irish 'An Clár', meaning the plain.

LAND AREA: 1,262 sq. miles (County's rank in size in the island of Ireland: 7).

COUNTY CAPITAL: Ennis.

MAIN TOWNS: Ennis, Kilkee, Killaloe, Kilrush, Shannon Town.

CENSUS DETAILS: Total population - 94,006 - a 3.4% increase since '91.

NUMBER OF SCHOOLS: 124 primary schools, 19 secondary schools, 1 college of art, 1 college of hotel management.

LOCAL ADMINISTRATION: See Public Administration Chapter.

LOCAL RADIO STATIONS & NEWSPAPERS: See Media Chapter.

THEATRES & ART GALLERIES: See Arts Chapter.

TOP 12 TOURIST ATTRACTIONS: Ailwee Caves, Bunratty Castle and Folk Park, the Burren National Park, Castles (Dromoland Castle, Dunguaire Castle, Dysert O'Dea Castle and its archaeology centre, Knappogue Castle, Newtown Castle), the Cliffs of Moher, Craggaunowen Bronze Age lake dwellings, Dolphin Watch at Carrigaholt (gives observers the chance to see Ireland's only resident group of bottlenose dolphins), Ennis Friary and Ennis Museum, Kilkee Bay (rated as one of the best diving locations in Europe), Lahinch (beach, Seaworld & Leisure Centre, golf course), Lisdoonvarna (with its matchmaking festival), Poulnabrone Dolmen (possibly the most famous dolmen in Ireland).

12 MOST FAMOUS NATIVES OF THE PAST: Sir Frederick Burton (painter and director of National Gallery, London, died 1900), Willie Clancy (Irish traditional multi-instrumentalist, died 1975), Michael Cusack (founding member of GAA, died 1906), John Philip Holland (created first commercially successful submarine, died 1914), Brian Merriman (wrote 'The Midnight Court', the most translated poem in gaelic, died 1805), Pat McDonald (US Olympic medalist shot-put, 1920), Edward Anthony Edgeworth MacLysaght (genealogist/scholar, died 1986), William Mulready (painter, died 1863), William Smith O'Brien (young Ireland leader/revolutionary, died 1864), Eugene O'Curry (celebrated Irish scholar, died 1862), Michael O'Gorman (founded first medical institution in Buenos Aires, died 1819), Harriet Smithson (actress/wife of the French composer Berlioz, died 1854).

COUNTY CORK (Province: Munster)

LOCATION: Located on the south-west coast of Ireland, Cork is Ireland's largest county. Long ridges of sandstone traverse the county, and the Rivers Blackwater, Lee and Bandon flow west to east along the fertile valleys between these limestone ridges, each turning sharply southwards to empty into the sea. The Gulf Stream touches Ireland first at Cork, providing warm, mild weather that ensures lush growth in the county's fertile farmlands. Little bays and harbours are indented all along the county's 680-miles long coastline (one-fifth of the national coastline), making Cork an ideal location for sailing. The oldest yacht club in the world is based in Cork at Crosshaven and dates back to 1720, and Ireland's only cable car service is in Cork, linking Dursey Island with the mainland at Beara peninsula.

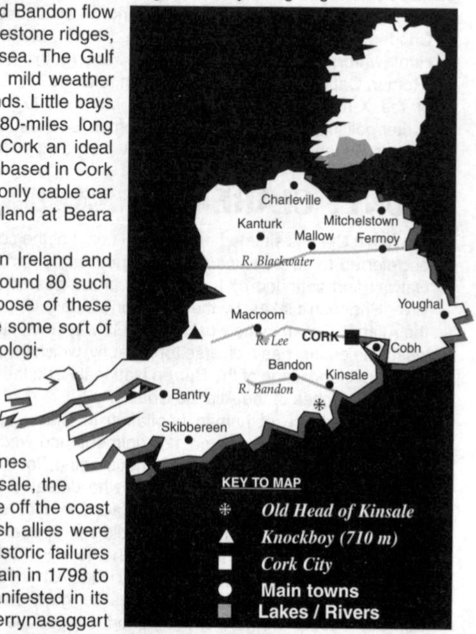

HISTORY: The heaviest concentration of stone circles in Ireland and Britain is to be found in the south-west region, with around 80 such monuments located in the Cork-Kerry area. The purpose of these ancient rings remains a mystery. It is certain they have some sort of ritualistic associations and could possibly have an astrological purpose. Cork's early Christian history centres around St. Finbarr who founded a church in the area of Cork city. Viking raiders attacked the region around AD 820 but later integrated with the local population. When the Anglo-Norman force attacked in 1172, the Danes and the McCarthy clan had to submit. The Battle of Kinsale, the event that heralded the end of Gaelic Ireland, took place off the coast of Cork in 1601, when the Irish along with their Spanish allies were defeated. Cork was also prominent in two other Irish historic failures - when the French entered Bantry Bay in 1689 and again in 1798 to aid the Irish. Cork's attachment to its Irish culture is manifested in its Gaeltacht region, an Irish speaking area near the Derrynasaggart Mountains. The county played a prominent role in all struggles for Independence, and Michael Collins, Ireland's best known revolutionary, came from Cork. Today, Cork is an established major tourist location (particularly West Cork) and an industrial location, with a wide range of small, indigenous companies and overseas-owned companies, including Apple Computers and Pfizer, which has established itself as a great success with its discovery and production of the drug, Viagra.

Map labels: Charleville, Kanturk, Mitchelstown, Mallow, Fermoy, R. Blackwater, Youghal, Macroom, R. Lee, CORK, Cobh, Bandon, Kinsale, Bantry, R. Bandon, Skibbereen

KEY TO MAP

* *Old Head of Kinsale*
▲ *Knockboy (710 m)*
■ *Cork City*
● **Main towns**
■ **Lakes / Rivers**

ORIGIN OF COUNTY NAME: Derived from the Irish 'Corcaigh', meaning marsh and referring to the swampy estuary of the River Lee upon which the city of Cork was founded.
LAND AREA: 2,878 sq. miles (County's rank in size in the island of Ireland: 1).
COUNTY CAPITAL: Cork City.
MAIN TOWNS: Bantry, Clonakilty, Cobh, Cork, Fermoy, Kinsale, Mallow, Mitchelstown, Skibbereen, Youghal.
CENSUS DETAILS: Total population - 293,323 (excluding Cork City) - a 3.6% increase since 1991.
NUMBER OF SCHOOLS: 311 primary schools, 63 secondary schools.
LOCAL ADMINISTRATION: See Public Administration Chapter.
LOCAL RADIO STATIONS & NEWSPAPERS: See Media Chapter.
THEATRES & ART GALLERIES: See Arts Chapter.
TOP 12 TOURIST ATTRACTIONS: Bantry House, Castles (Blarney Castle and the Blarney stone, Castle Curious - a folly tower, Desmond Castle, Dunmanus Castle, Roche Castle, Timoleague Abbey and Castle Gardens), Fota Wildlife Park, Gougane Barra National Park, Islands (Dursey Island, Garinish Island, Sherkin Island), Kinsale Town, Labbacallee (a huge prehistoric monument), Midleton (the home of Jameson Whiskey), the Queenstown Story (an exhibition that tells how Cobh was the embarkation point for many thousands of Irish emigrants), the Royal Gunpowder Mills in Ballincollig) Schull Planetarium, the West Cork Museum (contains many mementos of Michael Collins).
12 MOST FAMOUS NATIVES OF THE PAST: Leonara Barry (U.S. labour leader, born 1849), Ann Bonny (Caribbean female pirate, born 1700), Robert Boyle (chemist/physicist, died 1691), Francis Browne (Jesuit priest/photographer - famous for his photographs of the Titanic, died 1960), Michael Collins (revolutionary and statesman, died 1922), Thomas W. Croke (Roman Catholic Archbishop of Cashel/GAA patron, died 1902), Thomas Davies (Young Irelander/poet, died 1845), Jack Doyle (boxer/vaudeville artist, died 1978), Aloys Fleischmann (composer/teacher/author, born Munich, died 1992), John Holland (inventor of submarines, died 1914), Richard Hennessy (founded Hennessy Brandy Distillery in France in 1763, died 1800), Hugh Lane (art collector, died 1915), Sam Maguire (footballer, after whom the All-Ireland GAA cup is named, died 1927), Dr. Pat O'Callaghan (first Irish Olympic gold medalist, born 1905), Jeremiah O'Donovan Rossa (Fenian, 1915), Edel Quinn (Legion of Mary envoy to East Africa, died 1944), Christy Ring (hurler, died 1979), Edmund Spencer (late 16th century poet, 'The Faerie Queene'), Esmé Stuart Lennox Robinson (playwright, died 1958).

CORK CITY

LOCATION: Cork City, Ireland's third city after Dublin and Belfast, was established on the River Lee and gradually ascended up the steep banks of the river. The city can claim a distinct heritage, which stems from its origins as an important seaport. Indeed some of the Cork's main streets are built over channels where ships docked centuries ago.
HISTORY: The city began as a monastic site, founded by St. Finbarr in the sixth century. The settlement was raided by the Vikings and the Normans, but survived and thrived. Cork, and Cork City in particular, maintained its reputation for resistance and autonomy and came to be called 'Rebel Cork'. The city's reputation for stubborn resistance to the English overlords resulted from it being the base of the 19th-century Fenian movement and playing a pivotal role in the Irish struggle for independence.
ORIGIN OF COUNTY NAME: See County Cork.
LAND AREA: 15.5 sq. miles.
CENSUS DETAILS: Total population - 127,187 - a 0.1% decrease since 1991.
NUMBER OF SCHOOLS: 64 primary schools, 30 secondary schools, 1 university, 1 college, 1 school of music, 1 school of art and design,1 Institute of Technology.
LOCAL ADMINISTRATION: See Public Administration Chapter.
LOCAL RADIO STATIONS & NEWSPAPERS: See Media Chapter.
THEATRES & ART GALLERIES: See Arts Chapter.
MAJOR TOURIST ATTRACTIONS: Bishop Lucey Park; the Coal Quay, (an open air market steeped in Cork's folk culture); the Cork Heritage Park, Blackrock; Cork Opera House; the Crawford Municipal Art Gallery, (houses a fine sculpture collection, including some Rodins); the monument to Fr. Theobald Matthew, (a 19th-century temperance advocate); the Old English Market in Grand Parade; the old gaol in Sunday's Well; the riverside quadrangle at University College Cork; Shandon Church, (with its famous bells, clock and weathervane); St. Finbarr's Cathedral; St. Mary's Cathedral, (with its notable carvings);Triskel Arts Centre, Tobin Street.
TOP 10 TOURIST ATTRACTIONS: the Berwick Fountain (a monument to Irish patriots), Bishop Lucey Park, the Coal Quay (an open air market steeped in Cork's folk culture), the Cork Heritage Park, Blackrock, the monument to Fr. Theobald Matthew (a 19th-century temperance advocate), the Old English Market in Grand Parade, the old gaol in Sunday's Well, Patrick's Hill, the riverside quadrangle at University College Cork, Shandon Church (with its famous bells, clock and weathervane), St. Finbarr's Cathedral, St. Mary's Cathedral (with its notable carvings).
12 MOST FAMOUS NATIVES OF THE PAST: James Barry (artist who found fame for his mythical and historical scenes, b. 1741), Edward Hallran Bennett (diagnosed 'Bennett's fracture,' died 1907), George Boole (mathematician who first proposed 'Boolean Algebra,' died 1864), Richard Church (Liberator of Greece, died 1873), Frank Gallagher (first editor of Irish Press newspaper, died 1962), Tomas MacCurtain (Lord Mayor of Cork, assassinated 1920 allegedly by Crown forces), Terence MacSwiney (revolutionary, died 1920), Havelock Nelson (conductor/ composer, died 1996), Frank O'Connor (short story writer/novelist/translator, died 1966), Seán O'Faolain (short story writer/novelist, died 1991), Seán Ó Riada (arranger/composer/musician, died 1971),

George Salmon (mathematician/theologian, died 1904).

COUNTY DERRY (Province: Ulster)

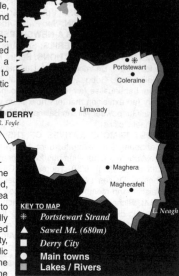

KEY TO MAP
- ✳ **Portstewart Strand**
- ▲ **Sawel Mt. (680m)**
- ■ **Derry City**
- ● **Main towns**
- ■ **Lakes / Rivers**

LOCATION: County Derry is situated on the north-west coast of Northern Ireland. It has a hilly terrain particularly in the south-west where the Sperrin Mountains are found. It is bordered on the west by the River Foyle, which flows into Lough Foyle, on the north by the Atlantic Ocean, on the east by County Antrim and on the south by County Tyrone and Lough Neagh.

HISTORY: The county's early Christian history is dominated by St. Columba, who died in 597 and who successfully advanced Christianity in both his native land and Scotland. He established a monastery in Derry 546, out of which Derry city grew, and went on to establish a large family of churches around Scotland's Atlantic seaboard. The O'Neills held sway over much of the county around the middle ages, although Richard de Burgh the 'Red Earl' of Ulster took control of the little port of Derry with a view to developing it as a stronghold at the beginning of the 14th century. However, he was defeated in battle by Edward Bruce in 1315 and lost control of Ulster for a time. The O'Neills assumed power during the 14th century and shared this power in Derry county with the O'Donnells and the O'Cahans in the 15th century. After the defeat of the native Irish at the Battle of Kinsale, Derry was selected, along with the rest of Ulster, to be planted in 1610. Most of the area included in the current County Derry was known as Coleraine prior to the plantation. Following the plantation, the area was formally assigned county status in 1613 and, along with the city, was renamed Londonderry after the intervention of the London-based society, which rebuilt the city after it was sacked. In 1641, the old Catholic landowners rose against the new Protestant planters in Ulster, but the rising was crushed by Cromwell when he arrived in 1649. During the Jacobite/Williamite war, many of the county's planter population sought refuge in Derry, which came under siege in 1689. The Williamites broke the siege, and the planters retained control of the county.

ORIGIN OF COUNTY NAME: Derived from the Irish 'Doire', meaning Oak Grove.

LAND AREA: 798 sq. miles (County's rank in size in the island of Ireland: 15).

LARGEST TOWN: Derry.

MAIN TOWNS: Coleraine, Derry, Dungiven, Limavady, Maghera, Magherafelt, Portstewart.

CENSUS DETAILS: 213,035 *(estimated)*.

NUMBER OF SCHOOLS: 72 primary schools, 23 secondary schools, 2 institutes of further and higher education.

LOCAL ADMINISTRATION: *See Public Administration Chapter.*

LOCAL RADIO STATIONS & NEWSPAPERS: *See Media Chapter.*

THEATRES & ART GALLERIES: *See Arts Chapter.*

TOP 12 TOURIST ATTRACTIONS*(by visitor numbers):* Portstewart Strand (133,080 - popular beach with over 2 miles of strand), Roe Valley Country Park (126,000 - contains riverside walks, Ulster's first domestic hydro-electric station and ruined linen water mills), Ness Wood Country Park (20,000 - woodland walks), Earhart Centre (11,000 - exhibition on Amelia Earhart, the first woman to fly the Atlantic solo and who finished her journey here), Bellaghy Bawn (2,905 - a restored fortified house dating back to 1618 and used in the writings of Bellaghy-born poet, Seamus Heaney), Plantation of Ulster Visitor Centre (1,921 - tells the story of the plantation of Ulster, including the Flight of the Earls), Garvagh Museum & Heritage Centre (850 - Stone Age artifacts and eel fishery), Mussenden Temple (situated on the cliffs at Downhill, built as a library by the eccentric earl-bishop of Derry in 1783), Mountsandel Fort (near the site of Ireland's oldest house, inhabited 9,000 years ago), the Wilson Daffodil Garden (a rare collection of Irish-bred daffodils and other narcissi in memory of daffodil breeder Guy Wilson), Downhill Castle (the palace ruins of the Earl-Bishop of Derry), Dungiven Priory and O'Cahan's Tomb (the tomb of an O'Cahan who died in 1385).

12 MOST FAMOUS NATIVES OF THE PAST: Liam Ball (international swimmer), Miciaih Browning (responsible for breaking 'the Boom' that ended The Siege of Derry 1689, died 1689), Willie Carson (photographer, died 1996), Henry Cooke (Presbyterian General Assembly Moderator 1862, died 1868), Fay Coyle (international footballer), George Farquhar (playwright, died 1707), William Hare (notorious murderer, died 1860), John Glendy (United Irishman/Commodore in US Navy, died 1832), Robert Lundy (Governor of Derry at time of Jacobite siege), James McCafferty (musician/choir master/musical director, died 1995), Norah McGuinness (painter, died 1980), William Scott (founded Derry shirt Industry 1831, born 1755).

DERRY CITY

LOCATION: Derry city is Northern Ireland's second largest city and the capital of the north-west region. The River Foyle effectively divides the city in two - the Waterside and the Cityside - the latter, containing the walls of Derry, built in the 17th century.

HISTORY: The city's existence can be traced back to pagan times when Calgach, a warrior, made his camp on the 'island' of Derry. St. Columb founded his first monastery in 546 in the vicinity. In 1164, the first bishop of Derry built a cathedral in the city near the monastic site, and Derry came to be known as Doire Columcille, in honour of St. Columb. During Norman times, the city was ruled over by the de Burgos, the earls of Ulster. The first defensive fortifications around the city were built by the English in 1566. These were breached in 1608 when Derry was sacked by Cahir O'Doherty. He was subsequently killed in Donegal and the rebellion he incited died. The city of London sent master builders and money between 1614 and 1619 to rebuild the ruined medieval city and construct its famous walls. During the 17th century, Derry endured a number of sieges - those of 1641, 1649 and the Great Siege of 1689, when the apprentice boys locked out the invading Jacobite forces. It was 105 days later that relief came when the Williamites broke the boom across the river. In the 18th century, Derry's reputation as a major port grew from the numbers embarking from its docks to emigrate from the county. Its industrial base in the 19th century as a centre for ship building and shirt manufacturing confirmed its status as an important trading port. During World War II, the city was one of the major naval bases for the Allied troops during the Battle of the Atlantic. Derry became a focal point for conflict during the troubles which started in 1969; it was the site of 'Bloody Sunday' in January 1972, when 13 civilians were shot dead by British army paratroopers during a civil rights march. One man died later from his injuries. Derry has been rejuvenated in recent years with major new building developments and community initiatives, but it still remains an unemployment black spot in Northern Ireland.

ORIGIN OF CITY NAME: See County Derry (the prefix London was added in 1613 when the city's second charter of incorporation changed its name to Londonderry).

LAND AREA: 3.4 sq. miles.

CENSUS DETAILS: 101,200.

NUMBER OF SCHOOLS: 8 nursery schools, 48 primary schools, 14 secondary schools, 1 college of further education, 1 university.

LOCAL ADMINISTRATION: *See Public Administration Chapter.*

LOCAL RADIO STATIONS & NEWSPAPERS: *See Media Chapter.*

THEATRES & ART GALLERIES: *See Arts Chapter.*

TOP 12 TOURIST ATTRACTIONS *(by visitor numbers):* St. Columb's Cathedral (31,954 - dating back to 1633, it was the first Protestant cathedral to be built after the Reformation; its stained glass windows depict scenes from the 1688/9 siege), Tower Museum, Derry (21,527 - a multi-award winning museum; its tunnels date from the 17th century), Guildhall (13,000 - built in 1890, it is the seat of local government in Derry), Foyle Valley Railway Museum (9,002 - tells of the narrow gauge railway that carried the Donegal, Londonderry and Lough Swilly railways), Harbour Museum (1,000 - narrates Derry's maritime history; contains a replica of St Columba's curragh in which he sailed to Iona in 563 AD), Derry's city walls and gates (the only intact city walls on the island of Ireland, these were built between 1613 and 1618), the Calgach Centre (on Butcher Street, contains a heritage library and genealogy centre), The Fifth Province (a interpretive centre that brings to life the history of the Celts), St. Eugene's Cathedral (dates back to 1873), the craft village (a centre for arts, crafts and design shops), Derry's murals and monuments, the Bloody Sunday memorial in the Bogside.

12 MOST FAMOUS NATIVES OF THE PAST: Liam Ball (international swimmer), Miciaih Browning (responsible for breaking 'the Boom' that ended The Siege of Derry 1689; died 1689), Willie Carson (photographer; died 1996), Henry Cooke (Presbyterian General Assembly Moderator 1862; died 1868), Fay Coyle (international footballer), George Farquhar (playwright; died 1707), William Hare (notorious murderer; died 1860), John Glendy (United Irishman/Commodore in U.S. Navy; died 1832), Robert Lundy (Governor of Derry at time of Jacobite siege), James McCafferty (musician/choir master/musical director; died 1995), Norah McGuinness (painter; died 1980), William Scott (founded Derry shirt Industry 1831; born 1755).

COUNTY DONEGAL (Province: Ulster)

LOCATION: Donegal can be found on the north-west seaboard of the country. Containing more beaches than any other county, Donegal's dramatic coastline includes the highest sea cliffs in Europe at Slieve League, with the cliff face at Bunglas towering more than 606 m above the ocean. Ireland's most northerly point - Malin Head - is located on the north coast of the county, on the Inishowen peninsula. Inland, the county's mountains and secluded glens are cast in an ever changing light, resulting from the sudden weather changes swept in by the Atlantic Ocean.

HISTORY: The inaccessibility of Donegal's highlands assisted in preserving its ancient Celtic culture and language and in remaining the last county to be taken over by the English - Cahir O'Doherty was the last chieftain in Ireland to be defeated in 1608. Donegal has numerous historical sites, including dolmens, souterrains, and 40 Bronze Age cairns. The most famous of these sites is the Grianan of Aileach, an ancient fortress and sun temple. Donegal's rich early Christian history centres around St. Column Cille (Columba of Iona) who gave his name to Glencolumkille and founded Derry.

ORIGIN OF COUNTY NAME: Derived from the Irish 'Dún na nGall', meaning the fort of the foreigners.

LAND AREA: 1,876 sq. miles (County's rank in size in the island of Ireland: 4).

COUNTY CAPITAL: Lifford.

MAIN TOWNS: Ballybofey, Ballyshannon, Buncrana, Bundoran, Carndonagh, Dungloe, Letterkenny, Lifford, Moville.

CENSUS DETAILS: Total population - 129,944 - a 1.5% increase since 1991.

NUMBER OF SCHOOLS: 180 primary schools, 24 secondary schools, 1 institute of technology, 1 tourism college.

LOCAL ADMINISTRATION: *See Public Administration Chapter.*

LOCAL RADIO STATIONS & NEWSPAPERS: *See Media Chapter.*

THEATRES & ART GALLERIES: *See Arts Chapter.*

TOP 12 TOURIST ATTRACTIONS: Ards Forest Park in Creeslough, the High Cross at Carndonagh (believed to be the oldest in Ireland), Donegal Castle (Donegal town), Donegal Railway Heritage Centre (tells the story of the Co. Donegal Railway, now defunct), Dunree Military Fort, Flight of the Earls Centre in Rathmullan, The Folk Village and Museum in Glencolumbkille, Glenveagh National Park, Grianan of Aileach, ancient fortress and sun temple, Lakeside Centre at Dunlewy, Lough Derg (known as St. Patrick's Purgatory where only pilgrims are allowed access), Slieve League (the location of Europe's highest sea cliffs).

12 MOST FAMOUS NATIVES OF THE PAST: William Allingham (poet, died 1889), Neil Blaney (politician, died 1995), Isaac Butt (leader of Irish parliamentary Party/founded Home Rule Movement, son of Donegal father, died 1879), St Columb Cille (patron saint/Scottish missionary, died 597), Patrick 'The Cope' Gallagher (promoter of the rural co-op, died 1964), Rory Gallagher (rock musician, 1970s), Ray McAnally (actor, died 1989), Patrick MacGill (author/poet, died 1963), Seosamh MacGrianna (novelist/short story writer, died 1990), Michael O'Cleary (chief scribe of historic Annals of the Four Masters, born 1575), Sir Cahir O'Doherty (the last Irish Chieftain, died 1608), Red Hugh O'Donnell (led Irish in Nine Years War, died 1602).

KEY TO MAP
* ✳ *Bunglas Sea Cliff (606m)*
* ▲ *Errigal Mt. (752m)*
* ■ *Lifford*   ● **Main towns**
* ■ **Lakes / Rivers**

COUNTY DOWN (Province: Ulster)

LOCATION: Down is situated on the north-east coast of Ireland and is bounded on three sides by water with more than 200 miles of coastline; the Irish Sea lies in the east, Belfast Lough in the north and Carlingford Lough in the south. The Mourne Mountains cover the southern part of the county. In the north-west lies the city of Belfast, with its industry and commerce, while in the east, the Ards Peninsula curves around to protect the waters of Strangford Lough, designated Northern Ireland's premier marine nature reserve, due to its marine wildlife, which is among the richest in Europe.

HISTORY: Humans have lived around the county's coast for around 9,000 years, and many ancient tales from the Ulster cycle are set in this region. St. Comgall founded a monastery in Bangor in A.D. 558, and monks from the monastery set sail to spread Christianity throughout Europe. The importance of this site in the Dark Ages was such that Bangor features on the famous Mappa Mundi, while London does not. John de Courcy, the Norman who gained control of east Ulster in the 12th century, pledged to bring the remains of Saints Patrick, Brigid and Columbanus to Bangor. Some believe that this pledge was based on the debt the Normans owed the Irish for keeping the Christian faith alive during the Dark Ages. The monastery was revived by St. Malachy in the 12th century but by 1469 was once more in ruins due to the dissolution of the Irish monasteries in the 1540s. The monastic lands were taken over by the O'Neills of Clandeboye and remained in their domain until they were divided by King James I between Hugh Montgomery and James Hamilton. As this shows, the lands in parts of Down were already in Scottish or English hands before the plantation of the rest of Ulster in 1610. During the 18th century, the coast from Newcastle to Greencastle became notorious for smuggling, and merchandise disappeared via mountainous trails, such as the Brandy Pad.

ORIGIN OF COUNTY NAME: Derived from the Irish 'an Dún', meaning Fort.

LAND AREA: 945 sq. miles (County's rank in size in the island of Ireland: 12).

LARGEST TOWN: Newtownards.

MAIN TOWNS: Ballynahinch, Bangor, Banbridge, Castlewellan, Donaghadee, Downpatrick, Dromore, Hillsborough,

KEY TO MAP
* ✳ *Strangford Lough (Marine Reserve)*
* ▲ *Slieve Donard (852m)*
* ■ *Bangor*
* ● **Main towns**
* ■ **Lakes / Rivers**

Holywood, Kilkeel, Newcastle, Newry, Newtownards, Portaferry.
CENSUS DETAILS: 454,411 *(estimated).*
NUMBER OF SCHOOLS: 191 primary schools, 46 secondary schools, 3 institutes of further and higher education.
LOCAL ADMINISTRATION: *See Public Administration Chapter.*
LOCAL RADIO STATIONS & NEWSPAPERS: *See Media Chapter.*
THEATRES & ART GALLERIES: *See Arts Chapter.*
TOP 12 TOURIST ATTRACTIONS *(by visitor numbers):* Pickie Family Fun Park (250,000), Tollymore Forest Park (203,800 - contains several stone follies and bridge, a giant sequoia tree and wildlife exhibits), Ulster Folk & Transport Museum (203,501), Scrabo Country Park (200,000), Castlewellan Forest Park (140,000), Murlough National Nature Reserve (134,000 - sand dune system with heath and woodland), Exploris (130,000 - an aquarium in Portaferry with thousands of species), Delamont Country Park (103,600 - a restored walled garden, heronry with hide and walks), Kilbroney Park, Rostrevor (100,000), Newry Arts Centre (75,000), Silent Valley, Kilkeel (70,497 - beautiful parkland and huge water reservoirs), Redburn Country Park (50,000).
FAMOUS NATIVES OF THE PAST: Thomas Andrews (chief designer of Titanic, died 1912), Patrick Brontë (father of novelists Anne, Charlotte and Emily Brontë, born 1777), Francis Rawdon Chesney ('father of Suez Canal', died 1872), St Columbanus of Luxeuil (established missions in France/Switzerland, died 615), Captain Francis Crozier (arctic explorer/discovered the North West Passage, 1796-1848), Lord Faulkner (Prime Minister of Northern Ireland 1971-72, died 1977), Harry Ferguson (engineer/inventor/built first Irish aeroplane 1909/invented tractors, died 1960), James Martin (invented aircraft ejector seat, died 1981), Sir Joshua Reynolds (portrait artist, died 1792), Sir Hans Sloane (naturalist/physician/founded British Museum in 1759, died 1753), John Butler Yeats (artist/essayist/father of W B Yeats, died 1922).

COUNTY DUBLIN (Province: Leinster)

LOCATION: County Dublin is located on the east coast of Ireland at the edge of the Irish Sea. It could be described, in geological terms, as the seaward extension of the central limestone plain lying to the west. The Liffey, the Dodder and the Tolka are its main rivers, and the county is bounded by granite mountains in the south and rich pastureland, bordered by river estuaries and a long sandy coast, in the north. The city dominates the county, having gradually subsumed many of the county's villages within its parameters. Roughly one-third of the Republic of Ireland's population now live in the Dublin region.

HISTORY: Dublin county had a strong early Christian presence; there are well-preserved round towers in Clondalkin and Swords, and monastic ruins can be found at Lusk, Tallaght, Newcastle and Saggart. The Vikings established a major settlement in Dublin, as reflected in town names such as Howth, but were finally defeated by Brian Boru at the Battle of Clontarf in Dublin on Good Friday, 1014. The county was part of the English Pale from the 12th to the 16th century. Its English past is reflected in the many stately homes and gardens and the model villages found throughout the county. However, Dublin has always been a hotbed of Irish political activity - the Easter 1916 Rising occurred here and paved the way for Irish Independence - and it was in Dublin that most Irish literary and artistic movements began and flourished.

ORIGIN OF COUNTY NAME: Derived from the Irish 'Dubh Linn', meaning black pool. The Irish for Dublin - Baile Átha Cliath - is translated as the town of the hurdle ford, which refers to barriers placed to prevent the Liffey flooding.

LAND AREA: 49 sq. miles *(Dun Laoghaire/Rathdown),* 173 sq. miles *(Fingal),* 86 sq. miles *(South Dublin)* (County's rank in size in the island of Ireland: 27).

COUNTY CAPITAL: *Dun Laoghaire/Rathdown* - Dun Laoghaire; *Fingal* - Dublin; *South Dublin* - Tallaght.

MAIN TOWNS: *Dun Laoghaire/Rathdown* - Blackrock, Dalkey, Dundrum, Dun Laoghaire, Shankhill and Stillorgan; *Fingal* - Balbriggan, Blanchardstown, Malahide, Skerries and Swords; *South Dublin* - Brittas, Clondalkin, Greenhills, Killakee, Lucan, Rathcoole, Rathfarnham, Saggart, Tallaght, Terenure.

KEY TO MAP
✳ *Phoenix Park*
▲ *Kippure Mountain (752m)*
■ *Dublin City*
● Main towns
■ Lakes / Rivers

CENSUS DETAILS: 189,999 - a 2.5% increase since 1991 *(Dun Laoghaire/Rathdown);* 167,683 - a 9.8% increase since 1991 *(Fingal);* 218,728 - a 4.8% increase since 1991 *(South Dublin).*
NUMBER OF SCHOOLS: 78 primary schools, 47 secondary schools, 1 college of art & design, 1 college of education, 1 university, 1 college of theology and philosophy, 2 Montessori colleges *(Dun Laoghaire/Rathdown).* 77

primary schools, 23 secondary schools, 1 institute of education, 2 colleges of education, 1 university, 2 colleges of theology and philosophy *(Fingal)*. 91 primary schools, 30 secondary schools, 1 Institute of Technology, 1 college of theology and philosophy*(South Dublin)*.

LOCAL ADMINISTRATION: *See Public Administration Chapter.*

LOCAL RADIO STATIONS & NEWSPAPERS: *See Media Chapter.*

THEATRES & ART GALLERIES: *See Arts Chapter.*

MAJOR TOURIST ATTRACTIONS: *Dun Laoghaire/Rathdown:* Dalkey Castle and Heritage Centre, Marlay Park & Craft Centre (Marlay House currently being renovated), Cabinteely House & Park, Leopardstown Racecourse, Booterstown Salt Marsh, Fernhill private gardens in Sandyford, The Old Oratory of the Sacred Heart Convent in Dun Laoghaire, The Dublin Mountains, Dun Laoghaire (the site of Ireland's first railway in 1831 and the National Maritime Museum of Ireland), the James Joyce Museum at Sandycove Martello Tower; Killiney Hill, Lambert Puppet Theatre & Museum in Monkstown. *Fingal:* Botanical Gardens in Glasnevin, Dunsink Observatory, Howth Head and Peninsula (provides a panoramic view of Dublin Bay), Howth Castle Gardens (boasts over 2,000 rhododendron varieties), Lambay Island (a noted bird sanctuary), Lusk Heritage Centre, Malahide Castle and the Fry Model Railway Museum, Marino Casino (a small folly house built in the 18th century), Marino Crescent (birthplace of Bram Stoker, the author of *Dracula)*, Newbridge House (an important 18th-century Georgian mansion in Donabate), Portrane House (once the home of Esther Johnson - Jonathan Swift's lover), Rush and Skerries seaside resorts. *South Dublin:* Corkagh Regional Park (Clondalkin), Dodder Valley Linear Park (Firhouse), Griffeen Valley Park (Lucan), Montpelier Hill (the location of the Hell Fire Club, where the first Earl of Rosse conducted Satanic rites with his friends in the 18th century), Rathfarnham Castle, Sean Walsh Memorial Park, Tymon Regional Park (Greenhills), Camac Valley Tourist Caravan and Camping Park, Grange Castle (Kilcarbery), the Dublin Mountains.

FAMOUS NATIVES OF THE PAST: Michael Balfe (opera composer, died 1870), Lucien Ball (inventor/pioneer of early cinematography, died 1972), Samuel Beckett (playwright, died 1989), Brian Boydell (composer/conductor, born 1917), Seán Lemass (politician/revolutionary, died 1971), Sr Catherine McAuley (founded Sisters of Mercy 1831, died 1841), Micheál O'Hehir (broadcaster/sports commentator, died 1996), Seán T. O'Kelly (President of Ireland 1945-59, died 1966), William Orpen (artist, died 1931), Patrick Pearse (revolutionary/writer/educationalist, died 1916), Bram Stoker (author of Dracula, died 1912).

DUBLIN CITY

LOCATION: Set in Dublin Bay at the confluence of the Liffey, Dodder, Poddle and Tolka Rivers, Dublin is the centre of Irish political, economic, social and cultural activity. The Liffey divides the city into two sides, the north side and the south side, a division that is as much social and economic as it is geographical. The city's architecture, although currently under threat from the many building developments that are taking place, reveals the wealth of Dublin's past, from its Viking underpinnings, its medieval lanes, its elegant Georgian Squares and the contemporary feel of the city's cultural quarter in the Temple Bar.

HISTORY: As with all of Ireland's major towns and cities, Dublin has had a tumultuous past. Evidence of human habitation appears to date back millennia. King Conor MacNessa gave the town a name - the town of the hurdle ford - when he built a ford to prevent flooding from the Liffey. The Vikings later sailed up the river, attacking monastic sites and establishing a settlement, the remains of which have been excavated at Wood Quay. The Vikings were defeated by Brian Boru at Clontarf in 1014 and subsequently integrated with the native Irish. By the time the Normans attacked, city walls had been built but were not strong enough to hold back Strongbow. The Normans took over Dublin, and an era of 700 years of foreign control began.

In the 18th century, the town was molded into a Georgian City, making it one of the most elegant and cosmopolitan cities of its day. Handel first performed the Messiah in Dublin in 1742. Dublin's reign as an English cosmopolitan centre ended in 1800 with the Act of Union, when Dublin ceased to be a political force. The 19th century saw increasing pressure to bring about Home Rule. This culminated in the 1916 Rising in Dublin, during which British gun boats sailed up the Liffey and bombed the city, and the War of Independence in 1921. These conflicts, along with the internecine turmoil that followed independence, left Dublin badly damaged. The city changed very little until the 1960s, when moves were made to address the conditions of the people who lived in Dublin's inner city tenements. The economic boom of the 1960s resulted in many changes for Dublin. Today it is the heart of Ireland's Celtic tiger, leading the way economically and culturally.

ORIGIN OF COUNTY NAME: *See County Dublin.*

LAND AREA: 44.5 sq. miles.

CENSUS DETAILS: Total population - 481,854 - 0.7% increase since 1991.

NUMBER OF SCHOOLS: 228 primary schools, 96 secondary schools, 1 university, 1 college of art & design, 1 institute of technology, 1 college of industrial relations, 1 college of education.

LOCAL ADMINISTRATION: *See Public Administration Chapter.*

LOCAL RADIO STATIONS & NEWSPAPERS: *See Media Chapter.*

THEATRES & ART GALLERIES: *See Arts Chapter.*

TOP 15 TOURIST ATTRACTIONS: the Brazen Head (Ireland's oldest pub), Churches & Cathedrals (including Christ Church Cathedral - built in 1038 by the Danish King Sitric of Dublin - St. Audoen's Church - one of Ireland's oldest surviving medieval parish churches - St. Michan's Church, St. Patrick's Cathedral), Dublin Castle (containing magnificent state apartments and the Chester Beatty Library), Dublinia (a permanent multi-media exhibition on Dublin's past), Dublin Writers Museum in Parnell Square, Dublin Zoo in Phoenix Park, the General Post

Office (where bullet holes from the 1916 Rising can still be seen), the Guinness Brewery, Kilmainham Gaol (where Ireland's revolutionaries were held and executed in 1916), the National Library, the National Museum of Ireland, the Natural History Museum, Phoenix Park (the biggest urban park in Europe), Trinity College (Ireland's oldest university and home to the Book of Kells), Waterways Visitor Centre on Grand Canal Quay.

MOST FAMOUS NATIVES OF THE PAST: Eamonn Andrews (broadcaster, died 1987), Sir Francis Bacon (artist, died 1992), Brendan Behan (author/poet/playwright, died 1964), Christy Brown (poet/novelist, *My Left Foot*, died 1981), Robert Emmet (United Irishman, died 1803), James Joyce (one of Ireland's foremost writers, 1882-1941), Phil Lynott (rock musician, died 1986), Sean O'Casey (playwright/prose writer, died 1964), Noel Purcell (actor, died 1985), George Bernard Shaw (playwright/polemicist, died 1950), Oliver St. John Gogarty (surgeon/poet/writer, died 1957), Jonathan Swift (political pamphleteer, died 1745), Katherine Tynan (poet/novelist/essayist, died 1931), Oscar Wilde (playwright/writer, died 1900).

COUNTY FERMANAGH (Province: Ulster)

LOCATION: Fermanagh is an inland county in the north-west of the island. The length of the county is spanned by the Erne River and Lake system, which stretches southwards for 50 miles. The system has recently been joined to the River Shannon via the Shannon-Erne Waterway. Both systems were previously linked by a canal, constructed in 1860. However, it closed to commercial traffic after nine years with the arrival of steam and railways. The county is also home to the extensive Marble Arch cave system, which can be navigated by boat during the drier seasons.

HISTORY: Fermanagh's ancient Celtic and early Christian heritage is revealed on the islands of its lakes and the Burren area near Belcoo, an area rich in archaeological monuments, such as portal tombs, wedge tombs and a court tomb. On Boa Island, there are two Celtic Janus (two-faced) statues, possibly dating from the first century; White Island is home to seven enigmatic statues, housed in an early Christian church; while Devenish Island contains a large monastic ruin, dating back to the sixth century. The monastery holds a 12th-century round tower, which monks used for spotting possible attackers. During medieval times, the Maguires held sway over the Fermanagh region and were said to police the Erne with a private navy of 1,500 boats. Their lands were confiscated after the 17th century wars and settled by English and Scottish planters. The many stately homes in the county date from this time onwards. These include the superb Castle Coole, home to the Earls of Belmore, which dates back to the 18th century, and the elegant Florence Court, with its graceful Rococo plasterwork, dating to the mid-18th century. Another location of historic note is Belleek Pottery - Ireland's oldest and most famous manufacturer of fine glazed porcelain. Enniskillen, the county capital, contains a wealth of historic sites, including the medieval Maguire Castle, the Museum of the Royal Inniskilling Fusiliers, the Watergate and Arcaded Barracks.

KEY TO MAP
※ *Marble Arch Caves*
▲ *Cuilcagh Mountain (667m)*
■ *Enniskillen*
● **Main towns**
■ **Lakes / Rivers**

ORIGIN OF COUNTY NAME: Derived from the Irish 'Fear Manach', the men of Manach.

LAND AREA: 647 sq. miles (County's rank in size in the island of Ireland: 25).

LARGEST TOWN: Enniskillen.

MAIN TOWNS: Enniskillen, Irvinestown, Lisnaskea and Roslea.

MAIN INDUSTRIES: Agriculture, craft & design, pottery making, quarrying, retailing, service industries, tourism.

CENSUS DETAILS: 54,033 *(estimated).*

NUMBER OF SCHOOLS: 47 primary schools, 15 secondary schools, 1 college.

LOCAL ADMINISTRATION: *See Public Administration Chapter.*

LOCAL RADIO STATIONS & NEWSPAPERS: *See Media Chapter.*

THEATRES & ART GALLERIES: *See Arts Chapter.*

TOP 12 TOURIST ATTRACTIONS*(by visitor numbers):* Belleek Pottery (177,824 - established in 1857 by John Caldwell Bloomfield, the factory is Ireland's oldest parian china factory), Castle Archdale Country Park (100,000 - located in Irvinestown), Marble Arch Caves (57,000 - one of the finest underground cave systems in the country), Drum Manor Forest Park, Cookstown (43,700), Florencecourt Forest Park (29,300), Florence Court House & Gardens (20,197 - one of the most important 18th-century houses in the country, built by the earls of Enniskillen), Enniskillen Castle (17,569 - a famous castle, once the stronghold of the Maguire chieftains), Lough Navar Forest Park (16,200 - offers incomparable views of Lower Lough Erne), Explore Erne Exhibition (14,000 - tells how Lough Erne was formed), Castle Coole (12,478 - the finest of the National Trust houses in Northern

Ireland, completed in 1798 with a Palladian facade), Crom Estate (12,396 - contains 1,900 acres of woods, lakes and farmland supporting a wide diversity of wildlife), Fermanagh Crystal (9,000).

FAMOUS NATIVES OF THE PAST: Robert Barton (wrote music for Australia's 'Waltzing Matilda'), Thomas Barton ('French Tom', set up the Barton wine business; born 1695), Kathleen Bridle (artist); Alan Francis Brooke Alanbrook (first viscount British Field Marshal, ninth child of Victor Brooke of Colebrook; died 1963), Sir Basil Brook (Lord Brookeborough, Northern Ireland Prime Minister 1943-1963/helped train U.V.F., died 1973), Denis Parsons Burkitt (African surgeon/discovered form of children's cancer 'Burkitt's Lymphoma'; died 1993), Gustavus Hamilton (founded 'The Enniskilleners', Williamite regiment; died 1723), Bobbie Kerr (athlete/represented Ireland/Canada Olympics 1908-1928; born 1882).

COUNTY GALWAY (Province: Connacht)

LOCATION: The second largest county in Ireland, Galway is set on the west coast. Its heavily indented Atlantic coastline provides a myriad of wide bays, sheltered harbours, deep fjords and island clusters. Lough Corrib, Ireland's second largest lake, divides the county in two - the fertile farmlands, with their traditional dry stone walls in the east, and mountainous Connemara, where the Irish culture and language thrives, in the west. At the mouth of Galway Bay lie the three Aran Islands - Inishmore, Inishmaan and Inisheer, whose inhabitants also maintain a distinctly Gaelic culture. Towering mountain ranges such as the Twelve Bens and the Maamturks fortify the west coast of the county. The land is bounded in the east by the Shannon and Suck Rivers.

HISTORY: Humans first inhabited the Galway Region over 5,000 years ago. Stone monuments on the Aran Islands date back as far as 2000 B.C. and include the famous Dun Aengusa, a stone fort situated at the edge of a sea cliff and dating back to around the time of Christ. With the arrival of Christianity, monasteries were built at Roscam, Inchagoill Island and Annaghdown. These monasteries attracted the attentions of the Vikings and Roscam was raided in 830. Around 1232, Richard de Burgo, a Norman Baron, attacked Connacht. Galway city expanded with the arrival of English, Welsh and Flemish settlers, but the native Irish regained their power as the Normans adopted the Irish language and tradition. Around this time, 14 prominent merchant families came to power and held this position until Cromwell's attack on the county. The Irish in Galway were finally routed at the Battle of Aughrim in 1691. Following this defeat, the native population lost most of their lands and suffered under the penal laws. They endured further suffering during the Great Famine and the population was decimated. Towards the close of the 19th century, Galway became the centre of the the Irish Literary Renaissance. Lady Gregory's home at Coole Park attracted many writers, and Lady Gregory herself, along with Yeats and Synge founded the Abbey Theatre in Dublin 1904.

ORIGIN OF COUNTY NAME: Derived from the Irish 'Abhainn na Gaillimhe' - the Galway River - which was named after Galvia, a mythological princess who supposedly drowned in the river.

LAND AREA: 2,349.79 sq. miles (County's rank in size in the island of Ireland: 2).

COUNTY CAPITAL: Galway.

MAIN TOWNS: Ballinasloe, Galway, Loughrea, Tuam.

CENSUS DETAILS: Total population - 131,613 (excluding the Galway Borough) - a 1.6% increase since 1991.

NUMBER OF SCHOOLS: 215 primary schools, 37 secondary schools.

LOCAL ADMINISTRATION: *See Public Administration Chapter.*

LOCAL RADIO STATIONS & NEWSPAPERS: *See Media Chapter.*

THEATRES & ART GALLERIES: *See Arts Chapter.*

TOP 12 TOURIST ATTRACTIONS: the Aran Islands and Dún Aenghus on Inishmore, Aughrim Interpretative Centre, Castles (Athenry Castle, Aughnanure Castle, Bunowen Castle - once the home of Grace O'Malley, Dunguaire Castle, Portumna Castle and Forest Park, Claregalway Abbey), Connemara National Park, Coole Park (the home of Lady Gregory and birthplace of the Irish Literary Renaissance), Dan O'Hara's Homestead in the Connemara Heritage & History Centre, Derrigimlagh Bog (the location of Marconi's 1907 telegraph station and landing site for Alcock and Brown in 1919 after their transatlantic flight), Killary Harbour (Ireland's best-known fjord and location of Kylemore Abbey), Rosmuck (with its memorial cottage in honour of 1916 Rebellion leader Padraig Pearse), Thoor Ballylee (the home of W.B. Yeats and inspiration for his poems in 'The Tower'), the Tropical Butterfly Centre in Costelloe.

12 MOST FAMOUS NATIVES OF THE PAST: Robert O'Hara Burke (leader of the first European expedition to cross Australia, died 1861), Eamonn Ceannt (revolutionary, died 1916), Lady Gregory (dramatist, founder of Abbey Theatre, died 1932), William Brook Joyce - Lord Haw Haw (propagandist/ broadcaster, born New York/educated Galway, died 1946), John Lynch (signatory of the American Declaration of Independence), Walter Macken

KEY TO MAP

✳   *Connemara National Park*

▲   *Benbaun (727 m)*

■   *Galway City*   ●   **Main towns**

(actor/novelist/playwright, died 1967), Máirtín Ó Cadhain (short story writer/novelist/teacher, died 1970), Liam O'Flaherty (novelist/short story writer, died 1984), Breandán Ó hEithir (journalist/writer/broadcaster, died 1991), Muiris Ó Súileabháin (writer, died 1950), Eoghan Ó Tuairisc (poet/novelist/playwright/soldier, died 1982), Oliver St. John Gogarty (surgeon/ writer).

GALWAY CITY

LOCATION: Galway City is one of the fastest growing cities in Europe and has a young population, two factors that contribute to it being regarded as Ireland's most vibrant city.

HISTORY: Galway as a city was already 500 years old when it was granted its charter in 1484 by Richard III. It had already assumed a commercial importance - Christopher Columbus visited the city while trading from Lisbon in 1477. Around this time 14 wealthy merchant families ruled the city, earning Galway the name of the 'City of the Tribes'. These families were proud of their status and created their own special coat of arms, often without heraldic authority, which they had carved on to the facades of their premises. The tribes held their position for the next 170 years, until 1651 when a Cromwellian force, under Sir Charles Coote, besieged the city. Galway surrendered, and the tribes lost all their power. Although Irish Catholics temporarily regained the city, they soon lost this control following the Battle of Aughrim. During the 18th century, Galway declined in status and in 1841, lost its classification as a city. Nonetheless, it still maintained strong trading links and many industries flourished. Queens College, Galway, was established in 1845. This was the time of the Great Famine, when many thousands died in the city and its environs. By 1899, the population of Galway had been halved. In 1916, a rising against the British was instigated by Liam Mellowes in the city but failed. It became an urban municipality once again in 1937. The fortunes of the city began to look up in the 1960s, with the expansion of industry and tourism in the country. It is now an industrial centre for the west, with a thriving arts scene.

LAND AREA: 18.75 sq. miles.

CENSUS DETAILS: Total population - 57,095 - a 12.6% increase since 1991.

NUMBER OF SCHOOLS: 26 primary schools, 11 secondary schools, 1 Institute of Technology, 1 university.

LOCAL ADMINISTRATION: *See Public Administration Chapter.*

LOCAL RADIO STATIONS & NEWSPAPERS: *See Media Chapter.*

THEATRES & ART GALLERIES: *See Arts Chapter.*

TOP 12 TOURIST ATTRACTIONS: the 17th-century Browne Doorway, the Claddagh district (inspired the popular Claddagh Ring), Kennedy Park-Eyre Square (with statues of Padraic O'Conaire and Liam Mellowes and the Quincentennial fountain), the leaping salmon statue at the Salmon Weir Bridge, Leisureland, the Lynch Memorial Window, Nora Barnacle House Museum, the restored Shoemaker and Penrice Towers, Salthill (one of Ireland's busiest seaside resorts), Shop Street (a medieval street that contains the 15th-century Lynch's Castle), Siamsa na Gaillimhe - the Spanish Arch, St. Nicholas Collegiate Church (which Christopher Columbus supposedly visited).

FAMOUS NATIVES OF THE PAST: Nora Barnacle (wife to James Joyce), Ellis Dillon (author, died 1993), Frank Harris (writer/journalist, died 1931), Gerard Anthony Hayes-McCoy (historian, died 1975), Dónall MacAmhlaigh (novelist/short story writer, died 1989), Liam Mellowes (leader of failed Galway rising in 1916), Pádraic Ó Conaire (short story writer/novelist, died 1928).

COUNTY KERRY (Province: Munster)

LOCATION: County Kerry is situated in the south-west of Ireland on the Atlantic seaboard. A great ridge of mountains dominates the county dividing it into the open countryside of the north and east, which extends into Ireland's Golden Vale, and the mountainous western region that consists of three jutting peninsulas. A county of superlatives, Kerry is home to Ireland's highest mountains, most westerly point and oldest tourist destination - Killarney - promoted by Lord Kenmare in the 18th century and still the most popular tourist centre in the country. The Gulf Stream washes the Kerry coast and brings with it several species of sub-tropical, marine mammals, many of which can be seen in the Dingle Sea Life Centre.

HISTORY: Kerry's history can be traced back to prehistoric peoples, who travelled across the county's peninsulas, seeking mineral treasures. Copper was extracted here and sent to Spain some 4,000 years ago by these peoples. The great forts and castles of the Celtic races and later groups are still highly visible, along with many fine early Christian sites, including the early Christian monastery on the Skellig Islands and the Gallarus Oratory, which at more than 1,000 years old is the oldest church in Ireland and is still structurally intact. Although the Normans arrived in the county in the 13th century, it was not until the wars of the 16th and 17th centuries that the county's native Irish came under direct threat. The county was formally demarcated in 1606. Nonetheless, it continued to maintain its unique and rich Irish culture. The Irish language is still spoken here, no doubt helped by the relative isolation imposed by the county's inaccessible mountains.

ORIGIN OF COUNTY NAME: Derived from the Irish 'Ciarraí', meaning Ciar's People and referring to an early Celtic tribe who settled in the county.

COUNTY CAPITAL: Tralee.

LAND AREA: 1,815.16 sq. miles (County's rank in size in the island of Ireland: 5).

MAIN TOWNS: Ballybunion, Castleisland, Cahirciveen, Dingle, Kenmare, Killarney, Killorglin, Listowel, Tralee.

CENSUS DETAILS: Total population - 126,130 - a 3.5% increase since 1991.

NUMBER OF SCHOOLS: 147 primary schools, 32 secondary schools, 1 Institute of Technology.

LOCAL ADMINISTRATION: *See Public Administration Chapter.*
LOCAL RADIO STATIONS & NEWSPAPERS: *See Media Chapter.*
THEATRES & ART GALLERIES: *See Arts Chapter.*
TOP 12 TOURIST ATTRACTIONS *(by visitor numbers):* Ring of Kerry (1.3 million), Killarney National Park (380,856), Tralee's Aqua Dome (215,966), Muckross House and Gardens (190,428), Blennerville Windmill (38,431), Steam Train (33,379), Dingle Sea Life Centre (98,000), Crag Cave (80,000 - located in Castleisland), Derrynane National Park (19,862 - the home of Daniel O'Connell), National Transport Museum (14,500 - in Killarney), Carrauntuohill (Ireland's highest mountain), Dingle (home of Fungi the Dolphin, and film location for *Ryan's Daughter* and *Far and Away*).
12 MOST FAMOUS NATIVES OF THE PAST: St. Brendan the Navigator (abbot/traveller, reputedly discovered America, died 577), Helen Blackburn (Women's Suffrage Movement pioneer, died 1903), Thomas Crean (Captain Scott's companion on Antarctic expedition, 1900s), Fr. Patrick Dinneen (priest/lexicographer/completed first Irish /English dictionary, died 1934), Lord Horatio Herbert Kitchener (British Field Marshal, died 1916), Daniel O'Connell (politician who fought for Catholic emancipation, died 1847), Tomás Ó Criomhthainn (writer /fisherman /stonemason, died 1937), Aodhagán Ó Rahataille (poet, died 1726), Eoghan Rua Ó Súileabháin (gaelic poet, died 1784), Peig Sayers (storyteller, died 1958), Daniel Spring (politician, father of Dick, died 1988), Austin Stack (revolutionary, died 1929).

KEY TO MAP
❋ Killarney National Park
▲ Carrauntohill (1041m)
■ Tralee ● Main towns
■ Lakes / Rivers

COUNTY KILDARE (Province: Leinster)

LOCATION: An inland county in the east of the country, Kildare is bounded by the Wicklow mountain range to the east, the foothills of which extend westwards to meet the unique plain known as the Curragh of Kildare, an area renowned for horse racing, training and breeding. The great Bog of Allen touches the west of Kildare, and Ireland's two canal systems, the Grand and the Royal canals, both flow through the county, as do the three major rivers of the Liffey, the Barrow and the Boyne. Kildare's river valleys, bogs, woodlands and canals are the preserve of wild fowl, birds and animals, with nature reserves at Pollardstown and Ballinafagh.

HISTORY: Kildare's history can be traced back to ancient times, with evidence of raths, earthworks and standing stones to be found around the Curragh. The early Christian era in the county is marked by Kildare's ties to St. Brigid, the sixth century saint who is one of the three patrons of Ireland. However, the legend of St. Brigid could originate from the fact that a pagan sanctuary commemorating the pagan goddess Brigda was located on the same site. The county has been associated with armies since the Anglo-Normans came to Ireland in the 12th century, and military garrisons have been sited here since the 18th century. The Curragh has been the main training base for the Irish army since Ireland gained its Independence and is the focal point of horse training and racing in Ireland.

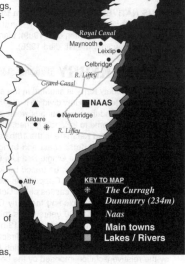

KEY TO MAP
❋ The Curragh
▲ Dunmurry (234m)
■ Naas
● Main towns
■ Lakes / Rivers

ORIGIN OF COUNTY NAME: Derived from the Irish 'Cill Dara', meaning Church of the Oak Tree, which alludes to St. Brigid's monastery beneath an oak tree.
LAND AREA: 654 sq. miles (County's rank in size in the island of Ireland: 24).
COUNTY CAPITAL: Naas.
MAIN TOWNS: Athy, Celbridge, Kildare, Leixlip, Maynooth, Naas, Newbridge (Droichead Nua).
CENSUS DETAILS: Total population - 134,992 - a 10.1% increase since 1991.
NUMBER OF SCHOOLS: 94 primary schools, 27 secondary schools, 1 university, 1 seminary, 1 military training college.
LOCAL ADMINISTRATION: *See Public Administration Chapter.*
LOCAL RADIO STATIONS & NEWSPAPERS: *See Media Chapter.*
THEATRES & ART GALLERIES: *See Arts Chapter.*

TOP 12 TOURIST ATTRACTIONS: the Butterfly farm in Straffan, Celbridge (Ireland's largest and finest Palladian House), Cross of Moone at Timolin, Japanese Gardens in Tully, Maynooth Castle, Mondello Park car racing circuit, National Irish Stud and Horse Museum in Tully, Peatland World Visitor Centre in Lullymore, Punchestown horse racing course, the Quaker Village of Ballitore (designed and built by Quakers and the location of the Quaker Museum), Straffan Steam Museum, Wonderful Barn Leixlip (an 18th century conical granary).

12 MOST FAMOUS NATIVES OF THE PAST: Paul Cullen (Ireland's first Cardinal/founder of U.C.D. 1854), Jack Dempsey (boxer, died 1895), John Devoy (founded *Irish Nation* and *Gaelic American* newspapers, died 1928), Lord Edward Fitzgerald (United Irishman, died 1798), Lord Thomas Fitzgerald ('Silken Thomas,' instigated a rising 1534), Arthur Guinness (founded Guinness brewery in 1759), John de Courcy Ireland (maritime historian/linguist/ author, born India/son of British Army Major from County, born 1911), Molly Keane (novelist/playwright, died 1996), Dame Kathleen Yardley Lonsdale (eminent crystallographer, born 1903), Domhnall Ó'Buachalla (Governor General Irish Free State 1932, died 1963), Ernest Henry Shackleton (antarctic explorer, died 1922), Theobald Wolfe Tone (United Irishman, died 1798).

COUNTY KILKENNY (Province: Leinster)

LOCATION: Kilkenny is an inland county in the south-east of the country. The great Barrow, Nore and Suir rivers drain its low lying hills and plains as they wend their way southwards. To the north-east of the county is the Castlecomer Plateau with its adjoining uplands of damp pasture layered on shale, sandstones and seams of anthracite coal. The county is also noted for its marble, a dark black stone, prized in Georgian and Victorian times, that led to Kilkenny being named the Marble City.

HISTORY: Kilkenny county is steeped in history, as evidenced by the ruined settlements left by the Celts, Vikings, Normans and the English. Kilkenny city itself was the medieval capital of Ireland and still retains much of its Norman origins and medieval structure. Dominating the city is Kilkenny Castle, which was built between 1192 and 1207 for Strongbow's son, William. The county's strong early Christian ties can still be seen in the abbeys at Jerpoint, Kilkenny and in Kells Priory. As Kilkenny was the country's medieval capital, many sessions of the Irish Parliament were held there, including the infamous one in 1366 that led to the unsuccessful Statute of Kilkenny, forbidding the Anglo-Irish to integrate with the Gaelic Irish, and the Confederation of Kilkenny in 1642, where Irish Catholics sided with Charles I. Kilkenny has long been a national centre for crafts and design.

ORIGIN OF COUNTY NAME: Derived from the Irish 'Cill Chainnigh', the Church of Cainneach, which was founded in Kilkenny City by St. Canice in the sixth century.

LAND AREA: 796 sq. miles (County's rank in size in the island of Ireland: 16).

COUNTY CAPITAL: Kilkenny.

MAIN TOWNS: Callan, Castlecomer, Graiguenamanagh, Kilkenny, Thomastown.

CENSUS DETAILS: Total population - 75,336 - a 2.3% increase since 1991.

NUMBER OF SCHOOLS: 79 primary schools, 16 secondary schools.

LOCAL ADMINISTRATION: *See Public Administration Chapter.*

LOCAL RADIO STATIONS & NEWSPAPERS: *See Media Chapter.*

THEATRES & ART GALLERIES: *See Arts Chapter.*

KEY TO MAP

* ✳   *Dunmore Cave*
* ▲   *Brandon Hill (516m)*
* ■   *Kilkenny*
* ■   **Main towns**
* ●   **Lakes / Rivers**

TOP 12 TOURIST ATTRACTIONS: the Black Abbey in Kilkenny, Bród Tullaroan and the Lory Meagher Heritage Centre, Duiske Abbey and Abbey Centre, Dunmore Cave (containing some of the best calcite formations found in any Irish cave), high crosses (at Kilree, Killamery and Kilkieran), Jerpoint Abbey at Thomastown, Kells Priory, Kilfane Glen and Waterfall, Kilkenny Castle, Kilkenny Design Centre, Rice House (the birthplace of Brother Edmund Rice in Callan), Shee Alms House.

MOST FAMOUS NATIVES OF THE PAST: George Berkeley (bishop/philosopher, died 1753), Daniel Bryan (colonel/founder of Military History Association of Ireland, died 1985), Hubert Marshall Butler (translator/essayist/ obtained visas for Nazi-fleeing Austrian jews, died 1991), Abraham Colles (surgeon, diagnosed 'Colles Fracture,' died 1843), Michael Cudahy (made first commercial use of refrigeration, died 1910), Richard Joseph Downey (youngest-ever Catholic Archbishop aged 47 years 1928, died 1953), Thomas Grubb (engineer, manufacturer of telescopes, died 1878), James Hoban (designed the White House, Washington, died 1831), Francis MacManus (novelist, died 1965), Edmund Rice (Brother Ignatius, founded Christian Brothers 1803, died 1844), James Stephens (founded Irish Republican Brotherhood, son of auctioneer's clerk from county, died 1901).

COUNTY LAOIS (Province: Leinster)

LOCATION: An inland county in the east of Ireland, Laois is the only county that does not border on another county touching the sea. It is largely bounded by raised bog, highlands and rivers - namely, the Barrow and Nore Rivers and the Slieve Bloom mountains. To the south-east of the county is the Castlecomer Plateau and its adjoining uplands, which are layered on Upper Carboniferous shales and sandstones, with some coal seams.

HISTORY: There are more than 1,000 historical sites and monuments in the county, some telling the story of the Mesolithic times of 8,500 years ago, others tracing the history of the Neolithic farmers. The county had a strong Christian establishment by the sixth century, but many of its monasteries fell prey to the Viking hordes, as evidenced by a re-discovered Viking longphort at Dunrally. The Normans gained control of the best land in the county by around 1325, but a gaelic revival occurred during the 14th century. This revival was summarily ended when the O'Mores had their lands confiscated by the English in the 16th century. Laois was established out of a number of unrelated Gaelic territories and earlier chiefdoms and referred to as the Queen's County by a parliamentary act in 1556, during the reign of Queen Mary. It, along with Offaly, became the first area to be planted in Ireland.

ORIGIN OF COUNTY NAME: Initially called 'Queen's County, it was renamed Laois after the War of Independence, in honour of the Loigis/Loigsi, late Iron Age Pict mercenaries who helped Welsh invaders (the Laigin) conquer Leinster.

LAND AREA: 664 sq. miles (County's rank in size in the island of Ireland: 23).

COUNTY CAPITAL: Portlaoise.

MAIN TOWNS: Abbeyleix, Mountrath, Mountmellick, Portarlington.

CENSUS DETAILS: Total population - 52,945 - a 1.2% increase since 1991.

NUMBER OF SCHOOLS: 69 primary schools, 13 secondary schools.

LOCAL ADMINISTRATION: *See Public Administration Chapter.*

LOCAL RADIO STATIONS & NEWSPAPERS: *See Media Chapter.*

THEATRES & ART GALLERIES: *See Arts Chapter.*

TOP 12 TOURIST ATTRACTIONS: Abbeyleix House and Gardens, Castles (Ballaghmore Castle, Kinnity Castle, Lea Castle, Dysart Castle, Srahan Castle and Moat), St Canice's Monastery, Emo Court and Gardens, the Great Heath of Maryborough (one of the most important archeological sites in Ireland), Heywood Gardens in Ballinakill, Killeshin Church (contains some of Ireland's finest medieval stonework), Mountmellick Quaker Museum, Rock of Dunamase, Slieve Bloom Environmental Park, Stradbally Steam Museum, Timahoe Church and Round Tower.

FAMOUS NATIVES OF THE PAST: Jacob Arthur (discovered eye membrane, died 1874), Patrick Cahill (prominent tenant-leader/first editor of Leinster Leader), Colonel James C. Fitzmaurice (aviator, died 1965), Oliver J. Flanagan (politician, died 1987), Liam Miller (publisher, died 1987), Kevin O'Higgins (politician, died 1927), Owny MacRory O'More (chieftain, died 1600), Roger O'More (17th-century rebel), Frank Power (acting British Consul in French Foreign Legion, died 1884).

KEY TO MAP
* ✳ *Slieve Bloom*
* ▲ *Arderin Mountain (528m)*
* ■ *Portlaoise*
* ● Main towns
* ■ Lakes / Rivers

COUNTY LEITRIM (Province: Connacht)

LOCATION: Leitrim is situated in the north-west of the country. Although mostly an inland county, a tiny stretch of Leitrim touches on the Atlantic coastline near Bundoran in Co. Donegal. Leitrim's northern borders are defined by Loughs MacNean and Melvin and the River Erne, and the county is divided by the great river Shannon. The two major rivers have recently been joined by a canal to form the Shannon-Erne Waterway.

HISTORY: The O'Rourke clan ruled most of the county in Celtic times but were supplanted by the Normans and later by the English, who imposed a policy of land confiscation and plantation on Leitrim at the beginning of the 17th century. Towns such as Carrick-on-Shannon, Manorhamilton and Jamestown were established and fortified during this time. Emigration from famine times onwards caused the population to dramatically drop from a high of 155,000 in the early 19th century to around 25,000 today.

ORIGIN OF COUNTY NAME: Derived from the Irish 'Liathdroim' , meaning the grey hillridge.

LAND AREA: 614 sq. miles (County's rank in size in the island of Ireland: 26).

COUNTY CAPITAL: Carrick-on-Shannon.

MAIN TOWNS: Carrick-on-Shannon, Drumshanbo, Manorhamilton.

CENSUS DETAILS: Total population - 25,057, - a 1.0% decrease since 1991.

NUMBER OF SCHOOLS: 43 primary schools, 9 secondary schools.

LOCAL ADMINISTRATION: *See Public Administration Chapter.*
LOCAL RADIO STATIONS & NEWSPAPERS: *See Media Chapter.*
THEATRES & ART GALLERIES: *See Arts Chapter.*
TOP 12 TOURIST ATTRACTIONS: the Barr Scenic Route, Miners Way (historical trail, long-distance walking route), Creevylea Abbey ruin (set on the banks of the Bonet river, Dromahair), cruising on the River Shannon, Drumcoura City Western Riding Farm in Ballinamore), Glencar Waterfall, the Leitrim Way/Slí Liatroma (a scenic walking route), Leitrim Heritage Centre, Lough Rynn House and Gardens and caravan park in Mohill, Parke's Castle in Dromahair, the Shannon-Erne Waterway, Sliabh an Iarain Visitor Centre in Drumshanbo.
FAMOUS NATIVES OF THE PAST: Charles Atlas (famous strong man), Rev. Peter Conefrey (did much to foster Irish culture in the 1930's), Anthony William Durnford (colonel/fought at Battle of Isandhlwana, died 1879), Seán Mac Diarmada (revolutionary, died 1916), Gus Martin (academic, died 1995), John McKenna (traditional musician, died 1947), Joe Mooney (established 'An Tostal' festival), Turlough O'Carolan (harpist), Thomas Parke (surgeon /first Irishman to traverse the African continent, died 1893), Robert Strawbridge (founded the Methodist Church in the US), Anthony Trollope (English writer, lived in Drumsna for a time), Gordon Wilson (senator/peacemaker, died 1995).

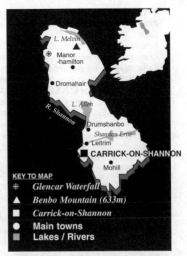

KEY TO MAP
✳ *Glencar Waterfall*
▲ *Benbo Mountain (633m)*
■ *Carrick-on-Shannon*
● Main towns
■ Lakes / Rivers

COUNTY LIMERICK (Province: Munster)

LOCATION: The county of Limerick is located on Ireland's south-west coast between Clare and Kerry. A fertile limestone plain constitutes the greater part of its north, central and east regions and is commonly referred to as the Golden Vale. The county is bounded by the wide mouth of the Shannon estuary to the north-west, the high peaks of the Galtee mountains to the south-east and Co. Kerry to the west.
HISTORY: Human habitation of the region can be traced back to around 3500 BC, with the megalithic remains at Duntryleague dating to this time. However, most of Limerick does not appear to have been settled until the fifth century, with the arrival of Christianity and the establishment of monasteries at Ardpatrick, Mungret and Killeedy. The Ardagh Chalice, which dates from this era, was found in a west Limerick ring fort. The Vikings launched attacks on the county, sailing up the Shannon Estuary in 922 and establishing a settlement on an island in the estuary, which was to form the origins of Limerick City. The Normans attacked in 1194, after Dónal Mór O'Brien, the King of Munster, died, and the county of Limerick was formally recognised in 1210. The Normans built hundreds of castles in the region - Limerick has more castles than any other county in Ireland. The Earls of Desmond, or the Geraldines as they were known, were at the centre of Norman power in Munster and led a revolt against the English in 1571. This rebellion was put down and the Geraldines' lands confiscated. The revolt was to be the start of centuries of wars and sieges centred around Limerick City. The native Irish suffered badly in the Great Famine, and Limerick endured waves of emigration. However, in the 1950s and 1960s, the region experienced an economic upturn as a result of the development of the Shannon Region and Shannon Airport.

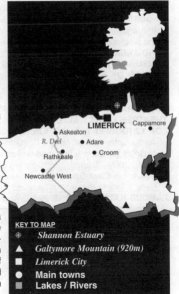

KEY TO MAP
✳ *Shannon Estuary*
▲ *Galtymore Mountain (920m)*
■ *Limerick City*
● Main towns
■ Lakes / Rivers

ORIGIN OF COUNTY NAME: The origin of the name of Limerick, or the Irish 'Luimneach', is unclear. One explanation given is that the name is derived from 'Luamanach', meaning a place covered in cloaks, and could possibly refer to cloaks or mantles observed floating on the Shannon after some prehistoric battle.
LAND AREA: 1,030 sq. miles (County's rank in size in the island of Ireland: 10).
COUNTY CAPITAL: Newcastle West.
MAIN TOWNS: Abbeyfeale, Kilmallock, Limerick, Newcastle West, Rathkeale.
CENSUS DETAILS: Total population (excluding Limerick Borough) - 113,003 - a 2.8% increase since 1991.
NUMBER OF SCHOOLS: 116 primary schools, 18 secondary schools.
LOCAL ADMINISTRATION: *See Public Administration Chapter.*
LOCAL RADIO STATIONS & NEWSPAPERS: *See Media Chapter.*
THEATRES & ART GALLERIES: *See Arts Chapter.*

TOP 12 TOURIST ATTRACTIONS: Abbeys (at Ardpatrick, Glenstal, Lislaughtin, Manister, Mungret and Killeedy), Adare Village and Heritage Centre, Castles (numbering more than 400 in total and including Askeaton Island Castle, Castle Matrix - where Edmund Spencer met Sir Walter Raleigh and where the potato was first grown in Ireland - Glenquin Castle, Glin Castle, Portrinard Castle), Croom Mills, the Celtic Park and Gardens in Kilcornan, Curraghchase Forest Park, the de Valera Museum at Bruree, Foynes Flying Boat Museum (tells the story of the early days of transatlantic flights), the Palatine Exhibition at Rathkeale, Lough Gur Interpretative Centre, Mitchelstown Caves, Reerasta Fort (where the Ardagh Chalice was found).

12 MOST FAMOUS NATIVES OF THE PAST: Dan and Tim Ahearne (brothers, triple jump olympic winners, 1908-1910), Thomas James Clarke (revolutionary, died 1916), Tomás de Bhaldraithe (scholar/lexicographer, died 1966), Philip Embury (with Barbara Ruttle Heck, co-founded Methodism in US 1768), Jim Kemmy (politician, died 1997), James Clarence Mangan (poet/writer, died 1849), Kate O'Brien (writer, died 1974), William Smith O'Brien (Irish freedom fighter; born 1848), Donogh O'Malley (politician, died 1968), Michael Maurice O'Shaughnessy (engineer, rebuilt much of San Francisco after 1906 earthquake, died 1934), Seán Ó Tuama (poet, late 18th century), Dáithí Ó Brudair (one of the last great Gaelic Bards 1625-98).

LIMERICK CITY

LOCATION: Limerick City is set in the north-east of County Limerick on the mouth of the Shannon estuary.

HISTORY: Its charter is 800 years old, making it older than London. The city's origins date back to when the Vikings sailed up the Shannon Estuary in 922 and founded a settlement on an island. With the arrival of the Normans in 1194, St. Mary's Cathedral and the great castle of King John were built. The Geraldines' rebellion against the English in 1571 was the first of many such wars and sieges centred around Limerick City, including the year-long siege against Oliver Cromwell in 1651 and the 1690 and 1691 sieges. The 1690 siege resulted in General Patrick Sarsfield leading the Jacobite cause, which was supported by the Catholic Irish. The end of this siege led to the signing of the Treaty of Limerick in 1691, the terms of which were dishonoured by the English parliament. The city's walls were taken down in the 18th century and the city developed westwards into an area known as Newtown Pery, famed for its elegant houses and wide streets.

Limerick City began to prosper in the 1950s and 1960s with the industrial development arising from Shannon Airport, the geographical location of which made it the first suitable landing site for long-distance air travel from and to America. Shannon Free Airport Development Company was established in 1959 to ensure that the region maintained its viability in air transport activity. The effects of this agency were quickly felt throughout the Shannon region, particularly in Limerick City. The success of the city today attests to the agency's initiatives.

LAND AREA: 7.9 sq. miles.

CENSUS DETAILS: Total population - 52,039 - a 0.1% decrease since 1991.

NUMBER OF SCHOOLS: 34 primary schools, 17 secondary schools, 1 college of education, 1 Institute of Technology, 1 university.

LOCAL ADMINISTRATION: *See Public Administration Chapter.*

LOCAL RADIO STATIONS & NEWSPAPERS: *See Media Chapter.*

THEATRES & ART GALLERIES: *See Arts Chapter.*

TOP 12 TOURIST ATTRACTIONS: Churches (the Dominican Church, Kilrush Church - dates back to 1201, St. John's Cathedral, St. Mary's Cathedral), the Exchange at Nicholas Street, the Granary in Michael Street, Hunt Museum (includes a fine medieval collection and more than 2,000 works of art donated by John and Gertrude Hunt), John's Square, King John's Castle, Limerick City Walls, Limerick Lace Making at the Good Shepherd Convent in Clare Street, Limerick Museum, the O'Connell Monument, the Rugby Heritage Centre at Thomond Park, Sarsfield Bridge, the Sarsfield Memorial, the Treaty Stone off Thomond Bridge.

FAMOUS NATIVES OF THE PAST: Andrew N Bonaparte-Wyse (public servant, died 1940), John Hunt (scholar/antiquarian, died 1976), Séan Keating (artist, died 1977), Jim Kemmy (politician, died 1997), Mick Mackey (hurler, died 1982), Lola Montez (adventuress/dancer, died 1861), Michael J O'Kelly (archaeologist, died 1982).

COUNTY LONGFORD (Province: Leinster)

LOCATION: An inland county set in the River Shannon basin and the upper catchment of the River Erne, Longford contains lakeland, bogland, pastureland and wetland. It is bordered to the west by the River Shannon and Lough Ree, while its largest lakes, Loughs Gowna and Kinale, both form the boundary between Longford and Cavan.

HISTORY: Longford's bogland contributes much to its history. A trackway of large oak planks was recently discovered in a bog at Corlea. This trackway is very important in archaeological terms, as it's the only find from Ireland that can be dated back to the early Iron Age. An exhibition centre, focusing on the Corlea Trackway, has now been built in the area. Longford figures in many Irish myths; the Black Pig's Dyke can be found near Granard, and the route of the Táin crosses through the county. Longford was ruled in the eleventh century by O'Farrell, a hero at the Battle of Clontarf (1014 A.D.), who marched westwards and took control of the region by force. The present county was established in 1547 by the Tudors. Some of the fiercest fighting of the 1798 rebellion occurred in the county, mainly around Ballinamuck. The Great Famine in 1847 took a heavy toll on the county's population, and during this time, a Longford-Argentine connection was established, resulting from the many families in the county emigrated to Argentina.

ORIGIN OF COUNTY NAME: Derived from the Irish 'Longford Ui Fearraill' - the stronghold of the O'Farrell family.

LAND AREA: 403 sq. miles (County's rank in size in the island of Ireland: 30).

COUNTY CAPITAL: Longford.
MAIN TOWNS: Ballymahon, Edgeworthstown, Granard, Longford.
CENSUS DETAILS: Total population - 30,166, - a 0.4% decrease since 1991.
NUMBER OF SCHOOLS: 43 primary schools, 10 secondary schools.
LOCAL ADMINISTRATION: *See Public Administration Chapter.*
LOCAL RADIO STATIONS & NEWSPAPERS: *See Media Chapter.*
THEATRES & ART GALLERIES: *See Arts Chapter.*
TOP 12 TOURIST ATTRACTIONS: Ardagh Heritage Village (built in the 1860s along a Swiss design), the Black Pig's Dyke (one of the most visible ancient boundary formations in the country), Carrigglas Manor, Cashel Museum in Newtowncashel, Castleforbes Demesne, the Cistercian Abbeys at Abbeylara and Abbeyshrule, Clondra's Teach Cheoil, Corlea Trackway Exhibition Centre, Goldsmith Country (maps out the countryside celebrated by the poet Oliver Goldsmith), Lilac Activity Centre in Lanesboro, Longford County Museum, Michael Casey's Bog Oak sculptures at Barley Harbour.
FAMOUS NATIVES OF THE PAST: John Keegan Casey (ballad poet, wrote 'The Rising of the Moon'), Pádraic Colum (poet/playwright, wrote the song 'She moves through the fair,' died 1972), Maria Edgeworth (author, born Oxfordshire, father from Longford, died 1849), Abbé Henry Edgeworth (confessor to King Louis XVI at his execution, died 1807), Oliver Goldsmith (writer/essayist/novelist, died 1774), Thomas Lefroy (Chief Justice of Ireland, said to be the person on whom Jane Austen's character D'Arcy is based), Seán MacEoin (Blacksmith of Ballinalee, Guerrilla leader in the War of Independence, died 1973), Augustin Magaidrin (wrote important 14th century hagiography, now in Oxford's Bodleian Library), Edward Pakenham (Earl of Longford, playwright/theatre producer, died 1961), James Bonterre O'Brien (chartist leader/journalist, died 1864), Edel Miro O'Farrell (former President of Argentina), Fr. Joseph Mullooly (19th century archaeologist, discovered ancient temple of Mithras, Rome).

KEY TO MAP
✳ *Corlea Bog Tracks*
▲ *Corn Hill (276m)*
■ *Longford*
● Main towns
■ Lakes / Rivers

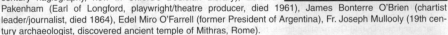

COUNTY LOUTH (Province: Leinster)

LOCATION: Louth, situated on the eastern seaboard, is the smallest county in Ireland. Despite this, it contains more than 30 miles of coastline. The underlying rock in the county, except the Cooley Peninsula, is limestone. The pressure of the Ice Age caused the surface to crumble and form rich and often deep soil with well-wooded areas and sandy beaches. Louth is in a prime location situated halfway between Belfast and Dublin.
HISTORY: The ancient and historic town of Drogheda straddles the River Boyne, Ireland's most historic river. In the 1970's, a 'flint', shaped in palaeolithic times, was found near the town and is believed to be the oldest of objects ever discovered in Ireland. According to the Táin, one of Ireland's great folk tales, it was in Ardee that the legendary folk hero Cuchulainn single-handedly defeated the armies of Ulster. In early Christian times, Monasterboice in south Louth was an important Christian centre. The Normans took power in the late 13th century and built the two main towns of Drogheda and Dundalk. The remnants of Dundalk's old walls still exist, despite Oliver Cromwell's attack on the city in 1649, when he murdered approximately 2,600 of the town's inhabitants. With the arrival of the Protestant ascendancy in the 17th century, the native Irish were dispossessed. However, the 19th century saw the demise of this landlord class and gave rise to the relatively small farms and fields that are evident in Louth today.
ORIGIN OF COUNTY NAME: Derived from the Irish 'Lú', referring to the River Lud or a hollow.
LAND AREA: 318 sq. miles (County's rank in size in the island of Ireland: 32).
COUNTY CAPITAL: Dundalk
MAIN TOWNS: Ardee, Drogheda, Dundalk.

KEY TO MAP
✳ *Carlingford Forest Park*
▲ *Slieve Foy (590m)*
■ *Dundalk*
● Main towns
■ Lakes / Rivers

CENSUS DETAILS: Total population - 92,166 - a 1.6% increase since 1991.
NUMBER OF SCHOOLS: 73 primary schools, 10 secondary schools, 1 Institute of Technology.
LOCAL ADMINISTRATION: *See Public Administration Chapter.*
LOCAL RADIO STATIONS & NEWSPAPERS: *See Media Chapter.*
THEATRES & ART GALLERIES: *See Arts Chapter.*
TOP 12 TOURIST ATTRACTIONS: Carlingford Forest Park, Dromiskin Cross, Dundalk Bird Sanctuary (one of the biggest in Ireland), Dundalk Motte and Bailey, Dun Dealgan, Dundalk Museum, King John's Castle at Carlingford, 'The Mint' (15th-century tower in Carlingford), Old Mellifont Abbey at Collon, Monasterboice's inscribed crosses and round tower, Proleek dolmen, Seatown Windmill (one of Ireland's largest surviving windmills),
FAMOUS NATIVES OF THE PAST: Fr. Nicholas J. Callan (invented the induction coil, died 1864), Brian Lenihan (politician, died 1995), Dorothy MacArdle (historian; died 1958), Sir Francis Leopold McClintock (arctic explorer, died 1907), Tom McCormack (professional boxer, born 1890), Sean MacEoin (Lieutenant-General, born 1910), Thomas D'Arcy McGee (Irish-Canadian politician/journalist, died 1868), Frank O'Reilly (Catholic Truth Society of Ireland, died 1957), Nano Reid (artist, died 1981), Tom Sharkey (world champion boxer, born 1873).

COUNTY MAYO (Province: Connacht)

LOCATION: Mayo is a maritime county on the west coast of Ireland and is the third largest county in Ireland. Its topography varies from the relatively flat land in east Mayo through the island-dotted lakes of Loughs Conn, Mask, Cullin and Carra to the bare quartzite mountains along Mayo's indented Atlantic coastline. The county is bounded by Lough Corrib and the fjord of Killary Harbour in the south; Killala Bay and Erris in the north; Achill Island, Clew Bay and the Mullet Peninsula in the west; and the counties of Sligo and Roscommon in the east.

HISTORY: North Mayo holds extensive tracts of blanket bog, under which have been recently discovered a system of corralled fields, enclosures and tombs - the Céide Fields - dating from about 5,000 years ago. The county's early Christian history shows significant associations with St. Patrick. The Normans took over Mayo in 1235, providing the county with some of its now familiar surnames. During Cromwellian times, native Irish who had their lands confiscated in the east were settled in Mayo. The French, under the leadership of General Humbert, landed at north Mayo on August 22, 1798, and overpowered the British. However, the Franco-Irish force were routed at Ballinamuck in Co. Longford, and many of those suspected of helping the French were executed. There was wide-scale emigration from Mayo from the famine times onwards. In 1879, Michael Davitt set up the Mayo Land League, which eventually became a national organisation and led to tenant farmers becoming landowners.
ORIGIN OF COUNTY NAME: Derived from the Irish 'Maigh Eo', meaning the plain of yew trees.
LAND AREA: 2,159 sq. miles (County's rank in size in the island of Ireland: 3).
COUNTY CAPITAL: Castlebar.
MAIN TOWNS: Ballina, Ballinrobe, Ballyhaunis, Castlebar, Charlestown, Claremorris, Crossmolina, Swinford, Westport.
CENSUS DETAILS: Total population - 111,524 - a 0.7% increase since 1991.
NUMBER OF SCHOOLS: 191 primary schools, 29 secondary schools, 1Institute of Technology.
LOCAL ADMINISTRATION: *See Public Administration Chapter.*
LOCAL RADIO STATIONS & NEWSPAPERS: *See Media Chapter.*
THEATRES & ART GALLERIES: *See Arts Chapter.*
TOP 12 TOURIST ATTRACTIONS: the Inishkea bird sanctuaries, Céide Fields near Ballycastle, Cong (famous for its cross and as the location of the film *The Quiet Man*), Croagh Patrick (one of the main pilgrimage points in Ireland), Downpatrick Head, Foxford Woollen Mills Visitor Centre, Knock Marian Shrine and Folk Museum, the new Mayo National Park in the Owenduff-Nephinbeg area (Ireland's sixth, with a visitors' centre at Ballycroy and encompassing some of the best Atlantic blanket bog in Europe), Michael Davitt Museum, Moore Hall, Rosserk Abbey, Westport House and Children's Zoo.
12 MOST FAMOUS NATIVES OF THE PAST: Louis Brennan (inventor of first helicopter, died 1932), William Brown (founded Argentine Navy, which was celebrated by a visit of a delegation of the Argentinian navy to the county in 1998, died 1857), Captain Charles Cunningham Boycott (land agent, died 1897), Michael Davitt (founded Irish National Land League 1879, died 1906), John Healy (journalist/broadcaster/author, died 1991), James Horan (Catholic priest who established Knock international airport, died 1986), John MacBride (revolutionary, father of

Seán/husband of Maud Gonne, died 1916), George A. Moore (writer, died 1933), William O'Dwyer (New York City Mayor/Mexican Ambassador), Grace O'Malley (pirate queen, died 1603), Antaine Ó Reaftaraí (gaelic bard), Margaret Burke-Sheridan (opera singer, died 1958).

COUNTY MEATH (Province: Leinster)

LOCATION: Situated in the eastern part of the country, Meath comprises a rich limestone plain that is the basis of the county's fertile farmlands. Meath is bordered by the Irish sea in the east and by County Dublin in the south. The two major rivers flowing through the county are the Blackwater and the history-steeped Boyne.

HISTORY: Once part of the ancient fifth province of Ireland, Meath has been inhabited for more than 8,000 years. The county is referred to as Royal Meath, as it was once home to the kings of pagan and early Christian Ireland at Tara and the place from which the ancient roads of Ireland radiated. In the Boyne Valley lie the celebrated megalithic burial grounds at Newgrange, Knowth and Dowth, the oldest Neolithic structures in Europe, predating the pyramids and Stonehenge. Newgrange could lay claim to being possibly the oldest astronomically aligned Stone Age structure in the world.

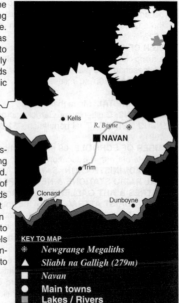

The Boyne Valley has been significant in most eras in Irish history from prehistory to the Battle of the Boyne in 1690, when King James II was vanquished by King William III for the crown of England. Arguably the most important early Christian artifact - The Book of Kells - came from Kells in Meath. Other important archaeological finds in the county include the Tara Brooch, found on the beach at Bettystown. The hill at Tara continued to play an important role in Irish history - it is said that St. Patrick was first given permission to convert Ireland to Christianity. The British army defeated Irish rebels during the 1798 rebellion at Tara, and Daniel O'Connell held a 'monster' rally here in 1843, leading an estimated one million people to protest against the Act of Union.

ORIGIN OF COUNTY NAME: Derived from the Irish 'An Mhí', meaning the middle.

LAND AREA: 905 sq. miles (County's rank in size in the island of Ireland: 14).

COUNTY CAPITAL: Navan.

MAIN TOWNS: Athboy, Dunshaughlin, Kells, Navan, Slane, Trim.

CENSUS DETAILS: Total population - 109,732 - a 4.1% increase since 1991.

NUMBER OF SCHOOLS: 103 primary schools, 19 secondary schools.

LOCAL ADMINISTRATION: *See Public Administration Chapter.*

LOCAL RADIO STATIONS & NEWSPAPERS: *See Media Chapter.*

THEATRES & ART GALLERIES: *See Arts Chapter.*

TOP 12 TOURIST ATTRACTIONS *(by visitor numbers):* Brú na Bóinne Visitor Centre (starting point for the visits to the megalithic tombs at Newgrange & Knowth), Hill of Tara (seat of the ancient high kings of Ireland), St. John's/Trim Castle (contains has the largest castle fortifications in Ireland and the location of the film *Braveheart*), Loughcrew (a series of hills with passage graves), Grove Gardens, Hill of Slane (where St Patrick lit the Pascal fire), Butterstream Gardens (at Fordstown, Kells), St. Mary's Abbey (where the Duke of Wellington was educated), Kells High Crosses, St. Colmcille's Hut in Kells, The Power & Glory Visitor's Centre at Trim, Sonairte - the National Ecology Centre in Laytown.

12 MOST FAMOUS NATIVES OF THE PAST: Francis Beaufort (devisor of the Beaufort Scale for measuring wind velocities, died 1857), Thekla Beere (founder member and president of An Óige/Irish Youth Hostel 1931, died 1991), Jim Connell (wrote the famous socialist song 'The Red Flag', died 1929), Kate Kennedy (formed America's first schoolteachers' union, died 1890), Francis Ledwidge (war poet, killed 1917 in the Great War), Mary Lavin (short story writer/ novelist, died 1996), Turlough O'Carolan (blind composer/harpist, died 1738), Charles Yelverton O'Connor (noted marine engineer in Australia, died 1881), Ambrosio O'Higgins (Viceroy in Peru, died 1801), Edward Lovett Pearce (architect/canal builder, died 1733), Horace Plunkett (founded Irish Co-op movement 1889, born Gloucestershire/related to Lord Dunsany, died 1932), St. Oliver Plunkett (Archbishop of Armagh, executed 1681).

COUNTY MONAGHAN (Province: Ulster)

LOCATION: An inland county, its rolling hilly landscape and myriad of lakes indicate that it is part of the drumlin belt in Ireland, a swath of small steep-sided hills that were formed by the melting glaciers of the Ice Age.

HISTORY: Monaghan was occupied before the bronze age, and its many low hills were natural sites for the tombs, forts and cairns of the county's early settlers. The county was part of the ancient Kingdom of Uladh or 'Ulster'. As the power of this kingdom declined, the Monaghan area was subsumed into the Oriel Kingdom and was ruled by the O'Carrolls. After the Normans invaded in 1169, the MacMahons rose to power, but they lost their grip on Monaghan to the English in the 17th century, and the town of Monaghan became a Scotts Calvinist town. The county was one of the three Ulster counties to be included in the Irish Free State in 1922.

ORIGIN OF COUNTY NAME: Derived from either the name of a ruling clan in Monaghan - the MacMahons - or from the Irish 'Muineachán', the place of the shrubs.

LAND AREA: 500 sq miles (County's rank in size in the island of Ireland: 28).

COUNTY CAPITAL: Monaghan Town.

MAIN TOWNS: Castleblaney, Carrickmacross, Clones, Monaghan.

CENSUS DETAILS: Total population - 51,266 - a 0.1% decrease since 1991.

NUMBER OF SCHOOLS: 69 primary schools, 11 secondary schools, 1 Institute of Further Education & Training.

LOCAL ADMINISTRATION: *See Public Administration Chapter.*

LOCAL RADIO STATIONS & NEWSPAPERS: *See Media Chapter.*

THEATRES & ART GALLERIES: *See Arts Chapter.*

TOP 12 TOURIST ATTRACTIONS: the antique lace exhibition at Clones, Castle Leslie in Glaslough, Clones Fort and Clones Medieval Abbey, the early Christian ruins at Donagh Graveyard, Fane River Park and River Walk, Heritage Centre at St. Louis Convent in Monaghan, Hope Castle, Lough Muckno Leisure Park, Monaghan County Museum (a centre that features archaeology, folk life, crafts, transport, coinage, industry and the arts), Patrick Kavanagh Rural and Literary Resource Centre at Iniskeen, Rossmore Forest Park, Tyrone Guthrie Centre (Annamakerrig House - a retreat for writers and artists to use as a working base).

FAMOUS NATIVES OF THE PAST: Lord Blayney (gave name to Castleblayney), Sir Charles Gavin Duffy (co-founded 'The Nation' newspaper/Australian statesman; died 1903), Thomas Lipton (founder of Liptons Teas; died 1931), John Joseph Lynch (first Archbishop of Toronto; died 1888), John R. Gregg (inventor of shorthand; died 1948), Tyrone Guthrie (theatre producer/benefactor, born Tunbridge Wells, left house to the state for writers/artists residence; died 1971), Patrick Kavanagh (poet; died 1967), Charles David Lucas (first recipient of Victoria Cross; died 1914), Canon Patrick Moynagh (organised mass emigration to Prince Edward Island, Canada, just before 1845), Eoin O'Duffy (Garda commissioner/General; died 1944), Sir William Whitla (physician; died 1933).

KEY TO MAP
✳ *Clones Fort*
▲ *Mullyash Mountain (320 m)*
■ *Monaghan*
● Main towns
■ Lakes / Rivers

COUNTY OFFALY (Province: Leinster)

LOCATION: Offaly, an inland county, is located at the heart of Ireland and is bordered by Slieve Bloom mountain range in the south-east and the River Shannon in the west. The county's Clara bog is one of the largest remaining relatively intact raised bogs in Western Europe and is now recognised as being of international importance. Offaly's bogs and wetlands are home to several species of native and migrant birds; a total of 87 species have been recorded to date.

HISTORY: In the past, the Shannon acted as the main route for the county. The Danes sailed up it to Clonmacnoise, one of the largest and most important monastic sites in Ireland, and raided it. The ruins of Clonmacnoise include a cathedral, three high crosses, two round towers and eight churches. In addition, Ireland's earliest Irish language manuscript was produced there and Ireland's last high king - Rory O'Connor - is buried here. After the English conquered the area, Offaly was known as King's County from 1556 and was, along with Laois, the first region in Ireland to be planted by the English. Other structures of historical note in the county include castles, the Martello Tower in Banagher and the Napoleonic fortifications at Lusmagh and Shannonbridge. One of the more spectacular castles in Ireland - Birr Castle Demesne - is sit-

KEY TO MAP
✳ *Clara Bog*
▲ *Arderin Mtn. (528m)*
■ *Tullamore*
● Main towns
■ Lakes / Rivers

uated in Offaly. Within its confines can be found a fabulous array of rare and exotic plants, as well as a giant telescope dating from 1845, once the largest in the world. A new telescope and observatory have recently been installed, and the demesne is the home of Ireland's new science museum.

ORIGIN OF COUNTY NAME: From the Irish 'Uíbh Fhailí', meaning Failghe's People.
LAND AREA: 771 sq. miles (County's rank in size in the island of Ireland: 18).
COUNTY CAPITAL: Tullamore.
MAIN TOWNS: Banagher, Birr, Edenderry, Ferbane, Tullamore.
CENSUS DETAILS: Total population - 59,080 - a 1% increase since 1991.
NUMBER OF SCHOOLS: 68 primary schools, 13 secondary schools.
LOCAL ADMINISTRATION: *See Public Administration Chapter.*
LOCAL RADIO STATIONS & NEWSPAPERS: *See Media Chapter.*
THEATRES & ART GALLERIES: *See Arts Chapter.*
TOP 12 TOURIST ATTRACTIONS: Clonmacnoise monastic ruins, Birr Castle and Demesne (with its newly opened science museum), Clonmacnoise and West Offaly Railway, Durrow Abbey and High Cross, Slieve Bloom Environment Park, Kinnitty Castle, Leap Castle at Clareen, Cloghan Castle, artillery fortifications at Shannonbridge and Lusmagh (from Napoleonic times), the Blackwater Bog (a raised bog of major significance near Clonmacnoise), the Martello Tower at Banagher, Tullamore Dew Heritage Centre.
FAMOUS NATIVES OF THE PAST: Charles Jervas (portrait artist in the courts of George I and II, died 1739), George Johnstone Stoney (first to propose existence of electrons, died 1911), John Joly (developed first practical colour photography system and radioactivity treatment for cancer, died 1933), Charles Parsons (invented the turbine, died 1931), Lawrence Parsons (brother of Charles, determined temperature of moon surface, died 1908), William Parsons (Earl of Rosse, astronomer, born New York/educated Offaly/Dublin, died 1867).

COUNTY ROSCOMMON (Province: Connacht)

LOCATION: Roscommon is an inland county in Connacht. Two-thirds of it is bounded by water, with the River Shannon and Lough Ree to the east, the River Suck to the west and Loughs Key, Gara and Boderg to the north. One-third of the county is under bog, mostly in the west.

HISTORY: Many traces of early colonisation are evident in Roscommon; the county has numerous burial mounds, megalithic tombs and ring forts. Rathcroghan, at the centre of the county, was home to the kings of Connacht from the earliest times and later became home to the high kings of Ireland. The O'Conors and the MacDermotts, two of Roscommon's great families, were among the leading Gaelic clans in medieval Ireland. Nearly all of the county's lands were confiscated during the various English plantations. These were subsequently reclaimed by the Irish Land Commission in the 1920s and 1930s.

ORIGIN OF COUNTY NAME: Derived from the Irish 'Ros', meaning a wooded or pleasant gentle height and 'Coman', the name of the county's famous Irish saint and the first bishop of the see.

LAND AREA: 984 sq. miles (County's rank in size in the island of Ireland: 11).

COUNTY CAPITAL: Roscommon.

MAIN TOWNS: Boyle, Castlerea, Elphin, Roscommon, Strokestown.

CENSUS DETAILS: Total population - 51,975 - a 1.1% increase since 1991.

NUMBER OF SCHOOLS: 95 primary schools, 11 secondary schools.

LOCAL ADMINISTRATION: *See Public Administration Chapter.*

LOCAL RADIO STATIONS & NEWSPAPERS: *See Media Chapter.*

THEATRES & ART GALLERIES: *See Arts Chapter.*

TOP 12 TOURIST ATTRACTIONS: Arigna Scenic Drive, Boyle Cistercian Abbey (9,240), Clonalis House in Castlerea, Dr. Douglas

KEY TO MAP
✳ **L. Key Forest Park**
▲ **Slieve Bawn (264m)**
■ **Roscommon**
● **Main towns**
■ **Lakes / Rivers**

Hyde Interpretive Centre in Frenchpark, Keadue Village (national tidy towns winner), King House in Boyle, Lough Key Forest Park, Rock of Doon near Boyle, Rathcroghan and Carnfree Ancient Celtic Sites, Roscommon Abbey and County Museum, Strokestown Park House and Famine Museum, the Old Schoolhouse Museum in Ballintubber.

12 MOST FAMOUS NATIVES OF THE PAST: James Dillon (politician, died 1986), George French (Lieutenant-Colonel/founded the Canadian Mounties 1873, born 1941), Percy French (painter/songwriter, died 1920), Douglas Hyde (academic/translator/former President of Ireland, died 1949), Sir Alferd Keogh (British Army Director-General, father county-born, died 1936), the King family (owned Rockingham demesne), the Mahons (notorious landlords of Strokestown), The O'Connors (high kings and the oldest family in Europe who can trace their ancestry back to 75 A.D.), Turlough O'Carolan (blind harpist), Maureen O'Sullivan (film actress/mother of Mia Farrow, born 1911), Patrick J. Whitney (founded St. Patrick's Foreign Missionary Society 1932, died 1942),

Sir William Wilde (surgeon/inventor of the ophthalmoscope/father of Oscar Wilde).

COUNTY SLIGO (Province: Connacht)

LOCATION: Sligo is a maritime county on the north-west coast of Ireland. Its Atlantic coast is dominated by the great bays of Killala, Sligo and Donegal. The county's topography is characterised by unusually shaped hills rising from steep valleys, including Benbulben at the prow of Kings Mountain; Knocknarea, the alleged burial site of Queen Maeve; and the ancient Ox Mountains, the oldest mountain range in Sligo at 600 million years old.

HISTORY: Evidence of human habitation in Sligo dates back nearly 6,000 years; one of the largest Stone Age cemeteries in Europe and one of the oldest in Ireland is situated to the west of Sligo town at Carrowmore. The remains of early Christian monasteries can be found on Inishmurray Island and at Drumcliffe. Near Drumcliffe, Saints Columcille and Finian fought a battle in the sixth century for the copy of a psalter that Columcille had secretly made. Columcille's self-imposed exile to Iona was a direct result of this battle, possibly the earliest battle over copyright. Most historical events in Sligo reflect the fact that the area was of strategic importance as one of the main conduits to the North. As a result, the region, but particularly Sligo town, suffered attacks from both the Northern chieftains and the English. The town of Sligo was established in Viking times, and an abbey and castle were founded by the Norman Maurice Fitzgerald during the 13th century. These were destroyed in 1641 by Sir Frederick Hamilton who burned the town and murdered its inhabitants. The town was subsequently rebuilt and became a prosperous port during the 19th century.

ORIGIN OF COUNTY NAME: Derived from the Irish 'Sligeach', meaning Shelly River.

LAND AREA: 709 sq. miles.

COUNTY CAPITAL: Sligo (County's rank in size in the island of Ireland: 21)

MAIN TOWNS: Ballymote, Grange, Sligo, Tubbercurry.

CENSUS DETAILS: Total population - 55,821 - a 1.3% increase since 1991.

NUMBER OF SCHOOLS: 75 primary schools,16 secondary schools, 1 Institute of Technology, 1 college of education.

LOCAL ADMINISTRATION: *See Public Administration Chapter.*

LOCAL RADIO STATIONS & NEWSPAPERS: *See Media Chapter.*

THEATRES & ART GALLERIES: *See Arts Chapter.*

TOP 12 TOURIST ATTRACTIONS: Carrowmably martello tower near Dromore West, the Caves of Keshcorran (where legend notes Diarmuid and Gráinne took refuge), the Glen (an area of botanical importance near Strandhill), Gleniff Horseshoe, Innismurray Island (with its early Christian remains), the Lake Isle of Innisfree on Lough Gill, Lissadell House (home to the Gore-Booth family), Sligo's Neolithic monuments (at Carrowmore, Carrowkeel, Creevykeel and Heapstown), Sligo Abbey, Rosses Point (a seaside resort with a world-renowned golf course and a metal man - an early 19th century navigational aid and one of four left in the world), Tobernalt (a holy well outside Sligo town), Yeats's grave at Drumcliffe.

12 MOST FAMOUS NATIVES OF THE PAST: Michael Coleman (traditional fiddler; died 1945), Mary Colum (critic/essayist/teacher; died 1957), Eva Gore-Booth (poet/dramatist/feminist/artist; died 1926), William Higgins (proposed existence of atoms 1789; died 1825), Maurice Fitzgerald (Norman founder of Sligo town), Countess Constance Markievicz (revolutionary, sister of Eva Gore-Booth, born London/reared Sligo; died 1927), James Morrison (fiddler/teacher/bandleader; died 1947), Tadhg Dall Ó hUiginn (bardic poet; died 1591), Susan Pollexfen (daughter of a shipping merchant/mother of Jack and William Butler Yeats), Nicholas Taaffe (Lieutenant-general of Australian army 1752; died 1769), William Butler Yeats (poet; died 1939), Jack Butler Yeats (artist/writer, born London/brother of William; died 1952).

KEY TO MAP

* ✳ *Carrowmore Megaliths*
* ▲ *Truskmore (647m)*
* ■ *Sligo*
* ● **Main towns**
* ■ **Lakes / Rivers**

Map labels: SLIGO, Lough Gill, Enniscrone, Easky Lough, Owenmore River, R. Moy, Templehouse Lake, Lough Arrow, Tobercurry, Ballymote, Lough Gara

COUNTY TIPPERARY (Province: Munster)

LOCATION: Located in the south of Ireland, Tipperary is Ireland's largest inland county. It is bordered by several mountain ranges - the Galtees and the Knockmealdowns in the south, the Silvermines and Arra Mountains in the west, Devilsbit mountain in the north and the Slieveardagh Hills and Slievenamon in the south-east. The River Suir cuts through the centre of the county and Lough Derg forms its boundary in the north-west. The great central-southern limestone plain in the county, which extends into County Limerick, is better known as the Golden Vale and is famed for its fertile farmlands. Tipperary's diverse geology has resulted in coal mines and slate quarries. It is the only county in Ireland that is divided into ridings. These divisions date back to 1838 when the English authorities decided that the county's large population (it was the third highest populated county at the time) and the alleged incidence of crime and lawlessness necessitated that the county be split, and it is still administered as the North Riding and the South Riding.

HISTORY: Tipperary contains a wealth of historical sites, the most prominent being the Rock of Cashel, which was the centre of ecclesiastical and secular life in Munster from the end of the fourth century until well into medieval times. The Kings of Munster ruled from Cashel until Brian Boru came into power, and in 1101, Muircheartach O'Brien gave the Rock of Cashel to the church. Tipperary was spared most of the ravages of the Viking attacks, and when the Normans arrived, the county was placed in the hands of the Butlers, whose royal patronage protected the county from all plantations except that of Cromwell. The Cromwellian Plantation had disastrous consequences for most of the native Irish in the county; some remained on as tenant farmers, while others moved to the bogland areas. Those who stayed on had to pay exorbitant rents, pushing them into joining the Whiteboy movement in the 18th century and carrying out violent reprisals against the English overlords. This ran concurrently with faction fighting that led the county to be christened 'Turbulent Tipperary'. By the middle of the 19th century, the county had a strong Fenian following. It defiantly elected John Mitchel, a Young Ireland transportee on two occasions and played a full political role in the formation of Ireland's fledgling state.

KEY TO MAP
✳ *Rock of Cashel*
▲ *Galtymore Mountain (920m)*
■ *Nenagh (Tipperary NR)*
■ *Clonmel (Tipperary SR)*
● **Main towns**
■ **Lakes / Rivers**

ORIGIN OF COUNTY NAME: Derived from the Irish 'Tiobraid Arann', the well of Era, referring to the River Ara.

LAND AREA: 1,647 sq miles (County's rank in size in the island of Ireland: 6).

COUNTY CAPITAL: Nenagh (North Riding), Clonmel (South Riding).

MAIN TOWNS: Cahir, Carrick-on-Suir, Cashel, Clonmel, Nenagh, Roscrea, Templemore, Tipperary, Thurles.

CENSUS DETAILS: Total population - 133,535 - a 0.8% increase since 1991.

NUMBER OF SCHOOLS: 173 primary schools, 36 secondary schools, 1 college of theology and philosophy, 1 garda training college.

LOCAL ADMINISTRATION: *See Public Administration Chapter.*

LOCAL RADIO STATIONS & NEWSPAPERS: *See Media Chapter.*

THEATRES & ART GALLERIES: *See Arts Chapter.*

TOP 12 TOURIST ATTRACTIONS: the Bianconi Coach Road (on Slieve na Muck), Cashel of Kings Heritage Centre, Bru Boru Heritage Centre, Fethard Augustinian Friary and Folk Farm and Transport Museum, Glen of Aherlow, GAA Museum (Lár na Pairce in Thurles), GPA Bolton Library (some of the collection of which dates from the beginning of the age of printing), Holycross Abbey (one of the most picturesque monasteries in Ireland), Mitchelstown Caves (containing some of Europe's finest calcite formations), Ormonde Castle in Carrick-on-Suir, the Rock of Cashel, the county museums at Tipperary and Clonmel.

12 MOST FAMOUS NATIVES OF THE PAST: John Joe Barry ('The Ballincurry Hare' - world record-holding athlete, born 1924), Charles Bianconi (operated transport services throughout county 1815, born Italy, died 1875), J.D. Bernal (scientist, died 1971), Dan Breen (revolutionary, died 1969), the Davins brothers (Tom, Maurice, Pat, athletes, died 1894, 1927, 1949), Pádraig De Brún (academic/poet/priest/translator, died 1960), Sir Henry Kellett (explorer, died 1975), Sean Kenny (set designer, died 1973), Charles Kickham (Fenian/ journalist/novelist, died 1882), Fr. Theobald Matthew (founded Temperance Society 1838, died 1856), Thomas McDonagh (revolutionary/poet, died 1916), Tom Semple (hurler/long puck exponent/GAA stadium named after him, died 1943).

COUNTY TYRONE (Province: Ulster)

LOCATION: An inland county, Tyrone is set in the centre of the province and is the largest county in Northern Ireland. The Sperrin mountains dominate the Tyrone skyline, and the county is bounded by Armagh, Derry, Donegal, Fermanagh, Monaghan and Lough Neagh.

HISTORY: Evidence of human settlement in the area dates back 6,000 years. The Beaghmore Stone Circles, near Cookstown, attest to this ancient inhabitation, as do other burial chambers, monuments and cairns found throughout the county. The hilltop enclosure of Tullyhogue Fort served for a time as the inauguration site for the Celtic kings of Ulster. Tyrone is rich in early Christian remains; examples of such remains include the Ardboe High Cross, which depicts biblical scenes, and Donaghmore High Cross. Tyrone is renowned for its connection with the O'Neills, the clan from which it takes its name. Their domain at one stage incorporated parts of Tyrone, Armagh, Derry and Donegal. They ruled over Ulster for more than four centuries and hindered the English in their attempts to colonise the region. After the defeat of the chieftains at the Battle of Kinsale in 1601, however, their power waned and they eventually left Ireland, an event that has been termed the 'Flight of Earls'. Their lands were forfeit to the crown, and in 1610, Tyrone, along with most of the counties in Ulster was planted by Scottish and English settlers. Many inhabitants of the area, particularly those of Presbyterian Scottish Stock, suffered religious persecution during the 18th century along with the native Irish and emigrated from Tyrone to America in the early 1700s. There is a strong connection culturally between Tyrone and the Appalachian mountain region in Virginia. In particular, the musical culture of the emigrants has had a formative influence on American folk music.

ORIGIN OF COUNTY NAME: Derived from the Irish 'Tír Eoghain', meaning the territory of Eoghan who was one of the sons of Niall of the Nine Hostages, St. Patrick's abductor.

LAND AREA: 1,211 sq. miles (County's rank in size in the island of Ireland: 8).

LARGEST TOWN: Omagh.

MAIN TOWNS: Augher, Castlederg, Clogher, Cookstown, Coalisland, Dungannon, Omagh, Strabane.

CENSUS DETAILS: 152,827 *(estimated)*.

NUMBER OF SCHOOLS: 169 primary schools, 30 secondary schools, 2 Further Education Institutes.

LOCAL ADMINISTRATION: *See Public Administration Chapter.*

LOCAL RADIO STATIONS & NEWSPAPERS: *See Media Chapter.*

THEATRES & ART GALLERIES: *See Arts Chapter.*

TOP 12 TOURIST ATTRACTIONS*(by visitor numbers)*: Ulster American Folk Park (118,758 - tells the story of 200 years of emigration to America), Tyrone Crystal (74,700), Benburb Valley Park (55,000 - contains ruins of Benburb Castle and walks along the River Blackwater), Parkanaur Forest Park (51,800 - home to a herd of white fallow deer and daffodil and rhododendron plantations), Drum Manor Forest Park (43,700 - with shrub gardens, walled butterfly garden and arboretum), Ulster History Park (41,448 - narrates the history of human settlement in Ulster), Gortin Glen Forest Park (34,500 - five-mile forest drive), An Creagan Visitor Centre (28,000 - tells archaeological history and stories of the Omagh area), Sperrin Heritage Centre (9,500 - containing natural history and gold-mining exhibits), Grant Ancestral Home (4,418 - the ancestral home of the 18th U.S. president in Ballygawley), Corn Mill Heritage Centre (tells the story of Coalisland's industrial history), Ardboe High Cross (richly decorated high cross dating back to the 10th century).

FAMOUS NATIVES OF THE PAST: Mrs Cecil Frances Alexander (celebrated hymn writer of 'All Things Bright and Beautiful'), William Carleton (writer, died 1869), John Crockett (father of Davy Crockett' - legendary 'King of the Wild Frontier', emigrated to US 1782), John Dunlap (printer - founded first US daily newspaper - printed 'The Declaration of Independence,' died 1812), Jimmy Kennedy (lyricist - 'Teddy Bear's Picnic'/'Hokey, Cokey'/'Red Sails in the Sunset', died 1984), Sir William McArthur (first Irish Lord Mayor of London, born 1809), Thomas McKeen and Thomas Nelson (signatories to Declaration of Independence 1776), Owen Roe O'Neill (led Ulster forces who rebelled supporting Charles I/nephew of Hugh, died 1649), Hugh O'Neill (Clan Chieftain/second Earl of Tyrone/gaelic leader, died 1616), Brian O'Nolan (writer, used the pseudonyms Flann O'Brien and Myles naGopaleen, died 1966), Dr. George Sigerson (zoologist/social reformer/writer; born 1836), James Wilson (emigrated to U.S. 1807, grandfather of Woodrow Wilson - President of US 1913-21).

● Strabane

● Castlederg ▲ Cookstown ● *L. Neagh*

✳

■ OMAGH

Dungannon ●

Augher ● Aughnacloy ●
Clogher ●

Fivemiletown ●

KEY TO MAP
✳   *Ulster American Folk Park*
▲   *Mullaghclogha (634m)*
■   *Omagh*
●   **Main towns**
■   **Lakes / Rivers**

COUNTY WATERFORD (Province: Munster)

LOCATION: Waterford is situated on the south-eastern seaboard. Its coast stretches from Youghal Bay to Waterford Harbour. The Comeragh, Knockmealdown, and Monavullagh mountain ranges dominate the landscape and border the county to the north and north-west. The River Blackwater and its tributary, the River Bride, carve out the western boundary and the River Suir defines the eastern boundary. The diversity of the landscape found in Waterford is based on the three main rock types - the old red sandstone of the mountain ranges, the shale found in the north and the limestone belt found in the south-west.

HISTORY: Waterford's history gives testament to the fact that it has been one of the few counties to successfully assimilate the three diverse races of the Gaels, the Vikings and the Normans. Because of Waterford Harbour's wide sea route into the heart of the country, the county was the focus of Viking, Norman and English activity. The city of Waterford was designated a royal city circa 1171 and became one of Ireland's major ports and merchant centres. The county has a unique feature for the east coast in that it has a surviving Gaeltacht area - Ring - located near Dungarvan. This is despite the county's subjection to four centuries of an active Viking presence, as reflected in many of the town names, and subsequent waves of Norman invasion and settlement. The ability to endure these attacks carried on through the turbulent events of the 18th and 19th centuries. Waterford's population showed a talent for surviving and prospering; Thomas Francis Meagher, a fervent nationalist, was sentenced to death in 1848, but he escaped to the U.S. and went on to become Governor of Montana.

ORIGIN OF COUNTY NAME: Derived from the Viking 'Vethrafjorthr', meaning weather haven. The Irish 'Port Láirge' means the Port of Laraig, Laraig being a tenth century Viking.

LAND AREA: 713.08 sq. miles (County's rank in size in the island of Ireland: 20).

COUNTY CAPITAL: Waterford City.

MAIN TOWNS: Dungarvan, Tramore, Waterford.

CENSUS DETAILS: Total population - 52,140 (excluding Waterford Borough) - a 1.6% increase since 1991.

NUMBER OF SCHOOLS: 59 primary schools, 11 secondary schools.

LOCAL ADMINISTRATION: See Public Administration Chapter.

LOCAL RADIO STATIONS & NEWSPAPERS: See Media Chapter.

THEATRES & ART GALLERIES: See Arts Chapter.

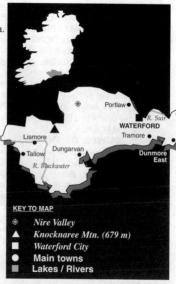

KEY TO MAP
- ✳ *Nire Valley*
- ▲ *Knocknaree Mtn. (679 m)*
- ■ *Waterford City*
- ● **Main towns**
- ■ **Lakes / Rivers**

TOP 12 TOURIST ATTRACTIONS: Dromana (a Hindu-Gothic gate lodge), Laserworld, the Master McGrath Monument (possibly the only public monument to a greyhound in Ireland), Mount Congreve Gardens in Kilmeadan, Mount Mellerey Abbey, the Nire Valley (a scenic area, with glens and waterfalls), Portlaw (a model village founded by a Quaker family), Tourin House and Gardens, the Vee (a spectacular scenic route through the Knockmealdown mountains), Waterford's Castles (King John's Castle at Dungarvan, Dunhill Castle, Knockmaun Castle), Waterford Crystal Factory, West Waterford Vineyards at Cappoquin.

FAMOUS NATIVES OF THE PAST: Robert Boyle ('The Father of Chemistry' who devised Boyle's law, died 1691), Sir Hubert de la Poer Gough (British General/Irish unionist, died 1963), John Hogan (sculptor/poet, 'the Bard of Dunclug,' died 1858), Master McGrath (greatest-ever racing greyhound), David Patrick Moran (author/journalist, died 1936), Tadhg Gaelach O'Suilleabháin (gaelic poet, died 1795), Tyrone Power (film actor, grandfather came from Kilmacthomas, born 1903), Ernest Thomas Sinton Walton (scientist, first achieved splitting of atoms/joint Nobel-laureate 1951, died 1995).

WATERFORD CITY

CENSUS DETAILS: Total population - 42,540 - a 5.5% increase since 1991.

NUMBER OF SCHOOLS: 19 primary schools, 10 secondary schools, 1 Institute of Technology, 1 college of Theology and Philosophy.

LOCAL ADMINISTRATION: See Public Administration Chapter.

LOCAL RADIO STATIONS & NEWSPAPERS: See Media Chapter.

THEATRES & ART GALLERIES: See Arts Chapter.

WHO WAS WHO: Noel Browne (politician/medical doctor; died 1997), Alexis Fitzgerald (lawyer/economist/senator; died 1985), Thomas Francis Meagher (part of 1848 Rising/Governor of Montana; died 1867), Richard Mulcahy (revolutionary/soldier/politician; died 1971), William Vincent Wallace (composed the opera *Maritana*).

COUNTY WESTMEATH (Province: Leinster)

LOCATION: An inland county at the heart of Ireland, Westmeath's northern regions are dotted with drumlins - small steep-sided hills that were formed by the melting glaciers of the Ice Age - while the central and southern regions of the county are flatter, with bogs and lakes. The southern part also contains a long line of low hills, or eskers, another feature dating from the Ice Age, formed from sand and rounded stones.

HISTORY: Westmeath has played a prominent role in Ireland's history, as one of its principal towns, Athlone, is a major crossing point on the River Shannon. Two centuries prior to St. Patrick's arrival, the county was home to the seat of the High King of Ireland at Uisneach, near Mullingar, which was also the meeting point of the five ancient provinces of Ireland. St. Patrick brought Christianity to Westmeath in the fifth century, and there are a number of notable, early monastic sites in the county, particularly that of Fore, established by St. Fechin. The Normans arrived in the region circa 1170, and their numerous mottes-and-baileys can still be seen. The county was originally part of the ancient province of Meath, but in 1542, an act of law by Henry VIII designated it as a separate county.

ORIGIN OF COUNTY NAME: Derived from the Irish 'an Iar Mhí', Iar meaning west and Mí the central place.

LAND AREA: 710 sq. miles (County's rank in size in the island of Ireland: 22).

COUNTY CAPITAL: Mullingar.

MAIN TOWNS: Athlone, Kilbeggan, Moate.

CENSUS DETAILS: Total population - 63,314 - a 2.3% increase since 1991.

NUMBER OF SCHOOLS: 78 primary schools, 17 secondary schools, 1 Institute of Technology, 1 business school, 1 agricultural college.

LOCAL ADMINISTRATION: *See Public Administration Chapter.*
LOCAL RADIO STATIONS & NEWSPAPERS: *See Media Chapter.*
THEATRES & ART GALLERIES: *See Arts Chapter.*
TOP 12 TOURIST ATTRACTIONS: Athlone Castle Interpretative Centre, the Catstone on Uisneach Hill, the Dower House of the Pollard Family at Castlepollard, An Dun Transport and Heritage Museum in Athlone, Fore Abbey, St. Fechin's Church, Gigginstown House and Mearescourt House in Mullingar, Locke's Distillery (one of the world's oldest licensed whiskey distilleries), the Military Museum at Columb Barracks, Mullingar Bronze and Pewter Visitor Centre, Tullynally Castle and Gardens in Castlepollard, Tyrrellspass Castle and Museum.
FAMOUS NATIVES OF THE PAST: Thomas St. George Armstrong (founded Argentine stock exchange/Buenos Aires Bank, emigrated 1817), Colonel Charles Howard Bury (commanded first British Everest expedition 1921, died 1963), Mary Josephine Hannon (one of first Irish female doctors), Count John McCormack (famous tenor, died 1945), Brinsley McNamara (author/dramatist), Thomas Power O'Connor (publisher, died 1929), Myles 'Slasher' O'Reilly (defended Finea 1646), Captain Richard Tyrrell (defeated Elizabethan army during Nine Years War), James Woods (Annals of Westmeath author).

KEY TO MAP
✳ *Hill of Uisneach* ▲ *Mullaghmeen*
(260m) ■ *Mullingar* ● **Main towns**

COUNTY WEXFORD (Province: Leinster)

LOCATION: Known as the 'Model County', Wexford is set in the south-east coast of Ireland and enjoys the best of Irish weather. It is bounded by the sea on the east - St. George's Channel - and by hills and the River Barrow on the west. The River Slaney, a noted salmon river, flows through the county.
HISTORY: The county's history has been shaped by the many invasions it has endured. The Vikings attacked and settled the main town of Wexford, from the 9th to the 12th centuries, to be followed by the Normans, who captured the town of Wexford after they landed in the country in 1169. The county suffered Cromwell's attacks in 1649, when he attacked the town and murdered 200 people. The men of Wexford were among the main instigators in the 1798 Rebellion. Their opposition to the English came to a head at the famous Battle of Vinegar Hill in Enniscorthy, the 200th anniversary of which was celebrated in 1998.
ORIGIN OF COUNTY NAME: Wexford is Viking in origin; the Irish 'Loch Garman' means inlet by the sea-washed bank.
LAND AREA: 909 sq. miles (County's rank in size in the island of Ireland: 13).
COUNTY CAPITAL: Wexford.
MAIN TOWNS: Bunclody, Enniscorthy, Gorey, New Ross, Wexford.
CENSUS DETAILS: Total population - 104,371 - a 2.3% increase since 1991.
NUMBER OF SCHOOLS: 103 primary schools, 20 secondary schools, 1 college of Theology and Philosophy.
LOCAL ADMINISTRATION: *See Public Administration Chapter.*
LOCAL RADIO STATIONS & NEWSPAPERS: *See Media Chapter.*
THEATRES & ART GALLERIES: *See Arts Chapter.*
TOP 12 TOURIST ATTRACTIONS: Craanford Mills, Dunbrody Abbey and Visitor Centre, Hook Lighthouse (one of the oldest lighthouses in Europe, dating from the 12th century), John F. Kennedy Park, (marks the birthplace of the late president's grandfather), Irish National Heritage Park at Ferrycarrig, Tintern Abbey, Wexford's Castles (Ballyhack Castle, Enniscorthy Castle, Ferns Castle, Johnstown Castle and Gardens, Rathmacknee Castle, Slade Castle), Wexford County Museum in Enniscorthy, Wexford's high crosses (at Arthurstown, Ballinaray, Carrick and Killesk), Wexford town (a designated heritage town), Wexford Wildfowl Reserve, Woodville Victorian Walled Garden in New Ross.
FAMOUS NATIVES OF THE PAST: James Annesley (title claimant, inspiration for Robert Louis Stevenson's *Kidnapped*, died 1760), Charles Blacker Vignoles (Ireland's first railway engineer-in-chief, died 1875), Brendan Corish (politician, died 1990), James A. Cullen (Jesuit priest, launched Pioneer Total Abstinence Association 1898, died 1921), James Dillon (politician, died 1986), Robert John Le Mesurier McClure (discovered Northwest

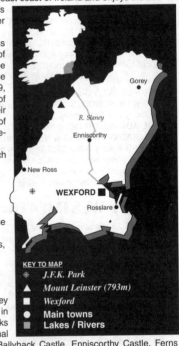

KEY TO MAP
✳ *J.F.K. Park*
▲ *Mount Leinster (793m)*
■ *Wexford*
● **Main towns**
■ **Lakes / Rivers**

Passage for Arctic expeditions, died 1873), Fr. John Murphy (led Wexford 1798 rising), John Redmond (led Parnellite fraction of Home Rule Party, died 1890), William Redmond (politician, died 1917), Jem Roche (boxer 1900's), Michael James Whitty (founded first U.K. Penny Daily Newspaper 1855, died 1873).

COUNTY WICKLOW (Province: Leinster)

KEY TO MAP

✳ *Powerscourt Waterfall*
▲ *Lugnaquilla (927m)*
■ *Wicklow* ● **Main towns**
■ **Lakes / Rivers**

LOCATION: A small maritime county on the east coast of Ireland, Wicklow is known as the 'Garden of Ireland'. A raised granite ridge runs through it, containing two of the highest passes in the country - the Sally Gap and the Wicklow Gap - which are major routes to the east and west for the county. To the north of this ridge is Dublin city, to the west lie the Blessington lakes and to the east is the tranquil valley of Glendalough, which was a centre of early Christianity in Ireland. In addition to lakes at Blessington and Roundwood, the county is criss-crossed by rivers.

HISTORY: The county's history is directly related to its physical setting. Glendalough was established as a monastic city from a sixth century hermitage set up by St. Kevin in the peaceful setting of 'the Glen of Two Lakes'. Although the county's highlands assisted in protecting the county's Gaelic heritage, the lowlands of the west and the east coast were more susceptible to the successive raids launched by the Vikings, the Normans and the English. Dermot McMurrough, a Wicklow chieftain and King of Leinster, invited the Normans to help him repossess his lands, and it was this act that led to English taking power and that ultimately directed the course of Irish history. Their sojourn in the county is marked by the many stately homes and gardens scattered around the county, the most notable of these being Powerscourt and Russborough House. Many of Wicklow's villages still reflect their English origins as estate villages. The Irish kept their hold on the highlands, providing refuge to rebels, and the people of Wicklow played a prominent role in the 1798 rebellion. However, after the rebellion, the British built the Military Road through the county to provide them with easier access to the rebel strongholds.

ORIGIN OF COUNTY NAME: Derived from 'Vykinglo' - the original Viking settlements founded in the county around the eighth century.

LAND AREA: 782 sq. miles (County's rank in size in the island of Ireland: 17).

COUNTY CAPITAL: Wicklow. Bray.

MAIN TOWNS: Arklow, Bray. Greystones, Wicklow.

CENSUS DETAILS: Total population - 102,683 - a 5.6% increase since 1991.

NUMBER OF SCHOOLS: 84 primary schools, 21 secondary schools.

LOCAL ADMINISTRATION: *See Public Administration Chapter.* ,

LOCAL RADIO STATIONS & NEWSPAPERS: *See Media Chapter.*

THEATRES & ART GALLERIES: *See Arts Chapter.*

TOP 12 TOURIST ATTRACTIONS: Arklow Pottery, Avondale House (the home of Charles Stewart Parnell), Blessington lakes, Glendalough (with its many monastic ruins), the Maritime Museum in Arklow, the National Aquarium at Bray, National Garden Exhibition Centre at Kilquade, Powerscourt Gardens (containing the impressive ruins of Powerscourt House), Russborough House (an 18th century Palladian mansion that houses the internationally renowned Sir Alfred Beit art collection), Wicklow Historic Gaol, Wicklow Mountains National Park, Wicklow's seaside resorts (Brittas Bay, Arklow, Clogga, Sliver Strand, Bray and Greystones).

FAMOUS NATIVES OF THE PAST: Robert Barton (signatory of Anglo-Irish Treaty, died 1975), Harry Bradshaw (golfer, died 1990), Robert Erskine Childers (writer/nationalist, born London, father of President Erskine Childers, died 1922), Dame Ninette de Valois (ballet dancer/choreographer, born 1898), Michael Dwyer (1798 rebellion leader), Captain Robert Charles Halpin (one of the greatest navigators of 19th century), Peter J. O'Connor (world record athlete 1901, born 1874), Cearbhall O'Dálaigh (President of Ireland, died 1978), Anna Parnell (sister of Charles, founded the Ladies Land League in 1881, died 1911), Charles Stewart Parnell (leader of the Home Rule Party, died 1891), Joshua Pim (only Irish Wimbledon Singles tennis champion 1893, born 1869).

The launch of the Euro: A black day for Ireland

By **Richard Douthwaite**

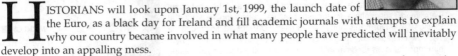

HISTORIANS will look upon January 1st, 1999, the launch date of the Euro, as a black day for Ireland and fill academic journals with attempts to explain why our country became involved in what many people have predicted will inevitably develop into an appalling mess.

They will find Brussels' two main motives for closing down Europe's national currencies easy to explain. The primary one, they will agree, is that a country's currency is one of its government's main levers of power and EU member-states had to be persuaded to give up their national levers because they stood in the way of the centralised management of an effective European super-state.

The second reason they will spot for the launch of the Euro is that it can be expected to displace the dollar as the world's preferred reserve currency. At present, 57% of the world's foreign exchange reserves are held in dollars, around three times the amount held in ecus, D-marks, French francs and sterling combined. Having a reserve currency gives a country an enormous advantage, because it means that other countries happily sell it their goods but don't use the money they receive to buy goods and services in exchange. Instead, they leave them sitting in their central banks. As a result, the US has, over the years, received billions of dollars worth of imports and given nothing in return apart from paper notes and electronic credits. The EU would very like a much bigger share of this wonderful system of trade and intends that the Euro will bring that about.

Both these motives are pretty unfamiliar to us, so what will historians make of the claims now being made in EU propaganda? For example, the claim that interest rates in Euroland will fall to current German levels? Or that the efficiency gained by not having to have people to convert money from one European currency to another will improve our competitiveness on international markets?

On interest rates, I believe future historians will say that although cuts were made initially, rates did not stay low very long as the new European Central Bank was unable to muster political support for controlling the money supply as tightly as the Germans had done. This will be because, with European unemployment rates rising rapidly as a result of the Russian, Latin American and Asian crises, most Euroland politicians will soon be calling for masses of money to be put into circulation. As a result, international investors will begin to fear that the Euro will be unable to maintain its exchange rate with the dollar, the Swiss franc, and even the yen and take their money out of Europe, forcing interest rates back up.

As for claims of greater efficiency leading to improved competitiveness, future historians will simply shake their heads at our stupidity and laugh. It will be obvious to them that no economy which leaves millions of people in unwanted idleness and scraps factories and equipment long before they are obsolete can be regarded as efficient, but this type of waste is exactly what the introduction of the Euro will bring about. Why? Well, the simultaneous removal of the mark, the franc, the lire and eight other currencies on January 1st will destroy the freedom to adjust to changing circumstances that the European economy has now. Consequently, when some part of

Europe becomes uncompetitive in the future - as it is bound to - many of its businesses will have to close down.

Until mid-1998, if the price level in a country which is now part of Euroland got out of line it could simply devalue its currency, restoring its competitiveness overnight. With the Euro established, however, devaluation is no longer possible and unless some equally effective alternative adjustment mechanism can be developed, a country which becomes uncompetitive will find itself locked into high levels of unemployment and poverty for a decade or more. So much social unrest could occur during this period that nationalist politicians might come to power promising to take their stricken countries out of the EU altogether. The whole European structure could come apart.

This lack-of-an-adjustment-mechanism problem could become particularly acute for us in Ireland, as our present prosperity and high growth rate are based on the government's success in attracting just two types of multinational companies - computers and pharmaceuticals - to locate here. Almost every significant computer firm in the world has an Irish plant serving the European and, often, the African market. These firms are doing so well that the country is running a big balance of payments surplus and the Irish pound is one of the strongest currencies in Europe. We are being locked into the Euro at a level that reflects this strength..

Supposing something goes wrong after January 1st. Suppose, for example, the computer firms located here decide to move their operations lock, stock and barrel to the Far East to take advantage of the very much lower prices the current Asian crisis has brought about. This is already happening to some extent and in the past few months: Seagate has closed its Irish hard-drive factory and shifted production to Asia, and Apple has done the same with its printed circuit assembly plant in Cork.

Under the Euro regime, large-scale closures in the Irish computer industry will lead to long-lasting unemployment because the high levels of wages and other costs which the current prosperity has generated will handicap government efforts to attract replacement industries. True, the unemployed could be pressured to accept lower wages to 'price themselves back into work,' but they will fight tooth and nail to avoid doing so because many have taken out mortgages and made other commitments on the basis of their present wage levels, and they would be unable to make ends meet at lower levels of pay. As a result, having lost the freedom to devalue, it could be years before this country is able to restore its competitiveness in relation to the rest of Europe and for its unemployment to begin to fall.

Since there are some pretty smart people in Brussels, we can be reasonably sure that this potentially serious problem has been anticipated and that the Eurocrats have an alternative adjustment mechanism to devaluation in mind. My hunch is that they want to establish regional (that is, subnational) currencies to replace national ones. These - so long as national governments didn't set them up - wouldn't give national governments any power. Moreover, they would fit in with the EU's 'Europe of the Regions' policy and provide even more economic flexibility than the present system. For example, they would have prevented the situation which arose in Britain under Mrs. Thatcher in which the London area was booming, while the North of England was on its knees after the closure of its coal mines and most of its heavy industries, such as shipbuilding. By allowing a North of England pound to fall in value compared with the London one, many of the businesses which closed would be operating today and a great deal of social distress would have been prevented.

What evidence do I have to back this hunch? Well, simply that the EU is currently financing experiments into what could develop into regional currencies in Scotland, the Netherlands, Spain and Ireland. The Irish test is being carried out in East Mayo and West Roscommon where a currency called the Roma will be in circulation by the time this almanac appears. The test is small-scale and low-key, but it could be a straw in the wind. Let's hope that the global economic wind does not get too cold and biting before satisfactory results with these experiments are achieved.

❐

The author is a writer and economist living in Westport, Co. Mayo.
He advises the EU currency experiments that he mentions above.

COMPANIES

REPUBLIC OF IRELAND: TOP 30 COMPANIES

Rank	Company	Nature of Business	Estimated Turnover (IR£ m)	Profit (IR£ m)	Number of Employees
1	Intel (Ireland)	Computer Manufacturing	3,300	n/a	3,600
2	Jefferson Smurfit Group	Paper / Packaging	2,594	201.1	25,353
3	Cement Roadstone Holdings	Building Materials	2,428	193.4	19,184
4	Avonmore Waterford Group	Dairy / Food Products	2,400	56.3	12,000
5	Dell	Computer Manufacturing	1,768	n/a	2,525
6	Microsoft (Ireland)	Software Manufacturing	1,600	n/a	800
7	Fyffes	Fruit & Vegetable Distribution	1,460	54.0	5,700
8	The Irish Dairy Board	Export Dairy Produce	1,311	22.1	2,062
9	Kerry Group	Food Processing	1,233	51.3	9,426
10	Telecom Éireann	Telecommunications	1,219	203.6	11,560
11	Dunnes Stores	Retailing	1,150	n/a	9,500
12	Electricity Supply Board	Electricity Supply	1,095	131.6	10,003
13	Musgrave	Wholesale Distribution	854	25.6	2,100
14	Tesco Ireland	Supermarket Retail	810	n/a	8,500
15	Aer Lingus	Air Transportation	766	40.9	5,617
16	Guinness (Ireland)	Brewing	764	163.0	2,300
17	Apple Computers	Computer Manufacturing	720	n/a	1,500
18	Irish Food Processors	Meat Processors / Export	680	n/a	2,950
19	Swords Laboratories	Pharmaceuticals Manufacturing	680	n/a	317
20	DCC	Industrial Holding Co.	628	35.3	2,170
21	Dairygold Co-op Society	Dairy Products	621	14.1	2,898
22	Irish Distillers Group	Distillers	616	51.2	2,010
23	Oracle Group	Software Manufacturing & Sales	600	n/a	520
24	IAWS Group	Agri Business	583	25.3	950
25	Golden Vale	Dairy Products	561	6.3	2,032
26	Janssen Pharmaceutical (Irl.)	Pharmaceuticals	550	n/a	350
27	Coca-Cola Atlantic	Soft Drinks	520	n/a	270
28	Pepsi Cola Manufacturing	Soft Drinks	510	n/a	150
29	EMC (Benelux) BV	Computer Data Storage	505	n/a	650
30	Glen Dimplex	Domestic Appliance Manufacturer	500	n/a	6,000

NORTHERN IRELAND: TOP 30 COMPANIES

Rank	Company	Nature of Business	Estimated Turnover (£STG m)	Profit (£STG m)	Number of Employees
1	NIE Plc.	Electricity Service	500.4	76.7	2,130
2	Short Bros. Plc.	Aircraft Manufacturers	358.0	30.1	8,492
3	Glen Electric Ltd.	Domestic Heating	347.8	23.2	3,473
4	Powerscreen International Plc.	Screening Equipment	304.8	42.3	1,974
5	F.A. Wellworth	Supermarket Proprietors	291.6	17.2	4,979
6	United Dairy Farmers	Dairy / Milk Products	261.9	0.7	716
7	F.G. Wilson Group	Electrical Generators	247.1	35.3	1,563
8	Dunnes Stores (Bangor) Ltd.	Supermarkets	223.0	18.1	1,615
9	Nortel (NI)	Telecommunications	215.5	25.7	1,186
10	John Henderson Ltd.	Grocery Wholesale	180.6	2.9	956
11	Harland & Wolff Group	Ship Building	178.3	(-1.5)	1,701
12	J. & J. Haslett Ltd.	Grocery Wholesale	173.0	7.0	904
13	Charles Hurst Ltd.	Vehicle Distributors	166.4	5.2	523
14	Stewarts Supermarkets Ltd.	Supermarkets	154.9	0.1	3,905
15	Nigen Ltd.	Electricity Supply	142.9	23.3	368
16	Moy Park Ltd.	Poultry Products	140.8	(-0.3)	2,758
17	Nacco Materials Handling (NI) Ltd.	Fork Lift Manufacturers	140.2	5.8	752
18	Premier Power Ltd.	Electricity Supply	128.0	6.3	392
19	Desmond & Sons Ltd.	Clothing Manufacturers	118.3	71.0	2,447
20	Alchem Plc.	Pharmaceuticals	113.1	1.7	238

Continued from previous page -

Rank	Company	Nature of Business	Estimated Turnover (£STG m)	Profit (£STG m)	Number of Employees
21	Leckpatrick Dairies Ltd.	Dairy Products	112.0	2.6	192
22	Maxol Oil Ltd.	Petroleum / Oil Distributors	110.5	(-0.9)	87
23	Daewoo Electronics UK Ltd.	Video Recorder Manufacturers	110.3	(-0.4)	854
24	NI Transport Holding	Transport	107.3	6.2	3,588
25	Boxmore International Plc.	Packaging Manufacturers	100.7	16.8	1,017
26	Andrews Holdings Ltd.	Animal Feeds & Flour	96.7	2.3	885
27	NI Co-Op Society Ltd.	Supermarkets	95.9	3.0	887
28	Lamont Textiles Ltd.	Textile Products	94.7	6.1	1,216
29	Rotary Group Ltd.	Electrical Engineers	93.1	3.8	2,023
30	Fayrefield Foods Ireland Ltd.	Dairy Products	92.8	0.4	18

REPUBLIC OF IRELAND: TOP TEN DOMESTIC ACQUISITIONS BY IRISH COMPANIES, 1997

Rank	Acquirer	Target Company	Nature	Value IR£000s
1	(merger)	Avonmore & Waterford Foods	Food & Drink	373,000
2	Bank of Ireland Plc.	New Ireland Assurance Ltd.	Financial Services	273,600
3	IAWS Plc.	Cuisine de France Ltd.	Food & Drink	51,000
4	MBO	Cable Management Ireland Ltd.	Communications	26,000
5	Dunloe Plc.	Property Portfolios	Property	22,000
6	United Drug Plc.	Dublin Drug Co.	Medical	15,100
7	MBO	Lifestyle	Retail	15,100
8	Kepak Ltd.	Agra Trading Ltd.	Food/Drink/Agribusiness	*13,500
9	MBO	Kartoncraft Ltd.	Print & Packaging	9,400
10	Porthos Ltd.	Impshire Thoroughbreds	Residual Assets	8,000

estimated

REPUBLIC OF IRELAND: TOP TEN FOREIGN ACQUISITIONS BY IRISH COMPANIES, 1997

Rank	Acquirer	Target Company	Nature	Value IR£000s
1	AIB Plc.	Dauphin Deposit Corporation (USA)	Financial Services	840,000
2	Elan Plc.	Sano Corporation Inc. (USA)	Medical	268,000
3	Treasury Holding Ltd.	Hermes Green Property Portfolio (UK)	Property	77,000
4	Musgraves Ltd.	Wellworths (UK)	Retail	67,000
5	CRH Plc.	CPM Development Corporation (USA)	Construction	62,700
6	Dana Petroleum Plc.	Seafield Resources Ltd. (UK)	Natural Resources	61,300
7	Avonmore Foods Plc.	Beni Foods (UK)	Food/Drink/Agribusiness	54,200
8	AIB Plc.	WBK Polish Bank	Financial Services	43,400
9	IWP Plc.	Constance Carroll Holdings (UK)	Cosmetics	38,500
10	Doyle Hotel Group Ltd.	Dupont Plaza Hotel (USA)	Property	28,500

REPUBLIC OF IRELAND: LOCATION OF ACQUISITIONS, 1994-97

Location	1994 (%)	1995 (%)	1996 (%)	1997 (%)
Republic of Ireland	41	51	40	36
UK	30	31	29	29
Other European Countries	11	8	12	10
United States	13	7	15	17
Rest of World	5	3	4	8
TOTAL:	100	100	100	100

REPUBLIC OF IRELAND: TOP TEN ACQUISITIONS INVOLVING IRISH COMPANIES, 1998*

Rank	Acquirer	Target Company	Nature of Company	IR£m
1	Elan Corporation	Neurex	Medical	498,000
2	Kerry Foods	Dalgety	Food/Drink/Agri-business	394,000

3	CBT Group	Forefront	Other	108,000
4	Elan Corporation	GWC Health	Medical	107,000
5	Greencore Plc.	Pauls Malt	Food/Drink/Agri-business	74,000
6	CRH Plc.	Assets of MA Segale	Construction	42,900
7	Independent Newspapers Plc.	London Independent	Media	32,500†
8	Dunloe Plc.	Ewart Plc.	Construction	31,000
9	CrossGroup	MTC Animal Health	Medical	30,000†
10	Grafton Group	British Dredging	Construction	30,000

Jan. to June 1998 † estimate

NUMBER OF OVERSEAS COMPANIES IN REP. OF IRELAND & NORTHERN IRELAND, 1997*

REPUBLIC OF IRELAND		NORTHERN IRELAND	
Company's Country of Origin	Number	Company's Country of Origin	Number
United States	455	North America	52
Rest of Europe	239	United Kingdom	47
United Kingdom	170	Rest of Europe	16
Germany	151	Republic of Ireland	14
Asia / Pacific	56	Asia / Pacific	13
Rest of World	46	Germany	10
TOTAL:	1,117	TOTAL:	152

* IDA Assisted   ** IDB Assisted*

TAXATION

REPUBLIC OF IRELAND: TAX TABLES, 1998/99

INCOME TAX

RATES:	Single	Married
24% on First	IR£10,000	IR£20,000

46% on Balance

MAIN ALLOWANCES:	IR£
Single Person	3,150
Married Couple	6,300
Widowed Person*	3,650
PAYE Allowance	800
Child Allowance *(Incapacitated)*	800
Dependent Relative Allowance	110
Age 65 or over *(single)*	400
Age 65 or over *(married)*	800

* Widow in year of bereavement - IR£6,300

RELIEFS:

VHI & BUPA Premiums
Relief for 1998-99 is available at 24% only for the premium paid in the preceding tax year.

Rented Accommodation
Relief is allowed at the standard rate of tax on the first £500 paid for private residential rented accommodation.

Pension Contributions
Relief is available for contributions to revenue-approved schemes at the marginal rate. Contributions are limited to 15% of net relevant earnings.

Mortgage Interest
Relief is at the standard rate of tax only (24%). The maximum relief is:

	Single	Married	Widow
Existing Mortgages	1,900	3,800	2,780
First-Time Buyer	2,500	5,000	3,600

Medical Expenses
Relief is available at the taxpayers' marginal rate for expenses paid in excess of £200 (£100 single person).

PRSI & LEVIES

	IR £	IR £	IR £
	0-24,200	24,200-29,000	over 29,000
Employees	6.75%	2.25%	2.25%
Employer*	12%	12%	Nil
Self-Employed	7.25%	2.25%	2.25%

* 8.5% if earning less than IR£14,040.

*The Income Levies are comprised of the **Health** levy and the **Employment** levy which are 1.25% and 1.0% on all income (less benefits in kind), respectively. Both levies apply only where annual income is over £10,750*

CORPORATION TAX

RATES:
Standard Rate*	32%
Manufacturing Rate	10%

* A rate of 25% applies to the first IR£50,000 of taxable income.

CAPITAL GAINS TAX

RATES:
Personal Exemption	£500
Standard Rate*	20%
Development Land Gain	40%

*A rate of 20% applies to disposals of shares in certain unquoted Irish companies.

CAPITAL ACQUISITIONS TAX

CLASS THRESHOLDS:
Relationship to Disponer:	IR£
Child, minor child of deceased child	188,400
Other blood relatives	25,120
None of the above	12,560

NORTHERN IRELAND: TAX TABLES, 1998/99

INCOME TAX

RATES: £STG
20% on first...4,300
23% on next...22,800
40% on balance

MAIN ALLOWANCES:
Personal Allowance.....................................4,195
Married Couple's Allowance*......................1,900
Additional Widows' Bereavement Allowance*.......1,900
Additional One-Parent Families' Allowance*.........1,900
Blind Person's Allowance................................1,330
Age Allowance 65-74 (single)............................5,410
Age Allowance 65-74 (married)..........................3,305
Age Allowance 75 and over (single)....................5,600
Age Allowance 75 and over (married)..................3,345

* Relief restricted to 15%
† Excess over basic allowances withdrawn by £1 for every £2 of income over £16,200.

RELIEFS

Personal Equity Plans (PEPs)

Annual Maximum £STG
Standard PEP...6,000
Single Company PEP.......................................3,000

Tax Exempt Special Savings Accounts (TESSAs)

Annual Maximum £STG
First Year..3,000
Subsequent Years..1,800
Investment cannot succeed..............................9,000
* PEPs and TESSAs will be replaced from 6th April 1999 by the new Individual Savings Account.

Pension Contributions
Relief for private pension contributions:

Age	PPP	RAP
	% of Net Relevant Earnings	
35 or under	17.5	17.5
36-45	20.0	17.5
46-50	25.0	17.5
51-55	30.0	20.0
56-60	35.0	22.5
61 or over	40.0	22.5

The general earnings cap is £STG 87,600.

Mortgage Interest:
Mortgage Interest Relief at Source is 10%. The maximum mortgage amount on which this may be claimed is £30,000.

National Insurance:
Earnings limits are as follows:

	Lower Earnings Limit - Annual (£STG)	Upper Earnings Limit - Annual (£STG)
Class 1 employee	3,328	25,220
Class 2 employee	3,590	25,220
Class 4 employee	7,310	25,220
Employer	3,328	"

Class 1 employees* rates:

Weekly Earnings £STG	First £64 %	Employees Balance %	Employers %
Below 64	0	0	0
64 - 109.99	2	10	3
110 - 154.99	2	10	5
155 - 209.99	2	10	7
210 - 485	2	10	10
Over 485	0	0	10

*Abatements apply to the above national insurance contribution rates for contracted-out employees with salaries between the upper and lower limits. For the employee, the abatement rate is 1.6%; for employers, the abatement rate is 3% for salary-related schemes and 1.5% for money-purchase schemes.

CORPORATION TAX

RATES	Percentage
Standard Rate	31%
Small Companies' Rate	21%
Small Companies Rate Limit	£300,000
Marginal Relief Limit	£1,500,000
Marginal Rate	33.5%

CAPITAL GAINS TAX

RATES	£STG
Individual Annual Exemption	£6,800
Trusts	£3,400

INHERITANCE TAX

RATES	£STG
Chargeable Value up to £223,000	0%
Chargeable Value over £223,000	40%

There are reduced charges on lifetime gifts within seven years of death:

Years Between Gift & Death	% of Death Rates
0-3	100%
3-4	80%
4-5	60%
5-6	40%
6-7	20%

REPUBLIC OF IRELAND: BUDGET HIGHLIGHTS, DECEMBER 1997

Changes in Rates	Old Rate %	New Rate %
Corporation Tax	36	32
Corporation Tax applicable to first £50,000 of profits	28	25
Capital Gains Tax	40	20
Standard rate of income tax	26	24
Top Income Tax Rate	48	46
Standard Rate of DIRT Tax	26	24
Vehicle Registration Tax on Cars	23.2	22.5
Relief from Inheritance Tax (to the value of the home of £150,000)	60	80

Other Changes	Amount
Increases in leaded petrol	4p per litre
Increase in packet of 20 cigarettes	10p
New Employers' PRSI ceiling	£29,000
New Employees' PRSI ceiling	£24,200
Increase in Social Welfare Payments	£3 per week
Increase in Old Age Pensions	£5 per week
Increase in Child Benefit - 1st and 2nd child	£1.50 per month
Increase in Child Benefit - 3rd and subsequent children	£3.50 per month
Increase in Family Income Supplement	£7 per week
Increase in PRSI Allowance	£20 per week
New income exemption limit (single person)	£4,100
New income exemption limit (married couple)	£8,200

N. IRELAND: BUDGET HIGHLIGHTS, MARCH 1998

Changes in Rates	Old Rate %	New Rate %
Stamp Duty for Houses worth more than £250,000	1.5	2
Stamp Duty for Houses worth more than £500,000	2	3
VAT Rate on Energy Saving Materials	17.5	5

Other Changes	Amount
Increase on Beer	1p per pint
Increase on Wine	4p per bottle
Increase on packet of 20 cigarettes	20p per packet
Increase in Unleaded Petrol	4.4p per litre
Increase in Leaded Petrol	4.9p per litre
Increase in Diesel	5.5p per litre
Increase in Child Benefit	£2.50 per week
Increase in Threshold on Inheritance Tax	£8,000 (to £223,000)

REPUBLIC OF IRELAND: TAXATION YIELDS, 1996-97

Sector	1996 IR£m	1997 IR£m
PAYE	3,894	4,357
Self-Employed	527	644
Income Tax from Non-PAYE Sources	158	208
VAT	3,109	3,707
Excise:	2,304	2,523
Excise Duty on Tobacco	533	573
Excise Duty on Alcohol	552	579
Tax on Motor Vehicles	353	396
Excise Duty on Hydrocarbons	795	895
Other Indirect Taxes	71	79
Corporation Tax	1,428	1,697
Stamp Duty	332	424
Residential Property Tax	14	3
Other Capital Taxes	166	221
Revenue Investigations and Audits	133	127
Other	31	52
TOTAL NET TAX RECEIPTS:	12,096	13,963

REPUBLIC OF IRELAND: TAXES COLLECTED, 1988-97

Year	Total Arrears	Taxes Collected IR£m	Year	Total Arrears	Taxes Collected
1988	IR£3,501m	IR£6,100m	1993	IR£2,215m	IR£8,524m
1989	IR£2,985m	IR£6,242m	1994	IR£2,057m	IR£9,427m
1990	IR£2,718m	IR£6,763m	1995	IR£1,978m	IR£9,870m
1991	IR£2,538m	IR£7,247m	1996	IR£1,690m	IR£11,468m
1992	IR£2,437m	IR£8,037m	1997	IR£1,329m	IR£12,794m

EXPORTS AND IMPORTS

CROSS-BORDER TRADE, 1990-97

Year	Imports by ROI from NI (IR£m)	Exports by ROI to NI (IR£m)
1990	500.1	816.1
1991	496.1	789.4
1992	468.2	825.1
1993	417.2	701.0
1994	536.8	721.9
1995	651.2	785.3
1996	642.4	822.6
1997	716.1	1,022.5

NORTHERN IRELAND: TRADE, 1992-97

Year	Imports (tonnes)	Exports (tonnes)	Year	Imports (tonnes)	Exports (tonnes)
1992	12,937	4,392	1995	14,952	5,083
1993	13,859	4,688	1996	14,918	4,981
1994	14,830	4,958	1997	14,175	5,142

REPUBLIC OF IRELAND: TRADE BY AREA, 1996-97

Area (£m)	1996 Imports	1996 Exports	1996 Balance	1997 Imports	1997 Exports	1997 Balance
European Union:						
Britain	7,155.6	6,654.3	-501.3	8,001.3	7,487.4	-513.9
Northern Ireland	642.4	822.6	180.2	716.1	1,022.5	306.4
Other Member States	4,927.4	13,327.8	8,400.4	5,525.6	14,766.0	9,240.4
Total: European Union	12,725.4	20,804.7	8,079.3	14,243.0	23,275.9	9,032.9
Other Countries	8,654.0	8,247.8	-406.2	10,601.3	10,548.8	-52.5
Country Unknown	249.9	488.0	238.1	126.8	394.1	267.3
Unclassified	800.1	866.5	66.4	888.6	808.3	-80.3
TOTAL:	22,429.4	30,407.0	7,977.6	25,859.7	35,027.1	9,167.4

REP. OF IRELAND: COMPOSITION OF IMPORTS & EXPORTS, 1996-97

Sector (£m)	Imports 1996	Imports 1997	Exports 1996	Exports 1997
Food & Live Animals	1,545.8	1,647.3	4,143.2	3,594.1
Beverages & Tobacco	233.4	276.5	517.8	549.3
Crude Materials, Inedible, except Fuels	407.3	447.2	556.7	584.9
Mineral Fuels, Lubricants & related Materials	823.7	894.3	116.6	150.2
Animal & Vegetable Oils, Fats & Waxes	82.3	82.5	28.0	28.0
Chemicals & Related Products	2,762.1	3,207.6	6,724.3	8,865.7
Manufactured Goods	2,422.8	2,665.2	1,358.4	1,370.4
Machinery & Transport Equipment	9,468.2	11,694.7	10,627.7	13,111.2
Miscellaneous	2,862.3	3,090.0	4,601.9	4,769.6
Other	1,821.5	1,854.4	1,732.4	2,003.7
TOTAL:	22,429.4	25,859.7	30,407.0	35,027.1

REPUBLIC OF IRELAND: EXPORT GROWTH AND PERFORMANCE, 1996-97

Sector	Export Growth %	Sector Value IR£m
Industrial:		
Machinery / Engineering	11	730
Electrical / Electronics	35	670
Aerospace	25	670
Building Supplies	12	620

Continued from previous page -

Sector	Export Growth %	Sector Value IR£m
Chemicals / Healthcare	6	600
Telecommunications	18	390
Packaging	3	220
Instrumentation	13	180
Total	123	4,080
Consumer:		
Textiles	4	430
General Consumer	4	360
Household Furnishings / Furniture	6	305
Giftware	21	210
Clothing / Footwear	3	175
Total	38	1,480
Services:		
Software	40	530
Construction Services	35	375
Financial Services	17	370
Consultancy / Training Services	10	245
Film Entertainment	17	150
Other Services	17	800
Total	136	2,470
TOTAL:	16	8,030

REPUBLIC OF IRELAND: VOLUME AND PRICE OF EXPORTS AND IMPORTS, 1990-97

Year	Volume Index Imports	Volume Index Exports	Price Index Imports	Price Index Exports
1990	100.0	100.0	100.0	100.0
1991	100.8	105.6	102.3	99.3
1992	105.6	121.1	100.2	96.6
1993	113.0	133.4	105.4	103.9
1994	127.9	153.2	108.1	103.8
1995	146.3	184.0	112.7	105.7
1996	161.2	201.4	111.5	105.1
1997	-	-	112.0	106.3

NORTHERN IRELAND: MANUFACTURING COMPANIES EXPORT SALES, 1992-97

	1992-93 (£STGm)	1993-94 (£STGm)	1994-95 (£STGm)	1995-96 (£STGm)	1996-97* (£STGm)
Total Sales	6,827	7,267	7,848	8,618	8,824
Northern Ireland	2,425	2,578	2,631	2,794	2,790
External Sales	4,402	4,689	5,217	5,824	6,034
Britain	2,422	2,514	2,614	2,811	3,023
Export Sales	1,980	2,175	2,603	3,013	3,011
Republic of Ireland	498	544	631	678	717
Rest of European Union	879	916	1,047	1,218	1,224
Rest of World	603	715	925	1,117	1,070

provisional

NORTHERN IRELAND: TOP FIVE EXPORT MARKETS BY SECTOR, 1996/97

Country (£m)	Textiles, Clothing & Leather	Food, Drink & Tobacco	Engineering	Other	Total
Republic of Ireland	86.3	165.4	53.5	246.9	552.1
Germany	9.7	29.1	133.9	91.5	264.2
United States	27.3	9.4	142.7	25.1	204.2
Asia	28.2	26.6	211.6	41.3	307.7
France	16.9	64.9	53.9	58.6	194.3
TOTAL:	**168.4**	**295.4**	**595.6**	**463.4**	**1,522.8**

NORTHERN IRELAND: SALES BY SECTOR, 1996-97

Sector (£m)	Sales	External Sales	Exports
Food, Drink & Tobacco	2,726	1,526	574
Textiles, Clothing & Leather	1,167	1,036	281
Electrical & Optical Equipment	829	773	502
Transport Equipment	742	687	342
Other Machinery & Equipment	671	558	368
Chemicals & Man-Made Fibres	600	494	407
Rubber & Plastics	502	390	211
Paper & Printing	440	183	105
Other Non-Metallic Mineral Products	364	103	65
Basic Metals & Fabricated Metal Products	330	112	70
Wood & Wood Products	286	87	40
Other Manufacturing	167	85	46
TOTAL:	8,824	6,034	3,011

FINANCE

REP. OF IRELAND: EXCHANGE RATE OF IR£, 1996-98

Year	US Dollar	Sterling	DM
1996	1.69	98.88	2.61
1997	1.42	86.64	2.56
1998†	1.36	81.11	2.51

† average for first quarter

REP. OF IRELAND: NOTE & COIN CIRCULATION, 1997

Coin	Number Million	% of Total	Value £ Million	% of Total	Note	Number Million	% of Total	Value £ Million	% of Total
1p	752.0	38.5	7.5	3.7	10/-	1.2	0.8	0.6	0
2p	445.5	22.8	8.9	4.4	£1	13.8	9.1	13.8	0.6
5p	284.6	14.6	14.2	7.0	£5	20.4	13.6	102.2	4.2
10p	172.4	8.8	17.2	8.5	£10	23	15.3	230.2	9.5
20p	137.9	7.1	27.6	13.7	£20	85.6	56.8	1711.3	70.8
50p	64.2	3.3	32.1	15.9	£50	6.1	.4	303.7	12.6
£1	94.6	4.9	94.6	46.8	£100	0.5	0.4	54.6	2.3
Total:	1,951.2	100.0	202.1	100.0	Total:	150.6	100	2,416.4	100

REPUBLIC OF IRELAND: NUMBER OF NOTES & COINS PRODUCED, 1997

Coin (millions)	1996	1997	Note (millions)	1996	1997
1p	41.5	62.7	£5	24.2	36.3
2p	32.5	18.1	£10	30.3	36.6
5p	40	45.9	£20	57.5	51.3
10p	12	17.2	£50	10.8	0
20p	10.6	17.4	£100	0.8	4.6
50p	0	0	Total:	123.6	128.8
£1	0	0			
Total:	136.6	161.3			

REPUBLIC OF IRELAND: BALANCE OF PAYMENTS - CAPITAL AND FINANCIAL ACCOUNT, 1990-97*

Year	Capital Transfers	Private Capital	Official Capital	Transactions of Credit Insts.	Official External Reserves	Total	Net Residual
1990	229	-1,862	59	727	-443	-1,290	1,514
1991	378	-1,141	254	-381	-280	-1,169	960
1992	463	-743	-167	-1,344	1,201	-589	269

Continued from previous page -

Year	Capital Transfers	Private Capital	Official Capital	Transactions of Credit Insts.	Official External Reserves	Total	Net Residual
1993	513	-471	542	-844	-1,756	-2,016	768
1994	251	-1,375	-1,335	140	102	-2,217	1,219
1995	511	-1,824	24	1,798	-1,443	-934	-136
1996	489	-594	38	-1,229	55	-1,241	379
1997	398	489	-1,595	-148	-647	-1,503	1,215

* First 3 Quarters of 1997

REPUBLIC OF IRELAND: BALANCE OF PAYMENTS - CURRENT ACCOUNT, 1990-97

Year (IR£m)	Merchandise	Services	Invisibles Factor Incomes	Transfers	Total	Current Balance
1990	1,797	-513	-2,921	1,412	-2,022	-225
1991	2,066	-668	-2,796	1,608	-1,856	210
1992	3,501	-1,217	-3,209	1,245	-3,181	320
1993	4,826	-1,366	-3,521	1,309	-3,578	1,248
1994	5,396	-1,978	-3,575	1,156	-4,397	999
1995	7,459	-2,991	-4,508	1,110	-6,390	1,070
1996	8,756	-3,782	-5,151	1,354	-7,580	1,176
1997	11,084	-4,690	-6,322	1290	-9,722	1,362

REP. OF IRELAND: CURRENT REVENUE 1997-98*

Sector	1997	*1998	% Change
Tax Revenue:			
Income Tax	5,194	5,522	6.3%
VAT	3,664	4,017	9.6%
Excise Duties	2,513	2,659	5.8%
Corporation Tax	1,684	1,926	14.4%
Stamp Duties	416	467	12.3%
Customs	180	176	-2.2%
Agricultural Levies	9	9	0%
Employment and Training Levy	177	193	9.0%
Capital Taxes	221	198	-10.4%
Motor Vehicle Duties	100	-	-
Non-Tax Revenue	333	330	-0.9%
TOTAL CURRENT REVENUE:	**14,491**	**15,497**	**6.9%**

* Post Budget-Estimate

REPUBLIC OF IRELAND: CAPITAL ACCOUNT 1996-2000

Sector	1996 (IR£m)	1997 (IR£m)	1998* (IR£m)	1999† (IR£m)	2000† (IR£m)
Capital Expenditure:					
Exchequer Capital Programme	1,458	1,609	1,946	1,908	1,845
Other (non programme)	78	70	56	63	147
Total: Capital Expenditure	1,536	1,679	2,002	1,971	1,992
Capital Resources:					
Exchequer Capital Resources	807	782	804	844	985
Exchequer Borrowing for Capital Purposes	729	-	-	-	-
EBR before Contingency	437	-278	-89	175	736
General Contingency Provision	-	-	-	180	450
EBR with contingency	437	-278	-89	-5	286
EBR as % of GNP	1.2%				
EBR as % of GNP before contingency	-	-0.7%	-0.2%	0.4%	1.4%
EBR as % of GNP after contingency	-	-0.7%	-0.2%	0.0%	0.6%

* Post Budget Estimate † Projection

REPUBLIC OF IRELAND: CURRENT EXPENDITURE 1998*

Sector	£m	% of Expenditure
Health	2,943	16.8
Security	1,300	7.4
Infrastructure	91	0.5
Service of Public Debt	2,596	14.8
Education	2,351	13.4
Social Welfare	4,866	27.8
Other Social Services	122	0.7
Economic Services (industry, agriculture, tourism)	1,322	7.6
Other	1,908	10.9
TOTAL:	**17,499**	**100.0**

* Post Budget Estimate

REPUBLIC OF IRELAND: NATIONAL DEBT, 1977-97

IR£m	1977	1987	1990	1996	1997
Domestic Debt	3,190	14,001	16,235	21,194	22,401
Foreign Debt	1,039	9,693	8,848	8,718	8,288
Total National Debt	4,229	23,694	25,083	29,912	30,689
General Government Debt	-	24,636	26,600	32,100	32,300

REP. OF IRELAND: CURRENT ACCOUNT 1996- 2000

Sector (IR£m)	1996	1997	*1998	1999†	2000†
Current Expenditure:					
Central Fund Services	3,161	3,505	3,403	3,571	3,617
Supply Services	9,501	10,367	10,985	11,502	11,922
Total Current Expenditure	12,662	13,872	14,388	15,073	15,539
Current Revenue:					
Taxation	12,520	14,158	15,167	16,006	16,925
Non Tax	434	333	330	369	357
Tota Current Revenue	12,954	14,491	15,497	16,375	17,282
Current Budget Surplus	292	619	1,109	1,302	1,743
% of GNP	0.8%	1.5%	2.5%	2.7%	3.4%

* Post-Budget Estimate   † Projection

REPUBLIC OF IRELAND: CURRENCY COMPOSITION OF FOREIGN DEBT, 1997

Currency	IR£m	%
US Dollar	1,712	20.7
Deutschemark	1,621	19.6
Swiss Franc	1,132	13.7
Yen	139	1.7
Sterling	2,185	26.4
Dutch Guilder	165	2.0
Ecu	178	2.1
French Franc	904	10.9
Others	253	3.0
Total:	**8,288**	**100**

REPUBLIC OF IRELAND: INTEREST COST OF NATIONAL DEBT, 1990-97

Year	Interest Cost IR£m	Year	Interest Cost IR£m
1990	2,109	1994	2,030
1991	2,132	1995	1,963
1992	2,106	1996	2,052
1993	2,076	1997	2,198

Interest figures for 1994-97 exclude the payments to the National Savings Interest Reserve.

REPUBLIC OF IRELAND: NATIONAL BORROWING TREND 1990-97

Year	Current Budget Deficit/Surplus (IR£m)	% of GNP	Exchequer Borrowing Requirement (EBR - IR£m)	% of GNP	Public Sector Borrowing Requirement (IR£m)	% of GNP
1990	(152)	(0.6)	462	1.9	588	2.4
1991	(298)	(1.2)	499	2.0	762	3.0
1992	(446)	(1.7)	713	2.7	910	3.4
1993	(379)	(1.3)	690	2.5	862	3.1
1994	15	0.1	672	2.2	782	2.6
1995	(362)	(1.1)	627	1.9	826	2.5
1996	292	0.8	437	1.2	531	1.5
1997*	604	1.5	235	0.6	-	-

* provisional

N. IRELAND: GROSS DOMESTIC PRODUCT, 1990-96

Industry (£ m)	1990	1991	1992	1993	1994	1995	1996
Agriculture, Fisheries & Forestry	435	477	513	526	582	627	651
Mining & Quarrying	47	51	52	55	71	84	88
Manufacturing	2,150	2,235	2,198	2,433	2,496	2,657	2,769
Electricity, Gas & Water	281	371	346	369	372	361	381
Construction	703	649	729	701	712	765	789
Distribution, Hotels & Catering	1,288	1,414	1,463	1,560	1,666	1,844	1,949
Transport & Communication	554	598	617	632	674	750	784
Financial & Business Services	1,511	1,653	1,901	2,095	2,306	2,396	2,530
Public Administration & H.M. Forces	1,498	1,648	1,751	1,822	1,707	1,715	1,751
Education & Health Services	1,547	1,814	1,942	2,066	2,359	2,493	2,555
Other Services	152	188	149	175	147	198	224
GROSS DOMESTIC PRODUCT	10,166	11,098	11,661	12,434	13,092	13,890	14,471
GDP per head (£)	6,396	6,930	7,205	7,620	7,974	8,423	8,700

NORTHERN IRELAND: LOCAL AUTHORITY EXPENDITURE: 1994-97

Sector (£STGm)	Current 94/95	Current 95/96	Current 96/97	Capital 94/95	Capital 95/96	Capital 96/97
Agriculture, Fisheries and Forestry	0	0	0	1	2	1
Energy	6	6	7	7	7	7
Roads & Transport	1	1	1	6	6	6
Environmental Services	102	106	115	17	18	20
Education, Arts and Libraries	56	57	63	18	18	19
TOTAL:	165	170	186	49	51	53

ECONOMIC STATISTICS, 1992-96

Year (£m)	1992	1993	1994	1995	1996
Northern Ireland: Gross Domestic Product	11,660	12,434	13,091	13,890	14,470
Consumer Spending	9,373	9,805	10,475	11,222	-
Personal Disposal Income	11,081	11,887	12,541	13,236	-
Republic of Ireland: Gross Domestic Product	29,980	32,218	34,844	38,638	42,104
Gross National Product	26,771	28,698	31,269	34,129	36,983

N. IRELAND: PUBLIC EXPENDITURE, 1994-2000

Sector (£STGm)	94-95	95-96	96-97	97-98*	98-99*	99-00*
Law, Order & Protection Services	959	934	901	929	912	923
National Agriculture & Fisheries Support	141	152	186	176	164	165
NI Agriculture, Forestry & Fisheries Support	160	132	151	152	137	137
Industry, Energy, Trade & Employment	432	430	474	488	459	444
Transport	177	174	172	165	161	161
Housing	226	246	248	243	243	240

Sector (£STGm)	94-95	95-96	96-97	97-98*	98-99*	99-00*
Environmental & Miscellaneous Services	208	217	243	205	171	160
Fire Service	40	42	43	44	44	44
Education, Arts & Libraries	1,295	1,355	1,401	1,376	1,383	1,401
Health & Personal Social Services	1,418	1,518	1,600	1,645	1,672	1,690
Social Security	2,232	2,380	2,586	2,652	2,750	2,854
Other Public Services	75	62	85	56	56	55
Euro-Regional Funded Expenditure	62	63	95	94	103	89
TOTAL:	**7,425**	**7,705**	**8,185**	**8,225**	**8,255**	**8,363**

forecast

BANKS AND POST OFFICES

REPUBLIC OF IRELAND: EMPLOYMENT IN BANKING, BUILDING SOCIETIES & INSURANCE, 1993-97*

Year (*as at December*)	Banks	Building Societies	Insurance	Total
1993	22,500	2,600	10,500	35,600
1994	23,000	2,800	10,500	36,300
1995	23,300	2,900	11,000	37,200
1996	24,600	3,000	10,600	38,200
1997*	26,100	3,100	11,200	40,400

September 1997 figures

N. IRELAND: BANKING STATISTICS, 1996-97

Bank	No. of Branches Agencies & Sub-Offices		Authorised Capital £STGm		Issued Capital £STGm		Paid Up Capital £STGm	
	1996	1997	1996	1997	1996	1997	1996	1997
Northern Bank Ltd.	119	112	100	100	88	88	88	88
Ulster Bank Ltd.	108	106	150	150	105	105	105	105
Bank of Ireland	46	46	1,074	1,081	497	502	497	502
First Trust Bank	76	72	20	145	20	145	20	145

NORTHERN IRELAND: CREDIT EXTENDED BY FINANCE HOUSES, 1992-96

Type of Purchase (£000s)	1992	1993	1994	1995	1996
Private Cars:					
New	88,513	109,964	124,883	121,267	121,942
Second-Hand	115,352	124,321	131,923	149,175	180,931
Commercial Motor Vehicles:					
New	27,816	36,657	40,845	57,113	41,893
Second-Hand	20,015	22,234	23,992	26,754	22,651
Farm Equipment:					
New	4,012	2,501	3,258	3,540	4,221
Second-Hand	1,095	2,237	2,757	3,436	2,911
Industrial Equipment:					
New	15,213	16,405	20,230	31,340	46,007
Second-Hand	7,900	10,065	9,398	11,290	15,820
Other	38,119	51,491	55,406	58,366	70,774
TOTAL:	**318,035**	**375,875**	**412,692**	**462,281**	**507,150**

NORTHERN IRELAND: PARCELFORCE STATISTICS

Operational Statistics	1994-95	1995-96
Traffic *(parcels)*	599,000	725,000
Revenue *(£STG)*	2,789,000	3,323,000

REPUBLIC OF IRELAND:
POST OFFICE STATISTICS, 1993-97

Operational Statistics	1993	1994	1995	1996	1997
Mail:					
Letter Post - items delivered (m)	518.1	551.7	559.8	578.0	646.6
Pieces of mail per capita	146.9	156.5	158.8	159.6	176.6
System Size:					
No. of delivery points (m)	1.178	1.208	1.232	1.261	1.296
Post Office Network:					
No. of company Post Offices	95	95	96	96	99
No. of Sub-Post Offices	1,876	1,854	1,838	1,825	1,818
Other Company Premises	38	38	40	41	42
No. of Motor Vehicles	2,147	2,208	2,214	2,239	2,275
Personnel:					
Headquarters	469	461	459	463	475
Savings Services	211	204	190	184	193
Remittance Services	75	71	68	67	71
Inspection	35	38	45	40	50
Postmen/Women	4323	4058	4066	3876	4045
Postal Sorters	530	648	766	759	888
Post Office Clerks	1165	1125	1154	1244	1246
Other Grades	827	765	737	718	729
Temporary	879	711	515	681	609
Total Group Employees	8,532	8,101	8,025	8,110	8,445
Postmasters engaged as Agents	1976	1854	1838	1825	1818
Financial: Operating Costs (IR£m)	273.0	287.1	297.8	319.1	354.8
Profit for the Financial Year (IR£m)	4.8	5.8	7.2	6.1	6.3
Letter Post Turnover (IR£m)	179.8	192.0	194.4	207.3	231.3
SDS Turnover (IR£m)	27.1	29.7	32.7	36.7	42.3

HOUSING AND PROPERTY

REPUBLIC OF IRELAND: HOUSE PRICES, 1995-97

Location	New IR£			Second-Hand IR£		
	1995	1996	1997	1995	1996	1997
Dublin	68,259	76,439	94,326	70,045	82,246	102,436
Cork	60,334	67,219	75,242	55,756	60,762	69,364
Galway	69,135	73,283	86,160	61,721	69,321	78,882
Limerick	57,766	65,589	71,188	48,119	55,969	61,180
Waterford	55,090	62,835	71,473	46,788	49,582	57,121
Other Areas	56,570	64,652	74,042	50,538	58,480	67,572
National Average	61,192	68,336	78,739	55,495	62,727	72,759

NORTHERN IRELAND:
NEW HOUSES - SALES AND PRICES, 1993-97

Year	Average Number of Sales	Average Price (£)
1993	4,811	53,000
1994	4,215	57,000
1995	4,991	61,000
1996	5,865	63,000
1997	4,921	67,000

N. IRELAND: HOUSE SALES & PRICES,1996

District Council Area	Sales	Average Price (£)	District Council Area	Sales	Average Price (£)
Antrim	452	48,870	Banbridge	335	46,759
Ards	977	50,415	Belfast	4,269	42,934
Armagh	299	43,780	Carrickfergus	616	45,428
Ballymena	652	47,672	Castlereagh	954	55,503
Ballymoney	140	48,831	Coleraine	515	54,649

District Council Area	Sales	Average Price (£)
Cookstown	150	44,010
Craigavon	897	35,993
Derry	822	47,035
Down	463	50,397
Dungannon	216	41,891
Fermanagh	396	50,617
Larne	368	42,301
Limavady	198	49,203
Lisburn	1,195	50,124

District Council Area	Sales	Average Price (£)
Magherafelt	182	48,452
Moyle	92	50,975
Newry & Mourne	454	40,740
Newtownabbey	1,033	48,153
North Down	1,344	60,069
Omagh	228	51,105
Strabane	146	41,390
Total:	**17,393**	**47,476**

NORTHERN IRELAND: NEW HOUSES STARTED AND COMPLETED BY OWNERS, 1994-97

Owners	1994-95		1995-96		1996-97	
	Starts	Completions	Starts	Completions	Starts	Completions
Northern Ireland Housing Executive	1,245	878	747	1362	1279	823
Housing Associations	810	504	771	896	958	787
Other Agencies	0	0	0	0	0	0
Total Public Sector	2,055	1,382	1,518	2,258	2,237	1,610
Total Private Sector	7,477	5,350	8384	6782	8335	7273
TOTAL ALL AGENCIES:	**9,532**	**6,732**	**9,902**	**9,040**	**10,572**	**8,883**

REPUBLIC OF IRELAND: HOUSE SALES, 1996-97 & COMPLETIONS, 1995-97

House Sales, 1996-97			Republic of Ireland: House Completions, 1995-97			
County Council Area	Sales 1996	Sales 1997	County Council Area	1995	1996	1997
Carlow	18	24	Carlow	359	403	656
Cavan	20	9	Cavan	287	325	440
Clare	34	49	Clare	735	966	1,435
Cork	74	94	Cork	2,171	2,461	3,222
Cork County Borough	59	73	Cork County Borough	966	859	1,132
Donegal	77	87	Donegal	1,232	1,548	1,507
Dublin County Borough	516	331	Dublin County Borough	4,285	4,125	3,427
Dun-Laoghaire/Rathdown	50	54	Dun-Laoghaire/Rathdown	903	1,053	712
Fingal	33	59	Fingal	1,936	2,024	2,707
Galway	93	37	Galway	997	1,093	1,295
Galway County Borough	38	30	Galway County Borough	793	1,047	1,223
Kerry	177	165	Kerry	1,087	1,024	1,242
Kildare	18	33	Kildare	1,635	1,900	2,095
Kilkenny	17	35	Kilkenny	671	562	628
Laois	20	25	Laois	346	404	399
Leitrim	17	13	Leitrim	179	221	265
Limerick	23	50	Limerick	617	800	903
Limerick County Borough	103	89	Limerick County Borough	833	539	946
Longford	6	18	Longford	185	316	292
Louth	179	101	Louth	977	969	1,191
Mayo	35	49	Mayo	1,001	1,097	1,431
Meath	27	29	Meath	923	1,154	1,318
Monaghan	41	36	Monaghan	277	334	295
Offaly	31	55	Offaly	398	347	382
Roscommon	8	11	Roscommon	333	332	292
Sligo	31	27	Sligo	525	563	666
South Dublin	103	97	South Dublin	1,699	2,244	2,479
Tipperary N.R.	22	58	Tipperary N.R.	298	520	749
Tipperary S.R.	137	96	Tipperary S.R.	420	407	478
Waterford	32	38	Waterford	373	393	539
Waterford County Borough	56	63	Waterford County Borough	464	433	574
Westmeath	17	32	Westmeath	400	702	929
Wexford	63	79	Wexford	840	992	1,446
Wicklow	109	93	Wicklow	1,030	1,168	1,147
TOTAL:	**2,284**	**2,139**	**TOTAL:**	**30,175**	**33,325**	**38,442**

% SHARE OF MORTGAGE MARKET, 1993-97

Year	Banks & Other Agencies	Building Societies	Local Authorities
1993	36.0	62.9*	1.1
1994	45.0	54.4*	0.6
1995	67.2*	32.4	0.4
1996	65.4*	34.3	0.3
1997	63.7*	36.1	0.2

includes Irish Permanent

NORTHERN IRELAND: HOUSING TENURE, 1992-97

Tenure (%)	1992-93	1993-94	1994-95	1995-96	1996-97
Owner Occupied	28	31	29	29	29
Owner Occupied with Mortgage	36	33	34	38	38
Rented (NIHE)	28	28	28	26	25
Rented Other	7	7	8	7	6
Rent Free	1	1	1	1	1

REPUBLIC OF IRELAND: TENURE OF BORROWERS FOR HOUSING, 1993-97

Year	Owner Occupied		Private Tenant		Local Authority Tenant		Parents' Residence		Other	
	New (%)	Second Hand (%)	New (%)	Second Hand (%)	New (%)	Second Hand (%)	New (%)	Second Hand (%)	New (%)	Second Hand (%)
1993	32.0	44.3	23.1	24.1	1.4	2.8	41.1	26.3	2.4	2.6
1994	35.5	45.3	26.4	21.1	2.4	4.9	33.9	25.8	1.9	2.8
1995	40.8	54.8	24.6	18.5	1.3	2.9	30.5	21.0	2.8	2.8
1996	46.4	60.3	22.8	16.5	1.1	3.3	27.3	17.2	2.4	2.7
1997	52.6	65.0	22.9	16.8	1.1	1.7	21.4	14.2	2.0	2.3

REPUBLIC OF IRELAND: PUBLIC CAPITAL EXPENDITURE ON HOUSING, 1993-97

Constituents (£m)	1993	1994	1995	1996	1997
Local Authority Housing	92.6	157.1	180.3	191.9	218.2
Voluntary Housing	20.5	27.5	33.8	33.0	27.3
Shared Ownership	35.0	44.4	50.0	50.0	43.1
House Purchase & Improvement Loans etc.	24.2	19.2	18.0	20.6	18.8
Private Housing Grants	15.3	26.5	33.9	26.7	36.6
Other Housing	2.0	4.0	3.0	4.0	4.1
TOTAL:	**189.6**	**278.7**	**319.0**	**336.2**	**348.1**

REPUBLIC OF IRELAND: INTEREST RATES, 1990-98

Year	* Mortgage Rate (%)	† Associated Banks Overdraft Rate (%)	Interbank Rate (%)
1990	11.00 - 11.70	10.50	11.10
1991	10.75 - 11.45	11.30	10.70
1992	13.75 - 14.45	19.00	18.00
1993	7.75 - 8.45	7.00 - 7.40	6.60
1994	6.85 - 7.25	6.21 - 6.25	5.75
1995	6.85 - 7.79	6.00 - 6.13	5.45
1996	6.50 - 6.75	5.73 - 5.75	5.20
1997	7.10 - 7.85	6.81 - 7.00	7.00
1998	7.10 - 7.85	6.62 - 6.74	6.63

The rates shown for 1996 are those for quarter two; for 1998, they are those for quarter one
* The mortgage rate refers to a building society annuity rate.
† The overdraft rates are percentages charged to large commercial borrowers for short-term borrowings

REPUBLIC OF IRELAND:
CONSUMER PRICE INDEX, 1990-98*

Year	Base: 1985 = 100	Increase (%)
1990	117.6	1.64
1991	121.4	3.18
1992	125.1	3.08
1993	126.9	2.14
1994	129.9	3.15
1995	133.2	1.14
1996	135.4	2.01
1997	137.4	1.54
1998*	138.8	1.01

Average for the quarter Jan - March '98

NORTHERN IRELAND:
CONSUMERS' EXPENDITURE, 1990-95

Industry (£m)	1990	1991	1992	1993	1994	1995
Food	1,085	1,143	1,208	1,241	1,266	1,336
Alcoholic Drink	414	457	479	526	575	583
Clothing & Footwear	607	753	776	696	710	776
Tobacco	251	296	327	342	362	405
Housing	910	1,021	1,160	1,309	1,463	1,557
Fuel and Power	390	429	426	426	429	441
Household & Services	570	602	645	646	689	791
Transport & Communications	1,607	1,609	1,582	1,633	1,719	1,775
Recreation, Entertainment, Education	635	618	646	742	863	955
Other Goods & Services	1,398	1,530	1,681	1,807	1,954	2,171
Household Expenditure Abroad	428	447	446	438	445	432
Consumers' Expenditure	8,295	8,905	9,376	9,806	10,475	11,222
Personal Disposable Income	9,166	10,230	11,081	11,887	12,541	13,236
Balance Saving	871	1,325	1,705	2,081	2,066	2,014
Saving Ratio (%)	9.5	13.0	15.4	17.5	16.5	15.2

INDUSTRY, ENERGY& TRANSPORT

Foreign Companies in Ireland - The Long Haul?

By **Kieran McGowan**, *outgoing Chief Executive, IDA Ireland*

IDA IRELAND'S aim is to contribute to Ireland's economic development by convincing international companies, in both manufacturing and traded services, to locate in Ireland and by encouraging the expansion of such companies already in Ireland.

Foreign-owned companies are a critical part of the Irish economy, employing about half of the manufacturing labour force and accounting for around 16% of GDP. There are over 1,100 such companies in Ireland assisted by IDA Ireland, employing over 108,000 people directly and generating a similar number of jobs indirectly in the economy. Together these companies have annual turnover of more than £19 billion, mainly in exports, and over £7 billion of this retained in the Irish economy.

The key sectors that have invested in Ireland include the Information Technology, Healthcare, and Pharmaceuticals sectors and certain internationally traded services sectors such as financial services, software, data processing, teleservices and back office projects.

Over the past twenty years or so we have become a significant player in a number of technology areas, disproportionately so for a country of our size, and particularly in the areas of computers, communications and electronics, software, pharmaceuticals and healthcare. In these sectors we are rapidly becoming a high skills and high value economy and this is an underlying objective within national economic and social strategy.

In computers, communications, and electronics Ireland is winning about 20% of new projects locating in Europe in recent years and a higher proportion of US projects. The sector now directly employs 54,000 people and we have the cream of the world's companies here in sub-sectors such as semiconductor design, telecoms, personal computers and peripheral products. Companies such as Intel, Analog Devices, 3COM, Nortel, Dell, EMC and IBM are amongst the most advanced in the world in terms of the technology they use and the management practices they operate and they offer highly challenging jobs and exciting career opportunities to employees.

In software, Ireland has become a leading player accounting for 40% of the output of packaged software being sold in Europe. The Irish Software Association in a recent report estimated that on the basis of current growth the software industry will employ over 40,000 people by the year 2002, up from the current employment of around 20,000. The only constraint to this growth is availability of sufficient people with the necessary skills. The companies located here look like a list from the Fortune 1,000. New opportunities are developing in network computing, multimedia and the Internet which are all at relatively early stages in their lifecycles. A key reason for our success in this area is that the third level educational institutions in Ireland moved relatively early, in international terms, to establish courses that treated computing as an applied science rather than an abstract theoretical subject.

Of the top ten pharmaceutical companies in the world, nine have very substantial operations in Ireland, which may continue to expand. Schering Plough, for example, has two facilities in Brinny, County Cork and Rathdrum, County Wicklow with an investment of £250m and employing 600, of which 45% are third level graduates. The Brinny facility is a centre of excellence for biotechnology production and is the sole source for world-wide markets for Interferon, an anti-cancer drug. Ireland is strong in biotechnology, which is an engine for future development in healthcare, pharmaceutical, food and other industries.

The healthcare sector includes medical and hospital product companies such as Abbot, Boston Scientific and Johnson & Johnson, each of which has a number of operations located throughout the country. Ten of the top fifteen medical companies in the world have major facilities in Ireland, exporting over £6 billion annually and accounting for 25% of all medical plastic disposables in the European market.

In financial services over 600 companies have been approved to operate from Dublin's International Financial Services Centre, including the major financial names in the world. Key sectors include international banking, asset finance and leasing, treasury activities, funds, captive insurance and life assurance.

In all sectors these companies came to Ireland to operate mainly into European markets because of the competitive strengths of the Irish economy: - a stable, well managed economy, with a young, well educated and flexible workforce, with competitive operating and labour cost structures. To convince companies of the potential in Ireland we also offer a low corporate tax regime and certain financial incentives.

As Ireland's industrial base continues to develop there is no doubt but that overseas companies will continue to be a key element of the economy, providing a good balance with the strong mix of indigenous enterprises, both large and small. As time goes on, however, there will be change and fluctuations in the industrial base.

This change is a necessary feature of the business world and, to a great extent, it reflects the changes that occur in world markets in technologies globally. As Ireland is not immune to the impact of such change then the industrial base will inevitably change over time. This means some job losses each year but based on our current activity these job losses are compensated for by three times that number in new jobs each year.

Change will also be reflected in the continuous re-balancing of IDA Ireland's business. For example, in recent years there has been a strong focus on new electronics and information technology businesses. As that sector shows some early signs of slowdown there is increased activity in other business sectors such as healthcare, pharmaceuticals, teleservices and back office projects. By keeping a good balance across key sectors internationally IDA Ireland expects that Ireland will cope with the fluctuations of various sectors, as they occur.

While jobs are being created in Ireland at a pace never seen before the possibility of achieving continued growth of the pace of recent years will depend to a great extent on the overall competitiveness of the Irish economy and on the situation in global markets. Our key advantage - the demographic structure - will continue to be the focus for future growth, with ongoing substantial investment in ensuring that the labour force has the education and skills to meet future needs. In addition, significant investment is continuing in infrastructure such as telecommunications, roads, ports and airports.

Taking all these factors into account I would argue that not only will the strong performance of overseas companies in Ireland continue, but these companies will also remain a critical element of Ireland's economy well into the future. ❏

INDUSTRY

REPUBLIC OF IRELAND:
PERSONS EMPLOYED BY SECTOR, 1996-97

Sector	1996 Males	Females	Total	1997 Males	Females	Total
Agriculture, Forestry & Fishing	123,000	15,000	138,000	123,000	12,000	135,000
Mining, Quarrying, Turf Production	5,000	-	5,000	6,000	-	6,000
Manufacturing	175,000	75,000	250,000	186,000	85,000	271,000
Building & Construction	82,000	4,000	86,000	92,000	5,000	97,000
Electricity, Gas & Water	12,000	2,000	14,000	10,000	2,000	12,000
Commerce, Insurance and Finance	155,000	120,000	275,000	155,000	125,000	280,000
Transport, Communication & Storage	63,000	18,000	81,000	66,000	18,000	84,000
Public Administration & Defence	48,000	29,000	77,000	46,000	28,000	74,000
Other	142,000	230,000	372,000	141,000	238,000	379,000
TOTAL:	**805,000**	**493,000**	**1,298,000**	**825,000**	**513,000**	**1,338,000**

NORTHERN IRELAND:
PERSONS EMPLOYED BY SECTOR, 1996-97

Sector	1996 Males	Females	Total	1997 Males	Females	Total
Agriculture, Hunting, Forestry & Fishing	16,470	2,340	18,810	16,400	2,250	18,650
Mining & Quarrying	1,700	160	1,860	1,770	170	1,940
Manufacturing	69,840	33,210	103,050	71,440	33,240	104,680
Electric, Gas & Water Supply	4,110	480	4,590	3,860	460	4,320
Construction	20,190	2,370	22,560	21,650	2,570	24,220
Wholesale & Retail Trade: Repairs	41,660	46,480	88,140	43,220	48,230	91,450
Hotels & Restaurants	10,700	17,390	28,090	11,180	17,780	28,960
Transport, Storage & Communications	16,910	5,140	22,050	17,480	5,410	22,890
Financial Intermediation	5,260	8,360	13,620	5,200	8,480	13,680
Real Estate Renting & Business Activities	14,750	17,670	32,420	15,550	19,060	34,610
Public Administration & Defence	35,630	23,860	59,490	35,040	23,930	58,970
Education	17,380	44,920	62,300	17,130	44,140	61,270
Health & Social Work	16,260	75,020	91,280	16,010	75,970	91,980
Other	13,470	12,300	25,770	13,810	12,660	26,470
TOTAL:	**284,330**	**289,700**	**574,030**	**289,740**	**294,350**	**584,090**

REPUBLIC OF IRELAND & NORTHERN IRELAND:
LABOUR FORCE STATISTICS, 1996-97

	Republic of Ireland 1996	1997	Northern Ireland 1996	1997
Civil Employment:				
Males	804,000	826,000	350,450	355,600
Females	494,000	513,000	301,250	310,250
Total	1,298,000	1,339,000	651,700	665,850
Unemployed:				
Males	139,000	131,000	65,000	50,000
Females	53,000	48,000	19,000	13,400
Total	192,000	179,000	84,000	63,400
Total in Labour Force:				
Males	943,000	957,000	415,450	405,600
Females	547,000	561,000	320,250	323,650
Total	1,490,000	1,518,000	735,700	729,250
Employment In:				
Agriculture	138,000	134,000	18,810	18,660
Industry	355,000	386,000	132,060	135,170
Services	804,000	818,000	423,160	430,290
TOTAL:	**1,297,000**	**1,338,000**	**574,030**	**584,120**

REPUBLIC OF IRELAND:
PUBLIC SECTOR EMPLOYMENT FIGURES, 1993-97

Sector*	1993 (000s)	1994 (000s)	1995 (000s)	1996 (000s)	1997 (000s)
Prison Officers	2.3	2.5	2.5	2.5	2.5
Non-Industrial: Civil Service	26.5	26.0	27.0	26.8	26.6
Industrial: Civil Service	1.8	2.0	2.0	1.9	1.8
Others: Civil Service	0.6	0.6	0.5	0.5	0.9
Defence	14.0	14.3	14.0	13.1	12.8
Garda Síochána	11.2	10.8	10.7	10.7	10.8
Education: Primary	21.5	21.4	21.5	21.7	21.7
Education: Secondary	16.8	17.4	17.7	18.0	18.1
Education: Third Level	7.9	8.1	9.0	9.4	9.8
VECs (Including RTCs)	16.9	16.7	17.7	18.2	18.7
Local Authorities	29.0	28.9	28.6	28.7	29.4
Other Regional Bodies	1.4	1.5	1.5	1.6	1.5
Commercial Semi-State Companies	56.6	55.6	55.0	54.0	53.7
Non-Commercial Semi-State Companies	7.8	7.9	7.9	8.1	8.3
Health Boards	39.7	40.8	41.8	42.0	†42.0
Voluntary Hospitals	22.1	23.2	23.4	23.7	†23.7
TOTAL:	276.1	277.7	280.8	280.9	282.3

Employment figures at December of each year; † Employment figures at December 1996

REPUBLIC OF IRELAND & NORTHERN IRELAND:
MANUFACTURING INDUSTRY EMPLOYMENT, 1992-97

Year	Republic of Ireland			Northern Ireland		
	Males	Females	Total	Males	Females	Total
1992	157,000	69,000	226,000	65,720	35,000	100,720
1993	160,000	65,000	225,000	64,320	34,250	98,570
1994	166,000	70,000	236,000	66,090	34,640	100,730
1995	172,000	76,000	248,000	69,260	34,330	103,590
1996	175,000	75,000	250,000	69,840	33,210	103,050
1997	186,000	85,000	271,000	71,440	33,240	104,680

REPUBLIC OF IRELAND: WOMEN AT WORK, 1971-96

Year	Single	Married	Other	Total
1971	212,600	38,300	24,600	275,500
1981	211,000	102,600	15,600	329,200
1991	191,700	173,800	20,800	386,300
1996	218,600	244,300	30,800	493,700

N. IRELAND: PUBLIC SECTOR EMPLOYMENT, 1994-97

Sector / Department	1994	1995	1996	1997
Agriculture	4,009	3,828	3,754	3,642
Economic Development	2,585	2,538	2,556	2,464
Education	618	590	597	612
Environment	9,027	8,505	8,435	8,025
Finance & Personnel	1,396	1,373	1,568	1,528
Fire Service	2,163	2,229	2,231	2,186
Health & Social Services	7,895	7,809	7,999	8,031
Prison Services	3,260	3,174	3,129	2,986
Royal Ulster Constabulary	16,629	16,758	16,519	16,439
Northern Ireland Assembly	9	10	9	10
Other Northern Ireland Central Government	1,489	1,546	1,493	1,556
Bodies under the aegis of NI Central Government	84,016	71,736	71,940	62,591
UK Central Government	6,283	6,221	6,193	6,073
Local Government	9,205	8,779	9,037	9,251
NI-based Public Corporations	8,045	7,635	7,527	7,270
UK-based Public Corporations	4,539	4,340	4,407	4,797
NHS Trusts	33,614	48,225	47,955	55,837
TOTAL:	194,782	195,296	195,349	193,298

NORTHERN IRELAND:
AVERAGE GROSS WEEKLY EARNINGS, 1996-97

Sector	1996 Males (£)	1996 Females (£)	1997 Males (£)	1997 Females (£)
Agriculture, Hunting & Forestry	180.3	-	179.9	-
Fishing	-	-	-	-
Mining & Quarrying	287.2	-	282	-
Manufacturing	300.1	195.2	314	205.2
Electricity, Gas & Water Supply	398.5	-	429.2	-
Construction	295.5	-	320.5	-
Wholesale & Retail Trade	287	191	299	208.6
Hotels & Restaurants	191.6	177	231.4	155.4
Transport, Storage & Communication	323.1	281.1	341.5	254.7
Financial Intermediation	531.9	297.3	509.4	305.7
Real Estate, Renting & Business Activities	301.1	212.7	335.5	219.4
Public Administration & Defence	423	264.2	445.2	266.2
Education	407.2	438.4	356.6	370.8
Health & Social Work	364.1	279.6	367.3	280.8
Other Industries	292.8	221.3	291.3	252.7
TOTAL:	337.4	256.9	356	265.4

REPUBLIC OF IRELAND: INDUSTRIAL WORKERS
WEEKLY EARNINGS, 1990-97

Year	Avg. Weekly Earnings (IR£)	Increase on Previous Year (%)	Average Hours Worked	Avg. Earnings Per Hour (IR£)
1990	225.16	4.0	41.4	5.43
1991	235.23	4.5	41.0	5.73
1992	244.27	3.8	40.6	6.01
1993	258.00	5.6	40.5	6.36
1994	265.13	2.8	41.0	6.47
1995	270.70	2.1	40.9	6.62
1996	278.68	2.9	40.9	6.82
1997*	284.07	1.9	40.8	6.96

Average figures for January - September 1997

NORTHERN IRELAND: ADULT EMPLOYEES GROSS
WEEKLY EARNINGS, 1992-97

Year	Average Weekly Earnings Male (£)	Increase on Previous Year (%)	Average Weekly Earnings Female (£)	Increase on Previous Year (%)
1992	298.2	9.5	224.2	11.2
1993	313.6	5.2	232.5	3.7
1994	319.2	1.8	236.7	1.8
1995	330.9	3.7	251.4	6.2
1996	337.4	2	256.9	2.2
1997	355.9	5.5	265.2	3.2

REPUBLIC OF IRELAND: COMPARISONS OF OUTPUT & WAGE COSTS INDEX, 1987-97

Year	Output per Hour	Unit Wage Costs
1987	115.9	97.0
1988	129.3	90.6
1989	141.3	86.3
1990	144.9	87.9
1991	149.7	89.8
1992	166.0	84.8
1993	175.8	84.7
1994	190.6	79.5
1995	215.8	71.8
1996	223.7	71.2
1997	235.0	69.0

Base: 1985 = 100

REPUBLIC OF IRELAND & NORTHERN IRELAND: SEASONALLY ADJUSTED UNEMPLOYMENT, 1992-97

	Republic of Ireland		Northern Ireland	
Year	Number	%	Number	%
1992	211,110	15.5	104,700	13.8
1993	215,592	15.6	103,700	13.7
1994	198,387	14.1	97,100	12.6
1995	175,558	12.2	88,100	11.4
1996	171,120	11.5	84,000	10.9
1997	156,251	10.3	63,200	8.2

REPUBLIC OF IRELAND: UNEMPLOYMENT BY AREA, 1996-97

	1996		1997	
Area	Persons	%	Persons	%
Border	34,610	12.8	34,042	13.7
Dublin	83,549	30.9	73,318	29.6
Mid-East	19,390	7.2	17,616	7.1
Midland	14,038	5.2	12,919	5.2
Mid-West	20,282	7.5	18,458	7.5
South-East	30,585	11.3	29,136	11.8
South-West	41,192	15.2	37,324	15.1
West	26,510	9.8	24,917	10.1
TOTAL:	270,156	100.0	247,730	100.0

NORTHERN IRELAND: UNEMPLOYMENT BY AREA, 1996-97

	1996		1997	
Area	Persons	%	Persons	%
Ballymena	1,864	6.0	1,391	4.8
Belfast	34,800	8.2	27,335	6.5
Coleraine	4,572	11.2	3,578	8.8
Cookstown	1,484	13.0	973	8.6
Craigavon	5,579	7.6	4,347	6.0
Derry	7,941	13.3	7,041	11.6
Dungannon	2,281	11.1	1,813	8.6
Enniskillen	2,780	11.1	2,350	9.2
Magherafelt	1,556	9.8	1,159	7.5
Newry	4,625	13.1	3,725	10.7
Omagh	2,364	10.9	1,993	9.2
Strabane	2,094	15.3	1,827	12.6
TOTAL:	71,940	9.3	57,532	7.5

INTERNATIONAL UNEMPLOYMENT COMPARISONS

Country	Month/Year	Rate (%)	Country	Month/Year	Rate (%)
Australia	Feb-98	8.1	Japan	Feb-98	3.6
Austria	Feb-98	4.4	Luxembourg	Feb-98	3.4
Belgium	Feb-98	9.0	Netherlands*	Jan-98	4.7
Canada	Feb-98	8.6	Norway*	Nov-97	3.8
Denmark	Feb-98	5.5	Portugal	Feb-98	6.6
Finland	Feb-98	12.5	Spain	Feb-98	20.0
France	Feb-98	12.1	Sweden	Feb-98	9.0
Germany	Feb-98	9.7	United Kingdom	Feb-April '98	6.3
Greece*	June-96	9.7	United States	Feb-98	4.6
IRELAND	Feb-98	9.6	Northern Ireland	Feb-April '98	8.0
Italy*	Jan-98	12.0	EU Average	Feb-98	10.3

latest statistics available

REP. OF IRELAND: INDUSTRIAL DISPUTES, 1997

Description	Public Sector	Private Sector	Totals
Number of Disputes	13	15	28
Official	8	14	22
Unofficial	5	1	6
Days Lost	31,093	43,415	74,508
Number of Firms	19	14	33
Number of Workers	4,111	1,253	5,364

REP. OF IRELAND: INDUSTRIAL DISPUTES, 1990-97

Year	Disputes	Workers Affected	Working Days Lost
1990	49	-	222916
1991	54	-	85513
1992	38	13,107	190,609
1993	47	12,764	61,312
1994	28	5,007	25,550
1995	34	31,654	130,300
1996	30	13,339	114,585
1997	28	5,364	74,508

NORTHERN IRELAND: INDUSTRIAL STOPPAGES, 1990-97

Year	Stoppages	Workers Affected	Working Days Lost
1990	24	12,479	18,322
1991	12	16,805	16,926
1992	5	3,905	7,734
1993	7	15,870	15,723
1994	14	3,849	4,949
1995	7	4,391	4,919
1996	3	4,660	20,201
1997	7	6,000	13,800

REPUBLIC OF IRELAND: IDA STATISTICS, 1993-97

Description	1993	1994	1995	1996	1997
New Jobs Filled	8,258	9,930	11,725	13,296	14,930
Number of Companies	878	914	968	1,051	1,117
Employment (F/T)	78,944	83,958	90,517	97,841	107,826
Net Change in Employment (F/T)	2,643	5,014	6,559	7,324	9,985
Losses	5,615	4,916	5,166	5,972	4,945

REPUBLIC OF IRELAND: IDA SUPPORTED EMPLOYMENT & NEW JOBS BY REGION, 1994-97

Region	Total Employment 1994	1995	1996	1997	New Jobs 1994	1995	1996	1997
North West / Donegal	6,910	7,122	6,947	6,936	459	411	297	279
West	7,779	8,571	8,993	9,855	1,059	1,039	954	1,434
Mid West	10,248	10,806	11,247	11,547	1,351	1,142	1,227	998
South West	11,841	12,404	13,060	13,699	1,032	1,477	1,176	1,510
South East	8,362	8,653	9,424	9,896	645	780	1,457	935
East	28,197	32,310	37,697	45,113	4,136	6,143	7,570	8,698
North East	4,781	4,960	4,378	4,484	726	432	85	440
Midlands	5,840	5,691	6,095	6,296	522	301	530	636
TOTAL:	83,958	90,517	97,841	107,826	9,930	11,725	13,296	14,930

N. IRELAND: IDB PROMOTED JOBS, 1990-96

Year	Jobs New to Northern Ireland	New Companies From Within NI	Expanding Companies	Total Jobs
1990	1,616	214	3,032	4,862
1991	1,098	91	3,113	4,302
1992	1,320	232	2,119	3,671
1993	2,234	185	1,945	4,364
1994	3,213	181	1,373	4,767
1995	3,317	-	1,811	5,128
1996	2,599	-	4,661	7,260

REPUBLIC OF IRELAND & NORTHERN IRELAND: COUNTRY OF ORIGIN OF OVERSEAS COMPANIES

REPUBLIC OF IRELAND (1997)* Country of Origin	Number of Companies	NORTHERN IRELAND (1997)* Country of Origin	Number of Companies
United States	455	North America	52
Germany	151	Germany	9
United Kingdom	170	Britain	47
Rest of Europe	239	Republic of Ireland	14
Asia / Pacific	56	Asia / Pacific	13
Rest of World	46	Rest of World	17
TOTAL:	1,117	TOTAL:	152

*IDA Assisted   * IDB Assisted*

REPUBLIC OF IRELAND: INDUSTRIAL PRODUCTION INDEX, 1990-96

Sector volume index (1985=100)	1990	1991	1992	1993	1994	1995	1996
Manufacturing Industries:							
Non-Metallic Mineral Products	116.5	109.5	113.7	109.7	121.2	132.4	145.5
Chemicals	149.3	182.3	212.8	234.3	279.8	324.1	384.3
Metals and Engineering	190.4	184.9	205.7	218.4	252.8	337.4	365.9
Food	130.8	136.5	149.1	156.5	168.5	186.9	188.6
Drink and Tobacco	117.0	122.8	122.3	122.2	129.5	136.1	143.2
Textile Industry	119.3	119.0	125.4	128.5	131.7	132.8	125.8
Clothing, Footwear and Leather	87.9	77.1	73.6	68.9	65.9	63.5	64.0
Timber and Wooden Furniture	117.7	117.6	120.3	121.7	134.5	141.8	153.3
Paper and Printing	139.5	151.1	165.2	176.6	180.3	199.9	200.8
Miscellaneous Industries	129.2	127.5	133.0	130.2	140.8	150.4	148.7
Total: Manufacturing Industries	149.4	154.2	169.6	178.8	201.6	242.2	262.2
Mining, Quarrying and Turf	115.1	106.9	98.3	113.7	115.6	136.1	140.0
Transportable Goods Industries	148.3	152.6	167.3	176.7	198.7	238.7	258.2
Electricity, Gas and Water	108.2	116.1	120.4	127.2	133.6	137.9	145.1
TOTAL:	143.9	148.6	162.2	171.3	191.7	227.9	246.0

NORTHERN IRELAND: INDUSTRIAL PRODUCTION, 1990-96*

Sector volume index (1990=100)	1990	1991	1992	1993	1994	1995	1996
Manufacturing Industries:							
Food, Drink and Tobacco	100.0	98.6	97.9	99.7	101.8	101.6	102.5
Textiles, Leather & Clothing	100.0	97.3	101.8	108.5	113.4	113.2	110.4
Wood and Wood Products	100.0	96.1	94.4	103.1	117.2	114.7	111.6
Pulp, Paper and Printing	100.0	101.2	103.6	101.2	104.9	110.7	111.3
Chemicals and Chemical Products	100.0	99.2	107.9	108.1	114.2	107.8	106.2
Rubber and Plastics	100.0	93.2	91.0	96.5	111.7	122.6	122.6
Non-Metallic Mineral Products	100.0	98.8	95.9	112.2	121.2	120.9	124.8
Basic Metals and Fabricated Metals	100.0	88.0	86.1	104.9	117.5	116.1	122.7
Machinery and Equipment	100.0	89.9	91.4	97.7	109.3	115.9	113.6
Electrical and Optical Equipment	100.0	103.5	99.2	108.4	129.5	164.5	183.6
Transport Equipment	100.0	106.5	106.9	85.9	91.4	106.8	107.9
Miscellaneous	100.0	98.3	97.0	106.1	117.1	127.1	128.2
Total: Manufacturing Industries	100.0	98.3	99.2	101.8	109.2	114.1	115.4
Electricity, Gas and Water	100.0	102.2	103.3	106.3	108.9	110.7	115.7
Mining and Quarrying	100.0	96.7	87.3	99.2	112.0	110.4	105.8
TOTAL:	100.0	98.8	99.5	102.4	109.2	113.6	115.3

* Seasonally Adjusted

REPUBLIC OF IRELAND & NORTHERN IRELAND:UNION MEMBERSHIP

Union Group	Republic of Ireland		Northern Ireland	
	Number of Unions	Union Members	Number of Unions	Union Members
General Unions	2	207,507	3	60,589
Public Service Unions	13	102,923	10	80,011
Postal & Telecommunications	2	20,556	2	6,540
Electrical, Engineering Unions	3	36,193	1	19,010
Construction Unions	4	19,989	1	2,800
Other Industry Unions	3	7,527	3	3,726
Distribution / Transport Unions	7	36,758	4	6,753
Professional / White Collar Unions	12	58,818	8	19,547
Others	6	893	-	-
TOTAL:	52	491,164	32	198,976

WORLD'S 20 MOST COMPETITIVE COUNTRIES, 1998

1998 Ranking	1997 Ranking	1998 Ranking	1997 Ranking
1 .... United States	(1)	11 .... Ireland	(15)
2 .... Singapore	(2)	12 .... Britain	(11)
3 .... Hong Kong	(3)	13 .... New Zealand	(13)
4 .... Netherlands	(6)	14 .... Germany	(14)
5 .... Finland	(4)	15 .... Australia	(18)
6 .... Norway	(5)	16 .... Taiwan	(23)
7 .... Switzerland	(7)	17 .... Sweden	(16)
8 .... Denmark	(8)	18 .... Japan	(9)
9 .... Luxembourg	(12)	19 .... Iceland	(21)
10 .... Canada	(10)	20 .... Malaysia	(17)

REP. OF IRELAND:FATAL ACCIDENTS AT WORK, 1997

Sector	Number	Sector	Number
Agriculture	15	Wholesale & Retail Services	2
Construction	15	Mining & Quarrying	1
Transport, Storage & Communications	6	Other	2
Fishing	5	**TOTAL:**	**48**
Manufacturing	2	Total for 1998 (Jan - Oct 5th)	50

REPUBLIC OF IRELAND:
TELECOMMUNICATIONS STATISTICS, 1995-97

Operational Statistics	1995-96	1996-97
Telephone Lines (million)	1.31	1.39
New Connections	163,000	171,300
Telephone Traffic Growth (%)	12	14
Data Lines	22,700	24,600
Mobile Lines	158,000	288,600
Chargecards	50,000	70,800
Voicemail	24,000	120,000
Public Payphones	6,500	7,200
Number of Employees	11,707	11,560

ENERGY

NORTHERN IRELAND:
MINE AND QUARRY PRODUCTION, 1995-97

	Quantity 000 Tonnes			Selling Value £000		
Category of Rock	1995	1996	1997	1995	1996	1997
Basalt and Igneous Rock *	7,564	6,974	6,286	18,751	17,007	16,570
Sandstone	4,779	4,941	6,042	11,151	12,023	14,493
Limestone	3,703	4,122	3,500	10,928	10,793	10,534
Sand and Gravel	5,262	7,684	5,138	10,730	16,880	10,542
Others	812	1,392	625	4,422	6,622	3,394
TOTAL:	22,120	25,133	21,591	55,982	63,325	55,533

* other than granite

NORTHERN IRELAND: PERSONS EMPLOYED
AT MINES AND QUARRIES, 1996-97

	Inside Pit or Excavation		Outside Pit or Excavation		Management/ Administration		Total Employed	
Mineral	1996	1997	1996	1997	1996	1997	1996	1997
Basalt and Igneous Rock *	152	137	220	259	108	104	480	500
Sandstone	97	143	137	124	72	96	306	363
Limestone	68	59	60	78	97	103	225	240
Sand and Gravel	109	101	93	100	99	106	301	307
Others	73	39	35	18	40	11	148	68
TOTAL:	499	479	545	579	416	420	1,460	1,478

* other than granite

REPUBLIC OF IRELAND:
ESB GENERATION BY POWER STATIONS, 1993-96

Generating Station	1993	1994	1995	1996
	Kilowatt hours (million)			
Hydro-Electric:				
Ardnacrusha	331	395	268	288
Erne	259	320	275	258
Lee	82	104	87	92
Liffey	46	50	37	47
Clady	15	15	16	4
Total	733	884	683	689
Pumped Storage:				
Turlough Hill	247	278	255	260
Total	247	278	255	260
Peat:				
Allenwood	-	-	-	-

Continued from previous page

Generating Station	1993	1994	1995	1996
		Kilowatt hours million		
Ferbane	223	201	171	162
Lanesboro'.	485	556	581	603
Cahirciveen	14	7	11	14
Gweedore	7	7	3	0
Rhode	286	282	393	366
Bellacorrick	181	159	239	220
Shannonbridge	639	655	578	779
Total	1,835	1,867	1,976	2,144
Coal / Oil:				
Moneypoint	6,567	6,662	6,995	6,963
Arigna	29	-	-	-
Great Island	86	200	221	244
Tarbert	1,631	1,846	1,688	2,147
Poolbeg	595	753	730	256
Total	8,908	9,461	9,634	9,610
Gas:				
Marina	302	695	634	791
Aghada	1,760	1,041	1,823	1,858
North Wall	710	835	669	921
Poolbeg	1,633	1,747	1,882	2,572
Total	4,405	4,318	5,008	6,142
TOTAL	16,128	16,808	17,556	18,845

NORTHERN IRELAND: POWER STATIONS BY TYPE AND CAPACITY, 1997

Name	Type	Capacity (MW)
Ballylumford	Gas / Gas Oil	1,067
Belfast West	Coal	240
Kilroot	Fuel Oil / Coal or Gas Oil	578
Coolkeeragh	Fuel Oil / Gas Oil	358

REPUBLIC OF IRELAND: ESB STATISTICS, 1996-97

Description	1996	1997
New Houses Connected	33,097	38,452
Turnover (£m)	1,104	1,191
Surplus (£m)	132	160
Sales (million units)	15,707	16,726
Customers	1,442,416	1,483,740

REP. OF IRELAND: ENERGY DEMANDS, 1995-97

Energy Source	1995 (%)	1996 (%)	1997 (%)
Peat	12	11	10
Coal	18	17	17
Oil	49	50	50
Hydro/Renewables	2	2	3
Natural Gas	19	20	20

NORTHERN IRELAND: PRIMARY ENERGY SUPPLY, 1992-96

Source	1992	1993	1994	1995	1996
			million therms		
Oil	1,361	1,472	1,373	1,296	1,258
Coal	643	647	688	716	691
TOTAL:	2,004	2,119	2,061	2,012	1,950

REPUBLIC OF IRELAND:
FUEL CONSUMPTION BY SOURCE, 1995-96

Source	TOE (Ton of Oil Equivalent) 1995	1996
Peat	1,214,000	1,069,000
Coal	1,000	-
Natural Gas	1,916,000	2,255,000
Hydro Power	63,000	61,000
Other	179,000	141,000
TOTAL:	**3,373,000**	**3,526,000**

NORTHERN IRELAND:
ENERGY CONSUMPTION BY SOURCE, 1993-96

Source	1993	1994 million therms	1995	1996
Coal	350	398	323	330
Gas	0	0	0	0
Electricity	216	221	226	237
Petroleum	528	550	526	483
TOTAL:	**1,094**	**1,169**	**1,075**	**1,050**

NORTHERN IRELAND:
ELECTRICITY STATISTICS, 1992-97

Description	1992-93	1993-94	1994-95	1995-96	1996-97
Sales (million kWh)	6,214.0	6,412.0	6,529.0	6,715.0	6,876.0
Consumers	624,200.0	633,647.0	643,776.0	654,625.0	665,000.0
Turnover (£ million)	453.2	481.9	497.7	524.7	560.9
Operating Costs (£ million)	121.6	117.8	113.9	114.2	129.6
Capital Expenditure (£ million)	58.5	41.9	58.5	66.5	64.5

REPUBLIC OF IRELAND:
AVERAGE PRICE OF PETROL YEARLY, 1987-97

Year	Premium Leaded	Regular Leaded	(PENCE PER LITRE) Unleaded Petrol	Diesel
1987	58.87	57.93	-	-
1988	58.19	57.06	-	-
1989	61.49	60.57	61.71	-
1990	63.02	59.92	60.90	-
1991	62.26	-	59.89	-
1992	59.04	-	58.27	-
1993	59.43	-	56.57	-
1994	59.77	-	56.03	-
1995	60.57	-	56.34	-
1996	63.69	-	59.14†	-
1997	66.68	-	59.86†	57.42

† Price relates to Unl95 (price for Unl98: 67.90)

NORTHERN IRELAND:
AVERAGE PETROL PRICES, 1987-97

Year	4 star	Super Unleaded	(PENCE PER LITRE) Unleaded	Derv
1987	37.9	-	-	34.58
1988	37.38	-	-	34
1989	40.39	-	38.29	36.18
1990	44.87	-	42.03	40.48
1991	48.47	47.31	45.06	43.81
1992	50.28	48.38	46.11	45.01

Year	4 star	Super Unleaded	(PENCE PER LITRE) Unleaded	Derv
1993	54.12	52.91	49.44	49.2
1994	56.87	55.98	51.56	51.53
1995	59.7	58.55	53.77	54.24
1996	61.63	63.67	56.52	57.71
1997	67.22	71.31	61.82	62.47

COAL SHIPMENTS INTO N. IRELAND, 1993-96

Use	1993	1994	1995	1996
Domestic	1,082	1,211	932	919
Industrial	147	190	206	246
Electricity	1,256	1,225	1,660	1,525
TOTAL:	2,485	2,626	2,798	2,690

REPUBLIC OF IRELAND: PEAT AND BRIQUETTE PRODUCTION AND SALES, 1989-98

Year	Milled Peat (M tonnes) Production	Sales	Briquette (000 tonnes) Production	Sales
1989/90	7.3	4.2	355	368
1990/91	5.9	4.5	403	399
1991/92	4.3	4.5	365	367
1992/93	2.7	4.2	394	374
1993/94	3.5	3.9	365	391
1994/95	3.6	3.9	365	363
1995/96	6.7	4.0	344	294
1996/97	5.0	4.0	291	283
1997/98	2.7	3.6	244	263

REPUBLIC OF IRELAND: BORD NA MÓNA PRODUCTION AND SALES STATISTICS, 1992-98

Description	1992/93	1993/94	1994/95	1995/96	1996/97	1997/98
Production:						
Machine Turf *(000 tonnes)*	135	123	94	77	62	52
Milled Peat *(000 tonnes)*	2,759	3,536	3,646	6,658	5,049	2,744
Briquettes *(000 tonnes)*	394	365	365	344	291	244
Horticulture *(000 cu metres)*	1,216	1,160	1,142	1,702	1,452	1,616
Total	4,504	5,184	5,247	8,781	6,854	4,656
Sales:						
Machine Turf to ESB *(000 tonnes)*	19	-	-	-	-	-
Machine Turf to Others *(000 tonnes)*	105	106	97	86	88	67
Milled Peat to ESB *(000 tonnes)*	3,259	2,944	2,994	3,145	3,284	3,005
Milled Peat to Bord na Móna:						
Factories *(000 tonnes)*	1,002	962	995	868	728	612
Briquettes *(000 tonnes)*	374	391	363	294	283	263
Horticulture *(000 cu metres)*	1,271	1,446	1,562	1,710	1,393	1,536
Total	6,030	5,849	6,011	14,653	5,776	5,483
Value of Sales:						
Machine Turf to ESB *(£000s)*	515	-	-	-	-	-
Machine Turf to Others *(£000s)*	3,357	3,264	3,224	2,581	2,363	2,088
Milled Peat to ESB *(£000s)*	57,613	56,406	54,926	57,613	56,477	52,071
Briquettes *(£000s)*	26,087	27,573	27,151	23,326	22,089	21,438
Coal *(£000s)*	-	-	-	9,073	11,069	9,906
Horticulture *(£000s)*	33,783	37,610	41,587	45,409	45,959	42,132
Environmental Products *(£000s)*	1,661	2,166	2,732	3,050	4,930	6,000
Total *(£000s)*	123,016	127,019	129,620	141,052	142,887	133,635

NORTHERN IRELAND: WATER SUPPLY, 1993-97

Description	1993	1994	1995-96	1996-97
Supply (million litres per day):				
Total Water Supplied	667.0	682.0	703.2	706.0
Water Supplied by Meter	177.4	176.2	174.5	186.9
Metered Water as % of Total Water	26.6%	25.8%	24.8%	26.4%
Supply (litres per head per day):				
by Meter	109	108	106	112
unmetered	300	310	321	312
Total: Supply	409	418	427	424

TRANSPORT

REPUBLIC OF IRELAND: BUS TRANSPORT

Coras Iompair Éireann (CIÉ)

The Irish Transport System - provides public transport in Ireland. It operates the two following subsidiaries:

Bus Éireann (Irish Bus)

Provides the national bus service outside the Dublin area. It operates a network of bus services between the larger towns and cities, in addition to servicing rural areas and the cities of Cork, Limerick, Waterford and Galway. Bus Éireann caters for more than 60 million passengers annually.

Bus Átha Cliath (Dublin Bus)

Operates the Dublin City bus services. It accounts for more than 160 million passenger journeys annually and covers an area of 1,000 sq. km of the Dublin area.

Bus Éireann (1997)

Revenue (IR£m)	102.2
Profit (IR£m)	3.4
Number of Passengers (million)	85.2
Vehicle Services (kilometres)	62,835
Number of Employees	2,521
Fleet:	
New Coaches	61
Mini Buses	25

Bus Átha Cliath (1997)

Revenue (IR£m)	102.5
Profit (IR£m)	1.5
Number of Passengers (million)	187.9
Vehicle Services (kilometres)	
Number of Employees	2,901
Fleet:	
New Buses	63
Mini Buses	3

NORTHERN IRELAND: BUS TRANSPORT

Ulsterbus and Citybus - provide the provincial and Belfast City bus services, respectively. Citybus operates mostly within the boundaries of the Belfast City Council area. In practice, both companies cater for Belfast's bus transportation requirements, as the actual built-up urban area of Belfast extends far beyond the council area boundaries. Ulsterbus operates inter-urban express services and rural services. It also provides the city services in Derry, together with urban services in virtually every town in Northern Ireland.

CITYBUS STATISTICS (1996/1997)

Kilometres Operated	11,800,000
Passenger Journeys	24,300,000
Bus Miles	7,300,000
Passenger Receipts	£16,900,000
Bus Fleet	270
Average Age of Buses	8.0 years
Number of Staff	727

ULSTERBUS STATISTICS (1996/1997)

Kilometres Operated	61,200,000
Passenger Journeys	53,900,000
Bus Miles	38,000,000
Passenger Receipts	£54,400,000
Bus Fleet	1,221
Average Age of Buses	9.9 years
Number of Staff	2,183

REPUBLIC OF IRELAND: RAIL TRANSPORT

Coras Iompair Éireann (CIÉ) - Irish Transport System - provides rail services throughout Ireland through its subsidiary company - **Iarnród Éireann (Irish Rail).** Iarnród Éireann operates rail services around Ireland and into Northern Ireland over its 1,900 route kilometres. It operates passenger and freight services, including the **DART** (see further on), and carries 26 million passengers annually.

Dublin Area Rapid Transport (DART) provides a passenger service to the mainly coastal areas of Dublin City, between Howth and Dun Laoghaire and to coastal parts of Co. Wicklow. It consists of 38 km of track and operates on electric motive power.

Revenue (IR£m)	129.0
Profit (IR£m)	1.8
Number of Passengers (IR£m)	29.4
Rail Freight Revenue (IR£m)	17.3
Number of Employees	4,939

GEOGRAPHICAL ANALYSIS OF PASSENGER REVENUE, 1997

Region	Revenue (IR£m)
South West	27.2
West	13.1
South East	4.3
Belfast	4.4
DART	14.6
Other Suburban	7.9
Branch Lines	0.8
Total:	**72.3**

NORTHERN IRELAND: RAIL TRANSPORT

Northern Ireland Railways (NIR) operates all public passenger railway services within Northern Ireland and a joint service with Iarnród Éireann on the Dublin-Belfast route. The NIR provides railway services from Belfast to the following destinations in Northern Ireland: Larne Harbour, Carrickfergus, Bangor, Portadown, Ballymena, Coleraine, Portrush, Derry City and intermediate stations and halts.

RAIL STATISTICS (1996/97)

Passenger Journeys	6,200,000
Passenger Receipts	£9,959,000
Number of Staff	726
Track Routes (miles)	211
Rolling Stock:	
Locomotives	43
Passenger Coaches	96
Tota Rolling Stock	139

IARNRÓD ÉIREANN: PASSENGER & RECEIPT STATISTICS, 1994-97

	1994	1995	1996	1997
Train Traffic (Passengers)	£61,274,000	£66,317,000	£69,955,000	£75,405,000
Train Traffic (Goods)	£18,412,000	£17,398,000	£17,413,000	£18,085,000
Total	**£79,686,000**	**£84,290,000**	**£87,368,000**	**£93,490,000**
Number of Passengers Carried	25,810,000	27,120,000	27,915,000	28,913,000

REPUBLIC OF IRELAND: SEA TRANSPORT

The Republic of Ireland's main passenger / car ferry ports are Rosslare, Dun Laoghaire, Cork and Dublin. Other smaller harbours are located throughout the country which deal in bulk cargoes. There are a number of car ferries currently operating services from Ireland, including Irish Ferries and Stena Sealink.

Shipping The process of shipping and cargo handling has developed rapidly in recent times, and Irish ports have expanded their facilities to accommodate these developments, as Ireland's external trade depends on shipping for 76% of its exports. Ireland's multi-modal ports are located in Dublin and Cork and deal with all cargoes, while Waterford Harbour is becoming the most up-to-date Lo/Lo handling port in Ireland.

REPUBLIC OF IRELAND: SEA TRANSPORT - PASSENGER MOVEMENT, 1990-97

	Britain		Other Places		Total	
Year	Outward	Inward	Outward	Inward	Outward	Inward
1990	1,419,000	1,445,000	197,000	198,000	1,617,000	1,643,000
1991	1,556,000	1,573,000	193,000	191,000	1,749,000	1,765,000
1992	1,579,000	1,581,000	193,000	191,000	1,772,000	1,772,000
1993	1,717,000	1,739,000	192,000	189,000	1,909,000	1,928,000
1994	1,807,000	1,815,000	191,000	189,000	1,998,000	2,004,000
1995	1,950,000	1,938,000	181,000	176,000	2,131,000	2,114,000
1996	1,977,000	1,954,000	158,000	158,000	2,135,000	2,112,000
1997	2,149,000	2,184,000	112,000	109,000	2,260,000	2,293,000

NORTHERN IRELAND: SEA TRANSPORT

Northern Ireland's main passenger / car ferry ports are located in the harbours at Belfast and Larne. Other sea ports operate shipping lines out of Northern Ireland. The car ferries currently operating services from Northern Ireland include Belfast Car Ferries, P & O Ferries and Stena Line Sealink.

Shipping Over 80 international shipping lines operate out of Northern Ireland's five commercial seaports. These ports handle 90% of Northern Ireland's total trade, and almost 50 % of the Republic of Ireland's freight traffic. There are 150 sailings weekly to Britain, as well as regular sailings to ports in the US, Continental Europe and the rest of the world. Over 55 % of Northern Ireland's seaborne trade is shipped through Belfast Port - the busiest port in the Island of Ireland - 5,500 ships carrying 11 million tonnes of cargo leave the port each year.

NORTHERN IRELAND: SEA TRANSPORT - PASSENGER STATISTICS, 1991-96

Year	Belfast Inward	Belfast Outward	Larne Inward	Larne Outward	Warrenpoint Inward	Warrenpoint Outward	Totals Inward	Totals Outward
1991	1,804	1,935	196,263	190,910	-	-	198,067	192,845
1992	43,536	43,868	180,087	174,241	627	141	224,250	218,250
1993	60,153	60,205	201,903	196,118	-	-	262,056	256,323
1994	57,723	57,927	215,578	208,959	-	-	273,301	266,886
1995	75,972	73,139	226,119	220,252	-	-	302,091	293,391
1996	201,899	193,489	98,186	95,779	-	-	300,085	289,268

REPUBLIC OF IRELAND: AIRLINE TRANSPORT

INTERNATIONAL AIRPORTS The three international airports - Cork, Dublin and Shannon - handle more than 13 million passengers and 94,000 tonnes of freight annually. Dublin International Airport, the busiest, has a throughput in excess of 10 million passengers annually. In addition to these three airports, Knock International Airport also handles flights from America and Britain.

AER LINGUS is the state airline. It operates flights to 27 cities in Britain, Europe and North America and caters for over 4 million passengers and 45,000 tonnes of freight annually.

OTHER AIRLINES offering flights to and from Ireland include CityJet, Ryanair and Translift Airways. Various passenger, freight and helicopter services operate within the country using the network of regional airports - Donegal, Galway, Kerry, Sligo and Waterford.

REPUBLIC OF IRELAND: AER RIANTA PASSENGER STATISTICS, 1993-97

Year	Transatlantic	Britain	Europe	Domestic	Transit	Total
1993	708,601	4,276,950	2,005,690	630,364	749,744	8,371,349
1994	829,918	5,000,251	2,304,924	654,939	525,571	9,315,603
1995	866,464	5,864,923	2,641,078	751,836	443,297	10,567,598
1996	991,300	6,789,638	2,884,820	804,873	485,635	11,956,266
1997	1,032,166	7,614,919	3,261,279	850,465	592,698	13,351,527

REPUBLIC OF IRELAND: AER LINGUS PASSENGER STATISTICS, 1994-97

Airport	(NO. OF PASSENGERS) 1994	1995	1996	1997
Dublin	6,980,983	8,024,898	9,091,296	10,333,203
Shannon	1,534,432	1,571,385	1,740,650	1,822,064
Cork	800,188	971,319	1,124,320	1,196,261
TOTAL:	9,315,603	10,567,602	11,956,266	13,351,528

R.O.I.: AIR PASSENGER MOVEMENT, 1990-97

Year	Dublin Airport (000s) Outward	Dublin Airport (000s) Inward	Cork Airport (000s) Outward	Cork Airport (000s) Inward	Shannon Airport (000s) Outward	Shannon Airport (000s) Inward	Shannon Airport In Transit	Total* (000s) Outward	Total* (000s) Inward
1990	2,399	2,362	253	252	543	520	417	3,337	3,270
1991	2,301	2,274	234	237	480	456	462	3,114	3,062
1992	2,548	2,524	253	258	569	537	415	3,441	3,388

Continued from previous page

Year	(000s) Dublin Airport Outward	(000s) Dublin Airport Inward	(000s) Cork Airport Outward	(000s) Cork Airport Inward	(000s) Shannon Airport Outward	(000s) Shannon Airport Inward	(000s) Shannon Airport In Transit	Total* Outward	Total* Inward
1993	2,645	2,621	276	277	586	571	403	3,569	3,530
1994	3,219	3,176	314	313	554	536	301	4,170	4,107
1995	3,737	3,670	388	385	596	579	240	4,824	4,736
1996	4,244	4,193	462	453	654	637	271	5,472	5,393
1997	4,826	4,744	494	482	653	633	350	6,105	5,989

* includes Connacht, Waterford Regional, Galway, Carrickfin and Kerry County Airports. Sligo Airport included from June 1990.

NORTHERN IRELAND: AIRLINE TRANSPORT

INTERNATIONAL AIRPORTS Belfast International Airport, situated 13 miles north-west of the city, provides direct services to more than 40 major British and European destinations with onward connections to centres worldwide. Outside London, it is the second largest freight airport in Britain. Belfast City Airport, five minutes from Belfast city, offers connections to most major British cities including London. In the north-west of Northern Ireland, the City of Derry Airport also provides links to a variety of destinations. With competing airlines, there are currently 24 scheduled flights daily between Belfast and London. Easy access to, and transfer at, London (and other major British airports) means that most European destinations can be easily reached.

FREIGHT SERVICES For air freight, eight International Air Transport Authority (IATA) agents in Northern Ireland act on behalf of all airlines and offer competitive rates to customers requiring direct consolidated or charter freight. Specialist airlines offer air freight services from both Belfast International and Belfast City Airports. The main passenger airlines also operate freight services.

NORTHERN IRELAND: TERMINAL PASSENGERS AT AIRPORTS, 1990-96

Year	Belfast International	Belfast City	City of Derry	Totals
1986	1,854,000	210,000	12,000	2,076,000
1988	2,176,000	400,000	13,000	2,589,000
1990	2,294,000	548,000	41,000	2,883,000
1992	2,241,000	612,000	28,000	2,881,000
1994	2,039,000	1,228,000	34,000	3,301,000
1995	2,346,000	1,280,000	64,000	3,691,000
1996	2,351,000	1,361,000	64,000	3,776,000

REPUBLIC OF IRELAND: CROSS-BORDER PASSENGER MOVEMENT, 1990-97

Year	Rail Outward	Rail Inward	Road bus scheduled services Outward	Road bus scheduled services Inward	Total rail and road bus scheduled services Outward	Total rail and road bus scheduled services Inward
1990	180,000	189,000	309,000	305,000	489,000	494,000
1991	226,000	238,000	386,000	387,000	612,000	625,000
1992	227,000	243,000	418,000	412,000	645,000	655,000
1993	255,000	280,000	417,000	412,000	671,000	692,000
1994	306,000	337,000	411,000	407,000	717,000	744,000
1995	377,000	415,000	430,000	427,000	807,000	842,000
1996	374,000	388,000	430,000	429,000	804,000	817,000
1997	344,000	374,000	517,000	516,000	861,000	890,000

NORTHERN IRELAND: LICENSED VEHICLES, 1991-96

Vehicle Type	1991	1992	1993	1994	1995	1996
Cycles	2,218	1,993	1,885	1,943	2,362	2,803
Motor-Hackneys	620	551	466	1,143	622	724
Agricultural Tractors & Engines	1,177	1,184	1,658	1,558	1,619	1,292
Goods Vehicles	8,892	8,707	9,061	9,576	10,292	10,724
Private Cars	63,739	62,777	65,360	70,765	73,718	77,817
Exempt from Duty	2,336	2,463	4,550	6,423	8,333	10,520
Total	78,982	77,675	82,980	91,408	96,946	103,880
Current Vehicle & Driving Licences:						
Cycles	9,684	9,023	8,634	8,775	9,142	10,026

Continued from previous page

Vehicle Type	1991	1992	1993	1994	1995	1996
Motor-Hackneys	2,887	2,744	2,679	3,078	2,092	2,090
Agricultural Tractors & Engines	7,199	6,892	7,201	7,317	7,318	5,911
Goods Vehicles	18,901	19,601	20,074	20,714	18,698	17,401
Private Cars	498,471	516,194	515,185	514,760	521,605	540,083
Other	21,176	23,858	32,552	41,307	52,707	63,775
Total	558,318	578,312	586,325	595,951	611,562	639,286
TOTAL LICENCES:	912,000	947,000	978,000	1,005,000	1,041,000	1,077,000

NORTHERN IRELAND: DRIVING LICENCES, 1991-97

Licences	1991-92	1992-93	1993-94	1994-95	1995-96	1996-97
Ordinary Licences:						
Provisional	133	133	136	135	143	148
Full	814	845	869	906	943	960
Total Ordinary Licences	947	978	1,005	1,041	1,086	1,108
Vocational Licences:						
Passenger Carrying Vehicles	-	4	14	11	12	12
Large Goods Vehicles	-	25	86	44	47	50
Total Vocational Licences	-	29	100	55	59	62

REP. OF IRELAND: LICENSED VEHICLES, 1992-97

Vehicle Type:	1992	1993	1994	1995	1996	1997
New Vehicles:						
Private Cars	67,861	60,792	77,773	82,730	109,333	125,818
Goods Vehicles	11,883	9,887	12,845	13,790	16,445	18,895
Tractors	1,598	1,338	1,830	2,108	2,233	1,848
Motor Cycles	2,884	1,914	1,837	1,911	2,412	2,717
Exempt Vehicles	1,306	1,261	1,178	1,489	1,887	2,042
Public Service Vehicles	683	596	906	1,039	1,100	1,051
Combine Harvesters	15	5	2	5	8	10
Excavators and Trench Diggers	113	79	178	207	272	313
Machines or Contrivances	80	61	94	144	209	323
Other Classes	55	31	42	56	65	69
Total New Vehicles	86,478	75,964	96,685	103,479	133,964	153,086
Second Hand Vehicles:						
Private Cars	17,631	26,560	38,863	41,865	44,500	41,554
Goods Vehicles	3,742	3,259	3,501	3,912	4,927	4,888
Tractors	4,377	3,483	3,814	3,627	3,627	3,065
Other Classes	2,467	2,587	3,335	3,715	4,138	4,263
Total Second Hand Vehicles	28,217	35,889	49,513	53,119	57,192	53,770
Total All Classes	114,695	111,853	14,618	156,598	191,156	206,856

REPUBLIC OF IRELAND: DRIVING LICENCES, 1996

Licensing Authority	Provisional Licences	Annual Licences	Triennial Licences	Ten-Year Licences	Total Licences
County Councils:					
Carlow	5,621	98	2,378	11,747	19,844
Cavan	6,080	109	3,230	17,534	26,953
Clare	10,114	229	4,861	30,755	45,959
Cork	48,917	852	20,202	141,740	211,711
Donegal	13,550	256	6,804	41,151	61,761
Dublin (City & County)	117,626	1,578	48,839	315,077	483,120
Galway (City & County)	21,482	284	8,755	59,887	90,408
Kerry	15,716	279	6,883	42,831	65,709
Kildare	16,142	239	5,282	42,175	63,838
Kilkenny	9,085	240	4,421	24,694	38,440
Laois	6,284	121	3,332	16,728	26,465
Leitrim	2,627	72	1,681	8,528	12,908
Limerick	13,641	292	5,953	39,206	59,092
Longford	3,512	89	1,867	9,553	15,021

Continued from previous page

Licensing Authority	Provisional Licences	Annual Licences	Triennial Licences	Ten-Year Licences	Total Licences
Louth	10,688	176	4,733	27,087	42,684
Mayo	11,618	233	4,862	35,022	51,735
Meath	13,153	201	5,223	36,233	54,810
Monaghan	5,862	121	3,649	17,338	26,970
Offaly	6,807	153	3,187	17,754	27,901
Roscommon	5,657	162	3,291	17,932	27,042
Sligo	6,235	121	3,315	18,841	28,512
Tipperary (North Riding)	7,272	85	3,576	20,697	31,630
Tipperary (South Riding)	9,700	206	4,837	24,158	38,901
Waterford	5,635	98	2,669	16,085	24,487
Westmeath	7,433	139	3,454	20,820	31,846
Wexford	12,941	482	5,114	33,680	52,217
Wicklow	13,113	257	4,760	32,611	50,741
County Borough:					
Limerick Corporation	5,958	54	2,099	12,161	20,272
Waterford Corporation	5,005	101	1,975	11,445	18,526
TOTAL:	**417,474**	**7,327**	**181,232**	**1,143,470**	**1,749,503**

REP. OF IRELAND: CAR REGISTRATION MARKS

Index Mark	From Jan. 1987	County	Council Office
C;	CW	Carlow	Athy Road, Carlow
ID;	CN	Cavan	Courthouse, Cavan
IE;	CE	Clare	Courthouse, Ennis
IF; PI; ZB; ZF; ZK; ZT;	C	Cork	Carrigrohane Road, Cork
IH; ZP;	DL	Donegal	County Building, Lifford
IM; ZM;	G	Galway	County Building, Galway
IN; ZX;	KY	Kerry	Moyderwell, Tralee
IO; ZW;	KE	Kildare	Friary Road, Naas
IP;	KK	Kilkenny	John's Green, Kilkenny
CI;	LS	Laois	County Hall, Portlaoise
IT;	LM	Leitrim	Priest's Lane, Carrick-on-Shannon
IU; IV;	LK	Limerick	O'Connell Street, Limerick
IX;	LD	Longford	Great Water Street, Longford
IY; ZY;	LH	Louth	The Crescent, Dundalk
IS; IZ;	MO	Mayo	Courthouse, Castlebar
AI; ZN;	MH	Meath	County Hall, Navan
BI;	MN	Monaghan	North Road, Monaghan
IR;	OY	Offaly	O'Connor Square, Tullamore
DI;	RN	Roscommon	Abbey Street, Roscommon
EI;	SO	Sligo	Cleveragh Road, Sligo
FI;	TN	Tipperary, N.Riding	Kickham Street, Nenagh
GI; HI;	TS	Tipperary, S.Riding	Emmet Street, Clonmel
KI;	WD	Waterford	Courthouse, Dungarvan
LI;	WH	Westmeath	County Buildings, Mullingar
MI; ZR;	WX	Wexford	County Hall, Wexford
NI;	WW	Wicklow	County Buildings, Wicklow
TI;	L	Limerick City	City Hall, Merchants Quay, Limerick
WI;	W	Waterford City	6-8 Lombard Street, Waterford
IK; RI; SI; YI; Z; ZA; ZC; ZD; ZE; ZG; ZH; ZI; ZJ; ZL; ZO; ZS; ZU; ZV;	D	Dublin	River House, Chancery Street, Dublin 7.

NORTHERN IRELAND: CAR REGISTRATION MARKS

Index Mark	County	Index Mark	County
IA; DZ; KZ; RZ;	Antrim	OI; XI; AZ; CZ; EZ; FZ; GZ; MZ;	
IB; LZ;	Armagh	OZ; PZ; TZ; UZ; WZ;	Belfast City
IJ; BZ; JZ; SZ;	Down	UI;	Derry City
IL;	Fermanagh	*Issued by: Dept. of the Environment for N. Ireland,*	
IW; NZ; YZ;	Derry	*The Vehicle Licensing Central Office, County Hall,*	
JI; HZ; VZ;	Tyrone	*Castlerock Rd, Coleraine, Co. Derry BT51 3HS.*	

REPUBLIC OF IRELAND: SPEED LAWS

Vehicle Type	MPH Built-up Areas	MPH Elsewhere	MPH Motorways
Cars (includes light goods vehicles & motorcycles)	30	60	70
Single Deck Buses - not carrying standing passengers	30	50	-
Single Deck Buses - carrying standing passengers	30	40	-
Double Deck Buses	30	40	-
Goods Vehicles (including Articulated vehicles) - gross vehicle weight in excess of 3,500 Kgs	30	50	-
Any vehicle towing another	30	50	-

NORTHERN IRELAND: SPEED LAWS

Vehicle Type	MPH Built-up Areas	MPH Elsewhere Single Carriage	Dual Carriage	MPH Motorways
Cars (including car-derived vans & motorcycles)	30	60	70	70
Cars towing caravans or trailers (including car-derived vans & motorcycles)	30	50	60	60
Buses and Coaches (not exceeding 12 metres in overall length)	30	50	60	70
Goods vehicles (not exceeding 7.5 tonnes maximum laden weight)	30	50	60	70*
Goods vehicles (exceeding 7.5 tonnes maximum laden weight)	30	40	50	60

* 60 if articulated or towing a trailer.

REPUBLIC OF IRELAND:
20 MOST POPULAR NEWLY LICENSED CARS, 1997

Car	Number	Car	Number
Ford	16,235	Mitsubishi	3,639
Volkswagen / Audi	15,771	Honda	3,304
Opel	14,656	Seat	2,839
Toyota	12,409	Hyundai	2,339
Nissan	11,917	Citroen	2,189
Fiat / Lancia	9,292	Mercedes	1,730
Renault	7,768	BMW	1,694
Peugeot / Talbot	5,426	Volvo	1,575
Mazda	4,414	Suzuki	1,348
Austin / Rover	3,937	Subaru	473

NORTHERN IRELAND: 20 MOST POPULAR NEWLY REGISTERED VEHICLES, 1997

Car	Number	Car	Number
Renault	7,945	Honda	1,271
Ford	6,533	Fiat	1,247
Vauxhall	6,149	Hyundai	1,146
Peugeot	3,505	Mazda	1,009
Rover	3,424	Audi	962
Volkswagen	3,403	Seat	879
Nissan	2,735	Mercedes	847
Citroen	2,499	Mitsubishi	752
Toyota	2,140	Volvo	577
BMW	1,430	Daewoo	468

REP. OF IRELAND: LENGTH OF PUBLIC ROADS, 1997

County (km)	National Primary	National Secondary	Regional	Local	Total
Carlow	23.40	53.60	157.70	980.80	1,215.50
Cavan	65.20	60.70	399.00	2,479.50	3,004.40
Clare	54.50	179.80	597.50	3,363.87	4,195.67

County (km)	National Primary	National Secondary	Regional	Local	Total
Cork	254.50	259.20	1,359.30	10,722.01	12,595.01
Donegal	150.00	153.70	688.30	5,360.92	6,352.92
Dublin	142.80	27.60	568.42	2,824.08	3,562.90
Galway	165.70	282.90	796.60	5,480.51	6,725.71
Kerry	94.80	332.60	460.30	3,890.80	4,778.50
Kildare	112.40	25.60	387.80	1,755.80	2,281.60
Kilkenny	146.40	67.90	313.30	2,560.60	3,088.20
Laois	83.50	79.40	280.80	1,664.90	2,108.60
Leitrim	56.50	0.00	334.20	1,774.60	2,165.30
Limerick	150.10	55.60	480.10	3,073.80	3,759.60
Longford	42.80	54.70	153.39	1,329.20	1,580.09
Louth	73.10	51.90	196.00	1,084.25	1,405.25
Mayo	133.60	265.90	586.24	5,314.48	6,300.22
Meath	121.80	76.20	474.70	2,458.49	3,131.19
Monaghan	72.90	31.00	289.30	2,106.45	2,499.65
Offaly	18.00	120.30	338.70	1,538.50	2,015.50
Roscommon	100.90	145.00	346.10	3,358.00	3,950.00
Sligo	108.20	47.80	221.80	2,380.60	2,758.40
Tipperary	185.40	139.40	768.14	4,628.42	5,721.36
Waterford	76.30	35.70	401.40	2,248.60	2,762.00
Westmeath	96.60	84.20	228.80	1,793.10	2,202.70
Wexford	149.80	15.10	438.70	2,800.63	3,404.23
Wicklow	53.70	42.00	423.70	1,637.50	2,156.90
TOTAL:	**2,732.90**	**2,687.80**	**11,690.29**	**78,610.41**	**95,721.40**

NORTHERN IRELAND:
LENGTH OF PUBLIC ROADS, 1997

Divisions/Council Areas	Motorway	Class I Dual Carriage	Single Carriage	Class II	Class III	Unclass- ified	Total
	km	km	km	km	km	km	km
Ballymena Division:	28.97	22.37	349.83	410.01	655.93	1,853.28	3,320.39
Belfast Division:	27.72	24.90	138.31	118.21	130.91	1,194.24	1,634.28
Coleraine Division:	0.00	12.21	357.23	524.98	580.74	1,828.37	3,303.54
Craigavon Division:	23.86	36.39	397.04	565.78	1,038.59	3,108.03	5,169.69
Downpatrick Division:	19.32	41.59	362.74	331.65	608.26	1,899.87	3,263.44
Omagh Division:	12.70	5.63	493.86	925.01	1,707.94	4,509.12	7,654.26
GRAND TOTAL:	**112.57**	**143.09**	**2,099.02**	**2,875.64**	**4,722.37**	**14,392.92**	**24,345.59**

REPUBLIC OF IRELAND:
NON-NATIONAL ROAD GRANTS, 1993-97

Year	Amount (£m)	Year	Amount (£m)	Year	Amount (£m)
1993	77.30	1995	125.95	1997	172.82
1994	109.50	1996	146.86		

TRANSPORT INFRASTRUCTURE - ROADS, 1997
Length of Public Roads in Republic of Ireland and Northern Ireland

REPUBLIC OF IRELAND, 1997	
Road	Length (kms)
National Primary	2,732.90
National Secondary	2,687.80
Regional	11,690.29
Local	78,610.41
TOTAL	**92,425**

NORTHERN IRELAND, 1997	
Road	Length (kms)
Motorway	110
Class I	2,240
Class II	2,880
Class III	4,720
Unclassified	14,390
TOTAL	**24,340**

REPUBLIC OF IRELAND:
MINIMUM AGE FOR DRIVING BY CATEGORY

Vehicle Type	Categories	Minimum Ages for Driving
Motorcycles	A, A1	18, 16
Cars	B, EB	17
Trucks	C, EC, C1, EC1	18
Buses	D, ED	21
Minibuses	D1, ED1	21
Work Vehicles/Tractors	W	16

NORTHERN IRELAND:
MINIMUM AGE FOR DRIVING BY CATEGORY

Vehicle Type	Categories	Minimum Ages for Driving
Motorcycles	A,	17
Moped	P	16
Cars	B, B1	17
Trucks	C+E, C, C1	21,18
Buses	D, D1	21
Other Vehicles/Tractors	F, G, H, B1, K	16

REPUBLIC OF IRELAND & NORTHERN IRELAND:
COSTS OF SELECTED CARS IN IRELAND, 1998

Make	Model	Type	Republic of Ireland (IR£)*	Northern Ireland (£Stg)*
Ford	Fiesta	5dr Encore 1.3(i)	10,750	8,315
Ford	Escort	5dr GLX 1.4 (i)	13,230	13,195
Ford	Mondeo	5dr LX 1.6 (i)	16,970	15,495
Honda	Civic	3dr 1.4 (i)	12,835	12,395
Honda	Accord	4dr 1.8 (i)	18,765	14,995
Mazda	323	5dr LX 1.5 (i)	14,640	13,220
Mazda	626	4dr LX 2.0 (i)	17,500	14,650
Nissan	Micra	3dr GX 1.0	10,475	9,320
Nissan	Almera	5dr GX 1.4	13,875	12,895
Nissan	Primera	5dr SLX 1.6	17,090	16,125
Opel / Vauxhall	Corsa	5dr GLS 1.0	12,140	10,645
Opel / Vauxhall	Astra	3dr Sport 1.8 (i)	16,585	14,245
Opel / Vauxhall	Vectra	5dr CDX 2.0	23,093	21,175
Peugeot	106	3dr XL 1.1	10,695	8,895
Peugeot	306	3dr L 1.4	12,395	11,230
Renault	Clio	3 dr 1.2	10,245	8,350
Renault	Megane	5dr RN 1.4	13,400	11,700
Renault	Laguna	5dr RT 1.6	16,750	14,020
Toyota	Starlet	3dr 1.3 (i)	11,010	7,995
Volkswagen	Polo	3dr 1.0	10,450	8,290
Volkswagen	Passat	4dr 1.6	17,225	15,460

refers to recommended retail price as of July / August 1998; (the price does not include extras or delivery)

NORTHERN IRELAND:
CARS IMPORTED BY COUNTRY OF ORIGIN, 1997

Country	Number	%
Used Cars (re-registered)	25,988	82.7
Republic of Ireland	2,650	8.4
Continent	2,790	8.9
TOTAL:	**31,428**	**100.0**

REPUBLIC OF IRELAND: USED CAR IMPORTS, 1997

Country of Origin	Cars	Car Vans	Commercials	Motorbikes	Others	Total
France	3,463	110	377	23	2	3,975
Belgium	47	1	21	2	0	71
Netherlands	69	3	39	4	0	115
Germany	3,434	42	809	48	20	4,353
Italy	512	2	220	227	6	967
Britain	17,060	470	10,574	381	39	28,524
Northern Ireland	2,857	38	336	38	0	3,269
Spain	139	0	10	1	0	150
Sweden	325	0	527	4	0	856
Others	16,922	216	953	2,236	154	20,481
TOTAL:	**44,828**	**882**	**13,866**	**2,964**	**221**	**62,761**

REPUBLIC OF IRELAND: USED CARS, 1997

Month	Quantity	Month	Quantity
January	3,369	July	3,634
February	3,501	August	3,288
March	3,544	September	3,453
April	3,969	October	3,537
May	3,739	November	3,380
June	3,132	December	3,008
		Total:	41,554

REPUBLIC OF IRELAND: COSTS OF KEEPING A CAR ON THE ROAD, 1998

Engine Capacity (cc)	Cost per Week (£)*
Up to 1,000	95.99
1,001 to 1,250	110.63
1,251 to 1,500	119.98
1,501 to 1,750	131.27
1,751 to 2,000	143.66
2,001 to 2,500	156.99
2,501 to 3,000	180.86
3,001 to 4,000	214.35

insurance, interest on capital, depreciation, petrol, tax and servicing.

RELIGION

Forgotten Heroes

By **Bishop Edward Daly**, *retired Bishop of Derry*

WHEN Irish people, in years to come, look back on the 1990s, Friday April 10th 1998 will be perceived as a very significant date. It was Good Friday, the day when the major political parties in the North together with the British and Irish Governments all signed an historic Agreement. It has become known as the Good Friday Agreement although some people, who seem to be uncomfortable with the term, Good Friday, now describe it as the Belfast Agreement. It was undoubtedly the most notable political or social achievement in Ireland in the last few decades. It was almost miraculous and all the more remarkable because it happened on that particular day.

However, there is another event which will forever highlight 1998 in Irish history. It occurred on the afternoon of August 15 in Omagh when a car bomb exploded in Market Street and killed 29 people and two unborn children and wounded countless others. It was the type and scale of atrocity which had been feared all during the 30 years of the Troubles. It was paradoxical that it came just when people had begun to believe that a permanent and lasting peace had been achieved. And it came in a place and at a time where one would least suspect it, in Omagh in County Tyrone in the midst of crowds of shoppers on a busy Saturday afternoon.

The clergy of all denominations distinguished themselves by their ministry to the victims and their families in the wake of the Omagh bombing. Ministry in the wake of a violent act is enormously difficult. The difficulty and complexity presented by such an atrocity and the enormous commitment required by clergy in pastoral ministry in situations of conflict are not fully appreciated by people at large.

Clergy from all the Churches have been engaged in this ministry here for the past 30 years. This ministry initially involves attending the scene of the atrocity, endeavouring to minister to the dead and to comfort the injured in the immediate aftermath. Attention then is moved to hospitals or the homes of families of victims. The unsuspecting families of the dead have to be formally notified of the death of their loved one. This daunting task is often entrusted to the clergy. Sometimes, clergy are asked to accompany family members to a morgue to identify the remains of a loved one. Then there are parents and relatives and children to be comforted, a task which requires great sensitivity and long periods of time. In the following days, there are the funerals to be arranged, services to be conducted and sermons to be prepared. There are considerable demands from the media which have to be met by clergy. These demands have multiplied greatly in recent years as the number of national and local radio stations and media outlets continues to grow. Sermons can be quite difficult to prepare at any time and it can be particularly frustrating when the preparation is punctuated by incessant telephone calls from the media and others. Funerals of victims of violence present clergy with a great challenge in the preparation of sermons or homilies. There should always be words to comfort the bereaved but it also may be found necessary to comment on the circumstances in which the victim died. It is a time when head must always rule heart and words must be carefully prepared and chosen.

After the funerals have ended and the crowds have dispersed and gone their way to take up their lives again, the clergy in the local parish or congregation are left to continue the work of 'binding up hearts that are broken' and being available to bereaved families for as long as such support is needed. And this may and often does go on for years.

In the media reports of events like Omagh. much credit is rightly given to the emergency services, firemen, ambulance personnel, police, nurses, doctors, first aid people etc. The clergy, however, are seldom mentioned for their role. Nor do they seek much mention.

It is important however, that their contribution should be noted, because it is a significant contribution. The Troubles have taken a considerable toll on clergy around the North who have been exposed to the worst of these atrocities. No matter how often such dreadful outrages occur, no matter how much training or preparation one has, it is impossible to become accustomed to such experiences or to be fully prepared for an atrocity. The ghastly first sight of the bodies of fellow human beings, murdered, dismembered or horribly wounded can test the spirit of even the strongest individual, clergy or lay person.

The repeated exposure to families broken by excruciating grief and filled with a mixture of incredulity, anger and anguish takes its own toll emotionally on those endeavouring to comfort them and travelling the long journey with them from darkness back to light. There are many times when emotional and physical resources are put to the test. There are even times when religious faith is tested and frustrated and when there is the temptation to cry out with Habakkuk 'How long, Lord, am I to cry for help while you will not listen!'.

In situations of conflict, people are at their very worst and also at their very best. Ministry in such situations, although difficult and demanding, is most fulfilling, challenging and worthwhile.

The clergy of all the Churches who ministered so well to the victims and their families in Omagh in August 1998 and throughout the North during the past 30 years are deserving of due recognition and credit for their unselfish service.

❐

The author is the retired Bishop of Derry

RELIGIOUS ORDERS - CONTACTS

THE CATHOLIC CHURCH

Catholic Press Office, 169 Booterstown Ave., Blackrock, Co. Dublin. Tel. (01) 2885043.

Organisation: The church's ecclesiastical capital is Armagh, and it is there that the Primate of All-Ireland resides. The church has four Ecclesiastical Provinces - Armagh, Dublin, Cashel and Tuam - each with its own archbishop.

Relevant Statistics: The church has 26 dioceses, approximately 1,367 parishes and about 4,000 Catholic priests.

THE CHURCH OF IRELAND

Central Office, Church Ave., Rathmines, Dublin 6. Tel. (01) 4978422

Organisation: The Church of Ireland is a self-governing church within the worldwide Anglican Communion of Churches. It is led by the Archbishop of Armagh, who is Primate of All Ireland, and the Archbishop of Dublin, who is Primate of Ireland.

Relevant Statistics: There are 12 dioceses in the Church of Ireland and 473 parishes. Like the Catholic Church, the Church of Ireland is heavily involved in education and has its own schools in the Republic of Ireland.

THE PRESBYTERIAN CHURCH

Church House, Belfast BT1 6DW. Tel. (01232) 322284

Organisation: The Presbyterian Church in Ireland has as its chief representative a Moderator, elected at a General Assembly of the Church, who serves for one year only. This Assembly, which meets annually, makes the rules of the church and decides policy.

Relevant Statistics: The church has a total of 639 ministers and approximately 557 congregations in Ireland Each congregation is entitled to representation at that Assembly. There are five regional Synods in the Presbyterian Church and within these, 21 regions each known as a Presbytery. The Ministry was opened to women in 1972.

THE METHODIST CHURCH

1 Fountainville Avenue, Belfast BT9 6AN. Tel. (01232) 324554

Organisation: The Methodist Church in Ireland is a democratic church, with authority invested in its annual conference whose president is elected for one year only.

Relevant Statistics: The church is divided into eight districts each of which has at its head a Chairman who, while elected annually, can serve up to six years. There are also 76 circuits, that is groups of congregations throughout the country, North and South, who work together. The Methodist Church has a 225 Churches and serves a total community of approximately 57,476.

MINOR RELIGIONS:
BAHÁ'Í FAITH
24 Burlington Road, Dublin 4. Tel. (01) 6683150.

Organisation: The Bahá'í Faith is an independent world religion founded over 150 years ago. It is governed by elected councils at local, national and international levels. The jurisdictions of these councils (spiritu-al assemblies) are contiguous with civil boundaries.

Relevant Statistics: There are 174 elected National Spiritual Assemblies, including one for the Republic of Ireland and one for the United Kingdom. In the Republic of Ireland, there are 20 elected local spiritual assemblies and 9 in Northern Ireland. National and local Assemblies have nine members and are elected annually. The Universal House of Justice (international level) has nine members and is elected every five years.

BAPTIST UNION OF IRELAND
117 Lisburn Road, Belfast BT9 7AF. Tel. (01232) 663108.

Organisation: The Baptist Union is an association of 109 autonomous local churches of the Baptist faith in Ireland (93 in Northern Ireland and 16 in the Republic of Ireland). Membership in the Union does not interfere with the autonomy of the local church. The operations of the Union are controlled by the Churches' Council, which is made up of at least two representatives from each church in the Union and meets at least twice a year. The Council acts through its Officers and Executive Committee. The Executive Committee is elected by the Churches' Council from among its members and its role is to supervise the work of the Union.

BUDDHISM
23 South Frederick Street, Dublin 2. Tel. (01) 6713187

Organisation: A number of Buddhist traditions are accounted for in Ireland (i.e. Tibetan, Theravadan and Zen forms) by way of groups which have regular meditation meetings.

Irish Centres: There are two centres in Ireland which accommodate teaching programmes, meditation meetings and retreats, situated in Cavan and Cork and a meditation / teaching centre in Dublin. The Western Buddhist Order is a worldwide Buddhist organisation which runs the far larger Friends of the Western Buddhist Order (estimated at 1 million). Founded in 1991, the Friends of the Western Buddhist Order - Tara Institute is Ireland's largest and fastest growing Buddhist organisation with a comparatively high number of Order Members per head of population.

THE CHURCH OF JESUS CHRIST OF LATTER-DAY SAINTS
The Willows, Glasnevin, Dublin 11. Tel. (01) 8306899

Organisation: The church is divided ecclesiastically into two Stakes (Belfast and Dublin) and one District (Cork). *Belfast:* The Belfast Stake caters for approximately 3,500 members across Northern Ireland. The Stake was organised in 1974 and has had three Presidents. There are a number of wards in Belfast and Bangor and other congregations in Derry, Omagh, Antrim, Coleraine, Newtownabbey, Lisburn and Portadown. Each is controlled by a Bishop (ward) or Branch President. *Dublin:* The Dublin Stake was created out of the Dublin District in 1995 and has around 1,800 members. There are four wards in Dublin City, and branches in Bray, Dundalk, Mullingar, Sligo and Galway. *Cork:* The Cork District has over 400 members with branches in Cork, Limerick, Waterford and Tralee. There are a number of missionaries serving both in

Ireland and abroad.

JEWISH COMMUNITY
Herzog House, Zion Road, Rathgar, Dublin 6.
Tel. (01) 4923751.

Organisation: The Jewish Community is centred mainly in Dublin. The Spiritual head of the Jewish Community in the Republic of Ireland is the Chief Rabbi, under whose supervision all congregations operate.

CHURCH OF SCIENTOLOGY
62-63 Middle Abbey Street, Dublin 1.
Tel. (01) 8720007

Organisation: The Church of Scientology - Mission of Dublin is the main congregation of Scientologists in Ireland. There are smaller informal groups in Cork, Belfast and elsewhere. The Dublin Mission was officially incorporated in early 1994 but has been in operation on a less formal basis since the late 1980s.

ISLAM
19 Roebuck Road, Clonskeagh, Dublin 14.
Tel. (01) 2603740.
38 Wellington Park, Belfast BT9 6DN.

Organisation: The Dublin Islamic Society was formed in 1959 by Muslim students from South Africa and Malaysia. In 1971, it was registered as a friendly society and later as a charitable organisation.
Relevant Statistics: The population of Muslims in Ireland is between approximately 8,000 and 9,000 persons with about 5,000 Muslims in the Dublin Metropolitan Area alone. Consequently, the main body is in Dublin with the next largest grouping in Belfast and smaller communities in Galway, Ballyhaunis, Craigavon and Cork, each of which is independently run.

LUTHERAN CHURCH
Luther House, 24 Adelaide Road, Dublin 2.
Tel. (01) 6766548.

CATHOLIC BISHOPS OF IRELAND

The Catholic Church in Ireland is divided into four provinces which are named after the four arch-dioceses: Armagh, Cashel, Dublin and Tuam.

PROVINCE OF ARMAGH

Diocese of Armagh: Most Rev. Sean Brady (Archbishop) and Primate of All-Ireland. Most Rev. Gerard Clifford (Auxiliary) and Titular Bishop of Geron.

Diocese of Meath: Most Rev. Michael Smith.

Diocese of Ardagh and Clonmacnois: Most Rev Colm O'Reilly.

Diocese of Clogher: Most Rev. Joseph Duffy.

Diocese of Derry: Most Rev. Seamus Hegarty. Most Rev. Francis Lagan (Auxiliary) and Titular Bishop of Sidnascestre.

Diocese of Down and Connor: Most Rev. Patrick Walsh. Most Rev. Michael Dallet (Auxiliary). Most Rev. Anthony Farquhar (Auxiliary) and Titular Bishop of Ermiana.

Diocese of Dromore (Down): Most Rev. Francis Gerard Brooks.

Diocese of Kilmore (Cavan): Most Rev. Francis McKiernan. Most Rev Leo O'Reilly (Coadjutor).

Diocese of Raphoe (Donegal): Most Rev. Philip Boyce.

PROVINCE OF DUBLIN

Diocese of Dublin: Most Rev. Desmond Connell (Archbishop) and Primate of Ireland. Most Rev. Martin Drennan (Auxiliary) and Titular Bishop of Acque Regie. Most Rev. Raymond Field (Auxiliary) and Titular Bishop of Ard Mor. Most Rev. James Moriarty (Auxiliary) and Titular Bishop of Bononia. Most Rev. Fiachra Ó Ceallaigh (Auxiliary). Most Rev. Eamonn Walsh (Auxiliary) and Titular Bishop of Elmhama.

Diocese of Ferns (Wexford): Most Rev. Brendan Comiskey.

Diocese of Kildare and Leighlin (Carlow): Most Rev. Laurence Ryan.

Diocese of Ossory (Kilkenny): Most Rev. Laurence Forristal.

PROVINCE OF CASHEL

Diocese of Cashel and Emly: Most Rev. Dermot Clifford, Archbishop of Cashel and Emly.

Diocese of Cloyne (Cork): Most Rev. John Magee.

Diocese of Cork and Ross: Most Rev John Buckley, Titular Bishop of Leptis Magna.

Diocese of Kerry: Most Rev. William Murphy.

Diocese of Killaloe (Clare): Most Rev. William Walsh.

Diocese of Waterford and Lismore: Most Rev. William Lee.

Diocese of Limerick: Most Rev. Donal Murray.

PROVINCE OF TUAM

Diocese of Tuam: Most Rev. Michael Neary (Archbishop).

Diocese of Achonry (Roscommon): Most Rev. Thomas Flynn.

Diocese of Clonfert (Galway): Most Rev. John Kirby.

Diocese of Elphin (Sligo): Most Rev. Christopher Jones.

Diocese of Galway: Most Rev. James McLoughlin.

Diocese of Killala (Mayo): Most Rev. Thomas A. Finnegan.

PAPAL NUNCIO

His Excellency Most Rev Dr Luciano Storero.
Born Italy, 1926. Ordained Priest June 29th 1949. Ordained Titular Archbishop of Tigimma February 1970. Appointed Apostolic Nuncio to Ireland November 15th 1995.

CHURCH OF IRELAND BISHOPS

There are 12 dioceses in the Church of Ireland, divided into two provinces - Armagh and Dublin.

PROVINCE OF ARMAGH

Diocese of Armagh: The Most Rev. Robin Eames, Archbishop of Armagh and Primate of All Ireland.

Diocese of Clogher: The Right Rev. Brian Hannon.
Dioceses of Derry and Raphoe: The Right Rev. James Mehaffey.
Dioceses of Down and Dromore: The Right Rev. Harold Miller.
Diocese of Connor: The Right Rev. James Moore.
Dioceses of Kilmore, Elphin and Ardagh (Cavan): The Right Rev. Michael Mayes.
Dioceses of Tuam, Killala and Achonry: The Right Rev. Richard Henderson.

PROVINCE OF DUBLIN

Dioceses of Dublin and Glendalough: The Most Rev. Walton Empey, Archbishop of Dublin, Archbishop of Dublin, Bishop of Glendalough and Primate of Ireland.
Dioceses of Meath and Kildare: The Most Rev. Richard Clarke.
Dioceses of Cashel and Ossory: The Right Rev. John Neill, Bishop of Cashel, Waterford, Lismore, Ossory, Ferns and Leighlin.
Dioceses of Cork, Cloyne and Ross: The Right Rev. Robert Warke.
Dioceses of Limerick and Killaloe: The Right Rev. Edward Darling, Bishop of Limerick, Ardfert, Aghadoe, Killaloe, Kilfenora, Clonfert, Kilmacduagh and Emly.

METHODIST CHURCH PRESIDENT AND CHAIRMEN

The Methodist Church in Ireland is divided into eight district synods, each headed by a Chairman.

President: Rev David J. Kerr.
Secretary: Rev Edmund T.I. Mawhinney.

CHAIRMEN OF DISTRICTS

Belfast District: Rev W.J. Rea.
Down District: Rev R.P. Roddie.
Dublin District: Rev T.M. Kingston.

Enniskillen and Sligo District: Rev I.D. Henderson.
Londonderry District: Rev P.A. Good.
Midlands and Southern District: Rev S.K. Todd.
North East District: Rev K.H. Thompson.
Portadown District: Rev S.R.F. Clelland.

PRESBYTERIAN MODERATORS

The Presbyterian Church has five Regional Synods.

General Assembly Moderator: Dr Samuel John Dixon.

SYNOD OF ARMAGH AND DOWN

Presbytery of Ards: Rev. D. Bradley.
Presbytery of Armagh: Rev. B.A. McDonald.
Presbytery of Down: Rev. M. Stanfield.
Presbytery of Dromore: Rev. D.J. Temple.
Presbytery of Iveagh: Rev. J.G. Trueman.
Presbytery of Newry: Rev. W.J. Carlisle.

SYNOD OF BALLYMENA AND COLERAINE

Presbytery of Ballymena: Rev. Dr D.G. McMeekin.
Presbytery of Carrickfergus: Rev. J.H. Wilson.
Presbytery of Coleraine: Rev. M. Goudy.
Presbytery of Route: Rev. J.T. Magowan.
Presbytery of Templepatrick: Rev. D. Bannerman.

SYNOD OF BELFAST

Presbytery of North Belfast: Rev. J.K. Doherty.
Presbytery of South Belfast: Rev. D.J. McKelvey.
Presbytery of East Belfast: Rev. Joan Scott.

SYNOD OF DERRY AND OMAGH

Presbytery of Derry and Strabane: Rev. R.L. Brown.
Presbytery of Foyle: Rev. N. Hunter.
Presbytery of Omagh: Rev. D.P. Kirkwood.
Presbytery of Tyrone: Rev. W.T. Bingham.

SYNOD OF DUBLIN

Presbytery of Donegal: Rev. P.A. McBride.
Presbytery of Dublin and Munster: Rev. R. Cobain.
Presbytery of Monaghan: Rev. N. Cubitt.

FORMER CATHOLIC CARDINALS OF IRELAND

Name	Born	Appointed Archbishop	Created Cardinal	By Pope	Died
Paul Cullen	1803	Armagh, 1850	22nd June 1866	Pius IX	1878
Edward McCabe	1816	Dublin, 1879	27th March 1882	Leo XIII	1885
Michael Logue	1840	Armagh, 1887	16th January 1893	Leo XIII	1924
Patrick O'Donnell	1856	Armagh, 1924	14th December 1925	Pius XI	1927
Joseph McRory	1861	Armagh, 1928	12th December 1929	Pius XI	1945
John D'Alton	1882	Armagh, 1946	12th January 1953	Pius XII	1963
William Conway	1913	Armagh, 1963	22nd February 1965	Paul VI	1977
Tomás Ó Fiaich	1923	Armagh, 1977	30th June 1979	John Paul II	1990
Cahal Daly	1917	Armagh, 1990	1991	John Paul II	-

CHURCH OF IRELAND BISHOPS, 1968-98

Province of Dublin			Province of Armagh		
Year	Diocese	Name	Year	Diocese	Name
1968	Cashel	J. W. Armstrong	1969	Armagh	G. O. Simms
1969	Dublin	A. A. Buchanan	1969	Clogher	R. P. C. Hanson
1970	Limerick	D. A. R. Caird	1969	Connor	A. H. Butler
1971	Killaloe	E. Owen	1969	Tuam	J. C. Duggan
1976	Meath and Kildare	D. A. R. Caird	1969	Derry	C. I. Peacocke
1976	Limerick and Killaloe	E. Owen	1970	Down and Dromore	G. A. Quin
1977	Dublin	H. R. McAdoo	1973	Clogher	R. W. Heavener
1977	Cashel and Ossory	J. W. Armstrong	1975	Derry	R. H. A. Eames
1978	Cork	S. G. Poyntz	1980	Armagh	J. W. Armstrong
1980	Cashel and Ossory	N. V. Willoughby	1980	Clogher	G. McMullan
1981	Limerick and Killaloe	W. N. F. Empey	1980	Down and Dromore	R. H. A. Eames
1985	Meath and Kildare	W. N. F. Empey	1980	Derry	J. Mehaffey
1985	Limerick and Killaloe	E. F. Darling	1981	Connor	W. J. McCappin
1985	Dublin	D. A. R. Caird	1981	Kilmore	W. G. Wilson
1987	Cork	R. A. Warke	1986	Armagh	R. H. A. Eames
1996	Dublin	W. N. F. Empey	1986	Clogher	B. D. A. Hannon
1996	Meath and Kildare	R. L. Clarke	1986	Down and Dromore	G. McMullan
1997	Cashel and Ossory	J. R. W. Neill	1986	Tuam	J. R. W. Neill
			1987	Connor	S. G. Poyntz
			1993	Kilmore	M. H. G. Mayes
			1995	Connor	J. E. Moore
			1997	Down and Dromore	H. C. Miller
			1998	Tuam	R. C. A. Henderson

PRESBYTERIAN MODERATORS, 1967-98

Year	Name	Assembly
1967	The Very Rev. William Boyd	Lisburn
1972	The Very Rev. R.V.A. Lynas	Larne
1976	The Very Rev. J. Weir	Belfast
1978	The Very Rev. David Burke	Bangor
1979	The Very Rev. William Craig	Portadown
1980	The Very Rev. R.G. Craig	Carrickfergus
1981	The Very Rev. John Girvan	Lurgan
1982	The Very Rev. E.P. Gardner	Ballymena
1983	The Very T.J. Simpson	Newtownards
1984	The Very Rev. Howard Cromie	Lisburn
1985	The Very Rev. Robert Dickinson	Tobermore & Draperstown
1986	The Very Rev. Prof. John Thompson	Belfast
1987	The Very Rev. William Fleming	Belfast
1988	The Very Rev. A.W.G. Brown	Ballycastle
1989	The Very Rev. James Matthews	Lurgan
1990	The Very Rev. Prof. R.F.G. Holmes	Helen's Bay
1991	The Very Rev. Rodney Sterritt	Newtownards
1992	The Very Rev. John Dunlop	Belfast
1993	The Very Rev. Andrew R. Rodgers	Dungannon
1994	The Very Rev. David J. McGaughey	Kilkeel
1995	The Very Rev. John Ross	Holywood
1996	The Very Rev. Harry Allen	Coleraine
1997	The Right Rev. Samuel Hutchinson	Lisburn
1998	Rev. Samuel John Dixon	First Antrim

PRESIDENTS OF THE METHODIST CHURCH IN IRELAND, 1965-98

Year	President	Year	President
1965	Rev. Robert A. Nelson	1969	Rev. George E. Good
1966	Rev. Samuel J. Johnston	1970	Rev. James Davison
1967	Rev. R.D. Eric Gallagher	1971	Rev. Charles H. Bain
1968	Rev. Gerald G. Myles	1972	Rev. Edward R. Lindsay

Continued from previous page

Year	President
1973	Rev. Harold Sloan
1974	Rev. R. Desmond Morris
1975	Rev. Hedley W. Plunkett
1976	Rev. Richard Greenwood
1977	Rev. Robert G. Livingstone
1978	Rev. John Turner
1979	Rev. Vincent Parkin
1980	Rev. W. Sydney Callaghan
1981	Rev. Ernest W. Gallagher
1982	Rev. Charles G. Eyre
1983	Rev. Cecil A. Newall
1984	Rev. Paul Kingston

Year	President
1985	Rev. Hamilton Skillen
1986	Rev. Sydney Frame
1987	Rev. William I. Hamilton
1988	Rev. T. Stanley Whittington
1989	Rev. George R. Morrison
1990	Rev. William T. Buchanan
1991	Rev. J. Winston Good
1992	Rev. J. Derek H. Ritchie
1993	Rev. Richard H. Taylor
1994	Rev. Edmund T.I. Mawhinney
1995	Rev. Christopher G. Walpole
1996	Rev. Kenneth Best
1997	Rev. Norman W. Taggart
1998	Rev. David J. Kerr

MEMBERSHIP OF MAIN IRISH CHURCHES

Religion	Members (000s)			Ministers			Church Buildings		
	1985	1990	1993	1985	1990	1993	1985	1990	1993
Catholic	3,341,949	3,257,776	3,241,566	3,950	3,926	4,281	2,626	2,646	2,656
Presbyterian	218,257	218,012	217,888	517	533	531	657	658	656
Anglican	221,200	220,860	220,570	605	535	514	1,186	1,080	1,000
Orthodox	475	502	522	3	3	3	3	3	3
Methodist	24,284	22,966	22,146	137	142	141	282	249	248
Independent	16,627	17,368	16,828	86	96	116	356	389	402
Baptist	8,921	9,270	9,485	109	120	121	112	123	127
Pentecostal	5,225	6,740	7,630	75	87	95	80	86	92
Other Churches	6,157	6,492	6,589	95	101	102	106	107	110
TOTAL	3,843,095	3,759,986	3,743,224	5,577	5,543	5,904	5,408	5,341	5,294

CHURCH OF IRELAND STATISTICS, 1998

Diocese	Incumbents	Curates	Parishes
Armagh	40	5	46
Clogher	27	1	35
Derry and Raphoe	43	4	50
Down and Dromore	69	19	78
Connor	71	17	78
Kilmore, Elphin and Ardagh	18	1	25
Tuam, Killala and Achonry	6	2	9
Dublin and Glendalough	50	8	54
Meath and Kildare	17	-	21
Cashel and Ossory	26	5	34
Cork, Cloyne and Ross	20	3	23
Limerick and Killaloe	14	2	20
TOTAL:	401	67	473

METHODIST CHURCH STATISTICS, 1998

District	Total Community	Number of Circuits	Number of Churches
Dublin	2,290	8	20
Midlands & Southern	2,050	10	27
Enniskillen & Sligo	3,330	9	32
Londonderry	3,545	6	27
North East	11,415	8	24
Belfast	17,423	14	29
Down	10,124	10	22
Portadown	7,299	11	44
TOTAL:	57,476	76	225

PRESBYTERIAN CHURCH STATISTICS, 1997

Synod	Presbyteries	Congregations	Ministers
Armagh & Down	6	162	186
Ballymena & Coleraine	5	118	155
Belfast	3	71	139
Derry & Omagh	4	117	96
Dublin	3	89	63
TOTAL:	21	557	639

CATHOLIC PARISHES, CHURCHES AND SCHOOLS, 1997

Diocese	Parishes	Catholic Population	Churches	Primary Schools Number	Secondary Schools Number	Primary Schools Population	Secondary Schools Population
Armagh	62	204,330	146	169	30	27,832	20,941
Dublin	200	1,041,100	238	513	197	-	-
Cashel	46	78,440	85	127	23	11,430	9,974
Tuam	56	116,201	131	240	38	29,433	9,500
Achonry	23	35,000	47	55	11	4,601	4,134
Ardagh	41	71,806	80	89	22	11,256	7,857
Clogher	37	85,022	86	97	20	12,757	8,573
Clonfert	24	32,600	47	49	8	6,800	3,200
Cloyne	46	119,672	106	131	32	16,002	14,485
Cork & Ross	68	215,500	124	189	49	-	-
Derry	53	213,525	104	136	31	25,820	21,011
Down & Connor	88	304,966	152	172	42	43,113	28,434
Dromore	23	63,300	48	51	14	10,874	9,506
Elphin	37	68,000	90	126	20	12,700	8,000
Ferns	49	99,000	101	96	22	17,000	10,000
Galway	40	87,258	71	96	20	12,046	6,770
Kerry	54	125,000	105	170	35	-	-
Kildare & Leighlin	56	174,454	117	174	45	26,194	19,927
Killala	22	37,412	48	78	12	5,593	4,242
Killaloe	59	107,817	133	157	24	16,394	11,966
Kilmore	36	55,465	97	89	15	8,215	5,850
Limerick	60	160,000	97	114	30	21,500	18,000
Meath	69	182,000	149	186	37	27,025	18,188
Ossory	42	73,875	89	91	16	11,263	7,150
Raphoe	31	82,260	71	104	20	12,255	13,151
Waterford & Lismore	45	133,162	85	100	30	17,472	12,931
ESTIMATED TOTAL:	1,367	3,967,165	2,647	3,599	843	387,575	273,790

NUMBERS OF CATHOLIC PRIESTS & RELIGIOUS, 1996

	Priests			Religious Orders	
	Active in Diocese*	Others†	Clerical	Brothers	Sisters
Armagh	166	22	61	47	380
Dublin	478	122	975	505	2,736
Cashel	120	15	57	27	248
Tuam	152	23	28	48	393
Achonry	49	13	3	1	68
Ardagh	73	19	5	10	325
Clogher	92	13	7	4	157
Clonfert	52	16	39	-	176
Cloyne	135	27	6	30	275
Cork & Ross	143	19	160	90	802
Derry	140	14	5	4	155
Down & Connor	221	24	68	67	355
Dromore	67	11	21	9	167
Elphin	80	12	6	5	204
Ferns	118	39	12	10	275
Galway	70	19	49	24	239
Kerry	113	33	11	23	361

Continued from previous page

	Priests		Religious Orders		
Active in Diocese*	Others†	Clerical	Brothers	Sisters
Kildare & Leighlin	108	25	87	68	391
Killala	46	16	3	3	81
Killaloe	122	23	26	25	320
Kilmore	97	4	14	0	85
Limerick	144	19	76	30	416
Meath	124	26	132	39	305
Ossory	80	25	20	40	262
Raphoe	76	22	12	7	76
Waterford & Lismore	116	9	149	65	532
ESTIMATED TOTAL:	3,182	610	2,032	1,181	9,784

* includes priests who are active in voluntary, secondary and state schools.
† priests of the diocese who are retired, sick, on study leave or working in other dioceses in Ireland and abroad.

APPLICANTS AND ENTRANTS TO CATHOLIC CHURCH

	1994		1996	
Religious Orders	Applicants	Entrants	Applicants	Entrants
Diocesan	193	98	131	52
Clerical Religious Orders	130	66	88	39
Sister Orders	63	33	48	19
Brothers Orders	18	4	11	1
TOTAL:	404	201	278	111

CATHOLIC CHURCH:NULLITY OF MARRIAGES, 1987-94

Year	Applications	Decrees	Year	Applications	Decrees
1987	882	209	1991	402	215
1988	926	188	1992	444	289
1989	915	212	1993	347	282
1990	1,043	216	1994	470	300

GOOD FRIDAY AGREEMENT: Taoiseach Bertie Ahern with British Prime Minister Tony Blair and Senator George Mitchell at Castle Buildings after they signed the historic Peace Agreement that will allow the people of Northern Ireland decide their own future.

PRESIDENT CLINTON IN IRELAND: President Bill Clinton visited Ireland in September to follow up on his initiative in pushing for Peace in Northern Ireland, stopping off in Belfast, Dublin, Armagh, Limerick and Omagh.

Omagh - August 1998

Samantha McFarland

Seán McLaughlin

Veda Short

Aidan Gallagher

Alan Radford

Anne McCombe

Fred White

Brenda Logue

Bryan White

Debra Cartwright

Esther Gibson

Breda Devine

Gareth Conway

Geraldine Breslin

James Barker

Elizabeth Rushe

Fernando Blasco

Brian McCrory

Rocio Abad Ramos

Oran Doherty

Sean McGrath

Philomena Skelton

Mary Grimes

Jolene Marlow

Olive Hawkes

Avril Monaghan

Lorraine Wilson

Julie Hughes

Maura Monaghan

McCOLGAN CASE ENDS: Keith, Sophia and Gerard McColgan, from Sligo, pictured at a press conference in Dublin after a settlement was reached in their case against the North West Health Board for negligence and breach of duty of care. The McColgans' case was described in court as one the worst instances of reported sexual abuse in the history of the State.

SHOCK DEATH OF DERMOT MORGAN:
One of Ireland's top comedians, Dermot Morgan, star of the hit TV series *Fr. Ted* died suddenly earlier this year. *Fr. Ted* had massive viewership both in Ireland and the UK.

GARDA BRIBED : Garda John O'Neill leaving Dublin's Central Criminal Court after admitting taking bribes worth £16,100 from criminals.

MICHELLE DE BRUIN BANNED: A tearful Olympic swimming champion Michelle de Bruin at a Press Conference in Dublin with her husband and coach, Eric de Bruin, and solicitor Peter Lennon. De Bruin rejected allegations levelled against her by FINA, accusing her of tampering with a urine sample.

IRISH DUO WIN GOLF WORLD CUP: Golfers Paul McGinley and Padraig Harrington with Taoiseach Bertie Ahern following their return from Kiawah Island, South Carolina, where they won the Golf World Cup.

TRIMBLE AND ADAMS MEET AT LAST: Ulster Unionist Party leader David Trimble and Sinn Féin leader Gerry Adams finally meet in the aftermath of the Good Friday Agreement . . . but no words were exchanged on this occasion.

U2 ROCK FOR PEACE: Politicians David Trimble and John Hume unite with Bono of U2 on stage in Belfast to promote a 'Yes' vote in the Referendum for the Good Friday Agreement.

Philip Allen   Damien Treanor

FRIENDS GUNNED DOWN IN POYNTZPASS: RUC officers investigate the murder scene of friends Damien Treanor (a Catholic) and Philip Allen (a Protestant). The two men were shot dead by Loyalists as they enjoyed a quiet night out in a local pub.

LOTTO MILLIONAIRE CELEBRATES: Michael Kelly who, with his wife Ann, won over £4million in the Lottery, performs the New Zealand 'hakka' outside the National Lottery Headquarters.

REPUBLIC OF IRELAND SCORE GREAT VICTORY: The Republic of Ireland had a surprise win over Croatia in the opening game of their European 2000 qualifiers.

MOWLAM MEETS PRISONERS: A resolute Secretary of State Dr. Mo Mowlam emerges from the Maze Prison after what she termed "useful talks" with Loyalist inmates.

SINN FÉIN VISIT DOWNING STREET: The Sinn Féin delegation, led by Gerry Adams and Martin McGuinness, pictured outside Number 10 Downing Street prior to meeting British Prime Minister Tony Blair. It was the first time a Sinn Féin delegation had met a British leader since Michael Collins led a deputation in December 1921.

BALLYBUNNION'S BIG DAY: US President Bill Clinton kept his promise to travel to Ballybunnion, Co. Kerry, for a game of golf. Standing with the President are golfer Christy O'Connor Snr, Charlie McCreevey - Minister for Finance, and former Tánaiste Dick Spring

TOUR DE FRANCE: After months of preparation, the Tour de France finally came to Ireland. Le Tour began in Dublin before making its way to the town of Enniscorthy, Co. Wexford (pictured left), for the second stage. Also included in the photograph is a guard of honour, formed by Enniscorthy's Pike men who took part in Co. Wexford's 1798 commemorations.

FRUIT OF THE LOOM JOBS IN TROUBLE: Giant US clothing manufacturer, Fruit of the Loom, announced huge lay offs from staff at their operations in Donegal and Derry. Pictured here is chief executive, Bill Farrelly.

MARY McALEESE SUCCEEDS MARY ROBINSON AS PRESIDENT: Mary McAleese arrives at Dublin Castle to accept her election as President, following her landslide victory. She is pictured with Taoiseach Bertie Ahern and her Director of Elections, Noel Dempsey.

GREAT YEAR FOR IRVINE: Irish Formula One driver, Eddie Irvine, enjoyed his most successful year. Driving for Ferrari, he had seven podium finishes, including two second places.

THREE CHILDREN MURDERED: The Troubles in Northern Ireland seemed to have reached new depths of depravity following the murders of the three young Quinn brothers as they slept in their home in Ballymoney, Co. Antrim.

BOORMAN WINS TOP AWARD: Irish-based film director John Boorman (L), fresh from his triumph at the Cannes Film Festival where he won Best Director, with actor Brendan Gleeson who plays Dublin criminal, Martin Cahill, in Boorman's film *The General*.

BRAVE IRISH FLOP AGAIN: Despite spirited performances in the Five Nations series, the Irish rugby team finished with the Wooden Spoon. Pictured are David Humphries and Paul Wallace putting in a tackle on Gordon Bulloch of Scotland.

REFUGEES IN IRELAND: A Bosnian woman pictured with her baby in Dublin. Refugees from Eastern Europe are making their way into Ireland, via France, and have sparked debate on their economic status and on Irish racism.

CLIFTONVILLE DELIGHT: Cliftonville F.C. bridged a 78-year gap by winning the Irish League. The North Belfast side, captained by Mickey Donnelly (R) secured a 1-1 draw with Glenavon and the defeat of arch rivals Linfield, on the same day, brought the Gibson Cup to North Belfast for the first time since the 1909/10 season.

NORTHERN IRELAND'S NEW LEADERS: Northern Ireland First Minister, David Trimble (UUP), shakes the hand of his Deputy First Minister, Seamus Mallon (SDLP). The two men were elected following the inaugural meeting of the new Northern Ireland Assembly.

'BLUE FLU' SHOOTING:
The scene at Ashford, Co. Wicklow, following a shoot out between Gardai and republicans in which one of the gang was shot dead after attempting to rob a security van. The incident occured the same day as gardaí staged an unofficial strike - the so-called 'blue flu' - protesting over wages.

IRISH GRAND NATIONAL WINNER:
Irish Grand National Winner Bobbyjo with trainer Tommy Carberry and his son, winning jockey Paul Carberry.

O'SULLIVAN BACK IN BRILLIANT FORM: Cork's Sonia O'Sullivan breaks the tape to win the first of two golds in the IAAF World Cross Country Championships in Morocco. Later in the season, O'Sullivan went on to win double gold in the European Track and Field Championships in Budapest.

SOARING PROPERTY PRICES: Massive publicity was generated around the sale of an end-of-terrace Victorian property on Sorrento Terrace, Co. Dublin, for the unprecedented sum of £5.9 million.

WRIGHT FUNERAL: The funeral of Loyalist Volunteer Force leader, Billy Wright, makes its way through Portadown to the Seagoe cemetery in the town. Wright was shot dead by an INLA inmate inside the Maze Prison.

DOHERTY'S BRAVE BID FAILS: Ireland's Ken Doherty reached the final of the World Snooker Championship for the second year running, but failed to retain his world title, losing to Scot John Higgins 18 frames to 12.

ROAD DEATH FIGURES MOUNT: Carnage continued on Irish roads with scores of people killed and injured in numerous accidents throughout the country.

JOY FOR JORDAN: The Jordan Formula One team celebrated in style following their 1st and 2nd placing in the Belgian Formula One Grand Prix. Pictured are race winner Damon Hill (L) and his colleague Ralf Schumacher (R) with team boss Eddie Jordan.

McKIERNAN WINS LONDON MARATHON: Cavan athlete Catherina McKiernan, competing in just her second marathon, raced to victory in the London Marathon, winning in a time of 2 hours 26 minutes and 24 seconds.

PETER SUTHERLAND'S RISING FORTUNE: Ireland's former Attorney General and EC Commissioner, Peter Sutherland, has become co-chairman of one of the world's top three oil companies following the merger of the British company, BP, and American oil giant, Amoco, in 1998. In addition, the proposed flotation of leading investment firm, Goldman Sachs could earn him up to £75 million.

EUROPEAN CUP GLORY FOR REPUBLIC: The Republic of Ireland's U-16 soccer team won the European Cup in Scotland in May when they defeated Italy in the final. Pictured here is team captain Shaun Byrne with the European trophy.

UNDER-18'S EUROPEAN CUP SUCCESS: The Republic of Ireland's U-18 soccer team became the second of Brian Kerr's underage teams to win the European Cup when they defeated Germany on penalties in the European Final in July. Holding aloft the European trophy after the game in Cyprus is team captain Barry Quinn, with manager Brian Kerr (L) and Noel O'Reilly (R).

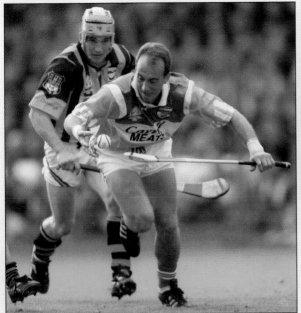

'BACK-DOOR' ALL IRELAND FOR OFFALY: Offaly hurlers won the All-Ireland title by defeating Kilkenny in the final. Kilkenny had earlier defeated the Offaly men in the Leinster final but new rules gave the Offaly men a second chance through the 'back-door'. They took it by defeating Clare after an epic three-match All-Ireland semi-final saga at Croke Park. Pictured above is Joe Dooley of Offaly pursued by Kilkenny's Pat O'Neill. *Top right: Offaly captain Hubert Rigney with the Liam McCarthy Cup.*

THE WEST'S AWAKE: Galway footballers caused a major shock by defeating hot favourites, Kildare, in the All-Ireland Senior Football Final following a first-class performance which left the Lilywhites trailing by four points at the final whistle. *Inset: Galway captain Ray Silke with the Sam Maguire Cup.*

Say hello to iMac

GalMac Computers Ltd
Liosbaun Estate
Tuam Road
Galway
Ireland

Phone: +091 755222
Fax :   + 091 744491

email: maureen@galmac.ie

AGRICULTURE, FORESTRY & FISHERIES

The Changing Face of Irish Agriculture

By **PJ Nolan,** *Irish Farmer's Journal*

B EFORE the next issue of this almanac is published, the future of Irish farming will be shaped by the negotiations on Agenda 2000, which is the latest round of reforms of the Common Agricultural Policy or CAP. Questions you could be forgiven for asking are why do we have the CAP and why does it need to be reformed. I will not bore you with figures that are much more accurately collated elsewhere in this publication, rather I will give a broad outline of the farming scene as it stands.

The CAP has become a victim of its own success, as the highly efficient European farmers not only made Europe self-sufficient but also managed to produce surpluses that were embarrassing, both politically and financially, for Europe. This meant supply controls in some products such as milk and cereals, but our international trading partners objected to large amounts of subsidised products being exported to third-world countries and affecting international trade.

The WTO, or world trade organisation, negotiations put further limits on subsidised exports, but now, internal pressures mean that the emphasis on farming in Europe will change from maximising output to controlling environmental and consumer-friendly production.

If that all sounds like too much jargon, I apologise, but the truth is that the average Irish farmer is now producing only a quarter of total household income from direct farming, another quarter comes from subsidies and the rest from off-farm income.

In money terms, about a billion pounds comes from subsidies, the same from direct farming income and the rest from non-farm income, such as alternative enterprises and part-time jobs plus income from members of the family outside the farm.

Sounds easy? Well, farming in Ireland is not the gravy train that is commonly imagined. The cost output squeeze is causing many farmers to consider their options and look outside farming. There is virtually no prospect of expansion in any of the main farm enterprises, and this has led to a stagnation that is very unhealthy. It now costs the equivalent of nine pounds a gallon to get into milk production in Ireland, a similar venture in the United States costs two pounds a gallon. It doesn't take too much inside knowledge to figure out where the expansion in dairy farming will come from in the future.

This raises another very fundamental question, who are the winners and losers in the world trade organisation talks? At those talks, there are maybe a dozen people representing the interests of 6 billion others, sometimes the lobbying power of giant conglomerates may overshadow the interests and long-term viability of whole sectors of industry.

Many countries complain that the EU has distorted world trade through subsidised third-world exports, but such distortions are not solely the province of Europe.

It is difficult to get a level playing pitch in world trade. The Americans, Australians and

Argentinians can all use growth enhancing hormones while animal husbandry practised in some new Zealand dairy herds would breach European animal welfare standards. There is a ban on European beef imports into Japan following a political trade off in the 1980s, and Chinese wheat imports are almost exclusively the property of the US.

Confused? Well I am, this summary may seem far away from irish farming but its important to know who is making the big moves internationally and why. So where does this leave ireland? We are lucky to have one of the most efficient agriculture industries in the world. Our farmers are the best grass growers in the Northern hemisphere and have a reputation for quality production. Milk is being produced here at world prices and our beef is top quality. The technical capability of Irish farmers stacks up against any of our competitors.

The greatest threats to our industry are political. The debt burden of Irish farming is very low, with Irish farmers owning 95% of total assets and their current assets exceeding their total liabilities threefold. This means that the industry is in a healthy state, with only a small number of farmers having a significant debt burden.

There are other structural challenges facing farming. The farming population is ageing; only three out of ten farmers have identifiable successors. The EU has introduced a farm retirement package which has helped to ease the burden on older farmers, but the incentive package for young farmers has been suspended since early 1997. The scheme was an important incentive for young farmers, as it allowed them to get a start in situations that were invariably undercapitalised.

The tax regime mitigates against on-farm investment, even for young farmers. This is in stark contrast with the French model, where there are a number of tax incentives to help preserve the structure of the industry. In a low margin business like farming, cash flow is critical and a vibrant young farming population is necessary in order to keep pace with the changes that are happening both in Europe and globally.

Another constraint to expansion is the high cost of land in Ireland. Farmland is regularly trading at £4,000 an acre without milk quota, which incidently can add up to £2,000 more onto the price; this is as a result of our Tiger economy, and because some farmers have got high prices for development land and want to reinvest in the business they are familiar with.

So in practical terms where are the opportunities for Irish farming in the next decade? Great efficiency through cost cutting and better us of resources is a must if farmers are to continue to stay profitable. The forestry sector offers good tax-free incentives for farmers with non-core land that may only be marginally profitable in other enterprises such as beef, sheep or tillage.

The Rural Environment Protection Scheme already has 40,000 participants and is worth £200 million each year to Irish farmers. This scheme gives farmers a subsidy of up to £5,000 a year to farm in an environmentally friendly way.

The maximising of direct payments for each farmer needs exact planning and often requires professional advice to find a way through the maze of forms that confront a farmer. Because the constraints of being a farmer in Europe are so absolute, it is their duty to get any benefits that ensue from that system and it is the duty of beaurocrats to ensure that payment methods are simple and timely.

Overall, Irish agriculture is facing major changes but if the resourcefulness of our farmers is matched by our politicians then there should be a reasonable living for all those who wish to stay on the land.

AGRICULTURE

REPUBLIC OF IRELAND & NORTHERN IRELAND:
AGRICULTURAL, FORESTRY & FISHING BODIES / ASSOCIATIONS

REPUBLIC OF IRELAND

Dept. of Agriculture, Food and Forestry - *Kildare Street, Dublin 2. Tel. (01) 6072000.*

An Bord Bia (Irish Food Board) - *Clanwilliam Court, Lower Mount Street, Dublin 2. Tel. (01) 6685155.*

An Bord Glas (Horticultural Development Board) - *8-11 Lower Baggot Street, Dublin 2. Tel. (01) 6763567.*

Bord Iascaigh Mhara (Irish Sea Fisheries Board) - *Crofton Road, Dun Laoghaire, Co. Dublin. Tel. (01) 2841544.*

Central Fisheries Board - *Balnagowan, Mobhi Boreen, Glasnevin, Dublin 9. Tel. (01) 8379206.*

Coillte (Irish Forestry Board) - *Leeson Lane, Dublin 2. Tel. (01) 6615666.*

Irish Dairy Board - *Grattan House, Mount Street Lower, Dublin 2. Tel. (01) 6619599.*

Irish Farmers' Association - *Irish Farm Centre, Bluebell, Dublin 12. Tel. (01) 4500266.*

Irish Fishermen's Organisation Ltd. - *Cumberland House, Fenian Street, Dublin 2. Tel. (01) 6612400.*

Irish Organic Farmers & Growers Association - *56 Blessington Street, Dublin 7. Tel. (01) 8307996.*

Teagasc (Agriculture & Food Development Authority) - *19 Sandymount Avenue, Ballsbridge, Dublin 4. Tel. (01) 6688188.*

NORTHERN IRELAND

Dept. of Agriculture - *Dundonald House, Upper Newtownards Road, Belfast, Co. Antrim BT4 3SB. Tel. (01232) 520100.*

British Wool Marketing Board - *20 Tirgracey Road, Muckamore, Co. Antrim BT41 4PS. Tel. (01494) 64919.*

Foyle Fisheries Commission - *8 Victoria Road, Derry BT47 2AB. Tel. (01504) 42100.*

Livestock and Meat Commission - *57 Malone Road, Belfast, Co. Antrim BT9 6SA. Tel. (01232) 381022.*

Milk Marketing Board for Northern Ireland - *456 Antrim Road, Belfast, Co. Antrim. Tel. (01232) 372237.*

Northern Ireland Agricultural Producers Association - *15 Molesworth Street, Cookstown, Co. Tyrone BT80 8NX. Tel. (016487) 65700.*

Pigs Marketing Board for Northern Ireland - *Bridgewater House, Bridge Street, Lisburn, Co. Antrim. Tel. (01846) 677070.*

Royal Ulster Agricultural Society - *Showgrounds, Balmoral, Belfast, Co. Antrim BT9 6GW. Tel. (01232) 665225.*

Ulster Farmers' Union - *475 Antrim Road, Belfast, Co. Antrim BT15 3BP. Tel. (01232) 370222.*

REPUBLIC OF IRELAND: LAND SALES, 1994-97

	1994	1995	1996	1997
Transaction Size (hectares)	18.4	12.9	14.5	13.1
Number of Transactions	1,014	1,598	1,265	627
Average Price per hectare (£)	4,215	4,399	5,279	5,130

REPUBLIC OF IRELAND:
NUMBER OF PERSONS FARMING, 1991

Category	Males	Females	Persons
Farmers (horse, pig or poultry)	224	46	270
Other Farmers	104,751	6,808	111,559
Farmers' sons (-in-law) & daughters (-in-law)	11,257	65	11,322
Farmers' other relatives assisting on farm	3,527	6,116	9,643
Farm Managers	1,152	96	1,248
Agricultural Labourers	13,610	835	14,445
Other Agricultural Workers	3,037	579	3,616
TOTAL:	**137,558**	**14,545**	**152,103**

NORTHERN IRELAND:
NUMBER OF PERSONS IN FARMING, 1993-96

Category	1993	1994	1995	1996
Farmers, Partners and Directors	34,408	35,377	34,309	34,408
Spouses of Farmers and Directors	5,790	5,489	6,019	6,022
Other Family Members	10,119	9,624	9,867	9,523
Hired Workers	9,307	9,117	9,482	9,128
TOTAL:	**59,624**	**59,607**	**59,677**	**59,081**

R.O.I. & N.I: AGRICULTURE IN RELATION TO POPULATION AND LABOUR FORCE, 1994-97

Persons (000s)	Republic of Ireland				Northern Ireland			
	1994	1995	1996	1997	1994	1995	1996	1997
Total Population	3,585.9	3,601.3	3,626.1	3,660.6	1,641.7	1,649.0	1,663.3	0
Total Labour Force	1,407	1,439	1,488	1,517	737.5	743.9	736.4	726.7
Total Unemployed	219	192	191	179	96.2	85.5	84.7	60.8
Total at Work	1,188	1,248	1,297	1,338	641.3	658.5	651.7	665.9
Agriculture	142	143	138	134	40.5	39.9	38.6	38.8
Agriculture as % of Total at Work	11.9%	11.5%	10.6%	10%	6.3%	6.1%	5.9%	5.8%

REPUBLIC OF IRELAND: FARMS BY SIZE AND NUMBER, 1993-95

Hectares	1993 (000s)	1994 (000s)	1995 (000s)
Less than 5	16.6	15.2	14.8
5 and less than 10	22.2	20.9	20.5
10 and less than 20	44.9	42.4	40.6
20 and less than 30	29.4	28.7	29.1
30 and less than 50	27.4	26.8	28.1
50 and less than 100	5.2	15.5	16.1
100 or more	3.7	3.9	4.1
TOTAL:	159.4	153.4	153.3

NORTHERN IRELAND: FARMS BY SIZE AND NUMBER, 1994-96

Hectares	1994 (000s)	1995 (000s)	1996 (000s)
Less than 10	32.7	32.1	30.7
10 and less 20	101.8	98	96.5
20 and less than 30	118.8	116.9	114.8
30 and less than 50	211.6	208.2	207.7
50 and less than 100	299.4	301.4	303.3
100 and less than 200	160.9	165.7	164.6
200 or over	81.3	81	82.6
Total:	1,006.5	1,003.3	1,000.2

REPUBLIC OF IRELAND & NORTHERN IRELAND: AGRICULTURAL WAGES, 1994-97

Minimum Weekly Wage Rate	1994 (£)	1995 (£)	1996 (£)	1997 (£)
Republic of Ireland	137.24	139.98	147.07	152.25
Northern Ireland	168.53	167.96	193.82	-

REPUBLIC OF IRELAND: VALUE OF AGRICULTURAL OUTPUT, 1994-97

Agricultural Products	1994 (£)	1995 (£)	1996 (£)	1997 (£)
Livestock:				
Cattle	1,282.6	1,321.8	1,147.4	1,097.3
Pigs	200.2	233.3	293.4	256.3
Sheep & Lambs	168.7	155.4	202	189.2
Other	174.1	174.6	202.8	214.6
Total	1,825.6	1,885.1	1,845.6	1,757.4
Livestock Products:				
Milk	1,138.9	1,212.5	1,210.5	1,112.6

Continued from previous page

Agricultural Products	1994 (£)	1995 (£)	1996 (£)	1997 (£)
Other	32.4	33.5	30.5	28.7
Total	1,171.3	1246	1241	1,141.3
Crops:				
Cereals	100.2	137.5	130.5	121.6
Root Crops	136.1	136.1	97.5	95.1
Other	165.6	176	199.7	194
Total	401.9	449.6	427.7	410.7
GROSS AGRICULTURAL OUTPUT:	**3,398.8**	**3,580.7**	**3,514.3**	**3,309.4**

NORTHERN IRELAND:
VALUE OF AGRICULTURAL OUTPUT, 1993-96

Description	1993 (£m)	1994 (£m)	1995 (£m)	1996 (£m)
Livestock & Other Products:				
Cattle & Calves	328.4	414.2	411.4	327.5
Sheep & Lambs	108.1	95.9	93.3	112.1
Pigs	79.8	83.9	98.8	112.8
Poultry	75.3	78.6	79.1	93.9
Eggs	34.8	34	38.2	44.6
Milk	281.1	288.9	341.3	343.1
Other	10	13.3	13.8	15.2
Total	917.5	1,008.8	1,075.9	1,049.2
Crops:				
Potatoes	14.9	24	34.3	15.3
Barley	10.5	10.5	14.2	15.9
Wheat	4.4	4.5	5.4	5.4
Oats	0.6	0.8	1	0.9
Other Crops	2.6	2.6	2.5	2.1
Total	33	42.4	57.4	39.6
Horticultural Products:				
Fruit	7.8	5.3	6.7	7.4
Vegetables	5.6	8.7	9.3	9.3
Mushrooms	26	27.2	27.8	29.4
Flowers	8	8.5	8.2	8.5
Total	47.4	49.7	52	54.6
GROSS AGRICULTURAL OUTPUT:	**997.9**	**1,100.9**	**1,185.3**	**1,143.4**

REPUBLIC OF IRELAND: SELECTED PRICES
OF AGRICULTURAL PRODUCTS, 1994-96

Price / unit	1994	1995	1996
Milk *(litre)*	0.218	0.232	0.233
Bullocks *(100kg lw)*	131	128.9	110.4
Heifers *(100 kg lw)*	122.3	118.6	103
Pigs *(kg head)*	27.1	33.1	35.8
Sheep *(kg head)*	46.3	44.4	53.6
Wheat *(tonne)*	94.1	117.9	95.6
Feed Barley *(tonne)*	88.7	106.7	90.7
Malting Barley *(tonne)*	95.8	126.9	110.9
Potatoes *(tonne)*	184	134	93
Sugar Beet *(tonne)*	44.4	40.2	40.9

NORTHERN IRELAND: SELECTED PRICES OF AGRICULTURAL PRODUCTS, 1994-96

Product £ / unit	1994	1995	1996
Milk *(litre)*	0.212	0.254	0.241
Finished Steers, heifers & young bulls *(kg dwt)*	2.23	2.22	1.84
Finished Sheep & Lambs *(kg dwt)*	2.16	2.04	2.54
Finished Clean Pigs *(kg dwt)*	0.95	1.11	1.31
Potatoes - ware maincrop *(tonne)*	118	172	76
Barley *(tonne)*	112	119	116
Wheat *(tonne)*	114	124	125
Mushrooms *(tonne)*	1,190	1,210	1,225
Apples *(tonne)*	119	138	158

REPUBLIC OF IRELAND: LAND USE, 1993-97

Product (000 hectares)	1993	1994	1995	1996	1997
Cereals:					
Wheat	79.2	74.1	70.7	85.7	93.9
Oats	20.2	20.9	19.9	20.9	20.6
Barley	180.8	169.7	178.6	181.4	189.8
Other	4.7	5.3	4.7	5.5	5.6
Total	284.9	270	273.9	293.5	309.9
Crops:					
Beans & Peas	6.1	5.6	4.8	4.8	4.8
Oilseed Rape	3.4	6.4	4.1	3.5	4.4
Potatoes	21.6	21.4	22.4	24.3	18.2
Sugar Beet	32.2	35.4	35.1	32.3	32.3
Turnips	5.2	5.6	5.3	5.4	5.2
Fodder Beet	10.9	9.8	8.9	9.9	9.1
Kale & Field Cabbage	1.8	1.8	1.5	1.6	1.7
Vegetables for Sale	4.6	4.8	4.7	4.6	4.7
Fruit	1.6	1.7	1.6	1.5	1.7
Nursery Stock, Bulbs & Flowers	1	1.3	1.2	1.1	1.2
Other	30.5	36.6	36	24	21
Total	118.9	130.4	125.6	113	104.3
Pasture:					
Silage	872.3	917.4	933.6	956.1	931.5
Hay	425.9	410.1	357.2	371.5	338.8
Pasture	2,202.5	2,201.3	2,238.9	2,178.4	2,273.0
Total	3,500.7	3,528.8	3,529.7	3506	3,543.3
Total: Cereals, Crops & Pasture	3,904.5	3,929.2	3,929.2	3,912.5	3,957.6
Rough Grazing in Use	499.7	461.5	459.5	429	473.9
TOTAL LAND IN USE:	4,404.2	4,390.7	4,388.7	4,341.5	4,431.6

NORTHERN IRELAND: LAND USE, 1994-97

Product (000 hectares)	1994	1995	1996	1997
Agricultural Crops:				
Oats	2	2	2	2
Wheat	7	7	7	7
Barley	34	34	34	37
Potatoes	9	9	9	8
Other	4	3	3	3
Horticulture Crops:				
Fruit	2	2	2	2
Vegetables	1	1	1	1
Grass	813	817	820	825
Rough Grazing	176	171	169	164
Woods and Plantations	8	8	8	8
Other Land	15	13	13	12
TOTAL LAND IN USE:	1,071	1,067	1,068	1,069

NORTHERN IRELAND: SUBSIDIES, 1994-96

Payments (£m)	1994	1995	1996
Cereals	4.7	7.7	8.2
Other Crops	0.4	0.2	0.1
Cattle Premiums:			
Beef Special Premium	35.5	36	44.7
Suckler Cow Premium	34.6	29.8	50.2
Extensification Supplement	15.0	15.1	16.4
Deseasonalisation Premium	4.6	0.5	-
Hill Livestock Compensatory Allowance	10.7	10.4	10.7
Beef Marketing Payment Scheme	-	-	4.5
Sheep Premiums	31.8	33.9	39.4
Other Subsidies	14.7	7.0	93.9
TOTAL:	**152.0**	**140.6**	**268.1**

REPUBLIC OF IRELAND: SUBSIDIES, 1994-97

Payments	1994 (£m)	1995 (£m)	1996 (£m)	1997 (£m)
Headage:				
Cattle Headage	93.8	80.2	81.4	88.8
Beef Cow Headage	19	17	11.3	13.4
Sheep Headage	20.8	20.4	22.5	23.9
Total	**133.6**	**117.6**	**115.2**	**126.1**
Livestock Premiums, Compensation Packages and Arable Aid:				
Suckler Cow Premium	89.9	112.2	157.7	121.3
Special Beef Premium	122.5	169.8	167.1	157.8
Deseasonalisation Premium	15.6	15	16.8	23.8
Ewe Premium	117.3	108	113.2	73.6
Extensification Premium	47.5	59.8	60.5	.67
Special BSE Compensation Package	0	0	.69	31.1
Agri-Monetary Compensation Package (Beef)	0	0	0	43.2
Agri-Monetary Compensation Package (Crops)	0	0	0	7.2
Arable Aid	66	82.5	88.6	95.7
Total	**458.8**	**547.3**	**672.9**	**620.7**
Disease Eradication Schemes	17.2	20.9	28.9	34.8
Milk Payments	36.6	18.4	17.3	38.9
Forestry Premium Scheme	1	4.2	12.6	10.9
Installation Aid for Young Farmers	2.3	4.2	6.5	.7
Rural Environment Protection Scheme	1.2	30.9	56.4	101.4
Others	15.8	4	0.7	0.3

REPUBLIC OF IRELAND: LIVESTOCK FIGURES, 1994-97

Livestock (000 heads)	1994	1995	1996	1997
Cattle:				
Cows	2,292.4	2,322.9	2,413.1	2,492.5
Heifers in Calf	295.7	326.7	340.9	362.2
Bulls	36.6	37.9	40.7	43.4
Other Cattle	4,439.9	4,434.6	4,628.2	4,761.6
Total	**7,064.6**	**7,122.1**	**7,422.9**	**7,659.7**
Sheep:				
Breeding Ewes	4,653.0	4,537.5	4,405.4	4,438.4
Rams	119.4	117.3	109.7	111.4
Other Sheep	3,661.0	3,714.8	3,418.9	3,635.3
Total	**8,433.4**	**8,369.6**	**7,934.0**	**8,185.1**
Pigs:				
Breeding Pigs	173.8	174.8	183.4	191.7
Other Pigs	1,361.4	1,375.6	1,437.5	1,507.8
Total	**1,535.2**	**1,550.4**	**1,620.9**	**1,699.5**
Poultry	13,726.0	12,898	13,171	13,433
Horses & Ponies	67	68	70	72

N. IRELAND: LIVESTOCK FIGURES, 1994-97

Livestock (000 heads)	1994	1995	1996	1997
Cattle:				
Dairy Cows	274	272	281	279
Beef Cows	309	309	316	324
Heifers in Calf	82	89	97	110
Other Cattle	1,022	1,030	1,065	1,019
Total	1,687	1,700	1,759	1,732
Sheep:				
Breeding Ewes	1,382	1,345	1,342	1,384
Other Sheep	1,439	1,408	1,412	1,496
Total	2,821	2,753	2,754	2,880
Pigs:				
Sows and Gilts	62	60	61	64
Other Pigs	517	504	504	553
Total	579	564	565	617
Poultry	14,602	16,003	15,898	15,608
Goats	4	4	4	3
Horses & Ponies	9	10	10	10

NORTHERN IRELAND: IMPORTS AND EXPORTS, 1993-97

Imported & Exported Stock (000 heads)	1993/94	1994/95	1995/96	1996/97
Cattle Imports from the Republic of Ireland:				
Steers, Heifers, Young Bulls	28.7	8.4	9.2	1.4
Store Cattle	13.4	7.3	9.1	10.4
Other Cattle	1.5	1.8	1.2	1.5
Total	43.6	17.5	19.5	13.3
Cattle Imports from Britain:				
Slaughter	-	-	7.6	0.1
Further Keep	-	-	15.4	3.5
Total	-	-	23	3.6
Cattle Exports to Britain & Other Countries	-	-	4.8	7.4
Sheep Imports from the Republic of Ireland:				
Slaughter	-	-	117.1	106.6
Further Keep	-	-	-	-
Total	-	-	117.1	106.6
Sheep Imports from Britain:				
Slaughter	-	-	4.6	12.3
Further Keep	-	-	4.8	7
Total	-	-	9.4	19.3
Sheep Exports to Britain & Other Countries	-	-	121.6	71

R. of IRELAND: EXPORTS OF LIVE CATTLE, 1994-96

Destination	1994	1995	1996
EU:			
France	15,000	9,000	3,000
Italy	20,000	24,000	9,000
Netherlands	32,000	14,000	11,000
Spain	39,000	39,000	17,000
Belgium	3,000	3,000	2,000
UK	18,000	18,000	10,000
Total	127,000	107,000	52,000
Non-EU:			
Egypt	256,000	176,000	106,000
Libya	6,000	79,000	33,000
Saudi Arabia	12,000	6,000	0,000
Total	274,000	261,000	139,000
TOTAL:	**401,000**	**368,000**	**191,000**

REP. OF IRELAND: CROP PRODUCTION, 1994-97

Crops (000 tonnes)	1994	1995	1996	1997
Cereals:				
Wheat	572	583	771	670
Oats	128	129	146	127
Barley	910	1,084	1,225	1,122
Total	1,610	1,796	2,142	1,919
Root Crops:				
Potatoes	642	618	733	490
Sugar Beet	1,390	1,547	1,495	1,408
Total	2,032	2,165	2,228	1,898
TOTAL CROPS:	3,642	3,961	4,370	3,817

NORTHERN IRELAND: CROP PRODUCTION, 1993-96

Crops (000 tonnes)	1993	1994	1995	1996
Cereals:				
Wheat	37.3	49.6	49.9	51.4
Oats	9.4	11.3	12.3	12.5
Barley	138.1	157.2	169	179.8
Total	184.8	218.1	231.2	243.7
Non-Cereal Crops:				
Potatoes	256.7	268.2	278.9	277.3
Oilseed Rape	0.9	1.5	.1	0.8
Total	257.6	269.7	279.9	278.1
Hay	292.2	228.2	269.7	257.8
Grass Silage	8,260.1	8,031.8	7631	8,215.9
TOTAL CROPS:	8,994.7	8,747.8	8,411.8	8,995.5

R. of IRELAND: IMPORTS AND EXPORTS, 1995-97

Products (£m)	Imports			Exports		
	1995	1996	1997	1995	1996	1997
Live Animals	56.6	64.6	61.4	170.8	149.4	62.4
Meat and Meat Products	142.2	142.1	110.9	1,251.9	1082	758.2
Dairy Products	133.8	143.5	119	994.1	757.2	640.1
Corn Crops and Processed Cereal Products	142.7	135.7	101	28.1	35.5	37.1
Vegetables and Fruit	192.6	209.1	141.8	86.9	91.6	76.1
Sugar Products	52.3	53	49.2	40.9	42.3	40.5
Animal Foodstuffs	168.2	152.6	94.4	49.9	47.5	27.9
Hides and Skins	3.2	4.3	4.2	71.3	66.2	50.1
Flax and Wool	26.4	22.7	16.9	24.2	22.6	11.8
Animal and Vegetable Materials	55.4	63	41.5	65.4	71.8	45.4
Lard, Oils and Fats	5.4	6.9	3.2	21.3	22.7	15.3
Casein and Caseinates	10	8.2	4.9	137.6	110.1	74.5
TOTAL:	988.8	1,005.7	748.4	2942.4	2,498.9	1,839.4

REPUBLIC OF IRELAND:
AGRICULTURAL IMPORTS AND EXPORTS, 1993-97

Products (000 heads)	1993	1994	1995	1996	1997
Cattle & Calves:					
Exports of Live Cattle:					
Fat Cattle	237	261	253	125	-
Store Cattle	75	83	61	24	-
Calves	70	68	55	42	-
Other	3	1	1	1	-
Total: Exports of Live Cattle	385	413	370	192	47
Slaughterings of Cattle & Calves	1,601	1,436	1,515	1,649	1,779
Imports of Fat & Breeding Animals	10	17	9	1	1
Change in Stocks	39	107	152	204	252
Total	2,015	1,939	2,028	2,044	2,077

Continued from previous page

Products (000 heads)	1993	1994	1995	1996	1997
Pigs:					
Exports of Live Pigs	120	135	199	547	513
Slaughterings of Pigs	3,070	3,086	3,003	2,926	3,047
Imports of Fat & Breeding Animals	275	234	222	283	116
Change in Stocks	63	-24	102	102	65
Total	2,978	2,963	3,082	3,292	3,509

Description (000)	1993	1994	1995	1996	1997
Sheep & Lambs:					
Exports of Live Sheep					
Fat Sheep	160	155	111	104	-
Lambs	139	124	87	91	-
Other	11	9	7	6	-
Total: Exports of Live Sheep	310	288	205	201	170
Slaughterings of Sheep & Lambs	4,701	4,417	4,298	4,367	3,776
Imports of Fat & Breeding Animals	38	36	35	241	201
Change in Stocks	-153	-237	-185	-61	250
Total	4,820	4,432	4,283	4,266	3,995

N. IRELAND: AGRICULTURAL TRADE, 1997

Commodity	Foreign (Tonnes)		Coastwise (Tonnes)	
	Inwards Import	Outwards Export	Inwards Import	Outwards Export
Unmilled Cereals	204,795	-	296,368	-
Milled Cereals & Cereal Preparations	-	-	-	-
Fresh Fruit & Vegetables	-	10,412	-	-
Other Fruit & Vegetables	-	-	-	1,380
Animal Feeding Stuffs	876,526	3,000	-	-
Sugar & Sugar Preparations	-	-	34,167	5,769
TOTAL:	**1,081,321**	**13,412**	**330,535**	**7,149**

EU COUNTRIES:
FULL-TIME AGRICULTURAL LABOUR FORCE, 1995

Country	Number (000s)	% Full-time	Country	Number (000s)	% Full-time
Austria	85.3	15.6	Italy	568.5	11.9
Belgium	54.7	44.8	Luxembourg	3.0	41.0
Denmark	73.7	52.2	Netherlands	136.9	49.6
Finland	122.4	41.3	Portugal	166.1	14.2
France	590.9	39.2	Spain	491.9	19.4
Germany	436.9	33.0	Sweden	45.1	27.5
Greece	138.4	9.1	United Kingdom	260.8	45.5
IRELAND	153.4	52.3	Total	3,328.0	21.8

FORESTRY

EU FOREST STRUCTURES: WOODED AREA AND TYPE OF OWNERSHIP

Country	Forest Area 000s ha	%	Ownership (%) Public	Private
Belgium	620	20	41.9	58.1
Denmark	466	11	39.1	60.9
France	13,110	24	25.7	74.3
Germany	10,490	29	56.2	43.8
Greece	2,512	19	93.4	6.6
IRELAND	**529**	**8**	**74.6**	**25.4**
Italy	6,750	22	39.7	60.3
Luxembourg	85	33	46.3	53.7
Netherlands	334	9	48.0	52.0
Portugal	2,755	31	24.0	76.0
Spain	8,388	17	33.5	66.5
UK	2,207	9	43.4	56.6

REPUBLIC OF IRELAND: AREA PLANTED BY COILLTE, 1989-97

Year	Area Planted (ha)	Year	Area Planted (ha)
1989	10,062	1994	10,614
1990	10,352	1995	11,734
1991	12,006	1996	10,548
1992	11,513	1997	9,984
1993	11,248		

NORTHERN IRELAND: AREA PLANTED AND REPLANTED, 1992-97

Description	1992-93	1993-94	1994-95	1995-96	1996-97
New Planting	422	365	296	158	140
Replanting	447	451	530	616	503
TOTAL:	869	816	826	774	643

REP. OF IRELAND:FORESTRY STATISTICS, 1996-97

Description	1996	1997
Area Planted (ha)	10,548	9,984
Timber Sold (million m³)	2.19	2.06
Plants Produced (million)	56	53
Forest Roads Built (km)	337	313
Employment	1,162	1,119

N.I: FOREST AND AREA RESOURCES, 1992-97

Description	1992-93	1993-94	1994-95	1995-96	1996-97
Forested Area (000 ha):					
State	61	61	61	61	61
Private	16	17	18	19	20
Total	77	78	79	80	81
Annual Planting Area (ha):					
State	869	816	826	774	643
Private	911	928	624	836	679
Total	1780	1744	1450	1610	1322
Timber Production from State Forests:					
Volume (000m³)³	200	222	222	223	230
Value (£000)	3,022	3,340	5,900	5,000	5,990

REP. OF IRELAND: FORESTRY STATISTICS, 1994-97

Region	1994	1995	1996	1997
Eastern Region:				
Land Planted (ha)	1,087	1,126	1,079	1,111
Timber Sold (m³)	400,000	354,000	340,000	264,127
Southern Region:				
Land Planted (ha)	1,575	1,590	1,614	2,576
Timber Sold (m³)	292,000	367,400	411,000	547,560
Mid-Southern Region:				
Land Planted (ha)	1,858	2,202	1,772	2,012
Timber Sold (m³)	292,000	367,400	411,000	547,560
Western Region:				
Land Planted (ha)	1,717	1,732	1,804	1,458
Timber Sold (m³)	201,000	261,000	245,000	228,216
North-Western Region:				
Land Planted (ha)	1,764	2,478	1,883	1,645
Timber Sold (m³)	293,000	265,000	297,000	290,006
Midlands Region:				
Land Planted (ha)	1,365	1,158	885	1,182
Timber Sold (m³)	256,000	232,000	263,000	255,318

N. IRELAND: AFFORESTATION BY COUNTY, 1997

Category	Antrim	Derry	Down/Armagh	Fermanagh	Tyrone	Total
Forested Area (ha):						
High Forest	10,740	9,466	6,165	18,281	12,564	57,216
Recreation	101	17	101	28	99	346
Amenity	107	121	341	26	220	815
Conservation	212	270	267	1,039	203	1,991
Research	139	27	18	198	69	451
Christmas Trees	13	16	21	9	43	102
Total (ha)	**11,312**	**9,917**	**6,913**	**19,581**	**13,198**	**60,921**
Other Unplanted Area (ha)	2,364	1,683	1,511	5,924	2,279	13,761
Plantable Reserve (ha)	0	5	2	43	75	125
Awaiting Replant (ha)	49	231	17	310	88	695
TOTAL AREA (ha):	**13,725**	**11,836**	**8,443**	**25,858**	**15,640**	**75,502**

NORTHERN IRELAND: PERSONS EMPLOYED IN FORESTRY, 1996/97

Sector	Numbers
Industrial:	
Forest Workers	246
Workshop Staff	18
Others	6
Total Industrial	270
Professional and Technical	77
Administrative (Headquarters)	30
Administrative (District Office)	24
OVERALL TOTAL	**401**

NORTHERN IRELAND: TIMBER PRODUCTION, 1991-97

Production (000m³)	1991-92	1992-93	1993-94	1994-95	1995-96	1996-97
Thinning	22.5	20.8	18.0	21.8	23.1	25.2
Clear Felling	166.0	174.5	191.6	191.4	200.9	200.0
Firewood	4.0	2.5	3.1	1.5	1.9	1.2
Scattered Windthrow	2.7	0.6	0.3	0.4	0.2	0.2
Clear Windthrow	0.8	1.3	9.9	6.8	5.7	4.3
TOTAL:	**196.0**	**199.7**	**222.9**	**221.9**	**231.8**	**230.9**

REPUBLIC OF IRELAND:
COILLTE - TOTAL PLANTATION BY SPECIES 1997

Species	Area Planted (ha)	Species	Area Planted (ha)
Conifers:		**Broadleaves:**	
Sitka Spruce	216,702	Beech	3,445
Lodgepole Pine	67,373	Oak	2,876
Norway Spruce	17,618	Ash	1,967
Larch	8,637	Birch	1,517
Scots Pine	8,624	Other Broadleaves	1,131
Douglas Fur	7,933	Sycamore	533
Other Conifers	5,432	**Total Broadleaves**	**11,469**
Total Conifers	**332,319**		

NORTHERN IRELAND: SPECIES PLANTED, 1992-97

Species (by % planted)	1992-93	1993-94	1994-95	1995-96	1996-97
Sitka Spruce	68	70	74	75	76
Lodgepole Pine	6	4	2	2	1
Larch	13	10	9	7	8
Norway Spruce	2	1	1	1	1
Other Conifers	3	4	3	4	4
Broadleaved Species	8	11	11	11	10
TOTAL:	**100**	**100**	**100**	**100**	**100**

NORTHERN IRELAND:
FORESTRY STATISTICS, 1992-97

Description	1992-93	1993-94	1994-95	1995-96	1996-97
Acquisitions	387	417	144	74	211
Disposals	287	198	124	172	155
Cost of Buying Land (£/ha)	1,307	1,219	1,760	2,739	2,665

FISHERIES

REPUBLIC OF IRELAND: LANDINGS AND VALUE OF SEAFISH AT THE TOP 20 IRISH PORTS, 1997

Rank	Port	County	Live Weight (Tonnes)	Landed Weight (Tonnes)	Value (IR£)
1	Killybegs	Donegal	114,627.7	114,290.0	28,459,524.38
2	Castletownbere	Cork	12,763.3	11,909.0	10,967,408.60
3	Dingle	Kerry	7,946.9	7,200.9	8,120,480.38
4	Howth	Dublin	5,963.9	4,580.6	7,937,852.25
5	Dunmore East	Waterford	10,598.0	10,020.7	5,974,550.22
6	Rossaveal	Galway	9,141.6	8,629.6	4,709,430.72
7	Greencastle	Donegal	4,092.6	3,804.0	4,638,285.81
8	Union Hall	Cork	2,911.8	2,654.4	3,214,247.50
9	Baltimore	Cork	3,509.7	3,406.8	2,737,355.00
10	Kilmore Quay	Wexford	1,625.8	1,481.0	2,629,259.00
11	Rathmullan	Donegal	8,563.7	8,563.7	1,972,376.25
12	Kinsale	Cork	1,614.4	1,444.0	1,808,519.00
13	Cobh	Cork	8,275.5	8,225.7	1,764,505.85
14	Valentia	Kerry	990.2	833.6	1,602,136.55
15	Skerries	Dublin	1,049.6	592.6	1,553,113.70
16	Bantry	Cork	2,945.7	2,905.5	1,551,411.00
17	Burtonport	Donegal	1,477.4	1,428.6	1,546,500.82
18	Clogherhead	Louth	1,039.9	638.4	1,488,167.70
19	Carlingford	Louth	2,670.0	2,670.0	1,353,000.00
20	Dungarvan	Waterford	851.2	851.2	1,288,754.70

REPUBLIC OF IRELAND: AQUACULTURE OUTPUT VALUE, 1986-1996

Year	£ 000s	Tonnes	Year	£ 000s	Tonnes
1986	7,790	12,828	1992	40,600	28,600
1987	15,275	18,626	1993	50,315	30,154
1988	24,885	18,327	1994	48,512	28,615
1989	27,599	21,090	1995	49,274	27,437
1990	29,900	26,560	1996	55,170	34,930
1991	39,316	27,699			

REPUBLIC OF IRELAND: FISH EXPORTS BY PRODUCTION, 1995-96

Product	1995 Value £m	%	1996 Value £m	%
Fish Live / Fresh / Chilled *(excl. fillets)*	59.4	27.9	56.0	22.2
Frozen Fish *(excl. fillets)*	53.8	25.2	67.1	26.5
Shellfish Live / Fresh / Chilled / Frozen	46.3	21.7	50.6	20.0
Fish Fillets Fresh / Chilled / Frozen	24.2	11.4	39.8	15.8
Fish & Shellfish Prepared / Preserved	10.7	5.0	17.6	7.0
Fish Dried Salted / Smoked etc.	9.5	4.5	10.1	4.0
Fish Meal / Oil etc.	9.2	4.3	11.3	4.5
TOTAL:	**213.1**	**100.0**	**252.5**	**100.0**

R. OF IRELAND: VALUE OF FISH EXPORTS, 1996

Country	£m	%
European Union:		
Britain	29.7	11.8
France	53.0	21.0
Germany	25.9	10.3
Italy	12.7	5.0

Continued from previous page

Country	£m	%
Spain	33.9	13.4
Netherlands	8.9	3.5
Northern Ireland	7.1	2.8
Other European Union	8.6	3.4
Total: European Union	179.8	71.2
Non-European Union:		
Japan	23.7	9.4
Lithuania	5.2	2.1
Russia	5.4	2.1
Other Non-European Union	38.4	15.2
Total: Non-European Union	72.7	28.8
TOTAL:	252.5	100.0

REPUBLIC OF IRELAND: GEOGRAPHICAL SPREAD OF EXPORT MARKETS, 1987-96

Country (£000)	1987	1990	1995	1996
European Union:				
Belgium / Luxembourg	2,003	2,149	1,983	2,871
Britain	13,966	10,797	20,972	29,681
Denmark	802	1,125	1,087	879
France	31,043	44,226	45,826	52,994
Germany	11,404	17,132	19,237	25,876
Greece	146	207	579	546
Italy	1,779	8,142	12,530	12,668
Netherlands	6,704	5,059	4,337	8,882
Northern Ireland	7,271	10,385	5,725	7,060
Portugal	64	196	414	713
Spain	8,993	21,026	36,540	33,852
Other European Union	-	-	2,723	3,607
Total	84,175	120,444	151,953	179,629
Non-European Union:				
Japan	18,343	14,965	16,699	23,687
Other Non-European Union	21,422	19,758	44,439	49,147
Total	39,765	34,723	61,138	72,834
TOTAL EXPORTS:	123,940	155,167	213,091	252,463

REPUBLIC OF IRELAND: PERSONS ENGAGED IN SEA FISHING, 1992-96

Personnel	1992	1993	1994	1995	1996
Full-Time	3,280	3,300	3,300	3,200	3,200
Part-Time	4,420	4,400	4,400	4,300	4,300
TOTAL:	7,700	7,700	7,700	7,500	7,500

REPUBLIC OF IRELAND: ALL LANDINGS, 1996-97

	1996 Live Weight (Tonnes)	1996 Landed Weight (Tonnes)	Value (IR£)	1997 Live Weight (Tonnes)	1997 Landed Weight (Tonnes)	Value (IR£)
Wetfish:						
Demersal	46,880.9	42,602.4	50,951,328.16	45,048.3	40,741.3	51,500,027.84
Pelagic	256,901.8	256,901.8	50,410,690.08	216,352.4	216,352.4	46,742,582.33
Shellfish	43,667.5	41,188.1	43,101,889.86	46,538.7	42,835.3	46,534,492.70
TOTAL:	347,450.2	340,692.3	144,463,908.10	307,939.4	299,929.0	144,777,102.87

REPUBLIC OF IRELAND:
FOREIGN LANDINGS BY IRISH VESSELS, 1996-97

	Live Weight (Tonnes)	1996 Landed Weight (Tonnes)	Value (IR£)	Live Weight (Tonnes)	1997 Landed Weight (Tonnes)	Value (IR£)
Wetfish:						
Demersal	3,299.5	3,213.3	4,750,155.00	3,286.5	3,215.8	5,407,686.40
Pelagic	41,020.1	41,020.1	14,889,794.00	63,938.6	63,938.6	12,689,358.80
Shellfish	65.3	64.5	168,300.00	94.8	94.2	269,617.20
TOTAL:	**44,384.9**	**44,297.9**	**19,808,249.00**	**67,319.9**	**67,248.6**	**18,366,662.40**

NORTHERN IRELAND: LIVEWEIGHT
& ESTIMATED VALUE OF FISH LANDED, 1993-96

Species	1993 tonnes	£000	1994 tonnes	£000	1995 tonnes	£000	1996 tonnes	£000
Wet Fish:								
Pelagic	4,247	397	4,096	428	5,680	588	10,667	1,386
Demersal	10,161	8,893	9,859	8,613	7,778	6,758	10,289	8,469
Shellfish	7,194	8,017	6,924	8,968	6,623	8,893	6,894	9,554
TOTAL:	**21,602**	**17,307**	**20,879**	**18,009**	**20,081**	**16,239**	**27,850**	**19,409**

N. IRELAND: LANDED FISH BY PORT, 1993-97

Port	1993	1994	1995	1996	1997
Ardglass:					
Tonnes	6,017	5,845	7,495	8,129	9,442
£000	2,638	2,960	3,131	3,195	4,074
Kilkeel:					
Tonnes	7,753	7,588	6,707	9,341	8,276
£000	7,088	7,368	6,432	8,751	9,199
Portavogie:					
Tonnes	5,919	6,119	5,094	5,451	6,231
£000	5,742	6,312	5,708	5,884	6,903
Other NI Ports:					
Tonnes	1,914	1,327	785	4,929	4,047
£000	1,839	1,369	968	1,579	1,815
Total: Landings at all Ports					
Tonnes	21,603	20,879	20,081	27,850	27,995
£000	17,307	18,009	16,239	19,409	21,992
Total: Landings by NI vessels in NI Ports					
Tonnes	21,103	20,225	19,898	22,189	-
£000	16,543	17,589	16,041	18,260	-

REPUBLIC OF IRELAND: SEA FISH LANDED
BY IRISH VESSELS INTO IRISH PORTS, 1993-96

Species	1993 Quantity (tonnes)	Value (£000)	1994 Quantity (tonnes)	Value (£000)	1995 Quantity (tonnes)	Value (£000)	1996 Quantity (tonnes)	Value (£000)
Wetfish:								
Demersal	33,427	37,719	35,826	38,370	43,428	45,448	44,162	48,246
Pelagic	219,301	31,180	225,851	32,861	305,472	40,306	256,901	50,409
Shellfish	33,962	28,368	33,257	35,096	44,166	40,667	43,666	43,100
GRAND TOTAL:	**286,690**	**97,267**	**294,934**	**106,327**	**393,066**	**126,421**	**344,729**	**141,755**

FISH LANDED BY NORTHERN IRELAND VESSELS OUTSIDE NORTHERN IRELAND, 1992-96

Country	1992	1993	1994	1995	1996
England & Wales:					
Tonnes	1,420	3,217	3,190	5,577	3,405
£000	1,025	1,500	1,137	1,727	1,227
Isle of Man:					
Tonnes	807	773	716	615	693
£000	149	114	125	86	184
Scotland:					
Tonnes	3,892	2,340	1,683	2,380	3,340
£000	1,036	1,127	973	1,809	2,022
Other Countries:					
Tonnes	2,687	2,563	2,366	2,991	3,298
£000	1,609	2,333	2,410	3,144	2,983
Total: All Countries					
Tonnes	8,806	8,893	7,955	11,563	10,736
£000	3,819	5,074	4,645	6,766	6,416

R.O.I: TRENDS OF FISH EXPORTS, 1985-96

Year	£m	Tonnes (000s)
1985	93.8	151.4
1986	94.4	141.5
1987	123.9	182.5
1988	136.7	190.9
1989	145.7	149.7
1990	152.2	168.6
1991	175.2	175.1
1992	175.7	183.6
1993	165.4	210.0
1994	179.8	232.6
1995	203.9	273.1
1996	241.2	269.8

TOURISM

Tourism in Northern Ireland: False Starts and Future Hopes

By Ian Henderson, Chief Executive Northern Ireland Tourist Board

T HE resilience of the tourism industry in Northern Ireland was again tested by the difficult summer of 1998 that culminated in the worst atrocity in thirty years of violence at Omagh.

Our industry has survived three decades of violence and instability and, indeed, from the late 1980s onwards had seen steady growth that peaked in 1995.

The number of false starts we have experienced since the boom of 1995 have led to an overall decline in visitor numbers in the years since, with some markets beginning to recover more quickly than others.

There is no doubt that we will see significant growth again, and the Northern Ireland Tourist Board will be working hard throughout 1999 to boost the confidence of those international tour operators who may have wavered.

The major possibilities that existed at the beginning of 1998 are still there. Indeed, for the first six months of the year, inquiry figures had increased by 10 per cent. While full figures for 1998 are still not available, the tragic events at Omagh and tension during the marching season will undoubtedly have had their effect.

Looking forward to the year ahead, what is clear is that those convinced about the appeal of Northern Ireland's unspoilt scenery, welcoming inhabitants and wide range of things to see and do for the visitor, will be out in the market place working doubly hard to convince the industry across the globe of these facts.

There have been many positive stories to tell the world over the past number of years. The hotel sector has shown phenomenal growth in a short space of time. The Hilton International, Stakis Park and McCausland Hotel projects for 1998 follow a long list of recent arrivals including Jurys, Choice International and Holiday Inn Express, all bringing with them great international marketing influence. The increase of locally owned hotels has also gone a long way to enhancing our tourism product.

Tourist accommodation premises across Northern Ireland have increased by 40% in only four years, while the total number of hotel rooms has increased by 30%. The number of bed and breakfast properties has also grown by 23%.

Following the introduction of the direct Brussels to Belfast service in June there has been growing interest from Belgian tour operators who plan to expand their programmes for 1999. Similarly, the increased frequency of flights between Amsterdam and Belfast has expanded the Northern Ireland content in Dutch programmes.

International access to Northern Ireland was again advanced with the recent announcement that Aer Lingus has extended its number of weekly flights on the New York and Boston to Belfast routes.

The willingness to promote Northern Ireland as a tourist destination exists across the globe and that goodwill must continue to be harnessed. Reassurance that the negative TV pictures are not the sum total of life here is all that most require.

Tourism is poised to grasp all the many opportunities that similar destinations have enjoyed in recent years. Tourism still contributes only 2% of GDP compared with 5 - 6% in Scotland or the Republic of Ireland.

Recommendations from the new strategy for tourism devised by the Northern Ireland Tourist Board are currently shaping most of what we do.

VISITORS TO REPUBLIC OF IRELAND AND EXPENDITURE BY COUNTRY OF ORIGIN, 1995-1997

Country of Origin	1995 Visitors 000s	1995 Expenditure £m	1996 Visitors 000s	1996 Expenditure £m	1997 Visitors 000s	1997 Expenditure £m
Britain	2,285	501.2	2,590	574.0	2,850	690.9
Mainland Europe:						
Germany	319	122.4	339	148.9	303	121.8
France	234	83.8	262	88.1	250	89.1
Italy	112	42.4	119	53.5	111	50.9
Netherlands	94	-	109	35.4	131	44.0
Belgium / Luxembourg	53	-	60	-	73	-
Spain	67	-	66	-	71	-
Denmark	22	-	23	-	28	-
Norway / Sweden	46	-	55	-	60	-
Switzerland	62	-	62	-	58	-
Other Europe	93	1,65.1	83	140.7	85	151.9
Total	1,102	4,13.7	1,178	466.6	1,170	457.7
North America:						
USA	587	*	660	*	718	n/a
Canada	54	*	69	*	60	n/a
Total	641	275.0	729	316.6	778	348.2
Rest of World:						
Australia / New Zealand	89	-	88	-	107	-
Japan	30	-	33	-	36	-
Other	85	96.5	65	93.8	71	99.7
Total	204	96.5	186	93.8	214	99.7
TOTAL:	4,232	1,286.4	4,683	1,451.0	5,012	1,596.5
Northern Ireland	590	82.6	600	85.0	550	101.0
Total incl. N. Ireland	4,822	-	5,283	-	5,562	-
Excursionist Revenue	-	8.0	-	8.0	-	14.5
Carrier Receipts	-	302.0	-	345.0	-	400.0
Total	-	1,679.0	-	1,889.0	-	2,112.0
Domestic Trips	6,924	610.9	6,170	578.8	6,850	670.8
Total Expenditure		2,289.9		2,467.8		2,782.8

VISITORS TO N. IRELAND BY COUNTRY, 1995-1997

Country of Origin	1995 Visitors 000s	1995 Expenditure £m	1996 Visitors 000s	1996 Expenditure £m	1997 Visitors 000s	1997 Expenditure £m
Britain:						
England & Wales	603	84.5	604	85.5	585	87.0
Scotland	207	23.5	221	25.5	214	26.0
Total	810	108.0	825	110.0	799	113.0

Country of Origin	1995 Visitors 000s	Expenditure £m	1996 Visitors 000s	Expenditure £m	1997 Visitors 000s	Expenditure £m
Europe:						
France	n/a	n/a	19	n/a	17	n/a
Germany	n/a	n/a	32	n/a	30	n/a
Holland	n/a	n/a	10	n/a	12	n/a
Italy	n/a	n/a	8	n/a	10	n/a
Other	n/a	n/a	27	n/a	36	n/a
Total	109	23.0	96	22.0	105	21.0
North America:						
USA	n/a	n/a	72	n/a	85	23.2
Canada	n/a	n/a	28	n/a	24	7.8
Total	118	26.0	100	29.0	109	31.0
Australia / New Zealand	n/a	n/a	29	n/a	39	9.0
Republic of Ireland	470	39.0	370	30.0	345	27.0
Other	50	18.0	15	15.0	18	7.0
TOTAL:	1,557	214.0	1,435	206.0	1,415	208.0

REPUBLIC OF IRELAND & NORTHERN IRELAND: TOURISTS CLASSIFIED BY ACCOMMODATION, 1997

Accommodation	Republic of Ireland (million nights)	Accommodation	Northern Ireland (million nights)
Hotels	5.1	Hotels	0.9
Guesthouses / B&Bs	8.1	Guesthouses / B&Bs	0.7
Rented	6.4	Rented	0.5
Caravan & Camping	1.7	Caravan & Camping	0.1
Friends / Relatives	14.1	Friends & Relatives	5.0
Other	7.2	Other	0.5
Total:	42.6	Total:	7.5

REPUBLIC OF IRELAND & NORTHERN IRELAND: ACCOMMODATION EXPENSES*

Type of Accommodation price range for a one-night stay	Republic of Ireland £	Northern Ireland £
Hotel (4/5 star)	46-185	52-165
Hotel (2 star)	24-95	25-96
Guest House	14-95	19-69

* approximate

REPUBLIC OF IRELAND: DESTINATION AND EXPENDITURE BY REGION, 1997

Region	Total Visitors 000s	£m	Overseas Visitors 000s	£m	Home Visitors 000s	£m	Northern Ireland Visitors 000s	£m
Dublin	3,685	567.4	2,586	476.4	989	77.0	110	14.0
Midlands / East	1,686	229.4	783	151.7	863	73.4	40	4.3
North-West	1,479	232.1	551	111.0	638	73.3	290	47.8
Shannon	1,857	283.7	1,010	188.1	827	91.8	20	3.8
South-East	2,107	243.8	854	137.6	1,243	104.8	10	1.4
South-West	2,834	467.9	1,499	309.9	1,315	149.6	20	8.4
West	2,297	344.0	1,134	221.8	1,073	100.9	90	21.3
TOTAL:	15,945	2,368.3	8,417	1,596.5	6,948	670.8	580	101.0

REPUBLIC OF IRELAND: VISITORS BY REASON FOR JOURNEY & BY COUNTRY OF ORIGIN, 1993-97

Country / Reason	1993 000s	1994 000s	1995 000s	1996 000s	1997 000s
County:					
Britain	1,887	2,087	2,365	2,698	3,025
Europe	924	970	1,085	1,164	1,175
USA and Canada	406	474	617	703	764
Other	116	150	190	174	201
TOTAL:	**3,333**	**3,681**	**4,257**	**4,739**	**5,165**
Reason:					
Business	497	547	597	757	785
Holiday	1,622	1,807	2,314	2,466	2,768
Visiting	980	1,031	1,014	1,139	1,231
Other	233	297	332	376	380
TOTAL:	**3,332**	**3,682**	**4,257**	**4,738**	**5,164**

VISITORS TO NORTHERN IRELAND BY REASON FOR JOURNEY & COUNTRY OF ORIGIN, 1997

Country	Business 000s	Holiday 000s	Visiting* 000s	Other 000s	Total 000s
Britain:					
England & Wales	227	37	305	16	585
Scotland	68	28	107	11	214
Total	295	65	412	27	799
Europe:					
France	2	9	3	3	17
Germany	3	15	8	4	30
Holland	2	5	3	2	12
Italy	2	6	2	1	11
Other	13	10	9	4	36
Total	22	45	25	14	106
North America:					
USA	11	37	29	8	85
Canada	2	7	14	1	24
Total	13	44	43	9	109
Australia / New Zealand	2	24	12	1	39
Other	3	4	9	1	17
Republic of Ireland	84	80	76	105	345
TOTAL:	**419**	**262**	**577**	**157**	**1,415**

* friends / relatives

VISITS ABROAD BY RESIDENTS FROM REPUBLIC OF IRELAND, 1995-97

Category	1995 Visits 000s	1995 Expenditure £m	1996 Visits 000s	1996 Expenditure £m	1997 Visits 000s	1997 Expenditure £m
Route of Travel:						
Air	1,200	621	1,398	725	1,570	793
Sea	512	169	458	133	491	145
Continental	689	468	725	501	830	567
Transatlantic	146	155	153	163	161	178
Total	2,547	1,413	2,734	1,522	3,052	1,683
Cross Border Visits	465	83	431	85	432	82
Total: Expenditure	-	1,496	-	1,607	-	1,765
Payments*	-	230	-	235	-	298
Total	-	1,266	-	1,372	-	1,467

Continued from previous page

Category	1995		1996		1997	
	Visits 000s	Expenditure £m	Visits 000s	Expenditure £m	Visits 000s	Expenditure £m
Reason for Journey:						
Business	451	326	551	393	530	357
Holiday	1,176	655	1,182	680	1,299	752
Visiting†	635	256	721	286	864	358
Other	285	176	278	162	360	216
Total	2,547	1,413	2,732	1,521	3,053	1,683

* passenger fares by Irish visitors abroad to Irish carriers † visiting friends and relatives

REPUBLIC OF IRELAND & NORTHERN IRELAND: MOST POPULAR VISITOR ATTRACTIONS, 1997

Republic of Ireland* (1997)		Northern Ireland (1997)	
Attraction *(County)*	**Attendance**	**Attraction**	**Attendance**
Brú na Bóinne (Meath)	220,300	Botanic Gardens (Belfast)	680,000
Rock of Cashel (Tipperary)	218,080	Cave Hill Country Park (Belfast)	390,000
Muckross House (Kerry)	214,402	Giant's Causeway Visitor Centre (Antrim)	378,481
Kilkenny Castle (Kilkenny)	161,372	Belvoir Park Forest (Belfast)	360,000
Clonmacnoise (Offaly)	142,765	Ulster Museum (Belfast)	328,823
Glendalough Visitor Centre (Wicklow)	112,504	Sir Thomas & Lady Dixon Park (Belfast)	300,000
Kilmainham Gaol (Dublin)	107,129	Pickie Family Fun Park (Down)	250,000
Glenveagh National Park (Donegal)	84,769	Belfast Zoo (Belfast)	206,362
Connemara National Park (Galway)	82,027	Tollymore Forest Park (Down)	203,800
Illnacullin - Garinish Island (Cork)	79,097	Ulster Folk & Transport Museum (Down)	203,501
Cahir Castle (Tipperary)	65,456	Scrabo Country Park (Down)	200,000
John F. Kennedy Park (Wexford)	61,924	Belleek Pottery (Fermanagh)	177,824
Céide Fields (Mayo)	40,156	Oxford Island Nature Reserve (Armagh)	155,000
Glenveagh Castle (Donegal)	39,948	Castlewellan Forest Park (Down)	140,000
Ionad an Bhlascaoid (Kerry)	39,646	Murlough Nature Reserve (Down)	134,000
Charles Fort (Cork)	35,362	Portstewart Strand (Derry)	133,080
Jerpoint Abbey (Kilkenny)	34,120	Exploris (Down)	130,000
Dunmore Cave (Kilkenny)	32,488	Carnfunnock Country Park (Antrim)	127,326
Donegal Castle (Donegal)	32,145	Roe Valley Country Park (Derry)	126,000
Parkes's Castle (Leitrim)	28,526	Gosford Forest Park (Armagh)	123,700

* Dúchas Heritage Sites only

REPUBLIC OF IRELAND & NORTHERN IRELAND: BEST KEPT TOWNS COMPETITION, 1998

The Best Kept Towns Competition is a joint venture organised by the Department of the Environment in the Republic of Ireland and the Amenity Councils in Northern Ireland. Results were announced by the two Ministers for the Environment, Noel Dempsey TD and Lord Dubs, in July 1998.

Title	Winner
Ireland's Best Kept Town	Loughgall (*Co. Antrim*)
Ireland's Best Kept Village	Loughgall (*Co. Antrim*)
Best Kept Small Town	Adare (*Co. Limerick*)
Best Kept Large Town	Enniskillen (*Co. Fermanagh*)

REPUBLIC OF IRELAND: TIDY TOWN AWARDS, 1998

The Tidy Town Awards were announced in Dublin Castle by the Minister for the Environment, Noel Dempsey TD, in September 1998.

Title	Winner
National Award Winner	Ardagh (*Co. Longford*)
Ireland's Tidiest Village	Ardagh (*Co. Longford*)
Ireland's Tidiest Small Town	Clonakilty (*Co. Cork*)
Ireland's Tidiest Large Town	Kilkenny (*Co. Kilkenny*)
40th Anniversary Special Award	Ennis (*Co. Clare*)

TIDY TOWN/VILLAGE AWARDS IN EACH COUNTY

County	Winner (Runners-up)	County	Winner (Runners-up)
Carlow	Rathvilly (Leighlinbridge, Ardattin)	Longford	Ardagh (Newtowncashel, Kenagh)
Cavan	Loch Gowna (Buttlersbridge, Cavan)	Louth	Tallanstown (Knockbridge, Greenore)
Clare	Mountshannon (Ennis, Kilkee)	Mayo	Westport (Belcarra, Aughagower)
Cork	Clonakilty (Rathbarry, Eyeries)	Meath	Moynalty (Slane, Trim)
Donegal	Malin (Dunfanaghy, Glenties)	Monaghan	Carrickmacross (Glaslough, Milltown)
Dublin	Skerries (Malahide, Rathcoole)	Offaly	Clonbullogue (Geashill, Tullamore)
Galway	Milltown (Mountbellew, Portumna)	Roscommon	Keadue (Cloontuskert, Ballintubber)
Kerry	Kenmare (Sneem, Killarney)	Sligo	Coolaney (Riverstown, Easkey)
Kildare	Kill (Johnstown, Narraghmore)	Tipperary NR	Terryglass (Garrykennedy, Silvermines)
Kilkenny	Kilkenny (Inistioge, Bennettsbridge)	Tipperary SR	Rossadrehid (Kilsheelan, Ballyporeen)
Laois	Castletown (Ballacolla, Errill)	Waterford	Stradbally (Lismore, Ardmore)
Leitrim	Dromod (Carrick-on-Shannon, Ballinamore)	Westmeath	Tyrrellspass (Finea, Glasson Village)
Limerick	Adare (Galbally, Athea Village)	Wexford	Blackwater (Ballymurn, Enniscorthy)
		Wicklow	Aughrim (Stratford-on-Slaney, Bray)

REPUBLIC OF IRELAND & NORTHERN IRELAND: BLUE FLAG BEACHES, 1998

Blue Flag Beach Awards are administered by the local authorities in association with An Taisce in the Republic of Ireland and with the Seaside Award Office - Tidy Britain Group (Norwich, England) - in Northern Ireland, following criteria set by the EU. The 1998 Blue Flag awards were presented to 74 beaches and 4 marinas in the Republic of Ireland and 7 beaches in Northern Ireland.

Antrim - 3 Blue Flag Beaches

Ballycastle, Portrush East Strand, Portstewart West Stand.

Clare - 6 Blue Flag Beaches*

Cappa Pier, Fanore, Lahinch, White Strand - Milltown Malbay, Mountshannon Marina, Kilrush Creek Marina.

Cork - 9 Blue Flag Beaches**

Claycastle - Youghal, Front Strand - Youghal, Garrylucas, Inchydoney, Garryvoe, Ownahincha, Tragumna, Warren Beach, Kinsale Yacht Club Marina.

Derry - 2 Blue Flag Beaches

Benone Strand, Portstewart Strand.

Donegal - 10 Blue Flag Beaches

Bundoran, Culdaff, Downings, Fintra, Lisfannon, Marble Hill, Murvagh, Portnoo / Naran, Portsalon, Rossnowlagh.

Down - 2 Blue Flag Beaches

Cranfield, Tyrella.

Dublin - 3 Blue Flag Beaches

Donabate, Killiney, Seapoint.

Galway - 7 Blue Flag Beaches

Cill Mhuirbthigh Aran, Traught Kinvara, Loughrea, Silver Strand, An Spideal - Trá na mBan, An Trá Mór - Caol Rua, Trá an Doilín - An Cheatru Rua.

Kerry - 12 Blue Flag Beaches

Ballinskelligs, Ballybunion North & South, Ballyheigue, Banna, Derrynane, Fenit, Inch, Kells, Magherabeg, Rossbeigh, Ventry, White Strand - Caherciveen.

Louth - 2 Blue Flag Beaches

Clogherhead, Shelling Hill - Templetown.

Mayo - 13 Blue Flag Beaches

Bertra, Carrowmore, Clare Island, Dooega, Dugort - Achill Island, Elly Bay - Belmullet, Golden Strand - Achill Island, Keel - Achill Island, Keem - Achill Island, Mullaghroe - Belmullet, Mulranny, Old Head, Ross.

Sligo - 3 Blue Flag Beaches

Enniscrone, Mullaghmore, Rosses Point.

Waterford - 3 Blue Flag Beaches

Bonmahon, Clonea, Counsellor's Strand - Dunmore East.

Westmeath - 2 Blue Flag Beaches

The Cut - Lough Lene, Lilliput - Lough Ennell.

Wexford - 4 Blue Flag Beaches**

Courtown, Curracloe, Duncannon, Rosslare, Kilmore Quay Marina.

Wicklow - 3 Blue Flag Beaches

Brittas Bay North, Brittas Bay South, Greystones.

*includes 2 marinas **includes 1 marina

HEALTH

Information Technology and Health

*By **Professor Jane Grimpson**, Trinity College, Dublin*

WE are now in the Information Age, thanks largely to the phenomenal developments in Information Technology and Telecommunications. In 1945, Thomas J. Watson, founder of IBM, predicted that there would be a world market for 15 computers; today it is estimated that there are over 200 million computers across the world connected to the Internet alone. The technology is ubiquitously supporting all sectors of the economy and is bringing with it major changes in they way we live and work.

Healthcare is an information-intensive industry generating enormous volumes of information every day in hospitals, GP surgeries, clinics and laboratories. Yet much of this data continues to be processed manually, in spite of decades of experience in the successful application of Information and Communications Technology (ICT) in other information intensive industries, such as banking and insurance. We take for granted the ability to be able to withdraw money from an Automatic Teller Machine located virtually anywhere in the world and are confident that our bank account back home will be securely, correctly and all too quickly debited.

Health has lagged behind other sectors in its use of ICT for many reasons, in particular, concerns about the security and confidentiality of patient data as well the complex nature of medical data itself. However, as these challenges are overcome, the health sector will catch up and the exploitation of ICT will bring with it major changes in the healthcare delivery system for both patients and healthcare professionals.

As one of the largest consumers of public funds, Health plays a major role in economic policy throughout the world. The major objectives of western governments in the health sector today are twofold - efficiency and effectiveness - with improved quality of care at the same or reduced cost. The application of Information and Communications Technology to medicine is no longer viewed as a peripheral issue but rather as a central means of achieving these ends.

At the same time, the delivery of healthcare today is undergoing a major change throughout the world. The provision of healthcare to an individual patient is no longer the sole responsibility of a single health professional, but rather is shifting to a team-based, or shared-care approach. Under shared-care, the patientís healthcare is managed by a group of health professionals representing all sectors, including primary, secondary and tertiary, all collaborating together. Such seamless healthcare depends crucially on the ability to share information efficiently between care providers.

Essentially, what is required is that everyone involved in the provision of healthcare to an individual patient has access to all the relevant information about that patient, i.e. the health care record. Ensuring that carers have the right information in the right place and at the right time is the key to providing better and more cost-effective healthcare.

These developments are taking place against a background of increasing computerisation throughout the healthcare domain, which has resulted in a diversity of heterogeneous, autonomous information systems, all containing patient-related health. These islands of information fail to communicate with each other, resulting in unnecessary duplication of tests, the retaking of a patient's history and, ultimately, a delay in delivering the appropriate care to the patient.

The technology is now sufficiently mature to be able to address the challenges of healthcare and to ensure the security and confidentiality of patient data. There have already been a number of successful pilot projects in Ireland, many of which have been funded by the European Union.

For example, as part of the Cardlink project, smartcards have been issued to 2000 patients in Bray, Co. Wicklow. The immediate availability of personal and medical information in cases of medical emergency helps to eliminate unnecessary clinical investigative procedures. The record will be electronically stored in a secure form on the smart card and may be accessed and updated by general practitioners, hospital specialists, pharmacists and authorised administrative staff. The card contains basic identification information about the patient together with key medical data, including allergies, vaccination and prescription information, major diagnoses and treatments. Today many people with life-threatening allergies wear special bracelets. In the future, it is likely that these patients and others suffering from chronic disease such as diabetes, for example, will carry a smart card containing key medical data about their condition and treatment.

Another project, Synapses, is developing the technology to allow healthcare professionals to share patient records and related data simply, consistently, comprehensively and securely. The ability to share information is a key factor in achieving integrated healthcare. Without it, patients are subjected to unnecessary repetitions of laboratory tests and other investigations, as well as being asked to repeat their personal information and medical history to each member of the healthcare team. This duplication of effort wastes resources, is frustrating to the healthcare professionals who waste valuable time trying to locate test results, patient charts, X-rays, and so on, and ultimately delays treatment.

A third project is aimed at raising the awareness among health professionals of the potential benefits from the appropriate application of Information and Communications Technology. In Ireland, we are perhaps fortunate in that we have not gone too far down the road in some respects as far as ICT in health is concerned so we are in a good position to benefit from experiences elsewhere and not to make the same mistakes. However, it is clearly accepted now that delivering the benefits promised by ICT depends crucially on the active involvement of users and the healthcare professionals themselves. It is they who should drive the exploitation of the technology and should determine how it should be used in health. However, if users are to get involved, then they need to understand both the potential benefits and the potential risks associated with the technology, and it is these sort of issues which the Awareness Programme is addressing. The Programme also seeks to enhance the visibility of the many success stories both in Ireland and elsewhere in Europe

The European model of Citizen-Centred-Care, where the informed citizen takes responsibility for his/her health and in which reliable services are accessible to all through a fully integrated health service is the way of the future. Information technology is the catalyst for this change. While the early applications of ICT in health sought to support administrative and business functions such as payroll, stock control, finance and budgeting, the emphasis now is much more on supporting clinical functions and the actual delivery of healthcare to the patient. The aim is to support healthcare professionals in the delivery of patient care, ensuring that they always have access to the relevant information about the patient when and where they need it. The result will be to improve the efficiency and effectiveness of healthcare delivery to the benefit of patients and health professionals alike.

The author is Dean of Engineering and System Sciences in TCD and is an expert in the field of Health Informatics.

REPUBLIC OF IRELAND: HEALTH BOARDS

EASTERN HEALTH BOARD - *(covers Dublin City and County, Co. Kildare & Co. Wicklow)*. Dr. Steevens Hospital, John's Road, Dublin 8. Tel. (01) 6790700.

MIDLAND HEALTH BOARD - *(covers Co. Laois, Co. Longford, Co. Offaly, Co. Westmeath)*. Arden Road, Tullamore, Co. Offaly. Tel. (0506) 21868.

MID-WESTERN HEALTH BOARD - *(covers Co. Clare, Limerick City and County, Co. Tipperary - North Riding)*. 31-33 Catherine Street, Limerick. Tel. (061) 316655.

SOUTH-EASTERN HEALTH BOARD - *(covers Co. Carlow, Co. Kilkenny, Co. Tipperary - South Riding, Co. Waterford, Co. Wexford)*. Lacken, Dublin Road, Kilkenny. Tel. (056) 51702.

NORTH-EASTERN HEALTH BOARD - *(covers Co. Cavan, Co. Louth, Co. Meath, Co. Monaghan)*. Navan Road, Kells, Co. Meath. Tel. (046) 40341.

NORTH-WESTERN HEALTH BOARD - *(covers Co. Donegal, Co. Leitrim, Co. Sligo)*. Manorhamilton, Co. Leitrim. Tel. (072) 55123.

SOUTHERN HEALTH BOARD - *(covers Cork City and County, Co. Kerry)*. Cork Farm Centre, Dennehy's Cross, Wilton Road, Cork. Tel. (021) 545011.

WESTERN HEALTH BOARD - *(covers Co. Galway, Co. Mayo, Co. Roscommon)*. Merlin Park Regional Hospital, Galway. Tel. (091) 751131.

NORTHERN IRELAND: HEALTH BOARDS

EASTERN HEALTH & SOCIAL SERVICES BOARD - Champion House, Linenhall Street, Belfast, Co. Antrim. Tel. (01232) 321313.

SOUTHERN HEALTH & SOCIAL SERVICES BOARD - 20 Seagoe Industrial Area, Portadown, Co. Armagh. Tel. (01762) 336611.

NORTHERN HEALTH & SOCIAL SERVICES BOARD - County Hall, Ballymena, Co. Antrim. Tel. (01266) 653333.

WESTERN HEALTH & SOCIAL SERVICES BOARD - 15 Gransha Park, Campsie, Co. Derry. Tel. (01504) 860086.

R.O.I: HEALTH PERSONNEL, 1996-97

Hospital Consultants	Numbers Practising	
	1996	1997
Accident & Emergency	14	14
Anaesthetics	176	191
ENT Surgery	27	28
General Surgery	134	135
Medicine	188	202
Obstetrics/Gynaecology	77	75
Ophthalmic Surgery	28	27
Orthopaedic Surgery	53	51
Paediatrics	60	64
Pathology	87	89
Psychiatry	168	167
Radiology	93	98
TOTAL:	**1,105**	**1,141**

R.O.I: HEALTH PERSONNEL, 1996-97

Hospital Consultants	Numbers Practising	
	1996	1997
Eastern Health Board	541	555
Midland Health Board	50	49
Mid-Western Health Board	66	69
North-Eastern Health Board	59	64
North-Western Health Board	56	60
South-Eastern Health Board	85	92
Southern Health Board	141	140
Western Health Board	107	112
TOTAL:	**1,105**	**1,141**

NORTHERN IRELAND: HOSPITAL-BASED STAFF

(March 1997) HSS Trust	Medical & Dental	Profess. & Technical	Nursing & Midwifery	Social Services	Admin. & Clerical	Ancillary & General	Works & Maint.	Total
Altnagelvin Group	166	147	715	1	186	65	0	1,280
Armagh & Dungannon	71	106	904	7	136	126	37	1,387
Belfast City Hospital	299	286	1,505	0	370	404	44	2,908
Causeway	92	111	567	1	131	184	0	1,086
Craigavon Area Hospital	163	102	864	8	151	46	30	1,364
Craigavon & Banbridge	9	6	88	0	17	0	0	120
Down / Lisburn	130	113	784	1	117	27	21	1,193
Foyle Community	5	26	418	12	22	11	0	494
Green Park Healthcare	68	198	915	0	205	12	37	1,435
Homefirst Community	40	35	300	1	53	71	0	500
Mater Infirmorum Hospital	73	84	350	0	146	139	16	808
Newry & Mourne	63	55	342	1	99	157	22	739
North & West Belfast	14	24	518	29	52	177	22	836
Royal Group of Hospitals	542	430	2,071	3	800	804	72	4,722
South & East Belfast	34	48	341	7	58	131	29	648
Sperrin Lakeland	90	107	962	0	158	163	0	1,480
Ulster, North Down & Ards	218	288	1,303	2	332	362	56	2,561
United Hospitals Group	209	271	1,436	0	438	488	91	2,933
TOTAL:	2,286	2,437	14,383	73	3,471	3,367	477	26,494

NORTHERN IRELAND: COMMUNITY-BASED STAFF

(March 1997) HSS Trust	Medical & Dental	Nursing & Midwifery	Social Services	Profession & Technical	Admin. & Clerical	Ancillary & General	Total
Armagh & Dungannon	26	207	134	57	100	88	612
Causeway	7	136	160	64	229	818	1,414
Craigavon & Banbridge	9	230	848	54	148	152	1,441
Down / Lisburn	18	302	344	89	203	267	1,223
Foyle	38	287	288	64	249	978	1,904
Homefirst	39	437	587	180	559	561	2,363
Newry & Mourne	11	146	176	41	100	131	605
North Down & Ards	14	265	397	92	180	334	1,282
North & West Belfast	42	271	462	120	206	392	1,493
South & East Belfast	17	558	524	139	279	473	1,990
Sperrin Lakeland	30	269	246	62	135	1,186	1,928
TOTAL:	251	3,108	4,166	962	2,388	5,380	16,255

R.O.I: HOSPITAL STATISTICS, 1995

Health Board	No. of Hospitals	Average In-beds Available	In-patients discharged / deaths	Average length of stay (days)	Average day beds available	Day Cases	Psychiatric Patients
Eastern	25	4,951	189,107	7.7	314	125,578	1,349
Midland	3	474	26,530	5.5	24	5,889	400
Mid-Western	6	784	40,739	6.1	47	13,872	483
North-Eastern	5	898	38,901	6.4	31	7,491	314
North-Western	3	668	34,653	5.3	15	15,016	268
South-Eastern	7	1,129	56,427	5.4	37	11,671	920
Southern	9	1,793	84,038	6.3	50	16,399	912
Western	5	1,256	58,423	6.4	25	11,332	702
TOTAL:	63	11,953	528,818	6.6	543	207,248	5,348

NORTHERN IRELAND: HOSPITAL STATISTICS, 1996

Trust	Hospitals	Average Beds Available
Altnagelvin Group HSS Trust	5	652
Armagh & Dungannon HSS Trust	7	726
Belfast City Hospital HSS Trust	3	767
Causeway HSS Trust	6	360
Craigavon Area Hospital HSS Trust	3	562
Craigavon & Banbridge Community HSS Trust	1	80
Down Lisburn HSS Trust	5	744
Foyle Community HSS Trust	2	247
Green Park Healthcare HSS Trust	4	550
Homefirst Community HSS Trust	2	390
Mater Infirmorum Hospital HSS Trust	1	215
Newry & Mourne HSS Trust	2	346
North & West Belfast HSS Trust	1	551
Royal Group of Hospitals HSS Trust	3	984
South & East Belfast HSS Trust	3	456
Sperrin Lakeland HSS Trust	5	720
Ulster, North Down & Ards Hospital HSS Trust	3	780
United Hospitals Group HSS Trust	5	925
TOTAL:	**61**	**10,055**

N. IRELAND: HOSPITAL STATISTICS, 1994-97

Programme of Care	Available Beds			Discharges		
	1994-95	1995-96	1996-97	1994-95	1995-96	1996-97
Acute Services	4,813	4,692	4,454	224,830	227,440	220,143
Maternity and Child Health	849	865	859	48,003	50,933	54,630
Elderly Care	2,340	2,137	1,931	14,168	14,164	13,758
Mental Health	1,495	1,521	1,447	8,352	9,095	9,260
Learning Disabilities	860	840	785	2,476	2,443	2,597
Day Cases	-	-	-	90,823	95,841	97,508
TOTAL:	**10,357**	**10,055**	**9,476**	**388,652**	**399,916**	**397,896**

REPUBLIC OF IRELAND & NORTHERN IRELAND: CAUSES OF DEATHS, 1994-96

Cause	Republic of Ireland			Northern Ireland		
	1994	1995	1996	1994	1995	1996
Blood Diseases	58	81	72	29	29	-
Circulatory System Diseases	14,067	13,963	13,949	7,011	6,929	6,633
Congenital Anomalies	199	184	151	145	168	-
Digestive System Diseases	313	281	268	424	449	-
Genitourinary Tract Diseases	407	420	440	250	251	-
Infectious & Parasitic Diseases	170	172	155	39	44	-
Injury & Poisoning	1,329	1,378	1,345	688	463	-
Malignant Neoplasms	7,362	7,492	7,306	3,595	3,491	3,623
Nervous System Diseases	13	2	12	278	302	-
Nutritional Deficiencies	363	377	416	144	180	-
Perinatal Conditions	102	128	113	69	93	-
Respiratory System Diseases	2,388	2,676	2,713	2,398	2,656	2,749
Other	4,105	4,491	4,574	44	55	2,213
TOTAL:	**30,876**	**31,645**	**31,514**	**15,114**	**15,110**	**15,218**

REPUBLIC OF IRELAND: INFANT MORTALITY RATES, 1993-96

Year (per 1,000 births)	Under 1 year of age	Under 4 weeks of age
1993	6	4
1994	6	4
1995	6	5
1996	6	4

NORTHERN IRELAND: INFANT MORTALITY, 1993-96

Description	1993	1994	1995	1996
Numbers:				
Infant Deaths *(under 1 year of age)*	176	147	169	142
Perinatal Deaths *(still births and under 1 week)*	220	236	250	232
Rates:				
Infant Deaths *(under 1 year of age)*	7*	6*	7*	6*
Perinatal Deaths *(still births and under 1 week)*	9†	10†	10†	9†

* per 1,000 live births; † per 1,000 live and still births

REPUBLIC OF IRELAND: INCOME & EXPENDITURE ON HEALTH SERVICES, 1993-96

Programme / Service	1993	1994	1995	1996
Community Protection	36,631	40,232	48,218	54,738
Community Health Services	343,142	371,626	405,948	434,048
Community Welfare	177,616	200,729	180,217	133,377
Psychiatric Service	209,381	215,850	227,852	233,199
Handicapped Service	202,203	222,756	257,742	267,519
General Hospital	1,097,451	1,146,609	1,226,510	1,276,548
General Support	94,144	92,856	99,231	107,586
Total: *(gross)*	2,160,568	2,290,658	2,445,718	2,507,015
Income	143,966	144,900	146,737	152,710
TOTAL: *(net)*	2,016,602	2,145,758	2,298,981	2,354,305

NORTHERN IRELAND: EXPENDITURE ON MEDICAL SERVICES, 1992-97

Payments to Doctors under Health Service:	1992-93	1993-94	1994-95	1995-96	1996-97
Expenditure (£000)	56,529	60,975	62,849	65,130	67,872
Receipts (£000)	251	996	1,107	1,105	1,139
TOTAL:	56,278	59,979	61,742	64,025	66,733

NORTHERN IRELAND: EXPENDITURE ON HEALTH SERVICES, 1992-97

Description	1992	1993	1994	1995-96	1996-97
Dental Services:					
Dental Estimates Paid:					
Gross Cost *(£000)*	47,701	43,904	46,318	48,780	51,512
Amount Paid by Patients *(£000)*	11,036	10,378	11,231	11,530	11,870
Total: Dental Estimates Paid	36,665	33,526	35,087	37,250	39,642
Ophthalmic Services (£000)	5,555	7,363	7,127	8,568	9,555
Pharmaceutical Services (£m)	141.343	159.463	166.764	191.324	213.95

N. IRELAND: ACCIDENT STATISTICS, 1993-97

Accidents	1993	1994	1995	1996	1997
Fire:					
Fatal	21	36	26	14	33
Non-Fatal	710	685	598	858	807
Total	731	721	624	872	840
Road:					
Fatal	53	61	52	62	60
Non-Fatal	1123	1148	1012	1282	1288
Total	1176	1209	1064	1344	1348
Other:					
Fatal	20	13	22	14	16
Non-Fatal	434	467	463	548	597
Total	454	480	485	562	613

R.O.I: ACCIDENT STATISTICS, 1993-96

Accidents	1993	1994	1995	1996
Factory:				
Fatal	30	23	28	34
Non-Fatal	2,888	3,413	3,252	3,510
Total: Factory	2,918	3,436	3,280	3,544
Railway:				
Fatal	3	11	7	8
Non-Fatal	6	7	8	7
Total: Railway	9	18	15	15
Road Traffic:				
Fatal	394	371	405	415
Total: Road Traffic	394	371	405	415
Shipping:				
Casualties on Board	35	74	39	51
Lives Saved	6	26	10	14
Casualties - no assistance	27	44	16	26
Lives Lost	2	4	13	11
Total: Shipping	70	148	78	102

NORTHERN IRELAND: ROAD ACCIDENTS, 1987-97

Year	Total Accidents	Killed	Seriously Injured	Slightly Injured	Total Casualties
1987	6,344	214	1,885	7,837	9,936
1988	6,943	178	1,969	8,820	10,967
1989	7,199	181	2,014	9,416	11,611
1990	7,159	185	1,993	9,583	11,761
1991	6,171	185	1,648	8,481	10,314
1992	6,650	150	1,841	9,273	11,264
1993	6,517	143	1,725	9,232	11,100
1994	6,783	157	1,648	10,289	12,094
1995	6,792	144	1,532	10,049	11,725
1996	7,093	142	1,599	10,834	12,575
1997	7,192	144	1,548	11,008	12,698

REP. OF IRELAND: ROAD ACCIDENTS, 1987-97

Year	Total Accidents	Persons Killed	Persons Injured	Total Casualties
1987	19,177	462	8,409	8,871
1988	19,436	463	8,437	8,900
1989	19,338	460	8,803	9,263
1990	19,926	478	9,429	9,907
1991	22,589	445	9,874	10,319
1992	22,674	415	10,188	10,603
1993	21,831	431	9,831	10,262
1994	22,737	404	10,229	10,633
1995	27,942	437	12,673	13,110
1996	30,348	453	13,319	13,772
1997	-	472	10,350	10,822
1998 *(Provisional- to September 31st)*	-	340	-	-

REPUBLIC OF IRELAND:
ROAD ACCIDENTS BY ROAD USER TYPE, 1993-96

Road User Type	1993	1994	1995	1996	1997
Pedestrians	136	121	113	115	-
Pedal Cyclists	24	26	28	22	-
Motor Cyclists	53	55	57	58	-
Car Users	187	178	193	218	-
Other	31	24	46	40	-
TOTAL:	431	404	437	453	-

NORTHERN IRELAND:
ROAD ACCIDENTS BY ROAD USER TYPE, 1993-97

Road User Type	1993	1994	1995	1996	1997
Motor Vehicle Drivers	5,053	5,505	5,448	5,883	5,965
Motor Cyclists	250	247	248	216	273
Pedal Cyclists	282	312	385	359	339
Pedestrians	1,275	1,271	1,229	1,256	1,202
Pillion Passengers	29	20	25	23	29
Passengers	4,175	4,683	4,334	4,764	4,823
Other	36	56	56	74	67
TOTAL:	11,100	12,094	11,725	12,575	12,698

REPUBLIC OF IRELAND: CASUALTIES
CLASSIFIED BY AGE AND GENDER, 1996

Age Group	Male	Female	Total
0-5	158	132	290
6-9	196	160	356
10-14	309	223	532
15-17	292	196	488
18-20	763	362	1,125
21-24	839	383	1,222
25-34	1,571	945	2,516
35-44	872	667	1,539
45-54	638	458	1,096
55-64	333	312	645
65 and over	322	330	652
Unknown	1,301	892	2,193
TOTAL:	7,594	5,060	12,654

NORTHERN IRELAND: CASUALTIES
CLASSIFIED BY AGE AND GENDER, 1997

Age Group	Male	Female	Total
0-5	151	121	272
5-10	430	292	722
11-15	383	329	712
16-19	828	676	1,504
20-24	1,089	721	1,810
25-34	1,943	1,316	3,259
35-44	1,168	762	1,930
45-54	630	557	1,187
55-59	184	189	373
60-64	121	149	270
65 and over	310	349	659
TOTALS:	7,237	5,461	12,698

EU COUNTRIES: COMPARISONS OF ROAD DEATHS

Country	Deaths per 10,000 Vehicles	Total Deaths	Injuries per 10,000 Vehicles
Australia	3	1,027	104
Belgium	3	1,356	113
Denmark	3	546	51
Finland	2	404	37
France	3	8,080	49
Germany	2	8,727	91
Greece	10	2,068	110
IRELAND	5	431	72
Italy	2	6,512	61
Netherlands	2	1,227	20
Norway	2	255	51
Spain	4	5,483	58

Sweden	2	572	43
United Kingdom	1	3,598	95

REP. OF IRELAND: DRUG TREATMENT CENTRES

Centre	Address	Telephone
Drug Treatment Centre	30-31 Pearse St., Dublin 2.	01 - 6771122
Coolmine Therapeutic Community	19 Lord Edward St., Dublin 2.	01 - 6793765 / 6794822
Talbot Centre	29 Upper Buckingham St., Dublin1.	01 - 8363434
Baggot Street Clinic	Haddington Rd., Dublin 4.	01 - 6602149
City Clinic	Amiens St., Dublin 1.	01 - 8749365
Aisling Clinic	Ballyfermot, Dublin 10.	01 - 6232200
Community Awareness of Drugs (CAD)	6 Exchequer St., Dublin 2.	01 - 6792681
Anna Liffey Drug Project	13 Lower Abbey St., Dublin 1.	01 - 8786899
Merchant's Quay Project	4 Merchant's Quay, Dublin 8.	01 - 6790044 / 6771128

REPUBLIC OF IRELAND: BUPA & VHI HEALTH INSURANCE COSTS

BUPA Ireland...............................*12 Fitzwilliam Square, Dublin 2*............*(01) 6627662*
Voluntary Health Insurance Board (VHI) ....*VHI House, Lower Abbey Street, Dublin 1.* ....*(01) 8724499*

VHI and BUPA are health insurances that are available in Ireland. Costs vary according to the medical requirements and both offer various plans that are best suited to each customer. The following table compares each insurance with different criteria.

Price (group rate)	VHI Plan B Option £	BUPA Essential Plus £	% Difference
Adult	315	259.08	22
Child	115	92.52	25
Full-Time Student	132	92.52	43
Family: 2 Adults & 2 Children	861	703.20	22
Family: 2 Adults & 2 children*	993	795.72	25

one student

EU COUNTRIES: LIFE EXPECTANCY AT SELECTED AGES†

Country	Year	Life Expectancy in years at ages							
		Males at				Females at			
		0 yrs	1 yrs	40 yrs	65 yrs	0 yrs	1 yrs	40 yrs	65 yrs
Australia	1994	73.4	72.8	35.6	15.1	79.7	79.2	41.0	18.6
Belgium	1994	73.4	72.9	35.7	14.8	80.1	79.5	41.4	19.1
Denmark	1994	72.7	72.2	34.7	14.3	78.1	77.5	39.3	17.7
Finland	1994	72.8	72.2	34.9	14.6	80.1	79.5	41.3	18.6
France*	1994	73.8	73.2	36.6	16.2	81.9	81.3	43.2	20.6
Germany	1994	73.1	72.5	35.1	14.7	79.6	78.9	40.8	18.4
Greece	1994	75.2	74.8	37.4	16.1	80.2	79.8	41.5	18.4
IRELAND	**1994**	**73.2**	**72.7**	**35.1**	**13.9**	**78.7**	**78.1**	**39.7**	**17.4**
Italy	1992	74.0	73.6	36.5	15.4	80.6	80.1	42.0	19.2
Luxembourg	1994	73.2	72.5	35.4	14.6	79.7	79.2	41.1	18.7
Netherlands	1994	74.6	74.1	36.2	14.8	80.3	79.7	41.5	19.1
Portugal	1994	71.6	71.2	34.9	14.4	78.6	78.2	40.4	17.9
Spain	1993	73.8	73.4	36.5	15.7	81.1	80.6	42.5	19.5
Sweden	1994	76.1	75.4	37.6	16.0	81.4	80.7	42.3	19.7
United Kingdom	1994	74.2	73.7	35.9	14.7	79.4	78.8	40.5	18.3
EU Average	1992	73.3	72.9	35.6	15.0	79.9	79.4	41.3	18.8

† *the number of additional years a person of a given age can expect to live;* * provisional*

REPUBLIC OF IRELAND: SUICIDES, 1991-97

Year	Female	Male	Total
1991	63	283	346
1992	59	304	363
1993	67	260	327
1994	73	280	353

1995	83	321	404
1996	69	323	392
1997	78	355	433

NORTHERN IRELAND: SUICIDES, 1990-96

Year	Female	Male	Total
1990	43	115	158
1991	36	93	129
1992	17	90	107
1993	26	103	129
1994	31	107	138
1995	31	91	122
1996	25	99	124

REPUBLIC OF IRELAND: PSYCHIATRIC PATIENTS, 1990-95

Region	1990	1991	1992	1993	1994	1995
Eastern	1,642	1,638	1,541	1,480	1,432	1,349
Midland	686	492	466	428	421	400
Mid-Western	705	620	520	508	485	483
North-Eastern	492	368	349	345	328	314
North-Western	536	375	321	319	279	268
South-Eastern	1,269	1,184	1,080	978	940	920
Southern	1,435	1,355	1,033	1,034	959	912
Western	1,042	968	864	815	797	702
TOTAL:	7,807	7,000	6,174	5,907	5,641	5,348

REPUBLIC OF IRELAND: AVERAGE AREA SERVED PER AMBULANCE STATION, 1998

Station Area	% Calls Answered within 20 mins.	Average Area per Station
Eastern Health Board	97%	240
Midland Health Board	58%	1,300
Mid-Western Health Board	78%	870
North Eastern Health Board	76%	1,270
North Western Health Board	53%	740
South Eastern Health Board	61%	851
Southern Health Board	86%	609
Western Health Board	56%	1,530
TOTAL:	87%	789

LAW & DEFENCE

The Road Forward for the RUC

By RUC Chief Constable Ronnie Flanagan.

A S we move towards a new millennium, the winds of change are sweeping across many aspects of life in Irish society, both north and south of the border. Few organisations have been subjected to as much change as the Royal Ulster Constabulary since its formation in 1922. Few organisations which I know have shown themselves to be more receptive to change either as a result of external factors or internal dynamics.

We in the RUC have no fear of real, improving change. But we would caution against change that is suggested simply for the sake of change; change that could be interpreted as mere tokenism; or change that is intended to remove one level of public disaffection without careful research to ensure it does not bring about a much greater level of disaffection.

The first step along this road must be a change in the environment in which the RUC operates. If we reach a point where the threat of violence faced by my officers and faced by the public is substantially reduced, then people will see a dramatic change in the way we go about our business.

For almost 30 years we have had to operate from fortified buildings; travel in armoured vehicles; patrol on foot wearing body armour, carrying weapons and often accompanied by military colleagues.

All of these things represent barriers between us and the people we serve - barriers most unwanted by police officers. When we can remove those barriers, and the conditions which made them necessary are absent, our relationships with all those we serve will improve dramatically.

Policing is much too important, much too impactive on all our lives, to be left to the police alone. If it is to work effectively, it must be conducted as a truly collaborative effort between police and the communities they exist to serve.

I say 'communities' in the plural sense quite deliberately because we clearly do not have, in Northern Ireland, a single, coherent, cohesive community. The reality is that there are many communities, some of them culturally based, others linked by geographic or economic conditions and, of course, religion.

All these communities have differing expectations and needs of the policing service. We must listen to these divergent demands; we must discern those differing needs and, working in partnerships with all the communities we exist to serve, we must do our utmost to match them.

The changing circumstances we face in Northern Ireland at the moment make such an objective more important than ever. If we are approaching a new and more peaceful era, as we all hope, it is quite appropriate that policing should be debated because it is something which impinges on the lives of everyone in our community tapestry.

No-one has done more to bring about the chance of such an era than the men and women of the RUC. Their sacrifice has been immense. More than 300 officers have been murdered, and many thousands more have been seriously injured in the terrorist campaign.

For 30 years now, the RUC has, quite simply, been the bulwark between anarchy and order. No-one should be under any illusions: this has not been a struggle between opposing sides, each with legitimate, if conflicting, views. This has been a struggle between right and wrong, between good and evil, whatever the political stand point of those who conducted terrorist campaigns.

The political climate is also witnessing dramatic change. If politicians have at last taken the opportunity with which we have provided them to implement a permanent agreement, no-one will be more pleased than the men and women of the RUC.

As I write this article, the Patten Commission is taking evidence from a whole range of groups before making recommendations on the future of policing in Northern Ireland. But already some recommendations from the Fundamental Review of policing which I conducted in 1994 are being implemented. In addition, a new Oath of Office is in place, changes have been made to rules governing the flying of the Union Flag and steps are being taken to reduce religious and gender imbalances in the composition of our organisation.

The RUC has co-operated fully with the Commission. Its establishment has presented us with perhaps the best opportunity we have had to counter the bombardment of propaganda levelled at us, often at an international level, with no basis in fact or evidence.

It has been my responsibility, and indeed my determination, to ensure that the facts in this regard are properly presented. The debate about policing is intense but, in the final analysis, an acceptable outcome for all of us will only be reached if communites engage in constructive dialogue.

I have no doubt that a Commission which has gathered evidence and weighed that evidence carefully and impartially to arrive at balanced conclusions will see the true value of what the men and women of the RUC have done, are doing and will continue to do.

RUC officers act fairly and impartially within the law to serve everyone in the community regardless of religion or creed. Alternative approaches such as 'restorative justice' and 'community policing' have their supporters. Great care should, however, be taken to avoid any risk that such models are abused by those with distorted concepts of justice as a means of social control. Paramilitary assaults, the so-called punishment beatings, are nothing more than a barbaric form of intimidation.

We will welcome conditions which facilitate and encourage policing to be more responsive, accountable and representative - with everyone in the community free and able to play a full part in reducing crime and its causes. We continue to examine approaches all over the world. We are prepared to draw on the best practice wherever it can be found although it has been my firm experience that we have at least as much to teach as to learn. For example, the 1998 Police Bill has set up the office of Police Ombudsman, giving Northern Ireland one of the most rigorous police complaints systems in the world.

The RUC stands for change - change which will make us more representative of all of our communites. We are also ready for change which will see us working in much closer relationships with those communites so that we can draw up and deliver policing arrangements best suited to their needs. Improved accountability and consultation are realistic objectives.

Our officers also yearn for and stand ready for the day when they can deliver a policing service without the need to bear arms.

I fervently hope that, as the winds of change sweep us towards a new millennium, all of our communites stand similarly ready.

The author has been the Chief Constable of the Royal Ulster Constabulary since 1996

REPUBLIC OF IRELAND: COURT SYSTEM

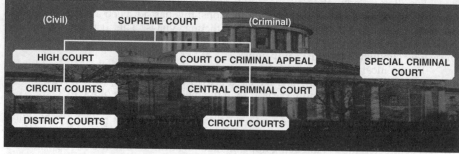

(Civil)	SUPREME COURT	(Criminal)	
HIGH COURT	COURT OF CRIMINAL APPEAL		SPECIAL CRIMINAL COURT
CIRCUIT COURTS	CENTRAL CRIMINAL COURT		
DISTRICT COURTS	CIRCUIT COURTS		

REPUBLIC OF IRELAND: JUDICIARY

JUDGES OF THE SUPREME COURT

Chief Justice The Hon. Mr. Justice Liam Hamilton
The Hon. Mr. Justice Hugh O'Flaherty
The Hon. Ms. Justice Susan Denham
The Hon. Mr. Justice Donal Barrington
The Hon. Mr. Justice Ronan Keane
The Hon. Mr. Justice Francis Murphy
The Hon. Mr. Justice Kevin Lynch
The Hon. Mr. Justice Henry Barron

JUDGES OF THE HIGH COURT

The Hon. Mr. Justice Frederick R. Morris - President of the High Court
The Hon. Ms. Justice Mella Carroll
The Hon. Mr. Justice Robert Barr
The Hon. Mr. Justice Richard Johnson
The Hon. Mr. Justice Vivian Lavan
The Hon. Mr. Justice Declan Budd
The Hon. Mr. Justice Fergus Flood
The Hon. Mr. Justice Paul Carney
The Hon. Mr. Justice Hugh Geoghegan
The Hon. Mr. Justice Dermot Kinlen
The Hon. Mr. Justice Brian McCracken
The Hon. Ms. Justice Mary Laffoy
The Hon. Mr. Justice Michael Moriarty
The Hon. Mr. Justice Peter Kelly
The Hon. Mr. Justice Thomas C. Smyth
The Hon. Ms. Justice Catherine McGuinness
The Hon. Mr. Justice Diarmuid B. O'Donovan
The Hon. Mr. Justice Philip O'Sullivan
The Hon. Mr. Justice Kevin C. O'Higgins
The Hon. Mr. Justice John Quirke
The Hon. Mr. Justice Matthew P. Smith

JUDGES OF THE CIRCUIT COURT

His Honour Judge Esmond Smyth - President of the Circuit Court
His Honour Judge Dominic Lynch
His Honour Judge Anthony G. Murphy
His Honour Judge Matthew F. Deery
His Honour Judge Patrick J. Moran
His Honour Judge Kieran O'Connor
His Honour Judge Liam Devally
His Honour Judge Cyril C. Kelly
His Honour Judge Harvey Kenny
His Honour Judge Sean A. O'Leary
His Honour Judge Anthony Kennedy

His Honour Judge Kevin Haugh
Her Honour Judge Alison Lindsay
His Honour Judge John F. Buckley
His Honour Judge Raymond Groarke
His Honour Judge Frank O'Donnell
His Honour Judge Michael White
Her Honour Judge Olive Buttimer
Her Honour Judge Elizabeth Dunne
His Honour Judge Joseph Gerard Matthews
His Honour Judge Patrick John McCartan
Her Honour Judge Jacqueline Linnane
His Honour Judge Carroll Moran
His Honour Judge John P. Clifford
His Honour Judge John D. O'Hagan
Her Honour Judge Yvonne Murphy

JUDGES OF THE DISTRICT COURT

District 1: John O'Donnell - (Buncrana, Carndonagh, Donegal, Glenties, Letterkenny).
District 2: Oliver McGuinness - (Ballyfarnon, Ballymote, Boyle, Collooney, Dowra, Drumkeerin, Easky, Grange, Inniscrone, Manorhamilton, Riverstown, Skreen, Sligo, Tubbercurry).
District 3: Daniel G. Shields - (Achill, Balla, Ballina, Ballinrobe, Ballycastle, Callycroy, Belmullet, Castlebar, Crossmolina, Foxford, Killala, Kiltimagh, Newport, Swinford, Westport).
District 4: Bernard M. Brennan - (Ballaghaderreen, Ballyhaunis, Carrick-on-Shannon, Castlerea, Charlestown, Claremorris, Dunmore, Elphin, Glenamaddy, Kilkelly, Roscommon, Rooskey, Strokestown, Williamstown).
District 5: Donal McArdle - (Arva, Bailieborough, Ballinamore, Ballyconnell, Ballyjamesduff, Belturbet, Cavan, Cootehill, Kingscourt, Mohill, Monaghan, Oldcastle, Virginia).
District 6: Flannan V. Brennan - (Ardee, Ballybay, Carlingford, Carrickmacross, Castleblayney, Drogheda, Dundalk, Dunleer).
District 7: John F. Garavan - (Carna, Clifden, Derreen, Derrynea, Galway, Headford, Kilronan, Letterfrack, Maam, Oughterard, Spiddal, Tuam).
District 8: James J. O'Sullivan - (Athlone, Ballinasloe, Ballyforan, Birr, Borrisokane, Eyrecourt, Loughrea, Moate, Mount Bellew, Kilcormac, Woodford).
District 9: Aidan O'Donnell - (Ballymahon, Ballynacargy, Castlepollard, Delvin, Edenderry,

Edgeworthstown, Granard, Kilbeggan, Killucan, Longford, Mullingar, Tullamore).
District 10: John Patrick Brophy - (Athboy, Ceanannus Mor, Dunshaughlin, Kilcock, Navan, Trim).
District 12: Albert Louis O'Dea - (Athenry, Corofin, Ennis, Ennistymon, Gort, Kildysart, Kilkee, Killaloe, Kilrush, Kinvara, Lisdoonvarna, Miltown Malbay, Shannon, Sixmilebridge, Scarriff, Tulla).
District 13: Mary A.G. O'Halloran - (Abbeyfeale, Adare, Askeaton, Bruff, Drumcologher, Kilfinane, Kilmallock, Listowel, Newcastle West, Rathkeale, Rath Luirc, Shanagolden, Tarbert).
District 14: Michael C. Reilly - (Cappamore, Cappawhite, Limerick City, Nenagh, Newport, Thurles).
District 15: Mary H. Martin - (Abbeyleix, Athy, Ballyragget, Carlow, Castlecomer, Mountmellick, Mountrath, Portarlington, Portlaoise, Rathdowney, Roscrea, Templemore, Urlingford).
District 16: Thomas J. Ballagh - (Baltinglass, Blessington, Bray, Droichead Nua, Dunlavin, Hacketstown, Kildare, Naas).
District 17: Humphrey P. Kelleher - (Annascaul, Cahirciveen, Castlegregory, Castleisland, Dingle, Kenmare, Killarney, Killorglin, Sneem, Tralee, Waterville).
District 18: Brendan Wallace - (Bandon, Bantry, Castletownbere, Clonakilty, Coachford, Dunmanway, Glengarriff, Kinsale, Macroom, Millstreet, Schull, Skibbereen).

District 19: Uinsin MacGruairc - (Cork City).
District 20: David Riordan - (Ballincollig, Blarney, Buttevant, Carrigaline, Castlemartyr, Castletownroche, Cobh, Fermoy, Kanturk, Mallow, Midleton, Mitchelstown, Riverstown).
District 21: Michael Pattwell - (Cahir, Cappoquin, Carrick-on-Suir, Cashel, Clogheen, Clonmel, Dungarvan, Killenaule, Lismore, Tallow, Tipperary, Youghal).
District 22: William Harnett - (Callan, Kilkenny, Kilmacthomas, Thomastown, Waterford).
District 23: Donnchadh O'Buachalla - (Arklow, Bunclody, Enniscorthy, Gorey, Muine Bheag, New Ross, Rathdrum, Shillelagh, Tullow, Wexford, Wicklow).
Dublin Metropolitan District: Peter A. Smithwick (President of the District Court), John J. Delap, Brian Kirby, Gillian M. Hussey, James Paul McDonnell, Desmond P. H. Windle, Thelma King, Timothy H. Crowley, Clare Leonard, Michael O'Leary, Catherine A. Murphy, Mary Collins, Constantine G. O'Leary, Miriam Malone.

MOVEABLE JUDGES OF THE DISTRICT COURT

John F. Neilan, Joseph Mangan, William G. J. Hamill, Thomas A. Fitzpatrick, Desmond P. Hogan, Gerard J. Haughton, J. W. Terence Finn, Murrough B. Connellan, Mary Fahy, William Early, Michael P. M. Connellan, John J. O'Neill.

REPUBLIC OF IRELAND: COURTS

SUPREME COURT AND HIGH COURT

Four Courts, Morgan Place, Dublin 7.

CIRCUIT COURTS

Cork Circuit
Towns: Bandon, Bantry, Clonakilty, Cork, Fermoy, Kanturk, Macroom, Mallow, Midleton, Skibbereen, Youghal. **Registrar:** Deirdre O'Mahony, Cork Courthouse.

Eastern Circuit
Town: Dundalk. **Registrar:** Mairead Ahern, Dundalk Courthouse.
Towns: Athy, Naas. **Registrar:** Eithne Coughlan, Naas Courthouse.
Town: Trim. **Registrar:** Maire Tehan, Trim Courthouse.
Town: Wicklow. **Registrar:** Breda Allen, Wicklow Courthouse.

Midland Circuit
Towns: Athlone, Mullingar. **Registrar:** Elizabeth Sharkey, Mullingar Courthouse.
Towns: Birr, Tullamore. **Registrar:** Patrick R. O'Gorman, Tullamore

Courthouse.
Towns: Boyle, Roscommon. **Registrar:** William Lyster, Roscommon Courthouse.
Town: Longford. **Registrar:** Imelda Branigan, Longford Courthouse.
Town: Portlaoise. **Registrar:** James E. Cahill, Portlaoise Courthouse.
Town: Sligo. **Registrar:** Kieran McDermott, Sligo Courthouse.

Northern Circuit
Towns: Buncrana, Donegal, Letterkenny. **Registrar:** Mary T. Devlin, Letterkenny Courthouse.
Towns: Carrick-on-Shannon, Manorhamilton. **Registrar:** Kevin Doherty, Carrick-on-Shannon Courthouse.
Towns: Castleblayney, Monaghan. **Registrar:** J. Duffy Monaghan Courthouse.
Town: Cavan. **Registrar:** Thomas P. Owens, Cavan Courthouse.

South Eastern Circuit
Town: Carlow. **Registrar:** John A. O'Gorman, Carlow Courthouse.
Towns: Clonmel, Nenagh, Thurles, Tipperary. **Registrar:** Mary Delehunty, Clonmel Courthouse.
Towns: Dungarvan, Waterford.

Registrar: Niall Robert Rooney, Waterford Courthouse.
Town: Kilkenny. **Registrar:** Mary N. Enright, Kilkenny Courthouse.
Town: Wexford. **Registrar:** Maurice J. Phelan, Wexford Courthouse.

South Western Circuit
Towns: Ennis, Kirush. **Registrar:** Enda Brogan, Ennis Courthouse.
Towns: Killarney, Listowel, Tralee. **Registrar:** Louise McDonough, Tralee Courthouse.
Towns: Limerick, Rathkeale. **Registrar:** Proinsias B. O'Gadhra, Limerick Courthouse.

Western Circuit
Towns: Ballina, Castlebar, Swinford, Westport. **Registrar:** Fintan J. Murphy, Castlebar Courthouse.
Towns: Galway, Loughrea. **Registrar:** Sean C. O'Domhnaill, Galway Courthouse.

Dublin Circuit
Town: Dublin. **Registrar:** Michael Quinlan, Áras Ui Dhalaigh, Inns Quay, Dublin 7.

For District Court Venues see Judiciary.

NORTHERN IRELAND COURT SYSTEM

The Superior Courts:

THE HOUSE OF LORDS (London)

THE SUPREME COURT OF JUDICATURE OF NORTHERN IRELAND

THE COURT OF APPEAL (BELFAST)

HIGH COURT (Belfast)

QUEENS BRANCH — **FAMILY BRANCH** — **CHANCERY DIVISION**

CROWN COURT
9 TOWNS IN NORTHERN IRELAND

NORTHERN IRELAND: JUDICIARY

THE LORD CHIEF JUSTICE OF NORTHERN IRELAND

The Right Honourable Sir Robert Douglas Carswell

JUDGES

The Right Honourable Lord Justice James Michael Anthony Nicholson

The Right Honourable Lord Justice William Paschal McCollum

The Right Honourable Mr Justice William Anthony Campbell

The Honourable Mr Justice John Joseph Sheil

The Honourable Mr Justice Brian Francis Kerr

The Honourable Mr Justice John Kenneth Pringle

The Honourable Mr Justice Malachy Joseph Higgins

The Honourable Mr Justice Frederick Paul Girvan

The Honourable Mr Justice Patrick Coghlin

LORD CHIEF'S JUSTICE OFFICE

Principal Secretary to the Lord Chief Justice: D.A. Lavery

SUPREME COURT OFFICES

Queen's Bench, Appeals and Clerk of the Crown in Northern Ireland: Master J.W. Wilson

Office of Care and Protection: Master F.B. Hall

Bankruptcy and Companies Office: Master C.W.G. Redpath

Chancery Office: Master R.A. Ellison

Probate and Matrimonial Office: Master N. Lockie Esq.

Taxing Office: Master J. C. Napier

Court Funds Office: Accountant General H.G. Thompson

RECORDERS

Belfast: His Honour Judge Hart QC

Derry: His Honour Judge Burgess

COUNTY COURT JUDGES

His Honour Judge Curran QC

His Honour Judge Gibson QC

His Honour Judge Petrie QC

His Honour Judge Smyth QC

His Honour Judge Markey QC

His Honour Judge McKay QC

His Honour Judge Brady QC

His Honour Judge Rodgers

His Honour Judge Foote QC

Her Honour Judge Philpott QC

His Honour Judge David Kennedy McFarland

CHIEF SOCIAL SECURITY COMMISSIONER

His Honour Judge Martin QC

DISTRICT JUDGES

Division of Belfast: District Judge Wells

Division of Derry and Antrim: District Judge Keegan

Division of Armagh & South Down and Fermanagh & Tyrone: District Judge Brownlie

Division of Craigavon & Ards: District Judge Wheeler

NORTHERN IRELAND: COURT VENUES

THE SUPREME COURT OF JUDICATURE

Royal Courts of Justice, Chichester Street, Belfast BT1 3JF.

MAGISTRATES' COURTS

Antrim Magistrates' Court: ....Clerk: Mr. T. Long. The Courthouse, Antrim.

Newtownards Magistrates' Court:.......................Clerk: Mr. P. Kelly. The Courthouse, Newtownards, Co. Down.

Armagh Magistrates' Court: ....Clerk: Mr. E. Strain. The Courthouse, Armagh.

Ballymena Magistrates' Court: ....Clerk: Mr. T. Long. The Courthouse, Ballymena, Co. Antrim.

Banbridge Magistrates' Court: ....Clerk: Mr. E. Strain. The Courthouse, Banbridge, Co. Down.

Belfast Magistrates' Court:..Clerk: Mr. B.W. Sinnamon. The Courthouse, Belfast.

Castlereagh Magistrates' Court: ....Clerk: Mr. P. Kelly. The Courthouse, Newtownards, Co. Down.

Craigavon Magistrates' Court: ....Clerk: Mr. J. Halliday. The Courthouse, Craigavon, Co. Armagh.

Down Magistrates' Court: ....Clerk: Mr. P. Kelly. The Courthouse, Downpatrick, Co. Down.

East Tyrone Magistrates' Court:....................Clerk: Mrs. M. Kilpatrick. The Courthouse, Cookstown, Co. Tyrone.
Fermanagh Magistrates' Court: ....Officer: Mrs. A. Harland. The Courthouse, Enniskillen, Co. Fermanagh.
Larne Magistrates' Court:...The Courthouse, Larne, Co. Antrim.
Limavady Magistrates' Court:..The Courthouse, Limavady, Co. Derry.
Lisburn Magistrates' Court: ....Clerk: Mr. J. Halliday. The Courthouse, Lisburn, Co. Antrim.
Londonderry Magistrates' Court: ....Clerk: Mr. G. Richardson, The Courthouse, Derry.
Magherafelt Magistrates' Court:..The Courthouse, Magherafelt, Co. Derry.
Newry and Mourne Magistrates' Court:.................Clerk: Mr. G. Strain. The Courthouse, Banbridge, Co. Down.
Newtownabbey Magistrates' Court:...Officer: Mr. R. Crossthwaite. The Courthouse, Newtownabbey, Co. Antrim.
North Antrim Magistrates' Court: (Ballymoney, Coleraine and Moyle):
....Officer in Charge: Mr. A. Cartwright. The Courthouse, Coleraine, Co. Derry.
North Down Magistrates' Court: ....Officer in Charge: Miss. C. Scollan. The Courthouse, Bangor, Co. Down.
Omagh Magistrates' Court:.......................Clerk: Mrs. M. Kilpatrick. The Courthouse, Omagh, Co. Tyrone.
Strabane Magistrates' Court:..............Officer in Charge: Ms. J. Devine. The Courthouse, Strabane, Co. Tyrone.

CROWN COURTS

Armagh Crown Court:..Manager: Mr. E. Strain. The Courthouse, Armagh.
Ballymena Crown Court:.............................Manager: Mr. T. Long. The Courthouse, Ballymena, Co. Antrim.
Belfast Crown Court: ....Manager: Mr. G.H. Keatley. The Courthouse, Belfast.
Craigavon Crown Court: ....Manager: Mr. J. Halliday. The Courthouse, Craigavon, Co. Armagh.
Downpatrick Crown Court: ....Manager: Mr. P. Kelly. The Courthouse, Downpatrick, Co. Down.
Enniskillen Crown Court: ....Manager: Mrs. M. Kilpatrick. The Courthouse, Enniskillen, Co. Fermanagh.
Londonderry Crown Court: ....Manager: Mr. G. Richardson. The Courthouse, Derry.
Newtownards Crown Court: ....Manager: Mr. P. Kelly. The Courthouse, Newtownards, Co. Down.
Omagh Crown Court: ....Manager: Mrs. M. Kilpatrick. The Courthouse, Omagh, Co. Tyrone.

COUNTY COURTS

Antrim County Court:Manager: ....Mr. T. Long. The Courthouse, Ballymena, Co. Antrim.
Ards County Court:Manager: ....Mr. P. Kelly. The Courthouse, Newtownards, Co. Down.
Armagh and South Down County Court:.............................Manager: Mr. E. Strain. The Courthouse, Armagh.
Belfast County Court: ....Mr. G.H. Keatley. The Courthouse, Belfast.
Craigavon County Court:............................Manager: Mr. J. Halliday. The Courthouse, Craigavon, Co. Armagh.
Fermanagh and Tyrone County Court: ....Manager: Mrs. M. Kilpatrick. The Courthouse, Omagh, Co. Tyrone.
Londonderry County Court:...................................Manager: Mr. G. Richardson. The Courthouse, Derry.

R.O.I. STRENGTH OF GARDA SÍOCHÁNA, 1996-97

Rank	1996	1997
Commissioner	1	1
Deputy Commissioners	2	2
Assistant Commissioners	9	9
Acting Surgeons	1	-
Chief Superintendents	44	44
Superintendents	163	163
Inspectors	251	263
Sergeants	1,862	1,844
Gardaí	8,484	8,642
TOTAL:	10,817	10,968

NORTHERN IRELAND: STRENGTH OF ROYAL ULSTER CONSTABULARY, 1996-97

Rank	1996	1997
Chief Constable	1	1
Deputy Chief Constable	1	1
Assistant Chief Constables	7	7
Chief Superintendents	22	16
Superintendents	132	137
Chief Inspectors	161	164
Inspectors	485	481
Sergeants	1,405	1,393
Constables	6,209	6,285
TOTAL:	8,423	8,485
RUC Reserve: (Full-Time)	2,929	2,982
RUC Reserve: (Part-Time)	1,473	1,324

REPUBLIC OF IRELAND:
GARDA SÍOCHÁNA REGIONAL STATISTICS, 1997

Description	Northern Region	Western Region	Eastern Region	Southern Region	South Eastern Region	Dublin Region
Population	311,551	431,635	599,894	701,216	440,533	1,041,259
Area (km²)	11,339	17,739	13,214	14,935	11,682	869
Primary / Secondary Roads (km)	745.2	1,328.2	1,117.6	1,152.7	906.5	153.5
Regional Crime	3,510	4,891	11,861	12,996	7,075	50,542
Crime per 1,000 Population	11.3	11.33	19.8	18.5	16	48.5
Road Traffic Offences	12,722	15,291	31,299	40,745	19,266	143,884
Garda Strength	1,073	1,026	1,280	1,648	874	3,847
Garda Vehicles	116	119	160	200	118	477
Garda Stations	108	144	127	162	117	43
Garda Districts	14	20	18	22	16	17

Regions:
Western: Clare, Galway, Roscommon, Mayo.
Southern: Kerry, Limerick, Cork.
Dublin: Dublin Area.
Northern: Sligo, Leitrim, Donegal, Cavan, Monaghan.
Eastern: Louth, Meath, Longford, Westmeath, Laois, Offaly, Carlow, Kildare.
South Eastern: Wexford, Tipperary, Waterford, Kilkenny.

NORTHERN IRELAND:
STRENGTH OF POLICE FORCE, 1991-96

Force	1991	1992	1993	1994	1995	1996
Royal Ulster Constabulary:						
Males	7,510	7,688	7,646	7,640	7,541	7,531
Females	707	790	818	853	899	897
Total Royal Ulster Constabulary	8,217	8,478	8,464	8,493	8,440	8,428
Royal Ulster Constabulary Reserves:						
Males: Part-time	1,089	1,014	964	996	953	949
Males: Full-time	2,980	3,046	3,063	3,056	2,787	2,778
Females: Part -time	429	419	424	495	528	524
Females: Full-time	62	114	121	143	151	151
Total RUC Reserves	4,560	4,593	4,572	4,690	4,419	4,402
TOTAL FORCE:	19,053	18,488	18,448	18,424	12,859	12,830

REPUBLIC OF IRELAND:
CRIME RATE PER GARDA DIVISION, 1992-97

Garda Division	1992 (%)	1993 (%)	1994 (%) (per 1,000 population)	1995 (%)	1996 (%)	1997 (%)
Dublin Metropolitan Area	49.9	53.6	-	56.3	56.4	48.5
Carlow / Kildare	15.4	16.5	16.9	17.2	19.1	20.7
Cavan / Monaghan	10.4	9.6	8.6	9.5	8.2	9.1
Cork City*	-	-	-	-	-	30.9
Cork East*	36.4	36.0	34.4	32.4	29.5	-
Cork North*	-	-	-	-	-	13.5
Cork West	11.2	9.5	9.7	9.7	9.1	9.7
Clare	7.9	7.9	8.8	11.8	11.5	12.1
Donegal	10.9	10.3	12.0	11.1	10.9	12.4
Galway West	19.8	21.8	19.8	19.3	17.6	15.7
Kerry	15.6	12.9	15.8	14.1	12.8	11.5
Laois / Offaly	10.7	11.4	14.3	13.3	11.9	13.0
Limerick	23.5	22.0	22.8	23.8	21.2	19.0
Longford / Westmeath	25.6	18.9	19.3	19.9	19.5	17.1
Louth / Meath	21.3	21.2	22.4	25.5	24.6	23.8
Mayo	7.5	7.4	7.6	8.0	8.1	8.5
Roscommon / Galway East	8.8	9.4	10.0	9.5	8.6	7.9
Sligo / Leitrim	10.2	11.2	11.9	10.0	11.5	12.7
Tipperary	16.4	14.5	13.7	12.8	11.2	11.8
Waterford / Kilkenny	14.0	15.8	17.6	17.3	17.8	20.1
Wexford	18.9	21.3	19.9	15.5	17.1	15.8

* in 1996, the division of Cork East gave way to two new divisions Cork City and Cork North.

REPUBLIC OF IRELAND: INDICTABLE OFFENCES, 1995-97

Offence	1995 Known	Detected	1996 Known	Detected	1997 Known	Detected
Non-Sexual Offences against the Person	7,324	2,458	7,339	2,332	5,777	2,039
Sexual Offences	923	768	836	709	1,015	871
Larcenies	49,483	18,517	47,943	18,473	42,533	16,969
Frauds	3,610	3,050	3,758	3,240	3,349	2,903
Burglaries	32,721	10,335	31,741	11,025	28,963	10,438
Criminal Damage	8,045	4,275	8,747	4,877	8,724	5,222
Other Offences	378	729	421	400	514	501
TOTAL OFFENCES:	**102,484**	**40,132**	**100,785**	**41,056**	**90,875**	**38,943**

REP. OF IRELAND: NON-INDICTABLE OFFENCES, 1996-97

Offence	1996 Proceedings Taken	Convictions	1997 Proceedings Taken	Convictions
Assaults	7,811	4,607	8,191	4,381
Cruelty to Animals	268	160	143	97
Offences against Traffic Accidents	268,572	122,404	263,207	107,426
Other Traffic Act Offences	122,910	53,051	112,613	48,317
Offences against Intoxicating Liquor Laws	12,642	8,516	16,110	10,213
Criminal Damage to Animals, Fences, etc.	2,393	1,594	3,276	2,172
Offences against Police Regulations	652	269	622	185
Criminal Law Sexual Offences Act, 1993	63	45	502	380
Criminal Justice (Public Order) Act, 1994	16,384	11,286	25,755	16,375
Offences against Revenue Laws	72	32	129	49
Offences against Street Trading Acts	640	192	710	247
Offences against Vagrancy Acts	242	123	526	394
Offences against Wireless Telegraphy Act, 1926	87	42	49	20
Offences against Firearms Acts	845	643	405	250
Firearms and Offensive Weapons Act, 1990	0	0	1,908	1,295
Offences in Relation to Explosives	5	0	5	1
Offences against Juries Act, 1976	169	122	284	148
Gaming and Lotteries Act, 1956	0	0	67	36
Prohibition of Incitement to Hatred Act, 1989	0	0	0	0
Other Offences	17,512	10,533	17,240	10,758
TOTAL:	**451,267**	**213,619**	**451,742**	**202,744**

REP. OF IRELAND: RECORDED CRIME, 1982-97

Year	Crime Recorded	Year	Crime Recorded
1982	97,626	1990	87,658
1983	102,387	1991	94,406
1984	99,727	1992	95,391
1985	91,285	1993	98,979
1986	86,574	1994	101,036
1987	85,358	1995	102,484
1988	89,544	1996	100,785
1989	86,792	1997	90,875

REPUBLIC OF IRELAND & NORTHERN IRELAND: FIREARMS AND EXPLOSIVES SEIZED, 1996-97

R.O.I.: Firearms and Explosives Seized			Northern Ireland: Firearms and Explosives Finds		
Description	1996	1997	Description	1996	1997
Firearms	696	638	Firearms	103	97
Explosives (kg)	104.2	36.7 kg	Explosives (kg)	2,462.6	661.7
Devices	677	1,104			
Litres	4.5	-			

NORTHERN IRELAND: PERSONS CONVICTED OF INDICTABLE OFFENCES AT COURT, 1990-97

Offence	1990	1991	1992	1993	1994	1995	1996	1997
Violence against the Person	1,750	1,634	1,558	1,674	1,498	1,685	1,597	1,550
Sexual Offences	275	193	184	126	148	182	184	130
Burglary	1,362	1,208	1,149	1,114	979	951	801	683
Robbery	220	162	202	159	168	195	161	137
Theft & Handling Stolen Goods	3,399	3,429	3,158	3,254	3,044	3,128	2,765	2,587
Fraud & Forgery	699	648	683	633	568	533	467	476
Criminal Damage	1,054	1,019	967	1,145	1,134	1,008	1,076	1,181
Offences against the State	233	195	187	184	137	166	147	174
Others	287	368	448	606	669	863	899	810
TOTAL PERSONS CONVICTED:	**9,279**	**8,856**	**8,536**	**8,895**	**8,345**	**8,711**	**8,097**	**7,728**

NORTHERN IRELAND: NOTIFIABLE OFFENCES RECORDED BY THE POLICE, 1991-97

Offence	1991	1992	1993	1994	1995	1996	1997
Violence against the Person	3,955	4,102	4,597	4,793	5,150	5,640	5,154
Sexual Offences	877	973	1,187	1,333	1,679	1,745	1,444
Burglary	16,563	17,117	15,735	16,902	16,457	16,114	14,306
Robbery	1,848	1,851	1,723	1,567	1,539	1,725	1,653
Theft & Handling Stolen Goods	32,033	34,256	33,161	33,233	33,472	32,772	29,543
Fraud & Forgery	4,811	5,486	5,553	5,100	4,884	4,081	3,818
Criminal Damage	2,394	2,502	2,856	3,077	3,772	4,847	4,692
Offences against the State	592	478	436	440	339	400	501
Others	419	767	980	1,441	1,516	1,225	1,111
TOTAL PERSONS CONVICTED:	**63,492**	**67,532**	**66,228**	**67,886**	**68,808**	**68,549**	**62,222**

REP. OF IRELAND: PRISON STATISTICS, 1992-97

Description	1992	1993	1994	1995	1996	1997
Average Daily Population:						
Male	2,146	2,127	-	-	-	-
Female	39	44	-	-	-	-
TOTAL:	**2,185**	**2,171**	**2,123**	**2,109**	**2,197**	**2,424**
Committal Trends:						
On Remand	5,078	5,255	-	-	-	-
For Trial	324	845	-	-	-	-
Sentenced	4,297	4,357	-	-	-	-
TOTAL:	**9,699**	**10,457**	**10,252**	**9,844**	**10,598**	**11,620**

NORTHERN IRELAND: PRISON POPULATION

Description of Prisoners		1992	1993	1994	1995	1996	1997
On Remand:	Male	400	418	427	312	318	333
	Female	13	8	12	5	8	9
Total:		**413**	**426**	**439**	**317**	**326**	**342**
Fine Defaulter:							
Male		33	30	27	28	24	24
Female		1	2	3	1	0	1
Total:		**34**	**32**	**30**	**29**	**24**	**25**
Description of Prisoners		**1992**	**1993**	**1994**	**1995**	**1996**	**1997**
Immediate Custody:							
Male		1,335	1,445	1,403	1,382	1,257	1,234
Female		27	30	26	29	21	20
Total:		**1,362**	**1,475**	**1,429**	**1,411**	**1,278**	**1,254**
Non-Criminal:							
Male		1	1	1	5	11	12
Female		0	0	0	0	0	0
Total:		**1**	**1**	**1**	**5**	**11**	**12**
TOTAL:		**1,810**	**1,934**	**1,899**	**1,762**	**1,639**	**1,633**

NORTHERN IRELAND: SECURITY SITUATION STATISTICS, 1995-97

Description	1995	1996	1997
Deaths:			
RUC	1	-	4
Army	-	1	1
UDR/RIR	-	-	-
Civilian	8	14	17
Total:	9	15	22
Injuries:			
Shootings	3	24	72
Assaults	217	302	156
Total:	220	326	228
Incidents:			
Shootings	50	125	225
Bombings	2	25	93
Incendiaries	10	4	9
Firearms Found	118	98	105
Explosives Found (kg)	5	1,677	1,258

NORTHERN IRELAND: BREAKDOWN OF PARADE STATISTICS, 1997

	Legal	Illegal	Re-routed	Other Conditions	Disorder	Total
Loyalist	2,585	1	10	11	6	2,613
Republican	230	6	1	8	-	245
Other	503	1	-	1	-	505
TOTAL:	3,318	8	11	20	6	3,363

BREAKDOWN OF PARADE STATISTICS, 1998*

	Legal	Illegal	Re-routed	Other Conditions	Disorder	Total
Loyalist	1,622	24	13	5	1	1,665
Republican	122	10	-	1	1	134
Other	273	-	-	-	-	273
Total	2,017	34	13	6	2	2,072

*1st January 1998 - 31st July, 1998

NORTHERN IRELAND: BANNED, RESTRICTED OR ILLEGAL PARADES, 1985-98

Year	Total	Banned	Illegal	Re-routed	Conditions Imposed	Disorder
1985	2,120	3	-	22	-	-
1986	1,950	1	-	9	-	-
1987	2,109	-	96	11	-	18
1988	2,055	-	8	11	-	21
1989	2,317	-	2	14	-	5
1990	2,713	-	1	10	-	1
1991	2,379	-	4	14	1	1
1992	2,744	-	-	16	16	-
1993	2,662	-	-	12	12	1
1994	2,792	-	-	29	29	-
1995	3,500	-	24	20	20	9
1996	3,162	-	19	25	7	15
1997	3,363	-	8	11	20	6
1998*	2,072	-	34	13	6	2

* Jan. - July 1998 (provisional)

REPUBLIC OF IRELAND: DEFENCE STAFF

Rank	Name	Stationed
Minister for Defence	Michael Smith, TD	Defence HQ, Dublin
Minister of State for Defence	Seamus Brennan, TD	Government Buildings
Chief of Staff	Lt. Gen. Dave Stapleton	Defence HQ, Dublin
Adjutant General	Maj. Gen. Bill Dwyer	Defence HQ, Dublin
Quartermaster General	Maj. Gen. Patrick Nowlan	Defence HQ, Dublin
Assistant Chief of Staff	Brig. Gen. E. Heskin	Defence HQ, Dublin
GOC Eastern Command	Brig. Gen. Colm Mangan	Cathal Brugha Bks., Dublin
GOC Western Command	Brig. Gen. John Martin	Custume Bks., Athlone
GOC Southern Command	Brig. Gen. Dave Taylor	Collins Bks., Cork
GOC Curragh Command	Brig. Gen. Frank Colclough	Curragh Camp, Kildare
Commandant Military College	Brig. Gen. Carl Dodd	Curragh Camp, Kildare
Flag Officer Commanding the Naval Service	Commodore John Kavanagh	Colaiste Caoimhín
GOC Air Corps / Director Military Aviation	Brig. Gen. Pat Cranfield	Baldonnel

NORTHERN IRELAND: DEFENCE STAFF

Rank / Force	Name
General Officer Commanding Northern Ireland	Lieutenant Gen. Sir Rupert Smith
Chief of Staff, Headquarters Northern Ireland	Brigadier Robin V. Brims
Commander, 3rd Infantry Brigade	Brigadier Roger Brunt
Commander, 8th Infantry Brigade	Brigadier Simon D. Young
Commander, 39th Infantry Brigade	Brigadier Mick Houghton
Commander, 107 (Ulster) Brigade	Brigadier Bigby O'Lone
Colonel in Chief, Royal Irish Regiment	HRH The Duke of York
Colonel of the Regiment, Royal Irish Regiment	Gen Sir Roger Wheeler
Colonel in Chief, The Royal Dragoon Guards	HRH The Prince of Wales
Colonel of the Regiment, The Royal Dragoon Guards	Lieutenant Gen Sir Anthony Mallens
Colonel in Chief, The Queen's Royal Hussars	HM Queen Elizabeth, The Queen Mother
Colonel of the Regiment, The Queen's Royal Hussars	Maj Gen R.E. Barron
Colonel in Chief, The Irish Guards	HM The Queen
Colonel of the Regiment, The Irish Guards	HRH The Grand Duke of Luxembourg

REP. OF IRELAND: DEFENCE HEADQUARTERS

Army, Air Corps and Naval Service - Parkgate, Dublin 8. ....(01) 8379911

Command Headquarters

Eastern Command - Cathal Brugha Barracks, Rathmines, Dublin 6. ....(01) 8046202
Southern Command - Collins Barracks, Cork. ....(021) 397577
Western Command - Custume Barracks, Athlone, Co. Westmeath ....(0902) 92631
Curragh Command - Curragh, Co. Kildare ....(045) 41301
Air Corps - Casement Aerodrome, Baldonnel, Dublin 22 ....(01) 4592493
Naval Service - Haulbowline, Cobh, Co. Cork. ....(021) 811246

NORTHERN IRELAND: DEFENCE HEADQUARTERS

The Army

Thiepval Barracks, Lisburn, Co. Antrim BT28 3SE............(01846) 665111
3rd Infantry Brigade - Mahon Barracks, Portadown, Co. Armagh ....(01762) 351551
8th Infantry Brigade - Ebrington Barracks, Derry BT47 1JU............(01504) 43211
39th Infantry Brigade - Thiepval Barracks, Lisburn, Co. Antrim BT28 3SE............(01846) 665111

Other Army Locations

Thiepval Barracks, Lisburn, Co. Antrim ....(01846) 665111
Palace Barracks, Holywood, Co. Down ....(01232) 425121
Abercorn Barracks, Ballykinler, Co. Down ....(01396) 613111
Lisanelly Barracks, Omagh, Co. Tyrone............(01662) 243194
Ebrington Barracks, Derry ....(01504) 43211
Shackleton Barracks, Ballykelly, Co. Derry............(01504) 763221
Mahon Barracks, Portadown, Co. Armagh ....(01762) 351551

Home Service Battalions *(Royal Irish Regiment)*

3rd Battalion (Co. Down & Armagh) - Mahon Road, Portadown, Co. Armagh............(01762) 351551
4th Battalion (Co. Fermanagh & Tyrone) - Grosvenor Barracks, Enniskillen, Co. Fermanagh ....(01365) 327540

5th Battalion (Co. Derry) - Shackleton Barracks, Ballykelly, Co. Derry.............................(01504) 763221
7th Battalion (City of Belfast) - Malone Centre, Windsor Park, Belfast, Co. Antrim ....(01232) 665244
8th Battalion (Co. Armagh & Tyrone) - Drumadd Barracks, Armagh, Co. Armagh ....(01861) 523821
9th Battalion (Co. Antrim) - Steeple Road, Antrim, Co. Antrim.............................(01849) 462402

Regimental Headquarters

Royal Irish Regiment - St. Patrick's Barracks, Ballymena, Co. Antrim BT43 7BH ....(01266) 652135
Royal Irish Rangers / Royal Ulster Rifles - 5 Waring Street, Belfast, Co. Antrim. BT1 2EW ....(01232) 232086
Royal Irish Fusiliers - Sovereign's House, The Mall, Armagh, Co. Armagh ....(01861) 522911
Royal Inniskilling Fusiliers - The Castle, Enniskillen, Co. Fermanagh ....(01365) 323142

Territorial Army

HQ 107 (Ulster) Brigade - St. Patrick's Barracks, Ballymena, Co. Antrim BT43 7BH ....(01266) 661298

Royal Navy

Palace Barracks, Holywood, Co. Down BT18 9RQ...(01232) 427040.

Royal Air Force

Aldergrove, Co. Antrim...(01849) 422051.

NORTHERN IRELAND: DEFENCE PERSONNEL, 1998*

Force	Number	Force	Number
Royal Air Force	1,200	Total RIR	5,000
Royal Navy	250	Others	10,500
Royal Irish Regiment (RIR):		TOTAL:	**16,950**
RIR (Full-time)	2,000		
RIR (Part-time)	3,000	* approximate	

REP. OF IRELAND: DEFENCE PERSONNEL, 1960-1997

Year	Permanent Defence Force	Reserve Defence Force
1960	8,965	24,569
1965	8,199	21,946
1970	8,574	20,253
1975	12,059	17,221
1980	13,383	19,249
1985	13,778	16,358
1990	13,233	15,982
1995	12,742	16,188
1996	12,107	15,795
1997	12,006	15,515

R.O.I.: STRENGTH OF PERMANENT DEFENCE FORCES (MALES AND FEMALES), JUNE 1998

Rank	Army	Air Corps	Naval Service	Total
Commissioned Officers:				
Lieutenant-General	1	0	0	1
Major-General	3	0	0	3
Brigadier-General	6	1	1	8
Colonel	32	1	3	36
Lieutenant-Colonel	114	11	10	135
Commandant	363	32	43	438
Captain	413	54	37	504
Lieutenant	107	13	18	138
2nd Lieutenant	42	14	9	65
TOTAL:	**1,081**	**126**	**121**	**1,328**
Non-Commissioned Officers:				
Sergeants-Major	32	5	6	43
Battalion Quartermaster Sergeant	41	4	5	50
Company Sergeant	137	48	53	238
Company Quartermaster Sergeant	283	15	16	314
TOTAL:	**493**	**72**	**80**	**645**

REPUBLIC OF IRELAND: NAVAL & AIR SERVICE

Description	Type
Naval Service Vessels:	
LE Deirdre	Offshore Patrol Vessel (OPV)
LE Emer	Offshore Patrol Vessel (OPV)
LE Aoife	Offshore Patrol Vessel (OPV)
LE Aisling	Offshore Patrol Vessel (OPV)
LE Eithne	Helicopter Patrol Vessel (HPV)
LE Orla	Coastal Patrol Vessel (CPV)
LE Ciara	Coastal Patrol Vessel (CPV)
Air Corps Aircraft:	
40 Aircraft	25 Fixed Wing & 15 Rotor Blade

REPUBLIC OF IRELAND & NORTHERN IRELAND: DRUGS SEIZED BY POLICE FORCES, 1997

REPUBLIC OF IRELAND		NORTHERN IRELAND	
Type of Drug	**Quantity**	**Type of Drug**	**Quantity**
Cannabis (g)	34,827	Cannabis - herbal & resin (kg)	486.5
Cannabis Resin (g)	1,247,875	Cannabis Plants	155
Cannabis Plants	753	Cannabis Joints	225
Heroin - Diamorphine (g)	8,211	Heroin (g)	196.5
Morphine (g)	3.28	Heroin (tablets)	1104
Morphine (tablets)	529	Heroine (ampoules)	20
LSD	1,851	L.S.D. (tablets)	111,851
Ecstasy (tablets)	17,516	L.S.D. (microdots)	18
Amphetamines (g)	102,894	Ecstasy (tablets)	78,108
Amphetamines (tablets)	3,889	Ecstasy (capsules)	158
Cocaine (g)	11,020	Ecstasy Powder (g)	1.25
Benzodiazepines (tablets)	4,942	Amphetamines (kg)	24
Benzodiazepines (g)	248	Amphetamines (tablets)	46
Methadone (litres)	34.6	Cocaine (g)	426
Methadone (tablets)	908	Cocaine (wraps)	4
Dihydrocodeme (tablets)	83		
Buprenorphine (tablets)	22		
Ephedrine (tablets)	2,918		
Ephedrine (g)	70.1		
Other (tablets)	115		
Other (g)	212		

REPUBLIC OF IRELAND: DRUG OFFENCES BY REGION, 1997

	Northern Region	Western Region	Eastern Region	Southern Region	South Eastern Region	Dublin Region	Total
				Prosecutions for Offences under the Misuse of Drugs Act			
Possession Only	181	221	315	910	313	3,926	5,866
Supplier / Dealer	13	24	89	212	62	1,214	1,614
Obstruction	1	5	3	26	6	317	358
Other	1	7	3	15	5	58	89
Total	**196**	**257**	**410**	**1,163**	**386**	**5,515**	**7,927**
By Gender:							
Male	179	238	394	1,081	369	3,925	6,186
Female	17	19	16	82	17	1,590	1,741
Total:	**196**	**257**	**410**	**1,163**	**386**	**5,515**	**7,927**

Regions:
Western: Clare, Galway, Roscommon, Mayo.
Southern: Kerry, Limerick, Cork.
Dublin: Dublin Area.
Northern: Sligo, Leitrim, Donegal, Cavan, Monaghan.
Eastern: Louth, Meath, Longford, Westmeath, Laois, Offaly, Carlow, Kildare.
South Eastern: Wexford, Tipperary, Waterford, Kilkenny.

NORTHERN IRELAND: ARRESTS MADE FOR DRUG RELATED OFFENCES, 1994-97

Year	No. of Arrests
1994	1,196
1995	1,558
1996	1,017
1997	909

REP. OF IRELAND: DOMESTIC VIOLENCE, 1996-97

Area	Incidents		Arrests		Persons charged		Persons injured		Persons convicted	
	1996	1997	1996	1997	1996	1997	1996	1997	1996	1997
Eastern Region	631	506	161	235	127	193	144	172	110	144
Dublin Region	2,996	2306	436	460	380	348	428	315	251	236
Northern Region	199	302	50	129	36	111	47	117	27	46
South Eastern Region	164	267	67	78	42	76	88	114	18	62
Southern Region	491	530	108	152	100	166	149	190	70	140
Western Region	164	273	38	81	40	53	67	84	30	45
TOTAL:	4,645	4,184	860	1,135	725	947	923	992	506	673

Regions:
Western: Clare, Galway, Roscommon, Mayo.   *Northern:* Sligo, Leitrim, Donegal, Cavan, Monaghan.
Southern: Kerry, Limerick, Cork.   *Eastern:* Louth, Meath, Longford, Westmeath, Laois, Offaly, Carlow, Kildare.
Dublin: Dublin Area.   *South Eastern:* Wexford, Tipperary, Waterford, Kilkenny.

REP. OF IRELAND: CLAIMS RECEIVED AND PROCESSED BY ARMY PERSONNEL, JULY 1997

Type of Claim	Number
Personal Injury claims received	7,200
Army Deafness cases processed	4,150

CONSTITUTION of IRELAND BUNREACHT na hÉIREANN

The Constitution of Ireland was approved by referendum on July 1, 1937, the Dáil having already approved it on June 14, 1937. It came into effect on December 29, 1937, replacing the Constitution of the Irish Free State (1922). The then Taoiseach, Éamon de Valera, played a large part in the drafting of the document which made the Free State a Republic in all but name.

Under the Constitution, the name of the state became Éire (Article 4), and it defined the national territory as "the whole island of Ireland, its islands and the territorial seas" (Article 2). It also stated that laws passed by the Dáil would have effect in the 26 counties only "pending re-integration of the national territory".

Under the heading of the State, the Constitution provided for the name and description of the State, stating Ireland to be a "sovereign, independent democratic state" (Article 5). The powers of government, the national flag, the position of Irish as the national language and the recognition of English as the second official language, citizenship and natural resources are also dealt with under the heading of the State.

The office and function of the President are enshrined in Articles 12 and 13, while the composition, regulation and functions of the Oireachtas (the National Parliament) and both houses therein, the Dáil and the Seanad (the houses of representatives and senate, respectively), are dealt with in Articles 15 to 19.

Articles 20 to 27 deal with the introduction, debate of and passing of legislation. Government, which according to Article 6 derives all legislative, executive and judicial powers from the people, is considered by Article 28, with reference to the exercising of that power, its responsibility to the Dáil, its powers during war or national emergency and the nomination and composition of the cabinet. Foreign Affairs and International Relations, as conducted by the Government, are provided for under Article 29 such as membership of the European Union.

Articles 34 to 39 deal with the Structure Organisation and Powers of the Courts; Articles 30 to 33 being concerned with the establishment of the Offices of the Attorney General, Comptroller and Auditor General and the creation of a Council of State to advise the President.

Articles 40 to 44 are concerned with the fundamental rights of the Citizen under the broad headings of Personal Rights (Article 40); The Family and Education (Articles 41 to 42); Private Property (Article 43); Religion (Article 44). Other unenumerated Rights have been granted by the Courts. Under these Articles, all Citizens are equal before the law and the law undertakes to protect the personal rights of all Citizens. Freedom of expression, assembly and association are guaranteed, subject to Public Order and Morality. The family is recognised as the fundamental unit of society and provision is made for mothers "not obliged by economic necessity to engage in labour to the neglect of their duties in the home" (Article 40.2.2). The institution of marriage was protected by the prohibiting of its dissolution, but with the introduction of the Family Law (Divorce) Act in 1997, this no longer the case.

The State will endeavour to educate its citizens but recognises and respects that the family is the "primary and natural educator of the Child" (Article 42.1). The right to own private property is guaranteed, as is the Freedom of Religious Conscience and Practice, and the State will not discriminate on grounds of Religious Belief (Article 44.2.3).

Article 45 contains the principles of social policy under which the state operates. Articles 46 and 47 deal with amendments to the Constitution which can only be done by referendum. Articles 48 to 63 deal with the Repeal of the 1922 Irish Free State Constitution and the transitory powers necessary until the new Constitution comes into effect.

EDUCATION

From Hedge
Schools to Computers:
The Importance of Education to Commercial and Professional Evolution

By **Senator Joe O'Toole,** *General Secretary Irish National Teachers' Organisation*

THERE has always been the inherent contradiction in our attitude as a nation of people to Education. The teacher whether referred to as Saoi, Professor, Brehon, or Teacher has invariably been respected and held in high esteem by the community. On the other hand there has always been a reticence about paying the financial price for a decent infra-structure. This was never more obvious in our history as when we began to establish the Great Universities of Trinity and Queens and others but ignored the need for a Primary school system which fed into it. There were resonances of this again in recent years when at a time Primary Education was absolutely strapped for resources, the Government of the day decided that money would be better spent on free Third level fees.

The paradoxes created by the differing directions of expressed commitment as between Valuing education, taking pride in our Scholarly past and wanting the best and most modern for our pupils was never as clearly manifest for me as during a visit some years ago, to Clonmacnoise National School, situated on a most beautiful sweeping bend of the Mid Shannon. The school was in an atrociously substandard condition at the time and parents, teachers, management and the INTO were in dispute with the Department of Education in an effort to get funding for the renovation and improvement of the school building. Meanwhile there were busloads of tourists disembarking from buses and boats to walk past the decrepit building which was the twentieth century Primary school in order to view the remains of St. Ciaran's Fifth Century Educational Institution, in which the state had invested millions to cre-ate an interpretative centre to explain to the world how much we valued our scholars. My most powerful residual image of my wet day visit, was the sight of the rain seeping through the hole in the roof, which the state would not replace and dripping on to the keyboard of the brand new computer which had been presented to the school by the parents and local community. It was difficult not to conclude that St. Ciaran was getting a better deal than our next generation.

The tension between Education and investment continues. Every schoolday sees a daily mir-acle take place in Irish schools. A half million Irish primary school pupils in the Republic con-gregate around twenty one thousand teachers in Europe's most overcrowded classrooms and manage not only to make progress but in fact to emerge close to the top in European studies on Literacy and Mathematics. It is extraordinary to marvel at the success of Irish Primary Education when it is objectively considered. It is quite stunning however when it is considered in the context of the fact that the Irish State has over many decades spent and invested less per Primary school pupil than any other Member State of the European Union.

Part of the difficulty in convincing the authorities to spend money on Primary and Post Primary education stems from the fact that such investment tends to be long or medium term and as long as there is no obvious gain during the course of the particular Government's period of office then they are slow to commit to it. The reality is, that there is an inextricable set of interconnections between Education, Qualification and Employment. Each is dependent on the other. Without Education there is only the slimmest of possibilities that a person may gain qualifications and without qualification there is only the slimmest of chances that a person may gain employment. It must be quite clear then that the pupil who fails at Primary level will be too far behind to make it at Post Primary and will not gain any meaningful qualification and will emerge from the Educational system almost unemployable and probably a cost on the Social Welfare budget. In many cases, additional support at Primary level either by way of Remediation or Special help could well have made the difference between a self-confident contributing member of the workforce and an anonymous member of the unemployed.

A generation ago there were many jobs of a repetitive nature which people without qualification or education could attain. Times have changed. Streets are brushed, and concrete is by machine. Assembly lines are operated by robots and most lifting, pushing and shoving functions are now automated. Apart from all that, the fact is that Irish parents do not aspire to getting their children jobs on an assembly line. Quite understandably they have higher aspirations, like every previous generation they would like their children to do a little better than themselves. Many of the jobs which have left Western Europe for the Far East are no great loss because the current generation would not want them. In fact if we live long enough we will see the same movement take place in the future from the Far East to Africa.

The debate about Education and Employment has focused overmuch on job attainment. It is a fact that the qualified person will gain employment. But what kind of person creates the jobs? It is a fact that if we are to share wealth we must first create it. What are the qualities of the person who creates employment? And where are those qualities developed and encouraged in the school system?

In my view, this is the point where the Education system fails the community. It must be a fact that the qualities of the successful entrepreneur would include traits such as risk taking, creativity, leadership, articulation, innovation, imagination, self-confidence etc., etc. It is also a fact that these find very little space in the subject based examination system. We reward and promote in the main those who rework and present the knowledge accumulated during the year's study. These go on to college and emerge as Honours students. But where have they ever shown the capacity to lead, to innovate, to organise, to strategise?

Surely the child who at five years of age covers a blank page with colour and then is encouraged to hold it up and explain what it is to teacher and classmates learns the importance of creativity?

Surely the child who captains the school football or chess team through both defeat and victory has learned about leadership?

Surely the child who takes the stage for the school play or concert and holds the attention of the audience has learned self-confidence?

Surely the child who has participated in school debates has learned the need for articulation and logical argument?

Surely the child who has selected and placed a team for a competition has learned the need to plan and strategise?

Surely these are the school activities which produce the people who will lead and energise the next generation of professionals, politicians, entrepreneurs etc.

These unfortunately are also the activities which get least public attention because they do not count for points.

The school system can deliver. There must however be an investment in it which reflects its importance as a key to future national success. ❐

STUDENT ENROLMENT

REPUBLIC OF IRELAND (School/College)	1985-86	1990-91	1995-96
Primary schools	567,064	543,744	478,692
Secondary schools	334,692	342,416	369,865
Tertiary Institutions	53,473	68,165	95,099
TOTAL:	**955,229**	**954,325**	**943,656**

NORTHERN IRELAND (School/College)	1987-88	1991-92	1996-97
Grant-aided Primary schools (incl. nursery)	187,346	190,988	192,305
Grant-aided Secondary schools	148,815	146,968	156,147
Special schools	3,811	4,106	4,680
Independent schools	1,119	1,052	925
Further Education	-	80,021	76,389
Higher Education	-	19,241	8,713
TOTAL:	**341,091**	**441,324**	**438,229**

NORTHERN IRELAND (1997-98)	Nursery	Primary	Secondary	Grammar	Special	TOTAL
Controlled	4,102	90,766	40,154	14,814	4,314	154,150
RC Maintained	1,431	88,620	46,165	-	250	136,466
Other Maintained	-	1,234	231	-	117	1,582
Controlled Integrated	-	725	358	-	-	1,083
Grant-maintained Integrated	-	3,121	3,950	-	-	7,071
Voluntary	-	-	-	50,800	-	50,800
Independent	-	-	-	-	-	1,213
Hospital Schools	-	-	-	-	-	197
TOTAL:	**5,533**	**184,466**	**90,858**	**65,614**	**4,681**	**352,562**

Source: DENI

REP. OF IRELAND: EXPENDITURE ON EDUCATION

Expenditure per Student	1985-86	1990-91	1995-96
Primary Level	£861	£1,095	£1,498
Secondary Level	£1,553	£1,822	£2,269
Third Level	£3,913	£3,743	£4,097
TOTAL:	**£6,327**	**£6,660**	**£7,864**

Expenditure per Education Level	1985-86	1990-91	1995-96
Primary Level	£435.7m	£552.1m	£747.0m
Secondary Level	£463.8m	£592.2m	£881.5m
Third Level	£208.9m	£312.6m	£544.4m
TOTAL:	**£1,108.4m**	**£1,456.9m**	**£2,172.9m**

PUPIL-TEACHER RATIOS

REPUBLIC OF IRELAND* Type of School	1985-86	1990-91	1995-96
Primary	26.8	25.8	22.7
Secondary**	17.4	18.1	17.7

* Ratios are based on the total enrolment in all national schools
** These figures relate to full-time teachers only and not the full-time equivalent of part-time teachers.

NORTHERN IRELAND Type of School	1987-88	1996-97	1997-98
Nursery	24.1	23.4	24.4
Primary*	23.5	19.8	19.9
All Secondary	14.8	14.5	14.5
Special	7.2	6.4	6.7
All Grant-aided schools	**18.4**	**16.7**	**16.8**

* These ratios include pupils and teachers in nursery classes.
Source: DENI

PARTICIPATION IN EDUCATION

REPUBLIC OF IRELAND % Persons in Education*	1985-86	1990-91	1995-96
5-12 years	100.0	100.0	99.5
13-15 years	97.0	98.0	98.7
16 years	82.1	92.5	89.8
17 years	64.6	74.2	78.3
18 years	40.8	47.6	60.6
19 years†	24.1	31.0	44.5
20+ years†	9.9	14.2	18.2

* These figures are based on provisional population estimates for each year.
† From 1993-94, these figures exclude students aged 25+ years.

NORTHERN IRELAND % Persons in Education	1992-93	1994-95	1995-96	1996-97
16 years	45.6	47.0	45.0	46.7
17 years	33.2	36.9	36.7	31.4
16 and 17 years	39.4	42.0	41.4	42.2

Source: DENI

PRIMARY SCHOOL STUDENTS BY YEAR GROUP

YEAR GROUP	REP. OF IRELAND (1995/6)	NORTHERN IRELAND (1997/8)†
Junior Infants / Nursery*	56,336	3008
Senior Infants / Reception*	54,580	2552
Year 1	54,014	24,513
Year 2	57,506	25,541
Year 3	59,207	25,925
Year 4	59,713	25,878
Year 5	61,052	26,062
Year 6	62,049	26,660
Other / Year 7	1,397	26,709
Pupils with special needs / in special units	12,838	973
TOTAL:	485,923**	187,821

†Source: DENI
* includes nursery and reception classes in primary schools only.
**Total includes pupils in private primary schools.

ATTENDANCE AT SECONDARY SCHOOLS

REPUBLIC OF IRELAND (School Category)	1985-86	1990-91	1995-96
Secondary Schools	214,640	213,047	223,605
Vocational Schools	81,431	86,428	94,809
Community & Comprehensive Schools	38,621	42,941	51,451
TOTAL:	334,692	342,416	369,865

NORTHERN IRELAND (School Category)	1987-88	1991-92	1997-98
Secondary Schools	92,534	87,525	90,858
Grammar (preparatory)	3,815	3,673	3,378
Grammar (secondary)	52,466	55,770	62,236
TOTAL:	148,815	146,968	156,472

Source: DENI

ATTENDANCE AT HIGHER EDUCATION

REPUBLIC OF IRELAND (Students by Institution Type)	1985-86	1990-91	1995-96
Colleges aided by Dept. of Education:			
HEA Institutions	32,388	39,837	55,850
Teacher Training Colleges	3,209	1,658	593
Technological Colleges	18,953	27,271	38,130
Others (National College of Industrial Relations)	-	-	526
Colleges Aided by Depts. of Justice & Defence	-	-	863
Others (non-aided)	-	-	6,700
TOTAL:	53,473	68,165	102,662

Continued from previous page

NORTHERN IRELAND (Students by Institution Type)	1988-89	1991-92	1996-97
Further Education Students	53,531	72,926	76,389
Higher Education Students	3,177	4,095	8,713
University Students*	15,976	19,245	26,106
Students on Teacher Training courses	1,816	1,938	1,988

* figures for Queens University and the University of Ulster.

Source: DENI

STAGE AT WHICH LEAVERS WITH NO FORMAL QUALIFICATIONS LEFT SCHOOL

REPUBLIC OF IRELAND: Level (1996)	Male	Female	Total
Estimated Number in Category	1,600	1,100	2,700
First Year Post-primary	16.0%	23.9%	19.0%
Second Year Post-primary	49.8%	49.3%	49.6%
Third Year Post-primary	32.5%	21.1%	28.2%
Other	1.7%	5.6%	3.2%

NORTHERN IRELAND: Persons with no Qualifications	1987-88	1991-92	1994-95	1996-97
Males with no GCSEs/GCEs	3,366	1,772	946	1,020
Females with no GCSEs/GCEs	1,869	976	409	571
Total with no GCSE/GCE qualifications*	5,235	2,748	1,355	1,591
Males with no formal qualifications	-	-	596	584
Females with no formal qualifications	-	-	227	345
Total with no formal qualifications	-	-	823	929
% School leavers with no GCSEs/GCEs (%)	21.5 %	12.3 %	5.5%	6.2%
% School leavers with no formal qualifications (%)	-	-	3.4%	3.6%

*Includes those who didn't take GCSE exams and those who obtained no graded results but who obtained other qualifications.

Source: DENI

STATUS OF 2nd-LEVEL SCHOOL LEAVERS

REPUBLIC OF IRELAND (1996)	Male	Female	Total
Estimated Number in Category	34,500	34,000	68,500
Employed	47.9%	40.1%	44.0%
Unemployed after loss of job	4.2%	4.0%	4.1%
(of which on schemes)	*(0.6%)*	*(0.3%)*	*(0.4%)*
Unemployed seeking first job	9.5%	7.6%	8.6l%
(of which on schemes)	*(1.9%)*	*(1.8%)*	*(1.9%)*
Students	34.7%	40.3%	37.5%
Unavailable for work	1.8%	4.2%	3.0%
Emigrated	1.8%	3.8%	2.8%
TOTAL:	100.0%	100.0%	100.0%

NORTHERN IRELAND (1996-97)	Male	Female	Total
Students (Higher Education Institutes)	3,203	4,044	7,247
Students (Further Education Institutes)	3,785	4,608	8,393
Employed/in training/seeking employment	5,905	3,770	9,675
Unknown	224	178	402
TOTAL:	13,117	12,600	25,717

Source: DENI

NUMBERS OF SCHOOLS AND COLLEGES

Republic of Ireland Type of School/College	1985-86	1990-91	1995-6
Primary Schools*	3384	3352	3317
Secondary Schools**	811	794	768
Third Level***	33	34	30

* includes ordinary national schools and schools for those with special needs.
** includes secondary, vocational, community and comprehensive schools.
*** includes HEA institutions, technical colleges, teacher training colleges, and the National College of Industrial Relations.

Northern Ireland Type of School/College	1987-88	1991-92	1996-97
Primary Schools (incl. nursery)	1,071	1,052	1,011
Secondary Schools	249	236	238
Special Schools	46	46	47
Independent Schools	16	18	19
TOTAL:	1,382	1,352	1,315

* This figure does not include primary schools.

Source: DENI

NORTHERN IRELAND (1997-98)	Nursery	Primary	Secondary	Grammar	Special	TOTAL
Controlled	65	456	76	18	44	659
RC Maintained	26	431	78	-	2	537
Other Maintained	-	11	1	-	1	13
Controlled Integrated	-	7	1	-	-	8
Grant-maintained Integrated	-	15	10	-	-	25
Voluntary	-	-	-	54	-	54
Independent	-	-	-	-	-	22
Hospital Schools	-	-	-	-	-	3
TOTAL:	91	920	166	72	47	1,321

Source: DENI

NUMBERS OF MULTI-DENOMINATION SCHOOLS

REPUBLIC OF IRELAND INTER-DENOMINATION SCHOOLS	1997-98
Number of Schools	319
Number of Pupils	148,479

NORTHERN IRELAND INTEGRATED SCHOOLS	1991-92	1996-97	1997-98
Number of Schools	11	21	22
Number of Pupils	1,226	3,512	3,809

Source: DENI

NUMBERS OF GAELSCOILEANNA (outside the Gaeltacht)

SCHOOL LEVEL (1997-98)	Leinster	Munster	Connacht	Ulster	TOTAL
Primary Schools					
No. of Schools	48	39	11	18	116
Pupil Enrolment	8961	6242	1900	1740	18843
*No. of Teachers**	382 (21)	260 (4)	81 (3)	82 (4)	805 (32)
Secondary Schools					
No. of Schools	11	12	2	2	27
Pupil Enrolment	2,857	1710	193	295	5055
*No. of Teachers**	170 (29)	143 (70)	38	16 (2)	367 (101)

* Numbers in parentheses: part-time teachers

Leinster (Carlow, Dublin, Kildare, Kilkenny, Laois, Louth, Meath, Offaly, Westmeath, Wexford, Wicklow,) **Munster** (Clare, Cork, Kerry, Limerick,Tipperary, Waterford) **Connacht** (Galway, Mayo, Sligo) **Ulster** (Antrim, Armagh, Cavan, Derry, Donegal, Down, Monaghan, Tyrone)

GROWTH IN GAELSCOILEANNA (1972-98)

SCHOOL LEVEL	1972	1982	1992	1997-98
Primary Schools	11	27	72	116
Secondary schools	5	9	16	27
TOTAL:	16	36	98	143

NUMBERS OF PRIMARY SCHOOL TEACHERS

REPUBLIC OF IRELAND	1988-89	1991-92	1995-96
Total Primary Teachers	20362	20,708	21,052

NORTHERN IRELAND	1987-88	1991-92	1996-97
Nursery	156	162	180
Primary	7678	8044	9099
Special	525	609	726

Source: DENI

NUMBERS OF SECOND-LEVEL TEACHERS

REPUBLIC OF IRELAND PERSONNEL	1985-86	1991-92	1995-96
Secondary Schools	-	12,034	13382
Vocational Schools	-	6,383	6432
Community and Comprehensive Schools	-	2,621	3289
TOTAL:	**19,278***	**21,038**	**23,103**

*This total includes full-time teachers only.

NORTHERN IRELAND PERSONNEL	1987-88	1991-92	1996-97
Secondary Schools	6,378	5,965	6,553
Grammar Schools			
Preparatory	155	116	173
Secondary	3,268	3,354	3,815
TOTAL:	**9,801**	**9,435**	**10,541**

* These figures do not include full-time teachers in hospital schools. † This total includes seconded teachers.
Source: DENI

NUMBERS EMPLOYED IN 3rd-LEVEL EDUCATION
REPUBLIC OF IRELAND (Full-time)* December 1997

Personnel Category	Males	Females	Total
Academic Staff	2,011	721	2,732
Non-academic Staff	1,783	2,104	3,887
TOTAL:	**3,794**	**2,825**	**6,619**

* Figures include contract staff.
Above totals include 7 Universities (see list), NCAD, St. Patrick's College, Mary Immaculate College of Ed.

NORTHERN IRELAND (Full-and part-time)

Instructor Grade	1988-89	1991-92	1996-97*
Further Education Teachers	2,448	2,304	2,144
Universities	1,775	1,930	1,635
Professors	162	186	259
Readers & Senior Lecturers	467	495	473
Lecturers, Assistant Lecturers,			
Demonstrators and Others	1,146	1,249	1,635

* Full-time only. Source: DENI

THIRD-LEVEL COLLEGES IN REPUBLIC OF IRELAND

UNIVERSITIES

University of Dublin Trinity College, Dublin 2. *(Founded 1592)* (01) 6772941
Dublin City University Glasnevin, Dublin 9. *(Founded 1980)* (01) 7045000
University of Limerick Plassey Technological Park, Limerick. *(Founded 1972)* (061) 333644
National University of Ireland, 49 Merrion Square, Dublin 2. 01 - 6767246

CONSTITUENT COLLEGES

University College Cork - National University of Ireland, Cork *(Founded 1854)* (021) 276871
National University of Ireland, Dublin (UCD) Belfield, Dublin 4. *(Founded 1845)* (01) 2693244
National University of Ireland, Galway (NUI Galway) Galway. *(Founded 1845)* (091) 524411
National University of Ireland, Maynooth Co. Kildare. *(Founded 1795)* (01) 6285222

INSTITUTES OF TECHNOLOGY (ITs)

Athlone IT Dublin Road, Athlone, Co. Westmeath. (0902) 72647
IT Carlow Kilkenny Road, Carlow. (0503) 70400
Cork IT Rossa Avenue, Bishopstown, Co. Cork. (021) 326100
Dundalk IT Co. Louth. (042) 34785
Dun Laoghaire Institute of Art, Design & Technology
Carriglea Park, Kill Ave., Dun Laoghaire, Co. Dublin. (01) 2801138
Galway-Mayo IT Dublin Road, Galway. (091) 753161
Letterkenny IT Port Road, Letterkenny, Co. Donegal. (074) 24888
Limerick IT Moylish Park, Limerick. (061) 327688

IT Sligo Ballinode, Sligo. ....(071) 55222
IT Tallaght Dublin 24. ....(01) 4042000
IT Tralee Clash, Tralee, Co. Kerry. ....(066) 24666
Waterford IT Cork Road, Waterford. ....(051) 302000
DUBLIN INST. OF TECHNOLOGY Fitzwilliam House, 30 Upper Pembroke Street, Dublin 2. ....(01) 4023000
DIT Aungier Street, Dublin 2. DIT Bolton Street,Dublin 1. DIT Cathal Brugha Street, Dublin 1.
DIT College of Music, Adelaide Road, Dublin 2. DIT Kevin Street, Dublin 8. DIT Mountjoy Square, Dublin 1.

COLLEGES OF EDUCATION

Church of Ireland College of Education 96 Upper Rathmines Road, Dublin 6. ....(01) 4970033
Froebel College of Education Sion Hill, Blackrock, Co. Dublin. ....(01) 2888520
Mary Immaculate College of Education South Circular Road, Limerick. ....(061) 314588
Mater Dei Institute of Education Clonliffe Road, Dublin 3. ....(01) 8376027
St. Angela's College of Education for Home Economics Lough Gill, Co. Sligo. ....(071) 42785
St. Catherine's College of Education for Home Economics Sion Hill, Blackrock, Co. Dublin. ....(01) 2884989
St. Mary's College of Education Griffith Avenue, Marino, Dublin 9. ....(01) 8335111
St. Patrick's College of Education Drumcondra, Dublin 9. ....(01) 8376191

THEOLOGY & DIVINITY COLLEGES

All Hallows College (Theology & Philosophy) Grace Park Road, Dublin 9. ....(01) 8373745
Holy Cross College (Theology & Philosophy) Clonliffe, Drumcondra, Dublin 3. ....(01) 8375103
Holy Ghost College (Theology & Philosophy) Kimmage Manor, Dublin 12. ....(01) 4504174
Milltown Institute of Theology & Philosophy Milltown Park, Dublin 6. ....(01) 2698802
Pontiffical University (Seminary) St. Patrick's College, Maynooth, Co. Kildare. ....(01)7083600
St. John's College (Theology & Philosopy) John's Hill, Waterford. ....(051) 874199
St. Patrick's College (Theology & Philosopy) Carlow. ....(0503) 31114
St. Patrick's College (Theology & Philosopy) Thurles, Co. Tipperary. ....(0504) 21201
St. Peter's College Wexford. ....(053) 42071

ADDITIONAL STATE COLLEGES

Cork School of Music 13 Union Quay, Cork. ....(021) 270076
Crawford School of Art & Design Sharman Crawford Street, Cork. ....(021) 966343
Garda College Training Centre, Templemore, Co. Tipperary. ....(0504) 31522
Military College Curragh Camp, Co. Kildare. ....(045) 41301
National College of Art & Design 100 Thomas Street, Dublin 8. ....(01) 6711203

ADDITIONAL COLLEGES

American College in Dublin 2 Merrion Square, Dublin 2 ....(01) 6768939
Burren College of Art Newtown Castle, Ballyvaughan, Co. Clare ....(065) 77200
Dublin Business School (DBS) 13-14 Aungier Street, Dublin 2...(01) 4751024
Griffith College South Circular Road, Dublin 8...(01) 4545640
Honorable Society of Kings Inns, Henrietta Street, Dublin 1 ....(01) 8744840
HSI College The Crescent, Limerick. ....(061) 317822
Institute of Public Administration 57 - 61 Lansdowne Road, Dublin 4. ....(01) 6686233
Irish Management Institute Sandyford Road, Clonard, Dublin 16. ....(01) 2956911
Mid-West Business Institute Rutland Street, Limerick. ....(061) 313833
Montessori College Mount St. Mary's Road, Dundrum, Dublin 6. ....(01) 2692499
Law Society of Ireland Blackhall Place, Dublin 7. ....(01) 6710711
LSB College Ltd. Balfe House, 6-9 Balfe St., Dublin 2. ....(01) 6794844
National College of Industrial Relations Sandford Road, Dublin 6. ....(01) 4060500
Portobello College South Richmond Street, Dublin 2. ....(01) 6715811
Royal College of Surgeons in Ireland 123 St. Stephen's Green, Dublin 2. ....(01) 4022100
Shannon College of Hotel Management Shannon, Co. Clare. ....(061) 471444
Skerries College Wellington House, 9 - 11 Patrick's Hill, Cork. ....(021) 507027
St Nicholas Montessori College Ireland 16 Adelaide Street, Dun Laoghaire, Co. Dublin. ....(01) 2806064
Tourism College Killybegs, Co. Donegal. ....(073) 31120

THIRD-LEVEL COLLEGES IN NORTERN IRELAND

UNIVERSITIIES & HIGHER EDUCATION INSTITUTES

Queen's University of Belfast Belfast, BT7 1NN ....*(Founded 1845)* ....(01232) 245133
University of Ulster University House, Cromore Rd., Coleraine, Derry.......*(Founded 1968)* ....(01265) 44141
University of Ulster *(Jordanstown)* Shore Rd., Newtownabbey, Antrim ...*(Founded 1968)* ....(01232) 365131
University of Ulster *(Magee College)* Northland Rd., Derry BT48 7JL.....................................(01504) 265621
University of Ulster *(at Belfast)* York St., Belfast BT15 1ED....................*(Founded 1968)* ....(01232) 328515
St. Mary's Teacher Training College 191 Falls Road, Belfast...(01232) 327678

Stranmillis Teacher Training College Stranmillis Road, Belfast...(01232) 381271

FURTHER EDUCATION INSTITUTES

Armagh College of Further Education Lonsdale Street, Armagh. ....(01861) 522205
Belfast Institute of Further and Higher Education Park Hse, 87-91 Great Victoria St., Belfast ..(01232) 265000
Castlereagh College of Further and Higher Education Montgomery Road, Cregagh, Belfast .(01232) 797144
Causeway Institute of Further and Higher Education Union St., Coleraine, Co. Derry................(01265) 54717
East Antrim Institute of Further and Higher Education 32-34 Pound St., Larne, Co. Antrim .....(01574) 272268
East Down Institute of Further and Higher Education Market Street, Downpatrick, Co. Down ..(01396) 615815
East Tyrone College of Further Education Circular Road, Dungannon, Co. Tyrone....................(01868) 722323
Fermanagh College Fairview, 1 Dublin Road, Enniskillen, Co. Fermanagh ....(01365) 322431
Limavady College of Further Education Main St., Limavady, Co. Derry.................................(015047) 62334
Lisburn College of Further and Higher Education 39 Castle Street, Lisburn, Co. Antrim..........(01846) 677225
Newry/Kilkeel College of Further Education Patrick Street, Newry. Co. Down ....(01693) 61071
North Down and Ards Institute of Further and Higher Education
Castle Park Rd, Bangor, Co. Down ....(01247) 271254
Northern Ireland Hotel & Catering College Ballywillan Road, Portrush, Co. Antrim...................(01265) 823768
North East Institute of Further and Higher Education Trostan Ave., Co. Antrim........................(01266) 652871
North West Institute of Further and Higher Education Strand Road, Derry..............................(01504) 266711
Omagh College of Further Education Mountjoy Rd., Omagh, Co. Tyrone ....(01662) 245433
Upper Bann Institute of Further and Higher Education
26 Lurgan Road, Portadown, Craigavon, Co. Armagh ....(01762) 337111

POINTS FOR ENTERING THIRD-LEVEL EDUCATION

NORTHERN IRELAND* (A-level results)**	REPUBLIC OF IRELAND LEAVING CERTIFICATE*** (Higher-level results)	(Ordinary-level results)
A=10 points	A1=100 points	A1=60 points
B=8 points	A2=90 points	A2=50 points
C=6 points	B1=85 points	B1=45 points
D=4 points	B2=80 points	B2=40 points
E=2 points	B3=75 points	B3=35 points
	C1=70 points	C1=30 points
	C2=65 points	C2=25 points
	C3=60 points	C3=20 points
	D1=55 points	D1=15 points
	D2=50 points	D2=10 points
	D3=45 points	D3=5 points

*Source: DENI
** Two or more A-levels are taken into consideration.
*** Six Leaving Certificate subjects are taken into consideration; Bonus points are awarded for maths by UL and DIT.

GRADES IN THE REPUBLIC OF IRELAND SCHOOL CERTIFICATES: A1=90-100% A2=85-89% B1=80-84% B2=75-79% B3=70-74% C1=65-69% C2=60-64% C3=55-59% D1=50-54% D2=45-49% D3=40-44% E=25-39% F=10-24% No Grade=0-9%

ENTRY POINTS FOR THIRD-LEVEL EDUCATION

	NORTHERN IRELAND (1996/7)* mean points	REPUBLIC OF IRELAND (1998) range for degree courses
Accountancy/Actuarial Studies	-	285-545
Agriculture & Related Subjects	15.4	380
Architecture, Building & Planning	19.9	500-566
Biological Sciences	19.9	375-505
Business/Commerce & related subjects	22.4	250-525
Combined Subjects	20.4	-
Communications/Journalism	-	455-475
Computing/Information Technology	-	300-455
Creative Arts & Design	19.9	-
Drama & Theatre		450
Education	21.9	405-475
Engineering & Technology	20.9	250-495
Food Sciences	-	365-500
Hotel/Catering Management		320-355
Humanities/Arts	20.5	170-540
Languages	21.6	320-475

Law (alone/with other subjects)	-	450-575
Librarianship & Information Science	22.4	-
Mathematical Sciences	18.8	410-540
Medicine & Dentistry	29.0	520-580
Medicine-related subjects	24.2	505-550
Music	-	295-470
Physical Sciences	18.6	340-535
Psychology	-	250-565
Sports/Physical Education	-	490
Social Studies	23.0	420-485
Veterinary Studies	-	550

*Source: DENI

HIGHER EDUCATION STUDENT NUMBERS

REPUBLIC OF IRELAND INSTITUTIONS	1986-87	1991-92	1995-96
University College Dublin	9,339	12,083	14,241
University College Cork	5,560	7,451	9,253
University College Galway	4,298	5,312	6,466
Trinity College Dublin	6,555	8,043	9,054
St. Patrick's College, Maynooth	1,520	2,571	3,505
Dublin City University	2,090	2,921	5,098
University of Limerick	2,484	4,251	7,525
National College of Art & Design	531	624	708
Thomond College of Education	656	-	-
Royal College of Surgeons in Ireland	863	904	-
Inst. of Technology/Other Vocational Colleges	19,481	29,648	38,130
Other Colleges	-	-	1,119
Part-time students	-	-	21,910
TOTAL:	**53,377**	**73,808**	**117,069**
NORTHERN IRELAND INSTITUTIONS	**1984-85**	**1990-91**	**1997-98***
University of Ulster	7,458	9,205	19,382
Queen's University	-	8,498	20,776
TOTAL:	**7,458**	**17,703**	**40,158**

Includes full-time and part-time students

Source: DENI

HIGHER ED. STUDENTS BY FIELD OF STUDY

REPUBLIC OF IRELAND (1st of March, 1996)*

Field of Study	Full-Time	Part-Time
Agricultural Science & Forestry	950	12
Architecture	289	16
Art & Design	629	9
Arts	16,367	1,608
Business, Economics & Social Studies	1,155	294
Combined Studies	988	7
Commerce	6,634	1,043
Communications & Information Studies	463	50
Dentistry	477	1
Education	3,404	520
Engineering	5,514	1,001
Equestrian Studies	148	2
European Studies	698	1
Food Science & Technology	640	-
Law	1,433	284
Medicine	4,324	438
Science	10,376	567
Social Science	1,009	27
Veterinary Medicine	377	3
TOTAL:	**55,875**	**5,883**

* These figures include undergraduates and post-graduates.

| NORTHERN IRELAND (1995-96)* | | |
Field of Study	Full-Time	Part-Time
Agriculture & Related Subjects	279	60
Architecture, Building & Planning	1,156	390
Biological Sciences	1,937	170
Business & Administrative Studies	4,491	4,926
Combined Subjects	2,564	1,219
Computer Science	1,349	378
Field of Study	Full-Time	Part-Time
Creative Arts & Design	1,322	277
Education	1,367	211
Engineering & Technology	2,255	818
Humanities	817	500
Languages	1,142	1,130
Law	543	53
Librarianship & Information Science	623	59
Mathematical Sciences	797	560
Medicine & Dentistry	1,008	7
Medicine-related Subjects	3,364	1,034
Physical Sciences	1,168	113
Social, Economic & Political Studies	1,908	2,494
TOTAL:	28,090	14,399

* These figures include undergraduates only. Source: DENI

NUMBERS OF SCHOOL CANDIDATES IN PUBLIC EXAMINATIONS

| REPUBLIC OF IRELAND | | | |
Examination	1985-86	1990-91	1995-96
Candidates sitting Junior Certificate*	76,038	65,394	68,064
Candidates sitting Leaving Certificate**	47,857	55,641	59,176

*Totals for 1985-86 and 1990-91 combine figures for the Group Certificate and Intermediate Certificate exams
**Leaving Certificate totals include figures for school repeat and external candidates

| NORTHERN IRELAND | | | |
Examination	1992-93	1994-95	1996-97
Candidates sitting 'A' levels	8,126	8,458	8,827
Candidates sitting GCSEs	22,183	24,623	24,969

Source: DENI

QUALIFICATIONS OF SCHOOL LEAVERS

| REPUBLIC OF IRELAND (1996) | | | |
Examination	Female	Male	Total
Junior Certificate Total*	33,752	34,312	68,085
Leaving Certificate*	28,015	26,603	54,618
Candidates sitting at least 5 subjects	27,542	26,185	53,727
Candidates with ≥ 5 Grade D3s at any level	25,727	23,460	49,187
Candidates with ≥ 2 Grade C3s or higher on higher papers	14,968	12,554	27,522
Candidates with ≥ 4 Grade C3s or higher on higher papers	9,854	7,229	17,083
Candidates with ≥ 6 Grade C3s or higher on higher papers	4,772	3,259	8,031
Candidates with ≥ 3 Grade B3s or higher on higher papers†	3,936	2,685	6,621
Candidates with ≥ 3 Grade A2s or higher on higher papers†	878	717	1,595
External Candidates	2,545	2,013	4,558
TOTAL:	30,560	28,616	59,176

* Totals include those who participated in Vocational Training Opportunities Schemes, but not those who were external candidates.
† These figures cover candidates who received a minimum of 6 Grade C3s on higher papers.

| NORTHERN IRELAND | | | | |
Examination	1987-88	1991-92	1994-95	1996-97
Males:	12,658	12,034	12,543	13,117
Candidates with ≥ 2 'A' levels	2,566	3,051	3,288	3,588
Candidates with 1 'A' level	390	321	314	257

Continued from previous page

NORTHERN IRELAND

Examination	1987-88	1991-92	1994-95	1996-97
Candidates with ≥ 5 GCSE higher grades	1,150	1,417	2,133	2,462
Candidates with 1-4 GCSE higher grades	2,573	3,146	3,095	3,256
Candidates with low grades	2,613	2,327	2,767	2,534
Examination	**1987-88**	**1991-92**	**1994-95**	**1996-97**
Those with no GCSE/GCE qualifications	3,366	1,772	946	1,020
Females:	**11,730**	**11,447**	**11900**	**12,600**
Candidates with ≥ 2 'A' levels	2,897	3,760	4,262	4,768
Candidates with 1 'A' level	481	431	344	272
Candidates with ≥ 5 GCSE higher grades	1,430	1,716	2,629	2,622
Candidates with 1-4 GCSE higher grades	3,026	2,943	2,676	2,729
Candidates with low grades	2,027	1,621	1,670	1,638
Those with no GCSE/GCE qualifications	1,869	976	409	571
All School leavers:	**24,388**	**22,326**	**24,533**	**25,717**
Candidates with ≥ 2 'A' levels	5,463	6,811	7,550	8,356
Candidates with 1 'A' level	871	752	658	529
Candidates with ≥ 5 GCSE higher grades	2,580	3,133	4,762	5,084
Candidates with 1-4 GCSE higher grades	5,599	6,089	5,771	5,985
Candidates with low grades	4,640	3,948	4,437	4,172
Those with no GCSE/GCE qualifications	5,235	2,748	1,355	1,591

Source: DENI

UNIVERSITY DEGREES AND DIPLOMAS OBTAINED

REPUBLIC OF IRELAND

Award	1994	1996
Primary Degrees	11,051	13,045
Higher Degrees	2,510	2,845
Certificates & Diplomas	9,928	10,851
Higher Diplomas in Education& Primary Education	1,006	940
Primary Degrees in Education	422	652
National Diploma	-	4,877
National/ 2 Yr Certificate	-	5,862
One Year Certificate	-	112
TOTAL:	**24,917**	**39,184**

NORTHERN IRELAND

Award	1987	1991	1995-96	1996-97
First Degrees (Honours)	2,588	3,448	5,103	5,450
First Degrees (Ordinary)	646	499	643	509
Higher Degrees	796	1,070	1,592	1,844
Diplomas, Certs & Other Qualifications	1,969	2,551	2,436	3,793
TOTAL:	**5,999**	**7,568**	**9,774**	**11,596**

Source: DENI

NUMBERS INVOLVED IN HIGH-TECH EDUCATION

REPUBLIC OF IRELAND *(includes students at UCD, UCC, UCG, Maynooth, Trinity College, DCU, UL)*

Subject Category (Student Numbers)	1986-87	1990-91	1995-96	% Change 86/7 - 95/6
Computer Science	-	-	2,887	-
Information Technology	-	-	752	-
Biosciences (Biotechnology, Genetics, Food Sciences)	250	345	1,402	460.0
Engineering	4,431	5,002	4,461	0.6
Physics/Maths	-	-	632	-
Other Science	6,183	7,184	7,712	24.7
TOTAL:	**10,864**	**12,531**	**17,846**	**64.2**

NORTHERN IRELAND *(includes universities and further education colleges)*				
Subject	1985-86	1995-96	1997-98	% Change 95/6 - 97/8
Biosciences	748	2,035	1,937	-4.8%
Males	322	638	576	-9.7%
Females	426	1397	1,361	-2.6%
Maths & Computing	825	1,886	2,146	13.8%
Males	543	995	1,467	47.4%
Females	282	891	679	-23.8%
Engineering & Technology	-	2,184	2,255	3.3%
Males	-	1908	1,924	0.8%
Females	-	276	331	19.9%

Source: DENI

FIRST DESTINATION:
HIGHER EDUCATION RESPONDENTS, 1996

REPUBLIC OF IRELAND (Primary & Higher Degree)	Male	Female	Totals
Further Study	1,274	1,298	2,572
Teacher Training	88	310	398
Other Vocational/Professional Training	492	681	1,173
Work Experience - Ireland	58	81	139
Seeking Employment - Ireland	208	233	441
Not available - Ireland	175	207	382
Obtained Full-Time Employment	3,445	3,547	6,992
Obtained Part-Time Employment	134	239	373
TOTAL:	**5,874**	**6,596**	**12,470**

Sub-degree Respondents	Male	Female	Totals
Further Study	1,917	1,685	3,602
Work Experience - Ireland	66	71	137
Seeking Employment - Ireland	122	133	255
Not available - Ireland	34	38	72
Obtained Full-Time Employment	1,265	1,099	2,364
Obtained Part-Time Employment	29	62	91
TOTAL:	**3,433**	**3,088**	**6,521**

N. IRELAND, 1995-96*	Undergraduate	Postgraduate	Total
Further Study/Training	1,745	129	1,874
Employed in the UK	2,486	812	3,298
Employed outside the UK	413	125	538
Not available for Study/Employment/Training	154	19	173
Assumed unemployed	401	53	454
Other	246	61	307
TOTAL:	**5,445**	**1,199**	**6,644**

* First destination information was returned for 84% of the target population of students (primarily full-time) from NI Higher Education Institutions. Source: DENI

GRADUATES' FIRST DESTINATION OCCUPATIONS

REPUBLIC OF IRELAND Sector in which graduates are working (%)	Male	Female	Total
Employed in Ireland			
Agriculture, Forestry & Fishery Sectors	39	26	65
Manufacturing & Other Non-service Sectors	1,155	664	1,819
Public Services	662	1,161	1,823
Private Services	1,629	1,842	3,471
Other	94	93	187
TOTAL:	**3,579**	**3,786**	**7,365**

Occupation	Male	Female	Total
Associate Professional & Technical employment	354	452	806
Clerical & Secretarial employment	115	242	357
Craft & Related employment	32	12	44
Managers & Administrators	299	377	676
Personal & Protective Service employment	63	134	197
Plant & Machine Operatives	22	19	41
Professional employment	1,124	1,366	2,490
Sales respresentatives	114	163	277
Other Employment	54	23	77
Unknown	4	1	5
TOTAL:	**2,181**	**2,789**	**4,970**

Source: DENI

USEFUL ADDRESSES

Central Applications Office Tower House, Eglinton Street, Galway. Tel: (091) 563318. Fax: (091) 562344. (The body which processes applications for entry to most third-level undergraduate courses.)

Department of Education Block 1, Irish Life Centre, Lower Abbey Street, Dublin 1. Fax: (01) 8734700. Fax: (01) 8729003.

Higher Education Authority Third Floor, Marine House, Clanwilliam Court, Dublin 2. Tel: (01) 6612748. Fax (01) 6610492.

National Council for Educational Awards 26 Mountjoy Square, Dublin 1. Tel: (01) 8556526. Fax: 8554250.

Teastas / The Irish National Certification Authority Marino Institute of Education, Griffith Avenue, Dublin 9. Tel: (01) 8376969. Fax: (01) 8376301.

Oscail / The National Distance Education Centre Dublin City University, Dublin 9. Tel: (01) 70454421. Fax: (01) 7045494. e-mail: ndec.it@dcu.ie

Aontas / The National Association of Adult Education 22 Earlsfort Terrace, Dublin 2. Tel: (01) 4754121. Fax: 4780084.

FÁS / The Training Authority 27 -33 Upper Baggot Street, Dublin 4.
Forbairt Glasnevin, Dublin 9. Tel: (01) 808200. Fax: (01) 8082020. (The body which promotes indigenous industry/science and technology.)

Department of Education Northern Ireland Rathgael House, Balloo Road, Bangor, Co. Down BT19 7PR. Tel: (01247) 279677. Fax: (01247) 279777.

Belfast Education & Library Board 40 Academy Street, Belfast. Tel: (01232) 564000.

Council for Cahtolic Maintained Schools 160 High Street, Holywood, Co. Down. Tel: (01232) 426972.

North Eastern Education & Library Board County Hall 182 Galgorm Road, Ballymena, Co. Antrim. Tel: (01266) 653333.

South Eastern Education & Library Board 18 Windsor Avenue, Belfast BT9 6EF. Tel: (01232) 381188.

Southern Education & Library Board 3 Charlemont Place, The Mall, Armagh. Tel: (01861) 512200.

Western Education & Library Board 1 Hospital Road, Omagh, Co. Tyrone. Tel: (01662) 564000.

CULTURE

IRISH LANGUAGE

FACTFILE ON THE IRISH LANGUAGE

THE STATUS OF IRISH: Irish is constitutionally recognised as the nation's first official language, although in practice, English is the first language of most of the population.

WHERE DID IRISH ORIGINATE: introduced by the Celts (who emerged as a racial entity in middle Europe towards the end of the second millennium BC) into ireland c. 600 BC, Irish originated from the Indo-European family of languages.

WHAT OTHER LANGUAGES IS IT RELATED TO: It is closely related to the other celtic languages of Scots Gaelic, Manx, Welsh, Cornish and Breton.

WRITTEN IRISH: Irish is one of the oldest written languages in Europe - beginning with Ogham

THE OGHAM ALPHABET: Most ogham inscriptions date back to the fifth and sixth centuries. It is a form of writing whereby the letters of the alphabet are represented by differing numbers of strokes and dots. It is though have been derived from the Latin alphabet (its relationship with latin is similar to that between morse code and the modern alphabet) and it may have later influenced the form of Irish orthography in the Latin alphabet. It would have been used primarily on stone monuments, but it could have also been used for short texts on wood and bone.

Right-hand side of tree: 'n' 5 strokes, 's' 4 strokes 'f' 3 strokes 'l' 2 strokes 'b' 1 stroke

Left-hand side of tree: 'q' 5 strokes, 'c' 4 strokes 't' 3 strokes 'd' 2 strokes 'h' 1 stroke

Diagonals through the tree: 'r' 5 strokes, 'z' 4 strokes 'ng' 3 strokes 'g' 2 strokes 'm' 1 stroke

Stops on the tree: 'i' 5 dots, 'e' 4 dots, 'u' 3 dots, 'o' 2 dots, 'a' 1 dot.

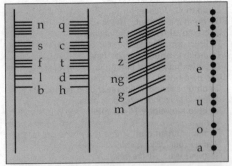

SUMMER COURSES: Around 60 Gael Linn-recognised summer colleges offer 3-week courses in Irish; the Department of Arts, Heritage, Gaeltacht and the Islands supports these courses, and in 1998, 20,000 people attended the summer courses.

THE GAELTACHT - IRISH-SPEAKING AREAS

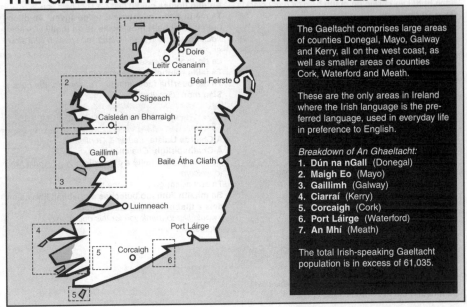

The Gaeltacht comprises large areas of counties Donegal, Mayo, Galway and Kerry, all on the west coast, as well as smaller areas of counties Cork, Waterford and Meath.

These are the only areas in Ireland where the Irish language is the preferred language, used in everyday life in preference to English.

Breakdown of An Ghaeltacht:
1. **Dún na nGall** (Donegal)
2. **Maigh Eo** (Mayo)
3. **Gaillimh** (Galway)
4. **Ciarraí** (Kerry)
5. **Corcaigh** (Cork)
6. **Port Láirge** (Waterford)
7. **An Mhí** (Meath)

The total Irish-speaking Gaeltacht population is in excess of 61,035.

USEFUL IRISH PHRASES (FRÁSAÍ ÚSÁIDEACHA)

Ó LÁ GO LÁ / DAY-TO-DAY

Dia Duit (singular) /daoibh (plural). *Hello.*
Dia 's Muire duit/daoibh. *Response to a greeting.*
Conas atá tú? *How are you feeling?*
Cad as duit? *Where are you from?*
Cad is ainm duit? *What's your name?*
Is mise . . . *My name is . . .*
An bhfuil Gaeilge agat? *Do you speak Irish?*
Tá/Níl. *Yes/No.*
Tá beagan Gaeilge agam. *I speak a little Irish.*
Is lá maith é. *It's a good day.*
Le do thoil. *Please.*
Go raibh maith agat. *Thank you.*
Gabh mo leithscéal. *Excuse me.*
Tá brón orm. *Excuse me.*
Tá droch lá ann. *It's a bad day.*
Tá sé te/ fuar/ tirim/ fliuch. *It's warm /cold /dry /wet.*
Cad é an t-am? *What's the time?*
Cá bhfuil an siopa/ leithreas/ oifig an phoist?
Where is the shop/ toilet/ post office?
An bhfuil tú réidh? Tá mé réidh. *Are you ready? I'm ready.*
Tá glao gutháin duit. *There is a phone call for you.*
Slán go fóill. *'Bye for now.*
Go n-éirí leat! *All the best!*

SIAMSAÍOCHT / ENTERTAINMENT

An bhfuil tú ag dul chuig an chéilí? *Are you going to the ceili?*
Ar mhaith leat damhsa? *Would you like a dance?*
Grúpa ceoltóirí *Group of musicians*
Ag seinm ceoil *Playing music*
Nach bhfuil an chraic go maith? *Isn't it great crack?*
Déan do dhícheall. *Try your best.*

SPÓRT / SPORT

Ag imirt peile *Playing football*
Liathróid Peile *Football*
Liathróid Leadóige *Tennis*
Raon rothaíochta *Cycling track*
Seomraí gléasta *Dressing rooms*
Cluiche *Game*
Cumann Gailf *Golf Club*
Galfchúrsa *Golf course*
Galf dha mhaide *Pitch & Put*
Rás fad-achair *Long distance race*
Comórtas cáiliúcháin *Qualifying competition*
Réiteoir *Referee*
Reathaí *Runner*
Iárionad Spóirt *Sports Complex*
Linn Snámha *Swimming Pool*
Ticéad Séasúir *Season Ticket*

SIOPADÓIREACHT / SHOPPING

An siopa *The shop*
Cé mhéad atá air seo? *How much does this cost?*
Ba mhaith liom . . . *I would like . . .*

Torthaí/ Glasraí *Fruit/ vegetables/ groceries/ meat counter*
Tá punt air. *It cost a pound.*
Tá punt agus deich pingin air. *It costs £1.10.*

GNÓ / BUSINESS

Dia Duit, (ainm an chomhairle) teo. *Hello, (name of the company) Ltd.*
Dia's Muire duit. *Response to a greeting.*
Cé atá ag caint? *Whose speaking?*
Cé atá uait, le do thoil? *Who do you want, please?*
An gnó pearsanta nó oifigiúil é? *Is it personal or official?*
Ar mhaith leat fanacht? *Would you like to hold?*
An bhfuil coinne agat? *Have you an appointment?*
B'fhearr coinne a dhéanamh. *It would be better to make an appointment.*
Scríobh d'ainm, do shloinne, do sheoladh agus an dáta. *Write your name, surname, address and the date.*
Níl freagra ón fholíne san am i láthair. *There is no reply from the extension at the moment.*
Tá sé/sí ag cruinniú. *He/she is at a meeting.*
Tá brón orm, ach . . . *I'm sorry, but . . .*
Níl sé/sí anseo. *He/she isn't here.*
Beidh sé/sí leat i gceann nóiméid. *He/she will be with you in a minute.*
An Rannóg Pearsanra/ Brainse na gCuntas a phléann leis. *The Personnel Section/ Accounts Branch deals with it.*
Tá an cruinniú ar athló go dtí . . . *The meeting is adjourned until . . .*
Leanfar den chruinniú ar . . . *The meeting will resume at . . .*
An dtig liomsa cuidiú leat? *May I help you?*
Tá mé buartha, níl morán Gaeilge agam. An dtiocfadh leat labhairt níos moille, le do thoil? *I'm sorry, I don't have much Irish. Could you speak a little slower please?*
Le do thoil. *Please.*
Tá fáilte romhat. *You're welcome.*
Tá mé buartha faoin mhoill. *I'm sorry for the delay.*
Slán mór. *Goodbye.*

AITHEASC FOIRMIÚIL / FORMAL ADDRESS

A Chairde Uaisle *Ladies & Gentlemen*
A Chathaoirligh *Chairman/woman*
Ba mhaith liom fáilte a chur roimh . . . *I would like to welcome . . .*
Tá súil agam go . . . *I hope that . . .*
Ba mhaith liom mo buíochas a ghabháil libh as an deis a thabhairt dom labhairt libh.
I would like to thank you for this opportunity to address you.

IRISH / NON-IRISH SPEAKERS BY PROVINCE

Region by Speakers	1861	1901	1926	1936	1946	1961	1971	1981	1996
Connacht									
Irish	409,482	245,580	175,209	183,082	154,187	148,708	137,372	155,134	201,195
Non-Irish	503,653	401,352	377,698	315,322	309,638	246,592	231,960	244,264	194,666
Leinster									
Irish	35,704	26,436	101,474	183,378	180,755	274,644	341,702	473,225	689,703
Non-Irish	1,421,931	1,126,393	1,047,618	966,434	1,017,491	964,383	1,055,160	1,202,292	1,052,000
Munster									
Irish	545,531	276,268	198,221	224,805	189,395	228,726	252,805	323,704	451,129
Non-Irish	968,027	799,920	771,681	668,030	672,660	576,613	573,308	612,526	484,670
Ulster* *(three counties)*									
Irish	86,370	71,426	68,607	75,336	64,388	64,342	57,550	66,350	88,178
Non-Irish	431,413	274,448	231,484	190,538	183,143	140,810	137,591	148,972	126,834
TOTAL									
Irish	1,077,087	619,710	543,511	666,601	588,725	716,420	789,429	1,018,413	1,430,205
Non-Irish	3,325,024	2,602,113	2,428,481	2,140,324	2,182,932	1,919,398	1,998,019	2,208,054	1,858,170

*This refers to Counties Cavan, Donegal and Monaghan only. According to the 1991 Northern Ireland Census, 142,003 people over the age of three - approximately 10% of Northern Ireland's population - claim to have some knowledge of Irish. This brings the total number of people with some knowledge of Irish in Ulster to approx. 230,181.

IRISH SPEAKERS IN GAELTACHT AREAS

County	1981	1991	1996	% in Gaeltacht area
Cork	2,681	2,686	2,756	79.9%
Donegal	19,209	17,574	17,788	76.5%
Galway	19,819	21,533	24,994*	72.7%
Kerry	6,264	5,945	6,132	78.1%
Mayo	8,457	7,096	7,481	67.3%
Meath	493	600	773	57.4%
Waterford	1,103	1,035	1,111	85.9%
Total Gaeltacht Areas:	**58,026**	**56,469**	**61,035**	73.8%

* includes Galway County Borough and Galway County.

FREQUENCY OF SPEAKING AND LISTENING TO IRISH

					Age Group					
Frequency	3-4	5-9	10-14	15-19	20-24	25-34	35-44	45-54	55-64	65+
Daily	4,812	78,109	117,565	82,227	8,149	13,463	17,660	13,468	8,471	9,739
Weekly	1,214	17,885	30,231	27,730	7,332	8,570	11,525	8,760	4,996	5,617
Rarely	1,570	19,211	37,057	62,479	65,539	81,764	88,918	71,081	45,397	51,632
Never	296	5,762	16,098	39,664	58,767	77,433	66,231	46,634	27,287	31,343
Not Stated	579	5,319	9,003	9,461	5,213	5,430	5,868	6,102	4,719	6,825
Total	8,471	126,286	209,954	221,561	145,000	186,660	190,202	146,045	90,870	105,156

IRISH SPEAKERS AS A % OF TOTAL POPULATION

Age Group	3-4	5-9	10-14	15-19	20-24	25-34	35-44	45-54	55-64	65+
% Irish Speakers	10%	48%	68%	68%	52%	37%	39%	37%	32%	27%

IRISH DANCE

FACTFILE ON IRISH DANCING

EARLIEST REFERENCE TO IRISH DANCING: A report on the Rínce Fada in 1569 by an English visitor and by Scotsman Arthur Young in 1776 in reference to Irish solo dancing, and references were made to set dancing in the late 18th and 19th centuries.

THE OLDEST DANCE: Possibly the renowned solo set dance - The Blackbird - and the St. Patrick's Day dance.

OTHER DANCE FORMS THAT HAVE INFLUENCED IT: Popular group set dancing grew from Quadrilles and Lancers, popular forms of dance in Europe, which were brought to Ireland in the 19th century by

Irish soldiers who fought with European armies

WHAT OTHER DANCE FORMS IS IT RELATED TO: Scottish Highland dancing, Appalachian Clog Dancing and the American Square Dancing, which in turn had an influence on American stage dancing.

WHEN WAS IRISH DANCING ORGANISED ON AN OFFICIAL LEVEL: Irish dancing was started on this level by the Gaelic League, founded in 1893.

THE MAIN BODY RESPONSIBLE FOR IRISH DANCE: An Coimisiúin Le Rincí Gaelacha, founded in 1929 by the Gaelic League to organise and develop the practice of Irish dancing, create and set standards for Feiseanna and preserve and promote it activity as an international organisation. It published the first handbooks detailing the movement of Ceilí dancing in 1939. The following refer to its activities:

OTHER COUNTRIES IN WHICH IRISH DANCING IS PRACTICED: Wherever Irish people have emigrated to and settled; this includes the England, Scotland, the US, Australia, Canada, New Zealand.

MAIN COMPETITIONS: The Regional Qualifying Championships (held worldwide) and the All-Ireland Dancing Championships - Oireachtas Rince na hÉireann - and World Dancing Championships - Oireachtas Rince na Cruinne established in 1969. *(To be held in Ennis, Co. Clare, in April 1999.)*

RATIO OF MALE TO FEMALE DANCERS: Over 5 to 1.

NUMBERS OF TEACHERS: 500 in Ireland and 600 in Canada, U.S., Australia, New Zealand and Britain (this compares to 100 teachers in 1950, which shows how popular Irish dancing has become, helped in no small way with the massive success of *Riverdance - The Show* and Michael Flatley's *Lord of the Dance* show). ❐

RESULTS of the WORLD DANCING CHAMPIONSHIPS - TORTHAÍ OIREACHTAS RINCE na CRUINNE 1998

COMPETITION	WINNER	DANCING SCHOOL
Men over 21	Gary Healy	Taylor, Glasgow
Overseas Award	Patrick Campbell	Masterson, Ohio
Men 19 - 21	Raymond Walls	McCaul Academy, Derry
Overseas Award	Jim Riordan	Trinity, Chicago
Men 17 - 19	Paul Cusick	O'Hare, Chicago
Overseas Award	Bill O'Hara	Harney Academy, California
Boys 15 - 17	Michael Belvitch	O'Hare, Chicago
Overseas Award	Ryan McCaffrey	Irwin, Canada
Boys 13 - 15	Alan Fox	Oirialla, Dundalk
Overseas Award	Craig Ashurst	Mulcahy, Melbourne
Boys 11 - 12	Eanna Ryan	Costello / O'Brien, Galway
Overseas Award	Shane Kelly	Broesler, New Jersey
Boys 10 - 11	Declan McHale	Doherty, Coventry
Overseas Award	Kevin Smith	Burke, Ohio
Women over 21	Paula McManus	Sean Éireann McMahon, Birmingham
Overseas Award	Kathleen Keady	Schade, New York
Women 19 - 21	Noelle Curran	Smith, New Jersey
Overseas Award	Amy Siegel	Smith, New Jersey
Girls 17 - 19	Róisín Turley Gibbons	Turley, Coventry
Overseas Award	Theresa Wall	Verlin, New York
Girls 16 - 17	Debbie O'Keeffe	Cowhie Ryab, Cork
Overseas Award	Nicole Rankin	Richens-Timm, Ohio
Girls 15 - 16	Erin Davidson	Oirialla, Dundalk
Overseas Award	Jaime Lynn Crowley	Davis, New Jersey
Girls 14 - 15	Eimear Murphy	Cadwell Cawte, BÁC
Overseas Award	Susan Hickey	Schade, New York
Girls 13 - 14	Stephanie Power	Costello / O'Brien, Galway
Overseas Award	Jillian Farmer	Schade, New York
Girls 12 - 13	Michelle Lawrence	Uí Nualláin, Limerick
Overseas Award	Meghan Reilly	Smith, New Jersey
Girls 11 - 12	Jordan Osborne	McLaughlin, Glasgow
Overseas Award	Mairead Masuda	Smith-Houlihan, Massachusettes
Girls 10 - 11	Elaine McConomy-Bradley	McConomy, Derry
Overseas Award	Ashley Smith	Smith-Houlihan, Massachusettes
Mixed Céilí under 13	Foireann A	Costello / O'Brien, Galway
Overseas Award	Foireann A	Doherty, Coventry
Girls Céilí under 13	Foireann B	NCOB, Drogheda
Overseas Award	Foireann A	Doherty, Coventry
Mixed Céilí 13 - 16	Foireann A	Kiely Walsh, Cork
Overseas Award	Foireann A	McLaughlin, Glasgow
Girls Céilí 13 - 16	Foireann A	Trinity, Chicago
Overseas Award	Foireann A	Sean Éireann McMahon, Birmingham

COMPETITION	WINNER	DANCING SCHOOL
Mixed Céilí over 16	Foireann A	Sean Éireann McMahon, Birmingham
Overseas Award	Foireann A	McLaughlin, Glasgow
Girls Céilí over 16	Foireann A	Setanta, Scotland
Overseas Award	Foireann A	McLaughlin, Glasgow
Rince Foirne mixed under 13	Foireann A	McLaughlin, Glasgow
Overseas Award	Foireann A	Reid, Belfast
Rince Foirne mixed under 13	Foireann A	Trinity, Chicago
Overseas Award	Foireann A	Doherty, Birmingham
Foirne mixed 13 - 16	Foireann A	McLaughlin, Glasgow
Overseas Award	Foireann A	Grif / Rod / O'Lough., London
Foirne Girls 13 - 16	Foireann A	Doherty, Coventry
Overseas Award	Foireann A	Scanlon, Birmingham
Foirne mixed over 16	Foireann A	McLaughlin, Glasgow
Damhasdráma	Foireann A	Gillan, Antrim
Overseas Award	Foireann A	O'Sioda Abbey, London

IRISH MUSIC

ORGANISATION: Comhaltas Ceoltóirí Éireann, the main body responsible for Irish traditional music and culture. The following statistics refer to its activities:

NO. OF BRANCHES: 400 (in every county in Ireland, Britain, US, Canada, Australia, Japan, Hungary, Sardinia and Italy).

NO. OF CLASSES: 600 per week

NO. OF IRISH MUSIC TEACHERS: 375 (qualified from TTCT).

QUALIFICATIONS AVAILABLE IN IRISH MUSIC: The TTCT - Diploma for traditional music teachers; Performance Certs Through Fás and City & Guilds for musicians, singers and dancers;

FLEADHANNA CHEOIL: 44 Fleadhanna Cheoil each year, with over 25,000 competitors taking part

CEOL AN GHEIMHRIDH (March) All-Ireland Finals for the inter-branch competitions held at county and provincial levels.

FLEADH NUA (to be held in Ennis, Co. Clare, 27-29 May, 1999) Dancing, exhibitions of traditional customs, e.g. wrenboys, biddy boys, etc.

FLEADH AMHRÁN & RINCE (June) Emphasis is on traditional singing and dancing and includes the inter-provincial set-dance competition.

FLEADH CHEOIL NA HÉIREANN (to be held in Enniscorthy, Co. Wexford, 27-29 August, 1999) The biggest fleadh, with competitors and onlookers coming from all over the world. Competitions in music, dance, singing and the Irish language.

CONCERT TOURS: Three main tours per year - in Ireland, Britain and North America (there are also regular tours to other countries).

VENUES: Cultúrlann, Dublin; Bru Boru, Tipperary;

SUMMER SCHOOLS: Scoil Éigse (held the week before the Fleadh Cheoil na hÉireann)

COMMON IRISH NAMES AND THEIR MEANING

Name	Pronounced	Meaning	English Versions
(M): Male, (f): Female, _: stress on pronunciation			
Aengus (m)	Ayn-gus	Celtic god; one choice	Angus
Aidan (m)	Ay-dan	Fire	Hugh
Ailis (f)	Ay-lish	One of Noble Birth	Adelaide
Aodh / Aodhagán (m)	Ay /Ay-gawn	Fire	Hugh
Aoibheann (f)	Ee-van	One who is fair of form	Yvonne
Aoife (f)	Ee-fa	Ancient Irish girl's name	Eva
Aideen / Eadaoin (f)	Ay-deen	Name of the Celtic goddess of beauty	Edwina
Áine (f)	Auw-nya	Ancient Irish girl's name	Ann
Aisling (f)	Ash-ling	Vision or dream	none
Airt (m)	Art	Bear	Aurthur
Bairbre (f)	Bar-bre	Greek in origin; meaning strange	Barbara
Bébhinn (f)	Be-vin	Melodious Lady	Vivienne
Bláithín (f)	Blaw-heen	Little Flower	none
Bran (m)	Bran	Raven	none
Briain (m)	Bry-an	High King of Ireland, defeated the Vikings	Brian
Bríd / Brigid (f)	Bridge-id	Strength; from patron saint - St. Brigid	Bridie / Biddy
Bronagh (f)	Bro-na	Sorrow; a queen who was held captive	Dolores
Cáit / Cáitlín (f)	Koytch - leen	Greek in origin; meaning pure	Kate / Kathleen
Caoimhe (f)	Kwee-va	Gentle, beauty, grace	Kevina
Caoimhín (m)	Kwee-veen	early Irish saint	Kevin
Caolán (m)	Key-lawn	Slender one	none
Cara (f)	Kara	Friend	none
Cathal (m)	Ka-hel	Mighty in battle	Charles
Catríona (f)	Catree-ona	a variation of Cáit	Katherina

Name	Pronounced	Meaning	English Versions
Cian (m)	Keen	Ancient one	none
Ciara (f)	Kee-yra	7th century Irish saint	none
Ciarán (m)	Keyar-awn	Black; early Christian Irish saint	none
Cillian (m)	Kill-eean	War; trouble	none
Clíodhna (f)	Clee-owna	tragic heroine from an old Irish legend	none
Clodagh (f)	Clo-da	name of an Irish river	none
Colm (m)	Kolum	Dove; linked with St. Colmcille	none
Conall (m)	Kon-al	High and mighty	none
Conn (m)	Con	Sense and reasoning powers	none
Conor (m)	Kon-or	High will or desire; linked with high kings	Cornelius
Cormac (m)	Kor-mak	Charioteer	none
Críosa (f)	Kree-osa	Christian	Christine
Críostóir (m)	Kris-stor	Christ-like	Christain, Christopher
Dabhnait (f)	Dav-net	poet	none
Dáire (m)	Daw-ra	From Doire - meaning oak	none
Daithí (m)	Da-hee	Swift and agile	David
Déaglán (m)	Deg-lawn	early Christian Irish saint	Declan
Deirdre (f)	Deer-dra	tragic heroine from old Irish legend	Deirdre
Deirbhle (f)	Derv-la	True desire	none
Desmond (m)	-	a native of south Munster	none
Diarmuid (m)	Jeer-mud	Freeman	Dermot
Dónal (m)	Doh-nal	Mighty one	Daniel
Donncha / Donagh (m)	Dunockah	Brown or strong fighter	Dennis
Dymphna (f)	See 'Dabhnait' above		
Éamon (m)	Ay-mun	Blessed protection	Edward
Eilís (f)	Ay-lish	Greek in origin; God has sworn	Elizabeth
Eileen (f)	Ay-leen	Greek in origin; meaning bright one	Helen, Elaine
Eithne (f)	Eth-na	Kernel	none
Emer (f)	Ee-mur	Ancient Celtic heroine	none
Enda / Eanna (m/f)	End-a	early Christian Irish saint	none
Eoin (m)	Own	Well born	John, Eugene
Felim (m)	Fay-lim	Always good	Philip
Ferdia (m)	Ferr-dee-a	From Irish legend; friend of Cú Chulainn	none
Fearghal (m)	Fur-gal	Manly	none
Fearghus (m)	Fur-gus	Best elected	none
Fíachra (m)	Fee-ackra	early Irish saint	none
Finian (m)	Fin-eean	Of fair birth	none
Fíona (f)	Fee-ona	fair	none
Fionn (m)	Fyun	Fair	none
Fionnbar (m)	Fin-bar	Of the fair head; early Irish saint	Barry
Fíonnuala (f)	Fin-ool-a	of the fair shoulder	none
Gearóid (m)	Gyar-oj	Great spear holder	Garrett, Gareth
Gobnait (f)	Gob-nayt	early Christian Irish saint	none
Gráinne (f)	Graw-nye	Grace, love	Grace
Iarla (m)	Eer-la	Western prince	Jarlath
Íde (f)	Eeda	early Christian Irish saint	Ita, Ida
Laoise (f)	Lee-sha		Louise
Liam (m)	Lee-yam	Protection	William
Lochlainn (m)	Lock-lan	Viking	none
Lorcan (m)	Lur-kan	Fierce	Lawrence
Máire (f)	Maw-re	Hebrew in origin	Mary, Miriam
Máirín (f)	Maw-reen	Hebrew in origin; little Mary	Mary
Mairéad (f)	Ma-raydth		Pearl, Margaret
Malachy (m)	-	Maolseachlann, servant of St Secundisus	none
Manus (m)		Norse - meaning Great	Magnus
Meadbh (f)	Mayv	1st century queen of Connacht	Maeve
Miles (m)	-	Great Chief	Myles
Muireadach (m)	Mur-a-dock	Lord of the Sea	Murray
Muireann (f)	Mwir-en	Of the long hair	Marion
Muiris (m)	Mur-ish		Maurice
Muirne (f)	Mwyr-ne	Soft and gentle	Myrna
Naoise (m)	Nee-sha	The only choice	Nicholas
Neasa (f)	Nya-se		none
Niall (m)	Ny-al	Ancient Ulster chieftain	none

Name	Pronounced	Meaning	English Versions
Niamh (f)	Nee-uv	Bright one; spellbinding heroine from Tír-na-nÓg	none
Noirín (f)	No-reen	Honorable one	Nora
Nuala (f)	See 'Fionnuala' above		
Odhrán (m)	O-ran	Pale green; early Irish saint	none
Oisín (m)	Usheen	Deer	none
Orlaith (f)	Or-la	Golden one	none
Oscar (m)	Oskar	Spear of God	none
Pádraig (m)	Paw-rick	Noble one	Patrick
Peadar (m)	Pa-dur	From the Latin Rock	Peter
Prionsias (m)	Prun-shees	French man	Francis
Ríonach (f)	Ree-nock	Queen	Regina
Risteárd	Rish-tard	From the German - tough rule	Richard
Róisín (f)	Ro-sheen	Rose	Rose
Rónan (m)	-	Seal-like	none
Ross (m)	-	Ancient Munster name	none
Ruaidhrí (m)	Roory	Red one	Rory, Roger
Saibh (f)	Sive	Goodness	none
Saoirse (f)	Seer-sha	Freedom	none
Seamus (m)	Shaymus	Supplanter	James
Seán (m)	Shawn	from the Hebrew gift of God	John
Shauna (f)	Shaw-na	Hebrew in origin; meaning gracious gift of God	Shawna
Síle (f)	Shee-la	Blind one	Sheila, Julia, Cecilia
Sinéad (f)	Shin-ayd		Jane, Jenny
Siobhán (f)	Shov-awn		Joan
Sorcha (f)	Sur-ka	Clear or bright	Claire
Tadhg (m)	Tyg	Philosopher, poet	Timothy
Tiarnan (m)	Tear-nan	Lord	none
Turlough (m)	Thur-lock		Terence
Treasa (f)	Tra-se	Strength	Theresa
Tríona (f)	See 'Catríona' above		
Uinsionn (m)	In-shun	Conqueror	Vincent
Úna (f)	Oona	Ancient Irish name	Winifred

IRISH FOLKLORE

FACTFILE ON IRISH FOLKLORE

ORIGINS: The cultural data transmitted in Irish folklore was accrued both from the indigenous Irish and the successive waves of invaders - Vikings, Normans, Scots and English - and was passed on through a special learned caste - the poets or filí - who where held in high esteem in Irish society. Their enjoyed patronage under the Gaelic chiefs and later, the Norman-Gaelic lords. Although their songs focused on stories and people, they were also thought to contain mystical knowledge that had magical effects.

LITERARY ROOTS: Irish folklore's literary roots date back to the 6th century AD and flourished until the 17th century, when the suppression of all native forms of learning was rigorously enforced by the British overlords.

TRANSMISSION: The early forms of transmission had an elaborate and highly rhetorical style while the oral tradition followed a distinctive highly stylised form, the rhythm and metre of which made it easy to remember for speaking. Indeed, many of the early poems were sung or chanted to the accompaniment of the harps on special occasions. Evidence also suggests that songs were created for everyday life (focusing on various events, work and laments), which were composed with a less complicated rhythm and metre.

During the medieval era, poets borrowed motifs freely from continental troubadour poetry, particularly on the themes of chivalry and love, and incorporated them into the native poems. From the 17th century onwards, the poet's place in society declined. The filí composed more popular stressed rhymes known as *amhrán* (meaning 'song') in Irish as they began to live among the Gaelic peasants. It was around this time, that poems of praise or satire (usually targeting those who were authoritarian, mean or pompous) became popular. A prime example of this type of satire (in this case, a social satire) is Brian Merriman's epic, *Cúirt an Mhean Oíche* - the Midnight Court, which seeks to deflate men's pomposity, dates to around this time (1780).

THEMES WITHIN IRISH FOLKLORE:

● **GENEALOGICAL DATA AND LITANIES** on the origins of various names and place names.
● **MYTHOLOGIC AND HISTORIC STORIES,** including the adventures of the famous seer-warrior, Finn Mac Cumhaill, his son Oisín, who was spellbound by a beautiful woman and lived with her for 300 hundred years in Tír na nÓg, the god Lugh, the hero warrior Cú Chulainn, in addition to a pantheon of other warriors and princesses.
● **LOCAL PATRON SAINTS,** whose feats could have been adapted from earlier Celtic deities, and whose

feast days are still celebrated at holy wells and other places of pilgrimage around the country (for example, the climbing of Croagh Patrick on the last Sunday in July).

● FAIRIES OR THE SÍ, who were created by the early Celts, possibly as explanations of the afterlife. Medieval literature refers to the fairies as the *Tuatha Dé Dannan* (the people of the Goddess Danu). Various phenomena in the country's topography were (and are still) attributed to the fairies - a prime example of this being raths, the ancient round forts that are found all over the country.

● INTERNATIONAL TALES, including stories of men who marry mermaids, and fairy women, changelings, trickster type tales and stories focusing on local animals and wildlife.

● TALES OF THE SUPERNATURAL, these are concerned with various spirits and ghosts (such as priests who have not celebrated a mass during their lifetime but are condemned to haunt a church or area until they celebrate it), but particularly the banshee, a female spirit which follows families who have an Ó or Mac in their surname. Her terrible keening crying portends the arrival of a death in these families.

As well as this strong emphasis on story and song, the Irish also celebrate festivals of saints; again these were probably adapted from earlier Celtic rituals. These include St Brigid's Day (the 1st of February), May Eve, St. John's Night (or Midsummer's Eve), Lughnasa (in August), Samhain (or Hallowe'en) and many more. *For further information on folklore, See Irish cultural organisations - Department of Irish Folklore, UCD.* ❐

IRISH CULTURAL ORGANISATIONS

BORD NA GAEILGE 7 *Merrion Square, Dublin 2. Tel. (01) 6763222.* **Profile:** A state board appointed to draft and advise the government on Irish language policies and to promote the language and all its aspects at all levels. Other work includes book distribution and community development projects.

AN COIMISIÚIN LE RINCÍ GAELACHA 6 *Harcourt Street, Dublin 2. Tel: (01) 4752220.* **Established:** 1929. **Profile:** The governing body in Irish dancing - it organises both the All-Ireland and World Irish Dancing Championships annually.

COMHALTAS CEOLTÓIRÍ ÉIREANN *Belgrave Square, Monks Town, Co. Dublin. Tel: (01) 2800295.* **Established:** 1951. **Profile:** An Irish cultural movement, it promotes Irish traditional music, song, dance and language, through education and performance, both nationally and internationally.

COMHCHOISTE NÁISIÚNTA NA GCOLÁISTÍ SAMHRAIDH 46 *Kildare Street, Dublin 2. Tel (01) 6794780.* **Profile:** The overall body representative of more than 60 summer colleges which organises three-week Irish courses over the summer months, mainly in the Gaeltacht areas.

COMHDHÁIL NÁISIÚNTA NA GAEILGE 46 *Kildare Street, Dublin 2. Tel: (01) 6794780.* **Established:** 1943. **Profile:** The steering council of the Irish language, it promotes over 20 different voluntary bodies, providing a forum for the exchange of ideas and information, politically and publicly.

COMHLACHAS NÁISIÚNTA DRÁMAÍOCHTA *Camus, Connemara, Co. Galway. Tel: (091) 574146/574155.* **Profile:** The National Council of Drama promotes drama in the Irish language through an advice centre, festivals, libraries of play texts and Irish drama courses.

AN CUMANN SCOILDRÁMAÍOCHTA 46 *Kildare Street, Dublin 2. Tel: (01) 6794780. Fax: (01) 6790214.* **Profile:** Involved in the promotion and development of the Irish language through drama and stage-craft in national schools. It organises an annual national schools' drama festival, *An Fhéile Scoildrámaíochta.*

CONRADH NA GAEILGE *Áras an Chonartha, 6 Harcourt Street, Dublin 2. Tel: (01) 4757401/2.* **Established:** 1893 - *See History Chapter.* **Profile:** A national organisation that provides support systems for Irish language schools, Irish language classes and other activities to further the use of Irish. It organises the Irish language festival, **An tOireachtas** (dating from 1897), and including literary, cultural, artistic and stage presentations and competitions.

CULTÚRLANN MACADHAMH Ó FIAICH 216 *Falls Road, Belfast, BT12 6AH. Tel: (01232) 239303*

DEPARTMENT OF IRISH FOLKLORE *University College Dublin, Belfield, Dublin.* **Profile:** The department has taken over the remit of the Irish Folklore Commission (set up by the government in 1935) which amassed a vast amount of folklore and ethnological data from around Ireland. Academics from the department are engaged in the study and collation of this data and are in continual co-operation with folklorists in other countries with regard to folklore around the world.

GAEL-LINN 6/27 *Merrion Square, Dublin 2. Tel: (01) 6767283. Fax: (01) 6767030. e-mail: info@gael-lin.iol.ie* **Established:** 1953. **Profile:** A non-political, non-governmental organisation working to promote and gain recognition for the Irish language and culture throughout Ireland. Its work covers four areas of activity: education, youthwork, the arts and its own traditional music label. It also organises the National Youth Arts and Music Festival, *Slógadh.*

GLÓR NA NGAEL *Áras na Comhdhála, 46 Kildare Street, Dublin 2. Tel: (01) 6794780. Fax: (01) 6790214.* **Profile:** It organises an annual competition encouraging communities to promote Irish culture and the use of Irish as a spoken language.

OIDEAS GAEL *Glenn Cholm Cille, Co. Donegal. Tel: (073) 30248. Fax: (073) 30348.* **Profile:** It organises Irish language courses together with cultural activities.

RAIDIÓ NA GAELTACHTA *Casla, Co. Galway. Tel: (091) 506677. Fax (091) 506688. Irish Radio station - see media chapter.*

RAIDIÓ NA LIFE 7 *Merrion Square, Dublin 2. tel (01) 6616333. Fax: (010) 6763966. Irish radio station - see media chapter.*

TAISCE CHEOL DÚCHAIS ÉIREANN 63 *Merrion Square, Dublin 2. Tel: (01) 6619699* **Established:** 1987. **Profile:** The Irish Traditional Archive acts as a

resource centre for collecting research and information on Irish traditional music. Collections of books, sound recordings, photographs and manuscripts have been made. access has been granted to the general public.
TEILIFÍS NA GAELIGE *Baile na hAbhann, Co. Galway. Tel: (091) 505050. Fax: (091) 505021.* **Profile:**

Ireland's television channel which broadcasts through the medium of Irish.
ÚDARÁS NA GAELTACHTA *Na Forbacha, Galway. Tel: (091) 503100.* **Profile:** A regional development agency responsible for establishing of economic, social and cultural development in the Gaeltacht regions. ◻

ARTS

Move Culture to Centre Stage

By *Michael D. Higgins* TD

MOST great advances in knowledge have come from acts of initial dissidence, made by someone brave enough to question the prevailing code. That act of dissent, even in the fields of science and technology, can often be rather artistic in nature: a hunch, an instinct, which may take years of hackwork to confirm. But the great scientific inventors of our modern world, Copernicus and Kepler as well as Smith and Keynes, were in that deepest sense artists. And they were productive.

The trite old mercantile image of the artist as a parasite, living off the surplus of more developed societies, needs to be rejected. Every artist, however humble, is a useful *producer*, and many great artists help to create the environments in which men and women of the future will live. A figure such a W.B. Yeats did not define creativity in solely personal terms; his project was a search for a unified culture, offering a 'fit' between socially defined goals and the expressive freedom of the individual. Now that information technology has become more calibrated to personal and domestic use, this ideal may seem more feasible. The solitary thinker at the keyboard may be able to launch counter-initiatives unthinkable to the worker who once stood on the production-line.

The 'fit' between personal and social fulfilment is never easily achieved. Keynes wisely observed that a reliance on market forces would never, of itself, have guaranteed the development of roads, street lighting, and so on.

Some government intervention is needed in areas of public utility. This is also true of the arts, especially in smaller countries whose private industries are never wealthy enough to offer major subsidies. Even in the massive United States, this can be so; American drama, even when written by radicals like Arthur Miller, remained old-fashioned in form because it was at the mercy of market forces. Yet, if government subventions become pervasive, they can smother creativity and compromise independence, something which happened in the countries of the Eastern Bloc before 1989. The need is for an arm's length relationship between "the state of the arts" and "the arts of the state"; otherwise self-censorship may ensue, the avoidance by artists of political topics which could embarrass the authorities, and the alternative pursuit of purely private themes. The balancing of these forces must include a separation of realms, and a recognition that that which seems audacious today may appear commonplace very soon. As Scott Fitzgerald sadly joked "an artist writes for the youth of today, the critics of tomorrow and the schoolmaster of ever after".

The vital importance of youth in all this is obvious. Subventions are often helpful in launching careers which, later on, acquire a momentum and a self-sufficiency of their own. This is precisely the reverse of the "learned dependency" which critics of government spending repeatedly claim to find among the chronic unemployed. And this is why Yeats was right to describe artists as producers, making a huge impact on their communities . . .

The recent Coopers & Lybrand Report on the Employment and Economic Significance of the Cultural Industries in Ireland has given us an idea of just how great that impact really is. Among the Report's principal findings were the following:

1. The cultural industries in ireland give employment to 33,800 people.
2. The value of the cultural industries amounts to IR£441 million per year.
3. Some 88% of income is earned by way of direct trading activity, and only 12% is provided by way of grants.
4. Cultural businesses employ slightly more women than men with a balance of 54% and 46%.
5. Almost seven out of every ten jobs in the cultural sector are full-time, mostly on a contract basis.

As has been indicated, we can have the enormous benefits of the cultural industries and inject creativity from the space of culture into the economy, practically and theoretically construed.

There is a new communications order on our planet, but one which works in a very uneven and unfair fashion. The great majority of the world's citizens are reduced by it to the condition of consumers - and what they mainly consume are visual images, sometimes woeful misrepresentations of themselves, coming from one particular part of the planet, the United States, and indeed from just one subsection of that mighty country. Some peoples, notably the French, have understandably sought to challenge this hegemony, to extend their own cultural space in the face of this invasion. But even their efforts, assisted by the *cordon sanitaire* of a distinctive and formidable language, have met with only partial success.

The choice is as to whether we become the consumers of images in a passive culture or the makers of images in an active culture in a democratic society. It will ultimately prove futile to seek to create boundaries, barriers and check-points in an age of transnational electronic media. The more optimistic approach is to invent and create alternative films, music, books, which can appeal over the heads of current market-leaders to the youth of America, many of whom are as likely as their European counterparts to tire of the prevailing blandness. The more unified and homogeneous our political structures become, the more will people turn to indigenous cultures for an expression of themselves . . . and it may even be that the role once played by the nation-state will be taken on by the culture industries. Here in Ireland, for instance, film-makers might do what an earlier generation of writers did under the leadership of Yeats: retell and reinvent Gaelic legends for new media, relying on the underlying integrity of the narrative to make a universal appeal (as has already been done so well in films such as *Into the West* or *My Left Foot*.)

The fact that Irish people use English is often cited as increasing our vulnerability to Anglo-American mass culture, but it also increases our opportunity in the vast English-speaking market, the most affluent in the world. There is also a huge Irish constituency overseas, to which works like *Dancing at Lughnasa* or films like *The Commitments* have appealed. Nor should this language facility prevent us from utilising the translation of English language products into Irish, of course, but also of our own English language works into other tongues. This is especially important given our many links with the post-colonial peoples, whose own leaders and artists, drew so much inspiration from the example of Ireland.

This in turn my help to clarify our role with in the European Union. Being a people with an experience of colonisation, we are uniquely equipped to represent the non-European world to the other peoples of Europe. By our success in extending our own culture space, we might once again provide a lead for other post-colonial peoples to follow. Nor can we forget some of our ancestors were part of the imperial adventure. But our mingled inheritance is what makes our culture so full of interesting tensions. If the key relationship of the next century will be, as the Brandt commission suggested, that between the Northern and Southern peoples, then there is a sense in which that is enacted every day within Irish communities and texts . . . in works like *Dancing at Lughnasa* or *The Commitments*. Once again, as a century ago, Ireland is a crucible of the modern, one of those fascinating points of pressure at which the future is being reimagined.

◻

Michael D. Higgins TD is a former Minister for Arts, Culture and the Gaeltacht.

Extract from the Keynote Speech given by Michael D. Higgins TD
at a European Symposium in Stockholm City Theatre, Stockholm, Sweden, 17-18 September, 1997.

ARTS COUNCIL OF IRELAND: EXPENDITURE, 1996

ARTS SECTOR	AMOUNT (% budget)	ARTS SECTOR	AMOUNT (% budget)
Literature	1,249,000 (6.4)	Multi-Disciplinary Arts	2,394,000 (12.3)
Visual Arts & Architecture	1,622,000 (8.3)	Local Authorities and Partnerships	531,000 (2.7)
Film	762,000 (3.9)	Aosdána	704,000 (3.6)
Drama	6,187,000 (31.8)	Capital	1,027,000 (5.3)
Dance	569,000 (2.9)	Sundry	696,000 (3.6)
Opera	1,009,000 (5.2)	Administration	1,270,000 (6.5)
Music	1,452,000 (7.5)	TOTAL:	19,472,000 (100)

STATE FUNDING OF ARTS COUNCIL OF IRELAND, 1992-96

Sources (£m)	1992	1994	1995	1996
Oireachtas Grant-in-aid	5.2	8.3	12.6	14.44
National Lottery	5.0	5.0	3.7	3.97
TOTAL:	10.2	13.3	16.3	18.3

BUSINESS SPONSORSHIP OF R.O.I. ARTS

SPONSORSHIP BY ARTFORM, 1997	
Artform	Amount (000s)
Community Arts & Centres	£0,417
Dance/mime	£0,078
Film arts	£0,883
Heritage	£0,398
Literature/publishing	£0,515
Multiple-discipline festivals	£0,994
Museums/libraries/archives	£0,598
Music	
Classical/contemporary	£1,380
Other	£1,073
Opera	£0,716
Theatre arts	£1,221

Visual arts	£1,388
TOTAL	£10,217

SPONSORSHIP BY ARTFORM, 1997	
Artform	Amount (000s)
Of which:	
All Arts Festivals	£2,755
Young People's Projects	£1,753

GROWTH IN SPONSORSHIP	
Year	Estimated Amount (000s)
1997	£10,217
1995	£6,263
1993	£5,200
1987	£1,498

SPONSORSHIP IN THE REGIONS, 1997	
Region	Estimated Amount (000s)
Multiple region events	£2,307
Dublin	£4,893
Southeast-East	£0,466
Southwest-South	£1,384
Northwest-North*	£0,987
Midlands	£0,181

Does not include Northern Ireland

SPONSORSHIP BY BUSINESS SECTOR, 1997	
Sector	Amount (000s)
Energy	£0,808
Financial & Insurance Institutions	£2,703
Food & Drink	£1,893
Hotel/catering/retailing	£0,467
Manufacturing/Construction/Property	£0,846
Telecommunications/Technology	£0,688
Transport & Motor Industry	£0,969
Services & Others	£0,674

ARTS COUNCIL OF IRELAND: ALLOCATED FUNDING 1998

Arts Sector	Amount
Literature	£846,500
Visual Arts & Architecture	£1,625,200
Film	£757,000
Drama	£7,690,800
Opera	£1,316,000
Music	£1,803,800
Dance	£713,500
Arts Centres	£1,597,000
Community Arts	£416,500
Festivals	£431,250
Arts & Disability	£103,000
Education, Children & Young People	£453,000
Local Authorities & Partnerships	£703,000
Aosdána	£840,000
TOTAL:	£19,296,550

Budget Allocation by government	£26m (25% increase)
Revenue funds	£23.5m
Capital provision	£2.5m
No. of arts bodies funded by Arts Council	over 300

Other Areas	Amount (increase)
Venues & buildings for the Arts	£7.3 m (13%)
Touring Companies	£1.6 m (17%)
Production companies	£8.7 m
Resource Organisations	£2.9 m (10%)
Arts in Irish	over £1 m
Cross-border initiatives	£0.25 m (30%)
Individual artists	£1,8 m (44%)
Literature	£120,000
Visual Arts and Architecture	£170,000
Film	£180,000
Drama	£75,000
Dance	£117,000
Opera & Music	£80,000
ARTFLIGHT	£190,000

ARTS COUNCIL OF NORTHERN IRELAND: ALLOCATED FUNDING, 1998-99

Arts Sector	Amount
Creative Arts	£987,647
Visual Arts	£600,320
Literature	£267,103
Traditional Arts	£120,224
Performing Arts	£3,456,350
Music & Opera	£1,781,000
Drama & Dance	£1,675,350

Arts Sector	Amount
Strategic Development	£1,129,903
Community Arts	£662,153
Education & Training	£155,250
Development	£312,500
Public Affairs	£53,200
Strategy	£107,200
Administration	£935,700
TOTAL	£6,670,000

LOTTERY FUNDING: N. IRELAND ARTS (1996/7)

Arts Sector	Awards Granted	Value (£000s)
Combined Arts	19	4,204.6
Community Arts	3	132.6
Dance	1	7.0
Drama	11	£183.5
Film Production	10	558.6
Film Development	5	70.9
Other Film	1	24.0
Literature	1	2.7
Music - Bands	79	1,122.8
Music - Other	6	64.0
Opera	3	134.3
Public Art	10	222.2
Visual Art	2	60.6

	Total	151	6,787.8
Project Type	Awards Granted		Value (£000s)
Building	8		2,923.8
Musical INstruments	81		1,115.9
Equipment	20		1,704.1
New Work	18		307.8
New to Northern Ireland	1		38.2
Feasibility Studies	7		56.0
Architectural Competitions	1		12.5
Film Production	10		558.6
Film Development	5		70.9
TOTAL	151		6,787.8

ARTS ECONOMIC PERFORMANCE, NORTHERN IRELAND (1993-94)

ARTS SECTOR	VALUE	NUMBERS EMPLOYED
Art Trade	£2.8 m	50
Broadcasting	£64.0 m	990
Cinema	£14.2 m	555

ARTS SECTOR	VALUE	NUMBERS EMPLOYED
Community Arts, Supportive Organisations and Creative & Performing Artists	£14.0 m	725
Design Trades	£14.5 m	1,010
Heritage	£3.0 m	430
Independent Films / Video	£8.0 m	380
Museums / Galleries	£10.0 m	560
Music Industry	£2.1 m	70
Performed Arts	£15.8 m	400
Publishing Industry	£1.4 m	35
TOTAL	£149.8 m	5,205

LITERATURE

FACTFILE: THE BOOK PUBLISHING INDUSTRY IN IRELAND

Persons employed in Irish publishing: 443 (1994)
Aid to Irish publishing industry: £420,000 (1997)

ESTIMATED RETAIL FOR IRISH-PUBLISHED BOOKS	1991 (IR£)	1994(IR£)
Educational books	23.3 million	25.37 million
General books	9.8 million	13.62 million
TOTAL:	33.1 million	38.99 million

BEST SELLING BOOKS IN IRELAND: OCTOBER 1997 - SEPTEMBER 1998

Type / Month	Title	Author	Publisher
Paperback Fiction:			
October 1997	Finbar's Hotel	Dermot Bolger (Editor)	New Island
November 1997	Finbar's Hotel	Dermot Bolger (Editor)	New Island
December 1997	Woman of the House	Alice Taylor	Mount Eagle
January 1998	Rachel's Holiday	Marian Keyes	Poolbeg
February 1998	The Partner	John Grisham	Century
	Rachel's Holiday	Marian Keyes	Poolbeg
March 1998	The Butcher Boy	Patrick McCabe	Pan
	Caroline's Sister	Sheila O'Flanagan	Poolbeg
	Love Like Hate Adore	Deirdre Purcell	Townhouse
April 1998	Love Like Hate Adore	Deirdre Purcell	Townhouse
	The Cold Mountain	Charles Frazier	Sceptre
May 1998	Mirror, Mirror	Patricia Scanlan	Poolbeg
	The Cold Mountain	Charles Frazier	Sceptre
	The God of Small Things	Arundhati Roy	Flamingo
	Scalpel	Paul Carson	Arrow
June 1998	Unnatural Exposure	Patricia Cornwell	Warner
	The God of Small Things	Arundhati Roy	Flamingo
July 1998	The God of Small Things	Arundhati Roy	Flamingo
	Unnatural Exposure	Patricia Cornwell	Warner
August 1998	The God of Small Things	Arundhati Roy	Flamingo
	Mirror, Mirror	Patricia Scanlan	Poolbeg
September 1998	The Horse Whisperer	Nicholas Evans	Corgi
	The God of Small Things	Arundhati Roy	Flamingo
Paperback Non-Fiction:			
October 1997	Angela's Ashes	Frank McCourt	Harper Collins
November 1997	Angela's Ashes	Frank McCourt	Harper Collins
December 1997	Angela's Ashes	Frank McCourt	Harper Collins
January 1998	Angela's Ashes	Frank McCourt	Harper Collins
February 1998	Little Book of Calm	Paul Wilson	Penguin
March 1998	Little Book of Calm	Paul Wilson	Penguin
April 1998	Little Book of Calm	Paul Wilson	Penguin
May 1998	Little Book of Calm	Paul Wilson	Penguin
	Veronica Guerin	Emily O'Reilly	Vintage
June 1998	Little Book of Calm	Paul Wilson	Penguin
	Longitude	Dava Sobel	Fourth Estate

Continued from previous page

Type / Month	Title	Author	Publisher
Paperback Non-Fiction:			
July 1998	Little Book of Calm	Paul Wilson	Penguin
August 1998	Angela's Ashes	Frank McCourt	Harper Collins
	Little Book of Calm	Paul Wilson	Penguin
September 1998	Snakes and Ladders	Fergus Finlay	New Island
	Little Book of Calm	Paul Wilson	Penguin
Hardback Fiction:			
October 1997	Love Like Hate Adore	Deirdre Purcell	Townhouse
	Unnatural Exposure	Patricia Cornwell	Little Brown
November 1997	Unnatural Exposure	Patricia Cornwell	Little Brown
December 1997	Unnatural Exposure	Patricia Cornwell	Little Brown
January 1998	Mirror, Mirror	Patricia Scanlan	Poolbeg
February 1998	Deja Dead	Kathy Reichs	Heinemann
Type / Month	**Title**	**Author**	**Publisher**
March 1998	Deja Dead	Kathy Reichs	Heinemann
	The Butcher Boy	Patrick McCabe	Picador
	The Solace of Sin	Catherine Cookson	Bantam
April 1998	The Street Lawyer	John Grisham	Century
May 1998	The Street Lawyer	John Grisham	Century
	The Eleventh Commandment	Jeffrey Archer	Harper Collins
June 1998	The Eleventh Commandment	Jeffrey Archer	Harper Collins
	Breakfast on Pluto	Patrick McCabe	Picador
July 1998	The Eleventh Commandment	Jeffrey Archer	Harper Collins
August 1998	Filth	Irvine Welsh	Jonathan Cape
	The Eleventh Commandment	Jeffrey Archer	Harper Collins
	The Street Lawyer	John Grisham	Century
September 1998	Tara Road	Maeve Binchy	Orion
Hardback Non-Fiction:			
October 1997	Diana:A Tribute to the People's Princess	Peter Donnelly	Bramley Books
	Diana, A Tribute	Tim Graham	Weidenfeld & Nicolson
	Anam Cara	John O'Donoghue	Bantam Press
November 1997	Anam Cara	John O'Donoghue	Bantam Press
	Diana: Her True Story	Andrew Morton	O'Mara Books
December 1997	Anam Cara	John O'Donoghue	Bantam Press
January 1998	Anam Cara	John O'Donoghue	Bantam Press
February 1998	Anam Cara	John O'Donoghue	Bantam Press
	Father Browne's Titanic Album	E. F. O'Donnell	Wolfhound
March 1998	Anam Cara	John O'Donoghue	Bantam Press
April 1998	Anam Cara	John O'Donoghue	Bantam Press
May 1998	Anam Cara	John O'Donoghue	Bantam Press
June 1998	Anam Cara	John O'Donoghue	Bantam Press
July 1998	Anam Cara	John O'Donoghue	Bantam Press
August 1998	Anam Cara	John O'Donoghue	Bantam Press
September 1998	Anam Cara	John O'Donoghue	Bantam Press
	Now is the Time	Sr. Stanilaus Kennedy	Town House

MAJOR PUBLISHING HOUSES IN IRELAND

Publisher	Founded	Address	Telephone	Director(s)
A & A Farmar	-	78 Ranelagh Village, Dublin 6	(01) 4963625	Anna Farmar
Adare Press	-	White Gables, Ballymoney, Co. Down	(018206) 23782	George McBride
Anvil Books	1964	45 Palmerstown Rd, D6	(01) 4973628	Rena Dardis
Appletree Press	-	19-21 Alfred St., Belfast BT2 8DL	(01232) 243074	John Murphy
Aran Books	1992	46 Charnwood, Bray, Wicklow	(01) 2842493	C Golden, Pat O'Loughlin
Argenta Publications	-	19 Mountjoy Square, Dublin 1	(01) 8748796	Uinseann Mac Eoin
Artcam Ireland Ltd	1996	Speenoge, Burt, Co. Donegal	(077) 68186	Pat McArt, Dónal Campbell
Ashfield Press	-	26 Eustace Street, Dublin 2	(01) 6773243	Gerard O'Connor
Attic Press Ltd	1988	29 Upper Mount Street, Dublin 2	(01) 6616128	Róisín Conroy
Ballinakella Press	-	Whitegate, Co. Clare	(061) 927030	Hugh Weir
Blackhall Publishing	-	26 Eustace Street, Dublin 2	(01) 6773243	Gerard O'Connor
Blackstaff Press	-	3 Galway Park, B'fast, BT16 0AN	(01232) 487161	Anne Tannahill

Boole Press......................26 Temple Lane, Temple Bar, Dublin 2 ....(01) 6797655 ....Paulene McKeever
Brandon..*See Mount Eagle*
Butterworths.................................26 Upper Ormond Quay, D7 ....(01) 8731555 ....Gerard Coakley
Careers & Educat. Pub.....Lwr James St, Claremorris, Co. Mayo ....(094) 62093 ....Eamonn O'Boyle
Children's Press...*See Anvil Books*
Cló Chaisil.....................179 Bóthar Ráth Maoinis Uachtarach, D6 .....(01) 4960586 .Dónal Ó Cuill, Róisín Uí Chuill
Cló Iar-Chonnachta ...1985.......Indreabhán, Connemara, Galway ......(091) 593307...............Micheál Ó Conghaile
Coiscéim ....Cosanic Teo, 91 Bóthar Bhinn Éadair, D13.......(01) 8322509 ....-
Collins Press ....1989..Carey's Lane, Huguenot Qrter, Cork ......(021) 271346......................Con Collins
Columba Press..........1985..... Spruce Ave. Stillorgan Ind. Park, Dublin ......(01) 2942556.......................Séan O'Boyle
Cork Uni. Press ....1925Crawford Business Park, Cross' Green, Cork ......(021) 902980....................Sara Wilbourne
C. J. Fallon.......................P.O. Box 1054, Palmerstown, D20 ......(01) 6265777.................Henry McNicholas
Dedalus Press ....24 The Heath, Cypress Downs, Dublin 6W ...(01) 4902582.......................John Deane
Dissident Editions ....71 Ballyculter Rd, Loughkeelan, Downpatrick ...(01396) 881364 ....Frederik Wolff
Eason.......................................66 Middle Abbey St, Dublin 1 ....(01) 8733811 ....Gordon Bolton
Edco.......................1910 .....Ballymount Rd, Walkinstown, D12 ....(01) 4500611 ....
Emperor Publishing.....-..................27-29 Washington St, Cork ......(021) 270559 ...................J.A. O'Connor
Field Day Public. ....Foyle Arts Centre, Lawrence Hill, Derry BT48 ...(01504) 360196 .Colette Nelis (Administrator)
Flyleaf Press ....1981.4 Spencer Villas, Glenageary, Dublin ......(01) 2806228 ....James Ryan
Folens.........................Broomhill Business Pk, Tallaght, D24 ......(01) 4515311 ....John O'Connor
Fortnight Ed. Trust.........-.........7 Lwr Crescent, Belfast BT7 1NR ...(01232) 236575 ....Chris Moffat
Four Courts Press.....1972.......Kill Lane, Blackrock, Co. Dublin ......(01) 2892922..................Michael Adams
Gallery Books ....1970.......Loughcrew, Oldcastle, Co. Meath ....(049) 41779 ....Peter Fallon
Gill & Macmillan ....1968.....Goldenbridge, Inchicore, Dublin 8 ......(01) 4531005.....................Michael Gill
Goldsmith Press.........1972..................Newbridge, Co. Kildare ......(045) 34648 ....Vivienne Abbott
Guildhall Press ....1979.41 Great James St, Derry BT48 7DF ...(01504) 364413 ....Adrian Kerr
Gúm, An......................-..................44 O'Connell Street, Dublin 1 ......(01) 8734700 Dónal Ó Cuill, Máire NicMhaoláin
HMSO..........................-.......16 Arthur Street, Belfast BT1 4GD ....-................................-
IPA..............................1957 ....Vergemount Hall, Clonskeagh, D6 ......(01) 2697011............ Jim O'Donnell
Irish Academic Press1974..........Kill Lane, Blackrock, Co. Dublin ......(01) 2892922..................Michael Adams
ITÉ.............................-................31 Fitzwilliam Place, Dublin 2 ......(01) 6765489 ....
Kestrel Books...................48A Main Street, Bray, Co. Wicklow ......(01) 2863402 ....Terry Rowan
Kingstown Press ....5 Marine Road, Dún Laoghaire, Dublin ......(01) 2803684 ....Henry O'Hagan
Lilliput Press..........1984.........62-63 Sitric Rd, Arbour Hill, D7 ......(01) 6711647 .... Antony Farrell
Longman, Brown & Nolan*See Edco (Educational Co. of Ireland)*
Mercier Press..........1944 ...PO Box 5, 5 French Church St, Cork ......(021) 275040...................John F. Spillane
Mount Eagle..............1997..............PO Box 32, Dingle, Co. Kerry ......(066) 51463................Steve MacDonogh
New Island Books.........-....2 Brookside, Dundrum Rd, Dublin 14 ......(01) 2989937 ....Edwin Higel
Oak Tree Press..........1992......Merrion Bldg, Lwr Merrion St, D2 ......(01) 6761600...................Brian O'Kane
O'Brien Press.............1974......20 Victoria Rd, Rathgar, Dublin 6 ......(01) 4923333.................Michael O'Brien
Oisín Publications ......-..................4 Iona Drive, Dublin 9 ....(01) 8305236....................Liam Ó hOisín
On Stream ....1992..........Currabaha, Blarney, Co. Cork ......(021) 385798....................Roz Crowley
Ossian Publications .....-......PO Box 84, 40 MacCurtain St, Cork ......(021) 502025 ....John Loesberg
Poolbeg Press ....1976 ...123 Baldoyle Industrial Estate, D13 ......(01) 8321477.............Philip MacDermott
Relay ....-..............Tyone, Nenagh, Co. Tipperary ......(067) 31734...................Donal Murphy
Roberts Rinehart......................Charleston Rd, Ranelagh, D6 ......(01) 4976860.................Jack Van Zandt
Round Hall Sweet & Maxwell......4 Uppr Ormond Quay, Dublin 7 ......(01) 8730101 ....-
Sáirséal Ó Marcaigh .....-.........13 Bóthar Crioch Mhór, Dublin 11 ......(01) 8738914 ....Caoimhín Ó Marcaigh
Salmon Publishing ....-...Knockeven, Cliffs of Moher, Co. Clare ....(065) 81621 ....Jossie Lendennie
Sporting Books ....4 Sycamore Rd, Mount Merrion, Co. Dublin ..(01) 2887914..................Raymond Smith
Town House ....1980..........Charleston Rd, Ranelagh, D6 ......(01) 4972399 ....Treasa Coady
Trident Media Ire...........-.......Station House, Clifden, Co. Galway ......(095) 22024 ....
Ulster Historical Found. Balmoral Bdgs, 12 College Sq East, B'fast(01232) 332288 ....Dr Brian Traynor
Veritas ....1969.......7-8 Lower Abbey St, Dublin 1 ....(01) 8788177 ....Fr. Sean Melody
Wolfhound Press ....68 Mountjoy Square, Dublin 1 ....(01) 8740354...............Seamus Cashman

DRAMA
THEATRES & THEATRE COMPANIES IN IRELAND

ANTRIM

Aisteoiri Aon Drama 216 Falls Rd., Belfast. Tel: (01232) 239303

Arts Theatre 41 Botanic Ave.,

Belfast. Tel: (01232) 316900

Belfast Theatre Co 207 Russell Court, Belfast. Tel: (01232) 241950

Belfast Waterfront Hall 2 Lanyon

Place, Belfast. (01232) 334400

Castleward Opera 61 Marlborough Pk. North, Belfast. Tel: (01232) 661090

Centre Stage 99 Fitzroy Ave, Belfast. Tel: (01232) 249119

Clotworthy Arts Centre Randalstown Rd, Antrim.

Dock Ward Community Theatre 20 Antrim Road, Belfast. Tel: (01232) 743334.

Grand Opera House 2-4 Great Victoria St., Belfast. Tel: (01232) 240411

Group Theatre, The Bedford St, Belfast. Tel: (01232) 329685

Kabosh Theatre Co. Old Museum Arts Centre, 7 College Sq. North, Belfast. Tel: (01232) 243343.

Lyric Theatre 55 Ridgeway St, Belfast BT9 5FB. Tel: (01232) 669660

Mad Cow Productions Ormeau Ave, Belfast. Tel: (01232) 313156

Old Museum Arts Ctre 7 College Sq North, Belfast

Opera Northern Ireland Stranmillis Rd, Stranmillis, Belfast.

Point Fields Theatre Co Cathedral Buildings, 64 Donegall St, Belfast. Tel: (01232) 314774

Prime Cut Productions McAvoy House, 17a Ormeau Ave, Belfast. Tel: (01232) 313156

Replay Productions Old Museum Ctre, 7 College Sq North, Belfast. Tel: (01232) 322724

Shanakee Productions 93 Kimberley Street, Belfast. Tel: (01232) 644276

Tinderbox Theatre Co McAvoy House, 17a Ormeau Ave, Belfast. Tel: (01232) 439313

Ulster Hall Bedford St, Belfast

Ulster Theatre Co Church Hall, Park Rd, Belfast. Tel: (01232) 645472

Virtual Reality Flat 3, 31 Wellington Park, Belfast. Tel: (01232) 666042

Who the Hell Thtre Co 63 Ardenvohr St, Belfast.

ARMAGH
Gateway Theatre Co 57 Gilford Rd., Portadown. Tel: (01762) 351313

Portadown Town Hall Theatre Edward Street, Portadown. Tel: (01762) 341199

CARLOW
Bridewell Lane Theatre Bridewell Lane, Tullow St, Carlow.

CLARE
Theatre Omnibus Business Centre, Francis St, Ennis. (065) 29952

CORK
Boomerang Theatre Co Teach Barra, Dean St, Cork. Tel: (021) 316826

Corcadorca Theatre Co 11 Marlboro St, Cork. Tel: (021) 278326

Cork Arts & Theatre Club 7 Knapps Sq, Cork. Tel: (021) 508398

Cork Opera House Emmet Place, Cork. Tel: (021) 274308

Craic Na Coillte Teo Scartagh, Clonakilty. Tel (021) 34555

Everyman Palace 15 MacCurtain St, Cork. Tel: (021) 501673

Firkin Crane Centre Shandon, Cork. Tel: (021) 507487

Graffiti Theatre Co Ltd 50 Popes Quay, Cork. Tel: (021) 505758

Meridian Productions Tel: (021) 276837

New Granary Theatre University College, Mardyke, Cork.

Schoolyard Theatre Old Limerick Rd, Charleville. Tel: (063) 81844

DERRY
Big Telly Theatre Co Flowerfield Centre, Coleraine Rd, Portstewart. Tel: (01265) 832588

Echo Echo Dance Co. 5 Artillery St, Derry. Tel: (01504) 262162

Field Day Theatre Co Foyle Arts Centre, Lawrence Hill, Derry.

Minkey Hill Theatre Co Foyle Arts Centre, Lawrence Hill, Derry. Tel: (01504) 373400

O'Casey Theatre Co The Playhouse, Artillery St, Derry. Tel: (01504) 374253

Playhouse, The Derry.

Rialto 5 Market St, Derry.

Ridiculusmus The Playhouse, Artillery St, Derry. Tel: (01504) 373800

Riverside Theatre University of Ulster, Cromore Road, Coleraine, Co Derry. (01265) 44141

Stage Beyond Thtre Co Play Resource Centre, Artillery Street, Derry.

St. Columb's Theatre and Arts Centre Orchard St, Derry. Tel: (01504) 262800

DONEGAL
Abbey Centre Trust Tir Connail St, Ballyshannon. Tel: (072) 51375

Balor Theatre Main St, Ballybofey. Tel: (074) 31840

DOWN
Ulster Theatre Co 54 Drumnaconagher Rd., Crossgar.

DUBLIN
Abbey Theatre Lower Abbey St, D1. Tel: (01) 8748741

Andrew's Lane Theatre Exchequer St, D2. Tel: (01) 6797760

Calypso Productions 7 South Great Georges St, D2. Tel: (01) 6704539

City Arts Centre 23-25 Moss St, D2. Tel: (01) 6770643

Co-Motion Theatre Co 1 Eden Quay, D1. Tel: (01) 8787928

Crypt Art Centre Dublin Castle, D2. Tel: (01) 6713387

Down-to-Earth Theatre High St, D8. Tel: (01) 6705734

Dublin Theatre Festival 47 Nassau St, D2. Tel: (01) 6778439

Dublin Youth Theatre 23 Gardiner St Upper, D1. Tel: (01) 8743687

Focus Theatre Co 6 Pembroke Place, D2. Tel: (01) 6763071

Gaiety Theatre South King St, D2. Tel: (01) 6773614

Gate Theatre 1 Cavendish Row, D1. Tel: (01) 8744045

Iomha Ildanach Thtre Co Crypt Arts Centre, Dublin Castle, D2. Tel: (01) 6713387

Lambert Puppet Theatre & Museum Clifton Lane, Monkstown. Tel: (01) 2800974

National Association of Youth Drama 34 Upper Gardiner St, D1. Tel: (01) 8781301

Olympia Theatre 72 Dame St, D2. Tel: (01) 6777744

Opera Theatre Co 18 St Andrew St, Temple Bar, D2. Tel: (01) 6794962

Opera Ireland 276 South Circular Road, D8. Tel: (01) 4535519

Pan Pan Theatre The Old School House, Eblana Ave, Dun Laoghaire. Tel: (01) 2800544

Passion Machine, The 30 Gardiner Place, D1. Tel: (01) 8788857

Peacock Theatre Tel: (01) 8787222

Pigsback Theatre Co Shamrock Chambers, D2. Tel: (01) 6704018

Point Theatre East Link Bridge, North Wall Quay, D1. Tel: (01) 8363633

Project Arts Centre 39 East Essex St, D2. Tel: (01) 6712321

Project @ the Mint Call save 1850 260027

RDS Simmonscourt Pavillion, Ballsbridge, D4. Tel: (01) 6680866

Rough Magic Ltd 5 South Great Georges St, D2. Tel: (01) 6719278

Samuel Beckett Theatre Trinity College, D2. Tel: (01) 7021239

Second Age Ltd 74 Dame St, D2. Tel: (01) 6798542

Smashing Times Co 5 Meeting House Lane, D7. Tel: (01) 872784

St. Anthony's Little Theatre Merchants Quay, D8. Tel: (01) 6777651

Sticks & Stones Co 19 Watkins Sq, D8. Tel: (01) 2807065

Storytellers' Theatre Co 3rd Floor, 5 Aston Quay, D2. Tel: (01) 6711161

Tallaght Civic Theatre *(Under Construction)*

Team Theatre Co 4 Marlborough Place, D1. Tel: (01) 8786108

Tivoli Theatre 135-138 Francis St, D2. Tel: (01) 4546349

FERMANAGH

Ardhowen Theatre Dublin Rd, Enniskillen, Co. Fermanagh BT74 6BR. Tel: (01365) 323233

GALWAY

Down to Earth Thtre Co Shantalla. Tel: (091) 529684

Druid Theatre Co Chapel Lane, Galway. Tel: (091) 568617

Galway Arts Centre 23 Nuns Island, Galway (091) 565886

Glenamaddy Townhall Creggs Rd, Glenamaddy.

Macnas Fisheries Field, Galway. (091) 561462

Mall Theatre The Mall, Tuam.

Punchbag Theatre Co 47 Dominick St, Galway. Tel: (091) 569481

Taibhdhearc n' Gaillimhe Sráid Lár, Galway. Tel: (091) 562024

Town Hall Theatre Courthouse Sq, Galway. Tel: (091) 569777

KERRY

Siamsa Tire Theatre Tralee. Tel: (066) 23055

St. John's Theatre Listowel.

KILDARE

The Grove Theatre Leinster St, Athy. Tel: (0507) 38375

Kilcullen Theatre Main Street, Kilcullen.

The Moat Club The Moat, Naas.

Properous Theatre Parish Centre, Prosperous.

Dunshane Hall c/o Camphills Community, Brannockstown, Naas.

KILKENNY

Barnstorm Theatre Co New St., Kilkenny. Tel: (056) 51266

Bickerstaffe Theatre Co

Cleere's Theatre Co. 28 Parliament St, Kilkenny. Tel: (056) 62573

Watergate Theatre Parliament St, Kilkenny. Tel: (056) 61674

LAOIS

Theatre under construction.

LEITRIM

Eggert Rodger Glenboy, Manorhamilton. Tel: (072) 55856

Corn Mill Theatre & Arts Centre Carrigallen.

LIMERICK

Belltable 69 O'Connell St, Limerick. Tel: (061) 319866

Island Theatre Co

Theatre Royal Upper Cecil St, Limerick. Tel: (061) 414224

LONGFORD

Backstage Theatre Farneyhoogan, Longford. Tel: (043) 47889

Bog Lane Theatre Bog Lane, Ballymahon, Longford.

LOUTH

Dundalk Town Hall Crowe St, Dundalk. Tel: (042) 32276

Footprint Productions Quay St Dundalk. Tel: (042) 27072

MAYO

Yew Theatre Co Cresent Hse,Casement St, Ballina. Tel: (096) 71238

MEATH

Duchas Folk Theatre Castle St, Trim.

MONAGHAN

Garage Theatre St Davnet's Complex, Armagh Rd, Monaghan.

SLIGO

Blue Raincoat Co Lwr Quay St (071) 70431

Hawk's Well Theatre Temple St, Sligo. Tel: (071) 61526

TIPPERARY

Galloglass Theatre Co Nelson St, Clonmel.

Magner's Theatre The Mall, Clonmel.

Phoenix Theatre Gas House Lane, Tipperary. Tel: (062) 33266

Regal Theatre Davis Rd, Clonmel.

TYRONE

Bardic Theatre Dungannon District Council, Dungannon.

WATERFORD

Forum Theatre The Glen, Waterford. Tel: (051) 871111

Garter Lane Theatre 22A O'Connell St,Waterford. Tel: (051) 877153

Red Kettle Theatre Co 33 O'Connell St., Waterford.

Theatre Royal The Mall, Waterford.

WEXFORD

Gorey Little Theatre Pearse St, Gorey. Tel: (055) 21608

Razor Edge Arts Theatre Paul Quay, Wexford.

St Michael's Theatre South St., New Ross. Tel: (051) 421255

Theatre Royal High St., Wexford.

WICKLOW

Dry Rain Perf. Arts Cntre An Lar Dargle Rd Lower, Bray.

□

AMATEUR DRAMATICS, 1998
THREE ACT FINAL

The following groups qualified to compete in the 46th Esso All-Ireland Drama Festival, which took place in May 1998 at Dean Crowe Hall, Athlone. Each company has to appear in at least six festivals prior to the All-Ireland (needing two wins out of the six).

GROUP (County)	PLAY	PLAYWRIGHT
Castleblaney Players, Monaghan	The Great Hunger	Tom McIntyre (adapted Patrick Kavanagh's poem)
Coolera, Sligo	The Steward of Christendom	Sebastian Barry
Cornmill Theatre Group, Leitrim	Belfry	Billy Roche
Enniscorthy Theatre Group, Wexford	Cavalcaders	Billy Roche
Hollywood Players, Down	A Man for All Seasons	Robert Bolt
Lifford Players, Donegal	The Barracks	Hugh Leonard (from the novel by John McGahern)
Moat Club, Kildare	Saint Oscar	Terry Eagleton
Palace Players, Cork	The Crucible	Arthur Miller
Sundrive Players, Dublin	Fathers & Sons	Brian Friel (after Turgenev)
Torch Players, Limerick	The Effect of Gamma Rays on Man-In-The-Moon Marigolds	Paul Zindel
Thurles Drama Group	Faith Healer	Brian Friel

AWARDS	GROUP
Esso Trophy for Winning Group	Corn Mill Theatre (1st time a Leitrim group has won)
Esso Trophy for Winning Group's Director	Killian McGuinness

Continued from previous page

AWARDS	GROUP
Best Director (other than winning group)	Michael Fieldhouse, Hollywood Players
Best Actor	Maurice Kehoe, Coolera Dramatic Society
Best Actress	Mary Harvey, Torch Players
Best Supporting Actor	Joe Kelly, Sundrive Players
Best Supporting Actress	Cathy Lawlor, Moat Club
Best Set	Eugene Finnegan, Corn Mill Theatre
Best Lighting	Cormac Carroll, Coolera Dramatic Society
Best Stage Manager	Terence Stewart, Holywood Players
Playwriting Competition Winner	*G. Men* by J.G. McEvoy, Dunmurray, Belfast

ONE ACT FINAL

The following groups qualified to compete in the All-Ireland One Act Festival, the Bell Table Theatre, Limerick, December, 1997

OPEN SECTION

GROUP (County)	PLAY	PLAYWRIGHT
Balally Players, Dublin	*Vinegar Tom*	Caryl Churchill
Blackrock Players, Cork	*Gum & Goo*	Howard Brenton
Carlow Little Theatre, Carlow*	*Tadgh Ó Cathain & the Corpse*	-
Donegal Theatre Group	*Roxencrantz & Guildenstern*	W.S. Gilbert
Estuary Players, Dublin	*The Valiant*	Hall & Middlemass
Haulbowline Drama Group, Cork	*Sing to me through Open Windows*	A. Koppit
Whitethorn Players, Mayo	*Audition for a Writer*	Doris M. Day

* Winner of the Open Section

CONFINED SECTION

GROUP (County)	PLAY	PLAYWRIGHT
Malthouse Players, Galway	*What's for Pudding*	David Tristam
Moate Drama Group, Westmeath	*Growing Pains*	Ian Armstrong
Stradone Players, Cavan	*A Pound on Demand*	Sean O'Casey
Wayside Players, Wexford	*The Briary Gap*	T.C. Murray

* Winner of the Confined Section

FACTFILE ON DRAMA

NORTHERN IRELAND
Number of Societies (1993-94): Drama: 100, Operatics: 17, Choirs: 73, Band / Orchestra: 220, Total: 410
Attendances at Performed Arts (1993-94): Concerts: 69,000, Plays: 131,000, Other theatre events: 256,000, Other Entertainment: 320,000, Total: 776,000

REPUBLIC OF IRELAND
Number of groups in the drama League of Ireland (DLI): 200
Number of performances given annually: 3,000
Estimated Audience totals: 400,000

ART

GALLERIES AND ART CENTRES

ANTRIM
Arches 2 Holywood Rd, Belfast.
The Arts Council 185 Stranmillis Rd, Stranmillis, Belfast. Tel: (01232) 381591
The Attic 6 Victoria St, Ballymoney.
Ballyearl 585 Church Rd, Newtownabbey.
The Bell 13 Adelaide Park, Belfast.
Catalyst 5 Exchange Place, Belfast. Tel: (01232) 313303
Cavehill 18 Old Cavehill Rd, Belfast. Tel: (01232) 776784
Clotworthy Arts Centre Castle Grounds, Randalstown Rd, Antrim.
Crescent 2-4 University Rd, Belfast. Tel: (01232) 242338

An Culturlann 216 Falls Rd, Belfast. Tel: (01232) 239303
Dalriada Crafts & Gallery 1 Market St., Ballymoney BT53 6EA. Tel: (012656) 62447
Eakin Gallery 237 Lisburn Rd, Belfast. Tel: (01232) 668522
Fenderesky, The Crescent Arts, 2-4 University Rd, Belfast.
Gallery, The 1 Market Place, Carrickfergus. Tel: (01960) 351083
Gilmore Charles 31 Church Rd, Holywood, Belfast.
Harmony Hill 54 Harmony Hill, Lambeg, Lisburn.
Jonathan Swift Gallery 114 Kilroot Business Park, Larne Road,

Carrickfergus.Tel: (01960) 367778
Magee 455 Ormeau Rd, Belfast
Old Museum 7 College Square North, Belfast. Tel: (01232) 235053
One Oxford St 1 Oxford St, Belfast. Tel: (01232) 310400
Orchard Arts & Crafts Castlecroft Centre, Main St., Ballymoney BT53 7ND. Tel: (012656) 67784
Ormeau Baths Gallery 18a Ormeau Ave., Belfast BT2 8HS. Tel: (01232) 321402
Seymour 20 Seymour St, Lisburn.
Stable Gallery 27 Ballywindland Rd., Ballymoney BT53 6QT. Tel: (012656) 65919
Trooperslane Art Gallery 2

Knockmore Park, Carrickfergus. Tel: (01960) 364754

Ulster Museum Botanic Gardens, Belfast. Tel: (01232) 383000

Village Gallery 4 Bendooragh Rd., Ballymoney BT53 7ND. Tel: (012656) 65528

ARMAGH

The Adam 28 Linenhall St., Armagh. Tel: (012657) 526908

Armagh Co. Museum The Mall East, Armagh. Tel: (01861) 523070

Hayloft Armagh.

The Peacock Craigavon.

Pineback House Arts Tullygally Rd, Craigavon. Tel: (01762) 41618

CAVAN

Cavan Co. Arts Service Cavan Town. Tel: (049) 62003

CARLOW

Pembroke Studio Carlow Town. Tel: (0503) 41562

CLARE

The Atlantis Kilshanny.

Burren Painting Centre Lisdoonvarna. Tel: (065) 74208

Dallán Ballyvaughan.

De Valera Library Ennis. Tel: (065) 21616

Clare Branch Library Ennistymon. Tel: (065) 71245

Seán Lemass Library Shannon.

CORK

Art Hive, The Thompson House, MacCurtain St, Cork. Tel: (021) 505228

Bantry Library Bantry.

Barn Gallery, The Garranes Sth, Drimoleague. Tel: (028) 31677

Beara Community Arts The Square, Castletownbere. Tel: (027) 70765.

Blackcoombe Cork. Tel: (021) 501319

Boole Library University College Cork.

Charleville Library Charleville.

Crawford Municipal Emmet Place, Cork.

Keane-on-Ceramics Pier Road, Kinsale. Tel: (021) 774553

Kent Gallery Quayside, Kinsale. Tel: (021) 774956

Lavit Gallery 5 Fr Matthew St, Cork. Tel: (021) 277749

O'Kane's Green Bantry

Riverside Gallery Riverside Hse, 40 Popes Quay, Cork. Tel: (021) 502730

Savoy Gallery The Savoy, Patrick St, Cork. Tel: (021) 502730

Sirius Trust Cobh. Tel: (021) 316899

Spiller's Lane Gallery Spiller's Lane, Clonakilty. Tel: (023) 34815

The Art Hive Cork City. Tel: (021) 505228

The Bandon Bandon

Triskel Arts Centre Tobin St., Cork City. Tel: (021) 272022

Vangard New St, Macroom. Tel: (026) 41198

West Cork Arts Centre North St, Skibbereen. Tel: (028) 22090

DERRY

Context Derry. Tel: (01504) 268027

Flowerfield 185 Coleraine Rd., Portstewart. Tel: (01265) 833959

Foyle Lawrence Hill, Derry. Tel: (01504) 266657

Gordon 7 London St., Derry. Tel: (01504) 374044

Orchard Orchard St, Derry BT48 6EG. Tel: (01504) 269675

The Playhouse 5-7 Artillery St, Derry. Tel: (01504) 264481

Riverside Coleraine. Tel: (01265) 51388

Town House Coleraine

Verbal Arts Centre Cathedral School Building, London St, Derry

DONEGAL

Bennetts Ardara. Tel: (075) 41652

Cristeph Gallery Port Road, Letterkenny. Tel: (074) 26411

Donegal Co. Arts Letterkenny

Donegal Co. Museum Letterkenny. Tel: (074) 24613

Dunfanaghy Tel: (074) 36224

Gallery, The Main St, Donegal. Tel: (073) 22686

Glebe House Churchill. Tel: (074) 37071

House on the Brae Arts Ramelton. Tel: (074) 51240

Port Letterkenny

Ram's Head Kilcar

Saturn Art Gallery Main St, Letterkenny. Tel: (074) 29475

Tullyarvan Mill Buncrana. Tel: (077) 61613

Ulster Cultural Institute Glencolumbcille

DOWN

Ards Arts Centre Town Hall, Conway Sq, Newtownards. Tel: (01247) 810803

Castle Espie Comber. Tel: (01247) 874146

Cleft Donaghadee. Tel: (01247) 888502

Down Centre 2-6 Irish St., Downpatrick. Tel: (01396) 615283

Dromore Community Centre Old Town Hall, Banbridge.

Grant Fine Art Newcastle. Tel: (013967) 22349

Kristyne Gallery Gilford Castle, Banbridge.

Lenaderg Lodge Gallery Tourist Information Centre, Banbridge.

Newcastle Newcastle. Tel: (013967) 23555

Newry Arts Centre Bank Parade, Newry BT35. Tel: (01693) 66232.

Newry & Mourne 1a Bank Parade, Newry. Tel: (01693) 66232

North Down Visitors & Heritage Centre Bangor

Priory Holywood

Salem Comber

Shambles Hillsborough

The Gallery Ards Arts Centre, Scrabo High School, Newtownards.

DUBLIN

Anye von Gosseln 11-13 Suffolk St, D2. Tel: (01) 6714079

Andrew's Lane Theatre 9 St Andrews Lane, D2. Tel: (01) 6797760

Architecture Centre

The Ark Eustace Street, Temple Bar, D2. Tel: (01) 6707788

Arts Council of Ireland, The 70 Merrion Square, D2. Tel: (01) 6611840

Arthouse Multimedia Curved Street, Temple Bar, D2. Tel: (01) 6056800

Black Church Print Studio 4 Temple Bar, D2.

Bobby Dawson 16 Georges St Upper, Dun Laoghaire.

Brock Ossory Business Park, D3.

Chester Beatty Library 20 Shrewsbury Rd, D4. Tel: (01) 2692386

Cill Rialaig 13 St Stephen's Green, D2. Tel: (01) 6707972

City Arts Centre 23-25 Moss St, D2. Tel: (01) 6770643

Combridge Fine Arts Ltd 24 Suffolk St, D2. Tel: (01) 6774652

The Courtyard 10A The Crescent, Monkstown. Tel: (01) 2807567

Crafts Council South William St, D2. Tel: (01) 6797383

Davis 11 Capel St, D1.

Designyard 12 East Essex St, D2.

Distinguished Artists 31 Molesworth St, D2. Tel: 6610541

Douglas Hyde Trinity College, Nassau St, D2. Tel: (01) 6081116

Dublin Photographic Centre

Dublin Public Libraries

Dublin Writers Museum 18 Parnell Sq, D1. Tel: (01) 8722077

Dun Laoghaire/Rathdown Arts Centre

European Fine Arts 6 Merrion Street Lr, D2. Tel: (01) 6762506

Fire Station Studios 9-11 Lower Buckingham St, D1. Tel: (01)

8555176
Frederick 24 Frederick St Sth, D2. Tel: (01) 6707055
Gallery of Photography Meeting House Sq, Temple Bar, D2. Tel: (01) 6714654
Terenure 95 Terenure Rd. North, Terenure. Tel: (01) 4902678
Gorry 20 Molesworth St., D2. Tel: (01) 6795319
Graphic Studio 8a Cope St, D2. Tel: (01) 6798021
Green on Red 58 Fitzwilliam Sq, D2. Tel: (01) 6613881
Guinness Hop Store St. James's Gate, D8. Tel: (01) 4538364
Hallward 65 Merrion Sq, D2. Tel: (01) 6621482
The Harrison 18 Stephens St Lwr, D2. Tel: (01) 4785580
Howth Harbour 6 Abbey St, Howth. Tel: (01) 8393366
Hugh Lane Municipal Parnell Sq Nth, D1. Tel: (01) 8741903
Irish Life Exhibition Ctre Lower Abbey Street, Dublin 1.
IMMA Royal Hospital, Kilmainham, D8. Tel: (01) 6129900
James Gallery 7 Railway Rd., Dalkey. Tel: (01) 2858703
Jo Rain Gallery 23 Anglesea St, D2. Tel: (01) 6779966
Kennedy 12 Harcourt St, D2. Tel: (01) 4751740
Kerlin Gallery Anne's Lane, D2. Tel: (01) 6709093
The Mansion House Dawson St., D2. Tel: (01) 6761845
Milmo-Penny Fine Art 55 Ailesbury Rd, D4. Tel: (01) 2693486
National Gallery Merrion Sq, D2. Tel: (01) 6615133
New Apollo 18 Duke St, D2.
New Art Studio Ltd 2 Mary's Abbey, D7. Tel: (01) 8730617
Oisín 44 Westland Row, D2. Tel: (01) 6611315
Oisín Fairview, D3. Tel: (01) 8333456.
Old Bawn Community School Tallaght, D24. Tel: (01) 4520566
Oriel 17 Clare St, D2. Tel: (01) 6763410
Original Print 4 Temple Bar, D2. Tel: (01) 6773657
Ormond Multi-media 16-18 Lower Ormond Quay. Tel: (01) 8723500
Phoenix Art Studio Lucan.
The Portrait 24 Glencarrig, D13.
Project Arts Centre 39 East Essex St, D2. Tel: (01) 6712321
RHA Gallagher Gallery 15 Ely Place, D2. Tel: (01) 6612558
Rubicon 10 St Stephen's Green,

D2. Tel: (01) 6708055
Sculptors' Society of Ireland 119 Capel Street, D2. Tel: (01) 8722296
Solomon Gallery Powerscourt Townhouse, D2. Tel: (01) 6794237
Stoneleaf Foundation 19 Manor St., D7. Tel: (01) 6707349
Swords Art & Craft Ctre 10 North St., Swords. Tel: (01) 8408258
Tallaght Community Art Centre Virginia House, Blessington Road, D24. Tel: (01) 4621501
Taylor Galleries 34 Kildare St, D2. Tel: (01) 6766055
Temple Bar Gallery 5 Temple Bar, D2. Tel: (01) 6710073
Village 47 Thomas Hand St, Skerries. Tel: (01) 8492236
The Waldock Blackrock Shopping Centre, Blackrock. Tel: (01) 2885657
Wyvern 41 Baggot St. Lower, D2. Tel: (01) 6789930
FERMANAGH
Ardhowen Dublin Rd, Enniskillen. Tel: (01365) 323233
Enniskillen Castle Ctre Castle Barracks, Enniskillen. Tel: (01365) 325000
GALWAY
Arcadia Antiques Castle St, Galway. Tel: (091) 561861
Artspace 49 Dominick St, Galway.
Ballinasloe Library Ballinasloe. Tel: (0905) 43464
Bridge Mills, The O'Briens Bridge, Galway. Tel: (091) 566231
Clifden Art Gallery Main St, Clifden. Tel: (095) 21788
Creative Force 12 Cross St, Galway. Tel: (091) 561086
Damhlann, An (Kenny Gallery) Spiddal Craft Centre, Spiddal. Tel: (091) 553733
Galway Arts Centre 47 Dominick St, Galway. Tel: (091) 65886
Grainstore, The University College Galway
Kenny Gallery Middle Street, Galway
Logan Gallery, The 4a St Anthony's Pl, Woodquay. Tel: (091) 563635
Maam Art Gallery Maam. Tel: (091) 571109.
West Shore Oughterard. Tel: (091) 552562.
KERRY
Artist Gallery, The 5 Plunkett St, Killarney. Tel: (064) 32273
Bín Bán 12 Lower Rock St, Tralee. Tel: (066) 22520
Brushwood Derryquin, Sneem. Tel: (064) 45108.
Cora's 3 Anadale Rd, Killorglin. Tel: (066) 61033

Crannóg Ballintaggart, Dingle. Tel: (066) 51666
Frank Lewis Killarney
Greenlane Gallery Green St, Dingle. Tel: (065) 52018
Iverni Kenmare
Kerry Branch Library Killarney. Tel: (064) 32972
Killarney, The Killarney.
Lewis Gallery 6 Bridewell Lane, Killarney. Tel: (064) 34843
Michael O'Shea 55 High St., Killarney. Tel: (064)34823
Sheeóg Langford St, Killorglin. Tel: (066) 61220
Siamsa Tire Theatre Town Park, Tralee. Tel: (066) 23055.
Simple Pleasures Dingle. Tel: (066) 51224
Tig Áine An Ghraig, Ballyferriter. Tel: (066) 56214.
St. John's Arts and Heritage Centre Listowel Square, Listowel. Tel: (068) 22566.
Tralee Library, Tralee.
Wellspring 16 Denny St, Tralee. Tel: (066) 21218
Woodland Woodland Gallery and Art Studio, Mount Eagle, Brosna.
KILDARE
Athy Library Athy.
Crookstown Mill Heritage Centre, Ballitore.
Kilcock Kilcock. Tel: (01) 6287619
Kildare Branch Library Celbridge.
Kildare Branch Library Naas.
Maynooth Exhibition Ctre Maynooth.
Tuckmil Naas. Tel: (045) 879761.
KILKENNY
Butler Gallery Kilkenny Castle, Kilkenny. Tel: (056) 61106
Kilkenny Co. Library Graiguenamanagh.
The Berkeley Thomastown.
LAOIS
Laois County Hall Portlaoise.
LEITRIM
Fionn MacCumhaill Centre Keshcarrigen.
Old Barrel Store Carrick-on-Shannon. Tel: (078) 20911
LIMERICK
AV University of Limerick.
Anne Fitzgerald Limerick. Tel: (061) 339995
Angela Woulfe 16 Perry Sq, Limerick. Tel: (061) 310164
Belltable 69 O'Connell St, Limerick. Tel: (061) 319866
Chris Doswell's Limerick.
Dolmen Honan's Quay, Limerick. Tel: (061) 417929
Hunt Museum The Custom House,

Limerick. Tel: (061) 312833
Gallery 75 75 O'Connell, Limerick. Tel: (061) 315650
Limerick Branch Library Foynes.
Limerick City Gallery Pery Square, Limerick. Tel: (061) 310633
McKenna Darren 46 Thomas St, Limerick. Tel: (061) 228552
Newcastle West Library
LONGFORD
Carroll Gallery Longford. Tel: (043) 41148
LOUTH
Artistic License Carlingford.
The Basement Dundalk.
County Museum Dundalk.
Droichead Arts Centre Stockwell St, Drogheda. Tel: (041) 33496
Holy Trinity Heritage Carlingford
Louth Branch Library Ardee. Tel: (041) 56080.
Tristann's Dundalk.
MAYO
Andrew Stone Gallery Bridge St, Westport. Tel: (098) 28870
The Aimhirgin Louisburgh
Art Studio Bridge St, Westport. Tel: (098) 26732
Ballinglen Foundation Main St, Ballycastle
Castlebar Public Library Castlebar. Tel: (094) 24444
Claremorris Claremorris
Foxford Exhibition Centre Foxford. Tel: (094) 56488
Joyce, John Ballina. Tel: (096) 71868
Kirk, The Castlebar.
Heinrick Böll Academy Achill

(opened December 1997).
The Linenhall Linenhall St, Castlebar. Tel: (094) 23733
Western Light Achill Island.
Westport Public Library Westport.
Wright, Sue Lower Quay, Westport. Tel: (098) 27343
Yawl Achill Island.
MEATH
Navan Library Navan
The Oriel Bedfort Place, Navan
Trim Library Trim
MONAGHAN
Market House Monaghan
Monaghan Co. Museum Monaghan. Tel: (047) 82928
Tyrone Guthrie Centre Newbliss, Co. Monaghan.
OFFALY
Offaly County Library Service Tullamore. Tel: (0506) 21419
SLIGO
Artist K Studios Lower Quay St, Sligo. Tel: (071) 42552
Hawk's Well Theatre Temple St, Sligo. Tel: (071) 61526
Sligo Art Gallery Yeats Memorial Building, Sligo.
Sligo County Library Stephen Street, Sligo (works of J.B. Yeats).
Model Arts Centre The Mall, Sligo. Tel: (071) 41405
Taylor's Castlebaldwin. Tel: (071) 65138
TIPPERARY
Carrick-on-Suir Heritage Carrick-on-Suir.
Nenagh District Heritage Nenagh.
Roscrea Heritage Centre Roscrea.

South Tipperary Clonmel. Tel: (052) 27877
Tipperary Co. Library Service Thurles. Tel: (0504) 21555
Tipperary (SR) Co. Museum Clonmel. Tel: (052) 25399
The Lucy Erridge Birdhill.
TYRONE
An Creagán Visitor Ctre Creggan, Omagh.
Gateway Museum Grange Court Complex, 21 Moyle Rd, Newtownstewart.
WATERFORD
Garter Lane 22a O'Connell St, Waterford. Tel: (051) 55038
Lismore Library Lismore. Tel: (058) 54128
The Pill Gallery 37b John St, Waterford. Tel: (051) 876445
WESTMEATH
Dolan Moore Athlone
Midland Arts Resource Centre Austin Friar St, Mullingar.
WEXFORD
Ladyship Oils Killurin.
Wexford Arts Centre Cornmarket. Tel: (053) 23764
Woodland Arts & Crafts Gorey.
The Chantry Bunclody.
WICKLOW
Aisling Newtownmountkennedy. Tel: (01) 2819112.
Craft Bray. Tel: (01) 2866728
The Hangman Bray. Tel: (01) 2866208
Renaissance III Wicklow.
Signal Bray. Tel: (01) 2864266 □

FACTFILE ON MAJOR IRISH ART GALLERIES

ARTHOUSE MULTIMEDIA *Arthouse, Curved Street, Temple Bar, Dublin 2.* **Tel:** 6056800 **Fax:** (01) 6056801 **e-mail:** bureau@arthouse.ie **Web:** www.arthouse.ie **Director:** Kieran Sweeney **Bureau of Arts Information:** Antoinette Uhlar. **Achievements:** Has recently released a CD-Rom, containing information on more than 700 Irish artists.

HUGH LANE MUNICIPAL *Parnell Square North, Dublin 1* **Tel:** (01) 8741903 **Director:** Barbara Dawson. **Curator:** Christina Kennedy. **Collection:** Largest collection of contemporary Irish paintings and sculptures. Paintings date from 1850 onwards and the collection contains many valuable impressionist paintings and paintings by Jack B. Yeats, which have become much sought after, some valued at over £1 million. The gallery holds four exhibitions annually.

IRISH MUSEUM OF MODERN ART *Royal Hospital, Military Road, Kilmainham, Dublin 8.* **Tel:** (01) 6129900 **Fax:** 6129999 **e-mail:** info@modernart.ie **Director:** Declan McGonagle **Senior Curator:**

(Exhibitions) Brenda McParland **Senior Curator:** (Collection) Catherine Marshall **Senior Curator:** (Education & Community) Helen O'Donoghue. **Best attended exhibitions, 1997-98:**
Andy Warhol *After the Party* - 160,000
Joseph Kosuth *New Installation & Survey* - 78,209
The Pursuit of Painting *Eurpean Painting of the 20th Century* - 130,220
Kiki Smith *Convergence* - 137,717
Once Is Too Much - 101,539
Brian Cronin *Fat Face with Fork* - 77,029

NATIONAL GALLERY OF IRELAND *Merrion Square, Dublin 2.* **Tel:** (01) 6615133 **Director:** Raymond Keaveney. **Senior Curator:** Sergio Benedetti **Most Valuable Paintings in the Museum:**
Carravagio - *the Taking of Christ*
Rembrandt - *Head of an Old Man* (yet to be confirmed; if verified could be worth as much as £20m)

RHA GALLAGHER GALLERY 15 Ely Place, Dublin 2. Tel: (01) 6612558. **Director:** Patrick T. Murphy

Curator: Patricia Moriarty **Exhibitions:** Holds many exhibitions, as well as the annual exhibition of RHA members. The exhibitions change monthly, and plans are underway to have them rotating every six weeks. Many prominent Irish artists have been members of the RHA, and the organisation has become reinvigorated in recent years.

ULSTER MUSEUM (est: 1881 as a museum, 1890 as a gallery) *Botanic Gardens,* Belfast BT9 5AB **Tel:** (01232) 383000 **Director:** Michael Houlihan **Best attended exhibitions, 1997-98: (in order of attendances)**
1- Friedemann Hahn (28/2/97-13/4/97)
2 - William John Leech (28/3/97-22/6/97)
3 - BP Portrait Awards (5/12/97-15/2/98)
4 - Royal Ulster Academy (10/10/97-16/12/97)
5 - John Keane (15/6/98-20/9/98)
6 - Royal Ulster Academy (1/10/98-25/10/98)
Most Valuable Paintings in the Museum:
J.M. Turner - *The Dawn of Christianity* (The Flight into

Egypt) (1841)
Morris Louis - *Golden Age* (1959)
Jean Dubuffet - *Feme et Bébé* (1956)
Francis Bacon - *Head II* (1949)
Thomas Gainsborough - *Arthur, 1st Marquess of Donegall* (c.1780)
Thomas Gainsborough - *Theodosia Magill,* afterwards Countess of Clanwilliam (1765)
Sir Joshua Reynolds - again *Theodosia Magill* (1765)

CRAWFORD MUNICIPAL ART GALLERY Emmet Place, Cork. Tel: (021) 273377. **Director:** Peter Murray **Curator:** Nuala Fenton. Exhibition: the gallery has a permanent exhibition with paintings from the late 19th century - early 20th century by prominent Irish artists, such as James Barry, Walter Osborne, Louis Le Brocquy and Jack B. Yeats. There are also rotating exhibitions, but these will be slowing down this year, due to renovations and building works on the gallery.

❐

ARTS COUNCIL OF IRELAND: WORKS OF ART PURCHASED, 1996

Artist	Title	Art Form	Price
Christopher Banahan	..*Icon from the House of the Tragic Poet*	Oil/Printed lace on Canvas	£1,250.00
Catherine Delaney	*Bridge Passage*	Bronze	£2,530.00
Fergus Feehily	*Scent*	Oil on Wood	£900.00
Martina Galvin	*Letter to Pope Paul III Nicholas Copernicus*	Resin & Paper	£300.00
Sarah Iremonger	*Untitled Blue Series I '94*	Oil on Canvas	£200.00
John Kelly	*Karvas Series No. 35*	Pencil on Paper	£800.00
Brian Kennedy	*Laganstown Panorama II*	Monoprint	£3,500.00
Dolores Lynne	*Connemara Day*	Oil on Canvas	£225.00
Alice Maher	*Nettle Jacket*	Nettles/pins/hanger	£3,000.00
Fergus Martin	*Untitled No. 9*	Acrylic on Cotton	£750.00
Jackie McNamee	*Hair Raising*	Lime wood/ paint	£700.00
Janet Mullarney	*Look Back in Anger*	Plaster/wood/metal/acrylic	£4,000.00
Kathlyn O'Brien	*Untitled No. 13*	Found Objects	£600.00
Nigel Rolfe	*Young Woman with a Rose 2/3*	B/W silver gelatin print	£200.00
John Noel Smith	*Bilocation*	Oil on Canvas	£6,860.00
Rachel Toomey	*Grave Dancing*	Video	£400.00
Katherine West	*Accumulation*	Glass/Porcelain	£350.00
TOTAL:			**£26,565.00**

WORKS OF ART PURCHASED, 1998			
Artist	Title	Art Form	Price
Mark Joyce	*The Entire City*	Oil on Canvas	£675
Margaret Fitzgibbon	*Specchio*	Cast/etched Bronze	£2,000
Eamonn Colman	*Wreckers Moon II*	Oil on Paper	£1,100
Helen Farrell	*Figure Study II*	Oil on Paper	£450
Colin Crotty	*Portrait by Window I*	Oil on Canvas	£600
Paul Seawright	*Bird, Night Shelter*	Photo Print	£2,000
Fionnuala Ní Chiosain	*Untitled 1998*	Mixed Media on Paper	£3,500

TOP TEN IRISH PAINTINGS AT AUCTION,1997/8

Painting	Artist	Value
Singing 'Oh, Had I The Wings of a Swallow' (1925)	Jack B. Yeats	£1,004,910 (£Stg881,500)
The Proud Galloper	Jack B. Yeats	£990,629 (£Stg870,500)
A Mere Fracture	Sir William Orpen	£988,770
A Farewell to Mayo	Jack B. Yeats	£885,500 approx. (£Stg805,000)
Skating at Wengen	Sir John Lavery	£691,410 (£Stg606, 500)
A Golfing Scene	Sir John Lavery	£620,000
The Expected	Jack B. Yeats	£595,000

Painting	Artist	Value
The Face in the Shadow............................	Jack B. Yeats...	£540,000
Lingering Sun, O'Connell Bridge	Jack B. Yeats...	£408,000
Beneath St Jacques, Antwerp	Walter Osborne	£345,000

DANCE

FACTFILE ON YOUTH DANCE & TRAINING

CURRENT STATUS: As yet, no national school exists in Ireland for training of professional dancers in classical ballet or modern dance since the demise of the Irish National Ballet in 1989, although the Firkin Crane is remedying this to a certain extent. The possible outcome of this is that the majority of young people studying theatre dance in Ireland study classical ballet, but the majority of young people entering professional vocational training in Ireland opt to study and work in the contemporary dance styles.

PRE-VOCATIONAL TRAINING:
● **Royal Academy of Dancing** (1996): 160 teachers, 2,923 pupils in exams both in the Republic of Ireland and Northern Ireland.
● **Irish Junior Ballet:** 18 pupils (10-18 yrs), Grants: £8,000 in 1997, £18,000 in 1998. Aims to give dance students the chance to meet and perform with students from other dance schools and give them a flavour of what it might be like to pursue a career on the stage.
● **Billie Barry School:** 40-45 senior students, privately run with no grant aid. Aims to produce an all-round performer with the ability to work in the musical theatre context.
● **Traditional Irish Dance:** _An Coimisiun le Rinci Gaelacha:_ 500 teachers in Ireland and 600 in Canada, U.S., Australia, New Zealand and Britain (this compares to 100 teachers in 1950, which shows how popular Irish dancing has become, helped in no small way by recent large Irish Dancing stage shows) 50,000 students. Aims to preserve and promote Irish dancing. _Siamsa na nÓg:_ 112 students (6-12 yrs). Aims to offer training in the traditional dance, music and story telling of the local region, having consistent links between the profession, training and the community. The course comprises two 3-year cycles with assessments and graduates usually going on to join Siamsa Tire in Tralee.
● **Shawbrook School of Ballet, Longford:** Summerschool, Funded through the Arts Council and the VEC.
● **Ulster Youth Dance Scheme:** 80 participants approx. (14-22 yrs), support from Arts Council

Northern Ireland and other funds. Aims to give young people in Northern Ireland the chance to participate in dance through the provision of experienced dance tutors and summerschools.

FULL-TIME VOCATIONAL TRAINING:
● **Gibson-Madden School of Dance, Cork:** 4 students (1997), fees payable
● **Firkin Crane, Cork:** 10 students (1997), funds available from VEC. Awards: National Council for Vocational Awards. Dance Course Coordinator: Donna Daly Blythe. _See Dance Venues below._
● **Inchicore School, Dublin:** 16 students, funds available from VEC. Awards: Royal Academy of Dancing, Student Teaching Cert.
● **Sallynoggin Senior College, Dun Laoghaire:** 23 students, funds from EU Social Fund, Awards: Dept of Education Foundation Course for full-time training.
● **The Irish World Music Centre, University of Limerick:** to start in 1999, MA in Contemporary Dance.
● **The Dance Studio, Bangor:** 6 students, fees payable (to be accredited for Council for Dance Education and Training) RAD Teaching Cert.
● **Abroad:** Due to lack of facilities in Ireland, most students of dance seek training abroad, applying for Arts Council bursaries to help fund their training. Although the Arts Council invested £71,600 between 1987 and 1995 in bursaries for 50 dance students (26 of whom are now working in the profession), very few dancers return to Ireland as their is a lack of work opportunities available for them, primarily due to the fact that most companies tend to re-employ dancers who have worked for them on previous occasions.
The four most popular courses among those who receive bursaries to train are as follows: Professional Performers Course at the Central School for Ballet, England; BA (Hons) in Dance Theatre at the Laban Centre for Movement & Dance, England; Laine Theatre Arts - Musical Theatre, Performers and Teachers Course, Epsom, England; BA (Hons) in Contemporary Dance at the London Contemporary Dance School, England.   ⌐

DANCE COMPANIES & VENUES IN IRELAND

Dance Theatre of Ireland: based in Dublin, Director: Robert O'Connor, Loretta Yurick

Daghda: based in University of Limerick, set up in 1988, Director: Mary Nunan

Irish Modern Dance Theatre: based in Dublin, Director: John Scott

Cois Ceim: based in Dublin, Director: David Bulger.

Firkin Crane: _Shandon, Cork. Tel: (021) 507487, Fax: (021) 501124, email: firkin@iol.ie_ Director: Mary Brady. Ireland's only dedicated dance venue. It houses a 240 seat theatre, rehearsal studios, workshop facilities, with attendant technical resources and qualified, professional personnel. It is a producing venue for new works, a presenting venue for national and international dance companies and a choreographic research centre; it provides studio facilities for Irish-based dance artistes and an informaton and advice service on dance touring programmes and funding sources; and it aims to create a dance library book, periodical library and a national database for dance.

Cork City Ballet: based in Cork, Director: Alan Foley

Project @ The Mint: based in Dublin. ❑

CLASSICAL / CONTEMPORARY MUSIC & OPERA

STATISTICS ON OPERA: In 1996 expenditure on opera was £1,009,000 (11% increase on 1995). This year also saw the establishment of the Opera Development Group. It is to endeavour to consolidate the revenue funding levels of the three production companies already funded, set up a fixed circuit of regional venues to be served by the Opera Theatre Co., set up a fund for commissioning new opera by Irish composers and librettists, provide bursaries and project awards to assist in the career development of Irish singers & other artists, support the National Chamber Choir as the core professional opera chorus, promote actively with government a new centre for the performing arts.

OPERA COMPANIES:
Wexford Festival Opera;
Opera Ireland (DGOS), based in Dublin, director: Dieter Kaegi;
Opera Theatre Company, based in Dublin
Opera South, based in Cork
National Chamber Choir, based in Dublin
Meridian Productions, based in Cork
Opera Northern Ireland

MOST POPULAR PRODUCTIONS, 1996
Opera Ireland with *Tosca* (Puccini), *The Magic Flute* (Mozart), *La Boheme* (Puccini), *l'Elisir d'amore* (Donizetti).
Opera Theatre Co. with *Zaide* (Mozart), *Amadigi* (Handel), *Katya Kabanova* (Janek).
Wexford Festival with *Parisina* (Donizetti), *l'Etoile du Nord* (Meyerbeer), *Sarka* (Zdenech Fibich)
Opera South with *Carmen* (Bizet) at the Cork Opera House
Pimlico Opera/Mountjoy Prisoners with *West Side Story* (Bernstein) at Mountjoy Prison.

STATISTICS ON CLASSICAL/CONTEMPORARY MUSIC: In 1996, expenditure on music by the Arts Council of Ireland was £1,452,000 (18% increase on 1995).

ORCHESTRAS

THE CLARE ORCHESTRA *College Road, Ennis, Co.Clare. (065) 41774 email: akr@tinet.ie* Conductor: Andrew Robinson, Members: 23
CORK SYMPHONY ORCHESTRA based in Cork.
DUBLIN YOUTH ORCHESTRAS *62 Ailesbury Grove, Dublin 16. Tel: (01) 2980680*
DUBLIN ORCHESTRAL PLAYERS
THE DUBLIN VIOLS Director: Andrew Robinson *35 Marlborough Road, Dublin 4. (01) 6685349email: akr@tinet.ie*
IRISH ASSOCIATION OF YOUTH ORCHESTRAS *6 Alexandra Place,Wellington Road,Cork. (021) 507412*

IRISH CHAMBER ORCHESTRA *Foundation Building, University of Limerick. email: ico@iol.ie* Members: 17. Founded 1970, by members of RTE orchestra and free-lance players. Relocated to Limerick, 1995. Artistic Director: Fionnuala Hunt, former co-leader of the RTE Symphony Orchestra. Perform in Ireland and abroad. Soloists include John O'Connor, Barry Douglas, Míchaél Ó Súilleabháin.
IRISH FILM ORCHESTRA *10 Beechpark Avenue,Castleknock, Dublin 15. (01) 8202581* Director: Catriona Walsh
MOSAIC MUSIC *Nationwide House, Bank Place, Ennis, Co. Clare. (065) 42480 email: cmmacto@iol.ie* Director: Tony Ovenen
NATIONAL CHAMBER CHOIR Conductor Colin Mawby.
NATIONAL SYMPHONY ORCHESTRA *Music Department - RTÉ, Donnybrook, Dublin 4. (01) 2082779 email: taylors@admin.rte.ie* Conductor: Alexander Anissimov. Founded Dublin, 1947, as the Radio Éireann Symphony Orchestra. Relaunched 1989 as National Symphony Orchestra. Conductors include: Michael Bowles, Tibor Paul, Albert Rosen, Colman Pearce, Bryden Thomson, János Fürst, George Hurst, Kasper de Roo.
NATIONAL YOUTH ORCHESTRA OF IRELAND *37 Molesworth Street, Dublin 2.*
THE OPERA THEATRE COMPANY *The Temple Bar Music Centre, Curved Street, Temple Bar, Dublin 2. (01) 6794962 email: otc@imn.ie*
RTÉ CONCERT ORCHESTRA *Music Department - RTÉ, Donnybrook, Dublin 4. (01) 2082779 e: taylors@admin.rte.ie* Head of Orchestras: Simon Taylor. Founded as the Radio Éireann Light Orchestra in 1948. Sister-company to what is now National Symphony Orchestra. Versatile small orchestra who work across musical spectrum of classical, pop, opera and musicals. Have performed several film scores.
RTÉ PHILHARMONIC CHOIR *Portobello Studios, Rathmines, Dublin 6. (01) 2082979 Web site: www.rte.ie*
RTÉ VANBRUGH STRING QUARTET *4 Tirol Avenue, Douglas, Cork. (021) 893027email: vanbrugh@iol.ie* Leader: Christopher Marwood
ST SEPULCHRES *35 Marlborough Road, Dublin 4. (01) 668 5349 email: akr@tinet.ie* Director: Andrew Robinson
ULSTER ORCHESTRA *Elmwood Hall, 89 University Road, Belfast BT7 1NF.* Principal Conductor: Dmitry Sitkovetsky.
ULSTER YOUTH ORCHESTRA *Chamber of Commerce Hse, 22 Great Victoria St., Belfast BT2 7LX. Tel: (01232) 2782877*

❑

POPULAR ARTS, OPERA AND MUSIC FESTIVALS

Name of Festival	Location	Contact	Month*
Aer Rianta Arts Festival	Dublin	-	-
AIB Music Festival in Great Irish Houses	Great Houses in Ir.	(01) 2782506	Jun.
Arklow Music Festival	Arklow, Wicklow	-	-
A Sense of Cork	Cork City	(021) 310597	Jun.
Aspects Celebration of Irish Writing	Bangor, Co. Down	(01247) 271200	Sep.
Belfast Festival at Queen's	Belfast	-	Nov.
Boyle Arts Festival	Boyle, Co. Roscommon	-	Jul.
Cat Laughs Comedy Festival	Kilkenny city	(056) 63837	May/Jun.
Clifden Arts Week	Clifden, Co. Galway	(095) 21162	Sep.
Cork Intern'l Choral Festival	Cork	-	-
Cork Film Festival Festival	Cork city	(021) 271711	Oct.
Dublin Festival of Early Music	Dublin	-	-
Dublin International Organ Fest	Dublin	-	-
Dublin Theatre Festival	Dublin city	(01) 6778439	Oct.
Éigse Carlow Arts Festival	Carlow town	(0503) 40491	Jun.
Ennis Arts Festival	Ennis, Co. Clare	(065) 43500	Jun.
Féile na Phobail	West Belfast	(01232) 313440	Aug.
Galway Arts Festival	Galway city	(091) 58300	Jul.
Galway Early Music Fest	Galway	-	May
Galway Film Fleadh	Galway city	(091) 751655	Jul.
Handelfest	Liberties, Dublin	-	Apr.
International Music Festival	Killaloe, Co. Clare	www.ul.ie/-iwmc/ico/home.html	Jul.
Kilkenny Arts Week	Kilkenny City	kaw@iol.ie	Aug.
Kilkenny Arts Week	Kilkenny city	(056) 63663	Aug.
Listowel Writers' Week	Listowel, Co. Kerry	(068) 21074	May
Portstewart Festival	Portstewart	-	-
Puck Fair	Killorglin, Co. Kerry	(066) 62366	Aug.
Rose of Tralee	Tralee, Co. Kerry	(066) 21322	Aug.
Seacat Storytelling Festival	Ulster Folk & Transport Museum, Co. Down	(01232) 428428	Jun.
Sligo Arts Festival	Sligo town	-	May/June
Sligo Contemporary Music	Sligo town	-	Nov.
Sonorities, Queen's University	Belfast	-	-
Two Cathedrals Festival	Derry	(01504) 377266	Oct.
UCC Contemporary Music Festival	Cork	(021) 902690	Apr.
West Cork Music Festival	Bantry, Cork	-	Jun.
Wexford Opera Festival	Wexford	(053) 22144	Oct/Nov.

*These dates are approximate, based on previous years. Contact local tourist offices or local authorities for correct dates.

SUMMER SCHOOLS

Name of Festival	Location	Contact	Month*
Achill Archaeological summer school	Achill	(0506) 21627	Jun.
Bard summer school	Clare Island, Co. Mayo	(086) 8302915	Jun./Jul.
Blas	University of Limerick	(061) 202047	Jul.
Bram Stoker summer school	Clontarf, Co. Dublin	(087) 2364829	Jul.
Byrne-Perry summer school	Gorey, Co. Wexford	(053) 59769	Jun.
Douglas Hyde Conference	Ballaghaderreen, Co. Roscommon	(0903) 37100	Jul.
Gerard Manley Hopkins sum. school	Monasterevin, Co. Kildare	(045) 525416	Jul.
General Humbert summer school	Ballina, Co. Mayo	(01) 4903963	Aug.
George Moore summer school	Claremorris, Co. Mayo	(094) 71830	Jul.
Glandore regatta & summer school	Glandore, Co. Cork	(021) 545333	Jul.
Goldsmith summer school	Ballymahon, Co. Longford	(0902) 32374	May
James Joyce summer school	Newman House, Dublin	(01) 7068323	Jul.
John Hewitt summer school	Carnlough, Co. Antrim	(01846) 662445	Jul./Aug.
Kerry Int'l sum.schl of Living Authors	Tralee, Co. Kerry	(066) 29370	Jul./Aug.
Kiltartan summer school	Gort, Co. Galway	(01232) 649010	Jul.
Lady Gregory Autumn Gathering	Gort, Co. Galway	(091) 521836	Sep.
Merriman summer school	Ennistymon, Co. Clare	(01) 4531818	Aug.
Parnell summer school	Avondale, Co. Wicklow	(01) 2874124	Aug.
Patrick McGill summer school	Glenties, Co. Donegal	(075) 51103	Aug.
Social Study Conference	Donegal town	(021) 293336	Jun.

Continued from previous page

Name of Festival	Location	Contact	Month*
Synge summer school	Rathdrum, Co. Wicklow	(0404) 46131	Jul.
William Carleton Summer School	Co. Tyrone	(01868) 767259	Aug.
Willie Clancy summer school	Miltown Malbay, Co. Cork	(065) 84148	Jul.
Women's Studies summer school	TCD Dublin	(01) 6609011	Jul.
Yeats Summer School	Sligo	(071) 42693	Aug.

*These dates are approximate, based on previous years. Contact local tourist offices or local authorities for correct dates.

FILM
IRISH OSCAR WINNERS 1929 -1993

The Motion Picture Academy Awards were instituted in 1928 for excellence in various aspects of cinema. Ireland has had numerous winners; they include the following:

Cedric Gibbons .... 11 Oscars for Best Art Direction 1929-1956

The Bridge of San Luis Rey (1929); *The Merry Widow* (1934); *Pride and Prejudice* (1940); *Blossoms in the Dust* (1941); *Gaslight* (1944); *The Yearling* (1946); *Little Women* (1949); Honorary Oscar for *'Consistent Excellence'* (1950); *An American in Paris* (1951); *The Bad and the Beautiful* (1952); *Julius Caesar* (1953); *Somebody Up There Likes Me* (1956).

George Bernard Shaw .... Best Screen Play *My Fair Lady* (Pygmalion) 1938
Greer Garson .... Best Actress *Mrs Miniver* 1942
Barry Fitzgerald .... Best Supporting Actor *Going My Way* 1944
Shane Connaughton .... Best Short Film *Bottom Dollar* 1981
Michele Burke .... Best Make-up *Quest For Fire* 1981
.... *Bram Stoker's Dracula* 1983
Josie McAvin .... Art Direction for *Out Of Africa* 1985
Daniel Day Lewis ....Best Actor *My Left Foot* 1989
Brenda Fricker .... Best Supporting Actress *My Left Foot* 1989
Neil Jordan .... Best Screenplay *The Crying Game* 1993

IRISH OSCAR NOMINATIONS 1939 -1998

Brian Donleavy .... Best Supporting Actor *Beau Geste* 1939
Greer Garson .... Best Actress *Goodbye Mr Chips* 1939
Geraldine Fitzgerald ....Best Supporting Actress *Wuthering Heights* 1939
Greer Garson ....Best Actress *Blossoms in the Dust* 1941
Sara Allgood ....Best Supporting Actress *How Green Was My Valley* 1941
Patricia Collinge ....Best Supporting Actress *Little Foxes* 1941
Greer Garson ....Best Actress *Madame Curie* 1943
Barry Fitzgerald ....Best Supporting Actor *Going My Way* 1944
Greer Garson ....Best Actress *Mrs Parkington* 1944
Greer Garson ....Best Actress *Valley of Decision* 1945
Richard Todd ....Best Actor *The Hasty Heart* 1949
Dan O'Herlihy ....Best Actor *The Adventures of Robinson Crusoe* 1953
Greer Garson ....Best Actress *Sunrise at Campobello* 1960
Peter O'Toole .... Best Actor *Lawrence of Arabia* 1962
Richard Harris ....Best Actor *This Sporting Life* 1963
Josie McAvin .... Best Set Designer *Tom Jones* 1963
Peter O'Toole .... Best Actor *Beckett* 1964
Josie McAvin ....Best Set Design *The Spy Who Came in From the Cold* 1965
Peter O'Toole .... Best Actor *The Lion in Winter* 1968
.... Best Actor *Goodbye Mr Chips* 1969
.... Best Actor The *Ruling Class* 1972
Louis Marcus ....Best Documentary *Páistí Ag Obair* (Children At Work) 1974
.... Best Documentary *Conquest Of Light* 1976
Peter O'Toole .... Best Actor *The Stunt Man* 1980
Peter O'Toole .... Best Actor *My Favourite Year* 1982
Clare Boylan ....Best Short Film *Making Waves* 1988
Kenneth Branagh ....Best Director *Henry V* 1989
.... Best Actor *Henry V* 1989
Daniel Day Lewis ....Best Actor *My Left Foot* 1989
Jim Sheridan .... Best Screenplay (with Shane Connaughton) *My Left Foot* 1989
....Best Director *My Left Foot* 1989

Gerry Hambling	Best Film Editor *The Commitments* 1989
Richard Harris	Best Actor *The Field* 1990
Kenneth Branagh	Best Short Film *Swan Song* 1992
Neil Jordan	Best Director *The Crying Game* 1992
	Best Film (as Producer) *The Crying Game* 1992
Kant Pan	Best Film Editor *The Crying Game* 1992
Stephen Rea	Best Actor *The Crying Game* 1992
Jaye Davidson	Best Supporting Actor *The Crying Game* 1992
Daniel Day Lewis	Best Actor *In the Name of the Father* 1993
Jim Sheridan	Best Screenplay (with Terry George) *In the Name of the Father* 1993
	Best Director *In the Name of the Father* 1993
	Best Film (as Producer) *In the Name of the Father* 1993
Liam Neeson	Best Actor *Schindler's List* 1993
Tim Loane	Best Live Action Short Film *Dance, Lexlie, Dance* 1998

TOP TEN FILMS IN REPUBLIC OF IRELAND, 1997

1	*The Full Monty*	5	*Ransom*	9	*Jerry Maguire*
2	*Men in Black*	6	*Sleepers*	10	*My Best Friend's Wedding*
3	*The Lost World*	7	*101 Dalmations*		
4	*Bean*	8	*Liar Liar*		

ROI FILM INDUSTRY PERFORMANCE INDICATORS

Categories	1993	1994	1995	3-yr avg
No. of Productions	12	13	22	15.6
Value of Productions	£50.5m	£133.1m	£100.1m	£94.6m
Foreign funds raised	£36.7m	82.3m	£45.1m	£54.7m
Foreign funds as % of total funds	73%	62%	45%	58%
Expenditure in Ireland	£30.6m	£57m	£64.1m	£50.6m
Irish funds as % of total funds	61%	43%	64%	53%
Total No. Employed	4,191	13,858	17,890	11,980
No. of Full-time Equivalent Jobs	480	1,291	1,266	1,012

INDIGENOUS BODIES' EXPENDITURE ON ROI FILM INDUSTRY, 1997

Organisation	Amount
Arts Council	£0.79m
Bord Fáilte	-
Bord Tráchtála	-
Dept of Arts, Heritage, Gaeltacht and the Islands	£11.30m
Forbairt	£0.28m
FÁS *(representing training input into the film industry)*	£0.37m
Irish Film Board	£3.40m
RTÉ *(representing 325 hrs of commissioned programmes)*	£8.60m
Teilifís na Gaeilge *(total budget for Irish-language commissions*	£7.50m
Údarás na Gaeltachta	£0.82m
TOTAL:	**over £33.06m**

FILM FUNDING - NORTHERN IRELAND

FUNDING - N. IRELAND FILM COMMISSION	
Department of Education	£300,000
Dept of Economic Development	£500,000
Other sources	£200,000
Total	£1,000,000

Development Funds for a single film project - **£15,000** (up to 50% of development costs)

Development Funds for a television series - **£40,000**

Funds offered by the NIFC in development loans since Aug.97 - Apr.98 - **£240,000**

ART COUNCIL AWARDS FOR FILM & VIDEO, 1998

Artist/Company	Title	Amount
Fir an Oileán	*The Parish*	£2,000.00
Tom Collins / De Facto Films	*Requim for Che*	£10,000.00
Marc Doyle / Olimundo Productions	*Fear of Flying*	£1,000.00
Laura Gannon / 3/1 Productions	*Parallel*	£5,000.00
Patrick Hodgkings	*Home*	£7,000.00
Jaki Irvine	*Italian Tales*	£8,500.00

Artist/Company	Title	Amount
Clare Langan	*The Search for the Sky*	£10,000.00
Stephen Rennicks	*Home*	£4,000.00
Moira Tierney	*To Your Health Mrs Tone*	£6,000.00
Ian Fitzgibbon & Michael Garland	*Stranded*	£7,000.00
Johnny O'Reilly / Lemoncut Productions	*The Terms*	£2,000.00
Martin Mahon / Hill 16 Films	*Another Day*	£2,500.00
TOTAL:		**£65,000.00**

IRISH & IRISH-RELATED FILMOGRAPHY, 1910-1999

The films entered in the filmography have either been filmed in Ireland or featured an Irish subject and actors.
An asterisk (*) indicates that more information on the film is provided in the selected film profiles.

Film	Country of origin	Year	Director
The Lad from Old Ireland	US	1910	Sidney Olcott
Arragh-na-Pogue	US	1911	Sidney Olcott
Rory O'More	US	1911	Sidney Olcott
The Colleen Bawn	US	1911	Sidney Olcott
The Colleen Bawn	Aus	1911	Gaston Mervale
The Fishermaid of Ballydavid	US	1911	Sidney Olcott
Ireland The Oppressed	US	1912	Sidney Olcott
The O'Neill	US	1912	Sidney Olcott
The Shaughran	Aus/Ire	1912	Sidney Olcott
You Remember Ellen	US	1912	Sidney Olcott
The Kerry Gow	US	1913	Sidney Olcott
Bunny Blarneyed	US	1914	Larry Trimble
Ireland A Nation	US	1914	Walter MacNamara
Broth of a Boy	US	1915	Carlton King
Fun at Finglas Fair	Ire	1915	F.J. McCormick
An Unfair Love Affair	Ire	1916	J. M. Kerrigan
Food of Love	Ire	1916	J.M. Kerrigan
Knocknagow	Ire	1916	Fred O'Donovan
Molly Bawn	Brit	1916	Cecil M. Hepworth
O'Neill of the Glen	Ire	1916	J.M. Kerrigan
Puck Fair Romance	Ire	1916	J. M. Kerrigan
The Eleventh Hour	Ire	1916	Fred O'Donovan
The Miser's Gift	Ire	1916	J.M. Kerrigan
Widow Malone	Ire	1916	J.M. Kerrigan
Woman's Wit	Ire	1916	J.M. Kerrigan
A Girl Of Glenbeigh	Ire	1917	J.M. Kerrigan
Blarney	Ire	1917	J. M. Kerrigan
Rafferty's Rise	Ire	1917	J.M. Kerrigan
The Byeways of Fate	Ire	1917	J.M. Kerrigan
The Irish Girl	Ire	1917	J. M. Kerrigan
The Upstart	Ire	1917	J. M. Kerrigan
When Love Came to Gavin Burke	Ire	1917	Fred O'Donovan
Rosaleen Dhu	Ire	1918	William Power
Willie Scouts While Jessie Pouts	Ire	1918	William Power
Paying the Rent	Ire	1919	John MacDonagh
In the Days of Saint Patrick	Ire	1920	Norman Whitten
Willie Reilly and his Colleen Bawn	Ire	1920	John MacDonagh
Cruiskeen Lawn	Ire	1922	John MacDonagh
The Casey Millions	Ire	1922	John MacDonagh
Wicklow Gold	Ire	1922	John MacDonagh
The Colleen Bawn	Brit	1924	W.P. Kelly
Land of Her Fathers	Brit	1925	John Hurley
Irish Destiny	Ire	1926	George Dewhurst
The Informer	Brit	1929	Arthur Robinson
By Accident	Ire	1930	J.N.G. Davidson
Juno and the Paycock	Brit	1930	Alfred Hitchcock
Song O' My Heart	Ire/Brit	1930	Frank Borzage
The Voice of Ireland	Ire	1932	Colonel Victor Haddick
General John Regan	Brit	1933	Harold Shaw

Title	Country	Year	Director
*Man of Aran	Brit	1934	Robert Flaherty
Some Say Chance	Ire	1934	Michael Farrell
Sweet Inniscarra	Ire	1934	Emmett Moore
Guests of the Nation	Ire	1935	Denis Johnston
Irish Hearts	Brit	1935	Brian Desmond Hurst
Jimmy Boy	Brit	1935	John Baxter
Luck of the Irish	Brit	1935	Donovan Pedelty
The Informer	US	1935	John Ford
The Irish in Us	US	1935	James Cagney
Irish and Proud of It	Ire	1936	Donovan Pedelty
The Plough and the Stars	US	1936	John Ford
Ourselves Alone	Brit	1936	Brian Desmond Hurst
Riders to the Sea	Brit	1936	Brian Desmond Hurst
*The Dawn	Ire	1936	Tom Cooper
The Early Bird	Ire	1936	Donovan Pedelty
Rose of Tralee	Brit	1937	Oswald Mitchell
Wings of the Morning	Brit	1937	Harold Schuster
Blarney	Ire	1938	Harry O'Donovan
Cheer, Boys, Cheer	Brit	1938	Walter Forde
Devil's Rock	Ire	1938	Germain Burger
Let's be Famous	Brit	1938	Walter Forde
Mountains O'Mourne	Brit	1938	Harry Hughes
Penny Paradise	Brit	1938	Carol Reed
The Islandman	Ire	1938	Patrick Keenan Heale
The Londonderry Air	Brit	1938	Alex Bryce
Uncle Nick	Ire	1938	Tom Cooper
Foolsmate	Ire	1940	Brendan Stafford
Little Nellie Kelly	US	1940	Norman Taurog
I See a Dark Stranger	Brit	1946	Frank Launder
Captain Boycott	Brit	1947	Frank Launder
Hungry Hill	Brit	1947	Brian Desmond Hurst
Odd Man Out	Brit	1947	Carol Reed
The Courtneys of Curzon Street	Brit	1947	Herbert Wilcox
My Hands are Clay	Ire.	1948	Lionel Tomlinson
The Greedy Boy	Brit	1949	Richard Massingham
The Strangers Came	Brit	1949	Alfred Travers
At a Dublin Inn	Ire	1950	Brendan Stafford
Everybody's Business	Ire	1951	Tony Inglis
Keep Your Teeth	Ire.	1951	Rex Roberts
No Resting Place	Brit	1951	Paul Rotha
Return to Glennascaul	Ire	1951	Hilton Edwards
The Promise of Barty O'Brien	US	1951	George Freedland
Jack of All Maids	Ire	1952	Tomás MacAnna
The Gentle Gunman	Brit	1952	Basil Dearden
*The Quiet Man	US	1952	John Ford
From Time To Time	Ire	1953	Hilton Edwards
Our Girl Friday	Brit	1953	Noel Langle
Stop Thief!	Ire	1953	Gerard Healy
Fr. Brown	Brit	1954	Robert Hamer
Happy Ever After	Brit	1954	Mario Zamp
The Art of Reception	Ire	1954	Gerard Healy
Captain Lightfoot	US	1955	Douglas Sirk
Untamed	US	1955	Henry King
Jacqueline	Brit	1956	Roy Baker
The March Hare	Brit	1956	George More O'Farrell
*Moby Dick	US	1956	John Huston
Pretty Polly	Ire	1957	Tony Inglis
Professor Tim	Ire	1957	Henry Cass
Rooney	Brit	1957	George Pollock
The Rising of the Moon	Ire	1957	John Ford
The Story of Esther Costello	Brit	1957	David Miller
Dublin Nightmare	Brit	1958	John Pomeroy
Sally's Irish Rogue	Ire	1958	George Pollock
Darby O'Gill and the Little People	US	1959	Robert Stevenson

Title	Country	Year	Director
Home is the Hero	Ire	1959	J. Fielder Cook
Larry	Ire	1959	R. Dawson / S. Richards
O'Hara's Holiday	Ire	1959	Peter Byran
Shake Hands with the Devil	Brit	1959	Michael Anderson
*Mise Eire	Ire	1959	George Morrison
The Big Birthday	Ire	1959	George Pollock
This Other Eden	Ire	1959	Murial Box
A Terrible Beauty	Brit	1960	Tay Garnett
Boyd's Shop	Ire	1960	Henry Cass
Gorgo	Brit	1960	Eugene Lourie
Johnny Nobody	Brit	1960	Nigel Patrick
Lies My Father Told Me	Ire	1960	Don Chaffy
Love and Money	Ire	1960	Ronald Liles
The Big Gamble	US	1960	Richard Fleischer
The Siege of Sidney Street	Brit	1960	Roy Baker, Monty Berman
The Trials of Oscar Wilde	Brit	1960	Ken Hughes
Middle of Nowhere/The Webster Boy	Ire	1961	Don Chaffy
Dead Man's Evidence	Brit	1962	Francis Searle
I Thank a Fool	Brit	1962	Robert Stevens
The Devil's Agent	Ire	1962	John Paddy Carstairs
*The Playboy of the Western World	Ire	1962	Brian Desmond Hurst
The Quare Fellow	Brit	1962	Arthur Dreifuss
Dementia 13/The Haunted and the Hunted	US/Ire	1963	Francis Ford Coppola
Never Put It in Writing	Brit	1963	Andrew L. Stone
Girl With Green Eyes	Brit	1964	Desmond Davis
I Was Happy Here	Brit	1965	Desmond Davi
Young Cassidy	Brit	1965	Jack Cardiff
*The Blue Max	US	1966	John Guillermin
*The Fighting Prince of Donegal	Brit	1966	Michael O'Herlihy
*The Spy Who Came in from the Cold	Ire	1966	Martin Ritt
Finnegan's Wake	US	1967	Mary Ellen Bute
Ulysses	Brit	1967	Joseph Strick
Bright Future	Ire	1968	George Morrison
Finian's Rainbow	US	1968	Francis Ford Coppola
30 is a Dangerous Age, Cynthia	Brit	1968	Joseph McGrath
Guns in the Heather	Brit	1969	Robert Butler
McKenzie Break	Brit	1969	Lamont Johnson
Paddy	Ire	1969	Daniel Haller
The Violent Enemy	Brit	1969	Don Sharp
Wedding Night/I Can't, I Can't...	Ire.	1969	Piers Haggard
Emtigon	Ire	1970	Joe Comerford
Philadelphia Here I Come!	Ire	1970	John Quested
*Ryan's Daughter	Brit	1970	David Lean
The Molly Maguires	Brit	1970	Martin Ritt
The Return of the Islander	Ire	1970	James Mulkerns
Quackser Fortune has a Cousin in the Bronx	US	1970	Waris Hussein
Flight of the Doves	Brit	1971	Ralph Nelson
But they Said it - Didn't They	Ire	1972	Joe McCarthy
Images	Ire./US	1972	Robert Altman
The Hebrew Lesson	Ire	1972	Wolf Mankowitz
Three Weeks in a Tower	Ire	1972	Maurice O'Kelly
A Quiet Day in Belfast	Can	1973	Milad Bassada
Dunhallow Home	Ire	1973	Colin Hill
The Mackintosh Man	Brit	1973	John Huston
*Barry Lyndon	Brit	1975	Stanley Kubrick
Caoineadh Airt Uí Laoire	Ire	1975	Bob Quinn
Hennessy	Brit	1975	Don Sharp
Cancer	Ire	1976	Deirdre Friel
Nano Nagle	Ire	1976	Desmond Forristal
The Last Remake of Beau Geste	Ire	1976	Marty Feldman
Wheels	Ire	1976	Cathal Black
Down the Corner	Ire	1977	Joe Comerford
Portrait of the Artist as a Young Man	Brit	1977	Joseph Strick
The Kinkisha	Ire	1977	Tommy McArdle

Title	Country	Year	Director
*The Purple Taxi	Ire./Ita./Fra	1977	Yves Boisset
A Child's Voice	Ire	1978	Kieran Hickey / Shane O' Neill
Exposure	Ire	1978	Kieran Hickey
On a Paving Stone Mounted	Brit	1978	Thaddeus O'Sullivan
*Poitín	Ire	1978	Bob Quinn
Revival - Pearse's Concept of Ireland	Ire	1979	Louis Marcus
The Flame is Love	Ire	1979	Michael O'Herlihy
The Newcomers	Can	1979	Eric Till
The Outsider	Neth	1979	Tony Lurasch
Criminal Conversation	Ire	1980	Kieran Hickey
Cry of the Innocent	Ire	1980	Michael O'Herlihy
*Excalibur	Ire	1980	John Boorman
It's Handy When People Don't Die	Ire	1980	Tommy McArdle
The Dream Factory	Ire	1980	Peter Finegan
Desecration	Ire	1981	Neville Presho
Fire and Sword	Ire./Ger	1981	Keith Von Fürstenberg
*Maeve	Brit	1981	Pat Murray
Our Boys	Ire	1981	Cathal Black
Summer of the Falcon	Ire	1981	Tom Donovan
*The Ballroom of Romance	Ire	1981	Pat O'Connor
Traveller	Ire	1981	Joe Comerford
*Angel	Ire	1982	Neil Jordan
*Educating Rita	Ire./Brit	1982	Lewis Gilbert
The Outcasts	Ire	1982	Robert Wynne-Simmons
The Writing on the Wall	Ire./Bel./Fra	1982	Armand Gatti
*The Year of the French	Ire	1982	Michael Garvey
At the Cinema Palace - Liam O'Leary	Ire	1983	Donald Taylor
Attracta	Ire	1983	Kieran Hickey
Caught in the Free State	Ire	1983	Peter Ormrod
John, Love	Brit	1983	John Davis
Night in Tunisia	Ire	1983	Pat O'Connor
Paradiso	Brit	1983	Colm Villa
One of Ourselves	Ire	1983	Pat O'Connor
Reflections	Brit	1983	Kevin Billington
The Best Man	Ire	1983	Joe Mahon
The Country Girls	Brit	1983	Desmond Davis
The Schooner	Ire	1983	Bill Miskelly
Withdrawal	Ire	1983	Joe Comerford
Absolution	Brit	1984	Niall Leonard
Anne Devlin	Ire	1984	Pat Murphy
A Second of June	Ire	1984	Francis Stapleton
*Cal	Brit	1984	Pat O'Connor
Hostage	Brit	1984	Aisling Walsh
Pigs	Ire	1984	Cathal Black
The Company of Wolves	Ire	1984	Neil Jordan
Waterbag	Ire	1984	Joe Comerford
Four Days in July	Brit	1985	Mike Leigh
*Lamb	Brit	1985	Colin Gregg
The Doctor and the Devils	Brit	1985	Freddie Francis
*The End of the World Man	Ire	1985	Bill Miskelly
Boom Babies	Ire	1986	Siobhán Twomey
*Eat the Peach	Ire	1986	Peter Ormrod
Fear of the Dark	Ire	1986	Tony Barry
The Fantasist	Ire	1986	Robin Hardy
Budawanny	Ire	1987	Bob Quinn
Clash of the Ash	Ire	1987	Fergus Tighe
*High Spirits	Ire	1987	Neil Jordan
Out of Time	Ire	1987	Robert Wynne-Simmons
*Reefer and the Model	Ire	1987	Joe Comerford
Riders to the Sea	Ire	1987	Ronan O'Leary
*The Dead	Ire./US/Brit./Ger	1987	John Huston
*The Lonely Passion of Judith Hearne	Brit	1987	Jack Clayton
The Scar	Ire/Brit	1987	Robert Wynne-Simmons
A Prayer for the Dying	Brit	1988	Mike Hodges

Da	US	1988	Matt Clark
Joyriders	Brit	1988	Aisling Walsh
Now I Know	Ire	1988	Robert Pappas
Taffin	Brit./US	1988	Francis Megahy
The Courier	Brit	1988	Joe Lee
The Dawning	Brit	1988	Robert Knights
Fragments of Isabella	Ire	1989	Ronan O'Leary
*Hush-A-Bye-Baby	Ire/Brit	1989	Margo Harkin
*My Left Foot	Ire/Brit	1989	Jim Sheridan
After Midnight	Ire	1990	Shani S Grewal
Dear Sarah	Brit	1990	Frank Cvitanovich
*December Bride	Ire./Brit	1990	Thaddeus O'Sullivan
*Fools of Fortune	Brit	1990	Pat O'Connor
Hard Shoulder	Ire	1990	Mark Kilroy
Hidden Agenda	Brit	1990	Ken Loach
*The Field	Brit	1990	Jim Sheridan
Diary of a Madman	Ire	1991	Ronan O'Leary
*Hear My Song	Brit	1991	Peter Chelsom
*The Commitments	Brit	1991	Alan Parker
*The Miracle	Brit	1991	Neil Jordan
Far and Away	US	1992	Ron Howard
Hello, Stranger	Ire	1992	Ronan O'Leary
*Into the West	Ire	1992	Mike Newell
Micha	Ire./Russia	1992	Gerad Michael MacCarthy
Patriot Games	US	1992	Phillip Noyce
The Bargain Shop	Ire./Ger	1992	Johnny Gogan
*The Crying Game	Brit	1992	Neil Jordan
*The Playboys	Brit	1992	Gillies MacKinnon
Bad Behaviour	Brit	1993	Les Blair
High Boot Benny	Ire	1993	Joe Comerford
*In the Name of the Father	Ire./Brit./US	1993	Jim Sheridan
The Railway Station Man	Brit	1993	Michael Whyte
*The Snapper	Brit	1993	Stephen Frears
*Widow's Peak	Brit	1993	John Irvine
Ailsa	Ger./Fra./Ire	1994	Paddy Breathnach
All Things Bright and Beautiful	Ire./Brit	1994	Barry Devlin
*An Awfully Big Adventure	Ire./Brit	1995	Mike Newell
*Braveheart	Ire	1994	Mel Gibson
Broken Harvest	Ire	1994	Maurice O'Callaghan
Moondance	Ire	1994	Dagmar Hirtz
The Bishop's Story	Ire	1994	Bob Quinn
*The Secret of Roan Inish	US	1994	John Sayles
*War of the Buttons	Brit./Ire	1994	John Roberts
Words Upon the Window Pane	Ire	1994	Mary McGuckian
*A Man of No Importance	Ire./Brit	1995	Suri Krishnamma
Bloodfist VIII - Trained for Action	Ire	1995	Rick Jacobson
*Circle of Friends	US/Ire	1995	Pat O'Connor
*Frankie Starlight	Ire	1995	Michael Lindsay-Hogg
*Guiltrip	Ire./Fra./Ita./Spain	1995	Gerry Stembridge
Korea	Ire	1995	Cathal Black
*Nothing Personal	Ire./Brit	1995	Thaddeus O'Sullivan
*The Run of the Country	Ire	1995	Peter Yates
Undercurrent	Ire	1995	Brian O'Flaherty
*A Further Gesture	Ire./Brit./Ger	1996	Robert Dornhelm
*Dance, Lexlie, Dance	Ire	1996	Tim Loane
Driftwood	Ire	1996	Ronan O'Leary
Drinking Crude	Ire	1996	Owen McPolin
It's Now or Never	Den	1996	Jon Bang Carlsen
*Last of the High Kings	Ire	1996	David Keating
*Michael Collins	Ire	1996	Neil Jordan
My Friend Joe	Ire	1996	Chris Bould
November Afternoon	Ire	1996	John Carney, Tom Hall
*Snakes and Ladders	Ire	1996	Trish McAdam
Space Truckers	Ire	1996	Stuart Gordon

Spaghetti Slow	Ire./Ita./Brit	1996	Valerie Jaiongo
*The Moon on My Back	Ire	1996	Jonathan White
*Some Mother's Son	Ire	1996	Terry George
The Boy from Mercury	Ire	1996	Martin Duffy
The Brylcreem Boys	Brit	1996	Terence Ryan
*The Disappearance of Finbar	Ire./Brit./Swe	1996	Sue Clayton
*The Eliminator	Ire	1996	Enda Hughes
*The Sun, The Moon and The Stars	Ire	1996	Geraldine Creed
*The Van	Ire	1996	Stephen Frears
This is the Sea	Ire	1996	Mary McGuckian
Trojan Eddie	Ire	1996	Gillies MacKinnon
*All Souls' Day	Ire	1997	Alan Gilsenan
Angela Mooney Dies Again	Ire	1997	Tommy McArdle
*Separation Anxiety	Ire	1997	Mark Staunton
*Bogwoman	Ire	1997	Tommy Collins
*Cycle of Violence (Crossmaheart)		1998	Don Boyd
*Dancing At Lughnasa	Ire	1997	Pat O'Connor
*Divorcing Jack	Ire	1998	David Caffrey
Double Carpet	Ire	1997	Mark Kilroy, Howard Gibbons
Element	Ire	1997	Catherine Tiernan
*Falling for a Dancer	Ire	1998	Richard Standeven
George Best: A Documentary	Ire	1998	Mary McGuckian
Gold in the Streets	Ire	1997	Elizabeth Gill
*Hooligans	Ire/Brit./Ger/Hol	1997	Paul Tickell
*How to Cheat in the Leaving Cert	Ire	1997	Graham Jones
Hugh Cullen	Ire	1997	Nicholas O'Neill
*Drinking Crude	Ire	1997	Owen McPolin
*I Went Down	Ire	1997	Paddy Breathnach
Johnny Jump Up	Ire./US	1997	Kieron J. Walsh
Just in Time	Ire	1997	John Carney, Tom Hall
Marie Curie: What Meets the Eye	Ire./Can	1997	Richard Mozer
Miracle at Midnight	Ire./US	1997	Ken Cameron
*Saving Private Ryan	Ire./US	1997	Steven Spielberg
*The General	Ire	1997	John Boorman
*Love and Rage	Ire	1997	Cathal Black
*Sunset Heights	N. Ire	1997	Colm Villa
*St. Ives (St. Ives)	Ire./Fra./Ger	1997	Harry Hook
Sweetly Barret	Ire	1998	Stephen Bradley
*The Boxer	Ire	1997	Jim Sheridan
*Titanic Town	N. Ire	1997	Roger Michell
*Resurrection Man	N. Ire	1997	Marc Evans
*The Butcher Boy	Ire	1997	Neil Jordan
The Closest Thing to Heaven	Ire	1997	Dorne Pentes
The Deadness of Dad	Ire	1997	Phillipa Cousins
*The Fifth Province	Ire	1998	Frank Stapleton
*The Last Bus Home	Ire	1998	Johnny Gogan
*The Mammy	Ire	1998	Jim Sheridan
*The Nephew	Ire	1998	Pierce Brosnan
The Wish	Ire	1998	Martin Duffy
*This is My Father	Ire	1998	Paul Quinn
Sparrow's Trap	Ire	1998	Brendan O'Connor
*The Chaps	N. Ire	1998	Robert Young
This Lime Tree Bower	Ire	1998/9	Rob Walpole
The Last September	Ire	1998/9	Yvonne Thunder
All About Adam	Ire	1998/9	Marina Hughes
Mad About Mambo	N. Ire	1998/9	John Forte
I Could Read the Sky	N. Ire	1998/9	Nicholas O'Neill
Aristocrates	N. Ire	1998/9	Kevin Menton
Wild Horses	Ire	1998/9	Tim Palmer

PROFILES OF SELECTED IRISH FILMS*

MAN OF ARAN (*Brit. 1934, Reprinted 1992*) **Director/Writer** *Robert Flaherty* **Cast** *Colman 'Tiger' King, Maggie Dirane, Michael Dillane, the Aran Islanders* **Production Co.** *Gainsborough Pictures/Gaumont-British Picture*

Corporation Ltd./The Rank Organisation **Cinematography** *Robert J. Flaherty* **Editing** *John Goldman* **Music** *John Greenwood* **Location** *the Aran Islands, Co Galway.*
Profile The film centres around a family's efforts to eke a living from the Aran islands and the surrounding sea. It focuses on a man and two other fishermen attempting to catch a huge shark. After a two-day struggle, the shark is finally caught and the fishermen go out again in search of more sharks but a storm blows up, forcing them to abandon their search. Returning to shore on this occasion is very difficult, and as the men disembark, a wave catches the currach and dashes it against the rocks, while the family watches wordless as their livelihood is destroyed.

THE DAWN *(Ire. 1936, 85 mins)* **Director/Producer** *Thomas Cooper* **Writers** *Thomas Cooper and Dr. D.A. Moriarty* **Cinematography** *James Lawlor* **Music** *Pat Crowley's Dance Band* **Production Co.** *Hibernia Films* **Cast** *Eileen Davis, Brian O'Sullivan, Thomas Cooper, Donal O'Cahill, Jerry O'Mahony, Bill Murray, Marian O'Connell, James Steel* **Location** *Killarney, Co Kerry.*
Profile Between 1933 and 1936, Killarney Garage Owner Tom Cooper and 250 locals - none of whom had any previous film-making experience - assembled an ambitious feature length film set during the Irish War of Independence. All filming was done on a single camera and virtually every other piece of equipment (lighting, microphone booms, editing facilities) was built from scratch while the local chemist was used as a film laboratory. Arguably the most significant "Irish" film in the 50 years preceding Neil Jordan's Angel.
The film is set in 1919, when Brian Malone, grandson of a local "traitor" is a member of the local IRA column. Because of his family's past, some members of the column have doubts about his loyalty and vote to exclude him. In a fit of anger, Brian joins the Royal Irish Constabulary but deserts just before a raid and goes to warn the IRA column. In doing so, however, he jeopardises the IRA's own ambush. The IRA ambush goes ahead successfully but in the aftermath, Brian's brother is shot dead by the local RIC. His father accuses the IRA of the murder but it emerges that Billy, Brian's brother, was the column's intelligence officer, responsible for its success.

THE QUIET MAN *(Ire./US 1952)* **Director** *John Ford* **Cast** *John Wayne, Maureen O'Hara, Barry Fitzgerald, Eileen Crowe, Jack McGowran, Arthur Shields* **Writer** *Frank Nugent* **Production Co.** *Republic, Argosy (John Ford, Merian C Cooper)* **Location** *Cong, Co Mayo.*
Profile Based loosely on a story by Maurice Walsh, it's a story of a boxer who leaves his home in America to return to a simpler life in Ireland. He becomes involved in a courtship with a fiery local girl. One of the many popular scenes in the film is the marathon fight with the local girl's aggressive, dowry-withholding brother.

MOBY DICK *(1956)* **Director** *John Huston* **Writer** *Ray Bradbury, John Huston (based on Herman Melville's novel)* **Production Co.** *Warner/Moulin (John Huston)* **Cast** *Gregory Peck, Richard Basehart, Leo Genn, Harry Andrews* **Location** *Youghal, Co Cork.*
Profile Science Fiction writer Ray Bradbury described his experience of writing the screenplay of Herman Melville's epic novel with Huston as 'hell.' The film tells the story of Captain Ahab's battle with the great white whale. The Captain and Ishmael team up in the whaling ship 'Piquod' to hunt down and kill the whale (ultimately unsuccessfully).

MISE EIRE - I AM OF IRELAND *(Ire. 1959, 120 mins, B/W)* **Director** *George Morrison* **Music** *Sean O'Riada* **Commentary** *Sean MacReamoinn* **Narrators** *Padraig O' Raghallaigh, Liam Budhaeir* **Recording** *Peter Hunt, Gene Martin* **Assistant Editors** *Louis Marcus, Sean O'Briain, Caitriona O'Briain* **Photography** *Vincent H. Corcoran* **Historical Consultant** *Tomas P. O'Neill.*
Profile Made by Gael Linn, an independent but state-aided Irish language and cultural organisation, "Mise Eire" was the first feature length Irish language film that recorded actuality. The producers were lucky to find composer Sean O'Riada; his lush Mise Eire score has subsequently become one of the classic pieces of 20th century Irish music, classical in form, yet undeniably Celtic in tone. Basically, the film traces the development of the revolutionary movement in Ireland between 1896 and 1918. It exclusively uses contemporary film footage (most of which had to be found outside Ireland) cleverly woven into the narrative.
Split into three eras - Awakening (1896-1915), The Rising (1916) and The Dawning of the Day (1917 -1918), the film covers the rise of Sinn Fein in the first decade of this century, noting too the rise of (unsuccessful) revolutionary wars against the British Empire in the same period. In 1916, the Easter Rising breaks out with fewer than 3,000 men and women on the Volunteer side. The Rising is swiftly crushed but as the leaders are executed afterwards, Irish public opinion, initially hostile, turns to support the rebels. In the closing segment of the film, Sinn Fein's political success at the 1918 general election is interpreted as evidence that the tide of history is turning towards Irish nationalism.

THE PLAYBOY OF THE WESTERN WORLD *(Ire. 1962)* **Director** *Brian Desmond Hurst* **Cast** *Siobhán McKenna, Gary Raymond, Liam Redmond, Elspeth March, Brendan Cauldwell, Niall Mcginnis.*
Profile The film version of J.M. Synge's play. The play is considered a classic but caused riots on its opening in 1907 as it seemed to mock the Irish people. In the film, Siobhán McKenna gave a remarkable performance as Pegeen Mike.

THE BLUE MAX *(US 1966)* **Director** *John Guillermin* **Production Co.** *TCF* **Writer** *David Pursall, Jack Seddon, Gerald Hanley* **Cast** *George Peppard, James Mason, Ursula Andress, Jeremy Kemp* **Location** *Ardmore Studios, Co Cork and Powerscourt House, Wicklow.*
Profile A World War I flying epic with amazing aerial stunts and an engaging plot. Shot by legendary cameraman Douglas Slocombe, Ireland passes faultlessly for Germany.

THE FIGHTING PRINCE OF DONEGAL *(Brit. 1966)* **Director** *Michael O'Herlihy* **Cast** *Peter McEnery, Susan Hampshire, Tom Adams, Gordon Jackson, Donal McCann, Peggy Marshall.*
Profile Features a young Donal McCann in one of his first films.

THE SPY WHO CAME IN FROM THE COLD *(1966)* **Director** *Martin Ritt* **Production** *Paramount/ Salem (Martin Ritt)* **Writer** *Paul Dehn, Guy Trosper* **Cast** *Richard Burton, Claire Bloom, Oskar Werner, Cyril Cusack* **Location** *Dublin and Ardmore Studios, Wicklow.*
Profile This gripping cold war spy film was partly shot in Dublin, with Smithfields Market doubling for Checkpoint Charlie. Shot in black and white, an air of post-war gloom pervades the film and manages to raise it out of the banality of most spy films. Richard Burton gives a brilliant portrayal as a jaded, alcoholic agent.

RYAN'S DAUGHTER *(Brit. 1970)* **Director** *David Lean* **Production** *MGM/Faraway (Anthony Havelock-Allen)* **Writer** *Robert Bolt* **Cast** *Sir John Mills, Sarah Miles, Robert Mitchum, Trevor Howard, Niall Tóibín, Donal Neligan, Des Keogh, Marie Kean.* **Location** *Dingle, Co Kerry.*
Profile The film is credited with bringing prosperity to the Dingle area, as many local people were hired as extras and labourers on the film.
Set around the time of the Rising, the village publican's daughter with romantic notions marries a kind, middle-aged schoolteacher, but falls for an English officer, who has been stationed in Ireland after being shellshocked in the battle fields of France. The climax of the film centres around rescuing German arms from a local beach during a storm. Earned Sir John Mills an Oscar for his performance as the village idiot.

BARRY LYNDON *(Brit. 1975)* **Director/Writer** *Stanley Kubrick* **Production** *Warner/Hawk/Peregrine (Stanley Kubrick)* **Cast** *Ryan O'Neal, Marisa Berenson, Patrick Magee, Hardy Kruger, Steven Berkoff, Marie Kean.* **Location** *Ardmore Studios, Wicklow.*
Profile One of the few films made by Stanley Kubrick outside his Shepperton studios. This tale of a rake's progress and decline was partly shot in Co. Wicklow and Ardmore Studios, and is luscious to look at. After allegedly receiving threats from terrorists, Kubrick moved the film set lock, stock and barrell to the Netherlands.

THE PURPLE TAXI *(Ire./Ita./Fra. 1977)* **Director** *Yves Boisset* **Cast** *Peter Ustinov, Fred Astaire, Charlotte Rampling, Mairín O'Sullivan, David Kelly, Niall Buggy.*
Profile Once again, the mountains of Wicklow act as a film backdrop to this modern tale which features Fred Astaire driving around in the eponymous purple taxi.

EXPOSURE *(Ire. 1978, 52 mins)* **Director** *Kieran Hickey* **Cast** *Catherine Schell, T.P. McKenna, Bosco Hogan, Niall O'Brien, Mairín O'Sullivan* **Producer** *Roland Hills* **Screenplay** *Philip Davison and Kieran Hickey* **Production** *BAC Films/Arts Council/RTE/National Film Studios of Ireland.*
Profile An ordnance survey team, Dan, Oliver and Eugene, arrives at a hotel on the west coast of Ireland, where they will spend a week mapping the area. There is one other guest at the hotel: Caroline, a German photographer. The four quickly establish a rapport over drinks in the bar. One of the men sets his sights on Caroline and they strike up a relationship over dinner, spending the night together in Caroline's room. However, the relationship becomes a source of tension amongst the men, and she ultimately leaves.

POITÍN *(Ire. 1978)* **Director** *Bob Quinn* **Cast** *Cyril Cusack, Niall Tóibín, Donal McCann, Mairéad Ní Chonghaile.*
Profile A tale of local skullduggery and smuggling in the Gaeltacht which ends in tragedy.

EXCALIBUR *(Ire. 1981)* **Director/Writer** *John Boorman* **Production** *Warner/Orion Rospo Pallenberg* **Cast** *Nicol Williamson, Nigel Terry, Cherie Lunghi, Gabriel Byrne, Helen Mirren, Nicholas Clay, Liam Neeson* **Location** *Powerscourt, the Wicklow Mountains, Cahir Castle, the Rock of Cashel and Derrynane, Co Kerry.*
Profile A gritty, realistic view of the rise to power of King Arthur, the forbidden love of Queen Guinevere and Sir Lancelot and the quest of the Knights of the Round Table for the Holy Grail. The film marks the beginning of English Director John Boorman's deep involvement in the Irish film industry and provided many young Irish actors with an international platform, including Gabriel Byrne and Liam Neeson.

MAEVE *(Brit. 1981)* **Director/Writer** *Pat Murray* **Cast** *Mark Mullholland, Bríd Brennan, Trudy Kelly, John Keegan, Mary Jackson* **Locations** *Belfast, Antrim Coast and Co. Down.*
Profile 1981 . . . Maeve Sweeney, a young women living in London returns home to visit her Catholic family in Belfast. Her visit prompts memories of her childhood in Northern Ireland. The story unfolds by skipping between Maeve as a young girl, as a teenager and in the present. As she enters her later teenage years, her boyfriend

pressures her to take a stance on the Troubles. Unwilling to take sides in the conflict, Maeve is finally unable to find a place for herself in Northern Irish society and escapes to England.

THE BALLROOM OF ROMANCE *(Ire. 1981, 65 mins)* **Director/Writer** *Pat O'Connor* **Producer** *Kenith Trodd* **Cinematography** *Nat Crosby* **Editor** *Maurice Healy* **Cast** *Brenda Fricker, John Kavanagh, Joe Pilkington, Cyril Cusack, Michael Lally, Pat Leavy, Niall Toibin, Joe Pilkington, Ingrid Craigie, Brid Brennan, May Ollis, Anita Reeves, Brendan Conroy, Bob Carrickford.* **Location** *Ballycroy, County Mayo.*
Profile Based on a William Trevor's short story, set in the late 1950s, the film focuses on the Ballroom of Romance, delivered in its original setting. The hall fills up with the Romantic Jazz Band and Bridie, a local woman, finds out that drummer Dano Ryan is lost to her: he's lodging with a widow woman. Friends try to console her, but it looks like the drunken, useless Bowser Egan is the only prospect to save her from eternal spinsterdom. The oldest woman in the place, Madge Dowding, is left alone after failing to persuade Bowser to go for a drink with her. Bridie reluctantly agrees to let Bowser have a go at her in the field on the way home from the dance - her last.
Awards the Silver Drama Award at the New York Festival, the BAFTA for the Best Single Play, the Jacobs' Ward for Best Director, Runner up in the Prix Italia.

ANGEL (Ire. 1982) **Director/Writer** Neil Jordan **Cast** Stephen Rea, Veronica Quilligan, Peter Caffrey, Honor Heffernan, Ray McAnally **Production** Irish Film Board, Palace Pictures.
Profile Marking Neil Jordan's feature film debut and possibly a milestone film in Irish cinema, Angel follows a troubled saxophonist's search for the murderer of a young girl. Set in the border counties of Ireland, the film narrative occurs against the backdrop of the Troubles. Stephen Rea begins his career as Jordan's on-screen, glum-looking doppelganger in this film.

EDUCATING RITA *(Ire./Brit. 1982)* **Director/Production** *Lewis Gilbert* **Writer** *Willy Russell* **Cast** *Michael Caine, Julie Walters, Michael Williams, Maureen Lipman* **Location** *Trinity College, Dublin.*
Profile A boozing, depressed English professor takes on a sharp-witted, eager-to-learn hairdresser, and each educates the other.

THE YEAR OF THE FRENCH *(Ire. 1982)* **Director** *Michael Garvey* **Cast** *Jeremy Clyde, Oliver Cotton, Jean-Claude Drouot, Keith Buckley.*
Profile The film version of Flanagan's epic novel which recounts the events of 1798, starting with the French landing at Killala, their routing of the English forces at Castlebar and their ultimate defeat.

CAL (Brit. 1984) **Director** Pat O'Connor **Cast** Helen Mirren, John Lynch, Ray McAnally, Donal McCann, John Kavanagh, Steven Rimkus.
Profile Based on a Bernard MacLaverty story, it tells of a young republican (John Lynch) on the run from Crown forces. He had participated in the murder of an RUC man, but later gets a job from the family of the dead officer. He begins an affair with the dead mans wife.

LAMB *(Ire./Brit. 1985, 100 mins)* **Director** *Colin Gregg* **Producer** *Neil Zeiger* **Producer** *Al Burgess* **Screenplay** *Bernard MacLaverty* **Music** *Van Morrison* **Production Co.** *Flickers Limehouse/Channel 4* **Cast** *Liam Neeson, Hugh O'Connor, Owen Kane, Ian Bannen, Frances Tomelty, Dudley Sutton.*
Profile The film opens at a school for difficult children run by Christian Brothers. Michael Lamb, a brother facing a crisis of faith absconds from the school with Owen Kane, an eight-year-old young offender with epilepsy. He flees to England only to find that the order has reported his act as a kidnapping. Returning to Ireland and with the police closing in, Michael feels under increasing pressure; he knows that if they are caught, Owen will be returned to a life of institutional misery. Michael takes the decision to kill Owen. Struck by remorse he then tries to drown himself but cannot. The film ends with Michael staring out across the sea.

THE END OF THE WORLD MAN *(Ire. 1985, 86 mins)* **Director** *Bill Miskelly* **Exec. Producer** *Tiernan MacBride* **Screenplay** *Marie Jackson & Bill Miskelly* **Music** *John Anderson* **Cast** *John Hewitt, Leanne O'Malley, Claire Weir, Ian Morrison, Rowan Moore, Anthony McClelland.*
Profile Set in Belfast in the mid-1980s, Paula and Clare play in "The Glen" an area of forest surrounded by housing estates. One day, they come upon a government official planning the building of a leisure centre and carpark on the Glen. Horrified by the threatened loss of their play area, the two girls start a campaign to prevent the building of the centre. Just when they appear to have lost the struggle, they discover that a government official has illegally profited from the building of the centre. It also emerges that the Glen is an ancient and valuable archaeological site. The site is declared a national treasure.

EAT THE PEACH *(Ire. 1986, 91 mins)* **Director** *Peter Ormond* **Screenplay** *Peter Ormond & John Kelleher* **Music** *Donal Lunny* **Production Co.** *Strongbow Production/Film Four International/ Bord Scannan na hEireann* **Cast** *Stephen Brennan, Eamonn Morrissey, Catherine Byrne, Niall Tobin, Tony Doyle, Joe Lynch* **Location** *the Bog of Allen, Counties Kildare, Dublin, Meath and Wicklow.*
Profile Vinnie lives with his wife (Nora) and daughter on the bog where he also works, repairing bog-cutting

machines. He and his brother-in-law, Arthur, who has just been made redundant, are inspired by watching Roustabout, an Elvis Presley movie about wall-of-death motorcycles riders. Vinnie decided to build his own wall on the bog. They fund the project with Arthur's redundancy money and extra revenue earned from smuggling for local businessman, Boss Murtagh. The project ultimately fails. Niall Toibín gives a great performance of the local wheeler dealer.

HIGH SPIRITS *(Ire. 1987, 96 mins)* **Director/Writer** *Neil Jordan* **Cast** *Peter O'Toole, Daryl Hannah, Steve Guttenberg, Beverly D'Angelo, Jennifer Tilly, Martin Ferrero, Liam Neeson, Ray McAnally, Donal McCann, Peter Gallagher, Mary Coughlan.*
Profile In a desperate attempt to hold onto his ancestral home in Ireland, Lord Peter Plunkett and his staff conspire to market the castle as a haunted hotel. The fake ghosts are quickly unveiled, and the guests decide to leave the next morning. At this point, the castle's real ghosts conspire to save the castle, prompting a mass haunting. Two of the guests, honeymooners Jack and Sharon falls in love with two of the ghosts, Mary Plunkett and Martin Brogan. Chaos ensues, but the ghost-human pairings unite and "live" happily ever after, and the castle's reputation as a haunted house is assured as is its financial survival. The film is regarded as the low point in Neil Jordan's directorial career.

REEFER AND THE MODEL *(Ire. 1987, 120 mins)* **Director** *Joe Comerford* **Cast** *Ian McElhinney, Carol Scanlan, Sean Lawlor, Ray MacBride, Eve Watkinson, Birdy Sweeney* **Screenplay** *Joe Comerford* **Music** *Johnny Duhan* **Production Co.** *Berber Films/Irish Film Board/RTE/Film Four/International Instant Photo* **Location** *Galway, Connemara and the Aran Islands.*
Profile Set on the west coast of Ireland, Reefer, a dissolute, ex-IRA man takes in Teresa (The Model), a woman who is (it emerges) pregnant. He allows her to share the boat he lives in with Spider (another IRA character) who is on the run and Badger, who is if not gay then bisexual. A relationship develops between Reefer and the Model but ultimately ends in tragedy.

THE DEAD *(Ire./U.S./Brit./Ger. 1987)* **Director** *John Huston* **Cast** *Anjelica Huston, Donal McCann, Dan O'Herlihy, Rachel Dowling.*
Profile Based on the story by James Joyce, this was John Huston's swan song film and is uncharacteristically reflective and gentle in tone.

THE LONELY PASSION OF JUDITH HEARNE *(Brit 1987)* Director *Jack Clayton* **Cast** *Bob Hoskins, Maggie Smith, Marie Kean, Alan Devlin, Prunella Scales, Niall Buggy, Kate Binchy.*
Profile Based on the novel by Brian Moore, the film tells the tragic story of an alchoholic spinster who falls for and is conned by an American.

HUSH-A-BYE-BABY *(Ire/Brit. 1989, 80 mins)* **Director** *Margo Harkin* **Cast** *Emer McCourt, Sinead O'Connor, Michael Liebman, Cathy Casey, Julie Rodgers* **Producer** *Tom Collins* **Screenplay** *Margo Harkin & Stephanie English* **Production Co.** *Derry Film & Video Workshop/Channel 4/British Screen/RTE/Arts Council.*
Profile Derry, 1984 . . . Goretti, a 15-year-old Catholic schoolgirl, lives a normal life. At the local disco, she encounters Ciaran, a boy she likes but who is initially too shy to talk to her. Days later, they meet at an extra-curricular Irish class and a relationship begins. Ciaran is arrested on suspicion of IRA membership, and Goretti discovers she is pregnant. After much soul searching, the film ends conveying a sense that Goretti will finally tell her parents she is pregnant.

MY LEFT FOOT *(Ire/Brit. 1989)* **Director/Writer** *Jim Sheridan* **Producer** *Noel Pearson* **Production Co.** *Ferndale Films* **Cast** *Daniel Day-Lewis, Brenda Fricker, Ray McAnally, Hugh O'Conor, Fiona Shaw, Adrian Dunbar.* **Locations** *Dublin, Killiney and Bray.*
Profile (Based on the book by Christy Brown) 1963 . . . Christy Brown is a guest at a fund-raising gala held in his honour. As he waits to be presented, the film follows his life. Born with cerebral palsy into a poor, large family in 1932, his parents are told by doctors that he will be a vegetable for the rest of his life. His father treats him accordingly, but his mother is unconvinced by the diagnosis. It is not until Christy is ten years old that he is able to communicate his intelligence. Christy begins to explore his artistic side, painting with his left foot. At the age of 19, he meets and falls in love with Eileen. He is heartbroken when she announces her engagement to the gallery owner who gives Christy his first public art exhibition. Frustrated with painting, Christy moves to writing and starts writing his biography. The film returns to the present; Christy asks Mary, his nurse, if she'll go out with him and she eventually agrees. A postscript discloses that they married in 1972. **Awards** Oscars - nominated in four categories, the film won two - Daniel Day Lewis and Brenda Fricker for Best Actor and Best Supporting Actress, respectively.

DECEMBER BRIDE *(Ire./Brit. 1990)* **Director** *Thaddeus O'Sullivan* **Cast** *Donal McCann, Saskia Reeves, Ciaran Hinds, Patrick Malahide, Brenda Bruce, Dervla Kirwin, Gabrielle Reidy.*
Profile Based on the novel by Sam Hanna Bell, and set amongst Northern Ireland's Presbyterian community, it tells the story of a servant girl who has a child by one of the sons of the farmer for whom she works. Her refusal,

over the years, to disclose the name of the father causes widespread alienation.

FOOLS OF FORTUNE *(Brit. 1990, 109 mins)* **Director** *Pat O'Connor* **Producer** *Sarah Radclyffe* **Screenplay** *Michael Hirst (Based on William Trevor's Novel)* **Cast** *Iain Glenn, Mary Elizabeth Mastrantonio, Julie Christie, Michael Kitchen, Niamh Cusack, Tom Hickey, John Kavanagh, Mick Lally, Niall Toibin, Sean T. McClory, Catherine McFadden* **Locations** *Counties Westmeath, Kildare and Galway.*
Profile Willie Quinton's life has fallen apart. During the War of Independence the Black and Tans murder his father and two younger sisters at their Big House. He and his mother Evie now live in quiet desperation in Dublin while the family's maid, Josephine, looks after them. Willie falls in love with his beautiful cousin Marianne Woodcombe. Evie commits suicide, and Marianne goes to Dorset with her mother but returns months afterwards, pregnant. The film ends with a reunion for a family that has never truly met.

THE FIELD *(Brit. 1990)* **Director** *Jim Sheridan* **Cast** *Richard Harris, John Hurt, Tom Berenger, Sean Bean, Frances Tomelty, Brenda Fricker, John Cowley, Ruth McCabe* **Production** *Noel Pearson* **Writer** *Jim Sheridan (Based on John B. Keane's play)* **Location** *Leenane, Co. Galway.*
Profile Set on the western seaboard in the middle of this century, a small farmer believes he has a natural right to the field which he has raised to fertility from bare rock. He kills, in a fit of rage the 'outsider,' Yank who wants to pour concrete on the field to gain access to a rich limestone mountain. This results in his desctruction and the end of his family line.

HEAR MY SONG *(Brit. 1991)* **Director** *Peter Chelsom* **Cast** *Ned Beatty, Shirley Ann Field, Adrian Dunbar, Tara Fitzgerald.*
Profile Based on the story of tenor Josef Locke, the film is a picaresque tale of the young manager who books him and of Locke's attempts to evade the Inland Revenue by fleeing to Ireland.

THE COMMITMENTS *(Brit. 1991)* **Director** *Alan Parker* **Cast** *Michael Ahern, Maria Doyle, Dave Finnegan, Bronagh Gallagher, Colm Meaney, Andrew Strong, Angeline Ball, Johnny Murphy.* **Screenplay** *Ian La Frenais, Dick Clement, Mark Abraham Location Dublin City and Bray, Co Wicklow.*
Profile: Based on Roddy Doyle's story, the film is a musical account of the rise and fall of a working-class, Dublin, soul band.

THE MIRACLE *(Brit. 1991)* **Director/Writer:** *Neil Jordan* **Production** *Steven Woolley/Palace* **Cast** *Beverley D'Angelo, Donal McCann, Niall Byrne, Lorraine Pilkington, Tom Hickey, Shane Connaughton, Mary Coughlan* **Location** *Dalkey, Co Dublin.*
Profile This sea-side coming of age film was shot outside director Neil Jordan's front door on the seafront. Jordan wanted to work at home after the difficulties of *We're No Angels* and he was able to walk to work every morning.

FAR AND AWAY *(US/Ire. 1992)* **Director** *Ron Howard* **Cast** *Tom Cruise, Nicole Kidman, Colm Meaney, Thomas Gibson, Cyril Cusack, Eileen Pollock, Niall Tóibín, Barry McGovern* **Locations** *Dublin, the Dingle Penninsula, Co Wicklow and Clogher Head, Co Louth.*
Profile The son of a poor 19th century West of Ireland tenant farmer pledges to avenge the death of his father, an event he blames on the local landlord. He and the landlord's daughter fall in love and elope to America.

INTO THE WEST *(Ire. 1992, 102 mins)* **Director** *Mike Newell* **Cast** *Gabriel Byrne, Ellen Barkin, Ciarán Fitzgerald, Ruaidhrí Conroy, David Kelly, Johnny Murphy, Colm Meaney, John Kavanagh, Brendan Gleeson* **Executive Producer** *James Mitchell* **Screenplay** *Jim Sheridan (based on a story by Michael Pearce).*
Profile Since the death of his wife, Papa Riley (once king of the travellers) lives among the settled community with his two sons, Ossie and Tito. A mysterious white horse forms an instant attachment to Ossie and moves into the family's Ballymun flat. The horse is removed by the police who then illegally sell it on. Ossie and Tito steal the horse back and set off across the country. Their father enlists the help of the travelling community to track down the boys. Eventually, the boys and the horse are cornered by the police on the edge of the Atlantic Ocean. Papa Riley arrives just in time to see Ossie and the horse submerge under the waves. Ossie re-emerges having finally met his dead mother under the sea. His sense of self-worth re-invigorated by his rediscovery of his old life, Papa vows to return to the travelling life.

THE CRYING GAME *(Brit./Ire. 1992, 110 mins)* **Director/Writer** *Neil Jordan* **Production** *Steven Woolley* **Cast** *Stephen Rea, Miranda Richardson, Forest Whitaker, Jaye Davidson, Adrian Dunbar, Tony Slattery* **Location** *Co Meath.*
Profile A British soldier is abducted by the IRA and held hostage on a farm by an IRA volunteer, who comes to respect and understand him. The film contains a unique twist in its treatment of political violence, race and sexuality, but it handles it in a way that does not alienate mainstream audiences. **Awards** 1993 Oscar for Best Screenplay (Neil Jordan).

THE PLAYBOYS *(Brit. 1992)* **Director** *Gillies McKinnon* **Cast** *Albert Finney, Aidan Quinn, Robin Wright, Milo*

O'Shea, Adrian Dunbar, Alan Devlin, Niamh Cusack. **Location** Redhills, Co. Cavan.
Profile In a remote Irish village in 1957, the Playboys were the travelling actors on whom the villagers relied for entertainment. A young woman, who has scandalised the village by having an illegitimate baby and refusing to name the father, begins a relationship with one of the actors.

IN THE NAME OF THE FATHER *(Ire./Brit./U.S.1993)* **Director** Jim Sheridan **Production** Hell's Kitchen **Writer** Jim Sheridan **Cast** Daniel Day-Lewis, Emma Thompson, Pete Postlethwaite, John Lynch, Mark Sheppard, Beatie Edney, Marie Jones, Tina Kellegher, Brian De Salvo, Bosco Hogan, Don Baker **Location** Dublin City and Kilmainham Jail.
Profile The film loosely tells the true story of the Guildford Four, particularly Gerry Conlon and his father, who were wrongfully imprisoned for a terrorist bombing in England and their search for fairness in the British justice system. **Awards** four Oscar nominations: Best Actor, Best Screenplay, Best Director and Best Film.

THE SNAPPER *(Ire./Brit. 1993)* **Director** Stephen Frears Cast Colm Meaney, Tina Kellegher, Ruth McCabe, Eanna MacLiam, Peter Rowen, Pat Laffan, Finnuala Murphy, Brendan Gleeson **Production** Linda Myles **Screenplay** Roddy Doyle (Based on his book).
Profile The Snapper is comedy, set among a working class family. The eldest daugher in the family is pregnant and refuses to reveal the identity of the father.

WIDOW'S PEAK *(Ire./Brit. 1993)* **Director** John Irvine Cast Mia Farrow, Joan Plowright, Natasha Richardson, Adrian Dunbar, Jim Broadbent, John Kavanagh **Location** Wicklow.
Profile Set in 1920's Ireland, it tells of a community of widows and single women who are permitted to live on this hill. This community is disrupted by the arrival of a spirited war widow who is immediately disliked by the women and takes up with the scion of the village's best family.

AN AWFULLY BIG ADVENTURE (Ire./Brit. 1995) **Director** Mike Newell **Cast** Hugh Grant, Alan Rickman, Peter Firth, Georgia Cates, Prunella Scales **Location** Dublin
Profile Set in Liverpool, this film was released in the euphoria after Four Weddings And A Funeral. Hugh Grant plays a sadistic theatre director.

BRAVEHEART *(Ire. 1994)* **Director** Mel Gibson **Production** Bruce Davey/Alan Ladd Jr./Mel Gibson **Cast** Mel Gibson, Sophie Marceau, Patrick McGoohan, Brendan Gleeson, John Kavanagh and members of the FCA **Location** Filmed on location at Curragh, Trim Castle, and Ardmore Studios, Co Wicklow.
Profile Based on Scotland's William Wallace, who rose from being a lowly Highland farmer in the late 13th century. After the loss of his first love,he galvanised a vast army of clansmen against King Edward I of England. He defeated the army at Stirling and took it upon himself to invade England.

THE SECRET OF ROAN INISH *(US 1994)* **Director/Writer** John Sayles **Cast** Mick Lally, John Lynch, Eileen Colgan, Richard Sheridan, Jennifer Courtney **Location** Donegal.
Profile The story follows the spiritual fortunes of an Irish fisherman's family who lose the old way of life when they abandon their island home. Also about myths and legends and their place in today's world.

WAR OF THE BUTTONS *(Brit./Ire. 1994)* **Director** John Roberts **Cast** Colm Meaney, Johnny Murphy, John Coffey, Gregg Fitzgerald, Gerard Kearney, Liam Cunningham, Paul Batt.
Profile Based in west Cork, the film tells the story of an ongoing war between two rival gangs of children from neighbouring villages and how they resolve their differences.

A MAN OF NO IMPORTANCE *(Ire./Brit. 1995)* **Director** Suri Krishnamma **Cast** Albert Finney, Brenda Fricker, Tara Fitzgerald, Michael Gambon, Mick Lally **Screenplay** Barry Devlin **Producer** Jonathan Cavendish.
Profile The story of a gay bus conductor in Dublin who is obsessed with Oscar Wilde.

CIRCLE OF FRIENDS *(US/Ire. 1995)* **Director** Pat O'Connor **Cast** Chris O'Donnell, Minnie Driver, Geraldine O'Rawe, Saffron Burrows, Colin Firth, Mick Lally, John Kavanagh, Ruth McCabe, Ciaran Hinds, Alan Cumming, Aidan Gillen **Producer** Arlene Sellers/Alex Winitsky/Frank Price **Screenplay** Andrew Davies (Based on the Maeve Binchy novel) **Location** Dublin City and Co. Kilkenny.
Profile: In a small village in 1950s Ireland, three girls, Benny, Nan and Eve, pledge everlasting friendship. The three are re-united at university in Dublin. Benny meets Jack, a handsome medical student and college rugby star, but her parents insist that she will marry the repulsive Sean, who works in her father's business. When her father suddenly dies, Benny must leave college and take over the shop. However, Jack and Benny are eventually re-united and begin their relationship again.

FRANKIE STARLIGHT *(Ire. 1995, 101 mins)* **Director** Michael Lindsay-Hogg **Cast** Ann Parillaud, Matt Dillon, Gabriel Byrne, Rudi Davies, Georgina Cates, Niall Tóibín Producer Noel Pearson **Screenplay** Chet Raymo/Ronan O'Leary (based from Raymo's novel The Dork from Cork).

Profile A 'literary dwarf' drops his memoirs on the desk of a book agent; it tells of his mother and her lovers: A beautiful 18-year-old Frenchwoman, Bernadette leaves her home in Normandy, stowing away on a U.S. troopship. She is dropped off in Ireland, pregnant. A married customs officer, Jack Kelly, looks after her until the birth of her son, Frankie. Jack and Bernadette become lovers, but are discovered. A handsome GI appears and takes the family back to the US.

GUILTRIP *(Ire./Fra./Ita./Spain 1995)* **Director/Writer** *Gerry Stembridge* **Cast** *Andrew Connolly, Jasmine Russell, Michelle Houlden, Peter Hanly, Pauline McLynn, Frankie McCafferty, Mikel Murfi* **Producer** *Ed Guiney* **Location** *Maynooth.*
Profile The film explores destructive relationships, focusing on the marriage of a bullying, violent soldier and his frightened wife who live in a small Irish garrison town.

NOTHING PERSONAL *(Ire./Brit. 1995) Director Thaddeus O'Sullivan* **Cast** *Ian Hart, John Lynch, James Frain, Gary Lydon, Michael Gambon, Jenifer Courtney Screenplay Daniel Mornin (based on his novel All Our Fault).*
Profile Belfast, 1975 - high-ranking paramilitaries agree a ceasefire, which 'loose cannon' Loyalist Ginger immediately breaks, viciously burning a Catholic to death. Ginger's squad leader, Kenny, is ordered to kill him. Single Catholic father, Liam, is stuck on the wrong side of the tracks after a riot. Kenny's patrol finds Liam and Kenny recognises him as a friend who he knows to be innocent of IRA activity. However, things go badly wrong as the film progresses and the narrative ends in tragic, senseless deaths.

THE RUN OF THE COUNTRY *(Ire. 1995, 108 mins) Director Peter Yates* **Cast** *Albert Finney, Matt Keeslar, Victoria Smurfit, Anthony Brophy, David Kelly, Dearbhla Molloy, Vinnie McCabe* **Screenplay** *Shane Connaughton from his own novel* **Location** *Redhills, Co. Cavan.*
Profile In Butlershill, Co. Cavan, on the border with Northern Ireland, young Danny argues with his father, the local Garda sergeant, after the death of his mother and moves in with his friend Prunty, who has the run of the country. Danny learns about life and the countryside from Prunty and finally musters up the courage to befriend Annagh Lee, a girl of his own age who lives across the border. He eventually becomes reconciled with his father and decides to go to university in Dublin instead of emigrating.

DANCE, LEXLIE, DANCE *(N. Ireland 1996)* **Director** *Tim Loane* **Writer** *Dave Duggan* **Producer** *Pearse Moore* **Production Co** *Raw Nerve Productions* **Cast** *B.J. Hogg, Kimberly McConkey.*
Profile The film tells the story of a lone father trying to bring up his daughter. His daughter becomes obsessed with Riverdance and Irish dancing, not an easy thing for her staunchly Protestant father to come to terms with.
Awards One of only five films nominated for the 1998 Academy Awards - Best Short Film: Live Action.

FLYING SAUCER ROCK 'N' ROLL *(N. Ireland 1996, 12 mins)* **Directors/Producers** *Enda and Michael Hughes* **Screenplay** *Mik Duffy* **Cast** *Ardal O'Hanlon, Joe Rooney.*
Profile A pastiche of 1950s B sci-fi movies but set in rural Ireland. Toe-tappin' rock 'n' roll rebel Ardal O'Hanlon encounters terror from another dimension. **Awards** Best Black & White Short at the 1997 Cork Film Festival; Best European Short Film at the Brussels International Film Festival; Jury Award at the 1998 Celtic Film & Television Festival.

LAST OF THE HIGH KINGS *(Ire. 1996)* **Director** *David Keating* **Cast** *Gabriel Byrne, Colm Meaney, Christine Ricci, Catherine O'Hara, Jared Leto, Renee Weldon, Peter Keating, Stephen Rea* **Screenplay** *David Keating/Gabriel Byrne* **Producer** *Tim Palmer.*
Profile A coming of age film, based in Dublin in the 1970s. A boy, in the summer holidays after his leaving certificate, negotiates the gap between boyhood and adulthood while trying to come to terms with his bohemian family.

MICHAEL COLLINS *(Ire. 1996) Director/Writer: Neil Jordan* **Cast** *Liam Neeson, Julia Roberts, Aidan Quinn, Alan Rickman, Stephen Rea, Ian Hart, Charles Dance, Brendan Gleeson, Stuart Graham, Gerard McSorley* **Producer** *Steven Woolley* **Location** *Dublin City, Grangegorman, Wicklow.*
Profile 1916 Easter Rising - Michael Collins, Harry Boland and Eamonn De Valera are amongst those surrending. De Valera is imprisoned but Collins and Boland, are released after a few months. Collins becomes the de facto military leader of the IRA and campaigns for Sinn Fein. He decides that the organisation will adopt guerrilla warfare in fighting the British. At the same time, he and Harry Boland compete for the favours of Kitty Kiernan, and Collins eventually wins out. De Valera is freed and goes to America to raise funds. In the meantime the guerrilla warfare continues. De Valera returns, and against Collins' advice, demands that the IRA engage the British in open warfare. The IRA sustain heavy losses but just as the rebels near exhaustion, the British agree to discuss a treaty to end the War of Independence. De Valera insists that Collins lead the Irish delegation to the British Government, arguing that Collins is their best weapon Collins goes and returns with a treaty that secures not a 26-county free state, the stepping stone to full independence. De Valera and his supporters refuse to accept the treaty, prompting civil war. Seeking to end the violence, Collins travels to west Cork to meet De Valera but is ambushed and is killed outright. The film closes with documentary footage of Collins' funeral.

THE MOON ON MY BACK *(Ire. 1996, 40mins, Irish Film Archive)* **Director** *Johnathan White* **Producer** *David Power* **Production Co.** *JDM Productions.*
Profile A biography of Pat Tierney based on his autobiography of the same title. A familiar figure to many Dubliners, he cited poetry on request in Grafton Street. Born in 1957, Tierney left for the US in the 1970s after a childhood spent in institutions and involvement with petty crime. While in the US, Tierney drank heavily and used a variety of drugs. He entered a detox programme when he was in Canada where he was diagnosed as having AIDS. When he returned to Ireland, Tierney went to live in Ballymun towers, a deprived high rise complex on Dublin's northside. He became involved in working with young people from the area and set up the Rhymers club where he shared his love of language and poetry with the local children. Tierney took his own life shortly after filming was completed.

SNAKES AND LADDERS *(Ire. 1996)* **Director/Writer** *Trish McAdam* **Cast** *Pom Boyd, Gina Moxley, Sean Hughes, Rosaleen Linehan, Pierce Turner, Catherine White* **Producers** *Lilyan Sievernich, Chris Sievernich.*
Profile The story of two friends on the arts fringe in Dublin and their complicated love lives. Sean Hughes is the wimpy boyfriend of one, who is cheated on and in turn sleeps with the other friend. Contains some nice vignettes of modern Irish life, particularly Joe Dolan belting out his top tunes to an audience of middle-aged women.

SOME MOTHER'S SON *(Ire. 1996)* **Director** *Terry George* **Cast** *Helen Mirren, John Lynch, Fionnuala Flanagan, Aidan Gillen, David O'Hara, Tom Hollander, Gerard McSorley, Ciaran Hinds, John Kavanagh.*
Profile The story of the hunger strikes in 1981, taken from a mother's perspective (Fionnuala Flanagan). Helen Mirren is a teacher who becomes embroiled in the unfolding tragedy.

THE DISAPPEARANCE OF FINBAR *(Ire./Brit./Swe. 1996)* **Director** *Sue Clayton* **Cast** *Jonathon Rhys-Myers, Lorraine Pilkington, Luke Griffin, Sean McGinley, Marie Mullan, Sean Lawlor, Tina Kellegher, Don Foley, Robert Hickey* **Producers** *Bertil Ohlsson and Martin Bruce-Clayton* **Screenplay** *Dermot Bolger and Sue Clayton (based on the novel* The Disappearance of Rory Brophy *by Carl Lombard)* **Locations** *Dublin, Sweden, Lapland.*
Profile Finbar belongs to a working-class Dublin suburb. With his father's dream of Country & Western stardom dead, his hopes are pinned on Finbar who has been talent spotted to play football in Zurich. Finbar can't handle it and resumes life in the dead-end working-class estate. Romantic difficulties lead to complications with best friend Danny. Finbar takes flight. The community is drawn together in an Action Committee to find him, yet three years pass before there is any confirmation that he is still alive. A late-night phonecall prompts Danny to go to Sweden. **Awards** the American Film Institute's choice for Irish Film of the Year (for 1997).

THE ELIMINATOR *(Ire. 1996, 83 mins)* **Writer/Director** *Enda Hughes* **Producers** *Enda Hughes, Denis O'Hare, Michael Hughes* **Music** *Stuart Neville* **Production/Designer/Visual** *Effects/Stunts Denis O'Hare* **Cast** *Barry Wallace, Michael Hughes, Mike Duffy, Edward Hughes, Paul McAvinchey, Donna Crilly* **Production Co.** *Cousins Pictures* **Location** *Keady, Co. Armagh.*
Profile This low budget sci-fi film is now a cult classic. A young Northern Irish man, John O'Brien - a member of The Organisation - is hard at work on plans for a terrifying, turbo-charged military vehicle, the VIPER, intended for urban warfare. After much fighting, gunfire, explosions, spectacular car chases, a soaring bodycount, zombies and the resurrected spirit of Saint Patrick, there is one last, apocalyptic explosion.

THE SUN, THE MOON AND THE STARS *(Ire. 1996, 92 mins)* **Director/Writer** *Geraldine Creed* **Producer** *Brendan McCarthy* **Music** *Noel Eccles* **Cast** *Jason Donovan, Angie Dickinson, Gina Moxley, Vinny Murphy, Elaine Cassidy, Aisling Corcoran* **Location** *Donabate, Co. Wicklow.*
Profile A coming-of-age story centred around three women of very different sorts. The story unfolds during that favourite setting of teenage fiction, the summer holiday, and the visual style of the whole is onsistently bright and breezy, with an emphasis on colourful settings and costumes.

THE VAN *(Ire. 1996, 92 mins)* **Director** *Stephen Frears* **Cast** *Colm Meaney, Donal O'Kelly, Brendan O'Carroll, Ger Ryan, Caroline Rothwell, Stuart Dunne, Jack Lynch, Moses Rowen* **Executive Producer** *Mark Shivas* **Screenplay** *Roddy Doyle (based on his novel)* **Production Co.** *BBC Films* **Location** *Dublin.*
Profile Bimbo becomes unemployed after losing his job at the bakery. After a night on the booze, Bimbo and his friend Jimmy Curley curse the absence of the Vietnamese chip van on which they were depending for dinner. The next morning Bimbo has the idea of using his redundancy money to buy a chip van and set up in business. Although the money begins to roll in, the business relationship begins to place pressures on their friendship. More pressure follows the arrival of a Health Board inspector demanding expensive hygiene changes be made. As their friendship teeters on the brink, Bimbo and Jimmy take the Van out on one last drunken drive, driving into the sea at Dollymount. The Van is abandoned forever, but their friendship saved.

I WENT DOWN *(Ire. 107 mins)* **Director** *Paddy Breathnach* **Producer** *Rob Walpole* **Screenplay** *Conor McPherson* **Cast** *Brendan Gleeson, Peter MacDonald, Peter Caffrey, Tony Doyle* **Music** *Dario Marianelli* **Locations** *Kildare, Offaly, Dublin* **Production Co.** *Treasure Films.*
Profile A road movie . . . Git Hynes is just out of jail, has lost his girlfriend and finds himself owing a debt to gang-

ster Tom French, who sends him on an 'easy ride' down South to pick up a criminal associate, Frank Grogan. Git finds himself stuck with Bunny Kelly, an older criminal with a bad attitude and they discover that French wants Grogan dead. Git and Bunny need to stick together, or they could find themeselves sharing an unmarked grave. But greed, betrayal and old secrets make for a dangerous, violent trip, leading to a shocking conclusion. **Awards** 1997 San Sebastian Film Festival - Winner of the New Director's Prize, Jury Prize & Best Screenplay Prize; 1997 Thessaleniki Film Festival - Best Director Prize.

ALL SOUL'S DAY *(Ire. 78 mins)* **Director/Writer** *Alan Gilsenan* **Producer** *David McLoughlin* **Cast** *Declan Conlon, Eva Birthistle, Jayne Snow, Tom Hickey, Michael McElhatton* **Music** *Robert Lockhart* **Locations** *Donegal, Dublin* **Production Co.** *Yellow Asylum Films.*
Profile A film about the interlinked themes of memory, trust, faith, forgiveness and redemption. The date was November 2nd - All Soul's Day - when Nicole's naked body was found on the beach. Seven years on, Nicole's mother Madie, obsessed with finding out what really happened on that day, visits her daughter's boyfriend Jim in prison. As memories unfold and secrets are unveiled in the search for truth, Madie and Jim stumble upon something more sinister. Shot in different formats, in colour and black and white, fragments of a tragic story emerge.

BOGWOMAN *(Ire. 84 mins)* **Director/Writer** *Tom Collins* **Producers** *Martha O'Neill, Tom Collins* **Cast** *Rachel Dowling, Peter Mullen, Sean McGinley, Maria McDermottroe* **Music** *Fiachra Trench* **Locations** *Donegal, Derry* **Production Co.** *De Facto Film & Video.*
Profile A poignant tale which follows Maureen, a young unmarried mother from an island off Donegal who moves to Derry in the late 1950s to marry. It is a film about a woman and her relationship with her past - her parents on her island home - and her future with her family and neighbours in the Bogside in Derry at the beginning of the 'Troubles' in the 1960s.

DRINKING CRUDE *(Ire. 84 mins)* **Director/Writer** *Owen McPolin* **Producers** *Kim Tapsell, Gerry Johnston* **Cast** *Andrew Scott, James Quarton, Eva Birthistle* **Music** *Bill Corkey* **Locations** *Dublin, London, Cork, Kerry* **Production Co.** *Sweetskin Productions.*
Profile Believing he has failed his final school exams, 18-year-old Paul leaves Kerry for a London squat and a job repairing tanks in oil refineries. While there, he forms an unlikely friendship with Al, an overbearing and loud Scottish labourer. When they return to Kerry on a job, his own community's reaction forces him to confront his own attitudes and prejudices.

THE FIFTH PROVINCE *(N. Ireland 93 mins)* **Director** *Frank Stapleton* **Producer** *Catherine Tiernan* **Screenplay** *Nina Fitzpatrick & Frank Stapleton* **Cast** *Brian F. O'Byrne, Lia Williams, Anthony Higgins, Ian Richardson* **Music** *Al Lethbridge* **Locations** *Cavan, Wicklow, Dublin* **Production Co.** *Ocean Films* **Awards** *Winner Best First Feature - Galway Film Festival 1997.*
Profile This surreal, comic fantasy and love story unfolds in an Ireland teetering on the edge of a Europe that is drawing ever closer. A contemporary fable of persecuted guest-house keeper Timmy Sugrue and his wild flight of imagination into a domain of 'magic, passion and possibility.'

HOOLIGANS *(Ire. 91 mins)* **Director** *Paul Tickell* **Producer** *Nicholas O'Neill* **Screenplay** *James Mathers* **Cast** *Darren Healey, Jeff O'Toole, Viviana Verveen, Mark Dunne* **Music** *Speedy J. and Red Snapper* **Locations** *Wicklow, Dublin* **Production Co.** *Liquid Films.*
Profile Just hours after his release from prison Neal takes his murderous revenge and ends up on the run with his old gang. But the gang he once considered his home from home is no longer his refuge and their days as urban cowboys riding the wild horses are numbered. Hooligans is 'The Four Horsemen of the Apocalypse' reset in the already vanishing 'pony club' subculture of Dublin's wild Northside. It tells the mythic but realistic tale of the last gang in town riding rough-shod and bare-back towards the millennium.

HOW TO CHEAT IN THE LEAVING CERTIFICATE *(Ire. 80 mins)* **Director** *Graham Jones* **Producers** *Graham Jones, Clara Flanagan* **Screenplay** *Graham Jones/Tadhg O'Higgins/Aislinn O'Loughlin* **Cast** *Eamon Morrissey, Aileen O'Connor, Garret Baker, Joe McKinney* **Music** *Giles Packham/Jurgen Simpson* **Locations** *Westmeath, Dublin* **Production Co.** *Graham Jones Prods.*
Profile Six students develop an complex masterplan to 'beat the system' by cheating in their final exams. This film has excited controversy and praise, with Irish politicians criticising it for inciting students to cheat. A host of Irish celebrities play cameo roles in the film, including Chris de Burgh.

THE LAST BUS HOME *(Ire. 93 minutes)* **Director/Writer** *Johnny Gogan* **Producer** *Paul Donovan* **Cast** *Annie Ryan, Brian F. O'Byrne, John Cronin, Donal O'Kelly, Anthony Brophy, Gemma Craven* **Music** *Cathal Coughlan* **Locations** *Dublin* **Production Co.** *Bandit Films.*
Profile Dublin 1979 - While everyone in Ireland embarks on a public mass to welcome the Pope, punkette Reena ducks out with the aid of her grandmother - a rebel from an older generation. In the deserted street of her suburb, she tracks down Jessop, a punk guitarist. Their attraction is immediate and by the time her parents return, renewed from the Pope's blessing, Reena and Jessop have sealed their unholy alliance in other ways. **Awards**

Winner of the Best Film Award - 1997 Irish and British Film Festival, Cherbourg.

SEPARATION ANXIETY *(Ire. 91 mins)* **Director** *Mark Staunton* **Producer** *Liam O'Neill* **Screenplay** *Shelagh Harcourt* **Cast** *Susan Collins, Kevin Gildea, Shelagh Harcourt, Conor Lambert, Michelle Reid, Brendan Dempsey* **Music** *Stephen McKeown* **Locations** *Dublin* **Production Co.** *Paradox Pictures / Dogtown Films.*
Profile A contemporary comedy of manners set against the backdrop of the first divorce case in Ireland. Kevin is a charming waster. Sally is his upwardly mobile but estranged wife and they are both trying to come to terms with the fact that their relationship is over. Their bawdy and irreverent twenty-something friends get involved as they struggle with committment and betrayal, lust and love and the old fashioned notion that perhaps a relationship can last forever.

THE BOXER *(Ire.)* **Director** *Jim Sheridan* **Producers** *Arthur Lappin, Jim Sheridan* **Screenplay** *Terry George* **Production Co.** *Hell's Kitchen* **Cast** *Daniel Day-Lewis.*
Profile Danny Flynn has just been released from prison having served 14 years after refusing to explode a bomb that might have injured women and children. Leaving the relative safety of jail, he returns to Belfast where the conflict follows him like a dark shadow. The faceless enemy is everywhere. Back in Belfast he is still 'the Boxer' and his return restores respect to the neighbourhood. Danny Boy is on a winning streak . . . Again Daniel Day-Lewis has immersed himself in his role, and had Barry McGuigan train him for the film.

DANCING AT LUGHNASA *(Ire.)* **Director** *Pat O'Connor* **Producer** *Noel Pearson* **Screenplay** *Frank McGuinness (Adapted from Brian Friel's play)* **Production Co.** *Ferndale Films* **Cast** *Meryl Streep, Bríd Brennan, Catherine McCormack, Kathy Burke, Michael Gambon.*
Profile Ballybeg in 1930's Donegal: Michael Mundy observes the lives of his mother, Christina and her four sisters in their closely knit family as secrets and sorrows begin to emerge. The arrival of Michael's father - a feckless Welshman and the women's older mad brother, a priest who has gone native while in Africa on the missions - to the family home unleashes repressed passion. The fine ensemble performance by the cast portrays the hopelessness that these women faced in their daily lives, as they become more and more imprisoned by poverty and religion.

THE GENERAL *(Ire.)* **Writer/Director/Producer** *John Boorman* **Executive Producer** *Kieran Corrigan* **Cast** *Brendan Gleeson, John Voight, Adrian Dunbar, Sean McGinley, Maria Doyle Kennedy, Angeline Ball* **Locations** *Dublin* **Production Co.** *Merlin Films*
Profile Based on the book by Paul Williams about the notorious Dublin gangland boss Martin Cahill. Cahill grew up in an area of Dublin where crime was the main occupation and toughness was the means by which you survived. For years he was Ireland's most dangerous and talented criminal and he managed to evade all attempts to pin anything on him, that is until he met his brutal end on the eve of the 1994 IRA ceasefire. The film was criticised for glamourising Cahill and crime. **Awards** 1998 Cannes Film Festival Competition - Best Director.

LOVE AND RAGE *(Ire.)* **Director** *Cathal Black* **Producers** *Rudolf Wichmann, Cathal Black* **Screenplay** *Brian Lynch* **Production Co.** *Cathal Black Films.*
Profile At the end of the 19th century in the Western Island of Achill, Agnes MacDonnell, a tough and determined Englishwoman meets her match in the dark and mysterious James Lynchehaun who persuades her to employ him as her land agent. A passionate and dangerous affair ensues despite their obvious differences.

SUNSET HEIGHTS *(N. Ireland)* **Writer/Director** *Colm Villa* **Producer** *Denis Bradley* **Production Co.** *Northland Films/Scorpio Productions* **Location** *Derry, Donegal.*
Profile In Derry, in the not-too-distant future, a two year ceasefire has existed between the two rival gangs that run the city. A series of child murders jeopardises the fragile peace and both sides work together to put an end to the brutal killings. Having found the guilty party the city breathes a sigh of relief, but then the murders begin again.

CROSSMAHEART *(aka Cycle of Violence, N. Ireland, 100 mins)* **Director** *Henry Herbert* **Producer** *Don Boyd* **Production Co.** *Lexington* **Screenplay** *Colin Bateman (based on his novel)* **Location** *Co. Down* **Cast** *Gerard Rooney, Maria Lennon, Ena Oates, Des Cave, Seamus Ball.*
Profile Although placed in the context of Northern Ireland and the Troubles, *Crossmaheart* is an off-beat black comedy. Kevin Miller, hapless bicycling reporter who works on the Crossmaheart Chronicle. His predecessor on the paper, Jamie Milburn, has dissappeared and is presumed dead but Jamie's girlfriend Marie thinks Jamie was killed because of a story he was working. Kevin sets out to investigate.

DIVORCING JACK *(N. Ireland)* **Director** *David Caffrey* **Screenplay** *Colin Bateman (based on his novel)* **Producer** *Robert Cooper* **Music** *Adrian Johnston* **Production Co.** *Scala Productions/BBC Films/ Winchester Films* **Cast** *David Thewlis, Rachel Griffiths, Jason Isaacs, Robert Lindsay, Bronagh Gallagher.*
Profile Set in 1999 in a Northern Ireland on the brink of independence, Divorcing Jack is a comedy-thriller with David Thewlis playing Dan Starkey, a cynical reporter up to his neck in trouble - his infidelity brings about a chain of events which lead him ultimately to choosing between saving his wife or the future of peace in Northern Ireland.

Premiéred at the 1998 Cannes Film Festival.

ALL FOR LOVE *(aka St. Ives N. Ireland/Fra./Ger.)* **Director** *Harry Hook* **Production Co** *Little Bird* **Cast** *Jean-Marc Barr, Miranda Richardson, Anna Friel, Richard E. Grant.*
Profile: A period story set in France and Scotland.

TITANIC TOWN *(N. Ireland)* **Director** *Roger Michell* **Production Co.** *Company Pictures* **Cast** *Julie Walters,* **Location** *Belfast, London.*
Profile Walters plays a peace crusader in the Belfast of the 1970s. *Premiéred at the 1998 Cannes Film Festival.*

RESURRECTION MAN (N. Ireland, 101 mins) **Director** Marc Evans **Cast** Stuart Townsend, James Nesbitt, John Hannah, Brenda Fricker.
Profile Based loosely on the true story of the Shankill Butchers, the film focuses on Victor Kelly, a loyalist thug who is obsessed with James Cagney. Adored by his mother, Victor spends his nights wielding terror with his stanley knife and rising through the ranks of the criminal fraternity.

FALLING FOR A DANCER *(Ire.)* **Director** *Richard Standeven* **Producer** *Alan Maloney* **Writer** *Deirdre Purcell (based on her popular novel)* **Production Co.** *Parallel Films*
Profile Shot in the breathtaking landscape of the Beara peninsula, this film tells the story of Elizabeth and her fall from fashionable society in Dublin, to the horror of a Magdalen Laundry leading ultimately to a self-imposed exile in a remote corner of County Cork.

A FURTHER GESTURE *(196 min.)* **Director** *Robert Dornhelm* **Producer** *Chris Curling* **Screenplay** *Ronan Bennett* **Cast** *Stephen Rea, Alfred Molina, Rosana Pastor, Brendan Gleeson, Pruitt Taylor Vince, Maria Doyle Kennedy* **Production Co.** *Colour A Channel 4 Films Production.*
Profile Rea, an imprisoned IRA man, takes part in a spectacular and violent jailbreak from the Maze prison. He is smuggled out to New York where he works as a dishwasher. He becomes friendly with a South American kitchen porter and is soon romantically involved with the man's sister. Both brother and sister are members of a revolutionary cell, dedicated to the overthrow of the repressive regime in their country but lack any basic military skills. Rea trains them and draws up a successful assassination blueprint for them, helps them execute it, and then attempts to escape with them. However, he must first meet up with another exiled IRA man. It emerges that the authorities have been tailing him, and there is a shootout in which Rea is killed.

THE BUTCHER BOY *(Ire.)* **Director** *Neil Jordan* **Cast** *Eamonn Owens, Eugene McCabe, Stephen Rea, Sinéad O'Connor* **Script** *Neil Jordan (Based on Eugene McCabe's novel).*
Profile The story of a young boy in a Monaghan town, who is left orphaned and despised by the community he lives in. Told from his perspective as he descends into madness and turns to murder, the black humour which Jordan successfully translates from the book lifts the film from what could be a dismal, depressing tale to an entertaining if somewhat disturbing narrative. Eamonn Owens as the young Francie Brady gives a remarkable performance.

THIS IS MY FATHER *(Ire. 1998)* **Director** *Paul Quinn* **Cast** *Aidan Quinn, James Caan, Eamon Morrisey, Stephen Rea, Gina Moxley, Moya Fairley, Donal Donnelly* **Cinematography** *Declan Quinn.*
Profile The US - James Caan, an embittered teacher, who doesn't know who his father was goes back to Ireland to find out about him. We are taken back to 1939, where a tragic love story unfolds.

SAVING PRIVATE RYAN *(Ire./U.S. 1997)* **Director** *Steven Spielberg* **Cast** *Tom Hanks, Ed Burns* **Location** *partly in Curracloe beach, Co. Wexford.*
Profile Steven Spielberg's World War II epic about the futility of war and the bravery of ordinary men. Set against the backdrop of the Normandy landings, an army captain, leads a team to rescue one soldier, who is the last surviving boy in his family after his three brothers are killed in action. Co. Wexford doubles as the beach heads at Normandy. The FCA were drafted in as extras in the film and according to the director, performed suberbly, some of them even enduring hypothermia as they waded in the cold waters of the Irish sea. The film is seen as an Oscar contender in 1999.

THE MAMMY *(Ire. 1998)* **Producer** *Jim Sheridan* **Cast** *Angelica Huston, Peter Ustinov. (Based On Brendan O'Carroll's novel).*
Profile: A comedy, the film is based around a mother and stall trader in Moore Street, Dublin, as she struggles against poverty to bring up her children. The film features performances from entertainers such as singer Tom Jones.

THE NEPHEW (Ire. 1998) **Producer** Pierce Brosnan **Cast** Donal McCann, Aislín McGuckan.

THE CHAPS (N. Ireland; 1998) **Director** Robert Young **Production Co** Menage A Trois.
Profile: Set in 1950s Ulster, this is a 'feelgood' film about a couple of misfit actors.   ❐

ENTERTAINMENT

Irish Music, and the Global Feast!

By **Kevin Courtney,** *Irish Times*

I F THE world is our oyster, then Irish music is enjoying a global feast. Back home, however, we still seem to be nibbling on scraps and missing out on the choicest cuts. Irish pop with a traditional flavour is now top of the menu all over the world, and the Celtic Tiger is evident in record shops from New York to Bangkok. The proliferation of Celtic themed compilations is testimony to the far-reaching popularity of Irish music, and any CD which bears the magic world 'celtic' on its cover is guaranteed to fly off the shelves. The biggest grossing movie of all time, *Titanic*, features traditional Irish music on its soundtrack, and the sight of Kate Winslet and Leonardo Di Caprio doing a jig below decks has raised the profile of Irish music around the world. Productions of *Riverdance* and *Lord of the Dance* are still thrilling audiences with their exuberance and energy.

Irish girl group B*Witched have made a big splash in the UK charts, hitting the Number One spot with their first two singles, *C'Est La Vie* and *Rollercoaster*. Two members of B*Witched, twins Edele and Keavy Lynch, are sisters of Boyzone's Shane Lynch, and it looks as though the girls will follow their big brother into teenage hearts everywhere. Dundalk band The Corrs, meanwhile, have topped the UK charts with their second album, *Talk on Corners*, and the combination of good looks, talent and a strong Irish lilt in their sound has made stars out of Andrea, Sharon, Caroline and Jim. Both B*Witched and The Corrs show that Irish pop music is overtaking its older, louder rock 'n' roll brother, and no new Irish rock act has managed to make that great leap forward into U2-style superstardom. Downpatrick band Ash remain Ireland's biggest rock export of the year, scoring another chart success with their second album, *Nu-Clear Sounds*. Meanwhile, The Divine Comedy, a.k.a. Neil Hannon, continues to blend rock, pop and classical music with his latest album, *Fin De Siecle*.

The Irish music industry likes to make a meal of our success abroad, but beneath all the table talk lurks the uneasy feeling that we're not making the most of what we've got. Many of our most successful exports have made it without much help from the homefront, and some have even had to escape the safe cocoon of the Irish scene before they could make their mark abroad. Irish record companies seem less savvy at spotting artists with the potential to become superstars, and when they do sign new bands, they often hype them up in an increasingly desperate attempt to justify the investment. Dublin was once known as the city of 1,000 bands, but now we've lost count: it seems as though every young male Dubliner between the ages of 18 and 25 wants to be a rock star. With the increasing number of bands comes a decline in standards, and few of the current crop have what it takes to break out to a wider audience.

There are still a few rock bands out there who are trying to kick down the the doors, and making some interesting sounds in the process. Bands like The Ultra Montanes from Dublin and The Young Offenders from Cork are influenced by the eras of glam-rock and punk, and their flamboyant styles are making people sit up and take notice. Guitar rockers The Hormones, led Dubliner Marc Carroll, were the guest stars on the U.S. sitcom *Friends*, playing the part of the band at Ross's wedding. And what did they play? A traditional-sounding Irish tune, of course. Let's hope Ross's relationship doesn't sink like the Titanic.

Older, more established Irish bands are also on the verge of cashing in on years of hard graft and exhaustive touring. Dublin band Aslan, for instance, have had their best-known song, *Crazy World*, remixed by local producer Hugh Drumm, and are finally starting to carve out a name for themselves in the UK. The Saw Doctors, who have been plugging away at their Tuam rock sound for almost a decade, are set to have their biggest success with their new album, *Songs From Sun Street*. Dublin band The Picture House are also hoping to generate some good vibes abroad with their new album, *Karmarama*.

While horizons expand overseas, the outlook at home seems to have narrowed in the past few years. The signs are, however, that opportunities are opening up again, and it will be interesting to see if the Irish music industry can make the most of these opportunities. The restrictive situation which forced concert promoters to seek planning permission to stage outdoor shows seems to be loosening up: the annual Slane festival was reinstated this year, and 80,000 young people filled the grounds of Slane Castle to watch The Verve, The Manic Street Preachers and Robbie Williams. The planning permission issue still needs to be resolved, and most pundits agree that a less cumbersome licensing system needs to be put in place. In anticipation of these changes, The Mean Fiddler have announced the return of the legendary Lisdoonvarna Festival in Clare for the year 2000. Perhaps the organisers can even persuade Christy Moore to come out of semi-retirement and perform his famous Lisdoonvarna anthem.

The Irish music industry is often hidebound by old fashioned musical values, and sometimes our traditional outlook can work against us. Record companies tend to be somewhat conservative in their choice of artists, touting bands who are safe and dull, and leaving the more innovative acts to strike out on their own. We have no shortage of local heroes who can rely on their home audience year in and year out, but how many of them can keep up with the changing face of international pop and the ever-progressing nature of modern rock?

Irish dance acts and DJs are moving with the times, and some of our most creative and forward-looking artistes are more likely to be spinning a turntable than strumming a guitar. Belfast DJ David Holmes has made a huge impression on the dance scene with his last album, *Let's Get Killed*, and DJs like Mark Kavanagh and Glen Brady are part of the new breed of club heroes. Tomorrow's talent is being spawned in the clubs and on the dancefloors, and Sony's recent dance compilation, *Irish Underground*, goes some way towards acknowledging this.

The Internet is also opening new avenues for Irish acts, and bands can now sell their own records and publicise their own music through the world wide web. The music industry is also catching onto the surfing wave, but we're still a cottage industry compared to the major players on the Net. When everyone from record distributors to t-shirt manufacturers have their own websites, then we can truly say that the Irish music industry has gone global.

MUSIC

IRISH NO. 1 ALBUM CHARTS, 1997-1998

Week beginning Day / mth	Album Title	Artist(s)	No. of weeks at No. 1	Record Label	Previous Highest Position	Country of Origin
04.10.97	Urban Hymns	The Verve	3	Virgin	*	England
25.10.97	Talk On Corners	The Corrs	3	Warner	*	Ireland
15.11.97	Spiceworld	Spice Girls	1	Virgin	3	England
22.11.97	Let's Talk About Love	Celine Dion	2	Sony	*	Canada
06.12.97	Faith Of Our Feathers	Dustin	4	EMI	2	Ireland
03.01.98	Urban Hymns	The Verve	5	Virgin	1	England
07.02.98	Titanic - O.S.T.	James Horner	9	Sony	5	Various
11.04.98	NOW 39	Various	2	EMI	*	Various
25.04.98	Mezzanine	Massive Attack	1	Virgin	*	England
02.05.98	NOW 39	Various	3	EMI	1	Various
23.05.98	Blue	Simply Red	1	Warner	*	England
30.05.98	Where We Belong	Boyzone	2	Polygram	*	Ireland
13.06.98	Adore	Smashing Pumpkins	1	Hut	2	USA
20.06.98	Talk On Corners	The Corrs	1	Warner	1	Ireland
27.06.98	Shame About Lucy Moonhead	Aslan	1	EMI	*	Ireland
04.07.98	Fresh Hits '98	Various	4	Sony	10	Various
01.08.98	Tracy Chapman	Tracy Chapman	1	Warner	2	USA
08.08.98	NOW 40	Various	4	EMI	*	Various
05.09.98	Tracy Chapman	Tracy Chapman	2	Warner	1	USA
19.09.98	This Is My Truth	Manic Street Preachers	2	Sony	*	Wales

* indicates album entered charts at number one.
Compiled by ChartTrack on behalf of IRMA. ©

IRISH NO. 1 SINGLE CHARTS, 1997-1998

Week Ending Day / mth	Song Title	Artist(s)	No. of weeks at No. 1	Record Label	Previous Highest Position	Country of Origin
04.10.97	Candle in the Wind	Elton John	5	Mercury	1	England
25.10.97	Barbie Girl	Aqua	4	MCA	3	Denmark
22.11.97	Good Lookin' Woman	Dustin & Joe Dolan	1	EMI	2	Ireland
11.01.98	Perfect Day	Various	7	Chrysalis	3	Various
17.01.98	All Around the World	Oasis	2	Creations	*	England
31.01.98	Dr. Jones	Aqua	2	MCA	2	Denmark
14.02.98	My Heart Will Go On	Celine Dion	6	Sony	*	Canada
28.03.98	It's Like That	Run DMC vs Jason Nevins	4	Profile	2	USA
25.04.98	All That I Need	Boyzone	3	Polygram	*	Ireland
16.05.98	Feel It	Tamperer featuring Maya	3	Zomba	3	England
06.06.98	C'est La Vie	B*witched	6	Sony	2	Ireland
18.07.98	Ghetto Superstar	Pras Michel, ODB & MYA	3	Universal	3	USA
08.08.98	No Matter What	Boyzone	6	Polygram	*	Ireland
19.09.98	Millennium	Robbie Williams	2	Chrysalis	2	England

* indicates single entered charts at number one.
Perfect Day (Various) - includes Irish artists: Bono, Boyzone and Shane McGowan.
Compiled by ChartTrack on behalf of IRMA. ©

(IRISH) TOP 30 ALBUM ENTRIES, 1997-1998

Week of Entry Day / mth	Album Title	Artist(s)	No. entered at	Highest position	Weeks spent in Top 30
04.10.97	Miss You Tonight	Brendan Keely	5	3	5
11.10.97	Heavenly	Vard Sisters	13	13	2
11.10.97	Forgiven, Not Forgotten	The Corrs	19*	15	4
11.10.97	The Best of Van Morrison	Van Morrison	30	30	1
18.10.97	The Christy Moore Collection Part 2	Christy Moore	7	4	15
25.10.97	Talk On Corners	The Corrs	1	1	50
01.11.97	Who Fears To Speak	Various	19	11	5
01.11.97	I Believe	Daniel O'Donnell	23	23	2
08.11.97	Paint the Sky with Stars, Best of	Enya	4	3	13
08.11.97	Here Comes Lucy Jones	Aslan	14	14	2
08.11.97	This One's For You	OTT	20	20	1
15.11.97	So Far . . . The Best of	Sinéad O'Connor	20	13	5
15.11.97	I Give My Heart	Finbar Wright	25	25	3
16.11.97	Gael Force	Various	26	10	7
22.11.98	Heavenly	Vard Sisters	28*	10	11
29.11.97	Faith Of Our Feathers	Dustin	2	1	11
29.11.97	I Believe	Daniel O'Donnell	28*	28	1
13.12.97	I Give My Heart	Finbar Wright	26*	26	3
20.12.97	Warmer For The Spark	Various	28	22	3
07.02.98	The Long Journey Home	Various	18	14	8
14.02.98	Paint the Sky with Stars, Best of	Enya	28*	28	1
21.02.98	Solas	Ronan Hardiman	21	15	3
14.03.98	Worse Than Pride	Kieran Goss	7	5	10
28.03.98	Forgiven, Not Forgotten	The Corrs	20*	20	1
04.04.98	Landmark	Clannad	20	20	4
04.04.98	Semi-Detached	Therapy?	22	22	1
11.04.98	Forgiven, Not Forgotten	The Corrs	29*	29	1
23.05.98	Junkster	Junkster	24	24	1
30.05.98	Where We Belong	Boyzone	1	1	18
30.05.98	Born	Hothouse Flowers	26	26	1
27.06.98	Shame About Lucy Moonhead	Aslan	1	1	12
27.06.98	The Philosopher's Stone	Van Morrison	26	26	1
11.07.98	The Mobile Phone - The Album	Ritchie Kavanagh	30	23	2
18.07.98	No Stranger	Sean Keane	11	8	6
01.08.98	Don't Get Me Wrong	Frances Black	12	9	4
15.08.98	No Mermaid	Sinead Lohan	3	3	7
15.08.98	The Water Is Wide	Various	11	2	7
29.08.98	Very Best Of - 23 Great Songs	Brendan Shine	17	17	4
29.08.98	Stop I'm Doing It Again	Kaydee	30	30	1
05.09.98	Fin De Siecle	Divine Comedy	6	4	4
05.09.98	The Unforgettable Fire	U2	30	30	1
19.09.98	Worse Than Pride	Kieran Goss	20	20	1
19.09.98	Coolfin	Donal Lunny	22	22	2
26.09.98	Karmarama	Picture House	8	8	1

In addition: *The Best Of* (Dolores Keane) spent nine weeks in Top 30 from 04.10.97; *Faith Of Our Fathers II* (Various) spent five weeks in Top 30 from 04.10.97; *Pop* (U2) spent three weeks in Top 30 from 04.10.97; *The Greatest GAA Album In The World Ever Vol. I* (Various) spent one week in Top 30 from 04.10.97; *A Better Man* (Brian Kennedy) spent one week in Top 30 from 04.10.97. For original date of entry of these albums see *The Irish Almanac & Yearbook of Facts 1998*.

Compiled by ChartTrack on behalf of IRMA. ©

(IRISH) TOP 30 SINGLES ENTRIES, 1997-1998

Week of Entry Day / mth	Song Title	Artist(s)	No. entered at	Highest position	Weeks spent in Top 30
11.10.97	Only When I Sleep	The Corrs	22	10	8
18.10.97	Heaven	Brendan Martin	24	24	1
18.10.97	A Life Less Ordinary	Ash	28	16	5
15.11.97	Good Lookin' Woman	Dustin	2	1	5
15.11.97	Hot Stuff	Who's Eddie	23	23	2
29.11.97	Baby Can I Hold You	Boyzone	4	2	13
29.11.97	The Mobile Phone	Richie Kavanagh	20	8	13
06.12.97	More Than I Can Say	Darren Holden	20	20	1
06.12.97	This Is A Rebel Song	Sinead O'Connor	29	29	1
06.12.97	The First Of May	Carter Twins	30	30	1
13.12.97	If God Will Send His Angels	U2	11	11	5
27.12.97	A Silent Night - Christmas 1915	Jerry Lynch	24	24	1
17.01.98	The Story Of Love	OTT	15	9	6
31.01.98	Waiting	The Devlins	21	21	1
07.02.98	Weatherman	Juniper	9	9	7
14.02.98	Out Of My Head	Kieran Goss	30	16	2
07.03.98	Out Of My Head	Kieran Goss	29	29	1
22.03.98	Wonderful Thing	Leslie Dowdall	19	9	3
28.03.98	What Can I Do	The Corrs	30	30	1
05.04.98	Give A Little Love	Daniel O'Donnell	10	5	7
11.04.98	Lucille	Kieran Goss	28	22	3
11.04.98	The Celtic Tiger	Brendan Shine	29	21	4
18.04.98	A Mother's Love	Jimmy Buckley	21	17	5
25.04.98	All That I Need	Boyzone	1	1	7
25.04.98	Blow Your Mind	Dove	19	19	1
25.04.98	Mr Sweeney	Kaydee	30	22	3
09.05.98	Dreams	The Corrs	11	6	9
16.05.98	Is Always Over Now	Dawn Martin	24	24	1
23.05.98	The World Is Dead	Juniper	20	19	2
30.05.98	C'est La Vie	B*witched	2	1	17
30.05.98	Breathing But There's No Air	Stand	23	23	3
06.06.98	Do You Love Me Boy?	Kerri Ann	2	2	11
13.06.98	This Is '98	Aslan	7	7	8
13.06.98	She Says	The Saw Doctors	17	17	3
13.06.98	Here To Stay	The Wild Swans	19	19	2
13.06.98	Whatever It Takes	Sinead Lohan	22	16	7
13.06.98	Don't Get Me Wrong	Francis Black	30	22	3
04.07.98	Theme From Green Machine	Green Machine	23	10	5
11.07.98	Seven Days	Kaydee	24	24	1
18.07.98	Candy Store / Showband Shuffle	Showband Show	27	27	1
08.08.98	No Matter What	Boyzone	1	1	8
08.08.98	Let's Go Dancing (Oh La La La)	Carter Twins	9	6	4
29.08.98	Sunburst	Picture House	25	18	5
29.08.98	Come On You Lilywhites	Sean Brennan	21	11	5
19.09.98	Running For A Reason	Kieran Goss	21	21	2
19.09.98	Generation Sex	Divine Comedy	24	24	2
19.09.98	The Rose Of Mooncoin	Darren Holden	28	28	1
26.09.98	Rollercoaster	B*witched	2	2	1
26.09.98	Crazy World '98	Aslan	23	23	1

In addition: *Please* (U2) spent seven weeks in Top 30 from 04.10.97; *Sam Maguire Is Coming Home To Mayo* (Tom Tom & Byrne's Babes) spent one week in Top 30 from 04.10.97; *Picture Of You* (Boyzone) spent one week in Top 30 from 04.10.97; *Turn Around* (Fab) spent one week in Top 30 from 04.10.97. For original date of entry for these singles see *The Irish Almanac & Yearbook of Facts 1998.*

Compiled by ChartTrack on behalf of IRMA. ©

IRISH EUROVISION SONG CONTEST ENTRIES 1965-1998

Year	Venue	Song Title (Ireland)	Irish Performer(s) & Placing	Winning Country
1965	Naples	I'm Walking the Streets in the Rain	Butch Moore (6th)	Luxembourg
1966	Luxembourg	Come Back to Stay	Dickie Rock (=4th)	Austria
1967	Vienna	If I Could Choose	Sean Dunphy (2nd)	United Kingdom
1968	London	Chance of a Lifetime	Pat McGeegan (4th)	Spain
1969	Madrid	The Wages of Love	Muriel Day & The Lindsays (=7th)	*
1970	**Amsterdam**	**All Kinds of Everything**	**Dana (1st)**	Ireland
1971	Dublin	One Day Love	Angela Farrell (11th)	Monaco
1972	Edinburgh	Ceol an Ghrá	Sandie Jones (15th)	Luxembourg
1973	Luxembourg	Do I Dream?	Maxi (=10th)	Luxembourg
1974	Brighton	Cross your Heart	Tina (=7th)	Sweden
1975	Stockholm	That's What Friends are For	Jimmy & Tommy Swarbrigg (9th)	Netherlands
1976	The Hague	When	Red Hurley (10th)	United Kingdom
1977	London	It's Nice to be in Love Again	The Swarbriggs Plus Two (3rd)	France
1978	Paris	Born to Sing	Colm C.T. Wilkinson (5th)	Israel
1979	Jerusalem	Happy Man	Cathal Dunne (5th)	Israel
1980	**The Hague**	**What's Another Year?**	**Johnny Logan (1st)**	Ireland
1981	Dublin	Horoscopes	Sheeba (5th)	United Kingdom
1982	Harrogate	Here Today, Gone Tomorrow	The Duskey's (11th)	Germany
1983	Munich	No Entry		Luxembourg
1984	Luxembourg	Terminal 3	Linda Martin (2nd)	Sweden
1985	Gothenburg	Wait Until the Weekend Comes	Maria Christian (6th)	Norway
1986	Bergen	You can Count on Me	Luv Bug (4th)	Belgium
1987	**Brussels**	**Hold me Now**	**Johnny Logan (1st)**	Ireland
1988	Dublin	Take him Home	Jump The Gun (8th)	Switzerland
1989	Lausanne	The Real Me	Klev Connolly &	
			The Missing Passengers (18th)	Yugoslavia
1990	Zagreb	Somewhere in Europe	Liam Reilly (=2nd)	Italy
1991	Rome	Could it be That I'm in Love	Kim Jackson (=10th)	Sweden
1992	**Malmö**	**Why Me?**	**Linda Martin (1st)**	Ireland
1993	**Cork**	**In your Eyes**	**Niamh Kavanagh (1st)**	Ireland
1994	**Dublin**	**Rock 'n' Roll Kids**	**Paul Harrington &**	
			Charlie McGettigan (1st)	Ireland
1995	Dublin	Dreamin'	Eddie Friel (14th)	Norway
1996	**Oslo**	**The Voice**	**Eimear Ouinn (1st)**	Ireland
1997	Dublin	Mysterious Woman	Marc Roberts (2nd)	United Kingdom
1998	Birmingham	Is Always Over Now	Dawn Martin (9th)	Israel

*Spain, UK, Netherlands, France

MAJOR CONCERT VENUES IN THE ISLAND OF IRELAND

Croke Park Dublin
Capacity: 68,000
Semple Stadium Thurles
Capacity: 59,000
Lansdowne Road Dublin
Tel: (01) 6689300.
Capacity: 50,000
Pairc Ui Chaoimh Cork
Capacity: 50,000
Point Depot Dublin
Tel: (01) 8366777. Capacity: 7,500
King's Hall Belfast
Tel: (01232) 665225
Capacity: 7,000
Neptune Stadium Cork
Tel: (021) 395873. Capacity: 2,500
Waterfront Hall Belfast
Tel: (01232) 334400
Capacity: 2,235
National Stadium Dublin

Tel: (01) 4533371. Capacity: 2,200
Olympia Theatre Dublin
Tel: (01) 4782153. Capacity: 1,300
Leisureland Galway
Tel: (091) 521455. Capacity: 1,250
National Concert Hall Dublin
Tel: (01) 6711533. Capacity: 1,200
R.D.S. Dublin
Tel: (01) 6680866. Capacity: 1,200
Ulster Hall Belfast
Tel: (01232) 323900
Capacity: 1,200.
City Hall Cork
Tel: (021) 966222. Capacity: 1,200
S.F.X. Centre Dublin
Tel: (01) 2841747. Capacity: 1,000
Cork Opera House Cork
Tel: (021) 270021. Capacity: 1,000
University of Limerick Concert Hall Limerick

Tel: (061) 331549. Capacity: 1,000
Seapoint Leisure Centre Galway
Tel: (091) 521716. Capacity: 1,000
Rialto Entertainment Centre Derry
Tel: (01504) 260516. Capacity: 950
Connolly Hall Cork
Tel: (021) 277466. Capacity: 800
Mean Fiddler Dublin
Tel: (01) 4758555. Capacity: 700
Bad Bob's Dublin
Tel: (01) 6792992. Capacity: 500
Rotterdam Warehouse Belfast
(01232) 352864. Capacity: 450
Riverside Theatre Coleraine
Tel: (01265) 324683. Capacity: 380

MAJOR CONCERTS HELD IN IRELAND 1998

Date	Artiste	Venue	Venue Capacity	Ticket price
20 Jan	Ocean Colour Scene	Leisureland, Galway	1,250*	£16.50+
31 Jan	Max Levinson	National Concert Hall, Dublin	1,200	£5.00+
04 Feb	Primal Scream	Olympia Theatre, Dublin	1,300	£13.50+
05 Feb	Primal Scream	Leisureland, Galway	1,250*	£12.50
05-12 Feb	Christy Moore	Olympia Theatre,	1,300	£15.00+
13 Feb	Ocean Colour Scene	The Point Theatre, Dublin	7,500	£16.50+
21 Feb	Childline 10th Birthday Celebration (various)	The Point Theatre, Dublin	7,500	£16.50
24 Feb	The Spice Girls	The Point Theatre, Dublin	7,500	
05-07 Mar	Christy Moore	Leisureland, Galway	1,250*	£16.50+
06 Mar	Massive Attack	Olympia Theatre, Dublin	1,300	£15.50+
08 Mar	Genesis	The Point Theatre, Dublin	7,500	£27.50+
17 Mar	Shane McGowan & The Popes / Kelly Family	The Point Theatre, Dublin	7,500	
17 Mar	Shane McGowan & The Popes / Kelly Family	The Point Theatre, Dublin	7,500	
24 Mar	Errol Brown	Olympia Theatre, Dublin	1,300	£18.50+
28/29 Mar	Gary Barlow / Kinane	Olympia Theatre, Dublin	1,300	
05 Apr	Echo & The Bunnymen	Olympia Theatre, Dublin	1,300	£14.50+
15/16 Apr	Massive Attack	Olympia Theatre, Dublin	1,300	£14.50+
16 Apr	The Mavericks	Ulster Hall, Belfast	1,200	£22.50
17 Apr	The Mavericks	Olympia Theatre, Dublin	1,300	£15.50+
19 Apr	Kieran Goss	Olympia Theatre, Dublin	1,300	
02 May	Texas	The Courtyard, Dublin Castle	-	
02 May	Kula Shaker / Junkster	Botanic Gardens	-	£17.50
03 May	Kula Shaker	The Courtyard, Dublin Castle	-	
03 May	Finley Quaye	Botanic Gardens, Belfast	-	
04 May	Finley Quaye	The Courtyard, Dublin Castle	-	
09 May	Celebrity Concert (Final Concert)	National Concert Hall, Dublin	1,200	£10.00+
15 May	Lighthouse Family	The Point Theatre, Dublin	7,500	£19.50+
19 May	U2 / Ash	The Waterfront Hall, Belfast	2,000†	Free
19/20 May	The Verve	Point Theatre, Dublin	7,500†	£22.50
22 May	Finbar Wright	Avondale Forest Park, Wicklow	-	
27 May	Elton John	Stormont Castle, Belfast	15,000†	£25.00+
29/30 May	Elton John / Billy Joel	Croke Park, Dublin	80,000†	
05 Jun	Aslan	Olympia Theatre, Dublin	1,300	£10.50+
13 Jun	Phil Coulter and his Orchestra	National Concert Hall, Dublin	1,200	
19 Jun	Bob Dylan / Van Morrison	Botanic Gardens, Belfast	-	£25.00+
26/27 Jun	Michael Flatley - Lord Of The Dance	RDS, Dublin	7,000	£19.50+
1-25 Jul	Grease	The Point Theatre, Dublin	7,500	£10.00+
7-8 Jul	Simple Minds	Olympia Theatre, Dublin	1,300	£20.00+
9 Jul	Ash	Olympia Theatre, Dublin	1,300	£14.50+
11 Jul	Big Day Out (various)	Castlegar Sportsground, Galway	20,000†	£29.50
14 Jul	Kodó / Donal Lunny Band	RDS Main Hall, Dublin	7,000	£15.50+
19 Jul	Sinead Lohan	Olympia Theatre, Dublin	1,300	£9.50+
19 Jul	Coolio	The Waterfront Hall, Belfast	2,235	£10.00+
27 Jul	B.B. King	The Point Theatre, Dublin	7,500	£28.50
28 Jul	B.B. King	The Waterfront Hall, Belfast	2,235	
31 Jul	Fun Lovin' Criminals	Killyleagh Castle, Down	-	£15.00+
01 Aug	Paul Weller / Fun Lovin' Criminals	The Point Theatre, Dublin	7,500	£22.50+
02 Aug	Ash	Killyleagh Castle, Down	-	£15.00+
04 Aug	Brian Kennedy	National Concert Hall, Dublin	1,200	
07/08 Aug	Paul Young	Olympia Theatre, Dublin	1,300	£14.50+
20 Aug	Ringo Starr & His All Star Band	The Point Theatre, Dublin	7,500	£22.50+
21 Aug	James Brown	The Point Theatre, Dublin	7,500	£20.00+
24 Aug	James Brown	The Waterfront Hall, Belfast	2,235	££19.50+
26 Aug	Robert Plant & Jimmy Page	The Point Theatre, Dublin	7,500	£23.00+
29 Aug	The Verve, Manic Street Preachers, Robbie Williams	Slane Castle	80,000	£29.50
29 Aug	Bee Gees	RDS, Dublin	7,000	
30 Aug	Manic Street Preachers	Ulster Hall, Belfast	1,200	
21 Sep.	The Mavericks	RDS Main Hall, Dublin	7,000	£19.50
22 Sep	The Mavericks / Havana Horns	The Waterfront Hall, Belfast	2,235	
24 Sep	Luka Bloom	Olympia Theatre, Dublin	1,300	
27 Sep	David Essex	The Waterfront Hall, Belfast	2,235	£18.00+

1,250 (standing), 1,050 (seated);   • Simmonscourt Pavilion (7,000), Concert Hall (1,200);   † concert attendance;

IRISH NATIONAL LOTTERY FACT FILE 1997

Chairman ....John Hynes (Chief Executive, An Post)	Lotto 5-4-3-2-1 sales (launched Feb. 1997) .....IR£9.6m
National Lottery Director ....Ray Bates	Instant game sales ....IR£101.1 million
Total sales ....IR£324.3 million	Instant game players winnings................IR£55 million
Total prizes ....IR£167 million	Total operating costs ....IR£50.1 million
Operating expenses ....IR£50.1 million	Allocated to sport ....IR£12.9 million
Surplus for beneficiary projects ....IR£107 million	Largest jackpot..IR£6.2 million
Lotto sales ....IR£213.7 million	Printing, marketing & distribution costs ....IR£8,842,435

LOTTERY GRANTS BY GOVERNMENT DEPT. 1987-96

DEPT.	1987	1988	1989	1990	1991	1992
Finance			28,946	107,538	71,202	366,000
OPW		1,736,913	1,497,000	2,441,000	1,366,000	1,296,000
Environment	350,000	6,122,795	5,335,678	4,948,123	6,536,151	5,964,969
Education	3,588,794	21,637,746	22,231,485	28,051,151	28,993,454	28,640,305
Defence			620,000	670,000	704,000	1,026,000
Foreign Affairs		319,186	529,883	438,096	422,521	212,864
Int. Co-operation		800,000			690,000	0
Social Welfare		850,000	900,000	750,000	2,360,000	3,485,000
Health	3,357,500	6,412,634	7,120,741	8,671,950	28,135,000	41,292,000
Arts/Cult./Gael.			2,948,000		0	0
Heritage Co.		109,093	273,236	596,514	1,020,753	1,435,504
National Gallery				99,216	36,794	231,373
Arts Council	1,800,000	1,880,000		4,948,000	4,988,000	4,988,000
Trans/Ener/Comm					0	2,965,000
Taoiseach	1,347,852	2,711,987	2,035,020	3,328,404	4,346,036	4,268,913
Tourism & Trans				558,000	442,000	0
Communications				500,000	999,391	0
Gaeltacht		836,937	3,370,563	4,111,650	3,912,449	0
Agriculture					940,581	0
TOTAL:	10,444,146	43,417,291	46,890,552	60,219,642	85,964,332	96,171,928

DEPT.	1993	1994	1995	1996	TOTAL
Finance	100,000	98,000	358,943	94,077	1,224,706
OPW	80,000	753,000	1,150,000	378,755	10,698,668
Environment	784,968	3,540,000	6,290,000	6,600,000	50,472,684
Education	30,406,537	36,969,383	33,008,475	36,027,295	269,554,625
Defence	1,078,000	1,050,000	1,194,000	1,328,000	7,670,000
Foreign Affairs	212,468	250,000	219,991	179,959	2,784,968
Int. Co-operation	0	0	0	1,000,000	2,490,000
Social Welfare	4,729,000	4,728,000	4,430,000	4,460,084	26,692,084
Health	29,436,000	30,012,000	22,181,000	22,144,000	198,762,825
Arts/Cult./Gael.	8,907,736	74,964,19	8,520,927	10,312,895	38,185,977
Heritage Co.	1,265,722	1,544,372	1,560,820	1,796,150	9,602,164
Nat Gallery	83,275	201,305	227,855	191,897	1,071,715
Arts Council	988,000	4,728,000	3,707,000	3,970,000	35,997,000
Trans/Ener/Comm	729,000	0	0	0	3,694,000
Taoiseach	0	0	0	0	18,038,212
Tourism & Trans	0	0	0	0	1,000,000
Communications	0	0	0	0	1,499,391
Gaeltacht	0	0	0	0	12,231,599
Agriculture	0	0	0	0	940,581
TOTAL:	86,800,706	91,370,479	82,849,011	88,483,112	692,611,199

IRISH NATIONAL LOTTERY FUND EXPENDITURE

Sector	1997 (IR£m)	1987-97 (IR£m)	1987-97 (%)
Youth, Sports, Recreational, Amenities	30.415	263.516	33
Arts, Culture, National Heritage	24.345	195.615	25
Health and Welfare	36.773	277.869	35
Irish Language	7.341	59.312	7
TOTAL:	98.874	796.132	100

MEDIA

A Good Year for the Media

By *Charlie Bird, RTÉ Special Correspondent*

WE can all bask, to some extent, in the reflected glory of the Nobel Peace Prize going to the SDLP leader, John Hume and the Unionist leader, David Trimble. In no small way the media in Ireland, and more especially the media in the North have a right to clap themselves on the back for getting the peace process to where it is today. A strong, vibrant and independent media is good for democracy and over the past few years the fourth estate has played an important role in questioning, cajoling and pushing the peace process forward.

For my journalist colleagues in the North the long days and nights spent outside Castle Buildings in Stormont were well worth it. All the waiting, all the exposure, all the analysis undoubtedly helped the democratic process.

In the past the coming together of the *Irish News* and the *Newsletter* to pen joint editorials were in themselves journalistic and, to some extent, historical landmarks which all of us should be proud of.

This year, as a journalist from the South, I happened to be on duty in Derry on the Sunday that the three Quinn children were burned to death in their home in Ballymoney. On that early Sunday morning, in the pouring rain, I watched many of my journalistic colleagues at work in the small housing estates where the vicious sectarian murder attack occurred. For many of them, hardened by years of reporting the tragedy of Northern Ireland, I could see the despair in their faces reporting the ghastly events of what happened in Ballymoney. There was no rivalry between the various media organisations that morning; we shared information, we helped one and other. The grim task of getting the names of the Quinn children right, their ages, all part of a days reporting. Who could forget, who should forget the names of Richard, Mark and Jason.

A few months later I found myself in Omagh, this time for the visit of President Clinton and Tony Blair to the site of the bomb blast where just a few short weeks before twenty nine people were murdered and scores others injured. It was a beautiful sunny day, and despite the earlier horror which had occurred, I felt a great sense of friendship with many of my colleagues from the North. Despite all the horrors they've been through, once again they were more than happy to share information, to point one, if necessary, in the right direction, to share a joke together and to laugh together.

It has surely been a good year for the media. Colleagues, on the day John Hume and David Trimble receive their Nobel Peace Prize in Stockholm, go into a pub and have a celebrity drink yourselves, you deserve it. Raise a glass also to absent friends and colleagues long gone, who over the years, reported faithfully the unfolding events in Northern Ireland.

If its been a good year for the media in the North, it hasn't been a bad year either for journalism in the South.

The body politic in the South has been going through a sort of catharsis what with the various financial scandals and the multitude of inquiries into them.

Most, if not all of these inquiries, have been prompted by media revelations. For many years most people felt that they were being hoodwinked by their local branch manager. Now they know it for sure. Its official, much of the evidence having being provided by the banks themselves.

Early in 1998 came the revelations from RTE that National Irish Bank had set up an off-shore scheme back in the early nineties to help some of its customers, who had bogus accounts, to evade paying tax.

In March came further revelations that, at least, half a dozen National Irish Bank branches had, in all but name, been stealing money from some of their own customers.

Further amazing media revelations followed. In April the *Sunday Independent* broke a story that the largest bank in the country, Allied Irish Banks, had a staggering fifty three thousand bogus non-resident accounts in their branch network in the late eighties and the early nineties. At the time the paper valued the money in these accounts in the region of 600 million pounds.

But worse was to follow. In October, the *Magill* Magazine got hold of internal Allied Irish Banks documentation which showed that the bank itself had accepted in 1991 that it had a liability, on behalf of its customers, to pay around one hundred million pounds in DIRT tax. The correspondence also revealed that a secret deal appeared to have been done between the bank and the Revenue Commissioners to turn a blind eye to the non payment of DIRT tax. The loss to the state coffers according to the banks own evidence was a whopping eighty six million pounds.

Not for the first time in the past few years had the media across the board brought valuable information to light on behalf of the ordinary citizen on the street.

An opinion poll in a Sunday newspaper towards the end of the year came up with a rather strange finding. Of those questioned it showed that journalists, believe it or believe it not, had more credibility with the public than any other group, including the clergy and yes, politicians. What a strange world we live in. Alas, we journalists must be careful not to take ourselves too seriously. But the digging and investigations should continue.

The two Tribunals which are already under way in the South, the Moriarty Tribunal into the murky financial affairs of the former Taoiseach Charles Haughey and former Government Minister, Michael Lowry and the Flood Tribunal into possible planning irregularities in the North County Dublin area - were both prompted by dogged journalistic digging by Correspondent's from *The Irish Times*, the *Sunday Independent* and the *Sunday Business Post*.

With these two Tribunals still bogged down in legal wrangling, journalists have been the told on more than one occasion that they should butt out and not continue chipping away and let the Tribunals do their work. But if the journalists had butted out in the first instance, then the scandals which these tribunals are now trying to get to the bottom of may never have come to light in the first place.

Keep up the good work lads and lassies. Everyone knows there is more to come out.

❑

The author is Special Correspondent with RTÉ, and, with colleague George Lee, was instrumental in exposing the National Irish Bank scandal earlier this year.

TELEVISION

NATIONAL TELEVISION STATIONS FACTFILES

RADIO TELEFÍS ÉIREANN:
Founded: 1961. **Number of channels:** (3) RTÉ 1, Network 2, TnaG (see profile below). **Address:** Donnybrook, Dublin 4. **Contact Numbers: Tel.:** (01) 2083111. Fax: (01) 2086080. **Chairman:** Farrel Corcoran. **Director-General:** Bob Collins. **Director of Television:** Joe Mulholland. **Director of News:** Edward Mulhall. **Output:** 200 hours per week - 50% home-produced. **RTÉ 1:** 24hrs x 7 days; **Network 2:** 18hrs x 7 days. **Number of Regional Studios:** 8. **International offices:** (3) London, Washington D.C., Brussels.

TEILIFÍS NA GAEILGE
Founded: 1996. **Address:** Baile na hAbhainn, Co. na Gaillimhe. **Contact Numbers: Tel.:** (091) 505050. Fax: (091) 505021. **Ceannasaí:** Cathal Goan. **Output:** 45 hours per week.

TV3 TELEVISION NETWORK LIMITED
Founded: 1998. **Address:** Unit 5, Westgate Business Park, Ballymount, Dublin 24. **Contact Numbers: Tel.:** (01) 4193333. Fax: (01) 4193300. **Chairman:** James Morris. **Managing-Director:** Rick Hetherington. **Director of Operations:** Peter Ennis. **Director of Sales:** Pat Kiely. **Director of News:** Andrew Hanlon. **Director of Television Programmes:** Michael Murphy. **Output:** 100 hours per week.

BRITISH BROADCASTING CORPORATION (N.I.)
Founded: 1924. **Number of channels:** (1) BBC Northern Ireland. **Address:** Broadcasting House, Ormeau Avenue, Belfast BT2 8HQ. **Contact Numbers: Tel.:** (01232) 338000. Fax: (01232) 338800. **Controller:** Patrick Loughrey. **Head of Broadcast:** Anna Carragher. **Head of Production:** Paul Evans. **Head of News & Current Affairs:** Tony Maddox. **Head of Drama:** Robert Cooper. **Total hours of output:** 657 (1996/97). **Number of other Studios:** (1) Foyle, Derry.

ULSTER TELEVISION PLC
Founded: 1959. **Number of channels:** (1) UTV. **Address:** Havelock House, Ormeau Road, Belfast BT7 1EB. **Contact Numbers: Tel:** (01232) 328122. Fax: (01232) 246695. **Managing Director:** J.D. Smyth. **Controller of Programming:** Alan Bremner. **Head of News and Current Affairs:** Rob Morrison. **Output:** 12 hours of home-produced programmes per week. **Other Studios:** (1) Derry.

REPUBLIC OF IRELAND CHANNEL PENETRATION

	RTÉ 1 %	N2 %	TnaG %	BBC 1 %	BBC 2 %	UTV %	C4 %	SKY 1 %	S. News %
Percentage Reception	100	100	59	10	4	10	4	3	9

AUDIENCE SHARE, R.O.I. AND N.I.

	RTÉ 1 %	N2 %	TnaG %	BBC 1 %	BBC 2 %	UTV %	C4 %	SKY 1 %	Others %
Republic of Ireland	44	16	1	10	4	10	4	3	9
Northern Ireland	-	-	-	26	10.4	39.4	11.3	-	12.5

TELEVISION LICENCES BY COUNTY 1998

County	Monochrome	Colour	Total
LEINSTER	5,443	486,749	492,192
Dublin	1,868	280,488	282,356
Carlow	326	12,783	13,109
Kildare	395	32,875	33,270
Kilkenny	281	13,444	13,725
Laois	375	12,798	13,173
Longford	278	7,186	7,464
Louth	359	26,753	27,112

Continued from previous page

County	Monochrome	Colour	Total
Meath	362	19,142	19,504
Offaly	367	15,386	15,753
Westmeath	312	20,314	20,626
Wexford	387	25,658	26,045
Wicklow	133	19,922	20,055
MUNSTER	**5,143**	**262,600**	**267,743**
Clare	592	17,153	17,745
Cork	2,127	101,028	103,155
Kerry	879	29,034	29,913
Limerick	766	53,276	54,042
Tipperary	550	30,020	30,570
Waterford	229	32,089	32,318
CONNACHT	**2,654**	**101,940**	**104,594**
Galway	1,109	41,876	42,985
Leitrim	234	7,725	7,959
Mayo	708	27,537	28,245
Roscommon	386	10,193	10,579
Sligo	217	14,609	14,826
ULSTER *(part of)*	**765**	**49,858**	**50,623**
Cavan	194	6,811	7,005
Donegal	444	33,972	34,416
Monaghan	127	9,075	9,202
TOTAL (R.O.I.)	**14,005**	**901,147**	**915,152**
NORTHERN IRELAND	**17,431**	**406,185**	**423,616**
TOTAL (all-island)	**31,436**	**1,307,332**	**1,338,768**

RTÉ 1 AND NETWORK 2: AVERAGE DAILY REACH, 1997

Month	Individuals*	Men 15+	Women 15+	Total Adults 15+	Children[†]	Housekeepers
January	72.0	70.4	73.2	71.9	72.7	81.1
February	72.0	69.6	73.7	71.7	73.3	81.7
March	70.5	69.0	71.9	70.5	70.7	79.5
April	68.7	67.9	72.1	70.1	63.6	77.7
May	67.4	67.1	69.8	68.5	63.3	76.3
June	66.1	65.8	67.9	66.9	63.3	73.6
July	62.0	62.3	65.1	63.7	55.7	70.6
August	61.6	62.2	63.6	62.9	56.5	69.4
September	66.9	66.3	69.6	68.0	62.2	75.4
October	69.8	69.2	71.3	70.2	67.8	76.9
November	71.8	69.8	73.6	71.8	72.0	79.3
December	71.3	69.7	72.0	70.9	73.2	76.4
Average	68.3	67.3	70.4	68.9	66.4	76.4

*A. C. Nielsen * Individuals (4+); † Children (4-14);*

30 MOST POPULAR RTÉ 1 PROGRAMMES, 1997

Rank	Programme	Type	Date	Number of viewers
1	Eurovision Song Contest	*Music*	3 May	1,119,000
2	The Late Late Show	*Talk Show*	12 Dec	1,111,000
3	Rose of Tralee	*Beauty Contest*	28 Aug	1,015,000
4	Speed	*Film*	25 Dec	1,020,000
5	Coronation Street	*Soap Opera*	25 Dec	994,000
6	Glenroe	*Soap Opera*	5 Jan	978,000
7	Crimeline	*Crime Solving*	20 Jan	951,000
8	Fair City	*Soap Opera*	25 Dec	947,000

Continued from previous page

Rank	Programme	Type	Date	Number of viewers
9	The Joy	Documentary	10 Feb	878,000
10	Winning Streak	Game Show	27 Dec	855,000
11	Home Alone 2: Lost in New York	Film	25 Dec	839,000
12	Kenny Live	Talk Show	18 Jan	819,000
13	Simpsons	Comedy	25 Dec	816,000
14	Forrest Gump	Film	21 Dec	815,000
15	Keeping Up Appearances	Comedy	27 Apr	802,000
16	Client	Film	30 Dec	802,000
17	Mrs. Doubtfire	Film	29 Mar	783,000
18	Only Fools and Horses	Comedy	30 Dec	780,000
19	Prime Time	Current Affairs	4 Jan	757000
20	Making the Cut	Drama	5 Oct	753,000
21	River Wild	Film	23 Dec	731,000
22	In the Line of Fire	Film	1 Jan	722,000
23	Vanishing	Film	5 Aug	720,000
24	The Sporting Year	Sport	3 Jan	711,000
25	Beverly Hills Cop	Film	9 Sep	707,000
26	Clear and Present Danger	Film	4 Aug	701,000
27	Thin Blue Line	Sitcom	3 Jan	700,000
28	The Boyz are Back	Music	25 Dec	697,000
29	Fame and Fortune	Game Show	20 Jan	696,000
30	Fawlty Towers	Comedy	3 Aug	691,000

30 MOST POPULAR NETWORK 2 PROGRAMMES, 1997

Rank	Programme	Type	Date	Number of viewers
1	Father Ted	Sitcom	23 Jan	928,000
2	Rep. of Ireland v Belgium	Sport	29 Oct	727,000
3	Home and Away	Soap Opera	20 Jan	709,000
4	Wales v Rep. of Ireland	Sport	11 Feb	663,000
5	Rep. of Ireland v Liechtenstein	Sport	21 May	645,000
6	Belgium v Rep. of Ireland	Sport	15 Nov	625,000
7	Friends	Sitcom	1 Dec	608,000
8	The Sunday Game	Sport	28 Sep	601,000
9	Rep. of Ireland v Lithuania	Sport	20 Aug	558,000
10	Romania v Rep. of Ireland	Sport	30 Apr	527,000
11	The Sunday Game	Sport	14 Sep	498,000
12	Lithuania v Rep. of Ireland	Sport	10 Sep	492,000
13	Jaws	Film	12 Feb	452,000
14	Dr. No	Film	8 Jan	445,000
15	Carlito's Way	Film	2 Jan	438,000
16	Money Pit	Film	26 Feb	433,000
17	X-Files	Drama	21 Jan	433,000
18	Champions League	Sport	5 Mar	420,000
19	G'day Summer Bay	Documentary	1 Jan	420,000
20	IRMA Music Awards	Music	24 Feb	419,000
21	Riverdance	Music	17 Mar	409,000
22	You Only Live Twice	Film	22 Jan	405,000
23	Ireland v Macedonia	Sport	2 Apr	398,000
24	Who Do They Think They Are?		28 Nov	394,000
25	Top Thirty Hits	Music	24 Nov	394,000
26	Roseanne	Sitcom	11 Feb	387,000
27	From Russia With Love	Film	15 Jan	384,000
28	Blackboard Jungle	Quiz Show	10 Feb	377,000
29	Diamonds are Forever	Film	5 Feb	371,000
30	Only Fools and Horses	Comedy	14 Dec	370,000

10 MOST POPULAR TnaG PROGRAMMES, WEEK BEGINNING 28TH SEPTEMBER 1998

Rank	Programme	Type	Date	Number of viewers
1	Féilte	-	28 Sep	43,000
2	Christy Ring	Documentary	29 Sep	41,000
3	Late Late Movie	Film	28 Sep	32,000
4	Nationwide	Current Affairs	19 Sep	27,000
5	Olé Olé	Sport	29 Sep	24,000
6	Ros na Rún	Soap Opera	4 Oct	23,000
	Late Late Movie	Film	30 Sep	23,000
7	Nationwide	Current Affairs	3 Oct	22,000
8	Pop TV Togha	Music	4 Oct	21,000
	Late Late Movie	Film	2 Oct	21,000
9	Cleamhnas	-	2 Oct	20,000
	Nuacht TnaG	News	3 Oct	20,000
	Late Late Movie	Film	3 Oct	20,000
10	Nuacht TnaG	News	28 Sep	19,000

TELEVISION ADVERTISING RATES

Station (Rate in bracket)	10 secs £	20 secs £	30 secs £	40 secs £	50 secs £	60 secs £
RTÉ1 and **Network 2** (prime rate)	2,250	4,000	5,000	6,650	8,350	10,000
RTÉ 1 and **Network 2** (bottom rate)	23	40	50	67	84	100
TnaG (single slot)	60	80	100	-	-	-
UTV (prime rate)	563-900	938-1500	1125-2025	-	-	-
UTV (bottom rate)	75-169	125-287	150-338	-	-	-

PRINT

PROFILE OF NATIONAL AND PROVINCIAL PAPERS

NATIONAL (DAILY) NEWSPAPERS

Title	Est'd.	Main Area Served	Circulation	Tel. No.	Editor
Belfast Telegraph*	1870	Northern Ireland	130,756	(01232) 264000	Edmund Curran
Examiner, The*	1841	Rep. of Ire.	56,900	(021) 272722	Brian Looney
Evening Echo*	1879	Cork	26,924	(021) 272722	Brian Feeney
Evening Herald*	1891	Rep. of Ire.	110,416	(01) 8731666	Paul Drury
Irish Independent*	1905	Rep. of Ire.	162,064	(01) 8731666	Vincent Doyle
Irish News*	1891	Northern Ireland	50,284	(01232) 322226	Tom Collins
Irish Times, The*	1859	Rep. of Ire.	111,243	(01) 6792022	Conor Brady
Newsletter, The*	1737	Northern Ireland	34,002	(01232) 680000	Geoff Martin
Star, The*	1988	Rep. of Ire.	88,676	(01) 4901228	Gerard O'Regan

NATIONAL (WEEKLY) NEWSPAPERS

Title	Est'd.	Main Area Served	Circulation	Tel. No.	Editor
Sunday Business Post*	1989	Rep. of Ire.	48,637	(01) 6799777	Damien Kiberd
Sunday Independent*	1906	Rep. of Ire.	309,320	(01) 8731666	Aengus Fanning
Sunday Life*		Northern Ireland	103,457	(01232) 330000	Martin Lindsay
Sunday Tribune*	1983	Rep. of Ire.	88,186	(01) 6615555	Matt Cooper
Sunday World †*	1973	Rep. of Ire.	305,105	(01) 4901980	Colm MacGinty
Ireland on Sunday*	1997	Rep. of Ire.	61,204	(01) 6718255	Liam Hayes
Irish Farmers' Journal	1948	Rep. of Ire.	73,979	(01) 4501166	Matt Dempsey
Irish Family, The	1994	Rep. of Ire.	8,000	(044) 42987	Richard Hogan

PROVINCIAL NEWSPAPERS

Title	Est'd.	Main Area Served	Circulation	Tel. No.	Editor
Alpha Newspaper Group*			30,902		
Anglo-Celt, The*	1846	Cavan	15,522	(049) 31100	Johnny O'Hanlon
Antrim Guardian	1970	Antrim	23,500	(01849) 462624	Liam Heffran
Argus, The*		Louth	9,036	(042) 34632	Kevin Mulligan

Title	Est'd.	Main Area Served	Circulation	Tel. No.	Editor
Armagh Observer	1929	Armagh		(018687) 22557	Desmond Mallon
Ballyclare Gazette*			3,025		
Ballymena Chronicle and Antrim Observer		Antrim		(018687) 22557	Desmond Mallon
Ballymena Guardian	1970	Antrim/Co. Derry	24,300	(01266) 41221	Maurice O'Neill
Banbridge Chronicle*	1870	Down	6,326	(018206) 62322	Bryan Hooks
Carrickfergus Advertiser and East Antrim Gazette*		Antrim	2,803	(019603) 63651	Ian Greer
Clare Champion	1903	Clare	20,113	(065) 28105	Gerry Collison
Coleraine Chronicle	1844	Derry	23,000	(01265) 43344	Grant Cameron
Coleraine Times*			6,372		
Connacht Sentinel, The*	1925	Galway	8,313	(091) 567251	John Cunningham
Connacht Tribune, The*	1909	Galway	29,908	(091) 567251	John Cunningham
Connaught Telegraph	1828	Mayo	15,261	(094) 21711	Tom Gillespie
Corkman, The*			6,078		
County Down Spectator	1904	Down	16,000	(01247) 270270	Paul Flowers
Craigavon Echo		Armagh	23,000	(01762) 350041	David Armstrong
Democrat, The		Tyrone		(018687) 22557	Desmond Mallon
Derry Journal (Tue. & Fri.)*	1772	Derry / Donegal	52,349	(01504) 272200	Pat McArt
Derry People/Donegal News*	1901	Donegal		(074) 21014	Columba Gill
Donegal Democrat*	1919	Donegal	16,952	(072) 51201	John Bromley
Donegal Peoples Press*	1932	Donegal	4,341	(074) 21842	Paddy Walsh
Down Recorder*		Down	11,993	(01396) 613711	Paul Symington
Drogheda Independent*	1884	Louth	15,056	(041) 38658	Paul Murphy
Dundalk Democrat*	1849	Louth	16,000	(042) 34058	T.P. Roe
Dungannon News and Tyrone Courier*		Tyrone	14,558	(018687) 22271	R. G. Montgomery
Dungannon Observer		Tyrone		(018687) 22557	Desmond Mallon
Dungarvan Leader and Southern Democrat	1938	Waterford	13,000	(058) 41203	Colm J. Nagle
Dungarvan Observer	1912	Waterford	10,500	(058) 41205	James Lynch
Enniscorthy Guardian Series*			5,824		
Fermanagh Herald		Fermanagh	10,800	(01365) 322066	Dominic McClements
Fermanagh News		Fermanagh		(018687) 22557	Desmond Mallon
Galway Advertiser	1970	Galway	32,000	(091) 567077	Ronnie O'Gorman
Herald and Post Newspapers		Fermanagh	159,000	(01232) 239049	Nigel Tilson
Imokilly People		Cork	8,000	(021) 613333	Patrick O'Connor
Inner City News		Dublin		(01) 8363832	John Hedges
Kerryman, The*		Kerry	28,381	(066) 21666	Ger Colleran
Kerry's Eye	1974	Kerry	17,500	(066) 23199	Padraig Kennelly
Kildare Nationalist		Kildare	10,000	(045) 432147	Eddie Coffey
Kilkenny People*	1892	Kilkenny	16,640	(056) 21015	John Kerry-Keane
Kingdom Newspaper		Kerry	17,924	(064) 31392	John O'Mahony
Laois Nationalist		Laois		(0502) 60265	Eddie Coffey
Larne Gazette Group*			5,828		
Larne Times*			13,539		Hugh Vance
Leader, The*		Down	4,361	(01846) 692217	Carlton Baxtor
Leinster Express	1831	Laois	18,684	(0502) 21666	Teddy Fennelly
Leinster Leader		Kildare	15,440	(045) 897302	Michael Sheeran
Leitrim Observer	1889	Leitrim	9,750	(078) 20025	Anthony Hickey
Liffey Champion		Kildare		(01) 6245533	Vincent Sutton
Limerick Chronicle	1766	Limerick	7,000	(061) 315233	Brendan Halligan
Limerick Leader*	1889	Limerick	26,640	(061) 400400	Brendan Halligan
Lisburn Echo		Antrim	22,614	(01846) 679111	Joseph Fitzpatrick
L'derry/Limavady Sentinel*		Derry	5,315	(01504) 267571	James Cadden
Longford Leader, The		Longford	13,500	(043) 45241	Eugene McGee
Longford News	1936	Longford	24,000	(043) 41147	Paul Healy
Lurgan and Portadown Examiner		Armagh		(018687) 22557	Desmond Mallon
Lurgan Mail*		Armagh	9,594	(01762) 327777	Richard Elliott
Mayo News		Mayo	11,500	(098) 25311	Seán Staunton
Meath Chronicle	1897	Meath	19,320	(046) 21442	Ken Davis

Title	Est'd.	Main Area Served	Circulation	Tel. No.	Editor
Midland Tribune, The*	1881	Offaly	12,000	(0509) 20003	John O'Callaghan
Mid-Ulster Mail*			11,904		
Mid-Ulster Observer		Tyrone		(018687) 22557	Desmond Mallon
Mourne Observer*	1949	Down	12,352	(013967) 22666	Terence Bowman
Munster Express, The*	1859	Waterford	17,909	(051) 872141	Kieran Walsh
Nationalist and Leinster Times	1883	Carlow	15,620	(0503) 31731	Eddie Coffey
Nationalist and Munster Advertiser*		Tipperary	15,788	(052) 22211	Tom Corr
Nenagh Guardian*		Tipperary	7,714	(067) 31214	Gerry Slevin
Newry Reporter, The	1867	Down	16,000	(01693) 67633	D. O'Donnell
Newtownards Spectator		Down	4,000	(01247) 270270	Paul Flowers
Northern Constitution	1876	Derry		(01265) 43344	Grant Cameron
Northern Standard		Monaghan	13,500	(047) 82188	Martin Smyth
Offaly Express		Offaly		(0506) 21744	Teddy Fennelly
Outlook, The		Down	7,500	(018206) 30202	Ken Purdy
People Newspapers*		Wexford	39,386	(053) 22565	Gerard Walsh
Portadown Times*		Armagh	11,804	(01762) 336111	David Armstrong
Roscommon Champion	1927	Roscommon	9,100	(0903) 25051	Paul Healy
Roscommon Herald	1859	Roscommon	15,995	(079) 62004	Christina McHugh
Sligo Champion	1836	Sligo	15,298	(071) 69222	Seamus Finn
Sligo Weekender	1983	Sligo	13,500	(071) 42140	Brian McHugh
Southern Star		Cork	15,600	(028) 21200	Liam O'Regan
Southside People, The		Dublin	59,000	(01) 2942494	Ken Finlay
Strabane Chronicle		Tyrone		(01662) 243444	Paddy Cullen
Strabane Weekly News*	1908	Tyrone	2,170	(01662) 242721	Wesley Atchison
Tipperary Star*	1909	Tipperary	9,842	(0504) 21122	Michael Dundon
Topic Newspapers Ltd.				(044) 48868	Dick Hogan
Tuam Herald	1837	Galway	10,500	(093) 24183	David Burke
Tullamore Tribune, The	1978	Offaly	6,000	(0506) 21152	Ger Scully
Tyrone Constitution, The*	1844	Tyrone	9,847	(01662) 242721	N.F. Armstrong
Tyrone Times*			3,509		
Ulster Farmer		Tyrone		(018687) 22557	D. Mallon
Ulster Gazette and Armagh Standard*	1844	Armagh	10,516	(01861) 522639	Richard Stewart
Ulster Herald	1901	Tyrone		(01662) 243444/5	Paddy Cullen
Ulster Star*		Antrim	13,299	(01846) 679111	David Fletcher
Waterford News & Star	1848	Waterford	16,000	(051) 74951	Peter Doyle
Western People, The	1883	Mayo	23,642	(096) 21188	Terry Reilly
Westmeath Examiner, The	1882	Westmeath	13,600	(044) 48426	Nicholas Nally
Westmeath & Offaly		Westmeath / Offaly	13,788	(0902) 72003	Margaret Grennan
Wexford People*			10,212		
Wicklow People*			17,975		

*refers to the latest figures available from ABC (Jan. to June 1998), all other figures refers to the latest available prior to this period.
† refers to Newspaper Groups.

PROFILE OF PERIODICALS, MAGAZINES, JOURNALS

Title	Est'd.	Published	(issues per yr.) Circulation	Tel. No.	Editor
Accountancy Ireland*	1969	Dublin	(6) 16,298	(01) 6680400	Charles O'Rourke
Administration	1953	Dublin	(4) 1,500	(01) 2697011	Tony McNamara
Afloat		Dublin	(12) 9,000	(01) 2846161	David O'Brien
Africa	1938	Wicklow	150,000	(0508) 73233	Rev. Gary Howley
Aisling Magazine, The		Galway	(4) 1,500	(099) 61245	D. Molloy & T. Harper
Amnesty International	1974	Dublin	(4) 12,000	(01) 6776361	Séamus Shiels
AMT Magazine	1979	Dublin	(12) 4,500	(01) 2800424	John McDonald
Apple Report		Dublin	(4) 6,000	(01) 8303455	Frank Quinn
Archaeology Ireland		Wicklow		(01) 2862649	Dr. Gabriel Cooney
Astronomy & Space	1994	Dublin	(12)	(01) 4598883	David Moore
AudIT	1990	Cork	(6) 750	(021) 313855	Ken Ebbage
Bakery World*		Dublin	(6) 2,004	(01) 2800000	Natasha Swords
Banking Ireland		Dublin	(4) 16,000	(01) 6793311	Sean McQuaid
Béaloideas		Dublin	(1) 1,000		Pádraig Ó Héalaí

Title	Est'd.	Published	(issues per yr.) Circulation	Tel. No.	Editor
Big Issues, The		Dublin	(26)	(01) 8553969	
Books Ireland	1976	Dublin	(9) 3,300	(01) 2692185	Shirley Kelly
Bord Altranais News		Dublin	(4) 50,000	(01) 6760226	Eugene Donoghue
Build		Dublin	(12) 4,000	(01) 6619236	John Low
Bulletin	1856	Dublin	(4) 12,000	(01) 8384164	Tom McSweeney
Business and Exporting	1994	Dublin	(12)	(01) 6713500	Neil Whoriskey
Business and Finance	1964	Dublin	(52) 11,000	(01) 6764587	John McGee
Business Contact	1988	Dublin	(12) 4,500	(01) 8550477	
Business Travel		Dublin	(4) 6,000	(01) 4502954	Michael Flood
Business Ulster		Belfast	(12)	(01232) 663247	Patricia Rainey
Car Driver		Dublin	(12) 9,135	(01) 2600899	Michael Flood
Carsport		Down	10,000	(01846) 619099	Patrick Burns
Catering and Licensing Review*	1975	Belfast	(12) 4,104	(01232) 231634	Kathy Jensen
Certified Accountant	1908	Cork	(12) 65,000	(021) 313855	Brian O'Kane
Checkout*	1966	Dublin	(12) 10,069	(01) 2808415	Mary Brophy
Church of Ireland Gazette		Antrim	(52) 5,000	(01846) 675743	Rev. C. Cooper
Circa Art Magazine		Dublin	(4) 7,000	(01) 6765035	Tanya Kiang
Clár na nÓg		Dublin	(12) 2,000	(01) 4784122	Eamonn Waters
Comhar	1942	Dublin	(12) 2,500	(01) 6785443	Tomás Mac Síomóin
Commercial Law Practitioner	1994	Dublin	(11)	(01) 8730101	Thomas B. Courtney
Communications Today		Dublin	(12) 7,500	(01) 2800424	Paul Golden
Communications Worker	1989	Dublin	(6) 18,000	(01) 8366388	Con Scanlon
ComputerScope	1985	Dublin	(10) 8,000	(01) 8303455	David Darcy
Constabulary Gazette		Belfast	(12) 4,000	(01232) 681371	W. Martin Williams
Construction*		Dublin	(10) 3,414	(01) 6719244	Fergus Farrell
Construction & Property News		Dublin	(24) 5,208	(01) 8556265	
Consultant, The		Dublin	(12)	(01) 6713500	
Consumer Choice		Dublin	(12) 11,000	(01) 6612442	Kieran Doherty
Cosantóir, An	1940	Dublin	(10) 6,000	(01) 8042690	Terry McLaughlin
CPA Journal of Accountancy		Dublin	(4) 3,250	(01) 6767353	Deirdre McDonnell
Dairy & Food Industries Magazine		Dublin	(12) 3,600	(01) 6760280	
Dairy Executive		Dublin	(4) 1,650	(01) 6761989	Noel Wardick
Doctrine and Life		Dublin	(12) 3,000	(01) 8721611	Bernard Treacy
Drystock Farmer		Cork	(4) 4,000	(021) 313855	
d'Side		Dublin	(4) 11,000	(01) 6684966	Melanie Morris
Economic & Social Review, The	1969	Dublin	(4)	(01) 6671525	Dr. Barry/Dr. Tovey
Education Magazine		Dublin	(6)	(01) 6719244	Ruth Walton
Education Today		Dublin	(3) 27,000	(01) 8722533	
Éigse: A Journal of Irish Studies		Dublin	(1)	(01) 7068133	Prof. P. Breatnach
Engineers Journal		Dublin	(12) 12,500	(01) 8550477	Hugh Kane
European Building Magazine		Dublin	(12)	(01) 6767018	
European Industry		Dublin	(11) 11,000	(01) 6603174	
Far East, The	1918	Meath	(8) 152,000	(046) 21525	Rev. Alo Connaughton
Feasta	1948	Cork	(12) 2,500	(01) 4757401	P. Mac Fhearghusa
Finance Magazine	1987	Dublin	(12) 3,000	(01) 6606222	Ken O'Brien
Flaming Arrows		Sligo	(1) 500	(071) 45844	Leo Regan
Fleet Management Magazine		Dublin	(12) 5,300	(01) 4976050	Andy Salter
Food & Wine Magazine, The		Dublin	(6)	(01) 2300322	Jason Cooke
Food Ireland*		Dublin	(12) 2,124	(01) 6719244	Bernard Potter
Fortnight	1970	Belfast	(11) 4,500	(01232) 232353	Robin Wilson
Forum		Dublin	(12) 3,500	(01) 2803967	Geraldine Meagan
Furrow, The		Kildare	(12) 8,000	(01) 6286215	Fr. Ronan Drury
Futura		Dublin	(12) 3,500	(01) 2836782	June Considine
Gaelic Sport	1958	Dublin	(12) 30,000	(01) 8374311	Tommy McQuaid
Gaelic World		Dublin	(12)	(01) 6798655	Mick Dunne
Gaelsport Magazine		Dublin	(12) 15,000	(01) 4784322	Owen McCann
Garage Trader		Armagh	(4) 10,000	(01762) 334272	Lorna Brown
Garda News		Dublin	(12) 5,000	(01) 8309188	Austin Kenny
Garda Review	1923	Dublin	(12) 6,500	(01) 8550477	Andy Needham
Gay Community News	1988	Dublin	(12) 12,000	(01) 6710939	Deborah Ballard
Gazette of the Law Society of Ireland		Dublin	(10) 6,200	(01) 8375018	Barbara Cahalane

Title	Est'd.	Published	(issues per yr.) Circulation	Tel. No.	Editor
Golfer's Companion		Dublin	(6) 7,500	(01) 2804077	Pat Ruddy
Guideline		Dublin	(5) 750	(01) 7083653	L. Jennings
Health and Nutrition		Dublin	(12) 6,000	(01) 6719566	Maura Henderson
Health and Safety		Dublin	(12)	(01) 6713500	
Health Services News	1989	Dublin	(4) 3,000	(01) 2697011	
History Ireland		Dublin	(4) 6,000	(01) 4535730	H. Morgan / T. Graham
Hospital Doctor of Ireland		Dublin	(12) 3,700	(01) 6719566	Jess O'Neil
Hot Press*		Dublin	(24) 20,698	(01) 6795077	Niall Stokes
Hotel and Catering Review	1974	Dublin	(12) 4,123	(01) 2800000	Frank Corr
House and Home		Dublin	(6) 18,000	(01) 8550477	Karen Hesse
ICCL News		Dublin	(3)	(01) 6779813	
.ie		Dublin	(6) 20,000	(01) 4784322	Sheila McDonald
Image*	1975	Dublin	(12) 22,504	(01) 2808415	Jane McDonnell
Incognito		Dublin	(4)	(01) 8532152	Christopher O'Rourke
In Dublin	1976	Dublin	(24) 15,000	(01) 4784322	John Regan
Industry and Commerce		Dublin	(12) 8,500	(01) 6713500	Carol Power
Inside Business	1991	Dublin	(6) 10,000	(01) 8550477	Claire Reilly
Inside Ireland	1978	Dublin	(4) 5,000	(01) 4931906	Brenda Weir
Intercom	1970	Dublin	(12) 7,500	(01) 8788177	K.H. Donlon
In Touch		Dublin	(10) 28,000	(01) 8722533	Sinead Shannon
IPU Review	1976	Dublin	(12) 1,600	(01) 4931801	David Butler
Ireland of the Welcomes	1952	Dublin	(6) 100,000	(01) 6024000	Letitia Pollard
Ireland's Eye		Westmeath	(12)	(044) 48868	
Ireland's Own	1902	Wexford	(52) 50,000	(053) 22155	M. Galvin
Ireland's Transport Journal Export & Freight		Armagh	(8) 8,000	(01762) 334272	
Irish Architect		Dublin	(12) 2,720	(01) 2958115	
Irish Banking Review, The		Dublin	(4)	(01) 6715311	Felix O'Regan
Irish Basketball Magazine		Dublin	(3) 10,000	(01) 2841067	
Irish Brides & Homes Magazine		Dublin	(4) 10,000	(01) 4905504	Ruth Kelly
Irish Bridge Player		Dublin	(12)	(01) 4973648	Eileen Davis
Irish Broker		Dublin	(12) 5,000	(01) 8360366	Frank McQuaid
Irish Building Services News		Dublin	(12) 2,500	(01) 2885001	Pat Lehane
Irish Car		Mayo	(6) 10,000	(096) 70941	
Irish Catholic, The	1888	Dublin	(52) 35,000	(01) 8555619	B. A. Ryan
Irish Competition Law Reports		Wicklow	(12)	(088) 557584	Peter Byrne
Irish Computer	1977	Dublin	(12) 7,400	(01) 2800424	Declan McColgan
Irish Construction Industry Magazine		Dublin	(12) 4,000	(01) 6760280	Tony Cantwell
Irish Criminal Law Journal	1991	Dublin	(2) 450	(01) 8730101	Ivana Bacik
Irish Cycling Review		Dublin	(10) 10,000	(01) 2841067	
Irish Doctor		Dublin	(12)	(01) 6713500	Paul Carson
Irish Electrical Review		Dublin	(12) 3,000	(01) 2836755	
Irish Emigrant	1987	Galway		(091) 569158	Liam Ferrie
Irish Farmers Monthly Journal		Dublin	(12) 24,000	(01) 2893305	Brian Gilsenan
Irish Field, The*		Dublin	(52) 11,309	(01) 6792022	Valentine Lamb
Irish Food		Dublin	(7)	(01) 2893305	Paul O' Grady
Irish Forestry	1942	Wicklow	(2) 600	(01) 2781874	Donal Magner
Irish Geography	1944	Dublin	(2)	(01) 7021143	
Irish Hardware Magazine*		Dublin	(12) 1,934	(01) 2800000	Bridget McAuliffe
Irish Health Professional		Dublin	(6) 5,000	(01) 4924034	Terry Gogan
Irish Historical Studies	1938	Dublin	(2) 1,000	(01) 7021578	Dr. C. Brady & Dr. K. Jeffery
Irish Homes Magazine		Dublin	(4) 18,000	(01) 8780444	Berenice Brindley
Irish Hospital		Dublin	(6) 3,000	(01) 4532497	Lindie Naughton
Irish Journal of Education	1967	Dublin	(1) 1,000	(01) 8373789	Thomas Kellaghan
Irish Journal of European Law	1991	Dublin	(2) 450	(01) 8730101	J. O'Reilly & A.Collins
Irish Journal of Medical Science	1832	Dublin	(4) 1,500	(01) 6767650	Thomas F. Gorey
Irish Journal of Psychological Medicine		Dublin	(4) 3,000	(01) 2803967	Brian Lawlor
Irish Journal of Psychology, The	1971	Belfast	(4)	(01232) 245133	Carol McGuinness
Irish Law Reports Monthly	1981	Dublin	(14) 750	(01) 8730101	Hilary Delany
Irish Law Times	1983	Dublin	(12) 750	(01) 8730101	Raymond Byrne

Title	Est'd.	Published	(issues per yr.) Circulation	Tel. No.	Editor
Irish Marketing Journal		Dublin	(12) 4,500	(01) 2950088	Norman Barry
Irish Medical Journal		Dublin	(8) 4,875	(01) 6767273	Dr. John Murphy
Irish Medical News*		Dublin	(52) 6,841	(01) 2960000	Niall Hunter
Irish Medical Times*	1967	Dublin	(52) 7,397	(01) 4757461	Maureen Browne
Irish Motor Industry		Dublin		(01) 2893305	Paul O'Grady
Irish Music		Dublin	(12) 8,500	(01) 6624887	Ronan Nolan
Irish Pharmacy Journal	1923	Dublin	(12) 2,100	(01) 6600699	Val Harte
Irish Planning and Environmental Law Journal	1994	Dublin	(4) 300	(01) 8730101	Eamon Galligan
Irish Political Studies	1986	Limerick	(1) 600	(061) 333644	R. Jay / B. Girvin
Irish Post	1970	Middlesex	(52) 75,000	(0181) 5610059	Donal Mooney
Irish Printer*		Dublin	(12) 1,866	(01) 2800000	Frank Corr
Irish Psychologist, The	1974	Dublin	(12) 1,000	(01) 8326656	Chris Morris
Irish Pub & Restaurateur		Dublin	(12)	(01) 2808880	
Irish Racquets Review		Dublin	(3)	(01) 2841067	
Irish Reporter, The		Dublin		(01) 8745158	
Irish Review, The	1986	Belfast	(2)	(01232) 273235	Kevin Barry
Irish Roots		Cork	(4)	(021) 500067	Tony McCarthy
Irish Rugby Review		Dublin	(12) 11,000	(01) 2841067	
Irish Runner		Dublin	(6) 10,000	(01) 4922413	Frank Greally
Irish Scientist, The		Dublin	(1) 8,000	(01) 2896186	Dr. C. Mollan
Irish Skipper, The	1964	Dublin	(12)	(01) 2960000	Fiacc O'Brolchain
Irish Soccer Magazine		Dublin	(12) 13,000	(01) 2841067	
Irish Social Worker		Dublin	(4) 700	(01) 6774838	Kieran McGrath
Irish Sword, The	1949	Dublin	(2) 1,000		Dr. H. Murtagh.
Irish Tax Review		Dublin	(6) 4,500	(01) 6688222	
Irish Theological Quarterly	1906	Kildare	(4) 1,000	(01) 6285222	Vincent Twomey
Irish Travel Trade News		Dublin	(12) 2,000	(01) 4502422	Michael Flood
Irish Tyre Trade Journal		Mayo	(4) 3,000	(096) 70941	
Irish University Review		Dublin	(2)		Anthony Roche
Irish Veterinary Journal		Dublin	(12) 2,300	(01) 2893305	Gemma Tuffy
Irish Wedding & New Home		Dublin	(4) 12,000	(01) 6719566	Vanessa Harris
Irish Woman		Louth	(4) 5,000	(041) 22119	James Creed
Irish YouthWork Scene		Dublin	(4) 600	(01) 8729933	Fran Bissett
IT Magazine (Irish Tatler)		Dublin	(12) 156,000	(01) 6623158	Morag Prunter
Journal of the Irish Dental Association		Dublin	(4)	(01) 2830499	Dr. Seamus O'Hickey
Law Society Gazette*		Dublin	(12) 83,732	(01) 6710711	Conal O'Boyle
Leabharlann, An		Wexford	(4) 1,100	(053) 42211	L. Ronayne & K. Quinn
Licensed and Catering News*	1994	Belfast	(12) 4,164	(01232) 230425	Geoff McCartney
Licensing World	1942	Dublin	(12) 4,000	(01) 2800000	Pat Nolan
Local Authority Times	1986	Dublin	(4) 3,000	(01) 6686233	E. MacCafferty
Magill	*1977	Dublin	(12)	(01) 6703488	John Ryan
Management	1954	Dublin	(12) 7,078	(01) 2800000	Sandra O'Connell
Manufacturing Ireland		Dublin	(12) 6,500	(01) 8744180	
Marketing*		Dublin	(12) 40,168	(01) 2807735	Michael Cullen
Meat Matters		Dublin	(4) 4,000	(01) 2893305	
Medical Missionaries of Mary Magazines		Dublin	(4) 15,000	(01) 2887180	Sr. Isabelle Smyth
Medicine Weekly		Dublin	(52) 5,000	(01) 6719566	
Medico-Legal Journal of Ireland	1995	Dublin	(3) 150	(01) 8730101	Dr. Denis Cusack
Metre		Dublin	(3) 750		J. Quinn & D. Wheatley
Milltown Studies	1978	Dublin	(2) 1,000	(01) 2698802	Gervase Corcoran
Modern Medicine of Ireland		Dublin	(12) 5,000	(01) 6719566	Maura Henderson
Modern Woman		Meath	(12) 29,331	(046) 21442	Margot Davis
Motoring Life	1946	Dublin	(12) 9,500	(01) 8780444	Fergal K. Herbert
New Engineering		Dublin	(4) 14,000	(01) 8550477	Hugh Kane
New Irish Optician		Dublin	(6) 4,000	(01) 2960000	Brian McCarthy
New Music News		Dublin	(3)	(01) 6612105	Eve O'Kelly
Northern Business Mail		Belfast	(6) 12,000	(01232) 319008	Joan Arthurs
Northern Ireland Legal Quarterly	1964	Belfast	(4) 700	(01232) 335224	Dr. Peter Ingram
Northern Woman		Belfast	(12) 10,000	(01232) 681914	Claire Shiells

Title	Est'd.	Published	(issues per yr.) Circulation	Tel. No.	Editor
Oblate Missionary Record	1891	Dublin	(12) 10,000	(01) 4542417	Fr. J. Archbold
Off Licence		Dublin	(6) 5,000	(01) 2800000	Natasha Swords
Outlook		Dublin	(6) 35,000	(01) 2881789	Rev. Brian Gogan
Patrol		Dublin	(12) 22,000	(01) 6719566	Karina Colgan
PC Live!	1994	Dublin	(12) 16,000	(01) 8303455	John Collins
Phoblacht, An/Republican News		Dublin	(52) 24,000	(01) 8733611	Mícheál Mac Donnaha
Phoenix*	1983	Dublin	(24) 21,013	(01) 6611062	Paddy Prendiville
Pioneer	1948	Dublin	(11) 16,500	(01) 8749464	
Plan-The Business of Building		Dublin	(12)	(01) 2958115	Emer Hughes
Plantman		Dublin	(12) 4,500	(01) 4520898	Patrick J. Murphy
Poetry Ireland Review		Dublin	(4) 1,000	(01) 6714632	Frank Ormsby
Presbyterian Herald	1943	Belfast	(10) 17,500	(01232) 322284	Rev. Arthur Clarke
Public Sector Times		Wicklow	(12) 17,000	(01) 2869111	James D. Fitzmaurice
Public Service Review		Dublin	(6) 6,000	(01) 6767271	Tom McKevitt
Reality	1935	Dublin	(11) 20,000	(01) 4922488	Fr. Gerard Moloney
Recover	1968	Dublin	(4)	(01) 2882873	Fr. G. Price
Religious Life Review		Dublin	(6) 3,000	(01) 8731355	Austin Flannery
Retail News*		Dublin	(10) 4,563	(01) 6719244	
RTÉ Guide*	1961	Dublin	(52) 155,896	(01) 2083111	Heather Parsons
Running Your Business		Dublin	(6) 30,000	(01) 2962244	
Runway Airports	1970	Dublin	(6) 5,500	(01) 7044170	Brian McCabe
Sacred Heart Messenger, The	1988	Dublin	(12) 180,000	(01) 6767491	Brendan Murray
Salesian Bulletin, The	1939	Dublin	(4) 20,000	(01) 4560921	Eddie Fitzgerald
Scouting Ireland / SAI News		Dublin	(5) 10,000	(01) 10,000	Fiona Sullivan
Scripture in Church		Dublin	(4) 5,200	(01) 8721611	Martin McNamara
Search		Dublin	(2) 7000	(01) 4972821	Rev. S. R. White
Security World		Dublin		(01) 2833500	A. Mortell
Seirbhís Phoilblí		Dublin	(2) 3,000	(01) 6767571	Breda Byrne
Shelflife	1975	Dublin	(12) 11,301	(01) 2800424	Colette O'Connor
SMA Magazine - The African Missionary	1914	Cork	(5) 39,000	(021) 292871	Fr. Peter McCawille
Social & Personal		Dublin	(12) 21,000	(01) 6620500	Nell Stewart-Liberty
Socialist Voice		Dublin	(24)	(01) 6711943	
Specify*	1979	Belfast	(6) 4,202	(01232) 231634	Brian Russell
Sporting Press		Tipperary	(52) 8,000	(052) 21422	Jerry Desmond
Sportsworld		Dublin	(12) 18,000	(01) 8721414	David Guiney
Steering Wheel		Dublin	(1) 15,000	(01) 4924034	Derek H. Farrell
Student Voice, The		Dublin	(8) 15,000	(01) 6710088	Anna Kenny
Studies		Dublin	(4)	(01) 6766785	Noel Barber
Technology Ireland		Dublin	(10) 5,000	(01) 8082287	T. Kennedy & M. Mulvihill
This is Ulster		Belfast	(12) 12,000	(01232) 681371	P. Rainey
Today's Farm	1990	Dublin	(6) 35,000	(01) 4515459	
Trade-Links Journal	1979	Dublin	(6) 3,750	(01) 4542717	Cathal Tyrrell
TV Week		Dublin	(52) 15,000	(01) 2840266	Ken Finlay
U Magazine	1979	Dublin	(12) 21,000	(01) 6623158	Maura O'Kiely
Ulster Business*	1987	Belfast	(12) 5,117	(01232) 231634	Richard Buckley
Ulster Business Journal		Belfast	(12) 5,000	(01232) 681671	
Ulster Countrywoman		Belfast	(12) 6,500	(01232) 301506	Mildred Brown
Ulster Farmer		Tyrone	(52)	(018687) 22557	D. Mallon
Ulster Grocer*	1972	Belfast	(12) 4,277	(01232) 231634	Brian McCalden
Ulster Tatler*		Belfast	(12) 12,378	(01232) 681371	R. M. Sherry
Unity & Socialist Voice		Dublin	(52)	(01) 6711943	James Stewart
Vintner, The		Dublin	(12)	(01) 2808880	
Walking World Ireland		Dublin	(6)	(01) 4923030	Martin Joyce
Wings Magazine	1974	Dublin	(4) 5,000	(01) 2804322	C. Mac Lochlainn
Woman's Way		Dublin	(52) 67,300	(01) 6623158	Celine Naughton
Women's Clubs Magazine		Dublin	(4) 10,000	(01) 4924034	June Cooke

Title	Est'd.	Published	(issues per yr.) Circulation	Tel. No.	Editor
Word, The	1953	Roscommon	(12) 35,000	(0903) 62608	Rev. Thomas Cahill
World of Irish Nursing		Dublin	(10) 21,000	(01) 2803967	Geraldine Meagan
WP Journal		Cavan	(6)	(049) 31640	Hannah D. Maguire
Xchange	1995	Dublin	(10) 17,000	(01) 7015057	Seán Creedon

* refers to the latest figures available from ABC (Jan. to June 1998), all other figures refers to the latest available prior to this period.

NATIONAL NEWSPAPER ADVERTISING RATES

Newspaper	Currency	Per Single Column Inch/cm (£)	Mono Full Pg (£)	Colour Full Pg (£)
Belfast Telegraph	Sterling	15	8,400	11,340
Examiner, The	Punt	45	8,700	10,400
Evening Echo	Punt	27	2,350	2,820
Evening Herald	Punt	66	5,900	6,500
Irish Independent	Punt	96	15,300	19,250
Irish News	Sterling	7.20	3,434	4,295
Irish Times, The	Punt	42	14,970	16,495
News Letter, The	Sterling	10.30	2,439	3,415
Star, The	Punt	58	5,640	7,500
Sunday Business Post	Punt	43	6,600	8,800
Sunday Independent	Punt	108	17,500	22,000
Sunday Tribune	Punt	63	10,466	15,188
Sunday World	Punt	98	9,140	13,600
Ireland on Sunday	Punt	40.50	6,350	7,760
Irish Farmers' Journal	Punt	52	4,210	7,370

SELECTED PROVINCIAL NEWSPAPER AD. RATES

(1998 Rates) Newspaper	Circulation	Per Single Column Inch (B/W) £	Half Pg. Mono £	Full Pg. Mono £	Full Pg. colour
Anglo Celt	15,434	12	800	1,500	N/A
Derry Journal (Irish Republic rate)	27,095	9.75	1,150	2,300	2,650
Donegal Democrat	17,075	9.50	950	1,900	2,250
Northern Standard	13,500	15	1,320	2,580	N/A
Clare Champion	20,113	16	1,300	2,600	3,000
Kerryman / Corkman	35,015	27.50	2,722	5,445	6,534
Limerick Leader	26,492	20	1,900	3,600	3,950
Tipperary Star	9,842	13	1,228	2,457	2,857
Waterford News & Star	16,000	11	1,089	2,178	3,000
Connacht Tribune	28,889	17	1,640	3,280	3,676
Leitrim Observer	9,750	14	1,000	2,000	2,800
Mayo News	11,500	11	528	1,056	N/A
Sligo Champion	15,298	10	750	1,450	1,700
Western People	23,642	14.50	1,370	2,740	3,040
Dundalk Democrat	16,000	9	720	1,440	N/A
Leinster Leader	15,440	15	1,150	2,300	2,800
Meath Chronicle	19,320	14.50	1,232	2,465	2,720
People Newspaper Group (6)	38,214	29.90	1,320	2,600	3,600

RADIO

NATIONAL RADIO STATIONS FACTFILES

RADIO TELEFÍS ÉIREANN.
Founded: 1926. *Number of channels:* (5) *Address:* Donnybrook, Dublin 4. *Contact Numbers:* Tel.: (01) 208 3111. Fax: (01) 208 3080.

RADIO 1 - *Founded:* 1926. *Address:* As above. *Director:* Helen Shaw. *Editor, Features/Arts:* Michael Littleton. *Editor, Arts and Drama:* Lorelei Harris. *Editor, Sport:* Ian Corr. *Frequency:* 88.5-95.2FM *Target Audience:* General. *Output:* 168 hours - 24 hrs x 7days.

2FM - *Founded:* 1979. *Address:* As above. *Contact Numbers:* Tel.: (01) 208 3111. Fax: (01) 208 3092. *Station Manager:* Bill O'Donovan. *Frequency:* 90.7-97.0FM. *Target Audience:* 15-34 yrs *Output:* 168 hours - 24 hrs x 7days.

RAIDIÓ NA GAELTACHTA - *Founded:* 1972. *Address:* Casla, Contae na Gaillimhe. *Contact Numbers:* Tel.: (091) 506677. Fax: (091) 506666. *Ceannaire:* Pól Ó Gallchóir. *Leas Ceannaire agus Eagarthóir Stiúrtha:* Tomas Mac Con Iomaire. *Frequency:* 92.9-102.7FM. *Target Audience:* Gaelic speakers.

RTÉ RADIO CORK - *Founded:* 1974. *Address:* Fr. Mathew Street, Cork. *Contact Numbers:* Tel.: (021) 805805. Fax: (021) 273829. *Head of Broadcasting:* Gerry Reynolds. *Frequency:* 89.2FM *Target Audience:* 30 - 50 yr. olds.*Output:* 38 hrs 30 mins - 5 hrs 30 mins daily.

FM3 - *Frequency:* 92.6-93.6 FM. *Target Aud.:* Classical music listeners. *Output:* 87.5 hrs - 12.5 hrs x 7days.

TODAY F.M. (formerly 'Radio Ireland')
Relaunched: 5 Jan 1998, as 'Today FM'. *Address:* 124 Upper Abbey Street, Dublin 1. *Contact Numbers:* Tel.: (01) 804 9000 Fax: (01) 804 9089. *Chairperson:* John McColgan. *Programme Controller:* Tom Hardy. *Frequency:* 100.102 FM. *Output:* 168 hrs. per wk. *Target Audience:* 25-44 yr. olds. *Staff:* Approx. 50.

BRITISH BROADCASTING CORPORATION (Northern Ireland)
Founded: 1924. *Address:* Ormeau Avenue, Belfast, BT2 8HQ. *Contact Numbers:* Tel.: (01232) 338000. Fax: (01232) 338800. *Controller:* Pat Loughrey. *Head of Broadcast:* Anna Carragher. *Number of studios:* 8. *Output:* 5,500 hrs. per year. *Target Audience:* General.

BBC RADIO ULSTER - *Founded:* 1924. *Address:* Ormeau Avenue, Belfast, BT2 8HQ. *Contact Numbers:* Tel.: (01232) 338000. Fax: (01232) 338800. *Frequency:* 92.4 - 95.4 FM.
BBC RADIO FOYLE - *Founded:* 1979. *Address:* 8 Northland Road, Derry BT48 7JD. *Contact Numbers:* Tel.: (01504) 262244. Fax: (01504) 378666. *Frequency:* 93.1 FM. *Station Manager:* Ana Leddy.

ATLANTIC 252
Founded: 1989. *Address:* Mornington Hse., Trim, Co. Meath. *Contact Numbers:* Tel.: (046) 36655. Fax: (046) 36704. *Chairperson:* Donnach O'Driscoll. *Station Manager:* Cathryn Geraghty. *Frequency:* 252 LW.*Output:* 168 hrs. per wk. *Target Audience:* UK - General. *Staff:* 30.

LOCAL RADIO STATIONS FACTFILES

Detailed profiles below feature the main Irish Local Radio Stations.

● C.K.R. FM
Franchise area: Carlow and Kildare. **Address:** Lismard House, Tullow Street, Carlow. Also: ACC House, 51 South Main Street, Naas, Co. Kildare. **Tel. No.:** (0503) 41044. **Main towns:** Carlow, Tullow, Haketstown, Bagnalstown, Leighlin-Bridge, Athy, Naas, Clane, Kill, Newbridge, Maynooth, Kilcock, Leixlip, Celbridge, Kildare. **Population 15+:** 130,000. **Chief Executive:** Hugh Browne. **Frequency(ies):** 97.3 MHz/97.6 MHz/104.4 MHz. **Target Audience:** 20+ Adults. **Average Quarter Hour listnership:** 9,313

(7%). **Weekly Reach:** 78,000 (60%). **Market Share:** 26%. **30 sec rate/R.O.D.:** £28.00

● CLARE FM
Franchise area: County Clare. **Address:** Abbey Centre, Francis Street, Ennis, Co. Clare. **Tel. No.:** (065) 28888. **Main towns:** Ennis, Kilkee, Kilrush, Killaloe, Ennistymon, Lahinch, Lisdoonvarna, Shannon, Miltown Malbay. **Population 15+:** 72,000. **Chief Executive:** John O'Flaherty. **Frequency(ies):** 96.4 MHz/95.5 MHz/95.9 MHz. **Target Audience:** 25-45 Adults. **Average Quarter Hour listenership:** 9,042 (13%). **Weekly Reach:** 60,000 (84%). **Market Share:** 53%. **30 sec rate/R.O.D.:** £23.00

● EAST COAST RADIO

Franchise area: County Wicklow. **Address:** 9 Prince Of Wales Terrace, Bray, Co. Wicklow. **Tel. No.:** (01) 2866414. **Main towns:** Bray, Wicklow Town, Arklow, Rathdrum, Blessington. **Population 15+:** 78,000. **Joint Chief Executives:** Sean Ashmore, Padraig O'Dwyer. **Frequency(ies):** 94.9 MHz/96.2 MHz/102.9 MHz/104.4 MHz (Arklow). **Target Audience:** 25-55 Adults. **Average Quarter Hour listenership:** 6,667 (9%). **Weekly Reach:** 50,000 (64%). **Market Share:** 30%. **30 sec rate/R.O.D.:** £21.00

● GALWAY BAY FM

Franchise area: Galway City and County. **Address:** Sandy Road, Galway. **Tel. No.:** (091) 770000. **Main towns:** Tuam, Ballinasloe, Athenry, Headford, Loughrea, Portumna, Moycullen, Oughterard, Spiddal, Clifden. **Population 15+:** 147,000. **Chief Executive:** Keith Finnegan. **Frequency(ies):** 95.8 MHz (City)/96.8 MHz (County). **Target Audience:** 22-50 Adults. **Average Quarter Hour listenership:** 10,500 (7%). **Weekly Reach:** 109,000 (74%). **Market Share:** 33%. **30 sec rate/R.O.D.:** £21.00

● HIGHLAND RADIO

Franchise area: Donegal North. **Address:** Pine Hill, Letterkenny, Co. Donegal. **Tel. No.:** (074) 25000. **Main towns:** Letterkenny, Buncrana, Carndonagh, Dungloe. **Population 15+:** 74,000. **Chief Executive:** Charlie Collins. **Frequency(ies):** 94.7 MHz/95.2 MHz/103.3 MHz. **Target Audience:** 20+ Adults plus 14-20 yr old programming. **Average Quarter Hour listenership:** 13,458 (18%). **Weekly Reach:** 64,000 (87%). **Market Share:** 78%. **30 sec rate/R.O.D.:** £22.00

● LM FM

Franchise area: Louth and Meath. **Address:** Boyne Centre, Drogheda, Co. Louth. **Tel. No.:** (041) 32000. **Main towns:** Dundalk, Drogheda, Ardee, Dunboyne, Navan, Trim, Ashbourne, Kells, Dunshaughlin. **Population 15+:** 152,000. **Chief Executive:** Michael Crawley. **Frequency(ies):** 95.8 MHz/104.9 MHz. **Target Audience:** 25+ Adults. **Average Quarter Hour listenership:** 10,313 (7%). **Weekly Reach:** 98,000 (65%). **Market Share:** 36%. **30 sec rate/R.O.D.:** £24.00

● MIDLANDS RADIO 3

Franchise area: Laois, Offaly, Westmeath. **Address:** Williams Street, Tullamore, Co. Offaly. **Tel. No.:** (0506) 51333. **Main towns:** Portlaoise, Portarlington, Mountmellick, Abbeyleix, Mountrath, Tullamore, Birr, Clara, Edenderry, Ferbane, Mullingar, Athlone, Moate, Kilbeggan, Kinnegad. **Population 15+:** 127,000. **Chief Executive:** Joe Yerkes. **Frequency(ies):** 103.5 MHz/102.1 MHz. **Target Audience:** 25-60 Adults. **Average Quarter Hour listenership:** 8,917 (7%). **Weekly Reach:** 79,000 (63%). **Market Share:** 33%. **30 sec rate/R.O.D.:** £18.00

● MID WEST RADIO & NORTH WEST RADIO

Franchise area: MWR FM - Mayo; NWR FM - Sligo, Leitrim North, Donegal South. **Address:** MWR FM - Abbey Street, Ballyhaunis, Co. Mayo. **Tel. No.:** (0907) 30553. **Address:** NWR FM - Market Yard, Sligo. **Tel. No.:** (071) 60108. **Main towns:** Castlebar, Westport, Ballina, Ballyhaunis, Claremorris, Foxford, Belmullet, Sligo, Tubbercurry, Ballymote, Manorhamilton, Bundoran, Ballyshannon, Donegal Town. **Population 15+:** 151,000. **Chief Executives:** Paul Claffey, Tommy Marren. **Frequency(ies):** MWR FM - 96.1 MHz/97.1 MHz/97.3 MHz/95.4 MHz. NWR FM - 102.5 MHz (Sligo) / 105.0 MHz (Donegal). **Target Audience:** 20+ Adults. **Average Quarter Hour listenership:** 19,500 (13%). **Weekly Reach:** 118,000 (78%). **Market Share:** 54%. **30 sec rate/R.O.D.:** £40.00

● RADIO KERRY

Franchise area: County Kerry. **Address:** Main Street, Tralee, Co. Kerry. **Tel. No.:** (066) 23666. **Main towns:** Tralee, Listowel, Ballybunion, Tarbert, Castleisland, Killarney, Killorglin, Cahirciveen, Dingle, Kenmare. **Population 15+:** 97,000. **Chief Executive:** Paul Sheehan. **Frequency(ies):** 97.0 MHz/97.6 MHz/96.2 MHz. **Target Audience:** 18+ Adults. **Average Quarter Hour listenership:** 12,021 (12%). **Weekly Reach:** 78,000 (80%). **Market Share:** 48%. **30 sec rate/R.O.D.:** £28.00

● RADIO KILKENNY

Franchise area: Kilkenny City and County. **Address:** Hebron Road, Kilkenny. **Tel. No.:** (056) 61577. **Main towns:** Kilkenny City, Gowran, Bennetsbridge, Thomastown, Callan, Kells, Castlecomer, Graiguenamanagh. **Population 15+:** 57,000. **Chief Executive:** John Purcell. **Frequency(ies):** 96.6 MHz/96.0 MHz. **Target Audience:** All Adults. **Average Quarter Hour listenership:** 7,813 (14%). **Weekly Reach:** 43,000 (75%). **Market Share:** 47%. **30 sec rate/R.O.D.:** £15.00

● SHANNONSIDE FM / NORTHERN SOUND

Franchise area: Shannonside FM - Roscommon, Longford, Leitrim South. Northern Sound - Cavan and Monaghan. **Address:** Shannonside FM, Minard House, Sligo Road, Co. Longford. **Tel. No.:** (043) 47777. **Main towns:** Longford Town, Granard, Edgeworthstown, Ballymahon, Roscommon Town, Strokestown, Castlerea, Ballaghaderreen, Boyle, Ballinamore, Mohill, Carrick-on-Shannon, Carrigallen, Kingscourt, Virginia, Killeshandra, Ballinagh, Swanlinbar, Ballyconnell, Belturbet, Cootehill, Cavan Town, Baileborough, Ballyjamesduff, Monaghan Town, Clones, Ballybay, Castleblaney, Carrickmacross. **Population 15+:** 151,000. **Chief Executive:** Richard Devlin. **Frequency(ies):** Shannonside FM - 104.1 MHz/95.7 MHz. Northern Sound - 94.8 MHz (Cavan)/96.3 MHz. **Target Audience:** 18-55 Adults. **Average Quarter Hour listenership:** 11,896 (8%). **Weekly Reach:** 94,000 (62%). **Market Share:** 40%. **30 sec rate/R.O.D.:** £32.00

● SOUTH EAST RADIO

Franchise area: County Wexford. **Address:** Custom House Quay, Wexford. **Tel. No.:** (053) 45200. **Main towns:** Wexford, Enniscorthy, New Ross, Gorey. **Population 15+:** 78,000. **Chief Executive:** Eamonn Buttle. **Frequency(ies):** 95.6 MHz/96.2 MHz/96.4 MHz.

Target Audience: 25-49 Adults with specialist programming. **Average Quarter Hour listenership:** 8,271 (11%). **Weekly Reach:** 66,000 (85%). **Market Share:** 57%. **30 sec rate/R.O.D.:** £23.00

● **TIPPERARY MID WEST RADIO**

Franchise area: Tipperary South West. **Address:** St. Michael Street, Tipperary. **Tel. No.:** (062) 52555. **Main towns:** Tipperary Town, Cashel, Cahir. **Population 15+:** 17,000. **Chief Executive:** Sean Kelly. **Frequency(ies):** 104.8 MHz. **Target Audience:** All Adults. **Average Quarter Hour listenership:** 1,479 (9%). **Weekly Reach:** 12,000 (71%). **Market Share:** 36%. **30 sec rate/R.O.D.:** £10.00

● **TIPP FM**

Franchise area: Tipperary North and South East. **Address:** Davis Road, Clonmel, Co. Tipperary. **Tel. No.:** (052) 25456. **Main towns:** Nenagh, Roscrea, Templemore, Borrisoleigh, Thurles, Clonmel, Carrick-on-Suir, Cahir. **Population 15+:** 83,000. **Chief Executive:** John O'Connell. **Frequency(ies):** 97.1 MHz/103.9 MHz/95.3 MHz. **Target Audience:** 24-55 Adults. **Average Quarter Hour listenership:** 9,875 (12%). **Weekly Reach:** 66,000 (80%). **Market Share:** 45%. **30 sec rate/R.O.D.:** £21.00

● **W.L.R. FM**

Franchise area: Waterford City and County. **Address:** The Radio Centre, Georges Court, Waterford. **Tel. No.:** (051) 77592. **Main towns:** Tramore, Dunmore East, Dungarvan, Cappoquin, Lismore, Kilmacthomas, Waterford City. **Population 15+:** 74,000. **Chief Executive:** Des Whelan. **Frequency(ies):** 97.5 MHz/95.1 MHz. **Target Audience:** 15-55 Adults. **Average Quarter Hour listenership:** 11,708 (16%). **Weekly Reach:** 62,000 (84%). **Market Share:** 62%. **30 sec rate/R.O.D.:** £20.00

Population: refers to population of area
Target Audience: refers to no. of population (listenership)

OTHER IRISH RADIO STATION PROFILES

REPUBLIC OF IRELAND

Station	Frequency	Main area Served	Tel. No.	Chief Executive
Anna Livia	103.8 FM	Dublin city/county	(01) 6778103	Eileen O'Gorman
FM 104	104.4 FM	Dublin city/county	(01) 6797104	Dermot Hanrahan
96 FM/County Sound	96.4 FM	Cork city/county	(021) 551596	Colm O'Conaill
98 FM	98.1 FM	Dublin city/county	(01) 6708970	Ken Hutton
95 FM	95.0 FM	Limerick city/county	(061) 400195	Scott Williams
Raidió na Life	102.2 FM	Dublin city/county	(01) 6616333	Finnouala Mac Aodha

NORTHERN IRELAND

Station	Frequency	Main area Served	Tel. No.	Manager
Belfast City Beat	96.7 FM	Greater Belfast	(01232) 438500	
Cool FM		Eastern N. Ireland	(01247) 815551	James Donnelly
Downtown Radio	102.4 FM	Ulster	(01247) 815555	James Donnelly
Q102 FM	102.9 FM	North West	(01504) 344449	David Austin

COMMUNITY RADIO STATIONS

Station	Frequency	Main area Served	Tel. No.	Manager
C.R. Castlebar	102.9 FM	Castlebar	(094) 25555	Patrick Staunton
C.R. Youghal	105.1 FM	Youghal	(024) 91199	James Fitzgerald
C.R. Connemara	106.1 FM	N.W. Connemara	(095) 41616	Mary Ruddy
Cork Campus Radio	97.4 FM	Cork city	(021) 902008	Sinéad Wlyde
Dublin South C.R.	104.9 FM	South Dublin	(01) 4930377	John O'Brennan
Dublin Weekend Radio	102.2 FM	Dublin city/county	(01) 7045203	Teresa O'Malley
Flirt FM	105.6 FM	Galway city	(091) 750445	Fiona MacNulty
Near	101.6 FM	N.E. Dublin city	(01) 8485211	Jack Byrne
West Dublin C.R.	104.9 FM	Dublin West	(01) 6261160	Celia Flanagan
Wired 103FM	103.8 FM	Limerick City	(061) 315103	Eoin Brady

AVERAGE WEEKDAY (YESTERDAY) LISTENERSHIP

Period: June '97 - June '98	National			National excl. Dublin / Cork			Co. Dublin			Co. Cork		
"JNLR / MRBI 1997/1998"	Wk. days	Sat	Sun	Wk. days	Sat	Sun	Wk. days	Sat	Sun	Wk. days	Sat	Sun
Listened at all*	89%	63%	60%	90%	65%	63%	87%	59%	51%	86%	64%	66%
Any RTÉ Radio	60%	35%	33%	63%	37%	34%	57%	32%	30%	52%	36%	35%
Any RTÉ Radio 1												
2FM / RTÉ Cork	56%	33%	30%	59%	34%	31%	55%	30%	29%	50%	35%	33%
RTÉ Radio 1	34%	18%	18%	32%	16%	15%	38%	22%	21%	30%	20%	20%
2FM	29%	15%	14%	33%	18%	17%	23%	10%	8%	24%	14%	12%

Period: June '97 - June '98	National			National excl. Dublin / Cork			Co. Dublin			Co. Cork		
	Wk. days	Sat	Sun	Wk. days	Sat	Sun	Wk. days	Sat	Sun	Wk. days	Sat	Sun
Any Local Radio......51%		...31%	....32%	54%	....34%	...36%	44%	....25%	...21%	57%	...36%	...43%
Home Local................-	...........-	.........-	47%	....29%	...30%	-........	.....-	.......-	-........	.....-	........-
98FM................-	...........-	.........-	-........	.....-	.......-	22%	....11%	...8%	-........	.....-	........-
FM104................-	...........-	.........-	-........	.....-	.......-	28%	....15%	...12%	-........	.....-	........-
RTÉ Radio Cork ....-	...........-	.........-	-........	.....-	.......-	-........	.....-	.......-	7%	.....4%	.....4%
96FM County Sound ..-.......	......-	.........-	-........	.....-	.......-	-........	.....-	.......-	56%	...34%	...41%

* Indicates the proportion tuning to the station at some time of the day

SHARE OF LISTENING (7am - 7pm)

Period: June '97 - June '98	National			National excl. Dublin / Cork			Co. Dublin			Co. Cork		
"JNLR / MRBI 1997/1998"	Wk. days	Sat	Sun	Wk. days	Sat	Sun	Wk. days	Sat	Sun	Wk. days	Sat	Sun
Any RTÉ Radio 53%	......47%	.....43%	52%	....46%	...40%	62%	....55%	...58%	41%	...39%	...36%
RTÉ Radio 1.............32%	......24%	.....25%	27%	....19%	...20%	45%	....40%	...43%	25%	...21%	...21%
2FM.......................21%	......23%	.....18%	25%	....27%	...20%	17%	....15%	...15%	12%	...14%	...11%
Any Local Radio......43%	......49%	.....53%	44%	....50%	...56%	35%	....41%	...39%	55%	...58%	...61%
Home Local.............-	.........-	.........-	38%	....43%	...48%	-........	.....-	.......-	-........	.....-	........-
98FM....................-	.........-	.........-	-........	.....-	.......-	15%	....16%	...14%	-........	.....-	........-
FM104....................-	.........-	.........-	-........	.....-	.......-	17%	....20%	...18%	-........	.....-	........-
RTÉ Radio Cork ....-	.........-	.........-	-........	.....-	.......-	-........	.....-	.......-	3%	.....3%	.....4%
96FM County Sound ..-.......	......-	.........-	-........	.....-	.......-	-........	.....-	.......-	54%	...56%	...59%

'TODAY FM' LISTENING PATTERNS

January to June 1998	National Weekdays	Dublin Weekdays
Average Weekday Yesterday Listnership...9%		.......7%
Market Share (7am - 7pm)..6%		.......4%

MAIN RADIO ADVERTISING RATES

Station *(Advert period in brackets)*	15 secs £	20 secs £	30 secs £	40 secs £	50 secs £	60 secs £
RTÉ Radio 1 (7:55 - 9:15a.m.)............744	889	1,111	1,478	1,855	2,222
RTÉ Radio 1 (5:00 - 7:00p.m.) 163	195	244	324	407	488
2 FM (7:00a.m. - 7:00p.m.) 185	221	276	367	461	552
2 FM (7:00p.m. - 7:00a.m.) 52	62	78	104	130	156
Raidió na Gaeltachta ....No commercial advertising carried					
Today FM (7:00a.m. - 7:00p.m.)* ....-	64	80	...............-	.............-	160
Today FM (7:00p.m. - 11:00p.m.)** ....-	...............26.5	35	...............-	.............-	70

* Based on Prime Time Package (21 spots) ** Based on Night Time Package (21 spots)

IMPORTANT IRISH WEBSITE ADDRESSES

Business	Address	Business	Address
Aer Lingus	www.aerlingus.ie	Central Statistics Office	www.cso.ie
Aer Rianta	www.aer-rianta.com	Church of Ireland	www.ireland.anglican.org
Allied Irish Bank Group	www.aib.ie	Cooperation North	www.co-operation-north.ie
An Post	www.anpost.ie	Directory of Irish sites	www.niceone.com
Bank of Ireland	www.boi.ie	Ednet Ireland	ireland.iol.ie/ednet
Bank of Ireland, Northern Ireland		Enterprise Ireland	www.irish-trade.ie
	www.bankofireland-ni.com	Eunet Ireland	www.eunet.ie
Bord Fáilte	www.ireland.travel.ie	First National Building Society	www.fnbs.ie
Bord Iascaigh Mhara	www.bim.ie	First Trust Bank	www.ftbni.com
Bord Gáis Éireann	www.bge.ie	Farmers Journal	www.farmersjournal.ie
British Olympic Association	www.olympics.org.uk	Electricity Supply Board	www.esb.ie

Business	Address	Business	Address
ENFO (Public Environment Information) ....www.enfo.ie		The Irish Times ....www.irish-times.com	
Environmental Protection Agency ....www.epa.ie		The Irish Trade Web...................................www.itw.ie	
Forfas ....www.forfas.ie		KPMG Ireland ....www.kpmg.ie	
Garda Síochána................................www.garda.ie		Music Site ....www.tinet.ie/muse	
Glasnevin Cemetary ....www.glasnevin-cemetery.ie		National Lottery ....www.lotto.ie	
Government of Ireland...........................www.irlgov.ie		National Safety Council...	
Government of Northern Ireland.....www.nics.gov.uk		....................................www.national-safety-council.ie	
Hibernian....................www.hibernian-group.ie		Northern Ireland Tourist Board ..www.ni-tourism.com	
ICC Bank...www.icc.ie		Northern Ireland Office ....www.nio.gov.uk	
IDA..www.ida.ie		Presbyterian Church in Ireland	
Indigo ....www.indigo.ie		....................................www.Presbyterian Ireland.org	
The Institute of Bankers in Ireland...www.instbank.ie		Revenue Commissioners ....www.revenue.ie	
Ireland On-Line ....www.iol.ie		RUC ....www.ruc.police.uk	
Irish Defence Forces ....www.military.ie		RTÉ (The Irish Broadcasting Service) ....www.rté.ie	
Irish Exporters Association ....www.itw.ie/exporter		Sports Council, Northern Ireland	
Irish Independent......................www.independent.ie		...................................www.sportscouncil-ni.org.uk	
Irish Internet Association..........................www.iia.ie		The Sunday Business Post.................www.sbpost.ie	
Irish Job Pages ....www.exp.ie		Telecom Internet...................................www.tinet.ie	
The Irish Management Institute.................www.imi.ie		TouristNET ....www.indigo.ie/ipress	
Irish National teachers Organisation ......www.into.ie		TSB Bank...www.tsbbank.ie	
Irish Music Network...................................www.imn.ie		2FM...www.2fm.ie	
The Irish News ....www.irishnews.com		Udaras na Gaeltacht.........................www.udaras.ie	
Irish Sport.................................www.failte.com/sport		Ulster Bank..................................www.ulsterbank.com	

IRISH MEDIA PERSONNEL

ADDIS, Jeremy: publisher *Books Ireland* magazine.

ALLEN, Liz: crime correspondent *Sunday Independent.*

AUSTIN, Wendy: news and current affairs presenter with BBC Northern Ireland.

BAXTER, Carlton: editor of *Ulster Business.*

BEACOM, Steve: sports journalist with the *Belfast Telegraph.*

BIRD, Charlie: RTÉ's special correspondent.

BOLAND, John: arts journalist with *Irish Independent.*

BOWMAN, John: chairman of RTÉ's current affairs programme *Questions and Answers.*

BRADFORD, Conor: newscaster BBC Northern Ireland.

BRADY, Conor: editor *The Irish Times.*

BRADY, Tom: security editor *Irish Independent.*

BREHENY, Martin: sports journalist with *Ireland on Sunday.*

BRIEN, Linda: sports editor, UTV.

BROWNE, Vincent: broadcaster and former editor/owner *Magill* current affairs magazine.

BUTLER, Pat: RTÉ journalist.

BYRNE, Gay: one of Ireland's most famous radio and television hosts. Host of the long running *Late Late Show* on RTÉ television and the *Gay Byrne Show* on RTÉ radio.

CADWALLADER Anne: radio and print journalist. Northern correspondent with *Ireland on Sunday.*

CAHILL, Des: Sports presenter with RTÉ television and radio.

CARRAGHER, Anna: Head of Broadcasting, BBC Northern Ireland.

CARRUTHERS, Mark: BBC Northern Ireland news and current affairs presenter.

CARTY, Ciaran: literary editor with *The Sunday Tribune.*

CLAFFEY, Una: political correspondent with RTÉ.

CLANCY, Paddy: newspaper columnist and broadcaster.

CLARKE, Liam: journalist with *The Sunday Times.*

CLARKE, Paul: presenter of *UTV Live At Six.*

CLAYTON-LEA, Tony: music journalist.

COGLEY, Fred: RTÉ's head of sport.

COLEMAN, Shane: business editor *The Sunday Tribune.*

COLLINS, Bob: Director-General of RTÉ.

COLLINS, Liam: business and finance journalist with *Sunday Independent.*

COLLINS, Stephen: political correspondent *The Sunday Tribune.*

COLLINS, Tom: editor *Irish News.*

CORCORAN, Jody: *Sunday Independent* correspondent.

COOPER, Matt: editor *The Sunday Tribune* and radio presenter with Today FM.

COOGAN, Tim Pat: historian, writer, and columnist with *Ireland on Sunday.*

CORR, Ian: RTÉ radio's sports editor.

COURTNEY, Kevin: music journalist with *The Irish Times.*

COWAN, Barry: senior presenter with BBC Northern Ireland.

CRONIN, Anthony: literary critic.

CROWLEY, Carrie: RTÉ television and radio presenter.

CROWLEY, Richard: current affairs presenter RTÉ radio. Co-presenter *Morning Ireland* on RTÉ Radio 1.

CURRAN, Edmund: editor *Belfast Telegraph.*

CUSACK, Jim: security correspondent with *The Irish Times.*

D'ARCY, Ray: television and radio presenter with RTÉ.

DAVIS, Derek: RTÉ television presenter.

DAVIN-POWER, David: RTÉ's Northern editor.

DE BRÉADÚN, Deaglán: Northern Editor with *The Irish Times.*

DELANEY, Frank: broadcaster and author.

DEMPSEY, Matt: editor *Irish Farmers' Journal.*

DERVAN, Cathal: editor of *Ireland on Sunday* sports section *The Title.*

DEVINE, John: northern editor *Irish Independent.*

DOHERTY, Moya: television producer, *Riverdance* Promoter and co-founder of Today FM.

DONAGHY, Kathy: journalist with *Ireland On Sunday.*

DOYLE, Vincent: editor *Irish Independent.*

DRURY, Paul: editor *Evening Herald.*

DUGGAN, Keith: sports journalist with *The Irish Times.*

DUFFY, Joe: RTÉ radio presenter.

DUIGNAN, Seán: RTÉ current affairs presenter, former RTÉ political editor and former government press secretary.

DUNNE, Mick: RTÉ sports broadcaster.

DUNPHY, Eamon: presenter of *The Last Word* on Today FM, television soccer pundit and author.

DUNSEITH, David: presenter of BBC Radio Ulster current affairs show *Talkback.*

EDGAR, Mike: presenter with BBC Radio Ulster.

FANNING, Aengus: editor *Sunday Independent.*

FANNING, Dave: radio and television presenter with RTÉ. Rock and film critic.

FARRELL, Brian: academic and television broadcaster. Chairman of the Arts Council.

FAHY, Jim: RTÉ's western correspondent.

FAY, Liam: music journalist with *Hot Press.*

FEENEY, Brian: editor *Evening Echo.*

FINUCANE, Marian: RTÉ television and radio presenter. Presenter of *Liveline* on RTÉ Radio 1.

FOLEY, Catherine: main correspondent with *The Irish Times* supplement *Education and Living.*

FULLERTON, Jackie: BBC Northern Ireland sports presenter and commentator.

GALVIN, Margaret: editor *Ireland's Own* magazine.

GILES, Johnny: television and radio soccer commentator and pundit.

GILLEECE, Dermot: golf correspondent with *The Irish Times.*

GLENNON, Chris: political correspondent *Irish Independent.*

GOAN, Cathal: ceannasaí (head) of Teilifís na Gaeilge.

GOGAN, Larry: radio presenter with 2FM.

GOLDEN, Tom: *The Sunday Business Post* technology editor.

GORMAN, Tommie: RTÉ's European correspondent.

GRIMASON, Stephen: BBC Northern Ireland political editor.

HALLORAN, Cathy: RTÉ's mid western correspondent.

HAND, Lise: columnist with *The Sunday Tribune.*

HANLY, David: journalist and co-presenter of *Morning Ireland* on RTÉ Radio 1.

HAYES, Liam: editor *Ireland on Sunday.*

HETHERINGTON, Rick: head of independent television channel TV3.

HOGAN, Richard: editor *Irish Family.*

HOLLAND, Mary: journalist, contributor to *The Irish Times* and *The Observer.*

HOLMES, Eamon: television presenter with GMTV in Britain.

HORAN, Liam: sports journalist *Irish Independent.*

HOSEY, Seamus: RTÉ radio producer.

HOWARD, Paul: sports journalist with *Sunday Tribune.*

HUMPHRIES, Tom: sports writer with *The Irish Times.*

KEANE, Fergal: journalist, author and BBC correspondent.

KEANE, Terry: social columnist with *Sunday Independent.*

KEARNS, John: television presenter with UTV.

KEENAN, Brendan: *Irish Independent* group business editor.

KEENAN, Mark: property editor *The Sunday Tribune.*

KELLY, Donal: RTÉ's political editor.

KELLY, Gerry: host of UTV chat show *Kelly.*

KELLY, John: journalist and presenter with To-day FM.

KELLY, Shirley: editor *Books Ireland.*

KENNEDY, Geraldine: political correspondent *The Irish Times,* former T.D.

KENNY, Pat: RTÉ television and radio presenter. Presenter of *Kenny Live* on RTÉ television, and *Today with Pat Kenny* on RTÉ Radio 1.

KERRIGAN, Gene: columnist with *Sunday Independent.*

KIBERD, Damien: editor *The Sunday Business Post.*

LAWLOR, Aine: co-presenter of RTÉ Radio 1 programme *Morning Ireland.*

LAWLOR, Eamon: presenter of RTÉ's current affairs programme *Prime Time.*

LEE, George: RTÉ Economics Editor.

LINDSAY, Martin: editor *The Sunday Life.*

LITTLE, Mark: RTÉ's Washington correspondent.

LOGAN, Adrian: sports presenter and commentator with UTV.

LOONEY, Brian: editor *The Examiner.*

LOUGHREY, Pat: controller BBC Northern Ireland.

MADDOX, Tony: Head of News and Current Affairs with BBC Northern Ireland.

MAGNIER, Eileen: RTÉ's north-west correspondent.

MARLOWE, Lara: feature writer with *The Irish Times.*

MARTIN, Geoff: editor *The Newsletter.*

MacSWEENEY, Tom: RTÉ's marine correspondent.

McCAFFERTY, Nell: columnist with *The Sunday Tribune.*

McCANN, Eamon: freelance journalist, author and broadcaster.

McCARTHY, Justine: features writer *Irish Independent.*

McDONALD, Frank: environment correspondent with *The Irish Times.*

McGEE, John: editor *Business & Finance* magazine.

McGINTY, Colm: editor *Sunday World.*

McGUINNESS, Mairead: television presenter and journalist with *Irish Farmers' Journal.*

McGURK, Tom: broadcaster and columnist with *The Sunday Business Post.*

McKEE, Seamus: news and current affairs presenter with BBC Northern Ireland.

McKINNEY, Fearghal: news and current affairs presenter with UTV.

McNIFFE, Mike: journalist with the *Sunday World.*

McWILLIAMS, Brendan: columnist with *The Irish Times.*

MILLAR, Frank: London Editor of *The Irish Times.*

MITCHELL, Frank: television presenter with UTV.

MOLONEY, Ed: *Sunday Tribune* northern political editor.

MORRISON, Rob: UTV's head of news and current

affairs.

MULHALL, Edward: Director of News at RTÉ.

MULHOLLAND, Joe: managing director of RTÉ television.

MULLOOLY, Ciaran: RTÉ's midlands correspondent.

MULRENNAN, Frank: business editor Irish Independent

MURPHY, Mike: radio and television presenter with RTÉ, arts critic.

MURRAY, Paddy: columnist with *The Star.*

MYERS, Kevin: historian, broadcaster, and columnist with *The Irish Times.*

NAUGHTON, Celine: editor *Woman's Way.*

NEILL, Rose: newscaster with BBC Northern Ireland.

NESBITT, Mike: news and current affairs presenter with UTV.

NOLAN, PJ: journalist with *Irish Farmers' Journal.*

Ó GALLCHÓIR, Pól: Ceannaire (head) of Raidió na Gaeltachta.

Ó MUIRCHEARTAIGH, Micheál: Gaelic games commentator and cathaoirleach Bord na Gaeilge.

O'BRIEN, Anne-Marie: journalist with *The Evening Echo.*

O'CALLAGHAN, Gareth: radio presenter on 2FM.

O'CALLAGHAN, Miriam: journalist and presenter of RTÉ's current affairs programme *Prime Time.*

O'CLERY, Conor: Asia correspondent for *The Irish Times.*

O'CONNELL, Brian: RTÉ's London correspondent.

O'CONNELL, Mark: political correspondent *The Sunday Business Post.*

O'CONNOR, Tim: head of sport at RTÉ television.

O'DOWD, Niall: editor of Irish American newspaper *The Irish Voice* facilitator in Northern Ireland peace process.

O'FAOLAIN, Nuala: writer and columnist with *The Irish Times.*

O'HANLON, Eilis: columnist with *Sunday Independent.*

O'MALLEY, Joseph: political correspondent *Sunday Independent.*

O'REAGAN, Gerard: editor of *The Star.*

O'REGAN, Eilish: health correspondent *Irish Independent.*

O'REILLY, Dr Tony: media magnate.

O'REILLY, Emily: political editor *The Sunday Business Post.*

O'RIORDAN, Tom: sports correspondent with the *Irish Independent.*

O'TOOLE, Fintan: journalist, author and columnist with

The Irish Times.

PARSONS, Heather: editor *RTÉ Guide* magazine.

POLLAK, Andy: education correspondent with *The Irish Times.*

POIRTEIR, Cathal: RTÉ radio producer.

POWER, Brenda: columnist with *The Sunday Tribune.*

PRUNTY, Morag: editor *IT* magazine.

RAFFERTY, Seán: presenter with BBC Radio 3.

RAPPLE, Colm: *The Sunday Business Post* economic editor.

REID, Ken: political correspondent with UTV.

ROCHE, Michael: managing director *Ireland's Own.*

ROSS, Shane: business editor *Sunday Independent,* former senator.

ROWAN, Brian: chief security correspondent BBC Northern Ireland.

RUANE, Brigid: *Late Late Show* senior researcher.

RYAN, Gerry: radio and television presenter with RTÉ. Presenter of *The Gerry Ryan Show* on 2FM.

RYAN, John: editor of *Magill* magazine.

SHAW, Helen: Director of RTÉ radio.

SHEEHY, Pascal: RTÉ's southern correspondent.

SMYTH, Sam: journalist with *Irish Independent,* columnist *The Sunday Tribune.*

STOKES, Niall: editor of *Hot Press.*

TAYLOR, Cliff: business editor *The Irish Times.*

THOMPSON, Noel: current affairs presenter with BBC Northern Ireland.

TIERNAN, Damien: RTÉ's south east correspondent.

TRAYNOR, Donna: newscaster with BBC Northern Ireland.

WALSH, Ann: producer RTÉ radio.

WALSH, David: sports journalist with *The Sunday Times.*

WALSH, Declan: journalist with *Sunday Business Post.*

WALSHE, John: education editor *Irish Independent.*

WATSON, Stephen: sports presenter on UTV.

WATTERSON, Johnny: sports writer with *The Irish Times.*

WHELAN, Ken: political correspondent with *Ireland on Sunday.*

WHELAN, Marty: RTÉ television presenter.

WILLIAMS, Paul: writer and crime correspondent for the *Sunday World.*

WOGAN, Terry: radio presenter with the BBC.

YEATES, Padraig: correspondent with *The Irish Times.*

❑

SPORT

Confidence Conquers Fear

By **Martin Breheny**, *Ireland On Sunday*

CONFIDENCE attracts success, fear invites failure. A touch too general, perhaps, but only just. For when the 1988 sporting year is contextualised for Ireland, the abiding theme is one where confidence, which is some cases was derived from the most trying circumstances, jostled its way past a whole variety of obstacles.

Sonia O'Sullivan's double triumph at the European Athletics championships in Budapest; Brian Kerr's double European triumph with the Irish U-16 and U-18 Republic of Ireland soccer teams; Team Jordan finally making it to the victory podium on the Formula One circuit; Galway's re-emergence as a Gaelic football force after 32 years in isolation and the absolute refusal by Offaly hurlers to accept that their championship dream was over all stand as memorable examples of the all-embracing influence of positive thinking.

Sonia O'Sullivan's disappointment in the 1996 Olympic Games in Atlanta was followed by an even deeper nightmare in the 1997 World championships. In the space of a miserable year, Sonia's status as an athlete had turned 180 degrees.

She was being written off by self-taught analysts who found no difficulty in explaining exactly why Sonia's star had spun out of its winning orbit. Sporting obituaries were penned as if Sonia's winning days were no more than golden memories from days long since past.

Had Sonia took any notice of them, she would have packed away her spikes for the last time and re-invented herself outside athletics. Thankfully she chose a different route, one which she located deep inside her own psyche and which drew its inspiration from a self-confidence which, while shaken, was never broken.

And so the long haul back to glory began. It was reached in Budapest in August when she galloped to two splendid victories in the European 5,000 and 10,000 metres finals. It was a double triumph which had only ever been achieved by athletics' very elite - now Sonia could rightfully claim her place amongst them.

For those who always believed that Sonia's dip in form was no more than a temporary setback, the sight of her in full flow in Budapest was as inspiring as it was thrilling. It was more than just a victory for Ireland's finest ever female athlete - it was a triumph for the power of self-belief and served as a fine example for people in every walk of life.

If Sonia O'Sullivan's return to her best was one of the most heartening developments of 1998, Catherina McKiernan's marathon exploits was one of the most satisfying. She, too, had to show remarkable degrees of self-confidence to take on the most gruelling athletic discipline of all but she did it with style and determination to emerge as one of the world's truly great marathon runners. The Olympics in Sydney may be some way off yet but not so far that Irish people can't begin to dream about a historic double for two of the finest athletes this country has ever produced.

It was ironic that on the very day when Sonia O'Sullivan was creating history by winning the second leg of her splendid double in August, the Galway football team were emerging from their very own desert to reach the All-Ireland final. A week later they were joined by

Kildare, setting up a final between two counties which were starved of success for so long.

Kildare hadn't won an All-Ireland final since 1928 while Galway's last success was in 1966 so when they clashed in the decider, Croke Park was filled with an emotion which had rarely been experienced in modern times. Victory went to a Galway team, fired by the inspirational confidence of youth.

Five of the Galway team were just 21 years old but Michael Donnellan, Padraig Joyce, John Divilly, Tomas Meehan and Derek Savage were very much at the heart of a splendid team effort. More than 200 years ago, Samuel Johnson defined youth as 'the confidence of 21.' Never was that a more apt description than in the All-Ireland football final.

Not that it is necessary to have reached 21 years of age before self-belief makes an important contribution in the sporting arena. Brian Kerr took the Republic of Ireland U-16 soccer team to Scotland in May for the European championships against a background of disappointment that the Irish senior team hadn't qualified for the World Cup finals.

The country's soccer public badly needed a lift and it was provided in the most dramatic circumstances as Ireland drew with Scotland and beat Finland, Spain, Denmark, Portugal and Italy (in the final) to take the European crown. It was a magnificent achievement by the youngsters and by Kerr, the man with the winning touch at this level.

Just over two months later, Kerr was on tour again, this time with the Republic's U-18 side in the European championships in Cyprus. Surely, he couldn't repeat the spectacular success, achieved with the U-16s.

Back to confidence again. Those who know Kerr talk passionately about the his capacity to instill self-belief into young players. He achieves it in a very natural way, never resorting to the pseudo-psychological babble in which some coaches indulge.

Beneath Kerr's straight-forward exterior lurks a sharp football brain and once again he out-foxed and out-witted the best European coaches to preside over another amazing triumph as the U-18s powered their way to glory. In the final against Germany, they seemed to have blown their chance when they conceded an equaliser in the very last minute of normal time.

Extra-time failed to separate the sides and so it came down to penalties. In a tense shoot-out, the young Irish lads held their nerve and it fell to Liam George to slot home the final penalty which won the match and the championship.

Success can come at a very early stage of their careers for the U-16 and U-18 soccer team, almost indeed before they had an opportunity to experience disappointment and frustration. Not so for Eddie Jordan, who has had to battle against all sorts of setbacks on the Formula One circuit.

There were times when those of a less obsessional nature might have quit but Jordan, ever the optimist, battled on and was rewarded in the Belgian Grand Prix in August when Damon Hill drove the Jordan car to its first ever Grand Prix win. Jordan's second driver, Ralf Schumacher, added to the Dubliner's delight by finishing in second place to complete a memorable 1-2.

Offaly hurlers finished second in the Leinster hurling championship, losing the final to Kilkenny but, under the new system, were allowed back into the All-Ireland championship at the quarter-final stage. A draw with Clare was followed by a three point defeat in a match which had to be re-fixed because the referee played two minutes short and, third time around, Offaly made no mistake, beating the defending All-Ireland champions by three points.

By now their sights were firmly set on the McCarthy Cup and they were not be deflected. Once again, Kilkenny stood in their way, only this time Offaly's confidence reserves were so high that nothing was going to stop them and they went on to take their fourth All-Ireland crown.

Like so many of the success stories in Irish sport in 1988, it was a triumph for confidence over fear.   ◻

The author is a sports journalist with Ireland On Sunday

TOP SPORTS STORIES OF THE YEAR

JOY IN SOLITUDE FOR CLIFTONVILLE April 18, 1998. Cliftonville won the Irish League for the first time since the 1909/10 season and secured entry to the preliminary round of the European Champions League. The oldest club in Ireland had its 78 year wait extended by an hour hoping the 1-1 draw with Glenavon would deliver the championship and old rivals Linfield (whose match had been delayed for an hour for what were described as 'security reasons') could not secure the result away to Coleraine which would extend the season to the last game. Linfield lost, and the usual Solitude celebrations at the demise of the old foe were dwarfed by the unrestrained outpouring of joy from the Cliftonville faithful. In the presence of former ballboy but now Irish Football Association President Jim Boyce, captain Mickey Donnelly was presented with the Gibson Cup by Irish League Vice President Jim Semple. Solitude had never in its 108 year history witnessed celebrations like it. Fans streamed onto the pitch, and the *Fields of Athenry* were once again sinned against.

THREE STRIKES AND YOU'RE OUT - NOT SO FOR OFFALY HURLERS Offaly's summer of hurling mediocrity ended with 70 glorious minutes in Offaly v Clare Part I. The resignation of Babs Keating after a Leinster final hurling lesson from Kilkenny and his replacement by little known Galway man Michael Bond turned a summer on its head. Tempers frayed in a Munster final replay in Thurles while New Offaly got to work. A workmanlike victory over Antrim was followed by a 1-13 apiece draw with Clare (Part I). That draw initiated an unparalleled sequence of events. Referee Jimmy Cooney prematurely ended Offaly v Clare Part II, apparently mistaking the length of a championship hurling half for 30 minutes, the game was declared void and a replay ordered for Thurles six days later. A weary Clare prepared for Part III (their third replay of the championship) and were beaten perhaps more convincingly than the 0-16 to 0-13 scoreline suggested. Cue an Offaly rematch with Kilkenny in the All-Ireland title decider. In the final the teamwork acquired in the three game series and the individual brilliance of Brian Whelahan secured victory leading captain Hubert Rigney to proclaim that while they may have entered by the back door, Offaly were leaving by the front.

FEAST OR FAMINE - GALWAY EAT OUT! For thirty-two years Galway and Connacht waited on Sam Maguire, while Kildare had waited 70. The Lilywhites of Kildare liberated from Leinster for the first time since 1956 defeated Dublin, Meath and Kerry, the 1995, '96, and '97 All-Ireland Champions respectively en route to the All-Ireland final. The Tribesmen defeated the most consistent team in the country in the previous two years, Mayo, in the first round of the Connacht championship in Castlebar, dismissed Leitrim in the semi final but stumbled against Roscommon in the Connacht decider. On final day a whiter-than-white Hill 16 looked like an advertisement for washing powder while the maroon and white on the Canal End were determined to give the old terrace a good send off. Initially Kildare's short passing game troubled Galway but poor shooting left them only a goal ahead at half-time. An unanswered goal and four points in the first ten minutes of the second half all but won the game for Galway. A last minute punched ball which rebounded off the post would have drawn Kildare level and possibly ended their famine, but it was Galway who tasted the sweet fruits of victory. Tens of thousands welcomed the victors back to the West lining the road from Ballinasloe through Moutbellew to Tuam and on to Galway. In Kildare the followers celebrated the achievement of getting there and winning their first Leinster Championship in 42 years but they must have worried about getting out of the Leinster in 1999.

WORLD CUP GOLF TRIUMPH Padraig Harrington and Paul McGinley joined an illustrious club when they won the 43rd Golf World Cup at Kiawah Island, South Carolina, scene of the 1991 Ryder Cup. Emulating the achievement of Harry Bradshaw and Christy O'Connor Senior, who won the then Canada Cup in 1958, Harrington and McGinley set a new tournament record of an aggregate 31 under par to claim the title. Five shots clear of second placed Scotland and a further shot ahead of the United States McGinley finished fourth overall and Harrington finished joint fifth. The pair moved from joint sixth after the first round, to joint second after the second round to outright second after the third round. Parallels with Ireland's 1958 victory are obvious but recompense in the intervening years has changed considerably. In 1958 Bradshaw and O'Connor Senior won £357 each with Bradshaw picking up a further £187 for finishing second overall in the individual competition. In 1997 McGinley and Harrington won $200,000 each, McGinley won a further $15,000 for finishing fourth in the individual competition while Harrington won $5,000 for equal fifth.

SONIA'S BIG BIG YEAR 1998 marked a watershed in the career of Sonia O'Sullivan, emerging from the debris of the previous two seasons she won two World and two European titles. Never had she enjoyed such a successful season in terms of major championships won, in previous years O'Sullivan proved all but unbeatable on the Grand Prix Circuit but did not always deliver in the major championships. Realising that few remember Grand Prix winners and the success of an athlete's career will ultimately be judged on their record at major championships she focused solely on these. Success came in the World Cross Country Championship in March where she won both the long course (7.6km) and short course (4 km) titles within 24 hours. A summer of fourths, fifths and sixths on the Grand Prix circuit dovetailed into an unprecedented 5,000m/10,000m double victory in the European Championships. The ghosts of championships past were well and truly exorcised in 1998.

CATHERINA THE MARATHON WOMAN Cavan woman Catherina McKiernan dominated road racing in the twelve months past. Having set the fastest ever marathon debut time of two hours 23 minutes and 44 seconds in winning the Berlin marathon in September 1997 she remained unbeaten in fourteen races until June 1998. In winning the London marathon in April McKiernan realised her huge potential in the event, London is after all, one of the most lucrative marathons on the international circuit and attracts a strong talented field. Despite her inexperience she beat the 1996 champion, Liz McColgan and the 1997 champion Joyce Chepchumba into second and third respectively and her time of two hours 26 minutes twenty six seconds was the seventh fastest time recorded in London. Success had often eluded McKiernan as evidenced by four consecutive silver medals at the World Cross Country Championships between 1992 and 1995 and under performance at major track championships but the switch to road running has already paid rich dividends. Already she is being touted as a possible Olympic champion in Sydney, but she hasn't turned her back completely on cross country. A clash between her and a certain Sonia O'Sullivan at the 1999 World Championships in Belfast is a mouth watering prospect indeed.

DOHERTY NARROWLY FAILS IN BRAVE TITLE DEFENCE In 1998, as in 1997, Ken Doherty saved his best form for the Crucible Theatre in Sheffield, the venue of the Embassy World Championships. Despite a good showing in the 1998 Irish Masters where he was beaten 9-3 by Ronnie O'Sullivan in the final (which he was later awarded when O'Sullivan failed a drugs test) Doherty went into the World Championships in a decidedly low key way. Attention was focused elsewhere on O'Sullivan, John Higgins, Stephen Higgins and the people's champion, Jimmy White. Doherty remained out of the limelight and after defeating Lee Walker, Stephen Lee and Matthew Stephens he faced Mark Williams in the semi-final. After Williams' high profile victories and Doherty's solid but not spectacular ones Doherty found himself in a familiar position. Underdog. Thriving on this Doherty beat Williams and faced John Higgins in the final. No previous first-time champion had successfully defended his title and so it proved for Doherty. He played well, but Higgins' game was flawless. Capitalising on virtually every scoring opportunity and punishing mistakes when they occurred he ran out winner on a scoreline of 18-12. Two world finals in two years, Doherty passed the mantle of champion gracefully, and he could afford to, as runner-up he collected a cool £132,000.

JORDAN'S COMING OF AGE Eddie Jordan turned 50 somewhere in Brazil on March 30th 1998. The Brazilian Grand Prix on the previous day had seen his team Ralf Schumacher crashed out, Damon Hill finished but was disqualified for having an underweight car and now here was a cake groaning under the weight of fifty candles. The season was only two races old, Jordan were well off the pace and McLaren were miles ahead of everyone, Ferrari, Williams, Bennetton couldn't live with them, no-one could. Worse lay ahead. The season was half finished before Ralf Schumacher scraped home in sixth at the British Grand Prix in July to score Jordan's first championship point. Reliability had proven elusive all season but the Silverstone sixth proved a turning point. Damon Hill finished fourth in consecutive races, Ralf Schumacher was scoring too. The Belgian Grand Prix on August 30 was Jordan's 126th race since entering Formula 1 in 1991. In heavy rain Hill and Schumacher survived a first corner crash. Restarted the rain caused problems for others, but not the Jordan team. Hill won, Schumacher was second and Eddie Jordan wept and whooped with delight. Jordan Grand Prix had finally come of age and were well on their way to their best season points tally ever.

LE TOUR DE FRANCE EN IRLANDE 1998 Men with shaved legs, bright jerseys and high-tech machines. Freshly tarred roads, Wicklow Gap and the peleton. *Le Grande Depart*, the caravan and French tricolours. After many years of lobbying, and then planning, the Tour de France arrived in Ireland in July. The drugs storm which later engulfed the Tour was but a distant cloud when Chris Boardman won the Prologue in Dublin City Centre on July 11th. The first stage proper rolled out of Dundrum, home of 1987 Tour winner Stephen Roche a spectacular trip over Wicklow gap was seen, we were assured, by hundreds of millions of people worldwide. The finish in the Phoenix park provided a spectacular crash. Top sprinter and one of the pre-race favourites Mario Cipollini crashed near the finish, the stage was won by Tom Steels while Cipollini, surrounded by his *domestiques*, trailed in over five minutes down. The second stage covered 200 kilometres from Enniscorthy to Cork travelling through Carrick-on-Suir, the home of Seán Kelly. The stage was won Jan Svorada but race leader Chris Boardman crashed out and failed to finish the stage and a young female spectator was also injured. The Tour and entourage then boarded three ferries and three aeroplanes and arrived in Roscoff for the start of the third stage.

TROUBLES FOR MICHELLE DE BRUIN It was an awful year for Irish swimming star, Michelle de Bruin. Since her glory days of Olympic success in Atlanta in 1996, there had been allegations and whispers about the reasons for that success. De Bruin eventually issued legal proceedings against a number of media outlets. However, it all reached a climax this year when she was banned by the international swimming body, FINA, for allegedly manipulating a urine sample. De Bruin has steadfastly rejected this finding, stating that she "will not go away" just to please the critics who want to believe her guilt. She is issuing proceedings against FINA to clear her name.

SPORTS CHRONOLOGY OF THE YEAR

02: Boxing WBO Super Middleweight champion Steve Collins announced his retirement from boxing. A tearful Celtic Warrior made his shock announcement in London 24 hours after his ninth title defence was cancelled on medical grounds.

04: Greyhound Racing Tom's The Best won the £50,000 Irish Derby at Shelbourne Park.

05: GAA Limerick beat Galway 1-12 to 1-9 in the National League Hurling final.

Cork easily won the All-Ireland Vocational Schools Hurling final beating Galway by 4-13 to 3-3.

Antrim side Dunloy won the Ulster Club Hurling final beating Derry champions Lavey 3-16 to 4-10.

07: Soccer The Republic of Ireland beat Northern Ireland 4-0 in an U18 friendly match at Tolka Park.

10: Soccer Romania beat the Republic of Ireland 2-0 in a European U21 qualifying match at Drogheda.

11: Boxing Antrim's Mark Winters beat Carl Wright on points to win the vacant British Light Welterweight title.

Soccer The Republic of Ireland finished second in group eight of the European World Cup qualifiers following a 1-1 draw with group winners, Romania. The Republic's qualification for the World Cup finals will be decided in a two-leg play-off.

Northern Ireland finished their qualifying group with a 1-0 defeat in Portugal.

12: Formula 1 Ferrari's Eddie Irvine finished third in the Japanese Grand Prix at Suzuka.

GAA Monaghan retained the All-Ireland Women's football title beating Waterford 2-15 to 1-16 in front of 15,501 spectators in Croke Park. Longford won the women's Junior football title beating Tyrone 2-12 to 1-11 in the Croke Park curtain raiser.

Golf Paul McGinley won the Smurfit Irish PGA Championship at Fota Island by one shot from David Higgins, John McHenry and Stephen Hamill.

16: Golf South Africa beat the Irish team of Paul McGinley, Darren Clarke and Padraig Harrington 2-1 in the opening round of the Dunhill Cup.

17: Golf Ireland lost 2-1 to Scotland in their second group match in the Dunhill Cup.

18: Golf Ireland won their final match of the Dunhill Cup by defeating Germany 2-1.

Horse Racing Mick Kinnane partnered Pilsudski to victory in the Dubai Stakes at Newmarket.

22: Soccer The Republic of Ireland U18s beat Azerbaijan 4-2 in Moldova.

23: Soccer Northern Ireland manager Bryan Hamilton was sacked by the IFA.

24: Boxing Steven Kirk won a bronze medal in the light heavyweight division at the World Championships when he was stopped in the second round of his semi-final by Russian Alexandr Lebziakin.

Soccer The Republic of Ireland U18s beat their Moldovan counterparts 1-0 in a European qualifying group match.

26: Formula 1 Eddie Irvine finished fifth in the final Grand Prix of the season, the European Grand Prix at Jerez, Spain. The Drivers' Championship was headed by Canadian Jacques Villeneuve with Irvine in

eighth place overall. The Constructors' Championship was won by Williams, the Jordan team finished fifth overall.

Golf Paul McGinley recorded his second ever European PGA Tour victory in winning the Oki Pro-Am in Madrid by four shots. His four round total of 266 was 22 shots under par.

Soccer Roy Keane (Senior Player), David Connolly (Young Player), Peter Hutton (National League) and Franz Beckenbauer (International Celebrity) were among the major winners at the 1997 FAI Opel Awards ceremony.

29: Soccer The Republic of Ireland were held to a 1-1 draw by Belgium in the World Cup play-off first leg match at Lansdowne Road. Denis Irwin scored the Republic's goal from a free kick in the eighth minute, Luc Nilis equalised for Belgium on 30 minutes.

31: Swimming Michelle deBruin was slightly injured in a car accident in Kilkenny which put her plans to compete in January's World Championships in Australia in doubt.

02: GAA Mickey Whelan's two year tenure as Dublin football manager ended when he announced his resignation after Dublin's 1-11 to 1-8 defeat to Offaly in the National League.

Golf Padraig Harrington finished second in the Volvo Masters at Jerez, Spain. Bad weather limited the tournament to three rounds.

Snooker Ken Doherty beat John Higgins 7-5 in the Malta Grand Prix Trophy final.

08: Rugby Connacht's European adventure ended when they lost 40-27 to French side Agen in the quarter-finals of the European Conference.

09: GAA Munster beat Leinster by 0-14 to 0-10 in the Railway Cup Hurling final at Ballinasloe. Louth won the All-Ireland B Football championship defeating Clare 1-11 to 1-8. Dungiven became Ulster Club football champions defeating Errigal Ciaran 0-14 to 1-8.

15: Rugby Ireland conceded seven tries and six penalties in the 63-15 defeat by New Zealand at Lansdowne Road.

Soccer The Republic of Ireland failed to qualify for the 1998 World Cup finals when they lost 2-1 to Belgium in the second leg play-off in Brussels. The Republic lost 3-2 on aggregate.

22: Soccer In the National League Premier Division Stephen Geoghegan celebrated a new milestone when scored his 99th and 100th goals in helping Shelbourne beat Kilkenny City 3-1.

23: Golf The Irish team of Padraig Harrington and Paul McGinley won the World Cup at Kiawah Island, South Carolina by five shots. They finished with record 31 under par aggregate. McGinley finished fourth on the individual leaderboard with Harrington in fifth. In 1958 Harry Bradshaw and Christy O'Connor collected £357 for their win (the competition was then known as the Canada Cup), this time around McGinley and Harrington collected $200,000 each.

27: Soccer George Best was voted the second best footballer of all time behind Pele in the International Hall of Fame.

30: Athletics Seamus Power retained his senior men's National Intercounties Cross Country title with the team title going to Dublin. In the women's event Teresa Duffy emerged victorious with Donegal winning the team title.

Rugby Ireland beat Canada 33-11 at Lansdowne Road, Kevin Nowlan from St Mary's College scored two of Ireland's five tries.

DECEMBER

02: Soccer Glenavon beat Coleraine 4-1 in the final of the Ulster Gold Cup.

03: GAA In his first budget the Minister for Finance, Charlie McCreevy, announced the allocation of £20 million to the GAA towards the redevelopment of Croke Park.

The 1997 Hurling All-Stars were announced. Clare had six representatives, Tipperary four, Kilkenny three (including DJ Carey's sixth in seven years), while Galway and Wexford received one apiece.

05: GAA The 1997 Gaelic Football All-Stars were announced. All-Ireland champions Kerry received five, Kildare three, Meath and Mayo two each and Derry, Cavan and Offaly one each.

06: GAA Sarsfields of Galway won the Connacht Club hurling title beating Tooreen of Mayo by 5-15 to 1-5.

07: Rallying Dessie Nutt and Elkin Robinson won the Killarney Historic Car Rally in a Porsche 911.

GAA Erin's Isle from Dublin won the AIB Leinster Club football championship while Clarecastle won the Munster Club hurling championship.

Soccer The Republic of Ireland beat Wales 3-0 in the women's UEFA Championship qualifiers.

08: GAA Tommy Carr was formally appointed as Dublin senior football manager.

14: GAA Castlehaven won the Munster Club football championship beating Fethard 1-14 to 1-8. Clarecastle comfortably beat St. Gabriel's in the All-Ireland Club hurling championship quarter final in London.

16: Horse Racing Tony McCoy set a new record for the fastest 150 winners in a season when winning on Deano's Beep at Bangor.

20: Boxing Darren Corbett won the Commonwealth Cruiserweight title when he beat England's Rab Norton on points.

Rugby Italy inflicted a third consecutive defeat on Ireland when they won 37-22 in Bologna.

21: Squash Derek Ryan won the National Championship when he beat Willie Hosey in straight sets. Madeline Perry won the women's Championship beating Anna McGeever 3-1 in sets.

23: Cricket Ireland lost to tournament favourites New Zealand in the quarter-final of the women's World Cup.

26: Horse Racing Kieran Gaule on Dardjini won the Denny Gold Medal Novice Chase at Leopardstown.

27: Horse Racing Time For a Run, the mount of Philip Fenton won the Paddy Power Chase at Leopardstown.

JANUARY

03: Athletics Catherina McKiernan won the 5.2 kms senior women's race in the IAAF Cross Country International in Durham.

04: Hockey Avoca won the National Indoor League,

beating Railway union 2-0 in the final which was held at the National Basketball Arena in Tallaght.

Tennis Owen Casey won the men's Irish Indoor Open Championship beating John Doran in three sets. Gina Niland won the women's title beating Laura McCracken by two sets to love.

10: Horse Racing Race favourite Graphic Equaliser won the Ladbroke Handicap Hurdle at Leopardstown by four lengths.

12: Swimming Adrian O'Connor and Colin Lowth finished 43rd and 45th respectively in the 200m Freestyle at the World Championships in Perth.

14: Swimming At the World Championships Colin Lowth set a new Irish record of 2:03.05 in the 200m Butterfly, he won his heat and was 26th overall. Nick O'Hare and Hugh O'Connor finished in 51st and 55th overall in the 100m Freestyle.

16: Swimming Colin Lowth set a personal best of 57.56 when finishing 49th overall in the 100m Butterfly in Perth.

18: Swimming At the World Championships in Perth brothers Adrian and Hugh O'Connor finished in 24th and 26th overall in the 200m Backstroke. Nick O'Hare finished 38th overall in the 50m Freestyle.

23: Boxing The National Senior Finals (amateur) were held in the National Stadium, winners and their weights were: Light fly - James Rooney; Fly - Martin Murphy; Bantam - Bernard Dunne; Feather - Pat O'Donnell; Light - Eugene McEneaney; Light welter - Mark Wickam; Welter - Neil Gough; Light middle - Michael Roche; Middle - Brian Magee; Light heavy - Alan Sheerin; Heavy - John Kiely; Super heavy - Stephen Reynolds.

24: Athletics Peter Matthews in fourth place was the top Irish finisher at the International Cross Country meeting held in Belfast. The race was won by Laban Chege of Kenya. In the women's event Maureen Harrington in fourteenth was best of the Irish and the race was won by Romanian Marianna Chirila.

Ten Pin Bowling P. Delany won the Irish Open Championship at Stillorgan with a score of 1835, N. Thienpondt was second on 1769. M. Goldwater won the women's event with a score of 1689 with I. Oien second on 1643.

25: Basketball Notre Dame beat Neptune 79-73 in the men's Sprite National Cup final while in the women's final Wildcats beat Naomh Mhuire 72-58.

Bowls Margaret Johnston beat Phillis Nolan in the National Indoor singles final.

27: Squash Derek Ryan beat Dan Jenson in four sets to win the Hartford Cup in Conneticut, his first ranking tournament victory.

28: Soccer The Republic of Ireland beat Scotland 2-0 in an U16 friendly at Richmond Park.

FEBRUARY

01: Athletics Catherina McKiernan won the 6,000m Rás na hÉireann at Dunleer, Seamus Power won the men's 10,000m event.

Badminton Title winners from the National Championships at Lisburn: M. Watt (men's singles), S. McGinn (women's singles), B. Topping & M. O'Meara (men's doubles), C. Henderson & J. Plunkett (women's doubles) and G. Henderson & J. Plunkett (mixed doubles).

Golf Padraig Harrington finished equal third in the Perth Classic, two shots behind winner Thomas Bjorn.

03: Awards The 1997 Texaco Awards were announced with Maurice Fitzgerald, Keith Wood, Ken Doherty and Michelle Smith among the winners.

04: GAA D.J. Carey shocked the sporting nation when he announced his retirement from hurling at the age of 27.

06: Boxing Ireland recorded a seven bouts to two victory in the annual Kuttner Shield Match with Scotland.

07: Rugby Ireland lost the opening game of the Five Nations Championship when Scotland beat them 17-16 at Lansdowne Road. Ireland led for most of the match but a 70th minute penalty gave the Scots a one point victory.

08: GAA Ulster beat Leinster 0-20 to 0-17 after extra time in the final of the football Railway Cup.

Horse Racing Dorans Pride comfortably won the Hennessy Gold Cup at Leopardstown beating Dun Belle by 15 lengths.

Squash Derek Ryan won the European Champions of Champions tournament in Oslo.

10: Skiing Pauli Patrick Schwarzacher-Joyce, Ireland's sole skier at the Winter Olympics, finished 21st in the slalom section of the men's combined competition.

11: Soccer A 44th minute goal from George O'Boyle gave Northern Ireland a 1-0 victory over the Republic of Ireland in a 'B' International at Tolka Park.

13: Athletics Marcus O'Sullivan became only the third athlete in history to run 100 sub four minute miles. The Cork man finished third, in a time of 3:58.10, in the Wannamaker Mile at the Melrose Games in New York. Mark Carroll won his third consecutive Melrose Games 3,000m title in a time of 7:49.37.

Skiing At the Winter Olympics in Nagano, Japan Pauli Patrick Schwarzacher-Joyce finished 27th in the Downhill section of the men's combined which earned him 16th position overall.

14: Athletics Ireland's men finished eighth overall at the European Cross Country Championships at Lisbon, the leading Irish finisher was Peter Matthews in 16th. The Irish women's team finished 10th overall with Valerie Vaughan in 42nd as their top finisher.

Basketball Star of the Sea's victory over Dugannon secured the men's Superleague title for them.

15: Athletics Some of the major winners in the men's competition from the National Indoor Championships (held in Nenagh) were: Neil Ryan, 60m; Gary Ryan, 200m; Stephen Fleming, 400m; James Nolan, 800m; Eugene O'Neill, 1,500m; J Daly, 3,000m; Mark Mandy, high jump; S Finnie, long jump; Dylan McDermott, pole vault; and Jason Flynn, shot putt. Major winners in the women's competition include: Lena Barry, 60m and 200m; Karen Shinkins, 400m; Freda Davoren, 800m and 1,500m; Aine Cuddihy, 60m hurdles; Sharon Foley, high jump; and Bridie Lynch, shot putt. Haile Gebrselassie (Ethiopia) broke Eamon Coghlan's 1987 indoor 2,000m world record.

Badminton The Irish men's team beat Brazil 5-0 while the women beat Spain, also on a 5-0 scoreline in the international competition in Norway.

17: Badminton Sweden beat Ireland 5-0 in the women's Uber Cup European Zone semi final.

Soccer Neil Ogden's 64 minute goal separated the sides as Sligo Rovers beat Shelbourne 1-0 in the League Cup final first leg at the Showgrounds. Linfield beat Crusaders 1-0 in the final of the County Antrim Shield.

19: Surfing Wild card entries Terence and Joe McNulty finished third and fourth overall in the Big Wave World Championships in Mexico to give Ireland an astounding second place overall. The quality of the result can be judged by the positions of other 'recognised' surfing nations, Brazil were first, the United States third and Australia fourth.

20: Bobsleigh Ireland 1 (Terry McHugh, G Power, Simon Linscheid and J Pamplin) finished 29th overall in the four man heats at the Nagano Winter Olympics.

22: Motor Sport Austin McHale and Brian Murphy won the Galway International Rally by over a minute from Bertie Fisher and Rory Kennedy.

23: Hockey Riet Kuper was appointed as the national ladies team new coach. Ms Kuper is a former Dutch international.

24: Rugby Brian Ashton resigned as the Irish national coach, within hours the IRFU announced that Connacht's New Zealand born coach Warren Gatland would take over coaching responsibilities for the remaining three games of the Five Nations Championship.

Soccer Sligo Rovers claimed the League Cup when they held Shelbourne scoreless in the second leg at Tolka Park. They won 1-0 on aggregate.

25: Athletics Sonia O'Sullivan won the 5,000m in the IAAF Grand Prix meeting in Melbourne. Marcus O'Sullivan finished third in the men's mile in another sub four minute time of 3:56.35

27: Swimming Irish winners from the Leisureland International meet included Nick O'Hare (whose time of 22.76 for the 50m Freestyle was a new Irish record). Niamh Cawley set a national junior record of 1.03.66 in winning the 100m backstroke.

28: Athletics Sonia O'Sullivan won the 1,500m in the IAAF Grand Prix in Sydney. Marcus O'Sullivan came third in the men's 1,500m.

Hockey Pegasus won the the women's Irish Senior Cup beating Old Alexandra 5-0 at Belfield. Harlequins won the Munster Senior League for women when they beat Belvedere 5-1.

Horse Racing Tony McCoy broke the record for the fastest 200 winners in a single National Hunt season.

MARCH

01: Athletics UCD athletes James Nolan and David Matthews finished fourth and fifth respectively in the 800m final at the European Indoor Championships.

Basketball In the last round of the men's Division One Championship Sligo beat Limerick 98-81 to win the title.

Swimming Michelle de Bruin set a new Irish record of 4:14.02 when winning the 400m freestyle at Galway.

02: Hockey Glynis Taylor was appointed assistant to national women's coach Riet Kuper.

04: Soccer The Republic of Ireland U18s drew 1-1 with France in Nice.

06: Soccer Republic of Ireland captain Andy Townsend announced his retirement from international football.

08: Formula 1 Eddie Irvine finished fourth in the first

Grand Prix of the year in Australia.

Soccer The Republic of Ireland beat Wales 4-0 in the women's World Cup qualifier at Bray.

14: Rowing Neptune won the men's Open Eights at the Tribesmen Head of the River event on Lough Corrib.

15: Athletics Catherina McKiernan won the Lisbon half-marathon in a time of one hour seven minutes 50 seconds.

Basketball Star of the Sea beat Notre Dame 92-74 in the men's Superleague Championship final while Wildcats beat Tolka Rovers 82-68 in the women's decider.

GAA Scotland beat Ireland 0-12 to 0-7 in the annual Shinty International which was held in Kilkenny.

17: GAA Corofin beat Erin's Isle by 0-15 to 0-10 in the All-Ireland football club championship final at Croke Park. In the hurling decider Birr, champions in 1995, proved too strong for Sarsfields, champions in 1993 and 1994, beating them 1-13 to 0-9.

Horse Racing The Aidan O'Brien trained Istabraq carried Charlie Swan to a twelve length victory in the Champion Hurdle. Ireland's French Ballerina won the opening race of meeting, the Supreme Novice's Hurdle.

18: Horse Racing Richard Dunwoody guided the Willie Mullins trained Florida Pearl to victory in the Royal & SunAlliance Chase on the second day of the Cheltenham festival. Alexander Banquet made it double for Ireland and Mullins when he won the Festival Bumper.

19: Horse Racing Tony McCoy rode the last three winners of the festival to claim the Jockey's Championship. Adrian Maguire was seriously injured in the Grand Annual Chase.

20: GAA DJ Carey announced his intention to return to hurling barely six weeks after announcing his retirement.

21: Athletics Sonia O'Sullivan became the first Irish woman to win the World Cross Country Championship when she completed the eight kilometre course, near Marakesh in Morocco, in a time of 25 minutes 39 seconds.

Rugby Twenty points from man-of-the-match Neil Jenkins led Wales to a 30-21 victory over Ireland in the Five Nations Championship. Despite leading 12-3 after 26 minutes and 15-13 at half-time Ireland, through a number of handling and defensive errors, fell behind early in the second half. An 80th minute Jenkins try put the Welsh on the right side of a somewhat flattering scoreline.

Soccer The Republic of Ireland drew 1-1 with Poland in an U15 international held at Newbridge.

22: Athletics Sonia O'Sullivan won the 4,000m short course World Cross Country Championship in Morocco.

24: Horse Racing Tony McCoy equalled Peter Scudamore's record of 221 winners in a season when winning the Court Selling Hurdle at Chepstow.

Soccer The Czech Republic beat the Republic of Ireland 3-0 in an U21 international in Drnovice.

25: Soccer The Republic of Ireland were beaten 2-1 by the Czech Republic in the friendly international in Olomouc. Gary Breen was the Republic's goalscorer. Slovakia provided the opposition at Windsor Park where

a 51st minute goal from captain Steve Lomas gave Lawrie McMenemy a winning start to his tenure as Northern Ireland manager.

The Republic of Ireland beat Greece 1-0 in the first leg of the UEFA U18 qualifying round play-off.

27: Boxing England beat Ireland 6-5 in the amateur boxing international held at the National Stadium.

28: Rowing Neptune won the men's Open Eights title in the Head of the River Race on the Liffey. Trinity College won the women's Open Eights race.

Swimming Michelle Smith set a new Irish record of 1:59.69 for the 200m freestyle at the Leinster championships.

29: Snooker Ronnie O'Sullivan won the Irish Masters final beating Ken Doherty 9-3 in the final. O'Sullivan picked up the winner's cheque of £75,000, Doherty won £34,000 plus £3,000 for the highest tournament break of 129.

APRIL

03: Rugby Ireland claimed two Triple Crowns courtesy of the U21 and Universities teams. Ireland U21 beat England U21 9-7 while the Irish Universities beat their English counterparts 80-30.

04: Golf Dublin won the All-Ireland intercounties final, beating Kerry 4-1 at Lahinch.

Hockey Harlequins beat UCC 4-3 in the women's Munster Senior Cup final.

In the final of the women's Irish Junior Cup Pembroke Wanderers seconds beat Old Alexandra's seconds 3-1.

Cork Church of Ireland beat Harlequins 4-3 on penalty strokes in the men's Munster Senior Cup final.

Rugby Ireland finished the Five Nations Championship pointless when they lost 35-17 to England at Twickenham in their last game of the championship. Denis Hickey with two tries and Eric Elwood with two conversions and a penalty were Ireland's scorers.

05: Cycling Tommy Evans won the 87 mile Des Hanlon Memorial Race at Carlow.

08: Soccer The Republic of Ireland's U18 team beat hosts Portugal 2-0 in the four nation invitational tournament in Lisbon.

09: Soccer The Republic's U18 team drew 0-0 with France in the quadrangular tournament in Portugal.

11: Soccer The Republic of Ireland beat Austria 2-1 in the final of the Oporto Tournament in Lisbon.

12: Basketball Ireland completed a clean sweep of victories to win the women's Four Countries International tournament when they beat Scotland 69-38.

Formula 1 Ferrari's Eddie Irvine finished third in the Argentinian Grand Prix at Buenos Aries.

Golf With rounds of 76, 73, 67 and 69 Darren Clarke finished in joint eighth in the US Masters at Augusta, Georgia. The tournament was won by Mark O'Meara.

Rugby Ireland beat France 18-0 to win the World U19 Championship. Paddy Wallace and Darragh Holt provided Ireland with a try apiece, Wallace also helped himself to a drop goal while Brian O'Driscoll kicked a penalty and a conversion.

13: Motor rallying Bertie Fisher provisionally won the Circuit of Ireland by 19 seconds from Austin McHale. The result was subsequently overturned when McHale had a 20 second penalty, which he incurred on the first day of the rally, quashed. His one second winning margin was the narrowest ever in the Circuit of Ireland.

14: Cycling The final days racing in the Tour of the North was abandoned due to bad weather and the leader after four stages, Andy Proffitt, was declared the winner.

Golf Noel Fox won the West of Ireland Amateur Championship in Enniscrone, beating Pat Lyons on a score of 2 and 1.

18: Hockey Cork Church of Ireland won their seventh consecutive Munster League title when they beat Harlequins 2-1.

Three Rock Rovers seconds beat Annadale's seconds 4-0 in the men's Irish Junior Cup final.

Soccer Cliftonville's 1-1 draw with Glentoran was enough to win the Irish League following Linfield's scoreless draw with Coleraine.

22: GAA Australia beat Ireland 56-51 in the U17 Compromise Rules test match at Croke Park.

Rugby Pat Whelan announced his resignation as manager of the national team. In his 20 games in charge Ireland won five, and lost 15.

Soccer In senior international friendlies the Republic of Ireland were beaten 2-0 by Argentina at Lansdowne Road while Northern Ireland recorded their second successive victory under new manager Lawrie McMenemie when they beat Switzerland 1-0 at Windsor Park.

23: Sports Minister Dr Jim McDaid announced the 1998 sports allocation by government of over £3.65 million.

25: Hockey Two late goals from Neil Cooke secured a 3-2 victory for Instonians over underdogs Three Rock Rovers in the Irish Senior Cup final.

Rugby Shannon beat Garryowen 15-9 in the final of the AIL held at Lansdowne Road. Four penalties and a dropped goal from man-of-the-match Andrew Thompson helped Shannon to their fourth successive AIL title.

26: Athletics Catherina McKiernan won the London marathon in a time of two hours 26 minutes and 26 seconds. This was her second marathon victory (from two starts) and fourteenth consecutive victory in road racing.

Formula 1 Eddie Irvine secured his second consecutive podium finish when he finished third in the San Marino Grand Prix behind David Coulthard and Michael Schumacher.

GAA Offaly won their first ever National Football League title when they beat Derry by 0-9 to 0-7 in heavy rain at Croke Park.

Tyrone won the All-Ireland vocational schools title when they beat Offaly by 2-17 to 1-5 also at Croke Park.

Soccer The Republic of Ireland drew 0-0 with Scotland in the UEFA U16 Championship finals in Scotland.

28: Soccer The Republic of Ireland beat Finland 2-0 in the U16 UEFA Championships in Scotland.

Swimming Allegations about Michelle de Bruin resurfaced when it emerged that a drugs test taken by her in January produced alleged evidence of 'physical manipulation.'

29: Snooker Ken Doherty beat Matthew Stevens 13-10 in the World Championship quarter-final at Sheffield.

30: Soccer A goal from David McMahon gave the Republic of Ireland a 1-0 victory over defending champions Spain in the UEFA U16 Championships.

MAY

01: Cricket Ireland were beaten by 115 runs by Glamorgan in the Benson & Hedges Cup match at Castle Avenue.

Hockey The Irish women's team drew 2-2 with Scotland.

Soccer St Patrick's Athletic won the FAI National League when they beat Kilkenny City 2-1 at Kilkenny. Shelbourne, two points clear at the top before the final round of matches, lost 2-1 away to Dundalk allowing St Pats to claim the title by a single point. Elsewhere Shamrock Rovers drew 2-2 with Cork City.

02: Hockey The Irish senior women's team drew 1-1 with Scotland while the U21s beat Germany 1-0.

Horse Racing Mick Kinane guided the Aidan O'Brien trained King of Kings to victory in the 2,000 Guineas at Newmarket.

Rugby The Irish women's team were beaten 21-0 by Australia in the Women's World Cup in Holland.

Snooker Ken Doherty beat Mark Williams 17-14 to qualify for the final of the World Championships at Sheffield.

Soccer Glenavon beat Glentoran 1-0 after extra time in the Bass Irish Cup final.

03: Soccer The Republic of Ireland beat Denmark 2-0 in the UEFA U16 Championship quarter final.

Tennis Ireland lost their Davis Cup tie 4-1 to Hungary in Budapest.

04: Athletics Tommy Hughes won the Belfast marathon and England's Jackie Newton won the women's race.

Cricket Essex beat Ireland by 171 runs in the Benson & Hedges Cup at Chelmsford.

Hockey Instonians won the men's All-Ireland Club Championship on goal difference from Cork Church of Ireland.

Snooker John Higgins beat Ken Doherty 18-12 in the final of the World Championships in Sheffield. Doherty did, however, collect the runner's up cheque of £132,000.

05: Cricket Middlesex beat Ireland by six wickets in their Benson & Hedges Cup match at Lord's.

Soccer The Republic of Ireland beat Portugal 2-0 in the semi-final of the UEFA U16 Championship in Perth, Scotland.

Tennis Bosnia-Herzegovina beat Ireland 2-1 in the Federation Cup in Turkey.

06: Tennis Ireland beat Estonia 2-1 in the Federation Cup with Gina Niland and Lesley O'Halloran winning their singles matches.

07: Tennis Ireland beat Moldova 2-1 in the Federation Cup

08: Hockey Three goals from Kim Mills helped the Irish women's team to a 5-1 victory over Italy in a four nations tournament at Belfield.

Soccer The Republic of Ireland U16 team won the European U16 Championship beating Italy 2-1 in the final in Scotland. The Irish goal scorers were Keith Foy and David McMahon.

Tennis Ireland were beaten 3-0 by Georgia in the Federation Cup in Turkey.

09: GAA Kerry beat Laois 2-8 to 0-11 in the All-Ireland U21 football final held in Limerick.

Hockey The Irish women's team beat France 5-0 at the Four Nations tournament at Belfield.

Tennis Ireland beat Iceland 3-0 in their final match in the Federation Cup but failed to progress to the next round.

10: Canoeing Ian Wiley won the K1 class at the Irish Open held on the Liffey near Lucan. Tadhg McIntyre won the C1 class.

Golf Nineteen year-old Michael Hoey won the Irish Amateur Open Strokeplay title at Royal Dublin by two shots from Gary Cullen.

Paul McGinley finished third in the Turespana Masters held in Majorca.

Hockey Ireland beat Wales 5-1 to claim top spot in the women's Four Nations tournament at Belfield.

Rugby At the Galway Sportsground Corinthians shocked Galwegians to win the Connacht Senior Cup 19-15.

Soccer The FAI Cup final at Dalymount Park between Cork City and Shelbourne finished scoreless.

14: Soccer The Republic of Ireland qualified for the European U18 Championships with a 2-0 victory over Greece (3-0 on aggregate).

15: Snooker It emerged that Benson & Hedges Irish Masters winner Ronnie O'Sullivan failed a random drugs test at Goffs in March when traces of cannabis were found in his sample. (O'Sullivan was stripped of his title and prize-money on July 6th.)

16: Rugby In the Munster Senior Cup final Shannon beat Young Munster 19-18 to record their second AIL/Munster Cup double in three years.

In the Leinster Senior Cup Lansdowne beat Skerries 23-17.

Soccer A 73rd minute goal from Derek Coughlan gave Cork City a 1-0 victory over Shelbourne in the FAI Cup final replay at Dalymount Park.

17: GAA Cork beat Waterford 2-14 to 0-13 in the NHL final held at Semple Stadium.

Golf Darren Clarke won the Benson & Hedges International at The Oxfordshire by three shots from Spaniard Santiago Luna.

Joe McDermott, originally from Clare but based in the US for the past 40 years, won the Irish Seniors Open at Woodbrook on the fifth sudden death play-off hole.

Soccer Thirty nine thousand fans attended Paul McGrath's testimonial match at Lansdowne road which saw the Republic of Ireland lose to an international selection. McGrath also made his final appearance in an Irish shirt.

18: Soccer The Republic of Ireland U21s beat Scotland 3-0 in the opening match of their triangular tournament at Ballybofey.

19: Basketball In the opening games of men's European basketball championship preliminary round Ireland beat Switzerland 88-80 but were beaten 57-56 by Cyprus.

Rugby Dungannon beat Malone 19-16 in the Ulster Senior Cup final at Ravenhill.

21: Soccer Northern Ireland drew 1-1 with Scotland in the U21 quadrangular tournament.

22: Soccer Northern Ireland won the quadrangular tournament thanks to a 1-0 victory over the Republic in Castlebar.

23: Golf Lillian Behan won the Irish Women's Amateur Close Championship at Clandeboye beating Oonagh Purfield at the nineteenth hole in the final.

Horse Racing Olivier Peslier guided Desert Prince to victory in the 1,000 Guineas at the Curragh leaving red hot favourite Second Empire three lengths back in third.

Soccer The Republic of Ireland drew 0-0 with Mexico in a friendly at Lansdowne Road.

24: Boxing Belfast middleweight Brian Magee claimed a silver medal at the European Championships when he was beaten in the middleweight final 10-2 by Hungarian Zsolt Erdei

Cycling The FBD Milk Rás was won by Waterford man Ciaran Power in a time of 29 hours, 44 minutes and 49 seconds. Tommy Evans from county Down made it a one-two for the Irish team 45 seconds behind Power. The ninth and final stage of the Rás was won by Michael Fitzgerald.

Formula 1 Eddie Irvine finished third in the Monaco Grand Prix. Despite finishing the race the Jordans of Damon Hill and Ralf Schumacher were well out of contention.

Horse Racing Seventeen year old Jamie Spencer rode Tarascon to victory in the 2,000 Guineas at the Curragh.

Snooker Ken Doherty beat Jimmy White 10-2 in the final of the Dr. Martens Premier League.

30: GAA A special congress convened to discuss the deletion of Rule 21 -the rule which prohibits members of the RUC and British Army from membership of the organisation and members of the GAA from attending functions organised by those forces- agreed to delete the rule when the provisions relating to policing set out in the Good Friday Agreement are implemented.

Rugby Ireland opened their tour of South Africa with a 48-35 victory over provincial side Boland.

31: Horse Racing Charlie Swan brought his ninth successive season at the head of the jockey's championship to a close with a win in Tralee.

JUNE

01: Golf Darren Clarke finished second in the Deutsche Bank Open in Hamburg, one shot behind winner Lee Westwood. Philip Walton finished fourth.

Snooker: TJ Dowling retained his National Snooker Championship title beating Douglas Hyde 8-4 in the final held at the Ivy Rooms in Carlow.

03: Rugby South-West District beat Ireland 27-20 in the second game of the South African tour in George.

Soccer Spain beat Northern Ireland 4-1 in Santander, Gerry Taggart was Northern Ireland's goalscorer.

05: Cricket Ireland beat Bangladesh by four wickets at Waringstown.

Horse Racing Mick Kinane guided the Aidan O'Brien trained Shahtoush to victory in the Oaks at Epsom.

06: Rugby Western Province beat Ireland 12-6 in Cape Town, with David Humphreys scoring two penalties for Ireland.

07: Athletics Catherina McKiernan comfortably won the Women's Mini Marathon in Dublin. Her time of 33 minutes 22.0 seconds was over a minute quicker than her nearest rival.

Irish records from Karen Shinkins in the 400m and Susan Smith in the 100m Hurdles were the outstanding results in a strong team performance at the

Europa Cup in Lithuania.

Formula 1 Ferrari's Eddie Irvine finished third in the Canadian Grand Prix.

Soccer The Republic of Ireland women's team were beaten 3-0 by Poland. The defeat ended their hopes of qualifying for the World Cup.

08: Motor cycling Joey Dunlop won the 250 cc Lightweight Race in heavy rain at the Isle on Man TT races.

09: Rugby Ireland were beaten 52-13 by Griqualand West in the fourth game of the South African tour.

10: Motor cycling Robert Dunlop won the Isle of Man TT 125cc Ultra-Lightweight race.

11: Swimming Larne's Andrew Reid set a new Irish long course record of 25.82 seconds for the 50m butterfly at the Scottish national championships.

13: Hockey Scotland beat Ireland 2-1 in a men's full international. Julian Stevenson scored the Irish goal.

Rugby Ireland lost the first of their two tests with South Africa by 37 points to 13. Three late unanswered tries tries gave the South Africans a 24 point victory margin which flattered them.

16: Rugby A try from Richard Wallace and seven penalties from David Humphreys helped Ireland beat North West Districts 26-18 in Pootchefstroom.

17: Golf Eddie Power from Kilkenny Golf Club beat Bryan Omelia from Newlands by one hole in the final of the Irish Amateur Close Championship.

19: Athletics Siobhan Hoey set a new national triple jump record of 12.38m at the Five Nations tournament in Estonia.

20: Rugby Ireland lost 33-0 to South Africa in a bad tempered final test in Pretoria.

21: Rallying Andrew Nesbitt and J. O'Brien won the Donegal International Rally by one minute seven seconds from Austin McHale.

23: Sailing The Jeep Cherokee yacht won the Round Ireland Yacht Race in a record time of 76 hours 23 minutes 57 seconds.

27: Athletics Sonia O'Sullivan set a new two miles World Record of 9 minutes 19.56 seconds at the Cork City sports.

28: Cycling R. Clarke won the Irish Road Race Championship covering the 110 miles in 4 hours 19 minutes 34 seconds. The junior race was won by Mark Scanlon, the women's race by S. O'Mara and the men's team event was won by Navan.

Formula 1 Eddie Irvine finished second to team mate Michael Schumacher in the French Grand Prix at Magny Cours.

Golf Royal County Down won the Irish Women's Senior Cup defeating Co. Louth 3½ to 1½ in the final.

Horse Racing American jockey Cash Asmussen guided the 2/1 favourite Dream Well to victory in the Budweiser Irish Derby. City Honour was second and Desert Fox third.

▌ JULY ▌

01: Cricket Ireland beat the English amateur XI by four runs in the their triple crown match in Scotland.

04: Cycling Aidan Duff won the Tour of the Mournes from Michael McNena in second and David Peelo in third.

05: GAA Kilkenny were crowned Leinster hurling champions when they beat Offaly 3-10 to 1-11.

Golf David Carter beat defending champion Colin Montgomerie at the first extra hole to win the Murphy's Irish Open. Ireland's John McHenry finished in joint third place.

Soccer Shamrock Rovers won the inaugural FAI Super Cup when they beat St Pat's 2-0 in the final at Tolka Park.

07: Hockey Ireland's women team drew 1-1 with Belarus in the European Nation's Cup qualifier in Helsinki.

09: Hockey The Czech Republic beat Ireland 2-1 on penalty strokes in the semi-final of the women's European Cup qualifiers.

10: Hockey Ireland beat Belarus 6-1 to qualify for the 1999 Europeans Nations' Cup finals.

11: Cycling Chris Boardman won the Prologue Time Trial of the Tour de France in Dublin city centre. He covered the 5.6 kilometre course in 6 minutes 12 seconds, Abraham Olano was second while Laurent Jalabert finished third.

GAA Galway eased past Roscommon in the Connacht SHC final scoring 2-27 to Roscommon's 3-13.

Tennis Owen Casey beat David Mullins 6-0, 6-1 in the Irish Close Championship men's singles final. In the women's final Gina Niland beat Claire Curran 4-6,6-4, 6-1.

12: Cricket South Africa beat Ireland by 63 runs at Castle Avenue.

Cycling Belgian Tom Steels won the first stage proper of the Tour de France covering the 180 kilometre course from Dublin through Wicklow and back to the Phoenix Park in 4 hours 29 minutes and 58 seconds. Briton Chris Boardman retained the yellow jersey but one of the pre-race favourites Mario Cipollini crashed seven kilometres from the finish.

Formula 1 Ralf Schumacher scored Jordan's first point of the season when finishing sixth at the British Grand Prix. The race was won by his brother Michael while Ireland's Eddie Irvine finished third. Damon Hill spun out of the race on lap 16.

Golf Ireland won the European Boys Team Championship beating Scotland 4-3 in the final which was held at Gullane in Scotland.

Horse Racing Winona and jockey Johnny Murtagh won the Irish Oaks at the Curragh from Kitza in second and Bahr in third.

13: Cycling Jan Svorada won the 200km Enniscorthy to Cork second stage of the Tour de France in a time of 5hours 45minutes 10seconds. Overall leader Chris Boardman crashed out of the Tour and was detained in hospital, his yellow jersey was taken Erik Zabel. A young girl was also detained in hospital after she was struck by a member of the peleton. The Tour then moved back to the continent with the third stage starting in Roscoff.

15: Athletics Seventeen year-old Emily Maher won the 100 metres in a time of 11.92 seconds at the World Youth Olympics in Moscow.

16: Athletics Emily Maher struck gold again in winning the 200m in a time of 24.16 seconds at the World Youth Olympics.

18: Rowing Neptune's men enjoyed a successful day at the National Championships winning the Senior Coxed and Coxless Fours, the Senior Pairs and the

Senior Double Sculls. The women of Commercial enjoyed a similar hegemony winning the Senior Fours, Senior Pairs and Senior Quads.

19: Athletics Catherina McKiernan won a 10km road race in Amsterdam in a time of 32 minutes 53 seconds.

Cricket Holland inflicted a five wicket defeat on Ireland at The Hague.

GAA An injury time goal from corner forward Joe Brolly handed Derry victory over Donegal by 1-7 to 0-8 in the Ulster SFC final.

In a torrid Munster SHC replay Clare ran out 2-16 to 0-10 victors over Waterford.

Rowing The men's National Senior Eights title was won by Neptune who beat Trinity by two lengths. The women's title was won by Commercial by one length from UCD.

Soccer In their opening match of the U18 European Championships in Cyprus the Republic of Ireland beat Croatia 5-2.

Tennis George McGill and John Doran completed an Irish whitewash of Monaco in the Davis Cup winning their reverse singles ties.

21: Cricket Denmark beat Ireland by three wickets in their European Championship match.

Soccer England beat the Republic of Ireland 1-0 in the U18 European Championships.

23: Cricket Scotland beat Ireland by 20 runs in the European Championships.

Soccer A 3-0 victory over hosts Cyprus and England's 3-0 defeat to Croatia helped the Republic of Ireland qualify for the European Youth Championships final.

24: Cricket Australia beat Ireland by 172 runs in the women's match held at College Park.

A four wicket defeat by Scotland saw Ireland finish fourth overall in the European Championships in Holland.

Swimming Colin Lowth set a national record of 2.00.33 for the 200m Butterfly.

25: Athletics Sonia O'Sullivan (women's 5,000m), Terry McHugh (men's Javelin) and Noel Berkely (men's 10,000m) were among the winners on the opening day of the National Athletic Championships at Santry Stadium.

Tennis Lucie Ahl won the Irish Women's Open Championship beating Petra Mandulla 7-6, 6-3.

26: Athletics James McIlroy (men's 1,500m), Mark Mandy (men's High Jump), Karen Shinkins (women's 400m) and Una English (women's 1,500m) were among the winners at the National Athletics Championships. Waterford's Susan Smith set a new record of 13.31 seconds in winning the 100m hurdles.

Formula 1 Eddie Irvine finished fourth in the Austrian Grand Prix while Jordan secured further championship points when Ralf Schumacher finished fourth.

Golf Darren Clarke finished second to Australian Stephen Leaney in the Dutch Open at Hilversum and collected a prize of £88,880.

Suzanne O'Brien won the Irish Women's Amateur Open which rain limited to 36 holes. O'Brien's 141 total was six shots clear of Lillian Behan in second.

Soccer The Republic of Ireland beat Germany 4-3 on penalties in the final of the European Youth Championships in Cyprus. One-all after full time and

then extra time a save from keeper Alex O'Reilly and converted penalties from Ryan Casey, Paul Donnolly, Barry Quinn and Liam George secured victory.

27: Cricket Women's World Champions Australia secured a 3-0 test series result when they beat Ireland by 95 runs.

29: Horse Racing Amlah, trained by Philip Hobbs and ridden by Brendan Powell won the centrepiece of the Galway Festival, the Compaq Galway Plate.

Soccer In the second leg games of the Champions League preliminary round Celtic beat St Pats 2-0 (2-0 on aggregate) at Tolka Park while Cliftonville were hammered 8-0 (13-1 on aggregate) by FC Kosice. In the UEFA Cup second leg games Rangers beat Shelbourne 2-0 (7-3 on aggregate) at Ibrox while Linfield beat Omonia 5-3 (lost 6-8 on aggregate) at Windsor Park.

AUGUST

01: GAA Galway sneaked past Roscommon in the Connacht SFC final replay. 0-11 apiece after 70 minutes Galway ran out winners 1-17 to 0-17 after extra-time.

02: Formula 1 Jordan enjoyed their best day of the 1998 season when drivers Damon Hill and Ralf Schumacher finished fourth and sixth respectively at the German Grand Prix. Eddie Irvine finished eighth.

GAA Defending All-Ireland champions Kerry proved too good for Tipperary in the Munster SFC final at Thurles. The men from te Kingdom won by 0-17 to 1-10. In the Leinster SFC final perennial under achievers Kildare beat neighbours Meath 1-12 to 0-10.

Golf At the Scandinavian Masters in Stockholm Darren Clarke finished second, three shots behind Sweden's Jesper Parnevik.

07: Golf Leinster won the women's golf interprovincial title with Ulster second, and Munster and Connacht joint third.

08: Hockey Belgium beat Ireland 1-0 in the men's senior international held at Belfield.

09: Athletics Susan Smith lowered her Irish 100m hurdles record to 13.12 seconds at the National League finals in Tullamore.

GAA All-Ireland champions Clare were rocked by a resurgent Offaly side in the All-Ireland SHC semi-final at Croke Park. A Johnny Pilkington goal followed by two points put Offaly in front in the 68th minute but 1997 hurler of the year Jamesie O'Connor equalised from a free on the stroke of full time to keep Clare's championship alive. The final score was 1-13 apiece.

Golf Welshman Brian Huggett beat Ireland's Eddie Polland at the first play-off hole in the British Seniors' Open at Royal Portrush. Both men had finished the tournament in a five under par score of 283.

A bogey on the last hole at the German Open in Berlin cost Padraig Harrington victory. His final round of 69 for a total of 281 saw him share second place with three other players.

Horse Racing Fourteen-to-one shot Lavery, ridden by Walter Swinburn won the Group One Heinz 57 Phoenix Stakes at Leopardstown.

Soccer Brian Kerr's remarkable underage success continued when his U16 charges beat England 3-2 in the final of the Nordic Cup in Iceland.

12: Athletics Susan Smith broke her second national

record in three days when she lowered her 400m hurdles mark to 54.31 in finishing seventh at the Weltklasse meeting in Zurich. Sonia O'Sullivan also finished seventh in the 1,500m at the same meeting.

13: Soccer In the Cup Winners' Cup qualifying round first leg Cork City beat CSKA Kiev 2-1 at Turners' Cross while Glentoran were beaten 1-0 by Maccabi Haifa at The Oval.

15: Cricket Strabane beat Ballymena by 24 runs in the Irish Senior Cup final at Beechgrove.

16: Formula 1 Team Jordan moved into fifth in the Constructors' Championship by virtue of Damon Hill's fourth place finish in the Hungarian Grand Prix.

GAA Leinster champions Kilkenny beat Munster runners-up Waterford by 1-11 to 1-10 in the 1998 Guinness All-Ireland SHC semi-final at Croke Park. In the curtain raiser Kilkenny qualified for the All-Ireland MHC final beating Galway on a scoreline of 2-10 to 1-12.

19: Athletics In her first ever race over the distance Sonia O'Sullivan claimed the European 10,000m title in a time of 31 minutes, 29.33 seconds. Karen Shinkins set a new national record of 52.13 seconds in qualifying for the 400m semi-final.

20: Athletics Niall Bruton finished twelfth in the final of the men's 1,500m at the European Championships in Hungary.

21: Athletics Susan Smith finished a disappointing eighth in the final of the 400m hurdles.

22: Athletics Mark Carroll won a superb bronze medal in the men's 5,000m at the European Championships.

GAA Controversy engulfed the All-Ireland SHC semi-final replay between Clare and Offaly when referee Jimmy Cooney blew the final whistle two minutes before full-time with the score standing at Clare 1-16, Offaly 2-10. A 90 minute protest by Offaly supporters on the pitch caused the U21 B All-Ireland hurling final to be postponed. The Games Administration Committee of the GAA ordered a replay for the following Saturday.

23: Athletics Sonia O'Sullivan secured an unprecedented double when she beat Romanian rival Gabriella Szabo to win the 5,000m at the European Championships. O'Sullivan's is now the reigning European champion at 3,000m, 5,000m and 10,000m. In the men's 800m James McIlroy finished outside the medals in fourth place while Sinead Delahunty finished ninth in the women's 1,500m final.

GAA Underlining the rise to prominence of Connacht football Galway qualified for the All-Ireland SFC final beating a lethargic Derry side by 0-16 to 1-8. In the All-Ireland MFC semi-final Tyrone defeated Leitrim 1-14 to 1-3.

Golf Swede Mathias Gronberg was a runaway ten shot winner of the Smurfit European Open at the K Club in Kildare collecting a first prize of £208,300. Darren Clarke was the leading Irish finisher eleven shots back in fourth place.

North of Ireland champion Paddy Gribben became the first Irishman to win the European Amateur Golf Championship finishing two shots clear of the field in Bordeaux.

27: Soccer CSKA Kiev beat Cork City 2-0 (3-2 in aggregate) in the European Cup Winners' Cup. Glentoran

were beaten 2-1 by Maccabi Haifa (3-1 in aggregate) also in the Cup Winners Cup.

28: Athletics Mark Carroll set a new Irish record for the 3,000m of 7:33.84 in finishing 5th at the IAAF Golden League meeting in Brussels.

29: GAA Offaly beat Clare by 0-16 to 0-13 at the third time of asking in the All-Ireland semi-final replay at Semple Stadium.

30: Cycling Mark Scanlon won the 490 miles eight day Credit Union Junior Tour by over three minutes from nearest rival England's Bradley Wiggins.

Formula 1 Jordan Grand Prix scored their first Grand Prix win when Damon Hill won in Belgium, Ralf Schumacher finished second.

GAA In the All-Ireland semi-final Kildare beat All-Ireland Champions Kerry by 0-13 to 1-9 to qualify for thier first final since 1935.

SEPTEMBER

01: Athletics Mark Carroll set a new Irish record of 13 minutes 3.93 seconds for the 5,000m in finishing seventh at the IAAF Grand Prix meeting in Berlin.

02: Soccer Jackie Blanchflower, former Northern Ireland international and 'Busby Babe', died aged 65. England beat the Republic of Ireland 5-0 in an U18 international played at Tolka Park.

04: Soccer The Republic of Ireland U21s drew 2-2 with Croatia in their opening European Championship match at Buckley Park, Kilkenny.

05: Canoeing The 39th annual Liffey Descent attracted 1,200 entrants. The men's K1 Class was won by Malcolm Banks and the K2 Class was won by Alan and Ian Tordoff. The women's K1 Class was won by Michelle Barry.

Soccer A penalty from Denis Irwin and a header from Roy Keane gave the Republic of Ireland a 2-0 victory over Croatia at Lansdowne Road. Croatia had two players sent off in the closing stages.

Northern Ireland were beaten 3-0 by Turkey in the opening game of Group Three.

06: Camogie Cork retained the All-Ireland Senior Camogie Championship beating Galway 2-13 to 0-15 at Croke Park.

Golf Swede Sophie Gustafson won the Irish Women's Open at Ballyliffin. The tournament was curtailed to three rounds as gales buffeted the Inishowen links.

Darren Clark collected £50,070 when he finished third in the European Masters taking his 1998 tournament earnings to £597,847.

Tennis Ireland won both the men's and women's Four Nations Senior International held at Cork, winning each of the matches against England, Scotland and Wales.

11: Golf Ireland lost 7-8 to England in the deciding match of the men's Home Internationals to finish second overall.

Ireland's women also finished second in the Home Internationals when they beat Wales 6-3.

12: Athletics Sonia O'Sullivan, representing Europe, won the 5,000m in the World Cup Championship in South Africa collecting $50,000.

13: Formula 1 Eddie Irvine finished second in the Italian Grand Prix at Monza behind Ferrari team mate Michael Schumacher. Jordan drivers Ralf Schumacher and Damon Hill finished third and sixth respectively to move within striking distance of Williams and Benetton in the Constructors' Championship

GAA Offaly created hurling history when they became the first side to win the All-Ireland title via the 'backdoor'. In the final the experience gained from three matches with Clare and the switch of Brian Whelahan from defence to attack overwhelmed a bemused Kilkenny side who had five points to spare over them in the Leinster decider only two months earlier. Led by a goal and six points from Whelahan Offaly ran out winners by 2-16 to 1-13.

Cork dismissed the challenge of Kilkenny in the minor final defeating them by 2-15 to 1-9.

17: Golf Warrenpoint beat Co. Sligo by one hole in the final of the Barton Shield at Athlone.

18: Golf At the National Cups and Shields finals held at Athlone Old Conna beat Tuam 3-2 to win the Junior Cup and Nenagh beat Woodbrook 3¹/₂-1¹/₂ to win the Pierce Purcell Shield.

19: Boxing Michael Carruth overcame Scott Dixon to win the WAA World Welterweight title at the National Basketball Arena.

Golf Cork beat Shandon Park 4-1 in the final of the national Senior Cup at Athlone while Moate beat Portumna 3¹/₂-1¹/₂ in the final of the Jimmy Bruen Shield.

27: Formula 1 Eddie Irvine finished fourth in the Luxembourg Grand Prix while the Jordan duo of Damon Hill and Ralf Schumacher failed to register championship points for the first time in six races.

GAA A second half western awakening saw Galway overturn a three point half time deficit to claim the All-Ireland Football Championship with four points to spare over Kildare on a scoreline of 1-14 to 1-10. Match winning displays from Jarlath Fallon and Michael Donnellan and indeed manager John O'Mahony saw Galway bridge a 32 year barren gap between All-Ireland victories and extended Kildare's 70 year wait by at least another twelve months.

Tyrone claimed the All-Ireland Minor football Championship beating defending champions Laois by 2-11 to 0-11. In an exceptional act of sportsmanship Laois formed a guard of honour and applauded the new champions off the pitch. ◻

GAELIC ATHLETIC ASSOCIATION
Cumann Lúthchleas Gael
Páirc an Chrócaigh, Baile Átha Cliath 3. Tel. (01) 8363222

Founded	1884
President	Joe McDonagh
Director General	Liam Mulvhill
Number of Provincial Councils	4
Number of Clubs	2,664
Number of Members	750,000
Number of Teams	20,000
Number of Coaches	2,000
Biggest Recorded Attendance	90,556 (Croke Park September 1961, Down v.Offaly)
Main Stadia	Croke Park (66,000), Semple Stadium Thurles (50,000)

1998 FINALISTS	HURLING		FOOTBALL	
	Winners	Runners Up	Winners	Runners Up
All-Ireland	Offaly	Kilkenny	Galway	Kildare
Connacht	Galway	Roscommon	Galway	Roscommon
Leinster	Kilkenny	Offaly	Kildare	Meath
Munster	Clare	Waterford	Kerry	Tipperary
Ulster	Antrim	Down	Derry	Donegal
National League	Cork	Waterford	Offaly	Derry
Railway Cup*	Munster	Leinster	Ulster	Leinster
All-Ireland Club	Corofin (Galway)	Erin's Isle (Dublin)	Birr (Offaly)	Sarsfields (Galway)

Top Scorer in 1998 Hurling Championship ....John Troy (Offaly) 2-31
Top Scorers in 1998 Football Championship .....Declan Browne (Tipperary) 2-29
1997 Player of the Year, Hurling .....James O'Connor (Clare)
1997 Player of the Year, Football .....Maurice Fitzgerald (Kerry)

*The Railway Cup Hurling result is from the 1997 season.

Attendances at GAA Championships 1996-98

1998 Total Championship Attendance	1,429,386
1997 Total Championship Attendance	1,337,345
1996 Total Championship Attendance	1,056,236

Provincial breakdown Figures in *italics* indicate number of fixtures played in each provincial championship

PROVINCE	1997		1998	
	FOOTBALL	HURLING	FOOTBALL	HURLING
Ulster	202,682...*11*	2,700...*2*	144,829...*8*	9,250...*4*
Connacht	71,000...*5*	2,500...*1*	119,000...*7*	2,000...*1*

PROVINCE	1997		1998	
	FOOTBALL	HURLING	FOOTBALL	HURLING
Leinster	338,454...14	124,677.....7	330,238...12	88,568.....5
Munster	62,651.....6	146,435.....5	84,725....5	221,689.....6
All-Ireland Series	182,042.....3	204,204.....5	169,457....3	259,630....7
Total	856,829 39	480,516 20	848,249 35	581,137 23

1998 Results

Guinness Hurling Championship

Connacht Final
11.07.98...Galway..........2-27   Roscommon.........3-13

Leinster Final
05.07.98...Kilkenny........3-10   Offaly 1-11

Munster Final
19.07.98...Clare.............2-16   Waterford ....0-10 (R)

Ulster Final
05.07.98...Antrim..........1-19   Derry....................2-13
(R)=Replay   † = Match unfinished, replay ordered.

All-Ireland Quarter Finals
26.07.98...Waterford......1-20   Galway.................1-10
26.07.98...Offaly 2-18   Antrim 2-9

All-Ireland Semi-Finals
09.08.98...Clare.............1-13   Offaly 1-13
16.08.98...Kilkenny.......1-11   Waterford 1-10
22.08.98...Clare.............1-16   Offaly ....2-10(R)†
29.08.98...Offaly 0-16   Clare ....0-13 (R)

All-Ireland Final
13.09.98...Offaly 2-16   Kilkenny 1-13

Bank of Ireland Football Championship

Connacht Final
01.08.98...Galway..........1-17   Roscommon....0-17(R)

Leinster Final
02.08.98...Kildare 1-12   Meath...................0-10

Munster Final
02.08.98...Kerry 0-17   Tipperary 1-10
(R)=Replay

Ulster Final
19.07.98...Derry...............1-7   Donegal 0-8

All-Ireland Semi-Finals
23.08.98...Galway..........0-16   Derry....................1-8
30.08.98...Kildare 0-13   Kerry 1-9

All-Ireland Final
27.09.98...Galway..........1-14   Kildare.................1-10

Church & General National Leagues

National Hurling League Final
17.05.98...Cork.............2-14   Waterford 0-13

National Football League Final
26.04.98...Offaly 0-9   Derry....................0-7

Railway Cup

Hurling Final (1997)
09.11.97...Munster 0-14   Leinster................0-10

Football Final
26.04.98...Ulster 0-20   Leinster.........0-17 aet

Allied Irish Banks All-Ireland Club Championships

Hurling Final
17.03.98...Birr................1-13   Sarsfields 0-9

Football Final
17.03.98...Corofin..........0-15   Erin's Isle 0-10

Eircell GAA All-Stars, 1997

FOOTBALL AWARDS: Declan O'Keefe (Kerry); Kenneth Mortimer (Mayo), Davy Dalton (Kildare), Cathal Daly (Offaly); Seamus Moynihan (Kerry), Glen Ryan (Kildare), Eamonn Breen (Kerry); Pat Fallon (Mayo), Niall Buckley (Kildare); Pa Laide (Kerry), Trevor Giles (Meath), Dermot McCabe (Cavan); Joe Brolly (Derry), Brendan Reilly (Meath), Maurice Fitzgerald (Kerry). *Player of the Year: M. Fitzgerald (Kerry).*

HURLING AWARDS: Damien Fitzhenry (Wexford); Paul Shelley (Tipperary); Brian Lohan (Clare), Wille O'Connor (Kilkenny); Liam Doyle (Clare), Sean McMahon (Clare); Liam Keoghan (Kilkenny); Colin Lynch (Clare), Tommy Dunne (Tipperary); James O'Connor (Clare), Declan Ryan (Tipperary), John Leahy (Tipperary); Kevin Broderick (Galway), Ger O'Loughlin (Clare) DJ Carey (Kilkenny). *Player of the Year: J. O'Connor (Clare)*

All-Ireland Championship, Past Winners

Hurling

27 Cork 1890, 1892, 1893, 1894, 1902, 1903, 1919, 1926, 1928, 1929, 1931, 1941, 1942, 1943, 1944, 1946, 1952, 1953, 1954, 1966, 1970, 1976, 1977, 1978, 1984, 1986, 1990.

25 Kilkenny 1904, 1905, 1907, 1909, 1911, 1912, 1913, 1922, 1932, 1933, 1935, 1939, 1947, 1957, 1963, 1967, 1969, 1972, 1974, 1975, 1979, 1982, 1983, 1992, 1993.

24 Tipperary 1887, 1895, 1896, 1898, 1899, 1900, 1906, 1908, 1916, 1925, 1930, 1937, 1945, 1949, 1950, 1951, 1958, 1961, 1962, 1964, 1965, 1971, 1989, 1991.

7 Limerick 1897, 1918, 1921, 1934, 1936, 1940, 1973.

6 Dublin 1889, 1917, 1920, 1924, 1927, 1938.
Wexford 1910, 1955, 1956, 1960, 1968, 1996.

4 Galway 1923, 1980, 1987, 1988.
Offaly 1981, 1985, 1994, 1998.

3 Clare 1914, 1995, 1997.

2 Waterford 1948, 1959.

1 Kerry 1891
Laois 1915
London 1901

Football

31 Kerry 1903, 1904, 1909, 1913, 1914, 1924, 1926, 1929, 1930, 1931, 1932, 1937, 1939, 1940, 1941, 1946, 1953, 1955, 1959, 1962, 1969, 1970, 1975, 1978, 1979, 1980, 1981, 1984, 1985, 1986, 1997.

22 Dublin 1891, 1892, 1894, 1897, 1898, 1899, 1901, 1902, 1906, 1907, 1908, 1921, 1922, 1923, 1942, 1958, 1963, 1974, 1976, 1977, 1983, 1995.

8 Galway 1925, 1934, 1938, 1956, 1964, 1965, 1966, 1998.

6 Cork 1890, 1911, 1945, 1973, 1989, 1990.
Meath 1949, 1954, 1967, 1987, 1988, 1996.

5 Cavan 1933, 1935, 1947, 1948, 1952.
Down 1960, 1961, 1968, 1991, 1994.
Wexford 1893, 1915, 1916, 1917, 1918.

4 Kildare 1905, 1919, 1927, 1928.
Tipperary 1889, 1895, 1900, 1920.

3 Louth 1910, 1912, 1957.
Mayo 1936, 1950, 1951.
Offaly 1971, 1972, 1982.

2 Limerick 1887, 1896.
Roscommon 1943, 1944.

1 Derry 1993.
Donegal 1992.

All-Ireland Football Final Results, 1887-1945

Year					Year				
1887	Limerick	1-4	Louth	0-3	1917	Wexford	0-9	Clare	0-5
1888	C'ship unfinished				1918	Wexford	0-5	Tipperary	0-4
1889	Tipperary	3-6	Laois	0-0	1919	Kildare	2-5	Galway	0-1
1890	Cork	2-4	Wexford	0-1	1920	Tipperary	1-6	Dublin	1-2
1891	Dublin	2-1	Cork	1-9*	1921	Dublin	0-6	Galway	0-4
1892	Dublin	1-4	Kerry	0-3	1922	Dublin	0-6	Galway	0-4
1893	Wexford	1-1	Cork	0-2	1923	Dublin	1-5	Kerry	1-3
1894	Dublin	0-5	Cork	1-2	1924	Kerry	0-4	Dublin	0-3
1895	Tipperary	0-4	Meath	0-3	1925	Galway	3-2	Cavan	1-2
1896	Limerick	1-5	Dublin	0-7	1926	Kerry	1-4	Kildare	0-4
1897	Dublin	2-6	Cork	0-2	1927	Kildare	0-5	Kerry	0-3
1898	Dublin	2-8	Waterford	0-4	1928	Kildare	2-6	Cavan	2-5
1899	Dublin	1-10	Cork	0-6	1929	Kerry	1-8	Kildare	1-5
1900	Tipperary	3-7	London	0-2	1930	Kerry	3-11	Monaghan	0-2
1901	Dublin	0-14	London	0-2	1931	Kerry	1-11	Kildare	0-8
1902	Dublin	2-8	London	0-4	1932	Kerry	2-7	Mayo	2-4
1903	Kerry	0-8	Kildare	0-2 (R)	1933	Cavan	2-5	Galway	1-4
1904	Kerry	0-5	Dublin	0-2	1934	Galway	3-5	Dublin	1-9
1905	Kildare	1-7	Kerry	0-5	1935	Cavan	3-6	Kildare	2-5
1906	Dublin	0-5	Cork	0-4	1936	Mayo	4-11	Laois	0-5
1907	Dublin	0-5	Cork	0-4	1937	Kerry	4-4	Cavan	1-7 (R)
1908	Dublin	1-10	London	0-4	1938	Galway	2-4	Kerry	0-7 (R)
1909	Kerry	1-9	Louth	0-6	1939	Kerry	2-5	Meath	2-3
1910	Louth	w.o.	Kerry		1940	Kerry	0-7	Galway	1-3
1911	Cork	6-6	Antrim	1-2	1941	Kerry	1-8	Galway	0-7
1912	Louth	1-7	Antrim	1-2	1942	Dublin	1-10	Galway	1-8
1913	Kerry	2-2	Wexford	0-3	1943	Roscommon	2-7	Cavan	2-2 (R)
1914	Kerry	2-3	Wexford	0-6 (R)	1944	Roscommon	1-9	Kerry	2-4
1915	Wexford	2-4	Kerry	2-1	1945	Cork	2-5	Cavan	0-7
1916	Wexford	2-4	Mayo	1-2					

* Goal outweighs any number of points. (R)=Replay.

All-Ireland Hurling Final Results, 1887-45

1887	Tipperary ....1-1....Galway 0-0	
1888	Championship unfinished	
1889	Dublin ....5-1....Clare...........................1-6	
1890	Cork...............1-6....Wexford 2-2	
1891	Kerry..............2-3....Wexford ....1-5 aet	
1892	Cork...............2-4....Dublin 1-1	
1893	Cork...............6-8....Kilkenny.....................0-2	
1894	Cork............5-20....Dublin 2-0	
1895	Tipperary ....6-8....Kilkenny...................1-10	
1896	Tipperary .....8-14....Dublin 0-4	
1897	Limerick........3-4....Kilkenny.....................2-4	
1898	Tipperary .....7-13....Kilkenny....................3-10	
1899	Tipperary .....3-12....Wexford 1-4	
1900	Tipperary ....2-5....London 0-6	
1901	London ....1-5....Cork 0-4	
1902	Cork............2-13....London ....0-0 (R)	
1903	Cork............3-16....London 1-1	
1904	Kilkenny........1-9....Cork 1-8	
1905	Kilkenny........7-7....Cork ....2-9 (R)	
1906	Tipperary .....3-16....Dublin 3-8	
1907	Kilkenny......3-12....Cork 4-8	
1908	Tipperary .....3-15....Dublin ....1-5 (R)	
1909	Kilkenny........4-6....Tipperary 0-12	
1910	Wexford ....7-0....Limerick.....................6-2	
1911	Kilkenny........3-3....Tipperary 2-1	
1912	Kilkenny........2-1....Cork 1-3	
1913	Kilkenny........2-4....Tipperary 1-2	
1914	Clare..............5-1....Laois...........................1-0	
1915	Laois..............6-2....Cork 4-1	
1916	Tipperary ....5-4....Kilkenny.....................3-2	
1917	Dublin ....5-4....Tipperary 4-2	
1918	Limerick ....9-5....Wexford 1-3	
1919	Cork...............6-4....Dublin 2-4	
1920	Dublin ....4-9....Cork 4-3	
1921	Limerick ....8-5....Dublin 3-2	
1922	Kilkenny.........4-2....Tipperary 2-6	
1923	Galway ....7-3....Limerick......................4-5	
1924	Dublin ....5-3....Galway 2-6	
1925	Tipperary ....5-6....Galway 1-5	
1926	Cork...............4-6....Kilkenny.....................2-0	
1927	Dublin ....4-8....Cork 1-3	
1928	Cork............6-12....Galway 1-0	
1929	Cork...............4-9....Galway 1-3	
1930	Tipperary ....2-7....Dublin 1-3	
1931	Cork...............5-8....Kilkenny................3-4 (R)	
1932	Kilkenny.........3-3....Clare...........................2-3	
1933	Kilkenny.........1-7....Limerick......................0-6	
1934	Limerick ....5-2....Dublin 2-6	
1935	Kilkenny.........2-5....Limerick......................2-4	
1936	Limerick ....5-6....Kilkenny.....................1-5	
1937	Tipperary .....3-11....Kilkenny.....................0-3	
1938	Dublin ....2-5....Waterford...................1-6	
1939	Kilkenny.........2-7....Cork 3-3	
1940	Limerick ....3-7....Kilkenny.....................1-7	
1941	Cork............5-11....Dublin 0-6	
1942	Cork............2-14....Dublin 3-4	
1943	Cork............5-16....Antrim.........................0-4	
1944	Cork............2-13....Dublin 1-2	
1945	Tipperary ....5-6....Kilkenny.....................3-6	

aet= after extra time.   (R)=Replay.

GAA Clubs in Britain and Overseas

Britain	Number of Clubs
Gloucestershire	7
Hertfordshire	12
Lancashire	10
London	50
Scotland	10
Warwickshire	26
Yorkshire	7

Worldwide	Number of Clubs
Australia	50
Canada	12
New York	42
New York (Minor Board)	6
North American Board	63

GAA Statistics - Inter County

County	Main Stadium	Approx. Capacity	No. of Clubs	Colours	All Ire. F	All Ire. H	NFL Title	NHL Title
CONNACHT	**Dr Hyde Park, Roscommon**	**30,000**	**280**		**13**	**4**	**15**	**6**
Galway	Tuam Park	22,000	88	Maroon & white	8	4	4	6
Leitrim	Pairc MacDiarmada	12,000	33	Green & gold	0	0	0	0
Mayo	McHale Park	30,000	52	Green & red	3	0	10	0
Roscommon	Dr. Hyde Park	30,000	56	Gold & blue	2	0	1	0
Sligo	Markevicz Park	13,000	51	White & black	0	0	0	0
LEINSTER	**Croke Park**	**68,000**	**1,091**		**43**	**42**	**18**	**16**
Carlow	Dr. Cullen Park	10,000	35	Red, green & yellow	0	0	0	0
Dublin	Parnell Park	10,000	270	Sky blue & navy	22	6	8	2
Kildare	Newbridge	15,000	70	White	4	0	0	0
Kilkenny	Nowlan Park	30,000	42	Black & amber	0	25	0	9
Laois	O'Moore Park	25,000	88	Blue & white	0	1	2	0
Longford	Pearse Park	8,000	52	Blue & gold	0	0	1	0
Louth	Drogheda	22,000	51	Red & white	3	0	0	0
Meath	Pairc Tailteann		145	Green & gold	6	0	7	0
Offaly	Pairc Úi Conchuir	25,000	65	Green, white & gold	3	4	1	1
Westmeath	Cusack Park, Mullingar	11,000	44	Maroon & white	0	0	0	0
Wexford	Wexford Park		178	Purple & gold	5	6	0	4
Wicklow	Aughrim	10,000	66	Blue & gold	0	0	0	0
MUNSTER	**Semple Stadium**	**50,000**	**710**		**43**	**64**	**19**	**43**
Clare	Cusack Park, Ennis	28,000	90	Saffron & blue	0	3	0	3
Cork	Pairc Úi Chaoimh	43,500	264	Red & white	6	27	4	14
Kerry	Fitzgerald Stadium	50,000	89	Green & gold	31	1	15	0
Limerick	Gaelic Grounds	36,000	117	Green & white	2	7	0	11
Tipperary	Semple Stadium	50,000	93	Blue & gold	4	24	0	16
Waterford	Walsh Park	17,000	57	White & blue	0	2	0	1
ULSTER	**St. Tiergnach's Park**	**33,000**	**583**		**12**	**0**	**10**	**0**
Antrim	Casement Park, Belfast	40,000	108	Saffron & white	0	0	0	0
Armagh	Athletic Grounds	18,000	55	Orange & white	0	0	0	0
Cavan	Breffni Park		59	Blue & white	5	0	1	0
Derry	Celtic Park, Derry	15,000	60	Red & white	1	0	4	0
Donegal	MacCumhaill Park, Ballybofey	15,000	63	Gold & green	1	0	0	0
Down	Pairc an Iúir, Newry	11,000	70	Red & black	5	0	4	0
Fermanagh	Brewster Park, Enniskillen		50	Green & white	0	0	0	0
Monaghan	Castleblayney	23,000	50	White & blue	0	0	1	0
Tyrone	Healy Park	20,000	68	White & red	0	0	0	0
Total			**2,664**		**111**	**110***	**63**	**66**

* *London have also won an All-Ireland Hurling title.*

1998 All-Ireland Football Final Statistics

Galway, Team and Scorers: Martin McNamara; Tomás Meehan, Gary Fahy, Tomás Mannion; Ray Silke (Captain), John Divilly, Seán Óg de Paor (0-2); Kevin Walsh, Seán Ó Domhnaill (0-1); Michael Donnellan (0-2), Jarlath Fallon (0-3), Shay Walsh; Derek Savage, Padraic Joyce (1-2), Niall Finnegan (0-4). **Sub:** Paul Clancy for S. Walsh (65 mins). **Manager:** John O'Mahony.

Kildare, Team and Scorers: Christy Byrne; Brian Lacey, Seamus Dowling, Ken Doyle; Anthony Rainbow, Glen Ryan (Captain), John Finn; Niall Buckley (0-1), Willie McCreery; Eddie McCormack (0-2), Declan Kerrigan (0-1), Dermot Earley (1-1); Martin Lynch, Karl O'Dwyer (0-2), Padraig Graven. **Subs:** Pauric Brennan (0-3) for P. Graven (46 mins); Brian Murphy for M. Lynch (58 mins). **Manager:** Mick O'Dwyer.

Half-time Score: Galway 0-5, Kildare 1-5; **Top Scorer:** Padraic Joyce (Galway, 1-2); **Man of the Match:** Michael Donnellan (Galway); **Referee:** John Bannon (Longford). **Booked:** Ken Doyle (48 mins), Glen Ryan (57 mins), Brian Lacey (59 mins) all Kildare. **Sent off:** None.

1998 All-Ireland Hurling Final Statistics

Offaly, Team and Scorers: Stephen Byrne; Simon Whelahan, Kevin Kinahan, Martin Hanamy; Brian Whelehan (1-6), Hubert Rigney (Captain), Kevin Martin; Johnny Pilkington (0-1), Michael Duignan (0-2); Johnny Dooley, Joe Errity (1-2), Gary Hanniffy; John Troy (0-3), Joe Dooley (0-2), Billy Dooley. **Subs:** Paudie Mulhare for G. Hannify (30 mins); Darren Hannify for B. Dooley (61 mins); John Ryan for J. Dooley (67 mins). **Manager:** Michael Bond.

Kilkenny, Team and Scorers: Joe Dermody; Tom Hickey (Captain), Pat O'Neill, Willie O'Connor; Michael Kavanagh, Canice Brennan, Liam Keoghan; Philip Larkin (0-1), Peter Barry; Brian McEvoy (0-3), Andy Comerford (0-1), DJ Carey (0-5); Ken O'Shea (0-2), PJ Delaney, Charlie Carter (1-1). **Subs:** Niall Moloney for K. O'Shea (61 mins); John Costelloe for M. Kavanagh (67 mins). **Manager:** Kevin Fennelly.

Half time score: Offaly 0-8, Kilkenny 1-7. **Top Scorer:** Brian Whelehan (1-6, 3 frees). **Man-of-the-Match:** Brian Whelehan (Offaly). **Referee:** Dickie Murphy (Wexford). **Booked:** Martin Hanamy (Offaly, 57 mins). **Sent off:** None.

Top All-Ireland Medal Winners

HURLING Name	County	Won	Between	FOOTBALL Name	County	Won	Between
1. Christy Ring	Cork	8	1941-54	1. Denis 'Ogie' Moran	Kerry	8	1975-86
2. John Doyle	Tipperary	8	1949-65	2. Páidí Ó Sé	Kerry	8	1975-86
3. Frank Cummins	Kilkenny	7 (+1)	1969-83	3. Ger Power	Kerry	8	1975-86
4. Noel Skehan	Kilkenny	6 (+3)	1963-83	4. Mikey Sheehy	Kerry	8	1975-86
5. Jimmy Doyle	Tipperary	6	1958-71	5. Seán Walshe	Kerry	7 (+1)	1976-86
				6. Charlie Neligan	Kerry	7	1978-86
				7. Dan O'Keefe	Kerry	7	1931-46
(Figure in brackets indicates medals won as a substitute).				8. John O'Keefe	Kerry	6 (+1)	1969-82

Top All Star Award Winners (Individual)

HURLING Name	County	Won	Between	FOOTBALL Name	County	Won	Between
1. Noel Skehan	Kilkenny	7	1972-83	1. Pat Spillane	Kerry	9	1976-86
2. Joe McKenna	Limerick	6	1974-81	2. Mikey Sheehy	Kerry	7	1976-86
3. Nicky English	Tipperary	6	1983-89	3. Jack O'Shea	Kerry	6	1980-85
4. DJ Carey	Kilkenny	6	1991-97	4. Ger Power	Kerry	6	1975-86
5. Joe Cooney	Galway	5	1985-90	5. John Egan	Kerry	5	1975-86
6. John Fenton	Cork	5	1983-87	6. John O'Keefe	Kerry	5	1973-79
7. Peter Finnerty	Galway	5	1985-90	7. Paidi Ó Sé	Kerry	5	1981-85
8. Pat Hartigan	Limerick	5	1971-75	**DUAL WINNERS**	**County**	**F**	**H**	**Total**
9. Ger Henderson	Kilkenny	5	1978-87	1. Jimmy Barry-Murphy	Cork	2	5	7
10. Joe Hennessy	Kilkenny	5	1978-87	2. Ray Cummins	Cork	2	3	5
11. Eddie Keher	Kilkenny	5	1971-75	3. Brian Murphy	Cork	2	2	4
12. Jimmy Barry-Murphy	Cork	5	1976-86	4. Liam Currams	Offaly	1	1	2

Top All Star Award Winners by County and (number)

HURLING 1. Kilkenny (85); **2.** Cork(72); **3.** Galway (59); **4.** Tipperary (46); **5.** Limerick (40); **6.** Offaly (32); **7.** Clare (29); **8.** Wexford (28); **9.** Antrim (5); **10.** Waterford (4).

FOOTBALL 1. Kerry (80); **2.** Dublin (67); **3.** Cork (45); **4.** Meath (36); **5.** Offaly (30); **6.** Derry (21); **7.** Mayo (20); **8.** Down (19); **9.** Galway (19); **10.** Roscommon (14).

Past Presidents

Year President	County	Year President	County	Year President	County
1884..Maurice Davin	Tipperary	1932..Seán McCarthy	Cork	1967..Seamus Ó Riain	Tipperary
1887..Eamonn Bennet	Clare	1935..Bob O'Keefe	Laois	1970..Pat Fanning	Waterford
1888..Maurice Davin	Tipperary	1938..Pádraig McNamee	Antrim	1973..Dr. Donal Keenan.Roscommon	
1889..Peter Kelly	Galway	1943..Seamus Gardiner	Tipperary	1976..Con Murphy	Cork
1895..Frank Dineen	Limerick	1946..Dan O'Rourke	Roscommon	1979..Paddy McFlynn	Down
1898..Michael Deering	Cork	1949..Michael Kehoe	Wexford	1982..Paddy Buggy	Kilkenny
1901..James Nowlan	Kilkenny	1952..Michael O'Donoghue.Waterford		1985..Dr. Mick Loftus	Mayo
1921..Daniel McCarthy	Dublin	1955..Seamus McFerran	Antrim	1988..John Dowling	Offaly
1924..Patrick Breen	Wexford	1958..Dr. J.J. Stuart	Dublin	1991..Peter Quinn	Fermanagh
1926..William Clifford	Limerick	1961..Hugh Byrne	Wicklow	1994..Jack Boothman	Wicklow
1928..Seán Ryan	Dublin	1964..Alf Murray	Armagh	1997..Joe McDonagh	Galway

Past General Secretaries

Year Secretary	County	Year Secretary	County	Year Secretary	County
1884-85....M. Cusack	Clare	1889-90....P.R. Cleary	Limerick	1929-64....P. Ó Caoimh	Cork
1884-85....J. McKay	Cork	1890-92....M. Moynihan	Kerry	1964-79....S. Ó Síocháin	Cork
1884-87....J.W. Power	Kildare	1891-94....P. Tobin	Dublin	1979-........L. Maolmhichíl..Longford	
1885-87....J.B. O'Reilly	Dublin	1894-95....D. Walsh	Cork		
1885-89....T. O'Riordan	Cork	1895-98....R. Blake	Meath		
1887-88....J. Moore	Louth	1898-1901 F. Dineen	Limerick	*Since 1964 the post has been*	
1888-89....W. PrendergastTipperary		1901-29....L. O'Toole	Dublin	*described as Director General.*	

SOCCER

The Football Association of Ireland
80 Merrion Square, Dublin 2. Tel. (01) 6766864

Founded	1921
President	Pat Quigley
General Secretary/Chief Executive	Bernard J. O'Byrne
Number of Affiliated Clubs	4,139
Number of Coaches	4,000 (at various levels)

1997/98 Champions	Winners	Runners Up
National League, Premier Division	St Patrick's Athletic	Shelbourne
National League, First Division	Waterford United	Bray Wanderers
Harp Lager F.A.I. Cup	Cork City	Shelbourne
FAI League Cup	Sligo Rovers	Shelbourne
Top Scorer 1997/98 National League Premier Division	17 (Stephen Geoghegan, Shelbourne)	
Main Stadium	Dalymount Park, capacity 18,000 (Lansdowne Road used for International games)	

INTERNATIONAL

National Manager	Mick McCarthy
Top International Goalscorer	Frank Stapleton (20 Goals)
Biggest Recorded Attendance	47,000
World Ranking	42nd
Most Capped Player	Paul McGrath (83)
1997 Senior Player of the Year	Roy Keane
Best World Cup Result	Quarter-finalists 1990 (beaten by Italy)

National League Premier Division Team Statistics

Club	Founded	Ground and Capacity	Colours	League Titles	FAI Cups	League Cups
Bohemians	1890	Dalymount Park (14,700)	Red & Black	7	5	2
Bray Wanderers	1942	Carlisle Grounds (7,500)	Green & White	0	1	0
Cork City	1984	Turner's Cross (7,000)	Green, Red & White	1	1	2
Derry City	1928	The Brandywell (7,500)	Red & White	2	2	4
Dundalk	1919	Oriel Park (13,600)	White & Black	9	8	4
Finn Harps	1954	Finn Park (8,000)	White & Blue	0	1	0
St. Patrick's Athletic	1929	Richmond Park (5,800)	Red & White	6	2	0
Shamrock Rovers	1901	Tolka Park (10,000)	Green & White	15	24	1
Shelbourne	1895	Tolka Park (10,000)	Red	8	6	1

Continued from previous page

Club	Founded	Ground and Capacity	Colours	League Titles	FAI Cups	League Cups
Sligo Rovers	1928	The Showgrounds (5,900)	Red & White	2	2	1
U.C.D.	1895	Belfield (6,000)	Sky Blue	0	1	0
Waterford United	1930	Regional Sports Centre (8,250)	Blue & White	6	2	2

National League First Division Team Statistics

Club	Founded	Ground and Capacity	Colours	League Titles	FAI Cups	League Cups
Athlone Town	1887	St. Mel's Park (10,200)	Blue & Black	2	1	3
Cobh Ramblers	1922	St. Colman's Park (7,000)	Claret & Blue	0	0	0
Drogheda United	1919	United Park (6,400)	Claret & Blue	0	0	1
Galway United	1937	Terryland Park (6,580)	Maroon & Blue	0	1	2
Home Farm Everton	1928	Whitehall (3,000)	Blue & White	0	1	0
Kilkenny City	1966	Buckley Park (6,900)	Black & Amber	0	0	0
Limerick F.C.	1937	Hogan Park (10,000)	Blue & White	2	2	2
Longford Town	1924	Strokestown Road (8,750)	Red & Black	0	0	0
Monaghan United	1979	Gortakeegan (5,600)	Blue & White	0	0	0
St. Francis	1958	John Hyland Park (2,000)	Green & White	0	0	0

League of Ireland All-Time Top Scorers

Name	No. of Goals	Name	No. of Goals	Name	No. of Goals
Brendan Bradley	235	Alfie Hale	153	Sean McCarthy	135
Turlough O'Connor	178	Pat Morley	143+97/98 goals	Mick Leech	132
Donal Leahy	162	Paul McGee	143	Eugene Davis	130
Johnny Matthews	156	Eric Barber	141	Jack Fitzgerald	130

League of Ireland Championship Winners

15 Shamrock Rovers 1922-23, 1924-25, 1926-27, 1931-32, 1937-38, 1938-39, 1953-54, 1956-57, 1958-59, 1963-64, 1983-84, 1984-85, 1985-86, 1986-87, 1993-94.

9 Dundalk 1932-33, 1962-63, 1966-67, 1975-76, 1978-79, 1981-82, 1987-88, 1990-91, 1994-95.

8 Shelbourne 1926-26, 1928-29, 1930-31, 1943-44, 1946-47, 1952-53, 1961-62, 1991-92.

7 Bohemians 1923-24, 1927-28, 1929-30, 1933-34, 1935-36, 1974-75, 1977-78.

6 St Patrick's Athletic 1951-52, 1954-55, 1955-56, 1989-90, 1995-96, 1997-98.
Waterford United 1965-66, 1967-68, 1968-69, 1969-70, 1971-72, 1972-73.

5 Cork United 1940-41, 1941-42, 1942-43, 1944-45, 1945-46.
Drumcondra 1947-48, 1948-49, 1957-58, 1960-61, 1964-65.

2 Athlone Town 1980-81, 1982-83.
Cork Athletic 1949-50, 1950-51.
Derry City 1988-89, 1996-97.
Limerick 1959-60, 1979-80.
St James' Gate 1921-22, 1939-40

1 Cork Celtic 1973-74
Cork Hibernians 1970-71
Dolphin 1934-35

Since the 1985-86 season the League of Ireland has been split into a Premier Division and First Division. Below is a list of First Division winners

2 Bray Wanderers 1985-86, 1995-96.
Drogheda United 1988-89, 1990-91.
Waterford United 1989-90, 1997-98.

1 Athlone Town 1987-88.
Derry City 1986-87.
Galway United 1992-93.
Kilkenny City 1996-97.
Limerick City 1991-92.
Sligo Rovers 1993-94.
U.C.D. 1994-95

FAI Cup Winners

24 Shamrock Rovers 1925, 1929, 1930, 1931, 1932, 1933, 1936, 1940, 1944, 1945, 1948, 1955, 1956, 1962, 1964, 1965, 1966, 1967, 1968, 1969, 1978, 1985, 1986, 1987.

8 Dundalk 1942, 1949, 1952, 1958, 1977, 1979, 1981, 1988.

6 Shelbourne 1939, 1960, 1963, 1993, 1996, 1997.

5 Bohemians 1928, 1935, 1970, 1976, 1992.

Drumcondra 1927, 1943, 1946, 1954, 1957.

2 Cork Athletic 1951, 1953.
Cork Hibernians 1972, 1973.
Cork United 1941, 1947.
Derry City 1989, 1995.
Limerick 1971, 1982.
St James' Gate 1922, 1938.
St Patrick's Athletic 1959, 1961.
Sligo Rovers 1983, 1994.
Waterford United 1937, 1980.

1 Alton United 1923.

Athlone Town 1924.
Bray Wanderers 1990.
Cork 1934.
Cork City 1998.
Finn Harps 1974.
Fordsons 1926.
Galway United 1991.
Home Farm 1975.
Transport 1950.
U.C.D. 1984.

F.A.I. National League Premier Division Final League Table 1997/98

	P	W	D	L	F	A	Pts
St. Patrick's Athletic	33	19	11	3	46	24	68
Shelbourne	33	20	7	6	58	32	67
Cork City	33	14	11	8	50	40	53
Shamrock Rovers	33	14	10	9	41	32	52
Bohemians	33	13	11	9	50	36	50
Dundalk	33	12	9	12	41	43	45
Sligo Rovers	33	10	14	9	46	49	44
Finn Harps	33	12	7	14	41	43	43
Derry City	33	10	10	13	30	31	40
U.C.D.	33	9	12	12	36	38	39
Kilkenny City	33	4	7	22	27	63	19
Drogheda United	33	2	9	22	20	55	15

Champions: **St Patrick's Athletic** *Relegated:* **Kilkenny City** *and* **Drogheda United.**

F.A.I. National League First Division Final League Table 1997/98

	P	W	D	L	F	A	Pts
Waterford United	27	18	6	3	35	17	60
Bray Wanderers	27	17	3	7	51	21	54
Limerick FC	27	14	8	5	41	25	50
Galway United	27	13	4	10	38	29	43
Home Farm/Everton	27	9	11	7	28	22	38
Cobh Ramblers	27	10	5	12	32	41	35
Athlone Town	27	8	7	12	31	37	31
St. Francis	27	7	8	12	29	40	29
Monaghan United	27	6	4	17	26	44	22
Longford Town	27	2	6	19	12	47	12

Promoted: **Waterford United** *and* **Bray Wanderers.**

1998 FAI Cup

Semi-Finals

Athlone Town .... 1 .... Cork City 3
Finn Harps .... 0 .... Shelbourne 0

Semi-Final Replay

Shelbourne .... 1 .... Finn Harps 0

Final

Cork City .... 0 .... Shelbourne 0

Final Replay

Cork City .... 1 .... Shelbourne 0

Top Republic of Ireland International Goalscorers

Player	No. of Goals
1. Frank Stapleton	20
2. Tony Cascarino	19
3. John Aldridge	19
4. Don Givens	19
5. Niall Quinn	16

Player	No. of Goals
6. Noel Cantwell	14
7. Gerry Daly	13
8. Jimmy Dunne	12
9. Liam Brady	9
10. Kevin Sheedy	9

Republic of Ireland International Squad

Name	Club	D.O.B.	Born	Caps	Goals
BABB, Phil	Liverpool	30.11.70	Lambeth	26	0
BRANIGAN, Keith	Bolton Wanderers	10.07.66	Fulham	1	0
BREEN, Gary	Coventry City	12.12.73	London	15	2
CARSLEY, Lee	Derby County	28.02.74	Birmingham	7	0
CASCARINO, Tony	A.S. Nancy	01.09.62	Kent	76	19
CONNOLLY, David	Wolves	06.06.77	Willesden	13	6
COYNE, Tommy	Dundee	14.11.62	Glasgow	22	6
CUNNINGHAM, Kenny	Wimbledon	28.06.71	Dublin	17	0
DELAP, Rory	Derby County	06.07.76	Donegal	3	0
DUFF, Damian	Blackburn Rovers	02.03.79	Dublin	3	0
EVANS, Michael	West Brom	01.01.73		1	0
FARRELLY, Gareth	Everton	28.08.75	Dublin	5	0
FLEMMING, Curtis	Middlesbrough	08.10.68	Manchester	10	0
GIVEN, Shay	Newcastle United	20.04.76	Lifford	18	0
HARTE, Ian	Leeds United	31.08.77	Drogheda	18	2
HOUGHTON, Ray	Reading	09.01.62	Glasgow	73	6
IRWIN, Denis	Manchester United	31.10.65	Cork	49	3
KAVANAGH, Graham	Stoke City	02.12.73	Dublin	1	0
KEANE, Robbie	Wolves	08.09.80	Dublin	4	0
KEANE, Roy	Manchester United	10.08.71	Cork	39	4
KELLY, Alan	Sheffield United	11.08.68	Preston	20	0
KELLY, David	Tranmere Rovers	25.11.65	Birmingham	26	9
KELLY, Gary	Leeds United	09.07.74	Louth	28	1
KENNA, Jeff	Blackburn Rovers	27.08.70	Dublin	25	0
KENNEDY, Mark	Wimbledon	15.05.76	Dublin	18	1

Name	Club	D.O.B.	Born	Caps	Goals
KILBANE, Kevin	West Brom	01.02.77	Preston	3	0
KINSELLA, Mark	Charlton Athletic	12.08.72	Dublin	3	0
MAYBURY, Alan	Leeds United	08.08.78	Dublin	1	0
McATEER, Jason	Liverpool	18.06.71	Liverpool	26	1
McLOUGHLIN, Alan	Portsmouth	20.04.67	Manchester	34	2
MOORE, Alan	Middlesbrough	25.11.74	Dublin	8	0
O'NEILL, Keith	Norwich City	16.02.76	Dublin	10	4
PHELAN, Terry	Everton	16.03.67	Manchester	38	0
QUINN, Niall	Sunderland	06.10.66	Dublin	63	16
STAUNTON, Steve	Liverpool	19.01.69	Drogheda	75	6
TOWNSEND, Andy	Middlesbrough	23.07.63	Maidstone	70	7

Information correct as of 5 September 1998.

FAI / Opel International Senior Player of the Year Recipients

Year	Name
1989	Kevin Moran
1990	Paul McGrath
1991	Paul McGrath
1992	John Aldridge
1993	Steve Staunton
1994	Ray Houghton
1995	Andy Townsend
1996	Alan McLoughlin
1997	Roy Keane

Presidents of the F.A.I.

W.H. Ritchie, Sir H. McLaughlin, J. Cunningham, O. Grattan-Esmond, Dr. W.F. Hooper, O. Traynor T.D., D. O'Malley T.D., N.T. Blaney T.D., D. O'Halloran, C.H. Walsh, F. Davis, C. Cahill, Dr. B. Menton, J.J. Farrell, D. Casey, P. O'Brien, F. Fields, M. Hyland, L.D. Kilcoyne, P. Quigley (current President).

Irish Football Association

20 Windsor Avenue, Belfast BT9 6EG. Tel. (01232) 669458

Founded	1880
President	Jim Boyce

1997/98 Season	Winners	Runners Up
Irish League, Premier Division Champions	Cliftonville	Linfield
Irish League, First Division Champions	Newry Town	Bangor
Irish Cup Winners	Glentoran	Glenavon
Nationwide Gold Cup	Glenavon	Coleraine
Main Stadium		Windsor Park (28,500)

INTERNATIONAL	
Northern Ireland Manager	Lawrie McMenemy
Top International Goalscorer	Colin Clarke (13 goals in 38 appearances)
Most Capped Player	Pat Jennings (119 caps)
Best World Cup Result	Quarter finalists (1958 World Cup in Sweden)

Irish League Premier Division Team Statistics

Club	Founded	Ground and Capacity	Colours	League Titles	Irish Cups
Ballymena United	1928	The Showgrounds (8,000)	Sky Blue & White	0	6
Cliftonville	1879	Solitude (8,000)	Red & White	3	8
Coleraine	1927	The Showgrounds (12,500)	Blue & White	1	4
Crusaders	1898	Seaview (9,000)	Red & Black	4	2
Glenavon	1889	Mourneview Park (10,900)	Royal Blue & White	3	5
Glentoran	1882	The Oval Grounds (30,000)	Green, Black & Red	19	17
Linfield	1886	Windsor Park (28,500)	Royal Blue & White	42	35
Newry Town	1923	The Showgrounds (5,000)	Blue & White	0	0
Omagh Town	1962	St. Julian's Road (8,000)	Black & White	0	0
Portadown	1924	Shamrock Park (15,000)	Red	3	1

Irish League First Division Team Statistics

Club	Founded	Ground and Capacity	Colours	League Titles	Irish Cups
Ards	1902	Castlereagh Park (10,000)	Red & Blue	1	4
Ballyclare Comrades	1919	Dixon Park (4,500)	Red & White	0	0
Bangor	1918	Clandeboye Park (5,000)	Gold & Royal Blue	0	1
Carrick Rangers	1939	Taylor's Avenue (5,000)	Amber & Black	0	1
Distillery	1879	New Grosvenor Stadium (7,000)	White & Dark Blue	6	12
Dungannon Swifts	1949	Stangmore Park (5,000)	Royal Blue & White	0	0
Larne	1900	Inver Park (12,000)	Red & White	0	0
Limavady United	1876	The Showgrounds (1,000)	Royal Blue & White	0	0

Irish Cup Champions

35 Linfield 1891, 1892, 1893, 1895, 1898, 1899, 1902, 1904, 1912, 1913, 1915, 1916, 1919, 1922, 1923, 1930, 1932, 1934, 1936, 1939, 1942, 1945, 1946, 1948, 1950, 1953, 1960, 1962, 1963, 1970, 1978, 1980, 1982, 1994, 1995.

17 Glentoran 1914, 1917, 1921, 1932, 1933, 1935, 1951, 1966, 1973, 1983, 1985, 1986, 1987, 1988, 1990, 1996, 1998.

12 Distillery 1884, 1885, 1886, 1889, 1894, 1896, 1903, 1905, 1910, 1925, 1956, 1971.

8 Belfast Celtic 1918, 1926, 1937, 1938, 1941, 1943, 1944, 1947.

Cliftonville 1883, 1888, 1897, 1900, 1901, 1907, 1909, 1979.

6 Ballymena 1929, 1940, 1958, 1981, 1984, 1989.

5 Glenavon 1957, 1959, 1961, 1992, 1997.

4 Ards 1927, 1952, 1969, 1974.

Coleraine 1965, 1972, 1975, 1977.

3 Derry City 1949, 1954, 1964.

Shelbourne 1906, 1911, 1920.

2 Crusaders 1967, 1968.

Queen's Island 1882, 1924.

1 Bangor 1993.

Bohemians 1908.

Carrick Rangers 1976.

Dundela 1955.

Gordon Highlanders 1890.

Moyola Park 1881.

Portadown 1991.

Ulster 1887.

Willowfield 1928.

Irish League Champions

42 Linfield 1890-91, 1891-92, 1892-93, 1894-95, 1897-98, 1901-02, 1903-04, 1906-07, 1907-08, 1908-09, 1910-11, 1913-14, 1921-22, 1922-23, 1929-30, 1931-32, 1933-34, 1934-35, 1948-49, 1949-50, 1953-54, 1954-55, 1955-56, 1958-59, 1960-61, 1961-62, 1965-66, 1968-69, 1970-71, 1974-75, 1977-78, 1978-79, 1979-80, 1981-82, 1982-83, 1983-84, 1984-85, 1985-86, 1986-87, 1988-89, 1992-93, 1993-94.

19 Glentoran 1893-94, 1896-97, 1904-05, 1911-12, 1912-13, 1920-21, 1924-25, 1930-31, 1950-51, 1952-53, 1963-64, 1966-67, 1967-68, 1969-70, 1971-72, 1976-77, 1980-81, 1987-88, 1991-92.

14 Belfast Celtic 1899-1900, 1914-15, 1919-20, 1925-26, 1926-27, 1927-28, 1928-29, 1932-33, 1935-36, 1936-37, 1937-38, 1938-39, 1939-40, 1947-48.

6 Distillery 1895-96, 1898-99, 1900-01, 1902-03, 1905-06, 1962-63.

4 Crusaders 1972-73, 1975-76, 1994-95, 1996-97.

3 Cliftonville 1905-06, 1909-10, 1997-98.

Portadown 1989-90, 1990-91, 1995-96.

1 Ards 1957-58.

Coleraine 1973-74.

Derry City 1964-65.

Queen's Island 1923-24.

Since the 1995-96 season the Irish League has been split into a Premier Division and First Division. Below is a list of First Division winners

First Division Winners

1 Ballymena 1996-97.

Coleraine 1995-96.

Newry Town 1997-98.

1997/98 Irish Cup

SEMI-FINALS			
Glenavon	3	Crusaders	1
Linfield	1	Glentoran	2

FINAL			
Glentoran	1	Glenavon	0 aet

Irish League Premier Division
Final League Table 1997/98

	P	W	D	L	F	A	Pts
Cliftonville	36	20	8	8	49	37	68
Linfield	36	17	13	6	50	19	64
Portadown	36	17	9	10	50	38	60
Glentoran	36	17	8	11	52	34	59
Crusaders	36	13	12	11	51	51	51
Ballymena United	36	14	9	13	54	55	51
Coleraine	36	11	10	15	41	47	43
Glenavon	36	9	12	15	47	56	39
Omagh Town	36	7	10	19	43	68	31
Ards	36	4	11	21	31	63	23

Champions: **Cliftonville** Relegated: **Ards**.

Irish League First Division
Final League Table 1997/98

	P	W	D	L	F	A	Pts
Newry Town	28	20	5	3	61	18	65
Bangor	28	18	4	6	51	26	58
Distillery	28	15	6	7	48	34	51
Dungannon Swifts	28	14	6	8	63	49	48
Ballyclare Comrades	28	13	3	12	47	45	42
Larne	28	8	2	18	30	58	26
Limavady United	28	6	2	20	29	60	20
Carrick Rangers	28	3	2	23	20	59	11

Promoted: **Newry Town**.

Top Northern Ireland International Goalscorers

Player	No. of Goals	Player	No. of Goals
Colin Clarke	13	Olphie Stanfield	11
Gerry Armstrong	12	Billy Bingham	10
Joe Bambrick	12	Johnny Crossan	10
Willie Gillespie	12	Jimmy McIlroy	10
Jimmy Quinn	12	Peter McParland	10
Iain Dowie	11		

Northern Ireland International Squad

Name	Club	D.O.B.	Born	Caps	Goals
DOWIE, Iain	Queens Park Rangers	09.01.65	Hatfield	50	11
FETTIS, Alan	Blackburn Rovers	01.02.71	Belfast	23	0
GILLESPIE, Keith	Newcastle United	18.02.75	Larne	22	1
HILL, Colin	Northampton Town	12.11.63	Uxbridge	27	1
HORLOCK, Kevin	Manchester City	01.11.72	Erith	14	0
HUGHES, Aaron	Newcastle United	08.11.79	Magherafelt	4	0
HUGHES, Michael	Wimbledon	02.08.71	Larne	43	3
JENKINS, Iain	Dundee United	24.12.72	Whiston	5	0
LENNON, Neil	Leicester City	25.06.71	Lurgan	23	1
LOMAS, Steve	West Ham United	18.01.74	Hanover	26	2
MAGILTON, Jim	Sheffield Wednesday	06.05.69	Belfast	39	5
McCARTHY, Jon	Birmingham City	18.08.70	Middlesbrough	7	0
McMAHON, Gerry	St. Johnstone	29.12.73	Belfast	17	2
MORROW, Steve	Queens Park Rangers	02.07.70	Bangor	33	1
MULRYNE, Philip	Manchester United	01.01.78	Belfast	6	1
NOLAN, Ian	Sheffield Wednesday	09.07.70	Liverpool	7	0
O'BOYLE, George	St. Johnstone	14.12.67	Belfast	12	1
PATTERSON, Darren	Dundee United	15.10.69	Belfast	11	1
QUINN, James	West Bromwich Albion	15.12.74	Coventry	13	1
ROWLAND, Keith	Queens Park Rangers	01.09.71	Portadown	14	0
TAGGART, Gerry	Leicester City	10.10.70	Belfast	45	7
WHITLEY, Jeff	Manchester City	28.01.79	Zambia	3	0
WHITLEY, Jim	Manchester City	14.04.75	Zambia	2	0

Information correct as of 5 September 1998.

Past Presidents

Lord Moyola, Captain Sir James Wilson, Austin Donnelly, Fred Cochrane, Joe McBride, Harry Cavan, Sammy Walker, Jimmy Boyce (current President).

RUGBY

Irish Rugby Football Union
62 Lansdowne Road, Ballsbridge, Dublin 4. Tel. (01) 6684601

Founded 1874
Number of Provincial Unions 4
Number of Clubs 250
Number of Members (men) 60,000
Number of Members (women) 500
President ....Niall Brophy
Secretary and Treasurer..P.R. Browne
Top Points Scorer 1997/98 A.I.L..Andrew Thompson (Shannon) 155 points
Top Try Scorer 1997/98 A.I.L..Denis Hickie (St Mary's) 12 tries
Oldest Club..Dublin University (founded 1854)
Biggest Recorded Attendance ....55,000 (in Five Nations Championship at Lansdowne Road)
Main Stadium..Lansdowne Road (capacity 49,638)

1997/98	Champions	Runners Up
All-Ireland League Division One	Shannon	Garryowen
All-Ireland League Division Two	Galwegians	Buccaneers
All-Ireland League Division Three	Portadown	Ballynahinch
All-Ireland League Division Four	County Carlow	Richmond
Provincial Series	Leinster	Munster

INTERNATIONAL

National Manager ....Donal Lenihan
National Coach ....Warren Gatland
Most Capped International..C.M.H. Gibson, 69 caps (1964-79)
Top International Points Scorer...M.J. Kiernan, 308 points (43 internationals)
Top International Try Scorer...B.J. Mullin, 17 (55 internationals)
First International Game...v. England, 1875
Best World Cup Performance ....Quarter-finalists (1987, 1991 and 1995)
Grand Slams 1 (1948)
Triple Crowns 6 (1894, 1899, 1948, 1949, 1982, 1985)
International Championships ....18 (including 10 outright wins)

All-Ireland League, Final Tables

DIVISION ONE	P	W	D	L	F	A	Pts
Shannon	13	12	0	1	367	142	24
Garryowen	13	9	1	3	361	224	19
Young Munster	13	9	1	3	244	176	19
St Mary's	13	9	0	4	409	274	18
Cork Constitution	13	8	0	5	289	217	16
Ballymena	13	7	0	6	344	287	14
Clontarf	13	7	0	6	276	266	14
Terenure College	13	5	1	7	241	263	11
Lansdowne	13	4	2	7	264	328	10
Blackrock College	13	4	1	8	249	326	9
*Dungannon	13	4	0	9	239	309	8
*Dolphin	13	3	2	8	227	345	8
*Old Crescent	13	4	0	9	168	298	8
*Old Belvedere	13	2	0	11	208	431	4

§ Promoted. * Relegated

DIVISION TWO	P	W	D	L	F	A	Pts
§Galwegians	13	13	0	0	336	164	26
§Buccaneers	12	11	0	1	311	102	22
Sunday's Well	13	7	2	4	252	227	16
City of Derry	13	8	0	5	277	255	16
UCC	13	6	1	6	204	282	13
Skerries	13	6	0	7	248	224	12
DLSP	13	6	0	7	280	269	12
Old Wesley	13	5	1	7	256	246	11
Greystones	13	5	1	7	204	212	11
Bective Rangers	13	5	1	7	210	233	11
Malone	13	5	0	8	210	255	10
Wanderers	12	5	0	7	200	252	10
*Monkstown	13	3	0	11	207	336	6
*Instonians	13	2	0	12	205	341	4

§ Promoted. * Relegated

I.R.F.U. Number of Affiliated Clubs

	Clubs	Commercial Clubs	Schools
Ulster	56	17	107
Munster	59	5	41
Leinster	71	8	75
Connacht	19	0	23
London Irish	1	-	-
	205	30	246

International Squad Factfile

Name	Club	D.O.B.	Born	Caps
BISHOP, Justin	London Irish	08.11.74	Sussex	2
BRENNAN, Trevor	St Mary's College	22.09.73	Kildare	2
CLARKE, Ciaran	Terenure College	08.03.69	Dublin	5
CLOHESSY, Peter	Young Munster	22.03.66	Limerick	20
CORKERY, David	Cork Constitution	06.11.72	Cork	25
CORRIGAN, Reggie	Greystones	10.11.70	Dublin	6
COSTELLO, Victor	St Mary's College	23.10.70	Dublin	13
DAWSON, Kieron	London Irish	29.01.75	Bangor	3
ELWOOD, Eric	Galwegians	26.02.69	Galway	27
ERSKINE, David	Sale	14.10.69	London	3
FITZPATRICK, Justin	Dungannon	21.11.73	Chichester	2
FULCHER, Gabriel	Lansdowne	27.11.69	England	21
GALWEY, Mick	Shannon	08.10.66	Kerry	23
HALVEY, Eddie	Shannon	11.07.70	Limerick	8
HENDERSON, Rob	Wasps	27.10.72	New Malden	7
HICKIE, Denis	St Mary's College	13.02.76	Dublin	12
HUMPHREYS, David	Dungannon	10.09.71	Belfast	10
JOHNS, Paddy	Saracens	19.02.68	Portadown	43
KEANE, Killian	Garryowen	14.08.71	Drogheda	1
MAGGS, Kevin	Bath	03.06.74	Bristol	9
McCALL, Mark	Dungannon	29.11.67	Bangor	13
McGUINNESS, Conor	St Mary's College	29.03.75	Dublin	7
McWEENEY, John	St Mary's College	26.05.76	Dublin	1
MILLER, Eric	Leicester	23.09.75	Dublin	8
NESDALE, Ross	Newcastle	30.07.69	New Zealand	7
NOWLAN, Kevin	St Mary's College	26.06.71	Dublin	3
O CUINNEAGAIN, Dion	Sale	24.05.72	South Africa	2
O'KELLY, Malcolm	London Irish	19.07.74	Essex	9
O'MEARA, Brian	Cork Constitution	05.04.76	Cork	4
O'SHEA, Conor	London Irish	21.10.70	Limerick	20
POPPLEWELL, Nick	Newcastle	06.04.64	Dublin	48
WALLACE, Paul	Saracens	30.12.71	Cork	20
WALLACE, Richard	Saracens	16.01.68	Cork	29

Ten Most Capped International Players

Mike Gibson	69
Willie John McBride	63
Fergal Slattery	61
Philip Orr	58
Brendan Mullin	55
Tom Kiernan	54
Donal Lenihan	52
Moss Keane	51
Nick Popplewell	48
Jackie Kyle	46

1997/98 Provincial Cup Results

Connacht Senior Cup Final

Corinthinans	41	Galwegians	15

Leinster Senior Cup Final

Lansdowne	23	Skerries	17

Munster Senior Cup Final

Shannon	19	Young Munster	18

Ulster Senior Cup Final

Dungannon	19	Malone	16

ATHLETICS

Bord Lúthchleas na hÉireann
11 Prospect Road, Glasnevin, Dublin 9. Tel. (01) 8309901

Founded 1967
President ....Nick Davis
Honorary Secretary ....Dermot Nangle
Number of Senior Clubs 144
Number of Junior Clubs 135
Total Membership 16,495
Principal Venues..........Morton Stadium, Dublin (10,000), Mardyke, Cork (8,000), Tullamore Harriers A.C. (5,000)
Biggest Recorded Crowd ....30,000 (1979. World Cross Country Championships, Limerick)

Track & Field, National Champions 1998

Event	Men's Champion	Performance	Women's Champion	Performance
100m	Neil Ryan	10.79	Lena Barry	11.83
200m	Gary Ryan	20.88	Ciara Sheehy	24.31
400m	Brian Forbes	47.72	Karen Shinkins	53.09
800m	James Nolan	1.47.75	Sinead Delahunty	2.05.19
1,500m	James McIlroy	3.49.83	Una English	4.14.21
5,000m	Martin McCarthy	14.02.43	Sonia O'Sullivan	15.20.16
10,000m	Noel Berkley	29.56.65	-	-
3,000m steeplechase	Eugene O'Neill	9.04.87	-	-
110m Hurdles	Peter Coghlan	14.20	-	-
100m Hurdles	-	-	Susan Smith	13.31*
400m Hurdles	Tom McGuirk	50.92	Orla Power	60.17
4x100m Relay	Dublin City Harriers	42.05	West Dublin	47.99
10,000m Walk	Pierce O'Callaghan	42.45.70	-	-
5,000m Walk	-	-	Gillian O'Sullivan	21.57.22
High Jump	Mark Mandy	2.10m	Orna Donoghoe	1.73m
Long Jump	Joseph Naughton	7.23m	Jacqui Stokes	5.96m
Triple Jump	Michael McDonald	14.62m	Siobhan Hoey	12.26m
Javelin	Terry McHugh	72.94m	Alison Moffitt	46.48
Hammer	Roman Linscheid	72.42	Olivia Kelleher	53.68m
Shot	John Dermody	16.85m	Emma Gavin	13.43m
Discus	John Menton	56.59m	Ailish O'Brien	47.93
Pole Vault	Neil Young	4.70m	M. O'Halloran	2.60m
56lbs Distance	John Menton	9.16m*	-	-

* Denotes National Record

Irish Cross Country Medalists at Major Championships

Year	Championships	Medal	Winner
1969	Junior International (Team)	Silver	J. Hartnett, E. Leddy, P. Gilsenan, D. Murphy
1971	Women's International C'ships (Team)	Bronze	A O'Brien, P. Mullen, D. Foreman, J. McNicholl
1971	Junior International	Gold	John Hartnett
1974	World Junior Championships	Bronze	John Treacy
1975	World Junior Championships	Bronze	John Treacy
1975	Junior Championships (Team)	Silver	J. Treacy, L. Kenny, G. Finnegan, G. Redmond
1978	World Championships	Gold	John Treacy
1979	World Championships	Gold	John Treacy
1979	World Championships (Team)	Silver	J. Treacy, D. McDaid, G. Deegan, M. O'Shea, D. Walsh, T. Brien
1992	World Championships	Silver	Catherina McKiernan
1993	World Championships	Silver	Catherina McKiernan
1994	World Championships	Silver	Catherina McKiernan
1994	European Championships	Gold	Catherina McKiernan
1995	World Championships	Silver	Catherina McKiernan
1997	World Championships (Team)	Bronze	C. McKiernan, S. O'Sullivan, V. Vaughan, U. English
1998	World Championships (7,600m)	Gold	Sonia O'Sullivan
1998	World Championships (4,000m)	Gold	Sonia O'Sullivan

BOXING

Irish Amateur Boxing Association

National Boxing Stadium, South Circular Road, Dublin 8. Tel. (01) 4533371

Founded 1911
President ....Breandán Ó Conaire
Honorary Secretary ....Seán Crowley
Number of Provincial Councils ....4 (Connacht, Leinster, Munster and Ulster)
Number of County Boards 26
Number of Clubs 330
Principal Venue...The National Boxing Stadium (capacity 2,000)

Irish Amateur Boxing Senior Champions 1997/98

Weight	Winner	Club
48kg Light Flyweight	James Rooney	Star, Belfast
51kg Flyweight	Martin Murphy	St Paul's, Waterford
54kg Bantamweight	Bernard Dunne	CIE
57kg Featherweight	Patrick O'Donnell	Dockers, Belfast
60kg Lightweight	Eugene McEnaney	Dundalk
63.5kg Light Welterweight	Mark Wickham	Enniscorty
67kg Welterweight	Neil Gough	St Paul's, Waterford
71kg Light Middleweight	Michael Roche	Sunnyside, Cork
75kg Middleweight	Brian Magee	Holy Trinity, Belfast
81kg Light Heavyweight	Adrian Sheerin	Swinford, Mayo
91kg Heavyweight	John Kiely	Corpus Christi, Limerick
91+kg Super Heavyweight	Stephen Reynolds	St Joseph's, Sligo

Irish Amateur Boxing Intermediate Champions 1997/98

Weight	Winner	Club
48kg Light Flyweight	James Moore	St Francis, Limerick
51kg Flyweight	Darren Campbell	Glin
54kg Bantamweight	Bernard Dunne	C.I.E.
57kg Featherweight	Anthony O'Donovan	Fr Horgan's
60kg Lightweight	Ian Hackett	Holy Family, Drogheda
63.5kg Light Welterweight	Patrick Jennings	C.I.E.
67kg Welterweight	James Moore	Arklow
71kg Light Middleweight	Terence McDermott	Bishop Kelly
75kg Middleweight	Jason McKay	H.M.L.
81kg Light Heavyweight	Seán O'Grady	St Saviours
91kg Heavyweight	Eanna Falvey	St Colmans
91+kg Super Heavyweight	John White	St Patrick's, Newry

Irish Amateur Boxing Junior Champions 1997/98

Weight	Winner	Club
48kg Light Flyweight	H. Cunningham	Saints
51kg Flyweight	D. Campbell	Glin
54kg Bantamweight	G. Brown	Crumlin
57kg Featherweight	D. Hamill	All Saints
60kg Lightweight	T. Hamill	All Saints
63.5kg Light Welterweight	C. Smithers	Bunclody
67kg Welterweight	P. Quinn	Ardnaree
71kg Light Middleweight	M. Lee	Oughterard
75kg Middleweight	L. Senior	Crumlin
81kg Light Heavyweight	M. Mellon	Newry
91kg Heavyweight	S. O'Hagan	Bishop Kelly
91+kg Super Heavyweight	D. Nevin	Dunboyne

Irish Medallists at European Championships

Name	Year(s)	Venue	Medal	Weight
Paul Griffin	1991	Sweden	Gold	57kg
Maxie McCullough	1949	Norway	Gold	60kg
Gerry O' Colmain	1947	Ireland	Gold	91kg
Jim Ingle	1939	Ireland	Gold	51kg
Paddy Dowdal	1939	Ireland	Gold	60kg
Brian Magee	1998	Belarus	Silver	75kgs
Terry Milligan	1953		Silver	63.5kg
John Kelly	1951		Silver	54kg
Peter Maguire	1947	Ireland	Silver	57kg
Damean Kelly	1995	Denmark	Bronze	51kg
Paul Griffin	1993		Bronze	57kg
Sean Casey	1985		Bronze	51kg
Kieran Joyce	1983		Bronze	71kg
Gerry Hawkins	1981		Bronze	48kg
Phil Sutcliffe	1977-79		Bronze	48kg + 51kg
Niall McLoughlin	1971		Bronze	51kg
Mick Dowling	1965-71		Bronze	54kg
Jim McCourt	1965		Bronze	60kg
Harry Perry	1959	Lucerne	Bronze	67kg
Colm McCoy	1959	Lucerne	Bronze	75kg
Fred Tiedt	1957	Prague	Bronze	67kg
Terry Milligan	1951		Bronze	63.5kg
David Connell	1949-51		Bronze	60kg

SWIMMING

Irish Amateur Swimming Association

House of Sport, Long Mile Road, Dublin 12. Tel. (01) 4501739

Founded 1893
Number of Provincial Branches ....4 (Connacht, Leinster, Munster and Ulster)
Number of Clubs 149
Number of Members 6,500
Number of Swimming Pools nationwide 219
President ....Mary O'Malley
Honorary Secretary ....Mrs. Pat Donovan
Honorary Treasurer ....Wally Clark
Number of Coaches 50
Number of Teachers 1,500
Biggest Recorded Attendance ....2,000 (Leisureland International Meeting, Galway March 1997)

1998 Irish National Swimming Champions

Event	Women's Champion	Club	Time	Men's Champion	Club	Time
50m Freestyle	C. Gibney	Trojan	26.01	N. O'Hare	Eastern Bay	22.76*
100m Freestyle	C. Gibney	Trojan	56.54	N. O'Hare	Eastern Bay	50.41
200m Freestyle	C. Gibney	Trojan	2.01.87	H. O'Connor	New Ross	1.50.99
400m Freestyle	N. Pepper	Cormorant	4.30.81	C. Lowth	Cormorant	4.04.27
800m Freestyle	L. Biargard	Iceland	9.03.92	-	-	-
1500m Freestyle	-	-	-	N. Cameron	Leander	16.13.06
50m Backstroke	N. Cawley	Claremorris	30.23	H. O'Connor	New Ross	26.2
100m Backstroke	E. Konradsdottir	Iceland	1.04.18	H. O'Connor	New Ross	55.52
200m Backstroke	N. Cawley	Claremorris	2.16.37§	H. O'Connor	New Ross	1.59.42
50m Breaststroke	L. Robinson	Bangor	33.66	M. Giles	Coolmine	29.44
100m Breaststroke	L. Robinson	Bangor	1.12.26	H. Gudmundsson	Iceland	1.04.61
200m Breaststroke	M. Corless	Tuam	2.35.50	M. Craig	Ards	2.18.01
50m Butterfly	E. Konradsdottir	Iceland	28.83	A. Reid	Larne	24.93
100m Butterfly	L. Kelleher	City of Cork	1.02.78§	A. Reid	Larne	55.67
200m Butterfly	L. Kelleher	City of Cork	2.17.52	C. Lowth	Trojan	2.00.33*
100m Individual Medley	L. Kelleher	City of Cork	1.06.12	H. O'Connor	New Ross	58.75
200m Individual Medley	L. Kelleher	City of Cork	2.21.26§	G. Beegan	Cormorant	2.06.30

Continued from previous page

Event	Women's Champion	Club	Time	Men's Champion	Club	Time
400m Individual Medley	L. Kelleher	City of Cork	5.03.32	A. Bree	Ards	4.33.96
4x100m Freestlye Relay	Iceland		3.55.78	New Ross		3.32.91
4x200m Freestyle Relay	-			Terenure		7.54.53
4x100m Medley Relay	Iceland		4.23.09	New Ross		3.48.31*

* Denotes Irish Senior record. § Denotes Irish Junior Record.

Irish National Records, Short Course

Event	Women's Record Holder	Time	Men's Record Holder	Time
50m Freestyle	Michelle Smith	25.85	Nick O'Hare	22.76
100m Freestyle	Michelle Smith	54.87	Nick O'Hare	50.02
200m Freestyle	Michelle Smith	1.59.69	Ken Turner	1.49.38
400m Freestyle	Michelle Smith	4.14.02	Ken Turner	3.53.82
800m Freestyle	Michelle Smith	8.44.06	Ken Turner	8.02.88
1500m Freestyle	Michelle Smith	16.46.75	Ken Turner	15.33.57
50m Backstroke	Niamh O'Connor	29.44	Adrian O'Connor	25.76
100m Backstroke	Michelle Smith	1.02.36	Adrian O'Connor	55.23
200m Backstroke	Michelle Smith	2.10.76	Hugh O'Connor	1.59.33
50m Breaststroke	Gina Galligan	32.47	Gary O'Toole	28.59
100m Breaststroke	Siobhan Doyle	1.10.71	Gary O'Toole	1.01.87
200m Breaststroke	Sharlene Brown	2.32.26	Gary O'Toole	2.11.35
50m Butterfly	Michelle Smith	28.15	Andrew Reid	24.67
100m Butterfly	Michelle Smith	59.99	Declan Byrne	55.41
200m Butterfly	Michelle Smith	2.07.04	Colin Lowth	2.00.65
100m Individual Medley	Michelle Smith	1.02.70	Standard	57.39
200m Individual Medley	Michelle Smith	2.13.46	Gary O'Toole	2.02.23
400m Individual Medley	Michelle Smith	4.36.84	Gary O'Toole	4.22.97
RELAYS				
4x50 Freestyle, Club	Trojan	1.50.91	Coolmine	1.32.93
4x100 Freestyle, Club	Trojan	3.59.60	Coolmine	3.25.47
4x200 Freestyle, Club	-	-	Glenalbyn	7.34.35
4x50 Medley, Club	Trojan	2.01.07	Coolmine	1.45.13
4x100 Medley, Club	Glenalbyn	4.22.99	New Ross	3.49.06
4x50 Freestyle, National	National Team	1.49.03	National Team	1.32.92
4x100 Freestyle, National	National Team	3.54.72	National Team	3.24.66
4x200 Freestyle, National	National Team	8.25.94	National Team	7.27.78
4x50 Medley, National	National Team	1.58.93	National Team	1.43.89
4x100 Medley, National	National Team	4.15.90	National Team	3.45.66

All records correct as of April 25, 1998.

HORSE RACING

Irish Horseracing Authority
Leopardstown Racecourse, Foxrock, Dublin 18. Tel. (01) 2892888

Founded	1994 (replaced the Racing Authority)
Chairman	Denis Brosnan
Chief Executive	Noel Ryan
Secretary	Paddy Walsh
Number of Meetings (1997)	256
Number of Races (1997)	1,794
Total betting (1997)	£552,728,300
On-course	£104,728 ,300
Off-course	£448,000,000
Total Prizemoney	£15,003,000
Total Attendances for 1997	1,164,724
Main tracks	The Curragh, Leopardstown, Fairyhouse, Punchestown and Ballybrit

NATIONAL HUNT	
Number of Races	1,102
Total Prizemoney	£7,131,000
Champion National Hunt Jockey (1996/97)	Charlie Swan (126 winners)
Champion National Hunt Trainer (1996/97)	Aidan O'Brien (76 winners)

1998 Winners	Winner	Jockey	Trainer
Jameson Grand National	Bobbyjo	Paul Carberry	Tommy Carberry
Powers Gold Cup	Delphi Lodge	Tommy Treacy	Tom Taafe
Hennessy Gold Cup	Dorans Pride	Richard Dunwoody	Michael Hourigan
Ladbroke Champion Hurdle	Graphic Equaliser	Conor O'Dwyer	Arthur Moore
A.I.G. Champion Hurdle	Istabraq	Charlie Swan	Aidan O'Brien
Compaq Galway Plate	Amlah	Brendan Powell	Philip Hobbs

FLAT	
Number of Races	692
Total Prizemoney	£7,872,000
Champion Flat Jockey (1997)	Christy Roche (93 winners)
Champion Flat Trainer (1997)	Aidan O'Brien (70 winners)

1998 Winners	Winner	Jockey	Trainer
Budweiser Irish Derby	Dream Well	Cash Asmussen	Pascal Bary
Heinz 57 Phoenix Stakes	Lavery	Walter Swinburn	Aidan O'Brien
Irish Oaks	Winona	Johnny Murtagh	John Oxx
Irish 2,000 Guineas	Tarascon	Jamie Spencer	Tommy Stack
Irish 1,000 Guineas	Desert Prince	Olivier Peslier	David Loder
Irish St. Leger	Kayf Tara	John Reid	S. Bin Suroor
National Stakes	Mus-if	Mick Kinane	Dermot Weld

GOLF

Golfing Union of Ireland

Glencar House, 81 Eglinton Road, Donnybrook, Dublin 4. Tel. (01) 2694111

Founded	1891
Number of Affiliated Clubs	367
President	Percy Shannon, Mallow
President Elect	Tom Grealy, Roscommon
Honorary Secretary	Gerard O'Brien, Clontarf
Number of Coaches	5
Number of Club Members	125,061
Oldest Club with a Continuous Existence	Royal Belfast (1881)

1998 Champion	Winners	Runners Up
East of Ireland Amateur Open	Garth McGimpsey (Bangor)	Enda McMenamin (Ballybofey)
North of Ireland Amateur Open	Paddy Gribben (Warrenpoint)	D. Gibson (Downpatrick)
West of Ireland Amateur Open	Noel Fox (Portmarnock)	Pat Lyons (Cork)
South of Ireland Amateur Open	Johnny Foster (Ballyclare)	Andrew McCormick (Scrabo)
Irish Amateur Open	Michael Hoey (Shandon Park)	G. Cullen (Beaverstown)
Irish Amateur Close	Eddie Power (Kilkenny)	Bryan Omelia (Newlands)

Irish Ladies Golf Union

1 Clonskeagh Square, Clonskeagh Road, Dublin 14. Tel. (01) 2696244

Founded	1893
President	Juliett McHugh
Secretary	M.P. Turvey
Number of Affiliated Clubs	333
Number of Club Members	42,500

1998 Champions	Winners	Runners Up
Irish Close Championship	Lillian Behan (The Curragh)	Oonagh Purfield (Co. Louth)
Irish OpenChampionship	S. Fanagan O'Brien (Milltown)	Lillian Behan (The Curragh)
Senior Cup Championship	Royal Co. Down	Co. Louth
Schools Championship	Laurel Hill College, Limerick	Santa Sabina, Sutton

Growth of Golf 1986-97

	No. of Clubs 1986	No. of Clubs 1997	No. of Members 1986	No. of Members 1997
Golfing Union of Ireland	248	367	123,000	200,000
Irish Ladies Golf Union	237	333	24,000	42,500

Based on the number of affiliated clubs and members of the respective organisations.

Irish Winners of International Professional Tournaments

Winner	Year	Tournament	Winner	Year	Tournament
Fred Daly	1946	Irish Open	Eddie Polland	1973	Penfold-Bournemouth Tournament
Fred Daly	1947	British Open	C. O'Connor Jnr.	1974	Zambian Open
Fred Daly	1947	PGA Matchplay Championship	Liam Higgins	1974	Kerrygold Classic
Harry Bradshaw	1947	Irish Open	C. O'Connor Jnr.	1975	Carrolls Open
Fred Daly	1948	PGA Matchplay Championship	C. O'Connor Jnr.	1975	Martini International
Fred Daly	1948	Dunlop Southport Tournament	Peter Townsend	1975	ICL Tournament
Fred Daly	1948	Penfold Tournament	John O'Leary	1975	Holiday Inns Championship
Harry Bradshaw	1949	Irish Open	John O'Leary	1975	Sumrie-Bournemouth Betterball
Fred Daly	1950	Lotus Tournament	Eddie Polland	1975	Sun Alliance Matchplay C'ship
Fred Daly	1952	PGA Matchplay Championship	C. O'Connor Jnr.	1976	Sumrie Betterball
Fred Daly	1952	Daks Tournament	John O'Leary	1976	Greater Manchester Open
Harry Bradshaw	1953	Dunlop Masters	Eddie Polland	1976	Spanish Open
Harry Bradshaw	1955	Dunlop Masters	Eamon Darcy	1977	Greater Manchester Open
C. O'Connor Snr.	1955	Swallow Penfold	Liam Higgins	1977	Kerrygold Classic
C. O'Connor Snr.	1956	Dunlop Masters	Liam Higgins	1977	Kenya Open
C. O'Connor Snr.	1956	Spalding Tournament	C. O'Connor Jnr.	1978	Sumrie-Bournemouth Betterball
C. O'Connor Snr.	1957	News of the World Matchplay	Eamon Darcy	1978	Sumrie-Bournemouth Betterball
Harry Bradshaw	1958	PGA Close Championship	David Jones	1978	PGA Club Pros' Championship
Harry Bradshaw	1958	Swallow-Penfold (tied)	Peter Townsend	1978	Caribbean Open
Norman Drew	1959	Yorkshire Evening News Tournament	Peter Townsend	1978	Zambian Open
Ernie Jones	1959	The Hennessy Tournament	Peter Townsend	1978	Moroccan Grand Prix
C. O'Connor Snr.	1959	Dunlop Masters	Peter Townsend	1978	Los Lagaratos Open
C. O'Connor Snr.	1959	Daks Tournament	Des Smyth	1979	European Matchplay C'ship
C. O'Connor Snr.	1960	Irish Hospitals Tournament	David Jones	1979	PGA Club Pros' Championship
C. O'Connor Snr.	1960	Ballantine Open	Eamon Darcy	1980	Air New Zealand Open
C. O'Connor Snr.	1961	Carling Caledonian	Des Smyth	1980	Newcastle Brown '900'
Hugh Boyle	1961	Yomiuri Tournament	Des Smyth	1980	Greater Manchester Open
Hugh Boyle	1961	Daks Tournamen	Eddie Polland	1980	Spanish Open
Ernie Jones	1961	The Coxmoore Tournament	Eamon Darcy	1981	Cock O'The North
C. O'Connor Snr.	1962	Irish Hospitals Tournament	Eamon Darcy	1981	West Lakes Classic
C. O'Connor Snr.	1963	Martini International (tied)	Des Smyth	1981	Coral Classic
C. O'Connor Snr.	1964	Martini International	Peter Townsend	1981	Laurent Perrier
C. O'Connor Snr.	1964	Carrolls International	John O'Leary	1982	Carrolls Irish Open
C. O'Connor Snr.	1964	Jeyes Tournament	Eamon Darcy	1982	Kenya Open
Ernie Jones	1964	Sportsman Inn Tournament	Ronan Rafferty	1982	Venezuelan Open
C. O'Connor Snr.	1965	Senior Service Tournament	Des Smyth	1983	Sanyo Open
C. O'Connor Snr.	1966	Carrolls Tournament	Eamon Darcy	1983	Spanish Open
C. O'Connor Snr.	1966	Ulster Open	Eamon Darcy	1984	Mufulira Open
C. O'Connor Snr.	1967	Carrolls Tournament	David Feherty	1984	ICL International
Peter Townsend	1967	Dutch Open	David Feherty	1986	Italian Open
Peter Townsend	1968	Chesterfield	David Feherty	1986	Bell's Scottish Open
Peter Townsend	1968	PGA Championship	Philip Walton	1986	Jack Mulcahy Classic
Peter Townsend	1968	Western Australia Open	Eamon Darcy	1987	Belgian Open
Peter Townsend	1968	Coca-Cola Young Professionals	Eamon Darcy	1987	Tretorn-Spalding Tournament
Hugh Jackson	1968	Picadilly Fourball	Liam Higgins	1987	Jack Mulcahy Classic
C. O'Connor Snr.	1968	Alcan International	Ronan Rafferty	1987	Nissan-Mobil N. Zealand Open
C. O'Connor Snr.	1968	Ulster Open	Des Smyth	1988	Jersey Open
Jimmy Martin	1968	Carrolls International	Ronan Rafferty	1988	Equity and Law Challenge Cup
C. O'Connor Snr.	1969	Ulster Open	Ronan Rafferty	1988	Australian Matchplay C'ship
Peter Townsend	1969	Caracas Open	David Jones	1988	Europcar Open
Paddy Skerrit	1970	Alcan International	C. O'Connor Jnr.	1989	European Airways Jersey Open
C. O'Connor Snr.	1970	John Player Classic	David Jones	1989	Kenya Open
C. O'Connor Snr.	1970	Sean Connery Pro-Am	David Feherty	1989	BMW International
Peter Townsend	1971	Swiss Open	Ronan Rafferty	1989	Volvo Masters
Peter Townsend	1971	Walworth Aloyco	Ronan Rafferty	1989	Lancia Italian Open
Ernie Jones	1971	Kenya Open	Ronan Rafferty	1989	Scandinavian Enterprises Open
Eddie Polland	1971	Parmeco Classic	Ronan Rafferty	1990	PLM Open
C. O'Connor Snr.	1972	Carrolls International	Ronan Rafferty	1990	Melbourne Classic
Jimmy Kinsella	1972	Madrid Open	Ronan Rafferty	1990	Ebel European Masters
Peter Townsend	1972	Los Lagaratos	C. O'Connor Jnr.	1990	Kenya Open
Paddy McGuirk	1973	Carrolls International	Eamon Darcy	1990	Emirates Airlines Desert Classic

Winner	Year	Tournament
Philip Walton	1990	Peugeot French Open
E. O'Connell	1990	Swedish Matchplay
E. O'Connell	1990	Torras Hostench-El-Prat
John McHenry	1990	Boggi Open
David Feherty	1991	Credit Lyonnais Cannes Open
Ronan Rafferty	1992	Portuguese Open
Ronan Rafferty	1992	Palm Meadows Cup
David Feherty	1992	Bell's Cup
C. O'Connor Jnr.	1992	Dunhill British Masters
Darren Clarke	1993	Alfred Dunhill Open
Ronan Rafferty	1993	Austrian Open
Des Smyth	1993	Madrid Open
Philip Walton	1995	Murphy's English Open
Philip Walton	1995	Catalonia Open
Darren Clarke	1996	Hinde German Masters
Paul McGinley	1996	Hohe Brucke Open
P. Harrington	1996	Peugeot Spanish Open
Paul McGinley	1997	Oki Pro-Am
Darren Clarke	1998	Benson & Hedges International

David Feherty	6
Harry Bradshaw	6
Eddie Polland	5
David Jones	4
Ernie Jones	4
John O'Leary	4
Liam Higgins	4
Philip Walton	4
Darren Clarke	3
Eoghan O'Connell	2
Hugh Boyle	2
Paul McGinley	2
Hugh Jackson	1
Jimmy Kinsella	1
Jimmy Martin	1
John McHenry	1
Norman Drew	1
Paddy McGuirk	1
Paddy Skerrit	1
Padraig Harrington	1

OVERALL INTERNATIONAL VICTORIES

Christy O'Connor Senior	24
Peter Townsend	15
Ronan Rafferty	13
Eamon Darcy	11
Fred Daly	9
Christy O'Connor Junior	8
Des Smyth	7

TEAM VICTORIES

World Cup* 1958 (H. Bradshaw, C. O'Connor)
1997 (P. McGinley, P. Harrington)
Dunhill Cup 1988 (R. Rafferty, E. Darcy, D. Smyth)
1990 (R. Rafferty, D. Feherty, P. Walton)

Known as Canada Cup in 1958.

BASKETBALL

Irish Basketball Association
National Basketball Arena, Tymon Park, Dublin 24. Tel. (01) 4590211

Founded	1945
Number of Clubs Affiliated to I.B.A.	300
Number of Local Area Boards	15
Number of Clubs Affiliated to Local Boards	1,200
Number of Registered Players (Men)	5,341
Number of Registered Players (Women)	5,896
Number of Registered Players (Schools)	80,000
President	Finn Ahern (until May 1998)
Chief Executive Officer	Scott McCarthy
General Secretary	Sheila Gilligan
Number of Coaches	1,100
Principal Venue	National Basketball Arena (capacity 2,500)

1997/98 Champions	Winners	Runners Up
Men's Superleague Champions	Star of the Sea, Belfast	Denny Notre Dame
Men's Cup Champions	Denny Notre Dame, Dublin	Neptune
Women's Superleague Champions	Snowcream Wildcats, Waterford	Naomh Mhuire
Women's Cup Champions	Snowcream Wildcats, Waterford	Naomh Mhuire
Men's National Team Coach		Enda Byrt
Women's National Team Coach		Gerry Fitzpatrick
Most Capped International (Men)		Mark Keenan (69 caps)
Most Valuable Player 1997/98 (Men)		Gareth Maguire, Star of the Sea
Most Valuable Player 1997/98 (Women)		Jillian Hayes, Snowcream Wildcats

1997/98 Final League Tables

MEN'S SUPERLEAGUE	P	W	L	Pts
Star of the Sea	18	17	1	52
Notre Dame	18	13	5	44
St Vincent's	18	10	8	38
Killester	18	10	8	38
Dungannon	18	9	9	36
Ballina	18	8	10	34
Marian	18	7	11	32
Killarney	18	6	12	30
Neptune	18	5	13	28
Tralee	18	5	13	28

MEN'S DIVISION ONE	P	W	L	Pts
Sligo	18	14	4	46
Waterford	18	13	5	44
Limerick	18	12	6	42
Tolka Rovers	18	10	8	38
MSB	18	10	8	38
Castleisland	18	8	10	34
Tridents	18	5	13	28
St Gall's	18	0	18	18

WOMEN'S SUPERLEAGUE	P	W	L	Pts
Wildcats	16	16	0	48
Naomh Mhuire	16	13	3	42
Tolka Rovers	16	12	4	40
Meteors	16	10	6	36
Blarney	16	10	6	36
Killester	16	7	9	30
Limerick	16	5	11	26
Castleisland	16	1	15	18
Tralee	16	1	15	18

BOWLING

Bowling League of Ireland
c/o 'Dookinelly', 13 Glenabbey Road, Mount Merrion, Co. Dublin. Tel. (01) 2880255

Founded	1912
Number of Clubs	21
President	R. J. O'Leary
Secretary	J. J. Burke
Number of Coaches	20
Number of Members	1,200
Senior Singles Champion 1998	B. Somers (Bray)
Senior Pairs Champions 1998	D. Lloyd & G. Darcy (CYM)
Senior Triples Champions 1998	B. Tormey, J. Kavanagh & T. Fitzpatrick (Leinster)
Junior Singles Champion 1998	J. Hayden (Greystones)
Junior Pairs Champions 1998	C. Cushen & P. O'Looney (Westmanstown)

Ladies' Bowling League of Ireland
c/o 17 Kimmage Road West, Dublin 12. Tel. (01) 4555302

President	Betty Kerrigan
Honorary Secretary	June Fincher
Number of Clubs	18
Number of Senior Coaches	6
Number of Club Coaches	10
Senior Pairs Champions 1998	M. Barber & P. Nolan (Blackrock)
Senior Triples Champions 1998	M. Murphy, P. Murphy & J. Nolan (Blackrock)
Junior Pairs Champions 1998	J. O'Looney & P. Ellis (Westmanstown)
Junior Triples Champions 1998	N. French, J. Kane & M. O'Farrell (IGB)
Junior Fours Champions 1998	K. Maume, J. Manning, J. Moore & A. Brophy (B of I)

Irish Indoor Bowling Association
c/o 204 Kings Road, Knock, Belfast BT5 7HX.

Founded	1962
President	R. McDermott
Secretary	D. Hunter
Number of Clubs	1,084
Number of Members	30,000+

GYMNASTICS

Irish Amateur Gymnastics Association
House of Sport, Long Mile Road, Dublin 12. Tel. (01) 4501805

Founded	1964
President	Pat O'Brien
Secretary (Finance)	Charles Appenzeller
Administration	Shay McDonald
Main Venue	National Basketball Arena, Tallaght
Number of Clubs	50
Number of Regions	7 (Midlands, North Dublin, North East, North West, South Dublin, South East & Southern)

GREYHOUND RACING
Bord na gCon (Irish Greyhound Board)
104 Henry Street, Limerick. Tel. (061) 316788

Founded 1958
Chairman ....Paschal Taggert
Chief Executive ....Michael J. Field
Number of Meetings (per annum)...1,800
Number of Races 16,300
Total Prizemoney...£2.2m
Betting (Tote & Bookmaker)..£29m
Main Tracks.......Shelbourne Park & Harolds Cross, Dublin; Cork; Limerick; Lifford; Dundalk; Tralee and Waterford
Irish Derby Winner...Eyeman 30.09secs. (550 yds.)
Irish Laurels Winner...Mr. Pickwick 29.29 secs. (525 yds.)

CAMOGIE
Cumann Camógaíochta na nGael,
Páirc an Chrócaigh, Áth Cliath 3. Tel. (01) 8554257

Founded 1904
President ....Fileas Ní Bhreasláin
Secretary...Síle De Bhailís
Number of Affiliated Clubs ....498 (including 28 abroad)
Number of Members 78,000

1998 Champions	Winners	Runners Up
All-Ireland, Senior	Cork	Galway
All-Ireland, Intermediate	Down	Cork
All-Ireland, Junior	Galway	Tipperary
All-Ireland, Minor	Cork	Derry
Most Senior All-Ireland Titles		Dublin (26)
Most Junior All-Ireland Titles		Galway (6)
Most Minor All-Ireland Titles		Cork (9)

CRICKET
Irish Cricket Union
45 Foxrock Park, Foxrock, Dublin 18. Tel. (01) 2893943

Founded 1923
President ....Enda McDermott
Chairman ....Gavin Craig
Honorary Secretary...John Wright
Number of Clubs Affiliated to I.C.U..170
Number of Teams 400
Number of Registered Players..9,000
Number of Coaches 70
Largest Attendance ....4,000 (July 1993, Ireland v. Australia in Dublin)
Highest Score Recorded ....198 (Ivan J. Anderson v. Canada XI, 1973)
Number of Provincial Unions ....4 (Munster, Leinster, North-West and North)
National Coach ....Mike Hendrick
Most Capped Player ...............................D.A. Lewis (121 caps between 1984 and 1997)
Most Runs ....4,275 (S.J.S. Warke, 1981-96)
Most Centuries ....7 (I.J. Anderson, 1966-85)
Most Wickets...326 (J.D. Monteith, 1965-84)
Best Bowling Analyses ....9-26 (F. Fee v. Scotland 1957)
Most Catches ....57 (A.J. O'Riordan)
Quickest Century ....51 minutes, 51 balls (J.A. Prior v. Warwickshire 1982)
Number International Matches played since 1855 502

1998 Champions	Winners	Runners Up
Royal Liver Irish Senior Cup	Strabane	Ballymena
Northern Cricket Union League	Ballymena	North of Ireland
North-West Cricket Union League	Limavady	Strabane
Munster Cricket Union League	Cork County	
Leinster Cricket Union League	Malahide	Merrion

World Ranking of the Irish Team 13th
Principal Grounds ....Malahide, Leinster, Clontarf, Downpatrick, Eglinton and North of Ireland Cricket Clubs

IRISH WOMEN'S CRICKET UNION
"Woodcroft", 50 St.Alban's Park, Sandymount, Dublin 4.

Founded 1982
President ....Hilary O'Reilly
Honorary Secretary...Ursula Lewis
Number of Provincial Unions...3 (South Leinster, North Leinster and Ulster)
Number of Clubs 17
Number of Registered Players..1,500
Number of Teams:
    League 39
    Interprovincial 13
    Schools..57
Number of Coaches..1
Most Capped Player ....Mary Pat Moore (46)
Most Runs ....956 (Mary Pat Moore)
Most Centuries.. 1 (Mary Pat Moore)
Most Wickets ....40 (Susan Bray)
Best Bowling Analyses ....5-27 (Susan Bray)
Biggest Attendance ....300 (July 1995, European Cup final)

CYCLING

Federation of Irish Cyclists
Kelly Roche House, 619 North Circular Road, Dublin 1. Tel. (01) 8551522

Founded 1988
President ....Pat McQuaid
Honorary Secretary ....Jack Watson
Number of Clubs 124
Number of Regions...4 (Connacht, Leinster, Munster & Ulster)
Total Membership (1997) 2,361
of which: Northern 744
            Western 248
            Southern 384
            Eastern 202
            Mid-Eastern 595
            South-Eastern 188

National Champions 1997

Race	Winner	Club
Senior Road Race	Morgan Fox	Cuchulainn C.C.
Junior Road Race	Dermot Nally	unattached
Veterans Road Race	Brian Holmes	V.C. Glendale
Ladies Road Race	Sue McMaster	Amev
Senior 40k TT	Scott Hamilton	Maryland Whs.
Senior 16k TT	Scott Hamilton	Maryland Whs.
Junior 16k TT	David Coughlan	Navan R.C.
Ladies 16k TT	Marie Reilly	Bohermeen C.C.
Senior 80k TT	Ian Chivers	Cyprus C.C.
Hill Climb	David Peelo	Sorrento C.C.
Senior Cyclo Cross (1996)	Robin Seymour	unattached
FBD Milk Rás	Andy Roche	Kerry
Junior Tour of Ireland	Alain Van Katwijk	Holland
Points Championship	David Peelo	Sorrento C.C.
Kilometre Championship	David Peelo	Sorrento C.C.
Sprint Championship	Keith Bannon	Bray Wheelers
Pursuit Championship	Simon Coughlan	Navan C.C.
U23 Men's Championships	Michael McNena	Thermo King C.C.
U23 Ladies Championships	Geraldine Gill	Navan R.C.

HOCKEY

Irish Hockey Union
6A Woodbine Park, Blackrock, Co. Dublin. Tel. (01) 2600087

Founded 1893
President...John Dennis
Honorary Secretary ....J. Andrew Kershaw
Number of Clubs 76
Number of Provincial Unions...3 (Ulster, Munster and Leinster)
Main Stadium ....University College Dublin, Belfield. Capacity 1,500

1998 Champions	Winners	Runners Up
Irish Senior Cup	Instonians	Three Rock Rovers
Irish League	Instonians	Cork Church of Ireland
Irish Junior Cup	Three Rock Rovers II	Annadale II
Irish Schools Cup	Bangor Grammar	St Andrew's College
Leinster Senior Cup	Pembroke Wanderers	Glenanne
Ulster Senior Cup (Kirk)	Lisnagarvey	Annadale
Ulster Senior Cup (Anderson)	Banbridge	Cliftonville
Munster Senior Cup	Cork Church of Ireland	Harlequins

INTERNATIONAL

Irish Senior Coach ....John Clarke
Number of Senior Coaches...19
Most Capped Player ....Marty Sloan (149 caps)
Top Scorer ....Jimmy Kirkwood
Biggest Attendance.......................................5,000 (1995, European Nations Cup finals)

Irish Ladies Hockey Union
95 Sandymount Road, Dublin 4. Tel. (01) 6606780

Founded 1894
President ....Grace Redmond
Honorary Secretary..Joan McCloy
Number of Clubs 126
Number of Provincial Unions ....5 (Ulster, Munster, Leinster, Connacht and South-East)
Number of Members ....30,000 (of which 20,364 are registered as players)
Main Stadium ....University College Dublin, Belfield. Capacity 1,500

1998 Champions	Winners	Runners Up
Irish Senior Cup	Pegasus	Old Alexandra
Irish League	Pegasus	Hermes
Irish Junior Cup	Pembroke Wanderers II	Old Alexandra II
Irish Junior League	Pembroke Wanderers II	Pegasus II
Irish Schools Cup	Regent House	Mount Mercy
Senior Interprovincial	Leinster	Munster
Leinster Senior Cup	Muckross	Loreto
Ulster Senior Cup	Pegasus	Randalstown
Munster Senior Cup	Harlequins	University College Cork
Connacht Senior Cup	N.U.I. Galway	Yeats County
Inter varsity	Trinity College, Dublin	

INTERNATIONAL

Irish Senior Ladies Coach ....Riet Kuper
Number of Coaches 8
Most Capped Player ....Mary Logue (108)
Top Scorer...Sarah Kelleher
International Ranking 14th
Biggest Attendance ....6,000 (August 1994, Women's Hockey World Cup final)
Biggest Recorded Victory.........................11-0 (v. Wales 28.02.1907 and v. Poland 18.04.1997)

MOTORCYCLING

Motor Cycle Union of Ireland
35 Lambay Road, Glasnevin, Dublin 9. Tel. (01) 8378090
7 St. Bennet's Avenue, Donaghadee, Co. Down. Tel. (01247) 883477

Founded 1902
Number of Centres ....2: Southern (i.e. Leinster, Connacht and Munster) and Ulster
Number of Clubs 66
Number of Members ....1,700 (Competition Licence Holders)
President..Sam McClelland
Secretary ....Andrew Campbell
Number of Coaches 2
Biggest Attendance...100,000 (at North-West 200 Road Races, Portrush Co. Antrim)
Main Venues (Short Circuit) ....Mondello Park, Naas; Nutts Corner, Co. Antrim; Bishopscourt, Downpatrick.
Main Venues (Road Racing) ....Cookstown, Tandragee, Portstewart, Skerries, Kells, Monaghan

IRISH CHAMPIONS 1998

Road Racing

125 c.c.	Owen McNally
200 c.c.	Ray Hanna
250 c.c.	Gary Dynes
Junior Class	Robert J. Hazelton
Supersport 600	Richard Britton
Senior Class	James Courtney
201-400 c.c. Support Class	Andrew McClean
401-750 c.c. Support Class	George Jeffers

Short Circuit

125 c.c.	Paul Robinson
250/350 c.c.	John Creith
600 c.c.	Kieran McCrory
Senior Class	Michael Swann
Sidecar	Charlie O'Neill/Peter O'Neill
125 Superking	Owen McNally
Regal 600	Richard Britton
Joe Lindsay Memorial Series	James Courtney

Irish Winners at the Isle of Man T.T. Races

Number of Wins	Name	Between
23	Joey Dunlop	1977-98
10	Stanley Woods	1923-39
9	Philip McCallen	1992-97
5	AlecBennett	1922-28
5	Robert Dunlop	1989-98
5	Brian Reid	1986-93
3	Tom Herron	1976-78
2	Manliff Barrington	1947-49
2	Artie Bell	1948-50
2	Con Law	1982-83

Number of Wins	Name	Between
2	Eddie Laycock	1987-89
2	Lowry Burton/Pat Cushnahan	1986-87
2	Steve Cull	1984-86
1	Reg Armstrong	1952
1	Norman Brown	1982
1	Ralph Bryans	1966
1	Charlie Johnston	1926
1	Cromie McCandless	1951
1	Johnny Rea	1989
1	Tommy Robb	1973
1	Henry G. Tyrell-Smith	1930

MOTOR RALLYING

Royal Irish Automobile Club

Motor Sport Department, 34 Dawson Street, Dublin 2. Tel. (01) 6775628

Founded..1901

Number of Clubs...35

Total Membership 2,800

Chairman Motor Sport Commission..Michael FitzSimons

Secretary...Alex Sinclair

Biggest Recorded Attendance...100,000 (Phoenix Park, 1929 Irish Grand Prix)

Main Venue ....Mondello Park, Naas, Co. Kildare

Irish Land Speed Record, flying kilometre..............179.31mph (20.08.94 Brendan O'Mahony in a Porsche 962)

1998 Circuit of Ireland Champion ....Austin McHale

1997 Motorsport Champion (Sexton Trophy)..Neil Shanahan

1997 Hillclimb Champion..Robbie Maybin

1997 Touring Car Champion...Ed O'Connor

1997 National Rally Navigation Champions ....Damien & Aiden Courtney

1997 Hewison Champion ....Peter Grimes

1997 Vard Rally Champions ....John Gileece/Michael Gibson

1997 Forestry Rally Champions ....John McKeown/Padraig Barry

1997 Rallycross Champion ....Dermot Carnegie

ROWING

Irish Amateur Rowing Union
House of Sport, Long Mile Road, Walkinstown, Dublin 12. Tel. (01) 4509831

Founded 1899
Number of Clubs 70
Number of Members 8,290
Number of Provincial Branches ....4 (Connacht, Leinster, Munster and Ulster)
President ....Thomas Fennessy
Honorary Secretary ....James Bermingham
Administrator...Peadar Casey
International Team Manager ....Dermot Henihan
Best International Result ....Niall O'Toole - Gold Medal, Mens Lightweight Single Scull (Vienna, 1991)

1998 NATIONAL CHAMPIONS: MEN		1998 NATIONAL CHAMPIONS: WOMEN	
Senior Eights	Neptune	Senior Eights	Commercial
Senior Coxed Fours	Neptune	Senior Coxless Fours	Commercial
Senior Coxless Fours	Neptune	Senior Coxless Pairs	Commercial
Senior Coxless Pairs	Neptune	Senior Quadruple Sculls	Commercial
Senior Quadruple Sculls	Commercial	Senior Double Sculls	Commercial
Senior Double Sculls	Neptune	Senior Single Sculls	Commercial
Senior Single Sculls	Neptune		
Senior Lightweight Single Sculls	St. Michaels		

SAILING

IRISH SAILING ASSOCIATION
3 Park Road, Dun Laoghaire, Co. Dublin. Tel. (01) 2800239

Founded 1946
Number of Branches ....4 (North, South, East and West)
Number of Category One Clubs 43
Number of Members (Category One) 16,000
President ....Neil Murphy
Honorary Secretary ....Riocard O'Tiarnaigh
Best International Result ....Silver Medal, 1980 Olympic Games (David Wilkins & Jamie Wilkinson)
1997 Senior Helmsman Champions ....David McHugh and Tom Fitzpatrick
1997 Junior Helmsman Champion ....Gerald 'Gerbil' Owens
Principle Venues ....Dublin Bay, Howth, Cork, Kinsale

Royal Yachting Association
Northern Ireland Council, House of Sport, Upper Malone Road, Belfast BT9 5LA. Tel. (01232) 381222

Founded 1875
Number of Clubs 35
President ....HRH Princess Anne, The Princess Royal
Chairman ....Patrick Knatchbull
Honorary Secretary...Harold Boyle
Number of Coaches ....250 (approx.)
Principal Venues ....Belfast Lough, Strangford Lough, Lough Neagh and Lough Erne

SURFING

Irish Surfing Association
Easkey Surf and Information Centre, Easkey, Co. Sligo. Tel. (096) 49020

Founded 1967
Number of Clubs 12
Total Number of Members (approx.) **Men** 1,150
Total Number of Members (approx.) **Women** 350
President..Brian Britton
Administrator..Zoë Lally
Number of Coaches 75
1997 National Champion (Men)..Joe McNulty
1997 National Champion (Women)...Zoë Lally
1996 Intercounty Champions ....Leitrim

European Ranking (Senior)..6th
European Ranking (Junior)..4th
World Ranking..18th
Best International Result (Team)...2nd in the 1998 Reef World Big Wave Challenge
Best International Result (Individual) ....Grant Robinson, 1987 and 1997 European Masters Champion
Principal Venues ....Portrush, Rossnowlagh, Bundoran, Strandhill, Lahinch, Ballybunion and Tramore

TENNIS

Tennis Ireland
Argyle Square, Morehampton Road, Donnybrook, Dublin 4. Tel. (01) 6681841.

Founded 1908
Provincial Councils ....4 (Connacht, Leinster, Munster and Ulster)
Number of Clubs 220
Total Number of Members 92,500
of which: Men 25,500
　　　　　　Women 21,000
　　　　　　U18s 46,000
President ....Ms Olwyn Raftery
Honorary Secretary..Mr Ciaran O'Donovan
Top Ranked Irish Player (men) ....Owen Casey (810 in world rankings)
Top Ranked Irish Player (women) ....Kelly Liggan (432 in world rankings)
Number of Coaches 191

1998 Champions	Men	Women
Irish Close, Senior	Owen Casey	Gina Niland
Irish Open, Senior	Ross Matheson	Julia Lutrova
Irish Indoor, Senior	Owen Casey	Gina Niland
Irish Open, Junior	Stephen Nugent	Catherine Lynch
Irish Indoor, Junior	Stephen Nugent	Catherine Lynch
Principal Venue		Riverview, Donnybrook

ANGLING

Irish Federation of Sea Anglers
27 Seafield Avenue, Dollymount, Dublin 3. Tel. (01) 8336218

Founded 1953
President..Capt. Christy O'Toole
Secretary ....Hugh O'Rorke
Number of Affiliated Councils ....4 (Connacht, Leinster, Munster and Ulster)
Number of Affiliated Clubs 182
of which:　Number in Connacht..16
　　　　　　Number in Leinster 64
　　　　　　Number in Munster 43
　　　　　　Number in Ulster 59

National Coarse Fishing Federation of Ireland
"Blaithin", Dublin Road, Cavan, Co. Cavan. Tel. (049) 32367.

Founded...1960's
President...Ned O'Farrell
Secretary ....Brendan Coulter
Number of Clubs...50-60
Number of Councils..4 (Connacht, Leinster, Munster and Ulster)

NETBALL

Northern Ireland Netball Association
Netball Office, House of Sport, Upper Malone Road, Belfast BT9 5LA. Tel. (01232) 383806

Founded 1949
President ....Maureen Drennan
Secretary ....Claire Curran
Number of Clubs 35

Number of Teams 54
Number of Members 1,000
Number of Coaches 40
National Senior Coach (international) ....Marion Lofthouse
Most Capped Players (internaltional) ....Elizabeth Rodgers
Top Scorer (international) ....Helen McCambridge
Biggest Recorded Attendance ....1,100 - N. Ireland v Jamaica, Maysfield Leisure Centre (Oct. 1996)
Best Result (international) ....Northern Ireland 44, England 54

BADMINTON

Badminton Union of Ireland

Baldoyle Badminton Centre, Baldoyle Industrial Estate, Grange Road, Baldoyle, Dublin 13. Tel. (01) 8393028.

Founded 1899
President ....Audrey E. Kinkead
General Secretary...John Feeney
Number of Clubs...600
Number of Branches...4 (Connacht, Leinster, Munster & Ulster)
Number of Teams...2,500
Number of Members ....Men (20,500); Women (21,000)
Senior Ladies Singles Champion...Sonya McGinn (Kadca)
Senior Men's Singles Champion ....Michael Watt (Alpha)
Senior Ladies Doubles Champions.................................Claire Henderson & Jayne Plunkett (Alpha)
Senior Men's Doubles Champions ....Bruce Topping (Alpha) & Michael O'Meara (Mt. Pleasant)
Senior Mixed Doubles Champions ....Bruce Topping (Alpha) & Michael O'Meara (Mt. Pleasant)
Junior Ladies Singles Champion...Sandra Lynch (UCD)
Junior Men's Singles Champion..Nigel Boyne (Kadca)
Junior Ladies Doubles Champions............................Pam Peard (Crawfordsburn) & Vera Marron (Ailesbury)
Junior Men's Doubles Champions.....................Mark Dempsey (Mt. Pleasant) & Mark Gogarty (Mt. Pleasant)
Junior Mixed Doubles Champions ....Mark Demsey (Mt. Pleasant) & Sandra Lynch (UCD)

TAEKWONDO

Taekwondo Association of Northern Ireland

c/o 20 Lester Avenue, Lisburn, Co. Antrim BT28 3QD. Tel. (01846) 604293

Founded 1978
Chairman ....Glen Culbert
Honorary Secretary ....Bertie Nicholson
Number of Clubs..16
Number of Teams...2
Number of Members (Northern Ireland) 600
Number of Coaches 15
All Time Record Attendanc at Taekwondo 650
National Senior Coach (international)..Paul Gibson
Most Capped Competitor (international)...Jason Creighton
Best Individual Result (international)...2 off silver Scottish International

EQUESTRIAN SPORT

Equestrian Federation of Ireland

Ashton House, Castleknock, Dublin 15. Tel. (01) 8387611

Founded 1931
Number of Organisations within the Federation 14
Total Number of Members 9,000
of which: Men 6,000
                Women 3,000
President..Lewis Lowry
Secretary General...Col. E. V. Campion
Number of Coaches..400
Biggest Recorded Attendance...................................150,000 (Punchestown 1991, European Three Day Event)
Principal Venues .....................................R.D.S. (7,000 seats), Millstreet (5,000 seats), Punchestown (21,000)

PITCH AND PUTT
The Pitch and Putt Union of Ireland
House of Sport, Long Mile Road, Walkinstown, Dublin 12. Tel. (01) 4509299

Founded 1961
Number of Clubs 155
Number of Provincial Councils...2
Total Number of Members 14,000
Number of Coaches..215
Honorary Secretary..Peg Smith
1998 Gents Matchplay Champion ....Ray Murphy (Templebreedy)
1998 Gents Strokeplay Champion ....Frank O'Donoghue (Templebreedy)
1998 Ladies Matchplay Champion ....Marion Byrne (St. Bridget's)
1998 Ladies Strokeplay Champion ....Bernadette Coffey (St. Bridget's)

ICE HOCKEY
Northern Ireland Ice Hockey
c/o 88 Coronation Park, Dundonald, Belfast BT16 0HF. Tel. (01232) 483859

Coach 1
Number of Teams................................6 (Coleraine - 1 senior & 2 junior); (Dundonald - 3 junior)
Capacity of Ice Hockey Venues ....Coleraine Jet Centre (300); Dundonald Ice Bowl (1,500)
Best International Tournaments....................Coleraine Jets at Peterborough (31st Jan. 1998)
....Coleraine Jets at Fort Lauderale, Florida (30th April 1998)

TUG OF WAR
Irish Tug of War Association
c/o Longhouse, Ballymore Eustace, Co. Kildare. Tel. (045) 864222.

Founded 1967
President ....Eddie Hubbard
Secretary ....Martha Buckley
Branches ..4 (Connacht, Leinster, Munster and Ulster)
Number of Clubs 41
Number of Members ....1,400 (approx)

Number of Coaches ....2 per club
Best International Result .Youth Team, Silver at 1997
European Championships (Jersey)
Most Capped Competitor Martin Keogh, won 13 gold
medals in European and World Championships
World Rankings ....Top 6

SQUASH
Irish Squash
House of Sport, Long Mile Road, Dublin 12. Tel. (01) 4501564

Founded ....1993 (amalgamation of Irish Squash Rackets and Irish Women's Squash Rackets Associations)
Number of Clubs 111
Total Number of Members...250
President ....Paddy McIlroy
Number of Provincial Associations 4
National Senior Mens Coach ....Eoin Ryan
National Senior Ladies Coach ....Elvy D'Costa
Ireland's European Ranking (women)..9th
Ireland's European Ranking (men) 10th
1997 Irish National Champion (women) ....Madeline Perry
1997 Irish National Champion (men)..Derek Ryan
Most Capped Competitor ....Derek Ryan (1998 European Champion of Champions Winner)
Top Ranked Irish Player (women) ....Aisling McArdle

Ulster Squash
House of Sport, 2a Upper Malone Road, Belfast, BT9 5LA. Tel. (01232) 381222

Founded ....1995 (amalgamation of Ulster men's and women's association)
Number of Clubs 49
Total Number of Teams 119
of which: men...88
           women 33

Total Number of Members 967
of which: men 706
            women 261
President ....David Irvine
Biggest Recorded Attendance ....300 (Maysfield Leisure Centre in 1992 for five nation tournament)
Principal Centre ....Centre of Excellence for Squash, Newtownards, Co. Down

CANOEING

Irish Canoe Union

House of Sport, Long Mile Road, Walkinstown, Dublin 12. Tel. (01) 84509838

President ....John Carolan
Secretary ....John Keogh
Number of Members 4,000
Number of Instructors 350
Number of Coaches (competitive canoeing) 23
Principal Venues ....Leixlip (Kildare), Liffey (Dublin), Lee (Cork), Avonmore (Wicklow), Boyne (Meath),
Inny (Longford), Barrow (Carlow/Kildare), Suir (Waterford), Nore (Kilkenny), Lahinch (Clare) and Bundoran (Donegal).

CROQUET

Croquet Association of Ireland

c/o Carrickmines Croquet & Lawn Tennis Club, Glenamuck Road, Carrickmines, Co. Dublin.

Founded 1900
President ....Niall McInerney
Secretary ....Jane Shorten
Number of Affiliated Clubs 6
Number of Associate Members 144

WRESTLING

Irish Amateur Wrestling Association

c/o 54 Elm Mount Drive, Beaumont, Dublin 9. Tel. (01) 8315522

Founded 1947
President ....Michael Whelan
Honorary Secretary ....Michael McAuley
Number of Recognised Wrestling Coaches ....20 (free-style)
Most Capped Competitor ....Joe Feeney (welterweight) won the British Title, 1957-64
Best International Result (team) ....1994 Small Nations Championships, Ireland won the team event
Best International Result (individual)..1994 Small Nations Championships, R. Dunleavy (1st), D. McLoughlin (2nd)

SPECIAL SPORTS

Special Olympics Ireland

Ormond House, Upper Ormond Quay, Dublin 7. Tel. (01) 8720300

Founded 1978
Chairman ....Cyril Freaney
Secretary ....Myra O'Leary
Number of Summer Sports .... 9 (Athletics, Basketball, Tenpin Bowling, Swimming,
                                        Table Tennis, Gymnastics, Soccer, Equestrian and Golf)
Number of Winter Sports ....2 (Polo Hockeyand Alpine Skiing)
Number of Clubs (*approx.*)...100
Number of Members (*approx.*)...12,000

BLIND SPORTS

Northern Ireland Blind Sports

12 Sandford Avenue, Belfast, BT5 5NW. Tel. (01232) 657156

Founded 1989
Secretary ....Lisa Royal
Number of Members (N.I.) 600
Sports Included........football, bowls, tandem cycling, golf, sailing, angling, water-skiing, athletics, ten pin bowling

BLIND SPORTS

Irish BlindSports
c/o 25 Turvey Close, Donabate, Co. Dublin. Tel. (01) 8436501

Founded	1989
President	Liam Nolan
Secretary	Catherine Walsh
Sports Included	athletics, judo, water-skiing, tenpin bowling, adventure weekends
Number of Members	300
1998 International Results	World Cross Country Championships (Bronze) and World Athletic Championships (Gold, Silver and Bronze)

OLYMPIC MEDAL WINNERS

Games	Name	Event	Medal
Amsterdam, 1928	Dr. Pat O'Callaghan	Hammer	Gold
Los Angeles, 1932	Dr. Pat O'Callaghan	Hammer	Gold
	Bob Tisdall	400m Hurdles	Gold
Helsinki, 1952	John McNally	Boxing (bantam weight)	Silver
Melbourne, 1956	Ronnie Delaney	1,500m	Gold
	Fred Tiedt	Boxing (welter weight)	Silver
	Freddie Gilroy	Boxing (bantam weight)	Bronze
	John Caldwell	Boxing (fly weight)	Bronze
	Tony Byrne	Boxing (light weight)	Bronze
Tokyo, 1964	Jim McCourt	Boxing (light weight)	Bronze
Moscow, 1980	David Wilkins & Jamie Wilkinson	Yachting (Flying Dutchman)	Silver
	Hugh Russell	Boxing (fly weight)	Bronze
Los Angeles, 1984	John Treacy	Marathon	Silver
Barcelona, 1992	Michael Carruth	Boxing (welter weight)	Gold
	Wayne McCullough	Boxing (bantan weight)	Silver
Atlanta, 1996	Michelle Smith	Swimming (400m Individual Medley)	Gold
	Michelle Smith	Swimming (400m Freestyle)	Gold
	Michelle Smith	Swimming (200m Individual Medley)	Gold
	Michelle Smith	Swimming (200m Butterfly)	Bronze

TOTAL: Gold 8, Silver 5, Bronze 6.

Irish Olympians, 1924-98

1924 PARIS *(Athletics):* John Kelly, W. J. Lowe, Sean Lavan, Norman McEachern, J. O'Connor, John O'Grady, Larry Stanley, J. J. Ryan. *(Boxing):* M. Doyle, Sgt. P. Dwyer, Pte. J. Flaherty, R. M. Hilliard, Pte. J. Kelleher, Pte. J. Kidley, Pte. M. McDonagh, W. J. Murphy. *(Lawn Tennis):* W. G. Ireland, E. D. McCrea, H. Wallis, P. Blair-White. *(Water Polo):* S. Barrett, J. Beckett, J. S. Brady, P. Convery, C. Fagan, M. A. O'Connor, N. M. Purcell.

1928 AMSTERDAM *(Athletics):* Pat Anglim, Alister F. Clarke, G. N. Coughlan, L. D. E. Cullen, Denis Cussen, Sean Lavan, Norman McEachern, Dr. Pat O'Callaghan, Con O'Callaghan, Theo Phelan. *(Cycling):* Bertie Donnelly, J. B. Woodcock. *(Boxing):* Garda J. Chase, Gda. Matt Flanagan, G. Kelly, P. J. Lenihan, Cpl. M. McDonagh, Gda. W. J. Murphy, Pte. W. O'Shea, Edward Traynor. *(Swimming):* J. S. Brady, W. D. Broderick, M. Dockrell, T. H. Dockrell, H. B. Ellerker, C. Fagan, N. Judd, T. McClure, J. A. O'Connor, M. A. O'Connor.

1932 LOS ANGELES *(Athletics):* Eamonn Fitzgerald, M. J. Murphy, Bob Tisdall, Dr. Pat O'Callaghan. *(Boxing):* John Flood, Patrick Hughes, James Murphy, Ernest Smith.

1936 BERLIN No Irish team travelled.

1948 LONDON *(Athletics):* J. J. Barry, Cummin Clancy,

Dan Coyle, Charles Denroche, Paul Dolan, Pat Fahy, Dave Guiney, Jimmy Reardon, Frank Mulvihill, Reggie Myles. *(Basketball):* H. Boland, Lt. P. Crehan, Lt. J. Flynn, Sgt. W. Jackson, Pte. T. Keenan, G. McLaughlin, Cadet J. R. McGee, Cpl. T. Malone, Cdt. F. B. O'Connor, Lt. D. O'Donovan, Sgt. D. Reddin, Pte. D. Sheriff, Pte. P. Sheriff, Sgt. C. Walsh. *(Boxing):* William E. Barnes, Peter Foran, Willie Lenihan, Maxie McCullagh, Mick McKeon, Kevin Martin, Gearoid O'Colmain, Hugh O'Hagan. *(Equestrian):* Cmdt. Fred Ahern, Cmdt. Dan J. Corry, Lt. Col. John J. Lewis. *(Fencing):* Dorothy Dermody, Patrick Duffy, T. Smith, Nick Thuillier, Owen Tuohy. *(Football):* W. Barry, W. Brennan, J. Cleary, F. Glennon, P Kavanagh, P. Lawlor, P. McDonald, Lt. P. McGonagle, E. McLoughlin, W. O'Grady, B. O'Kelly, W. Richardson, R. Smith. *(Rowing):* H. R. Chantler, P.G. Dooley, T. G. Dowdall, S. Hanley, P. D. Harrold, D. Lambert-Sugrue, B. McDonnell, E. M. A. McElligott, J. Nolan, W. J Stevens, R. W. R. Tamplin, D. B. C. Taylor. *(Yachting):* R.H. Allen, A.J. Mooney.

1952 HELSINKI *(Athletics):* Paul Dolan, Joe West. *(Boxing):* Peter Crotty, William Duggan, John Lyttle, John McNally, Kevin Martin, Terry Milligan, Andrew Reddy, Thomas Reddy. *(Equestrian):* Capt. Mark Darley, Harry Freeman-Jackson, Ian Hume-Dudgeon.

(Fencing): George Carpenter, Paddy Duffy, Harry Thuillier, Tom Rafter. (Wrestling): Jack Vard. (Yachting): Dr. Alf Delaney.

1956 MELBOURNE (Athletics): Ronnie Delany, Eamonn Kinsella, Maeve Kyle. (Boxing): Anthony Byrne, John Caldwell, Freddie Gilroy, Harry Perry, Patrick Sharkey, Martin Smyth, Fred Tiedt. (Equestrian): Capt. Kevin Barry, Harry Freeman-Jackson, Ian Hume-Dudgeon, Lt. Patrick Kiernan, William Mullin, Lt. William Ringrose. (Wrestling): Gerald Martina. (Yachting): John Somers-Payne.

1960 ROME (Athletics): Ronnie Delany, Willie Dunne, Michael Hoey, Maeve Kyle, John Lawlor, Patrick Lowry, Gerald McIntyre, Bertie Messitt, Frank O'Reilly. (Boxing): Joseph Casey, Patrick Kenny, Adam McClean, Colm McCoy, Eamonn McKeon, Bernard Meli, Danny O'Brien, Harry Perry, Ando Reddy, Michael Reid. (Cycling): Peter Crinion, Anthony Cullen, Seamus Herron, Michael Horgan, Martin McKay. (Equestrian): Lt. John Daly, Lt. Edward O'Donohoe, Capt. William Ringrose. (Eventing): Anthony Cameron, Ian Hume Dudgeon, Harry Freeman-Jackson, Edward Harty. (Fencing): Shirley Armstrong, Chris Bland, George Carpenter, Brian Hamilton, Tom Kearney, Harry Thuillier. (Weightlifting): Sammy Dalzell, Tommy Hayden. (Wrestling): Dermot Dunne, Joseph Feeney, Gerry Martina, Sean O'Connor. (Yachting): Dr R. G. Benson, Charles Gray, Jimmy Hooper, Dr A. J. Mooney, Dr D. A. Ryder, John Somers-Payne.

1964 TOKYO (Athletics): Noel Carroll, Basil Clifford, Jim Hogan, Maeve Kyle, John Lawlor, Derek McCleane, Tom O'Riordan. (Boxing): Brian Anderson, Paddy Fitzsimons, Sean McCafferty, Jim McCourt, Chris Rafter. (Fencing): John Bouchier-Hayes, Michael Ryan. (Judo): John Ryan. (Wrestling): Joseph Feeney, Sean O'Connor. (Yachting): Robin D'Alton, Johnny Hooper, Eddie Kelliher, Harry Maguire. (Equestrian): Tommy Brennan, Tony Cameron, John Harty, Harry Freeman-Jackson.

1968 MEXICO (Athletics): Noel Carroll, John Kelly, Pat McMahon, Mick Molloy, Frank Murphy. (Boxing): Mick Dowling, Brendan McCarthy, Jim McCourt, Eamonn McCusker, Martin Quinn, Eddie Tracey. (Cycling): Peter Doyle, Morrison Foster, Liam Horner. (Fencing): John Bouchier-Hayes, Finbarr Farrell, Colm O'Brien, Michael Ryan. (Shooting): Dr. Gerry Brady, Dermot Kelly, Arthur McMahon. (Swimming): Liam Ball, Anne O'Connor, Donnacha O'Dea, Vivienne Smith. (Equestrian): Tommy Brennan, Capt. Ned Campion, Diana Conolly-Carew, Juliet Jobling-Purser, Ada Matheson, Penny Moreton, Diana Wilson.

1972 MUNICH (Athletics): Phil Conway, Neil Cusack, John Hartnett, Mike Keogh, Eddie Leddy, Danny McDaid, Dessie McGann, Fanahan McSweeney, Frank Murphy, Margaret Murphy, Mary Tracey, Claire Walsh, Donie Walsh. (Boxing): Mick Dowling, Christy Elliott, Neil McLaughlin, James Montague, Charlie Nash, John Rodgers. (Canoeing): Gerry Collins, Ann McQuaid, Brendan O'Connell, Howard Watkins. (Cycling): Peter Doyle, Liam Horner, Kieran McQuaid, Noel Taggart. (Equestrian): Bill Butler, Patrick Conolly-Carew, Juliet Jobling-Purser, Bill McLernon, Ronnie McMahon. (Fencing): John Bouchier-Hayes.

(Judo): Anto Clarke, Liam Carroll, Matthew Folan, Patrick Murphy, Terry Watt. (Rowing): Sean Drea. (Clay Pigeon Shooting): Dr. Gerry Brady, William Campbell, Arthur McMahon, Dermot Kelly. (Swimming): Liam Ball, Brian Clifford, Christine Fulcher, Andrew Hunter, Brenda McGrory, Ann O'Connor, Aisling O'Leary. (Weighlifting): Frank Rothwell. (Yachting): Harry Byrne, Harold Cudmore, Owen Delaney, Robert Hennessy, Kevin McLaverty, Richard O'Shea, David Wilkins, Sean Whittaker.

1976 MONTREAL (Archery): Jim Conroy. (Athletics): Eamonn Coghlan, Neil Cusack, Eddie Leddy, Danny McDaid, Jim McNamara, Niall O'Shaughnessy, Mary Purcell. (Boxing): Brian Byrne, Brendan Dunne, Gerry Hammill, Dave Larmour, Christy McLaughlin. (Canoeing): Declan Burns, Ian Pringle, Brendan O'Connell, Howard Watkins. (Cycling): Alan McCormack, Oliver McQuaid. (Equestrian): Eric Horgan, Ronnie McMahon, Gerry Sinnott, Norman Van der Vater. (Rowing): Sean Drea, Martin Feeley, Ian Kennedy, Andrew McDonough, James Muldoon, Christopher O'Brien, Liam Redmond, James Renehan, Michael Ryan, William Ryan. (Clay Pigeon Shooting): Richard Flynn. (Swimming): Miriam Hopkins, Robert Howard, Deirdre Sheehan, Kevin Williamson. (Yachting): Robert Dix, Peter Dix, Derek Jago, Barry O'Neill, James Wilkinson, David Wilkins.

1980 MOSCOW (Archery): Jim Conroy, Hazel Greene, Willie Swords. (Athletics): Eamonn Coghlan, Sean Egan, Ray Flynn, Pat Hooper, Dick Hooper, Mick O'Shea, John Treacy. (Boxing): Martin Brerton, P. J. Davitt, Sean Doylelt, Gerry Hawkins, Barry McGuigan, Hugh Russell, Phil Sutcliffe. (Canoeing): Declan Burns, Ian Pringle. (Clay Pigeon Shooting): Nicholas Cooney, Thomas Hewitt, Albert Thompson. (Rifle & Pistol Shooting): Ken Stanford. (Cycling): Billy Kerr, Tony Lally, Stephen Roche. (Judo): Alonzo Henderson, Dave McManus. (Modern Pentathlon): Mark Hartigan, Jerome Hartigan, Sackville Curry. (Rowing): Christy O'Brien, Frances Cryan, Noel Graham, Pat Gannon, David Gray, Iain Kennedy, Pat McDonagh, Willie Ryan, Ted Ryan, Denis Rice, Liam Williams. (Swimming): David Cummins, Catherine Bohan, Kevin Williamson. (Yachting): David Wilkins, James Wilkinson.

1984 LOS ANGELES (Archery): Hazel Greene, Mary Vaughan. (Athletics): Ray Flynn, Declan Hegarty, Dick Hooper, Monica Joyce, Regina Joyce, Jerry Kiernan, Conor McCullough, Carey May, Caroline O'Shea, Marcus O'Sullivan, Frank O'Mara, Paul Donovan, Liam O'Brien, Mary Parr, Roisin Smith, John Treacy, Patricia Walsh. (Boxing): Tommy Corr, Paul Fitzgerald, Gerry Hawkins, Kieran Joyce, Sam Storey, Phil Sutcliffe. (Canoeing): Ian Pringle. (Cycling): Philip Cassidy, Seamus Downey, Martin Earley, Paul Kimmage, Gary Thompson. (Equestrian): Capt. David Foster, Sarah Gordon, Margaret Tolerton, Fiona Wentges, Capt. Gerry Mullins. (Judo): Kieran Foley. (Clay Pigeon Shooting): Roy Magowen, Albert Thompson. (Swimming): Carol-Anne Heavey, Julie Parkes. (Yachting): Bill O'Hara.

1988 SEOUL (Archery): Noel Lynch, Joe Malone, Hazel Greene-Pereira. (Athletics): Marcus O'Sullivan, Gerry O'Reilly , Ann Keenan-Buckley, Brendan Quinn,

Eamonn Coghlan, Frank O'Mara, John Doherty, John Treacy, John Woods, Dick Hooper, Marie Murphy-Rollins, Ailish Smyth, Conor McCullough, Terry McHugh, Carlos O'Connell, Jimmy McDonald, T. J. Kearns , Barbara Johnson. *(Boxing):* Wayne McCullough, Joe Lawlor, Paul Fitzgerald, John Lowey, Michael Carruth, Billy Walsh, Kieran Joyce. *(Canoeing):* Alan Carey, Pat Holmes, Pete Connor, Declan Bums. *(Cycling):* Phil Cassidy, Cormac McCann, Paul McCormack, John McQuaid, Stephen Spratt. *(Equestrian):* Cmdt. Gerry Mullins, Capt John Ledingham, Paul Darragh, Jack Doyle, Capt. David Foster, John Watson, Shea Walsh. *(Judo):* Eugene McManus. *(Rowing):* Frank Moore, Pat McDonagh, Liam Williams. *(Swimming):* Michelle Smith, Stephen Cullen, Aileen Convery, Richard Gheel, Gary O'Toole. *(Tennis):* Owen Casey, Eoin Collins. *(Wrestling):* David Harmon. *(Yachting):* Bill O'Hara, David Wilkins, Peter Kennedy, Cathy McAleavy, Aisling Byrne.

1992 BARCELONA *(Archery):* Noel Lynch. *(Athletics):* Sonia O'Sullivan, Catherina McKiernan, Marcus O'Sullivan, Paul Donovan, John Doherty, Frank O'Mara, Noel Berkeley, Sean Dollman, John Treacy, Andy Ronan, Tommy Hughes, Victor Costello, Paul Quirke, Terry McHugh, Nicky Sweeney, Perri Williams, Bobby O'Leary, Jimmy McDonald, T. J. Kearns. *(Boxing):* Paul Buttimer, Wayne McCullough, Paul Griffin, Michael Carruth, Paul Douglas, Kevin McBride. *(Canoeing):* Ian Wiley, Mike Corcoran, Pat Holmes, Conor Holmes, Alan Carey. *(Cycling):* Paul Slane, Mark Kane, Kevin Kimmage, Robert Power, Conor Henry. *(Equestrian):* Mairead Curran, Melanie Duff, Olivia Holohan, Eric Smiley, Anna Merveldt, Peter Charles, Francis Connors, Paul Darragh, James Kernan, Eddie Macken. *(Fencing):* Michael O'Brien. *(Judo):* Keith Gough, Ciaran Ward. *(Rowing):* Niall O'Toole. *(Swimming):* Gary O'Toole, Michelle Smith. *(Tennis):* Owen Casey, Eoin Collins. *(Yachting):* David Wilkins, Peter Kennedy, Mark Mansfield, Tom McWilliams, Denise Lyttle.

1992 ALBERTVILLE *(Bobsleigh):* John Farrelly, Gerard Macken, Pat McDonagh, Terry McHugh, Gary Power, Malachy Sheridan.

1996 ATLANTA *(Athletics):* Neil Ryan, Gary Ryan, Eugene Farrell, David Matthews, Niall Bruton, Shane Healy, Marcus O'Sullivan, Cormac Finnerty, Sean Dollman, T.J. Kearns, Sean Cahill, Tom McGuirk, Jimmy McDonald, Mark Mandy, Nicky Sweeney,Terry McHugh, Roman Linscheid, Sinead Delahunty, Sonia O'Sullivan, Kathy McCandless, Marie McMahon, Catherina McKiernan, Susan Smlth, Deirdre Gallagher. *(Boxing):* Damaen Kelly, Brian Magee, Francis Barrett, Cathal O'Grady. *(Canoeing):* Ian Wiley, Michael Corcoran, Andrew Boland, Stephen O'Flaherty, Conor Moloney, Gary Mawer. *(Clay Pigeon Shoot):* Thomas Allen. *(Cycling):* Declan Lonergan, Philip Collins, Martin Earley, Alister Martin, David McCann. *(Equestrian):* Jessica Chesney, Capt John Ledingham, Eddie Macken, Peter Charles. *(Three Day Event):* Mick Barry, Alfie Buller, David Foster, Virginia McGrath, Eric Smiley. *(Dressage):* Heike Holstein. *(Gymnastics):* Barry McDonald. *(Rowing):* Brendan Dolan, Niall O'Toole, John Holland, Neville Maxwell, Tony O'Connor, Sam Lynch, Derek Holland. *(Yachting):* Mark Lyttle, Mark Mansfield, David Burrows, Marshall King, Dan O'Grady, Garrett Connolly, Denise Lyttle, Louise Cole, Aisling Bowman, John Driscoll. *(Judo):* Kieran Ward. *(Swimming):* Marion Madine, Michelle Smith, Earl McCarthy, Adrian O'Connor, Nick O'Hare. *(Shooting):* Gary Duff, Ronagh Barry. *(Tennis):* Eoin Casey, Scott Barron.

1998 NAGANO *(Bobsleigh):* Peter Donohoe, Simon Linscheid, Terry McHugh, Nessan O'Carroll, Jeff Pamplin, Gary Power. *(Skiing):* Pauli Patrick Schwarzacher-Joyce.

◘

USEFUL INFORMTION

PASSPORTS

Demand at home for Irish passports increased by 16% during 1997, from 228,806 to 264,678. 60% of those were administered through the *Passport Express* service which is available at over 900 post offices nationwide. Over 88% of applications were processed in ten working days or less. A further 63,000 Irish passports were issued through Embassies and Consulates overseas.

REPUBLIC OF IRELAND REQUIREMENTS

• Two Passport-size photographs (35 mm x 45 mm)
• Long form of Birth Certificate or most recent Irish Passport (which ever is applicable).

Application forms are available at all Garda Stations and Post Offices in the Republic of Ireland. Passports can be obtained by post (via the *Passport Express* service, at an extra charge of £3) or by travelling in person to the Passport Office *(see address below)*.

Completed application forms must be signed in the presence of a Garda. The Garda must also sign the photographs after first ensuring the applicants likeness.

Irish Passports are available to anyone born in the thirty-two counties and to anyone who can produce evidence of an entitlement to Irish Citizenship. Children under 16 can be included on their parent's passport. Passports are usually valid for ten years, exceptions being those issued to those who are under 18 or over 65. Such passports are valid for 3 years.

Irish Passport Fees:
Standard Passport (valid for ten years): £45.
Large Passport (valid for ten years): £55.
Three-year Passport: £10.

NORTHERN IRELAND REQUIREMENTS

Residents from Northern Ireland can hold an Irish or a British Passport.

British Passport Fees:
Standard Passport (valid for 10 years): £21.
Large Passport (valid for 10 years): £31.

Applications for either can be made to:

Passport Office, Setanta Centre, Molesworth Street, Dublin 2. Tel. (01) 6711633 Fax. (01) 6711092.

Passport Office, Hampton House, 47 High Street, Belfast BT1. Tel. (01232) 236767.

SUMMARY OF BASIC APPLICATIONS

DIVORCE

Republic of Ireland - Clients can obtain appropriate forms from their local Circuit Court Office and file them with the Circuit Court, Family Law Division. However, because most divorces involve complex financial, legal and personal issues, most parties opt to act through a solicitor.
Grounds for divorce: Under Section 5 of the Family Law (Divorce) Act 1996, the applicants must be separated for at least four years during the previous five years, and there must be no reasonable prospect of a reconciliation. (Other grounds are outlined under the 1989 Judicial Separation Act).

Northern Ireland - Clients can obtain appropriate forms free of charge from the Matrimonial Office, first floor of the High Court, Chichester Street, Belfast. Clients should bring with them all relevant documents such as the long version of birth certificates, including those of any children; marriage certificates; previous court orders.
Grounds for divorce: adultery, unreasonable behaviour, desertion, separation for two years with consent or five years without consent.

SOCIAL WELFARE BENEFITS

Republic of Ireland - Applicants applying for social welfare benefits (i.e. unemployment, sickness etc.) can contact their local social welfare office or The Head Office, Department of Social, Community & Family Affairs, Áras Mhic Dhiarmada, Store Street, Dublin 1. Tel. (01) 8748444.

Northern Ireland - Applicants can contact their local D.H.S.S. office or Head Office, Department of Health & Social Services, Castle Buildings, Stormont, Belfast. Tel. (01232) 520500, freephone (0800) 616757.

TELEVISION LICENCE

Republic of Ireland - Television licences are valid for one year and can be obtained and paid for at local post offices. The cost of the licences are Black & White (£52) and Colour (£70).

Northern Ireland - Television licences are valid for one year and can be obtained and paid for at local post offices. The cost of the licences are Black & White (£32.50) and Colour (£97.50).

DRIVING LICENCE

Republic of Ireland - Application forms are available from local county council offices, Garda stations, libraries and post offices. A provisional licence (issued for a two year period to enable a person to learn to drive and to apply for a driving test) costs £12. A full licence (issued for a ten year period) costs £20. *Other cate-*

gories of full licenses are available.

Northern Ireland - Application forms are available from local vehicle licensing offices. A provisional licence

(issued for one year to enable a person to learn to drive and to apply for a driving test) costs £12. A full licence (issued for a ten year period) costs £12.

WEIGHTS, MEASURES AND FORMULAE

LENGTH	
1 centimetre (cm) ...10 millimetres (mm) ....0.3937 inch	
1 metre (m)..............100 cm ....1.0936 yards	
1 kilometre (km)......1000 m ....0.6214 mile	
1 inch (in.)..2.54 cm	
1 foot (ft) ....12 in ....30.48 cm	
1 yard (yd) ....36 in ....0.9144 m	
1 mile....................1760 yards ....1.6093 km	

To Convert	Multiply by
Feet to metres..0.3048
Metres to Feet...3.2808
Yards to Metres...0.9144
Metres to Yards...1.09361
Miles to Kilometres 1.60934
Kilometres to Miles 0.621371

SURFACE / AREA	
1 sq. cm..................100 sq. mm................0.1550 sq. in	
1 sq. m....................10,000 sq. cm.......1.196 sq. yards	
1 hectare (ha)........10,000 sq. m ....2.4711 acres	
1 sq. km..................100 ha ....0.3861 sq. mile	
1 sq. foot................144 sq. in .... 0.0929 sq. m	
1 sq. inch..6.4516 sq. cm	
1 sq. yard...............9 sq. feet ....0.8361 sq. m	
1 sq. mile ....640 acres ....2.59 sq. km	
1 acre ....4840 sq. yards..........4046.9 sq. m	

AREA	
Sq. inches to sq. centimetres............................6.4516
Sq. centimetres to sq. inches.............................0.155
Sq. metres to sq. feet....................................10.7639
Sq. feet to sq. metres.................................0.092903
Sq. yards to sq. metres.................................0.83613
Sq. metres to sq. yards.................................1.19599
Sq. miles to sq. kilometres............................2.58999
Sq. kilometres to sq. miles...........................0.386102
Acres to hectares 0.40469
Hectares to acres 2.47105

VOLUME / CAPACITY	
1 cu decimetre (dm) ..1,000 cu cm.............0.0353 cu ft	
1 cu centimetre......................................0.0610 cu inch	
1 cu metre ....1000 cu dm ....1.308 cu yd	
1 litre (l) ....1 cu decimetre ....0.22 gallons	
1 hectolitre ....100 litre ....21.997 gallons	
1 cu inch...16.387 cu cm	
1 cu yard..................27 cu ft................0.7646 cu m	
1 pint......................20 fluid ounces ....0.5683 litre	
1 gallon ....8 pints ....4.5461 litres	

CAPACITY	
Cu inches to cu Centimetres 16.3871
Cu centimetres to cu Inches...........................0.06102
Cu feet to cu Metres 0.02832
Cu metres to cu Feet......................................35.3147
Cu yards to cu Metres 0.7646
Cu metres to cu Yards 1.308
Cu inches to Litres...0.01639
Litres to cu inches...61.0237
Gallons to litres..4.546
Litres to gallons 0.22

WEIGHT	
1 gram ....1000 milligrams........0.0353 ounce	
1 kilogram...............1000 grams ....2.2046 pounds	
1 tonne ....1000 kilograms ....0.9842 ton	
1 ounce ....437.5 grains 28.35grams	
1 pound ....16 ounces ....0.4536 kg	
1 stone ....14 pounds ....6.35 kg	
1 ton ....2240 pounds ....1.016 tonnes	

WEIGHT	
Grains to grams 0.0648
Grams to grains 15.43
Ounces to grams 28.3495
Grams to ounces 0.03527
Pounds to grams 453.592
Grams to pounds 0.0022
Pounds to kilograms 0.4536
Kilograms to pounds 2.2046
Tons to kilograms..1016.05
Kilograms to tons..0.0009842

CONVERSION TABLE	
To Convert	Multiply by
LENGTH	
Inches to centimetres 2.54	
Centimetres to inches..0.3937	

DIPLOMATIC MISSIONS ACCREDITED TO IRELAND: DUBLIN, LONDON & PARIS

There are 93 embassies accredited to Ireland, 42 of which are resident in Ireland, 51 are resident in London and one resident in Paris. *(The years below refers to when the embassy was founded or raised to the status of embassy)*

DUBLIN

APOSTOLIC NUNCIATURE H.E. The Most Rev. Luciano Storero, Dean of the Diplomatic Corps, 183

Navan Road, Dublin 7. Tel. (01) 8380577

ARGENTINA (1964) H.E. Mr. Victor E. Beaugé, 15 Ailesbury Drive,

Ballsbridge, Dublin 4. Tel. (01) 2691546

AUSTRALIA (1946) H.E. Mr. Edward John Stevens, 2nd Floor,

Fitzwilton House, Wilton Terrace, Dublin 2. Tel. (01) 6761517.

AUSTRIA (1966) H.E. Dr. Michael Breisky, 15 Ailesbury Court, 93 Ailesbury Road, Dublin 4. Tel. (01) 2694577.

BELGIUM (1958) H.E. Mr. Louis H.M.A. Fobe, 2 Shrewsbury Road, Dublin 4. Tel. (01) 2692082.

BRAZIL, FEDERATIVE REPUBLIC OF (1974) Vacant, Europa House, Block 9, Harcourt Centre, 41-45 Harcourt House, Dublin 2. Tel. (01) 4756000.

BRITAIN (1939) H.E. Veronica Evelyn Sutherland (due to step down in January 1999), Ivor Roberts (due to take up office in February 1999), 29 Merrion Road, Dublin 4. Tel. (01) 2695211.

BULGARIA, REPUBLIC OF (1991) H. E. Mr. Peter Poptchev (Chargè d'Affaires), 22 Burlington Road, Dublin 4. Tel. (01) 6603293.

CANADA (1940) H.E. Mr. Michael B. Phillips, 4th Floor, 65-68 St. Stephen's Green, Dublin 2. Tel. (01) 4781988.

CHINA, PEOPLE'S REPUBLIC OF (1980) H.E. Mr. Zheng Jinjiong, 40 Ailesbury Road, Ballsbridge, Dublin 4.Tel. (01) 2691707.

CYPRUS, REPUBLIC OF (1997) H.E. Mr. Andreas D. Mavroyiannis, 71 Lower Leeson Street, Dublin 2. Tel. (01) 6763060.

CZECH REPUBLIC (1993). H.E. Dr. Lubos Novy, Ambassador Extraordinary & Plenipotentiary, 57 Northumberland Road, Dublin 4. Tel. (01) 6681135.

DENMARK (1973) H.E. Ulrick A. Federspiel, 121-122 St. Stephen's Green, Dublin 2. Tel. (01) 4756404.

EGYPT, ARAB REPUBLIC OF (1975) H.E. Hassan Wafik Salem, 12 Clyde Road, Ballsbridge, Dublin 4. Tel. (01) 6606566.

ESTONIA, REPUBLIC OF Mr. Juri Seilenthal, Chargé d'Affaires a.i., 24 Merlyn Park, Ballsbridge,

Dublin 4. Tel. (01) 2691552.

FINLAND (1962) H.E. Mr. Timo Jussi Jalkanen, Russel House, Stokes Place, St. Stephen's Green, Dublin 2. Tel. (01) 4781344.

FRANCE (1930) H.E. Mr. Henri Benoit de Coignac, 36 Ailesbury Road, Dublin 4. Tel. (01) 2694777.

GERMANY, FEDERAL REPUBLIC OF (1951) H.E. Dr. Hartmut Hillgenberg, 31 Trimleston Avenue, Booterstown, Blackrock, Co. Dublin. Tel. (01) 2693011.

GREECE (1977) H.E. Ms. Maria Zografou, 1 Upper Pembroke Street, Dublin 2. Tel. (01) 6767254.

HUNGARY, REPUBLIC OF (1977) H.E. Mr. László Mohai, 2 Fitzwilliam Place, Dublin 2. Tel. (01) 6612902.

INDIA (1951) H.E. Mr. Surendra Kumar, 6 Leeson Park, Dublin 6. Tel. (01) 4970843.

IRAN, ISLAMIC REPUBLIC OF (1976) H.E. Mr. Hossein Amin-Rad, 72 Mount Merrion Avenue, Blackrock, Co. Dublin. Tel. (01) 2880252.

ISRAEL (1994) H.E. Mr. Zvi Gabay, Carrisbrook House, 122 Pembroke Road, Dublin 4. Tel. (01) 6680303.

ITALY (1937) H.E. Dr Ferdinando Zezza, 63-65 Northumberland Road, Ballsbridge, Dublin 4. Tel. (01) 6601744.

JAPAN (1964) H.E. Mr. Takanori Kazuhara, Nutley Building, Merrion Centre, Nutley Lane, Dublin 4. Tel. (01) 2694244.

KOREA, REPUBLIC OF (1983) H.E. Suk Hyun Kim, 15 Clyde Road, Ballsbridge, Dublin 4. Tel. (01) 6608800.

MEXICO (1980) H.E. Mr. Daniel Dultzin Dubin, 43 Ailesbury Road, Ballsbridge, Dublin 4. Tel. (01) 2600699.

MOROCCO, KINGDOM OF (1959) (Mrs. Najat Zhor Dine, Chargé

d'Affaires a.i.), 53 Raglan Road, Dublin 4. Tel. (01) 6609449.

NETHERLANDS (1956) H.E. Mr. Peter van Vliet, 106 Merrion Road, Ballsbridge, Dublin 4. Tel. (01) 2693444.

NIGERIA, FEDERAL REPUBLIC OF (1963) H.E. Chief Elias Nathan, 56 Leeson Park, Dublin 6. Tel. (01) 6604366.

NORWAY (1950) H.E. Mr. Helge Vindenes, 34 Molesworth Street, Dublin 2. Tel. (01) 6621800.

POLAND, REPUBLIC OF (1990) H.E. Mr. Janusz Skolimowski, 5 Ailesbury Road, Ballsbridge, Dublin 4. Tel. (01) 2830855.

PORTUGAL (1965) H.E. Mr. Manuel Lopes da Costa, Knocksinna House, Knocksinna Road, Foxrock, Dublin 18. Tel. (01) 2894416.

ROMANIA (1995) Vacant, 47 Ailesbury Road, Ballsbridge, Dublin 4. Tel. (01) 2692852.

RUSSIAN FEDERATION (1974) H.E. Mr. Evgueni N. Mikhailov, 184-186 Orwell Road, Rathgar, Dublin 14. Tel. (01) 4922048.

SLOVAK REPUBLIC (1993) Mr. Miroslan Jenca, Chargè d'Affaires, 20 Clyde Road, Ballsbridge, Dublin 4. Tel. (01) 6600012.

SOUTH AFRICA, REPUBLIC OF (1995) H.E. Mr. Pieter Roelof Dietrichsen, 2nd Floor, Alexandra House, Earlsfort Centre, Earlsfort Terrace, Dublin 2. Tel. (01) 6615553.

SPAIN (1950) H.E. Mr. José Maria Sanz-Pastyor Mellado, 17a Merlyn Park, Ballsbridge, Dublin 4. Tel. (01) 2838827.

SWEDEN (1959) H.E. Mr. Peter Osvald, 13-17 Dawson Street, Dublin 2. Tel. (01) 6715822.

SWITZERLAND (1939) H.E. Mr. Willy Hold, 6 Ailesbury Road, Ballsbridge, Dublin 4. Tel. (01) 2692515.

TURKEY, REPUBLIC OF (1972) H.E. Mr. N. Murat Ersavci, 11

Clyde Road, Ballsbridge, Dublin 4. Tel. (01) 6685240.

UNITED STATES OF AMERICA (1950) Jean Kennedy-Smith. (incoming) H.E. Mr. Michael Sullivan, 42 Elgin Road, Ballsbridge, Dublin 4. Tel. (01) 6688777.

LONDON

ALBANIA (1996) Vacant, 4th Floor, 38 Grosvenor Gardens, London SW1 WOEB. Tel. (0171) 7305709.

ALGERIA (1983) H.E. Mr. Ahmed Benyamina, 54 Holland Park, London W11 3RS. Tel. (0171) 2217800.

AZERBAIJAN REPUBLIC H.E. Mr. Mahmud Mamed-Kuliyev, 4 Kensington Court, London W8 5DL. Tel. (0171) 9376463.

BAHRAIN, STATE OF (1981) H.E. Sheikh Abdulaziz bin Mubarak al-Khalifa, 98 Gloucester Road, London SW7 4AU. Tel. (0171) 3705132.

BANGLADESH, PEOPLE'S REPUB-LIC OF H.E. Mr. A. H. Mahmood Ali, 28 Queen's Gate, London SW7 5JA. Tel. (0171) 5840081.

BELARUS, REPUBLIC OF (1996) H.E. Mr. Vladzimir R. Shchasny, 6 Kensington Court, London W8 5DL. Tel. (0171) 9373288.

BRUNEI (1987) H.E. Pehin Dato Haji Jaya Abdul Latif, 19 Belgrave Square, London SW1X 8PG. Tel. (0171) 5810521.

BULGARIA, REPUBLIC OF (1991) H.E. Mr. Valentin Dobrev, 186-188 Queens Gate, London SW7 5HL. Tel. (0171) 5849400.

CHILE (1992) H.E. Mr. Mario Artaza, 12 Devonshire Street, London W1N 2FS. Tel. (0171) 5806392.

CROATIA, REPUBLIC OF (1996) H.E. Mr. Andrija Kohakovic, 19-21 Conway Street, London W1P 5HL. Tel. (0171) 3782022.

ESTONIA, REPUBLIC OF (1994) H.E. Raul Mälk, 16 Hyde Park

Gate, Kensington, London SW7 5DG. Tel. (0171) 5893428.

ETHIOPIA (1994) H.E. Dr. Solomon Gidada, 17 Prince's Gate, London SW7 1PZ. Tel. (0171) 5897212.

GEORGIA H. E. Mr. Teimuraz Mamatsashvili, 3 Hornton Place, London W8 4LZ. Tel. (0171) 9378233.

GHANA, REPUBLIC OF H.E. Mr. James E. K. Aggrey-Orleans, 13 Belgrave Square, London SW1X 8PN. Tel. (0171) 2354142.

ICELAND (1951) H.E. Mr. Benedikt Asgeirsson, 1 Eaton Terrace, London SW1 W 8EY. Tel. (0171) 5901100.

INDONESIA (1984) H.E. Rahardjo Jamtomo, 38 Grosvenor Square, London W1X 9AD. Tel. (0171) 4997661.

IRAQ, REPUBLIC OF Vacant, 21 Queen's Gate, London SW7 5JG. Tel. (0171) 5847141.

JORDAN, HASHEMITE KINGDOM OF (1984) H.E. Mr. Fouad Ayoub, 6 Upper Phillimore Gardens, Kensington, London W8 7HB. Tel. (0171) 9373685.

KENYA, REPUBLIC OF (1984) H.E. Mr. Mwanyengela Ngali, 45 Portland Place, London W1N 4AS. Tel. (0171) 6362371.

KUWAIT, STATE OF (1996) H.E. Mr. Khaled Abdul Aziz Al-Duwaissan, 2 Albert Gate, Hyde Park House, Knightsbridge, London SW1X 7JU. Tel. (0171) 5903400.

LATVIA, REPUBLIC OF (1994) Mr. Norman Penke, 45 Nottingham Palace, London W1M 3FE. Tel. (0171) 3120040.

LEBANON (1974) H.E. Mr. Mahmoud Hammoud, 21 Palace Garden Mews, London W8 4QM. Tel. (0171) 2297265.

LITHUANIA (1996) H.E. Mr. Justas V. Paleckis, 184 Gloucester Place, London W1H 3HN. Tel. (0171) 4866401.

PEOPLE'S LIBYAN ARAB

JAMAHIRIAYA Vacant.

LUXEMBOURG (1973) H.E. Mr. Joseph Weyland, 27 Wilton Crescent, London SW1X 8SD. Tel. (0171) 2356961.

MACEDONIA, FORMER YUGOSLAV REPUBLIC OF (1996) H.E. Mr. Stevo Crvenkovski, 10 Harcourt House, 19-19a Cavendish Square, London W1M 9AD. Tel. (0171) 4995152.

MALAYSIA (1969) H.E. Dato Mohamed Amir bin Jaafar, 45/46 Belgrave Square, London SW1X 8QT. Tel. (0171) 2358033.

MALTA (1990) Vacant, 36/38 Piccadilly, London W1V 0PQ8. Tel. (0171) 9381712.

NAMIBIA (1996) H.E. Mr. Ulenga Benjamin Ulenga, 6 Chandos Street, London W1M 0LQ. Tel. (0171) 6366244.

NEW ZEALAND (1966) H.E. Dr. Richard Sturge Grant, New Zealand House, Haymarket, London SW1 4TQ. Tel. (0171) 9308422.

OMAN, SULTANATE OF (1988) H.E. Mr. Hussain bin Ali bin Abdullatif, 167 Queens Gate, London SW3 1HY. Tel. (0171) 2250001.

PHILIPPINES (1984) Vacant, 9a Palace Green, London W8 4QE. Tel. (0171) 9371600.

QATAR, STATE OF (1976) H.E. Mr. Ali Jaidah, 1 South Audley Street, London W1Y 5DQ. Tel. (0171) 4932200.

RWANDA, REPUBLIC OF H.E. Dr. Zac Nsenga, Uganda House, 58-59 Trafalgar Square, London WC2N 5DX. Tel. (0171) 9302570.

SAUDI ARABIA (1981) H.E. Dr. Ghazi Abdulrahman Algosaibi, 30 Charles Street, London W1X 7DM. Tel. (0171) 9173000.

SINGAPORE, REPUBLIC OF (1975) H.E. Mr. Joseph Yuvaraj Pillay, 9 Wilton Crescent, London SW1X 8SA. Tel. (0171) 2358315.

SLOVENIA, REPUBLIC OF (1996) H.E. Mr. Marjan Setinc, Suite 1, Cavendish Court, 11-15 Wigmore Street, London W1H 9LA. Tel. (0171) 4957775.

SRI LANKA, DEMOCRATIC REPUBLIC OF H.E. Mr. Sarath Kusum Wickremesinghe, 13 Hyde Park Gardens, London W2 2LU. Tel. (0171) 2621841.

SUDAN, REPUBLIC OF H.E. Omer Yousif Bireedo, 3 Cleveland Row, St. James's, London SW1A 1DD. Tel. (0171) 8398080.

TANZANIA, UNITED REPUBLIC OF (1979) H.E. Dr. Abdul Kader A. Shareef, 43 Hertford Street, London W1Y 8DB. Tel. (0171) 4998951.

THAILAND (1976) H.E. Mr. Vidhya Rayananonda, 29/30 Queen's Gate, London SW7 5JB. Tel. (0171) 2595005.

TUNISIA, REPUBLIC OF (1978) H.E. Prof. Mohamed Ben Ahmed, 29 Prince's Gate, London SW7 1QG. Tel. (0171) 5848117.

UGANDA (1996) H. E. Mr. George Barnabas Kirya, 58-59 Trafalgar Square, London WC2N 5DX. Tel. (0171) 8395783.

UKRAINE (1996) Vacant, 78 Kensington Park Road, London W11 2PL. Tel. (0171) 7276312.

UNITED ARAB EMIRATES (1990) H.E. Easa Saleh Al-Gurg, 30 Princes Gate, London SW7 1PT. Tel. (0171) 5811281.

URUGUAY, ORIENTAL REPUBLIC OF (1996) H.E. Mr. Augustín Espinosa Lloveras, 2nd Floor, 140 Brompton Road, London SW3 1HY. Tel. (0171) 5848192.

VENEZUELA (1981) H.E. Mr. Roy Chaderton-Matos, 1 Cromwell Road, London SW7. Tel. (0171) 5844206.

YUGOSLAVIA, FEDERAL REPUBLIC OF H.E. Dr Milos Radulovic, 5 Lexham Gardens, London W8 5JJ. Tel. (0171) 3706105.

ZAMBIA (1983) H.E. Mr. Moses Musonda, 2 Palace Gate, Kensington, London W8 5NG. Tel. (0171) 5896655.

ZIMBABWE, REPUBLIC OF (1984) H.E. Dr Ngoni Togarepi Chideya, 429 The Strand, London WC2R OSA. Tel. (0171) 836 7755.

PARIS

PAKISTAN (1962) Vacant, 18 Rue Lord Byron, 75008 Paris. Tel. (00331) 45622332.

DIPLOMATIC & CONSULAR MISSIONS ACCREDITED TO THE REPUBLIC OF IRELAND: ABROAD

There are 40 Diplomatic and Consular Missions / Embassies accredited to Ireland abroad, representing several other countries of secondary accreditation. *(The countries below in brackets refers to countries of secondary accreditation in relation to the primary country)*

ARGENTINA *(CHILE, URUGUAY & VENEZUELA)* Embassy of Ireland, Suipacha 1380, 2nd Floor, 1011 Buenos Aires. Tel. (00541) 3258588.

AUSTRALIA *(INDONESIA & NEW ZEALAND)* Embassy of Ireland, 20 Arkana Street, Yarralumla, A.C.T. 2600. Tel. (00616) 2733022.

AUSTRIA *(SLOVAK REPUBLIC & SLOVENIA)* Embassy of Ireland, Hilton Centre, Landstrasse Haupstrasse 2A,1030 Vienna. Tel. (00431) 7154246.

BELGIUM Embassy of Ireland, 89-93 Rue Froissart, B-1040 Brussels. Tel. (00322) 2305337.

BRITAIN Embassy of Ireland, 17 Grosvenor Place, London SWIX 7HR. Tel. (0171) 2352171.

CANADA *(JAMAICA)* Embassy of Ireland, Suite 1105, 130 Albert Street, Ontario, Ottawa K1P 5G4. Tel. (001613) 2336281.

CHINA, PEOPLES REPUBLIC OF *(PHILIPPINES)* Embassy of Ireland, No. 3 Ri Tan Dong Iu, Beijing 100600. Tel. (008610) 65322914.

CZECH REPUBLIC *(UKRAINE)* Embassy of Ireland, Velvyslanectví Irska, Trziste 13, 11800 Praha 1, Czech Republic. Tel. (004202) 57530061.

DENMARK *(ICELAND & NORWAY)* Embassy of Ireland, Ostbanegade 21, 2100 Copenhagen. Tel. (0045) 31423233.

EGYPT *(JORDAN / WEST BANK / GAZA, LEBANON, SYRIA & SUDAN)* Embassy of Ireland, 3 ABU EL FIDA Street (7th Floor), Zamalek, Cairo. Tel. (00202) 3408264. (Postal Address: *Embassy of Ireland, P.O. Box 2681, Zamalek, Cairo).*

ETHIOPIA Embassy of Ireland, House No. 413, Higher 24, Kebele 13. Tel. (002511) 710835.

PERMANENT REPRESENTATION OF IRELAND TO THE EURO-PEAN UNION 89/93 Rue Froissart, 1040 Brussels. Tel. (00322) 2308580.

FINLAND *(ESTONIA)* Embassy of Ireland, Erottajankatu 7 A, 00130 Helsinki. Tel. (003589) 646006.

FRANCE Embassy of Ireland, 12 Avenue Foch, 75116 Paris. Tel. (00331) 44176700.

GERMANY Embassy of Ireland, Godesberger Allee 119, 53175 Bonn. Tel. (0049228) 959290.

GREECE *(ALBANIA, CYPRUS, ROMANIA & FEDERAL REPUB-LIC OF YUGOSLAVIA)* Embassy of Ireland, 7 Leoforos Vasileos, Konstantinou, GR 106 74 Athens. Tel. (00301) 7232771.

HOLY SEE Embassy of Ireland, Villa Spada, Via Giacomo Medici 1, 00153 - Rome. Tel. (003906) 5810777.

HUNGARY (*BULGARIA*) Embassy of Ireland, H-1054 Budapest, Szabadság tér 7. Tel. (00361) 3029600. (*Postal Address: Bank Centre, Granite Tower, Szabadság tér 7, 1944 Budapest*).

INDIA (*BANGLADESH, SINGAPORE & SRI LANKA*) Embassy of Ireland, 230 Jor Bagh, New Delhi 110003. Tel. (009111) 4626733.

IRAN (*PAKISTAN*) Embassy of Ireland, Avenue Mirdamad, Khiaban Razane Shomali No. 10, Tehran 19116. Tel. (009821) 2227672.

ISRAEL Embassy of Ireland, The Tower, 17th Floor, 3 Daniel Frish Street, Tel Aviv 64731. Tel. (009723) 6964166.

ITALY (*LIBYA, MALTA, SAN MARINO & TURKEY*) Embassy of Ireland, Piazza di Campitelli 3, (Scalla A, int. 2), 00186 Rome. Tel. (003906) 6979121.

JAPAN Embassy of Ireland, Ireland House 5F, 2-10-7 Kojimachi, Chiyoda-Ku, Tokyo 102. Tel. (00813) 32630695.

KOREA Embassy of Ireland, Daehan Fire and Marine Insurance Building, 15th Floor, 51-1 Namchang-Dong, Chung-Ku, 100-060 Seoul. Tel. (00822) 7746455.

LESOTHO Consulate General of Ireland, Christie House, Plot No. 856, Maseru. Tel. (00266) 314068.

LUXEMBOURG Embassy of Ireland, 28 Route D'Arlon, L-1140 Luxembourg. Tel. (00352) 450610.

MALAYSIA (*BRUNEI, VIETNAM & THAILAND*) Embassy of Ireland, No. 4 Jalan Penggawa, Off Jalan U Thant, 55000 Kuala Lumpur, Malaysia. Tel. (00603) 4563763.

MOZAMBIQUE Embassy of Ireland, Rua Don Juau 213, Maputo. Tel. (00258) 1491440.

NETHERLANDS Embassy of Ireland, Dr. Kuyperstraat 9, 2514 BA The Hague. Tel. (003170) 3630993.

NIGERIA (*GHANA*) Embassy of Ireland, P.O. Box 2421, 34 Kofo Abayomi Street, Victoria Island, Lagos. Tel. (002341) 2617567. (*Postal Address: Embassy of Ireland, P.O. Box 2421, Lagos*).

O.E.C.D. Embassy of Ireland, 12 Avenue Foch, 75116 Paris. Tel. (00331) 44176700.

DELEGATION OF IRELAND TO THE O.S.C.E. Hilton Centre, 1030 Vienna, Austria. Tel. (00431) 7157698.

POLAND (*LATVIA & LITHUANIA*) Embassy of Ireland, ul. Humanska 10, 00-789 Warsaw. Tel. (004822) 496633.

PORTUGAL (*BRAZIL & MOROCCO*) Embassy of Ireland, Rua da Imprensa a Estrela 1-4, 1200 Lisbon. Tel. (003511) 3929440.

RUSSIA (*ARMENIA, AZERBAIJAN, BEL- ARUS, GEORGIA, KAZAKHSTAN & UZBERKISTAN*) Embassy of Ireland, Grokholski Pereulok 5, Moscow 129010. Tel. (007095) 7420907.

SAUDI ARABIA (*BAHRAIN, KUWAIT, OMAN, QATAR & UNIED ARAB EMIRATES*) Embassy of Ireland, Diplomatic Quarter, Riyadh. Tel. (009661) 4882300.

SOUTH AFRICA (*BOTSWANA, NAMIBIA & ZIMBABWE*) Embassy of Ireland, Delheim Suite, Tulbach Park, 1234 Church Street, 0083 Colbyn, Pretoria. Tel. (002712) 3425062. (*Postal Address: P.O. Box 4174, Pretoria 0001*).

SPAIN (*ALGERIA, ANDORRA & TUNISIA*) Embassy of Ireland, Ireland House, Paseo de la Castellana 46-4, 28046 Madrid. Tel. (003491) 5763500.

SUDAN Irish Aid Office, P.O. Box 299, Wad Medani. Tel. (00249) 512279.

SWEDEN Embassy of Ireland, Ostermalmsg-atan 97, P.O. Box 10326, 100 55 Stockholm. Tel. (00468) 6618005.

SWITZERLAND (*BOSNIA-HERZEGOVINA, CROATIA, LIECHTENSTEIN, FORMER YUGOSLAV REPUBLIC OF MACEDONIA*) Embassy of Ireland, Kirchenfeldstrasse 68, CH-3005 Berne. Tel. (004131) 3521442.

TANZANIA Embassy of Ireland, 1131 Msasani Road, Oysterbay, Dar-es-Salaam. Tel. (0025551) 667816.

UGANDA (*BURUNDI & RWANDA*) Embassy of Ire., P.O. Box 7791, Kampala. Tel. (0025641) 344344.

UNESCO Embassy of Ireland, 12 Avenue Foch, 75116 Paris. Tel. (00331) 44176700.

UNITED NATIONS NEW YORK Permanent Mission of Ireland to the United Nations, 1 Dag Hammarskjold Plaza, 885 Second Avenue, 19th Floor, New York, N.Y. 10017. Tel. (001212) 4216934.

UNITED NATIONS GENEVA Permanent Mission of Ireland to the United Nations, 45-47 Rue de Lausanne, 1202 Geneva 2. Tel. (004122) 7328550.

UNITED STATES OF AMERICA (*MEXICO*) Embassy of Ireland, 2234 Massachusetts Avenue N.W., Washington D.C. 20008. Tel. (001202) 4623939.

NEW YORK Consulate General, Ireland House, 345 Park Avenue, 17th Floor, New York, N.Y. 10154-0037. Tel. (001212) 3192555.

BOSTON Consulate General, Chase Building, 535 Boylston Street, Boston Mass. 02116. Tel. (001617) 2679330.

CHICAGO Consulate General, 400 North Michigan Avenue, Suite 911, Chicago, Illinois 60611. Tel. (001312) 3371868.

SAN FRANCISCO Consulate General, 44 Montgomery Street, Suite 3830, San Francisco, C.A. 94104. Tel. (001415) 3924214.

ZAMBIA Embassy of Ireland, 6663 Katima Mulilo Road, P.O. Box 34923, 10101 Lusaka. Tel. (002601) 290650.

TELEPHONE CODES

Direct telephone codes within Ireland (Republic of Ireland and Northern Ireland). To phone from the Republic of Ireland to Northern Ireland use the prefix 08 before the dialling code. To phone from Northern Ireland to the Republic of Ireland, use the prefix 00353 and drop the 0 from the start of the dialling code.

A

Abbeydorney	066
Abbeyfeale	068
Abbeyleix	0502
Achill Sound	098
Adare	061
Aghadowey	01265
Aghalee	01846
Ahoghill	01266
Annaghmore	01762
Annagry	075
Annalong	013967
Antrim	01849
Ardara	075
Ardee	041
Ardglass	01396
Ardmore (Waterford)	024
Arklow	0402
Armagh	01861
Armoy	012657
Ashbourne	01
Ashford	0404
Askeaton	061
Athboy	046
Athenry	091
Athlone	0902
Athy	0507
Aughafatten	01266
Aughnacloy	016625

B

Bailieborough	042
Bailies Mills	01846
Balbriggan	01
Balla	094
Ballaghaderreen	0907
Ballina	096
Ballinmallard	01365
Ballinamore	078
Ballinasloe	0905
Ballinaskeagh	018206
Ballincollig	021
Ballingarry (Limerick)	069
Ballingarry (Nenagh)	067
Ballingarry (Waterford)	052
Ballingeary	026
Ballinrobe	092
Ballybay	042
Ballybofey	074
Ballybunion	068
Ballycastle (Antrim)	012657
Ballyclare	01960
Ballyconneely	095
Ballycotton	021
Ballycumber	0506
Ballydehob	028
Ballydesmond	064
Ballyferriter	066
Ballygally	01574

Ballygar	0903
Ballygawley	016625
Ballygowan	01238
Ballyheigue	066
Ballyjamesduff	049
Ballykinler	01396
Ballymahon	0902
Ballymakeera	026
Ballymena	01266
Ballymoney (Antrim)	012656
Ballymore	044
Ballymore Eustace	045
Ballymote	071
Ballynahinch	01238
Ballynoe	058
Ballyporeen	052
Ballyronan	01648
Ballyshannon	072
Ballyvaughan	065
Ballywalter	012477
Ballyward	018206
Baltinglass	0508
Banagher	0509
Banbridge	018206
Bandon	023
Bangor	01247
Bangor Erris	097
Bantry	027
Bawnboy	049
Belcoo	01365
Belfast	01232
Bellaghy	01648
Bellarena	015047
Belleek	013656
Bellewstown	041
Belmullet	097
Belturbet	049
Benburb	01861
Beragh	016627
Bessbrook	01693
Birr	0509
Blackwater	053
Blarney	021
Blessington	045
Borris	0503
Borris-in-Ossory	0505
Borrisokane	067
Borrisoleigh	0504
Boyle	079
Bray	01
Bready	01504
Brittas	01
Brittas Bay	0404
Brookeborough	013655
Broughshane	01266
Bruree	063
Bunbeg	075
Bunclody	054

Buncrana	077
Bundoran	072
Burrin	065
Burtonport	075
Bushmills	012657

C

Cahir	052
Cahirciveen	066
Caledon	01861
Callan	056
Campsie	01504
Cappamore	061
Cappawhite	062
Cappoquin	058
Carbury	0405
Carlingford	042
Carlow	0503
Carnlough	01574
Carrickfergus	01960
Carrickmacross	042
Carrickmore	016627
Carrick-on-Shannon	078
Carrick-on-Suir	051
Carrigaline	021
Carrigart	074
Carryduff	01232
Cashel	062
Castlebar	094
Castleblayney	042
Castlecomer	056
Castledawson	01648
Castlederg	016626
Castledermot	0503
Castlegregory	066
Castleisland	066
Castlemahon	069
Castlepollard	044
Castlerea	0907
Castlereagh	01232
Castlerock	01265
Castletownbere	027
Castlewellan	013967
Cavan	049
Celbridge	01
Charlestown	094
Charleville	063
Clane	045
Clara	0506
Clare Island	098
Claremorris	094
Claudy	01504
Clear Island	028
Clifden	095
Clogher	016625
Clonakilty	023
Clones	047
Clonmany	077
Clonmel	052

Cloughjordan.....................0505
Cloughmills.....................012656
Coachford.........................021
Coagh.............................016487
Coalisland.......................01868
Cobh..............................021
Coleraine.......................01265
Collooney.........................071
Comber..........................01247
Cong..............................092
Cookstown....................016487
Cootehill.........................049
Cork..............................021
Corofin...........................065
Courtown Harbour.........055
Craigavon.....................01762
Craughwell.......................091
Cross (Derry)................01504
Crossgar........................01396
Crosshaven......................021
Crossmaglen.................01693
Crossmolina.....................096
Crumlin (Antrim).............01849
Cullybackey...................01266
Curragh...........................045
Cushendall....................012667
Cushendun....................012667

D

Daingean........................0506
Derry.............................01504
Derryadd.......................01762
Derrygonnelly................013656
Derrylin........................013657
Dervock........................012657
Dingle............................066
Donaghadee...................01247
Donaghmore...................01868
Donard............................045
Donegal...........................073
Downpatrick...................01396
Draperstown...................01648
Drogheda.........................041
Dromara........................01238
Dromard..........................071
Dromore (Down)..............01846
Dromore (Tyrone)............01662
Dromore West...................096
Drumbo..........................01232
Drumlish..........................043
Drumquin.......................01662
Drumshanbo......................078
Dublin.............................01
Dunamanagh...................01504
Dunboyne..........................01
Dundalk...........................042
Dundonald.......................01232
Dundrod........................01232
Dundrum (Down)...............013967
Dungannon.....................01868
Dungarvan........................058
Dungiven.......................015047
Dungloe..........................075
Dún Laoghaire....................01
Dunlavin..........................045

Dunleer...........................041
Dunloy.........................012656
Dunmanway......................023
Dunmore East...................051
Dunshaughlin.....................01
Durrow...........................0502

E

Edenderry.......................0405
Edgeworthstown.............043
Edmondstown...................041
Eglinton.........................01504
Elphin............................078
Enfield..........................0405
Ennis.............................065
Enniscorthy.......................054
Enniskerry.........................01
Enniskillen.....................01365
Ennistymon........................065

F

Feakle............................061
Feeny...........................015047
Ferbane..........................0902
Fermoy............................025
Ferns.............................054
Fethard (Tipperary)............052
Fethard (Wexford)..............051
Fintona.........................01662
Fivemiletown..................013655
Florencecourt.................01365
Forkhill........................01693
Foulksmills.......................051
Foxford...........................094
Freshford.........................056

G

Galway............................091
Garristown.........................01
Garvagh.........................012665
Gilford (Armagh)..............01762
Glarryford......................01266
Glaslough.........................047
Glenbeigh.........................066
Glencar...........................066
Glendalough.....................0404
Glenanne........................01861
Glenarm.........................01574
Glengariff........................027
Glengormley....................01232
Glenties..........................075
Glenwherry.....................01266
Gorey............................055
Gormanstown......................01
Gort.............................091
Gortin.........................016626
Gowran............................056
Graiguenamanagh.............0503
Granard...........................043
Greyabbey......................012477
Greystones.........................01

H

Hacketstown.....................0508
Headford (Galway)..............093
Headford (Kerry)...............064
Helen's Bay....................01247
Hillsborough...................01846

Holywood.......................01232
Holycross.......................0504

I

Inniskeen.........................042
Irvinestown...................013656
Islandmagee....................01960

J

Jerrettspass...................01693
Johnstown........................056

K

Kanturk...........................029
Katesbridge...................018206
Keady...........................01861
Kells (Antrim).................01266
Kells (Meath)....................046
Kenagh...........................043
Kenmare..........................064
Kerrykeel.........................074
Kesh...........................013656
Kilbeggan......................0506
Kilcock...........................01
Kildare...........................045
Kilfinnan.........................063
Kilkee.............................065
Kilkeel.........................016937
Kilkelly..........................094
Kilkenny..........................056
Kill..............................045
Killala............................096
Killaloe..........................061
Killarney.........................064
Killeavy........................01693
Killenaule........................052
Killeshandra......................049
Killinchy.......................01238
Killorglin........................066
Killucan..........................044
Killybegs.........................073
Killyleagh......................01396
Kilmacthomas.....................051
Kilmallock........................063
Kilmihill..........................065
Kilmore Quay......................053
Kilrea.........................012665
Kilronan..........................099
Kilrush...........................065
Kingscourt........................042
Kinnegad..........................044
Kinsale...........................021
Kinvara...........................091
Kircubbin......................012477
Knock............................094
Knocknagoshel....................068

L

Lahinch...........................065
Lanesboro.........................043
Larne...........................01574
Letterkenny.......................074
Lifford...........................074
Limavady.......................015047
Limerick..........................061
Lisbellew.......................01365
Lisburn.........................01846
Lisdoonvara.......................065

MILEAGE AND KILOMETRE TABLE

	1	2	3	4	5	6	7	8	9	10	11	12
1. Athlone	-	85m	136m	70m	87m	136m	144m	112m	79m	88m	69m	56m
2. Ballina	136k	-	167m	155m	170m	184m	123m	76m	154m	143m	108m	74m
3. Belfast	218k	267k	-	156m	205m	262m	74m	116m	103m	51m	205m	187m
4. Carlow	112k	248k	250k	-	56m	116m	184m	177m	51m	104m	115m	117m
5. Clonmel	140k	272k	328k	90k	-	60m	225m	199m	102m	154m	72m	115m
6. Cork	218k	294k	419k	186k	96k	-	271m	245m	159m	209m	83m	128m
7. Derry	230k	197k	118k	294k	360k	434k	-	47m	147m	99m	207m	173m
8. Donegal	180k	122k	186k	283k	318k	392k	75k	-	141m	102m	168m	126m
9. Dublin	126k	246k	165k	82k	163k	253k	235k	226k	-	52m	147m	135m
10. Dundalk	141k	229k	82k	166k	246k	333k	158k	163k	83k	-	157m	145m
11. Ennis	110k	173k	328k	184k	115k	133k	331k	269k	235k	251k	-	42m
12. Galway	90k	118k	299k	187k	184k	205k	277k	202k	216k	232k	67k	-
13. Kilkenny	115k	251k	278k	38k	50k	146k	322k	294k	114k	197k	147k	171k
14. Killarney	226k	307k	443k	234k	146k	85k	456k	405k	302k	366k	146k	205k
15. Limerick	117k	198k	334k	138k	78k	101k	347k	296k	203k	250k	37k	104k
16. Mallow	178k	259k	400k	166k	78k	35k	408k	357k	235k	318k	98k	157k
17. Mullingar	46k	163k	176k	99k	160k	234k	208k	173k	86k	94k	157k	136k
18. Portlaoise	70k	206k	243k	37k	99k	173k	275k	242k	83k	154k	150k	142k
19. Sligo	115k	58k	208k	181k	254k	328k	139k	64k	216k	168k	205k	138k
20. Tipperary	139k	245k	346k	114k	38k	85k	358k	310k	178k	258k	75k	142k
21. Tralee	119k	204k	440k	251k	171k	117k	453k	398k	304k	346k	142k	202k
22. Waterford	163k	299k	326k	75k	48k	123k	370k	334k	162k	245k	163k	232k
23. Wexford	182k	318k	299k	77k	109k	184k	370k	360k	134k	202k	224k	251k
24. Wicklow	170k	294k	213k	86k	178k	250k	283k	274k	51k	131k	275k	259k

The digits across correspond to the towns numbered down the side. To find the mileage of your journey, find the number of the town across the top and simply go down the column to where it intersects with the specified town on the side of the chart.

TELEPHONE CODES *Continued from previous page*

Lismore	058
Lisnaskea	013657
Listowel	068
Longford	043
Loughgall	01762
Loughgiel	012656
Loughrea	091
Louisburgh	098
Louth	042
Lucan	01
Lurgan	01762

M

Macroom	026
Maghera	01648
Magherafelt	01648
Malahide	01
Mallow	022
Manorcunningham	074
Manorhamilton	072
Markethill	01861
Martinstown	012667
Maynooth	01
Mayobridge	01693
Maze	01846
Midleton	021
Millisle	01247
Millstreet	029
Miltown Malbay	065
Mitchelstown	025
Moate	0902

Mohill	078
Moira	01846
Monaghan	047
Monasterevin	045
Moneymore	016487
Moone	0507
Mostrim	043
Mount Bellew	0905
Mountfield	016627
Mountmellick	0502
Mountrath	0502
Moville	077
Moy	01868
Moycullen	091
Moyglass	0509
Moynalty	046
Moyvore	044
Muine Bheag	0503
Mullingar	044
Mulrany	098
Multyfarnham	044

N

Naas	045
Naul	01
Navan	046
Nenagh	067
Newbridge	045
Newcastle (*Down*)	013967
Newcastle West	069
New Inn (*Galway*)	052

New Inn (*Tipperary*)	052
Newmarket	029
Newmarket-on-Fergus	061
Newport (*Mayo*)	098
Newport (*Tipperary*)	061
New Ross	051
Newry	01693
Newtownards	01247
Newtownbutler	013657
Newtowngore	049
Newtownhamilton	01693
Newtownmountkennedy	01
Newtownstewart	016626
Nobber	046

O

Oldcastle	049
Oldtown	01
Omagh	01662
Oranmore	091
Oughterard	091

P

Patrickswell	061
Pomeroy	01868
Portadown	01762
Portaferry	012477
Portarlington	0502
Portavogie	012477
Portglenone	01266
Portlaoise	0502
Portrush	01265

MILEAGE AND KILOMETRE TABLE

13	14	15	16	17	18	19	20	21	22	23	24	
72m	141m	73m	111m	29m	44m	72m	87m	137m	102m	114m	106m	1. Athlone
157m	192m	124m	162m	102m	129m	36m	153m	190m	187m	199m	184m	2. Ballina
174m	277m	209m	250m	110m	152m	130m	216m	275m	204m	187m	133m	3. Belfast
24m	146m	86m	104m	62m	23m	113m	71m	157m	47m	48m	54m	4. Carlow
31m	91m	49m	49m	100m	62m	159m	24m	107m	30m	68m	111m	5. Clonmel
91m	53m	63m	22m	146m	108m	205m	53m	73m	77m	115m	156m	6. Cork
201m	285m	217m	255m	130m	172m	87m	224m	283m	231m	231m	177m	7. Derry
184m	253m	185m	223m	108m	151m	40m	194m	249m	209m	225m	171m	8. Donegal
71m	189m	127m	147m	54m	52m	135m	111m	190m	101m	84m	32m	9. Dublin
123m	229m	156m	199m	59m	96m	105m	161m	216m	153m	136m	82m	10. Dundalk
92m	91m	23m	61m	98m	94m	128m	47m	89m	102m	140m	172m	11. Ennis
107m	128m	65m	98m	85m	89m	86m	89m	126m	145m	157m	162m	12. Galway
-	122m	69m	80m	73m	30m	144m	47m	132m	30m	50m	80m	13. Kilkenny
195k	-	68m	42m	163m	139m	213m	83m	20m	121m	159m	202m	14. Killarney
110k	109k	-	41m	93m	70m	145m	24m	63m	79m	117m	149m	15. Limerick
128k	67k	66k	-	134m	96m	183m	41m	51m	79m	117m	160m	16. Mallow
117k	261k	149k	214k	-	42m	85m	95m	159m	100m	112m	88m	17. Mullingar
48k	222k	112k	154k	67k	-	116m	59m	133m	60m	70m	71m	18. Portlaoise
230k	341k	232k	293k	136k	186k	-	154m	211m	174m	186m	165m	19. Sligo
75k	133k	38k	66k	152k	94k	246k	-	83m	54m	92m	125m	20. Tipperary
211k	32k	101k	82k	254k	213k	338k	133k	-	130m	179m	212m	21. Tralee
48k	194k	126k	126k	160k	96k	278k	86k	208k	-	38m	88m	22. Waterford
80k	254k	187k	187k	179k	112k	298k	147k	286k	61k	-	54m	23. Wexford
128k	323k	238k	256k	141k	114k	264k	200k	339k	141k	86k	-	24. Wicklow

TELEPHONE CODES *Continued from previous page*

Portstewart............01265
Portumna............0509
Poyntzpass............01762

R
Ramelton............074
Randalstown............01849
Raphoe............074
Rasharkin............012665
Rathangan............045
Rathcoole............01
Rathdowney............0505
Rathfriland............018206
Rathkeale............069
Rathlin............012657
Rathmore............064
Rathoath............01
Recess............095
Rhode............0405
Richhill............01762
Rochford Bridge............044
Rooskey............078
Roscommon............0903
Roscrea............0505
Roslea............013657
Rosscarbery............023
Rosses Point............071
Rosslare............053
Rostrevor............016937
Roundwood............01
Rush............01

S
Saintfield............01238
Scarriff............061

Scotstown............047
Seaforde............01396
Shannon............061
Sion Mills............016626
Slane............041
Skerries............01
Skibbereen............028
Sligo............071
Sneem............064
Spiddal............091
Springfield............01365
Stewartstown............01868
Stoneyford............01846
Strabane............01504
Stradbally (*Laois*)............0502
Stradbally (*Waterford*)............051
Straffan............01
Strandhill............071
Strangford............01396
Strokestown............078
Summerhill............0405
Swanlinbar............049
Swatragh............01648
Swinford............094
Swords............01

T
Tandragee............01762
Tarbert............068
Templemore............0504
Templepatrick............01849
Tempo............013655
Thomastown............056
Thurles............0504

Tinahely............0402
Tipperary............062
Toomebridge............01648
Tory Island............074
Tralee............066
Tramore............051
Trillick............013655
Trim............046
Tuam............093
Tubbercurry............071
Tullamore............0506
Tullow............0503
Tulnacross............016487
Tyrrellspass............044

V
Valentia............066
Virginia............049

W
Waringstown............01762
Warrenpoint............016937
Waterford............051
Waterville............066
Wellington Bridge............051
Westport............098
Wexford............053
Whiteabbey............01232
White Gate............021
Whitehead............01960
Wicklow............0404
Woodford............0509

Y
Youghal............024

INTERNATIONAL TELEPHONE CODES TO REPUBLIC OF IRELAND & NORTHERN IRELAND

Country	Republic of Ireland	Northern Ireland	Country	Republic of Ireland	Northern Ireland
Australia	0011353	001144	Luxembourg	00353	0044
Austria	00353	0044	Malta	0353	0044
Bahrain	00353	0044	Mexico	n/a	9844
Belgium	00353	0044	Morocco	00353	0044
Brazil	00353	0044	Netherlands	00353	0044
Britain	00353	-	New Zealand	00353	0044
Canada	011353	01144	Nigeria	009353	00944
China	00353	0044	NORTHERN IRELAND	00353	-
Czech Republic	00353	0044	Norway	00353	0044
Denmark	00353	0044	Pakistan	00353	0044
Egypt	00353	0044	Poland	00353	0044
Finland	00353	0044	Portugal	00353	0044
France	00353	0044	Russian Federation	810353	81044
Germany	00353	0044	Saudi Arabia	00353	0044
Greece	00353	0044	Singapore	00353	0044
Hong Kong	001353	00144	Slovak Republic	n/a	0044
Hungary	00353	0044	South Africa	n/a	0944
India	00353	0044	Spain	00353	0044
Iran	00353	0044	Sweden	00353	0044
IRELAND	-	08	Switzerland	00353	0044
Israel	00353	0044	Taiwan	00353	00244
Italy	00353	0044	Trinidad & Tobago	00353	01144
Japan	001353	(KDD)* 00144	Tunisia	00353	0044
		(IDC)* 06144	Turkey	00353	0044
Kuwait	00353	0044	USA	0011353	01144

To make an international call to Belfast, Northern Ireland from France:
Belfast area code: **01232**; International code: **0044 + 232 + phone number.** *(Drop the 01 from the area code)*
* Japan has two telephone companies; **KDC** and **IDC**; use the appropriate code depending on which company you are with.

INTERNATIONAL TELEPHONE CODES

Country	Access Code	Country Code	Country	Access Code	Country Code
Australia	00	61	Malta	00	356
Austria	00	43	Mexico	00	52
Bahrain	00	973	Morocco	00	212
Belgium	00	32	Netherlands	00	31
Brazil	00	55	New Zealand	00	64
Canada	00	1	Nigeria	00	234
China	00	86	Norway	00	47
Czech Republic	00	420	Pakistan	00	92
Denmark	00	45	Poland	00	48
Egypt	00	20	Portugal	00	351
Finland	00	358	Russian Federation	00	7
France	00	33	Saudi Arabia	00	966
Germany	00	49	Singapore	00	65
Greece	00	30	Slovak Republic	00	421
Hong Kong	00	852	South Africa	00	27
Hungary	00	36	Spain	00	34
India	00	91	Sweden	00	46
Iran	00	98	Switzerland	00	41
IRELAND	00	353	Taiwan	00	886
Israel	00	972	Trinidad & Tobago	00	1868
Italy	00	39	Tunisia	00	216
Japan	00	81	Turkey	00	90
Kuwait	00	965	UK	00	44
Luxembourg	00	352	USA	00	1

WHO IS WHO 1998

Listed below, in alphabetical order, are persons who are major decision makers or of serious influence in their particular sphere in society on the island of Ireland.

POLITICS

ADAMS, Gerry (1949-) b. Belfast, president of Sinn Féin since 1983, MP (1983-92) and MP for West Belfast since 1997, interned (1971-72 and 1973-77). A noted writer, his works include *Falls Memories, The Politics of Irish Freedom* and the autobiographical *Before the Dawn.*

AHERN, Bertie (1951-) b. Dublin, elected Taoiseach June 1997. Leader of Fianna Fáil since 1994, TD since 1977. *See biographies of Taoisigh.*

AHERN, Dermot (1955-) b. Louth, Minister for Social, Community and Family Affairs since June 1997. Fianna Fáil TD since 1987, previously government chief whip (1991-92).

AHERN, Nuala MEP for Leinster. Member of the Green Party.

ALDERDICE, Lord John (1955-) b. Ballymena, speaker at the Northern Ireland Assembly. Former leader of the Alliance Party of Northern Ireland (1987-98) former Belfast City councillor, created a life peer in 1996.

ANDREWS, David (1935-) b. Dublin, appointed Minister of Foreign Affairs (8th October, 1997) after Ray Burke retired. Fianna Fáil TD since 1965, has held various ministerial portfolios, including Defence (June-October 1997), Foreign Affairs (1992-93) and Defence (1993-94).

ANDREWS, Niall b. Dublin, MEP for Dublin. Member of Fianna Fáil.

BANOTTI, Mary (1939-) b. Dublin, MEP for Dublin since 1984. Member of Fine Gael and party candidate for 1997 Presidential Elections. Grand niece of Michael Collins. Played an active role in campaigning for Elaine Moore's release when she was arrested in London in 1998.

BEGGS, Roy (1936-) Ulster Unionist Party MP since 1983.

BHREATHNACH, Lucilita General Secretary of Sinn Féin.

BRENNAN, Séamus (1948-) b. Galway, Minister of State at Departments of the Taoiseach and Defence and Government Chief Whip since June 1997. Fianna Fáil TD since 1981, Senator (1977-81).

BRUTON, John (1947-) b. Dublin, former Taoiseach (1994-1997). Leader of Fine Gael since 1990. *See biographies of Taoisigh.*

BYRNE, Hugh (1943-) b. Wexford, Minister of State at the Department of the Marine and Natural Resources (with special responsibility for aquaculture and forestry) since July 1997. Fianna Fáil TD (1981-89 and since 1992), Senator (1989-92).

CHICHESTER-CLARK, James *Lord Moyola* (1923-) b. Derry, former Prime Minister of Northern Ireland. *See Biographies of Northern Ireland Prime Ministers.*

COLLINS, Gerard (1938-) b. Limerick, member of Fianna Fáil and MEP for Munster since 1994. Was a

TD (1967-97), holding the ministerial posts of Justice (1977-81 and 1987-89), Post & Telegraphs (1970-73), Foreign Affairs (1982 and 1989-92).

COSGRAVE, Liam (1920-) b. Dublin, former Taoiseach (1973-77) and leader of Fine Gael (1965-77). *See biographies of Taoisigh.*

COWEN, Brian (1960-) b. Offaly, Minister for Health and Children since June 1997. Fianna Fáil TD since 1984, formerly Minister for Labour (1992-93) and Transport, Energy and Communications (1993-94).

COX, Pat (1952-) MEP for Munster since 1989. A registered PD, he is leader of the Liberal Group in the European Parliament since September 1998. Was a TD (1992-94).

CROWLEY, Brian MEP for Munster.

CUSHNAHAN, John (1948-) Fine Gael MEP since 1989. Former leader of the Alliance Party of Northern Ireland (1984-87).

CULLEN, Martin (1954-) b. Waterford, Minister of State at the Department of Finance (with special responsibility for the OPW) since July 1997. Progressive Democrat TD (1987-89 and since 1992).

DAVERN, Noel (1945-) b. Tipperary, Minister of State at the Department of Agriculture and Food (with special responsibility for livestock, breeding and horticulture) since July 1997. Fianna Fáil TD (1969-81 and since 1987).

DEMPSEY, Noel (1953-) b. Meath, Minister for Environment and Local Government since June 1997. Fianna Fáil TD since 1987, previously a Minister of State.

De ROSSA, Proinsias (1940-) b. Dublin, founding member of Democratic Left (1992) and party leader; TD since 1982; MEP (1989-92); Minister for Social Welfare (1994-97); leader of The Workers' Party (1988-92).

De VALERA, Síle (1954-) b. Dublin, Minister for Arts, Heritage, Gaeltacht and the Islands since June 1997. Fianna Fáil TD (1977-81 and since 1987), granddaughter of Éamon de Valera.

DONALDSON, Jeffrey (1963-) Ulster Unionist MP since 1997, Assistant Grand Master of the Orange Lodge of Ireland since 1994.

DUBS, Lord (1932-) b. Czechoslovakia, Northern Ireland Parliamentary Under Secretary of State, responsible for Departments of Environment and Agriculture, as well as community relations and employment equality. Labour MP (1979-87), created life peer in 1994, answers on Northern Ireland matters in the House of Lords.

DUKES, Alan (1945-) b. Dublin, Fine Gael TD since 1981. Former leader of Fine Gael (1987-90), has held various ministerial portfolios including Finance (1982-86) and Justice (1986-87).

EMPEY, Reg (1947-) b. Armagh, member of the Ulster Unionist Party and member of Belfast city council since 1985. Also member of the Northern Ireland

Assembly.

ERVINE, David (1953-) b. Belfast, joined Progressive Unionist Party (1981), spokesperson. Involved in brokering the Loyalist Ceasefire of 1994, elected Belfast city councillor in 1997. Also member of the Northern Ireland Assembly.

FAHEY, Frank (1951-) b. Dublin, Minister of State at the Department of Health and Children (with special responsibility for children) since July 1997. Fianna Fáil TD (1982-92 and since 1997), Senator (1993-97).

FITZGERALD, Dr. Garrett (1926-) b. Dublin, former Taoiseach (1981-82, 1982-87) and leader of Fine Gael (1977-87). *See biographies of Taoisigh.*

FITZSIMMONS, Jim (1936-) b. Navan, MEP for Leinster since 1984. Was also a Fianna Fáil TD (1977-87).

FLOOD, Chris (1947-) b. Westmeath, Minister of State at the Department of Tourism, Sport and Recreation (with special responsibility for local development) since July 1997. Fianna Fáil TD since 1987, also responsible for National Drugs Strategy team.

FLYNN, Pádraig (1939-) b. Mayo, Commissioner to the EU since 1993 with responsibility for Social Affairs. Fianna Fáil TD (1977-93) holding various ministries.

FORSYTHE, Clifford (1929-) Ulster Unionist Party MP since 1983.

GALLAGHER, Pat the Cope (1948-) b. Donegal, FF MEP for Connacht-Ulster since 1994. Was a TD (1981-97).

GILLIS, Alan MEP for Leinster. Member of Fine Gael.

GREGORY, Tony (1947-) b. Dublin, independent TD since 1982; prominent on local issues for his Dublin constituency.

HANAFIN, Des (1930-) b. Tipperary, FF Senator (1969-92). Leading figure in Anti-Divorce and Pro-Life organisations.

HARNEY, Mary (1953-) b. Galway, Tánaiste and Minister for Enterprise, Trade and Employment since June 1997. TD since 1981, Senator (1977-81). Formerly a member of Fianna Fáil; founding member of the PDs in 1985 and the party's leader since 1993.

HAUGHEY, Charles (1925-) b. Mayo, former Taoiseach and leader of Fianna Fáil. *See biographies of taoisigh.*

HIGGINS, Michael D. (1941-) b. Limerick, Labour Party TD (1981-82 and since 1987). Minister for Arts, Culture and the Gaeltacht (1993-97), author of poetry collections *Betrayal* (1990) and *The Season of Fire* (1993).

HILLERY, Patrick (1923-) b. Clare, former Fianna Fail government minister and President. *See biographies of Irish Presidents.*

HOWLIN, Brendan (1956-) b. Wexford, Labour Party TD since 1987; Minister for Health (1993-94) and Minister for the Environment (1994-97).

HUME, John (1937-) b. Derry, founding member (1970) and Leader of Social Democratic and Labour Party since 1979. MP since 1983, MEP since 1979, was prominent in civil rights movement, enjoys a high international profile. Also member of the Northern Ireland Assembly.

HUTCHINSON, Billy press officer of the Progressive Unionist Party, elected Belfast city councillor in 1997. Former loyalist prisoner. Also member of the Northern

Ireland Assembly.

HYLAND, Liam (1933-) b. Laois, FF MEP for Leinster. Was a TD (1981-97) and a Senator (1977-81).

INGRAM, Adam (1947-) b. Scotland, Labour MP since 1987. Minister of State at the Northern Ireland Office responsible for security, Economic Development and North/South co-operation

JACOB, Joe (1939-) b. Clare, Minister of State at the Department of Public Enterprise (with special responsibility for Energy) since July 1997. Fianna Fáil TD since 1987.

KILLILEA, Mark (1939-) b. Galway, MEP for Connacht-Ulster since 1987. Was a FF TD (1977-82) and a Senator (1969-77 and 1982-87).

KITT, Tom (1952-) b. Galway, Minister of State at the Department of Enterprise, Employment and Trade (with special responsibility for labour affairs, consumer rights and international trade) since July 1997. Fianna Fáil TD since 1987.

LOWRY, Michael (1954-) b. Tipperary, TD since 1987. Former minister (1994-96), resigned following revelations of irregular payments to him. Left Fine Gael in 1997, ran as an independent and topped the poll.

LYNCH, Jack (1917-) b. Cork, former Taoiseach and leader of Fianna Fáil. *See Biographies of Taoisigh.*

McALEESE, Mary (1951-) b. Belfast, President of Ireland. *See biographies of Irish Presidents.*

McALISKEY, Bernadette Devlin (1947-) b. Tyrone, founder of IRSP (1974). Youngest person to be elected to Westminster, civil rights activist and MP (1969-74), survived loyalist gun attack in 1981. Recently involved in the campaign to ensure that her daughter Roisín was not extradited to Germany from Britain.

McCARTIN, Joe (1939-) b. Leitrim, MEP for Connacht-Ulster. Member of Fine Gael. Was a TD (1981-82 and 1982-87), Senator (1973-81) and Leas Chathaoirleach (1977-79).

McCARTNEY, Bob (1936-) b. Belfast, leader of the United Kingdom Unionist Party. MP since 1995, expelled from UUP in 1987. Also member of the Northern Ireland Assembly.

McCREEVY, Charlie (1949-) b. Kildare, Minister for Finance since June 1997. Fianna Fáil TD since 1977, has previously been Minister for Social Welfare (1992-1993) and Tourism and Trade (1993-94).

McDAID, Dr. Jim (1949-) b. Donegal, Minister for Tourism, Sport and Recreation since June 1997. Fianna Fáil TD since 1989.

McFALL, John Labour MP and Parliamentary Under Secretary of State for Education, Health and Social Services at the Northern Ireland Office.

McGRADY, Eddie (1935-) b. Co. Down, SDLP MP since 1987. Also member of the Northern Ireland Assembly.

McGUINNESS, Martin (1950-) b. Derry, Mid-Ulster MP since May 1997. Sinn Féin's chief negotiator in talks with representatives of the British government, senior Sinn Féin strategist. Currently engaged in negotiations on arms decommissioning. Also member of the Northern Ireland Assembly.

McKENNA, Patricia MEP for Dublin since 1994. Member of the Green Party.

McMICHAEL, Gary (1971-) b. Antrim, leader of the Ulster Democratic Party since 1994. Member of

Lisburn Borough Council since 1993.

McSHARRY, Ray (1938-) b. Sligo, Fianna Fáil TD (1969-89). Held ministerial portfolios of Agriculture (1979-81), Finance (1982, 1987-88) and Tánaiste (1982). MEP (1984-87) and EU Commissioner for Agriculture (1989-93).

MAGINNIS, Ken (1938-) Ulster Unionist Party MP since 1983.

MALLON, Seamus (1942-) b. Armagh, deputy leader of the SDLP since 1978 and Deputy First Minister of the New Assembly. MP since 1986, Senator (1981-82). Also member of the Northern Ireland Assembly.

MALONE, Bernie MEP for Dublin since 1994. Member of the Labour Party.

MANSERGH, Martin (1947-) b. England, influential adviser to Albert Reynolds and now to Taoiseach Bertie Ahern on matters relating to Northern Ireland.

MARTIN, Micheál (1960-) b. Cork, Minister for Education and Science since June 1997. Fianna Fáil TD since 1989, was Lord Mayor of Cork (1992-93).

MOFFAT, Tom (1940-) b. Mayo, Minister of State at the Department of Health and Children (with special responsibility for food safety and older people) since July 1997. Fianna Fáil TD since 1992.

MOLLOY, Bobby (1936-) b. Galway, Minister of State to the Government and at the Department of the Environment and Local Government (with special responsibility for housing and urban renewal) since July 1997. TD since 1965, left Fianna Fáil in 1986 to join the Progressive Democrats.

MOLYNEAUX, Sir James (1920-) b. Antrim, MP (1970-97). Leader of Ulster Unionist Party (1979-95). Elevated to the peerage as Lord Molyneaux of Killead in 1997.

MOWLAM, Dr Mo (Marjorie) (1949-) b. Coventry, Secretary of State for Northern Ireland since May 1997. Labour MP for Redcar since 1987. Instrumental in pushing through the Good Friday agreement, visiting loyalist prisoners when the peace process was in stalemate. Known to be forthright in negotiations.

MURPHY, Paul (1948-) b. Wales, Minister of State at the Northern Ireland Office responsible for political development, Finance and Personnel and information and the EU. Labour MP since 1987.

NICHOLSON, Jim Ulster MEP. Member of the Ulster Unionists.

NOONAN, Michael (1943-) b. Limerick, Fine Gael TD since 1981, holding various ministerial portfolios including Justice (1982-86) and Health (1994-97).

O'BRIEN, Conor Cruise (1917-) b. Dublin, United Kingdom Unionist. Before his conversion to unionism, was a Labour TD (1969-77), Minister for Posts and Telegraphs (1973-77).

O'CAOLAIN, Caoimhghin (1953-) b. Monaghan, Elected to Dáil Éireann in June 1997 becoming the first Sinn Féin TD to take his seat in Leinster House since 1922.

Ó CUIV, Éamon (1950-) b. Dublin, Minister of State at the Department of Arts, Culture, Gaeltacht and the Islands (with special responsibility for the Gaeltacht and the islands) since July 1997. Fianna Fáil TD since 1992, Senator (1989-92), grandson of Éamon de Valera.

O'DEA, Willie (1952-) b. Limerick, Minister of State at

the Department of Education and Science (with special responsibility for adult education, youth affairs and school transport) since July 1997. Fianna Fáil TD since 1982.

O'DONNELL, Liz (1956-) b. Dublin, Minister of State at the Department of Foreign Affairs (with special responsibility for overseas development assistance and human rights) since July 1997. Progressive Democrat TD since 1992.

O'DONOGHUE, John (1956-) b. Kerry, Minister for Justice, Equality and Law Reform since June 1997. Fianna Fáil TD since 1987.

O'KEEFE, Ned (1942-) b. Cork, Minister of State at the Department of Agriculture and Food (with special responsibility for food) since July 1997. Fianna Fáil TD since 1982, Senator May-November 1992.

O'MALLEY, Des (1939-) b. Limerick, founder of the Progressive Democrats 1985 and former leader of that party (1985-93). TD since 1968, holding a number of ministerial portfolios, expelled from Fianna Fáil 1985.

O'ROURKE, Mary (1937-) b. Westmeath, Minister for Public Enterprise since 1997. TD since 1982, Senator (1981-82), has held several portfolios including Education (1987-91), deputy leader of Fianna Fáil since 1994.

OWEN, Nora (1945-) b. Dublin, deputy leader of Fine Gael since 1993, TD (1981-87 and since 1989). Former Minister for Justice (1994-97). Grand niece of Michael Collins.

PAISLEY, Rev. Dr. Ian (1926-) b. Armagh, founder and leader of the Democratic Unionist Party (1971). MP since 1971, MEP since 1979, established Free Presbyterian Church (1951). Also member of the Northern Ireland Assembly.

PATTISON, Séamus (1936-) b. Kilkenny, elected Ceann Comhairle, June 1997. Labour Party TD since 1961 and father of the Dáil.

QUINN, Ruairí (1946-) b. Dublin, leader of the Labour Party since 1997. TD (1977-81 and since 1982), Senator (1981-82), deputy leader of Labour Party 1989-97. Has held various ministerial portfolios including Labour (1983-87) and Finance (1994-97).

REID, Rev. Alex Catholic priest. Key negotiator in 1994 IRA ceasefire.

REYNOLDS, Albert (1932-) b. Roscommon, former Taoiseach and leader of Fianna Fáil. *See Biographies of Taoisigh.*

ROBINSON, Mary (1944-) b. Mayo, former President of Ireland (1990-97) and current UN High Commissioner of Human Rights. *See Biographies of Presidents.*

ROBINSON, Peter (1948-) b. Belfast, MP since 1979. Deputy Leader of the Democratic Unionist Party. Also member of the Northern Ireland Assembly.

ROCHE, Adi (1955-) b. Tipperary, aid worker and anti-nuclear campaigner. Founder of the Cork based Chernobyl Children's Project (1990). Labour party candidate for 1997 Presidential Elections.

RODGERS, Bríd b. Donegal, former General Secretary of SDLP (1981-83). Chairperson (1978-80), current spokesperson on Women's Issues and Irish Language. Also member of the Northern Ireland Assembly.

ROSS, William (1936-) Ulster Unionist Party MP since

1974.
SMITH, Michael (1940-) b. Tipperary, Minister of Defence. Fianna Fáil TD (1969-73, 1977-82 and since 1997).
SMYTH, Hugh (1941-) b. Belfast, founding member and leader of the Progressive Unionist Party. Belfast City Councillor, Lord Mayor of Belfast (1994/95).
SMYTH, Rev. Martin (1931-) Ulster Unionist Party MP since 1982. Grand Master of the Orange Lodge of Ireland (1972-96).
SPENCE, Gusty (1933-) b. Belfast, former member of the UVF and current co-ordinator of the Progressive Unionist Party.
SPRING, Dick (1950-) b. Kerry, former Tánaiste (1982-87 & 1993-97). Former leader of the Labour Party (1982-97), TD since 1981 has held various ministerial portfolios including Foreign Affairs (1993-97), was chief negotiator for the Irish government on Northern Ireland.
TAYLOR, John (1937-) b. Armagh, deputy leader of the Ulster Unionist Party since 1995. MP since 1983, MEP (1979-89), survived republican gun attack in 1972. Also member of the Northern Ireland Assembly.
THOMPSON, William (1939-) member of the Ulster Unionist Party, in 1997 he became the first MP elected by the new constituency of West Tyrone.
TREACY, Noel (1952-) b. Galway, Minister of State at the Departments of Education & Science and Enterprise, Trade & Employment (with special responsibility for Science and Technology). FF TD since 1982.
TRIMBLE, David (1944-) b. Co. Down, First Minister of the Northern Ireland Assembly and leader of the Ulster Unionist Party since 1995. MP since 1990, former deputy leader of the Vanguard Ulster Progressive Party (1975-77). Although he played a prominent role in Orange Order parades at Drumcree in 1996, he is strongly associated with the Good Friday agreement has entered into negotiations with Sinn Féin leader, Gerry Adams.
WALKER, Cecil (1924-) Ulster Unionist Party MP since 1983.
WALLACE, Danny (1942-) b. Cork, Minister of State at the Department of the Environment and Local Government since July 1997. Fianna Fáil TD since 1982.
WALLACE, Mary (1959-) b. Dublin, Minister of State at the Department of Justice, Equality and Law Reform (with special responsibility for equality and disabilities) since July 1997. Fianna Fáil TD since 1989, Senator (1987-89).
WALSH, Joe (1943-) b. Cork, Minister for Agriculture and Food since June 1997. Fianna Fáil TD (1977-81 and since 1982), Senator (1981-82), Minister for Agriculture (1992-94).
WOODS, Michael (1935-) b. Wicklow, Minister for the Marine and Natural Resources since June 1997. Fianna Fáil TD since 1977, has held various ministerial portfolios including Social Welfare (1979-81, 1982, 1987-91 and 1993-94) and Agriculture and Food (1991-92).

ARTS

BALLAGH, Robert (1943-) b. Dublin, renowned artist and designer. Qualified architect. Produced stage designs for much lauded plays and shows, including *Riverdance*. Completed government commissions for currency designs and postal stamps, also designed book covers.
BEHAN, John (1938-) b. Dublin, sculptor. Helped shape contemporary Irish painting and sculpture. Exhibited in all major Irish exhibitions from 1960. Commissions include major corporate sculptures, religious sculptures and works for the collections of the US. President of prominent galleries in Ireland.
BELTON, Liam Keeper of the RHA
BEWICK, Pauline (1935-) b. England, reared Kerry, prolific artist. Studied at NCAD and has since exhibited worldwide in private and public collections. Elected to the Royal Irish Academy of the Arts (1986). Produced two well-known books: *The South Seas and a Box of Paint* and *The Yellow Man*.
BLACKSHAW, Basil (1932-) b. Glengormley, artist. Exhibited widely in Ireland and abroad. Designed posters for all Field Day Productions (1986-90), and the Belfast '91 Calendar. Contributor to the *Great Book of Ireland*, IMMA. (1991). Honorary Member of the RHA.
BOURKE, Brian (1936-) b. Dublin, painter. Noted as an outstanding draughtsman and colourist. Represented Ireland at the *Paris Biennale* and the *Lugano Exhibition of Graphics*.
BOURKE, Fergus (1934-) b. Wicklow, photographer. Works included in *Famine Commemoration Exhibition*, Clifden (1995). Seven of his photographs are in permanent exhibition at New York's Museum of Modern Art.
BOLAY, Veronica Associate Member of RHA.
BRADY, Charles (1926-) b. New York, moved to Ireland (1961), artist. Works included in many collections - the Arts Council, the Hugh Lane Municipal Gallery and the Derek Hill Collection. Regular contributor to exhibitions at the RHA.'
BRENNAN, Cecily (1955-) artist. Deeply involved in Ireland's arts. Solo exhibitions held in Project Arts Centre, Taylor and Douglas Hyde Galleries. Included in the collections of the Arts Council, the Bank of Ireland and UCD.
BROWNE, Deborah (1927-) painter, has developed an interest in fibreglass (1965). Produced three-dimensional free standing-sculptures.
BROWNE, Vincent (1947-) b. Dublin, sculptor. Represented Ireland at the *7th International Small Sculpture Show* in Hungary (1987). Contributed to *The Great Book of Ireland* (1991). Won the Irish Concrete Society Award for *Maritime Piece*, Co. Wicklow (1993).
BRUEN, Gerald Member of the RHA
BUICK, Robin Associate Member of the RHA.
BULFIN, Michael (1939-) b. Offaly, renowned sculptor. Completed many major commissions, including *A Walk Among Stone*, Ballymun (1990). Chairman of the Sculptors' Society of Ireland (1983-91). Member of the committees on Living Art, the Oireachtas

Exhibition and the Municipal Gallery.

BURKE, John (1946-) b. Tipperary, sculptor. Works featured in many private and public collections. Participated in major annual group shows, including *Artists 77*, New York, and *18 European Sculptors*, Munich (1978).

CAFFREY, Elizabeth b. Co. Meath, ceramic sculptor. Involved in many major exhibitions - the Achill Island Sculpture Symposium and the 1997 Irish Contemporary Ceramic Touring Exhibition. Won the 1997 IONTAS sculpture award and Adjudicators' award - the first time a sculptor has been presented with the award - and exhibited her new works in May 1998.

CAMPBELL, George (1917-) b. Arklow, painter and stained-glass artist. Co-founded Irish Exhibition of Living Art (1943). Best remembered for powerful images of his paintings and drawings made in Spain.

CARR, Eithne Member of the RHA.

CARR, Tom (1909-) b. Belfast, artist. One of Northern Ireland's most respected painters. Produces figurative and landscape work. Widely exhibited in Ireland and abroad. Awarded the *Royal Ulster Academy* gold medal (1973) and the *Oireachtas Landscape* award (1976). Honorary Member of the RHA.

CARRICK, Desmond Member of the RHA.

CARRON, William Associate Member of RHA.

CLARK, Carey Member of the RHA

COLEMAN, James (1941-) b. Roscommon, artist. Acclaimed at home and abroad. Featured in prestigious group exhibitions, including *Hall of Mirrors: Art and Film since 1945*, Los Angeles, and *EV+A 96*, Limerick (1996).

COLEMAN, Eamon (1957-) b. Dublin, painter. Was president of the European Council of Artists. Held an exhibition in February 1998 in the RHA Gallery, entitled 'Postcards Home.'

COLLIS, Peter Treasurer of the RHA

CONNOR, Patrick ceramic sculptor. Regarded as one of the fine group of artists and craftspeople produced by the NCAD in the early 1970s, he is seen as an outstanding draughtsman and world-class ceramicist.

COOKE, Barrie (1931-) b. England, moved to Ireland (1954), painter. Featured in many major collections. Illustrated poetry books by Seamus Heaney and Ted Hughes.

COSTELLOE, Paul (1945-) b. Dublin, fashion designer. Worked in Milan, Paris and New York, now working in England. His designs were favoured by Princess Diana at one stage. Wrote a controversial attack on the fashion sense of Irish women in the *Sunday Times* magazine, September 1998. Told them to look to Maureen O'Hara in *The Quiet Man* for inspiration. Has recently designed a range of table ware.

COTTER, Maud (1954-) stained-glass artist. Exhibiting since 1974, perfecting the craft and technique of glass with James Scanlon.

COYLE, John Professor of Painting RHA

CROFT, Richard artist and teacher. Recognised as a talented painter, calligrapher and print maker, he has also experimented widely with sculpture and mixed media .

CRONIN, Brian (1958-) b. Dublin, painter and illustrator. Emigrated to the US (1985) to continue his career. His 1998 exhibition *Fat Face with Fork* is a selection of 12 years of commissioned work, given in the IMMA was very successful (attendance figures: 77,000).

CROSS, Dorothy (1956-) b. Cork, artist. Included in acclaimed exhibitions in England, the US and Ireland. Won the *Marten Toonder* Award and the *Pollock/Krasner* Award (1990).

CROZIER, William (1930-) b. Scotland, closely associated with Ireland, artist. Included in major national collections in Ireland, Britain, the US and across Europe. Featured in group exhibition *Contemporary Artists from Ireland*.

CULLEN, Charles (1939-) b. Longford, artist and current NCAD Head of Painting. Paintings exhibited in The Arts Council, the Hugh Lane Municipal Gallery and Trinity College, Dublin.

CULLEN, Michael (1946-) b. Wicklow, artist. Has had many solo exhibitions. Included in high profile group exhibitions: *Gateway to Art*, Dublin Airport (1990), *Art for Film*, Dublin Catalogue; and *Irish Potato Famine*, New York (1995).

de BUITLÉAR, Róisín contemporary glass artist. She uses both glass blowing and working in solid sheet glass. Originally trained in the NCAD has worked in studios in Denmark, Britain and Japan.

de CHENU, Noel Professor of Architecture RHA

de FOUW, Jan b. Holland, print artist. Came to Ireland more than 30 years ago with other Dutch graphic designers and worked as a commercial artist and designer. An early member of the Graphic Studio, he is now associated with the Black Church Print Studio, where he both works and teaches.

DELANEY, Edward (1930-) b. Mayo, sculptor. Has exhibited at such prestigious shows as the *Paris Biennale* (1959, 1961). Received high profile commissions, including Wolfe Tone's statue, St. Stephen's Green, Dublin. Member of RHA.

DONNELLY, Anne member of the RHA

DOYLE, Kay watercolour artist. Has served for many years on the committee of the Watercolour Society of Ireland and was its president in 1997. Notable works include *At the House of César Manrique*.

EGAN, Felim (1952-) b. Tyrone, painter and sculptor. Work featured in *A Sense of Ireland*, London, *ROSC 84*, Dublin, *Aspects of Irish Painting 1960s -1990s*, I.M.M.A. Dublin, *L'Imaginaire Irlandais*, Paris (1996). Won the *UNESCO* Prize for the Arts (1993).

FALLON, Conor (1939-) b. Wexford, self-taught painter who has turned to sculpture. Has received numerous public commissions including ones from UCD, St. Patrick's Hospital, The Arts Council and Irish Life, Dublin. Member of RHA

FARRELL, Brian chief art critic for the *Irish Times* for 35 years, retired in 1998.

FARRELL, Dr. Brian (1929-) b. Manchester, chairman of Arts Council (appointed 15th June 1998), broadcaster and professor of politics at UCD. Won a scholarship to Harvard University (1953), appointed to the politics department at UCD in the late 1960s, retired from academic life in 1994, has written several books and articles and presented RTÉ current affairs programme *Prime Time*.

FARRELL, Michael (1940-) b. Meath, painter.

Exhibited many times at the Dawson, Douglas Hyde and Taylor Galleries in Dublin, as well as at galleries in Munich, Sydney, Paris and Sweden.

FITZGERALD, Mary (1956-) b. Dublin, artist. Featured in prestigious solo and group exhibitions, including those at *EV+A*, Limerick, *'88 ROSC Exhibition* and the RHK, Dublin (1987), *The Abstract Irish*, B4A Gallery and South Bank Gallery, New York, and *L'Imaginaire Irlandais* (1996).

FLANAGAN, T.P. (1929-) b. Enniskillen, landscape artist. Exhibited in *Irish Art (1943-1973) - Rosc'80*, Northern Ireland Arts Council (1977), Ulster Museum (1995). Included in Hugh Lane Gallery, IMMA and Ulster Museum, Belfast, collections. Member of RHA.

FOLAN, Andrew Associate Member of the RHA.

GAYER, Terence artist and teacher. Seen to represent a link with schools of Ruskin and Morris and taught in the NCAD. Rarely exhibits and only in group exhibits.

GALE, Martin (1949-) b. England, reared Ireland, painter. Participated in Arts Council Touring Exhibition (1981-82) and *Sense of Ireland* Festival in London, XIe Biennale de Paris (1980), *Images from Ireland* in Brussels (1990), *Gateway to Art* at Dublin Airport. Member of RHA.

GEOGHEGAN, Trevor (1946-) b. London, moved to Ireland (1971), landscape artist. Lecturer at NCAD. Represented Ireland at *25th International Festival of Painting* in Cagnes-sur-Mer, France (1989).

GIBNEY, Arthur president of the RHA

GORMAN, Richard (1949-) b. Dublin, artist. Exhibited at the *GPA* Awards Exhibition (1981), *EV+A*, Limerick, *UNESCO* International Exhibition, Paris (1986), *L'Imaginaire Irlandais*, Paris (1996). Received the Open Award at the *EV+A*, Limerick (1987), and the *Pollock/Krasner* Award (1996). Member of the RHA.

GOULDING, Tim (1945-) b. Dublin, self-taught painter. Represented Ireland at various arts exhibitions, including *Young Artists from around the World*, New York (1970), Paris Biennale (1971), *Landscapes: American and European Perspectives*, Washington (1989), *Aspects of Irish Painting 1960-1990*, IMMA (1991).

GOULET, Yann Renard (1914-) b. Brittany, moved to Ireland (1947), sculptor and painter. Widely exhibited. Appointed Professor of Sculpture RHA. Received numerous public and private commissions.

GRAHAM, Patrick (1943-) b. Mullingar, visual artist. Featured in *Four Irish Expressionist Painters* in the US, the *Festival Celtique* in France, *Censorship USA* in Los Angeles, *The Famine* - International Touring Exhibition (1995). Books include *I am of Water*, *Works 5 - Patrick Graham* and *Art In America*.

HALL, Patrick (1935-) b. Tipperary, artist. Exhibitions include *Making Sense* - The Arts Council touring exhibition (1982-83), *Irish Art - The European Dimension*, RHA Gallagher Gallery (1990), *New Works* at selected galleries in Los Angeles, Belfast, Dublin and Limerick.

HAMILTON, Letitia (1876-) b. Meath, painter. Widely exhibited throughout Ireland. Founder member of Society of Dublin Painters. Work included in collections of the National Gallery of Ireland, Hugh Lane Gallery and the Ulster Museum, Belfast. Member of RHA.

HANRATTY, Alice b. Dublin, artist. Has worked in East Africa and Ireland. Participated in important national group shows in Ireland and abroad, including the London *Original Print Fair* (1995), *Ten Years of Invited Artists' Prints* - Dublin (1994), *International Impact Exhibition* - Japan (1989), *Irish Women Artists The 18th Century* - 1987 - Dublin.

HAPASKA, Siobhan (1963-) b. Belfast, sculptor. Noted for creating shiny, futuristic abstract fibreglass objects, as well as waxworks. A graduate of Goldsmith's College, London, she is the winner of the 1998 Glen Dimplex Award.

HARPER, Charles (1943-) b. Valentia Island, artist. Head of Fine Art Faculty, Limerick School of Art and Design. Founded EVA, Limerick, in 1975 and a founder member of Aosdána in 1981. Works featured in the *International Miniature Art Exhibition* - Toronto (1986), the *Great Book of Ireland* - IMMA (1991), *Gateway to Art* at Dublin Airport (1991), *Iontas* in Sligo (1991-92). A retrospective of his works was held in April 1998. Associate Member of RHA.

HARRISON, Colin member of RHA

HICKEY, Patrick (1927-) b. India, moved to Ireland (1948). Painter, lithographist, etcher, architect and designer. Honorary Member of RHA.

HIGGINS, Leo sculptor. Contributed to Irish sculpture, not only through his work, but also through his foundry - several of the country's finest sculptors have worked with him.

HIGGINS, Noelle contemporary glass artist. Recently worked with the foremost figure in the glass world, Dale Chihuly, on his work *Over Venice* - he and his team made giant chandeliers in different countries and suspended them over a canal for the Venice Biennale.

HILL, Derek b. England, portrait and landscape artist and collector. Arrived on Tory island in 1956 and returned repeatedly to paint the island. Set up the Glebe House and Gallery, Churchill (now run by the OPW). His collection features Donegal folk art (see PATSY DAN RODGERS) in addition to works by Picasso, Bonnard, Kokoschka, YEATS, Japanese and Islamic art and William Morris's textiles. Honorary Member of RHA. Granted honorary citizenship of Ireland on 9th September, 1998.

HONE, David Member of the RHA

HUTSON, Marshall C. Member of the RHA.

JORDAN, Eithne (1954-) b. Dublin, artist. Founder member of the Visual Arts Centre (a co-operative space for artists). Her work has featured in Arts Council collections. Developed towards painting more 'realistic' scenes - landscapes, interiors, gardens and nature in general. Gave a 1998 show at the Rubicon Gallery.

KANE, Michael (1935-) b. Dublin, painter. Worked for extended periods in UK, Switzerland and Spain. Features in major group exhibitions in Ireland and abroad, including *Gateway to Art* at Dublin Airport, *European Large Format Printmaking*, Hop Store, Dublin (1991), *Euroamerican Printmaking*, Spain (1992).

KEARNEY Declan b. Tyrone, fashion designer. Winner of the 1997 Smirnoff International Fashion Awards - the first time the title has come to Northern Ireland -

competing against 27 other countries. Also won the Guinness Student Designer Awards and the Satzenbrau Fashion Awards.

KELLY, John (1932-) b. Dublin, artist and lecturer in printmaking. Exhibited at *Dante Graphics Exhibition* in New York (1965), *NCAD Decade Show* (1986), *Four x Fore* at the Project Arts Centre (1992). Member of RHA.

KERR, Helen textile artist. Not only a talented textile artist, but also teaches the craft to many young artists in Northern Ireland.

KINDNESS, John artist. A graduate of the Belfast College of art, works in a variety of media and his unique use of materials has won him awards and admiration in Ireland, Europe and the US.

KING, Brian (1942-) b. Dublin, sculptor. Has lived and worked in Ireland, London and New York. Head of Sculpture at the NCAD. Exhibited widely in Ireland and abroad, recent exhibitions including *EV+A in Limerick* (1996) and *Innovation from Tradition,* Brussels (1996).

KINGSTON, Richard Member of the RHA.

LAMBERT, Gene (1952-) b. Dublin, artist. Exhibited at Irish Exhibition of Living Art, *the Independent Artists, the Figurative Image and the Guinness Peat Aviation Awards* Exhibition. Represented Ireland at the *14th International Festival of Painting* in Cagnes-sur-Mer. Associate Member of RHA.

LANDWEER, Sonja (1933-) b. Amsterdam, moved to Ireland (1960s), ceramicist. Evolved a batiked-ceramic technique and worked for Kilkenny Design Workshops. Her ceramics and jewellery are widely exhibited in Ireland and abroad.

le BROCQUY, Louis (1916-) b. Dublin, self-taught artist, widely acclaimed in Ireland and abroad. Elected Saoi by members of Aosdána (1992). Perhaps best known for his illustrations of *The Táin* (translated by THOMAS KINSELLA - 1969). Honorary Member of RHA.

le BROCQUY, Melanie (1919-) b. Dublin, artist. Held many prestigious solo and group exhibitions. Won many awards, including the *Silver Medal of the Oireachtas* (1983) and the *RHA Annual Exhibition Prize* (1995). Honorary Member of the RHA.

LENNON, Ciarán (1947-) b. Dublin, artist. Exhibits widely in Ireland and Europe. Exhibitions include *Irish Exhibitions of Living Art, Sense of Ireland* Festival in London (1980), *Images from Ireland,* Brussels (1990).

LOHAN, Mary member of the RHA.

LONG, John Director of the Tyrone Guthrie Centre at Annaghmakerrig, Co. Monaghan, since 1981. The centre is primarily a workplace for artists.

LOUGHLAN, Bernard Associate Member of the RHA.

MacRUAIRI, Tomas b. Armagh, president of Conradh na Gaeilge (appointed 9th May 1998). Former worker with the Irish Press Group, now runs a court reporting agency.

MADDEN, Anne b. London, reared Ireland, artist. Represented in permanent exhibitions worldwide, including the IMMA, the Ulster Museum, the Pompidou Centre, and the Musée Picasso in Antibes. Subject of two documentaries - *Anne Madden,* Cinematon, Paris; *L'Artiste Anne Madden,* Radio Television Luxembourg.

MADDEN, Bernadette batik artist. Has been a leading exponent of batik as an art form in Ireland. Has also served on the Craft Council and NCAD boards.

MAGILL, Elizabeth member of the RHA

MAGUIRE, Brian (1951-) b. Wicklow, visiting artist at main Irish art colleges and artist-in-residence in prisons throughout Ireland, Canada and the US.

MAHER, Alice (1956-) b. Tipperary, artist. Exhibited widely in US and Europe. Represented Ireland at the *1994 Sao Paulo Bienal.*

MAHON, Sir Denis donated eight baroque paintings, principally from the Bolognese school, to the National Gallery of Ireland in 1997, including Guercino's *Jacob blessing the Sons of Joseph,* Luca Giordano's *Venus, Mars and the Forge of Vulcan,* and an early Guido Reni of Cleopatra.

McENTAGART, Brett Secretary of the RHA

McKENNA, James (1933-) b. Dublin, sculptor. Exhibited at many international sculpture shows. Commissions include *Female Figure and Tree* in Sandyford, the Gerard Manley Hopkins monument in Monasterevin, and a suite of wood sculptures at Hazelwood in Co. Sligo.

McKENNA, Mary architect for the Office of Public Works, designed the European award-winning interpretative centre for the Céide fields which also won the RIAI's Gold Medal.

McKENNA, Stephen painter. Curator of the IMMA's very popular 1997 exhibition - 'The Pursuit of Painting' (attendance figures: 130,220) and has recently exhibited at the Kerlin Gallery. Member of RHA

McNAB, Theo (1940-) b. Dublin, self-taught artist. Represented Ireland at a number of international exhibitions, including *Cagnes-sur-Mer Festival,* France, *Impact Arts Festivals,* Kyoto, Japan (1981-84), *Irish Graphics in China (1985)* and the Edinburgh Festival (1985).

McSWEENEY, Sean (1935-) b. Dublin, painter. A student of Terence Gayer, his work seen as a continuation of Romantic Irish tradition. Also a teacher and organiser of the arts in his local area. Works included in many public and private collections, including AIB, Aer Lingus, the Arts Council, Dublin City University and the Hugh Lane Gallery. Notable works include his recent paintings based on seabogs and scapes around his home in Ballyconnell, Co. Sligo.

MELLET, Laurent sculptor, renowned for the kinetic, fire and water-spitting figures - an amalgam of robotics, solenoid valves, pneumatics, motors, steam and fire - created for Dublin's St Patrick's Day parade over the past three years.

MOLONEY, Helen (1926-) b. Dublin, stained-glass artist. Designed crosses, doors, altar panels and wall hangings for many churches across England and Ireland.

MULHOLLAND, Carolyn (1944-) b. Lurgan, sculptor. Exhibited throughout Ireland. Completed commissions for the Arts Council of Northern Ireland, Jefferson Smurfit and Irish Life. Member of RHA.

MULLARNEY, Janet (1952-) b. Dublin, sculptor. Trained in Florence as an artist and did not show in Ireland, so is regarded as outside mainstream Irish art. Wood figures largely in her works, and animals, birds and people figure as symbols in her work. Stresses the importance of Romanesque and

Renaissance art in her work. Was shortlisted for 1998 Glen Dimplex Award.

MURPHY, Mike (1941-) b. Dublin, TV and radio presenter. Currently hosts the popular and eclectic Arts Programme on RTÉ radio. Recently wrote his autobiography.

NAPIER, Philip (1965-) b. Belfast; artist. Regarded as mercurial installation artist dealing with Northern Irish political themes. Was shortlisted for 1998 Glen Dimplex Award; nominated for Gauge - an installation commemorating the 25th Anniversary of Bloody Sunday.

NÍ CHIOSÁIN, Fionnuala artist. Her work is dominated by translucent paintings, created through a process of layering films of paint. Featured in *L'Imaginaire Irlandais* (1996), A Century of Irish Painting (1997). Exhibitions include the City Centre Gallery (1991), the Trial Ballon in New York, the IMMA, the Hugh Lane Gallery, Waterford IT, Irish Arts Society and the State Collection in Government Offices. Exhibited April 1998 in the Kerlin Gallery, Dublin.

NISBET, Tom Member of the RHA.

NOLAN, James Member of the RHA.

OAKLEY, George watercolourist. Set up his own commercial silk-screen printing factory, but since retiring, has devoted himself full-time to painting. Notable works include the oil painting - *Shoppers, Henry Street*.

O'CONNELL, Eilís (1953-) sculptor. Recent showings include *Appetites of Gravity* in Sussex, *Recent Sculpture* in Green on Red Gallery, *Irish Women Artists* - Drogheda and *Tradition and Innovation*, Brussels.

Ó COFAIGH, Eoin (1956-) new president of the Royal Institute of Architects in Ireland (RIAI).

O'DEA, Michael Member of the RHA.

O'DOWD, Gwen (1957-) b. Dublin, artist. Included in the collections of the Arts Council, IMMA, the AIB and the Financial Services Centre, Dublin. Recent exhibitions include the *Poetic Land - Political Territory* NCCA Tour of England and *L'Imaginaire Irlandais* (1996). Member of RHA.

O'MALLEY, Tony (1913-) b. Kilkenny, artist. Widely exhibited in Ireland and abroad. Participated in *Arts Hibernia* - London (1985), *Images of Ireland* - Brussels, *30th Anniversary Exhibition, Erin Cara* - touring Canada and *Irish Art 1770-1995, History and Society*, touring the US. Honorary Member of RHA.

Ó MÓRÁIN, Donall (1923-) b. Kerry, founder and chief Executive of Gael Linn (1963), former chairman of RTÉ Authority (1970-72).

Ó MUIRCHÚ, Labhras (1939-) b. Tipperary, Ardstiúrthóir (director) of Comhaltas Ceoltóirí Éireann.

O'NEILL, Liam renowned woodturner. Apprenticed in the craft to John Shiel of Carlow (1968). Obtained a scholarship to the US and became a founder member of the American Association of Woodturners. Returned to Ireland and opened a gallery in the Spiddal Craft Centre (1992). Has a major permanent exhibition "Sculpture in Wood" at the Phoenix Park Visitor Centre featuring vessels made from 100 different species of tree in the park, including a giant California redwood.

O'SULLIVAN, Patrick (1940-) b. London, moved to Cork (1971), artist. Works in marble, wood and bronze. Exhibited and taught widely. Has received several awards.

PATTON, Eric Member of the RHA.

PRENDERGAST, Kathy (1958-) b. Dublin, artist. Exhibited at many prestigious shows, including the Henry Moore Foundation Fellowship Exhibition in London (1986) and the Unit 7 Gallery, London.

PYE, Patrick (1929-) b. Dublin, stained glass artist. Frequent exhibitor at the David Hendriks Gallery, Dublin. Fulfilled commissions for numerous churches throughout Ireland. Created more than 20 triptychs on sacred themes. Member of RHA.

QUINN, Patricia (1959-) b. Dublin, director of Arts Council since 1996 (its first woman director). Joined the Arts Council as music and opera officer in 1984, later becoming development officer; organised the first major Irish conference on arts management 'The Art of Managing the Arts' (1991). Former Cultural Director of Temple Bar Properties in (1992-96).

RAE, Barbara member of the RHA

ROBINSON, Markey b. Belfast, artist. Exhibits in the Oriel Gallery

ROCHA, John b. Hong Kong, settled in Ireland, internationally renowned fashion designer based in Ireland.

ROCHE, Vivienne Associate Member of RHA.

RODGERS, Patsy Dan b. Donegal, King of Tory Island, (Rí Thoraí). One of the more famous members of the island's Naive painting school, discovered by Derek Hill who first visited the island in 1956. There is now a permanent gallery on the island displaying their works.

RYAN, Thomas Member of RHA.

SCANLON, James (1952-) b. Kerry, widely exhibited artist. Works include paintings, drawings, sculpture and stained glass. His stained glass work represented Ireland at the Garden Festival in Japan.

SCOTT, Patrick (1921-) b. Cork, painter whose works are included in many public and private collections, including the Municipal Gallery, Dublin, the Gulf Oil Corporation - Pittsburg and the Ulster Museum, Belfast. Honorary Member of RHA.

SHAWCROSS, Neil member of RHA

SHELBOURNE, Anita Associate Member of RHA.

SHERIDAN, Noel (1936-) b. Dublin, painter and art critic. Works widely exhibited in Ireland, Europe, the US and Australia. Director of NCAD and the Perth Institute of Contemporary Arts, Western Australia.

SHINNORS, John artist. A lecturer in the Limerick School of Art & Design and member of the RHA, his work is noted for its simplicity and great skill.

SIMONDS-GOODING, Maria (1939-) b. India, moved to Kerry (1947), artist. Exhibited widely in Ireland and abroad. Regular contributor to Oireachtas Exhibitions, the RHA, and Living Art.

SOUTER, Camille (1929-) b. England, moved to Ireland (1956), widely exhibited painter. Group exhibitions include *12 Irish Painters* - New York (1963), *the Delighted Eye* - Ireland and London (1980), *Irish Art in the Eighties* - Douglas Hyde Gallery (1991) and *Figurative Image*, Dublin (1991).

STEPHENSON, Sam (1939-) b. Dublin, architect,

whose buildings include the Central Bank, ESB Offices and Bord na Móna Offices in Dublin. Associate Member of the RHA.

STUART, Imogen b. Berlin, moved to Ireland (1950), sculptor. Works in wood, stone, bronze, steel, clay, plaster and terracotta. Sculptures can be seen in churches and public places throughout Ireland, England and Rome. Work featured in the *Great Book of Ireland* and *Baedecker Guide to Ireland*. Member of the RHA.

TAGGART, Elizabeth member of RHA

TREACY, Philip (1967-) b. Galway, milliner, most famous hat designer in Europe. Worked with prominent couture houses in Europe, particularly Chanel.

TUACH, Rod (1945-) b. Dublin, widely exhibited photographer. Represented at group exhibitions - *Six Photographers* touring Ireland, *Contemporary Irish Photography* Guinness Hop Store (1987) and *Fetes Irlandaises* Montreal World Trade Centre (1992).

TYRRELL, Charles (1950-) b. Meath, artist. Lives and works on the Beara Penninsula, Co. Cork. Recent exhibitions include *Famine*, Claremorris and Boston (1995) and *L'Imaginaire Irlandais*, Paris (1996).

Van STOCKUM, Hilda member of the RHA

VIALE, Patrick painter. Works as a school teacher, and although only started painting around ten years ago, his pictures are lauded as being reminiscent of Cezanne and Van Gogh. Notable works include *Mantelpiece*.

WALKER, Brian (1947-) b. Belfast, chairman of the Arts Council of Northern Ireland (appointed 5th August 1998, succeeding Mr. Donal Deeney QC 1993-98). Member of the Arts Council of Northern Ireland since 1996, serving as chairman of its Creative Arts Panel since 1997. Has been Director of the Institute of Irish Studies at QUB since 1993. Served on the Northern Ireland Museums Council (1993-97) and president of the Board of Governors of the Linen Hall Library (1995-98).

WALLACE, Dr. Patrick b. Limerick, archaeologist and current director of the National Museum of Ireland since 1988.

WARREN, Barbara (1925-) b. Dublin, painter. Work represented in many public and private collections in Ireland and abroad. Exhibited at the Taylor Galleries - Dublin, *Irish Women Artists* - Hugh Lane Gallery (1987), and at the RHA's annual and banquet exhibitions.

WARREN, Michael (1950-) b. Wexford, sculptor. Commissions including RTÉ, Olympic Sculpture Park in Seoul (1988) and Utsukushi-ga-hara Open Air Museum, Japan (1989). Member of RHA.

WEIR, Grace sculptor/multi-media installation artist and lecturer at the NCAD. Science plays a big role in her art, and many of her shows allude to chaos theory and the butterfly effect. In her recent digital art exhibition *"and"* she created virtual panoramic images that played with perspective.

WYNNE JONES, Nancy Honorary Member of RHA.

YEATS, Anne b. Dublin, artist. Work represented in public and private collections worldwide. Was Abbey Theatre's chief stage designer.

BUSINESS

AIKEN, Jim (1932-) b. Belfast, successful concert promoter. Has brought many of worlds top acts to Ireland, including The Rolling Stones, U2, Bruce Springsteen, Bob Dylan and David Bowie.

BARRY, Oliver (1940-) b. Cork, concert promoter. Originally showband manager. Brought acts including John Denver, Michael Jackson, James Last, Prince and Frank Sinatra to Irish venues.

BATES, Ray Director of National Lottery since 1987.

BEGG, David (1950-) b. Dublin, chief executive of Concern. Succeeding Fr. Aengus Finucane (May 1997), former general secretary of Communications Workers' Union (1985-97), appointed to the board of the Central Bank in 1995.

BOWLER, Gillian travel business executive. Made cheap foreign holidays accessible to the masses with her company Budget Travel, which she sold to Granada group eleven years ago and which was subsequently sold onto the huge British travel business, Thompson.

BREWER, Stephen (1947-) b. England, chief executive of Eircell. Former Commercial Director with France Telecom Mobile, former Sales and Marketing Director at Cellnet.

BROSNAN, Denis (1944-) b. Kerry, managing director of Kerry Group plc. Joined Golden Vale as production manager, general manager of North Kerry Milk Products (1972). Founding partner of Kerry Co-operative, horse breeder, chairman of the Irish Horseracing Authority (IHA).

BUCKLEY, Michael (1945-) b. Cork, director of AIB Group (appointed 1995). Chef de Cabinet to President of the European Court of Auditors (1977-81). Director, later managing director NCB Stockbrokers (1986-91). Member of Custom House Docks Development Authority, chairman of review body on Higher Remuneration in the Public Service.

BUTLER, Brendan (1956-) director of Small Firms Association (SFA) since 1994, civil servant for 15 years. Former Industrial Relations Executive with the Federated Union of Employers - now IBEC - (1988-94).

CASSELLS, Peter (1950-) general secretary of Irish Congress of Trade Unions since 1989. Joined ICTU (1973) as a training officer, becoming Legislative Officer (1975) and Economic and Social Affairs Officer. Appointed Assistant General Secretary (1987).

CASSIDY, Angela (1955-) b. Roscommon, President of the Civil and Public Service Union, Works for the Revenue Commissioners.

COLLINS, Bob (1947-) b. Limerick, Director General of RTÉ (appointed January 1997). Secretary to RTÉ Authority (1975), Deputy controller for RTÉ 1 and Network 2 (1982), Director of TV programmes (1986); former Assistant Director General of RTÉ (March 1996-January 1997); Director of the Merriman Summer School (1981-87). Credited with overturning structures that had been in place for years. In 1997, RTÉ made a surplus of £5.8 million (most of which came from earnings from Riverdance).

CONN, David managing director of Xtra-Vision.

COONEY, Marie managing director of Tipperary Natural Mineral Water.

CORKERY, Sean (1958-) b. Cork, vice-president of Worldwide Operations at AST - one of the top 10 PC makers (appointed in 1997). Joined Apple (1984) and helped set up its replenishment programme in 1988. Manager of AST in Limerick (1994-97), appointed to Information Society Commission, heading the commission enterprise sub-group.

CULLEN, Gary (1945-) b. Wicklow, new chief executive of Aer Lingus (appointed 24th September, 1998, took up office 1st October, 1998), succeeding Gary McGann. Was chief operations officer for Aer Lingus.

DE BRÚN, Garech (1939-) b Dublin, record producer. Founded Claddagh Records ('59), to record traditional Irish artists and music. Led to formation of world-famous traditional band The Chieftains ('63).

DESMOND, Denis b. Cork, concert promoter. Founded MCD. Promotions include Féile, Gael Force, REM, Oasis, U2.

DILGER, David (1957-) b. Dublin, chief executive of Greencore (joined in 1991). Former accountant with Stokes Kennedy Crowley (now KPMG), former finance director of Woodchester Investments.

DOHERTY, Moya (1958-) born Donegal, former television producer. Promoter of *Riverdance,* Co-founder and on the board of directors of Radio Ireland.

DORGAN, Sean (1952-) b. Cork, chief executive Designate of the IDA appointed September 1998, to take up office in January 1999, succeeding KIERAN McGOWAN. Chief Executive, Institute of Chartered Accountants in Ireland since 1995. Was 22 years in the Civil Service - former secretary general of the Department of Tourism and Trade (1993-95), secretary general of the Department of Industry and Commerce (1991-93). Member, National Economic and Social Council (1988-95).

DOWNES, Margaret (1934-) b. Mayo, first female director on the board of the Bank of Ireland. Chairwoman of BUPA Ireland, became partner in Coopers & Lybrand (1968), first woman in Ireland to be elected to the Institute of Chartered Accountants (1974) and became its first female president (1983).

DOYLE, Ray (1946-) b. Wexford, managing director of Cable Management Ireland since 1990. Former journalist with Independent Newspapers and chief news editor for three titles from 1970, as well as managing director of People Newspapers in Wexford (1980).

DUFFY, Michael chief executive of Bord Bia.

DUGGAN, Noel C. (1933-) b. Cork, businessman. Developed family hardware business into a lucrative structural steel trade, built equestrian centre - Green Glens - which hosts international showjumping and entertainment events. Succeeded in bringing the 1993 Eurovision Song Contest to Millstreet.

DULLY, John (1946-) b. Westmeath, director general of Bord Fáilte, appointed 21st August, 1998, after the resignation of Matt McNulty (April 1998). Was assistant secretary at the Department of Tourism, Sport and Recreation and former chairman of the monitoring committee for the EU Operational Programme.

DUNNE, Ben (1949-) b. Cork, former joint managing director and chief executive of Dunnes Stores, came to prominence again during the 'Payments to Politicians' Tribunal, after allegedly making contributions to CHARLIE HAUGHEY and MICHAEL LOWRY. Invested into the Westpoint Leisure centre (Co. Dublin) and residential property.

FITZPATRICK, Sean (1949-) chief executive of Anglo Irish Bank since 1986. A chartered accountant, he was financial accountant with the Irish Bank of Commerce from 1974 and joined Anglo Irish Bank in 1980.

FLINTER, Dan (1950-) b. Kildare, chief executive of Enterprise Ireland (the newly created state body consisting of Forbairt, The Irish Trade Board and the industrial training division of FÁS) officially appointed July 1st, 1998. Was chief executive of Forbairt (1994-98), joined IDA as a researcher (1973), took overall responsibility for planning (1986) and appointed executive director at IDA (1987). Managed the inward investment side of the IDA (1990-94).

FLOOD, Finbar (1938-) chairman of the Labour Court (appointed 1998). Former managing director with Guinness (1989-94), appointed Deputy Chairman of the Labour Court (1994).

FLYNN, Phil (1940-) b. Louth, chairman of ICC Bank. Board member of VHI, chairman of the Devolution Commission, board member of the National College of Industrial Relations, rights commissioner and trustee of Common Purpose, Consultant in Industrial Relations, including mediation and change management, former general secretary of IMPACT.

FOLEY, Carmel b. Westmeath, chief executive of the Employment Equality Agency since 1993. former chief executive of the Council for the Status of Women. Worked previously in the diplomatic corps in Luxembourg and Washington.

GERAGHTY, Des (1944-) vice-president of SIPTU (appointed 1997). Responsible for SIPTU's industrial relations strategy, including power to sanction strikes. Former Workers Party activist and Democratic Left MEP for Dublin. Has written books on various subjects including European Works Councils and singer Luke Kelly.

GILL, Caroline b. Dublin, the Insurance Ombudswoman (succeeded Paulyn Marrinan Quinn in August 1998). Chief executive of the Consumers' Association from 1991.

GILLESPIE, Alan chairman of the IDB and merchant banker. Appointed chairman of the IDB in January 1998, succeeding John McGuckian. Managing director of UK operations of Goldman Sachs.

GOAN, Cathal (1954-) b. Belfast, Ceannasaí of Teilifís na Gaeilge (chief executive and controller of programmes) which was launched October 31st 1996 by RTÉ) since 1996. Joined the Irish Placenames Commission before going to RTÉ in 1979. Worked as a producer on *Today at Five* and *The Pat Kenny Show.* Moved to television in 1988, where he produced *Today Tonight,* RTÉ's current affairs programme (1988). Edited *Cúrsaí,* the Irish language current affairs and arts programme. Appointed editor of Irish language programmes in 1990, involved in bringing the Irish language soap, *Ros na Rún,* to the RTÉ in 1993, currently being shown on TnaG.

GOODMAN, Larry (1939-) b. Louth, chief executive of

Irish Food Processors. In the mid-1980s, his company, Goodman International was the largest processor and exporter of beef in Europe. In 1992 the group went into examinership with debts of over £500 million and subsequently came under intense scrutiny from the beef tribunal. Goodman later regained control of the group through an agreement with its creditors.

GOVERNEY, Michael (1939-) general manager with the Conrad Hotel since 1990. Has been in the hotel business for 40 years, spending 11 years at the flagship of the Doyle Chain of hotels. Has now set up his own consultancy business.

HANLON, Noel (1940-) b. Longford, chairman of VHI and Aer Rianta (since 1992), chairman of VHI, former factory owner and car dealer. Chairman of Great Southern Hotels since 1995, appointed chair of Aer Lingus (1980), also director of the state bank.

HASKINS, Chris (1937-) b. Wicklow, non-executive chairman of Northern Foods (the largest food supplier to the UK retail market).

HASTINGS, Billy (1928-) b. Belfast, hotelier and chairman of Hastings Hotels Group which owns seven hotels in Northern Ireland.

HEALY, Tom (1950-) general manager and chief executive of the Irish Stock Exchange for the past 10 years. Worked with the Irish Trade Board, the IDA, the Civil Service. Deputy Chairman of The Committee of Chief Executives of the Federation of European Stock Exchanges

HEFFERNAN, Margaret (1943-) b. Cork, chief executive of Dunnes Stores, chain store founded by Ben Dunne Snr. (her father) in Cork and now allegedly worth in excess of £600 million. Her ownership of the business came from being a beneficiary of the Dunnes Trust. Together with her brother Frank, she has taken control of the running of the company since their brother Ben was sacked as chairman in 1994.

HESKETH, Ted managing director of Translink (Ulsterbus, Citybus & Northern Ireland Railways). joined Ulsterbus (1971) and appointed managing director of Ulsterbus, Citybus & Flexibus in 1988. Past President of the Bus and Coach Council (Scotland), the Confederation of Passenger Transport (UK), the Belfast chamber of Trade and Commerce.

HETHERINGTON, Rick (1947-) managing director and chief executive of TV3 (which came on air, September 1998). Joined CanWest (Canadian TV group) in 1992 and was its station manager (1994-98).

HOARE, Richard (1955-) general manager of First National Building Society (appointed in January 1998 with responsibility for retail banking). Former managing director of Bank of Ireland Finance, appointed general manager of Bank of Ireland Finance in 1996 after five years in group sales and marketing, appointed retail sales director in 1990, helped set up Lifetime Assurance in 1987. Former marketing director of Maguire and Patterson (1983-87).

HUGHES, Paddy (1939-) b. Laois, managing director of Bord na Móna since 1995. Began working in Bord na Móna as a clerk and laboratory assistant, working in departments such as fuel and horticulture division. Was chief executive of the peat energy division and chief operations officer.

HUSSEY, Derry (1935-) b. Dublin, chairman of VHI since 1997. Chartered Accountant. formerly worked with Dunlop Tyres and Massey Ferguson.

JOYCE, Brian (1941-) b. Galway, chairman of CIÉ since November 1995. Former accountant with RTÉ, former Chief Executive of An Bord Bainne (1978-89) and runs his own consultancy firm, Joyce Marketing, in addition to holding several directorships. Chairman of Norish, the Mater Private Hospital and Allegro Ltd. and non-executive director of EBS and Nutricia Ireland (baby foods group). Also chairman of IDACO, an international consultancy firm.

JOYCE, Gary b. Kilkenny, chairwoman of the state-owned ACC Bank since 1996. Originally marketing executive having previously set up her own advertising company.

KANE, Alfie (1945-) b. Derry, chief executive of Telecom Éireann. Formerly chief executive of British Telecom Northern Ireland, BT's district general manager for Manchester and head of BT's worldwide networks.

KEANE, Maurice (1946-) chief executive with Bank of Ireland

KELLY, Paul managing director with the Brown Thomas Group which includes Brown Thomas in Dublin, Cashs of Cork and Todds of Limerick. Former general manager, A-wear.

KEOGH Patrick chief executive at Bord Iascaigh Mhara. Former deputy chief executive, former worker with the Economic and Social Research Institute (ESRI).

KEOGH, Paul (1958-) managing director of Polygram Ireland. Worked with the Irish Productivity Centre, joined Polygram as managing director almost ten years ago. Now serving second term as chairman of The Irish Recorded Music Association. Polygram artists include Boyzone, U2, Pavarotti and Hanson.

LAMONT, Owen (1953-) b. Dublin, managing director of Cabletel Northern Ireland.

LYNCH, John (1942-) chief executive of FÁS, the state training agency. Former engineer with Dublin Gas, former chief executive of Bord Gáis, former chief executive of the Irish Productivity Centre, Former Director of Business Policy with the Confederation of Irish Industry (now IBEC).

LYNCH, Philip (1946-) chief executive of IAWS (Irish Agricultural Wholesale Society). Technical sales representative for Odlums, former chairman of An Post, chairman of An Bord Bia.

McCABE, Frank (1937-) b. Monaghan, general manager of Intel Ireland. Joined Intel in 1994 as vice-president, technology and manufacturing, was a former manager director of Digital's European operation.

McCANN, Eamon Concert promoter. Founded Wonderland Promotions. Has brought major rock events to Belfast, including Popmart (U2) in the Botanic Gardens, and also the May '98 U2/Ash Belfast Gig in support of the Belfast Agreement.

McCANN, Neil (1924-) b. Louth, chairman and chief executive of Fyffes plc. (Fyffes is the largest fruit importing and distributing business in Ireland and Spain and a major operator in other markets).

McCARTER, Willie (1947-) born Derry, current chairman of International Fund for Ireland since 1989. Former Managing Director at Fruit of the Loom (1987-

1997).

McCOLGAN, John director and chairman of Today FM (formerly Radio Ireland), director of Abhann Ltd, Tyrone Productions and *Riverdance*. Former head of entertainment at RTÉ, former controller of programmes at TV AM in London.

McCUMISKEY, Edward (1943-) chief executive of the Advertising Standards Authority for Ireland (ASAI) appointed July 1997. Joined the Civil Service as an Executive Officer (1959), working in the Office of the Revenue Commissioners, Departments of Finance and of Social Welfare (was director general of the Services Offices within the Department of Social Welfare in the mid 1980s) and appointed secretary general in the department in 1989.

McDONNELL, John b. Cork, general secretary of SIPTU - appointed April 1998.

McGOWAN, Kieran (1944-) b. Dublin, chief executive IDA Ireland since 1990, due to step down at end of 1998, joined Industrial Development Authority in 1967. Director of An Post National Lottery Board.

McGUINNESS, Paul (1951-) b. Germany. Manager of rock-group U2. Joined forces with the band in 1979 and has been associated with their phenomenal success ever since. A respected figure in music management worldwide. His Principle Management company also manages top acts such as P.J. Harvey.

MACKEY, Paddy (1942-) president of the Irish Trade Protection Association. A chartered accountant, he joined the Fianna Fáil party, elected to National Executive 1969-70 and later became vice-chairman and joint honorary auditor of Dublin North Central constituency. Expelled from Fianna Fáil, he was founder member of the Progressive Democrats in December 1985, of which he is treasurer and trustee. Helped set up AA Finance in 1988.

MAGAHY, Laura (1961-) b. Dublin, managing director of Temple Bar Properties. Joined as cultural and financial director (1991), becoming chief executive in 1994. Former chief executive of the Irish Film Centre.

MAGNIER, John (1952-) owner of Coolmore Stud in partnership with Vincent O'Brien and Robert Sangster, which controls about 42% of British and Irish thoroughbred horse breeding. Son-in-law of legendary trainer Vincent O'Brien. Operates in international finance markets with J.P. McManus and Joe Lewis. Former director of Irish Thoroughbred Marketing, member of the Turf Club, member of the Irish Horseracing Authority (IHA), former member of Seanad Éireann.

MAHER, Anne (1945-) b. Tipperary, chief executive of the Pensions Board since 1996. Former associate director of Corporate Business, Irish Life Plc. Former chairman of the Irish Association of Pension Funds. Member of the National Economic and Social Council and of the Commission on Public Service Pensions.

MALONE, Peter (1944-) b. Louth, managing director and chief executive of Jurys since 1989. Announced his retirement in April 1998, but will remain for another 16 months.

MANSWORTH, John President of the Vintners' Federation of Ireland since April 7th, 1998, succeeding Paul O'Grady.

MOLLOY, Pat (1938-) group chief executive of the

Bank of Ireland since 1991. Appointed manager of the group marketing department in 1971, manager of branch banking in 1973. Appointed managing director for the north, Britain and of group personnel in 1983 and head of the bank's retail division in 1988.

MORAN, Shay b. Galway, managing director and leading shareholder of Indigo. Manufacturer and former head of hi-tech security firm - Huet Security in 1975. Started a mobile phone company called Motorphones.

MORRIS, James (1948-) Chairman of TV3, Windmill Lane Pictures and The Mill.

MULHOLLAND, Joe (1940-) b. Donegal, managing director of television at RTÉ since April 1997. Joined RTÉ in 1969 as a producer-director; appointed head of current affairs (1980 was former editor of *Today Tonight*). Appointed controller of TV productions (1986), Director of News at RTÉ (1990). Former regular contributor to the French newspaper *Le Monde*.

O'BRIEN, Denis (1959-) chairman of Esat Telecom, founded in 1991. Started a home shopping channel on satellite television in (1988-90), won a licence to operate an independent local radio station in Dublin in 1989. Was personal assistant to Guinness Peat Aviation boss, Tony Ryan. Chairs a company called National Utilities and has a share in the broadcasting company, Communicorp.

O'CONNOR Brian (1949-) chairman of EWART (the Belfast-based property company). Founded CrestaCare (the British private nursing home group) in 1995. Chief executive of a Hong Kong-based services, property and industrial holding company - Allied Group (1992-95) Founded healthcare firm Quality Healthcare Asia, which owns IPNS Healthcare (a nursing agency) and Ultronics (a medical equipment company).

O'CONNOR, Marie (1954-) b. Dublin, first female partner in Price Waterhouse (joined in 1974), chartered accountant and barrister.

O'DRISCOLL, Sean (1957-) b. Cork, chief executive of Glen Dimplex. Worked for KPMG and joined Glen Dimplex in late 1989 as group finance director. Appointed deputy chief executive in 1996.

Ó GALLCHÓIR, Pól Ceannaire (Head) of Raidío na Gaeilge.

O'HARA, Ken (1939-) b. Dublin, chief executive of ESB since September 1997. Joined ESB in 1961, working as an engineer in Cork and Galway. Appointed district manager for Cork in 1979, regional manager of south west region (1985-87), director of customer operations in 1987 and managing director of Power Generation 1993-97.

O'KEEFFE, Michael chief executive of the Independent Radio and Television Commission. Joined IRTC in 1988 and has just been appointed for another seven-year period.

O'LEARY, Michael (1961-) chief executive of Ryanair. Was recently in the news for the industrial dispute with Ryanair's baggage handlers, which brought Dublin airport to a standstill early in 1998 and for disputes with Aer Rianta.

O'NEILL, Pat chief executive at Waterford-Avonmore. Joined Avonmore in 1973, becoming chief executive in 1984.

O'REILLY, Patrick (1942-) chief executive of Educational Building Society since 1992. Joined EBS in 1988. Formerly with Ulster Bank and Irish Merchants. Worked in the ICC Bank (1973-88) and was Head of Lending at ICC. Chairman of the Financial Services Industry Association and Council Member with Irish Red Cross.

O'REILLY, Tony (1936-) b. Dublin, chief executive of Heinz International, largest individual shareholder in Independent Newspapers, the investment company Fitzwilton and the mining operation Arcon. Married to Chryss Goulandris, a shipping heiress. A former rugby player, he won of 29 international caps in his record breaking 16 year career (1955-70).

O'ROURKE, Martin b. Limerick, managing director of BUPA Ireland (appointed in May 1996). Joined BUPA in 1994 after working for VHI for 25 years, of which he was assistant chief executive. Also independent management consultant (1995-96).

POWER, John (1946-) b. Limerick, chief executive of the Irish Hotels Federation (IHF) - the representative body of 750 hotels and guest houses throughout the Republic. Fellow of the Chartered Institute of Secretaries and Administrators, worked for Ryan Hotels for 27 years, where he was group company secretary and director.

PRATT, Maurice (1956-) managing Director Tesco Ireland since March 1997, joined Quinnsworth in 1982 as Marketing Manager became Managing Director Quinnsworth (1996).

QUINN, Feargal (1936-) b. Dublin, managing director of Superquinn Grocery Chain and member of the Seanad since 1993 (Independent). Opened his first store in Dundalk (1960). Former chairman of An Post (1979-90), the Irish Management Institute, Irish Quality Association, Finance Committee of Dublin Archdiocese and Governor of Dublin Skin and Cancer Hospital since 1972.

QUINN, Lochlan (1942-) chairman of Allied Irish Bank. Has a 26% share of Glen Dimplex, the domestic appliance maker. Has a 25% share in the Merrion Hotel in Dublin with his partner in Glen Dimplex, Martin Naughton. Brother of Ruari Quinn, leader of the Labour party.

QUINN, Michael (1947-) managing director of ICC Bank. Qualified as a management accountant and moved to ICC Bank in 1972. Headed Cork Office in 1980 for five years then returned to Dublin. Appointed Assistant General Manager in 1987 and managing director in 1991. Was an intercounty footballer and hurler with Westmeath.

QUINN, Sean (1946-) b. Fermanagh, head of Seán Quinn Group Ltd. (includes quarrying and cement products, an hotel and leisure division - consisting of pubs and hotels in Ireland and the UK - and a direct insurance division). In 1973, founded a company based on shale reserves under family farm. Net worth now estimated at £130 million.

REDMOND, Dr Mary (1951-) Founder of the Irish Hospice Foundation in 1985, which promotes Hospice care in Ireland. Also a director with Bank of Ireland and the first woman non-executive director with the Jefferson Smurfit Group.

ROBINSON, Gerard (1948-) b. Donegal, chairman of Granada television (LWT and ITN) and outgoing chairman of British Sky Broadcasting (BSkyB). Also chief executive of the media and leisure group Granada. Appointed chairman of the Arts Council of England (January 1998, taking up office in April 1998) also chairs development of the Royal Court Theatre.

RYAN, Tony (1936-) b. Tipperary, non-executive chairman of Ryanair (the independent airline controlled by his sons Cathal, Declan and Shane) since 1996. Founded Ryanair (1985), and Guinness Peat Aviation, now General Electric Capital Aviation Services (1975). Governor of the National Gallery of Ireland.

SHAW, Helen (1960) b. Dublin, RTÉ's director of radio. Formerly BBC Northern Ireland editor of radio current affairs.

SHERIDAN, Vincent (1948-) group general manager of Norwich Union (Ireland) since May 1991. A chartered accountant with Reynolds McCarron (1969-73), joined Norwich Union Insurance Group in May 1973, was made financial controller (1979), assistant manager (1982), general manager (1988).

SMURFIT, Michael (1936-) director and chief executive of Jefferson Smurfit (a worldwide packaging company) since 1977. Through his initiative and drive, Smurfits developed from a relatively small family business to a major multinational in packaging, print and financial services. Former chairman of Telecom Éireann, former chairman of the Racing Board and currently honorary counsul for Ireland in Monaco.

SMYTH, Desmond (1950) b. Co. Derry, managing director of Ulster Television since 1983. Joined UTV in 1975. Director of Northern Ireland Electricity.

SMYTH, Tony (1953-) General Secretary of the Irish League of Credit Unions (1996-). A former civil servant, he worked in various government departments such as agriculture, finance and the Comptroller and Auditor General's office.

SOMERS, Jimmy (1940-) b. Dublin, president of SIPTU. Became full-time trade union official with ITGWU (1960), appointed national group secretary for the food, drink, catering and chemicals sectors (1983) and became one of the union's assistant national executive officers when SIPTU was formed (elected vice-president of SIPTU - 1994).

STANLEY, Jim managing director of Bula Resources since April 1997. Joined the Mining Company Bula Ltd. in 1978 as as accountant and moved over to Bula in 1981 becoming secretary and later finance director.

SULLIVAN, Ned (1948-) chief executive of Avonmore Waterford Group, he succeeds Pat O'Neill. Was manager of food section - Coras Trachtala (1973-79), ACC's marketing development manager (1979-80), chief executive of Baileys (1980-95).

SUTHERLAND, Peter (1946-) b. Dublin, chairman of Goldman Sachs group (which is in line for a proposed flotation) since 1995 and chairman of BP. Former Attorney General (1981-82, 1982-84) in Fine Gael-Labour coalition governments, former European Commissioner (1985-89), former chairman of AIB (1989-93). Director General of the World Trade Organisation, appointed Director General of GATT in June 1993.

WALSH, Louis b. Dublin. Manager of Boyzone. Guided

band to unprecedented level of worldwide success for an Irish pop group.

WENT, David (1957-) b. Dublin, managing director of Irish Life. Chief executive of NatWest's Coutts Group in London since 1994, former chief executive of Ulster Investment Bank.

WHITAKER, Ken (1916-) born Down, author of the 1958 *Programme for Economic Expansion*. Governor of the Central Bank (1969-76)and president of ESRI. (1974-87).

WILSON, Martin (1950-) Chief Executive of the Ulster Bank (appointed 16th April 1998 to succeed Ronnie Kells). Qualified as a chartered accountant (1974) and was senior audit manager with Stokes Kennedy Crowley (now KPMG, 1975-78). Joined Ulster Bank in 1980 as financial controller of its investment subsidiary. Former chief accountant at Bell lines, becoming group treasurer, promoted to group treasurer of Ulster Bank (1989). Appointed to the bank's Board (1991), chief executive of Ulster Bank markets (1995) and deputy chief executive of Ulster Bank (1997).

WILSON, Ronnie (1948-) owner of Monaghan Mushrooms, Europe's largest mushroom business.

LAW & DEFENCE

BYRNE, Pat (1945-) b. Cork, Garda Commissioner (appointed in July 1996 for a seven year term succeeding Patrick Culligan). Joined the Garda Siochána in 1965 and was Deputy Commissioner (1994-96).

FLANAGAN, Ronnie (1950-) b. Belfast, Chief Constable of the RUC (since November 1996, succeeding Sir Hugh Annesly). Joined the RUC in 1970, appointed as a Detective Inspector in Special Branch in 1982. Promoted to Chief Inspector in 1983, Detective Superintendent in 1987, Chief Superintendent in 1990. Appointed to the Police Staff College at Bramshill, made Assistant Chief Constable in 1992 and Acting Deputy Chief Constable in 1995. As Deputy Chief Constable in 1996, conducted a fundamental review of the structure and organisation of the RUC. Awarded an OBE in 1996.

DENHAM, Mrs Justice Susan the first woman judge of the Supreme Court. Chairperson of the Courts Commission.

HALWARD, Robin (1957-) director general of Prison Services in Northern Ireland (appointed August 1998, succeeding Alan Shannon). Former governor of Strangeways Prison, currently head of the Secretariat to the Metropolitan Police Committee in the home Office.

HAMILTON, The Hon. Liam (1928-) b. Cork, Chief Justice of the Supreme Court (since 1994, due to retire in the year 2000). Called to the Bar in 1956, appointed to the Supreme Court in September (1994) and the High Court (1974). Former Labour Party candidate in the 1958 local elections in Dublin.

McMAHON, Lieutenant General Gerry b. Limerick, former Chief-of-Staff of Defence Forces (February 1995-August 1998).

NALLY, Derek (born Tipperary, 1936) Founder and Honourary President of the Irish Association of Victim Support. Former General Secretary of the Association of Garda Sergeants and Inspectors.

NOLAN, Phyllis the first female Garda superintendent.

NUGENT, James (1944-) b. Dublin, Chairman of the Bar Council since 1995. Barrister (called to the Bar in 1969). Senior Counsel to the hepatitis C inquiry (1997).

PHILPOTT, Corinne (1954-) first woman County Court Judge in Northern Ireland (appointed 24th April 1998). Called to the Bar in 1977 and took Silk as Queen's Counsel (1993).

SMYTH, Esmonde (1945-) President of the Circuit Court (appointed on March 31st 1998, succeeding Mr. Justice Diarmuid Sheridan and Mr. Justice Frank Spain). A Judge since June 1992, formerly of the Special Criminal Court and the Circuit Court. Member of the Board of the Judicial Studies Institute and of the Working Group on a Courts Commission.

STAPLETON, Lieutenant General Dave (1937-) b. Tipperary, newly Appointed Defence Forces Chief-of-Staff (succeeding Lieut-Gen GERRY McMAHON, 22nd August, 1998). Was Force Commander of the UN Disengagement Observer Force. Joined the Defence Forces as an officer cadet (1955), served with the UN in Congo (1962), Syria (1972), Lebanon (1985), Namibia (1989).

LITERATURE

BANVILLE, John (1945-) b. Wexford, novelist & literary editor of *The Irish Times*. Works include *Long Lankin* (1970), *Doctor Copernicus* (1976), *The Newton Letter* (1982), *Mefisto* (1986), *The Book of Evidence* (1989), *Ghosts* (1993), *Athena* (1995).

BARDWELL, Leland (1928-) b. India, reared Kildare; poet, novelist and playwright. Works include *The Mad Cyclist* (1970), *The Fly and the Bed Bug*, *Girl on a Bicycle*, *That London Winter*, *There We Have Been*, *Thursday*, *Open Ended Prescription*.

BARRY, Sebastian (1955-) b. Dublin; poet, novelist, playwright. One of the country's best playwrights, his dramatic works *The Steward of Christendom*, with DONAL McCANN in the lead role, and more recently *Our Lady of Sligo*, have garnered much critical acclaim in both the UK, US and Ireland. His novels include *Macker's Garden* (1982), *The Water Colourist* (1983), *Elsewhere* (1985), *The Engine of Owl-Light* (1987), *The Rhetorical Town* (1985) and *The Wanderings of Eneas McNulty* (1997).

BATEMAN, Colin (1962-) b. Northern Ireland, novelist. Formerly a journalist, his works include *Divorcing Jack* (1994), *Cycle of Violence* (1995), *Of Wee Sweetie Mice and Men* (1996). He has written the film screenplays of his first two novels, which were released in 1998 and is adapting another novel *Empire State* (1997) for film as well as writing original screenplays for filming.

BECKETT, Mary (1926-) b. Belfast, short-story writer and novelist; works include *A Belfast Woman*, *A Literary Woman* (1980), *Give Them Stones* (1987), and children's fiction *Hannah or Pink Baloons* (1995).

BELL, Sam Hanna (1910-) b. Glasgow, writer and radio producer. Works include *December Bride* (1951) and *The Hollow Ball* (1961) about urban poverty.

BINCHY, Maeve (1940-) b. Dublin, best-selling writer and columnist for *The Irish Times*. Works include

Light a Penny Candle, Echoes, Circle of Friends (made into film) Number one Bestsellers: *The Copper Beach, Firefly Summer, Glass Lake, Evening Class.*

BOLAND, Eavan (1944-) born Dublin, poet. Works include *New Territory* (1967), *The War Horse* (1975), *In Her Own Image* (1980), *Outside History* (1990).

BOLGER, Dermot (1959-) b. Dublin; writer, publisher and poet. Works include *Night Shift* (1985), *The Journey Home* (1990), *A Second Life* (1994); *Internal Exiles* (1986), *A Dublin Quartet* (1992) and *Finbar's Hotel* (1997), a book of short stories which he edited.

BORAN, Pat (1963-) b. Portlaoise, poet and playwright. Works include *The Unwound Clock* (1989), *History and Promise* (1990), *Strange Bedfellows* (1991).

BOYLAN, Clare (1948-) b. Dublin, novelist and journalist. Received an Oscar nomination for Best Short Film for her story *Making Waves* (1988). Works include *Holy Pictures, Last Resorts* (1984), *Black Baby* (1988), *Home Rule* (1993), *That Bad Woman* (1995),

BURROWS, Wesley (1930-) b. Belfast, popular writer for theatre and TV. Works include RTÉ's *The Riordans, Bracken, Glenroe.*

CASEY, Philip (1950-) poet, writer and playwright. Works include *Those Distant Summers* (1980), *The Year of the Knife* (1991), *Cardinal* (1990), *The Fabulists* (1994), *The Water Star* (1997).

CONNOR, Patrick Rearden (1907-) b. Dublin, novelist who writes under the pen-name Peter Malin. Best known for *Shake Hands with the Devil* (1933), later a film (1959). Works include *A Plain Tale from the Bogs* (1937), *The Singing Stone* (1951), *The House of Cain* (1952).

CONLON-MCKENNA, Marita (1956-) b. Dublin, popular children's author. Works include *The Hawthorn Tree* (1990), *Wildflower Girl* (1991), *Little Star* (1993), *No Goodbye* (1994), *Fields of Home* (1996).

CRONIN, Anthony (1928-) b. Wexford; poet, playwright and writer. Works include *The Life of Riley* (1964), *Dead as Doornails* (1976), *The End of the Modern World* (1989), *No Laughing Matter: The Life and Times of Flann O' Brien* (1989), *Samuel Beckett: The Last Modernist* (1996).

DALY, Ita (1944-) b. Leitrim, novelist and short story writer. Works include *The Lady with the Red Shoes* (1980), *A Singular Attraction* (1987), *All Fall Down* (1992), *Unholy Ghost* (1996).

D'ARCY, Margaretta (1934-) b. London, writer and playwright. Works include *Tell them Everything* (1961), *Awkward Corners, Prison-voice of Countess Markievicz* (1995), *Galway's Pirate Women, a Global Trawl* (1996).

DAWE, Gerald (1952-) b. Belfast; poet, literary journalist and lecturer. Works include *Heritages* (1976), *The Lundys Letter* (1985), *The Water Table* (1990), *Sunday School* (1991), *Heart of Hearts* (1995).

DEANE, Seamus (1940-) b. Derry; poet and novelist, head of Irish Studies at the University of Notre Dame, Indiana. Educated at QUB and Cambridge. English Literature Professor at UCD (1980-93). Author of *Rumours* (1977), *Celtic Revivals: Essays In Modern Irish Literature 1880-1980, A Short History Of Irish Literature and The French Revolution and Enlightenment In English Literature 1789-1832.* General Editor of the *Field Day Anthology Of Irish*

Writing. His semi-autobiographical *Reading In The Dark* (1996) was nominated for the 1996 Booker Prize and won the 1997 *Irish Times* International Fiction Prize and Irish Literature Prize: Fiction.

DELANEY, Frank (1942-) b. Tipperary; novelist, literary critic and broadcaster. Works include *My Dark Rosaleen* (1988), *The Sins of the Mothers* (1992), *Telling the Pictures* (1986).

DONLEAVY, James Patrick (1926-) b. New York of Irish parents, novelist. After serving in the U.S. navy in WWII, he studied in Trinity College Dublin and became friendly with Brendan Behan. His first and best-known book, *The Gingerman* (1955), was a picaresque tale. Became an Irish citizen in 1967 and has written several novels and plays.

DORCEY, Mary (1950-) b. Dublin, poet and novelist. Works include *Kindling* (1982), *Scarlett O'Hara* (1989), *A Noise from the Woodshed* (1989), *The Tower of Babel* (1996).

DORGAN, Theo (1953-) b. Cork, poet and broadcaster. Director of *Poetry Ireland.* Works include *Slow Air* (1975), *A Moscow Quartet* (1989), *The Ordinary House of Love* (1990), *Rosa Mundi* (1995).

DOYLE, Carol (1960s-) b. Dublin, screenwriter. Moved to Los Angeles and started writing. Her screenplay *Comfort Zone* is to star Will Smith and Harry Belafonte. Her screen adaptation of the Henry James novel, *Washington Square,* has been filmed while her screenplay of Veronica Guerin's life is being developed by Jerry Bruckheimer, a producer known for his work on Hollywood blockbusters.

DOYLE, Roddy (1958-) b. Dublin, novelist who focuses on working-class Dublin. Had major successes with The Barrytown Trilogy *(The Commitments, The Snapper* and *The Van* which were made into films), the 1993 Booker Prize-winning *Paddy Clarke Ha Ha Ha* and *The Woman who Walked into Doors.,* recently adapted for radio. Wrote TV series *The Family* and stage-plays *Brownbread* and *War.* Awarded an honorary doctorate by DCU in March 1998.

DURCAN, Paul (1944-) b. Dublin, poet and literary critic. Works include *The Berlin Wall Cafe* (1985), *Crazy About Women* (1991), *A Snail in my Prime* (1993), *Christmas Day* (1996).

EGAN, Desmond (1936-) b. Athlone; publisher, poet and teacher. Formed Goldsmith Press (1972). Works include *Midland* (1972), *Woodcutter* (1978), *A Song for my Father* (1989), *Snapdragon* (1992), *In the Holocaust of Autumn* (1994).

FARRELL, Bernard (1941-), b. Dublin, playwright. Worked for Sealink and began travelling and writing plays. His works have been compared to those of Alan Ayckbourn - both deal with the foibles and pretensions of the middle class. His plays feature as some of the most popular in Irish theatre and include *I Do Not Like Thee, Dr Fell* (1979), *All in Favour Said No!* (1981), *Petty Sessions* (1983), *Don Juan* (1984), *Then Moses Met Marconi* (1984), *Foreign Bodies* (1985-88), *Forty-Four Sycamore* (1992), *The Last Apache Reunion* (1993), *Happy Birthday Dear Alice* (1994) His latest play *Kevin's Bed* opened in 1998 in the Abbey.

FIACC, Pádraic (1924-) b. Belfast, poet and writer. Works include *Woe to the Boy* (1957), *By the Black*

Stream (1969), *Odour of the Blood* (1973, 1983), *Nights in the Bad Place* (1977), *Missa Terribilis* (1986), *Ruined Pages* (1994).

FLYNN, Mannix b. Dublin, actor and writer. After a turbulent childhood and teenage years, which included a spell in prison, became successful as an actor. However, heavy drinking interrupted his career. Has written an autobiography and performed his one man show, *Talking To The Wall*, during the 1997 Dublin Fringe Theatre Festival to much critical acclaim.

FRIEL, Brian (1929-) b. Tyrone, one of the world's foremost English language dramatists. Works include *Philadelphia, Here I Come!* (1964), *The Loves of Cass McGuire* (1966), *The Freedom of the City* (1973), *Faith Healer* (1979), *Translations* (1980),*Wonderful Tennessee* (1993). He founded the Field Day Theatre Co. in Derry with actor Stephen Rea to stage *Translations. Dancing at Lughnasa* (1990) was a huge success both critically and financially in theatres in Ireland, the UK and on Broadway, and was made into a critically acclaimed film by Pat O'Connor, released in 1998 and starring Meryl Streep.

GALVIN, Patrick (1927-) b. Cork, writer and playwright. Works include *And Him Stretched, Cry the Believers, The Devil's Own People, My Silver Bird;* Poetry: *The Wood-Burners, Man on the Porch* (1980), *The Death of Art O'Leary* (1994), *New and Selected Poems* (1996); Autobiography: *Song for a Poor Boy* (1991) and *Song for a Raggy Boy* (1992).

GÉBLER, Carlo (1954-) b. Dublin, novelist. His novels include *The Eleventh Summer* (1985), *Driving Through Cuba* (1988) - a non-fiction travel book,*The Cure* (1994) and *How To Murder a Man* (1998) about the violence of the Ribbonmen in Monaghan in 1854. Wrote translations of Strindberg's*The Dance of Death Part I* and *The Dance of Death Part II.* Films include*Country and Irish* (1982), *Francis Stuart* (1985), *The Glass Curtain: Inside an Ulster Community* (1991), *A Little Local Difficulty* (1995) and *The Base* (1997). Directed *Baseball in Irish History* (1996). Son of writers EDNA O'BRIEN and ERNEST GÉBLER.

GREACEN, Robert (1920-) b. Derry, poet and writer. Works include *The Bird* (1941), *One Recent Evening* (1944), *Even Without Irene* (1969), *A Garland for Captain Fox* (1975), *I, Brother Stephen* (1978), *Carnival at the River* (1990), *Collected Poems* (1995); *Even Without Irene* (1969, 1985).

HARTNETT, Michael (1941-) b. Limerick, poet and translator. Has written books of English and Irish poetry, including *Anatomy of a Cliché* (1968), *The Retreat of Ita Cagney/Cúlú Ide* (1975), *A Farewell to English* (1975), *Prisoners* (1977), *Maiden Street Ballad* (1980), *A Necklace of Wrens* (1987), *The Naked Surgeon* (1991), *The Killing of Dreams* (1992).

HEALY, Dermot (1947-) b. Westmeath, writer and poet. Works include *Fighting with Shadows* (1984), *The Long Swim* (1988), *Blood Wedding* (1989), *Curtains* (1990), *On Broken Wings* (1992), *The Ballyconnell Colours* - poetry (1992), *A Goat's Song* (1994) shortlisted for the Booker Prize, *The Bend for Home* (1996). Also edited the arts journal *Force 10.*

HEANEY, Seamus (1939-) b. Co. Derry, poet and Nobel laureate. Studied at QUB. Has held numerous lecturing posts - at Dublin, Belfast, Berkeley, Oxford and Harvard. Renowned for poems such as *Wintering Out* (1972). *Station Island* (1985). Won 1995 Nobel Prize for Literature. Created Saoi, the highest honour that can be bestowed on an Irish artist by his/her peers in 1998 and spoke eloquently on the tragedy of the Omagh bombing. Works include *Death of a Naturalist* (1966), *Door into the Dark* (1969), *Wintering Out* (1972), *North* (1976), *Preoccupations* (1980), *Station Island* (1984), *Seeing Things* (1991), *The Redress of Poetry* (1995), *The Spirit Level* (1996).

HIGGINS, Aidan (1927-) b. Kildare, writer. Works include *Asylum & Other Stories* (1960), *Langrishe, Go Down* (1966), *Images of Africa* (1971), *Balcony of Europe* (1972) shortlisted for Booker Prize, *Scenes From a Receding Past* (1977), *Bornholm Night-Ferry* (1983), *Ronda Gorge & Other Precipices* (1989), *Lions of the Grunewald* (1993), his autobiographical *Donkey's Years* (1995), *Flotsam and Jetsam* (1997).

HIGGINS, Rita Anne (1955-) b. Galway, poet and playwright. Works include *Goddess on the Mervue Bus* (1986), *Witch in the Bushes* (1988), *Philomena's Revenge* (1992), *Higher Purchase* (1996).

INGOLDSBY, Pat b. Dublin, playwright and poet. Plays include *Rhymin' Simon* (1979), *Spotty Grousler* (1982), *When Am I Gettin' My Clothes?*, *The Full Shilling.* Poetry: *You've Just Finished Reading This Title.*

JOHNSTON, Jennifer (1930-) born Dublin, novelist and playwright, daughter of writer Dennis Johnston. Works include *The Captains and the Kings* (1972), *The Gates* (1973), *How Many Miles to Babylon?* (1974), *The Railway Station Man* (1984 - later a film), *Shadows on our Skin* (1992) nominated for the Booker Prize.

KEANE, John B. (1928-) b. Kerry, playwright and novelist. Has lived for most of his life in Listowel, Co. Kerry, and his works focus around his native place. His plays are among some of the most popular on Irish stage, although he has been ignored by the critics. His plays enjoyed a revival during the 1980s and *The Field* was made into a major film, starring Richard Harris. Works include the popular plays Sive, *The Year of the Hiker, The Field* (also screenplay), *Big Maggie, Moll;* Novels: *The Bodhran Makers, A High Meadow,* the *Letters* Series, as well as his autobiography, *Man of the Triple Name.*

KEENAN, Brian (1950-) b. Belfast; writer, teacher and former Beruit hostage (1986-90). Won the *Irish Times* Prize for non-fiction (1993), among other accolades, for his book *An Evil Cradling* (1992).

KENNELLY, Brendan (1936-) b. Kerry, poet and academic. Has lectured on English literature in TCD as well as in colleges in the US. Works include *My Dark Fathers, Good Souls to Survive, Love Cry, The Voices, Islandman, The House that Jack Didn't Build, The Boats are Home, Cromwell, Judas.*

KEYES, Marion (1963-) best-selling novelist. Debut novel *Watermelons* (1995), followed by *Lucy Sullivan is Getting Married* (1997). Lives and works in London.

KIBERD, Declan (1951-) b. Dublin; lecturer and writer. Appointed chair of Anglo-Irish Literature at UCD in 1997, he has lectured on Irish culture in over 20 countries and has prepared literary scripts for the BBC. Wrting both in English and Irish, his books include *Synge and the Irish Language, Men and Feminism in Modern Literature* and *Idir Dhá Chultúr*. His *Inventing Ireland* places literary analysis within its historical/political context and has won the 1997 *Irish Times* Irish Literature Prize for non-fiction.

KIELY, Benedict (1919-) b. Tyrone, journalist and writer. Works include *Counties of Contention: a Study of Irish Partition* (1945),*Call for a Miracle* (1950), *The Cards of the Gambler: a Folktale* (1953), *There was an Ancient House* (1955), *The Captain with the Whiskers* (1960), *Dogs Enjoy the Morning* (1968), *A Cow in the House* (1978), *A Letter to Peachtree* (1987), *The Trout in the Turn Hole* (1995).

KILROY, Thomas (1934-) b. Co. Kilkenny, playwright and writer. Initially an academic but resigned to devote himself full time to writing. Works include *The O'Neill, The Death and Resurrection of Mr. Roche, Tea and Sex and Shakespeare, Talbot's Box* (1977), *Double Cross*(1986), *Wife to Mr. Wilde, Farmers* (TV), *Gold in the Streets* (film 1997), *The Big Chapel* shortlisted for the 1971 Booker Prize, a much-lauded translation of Chekhov's *The Seagull* (1981), a version of Pirandello's *Six Characters in Search of an Author* (1996) and *The Secret Fall of Constance Wilde* which ran at the Abbey Theatre in 1998 to critical acclaim.

KINSELLA, Thomas (1928-) b. Dublin, poet. Worked for a time as a civil servant, left to lecture in the US. Also set up publishing houses. remembered for *Another September* and *Butcher's Dozen*, a poem reflecting on Derry's Bloody Sunday in 1972. Works include an acclaimed translation of *The Táin* (1969), *Vertical Man* (1973), *One* (1974), *Fifteen Dead* (1979), *Blood and Family* (1988), *From Centre City* (1990), *Open Court* (1993)

LEONARD, Hugh columnist and playwright. Works include *Da,* which was made into a film (1988) starring Martin Sheen. Retired from writing his long-running column for the *Sunday Independent* in October 1998.

LIDDY, James (1934-) poet and writer. Professor of English at University of Wisconsin, Milwaukee. Works include *In a Blue Smoke* (1964), *A Munster Song of Love and War* (1971), *Comyn's Lay* (1978), *Chamber Pot Music* (1982), *At the Grave of Fr. Sweetman* (1984), *Young Men Go Out Walking* (1986), *A White Thought in a White Shade* (1987), *Collected Poems* (1994).

LONGLEY, Michael (1939-) b. Belfast, one of Ireland's most important contemporary poets. Worked as a poetry critic for The *Irish Times.* Has not shirked his Northern heritage, his poetry addressing head on the terrors of the Northern conflict. Poetry collections include *No Continuing City* (1969), *An Exploded View* (1973), *Man Lying on a Wall* (1976), *The Echo Gate* (1979), *Gorse Fires, The Ghost Orchid, Poems 1963-1983, Tuppeny Stung.*

McCABE, Eugene (1930-) b. Glasgow, playwright and novelist. Works include the *Victims* trilogy of TV plays based on the North - *Heritage, Siege and Cancer* - for RTÉ, *The King of the Castle* (1964), *Breakdown* (1966), *Swift* (1969), *Pull Down a Horseman* (1979), *Roma* (1979), *Death and Nightingales* (1992).

McCABE, Pat (1955-) b. Clones, writer and script-

writer. Works include the novel*The Butcher Boy* (1992) which was nominated for the Booker Prize and made into a successful film by Neil Jordan, *Music on Clinton Street* (1986), *The Dead School* (1995) and *Breakfast on Pluto,* nominated for the 1998 Booker Prize.

McCAFFERTY, Nell (1944-) b. Derry, journalist. Reporter with *The Irish Times* (1970-80), *Hot Press* columnist and regular broadcaster. Known for feminist and nationalist views. Works include *In the Eyes of the Law* (1981), *A Woman to Blame* (1985),*Goodnight Sisters... (1988), Peggy Deery* (1989).

McCARTHY, Thomas (1954-) b. Waterford, poet and writer. Works include *The First Convention* (1978), *The Sorrow Garden* (1981), *Seven Winters in Paris* (1989), *Without Power* (1991), *Asya and Christine* (1992), *The Lost Province* (1996).

McCOURT, Frank b. US, reared Limerick, retired school teacher who won international acclaim for the 1997 Pulitzer-winning *Angela's Ashes,* which is being filmed in Ireland.

McDONAGH, Martin (1971-) b. London of Irish parents, playwright. Best known for the *Leenane Trilogy* of plays, first staged in Galway by the Druid Theatre and then transferred to London. He was nominated, along with the Irish cast of *The Beauty Queen of Leenane,* for a Tony Award - the top award in US theatre. It was the first new play to receive six nominations. The play won four Tony's. His plays deal with the brutal and violent side of human nature and have an dark humour and an innate feel for the vernacular of Connemara.

McGAHERN, John (1934-) b. Dublin, novelist and playwright. Works include *The Barracks* (1963), *The Dark* (1965), *Nightlines* (1970), *Getting Through* (1978), *The Pornographer* (1980), *The Rockingham Shoot* (1987), *Amongst Women* (1990) recently shown as a four-part drama series on RTÉ and BBC, *The Power of Darkness* (1991), *Collected Stories* (1992).

McGUCKIAN, Medbh (1950-) b. Belfast, writer and poet. Works include *The Flower Master* (1982), *Venus and the Rain* (1984), *The Big Striped Golfing Umbrella* (1985), *On Ballycastle Beach* (1988), *The Grateful Muse* (1997).

McGUINNESS, Frank (1953-) b. Buncrana, playwright and lecturer at Maynooth. Works include *The Factory Girls* (1983), *Observe the Sons of Ulster Marching Towards the Somme* (1985), *Scout* (TV 1987), *The Hen House* (TV 1989), *The Bread Man* (1990), *Someone Who'll Watch Over Me* (1992), *The Bird Sanctuary* (1994), *A Doll's House* (translation 1996). Wrote the screenplay for the film version of Brian Friel's *Dancing at Lughnasa* (1997).

MacINTYRE, Tom (1931-) b. Cavan, poet and writer. Works include *The Charollais* (1969), *Through the Bridewell Gate* (Documentary 1971), *Dance For Your Daddy* (1987), *Fleur-de-lit* (1990), *Kitty O'Shea* (1992), *Chichadee* (1993),*Good Evening, Mr. Collins* (1995).

MacLAVERTY, Bernard (1942-) b. Belfast, writer for radio, TV, film. Works include *Secrets* (1977), *Lamb* (1980), *A Time to Dance* (1982), *Cal* (1983) - all produced for the screen; *The Great Profundo* (1987), *The Real Charlotte* (1991). His book *Grace Notes* (1997) has been released to wide acclaim.

McPHERSON, Conor (1972-) b. Dublin, scriptwriter and playwright. Plays: *The Good Thief, This Lime Tree Bower, St. Nicholas* and *The Weir.* Screenplays: *I Went Down* (1997), which won the best screeplay at the San Sabastian Film Festival).

MAHON, Derek (1941-) b. Belfast; poet. He worked as a teacher and journalist. Among his influences are Louis MacNeice and WH Auden. Works include *Twelve Poems* (1965), *Poems 1962-1978* (1979), *The Hunt by Night* (1982), *A Kensington Notebook* (1984),*Selected Poems* (1990), *The Bacchae* (1991), *The Hudson Letter* (1995), *Racine's Phaedra* (1996).

MARCUS, David (1929-) journalist, editor and writer. Former editor of *Irish Writing* (1946-54) and *Poetry Ireland* (1948-54). Literary editor of *Irish Press* (1968-85).

MEEHAN, Paula (1955-) born Dublin, poet. Works include *Return and No Blame* (1984), *Reading the Sky* (1986), *The Man Who Was Marked by Winter* (1991), *Pillow Talk* (1994).

MHAC an tSAOI, Máire (1922-) b. Dublin, Irish language poet. Works include *Dhá Scéal Artúraíochta* (1946), *Margadh na Saoire* (1956), *A Heart Full of Thought* (1959), *Codladh an Ghaiscígh* (1973), *An Galar Dubhach* (1980) and *An Cion go dtí Seo* (1987).

MONTAGUE, John (1929-) b. New York, reared Tyrone; poet and writer. Works include *Poisoned Lands* (1961), *Death of a Chieftain* (1964, 1978), *A Chosen Light* (1967), *The Rough Field* (1972), *The Great Cloak* (1978), *The Dead Kingdom* (1984), *Mount Eagle* (1988), *Time in Armagh* (1993), *Collected Poems* (1995).

MOORE, Brian (1921-) b. Belfast, writer, published more than 20 novels. Although he moved to Canada and then North America as a young man, his books continue to deal with his Irish culture. Works include *The Lonely Passion of Judith Hearne* (1955 - later a film 1987),*The Luck of Ginger Coffey* (1960), *The Emperor of Ice-Cream* (1965), *I am Mary Dunne* (1968), *Fergus* (1970), *Catholics* (1972) later a film, *The Doctor's Wife* (1976), *The Mangan Inheritance* (1979), *Cold Heaven* (1983), *Black Robe* (1985 - also a film), *The Colour of Blood* (1987), *Lies of Silence* (1990),*The Statement* (1995), *The Magician's Wife* (1997). Has won numerous awards and nominated three times for the Booker Prize.

MULDOON, Paul (1951-) b. Portadown, poet. His first collection of poems was published while he was a university student. Worked as a radio producer for BBC Northern Ireland (1973-86), moved to the US and has held various university teaching posts - currently the director of the Creative Writing Program at Princeton. Won the 1995 T.S. Eliot Poetry Prize for *The Annals of Chile.* Works also include *New Weather* (1973), *Mules* (1977), *Why Brownlee Left* (1980), *Quoof* (1983), *Meeting the British* (1987), *Madoc: A Mystery* (1990). His *New Selected Poems - 1968-1994*, with its intellectual wordplay and literary cross-references, won the 1997 *Irish Times* Irish Literature Prize: Poetry.

MULKERNS, Val (1925-) b. Dublin, novelist. Associate editor of *The Bell.* Columnist for the *Evening Press* (1968-83). Works include *Antiquities* (1978), *An Idle Woman* (1980), *The Summerhouse* (1984), *Very Like*

a Whale (1986), *A Friend of Don Juan* (1988).

MURPHY, Dervla (1931-) b. Waterford, travel writer and literary critic. Works include *Full Tilt: Ireland to India on a Bicycle* (1965), *A Place Apart* (1978), *Eight Feet in the Andes* (1983), *Transylvania and Beyond* (1992), *The Ukimwi Road* (1993).

MURPHY, Tom (1935-) b. Tuam, playwright and novelist. A prolific writer, he has written over 15 plays, which are regularly produced on Irish stage. Works include *The Morning After Optimism* (1971), *A Whistle in the Dark, Famine, Conversations on a Homecoming, The Patriot, The Gigli Concert* (1983), *Bailegangaire* (1985), *The Seduction of Morality, She Stoops to Folly* (1995), *The Wake* (1996).

Ní CHUILLEANÁIN, Eiléan (1942-) b. Cork, writer. Founder editor of *Cyphers.* Works include *Acts and Monuments* (1972), *Site of Ambush* (1975), *The Second Voyage* (1977), *The Rose-Geranium* (1981), *The Magdalene Sermon* (1989), *The Brazen Serpent* (1994).

Ní DHOMHNAILL, Nuala (1952-) b. England, reared Ireland. Gaelic poet, playwright and broadcaster. Works include *An Dealg Droighin* (1981), *Féar Suaithinseach* (1984), *Rogha Dánta/Selected Poems* (1986, 1988, 1990), *The Astrakhan Cloak* (1992), *Cead Aighnis* (1997), Screenplays; *An Gobán Saor* (1993), *An t-Anam Mothála/The Feeling Soul* (1994).

NOLAN, Christopher (1965-) poet and short story writer. Born severely brain-damaged and physically disabled. Created a poignant collection of short stories and poems *Dam-burst of Dreams* (1981). He mastered typing with a stick strapped to his forehead. Autobiography *Under the Eye of the Clock* (1987) has won widespread critical acclaim. His latest novel is due out in 1999.

O'BRIEN, Edna (1932) b. Clare, writer and playwright. Her books were the first to broach the contemporary themes of women in the Ireland of the 1960s and were very controversial at the time. Works include *The Country Girls* (1960), *Girl with Green Eyes* (1962), *Girls in their Married Bliss* (1964), *August is a Wicked Month* (1965), *Johnny I Hardly Knew You* (1977), *Returning* (1982), *A Fanatic Heart* (1985).

O'BRIEN, Patrick novelist and translator. His writing is characterized by heavily researched books. Best known for his Aubrey Maturin tales. His book, *The Yellow Admiral*, was a best-seller in Britain. Has written around 30 books of fiction and 30 translations (translated the blockbuster *Papillon* from the original French into English).

O'CARROLL, Brendan (1955-) b. Dublin; author, script-writer and comedian. Has had two successful radio series and three best selling books *The Mammy* (1994),*The Chisellers* (1995),*The Granny* (1996). Presents RTÉ's quiz *Hot Milk and Pepper* wrote and directed two stage-plays -*The Course* (1995), *Grandad's Sure Lily's Still Alive* (1997). Film versions made in 1998 of *The Mammy,* starring Angelica Huston, and his latest novel *Sparrow's Trap*

Ó COISTEALBHA, Seán (1932-) b. Galway, actor, poet and playwright. Works include *Aon Phionta Uisge* (1966), *An Tinceára Buí* (1967), *Ortha na Seirce* (1967), *An tÉan Cuaiche* (1968), *A Book of Poetry and Verse* (1987), *An Mhéir Fhada* (1993).

O'CONNOR, Joseph (1963) b. Dublin, writer and playwright. Debut novel *Cowboys and Indians* (1991) short-listed for Whitbread Prize. Works include *Desperados* (1994), *True Believers, Even the Olives are Bleeding* (1986), *The Secret World of the Irish Male* (1994), *Sweet Liberty: Travels in Irish America* (1996).

O'CONNOR, Ulick (1929-) b. Dublin, playwright, poet and writer. Works include *The Dream Box* (1972), *Lifestyles* (1973), *The Dark Lovers* (1975), *The Emperor's Envoy* (1976), *The Grand Inquisitor*, (1977), *Irish Tales and Sagas* (1981), *Execution* (1985), *A Trinity of Two* (1988), *Joyicity* (1989), *One is Animate* (1990).

O DIREÁIN, Máirtín (1910-) b. Aran Islands, poet. Works include *Rogha Dánta* (1949), *Ó Mórna agus Dánta Eile* (1957), *Feamainn Bhealtine* (1961), *Ar Ré Dhearóil* (1962), *Cloch Choirnéil* (1967), *Crainn is Cairde* (1970), *Ceacht an Éin* (1984), *Tacar Dánta/ Selected Poems* (1984), *Craobhóg: Dán* (1986).

O'DRISCOLL, Denis (1954-) b. Thurles, poet and former editor of *Poetry Ireland Review*. Works include *Kist* (1982), *Hidden Extras* (1987), *Long Story Short* (1993), *The Bottom Line* (1994).

Ó FAOLÁIN, Nuala (1932-) b. London, novelist. Her novel, *Are You Somebody*, dominated the best-seller lists in Ireland in 1997.

Ó FLOINN, Críostóir (1927-) b. Limerick; playwright, writer and poet. Works include *In Dublin's Fair City* (1959), *Is É Dúirt Polonius* (1967), *Oineachlann* (1968), *Ó Fhás go hAois* (1969), *Sanctuary Island* (1971), *Banana* (1979), *An Spailpín Fánach* (1988), *A Poet in Rome* (1992), *Seacláidí Van Gogh* (1996).

O'GRADY, Desmond (1935-) b. Limerick, poet and translator. Works include *Chords and Orchestrations* (1956), *Reilly* (1961), *The Dark Edge of Europe* (1967), *The Dying Gaul* (1968), *Hellas* (1971), *Separations* (1973), *Alexandria Notebook* (1989), *Tipperary* (1991), *My Fields this Springtime* (1993).

ORMSBY, Frank (1947-) b. Enniskillen, poet and Northern Irish poetry editor. Poetry collections include *Ripe for Company* (1971), *Spirit of Dawn* (1973), *A Store for Candles* (1977), *Being Walked by a Dog* (1978), *A Northern Spring* (1986), *The Ghost Train* (1995).

Ó SEARCAIGH, Cathal (1956-) b. Donegal, Irish language poet and playwright. Works include *Mion Tragóide Chathrach* (1976), *Tuirlingt* (1979), *Súile Shuibhne* (1983), *Mairimid Leis na Mistéirí* (1989), *Tóin ag Titim as as tSaol* (1991), *An Bealach 'na Bhaile / Homecoming* (1993), *Na Buachaillí Bána* (1996).

Ó SIADHAIL, Mícheál (1947-) b. Dublin, distinguished bilingual poet. Works include *Spring Night* (1983), *The Image Wheel* (1985), *The Chosen Garden* (1990), *Hail! Madam Jazz: New and Selected Poems* (1992), *A Fragile City* (1995).

PAULIN, Tom (1949-) b. Leeds, reared Belfast, poet, playwright and academic. Works include *A State of Justice* (1977), *Personal Column* (1978), *The Strange Museum* (1980), *Liberty Tree* (1983), *Fivemiletown* (1985), *Walking a Line* (1994).

PLUNKETT, James (1920) b. Dublin, novelist and playwright. Works include *The Trusting and the Maimed*,

Strumpet City (later a TV series), *Farewell Companions, The Gems She Wore, The Risen People, Collected Short Stories, The Boy on the Back Wall, The Circus Animals*.

PURCELL, Deirdre (1945-) b. Dublin, novelist and formerly an RTÉ news presenter. Has written five best sellers - *A Place of Stones* (1991), *Falling For a Dancer* (1993, made into a TV drama series in 1998), *Francey* (1994), *Sky* (1995), *Love, Like Hate Adore* (1997). Collaborated on *The Time of My life: An Autobiography* (1989) with Gay Byrne.

REID, Christina (1942-) b. Belfast, playwright. Works include *Did You Hear the One About the Irishman...?* (1980),*The Belle of Belfast City*, *Joyriders*, *The Last of a Dying Race* (1986), *My Name, Shall I Tell You My Name?* (1987).

SCANLAN, Patricia (1956-) born Dublin, popular fiction writer. Works include *City Girl* (1990), *Apartment 3B* (1991), *Finishing Touches* (1992), *City Woman* (1993), *Foreign Affairs* (1994), *Promises, Promises* (1997).

SCOTT, Michael b. Dublin, writer, published over 60 books since 1981 on celtic mythology, horror and the supernatural. Works include *The Last of the Fianna, The Seven Treasures, House of the Dead, October Moon, Wolf Man, Gemini Game*.

SIMMONS, James (1933-) b. Derry, poet and playwright. Founded *The Honest Ulsterman* (1968). Works include *Late but in Earnest* (1967), *Judy Garland and the Cold War* (1976), *Constantly Singing* (1980), *From the Irish* (1985), *The Cattle Rustling* (1992), *Mainstream* (1995).

SIRR, Peter (1960-) b. Waterford, poet and editor. Irish Writers' Centre Director. Works include *Marginal Zones* (1984), *Talk, Talk* (1987), *Ways of Falling* (1991), *The Ledger of Fruitful Exchange* (1995).

SMITH, Paul (1935-) b. Dublin, novelist and playwright. Works include *Esther's Altar* (1959), *The Countrywoman* (1961), *The Stubborn Season* (1962), *Stravaganza* (1963), *Annie* (1972), *Miss Lemon* (1986), *Trudy on Sunday* (1987).

STUART, Francis (1902-) b. Australia; writer, poet and playwright. Works include *We Have Kept the Faith* (1923), *Women and God* (1931), *The Angel of Pity* (1935), *The Pillar of Cloud* (1948), *Redemption* (1949), *The Flowering Cross* (1950), *The Pilgrimage* (1955), *Black List, Section H* (1971), *Memorial* (1973), *A Hole in the Head* (1977), *States of Mind* (1983), *Faillandia* (1985), *A Compendium of Lovers* (1990), *Collected Poems* (1992). Although elected Saoi, one of the highest honours that can be bestowed on an Irish writer, controversy has dogged him, with allegations of anti-Semitism being levelled at his work.

SWEENEY, Matthew (1952-) b. Donegal, poet and children's writer. Works include *A Dream of Maps* (1981), *A Round House* (1983), *The Lame Waltzer* (1985), *The Chinese Dressing Gown* (1987), *Blue Shoes* (1989), *Fatso in the Red Suit* (1995).

TAYLOR, Alice (1938-) b. Cork, writer. Works include *To School through the Fields* (1988), *Quench the Lamp* (1990), *Secrets of the Oak* (1991), *The Village* (1992), *The Woman of the House* (1997).

TÓIBÍN, Colm writer. Works include *Walking Along the Border* (1987)*The South* (1990), *Homage to*

Barcelona (1990), Dubliners (1990), The Heather Blazing (1992), The Sign of the Cross: Travels in Catholic Europe (1994), The Story of the Night (1996).

TREVOR, William (1928-) b. Cork, Author. Works include The Old Boys, The Ballroom of Romance (later a film 1981), Excursions in the Real World (1993).

WALL, Mervyn (1908-) b. Dublin, writer and playwright. Works include Alarm Among the Clerks (1940), The Unfortunate Fursey (1946), Leaves for the Burning (1952), No Trophies Raise (1956), Forty-Foot Gentlemen Only (1963), Hermitage (1982), The Garden of Echoes (1982).

WOODS, Macdara (1942-) born Dublin; poet, editor and translator. Works include Drinks in a Bar in Marrakesh (1970), Early Morning Matins (1973), The Hanged Man Was Not Surrendering (1990), Notes from the Countries of Blood-Red Flowers (1994), Selected Poems (1996).

MUSIC

Rock / Pop

ASLAN Formed Dublin (1982). Enduring rock band in Ireland. Band members: Christy Dignam, Billy McGuinness, Tony McGuinness, Alan Downey, Joe Jewell. Albums: Feel No Shame ('88 - Irish No. 1); Goodbye Charlie Moonhead ('94 - Irish Top 10); Here Comes Lucy Jones ('97). Major singles: This Is ('86); Crazy World ('93 - Single of the Year in 1993 Hot Press Awards); Lucy Jones Part 2 ('97); Hurt Sometimes ('97); This Is 98 ('98). Band split up in 1988. Dignam went solo, reformed as Aslan in 1993.

ASH Formed Downpatrick (1991). Band influenced by new-wave punk. Band members: Tim Wheeler, Mark Hamilton, Rick McMurray, Charlotte Hatherley. First Irish rock band to have debut album premiere at No. 1 in UK charts. Albums: 1977 ('96 - Irish and UK No. 1); Nu-clear Sounds ('98) and debut mini-album Trailer ('94). Major singles: Kung Fu ('95); Girl from Mars ('95); Goldfinger ('96); Oh Yeah ('96) - 'Best Irish Single' at 1996/7 Hot Press Awards; A Life Less Ordinary ('97) - won 'Best Irish Single' at 1998 Hot Press Awards, having been awarded Best Irish Band in '96 and '97; Jesus Says ('98).

BOOMTOWN RATS Formed Dublin (1975). Ireland's punk pioneers. Band members: BOB GELDOF, Johnnie Fingers, Gerry Cott, Pete Briquette, Gerry Roberts, Simon Crowe. Albums include: The Boomtown Rats ('76), A Tonic for the Troops ('78),The Fine Art of Surfacing ('79), Mondo Bongo ('80). Major singles: Looking After No. 1 ('77), Rat Trap (UK No. 1 - '78), I Don't Like Mondays (UK No. 1 - '79).

BOYZONE Formed Dublin (1993). Most successful pop/boy-band in Irish music, dominating teenage music market in Ireland and UK. Band members: RONAN KEATING, Keith Duffy, Steven Gately, Mikey Graham, Shane Lynch. Accumulated numerous No. 1 album and singles in Ireland and UK in last five years. Albums: Said And Done; A Different Beat; Where We Belong ('98: Irish and UK No. 1). Major singles: Love Me for a Reason ('94); Working My Way Back to You ('94); Key to My Life ('95); A Different Beat; All That I

Need ('98); No Matter What ('98 - No. 1).

B*WITCHED Founded Dublin. All-girl pop band, first Irish band ever to have a UK No. 1 with a début single, and youngest girl group ever to have UK No. 1. Second single release Rollercoaster also reached No. 1 in Britain. Band Members: Lindsay Armaou, Sinéad O'Carroll, Edele and Keavy Lynch. Singles: C'est La Vie ('98 - Irish No. 1), Rollercoaster ('98 - Irish No. 2).

CORRS, The Formed Louth (1990s). Band members: Andrea, Sharon, Caroline and Jim Corr. Hugely successful pop/soft-rock band who have achieved commercial success in Ireland, UK, Australia, Spain, Japan etc. Albums (both Irish No. 1s): Forgiven Not Forgotten ('95), Talk on Corners (UK No. 1 - '97). Major singles: Runaway; Love To Love You; Forgiven, Not Forgotten ('95); Only When I Sleep; What Can I Do; I Never Loved You Anyway; Dreams (entered UK Charts at No. 6 - '98).

CRANBERRIES, The Formed Limerick (1990). One of Ireland's most commercially successful musical exports since U2. Band members: Dolores O'Riordan, Noel Hogan, Mike Hogan, Fergal Lawler. Albums: Everybody Else Is Doing it, So Why Can't We? (UK No. 64, US No. 18 - '94); No Need To Argue (UK No. 2, US No. 6 - '94); To The Faithful Departed ('96). Major singles: Dreams ('92), Linger (US No. 8 - '93), Zombie (UK No. 14 - '94).

DEVLINS, The Founded Dublin (1990s). Soft-rock band, critically acclaimed in America. Band members: Colin Devlin, Peter Devlin, Sean Devitt. Two studio albums: Drift; Waiting ('97). Major singles: I Almost Made You Smile, Waiting.

DIVINE COMEDY, The See NEIL HANNON.

FRANK & WALTERS, The Formed Cork (1990). Idiosyncratic alternative pop band. Band members: Paul Lineham, Niall Lineham, Ashley Keating.Two studio albums: Trains, Boats and Planes ('92); Grand Parade ('97). Major single: This Is Not A Song ('92).

HORSLIPS, The Formed Dublin (1970). Legendary Celtic-rock band, enjoyed massive critical and commercial success in Ireland with a huge live following in Ireland, Europe and the US. Band members: Charles O'Connor, John Fean, Barry Devlin, Jim Lockhart, Eamon Carr. Line-up originally also included Declan Synott. Albums: Happy to Meet, Sorry to Part ('73); The Tain (73); Dancehall Sweethearts ('74); Unfortunate Cup of Tea ('75); Drive the Cold Winter Away ('75); The Book of Invasions (UK Top 40 hit - '76); Aliens ('77); The Man Who Built America ('79); Short Stories / Tall Tales ('80). Major singles: Johnny's Wedding ('72); Green Gravel ('72); The Man Who Built America ('77). Also:The Belfast Gigs - live ('90). Several compilations have been released including: Horslips Story - Straight From The Horse's Mouth ('89). Disbanded 1980.

HOTHOUSE FLOWERS Formed Dublin (1985). Traditional-rock band who enjoy considerable commercial success in Ireland and UK. Band members: Liam Ó Maonlaí, Fiachra Ó Braonáin, Peter O'Toole. Original line-up included: Leo Barnes, Jerry Fehily. Disbanded 1993, reformed 1997. Albums (all Irish No. 1s except Born): People (UK No. 2 - '88); Home (UK No. 5 - '90); Songs From the Rain (UK No. 7 - '93); Born ('98). Major singles: Love Don't Work This Way

('87); *Don't Go* ('87); *I Can See Clearly Now* ('90); *You Can Love Me Now* ('98).

SAWDOCTORS, The Formed Tuam (1989), one of Ireland's best loved traditional-rock band with big live following here and in UK. Band members: Davy Carlton, Leo Moran, Pearse Doherty, John Donnelly. Original line-up included John Burke and Tony Lambert. Albums: *If This Is Rock and Roll I Want My Old Job Back* ('90); *All The Way From Tuam* ('92); *Songs From Sun Street* ('98). Major singles: *N17* (debut single - '91), *I Useta Love Her* (Irish No. 1 - '90).

STIFF LITTLE FINGERS Formed Belfast (1977), agit-punk band, lyrically influenced by The Troubles. Band members: Jake Burns, Henry Cluney, Ali McMordie, Brian Faloon. Albums: *Inflammable Material* ('79); *Nobody's Heroes* (UK number nine - '80), *Go For It* ('81), *Now Then* ('82). Major singles: *Alternative Ulster* ('78), *At The Edge* ('80). Also: *Hanxi -live* ('80). Disbanded 1982, reformed recently.

THERAPY? Formed Belfast (1989), grunge-metal band. Band members: Andy Cairns, Michael McKeegan, Fyfe Ewing. Also: Martin McCarrick, Graham Hopkins replaced Fyfe Ewing. Albums: *Babyteeth* ('91); *Pleasure Death* ('92); *Nurse* ('92); *Troublegum* ('94); *Infernal Love* ('95); *Semi-Detached* ('98). Major singles: *Teethgrinder* ('92); *Screamager* ('93) on Shortsharpshock EP; *Stories* ('95); *Church Of Noise* ('98); *Lonely, Crying Only* ('98).

THIN LIZZY Formed Dublin (1969). Ground-breaking internationally famous Celtic hard-rock band, founded by Lynott. Band members: PHIL LYNOTT, Brian Downey, Eric Bell, Eric Wrixon. Line-up also included Scott Gorham, Brian Robertson and Gary Moore. Albums: *Thin Lizzy* ('71); *Shade of a Blue Orphanage* ('72); *Vagabonds of the Western World* ('73); *Nightlife* ('74); *Fighting* ('75); *Jailbreak* ('76); *Johnny the Fox* ('76); *Bad Reputation* ('77); *Black Rose* ('79); *Chinatown* ('80); *Renegade* ('81); *Thunder and Lightning* ('83). Live albums: *Live and Dangerous* ('78); *Life* ('83). Major singles: *Whiskey in the Jar* (UK number 6 - '72); *Dancing in the Moonlight* ('77); *Waiting for an Alibi* ('79); *The Boys are Back in Town* ('76); *Chinatown* ('80). Disbanded 1983.

U2 Formed Dublin (1976). Arguably biggest rock group in the world. Band members: Bono *Paul Hewson* (1960-), The Edge *Dave Evans* (1961-), Adam Clayton (1960-), Larry Mullen Jnr. (1961-). All albums have reached No. 1 in Ireland since *Boy* ('80), in UK since *War* ('83), in US since *The Joshua Tree* ('87). Albums: *Boy* ('80); *October* ('81); *War* ('83); *The Unforgettable Fire* ('84); *The Joshua Tree* ('87); *Rattle and Hum* ('88); *Achtung Baby* ('91); *Zooropa* ('93); *Pop* ('97). Mini LPs: *Under a Blood Red Sky* ('83); *Wide Awake In America* ('85). Also: *Passengers* ('95) with Brian Eno and guests. Major singles: *Another Day* (first Irish No. 1 - '80); *With or Without You* (first US number one - '87); *I Still Haven't Found What I'm Looking For* (US No. 1 - '87); *Desire* (first UK No. 1 - '88); *The Fly* ('91); *One* ('92); *Numb* ('93); *Discotheque* (Irish and UK No. 1. - '97). Popmart ('97) biggest grossing live show in the world. Dominated Hot Press Reader's Poll 1998. Solo projects include: *Captive* ('86) - soundtrack by The Edge featuring Sinead O'Connor, also *Heroine* ('86); *Mystery Girl*

('88) co-written by Bono and Edge for last Roy Orbison studio album; soundtrack for Jim Sheridan film *In the Name of the Father* ('93) by Bono with Gavan Friday; *I've Got You Under My Skin* ('93) - duet by Bono with Frank Sinatra; *Golden Eye* ('95) - theme tune for James Bond film of same name co-written by Bono and The Edge; *Hold Me, Thrill Me, Kiss Me, Kill Me* ('95) theme for film *Batman Forever;* theme tune for film *Mission Impossible* by Larry Mullins Jnr. and Adam Clayton.

UNDERTONES, The Formed Derry (1970s). Punk-pop band, enjoyed much chart success in Ireland and UK. Band members: Feargal Sharkey, Damien O'Neill, John O'Neill, Michael Bradley, Billy Doherty. Albums: *The Undertones* ('79); *Hypnotised* ('80); *The Positive Touch* ('81); *The Sin of Pride* ('83). Major singles: *Teenage Kicks* (debut - '78); *Jimmy Jimmy* ('79); *Here Comes The Summer* ('79); *My Perfect Cousin* (number nine UK - '80). Disbanded 1983. Sharkey embarked on solo career with album titled *Fergal Sharkey* ('85) and has since become a music industry executive. Major singles *A Good Heart* (Irish and UK number one - '85); *You Little Thief* ('85). O'Neill brothers formed That Petrol Emotion (1984).

Solo Artistes/Songwriters

BAKER, Don (1950-) b. Dublin. Blues singer/musician, actor. Albums including: *Just Don Baker* ('98). Debut performance as an actor in Jim Sheridan film *In The Name Of The Father* (1994).

BLACK, Frances b. Dublin. One of Ireland's top selling solo artists. Younger sister of Mary. Began career in 1986 with The Black Family, recording albums *The Black Family* ('86) and *Time For Touching Home* ('89). Joined Arcady, recorded album *After The Ball* ('91), followed by a successful best-selling partnership with singer/songwriter **Kieran Goss**, recording album *Frances Black & Kieran Goss* ('92). Launched solo career ('93) following massive success of the collaborative album *A Woman's Heart* ('93), featuring the best of Ireland's female singers. Solo albums: *Talk To Me* ('94); *The Sky Road* ('95); *The Smile On Your Face* ('96); *Don't Get Me Wrong* ('98). Major singles: *All The Lies That You Told Me* ('94); *When You Say Nothing At All* ('96); *Stranger On The Shore* ('96); *Don't Get Me Wrong* ('98).

BLACK, Mary (1955-) b. Dublin. Hugely successful solo-singer. Enjoys huge success in Ireland and has a listenership in Europe, the US and Japan. Joined traditional band DE DANNAN (1983) as singer, recording two albums. Solo albums: *Mary Black* ('83); *Collected* ('84);*Without the Fanfare* ('85); *By The Time It Gets Dark* ('87); *No Frontiers* ('89); *Babes in the Wood* ('91); *The Collection* ('92);*The Holy Ground* ('93); *Circus* ('95); *Looking Back* ('95) *Shine* ('97). Major singles: *No Frontiers* ('89); *Beautiful* ('98). Among many accolades, voted Best Female Artist in Irish Rock Music Awards ('87, '88, '92, '94, '96).

BLOOM, Luka *Barry Moore.* b. Kildare. Singer/songwriter. Brother of Christy Moore. Albums: *Turf; The Acoustic Motorbike; Salty Heaven* ('98).

BOWYER, Brendan Formed The Royal Showband in Waterford (1957) with Tom Dunphy, Charlie Matthew, arguably Ireland's most successful showband of the 1960s. Nine Irish No. 1's, forever associated with The

Hucklebuck, as well as *Kiss Me Quick* and *No More*. Established themselves in Las Vegas, in the US from 1967. Broke up in1971, Boyer went on to found The Big 8 Showband with Tom Dunphy, based in Las Vegas since then.

BRADY, Paul (1947-) b. Tyrone. Chart-topping folk-rock singer/songwriter. His songs have been recorded by Tina Turner, Dave Edmunds and Bonnie Rait. Joined ballad group The Johnstons (1967), with whom he recorded seven albums. Returned from New York (1974) to join PLANXTY. Later with Andy Irvine formed a partnership ('76-'78) which produced album *Andy Irvine and Paul Brady*. Solo albums: *Welcome Here Kind Stranger* ('78); *Hard Station* (81); *True For You* (80's); *Back To The Centre* ('80's); *Primitive Dance* ('80's); *Trick Or Treat* ('91); *Spirits Colliding* ('95). Compilation album: *Songs And Crazy Dreams* ('93). Major singles: *The Island; Nothing But the Same Old Story* ('82); *Nobody Knows* ('91); *The World Is What You Make It* ('95).

COUGHLAN, Mary (1957-) b. Galway. Blues and folk singer. Albums include: *Tired and Emotional; Under the Influence; Uncertain Pleasures; Sentimental Killer, After The Fall*.

COULTER, Phil (1942-) b. Derry. Pianist, composer and record producer. Began career in 1963 working as pianist/arranger for VAN MORRISON, Tom Jones and Chet Atkins. Wrote 1968 Eurovision Song Contest winning entry *Puppet On A String* ('67) sung by Sandy Shaw and *Congratulations* ('69) sung by Cliff Richards. Also wrote for Elvis Presley, The Bay City Rollers, The New Seekers, James Last, and Waylon Jennings. Produced albums for PLANXTY, THE DUBLINERS and The Fureys. Major songs: *Saturday Night; Scorn Not His Simplicity; The Town I Love So Well*. Albums include: *Classic Tranquillity* ('84); *Sea Of Tranquility* ('84); *Peace And Tranquility* ('85); *Serenity* ('86); *Forgotten Dreams* ('88); *Words And Music* ('89); *Local Heroes* ('90); *American Tranquility* ('94); *Celtic Panpipes* ('95); *Celtic Tranquility* ('96); *Legends* ('97).

CUNNAH, Peter (1968-) b. Derry, lead singer with group D:ream. Album: *World* (1994). Major singles: *Things Can Only Get Better* (Irish and UK No. 1 '94, used by UK Labour Party as its 1997 election campaign theme), *You're the Best Thing, Blame It On Me*.

DANA *Rosemary Brown* (1951-) b. Derry, first Irish winner of Eurovision Song Contest with *All Kinds of Everything* ('70). Albums: *Everything is Beautiful* ('81); *Please Tell Him I Said Hello* ('84); *Let there be Love* ('85). Major singles: *All Kinds of Everything* ('70); *It's Gonna be a Cold, Cold Christmas; Fairy Tale; Who Put the Lights Out?*. Based in US for many years. Unsuccessful candidate in 1997 ROI Presidential elections.

De BURGH, Chris (1948-) b. Argentina, international singer/songwriter. Major world-wide hit with single *The Lady In Red* ('86). Albums: *Far Beyond These Castle Walls* ('75); *Spanish Train And Other Stories* ('75); *At The End Of A Perfect Day* ('77); *Crusader* ('79); *Eastern Wind* ('80); *The Getaway* ('82); *Man On The Line* ('84); *Into The Light* ('86); *Flying Colours* ('88); *The Power Of Ten* ('92); *This Way Up* ('94); *Beautiful Dreams* ('95). Compilation albums: *Best Moves* ('81); *The Very Best Of Chris DeBurgh* ('84);

Spark To A Flame ('89); *The Love Songs* ('97). Live albums: *Live In South Africa* ('79); *High On Emotion-Live From Dublin* ('90). Major singles: *Turning Around* ('75); *A Spaceman Came Travelling* ('75); *Patricia the Stripper* ('75); *Don't Pay The Ferryman* ('82); *The Lady In Red* ('86).

DOLAN, Joe b. Mullingar, popular showband-style singer. Began career as Joe Dolan & The Drifters. Solo career successful both commercially and in terms of live following. Numerous albums, including *Endless Magic* ('97); *Joe's Nineties* ('98). Major singles: *The Answer To Everything; Pretty Brown Eyes; Tar and Cement; Make Me An Island* ('69); *Teresa* ('69); *Good Looking Woman* ('69); *Sweet Little Rock 'n' Roller* ('74); *Lady In Blue* ('74); *Good Looking Woman* (No. 1 - '97) - with Dustin; *The Universal* ('98).

DOWDAL, Leslie former lead singer with popular 1980s band In Tua Nua. After a spell spent doing various odd jobs, including waitressing, she has made a comeback doing projects with other artistes and is carving a successful solo career, having recently had a hit with the single, *Wonderful Thing*.

ENYA *Eithne Ni Bhraonoin* (1961-) b. Gweedore, Celtic-New Age singer / musician (has sold more than 40 million records). Youngest member of Brennan family CLANNAD. With producers Nicky and Roma Ryan, pioneered instantly recognisable atmospheric sound. Albums: *The Celts* (recorded '86, released '87 and '92); *Watermark* ('88); *Shepherd Moons* (Irish, UK No 1 - '91); *The Memory of Trees* ('95). Major singles: *Orinoco Flow* (Irish, UK No. 1, US No. 24 - '88); *Caribbean Blue* ('91). Compilation album: *Paint The Sky With Stars* ('97).

FRIDAY, Gavin *Fionan Hanvey* (1959-) b. Dublin, singer/songwriter with performance-art, gothic style. Founded The Virgin Prunes (1977). Albums: *If I Die, I Die* ('82); *Heresie* ('83); *Over The Rainbow* ('85); *The Moon Looked Down And Laughed* ('86);*The Hidden Lie - Live in Paris* ('87); *Lite Fantastic* ('88); *Nada* ('89). With Man Seezer released *Each Man Kills The Thing He Loves* ('89). Solo albums: *Adam 'N' Eve* ('92); *Shag Tobacco* ('95). Other projects: collaborated with Bono on soundtrack for Jim Sheridan film *In the Name of the Father* and with Maurice Seezer produced soundtrack for Jim Sheridan film *The Boxer*.

GELDOF, Bob Formed Ireland's punk pioneer band the BOOMTOWN RATS. In 1984 Geldof assembled top stars of the day for famine-relief record *Do They Know It's Christmas* ('84) and for Live Aid concert ('85), raising over £100m in the process. Disbanded Boomtown Rats in 1986, given an honorary knighthood same year. Nominated for Nobel Peace Prize ('86). Published best-selling autobiography *Is That It?* ('86), producer and creator of Channel 4's *The Big Breakfast* and up and coming media mogul. In 1997, was involved in a high-profile divorce with ex-wife Paula Yates.

GOSS, Kieran singer/songwriter. Successful partnership with Frances Black, before going solo. Albums: *New Day* ('94), *Worse Than Pride* ('98). Major singles: *Out Of My Head* (Irish Top 20 hit - '98).

HANLY, Mick (1949-) b. Limerick, commercially successful singer-songwriter. Member of Moving Hearts, formed Rusty Old Halo, released critically acclaimed

Still Not Cured ('86). Embarked on solo career. Solo albums: *All I Remember* ('89), *Warts & All* ('91), *Happy Like This* ('93). Received BMI award for most played country song on American radio for the Hal Ketchum recording of his song *Past The Point Of Rescue* (US No. 2 - '92).

HANNON, Neil b. Enniskillen, singer/songwriter and frontman with THE DIVINE COMEDY, acclaimed for quirky lyrical and musical arrangements, many of which involve orchestral backing. Albums: *Liberation; Promenade; Casanova* ('96); *A Short Album About Love* ('97); *Fin De Siécle* ('98). Major singles: *Something For the Weekend; Becoming More Like Alfie; The Frog Princess; Everybody Knows (Except You) ('97); Generation Sex* ('98). Wrote theme music - *Songs Of Love* ('96) - for top TV sitcom *Father Ted.*

HOLMES, David b. Belfast, DJ and dance-act musician. Albums: *This Film's Crap, Let's Slash The Seats; Let's Get Killed* ('97). Major singles: *My Mate Paul* ('98). Topped 1998 Hot Press Reader's Poll Results for Best Dance Act and Album.

KAVANAGH, Niamh singer and former bank clerk. Won the 1993 Eurovision Song Contest for Ireland in Millstreet, Cork, with the song *In your Eyes.*

KEATING, Ronan (1977-) b. Dublin, Lead singer with BOYZONE. Co-presented the 1997 Eurovision Song Contest with Carrie Crowley, Presented the MTV Awards (1997), presented the National Entertainment Awards in December 1997 and voted 'Entertainer of the Year'.

KELLY, Nick critically acclaimed singer/songwriter. Formed Fat Lady Sings (mid-'80s). Albums include: *Twist* ('91); *John Son* ('93). Major singles: *Arclight* ('89), *Twist* ('91), *Deborah* (91). Went solo. Solo album: *Between Trapezes* ('97).

KENNEDY, Brian (1960-) b. Belfast, successful singer, associated with VAN MORRISON with whom he has collaborated. Solo albums: *Great War of Words* ('92); *A Better Man* ('96). Major singles: *Captured; Put the Message in the Box; Life, Love & Happiness.* Voted Best Male Singer by Hot Press Readers' Poll 1997.

KENNEDY, Kieran b. Cork. Singer/songwriter. Founded The Black Velvet Band. Solo albums include *Pagan Irish* ('94), *Foxymoran* ('97).

LOCKE, Josef *Joseph McLaughlin* (1917-) b. Derry. tenor and music-hall performer. Enjoyed stage success in the UK (1944-58). Broke records by playing 19 consecutive seasons in Blackpool. Major songs: *Hear My Song* ('47); *I'll Take You Home Again Kathleen; Galway Bay; Goodbye; Cara Mia; The Town I Love So Well.* Left the UK in 1958 following tax problems and retired to Ireland. Inspired film *Hear My Song* ('92).

LOGAN, Johnny Eurovision Song Contest winner in 1980 and 1987. Also wrote Linda Martin's Eurovision winning song *Why Me* in 1992. Major singles: *What's Another Year* ('80); *Hold Me Now* ('87).

LOHAN, Sinéad (1971-) b. Cork, singer-songwriter. Signed in 1998 by US record label in one of biggest first-album record deals ever by Irish act. Albums: *Who Do You Think I Am* ('95), *No Mermaid* ('98). Major singles: *Bee in the Bottle* ('95), *To Ramona* ('96), *Whatever It Takes* ('98 - No. 16).

McCARTHY, Jimmy b. Cork, one of Ireland's most successful singer-songwriters. His songs were covered by Christy Moore *Ride On* ('84) and Mary Black *No Frontiers* ('89). Solo albums: *The Song Of The Singing Horseman* ('91 - No. 5), *The Dreamer* ('94), *Warmer For The Spark* ('97).

McEVOY, Eleanor classically trained singer/songwriter. A violinist in National Symphony Orchestra for four years, she went solo (1992) to develop songwriting career. Wrote, recorded and performed title track of chart-topping album *A Woman's Heart* ('93). Solo albums: *Eleanor McEvoy* ('93), *What's Following Me* ('96).

McGOWAN, Shane (1957-) b. Tipperary, critically acclaimed songwriter. He enjoyed commercial and critical success as frontman with London-Irish traditional-punk band The Pogues (formed 1981). Albums: *Red Roses for Me; Rum, Sodomy and the Lash; Poguetry in Motion; If I Should Fall From Grace with God; Peace and Love; Hell's Ditch.* Major singles: *The Sick Bed of Cúchulaínn* ('85); *Dirty Old Town* ('85); *A Pair Of Brown Eyes* ('85); *Fairytale Of New York* ('87); *If I Should Fall From Grace With God* ('88); *A Rainy Night In Soho* ('91). Left Pogues (1991). Formed The Popes. Albums: *The Snake, The Crock Of Gold.* Major single: *The Snake With Eyes Of Garnet.*

MARTIN, Linda won the 1992 Eurovision Song Contest for Ireland in Malmö with the song *Why Me?* written by JOHNNY LOGAN.

MOORE, Christy (1945-) b. Kildare, singer/songwriter renowned for innovative song writing which often reflects on social and political issues. Has a massive following in Ireland. Founded folk group PLANXTY (1972) and much acclaimed Moving Hearts (1981). Solo since 1982. Albums: *Paddy On The Road* ('69); *Prosperous* ('72); *Christy Moore* ('75); *Whatever Tickles Your Fancy* ('75); *The Iron Behind The Velvet* ('78); *Christy Moore And Friends* ('81); *The Time Has Come* ('83); *Ride On* ('84); *The Spirit Of Freedom* ('85); *Ordinary Man* ('85); *Nice 'n Easy* ('86); *Unfinished Revolution* ('87); *Voyage* ('89); *Smoke And Strong Whiskey* ('91); *King Puck* ('93); *Graffiti Tongue* ('96). Compilation albums: *Christy Moore Folk Collection* ('73-'78); *Christy Moore* ('88); *The Christy Moore Collection* ('91); *Collection Part 2* ('97). Live albums: *Live In Dublin* ('79); *Christy Moore - Live At The Point* ('94). Major singles: *Nancy Spain; Lisdoonvarna; Ordinary Man; Voyage; Don't Forget Your Shovel.* Retired from live circuit in 1998 due to heath problems.

MOORE, Gary (1952-) b. Belfast, blues guitarist. Played with Skid Row ('69-71) and THIN LIZZY ('74-75, '77, '78-80) and his own Gary Moore Band; and G-Force. Embarked on a successful solo career. Teamed up with PHIL LYNOTT for *Parisienne Walkways* (UK No. 8 - '79) and *Out in the Fields* (UK No. 5 -'85).

MORRISON Van (1945-) b. Belfast, legendary rock-jazz influenced singer-songwriter and musician. Formed beat-band Them in 1963, hit singles with *Gloria* ('64); *Here Comes The Night* ('65). Left in 1966 and signed solo-artist deal in 1967. Albums (all charted in Ireland, UK and US): *Astral Weeks* ('68), *Moondance* (US No. 29 - '70), *Tupelo Honey* ('71), *Hard Nose the Highway* ('73), *A Period of Transition* ('77), *Beautiful Vision* ('82); *Days Like This* ('95). Major singles include: *Brown Eyed Girl* (US No. 10 - '67),

Domino (US No. 9 - '70), *Jackie Wilson Said* ('72), *Whenever God Shines His Light* ('89), *Days Like This* ('95), *No Religion* ('95). Live albums: *It's Too Late To Stop Now* ('74) and *Live at The Grand Opera House, Belfast.* Compilations: *The Best of Van Morrison* ('90) and *The Philosopher's Stone* ('98). Awarded OBE and inducted into Rock 'n' Roll Hall of Fame (1996). Awarded Commander dans L'Ordre des Arts et des Lettres (France's highest arts award) in recognition of his contribution to music in July 1998.

O'CONNOR, SINÉAD (1966-) b. Dublin, internationally successful rock singer. At least as well-known for controversial views on religion, abortion and The Troubles. Albums: *The Lion and the Cobra* (US and UK Top 40 - '87), *I Do Not Want What I Have Not Got* (Irish, UK and US No. 1 - '90), *Am I Not Your Girl* ('92), *Universal Mother* ('94), *Gospel Oak* (EP - '97). Major singles: *Mandinka* ('87), *Nothing Compares 2 U* (No. 1 in 17 countries, including Ireland, UK, US - '90), *Thank You For Hearing Me* ('94), *This Is A Rebel Song* ('97). Compilation album: *So Far, The Best Of* ('97). Contributed to a number of soundtracks, including single *You Made Me The Thief Of Your Heart* ('94) for the film *In The Name Of The Father*. Winner of Best Female Singer Award in 1998 Hot Press Awards.

O'DONNELL, Daniel b. Donegal (1961-). Internationally successful country/MOR singer, massive live following. Major singles: *Donegal Shore, I Just Want to Dance With You, Destination Donegal, Give A Little Love.*

QUINN, Eimear b. Dublin, singer. Classically trained, winner of 1996 Eurovision Song Contest with *The Voice*, written by Brendan Graham. Previously soloist with ANUNA. Founder member of early music chamber choir Zefiro.

STEWART, Louis (1944-) b. Waterford, jazz musician. Achieved international status winning the *Montreux Jazz Festival Grand Prix* ('69). Has toured and recorded with jazz greats Benny Goodman, Spike Robinson, Tubby Hayes, Ronnie Scott and Irish singer Honor Heffernon.

TURNER, Pierce b. Wexford, New York-based singer-songwriter. Albums: *It's Only A Long Way Across* ('87); *The Sky And The Ground* ('89); *Now Is Heaven* ('91); *Angelic Language* ('98). Compilation album: *Pierce Turner: The Compilation* ('98). Also soundtrack to *Snakes And Ladders* ('96).

WILKINSON, Colm singer. Sung Ireland's entry, *Born to Sing*, in the 1978 Eurovision Song Contest in Paris (where he came 5th). Embarked on a very successful stage singing career, most famous for singing the lead role in *Les Miserables*.

Traditional / Folk

ALTAN Formed Donegal, one of Ireland's top traditional groups. Band members: Mairéad Ní Mhaonaigh, Ciaran Tourish, Ciaran Curran, Dermot Byrne, Dáithí Sproule, Mark Kelly. Line-up also included late Frankie Kennedy (*d.* 1994, Mairéad's husband). Albums: *Altan; Horse With A Heart; The Red Crow; Harvest Storm; Island Angel; Blackwater; Runaway Sunday* ('97). Compilations: *The First Ten Years*.

ANÚNA New-age Celtic-folk group. Came to prominence as musical introduction to Riverdance at 1994 Eurovision. Album: *Behind The Closed Eye* ('97) with the Ulster Orchestra and saxophonist Kenneth Edge. Albums mostly written and arranged by Michael McGlynn, director and solo vocalist.

CLANCY BROTHERS & Tommy MAKEM Formed 1960's, Irish folk group. Adopted and introduced American folk, coupled with Irish traditional material. Band members: Paddy, Tom and Liam Clancy (from Carrick-on-Suir, Co. Tipperary) and Tommy Makem (Co. Armagh). Toured extensively. Disbanded (1969). Liam and Tommy continued as international duo and later soloists.

CLANNAD formed Donegal (1970), New-age group with haunting Celtic sound. Band members: Maire, Pol and Ciaran Ó Braonain, Padraig Ó Dugain, Noel Ó Dugain. Line up also included ENYA ('80-82). Albums: *Clannad* ('73); *Clannad II* ('74); *Dulaman* ('76); *Crann Ull* ('78); *Fuaim* ('82); *Magical Ring* ('83); *Legend* ('84); *Macalla* ('85); *Sirius* ('88); *The Angel And The Soldier Boy* ('89); *Anam* ('90); *Banba* ('93); *Lore* ('96); *Landmarks* ('98). Also: *Atlantic Realm* ('89) - BBC television series soundtrack, *Themes*. Major singles: *Theme From Harry's Game* ('82); *Robin, The Hooded Man* ('84); *In A Lifetime* (featuring Bono - '86, '89). Compilations include: *The Collection* ('88); *Past Present* ('89); *Rohga, The Best of Clannad* ('96). Live albums include: *Clannad in Concert* ('79).

CHIEFTAINS, The Formed Dublin (1963), traditional Celtic-folk band, have enjoyed a worldwide reputation for over 30 years. Band members: PADDY MOLONEY, Sean Potts, Martin Fay, Sean Keane, Derek Bell, Kevin Conneff, Matt Molloy. Line-up also included Mick Tubridy, David Fallon, Peadar Mercier, Ronnie McShane, Dolores Keane. Collaborated with many of music industry's major stars: Elvis Costello, Marianne Faithful, Nanci Griffith, Paul McCartney, Art Garfunkel, Mick Jagger, Mark Knopfler and VAN MORRISON. Albums include: *The Chieftains 1* ('65); *The Chieftains 2* ('69); *The Chieftains 3* ('70); *The Chieftains 4* ('73); *The Chieftains 5* ('75); *Bonaparte's Retreat* ('75); *The Chieftains 7* ('77); *The Chieftains 8* ('78); *Boil The Breakfast Early* ('80); *The Chieftains 10* ('81); *James Galway and The Chieftains In Ireland* ('87); *Celtic Wedding* ('87); *A Chieftains Celebration* ('89); *The Celtic Connection* ('90); *The Bells of Dublin* ('91); *Another Country* ('92); *The Celtic Harp* ('93); *The Long Black Veil* ('95). Soundtracks: *Ballad of the Irish Horse* ('85); *The Year of the French* ('88). Live albums: *The Chieftains Live* ('77); *Live in China* ('85); *An Irish Evening - Live at the Grand Opera House* ('92). Compilations: *The Best of the Chieftains* ('92).

DERVISH formed in Sligo, acclaimed traditional group. Band members: Brian McDonagh, Cathy Jordan, Liam Kelly, Shane McAleer, and Sheimí O'Dowd. Albums: *Harmony Hill; Playing With Fire; At The End Of The Day; Live in Palma* ('97).

DUBLINERS, The formed Dublin (1962), one of Ireland's longest surviving and most popular folk groups. Initially known as the Ronnie Drew Group. Original line-up of Ronnie Drew, Luke Kelly, Barney McKenna, Kieron Bourke and later John Sheehan. Toured extensively and enjoyed much success all over Europe. Most recent line-up included Sheehan, Drew, McKenna and Eamon Campbell.

HARDIMAN, Ronan (1962-) b. Dublin, composer.

Wrote musical score for Michael Flatley's hugely successful *Lord Of The Dance* ('96) which topped the Billboard World Music charts. Was very involved in the 1980's Dublin rock scene, decided to concentrate on writing instrumental music and composed the music to the very popular *Waterways* TV documentaries. His album, *Solus* (1997), combines traditional, classical, pop, and rock music and has Leslie Dowdall singing on a number of tracks.

HAYES, Martin b. Ennis, east Clare-style fiddler. Began acclaimed duet with Dennis Cahill in early '95.

LUNNY, Donal (1947-) b. Offaly. Instrumentalist, composer and record producer. Founder member of PLANXTY ('72), Bothy Band ('75) and Moving Hearts ('81). Established the bouzouki as a prominent instrument in Irish music. Has had pivotal role in development of ensemble traditional music in Ireland. Released solo album *Coolfin* ('98).

MOLONEY, Paddy (1938-) b. Dublin, founding member of THE CHIEFTANS (1961). Uilleann pipes and tin whistle player with the band. Notable solo projects: *Long Journey Home* ('98) arranged and produced by Moloney.

PLANXTY formed Dublin (1972), popular 1970's group. Band Members: CHRISTY MOORE, DONAL LUNNY, Liam O'Flynn, Andy Irvine. Line-up also included: Johnny Moynihan, PAUL BRADY, Matt Molloy, Noel Hill, Tony Linnane, BILL WHELAN, James Kelly, Nollaig Casey, Eoghan O'Neill. Albums: *Planxty* ('72); *The Well Below The Valley* ('73); *Cold Blow And The Rainy Night* ('74); *After The Break* ('79); *The Woman I Loved So Well* ('80); *Words & Music* ('82). Compilation albums: *The Planxty Collection* ('74); *Arís* ('74). Major singles: *Cliffs of Dooneen* ('72); *Timedance/Nancy Spain* ('81).

STOCKTON'S WING Formed (1977), internationally acclaimed folk group. Band Members: Paul Roche, Maurice Lennon, Kieran Hanrahan, Tommy Hayes and Tony Callinan. Also: Steve Cooney, Peter Keenan, Fran Breen, Davey McNevin, Eamonn McElholm. Albums: *Stockton's Wing* ('77); *Take A Chance* ('80); *Light In The Western Sky* ('82); *Full Flight* ('86), *Celtic Roots Revival* ('86); *The Crooked Rose* ('92). Compilation album: *American Special* ('84); *The Stockton's Wing Collection* ('91). Live albums: *Take One* ('85). Major singles: *Beautiful Affair* ('82); *Walk Away* ('82); *Why Wait Until Tomorrow* ('86); *America* ('86); *New Clare Revival* ('86); *So Many Miles* ('86).

O'FLYNN, Liam (1945-) b. Kildare, master uileann piper, played on Comhaltas' album *The Rambles of Kitty* and the CHRISTY MOORE album *Prosperous* ('71). Formed PLANXTY with Moore, Irvine and DONAL LUNNY (1972). Solo albums: *Out To An Other Side* ('93); *The Given Note* ('95); *The Piper's Call* ('98). Central performance on composer Shaun Davey's orchestral suites *The Brendan Voyage* ('83); *Granuaile* ('85); *The Relief Of Derry* ('90). Has contributed to a number of film scores, including *Cal* ('84), *The Field* ('90); *A River Runs Through It*. Guested on recordings by the Everly Brothers, Kate Bush, Mark Knopfler, ENYA and Mike Oldfield.

SHANNON, Sharon b. Clare. Acclaimed traditional instrumental musician.

WHELAN, Bill (1950-) b. Limerick, composer, record producer and songwriter. Keyboard player with PLANXTY ('79-81), composer for Abbey Theatre ('89-94), composed music for massively successful *Riverdance* ('94). TV and film credits include *Bloomfield* ('70), *Lamb* ('84), RTÉ's thriller *Twice Shy; Some Mother's Son* ('96). Other compositions include *The Ó Riada Suite* ('87); *The Seville Suite* ('92); *The Spirit of Mayo* ('93). Produced albums for Andy Irvine, Patrick Street, STOCKTON'S WING and Davy Spillane. Has worked with U2, PAUL BRADY and VAN MORRISON.

Classical ▮▮▮▮▮▮▮▮▮▮

AGNEW, Elaine (1967-) b. Co. Antrim, composer. Attended the Royal Scottish Academy of Music and Drama and studied composition with James MacMillan. Has worked in music education in Scotland, Northern Ireland, Iceland, Indonesia and America. Her works have been performed in Ireland, Scotland, England, Romania and Iceland. Won the 1996 RTÉ Musician of the Future Composer's Prize for *Philip's Peace* (1994). Works include four compositions for orchestra, nine works for chamber orchestra, and three works for vocal and choral performance.

ALCORN, Michael (1962-) composer. Senior lecturer in music at QUB, active in promoting new music technologies and chairman of the Irish Electro-acoustic Music Association. His compositions have been played in the UK, Europe, North and South America and the Far East. Works include three compositions for orchestra, seven works for chamber orchestra, two works for vocal and choral performance and seven electro-acoustic works.

BARRY, Gerald (1952-) composer. Studied composition with Stockhausen and Mauricio Kagel. Works include *Chevaux-de-frise* for the 1998 BBC Proms, *Hard D* for Orkest de Volharding and *The Conquest of Ireland* for the BBC Symphony Orchestra. Operas include *The Intelligence Park* (1981-89), performed at the 1990 Almeida Festival, and *The Triumph of Beauty and Deceit* (1991-92).

BODLEY, Seóirse (1933-) b. Dublin, composer. Associate Professor in UCD's music department and a founder member of Aosdána, his works have been performed and broadcast in Ireland, Europe, Australia, North America and China. Awarded the Arts Council Prize for Composition, the Macaulay Fellowship in Music Composition and the Marten Toonder Award. Works include five symphonies for full orchestra, two chamber symphonies and numerous orchestral, choral, vocal and chamber pieces.

BOYDELL, Brian (1917-) b. Dublin, composer. After studying at Cambridge, Heidelberg and Dublin, awarded a DMus at Dublin University (1959), was created Professor of Music at Trinity College (1962-82) and is now a Fellow Emeritus of the college. Has frequently been a guest conductor with the RTÉ Symphony Orchestra and is a member of Aosdána. His works are written for a wide range of media and include 7 compositions for orchestra, 11 works for chamber orchestra, and 11 works for vocal and choral performance.

BUCKLEY, John (1951-) b. Co. Limerick, composer. Studied flute with Doris Keogh and composition with Alun Hoddinott and James Wilson. His works have been performed and broadcast in Ireland and more than 30 countries. Very successful film composer, with noted compositions for this medium including his score for *The Woman who Married Clark Gable*. Other works include his opera *The Words upon the Window Pane*, the cantata *De Profundis* (1993), *Rivers of Paradise* (1993) for speakers and orchestra and the *Maynooth Te Deum* (1995), *Saxophone Quartet* (1996), *Two Songs* (1997), *Airflow* (1998).

CLARKE, Rhona (1958-) awarded a PhD in 1996 at QUB, became interested in electro-acoustics. Won the Varming Prize (1986) and the Music for the Movies Award at the Dublin Film Festival (1992). Works include *Pied Piper* (1994), *Gleann Dá Loch* (1995), *Inside Out* (1995) and *Bovine* (1996), a film score.

CLEARY, Siobhán (1970-) b. Dublin, composer. Finalist in the 1993 RTÉ Musician of the Future Composer's Competition, won the 1997 Arklow Music Festival Composers' Competition. Vienna Modern Masters performed her orchestral work, *Threads* (1992 rev. 1994), at the Second International Festival of New Music for Orchestra and for release on CD.

CORCORAN, Frank (1944-) b. Co. Tipperary, composer. Worked as a music inspector in Ireland (1971-79). Has been professor of composition and theory in the Staatliche Hochschule für Musik und darstellende Kunst, Hamburg since 1983 and is a member of Aosdána. Works include *Buile Suibhne* (1996), 9 compositions for orchestra, 13 works for chamber orchestra, 6 works for vocal and choral performance and 2 electro-acoustic pieces.

DAVEY, Shaun (1948-) b. Dublin. Composer. Best known for critically acclaimed arrangement to *The Brendan Voyage* ('83).

DEANE, Raymond (1953-) b. Co. Galway; composer, pianist, author and member of Aosdána. Studied composition with Gerald Bennett, Karlheinz Stockhausen and Isang Yun and now works in Dublin. Has won many awards, including the Varming Composition Prize and the Marten Toonder Award. Works include 8 compositions for orchestra, 17 works for chamber orchestra, 4 works for vocal and choral performance.

De BARRA, Séamus (1955-) composer. Studied at UCC under Aloys Fleischmann, awarded a BMus (1977) and an MA (1980). In addition to orchestral and chamber compositions, has written numerous vocal and choral works, including *Magnificat* (1983) and *Song of Pan* (1989), commissioned for the Cork International Choral Festival, *Canticum in Laudibus* (1988) for the Irish Youth Choir, *Tibi laus, tibi gloria* (1993) for the Choir of Christ Church Cathedral.

De BROMHEAD, Jerome (1945-) b. Waterford, composer. Studied with A.J. Potter, James Wilson, Seóirse Bodley and Franco Donatoni. Senior music producer with RTÉ Radio One. His compositions have been performed and broadcast in many countries, particularly the harpsichord piece *Flux*, performed at the ISCM World Music Days, Germany (1987). Works include 5 compositions for orchestra, 10 for chamber orchestra and 3 works for vocal and choral performance.

DENNEHY, Donnacha (1970-) b. Dublin, composer. Lecturer in music and media technology at TCD. His awards include the Kate Neal Kinley Prize and the Presser Music Award. His approach is influenced by the practice of algorithmic composition. Compositions include 6 works for acoustic and electronic media as well as 4 works for chamber orchestra and 3 works for vocal and choral performance.

DOYLE, Roger (1949-) b. Dublin, composer. Studied composition at RIAM and the University of Utrecht's Institute of Sonology. Specialises in electro-acoustic music and has produced many compositions for theatre, film and dance media. *The Babel Project*, his major, ongoing work, incorporates live and electronic music, dance and architecture and was first shown in the IMMA. In addition to this project, he produced music for Steven Berkoff's *Salomé*, the film score for *Budawanny* (1986) and *Thalia* (1976). His *Spirit Levels I-IV* (1993-97) won the Programme Music Prize at the 1997 Bourges International Electro-Acoustic Music Competition.

DOUGLAS, Barry b. Belfast, successful solo pianist, who tours extensively here and abroad. Has won several international competitions.

DWYER, Benjamin (1965-) b. Dublin, composer and guitarist. His works are performed and broadcast regularly and include 11 pieces for chamber combinations and 3 vocal and choral pieces, including *Winter Psalms* (1995 rev. 1997).

FARRELL, Eibhlis (1953-) b. Rostrevor, composer and Head of Music and Drama at Dublin Institute of Technology's Conservatory of Music. Compositions include 4 works for orchestra, 14 for chamber orchestra and 11 works for vocal and choral performance, including *Time Drops* (1989) and *Estampie* (1994).

FLOOD, Philip (1964-) b. Belfast, composer. Studied composition with Robert Saxton and Simon Emmerson and has collaborated with many leading performers and groups, including Rolf Hind, Nicola Walker Smith, Fine Arts Brass Ensemble and the BBC Singers. Deeply involved in educational activities and with dance. Compositions include 2 works for orchestra, 9 works for chamber orchestra, 3 works for vocal and choral performance and 2 works for acoustic and electronic media.

GARDNER, Stephen (1958-) b. Belfast, composer. Awarded a Vaughan Williams Scholarship and a Draper's Fellowship. His music has been performed and broadcast by the RTÉ Concert Orchestra, the Ulster Orchestra, the National Symphony Orchestra of Ireland and Ulster Youth Orchestra. Works include *Strange Fish* (1993) and *Trane* (1996), commissioned by Concorde, and *The Milesian Equation* (1993), commissioned by the Sculptors' Society of Ireland.

GALWAY, James (1939-) b. Belfast. Internationally renowned flautist. Graduate of the Guildhall School of Music, London, and Conservatoire National Supérieur de Musique, Paris. Principal flute with London Symphony Orchestra (1966) and Royal Philharmonic Orchestra (1967-69) and Berlin Philharmonic Orchestra (1969-75). Embarked on solo career 1975.

GIBSON, John (1951-) b. Dublin, concert pianist and composer. He studied composition with A.J. Potter at the RIAM and with Prof. Valentyna Schubinskaya in Moscow. Has performed extensively and is a lecturer in piano at the Cork School of Music. His music has been performed in Ireland, England, the US, Germany, France, Poland, Romania and Israel. Was awarded the Nijinsky Medal by the Polish Ministry of Arts in 1997 for his piano piece *Nijinsky* (1980). Other significant works include *String Quartet No. 2* (1976).

GREEVY, Bernadette (1940-) b. Dublin, internationally famous mezzosoprano. Operatic début at Wexford Festival (1962). Covent Garden début (1982) in *Pelléas et Mélisande* by Debussy. Celebrated as an exponent of the music of Elgar and of Mahler, recordings also cover the works of composers Handel, Brahms, Haydn, Berlioz and Duparc. Performances include many works by Irish composers.

GRIBBIN, Deirdre (1967-) b. Belfast, composer. Her music has been performed in Ireland and Europe. Has collaborated on education projects with the London Sinfonietta, Opera Factory, Ondine Ensemble in London and Estonia. Works include *Two Songs from Childhood* for the *Rainbow across Europe* Festival in England, France and the Netherlands. Other works include *Venusian Year* (1993) which won 1995 IMRO/Feis Ceoil Composers' Competition.

GUILDFOYLE, Ronan (1958-) jazz bass player. Has performed widely in Europe, the US and Asia and is director of the jazz department at Newpark Music Centre, Dublin. Has lectured abroad for UNESCO's International Music Council on improvisation and has written music for theatre, television, film and many jazz groups. Works include 2 orchestral pieces and 14 works for chamber ensembles.

HAMMOND, Philip (1951-) pianist, broadcaster, composer and currently Arts Council of Northern Ireland's Director of Performing Arts. Has written music in a range of media for musicians in both Ireland and Britain. Compositions include 2 works for orchestra, 12 works for chamber orchestra, 10 works for vocal and choral performance and 1 electro-acoustic work.

HAYES, Paul (1951-) b. Dublin, composer. Studied composition with James Wilson at RIAM and Seóirse Bodley in UCD. Fulfilled many commissions for Irish groups but is now living in Japan. Works include *The Love Sonata* (1991-92), commissioned by RTÉ, and *Mass Production* (1993), an electro-acoustic work, commissioned by RTÉ (for the 1993 Prix Italia).

HOLOHAN, Michael (1956-) b. Dublin, composer. Studied at UCD and QUB and presented with travel awards for masterclasses with Messiaen, Xenakis, Boulez and Berio. Works (premiered by the RTÉ Concert Orchestra) include *Cromwell* (1994), *Building Bridges* (1995), *Leaves of Glass* (1995) and *The Lost Land* (1996), performed as part of the orchestra's *Spirit of Ireland* tour in North America Worked with Seamus Heaney on projects, including the *No Sanctuary* concert and the TV programme - *A Nobel Tribute to Seamus Heaney*.

HURLEY, Donal (1950-) b. Dublin, composer. Studied music at UCD and lectures in music at the Mater Dei Institute of Education. Interested in electro-acoustic music and music for dance. Has worked closely with the Irish Youth Dance Company and the annual New Music-New Dance Festival. Works include orchestral compositions, 8 works for chamber orchestra, 9 works for vocal and choral performance and 12 electro-acoustic works.

INGOLDSBY, Marian (1965-) b. Carrick-on-Suir, composer. The first person to win the prestigious Elizabeth

Maconchy Composition Fellowship, tenable at the University of York. Works include choral music, songs, chamber and piano music and her first opera, *Hot Food with Strangers*.

JOHNSTON, Fergus (1959-) b. Dublin, composer. Studied at TCD and the RIAM where he studied composition with James Wilson. Works include 3 works for orchestra, chamber orchestral pieces and a short opera, *Bitter Fruit*, commissioned by the Opera Theatre Co. who toured it in Ireland in 1992.

KINSELLA, John (1932-) b. Dublin, composer. RTÉ's Head of Music, retired (1988) to compose. Has written five symphonies, Nos. 2, 3, 4, 5 and 6; a Second Violin Concerto; a Fourth String Quartet and is completing his Seventh Symphony. Notable works include *Festive Overture* (1995), commissioned by RTÉ to celebrate 70 years of broadcasting, and *The Wayfarer: Rhapsody on a poem of P.H. Pearse* (1979), commissioned by the Irish Government to mark Pearse's centenary of birth.

MCGLYNN, Michael (1964-) b. Dublin, composer. In the late 1980s, founded the vocal-instrumental group, *Anúna*, which has achieved international popularity, particularly through its association with *Riverdance*. Main influences are traditional and medieval music. Commissioned by, among others, the Ulster Orchestra, the RTÉ Concert Orchestra and Anúna. Has also acted as musical director for a production of Chekov's *Three Sisters* and for Jim Sheridan's production of *The Risen People*.

MARTIN, Philip (1947-) b. Dublin, pianist, teacher and composer. Awarded the UK-US Bicentennial Arts Fellowship and was a guest at Boston Symphony Orchestra's Tanglewood Summer School. Currently teaches piano and composition at Birmingham Conservatoire and is a member of Aosdána. Works include *Sonata* (1997 rev. 1998), *Beato Angelico* (1990), *Piano Concerto No. 2* (1991), *Harp Concerto* (1993) and *Serendipity* (1993), commissioned by the Crawford Piano Trio.

MAWBY, Colin (1936-) choral conductor and composer. Worked with many prestigious choirs - was Westminster Cathedral's Master of Music, London, choral director at RTÉ and at present, is director of Ireland's National Chamber Choir. Has been much influenced by plainchant. His works include *A Light Entertainment* (1997), 17 masses, 5 song cycles and numerous settings for choir.

MILLS, Alan (1964-) b. Belfast; pianist and composer and lectures in London and abroad. Studied composition with Hugh Wood and Robin Holloway at Cambridge. Influences: 20th-century French music, neo-classicism and modern jazz. Has broadcast for the BBC, Radio France and Dutch TV. Works include 11 compositions for chamber orchestra and 16 vocal and choral pieces.

MORRIS, David (1948-) b. London, composer. Studied with the Australian composer David Lumsdaine. Moved to Northern Ireland (1981) and now teaches at the University of Ulster. Current influences include those of jazz and minimalism. Has been awarded several prizes, including the International Lutoslawski Competition 1990-91. Works include 4 orchestral pieces, 9 compositions for chamber orchestra and an electro-acoustic piece.

MULVEY, Gráinne (1966-) b. Dún Laoghaire, composer. Studied composition at the University of York under Nicola LeFanu. Won the 1994 RTÉ Musician of the Future Composers' Prize for her *Rational Option Insanity*. Her work has been performed in Ireland, Britain and abroad. Notable commissions include *Sextet Uno* (1997) for Concorde and *Soundscape* (1996), which has been released on CD.

MURPHY, Suzanne one of Ireland's leading sopranos.

O'CONNELL, Kevin (1958-) b. Derry, composer and member of Aosdána. Composing since 12 years old, won the RTÉ Musician of the Future Composers' Prize while still a student. His music has been played in Ireland and Britain. Is regularly broadcast by the BBC. Works include *North* (1997/98), *From the Besieged City* (1989), *Sonata for Saxophone and Piano* (1988), *Concerto for Violin and Chamber Orchestra* (1990), his chamber opera *Sensational!* (1992), *Sonata for Cello and Piano* (1993-94) and *My Love, My Umbrella* (1997), based on JOHN McGAHERN's short stories.

O'CONNOR, John (1947-) b. Dublin. Pianist. A graduate of Hochschule für Musik, Vienna. Professor of Piano and a Director at RIAM. Came to prominence having won the Beethoven piano competition (1973) and Bösendorfer piano competition (1975). Has performed internationally with leading orchestras. Recordings include the works of Beethoven, Mozart and JOHN FIELD. In 1988 founded, and is director of, the GPA Dublin International Piano Competition. Trying to establish a conservatory / national music centre, based in the National Concert Hall.

O'LEARY, Jane (1946-) b. Connecticut, composer. Moved to Ireland (1972) and is based in Galway. Her music is widely performed in Ireland and abroad. A leading figure in Ireland both as artistic director of Ireland's leading contemporary music group, Concorde, and as chairperson of the Contemporary Music Centre (1989-97). Works include *Islands of Discovery*, an orchestral work commissioned by RTÉ.

O'LEARY, Martin (1963-) b. Dublin, pianist and composer. Lectures in music at St. Patrick's College, Maynooth, and has been course director of the Ennis/IMRO Composition Summer School. Works include 4 compositions for orchestra, 17 works for chamber orchestra and 9 vocal and choral pieces.

Ó SÚILLEABHÁIN, Mícheál (1950-) b. Tipperary. Pianist, composer. Professor of Music at University of Limerick, set up Irish World Music Centre (1994), which is one of the the the most active centres in Ireland for new music and new dance activity. Principle recordings feature Irish Chamber Orchestra under his direction performing compositions and arrangements by him which frequently bring classical and traditional music streams together. Scripted and presented TV series *A River of Sound* ('95), tracing the changing course of Irish traditional music. Recordings include: *The Dolphin's Way, Oileán/Island, Casadh/Turning, Gaiseadh/Flowing, Lumen, Between Worlds, Becoming* (1998) and *Irish Destiny* (1998). He is currently involved in setting up a new College of Performing arts. Played for President Clinton when he visited Limerick in 1998.

PATTERSON, Frank (1941-) b. Tipperary. Ireland's leading tenor, has toured extensively in Europe and America, where he enjoys much success.

PEARSE, Colman (1938-) b. Dublin, conductor, composer and pianist. Has guested as a conductor all over the world. Principal Conductor with RTÉ Symphony Orchestra (1981-83), Principal Guest Conductor with Bilbao Symphony Orchestra (1984-87), Principal Conductor and Musical Director with Mississippi Symphony Orchestra (1987).

SWEENEY, Eric (1948-) b. Dublin, composer. Studied in Ireland and all over Europe. Started composing in the 1960s. Influences include Bartók, Messiaen, John Adams and Steve Reich. His works have been broadcast in Ireland, the US and Europe. Represented Ireland at the International Rostrum of Composers in Paris five times. Lectured in TCD, was choral director at RTÉ (1978-81) and is currently head of the Waterford IT's Music Department. Works include a Concerto for Four Violins and Chamber Orchestra.

VOLANS, Kevin (1949-) b. South Africa, composer. Initially part of the 'New Simplicity' school, but began using African compositional techniques for a series of works, establishing himself as a unique voice on the European circuit. Now an Irish citizen and living in Dublin. Works include 3 orchestral pieces, 18 works for chamber orchestra, 1 chamber opera and 4 band compositions and 2 electro-acoustic works.

WILSON, Ian (1964-) b. Belfast, composer. His works have been performed and broadcast throughout Ireland, Europe, the US, Israel and the Far East. Works include *Rise* (1993), commissioned by the University of Ulster to mark its 10th founding anniversary; *Running Thinking, Finding* (1989), which received the 1991 Oslo Ultima festival's composition prize; *Winter's Edge* (1992), performed by the Vanbrugh Quartet and released on CD.

WILSON, James (1922-) b. London, composer and member of Aosdána. A self-taught composer, most of his works have been broadcast by RTÉ. He moved to Ireland in the late 1940s and has worked extensively here and in Denmark. Of his music, he regards *Menorah,* a viola concerto commissioned by Rivka Golani, to be his best to date.

Information on contemporary composers provided by the Contemporary Music Centre.

RELIGION

BEST, Rev. Kenneth Former President of Methodist Church in Ireland (1996-97), influential in negotiating Loyalist ceasefire in 1994.

BRADY, Seán (1939-) b. Cavan, Archbishop of Armagh and Primate of All-Ireland since 1996. Ordained (1964), was awarded a doctorate in Canon Law and taught languages at St. Patrick's College, Cavan, until 1980. Appointed vice-rector of the Irish College in Rome (1980) and rector (1987). Made parish priest of Ballyhaise, Co. Cavan (1994) and within a year, was appointed co-adjutor Archbishop of Armagh. Appointed Primate (Oct. 1996). former member of the executive of the National Council of Priests.

CASEY, Bishop Eamon (1927-) b. Kerry, Former Roman Catholic Bishop. Resigned in 1992 following the revelation that he had a son by American, Annie Murphy. Worked in South America and returned to live in England in 1998 amid much speculation about his return to Ireland.

CONNELL, Archbishop Desmond (1926-) Roman Catholic Archbishop of Dublin and Primate of Ireland since 1988.

DIXON, Samuel John (1943-) b. Monaghan, Moderator of the Presbyterian Church (1998-1999,succeeding the Rev. Sam Hutchinson). Ordained an Assistant Minister (1968), Minister in Rathfriland (1970-80), Minister of First Antrim since 1980.

EAMES, Archbishop Robert (1937-) b. Belfast, Church of Ireland Archbishop of Armagh and Primate of All Ireland since 1986. Ordained deacon (1963), ordained Bishop (1975), Bishop of Derry and Raphoe (1975-80), Bishop of Down and Dromore (1980-86), created a Life Peer (1995).

EMPEY, Archbishop Walton (1934-) Church of Ireland Archbishop of Dublin and Glendalough and Primate of Ireland since 1996.

FAUL, Mgr. Denis (1932-) b. Louth, Catholic priest. Prison chaplain at Long Kesh during the 1981 hunger strike. President of St. Patrick's Academy.

FLANNERY, OP, Austin (1925-) b. Tipperary, Religious editor and writer, entered Dominican Order (1943), Ordained Priest (1950), editor of the Dominican journal *Doctrine and Life* (1957-88).

HURLEY, SJ, Rev Michael Jesuit priest, founder of Irish School of Ecumenics and Columbanus Ecumenical Society.

KERR, Rev. David (1937-) b. Belfast, President of the Methodist Church in Ireland since June 1998. Trained for the Ministry at Edgehill Theological College; ordained in 1964; appointed superintendent minister in Limerick (1969); appointed superintendent minister at Ballyholme, Bangor, Co. Down (1975); Superintendent Methodist Minister of the Churches Central Mission in Belfast since 1987; former methodist advisor to the BBC religious programmes department.

McCURTAIN, OP, Sr. Margaret (1929-) Historian and religious writer, Professor of History at UCD until 1994.

McDONAGH, Rev. Enda (1930-) b. Mayo, writer and current President of the National Council of Priests of Ireland.

McKENNA, Sr. Breige Spiritual healer and writer.

MAGEE, Rev. Roy (1930-) b. Antrim, Presbyterian Minister. Negotiator in Loyalist Ceasefire (1994).

SPORT

Athletics

BRUTON, Niall (1972-) b. Dublin, athlete. Irish 1,500m Champion 1993, 94, 96, 97. 1996 Wannamaker Mile (indoor) winner. World Student Games 1,500m Gold Medallist 1991. 1,500m semi-finalist 1996 Olympic Games and 1997 World Championships. Twelfth in 1,500m at 1998 European Championships.

CARROLL, Mark b. Cork, athlete. Irish 1,500m Champion 1995. Gold Medallist 5,000m at 1991 European Junior Championships. Set new Irish records for 3,000m and 5,000m in 1998. Bronze Medallist 5,000m at 1998 European Championships. Melrose Games 3,000m Champion (Indoor) 1996, 97, 98.

McHUGH, Terry (1963-) b. Tipperary, athlete. Irish Javelin Champion (1984-98) and national record holder. Olympian in 1988, 1992, 1996 (team captain in 1996). Seventh in 1994 European Championships, eighth in 1993 World Championships. Represented Ireland in Bobsleigh at 1992 and 1998 Winter Olympic Games.

McKIERNAN, Catherina (1969-) b. Cavan, athlete. Irish 3,000m Champion (1990-94 and 1996) and national record holder at 10,000m. Silver medallist at World Cross Country Championships (1992-95), Gold Medallist European Cross Country Championships 1994. Competed in 1992 and 1996 Olympic Games. Won Berlin marathon in 1997, setting fastest ever time for a debutant and holds national record for the marathon. 1998 London marathon winner.

MAHER, Emily (1981-) b. Kilkenny, athlete. Gold Medallist in the 100m and 200m at the inaugural World Youth Olympics in Moscow in July 1998.

O'SULLIVAN, Marcus (1961-) b. Cork, athlete. Irish 800m Champion (1985, 86 and 92), 1,500m Champion 1984 and national 2,000m record holder (outdoors) and 1,000m and 1,500m (indoors). Gold medallist in 1,500m in (1987, 89 and 93) World Indoor Championships, 1,500m silver medallist 1985 European Indoor Championships. Winner of Wannamaker Mile six times. Olympian (1984, 88, 92, 96). Recorded his 100th sub-four minute mile on 13th February, 1998, in the Wannamaker Mile becoming only the third man to do so (prior to 1954 a sub-four minute mile was thought to be beyond human capability).

O'SULLIVAN, Sonia (1969-) b. Cork, athlete. Irish 800m champion 1992, 1,500m Champion (1987, 90, 95, 96 and 98) and national record holder at 800m, 1,000m, 1,500m, mile, 2,000m, 3,000m and 5,000 and indoor 3,000m and 5,000m. Gold Medallist 1,500m at 1991 World Student Games, the 1994 European Championships 3,000m, the 1995 World Championships 5,000m. Silver Medallist 1991 World Student Games 3,000m, 1993 World Championships 1,500m; 1997 World Indoor Championships 3,000m. Bronze Medallist with Irish team in 1997 World Cross Country Championships. Recovered from disappointing performances in 1996 Olympic Games and 1997 World Championships to enjoy her most successful year ever in 1998. Gold Medallist in both the long and short course events at the World Cross Country Championships in Morocco in March 1998. Gold Medallist in 5,000m and 10,000m at European Championships in Budapest in August (an achievement without precedent in women's athletics). Gold Medallist in 5,000m at World Cup in South Africa in September. Achieved the world record over 2 miles in Cork, June 1998, with a time of 9 mins 19.56 seconds.

SMITH, Susan (1971-) b. Waterford, athlete. Irish 100m Hurdles Champion (1989, 90, 91, 92, 95 and 98), Irish 400m Hurdles Champion (1992, 96 and 97). Set new Irish records for the 100m and 400m in August 1998 holds Irish 60m hurdles (indoor) record. Finished seventh in 400m hurdles at 1997 World Championships and eighth in 400m hurdles final at 1996 European Championships.

Boxing

BARRETT, Francie (1976-) b. Galway, amateur boxer. Irish light-welterweight champion 1996, became the first member of the travelling community to represent Ireland in the Olympic Games. Runner-up in Irish welterweight final 1998.

CARRUTH, Michael (1967-) b. Dublin, professional boxer. Irish lightweight champion (1987 and 1988), light welterweight champion 1990 and welterweight champion 1992. 1992 Olympic welterweight champion. Defeated on points by Romanian Michael Loewe in WBO welterweight title fight September 1997. Won World Athletic Association welterweight title, September 1998 beating Scott Dixon.

COLLINS, Steve (1964-) b. Dublin, professional boxer. Former WBO super-middleweight champion, retired in October 1997. Won the WBO middleweight world title in 1994, won the super middleweight title in 1995 beating Chris Eubank and then Nigel Benn. Successfully defended his title eight times. His professional record was 35 wins in 38 bouts.

GOGARTY, Deirdre b. Louth, professional boxer. Ireland's first female boxing world champion, she won the WIBF super-featherweight world title in March 1997.

KIRK, Stephen b. Belfast, amateur boxer. Irish light heavyweight champion 1995-97. Bronze medallist at 1997 World Championships.

McCULLOUGH, Wayne (1970-) b. Belfast, professional boxer. Irish light flyweight champion 1988, flyweight champion 1990 and bantamweight champion 1992. 1990 Commonwealth Games flyweight champion. Represented Ireland at 1988 Olympics and was 1992 Olympic bantamweight silver medallist. Turned professional 1993. Former WBC super-bantamweight World Champion he lost his title to Mexican Daniel Zaragoza in January 1997, the first defeat of his professional career.

MAGEE, Brian (1975-) b. Belfast, amateur boxer. Irish middleweight Champion since 1995. Represented Ireland at the 1996 Olympics. Silver medallist at 1998 European Championships.

GAA

BOYLE, Tony (1970-) b. Donegal, Gaelic footballer. All-Ireland medallist with Donegal in 1992. All-star award winner 1992.

BOND, Michael b. Galway, hurling manager. Manager of 1983 All-Ireland U21 hurling championship winners, Galway. Took over as Offaly manager in July 1998. Manager of 1998 All-Ireland Senior Hurling Champions, Offaly.

BROLLY, Joe (1970-) b. Derry, Gaelic footballer. Holds one All-Ireland Senior Football Championship medal (1993), two National Football League (1995 and 1996) and All-Star awards in 1996 and 1997.

BUCKLEY, Niall (1973-) b. Kildare, gaelic footballer. All-star award winner 1997, midfielder with 1998 All-Ireland finalists Kildare.

CANAVAN, Peter (1971-) b. Tyrone, Gaelic footballer. All-Star award winner 1995 and 1996, Player of the Year 1995. Won two Ulster Senior Football Championship medals (1995 and 1996).

CAREY, D.J. (1971-) b. Kilkenny, hurler. Holder of two All-Ireland Senior Hurling Championships (1992 and 1993), 2 National Hurling League (1990 and 1995) six All-Star awards (1991-95 and 1997) and 21 All-Ireland handball titles. Announced retirement - February 1998 - but returned for 1998 Championship. Considered the outstanding player of his generation.

DALY, Anthony (1970-) b. Clare, hurler. Holder of two All-Ireland Senior Hurling Championships (1995 and 1997) when he captained Clare. All-Star award winner three times.

DONNELLAN, Michael (1977-) b. Galway, gaelic footballer. Holder of one All-Ireland Senior Football Championship (1998), man of the match 1998 All-Ireland football final.

DOOLEY, Joe (1963-) b. Offaly, hurler. Holder of three All-Ireland Senior Hurling Championship (1985, '94 and '98) and one National Hurling League (1991). His brothers Billy and Johnny were also members of the 1994 and 1998 All-Ireland Senior Hurling Championship and 1991 National Hurling League winning Offaly teams.

DOWD, Tommy (1969-) b. Leicester, Gaelic footballer. Holds one All-Ireland Senior Football Championship (1996) when he captained Meath, and two National Football Leagues (1990 and 1994). Winner of three All-Star awards (1991, 95 and 96).

FALLON, Jarlath Ja (1973-) b. Galway, Gaelic footballer. Holder of one All-Ireland Senior Football Championship (1998). All-star award winner 1995. An accomplished rugby player, he has represented Connacht.

FENNELLY, Kevin (1954-) b. Kilkenny, hurling manager. Won one All-Ireland Senior Hurling Championship medal (1979) and three All-Ireland Club Senior Hurling Championships (1981, 84 and 90) with Ballyhale Shamrocks as a player. Manager of the Kilkenny team who were beaten in the 1998 All-Ireland Senior Hurling Championship final by Offaly.

FITZGERALD, Maurice (1970-) b. Kerry, Gaelic footballer. Holds one All-Ireland Senior Football Championship (1997), one National Football League (1997), three All-Star awards (1988, 95, 97). Man of the match in 1997 All-Ireland final and 1997 Player of the Year. In 1989 won the world long-kicking competition beating professionals from rugby, American football, soccer and Australian Rules.

GILES, Trevor (1976-) b. Meath, Gaelic footballer. Holder of one All-Ireland Senior Football Championship (1996), two All-Star awards (1996 and 1997). Player of the Year 1996.

KIRBY, Gary (1966-) b. Limerick, hurler. Holds two National Hurling League medals (1992 and 1997). All-Star award winner (1991, 94, 95, 96). Twice a beaten All-Ireland finalist (1994 and 1996).

LOUGHNANE, Ger (1954-) b. Clare, hurling manager. Holder of two National Hurling League as a player (1977 and 1978) and two All-Star awards (1974 and 1977) becoming the first Clare man to do so. Manager of the Clare teams which won the All-Ireland Senior Hurling Championship in 1995 (their first win since 1914) and 1997. Outspoken and fiercely loyal to his players.

LOHAN, Brian (1971-) b. Clare, hurler. Holder of two All-Ireland Senior Hurling Championships (1995 and 1997), three All-Star awards (1995, 96, 97) at full back. Player of the Year 1995.

McCARTHY, Ger (1947-) b. Cork, hurling manager. Won four All-Ireland Senior Hurling Championships (1970, 76, 77 and 78) and two National Hurling League (1969 and 1972) as a player with Cork. Won two All-Ireland Club Senior Hurling Championships (1975 and 1978) with St Finbarr's and was awarded an All-Star in 1975. Managed Cork when they were beaten in the 1982 All-Ireland Senior Hurling Championship final. Manager of a resurgent Waterford team who qualified for the National Hurling League final in 1998 and were beaten in the 1998 All-Ireland hurling final.

McDONAGH, Joe (1954-) b. Galway, GAA administrator. President of Cumann Lúthchleas Gael since 1997.
Holds one All-Ireland Senior Hurling Championship (1980) and an All-Star award (1976). When Galway won their breakthrough All-Ireland in 1980 McDonagh led a rendition of 'The West's Awake' from the steps of the Hogan Stand.

MAUGHAN, John (1962-). b. Mayo, Gaelic football manager. Managed Clare to Munster Senior Football Championships in 1992. Manager of Mayo team beaten in 1996 and 1997 All-Ireland Senior Football Championship finals.

MULVIHILL, Liam (1946-) b. Longford, GAA administrator. Director General of the GAA since 1979. Presided over GAA 's modernisation through the ongoing development of Croke Park and various provincial grounds and a better marketing of the games in general.

O'CONNOR, James (1972-) b. Clare, hurler. Holder of two All-Ireland Senior Hurling Championships (1995 and 1997), two All-Star awards (1995 and 1997). Player of the Year 1997, man of the match 1997 All-Ireland final and top scorer 1997 hurling championship.

O'CONNOR, Willie (1967-) b. Kilkenny, hurler. Holder of two All-Ireland SENIOR HURLING CHAMPIONSHIPS (1992 and 1993), two National Hurling Leagues (1990, 1995), two All-Star award (1992 and 1997), one All-Ireland Club Senior Hurling Championship (1991) with Glenmore. Corner back with 1998 All-Ireland finalists.

O'DWYER, Mick (1936-) b. Kerry, Gaelic football manager. Won four all-Ireland Senior Football Championships (1959, 62, 69 and 70) and eight National Football League (1959, 61, 63, 69, 71, 72, 73, 74) as a player. Managed Kerry to eight All-Ireland Senior Football Championships (1975, 78, 79, 80, 81, 84, 85, and 86) and three National Football Leagues (1977, 82 and 84). Manager of Kildare 1990-93 and since 1997 in 1998 he guided them to their first All-Ireland final since 1935.

O'MAHONY, John gaelic football manager. Guided Mayo to 1989 All-Ireland Senior Football Championship final, Leitrim to 1994 Connacht Senior Football Championship. Manager of the Galway team who won the 1998 All-Ireland Senior Football Championship.

Ó MUIRCHEARTAIGH, Mícheál Gaelic games broadcaster, cathaoirleach (Chairman) of Bord na Gaeilge.

O'NEILL, Pat (1971-) b. Kilkenny, hurler. Holder of two All-Ireland Senior Hurling Championships (1992 and 1993), one National Hurling League (1995) and one All-Star award (1992). Man of the match 1992 All-Ireland hurling final.

Ó SÉ, Páidí (1955-) b. Kerry, Gaelic football manager. Holder of eight All-Ireland Senior Football Championships (1975, 78, 79, 80, 81, 84, 85, and 86). Captain of Kerry in 1985. Holder of four National Football Leagues (1974, 77, 82 and 84) and five successive All-Star awards 1981-85. Manager of the Kerry team which won the All-Ireland Senior Football Championship and National Football League in 1997.

PILKINGTON, Johnny (1969-) b. Offaly, hurler. Holder of two All-Ireland Senior Hurling Championships (1994 and 1998), one National Hurling League (1991), two All-Ireland Club Senior Hurling Championships with Birr (1995 and 1998).

RYAN, Glen (1972-) b. Kildare, Gaelic footballer. Captain of 1998 All-Ireland finalists, Kildare. All-Star award winner 1997.

SHERLOCK, Jason (1975-) b. Dublin, Gaelic footballer, basketballer, soccer player. Holder of one All-Ireland Senior Football Championship (1995). Has represented Ireland in international basketball and currently plays in the FAI National League with Shamrock Rovers.

SILKE, Ray (1971-) b. Galway, Gaelic footballer. Holder of one All-Ireland Senior Football Championship (1998), he was the Galway captain. Captained his club, Corofin, to All-Ireland Club Senior Football Championship in 1998 (the first Connacht team to win the title).

STOREY, Martin (1964-) b. Wexford, hurler. Holds one All-Ireland Senior Hurling Championships (1996) when he captained Wexford to first title since 1968. All-star award winner 1993 and 1996. Player of the Year 1996.

TOHILL, Anthony (1971-) b. Derry, Gaelic footballer. Holds one All-Ireland Senior Football Championship (1993), three National Football League (1992, 95 and 96). All-star award winner in 1992, 93 and 95. Played Australian Rules football in Melbourne, and has played soccer for Derry City in the National League.

WHELEHAN, Brian (1971-) b. Offaly, hurler. Holder of two All Ireland Senior Hurling Championships (1994 and 1998), one National Hurling League (1991), two All-Ireland Club Senior Hurling Championships (1995 and 1998) with Birr, All-Star award winner 1993 and 1995. Man of the match and top scorer in the 1998 All-Ireland hurling final. His younger brother Simon was also a member of the 1998 All-Ireland winning team.

Golfing

CLARKE, Darren (1968-) b. Tyrone, professional golfer. Only Irish member of 1997 winning European Ryder Cup team. Winner of three European PGA tour events, Dunhill Open (1993), German Masters (1996) and Benson & Hedges International Open (1998). Second in 1997 British Open (his best finish in a major). Finished fourth overall in European Order of Merit in 1997. As an amateur he won the 1989 East of

Ireland Championship and in 1990 won the Irish Close, North of Ireland and South of Ireland Championships.

D'ARCY, Eamonn (1952-) b. Wicklow, professional golfer. Played in the Ryder Cup four times (1975, 77, 81 and 87) and was member of the 1988 Irish team which won the Dunhill Cup. Won eleven European PGA events including the 1983 Spanish Open and the 1990 Desert Open.

HARRINGTON, Padraig (1971-) b. Dublin, professional golfer (turned professional 1995). Won 1996 Spanish Open. Partnered Paul McGinley to win the 1997 World Cup for Ireland in South Carolina. As an amateur he won the West of Ireland Championship in 1994 and the Irish Open and Irish Close Championships in 1995. Member of the Walker Cup team in 1991, 93 and 95 (when Britain and Ireland beat the US at Royal Portcawl).

McGIMPSEY, Garth (1955-) b. Co. Down, amateur golfer. North of Ireland Championship winner 1978, '84, '91, '92 and '93; West of Ireland Championship winner 1984, '88, '93 and '96; East of Ireland Championship winner 1988, '94 and '98. He also won the 1988 Irish Close Championship and the 1985 British amateur Championship. Has played on three Walker Cup teams, 1985, '89 (when Britain and Ireland beat the United States for the first time in America) and '91.

McGINLEY, Paul (1967-) b. Dublin, professional golfer. Turned professional 1991 and has won two European PGA Tour events, the Austrian Open (1996) and the Oki Pro-Am (1997). Partnered Padraig Harrington to victory in the 1997 World Cup at Kiawah Island, South Carolina. As an amateur he won the 1989 Irish Close Championship and the 1991 South of Ireland Championship. He represented Britain and Ireland in the 1991 Walker Cup.

O'CONNOR JNR, Christy (1948-) b. Galway, professional golfer (turned professional 1965) and has won eight competitions on the European tour including the 1975 Irish Open, the 1989 Jersey Open and the 1992 British Masters. A member of the 1975 and 1989 Ryder Cup teams.

WALTON, Philip (1962-) b. Dublin, professional golfer (turned professional 1983) and has four European Tournament wins including the 1990 French Open and the 1995 English Open. A member of the victorious European Ryder Cup team in 1995. Won the 1982 Irish Close Championship as an amateur and was a member of the Walker Cup teams of 1981 and 1983.

Horse Racing

DUNWOODY, Richard (1960-) b Co. Down, national hunt jockey. Counts two Aintree Grand Nationals (with West Tipp, 1986 and Minnehoma, 1994), one Cheltenham Gold Cup (with Charter Party, 1988) and one Irish Grand National (with Desert Orchid, 1990) among his many winners. A former champion National Hunt jockey in Britain. Won the 1998 Hennessy Gold Cup with Doran's Pride.

EDDERY, Pat (1952-) b. Dublin, flat jockey. Has had in excess of 4,000 winners in a career stretching back to 1969. His 14 English Classic winners include Grundy (1975 Derby), Lomond (1993 2,000 Guineas) and Lady Carla (1996 Oaks). Ten Irish Classic winners include Law Society (1985 Derby), Tirol (1990 2,000 Guineas) and Bolas (1994 Irish Oaks). Has also won the Prix de l'Arc de Triomphe and the French Derby. Eddery is the most successful Irish jockey of all time and one of the most outstanding Irish sportsmen ever.

FALLON, Kieren b. Clare, flat jockey. Champion flat jockey in Britain 1997, has ridden in excess of 100 winners in each season since 1996. English Classic winners include Reams of Verse (1997 Oaks) and Sleepytime (1997 1,000 Guineas).

KINANE, Mick (1959-) b. Tipperary, flat jockey. Irish Champion Flat Jockey a record ten times between 1983 and 1994, has had Classics wins in Ireland, England, France, Italy, America and Australia. Perhaps his finest race (certainly his most famous) was in winning the 1993 Melbourne Gold Cup on Vintage Crop. His 15-year partnership with trainer Dermot Weld has served both well. In 1998 he won the English 2,000 Guineas with King of Kings, the Epsom Oaks on Shahtoush and the Irish National Stakes on Mus-if.

O'BRIEN, Aidan (1969-) b. Wexford, horse trainer. Irish Champion trainer (National Hunt) 1993/94-1997/98. A former champion amateur jockey, has enjoyed considerable success on the flat training three Irish Classic winners in 1997, Desert King (Derby and 2,000 Guineas) and Classic Park (1,000 Guineas). In 1998 he trained the Cheltenham Champion Hurdle winner, Istabraq, and the English Classic winners, Shahtoush and King of Kings, in the Oaks and the 2,000 Guineas, respectively.

SWAN, Charlie (1968-) b. Tipperary, national hunt jockey. Rode his 1,000th winner at Listowel in September 1997. Irish National Hunt Champion Jockey nine times (and the seventh consecutive year). Has Irish Grand National and Galway Plate wins to his credit. Rode Istabraq to victory in the 1998 Cheltenham Champion Hurdle.

Motor Sports

JORDAN, Eddie (1948-) b. Dublin, Formula 1 team owner. Irish Kart Champion in 1971, won the Irish Formula Atlantic Championship in 1978. Established Eddie Jordan Racing (1979); the team competed in British Formula 3 championships throughout the 1980s. Established Jordan Grand Prix (1991); the team finished fifth in the Constructors' championship (1991, 93 and 96). In 1998 Irish-based driver, Damon Hill, won the team's first Grand Prix at the Belgian Grand Prix.

IRVINE, Eddie (1965-) b. Co. Down, Formula 1 driver. A member of the Ferrari team since 1996 Irvine is assured fourth place in the 1998 Formula 1 Drivers' Championship, having scored 41 points and securing two 2nd place and five 3rd place finishes. Made his Formula 1 debut with Jordan (1993), has competed in 80 races, 48 of which have been with Ferrari. Prior to Formula 1, raced Formula 3000 in Europe and Formula Nippon in Japan.

DUNLOP, Joey (1952-) b. Ballymena, motorcyclist. World TT Formula 1 championship winner (1982, 83, 84, 85 and 86). Overcame injury to win his 23rd Isle of Man TT race in 1998. His brother Robert won his fifth Isle of Man TT in 1998.

Rugby

COSTELLO, Victor (1970-) b. Dublin, international rugby player. Member of the All-Ireland League Division 1 side St Mary's, has 13 full international caps and scored two international tries. Has represented Leinster at interprovincial level. Irish National Shot Putt champion (1988, 89, 90 and 91) he is a former Irish senior record holder, holds the Irish Junior record and competed in the 1992 Olympic Games.

ELWOOD, Eric (1969-) b. Galway, international rugby player. Member of the Galwegians who compete in the All-Ireland League Division One. Has won 28 Irish caps and scored in excess of 200 points. Was capped by the Barbarians and represented Connacht at interprovincial level.

GATLAND, Warren (1963-) b. New Zealand, international rugby coach for Ireland (appointed in February 1998 following Brian Ashton's resignation). As a player, he represented his province Waikato and made 17 representative appearances for the All-Blacks but never won a full cap. Player/coach with Galwegians (1989-93), managed the Connacht team (1996-98) guiding them to the 1997 European Shield quarter-final.

JOHNS, Paddy (1968-) b. Portadown, international rugby player. Member of the Saracens club in England, has 43 international caps and scored two tries. Represented Ulster at interprovincial level. Captain of the Irish team on their 1998 tour of South Africa.

LENIHAN, Donal (1959-) b. Cork, international rugby manager. Won 52 international caps (1981-92), member of 1982, 83 and 85 Triple Crown winning sides (when Ireland also won the International Championship). Nominated as a selector during the 1998 Five Nations campaign, appointed Irish manager for the 1998 summer tour to South Africa and appointed to the post for the forthcoming season on his return.

O'SHEA, Conor (1970-) b. Limerick, international rugby player. Member of the London Irish club, has won 20 international caps at full back and scored 14 points. Has represented Munster at interprovincial level.

WALLACE, Paul (1971-) b. Cork, international rugby player. Member of the Saracens club, plays in the English Premiership One. Won 20 international caps since his debut in the 1995 World Cup and scored two tries. Represented Munster at interprovincial level and won three caps on the successful 1997 Lions tour of South Africa.

WOOD, Keith (1972-) b. Limerick, international rugby player. Member of the Harlequins club who compete in the English Premiership One, has won 17 international caps and scored two tries (both against New Zealand). Irish captain for the 1997/98 season (excluding South African tour), has been capped by the Barbarians and won two caps with the Lions on the 1997 tour to South Africa.

Snooker

DOHERTY, Ken (1969-) b. Dublin, professional snooker player (turned professional 1990). World Snooker Champion in 1997 (beating Stephen Hendry 18-12 in the final), but was beaten 18-12 by John Higgins in the 1998 final. Irish Amateur Champion in 1987 and 1989,

was World Amateur Champion in 1989. Beaten 9-3 by Ronnie O'Sullivan in the final of the 1998 Irish Masters but was awarded the title when it emerged that O'Sullivan failed a drugs test.

HIGGINS, Alex (1949-) b. Belfast, professional snooker player (turned professional in 1971). Known as 'Hurricane', won the 1972 World Championship beating John Spencer 37-32 in the final, won the 1982 World title beating Ray Reardon 18-15. The 1983 UK Championship, the 1978 and 1981 Benson & Hedges Masters and the 1989 Irish Masters are among the most prominent of his many wins. Has retired from the sport and is in poor health.

TAYLOR, Denis (1949-) b. Tyrone, professional snooker player. Won the 1985 World Snooker Champion, beating Steve Davis 18-17 on the black ball in the final frame to win the most dramatic final ever. Won the 1984 Rothman's Grand Prix and the 1987 Benson & Hedges Masters. Announced his intention to retire at the end of the 1998/99 season.

Soccer

ARKINS, Vinny (1970-) b. Dublin, Irish League soccer player. Plays with Portadown in the Irish League Premier Division. Finished the 1997/98 season as the league's top goal scorer with 22 goals. Capped by the Republic of Ireland at 'B' U21 and U18 levels.

BREEN, Gary (1973-) b. London, international soccer player. Plays with Coventry City in the English Premiership. Won 15 caps, scoring two international goals for the Republic of Ireland since his 1996 debut.

CASCARINO, Tony (1962-) b. Kent, international soccer player. Plays with AS Nancy in the French League. Capped 76 times by the Republic of Ireland. With 19 goals he is one goal short of Frank Stapleton's Irish goal scoring record. Irish squad member at the 1998 European Championships and the 1990 and 1994 World Cup finals.

CUNNINGHAM, Kenny (1971-) b. Dublin, international soccer player. Plays with Wimbledon in the English Premiership, has won 17 caps for the Republic of Ireland.

DONNELLY, Michael (1968-) b. Belfast, Irish League soccer player. Captain of Cliftonville (team which won the 1997/98 Irish League Premier Division), has been with the club since 1987.

DOWIE, Iain (1965-) b. Hatfield, international soccer player. Plays with Queens Park Rangers in the English First Division, has been capped 50 times by Northern Ireland. With eleven international goals to his credit, is two goals shy of the Northern Ireland record.

DUFF, Damian (1979-) b. Dublin, international soccer player. Plays with Blackburn Rovers in the English Premiership, has won three caps for the Republic of Ireland. A member of the Irish team which finished third in the U20 World Cup in 1997.

GEOGHEGAN, Stephen (1971-) National League soccer player. Striker with Shelbourne in the National League Premier Division, has been the league's top goal scorer in the 1993/94, 95/96, 96/97 and 97/98 seasons. Winner of two FAI Cup winners' medals with Shelbourne (1996 and 1997).

GILLESPIE, Keith (1975-) b. Larne, international soccer player. Plays with Newcastle United in the English

Premiership, has been capped 22 times and scored one goal for Northern Ireland.

GIVEN, Shay (1976-) b. Donegal, international soccer player. Goalkeeper with Newcastle United in the English Premiership, has been capped 18 times by the Republic of Ireland.

HOUGHTON, Ray (1962-) b. Glasgow, international soccer player Plays with Reading in the English Second Division, has won 73 caps and scored six international goals for the Republic of Ireland. A member of the Irish European Championship squad in 1988 (where the goal he scored to beat England assures him sporting immortality), also played in the 1990 and 1994 World Cup finals (where his goal against Italy gave Ireland a shock victory and revenge for elimination by Italy in 1990). Voted FAI Player of the Year in 1994.

HUGHES, Michael (1971-) b. Larne, international soccer player. Plays with Wimbledon in the English Premiership, has won 43 caps and scored three goals for Northern Ireland.

IRWIN, Denis (1965-) b. Cork, international soccer player. Plays with Manchester United in the English Premiership, has scored three goals in his 49 international appearances for the Republic of Ireland. A member of the Irish World Cup squad at the 1994 World Cup finals.

KEANE, Robbie (1980-) b. Dublin, international soccer player. Plays with Wolverhampton Wanderers in the English First Division, won four international caps for the Republic of Ireland. A member of the Irish team which won the U18 European Championship in 1998.

KEANE, Roy (1971-) b. Cork, international soccer player. Captain of Manchester United in the English Premiership, also the current Irish captain. Has won 39 caps and scored four goals for the Republic of Ireland. FAI Player of the Year in 1997. Member of the Irish squad in the 1994 World Cup.

KELLY, Gary (1974-) b. Louth, international soccer player. Plays with Leeds United in the English Premiership, won 28 international caps and scored one goal for the Republic of Ireland since his debut in 1994. A member of the Irish team which qualified for the second round of the 1994 World Cup.

KERR, Brian (1953-) b. Dublin, international soccer manager. As manager of all Republic of Ireland youth teams (U15, U16, U18 and U20), has had unprecedented success. The U20 team finished third in 1997 World Cup in Malaysia, the U16 team won 1998 European Championships and the U18 team won the 1998 European Championships. Also the FAI's Technical Director.

LOMAS, Steve (1974-) b. Hanover, Germany, international soccer player. Plays with West Ham United in the English Premiership, won 26 caps and scored two international goals for Northern Ireland.

McCARTHY, Mick (1959-) b. Barnsley, international soccer manager. As a player - won 57 international caps for the Republic of Ireland, was a member of the Irish squad at the 1988 European Championships and Irish captain in the 1990 World Cup. Manager of the Republic of Ireland (since February 1996), almost brought the team to the 1998 World Cup finals (only losing in a play-off), but has had a promising start to the European 2000 qualifiers.

McGRATH, Paul (1959-) b. Ealing, international soccer player (now retired). Played as a defender, was capped 82 times by the Republic and scored six international goals. FAI Player of the Year (1990 and 1991). A member of the Republic of Ireland World Cup squads in 1990 and 1994 and the European Championship squad in 1988. Awarded a testimonial by the FAI in May 1998.

McMENEMY, Lawrie (1936-) b.Gateshead, international soccer manager. Manager of Northern Ireland (since February 1998), assisted by Pat Jennings and Joe Jordan. England assistant manager (1990-93), has also coached Sheffield Wednesday and managed Southampton and Sunderland.

MULRYNE, Philip (1978-) b. Belfast, international soccer player. Plays with Manchester United in the English Premiership. Won six international caps and scored one goal for Northern Ireland.

O'HERLIHY, Bill b. Cork, sports presenter on RTÉ covering most live sporting action. Worked in the *Cork Examiner* before joining RTÉ. Chief executive of the public relations consultancy, Bill O'Herlihy Communications Group. Main presenter of the soccer programme *The Premiership* with Eamon Dunphy and Johnny Giles.

QUINN, Niall (1966-) b. Dublin, international soccer player. Plays with Sunderland in the English First Division. Won 63 caps with the Republic of Ireland. Fifth on the Republic's all-time top scorers list, with 16 goals to his name. A member of the Republic of Ireland squad who were quarter finalists in the 1990 World Cup, injury kept him out of the 1994 World Cup squad. Played as a forward on the Dublin team which was beaten in the 1983 All-Ireland Minor Hurling final.

STAUNTON, Steve (1969-) b. Drogheda, international soccer player. Plays with Liverpool in the English Premiership. Won 75 caps and scored six goals for the Republic of Ireland. FAI Player of the Year in 1993 and a member of the Republic of Ireland World Cup squads in 1990 and 1994.

Other

DE BRUIN, Michelle (1969-) b. Dublin, swimmer. Gold medallist 200m Butterfly and 200m Individual Medley and silver medallist in 400m Individual Medley at 1995 European Championships. Gold Medallist 400m Freestyle, 200m Individual Medley, 400m Individual Medley and Bronze medallist 200m Butterfly at 1996 Olympic Games. Gold Medallist 400m Individual Medley and 200m Freestyle and silver medallist in the 200m Freestyle and 200m Butterfly at 1997 European Championships. Holds 14 short-course and 13 long-course records in freestyle, backstroke, butterfly and individual medley events. Banned for four years by the international swimming body FINA for allegedly manipulating a urine sample. Has appealed the ban.

JOHNSTON, Margaret (1943-) b. Derry, international bowls player. Commonwealth gold medallist 1986 and 1994, World Singles Champion 1992, World Pairs Champion (with Phylis Nolan) 1988, '92 and '96. Has also won numerous Irish and British Isles titles.

McNULTY, Joe (1969-) b. California, surfer. A longboarder, came 2nd with brother Terence at Big Wave World Championship 1998. Twice WSA West Coast

Men's Champion, was ranked 4th in Professional Surfing Association of America and was 1997 Irish Men's champion.

STYNES, Jim (1966-) b. Dublin, professional Australian Rules player. Winners of Brownlow medal (Best and Fairest Player of the Year) in 1991. Played with Melbourne and set an Australian record of 244 consecutive games. Retired from competitive football at end of 1998 season. Represented Ireland (one tour) and Australia (two tours) in International Rules series.

WILEY, Ian (28-years-old) b. Dublin, canoeist in the men's Slalom K1 Class. Currently ranked No. 2 in the World Cup series, 5th in the Atlanta Olympics, is seen as a medal prospect in the Sydney Olympics. Trains with the Liffey Valley Canoe Club.

THEATRE / FILM / TV

ALLEN, Dave (1936-) b. Dublin, comedian. Described as an anarchic wit - he introduced acts on the pop show circuit in London in the 1960s, emigrated to Australia and did his first one-man TV show in 1963, returned to England and has regularly appeared there in his unique one-man TV comedy shows.

BERGIN, Joan film costume designer. Designed the costumes for the Oscar winning My Left Foot (1989), and Pat O'Connor's Dancing at Lughnasa (1997).

BERGIN, Patrick (1953-) b. Dublin; film actor, playwright, producer and director. Had lead roles in Bob Rafelson's Mountains of the Moon (1990), Sleeping with the Enemy (1991), Robin Hood (TV 1991). His latest film is Angela Mooney Dies Again (1997).

BLACK, Cathal (1952-) director and writer. Films include Wheels (1976), Our Boys (1980), Pigs (1984), Korea (1995).

BOORMAN, John (1933-) b. London, director. Living in Ireland for nearly 30 years, has made controversial films, the latest being The General about the Dublin gang-land boss Martin Cahill for which he won the Best Director Award at the 1998 Cannes Film Festival. Other works include Point Blank (1966), Hell In The Pacific (1969), Deliverance (1972) and Excalibur (1980), Hope & Glory (1987).

BRANAGH, Kenneth (1960-) b. Belfast, shakespearean actor, leader of Renaissance Theatre Company and film director. Gained international recognition as director/star of screen version of Henry V (1989). Received Oscar-nomination for his short Swan Song (1992), directed and starred in screen adaptation of Much Ado About Nothing (1993) and Hamlet (1996). Other films include High Season (1987) and A Month in the Country (1987), Frankenstein and The Gingerbread Man (1997).

BRENNAN, Bríd Films include Anne Devlin (1984), Four Days in July (1985), Trojan Eddie (1996), Dancing at Lughnasa (1997).

BROSNAN, Pierce (1953-) b. Meath, actor. Gained recognition in TV series Remington Steele (1982-87). Film debut in The Long Good Friday (1980). Other films: Mrs Doubtfire (1993), disaster film Dante's Peake (1997) and as the fifth James Bond in Goldeneye (1996). His production company has filmed The Nephew (1997) in Ireland and has two more future projects.

BUGGY, Niall Films include Purple Taxi (1977), Portrait of an Artist as a Young Man (1977), Upwardly Mobile (TV sitcom), The Lonely Passion of Judith Hearne (1987).

BYRNE, Gabriel (1950-) b. Dublin, actor. TV debut in RTÉ's The Riordans (1979) and Bracken. Film debut in On a Paving Stone Mounted (1978). Went on to star in the Coen brothers' gangster drama, Miller's Crossing (1990). Was married to actress Ellen Barkin, opposite whom he starred in Siesta (1987). Other films include Defence of the Realm (1985), Into the West (1991) and The Usual Suspects (1995). Collaborated on film projects with Áine O'Connor, including Draíocht. Also an accomplished writer.

BYRNE, Gay (1934-) b. Dublin, Broadcaster, presenter and executive producer of The Late Late Show since 1962. Radio presenter of The Gay Byrne Show since 1972. Ireland's most influential broadcaster, responsible for opening many topical issues of the day for general discussion, which would have previously been considered taboo. Is to resign from his radio show on Christmas Eve 1998 and will retire from his TV show in 1999, but his place in history books has been assured with the Late Late Show being the world's longest-running live television talk show.

COLLINS, Tommy b. Derry, film-maker. Produced documentaries A Long Way to Go, the journey home of Johnny Walker of the Birmingham Six. Produced Margo Harkin's film Hush-A-Bye-Baby (1989) and More Than a Sacrifice (1995), a documentary for Channel 4 about the IRA's first ceasefire. Made his directorial debut with the Derry/Donegal-based Bogwoman (1997).

COMERFORD, Joe (1949-) director, made the first Irish language film Caoineadh Airt Ui Laoire (1975) - Lament for Art O'Leary. Other films include Emtigon (1977), Traveller (1981), Waterbag (1984), High Boot Benny (1993). Won Europa Prize for Reefer and the Model (1987).

CONNAUGHTON, Shane b. Cavan, actor turned scriptwriter. Nominated with Jim Sheridan for Best Adaptation Screen-play for My Left Foot (1989). Won an Oscar for writing The Bottom Dollar (1981). Films include A Border Station (1989), The Miracle (1991) and The Playboys (1992), co-written with Adrian Dunbar.

CRAVEN, Gemma (1950-) b. Ireland, actress, whose films include The Slipper and the Rose (1976), Double X (1992), Words Upon The Window Pane (1994) and the critically acclaimed Denis Potter TV series Pennies from Heaven (1977).

CUSACK, Sinéad (1948-) b. Dublin, actress. Films include David Copperfield (1969), The Last Remake of Beau Geste (1977), and Bad Behaviour (1993). Daughter of Cyril and sister of Sorcha (of the BBC TV series Casualty) and Niamh (The Playboys - 1992 and formerly of the ITV series Heartbeat).

DAY LEWIS, Daniel (1958-) b. London, actor and son of the poet-laureate, Cecil Day Lewis. Acclaimed in Stephen Frears' My Beautiful Laundrette and Merchant- Ivory's A Room with a View (1985). Lead role in My Left Foot (1989) for which he won an Oscar. His portrayal of Gerry Conlon - In the Name of the Father (1993) - earned him an Oscar nomination.

Films include *The Bounty* (1984), *The Unbearable Lightness of Being* (1988), *The Last of the Mohicans* (1992), *The Crucible* (1996), *The Boxer* (1997).

DOOLAN, Lelia artistic director of the Abbey Theatre and RTÉ's head of entertainment. Former chairperson of the Irish Film Board.

DUNBAR, Adrian (1958-) b. Fermanagh, actor and script-writer. Films include *A World Apart* (1987), *The Dawning* (1988), *My Left Foot* (1989), *Hear My Song* (1991), *The Playboys* (which he co-scripted 1992), *Widow's Peak* (1993).

DUNPHY, Eamon (1945-) b. Dublin, journalist and former footballer. Played for York, Milwall, Charlton, Reading, Shamrock Rovers, capped 23 times for Republic of Ireland. Journalist since 1978, Worked for the *Sunday Independent* and now working for Today FM, presenting the current affairs programme, *The Last Word*. Panelist on *The Premiership* with Johnny Giles, presented by Bill O'Herlihy (a Network 2 sports programme covering English premiership football).

FANNING, Dave (1955-) b. Dublin, TV and radio broadcaster. Began career on pirate radio, edited music journal *Scene*, moved to 2FM (1978). Closely associated with U2. Fanning's radio show remains invaluable source of exposure for emerging Irish acts. Television credits include Network 2 music show *2TV* and *The Movie Show*.

FINUCANE, Marian (1950-) b. Dublin, RTÉ radio and television presenter since 1974, presenter of *The Marian Finucane Show* on radio, and co-presenter of *Crimeline* on television.

FITZGERALD, Geraldine (1914-) b. Dublin, actress, appeared in several British films. Her Hollywood debut was in *Dark Victory* (1939). Best known for her Oscar-nominated role in *Wuthering Heights* (1939). Films include *The Mill on the Floss* (1937), *'Til We Meet Again* (1940), *The Last American Hero* (1973), *The Mango Tree* (1977), *Arthur* (1981), *Poltergeist II* (1986). Mother of director Michael Lindsay-Hogg.

FRICKER, Brenda (1944-) b. Dublin, actress. Was in the National Theatre, the Royal Shakespeare Company and the Court Theatre Company. Famed for Oscar-winning supporting performance as Christy Brown's mother in *My Left Foot* (1989). Moved to Hollywood in 1990s, starred in *Home Alone 2: Lost in New York* (1992) and *So I Married an Axe Murderer* (1993). Prominent roles BBC's TV series *Casualty* (1986-1990) and *Brides of Christ* mini-series (1992). Other films include *Of Human Bondage* (1964), *The Ballroom of Romance* (1981), *The Field* (1990), *A Man of No Importance* (1995), *Swann* (1997).

GALLAGHER, Bronagh Films include *Dear Sarah* (1990), *The Commitments* (1991), *Pulp Fiction* (1994) and Northern Irish film, *Divorcing Jack* (1997).

GARSON, Greer (1908-) b. Co. Down, actress. Spotted by Louis B. Mayer, signed up and given role in Sam Wood's *Goodbye Mr Chips* (1939). Nominated for six Best Actress Oscars and collected one as *Mrs Miniver* (1942). Films include *Pride and Prejudice* (1940), *The Valley of Decision* (1945), *Julius Caesar* (1953), *The Singing Nun* (1966), *The Happiest Millionaire* (1967).

GLEESON, Brendan Films include *Into the West* (1992), *The Snapper* (1993), *Braveheart (1994)*, *Michael Collins* (1996), *Trojan Eddie* (1996), *A Furtive*

Gesture (1996), *Angela Mooney Dies Again* (1997) and the lead role of Martin Cahill in JOHN BOORMAN'S *The General* (1997), which won him widespread acclaim for his portrayal of the Dublin gangster.

GUINEY, Ed managing director of *Temple Films*. Producer of *Guiltrip* (1995). Currently working on *Sweetly Barret* (1998) the first feature by writer/director Stephen Bradley.

HARRIS, Richard (1932-) b. Limerick, actor/director. Debuted in *The Quare Fellow* (1956). Acclaimed for his performance in *This Sporting Life* (1963), winning the Cannes Festival Acting Award and an Oscar nomination for Best Actor. Also an Oscar nominee for Best Actor in *The Field* (1990). Films include *Shake Hands with the Devil* (1959), *Mutiny on the Bounty* (1962), *Camelot* (1967), *A Man Called Horse* (1970), *The Molly Maguires* (1970), *Patriot Games* (1992), *Unforgiven* (1992). Regularly returns to theatre.

HILL, George Roy (1922-) film director and former actor with Cyril Cusack's Abbey Theatre company. Achieved major success with Paul Newman and Robert Redford in *Butch Cassidy and the Sundance Kid* (1969) and *The Sting* (1973), the latter earning Hill an Oscar for best direction and the former a nomination for Best Director. Other films include *Thoroughly Modern Millie* (1967), *Funny Farm* (1988) and The *World According To Garp* (1982).

HOBSON, Valerie (1917-) b. Larne, actress. Invited to Hollywood (1935), played leads in horror and thriller films. Retired from film (1954) after marriage to politician John Profumo. Supported him during infamous Christine Keeler sex scandal which toppled the British cabinet. Films include *Bride of Frankenstein* (1935), *Werewolf of London* (1935), *Great Expectations* (1946).

HOGAN, Bosco Films include *Portrait of an Artist as a Young Man* (1977), *The Outsider* (1979), *Jack B. Yeats Assembled Memoirs 1871-1957* (1980), *Anne Devlin* (1984), *In the Name of the Father* (1993).

HOGG, B.J. (1955-) actor. Remained in Northern Ireland during his 20-year career as an actor. Usually cast as a hard man (*Resurrection Man, Titanic Town* and *Divorcing Jack*), departed from type to play a lone father trying to bring up his daughter in the Oscar-nominated short film *Dance Lexie Dance*.

HYNES, Garry (1953-) b. Roscommon, theatre director and founder of the Druid Theatre Co. Set up the theatre with Marie Mullen and MICK LALLY (The Druid is unique in Irish theatre - setting as it does a precedent for companies outside Dublin to put on professional productions. It has not been afraid to stage new ground-breaking works, which have ultimately led to its continued success). Artistic Director with the Abbey Theatre (1990-93), has also directed the RSC in England but returned to the Druid. Her association with MARTIN MCDONAGH'S *Leenane Trilogy* has brought much acclaim to both herself, the Druid and the playwright. In 1998, the cast of *The Beauty Queen of Leenane* was nominated for six Tony Awards - the top award in US theatre. It won four, with Garry Hynes winning best director, the first woman to do so in the history of the Tony's.

JORDAN, Neil (1950-) b. Sligo, director, screen-writer and novelist. Script consultant on JOHN BOORMAN'S

Excalibur (1981). His best-known British feature was Mona Lisa (1986). Hollywood credits include High Spirits (1988) and We're No Angels (1989). Published three novels:The Past (1980), The Dream of a Beast (1983) and Sunrise with Seamonster (1995), plus a collection of short stories, Night in Tunisia (1978), upon which his film The Miracle (1991) was based. Most famed for The Crying Game (1992), which earned six Oscar nominations, collecting one for original screenplay. Directed Angel (1982), The Company of Wolves (1984), Interview with the Vampire (1995), Michael Collins (1996) and Pat McCabe's The Butcher Boy (1997) which has won a number of prizes including the Berlin Festival's prize and the Chrystal award from the 1998 Brussels International Film festival.

KAVANAGH, John films include Paddy (1969), Revival - Pearse's Concept of Ireland (1979), The Ballroom of Romance (1981), Caught in the Free State (1983), The Country Girls (1983), Cal (1984), Into the West (1992), Widow's Peake (1993), Braveheart (1994), Circle of Friends (1995), Some Mother's Son (1996).

KEAN, Marie films include Girl with Green Eyes (1964), I was Happy Here (1965), Ryan's Daughter (1970), Barry Lyndon (1975), The Lonely Passion of Judith Hearne (1987).

KELLEGHER, Tina films include In the Name of the Father (1993), The Snapper (1993), Undercurrent (1995), The Disappearance of Finbar (1996), Ballykissangel (TV series).

KIRWAN, Dervla films include December Bride (1990); TV series include Goodnight Sweetheart, and the highly popular TV series, Ballykissangel, which she left this year.

KILLANIN, Lord Michael (1914-) b. Melbourne, producer with director John Ford. Together, with Tyrone Power, they formed Four Provinces Films. Filmed The Rising of the Moon (1957), Young Cassidy (1964) and The Playboy of the Western World (1962). Father of producer Redmond Morris. Former President of the International Olympic Committee.

LALLY, Mick Films include Our Boys (1981), Night in Tunisia (1983), The Fantasist (1986), The Secret of Roan Inish (1994), A Man of No Importance (1995), Circle of Friends (1995), Glenroe (T.V. series). Founding member of the Druid Theatre Co. with GARRY HYNES and Marie Mullen. An accomplished theatre actor, appears regularly with the Druid Theatre, most recently in Martin McDonagh's A Skull in Connemara, from the Leenane Trilogy.

LINEHAN, Rosaleen b. Dublin, actress. Educated UCD, a veteran of the London and Dublin stage. She has play Winnie in Beckett's Happy Days, Mommo in TOM MURPHY'S Bailegangaire, Mary Tyrone in Eugene O'Neill's Long Day's Journey into Night and was highly acclaimed in BRIAN FRIEL'S Dancing at Lughnasa in the early 1990s. Her film and TV work includes Sharpe's Gold, Suddenly Last Summer and the Irish films Snakes and Ladders and The Butcher Boy.

McAVIN, Josie set designer. Nominated for an Oscar for Best Set Designer Tom Jones (1963) and won an Oscar for her art direction in Out Of Africa (1985).

McCANN, Donal Films include The Fighting Prince of Donegal (1966), Philadelphia Here I Come! (1970),

Poitín (1978), Angel (1992), Cal (1984), Budawanny (1987), The Dead (1987), December Bride (1990), The Miracle (1991), The Bishop's Story (1994), Trojan Eddie (1996), The Nephew (1998). Also an accomplished stage actor, particularly acclaimed for his performances in SEBASTIAN BARRY'S The Steward of Christendom. A special retrospective of his work was given at the 1998 Galway Film Fleadh.

McGINLEY, Sean b. Ballyshannon, worked with the Druid Theatre. Films include A Furtive Gesture (1996), The Disappearance of Finbar (1996), Trojan Eddie (1996), Bogwoman (1997). Has also appeared in many TV series, most notably as Charlo in Roddy Doyle's The Family.

McGUCKIAN, Mary director; films include Words Upon the Window Pane (1994), This is the Sea (1997), George Best (1998).

McLYNN, Pauline actress and comedian. Films include Guiltrip (1995), My Friend Joe (1996) and the TV series Father Ted, in which she played the long suffering housekeeper, Mrs. Doyle. Recorded Roddy Doyle's The Woman who Walked into Doors for RTÉ radio.

McSORLEY, Gerard films include Withdrawal (1983), The Scar (1988), Words Upon the Window Pane (1994), Some Mother's Son (1996), Michael Collins (1996).

MARCUS, Louis (1936-) b. Cork, chairperson of the Irish Film Board, documentary film-maker for cinema and TV. Made over 60 films, including Capallogy (1968), Poc Ar Buile (1973), earning Oscar nominations for both Páistí ag Obair (1973) and Conquest of Light (1975).

MEANEY, Colm Films include Far and Away (1992), The Commitments (1991), Into the West (1992), The Snapper (1993), War of the Buttons (1994), The Last of the High Kings (1996), The Van (1996) as well as the The Next Generation TV series of Star Trek.

MITCHELL, James managing director of Little Bird Films. Produced December Bride (1990), Into the West (1992), St. Ives (1997).

MURRAY, Johnny films include Desecration (1981), Hard Shoulder (1990), The Commitments (1991), Into the West (1992), War of the Buttons (1994).

MURPHY, Pat (1951-) b. Dublin, director and scriptwriter. Co-directed two feature films with John Davis, Maeve (1981) and Anne Devlin (1984).

NEESON, Liam (1952-) b. Ballymena, actor. Made his first amateur dramatic performance (1968) and his first professional theatre performance in The Risen at the Lyric Theatre, Belfast (1975). Joined the Abbey Theatre, Dublin (1977). Film debut in JOHN BOORMAN'S Excalibur (1981)Made his Hollywood debut in Darkman (1990). Roles followed in British productions, The Bounty (1984) and The Mission (1986). Performance in Broadway production of Eugene O'Neill's Anna Christie with his now wife Natasha Richardson (1993). Impressed director Stephen Spielberg who offered Neeson the lead in Schindler's List (1993) for which he received an Oscar nomination (1993). Played the lead in NEIL JORDAN'S Michael Collins (1996). Films include Excalibur (1981), Lamb (1985), A Prayer for the Dying (1987), Suspect (1987), The Dead Pool (1988), Darkman (1990), Husbands and Wives (1992), Revolver (1992), Shining Through (1992), Under Suspicion (1992), Deception (1993), Ethan Frome (1993) Rob Roy (1995) Nell. Played OSCAR WILDE in The Judas Kiss in Broadway (1998).

NEILL, Sam (1948-) b. Northern Ireland, reared New Zealand, actor. Gained acclaim in Gillian Armstrong's My Brilliant Career (1979), Hollywood debut as Damien in the third of the Omen films, The Final Conflict (1981). Starred opposite Meryl Streep in A Cry in the Dark (1988) and Plenty (1985). Lead roles in TV mini-series Kane and Abel (1985) and Amerika (1987). Co-starred in The Piano (1993), which won the Palme d'Or at Cannes. Films include Dead Calm (1989), The Hunt for Red October (1990), Jurassic Park (1993).

O'CONNOR, Carroll (1925-) b. New York, actor. Stage debut with Dublin's Gate Theatre. Gained worldwide fame as Archie Bunker in All in the Family. Films include Cleopatra (1963), What Did You Do in the War, Daddy? (1966), Kelly's Heroes (1970), Acting: Lee Strasberg and the Actor's Studio (1981).

O'CONOR, Hugh actor, films include Lamb (1985), Fear of the Dark (1986), Da (1988), My Left Foot (1989), The Boy From Mercury (1996) and The Young Poisoner.

O'CONNOR, Pat (1943-) b. Waterford, film director. Began career with RTÉ (1970), producing documentaries on Northern Ireland before turning to drama - The Riordans (1979), Miracles (1979). He won BAFTA Award for Best Single Play and Jacob's Award for Best Director for The Ballroom of Romance (1981). Films include Cal (1984), A Month in the Country (1986), Stars and Bars (1988), Circle of Friends (1996), Dancing at Lughnasa (1997).

O'HARA, Maureen Maureen FitzSimmons (b. Dublin, 1920-) actress. Flame-haired beauty who played fiery heroines. Best remembered for John Ford films - How Green was my Valley (1941) and opposite John Wayne in The Quiet Man (1952). Retired but returned in the comedy Only the Lonely (1991). Other films include Song O' My Heart (1930), The Black Swan (1942), Buffalo Bill (1944), Miracle on 34th Street (1947), The Redhead from Wyoming (1955), The Parent Trap (1961).

O'HERLIHY, Dan (1919-) b. Wexford, actor. Emigrated to US, joined Orson Welles's Mercury Theatre, acted in stage and screen versions of Macbeth (1948). Was nominated for a Best Actor Oscar for The Adventures of Robinson Crusoe (1952). Films: Odd Man Out (1947), How to Steal the World (1968), Halloween III (1982), Robocop (1987), The Dead (1988).

O'HERLIHY, Michael (1929-) director. Films: The Fighting Prince of Donegal (1966), Smith! (1969), The Flame is Love (TV 1979), Cry of the Innocent (TV 1980), I Married Wyatt Earp (TV 1983), Hoover vs the Kennedys: The Second Civil War (TV 1987).

O'LEARY, Ronan director. Films: Fragments of Isabella (1989), Diary of a Madman (1991), Hello, Stranger (1992), Driftwood (1996).

O'NEILL, Nicholas managing director of Liquid Films. Films include Hooligans (1997/98), Hugh Cullen (1998)

O'SHEA, Milo (1925-) actor. Film debut (1960) after lengthy stage career with Dublin's Abbey Players.

Impressive in screen adaptation of Joyce's Ulysses (1967). Films include You Can't Beat the Irish (1951), Barbarella (1968), The Verdict (1982), The Purple Rose of Cairo (1985), Only the Lonely (1991), The Playboys (1992), The Butcher Boy (1997).

O'SULLIVAN, Thaddeus (1948-) b. Dublin, director and cameraman. Debut film A Pint of Plain (1975), feature film On a Paving Stone Mounted (1978), debut short The Woman who Married Clark Gable (1985) with BRENDA FRICKER and Bob Hoskins. Films include December Bride (1990), In the Border Country (1991), Nothing Personal (1995).

O'TOOLE, Peter (1932-) b. Connemara, reared Leeds, actor. Film debut in Disney's Kidnapped (1960), his work with the Royal Shakespeare Company got him the lead in David Lean's Lawrence of Arabia (1962). Starred in and co-produced Becket (1964) and Lord Jim (1965). Career slumped in 1970s but made a comeback in The Stunt Man (1980), receiving the US Film Critics Award. Starred in Bertolucci's award-winning epic, The Last Emperor (1987). Most Oscar-nominated best actor (1962-82, six times) but as yet to receive one. Films include The Lion in Winter (1968), Goodbye Mr Chips (1969), My Favourite Year (1982), Supergirl (1984), High Spirits (1988), The Seventh Coin (1992). Also writer, has published a second volume of memoirs The Apprentice (1997) and was praised for his stage performances in Jeffrey Bernard in Unwell.

PILKINGTON, Lorraine actress. Films include The Miracle (1991), All Things Bright and Beautiful (1994), The Disappearance of Finbar (1996), Gold in the Streets (1997), The Nephew (1997).

POTTER, Maureen (1925-) b. Dublin, stage actress and comedienne. Performing since childhood - she joined the Jack Hilton Show at 12 - had the curious distinction of performing before Hitler. Began her career with Jimmy O'Dea in Olympia Theatre in 1953 until his death in 1965. Had her own radio show and introduced a number of comic characters to Irish audiences. Was a regular contributor to the Irish cabaret and pantomime circuit until recently, when health problems forced her to retire.

QUINN, Aidan (1959-) b. Chicago, reared and educated in Ireland, actor. First gained attention for his role in Desperately Seeking Susan (1985). Films include The Mission (1986), Stakeout (1987), The Handmaid's Tale (1990), At Play in the Streets of the Lord (1991), The Playboys (1992), Benny & Joon (1993), Legends of the Fall (1994), Michael Collins (1996) and This is My Father (1997), which was directed and filmed by his brothers.

QUINN, Bob (1935-) b. Dublin, film producer/director, writer and photographer. Made over 100 films, ranging from drama and documentary to experimental. Films include Caoineadh Áirt Uí Laoire (1974), Self-Portrait with Red Car (1976), Poitín (1977), The Family (1979), Budawanny (1987), Pobal (1988-90), The Bishop's Story (1993), Graceville (1996).

REA, Stephen (1949-) b. Belfast; actor, a director of Field Day Theatre Company based in Derry (which he co-founded with BRIAN FRIEL). His film debut was in NEIL JORDAN'S directorial debut, Danny Boy/Angel (1982). His work in Jordan's The Crying Game (1992) earned him an Best Actor Oscar nomination. West End and Broadway performance in *Someone to Watch Over Me* (1982). Films include *The Company of Wolves* (1984), *Life is Sweet* (1991), *Bad Behaviour* (1993), *Interview with a Vampire* (1994), *Prêt a Porter* (1996), *Trojan Eddie* (1996), *The Butcher Boy* (1997).

RYAN, Gerry (1956-) Popular RTÉ TV and radio personality. Presenter of the *Gerry Ryan Show* on 2FM since 1988, one of Ireland's most popular morning radio programmes. Also presented his own TV programme for a time.

SHAW-SMITH, David (1939-) b. Dublin, independent film-maker (1970). Made more than 80 documentaries. Films include *Connemara and its Ponies* (1971), *Hands* (TV series), *Patterns* (series), *Dublin - a Personal View* (series), *Irish Arts Series* (series), *The Angling Experience* (series), *English Silk* (C4/RTÉ).

SHAW, Fiona (1958-) actress. Films include *My Left Foot* (1989), *Mountains of the Moon* (1989), *Three Men and a Little Lady* (1990) and *The Butcher Boy* (1997).

SHERIDAN, Jim (1949-) b. Dublin, director/playwright. Had eight of his own plays produced. Oscar nominated for Best Director and Best Screenplay with *My Left Foot* (1989). First Irish production to be nominated for five Oscars (only to be exceeded in 1995 by Jordan's *The Crying Game*). Wrote screenplay for and directed *The Field* (1990), wrote screenplay for Mike Newell's *Into the West* (1993). Re-teamed with DANIEL DAY-LEWIS for *In the Name of Our Father* (1993), receiving Oscar Nominations for Best Director, Screenplay and Film, and again for *The Boxer* (1997). Critics have likened the Sheridan-Day Lewis pairing to that of Scorsese and De Niro.

TODD, Richard (1919-) b. Dublin, leading man in British and US films. Stage debut (1937). Film career developed in late 1940s. Best known for The *Hasty Heart* (1949) for which he received an Oscar nomination. Films: *Stage Fright* (1950), *The Story of Robin Hood and his Merry Men* (1952), *Rob Roy* (1954), *The Virgin Queen* (1955), *Saint Joan* (1957), *Chase a Crooked Shadow* (1958).

TÓIBÍN, Niall (1929-) b. Cork, comedian and actor, currently starring in BBC's hugely popular *Ballykissangel*. Films include *Bright Future* (1968), *Philadelphia Here I Come!* (1970), *Ryan's Daughter* (1970), *Poitín* (1978), *Summer of the Falcon* (1981), *Fools of Fortune* (1990). ◻

WHO WAS WHO

HISTORY

ALEXANDER, Harold R. (1891-1969) b. Tyrone, British army officer in both World Wars, made Field Marshal in 1944, played vital role in expelling Axis forces from North Africa in WWII. Governor-General of Canada (1946-52); elevated to the peerage 1959.

ANDREWS, John Miller (1871-1956) b. Co. Down, Prime Minister of Northern Ireland (1940-43). *See Biographies of Northern Ireland Prime Ministers.*

ANNESLEY, James (1715-60) b. Co. Wexford. Claimant to the earldom of Anglesea and inspiration for Robert Louis Stevenson's *Kidnapped.*

ASHE, Thomas (1885-1917) b. Kerry, veteran of 1916 Rising; force fed, he died on hunger strike protesting his right to be treated as a prisoner of war.

AUCHINLECK, Claude (1884-1981) b. Tyrone, served as a British army officer in World War I. A general during World War II; promoted to field-marshal in 1946.

BALLANCE, John (1839-93) b. Antrim, Prime Minister of New Zealand (1891-93).

BARNARDO, Thomas (1845-1905) b. Dublin, set up Dr. Barnardo's homes for homeless children (1867).

BARRINGTON, Sir Jonah (1760-1834) b. Co. Laois, Protestant judge and memorialist who was found to be pilfering court funds. Settled in France, where he wrote the racy *The Rise and Fall of the Irish Nation* (1833).

BARRY, John (1745-1803) b. Wexford, known as the 'Father of the American Navy'. Active during the War of Independence, he presided over the US navy from 1782 until his death.

BARRY, Kevin (1902-20) b. Dublin, medical student and member of the IRA, captured and hanged. His extreme youth at his death aroused widespread condemnation and led to many students joining the IRA.

BARRY, Tom (1897-1980) b. Cork, IRA 'flying column' leader during War of Independence.

BARTON, Robert (1881-1975) b. Wicklow, signatory of the Anglo-Irish Treaty.

BERGIN, Osborn (1873-1950) b. Cork, gaelic scholar and professor of Early and Medieval Irish at UCD.

BIANCONI, Charles (1786-1875) b. Italy and arrived in Ireland (1786), set up the road-car service. Became a naturalised Irish citizen.

BING, Geoffrey (1909-77) b. Down, lawyer and politician, opposed the Stormont administration and raised many questions about civil liberties in Northern Ireland. His pamphlet *John Bull's Other Ireland* (1950) on these issues was a best-seller.

BLACKBURN, Helen (1842-1903) b. Knightstown, Co. Kerry. Secretary of the National Society for Women's Suffrage in England (1874-95), she published many books on women's suffrage.

BLANEY, Neil T. (1922-95) b. Donegal, a TD (1948-95) and MEP (1979-84 & 1989-94), held various ministries in Fianna Fáil. Charged with gunrunning in 1970 but had charges dismissed.

BLYTHE, Ernest (1889-1975) b. Antrim, MP and TD (1918-33); held various ministries in CUMANN NA NGAEDHEAL governments; supporter of the restoration of the Irish language.

BLOOD, Thomas *'Captain Blood'* (c. 1618-1680) adventurer who plotted to seize Dublin Castle but was found out. In 1671, he stole the crown and orb from the Tower of London, was captured but pardoned.

BÓRÚ, Brian (c. 926-1014) high king of Ireland (1002-14). His forces were victorious in the decisive defeat of the Vikings in Ireland at the Battle of Clontarf, but he himself was killed.

BOYCOTT, Captain Charles Cunningham (1832-97) gave the word 'boycott' to the English Language. The tenants of the Mayo estate where he was a land agent protested at his refusal to reduce rents by not working the land.

BRACKEN, Thomas Irish born poet who wrote the National Anthem of New Zealand - *God Save New Zealand.*

BRENNAN, Robert (1881-1964) b. Wexford, leader of 1916 Rising in Wexford. Irish Ambassador to the US during WWII.

BROOKE, Alan Francis *1st Viscount Alanbrooke* (1883-1963) b. Fermanagh, British field marshal. Chief of Imperial General Staff in 1941, regarded as Churchill's most trusted military adviser, accompanied him to the Allied Forces conferences in 1943.

BROOKE, Sir Basil (1888-1973) b. Fermanagh, Prime Minister of Northern Ireland (1943-63). *See Biographies of Northern Ireland Prime Ministers.*

BROWN, William (1777-1857) b. Mayo, founder of the Argentine navy (1813) and veteran of the Royal Navy.

BROWNE, Noël (1915-1997) b. Waterford, TD (1948-82). Minister at the centre of controversial 'mother and child scheme' in 1951. Implemented a radical plan to eliminate TB (prepared by Dr. James Deeny) which greatly reduced the occurrence of the disease.

BROWNING, Miciaih (d. 1689) b. Derry, his vessel ended the Siege of Derry (1689) by breaking the boom across the Foyle.

BROY, Eamonn (1887-1972) b. Kildare, Garda Commissioner (1932-38). Enlisted former IRA members (the BROY HARRIERS) to counter the Blueshirts.

BRUGHA, Cathal (1874-1922) b. Dublin, veteran of 1916 Rising. TD (1918-22), Minister for Defence (1919-22); fought with anti-treaty forces during the civil war and was killed.

BURKE, Edmund (1729-97) b. Dublin, MP (1765-97); author of *Reflections on the Revolution in France* (1790) which condemned the revolution; advocated reform of the penal laws and Irish self-government.

BURKE, Robert O'Hara (1820-61) b. Galway, one of the first white men to cross Australia but died of starvation on his return journey.

BURKE, William (1792-1829) with his partner William Hare (1790-1860) he committed a series of murders in Edinburgh to supply dissection cadavers to Dr Robert Knox, the anatomist. Was hanged.

BUTT, Isaac (1813-79) b. Co. Donegal, politician and advocate for HOME RULE. Called to he Irish bar in

1838, he soon became active in politics. Led the Irish Parliamentary Party in the House of Commons (1871-79), espousing Home Rule in the House of Commons with little success.

CADE, Jack (d. 1450) leader of the 1450 insurrection. Worked in Kent as a physician. Marched on London and defeated the king's forces. Lost control over his men and was killed in Sussex.

CARSON, Sir Edward (1854-1935) b. Dublin, a barrister, leader of Irish Unionists at Westminster (1910-21). Supported the formation of the ULSTER VOLUNTEER FORCE, led 218,000 Ulster unionists in the signing of the Solemn League and Covenant in 1913. Prosecuted the homosexual writer OSCAR WILDE. Elevated to the peerage in 1921 as Lord Carson of Duncairn.

CASEMENT, Roger (1864-1916) b. Dublin, knighted in 1911 for his work with the British colonial service. A member of the IRISH VOLUNTEERS, he secured some German weapons for the 1916 Rising but was captured at Banna Strand, Co. Kerry, tried for treason and hanged. His remains were re-interred in Dublin in 1965.

CEANNT, Eamonn (1881-1916) b. Galway, veteran of 1916 Rising and signatory of the Proclamation of the Republic. Executed by firing squad.

CHILDERS, Erskine (1905-74) b. London, president of Ireland from 1973 until his death. *See Biographies of Irish Presidents.*

CHILDERS, Robert Erskine (1870-1922) b. London, veteran of Boer War, wrote the successful spy novel *The Riddle of the Sands* (1903), involved in Howth gun-running in 1914. Served in the British navy during WWI, secretary to the Irish delegation at Anglo-Irish treaty negotiations, executed by Free State authorities.

CHURCH, Sir Richard (1785-1873) b. Cork, led the revolution in Greece. Took part in the Greek War of Independence (1821-32), appointed generalissimo of the Greek insurgent forces, earning the title 'Liberator of Greece' and becoming a Greek citizen.

CLARKE, Thomas James (1858-1916) b. Isle of Wight, revolutionary. Credited with a huge influence on the Easter Rising in 1916, after which he was court-martialled and shot.

CLUSKEY, Frank (1930-98) b. Dublin, Labour Party Politician. In government from 1973, introduced wide-ranging social welfare reforms. Resigned his ministerial post over the controversial supply of natural gas from Kinsale.

COBBE, Frances Power (1822-1904) b. Newbridge, a supporter of women's rights and prominent anti-vivisectionist. Travelled in Italy and the East and wrote *Cities of the Past* (1864) and *Italics* (1864).

COLLEY, George (1925-83) b. Dublin, politician. Elected a TD (1961) and held various ministerial posts, was a candidate for the leadership of Fianna Fáil (against Charles Haughey)

COLLINS, Michael (1890-1922) b. Cork, veteran of the 1916 Rising. Leader of the IRISH REPUBLICAN BROTHERHOOD during War of Independence. Elected to the first Dáil, Minister of Finance in the Republican government, signatory of the Anglo-Irish Treaty 1921. Chairman of the Provisional government (January-

August 1922), Commander-in-Chief of the Free State army during the civil war. Killed in an ambush.

CONNELL, Jim (c.1850-1929) b. Meath, wrote the famous socialist song *'The Red Flag'*.

CONNOLLY, James (1868-1916) b. Edinburgh of Irish parents, revolutionary socialist. Founded Independent Labour Party of Ireland in 1912, founded Citizen's Army in 1913 to protect workers from police attacks during the Dublin Lockout, joined Irish Republican Brotherhood 1915. A signatory of the Proclamation of the Republic, he served as commanding officer in the General Post Office during the 1916 Rising. Executed while in a chair (tied to it because of his wounds).

COSGRAVE, William Thomas (1880-1965) b. Dublin, President of Executive Council (1922-32). *See Biographies of Taoisigh.*

COSTELLO, John A. (1891-1976) b. Dublin, Taoiseach (1948-51 and 1954-57). Died *See Biographies of Taoisigh.*

COUSINS, Margaret (1878-1954) b. Roscommon, major figure in Irish suffragette movement. Emigrated to India 1915 where she became that country's first female magistrate.

CRAIG, Sir James (1871-1940) b. Belfast, Prime Minister of Northern Ireland (1921-40). *See Biographies of Northern Ireland Prime Ministers.*

CROKE, Thomas W. (1824-1902) b. Cork, Roman Catholic Archbishop of Cashel from 1875 and Patron of the Gaelic Athletic Association who named their headquarters after him.

CROKER, Thomas Wilson (1780-1857) b. Galway; politician and essayist. In 1802, he was called to the Irish bar and his two essays produced around this time were brilliant successes as was his pamphlet advocating Catholic Emancipation.

CROKER, Richard 'Boss' (1841- 1922) b. Cork; politician infamous for his control of the Tammany Hall political machine. He entered New York City politics in 1862. As 'Boss Croker' he controlled Democratic party politics for the next 16 years. After political reforms in 1901, he left the US and lived out his life in Ireland.

CROZIER, Captain Francis (1796-1848) b. Banbridge, Co. Down, naval explorer. Died in an ill-fated polar expedition searching for the North-West Passage.

CUSACK, Michael (1847-1906) b. Clare, founding member of the GAA in 1884. A stand is named after him in Croke Park.

DARCY, Patrick (1598-1668) b. Galway, constitutional nationalist, who argued before the Commons that no law of the English parliament can have any force in Ireland unless enacted by the Irish Parliament.

DAVIES, Christian 'Mother Ross' (1667-1739) b. Dublin, woman soldier who served for many years in the army as a man, fighting in the battle of Blenheim and other battles.

DAVIS, Thomas (1814-45) b. Cork, Young Irelander and founding member of its newspaper *The Nation*. A noted poet, he wrote *A Nation Once Again* and *The West's Awake*.

DAVITT, Michael (1846-1906) b. Mayo, founder of the Irish NATIONAL LAND LEAGUE in 1879. Imprisoned in England as a Fenian in 1870, released in 1877.

de VALERA, Éamon (1882-1975) b. New York, Taoiseach and President of Ireland. *See Biographies* *of Taoisigh and Irish Presidents.*

DEVLIN, Anne (c. 1778-1851) devoted servant of Robert Emmet who carried messages between him and his friends after the failure of the rising in 1803. Arrested and tortured, she refused to reveal any information.

DEVLIN, Joe (1871) b. Belfast, MP (1902-34) at Westminster and Stormont. Member of IRISH PARLIAMENTARY PARTY, president of ANCIENT ORDER OF HIBERNIANS (1905-34). Died 1934.

DEVOY, John (1842-1928) b. Kill, Co. Kildare, journalist and nationalist. A member of IRB, later an influential figure in Clan na Gael, he raised finance for republican groups in Ireland. Wrote the *Recollections of an Irish Rebel* (1928).

DILL, Sir John (1881-1944) b. Armagh, Boer War and World War I veteran. Field Marshal and Chief of Staff of the British army 1940.

DILLON, John (1851-1927) b. Dublin, MP (1885-1918). Exponent of HOME RULE and leading figure in IRISH PARLIAMENTARY PARTY.

DONNELLY, Charles (1910-37) b. Tyrone, poet who fought and died with the 15th International Brigade in the Spanish Civil War.

DUFFY, Charles Gavan (1816-1903) b. Monaghan, member of Young Ireland movement. Co-founded *The Nation* in 1842, Prime Minister of Victoria, Australia (1871-72); knighted 1873.

DUGGAN, Eamonn (1874-1936) b. Meath, TD (1918-33). Signatory of Anglo-Irish Treaty.

DUNLAP, John (1747-1812) b. Tyrone, founded the first daily newspaper in North America, the *Pennsylvania Packet*; was first to print the US Declaration of Independence.

EMMET, Robert (1778-1803) b. Dublin, leader of an abortive rebellion in Dublin in 1803. remembered for his speech from the dock; hanged and beheaded.

EDGEWORTH (de Firmont), Henry Essex (1745-1807) b. Edgeworthstown, Co. Longford, known as the 'Abbé Edgeworth'. Son of a Protestant rector, ordained a Jesuit priest and became confessor to both Louis XVI and his sister. Narrowly escaped death during the Revolution.

FAIR, James G. (1831-1894) b. Tyrone, gold prospector in California. Founded Bank of Nevada, American Senator (1881-87).

FAULKNER, Brian (1921-77) b. Co. Down, Prime Minister of Northern Ireland (1971-72). *See Biographies of Northern Ireland Prime Ministers.*

FITZGERALD, Lord Edward (1763-98) b. Kildare, veteran of the American War of Independence. Leading member of the UNITED IRISHMEN, captured May 1798, he died from his wounds before he could be tried.

FITZGERALD, Thomas Lord Offaly *Silken Thomas* (1513-37) b. Kildare, appointed Lord Deputy in 1534. Instigated a rebellion almost immediately; surrendered in 1535, assured of a pardon but was hanged, drawn and quartered.

FITZMAURICE, James C. (1898-1965) b. Dublin, veteran of WWI. Subsequently officer in the Irish Air Corps, accompanied by two Germans he completed the first east-west crossing of the Atlantic by air in 1928.

FLOOD, Henry (1723-91) b. Kilkenny, MP in Irish House of Commons, leader of Patriot Party which agi-

tated for legislative independence. Appointed vice-treasurer of Ireland in 1775 but removed in 1781 for being strongly nationalist.

GLENDY, John (1778-1832) b. Derry, Presbyterian minister and member of UNITED IRISHMEN, emigrated to the US and became a Commodore in the US navy.

GOUGH, Sir Hubert de la Poer (1870-1963) b. Waterford, veteran of the Boer war, served as Lieutenant-General during World War I.

GRATTAN, Henry (1746-1820) b. Dublin; statesman. Became an active supporter of HENRY FLOOD, who led the Irish independence movement, and left law in 1775 to enter into the Irish parliament. Secured the abolition of all claims by the British parliament to legislate for Ireland in 1782 but could not prevent the ACT OF UNION (1800) and sat in the parliament at Westminster until his death.

GRAVES, Thomas (1747-1814) b. Derry, Admiral in the British navy (1812-14).

GRIFFITH, Arthur (1871-1922) b. Dublin, founded SINN FÉIN 1905, proposed Irish abstentionism from Westminster and establishment of indigenous assembly; MP (1917-22). Served as Minister for Justice and Minister for Foreign Affairs, signatory of 1921 Anglo-Irish Treaty, President of Dáil Éireann (January-August 1922).

GUINNESS, Arthur (1725-1803) b. Kildare, founded Guinness brewery at St James' Gate in 1759. Under his grandson's stewardship (Sir Benjamin Lee Guinness), the brewery's stout became famous and the business grew into the largest of its kind in the world.

HAMILTON, Gustavus (1639-1723) b. Fermanagh, founded the 'Enniskilleners'- a Williamite regiment; fought at the Battle of the Boyne.

HEALY, Cahir (1877-1970) b. Donegal, nationalist representative at Stormont from 1925-65 for Fermanagh South and MP for Fermanagh and South Tyrone 1950-55 at Westminster.

HEALY, Timothy (1855-1931) b. Cork, MP (1880-1918). Governor-General of Irish Free State (1922-28).

HENNESSY, Richard (1720-1800) b. Cork, fought with Irish regiments on continental Europe. Founded the Hennessy Brandy distillery in 1763.

HILL, Wills (1718-93) b. Co. Down, minister in various British governments. Became Marquis of Downshire in 1789, rebuilt Hillsborough castle.

HINCKS, Francis (1807-85) b. Belfast, Prime Minister of Canada (1851-54). Subsequently Governor of Barbados.

HOBSON, Bulmer (1883-1969) b. Co. Down, founding member of Fianna Éireann (1909), member of the IRB but opposed the 1916 Rising.

HUGHES, Desmond (1919-1992) b. Belfast, fighter pilot and veteran of WWII. Deputy commander of British forces in Cyprus (1972-74).

HUSSEY, Thomas (1741-1803) b. Meath, noted for his diplomatic skills in the service of George III in continental Europe. First president of Maynooth College and later Bishop of Waterford and Lismore.

HYDE, Douglas (1860-1949) b. Castlerea, Co. Roscommon, President of Ireland (1938-45). *See Biographies of Irish Presidents.*

KANE, Richard (1666-1736) b. Antrim, Governor of Gibraltar and Minorca (1720-25).

KEARNEY, Peadar (1883-1942) b. Dublin, wrote the words to the Irish national anthem, *Amhrán na bhFiann*. Veteran of 1916 Rising.

KENNEDY, Arthur (1810-1883) b. Co. Down, Governor of Hong Kong (1872-77) and Queensland (1877-83).

KING, John (1838-72) b. Tyrone, explorer. Was the first white man to travel across Australia, accompanying the Burke and Wills expedition (1860), and survive. The other members of the expedition died on the return journey, but King was rescued by the Aborigines and survived.

KITCHENER, Horatio Herbert (1850-1916) b. Ballylongford, Co. Kerry. General in WWI and statesman. Appointed secretary for war in 1914, raised a huge army before he went down with the HMS Hampshire off Orkney in 1916.

LACY, Count Peter (1678-1751) b. Limerick, field marshal in Russia. In 1691, served in the Irish Brigade and joined the army of Peter the Great in 1698, fought in the Swedish war and wounded. Appointed governor of Latvia (1728) and promoted to field marshal (1736).

LARKIN, Jim (1876-1947) b. Liverpool, founding member of Irish Transport and General Workers Union (1908). Charismatic workers' leader during the Dublin Lock-out (1913-14), founded Workers' Union of Ireland (1924), TD (1928-32, 1937-38 & 1943-44).

LEMASS, Seán (1899-1971) b. Dublin, Taoiseach (1959-66). *See Biographies of Taoisigh.*

Le MESURIER MCCLURE, Robert John (1807-73) b. Wexford, discovered the North-west Passage - the link between the Pacific and Atlantic via the Arctic Ocean.

LENIHAN, Brian (1930-95) b. Louth, TD (1961-73 & 1977-95), MEP (1973-79); held various ministries in Fianna Fáil governments. Defeated candidate in 1990 Presidential election.

LESTER, Seán (1888-1959) b. Antrim, Irish Free State representative to League of Nations, appointed Acting Secretary General of the League in 1940.

LOGAN, James (1674-1751) b. Armagh, appointed Governor of Pennsylvania 1736.

LOWE, Sir Hudson (1769-1844) b. Galway, soldier and diplomat. Fought with the British army during the Napoleonic wars and was made governor of Santa Maura, Ithaca and Cephalonia. Afterwards, was attached to the Prussian army of Blücher, and in 1816, was made governor of St Helena were he kept guard over Napoleon.

LUNDY, Robert Governor of Derry when King James and his army lay siege to the city in 1689. Removed from office by the citizens of Derry when suggested surrendering. Escaped but was later imprisoned in the Tower of London. His effigy is burned annually.

MacBRIDE, John (1865-1916) b. Mayo, fought in the Boer War against the British. Fought in the 1916 Rising and was executed. Married Maude Gone.

MacBRIDE, Maude Gonne (1865-1953) Irish nationalist and muse for the poet W.B. YEATS. Espoused the cause of Irish independence and edited a nationalist newspaper, *L'Irlande libre*, in Paris. Married Major John MacBride. After his death she became an active Sinn Féiner in Ireland. A celebrated beauty, Yeats pur-

sued her for many years. Her son Sean founded Amnesty International.

MacBRIDE, Seán (1904-88). b. Dublin, fought with republicans during the civil war. Chief-of-staff of the IRA (1936-37), founder and leader of the republican party CLANN NA POBLACHTA (1946-65), TD (1947-1957), Minister for Foreign Affairs (1948-51), UN commissioner for Namibia (1973-75), chairman of Amnesty International 1973-76. Awarded Nobel Prize for Peace (1974) and Lenin Peace Prize (1978).

McClure, Sir Robert John le Mesurier (1807-73) b. Wexford; Arctic explorer. He participated in two Arctic expeditions in 1836 and 1848. As commander of a ship in the Franklin expedition (1850-54), he penetrated eastwards and was officially accredited with the discovery of the North-west Passage (subsequently attributed to Sir John Franklin) for which he won a parliamentary award.

McCRACKEN, Henry Joy (1767-98) b. Belfast, Presbyterian and founding member of the UNITED IRISHMEN. Led the United Irishmen rebellion in Antrim in 1798 and was captured and hanged.

MacDIARMADA, Seán (1884-1916) b. Leitrim, revolutionary. Joined the IRB and was responsible for organising IRB infiltration into other organisations. Crippled after contracting polio (1912). After participating in the 1916 Rising, was court-martialled and shot.

McDONAGH, Thomas (1878-1916) b. Tipperary, poet and revolutionary. Published much highly acclaimed poetry and translations from Irish. Was active in the IRISH VOLUNTEERS and belatedly joined the preparations for the 1916 Rising, taking command of Jacob's Factory during the fighting for which he was executed.

MacEOIN, Seán (1893-1973) b. Longford, the most successful guerrilla leader in the War of Independence. Supported the Treaty and became Chief-of-Staff of the Free State army. Later a Government Minister in two Coalition Governments.

MacMURCHADA, Diarmait (1110-71) b. Wicklow, king of Leinster. Banished by high king Ruaidrí Ua Conchobair in 1166, solicited help from Henry II of England, succeeded in attracting Richard de Clare (Strongbow) to Ireland by offering him his daughter in marriage and succession to the kingship of Leinster.

MacNEILL, Eoin (1867-1945) b. Antrim, co-founder of the GAELIC LEAGUE (1893) and Irish Volunteers (1913). TD (1918-27), Minister for Education (1922-25). Irish representative to the Boundary Commission (1924-25) but resigned. Noted Gaelic scholar.

MacNEILL, James (1869-1938) b. Antrim, Governor-General of Irish Free State (1928-32).

MacSWINEY, Terence (1879-1920) b. Cork, prominent member of the Irish Volunteers. Elected Lord Mayor of Cork in 1920. Imprisoned in August 1920, commenced a hunger strike and died after 74 days.

MARKIEWICZ, Constance Georgine *née* Gore-Booth (1868-1927) b. London, reared in Sligo, nationalist. While studying art at the Slade School in London, met and married Count Casimir Markiewicz. The couple settled in Dublin. Became involved in SINN FEIN and met MAUD GONNE MACBRIDE. She and her husband parted in 1913. Fought in the 1916 Rising and was sentenced to death but sentence reprieved. The first woman MP elected (1918) to the English parliament, but never took her seat. Elected to Dail Éireann (1919) and assigned the labour portfolio, but was arrested twice. After the Civil War, was a member of the Dail from 1923.

MARTIN, Richard (1754-1834) b. Dublin, lawyer and humanitarian. As MP for Galway (1801-26), pushed a bill to proscribe the cruel treatment of cattle. Through his work the Royal Society for the Prevention of Cruelty to Animals (RSPCA) was founded.

MEAGHER, Thomas Francis (1823-1867) b. Waterford, deported to Van Diemen's land for his part in the abortive Rising of 1848. Escaped and went to the US. Became a general in the Union Army in the American Civil War and later Governor of Montana.

MITCHEL, John (1815-75) b. Co. Derry; patriot. Founded the UNITED IRISHMAN (1848) and was arrested and tried for treason-felony. Transported to Van Diemen's Land, escaped to the US, published his famous *Jail Journal* (1854). Returned to Ireland and elected as MP for Tipperary, but was not allowed to take his seat and died the same month.

MULCAHY, Richard (1886-1971) b. Waterford, veteran of 1916 Rising. Fought with the Free State forces during the civil war becoming Commander-in-Chief following the death of Michael Collins. TD (1918-37, 1938-43 & 1944-61), member of CUMANN NA NGAEDHEAL and FINE GAEL, served in various government ministries.

MURPHY, Fr. John (1753-98) b. Wexford, Leader of Rising of 1798. Led the rebellion against British, taking the towns of Enniscorthy, Wexford and Ferns. Captured by the British following defeats at Arklow and Vinegar Hill and hanged.

Ó BUACHALLA, Domhnall (1866-1963) b. Kildare, 1916 veteran, Governor-General of the Irish Free State (1932-37).

Ó CEALLAIGH, Seán T. (1882-1966) b. Dublin, President of Ireland (1945-59). *See Biographies of Irish Presidents.*

O'CONNELL, Daniel *'The Liberator'* (1775-1847) b. Kerry, founded CATHOLIC ASSOCIATION in 1823 to lobby for Catholic Emancipation which was achieved in 1829. In 1828, became first Roman Catholic elected to the House of Commons. Lobbied for the repeal of the Act of Union but was unsuccessful.

Ó DALAIGH, Cearbhall (1911-78) b. Wicklow, President of Ireland (1974-76). *See Biographies of Irish Presidents.*

O'DONNELL, Red Hugh (c. 1571-1602) b. Donegal, inaugurated Chief of O'Donnell Clan in 1592. Allied with HUGH O'NEILL, he engaged in the 'Nine Years' War'. Left Ireland after the Battle of Kinsale in 1602 to obtain further Spanish aid, but was poisoned at the Spanish court.

O'DOHERTY, Cahir (1587-1608) b. Donegal, the last Irish Chieftain. Was killed after attacking Derry and Strabane.

O'DUFFY, Eoin (1892-1944) b. Monaghan, Garda Commissioner (1922-33). Previously Chief-of-Staff of the Free State Army. Founded the ARMY COMRADES ASSOCIATION (Blueshirts) in 1932; founding member and first leader of Fine Gael (1933-34). Leader of an Irish Brigade (1936-38) which fought in the Spanish civil war on the side of General Franco's fascists.

O'HIGGINS, Kevin (1892-1927) b. Laois, TD (1918-27) Supported Anglo-Irish Treaty. Minister for Justice in first Free State government, 77 anti-treaty IRA members were executed in reprisals by this government during the civil war. Influential in establishing the Garda Síochana, he was assassinated.

O'LEARY, John (1830-1907) b. Tipperary, Fenian. Studied law and medicine but never qualified. Became strongly associated with the Fenian movement. Edited the *Irish People,* a newspaper voicing Fenian views, but was betrayed and arrested in 1865, sentenced to 20 years but released after nine and banished from the country, returning in 1885. A strong influence on the poet W.B YEATS.

O'MALLEY, Donogh (1921-1968) b. Limerick, TD (1954-68), as minister for education he introduced free post primary education in 1966.

O'MALLEY, Grace *Gráinne Ní Mháille* (c. 1530-1603) b. Mayo, legendary pirate queen along the Mayo coast. Allegedly visited Queen Elizabeth in London, speaking to her as one queen to another. Married twice, was seized after the death of her second husband. Managed to escape to Ulster and stayed with the O'Neill, was pardoned by Queen Elizabeth.

O'NEILL, Hugh (1550-1616) b. Tyrone, Earl of Tyrone and chief of the O'Neill Clan from 1583; his forces and the forces of RED HUGH O'DONNELL engaged the English in the Nine Years War, culminating in his surrender and the Treaty of Mellifont in 1603. Unable to adapt to the new circumstances, fled Ireland with other Gaelic chieftains in the 'Flight of Earls' in 1607.

O'NEILL, Owen Roe (c. 1590-1649) b. Tyrone, nephew of Hugh. Served with distinction in Spanish army, arrived in Ulster in 1642 and became military leader of the rebellion. Was victorious over Monro at Battle of Benburb.

O'NEILL, Phelim (1604-1653) leader of the 1641 Rising, he was executed for that role.

O'NEILL, Terence (1914-90) b. London, Prime Minister of Northern Ireland (1963-69). *See Biographies of Northern Ireland Prime Ministers.*

O'SHEA, Katharine (1845-1921) Charles Stewart Parnell's mistress, she married him after he was ousted from the leadership of the Irish Parliamentary Party.

PARKER, Debra (1882-1963) b. Derry, MP (1921-29 & 1933-60); Minister of Health (1949-57), the only woman to be a minister in the Northern Ireland government.

PARNELL, Anna (1852-91) b. Wicklow, sister of CHARLES STEWART PARNELL, established Ladies Land League in Ireland, January 1881. First radical female agitator in Irish history. The league's activities were suppressed by her brother.

PARNELL, Charles Stewart *'the uncrowned king of Ireland'* (1846-91) b. Wicklow, leader of Home Rule Movement from 1877 and leader of IRISH PARLIAMENTARY PARTY (1880-90). Lobbied the House of Commons successfully for land reform and manoeuvred Irish public opinion in favour of Home Rule. Ousted from leadership of the IPP in 1890 when cited as co-respondent in a divorce petition. Married divorcee Katherine O'Shea in 1891.

PEARSE, Pádraig (1879-1916) b. Dublin, poet and veteran of 1916 Rising. Founded the all-Irish Scoil Éanna (1908), founding member of Irish Volunteers (1913) member of the IRISH REPUBLICAN BROTHERHOOD. Commander-in-Chief of the Volunteers during the Rising, President of the Provisional Government and signatory of the Proclamation of the Republic, executed for his role in the Rising.

PLUNKETT, Joseph Mary (1887-1916) b. Dublin, poet and veteran of 1916 Rising. Member of IRISH REPUBLICAN BROTHERHOOD and the IRISH VOLUNTEERS. Chief military strategist for the Volunteers during the Rising, signatory of Proclamation of the Republic, executed for his role in the Rising.

REDMOND, John (1856-1918) b. Wexford, MP (1881-1918), leader of IRISH PARLIAMENTARY PARTY (1900-18). A major figure in the passage of the 1912 HOME RULE BILL (1914), called on the Irish Volunteers to join British Army - almost 200,000 did.

RYAN, Frank (1902-44) b. Limerick, fought with anti-treaty IRA during civil war. Founded Saor Éire, led 200 Irish volunteers to fight with the socialists in the Spanish civil war (1936-37).

SANDS, Bobby (1954-81) born Belfast, IRA member imprisoned in 1977, commenced hunger strike (March 1, 1981) to regain political status. Elected MP for Fermanagh & South Tyrone on April 9, died after 66 days without food.

SARSFIELD, Patrick (d. 1693) born Dublin, Brigadier General in army of James II. Signed the TREATY OF LIMERICK which allowed him and his men safe passage to join James in France. Killed at Battle of Landen.

STRONGBOW - *Richard Fitz Gilbert de Clare* (d. 1176) b. Wales; Norman adventurer who arrived in 1170 at the request of DIARMAIT MACMURCHADA. MacMurchada promised him his daughter in marriage and succession to the kingship of Leinster; king of Leinster from 1171.

TANDY, James Napper (1740-1803) b. Dublin, founding member of UNITED IRISHMEN, leader of French expeditionary force in 1798 which landed in Donegal but retreated. Captured and sentenced to death, Napoleon demanded and obtained his extradition in 1802.

TAYLOR, George (b. 1716) member of American Continental Congress, he was a signatory of the American Declaration of Independence.

WOLFE TONE, Theobald (1763-98) b. Dublin, founding member of the SOCIETY OF UNITED IRISHMEN in 1791. Solicited French aid for the 1798 rebellion. Captured at Buncrana, he was found guilty of treason and sentenced to be hanged. Committed suicide while awaiting execution.

ART

ANTRIM, Lady (1911-1974) b. Yorkshire, sculptor and cartoonist. Former Governor of the Ulster College of Art. Commissions include bronze sculptor and stained glass, Moyle Hospital, Larne; stone sculptors for St. Joseph's Church, Ballygally; the parliament buildings, Newfoundland.

ARMSTRONG, Arthur (1921-1996) b. Carrickfergus, self-taught landscape painter. Featured in collections worldwide. Former member of the RHA. Exhibited widely in Ireland, Europe and US.

BACON, Francis (1909-92) b. Dublin, one of the most important artists of the 20th century. His father forced him to leave home at an early age. Moved to London and worked as an interior designer and started painting with no formal training. Initially inspired by Surrealism but borrowed imagery from the old masters. Made a major impact with the painting *Three figures at the Base of a Crucifixion*. Best known for his disjointed, violent figures. His heir announced in 1998 that he will make a gift of Bacon's studio to the Hugh Lane Gallery, Dublin.

BARRY, James (1741-1806) b. Cork, historical painter. A protégé of Edmund Burke, he was appointed professor of painting of the Royal Academy. His most celebrated paintings are *Adam & Eve* (1771) and *Venus Rising from the Waves* (1772). Many of his works are on display in Cork's Crawford Gallery.

BEATTY, Sir Chester (1875-1968) b. New York, philanthropist and art collector. Amassed the greatest collection of oriental manuscripts ever held by a private collector. Left this collection to the Irish nation. Was made an honorary citizen of Ireland - the first to be given this honour.

BEIT, Sir Alfred (1903-94) philanthropist and art collector. Restored Russborough House, Co. Wicklow, using the family wealth (made from gold and diamond trading in South Africa). His art collection was at one time the most valuable private collection in the world. A governor of the National Gallery, established a trust for the house and the lands. Donated 17 Old Masters to the National Gallery but they were stolen (by the infamous Martin Cahill) before they were transferred - all but three were recovered. Made an honorary citizen of Ireland with his wife in 1993.

BIGGS, Michael (1928-1993) sculptor. Primarily known for stone carving and letter cutting. Created many public and private inscriptions in stone, wood and bronze between 1950-1992.

BINDON, Francis (d. 1765) b. Clare, portrait painter and architect. Many contemporaries, including Swift, sat for him. Worked with acclaimed architect Richard Cassels in designing Russborough House, considered the most important Palladian mansion in the country.

BRANDT, Muriel (1909-1981) b. Belfast, painter and portrait artist. Commissions include a series of decorative murals in the Franciscan Church of Adam and Eve, Dublin. Member of RHA. Mother of artist Ruth Brandt.

BRANDT, Ruth (1936-1989) b. Dublin, artist and lecturer at NCAD (1976-1988). Participated in the *Irish Exhibition of Living Art*. Commissions include the Glasnevin Met Office and stained-glass windows at Artane Oratory, Dublin. Solo exhibits throughout Ireland.

BROWN, Fr. Francis (1923-1989) b. Cork, photographer and Jesuit priest. His photographs of the Titanic (as it departed on its maiden voyage) were sent around the world after the ship sunk. More than 42,000 of his negatives were found in 1985, chronicling his travels in Australia, Ireland and Britain.

BYRNE, Michael (1923-1989) painter. Worked for the Arts Council and NCAD. Founder member of the

Independent Artists. Committee member of the Project Arts Centre, Dublin.

CAMPBELL, George (1917-79) b. Co. Wicklow, artist. Founding member of the Living Art Exhibition (after WWII), won many awards, his finest works are considered his paintings of Spain.

CLARKE, Harry (1889-1931) b. Dublin, illustrator and stained-glass artist. Possibly the country's best-known stained glass artist. His style evidences influences from the Art Noveau work of Aubrey Beardsley as well as Celtic dawn influences, which had come into vogue at the beginning of the century. Works represented in the Honan College Chapel, Cork; St. Patrick's Basilica, Lough Derg; the Catholic parish churches of Ballinrobe and Carrickmacross. Established stained glass business with brother Walter - Harry Clarke Studios (1930).

COLLINS, Patrick (1910-1994) b. Co. Sligo, painter. Featured in numerous public and private collections worldwide. Elected Saoi, one of the highest honours that can be bestowed on an Irish artist (1987).

CONNOR, Jerome (1876-1943) b. Kerry, sculptor. Commissions included the Walt Whitman Memorial and Robert Emmet statue for the Smithsonian Institution, Washington.

CONOR, William (1884-1968) b. Belfast, painter. First exhibited as war artist followed by portraits of city scenes and shipyard workers. Member of RHA. His works are on permanent exhibition in the Ulster Folk Museum. Awarded an OBE in 1952.

DANBY, Francis (1793-1861) b. Co. Wexford, landscape artist. Was a regular exhibitor at the Royal Academy in England but was never made a full member. Patented a new type of ship's anchor in 1861.

DEANE, Sir Thomas Newenhan (1828-99) b. Co. Cork, architect. Some of his best known works include The National Library and National Museum in Kildare Street, Dublin.

DILLON, Gerard (1916-1971) b. Belfast, artist. Worked with oils, tapestry and murals. Set designer for Abbey Theatre. Best known for Connemara landscapes. Represented Ireland at the *Guggenheim International Exhibition*.

DOYLE, John (1797-1868) b. Dublin, political cartoonist. Espoused Catholic emancipation. His caricatures revolutionised the art of the cartoon, moving them way from grotesques to likenesses of subjects. Created the persona of 'John Bull' to embody public opinion. His sons were also artists, and his grandson was Arthur Conan Doyle, creator of Sherlock Holmes.

DUNLOP, Ronald Ossary (1894-1973) b. Dublin, painter. A member of the London group, he is best remembered for his palette-knife paintings with their rich colours. Works on view in the Tate Gallery, London, in addition to many other public galleries. His writings on art include *Landscape Painting* (1954) and *Struggling with Paint* (1956).

FOLEY, John Henry (1818-74) b. Dublin, sculptor. Produced statues of public figures, including one of Prince Albert for the Albert Memorial. Other commissions include Edmund Burke and GOLDSMITH at Trinity College and Henry Grattan on College Green, Dublin.

FOWKE, Captain Francis (1823-65) b. Belfast, appointed architect and engineer to the British depart-ment of science and art, he designed many of the major museums in Britain, including the Albert Hall in London, the Victoria & Albert Museum in London (later completed by Sir Aston Webb) and the National Gallery of Ireland in Dublin..

FURNISS, Harry (1854-1925) b. Wexford, caricaturist. Emigrated to London and worked as a caricaturist on the *Illustrated London News* (1876-84) and *Punch* (1884-94). Illustrated Lewis Carroll's *Sylvie and Bruno* and editions of Dickens and Thackeray. Embarked on a career in film with Thomas Edison, pioneering animated cartoons (1914).

GANDON, James (1743-1823) b. London, architect who designed some of the finest buildings in 19th-century Dublin, including the Custom House, the Four Courts and King's Inns.

GIBBINGS, Robert John (1889-1958) b. Cork, illustrator and writer. Revived the art of wood engraving and was the first artist to use diving equipment and make underwater drawings. Famous works include the river books - *Sweet Thames Run Softly* (1940), *Lovely is the Lee* (1945), *Sweet Cork of Thee* (1951).

HARRISON, Celia (1863-1941) b. Co. Down, painter and advocate for women's rights.

HEALY, Michael (1873-1941) b. Dublin, illustrator and stained-glass artist. Commissions included illustrations for the Dominican's journal *Irish Rosary* and windows for Loughrea Cathedral, Galway, among many other church buildings throughout Ireland.

HENRY, Paul (1877-1958) b. Belfast, oil painter. Best remembered for his evocative and bold west of Ireland landscapes, with their strong blocks of colour and defined shapes. Member of RHA. (1929). Received poster commissions for the Irish Tourist Board and London & Scottish Railway. His work is very popular and his paintings are in great demand at auction.

HERON, Hilary (1923-1977) b. Dublin, artist. Awarded the first MAINIE JELLETT memorial travelling scholarships (1947) for work in carved wood, limestone and marble. Exhibited at the *Irish Exhibition of Living Art*. Represented Ireland with LOUIS LE BROCQUY at the *Venice Biennale* (1956).

HOBART, Henry (1858-1938) b. Co. Down, noted Ulster architect.

HOBSON, Florence (1881) b. Kildare, Ireland's first female architect (qualified 1893).

HONE, Evie (1894-1955) b. Dublin, painter and stained-glass artist. Overcame polio and joined her friend MAINIE JELLETT to study in Paris. Become one of the foremost Irish stained glass artists of the 20th century. Produced many stained glass windows, including *My Four Green Fields* and a number of oils and watercolours.

HONE, Nathaniel (1831-1917) b. Dublin, landscape artist. Studied in Paris and moved to Barbizon and worked closely with Millet, painting landscapes. Returned to Dublin (1875) and was elected to RHA (1880). Held an exhibition with John Butler Yeats. Some 500 oil paintings and 900 watercolours were bequeathed to the National Gallery by his widow.

JELLETT, Mainie (1897-1944) b. Dublin, abstract artist. One of Ireland's leading modern artists, studied in Paris with EVIE HONE, joined the cubist integral movement. Moved back to Ireland (1930) and was a founder member of the Irish Exhibition of Living Art (1943).

JERVAS, Charles (c.1675-1739) b. Offaly, a member of the Courts of George I and II of England, was an official portrait artist.

KEATING, Sean (1889-1977) b. Limerick, artist. Studied Dublin, Aran Islands and London. Elected to RHA (1923) and its president (1949-62), was a professor of painting and made many visits to US. Completed many government commissions, including one for the World's Fair, New York (1939) and a mural for International Labour Office, Geneva.

KING, Cecil (1921-1986) b. Dublin, self-taught artist and sculptor. Featured in many public and private collections. Co-founded the Contemporary Irish Art Society. Commissions include the brilliant yellow structure outside the UCG science block.

LAMB, Charles (1893-1964) b. Armagh, landscape painter and member of RHA.

LANE, Sir Hugh Percy (1875-1915) b. Cork, art critic and collector. Amid great controversy, founded a gallery of modern art in Dublin at the beginning of the 20th century and championed contemporary Irish artists of the time, including JACK B YEATS and WILLIAM ORPEN. Was director of the National Gallery of Ireland in 1914 but drowned on the Lusitania when it was torpedoed in 1915. A number of French impressionist paintings were reputed to be in his keeping on the boat when it went down, and there is ongoing controversy surrounding their recovery.

LAVERY, Sir John (1856-1941) b. Belfast, painter. After studying in Glasgow, London and Paris, became a portrait painter and enjoyed great success with his paintings of women. Famous works include a portrait of his wife, Hazel (used on Irish banknotes for half a century and still used as the watermark on Irish currency notes) and MICHAEL COLLINS lying in state. Knighted in 1918. Wrote an autobiography (1940).

LEECH, William (1881-1968) b. Dublin, impressionist artist. Studied in Dublin under WALTER OSBORNE and in Paris. Moved to France but exhibited in Dublin and was elected to the RHA (1910) and was associated with the group that included AE and COUNTESS MARKIEVICZ, moved to England (1916) but was still a regular contributor to Irish exhibitions.

LOVER, Samuel (1797-1868) b. Dublin; artist, writer and songwriter. Established himself in Dublin as a marine painter and miniaturist. Assisted Dickens in founding Bentley's Miscellany.

McCORMICK, Liam (born Derry, 1916) internationally acclaimed church architect. Died 1996.

McGUIRE, Edward (1932-1986) b. Dublin, painter. Participated in many prominent group exhibitions. Received numerous awards for his work. Works displayed at Ulster Museum, Belfast, National Gallery of Ireland, Hugh Lane Gallery, Dublin and Dublin City University.

MacLISE, Daniel (1806-70) b. Cork, painter. After studying at the Royal Academy in London, painted the Royal Gallery frescoes in the House of Lords. Most famous works are *The Meeting of Wellington and Blücher* (1861) and *The Death of Nelson* (1864). Also illustrated books for Tennyson and Dickens.

McWILLIAM, F.E. (1902-92) b. Banbridge, Co. Down;

sculptor. Studied in London and Paris - a fine example of his work - 'Legs Static' (1978) - is on public display in Banbridge Civic Building grounds.

ORPEN, Sir William (1878-1931) b. Dublin, artist. Studied at the Slade, London, received many commissions, elected as an associate of the Royal Academy and as a member of the RHA (1908). Taught in Ireland and in London with Augustus John. Was an official war artist (1917-19) - his paintings from this time hang in the Imperial War Museum, also painted the Treaty at Versailles. Afterwards was a popular portrait artist. His work approaches that of Jack B. Yeats in its popularity at the moment, with some of his paintings selling for close to £1 million at auction.

OSBORNE, Walter (1859-1903) b. Dublin, impressionist artist. Studied in Ireland at RHA and in Antwerp under a scholarship, mastering both oils and watercolours. Painted English and Irish landscapes, elected to the RHA and taught there, influencing the generation of young artists who studied under him. Many of his paintings can be seen at the National Gallery. His works have become increasing popular at auction Acclaimed works include *Beneath St Jacques, Antwerp.*

POWERS, Mary Farl (1948-92) b. Minnesota, artist. Known for printmaking and working with paper. Former director of the Graphic Studio, Dublin.

PURSER, Sarah (1848-1943) b. Dun Laoghaire, artist. Studied in Dublin and in Paris. In London, received many portrait commissions from the aristocracy. Became a wealthy woman from investing her earnings and helped purchase the building that is now the Hugh Lane Gallery. Her best-known paintings are those of her famous Irish contemporaries such as MAUD GONNE MACBRIDE.

REID, Nano (1905-81) b. Louth, noted landscape artist.

RUSSELL, George *'AE'* (1867-1935) b. Co. Armagh, artist and poet. Went to art school in Dublin where he met and became a lifelong friend of YEATS. Broadened his interests and became involved in theosophy. Wrote on a wide variety of subjects including the agricultural co-operative movement. Hosted meetings for those interested in the arts and economic future of Ireland. Published *Collected Poems* (1913) and was editor of the *Irish Homestead* and the *Irish Statesman.*

VANSTON, Dáirine (1903-88) painter who exhibited widely in Ireland and abroad. Work featured in *Horizon* magazine. Details of her work and career given to the Archives of Modern European Art, Venice.

WEJCHERT, Alexandra (1920-95) b. Poland, architect. Moved to Ireland in 1965. Worked here until her death.

YEATS, Jack Butler (1871- 1957) b. London, artist and writer. Brother of W.B. YEATS. Regarded as one the most influential and talented artists in Ireland. Illustrated many pen-and-ink drawings for journals and books - known as *W. Bird* for cartoon work in *Punch* magazine (1910-48). Famous works include *At the Galway Races, On Drumcliffe Strand* and *Memory Harbour.* Retrospectives of work mounted in London (1942, 1948), Dublin (1945) and the US (1951-52). Literary works include *Sailing, Sailing Swiftly* (1933) and *Ah Well* (1942). His works are the most popular In Irish art - at auction in 1998, his painting, *Singing 'Oh, Had I The Wings of a Swallow'* (1925) attained over £1 million, the most given for any Irish painting.

BUSINESS

ANDREWS, Christopher Stephen 'Todd' (1901-85) b. Dublin, leader in the semi-state sector. Placed in charge of turf development in 1932, set up a structured commercial enterprise - Bord na Móna - which thrived under his stewardship. Also headed CIE and RTÉ.

BEDDY, James (1900-76) b. Cobh, public servant. Managing director of the Industrial Credit Company (1952). Was the first chairman of both the IDA and An Foras Tionscal and made a valuable contribution to the financing and development of industry in Ireland.

BEERE, Thekla (1902-91) b. Kells, public servant. Rose through the ranks of the civil service, an expert on shipping and rail transport and on labour relations - eventually made Secretary of the Department of Transport and Power - the first woman to be appointed head of a government department. Was president of a number of societies and organisations.

CANTILLON, Richard (1680-1734) b. Co Kerry, the father of political economy. An English translation of his book on economy (which was never found) was quoted by many leading economists including Adam Smith and Condillac.

DOYLE, Vincent (1923-88) b. Donegal, hotelier. First to recognise an emerging affluent middle class and built hotels accordingly, including the Montrose and the Burlington among others. Became extremely successful and bought hotels in the US and Britain. Appointed chairman of Bord Fáilte (1973) and was retained in the post for several terms.

EASON, John (1880-1976) b. Dublin, businessman. Managing director of the family firm of Eason and Son - wholesale newsagents and book distributors (1926-50), played a prominent role in getting the business community to become reconciled with the nascent Irish State.

GALLAGHER, Pat 'the Cope' (1873-1964) b. Donegal, set up an extremely successful co-operative society in Dungloe, senior figure in the Irish Agricultural Organisation Society.

HARLAND, Edward (1831-1895) b. Yorkshire, established Harland and Wolff shipyard in Belfast in 1862 and was an MP (1889-95).

LITERATURE

ALLINGHAM, William (1824-1889) b. Ballyshannon, poet. Became involved with the pre-Raphaelites - his poetry collection *Day and Night Songs* was illustrated by Rossetti and Millais - best remembered for poem *The Fairies* which opens with 'Up the airy mountains, down the rushy glen...'

BALL, Francis Elrington (1863-1928) b. Dublin, historian. The son of a Lord Chancellor, educated privately because of poor health. His treatise *The Judges in Ireland 1221-1921* is now an important source as much of the information in it was based on documents in the Irish Record Office which was destroyed in 1922.

BANIM, John (1798-1842) b. Kilkenny, novelist and playwright who collaborated with his brother Michael (1796-1874) on the *Tales of the O'Hara Family* (1826) portraying humble Irish folk.

BECKETT, Samuel (1906-1989) b. Dublin - writer, poet, playwright and translator. Educated in Enniskillen and TCD, graduated with a 1st class in Modern Literature. Taught in Paris and became friendly with JOYCE. During the war, was involved with the French Resistance and awarded the Croix de Guerre for his participation. Usually wrote in French and made the translation in English. Works include *Dream of Fair to Middling Women* (1932), *More Pricks than Kicks* (1934), *Murphy* (1938), the trilogy *Molloy, Malone Dies* and *The Unnamable* (1950), *Waiting for Godot* (1952), *Endgame* (1957), *Krapp's Last Tape* (1958), *Happy Days* (1961), *Worstward Ho* (1983), *Collected Poems* (1984). Awards include the Nobel Prize for Literature (1969).

BEHAN, Brendan (1923-1964) b. Dublin; celebrated wit, dramatist, author and poet. His family was steeped in Irish literature and song, joined the IRA and was arrested and sent to a Borstal for possession of explosives in Liverpool. Returned to Dublin and again arrested for shooting at policeman. Learned Irish from native speakers in the Curragh prison and began to write. Worked with Joan Littlewood to produce plays, the most famous of which include *The Quare Fellow* (1954) and *An Giall/The Hostage* (1958), his autobiographical *The Borstal Boy* (1958). Remembered for wit and conversation. His drinking was legendary and eventually led to his death.

BEHAN, Dominic (1928-89) b. Dublin, writer and folklorist. A brother of BRENDAN BEHAN, emigrated and wrote scripts for the BBC. His songs include *The Patriot Game* and *Liverpool Lou*. His works include *Posterity Be Damned, My Brother Brendan* (1965), the *Folk Singer* (1972), *Teems of Times* (1979) and the novel *The Public Life of Parable Jones*.

BICKERSTAFFE, Isaac (c. 1735-1812) b. Dublin, playwright. An officer in the marines, he was dismissed and had to flee the country in 1772. The best known of his plays is *The Maid of the Mill*.

BOUCICAULT, Dion Lardner (c.1820-90) b. Dublin,dramatist. He is credited with writing around 150 plays (incl. translations and adaptations), the most notable of these being the *Colleen Bawn* (based on Griffin's *The Collegians*) which is still produced on stage, the most recent production given in 1998.

BOWEN, Elizabeth (1899-1973) b. Dublin, novelist in Anglo-Irish literary genre. Works include *The Last September* (1929), *The Death of the Heart* (1938), *A World of Love* (1955).

BRODERICK, John (1927-89) b. Athlone, novelist. Travelled extensively and met Ernest Hemmingway and Gore Vidal. His first novel, *The Pilgrimage* (1961), was banned in Ireland. Other works include *An Apology for Roses* (1973), *Oh, What a Beautiful City* (1974), *The Irish Magdalene* (1991).

BROOKE, Henry (1703-83) b. Co. Cavan, dramatist and novelist. Was friendly with the poet Alexander Pope and married his ward. His novel *The Fool of Quality* (1766) is the sole survivor of his reputedly numerous works.

BROWN, Christy (1932-1981) b. Dublin, writer. Despite

suffering from cerebral palsy, completed his autobiography *My Left Foot* (1964) - made into an Oscar-winning film - and *Down all the Days* (1970). Poetry includes *Come Softly to My Wake* (1971).

CARBERY, Ethna (1866-1911) b. Co. Antrim, writer. Her contributions to nationalist papers did much to contribute to Sinn Féin's cause.

CARLETON, William (1794-1869) b. Co. Tyrone; novelist. Of peasant stock, became a tutor and writer and went on to contribute pieces to the *Christian Examiner*, reprinted as *Traits and Stories of the Irish Peasantry* (1830). Also published a number of novels.

CENTLIVRE, Susanna (1667-1722) b. Co. Tyrone, dramatist. Wrote many successful comedies, including *The Wonder! A Woman Keeps a Secret* (1714) which gave the actor Garrick one of his best roles.

CLARKE, Austin (1896-1974) b. Dublin, poet and dramatist. Worked in England as a literary critic and journalist before returning to Dublin in 1937. The first of his 18 books, *The Vengeance of Fion*, was published in 1917. Famous poems include *The Planters Daughter* and *Lost Heifer*. Works include *Flight to Africa* (1963), *A Penny in the Clouds* (1968), *Collected Poems* (1974).

COFFEY, Brian (1905-1995) b. Dublin; poet, translator and editor. Works include *Third Person* (1938), *The Big Laugh* (1976), *Death of Hektor* (1984), *Advent* (1986).

COLUM, Patrick (1881-1972) b. Longford; primarily a poet, wrote the famous haunting song *She Moved Through the Fair*. Works include the biography of ARTHUR GRIFFITH - *Ourselves Alone* (1959) and a collection of anecdotes about Joyce - *Our Friend James Joyce* (1958).

CONGREVE, William (1670-1729) dramatist and poet who was educated at Kilkenny School and Trinity where he was a fellow student of Swift. His masterpiece *Love for Love* was first produced in 1695. Died after a coach accident and is buried Westminster Abbey.

CORKERY, Daniel (1878-1964) b. Cork, writer and cultural leader. His book, *The Hidden Ireland* (1925), criticized the literary historians who saw Ireland in terms of the 18th-century ascendancy. Had a profound influence on writers such as SEAN O'FAOLAIN and FRANK O'CONNOR. Also a member of Seanad Eireann.

DAY-LEWIS, Cecil (1904-72) b. Co. Mayo; poet and writer. Educated at Oxford, published his first book of poetry in 1925. Became associated with the poetry movement of the 1930s with Auden and Spender and espoused left-wing causes, becoming a member of the Communist party (which he later renounced). After WWII, was a professor of poetry at Oxford (1951-56) and Harvard (1964-65) and was made Poet Laureate in 1968. Also wrote literary criticism, translations and detective novels (under the pseudonym Nicholas Blake). Father of film star Daniel Day-Lewis.

DENHAM, Sir John (1615-69) b. Dublin, poet. Published *Cooper's Hill* (1642), a topographical poem which Pope imitated in *Windsor Forest*. Buried in Poets' Corner in Westminster Abbey.

De VERE WHITE, Terence (1912-1994) writer and literary editor for *The Irish Times* (1961-77). Works include *Kevin O'Higgins* (1948), *A Fretful Midge*

(1957), *Lucifer Falling* (1965), *The Parents of Oscar Wilde* (1967), *The Anglo-Irish* (1972), *Chimes at Midnight* (1977), *Chat Show* (1987).

DILLON, Eilís (1920-1994) b. Galway, adult/children's novelist and playwright. Works include *The Island of Horses* (1956), *A Page of History* (1966), *Across the Bitter Sea* (1973), *Blood Relations* (1977), *The Cats' Opera* (1981), *Wild Geese* (1981), *Down in the World* (1983), *Children of Bach* (1993).

DUNSANY, Edward John 18th Baron (1878-1957) b. London, poet and playwright. Fought in the Boer War and afterwards, settled in Dunsany Castle, Meath. At W.B. YEATS'S request, he wrote many plays for the ABBEY THEATRE, including *The Glittering Gate* (1909) and *The Laughter of the Gods* (1919). His poetry includes *Fifty Poems* (1930) and *Mirage Water* (1939).

EDGEWORTH, Maria (1767-1849) b. Oxfordshire, novelist. After an education in England, returned to Longford to help her father raise his many children. Published her first novel *Castle Rackrent* (1800) to immediate acclaim and went on to publish a series of social novels on Irish life.

ERVINE, St. John Greer (1883-1971) b. Belfast, playwright and novelist. Drama critic for the *Observer* until 1939. Works include *Boyd's Shop* (1936) and *Friend and Relations* (1941), as well as biographies of *Charles Stewart Parnell* (1925), *Sir James Craig* (1949) and *George Bernard Shaw* (1956).

FARQUHAR, George (c. 1677-1707) b. Derry, playwright. Educated at Trinity and an actor in Dublin, the accidental wounding of another actor shocked him into leaving. Wrote his first work, *Love and a Bottle* in 1698. His most famous plays, *The Beaux' Strategem* and *The Recruiting Officer*, were written during his final illness. He died in poverty.

GÉBLER, Ernest (1915-1998) b. Dublin, novelist. The son of an Austro-Hungarian itinerant musician, his novel *The Voyage Of The Mayflower* (1950) was a hugely successful blockbuster, selling 4 million copies in the US. Married to writer EDNA O'BRIEN, he separated from her in 1961, soon after her book *The Country Girls* was published. Screenplays include *Call Me Daddy, The Lonely Girl (Girl with Green Eyes), Women can be Monsters, Why Aren't You Famous?* and *A Little Milk of Human Kindness*.

GOGARTY, Oliver St. John (1878-1957) b. Dublin, poet and surgeon. Friendly with JAMES JOYCE. Works include *An Offering of Swans* (1923) and *Elbow Room* (1939).

GOLDSMITH, Oliver (1728-1774) b. Longford, poet and author. Studied medicine, but began writing. Became known in literary spheres and associated with Samuel Johnson. Works include *The Citizen of the World* (1762), the acclaimed *The Vicar of Wakefield* (1766), his most famous verse being *The Deserted Village* (1770). Plays include *The Good-Natur'd Man* (1768) and the still successful *She Stoops to Conquer* (1773).

GRAVES, Alfred (1846-1931) b. Dublin; writer and educationist. An inspector of schools in England, he was a leader of the Celtic Revival, writing a good deal of Irish folk verse and songs. He also wrote an autobiography *To Return to All That* (1930).

GREGORY, Lady Isabella Augusta (1852-1932) playwright and founder of the Irish Theatre movement. After her marriage to Sir William Gregory, governor of Ceylon, met and became friendly with WB YEATS, founding the ABBEY THEATRE and the Irish Players. Wrote many short plays including *Spreading the News* (1904) and *The Rising of the Moon* (1907). Also transcribed Irish legends and translated Molière.

GRIFFIN, Gerald (1803-40) b. Limerick, novelist. Travelled to London and published short stories of Irish life. His book, *The Collegians* (1829), was used as the basis of Boucicault's *Colleen Bawn*. In 1838 he destroyed his manuscripts and entered a monastery.

HANLEY, Gerard (1916-1992) b. England, writer. Works include *The Consul at Sunset* (1951), *The Year of the Lion, Gilligan's Last Elephant, See You in Yasukuni* and the screenplay *The Blue Max*. (1966).

JAMESON, Anna Brownell (1794-1860) b. Dublin, art critic and author. Her writings include *Diary of an Ennuyée* (1826), *Characteristics of Shakespeare's Women* (1832), *Beauties of the Court of Charles II* (1833) and works on art.

JOHNSTON, Denis (1901-84) b. Dublin, playwright. Educated in Dublin, Edinburgh, Cambridge and Harvard. Joined the English and Northern Ireland bars. His works include *The Old Lady Says 'No'* (1929) and *The Moon on the Yellow River* (1931). Autobiographical works include *Nine Rivers from Jordan* (1953), which tells of his years as a war correspondent. His daughter JENNIFER JOHNSTON is also a novelist.

JOYCE, James Augustine Aloysius (1882-1941) b. Dublin, writer. Educated at Clongowes, Belvedere and University College, Dublin. A linguist and a prolific reader, he corresponded with Ibsen. The Catholic Church's hold on Ireland compelled him to move to Paris. Returned briefly after his mother's death and returned to exile from Ireland with Nora Barnacle who was to be his partner for the rest of his life. Had written two books by the end of WWI, *Chamber Music* (1907) and *Dubliners* (1914), a collection of short stories. Ezra Pound became his champion and the autobiographical *A Portrait of the Artist as a Young Man* appeared in instalments in *The Egoist* (1914-15). Pound and W.B. YEATS petitioned on Joyce's behalf and he obtained a grant from the Royal Literary Fund in 1915. However, his eyesight was failing. Was also deeply disturbed by his daughter's schizophrenia. Published his most famous work, *Ulysses* (1922), in Paris to much criticism. Now regarded as a watershed in literature, it narrates a day in the life of Leopold Bloom as he wanders through Dublin (Bloomsday is now celebrated every year in Dublin). His subsequent work, *Finnegan's Wake*, was published in 1939.

KAVANAGH, Patrick (1905-67) b. Monaghan, poet and novelist. Left Monaghan for Dublin (1939) to pursue a literary career. Arguably his best work is *The Great Hunger* (1942), a poem which exposes the harsh reality of farming. In 1948, wrote the autobiographical *Tarry Flynn*. His antisocial, unorthodox lifestyle was anonymously written about in the press and led to a libel action, from which he never recovered. Works include *Collected Poems* (1964).

KEANE, Molly (1904-1996) b. Kildare, novelist. Used her anglo-Irish ascendancy background as the basis for her books. Adopted the pen-name MJ Farrell and wrote her first book, *The Knight of Cheerful Countenance*. Wrote ten books between 1928 and 1952, stopping when her husband died. However, resumed writing and her book, *Good Behaviour* (1981), was shortlisted for the Booker Prize.

KEATING, Geoffrey also known as Seathrún Céitinn (c. 1570-1645) b. Tipperary; historian. His chief work, *Foras Feasa ar Éirinn* (History of Ireland) was allegedly written in a cave. Supposedly killed in a church by Cromwellian soldiers.

KICKHAM, Charles (1828-82) b. Tipperary, Fenian, journalist and novelist. Editor of Fenian newspaper, *The Irish People*. Best known for novels *Sally Kavanagh* and *Knocknagow* (1879) and poem *Rory of the Hill*.

LAVIN, Mary (1912-96) b. Massachusetts (returned to Ireland as a child), best-known as a short story writer. Her first short story *Miss Holland* was published in the *Dublin Magazine*. Other works include *Tales from Bective Bridge* (1942), *Mary O'Grady* (1950), *A Memory and other Stories* (1972), *The Shrine and Other Stories* (1977) and *A Family Likeness* (1985). Was awarded the Katherine Mansfield prize and the Gregory Medal.

LECKY, William Edward Hartpole (1838-1903) b. Dublin, philosopher and historian. Educated at TCD and recognised as a great historian, his works include *History of Rationalism* (1865), *History of England in the 18th Century* (1878), *Democracy and Liberty* (1896) and *The Map of Life* (1899).

Le FANU, Joseph Sheridan (1814-73) b. Dublin, gothic horror novelist and journalist. Left law to take up journalism and went on to become owner and editor of the *Dublin University Magazine* as well as three other Dublin newspapers. His novels are marked by their preoccupation with the supernatural. His 14 works include The *House by the Churchyard* (1863), *Uncle Silas* (1864) and *In a Glass Darkly* (1872).

LESLIE, Sir Shane (1885-1971) b. Co. Cavan, writer. Born into the Protestant ascendancy, converted to Roman Catholicism and espoused nationalism. Wrote *The End of a Chapter*, an analysis of the pre-WWI generation, and followed it with *The Celt and the World, Doomsland, The Oppidan* and *The Cantab*.

LEWIS, C.S. (1898-1963) b. Belfast - writer, academic and Christian apologist. Was professor of medieval and Renaissance English at Cambridge from 1954. His first book *Dymer* (1926) is a narrative poem that is both satirical and idealistic - a quality that suffuses most of his work. Other works include *Allegory of Love* (1936), *The Screwtape Letters* (1942), *The Problem of Pain* (1940), *Beyond Personality* (1944) and *Mere Christianity* (1952). Has also written science fiction and children's books, the most famous of which are *The Chronicles of Narnia*.

LYNCH, Liam (1937-96) b. Dublin, writer and playwright. Works include *Do Thrushes Sing in Birmingham?* (1962), *Soldier* (1969), *Strange Dreams Unending* (1974), *Krieg* (1982), *Voids* (1982), *Shell Sea Shell* (1983).

LYNCH, Patricia (1900-72) b. Cork, popular children's author. Published more than 50 children's books including *The Turf Cutter's Daughter* (1934), *The Grey*

Goose of Kilnevan (1941), *Story Teller's Holiday* (1947) plus the *Brogeen* series from 1947.

LYONS, Francis Stewart (1923-83) b. Derry; historian and writer Educated at Trinity and taught there until appointed professor of history at the University of Kent (1964). Returned to Trinity and was made provost (1974-81). His works include The *Fall of Parnell* (1960), *John Dillon* (1968), *Ireland Since the Famine* (1971), *Charles Stewart Parnell* (1977) and *Culture and Anarchy in Ireland 1890-1939* (1978). Was working on the official historical biography of WB YEATS when he died.

McDONAGH, Donagh (1912-68) b. Dublin, playwright. Son of the revolutionary Thomas McDonagh, edited *The Oxford Book of Irish Verse* with Lennox Robinson. Plays include *Happy as Larry* (1946), *God's Gentry* (1951) and *Step-in-the-Hollow (1957)*.

McGEE, Thomas D'Arcy (1825-68) b. Co. Louth, writer and politician. Emigrated to Canada in 1842 and espoused numerous nationalist causes. Published Romantic poetry, as well as *A History of the Irish settlers in North America* (1851), *A Popular History of Ireland* (1862-69) and *Poems* (1869). Elected an MP, was assasinated in Ottawa for opposing a proposed Fenian invasion of Canada.

McMAHON, Brian (1909-1998) b. Listowel, writer and playwright. Works include *The Bugle in the Blood, The Song of the Anvil, The Honey Spike, The Death of Biddy Early, The Lion Tamer, Children of the Rainbow, Red Petticoat, The Sound of Hooves* (1985), *The Master* (autobiography 1992),*The Tallystick* (1994).

MacGILL, Patrick (1890-1963) b. Donegal, poet and novelist. Worked in Scotland as a farm-labourer and navvy. Works include *Children of the Dead End* (1914) and *The Rat-Pit* (1914), among many other books. Emigrated to the US (1930) and died there in poverty.

MacNEICE, Louis (1907-63) b. Belfast, poet. A lecturer in the classics, became aligned with left-wing British poets of the 1930s, particularly Auden. Works include *Blind Fireworks* (1929), *Collected Poems* (1949), *Autumn Sequel* (1954), *Eighty-Five Poems* (1961) and *Solstices* (1961). Also renowned for his radio plays and his literary criticism.

MACKEN, Walter (1915-67) b. Galway; novelist, actor and playwright. Remembered for historical trilogy *Seek the Fair Land* (1959), *The Silent People* (1962) *The Scorching Wind* (1964) and *Brown Lord of the Mountain.*

MALONE, Edmund (1741-1812) b. Dublin, editor of Shakespeare. Called to the Irish bar but worked in the London literary sphere. Wrote an eleven-volume edition of Shakespeare (1790) and was one of the first people to discredit Chatterton's Rowley poems and denounced William Henry Ireland's Shakespeare forgeries. The Malone Society was formed in 1907 in his honour.

MANGAN, James Clarence (1803-49) b. Dublin, poet. His life was marked by failed love, poverty and alchoholism. Published translations of Irish poetry in *The Poets and Poetry of Munster* (1849), which includes *My Dark Rosaleen, The Nameless One* and *The Woman of Three Cows.* Also published translated German poetry - *Anthologia Germanica* (1845).

MERRIMAN, Brian (1747-1805) b. Ennistymon, Co.

Clare, Gaelic poet. His poem *Cúirt an Mheáin Oidhche* (The Midnight Court) is the most translated poem in the Irish language. A bawdy epic, it mocks sexual morals, celibacy, the clergy and male chauvinism. The poem had the notable distinction of being banned in English but allowed in its original Irish (as Irish was deemed to be incapable of corruption).

MOORE, Thomas (1779-1852) b. Dublin, poet and socialite, most notably in Regency London. Published many works, including his *Irish Melodies* (1807-1834) with accompanying music, some of which he composed himself. Also wrote satires and prose.Noted for his wit, charm, liberalism and singing voice - was a close friend of Lord Byron. Other works include *Lalla Rookh* (1817) and *Life of Byron* (1830). Melodies include *Believe Me If All those Endearing Young Charms, The Harp that Once through Tara's Halls* and *The Time I've Lost in Wooing.*

O'BRIEN, Flann / Myles na gCopaleen Brian O'Nolan (1911-66) b. Co. Tyrone, playwright and novelist. Wrote a satirical column *An Cruiskeen Lawn* in *The Irish Times* for two decades. Works include *At Swim-two birds* (1939), *The Third Policeman* (1940/67), *An Béal Bocht* (1941), *The Hard Life* (1961), *Faustus Kelly* (1943), *The Dalky Archive* (1964).

O'CADHAIN, Máirtín (1906-70) b. Galway, noted Irish language writer. Most famous for novel *Cré na Cille* (1949), translated into several European languages. First Irish-writer elected to the Irish Academy of Letters.

O'CASEY, Seán (1880-64) b. Dublin, dramatist. Best remembered for the trilogy of plays dealing with struggle for Irish Independence: *The Shadow of a Gunman* (1923), *Juno and the Paycock* (1924) and *The Plough and the Stars* (1926), which remain among the most popular of productions on the Irish theatre circuit. *The Silver Tassie*, his next play, was rejected by the ABBEY THEATRE and O'Casey moved to London, wrote more plays and a six-volume autobiography.

Ó CLÉIRIGH, Mícheál (1575-1643) b. Donegal, Compiled the *Annals of the Four Masters* in Irish, assisted by Cuigcoigriche Ó'Duigeanáin, Fearfeasa Ó'Maolconaire, and Cuigcoigriche Ó'Cléirigh.

Ó CONAIRE, Pádraic (1883-1928) b. Galway, Irish language novelist and short story writer. Best known for *M'Asal Beag Dubh* and *Fearfasa MacFeasa* (1930).

O'CONNOR, Frank (1903-66) b. Cork, novelist, short story writer and translator. Best known for short stories, collected in volumes such as *Guests of the Nation* (1931) and *Crab Apple Jelly* (1944). Works include *Bones of Contention* (1936), *The Saint and Mary Kate* (1932), *Dutch Interior* (1940), *An Only Child* (1961), *My Father's Sons* (1968), *The Backward Look* (1967).

Ó CRIOMHTHAIN, Tomás (1856-1937) b. Great Blasket Island, Kerry. Best known for the diary, *Allagar na h-Inise* (1928) and the autobiography *An t-Oileánach* (1929).

Ó DOIRNÍN, Peadar (1682-1769) b. Louth, poet. Best known for works as political and humourous verse writer.

O'DONNELL, Peadar (1893-1986) b. Donegal, novelist and playwright. Works include *Storm* (1925), *Islands* (1928), *The Knife* (1930), *The Gates Flew Open*

(1932), *On the Edge of the Stream* (1934), *Salud: An Irishman in Spain* (1937), *The Big Windows* (1955), *There Will Be Another Day* (1963), *Proud Island* (1975).

O'FAOLÁIN, Seán (1900-91) b. Cork, novelist. Works include *Midsummer Night Madness* (1932), *King of the Beggars* ; (1938), *De Valera* (1939), *Come Back to Erin* (1940), *The Great O'Neill* (1942), *Constance Markievicz* (1943), *Vive Moi!* (1964), *Foreign Affairs* (1976), *Collected Stories* (1980-82).

O'FLAHERTY, Liam (1896-1984) b. Inishmór, novelist. Works include *The Black Soul* (1924),*The Assassin* (1928), *Skerrett* (1932), *Famine* (1937), *The Short Stories of Liam O'Flaherty* (1937), *Duil* (1953), *The Pedlar's Revenge and Other Stories* (1976).

O'GRADY, Standish (1846-1928) b. Cork, a writer of historical novels. Works include *The Heroic Period* (1878) and *Red Hugh's Captivity* (1889).

Ó GRIANNA, Séamus (1891-1969) b. Donegal, novelist and short story writer, known by pen-name *Máire*. Best known for *Cith is Dealain* (1926) and *Caislean Óir* (1924).

Ó RATHAILLE, Aodhagán (1670-1726) b. Kerry, Irish language poet.

Ó SÚILLEABHÁIN, Eoghan Rua (1748-84) b. Kerry, poet. Wrote in Irish about experiences as a school teacher, seaman and wandering labourer.

Ó SÚILLEABHÁIN, Muiris (1904-50) b. Great Blasket Island, Kerry; Irish-language writer. Best known for autobiography *Fíche Blian ag Fás - Twenty Years a-Growing* (1933).

Ó TUAIRISC, Eoghan (1919-82) b. Ballinasloe; poet, writer, playwright and translator. Works include *L'Attaque*, *Dé Luain*, *An Lomnochtán*, *Rogha na Fhile*, *Dialann sa Diseart*, *Na Mairnéalaigh*, *La Fhéile Mhichíl*, *An Hairyfella in Ifreann*, *Fornocht do Chonac*.

Ó hUIGINN, Tadhg Dall (1550-91) b. Sligo, bardic poet who dedicated his poems to the Gaelic lords in his surrounding area.

PARKER, Stewart (1941-88) b. Belfast, playwright. Works include *The Casualty Meditation* (1966), *Spokesong* (1975), *Catchpenny Twist* (1977), *Nightshade* (1985), *Northern Star* (1985).

REID, Forrest (1875-1947) b. Belfast, novelist and literary critic. Works include *The Kingdom of Twilight* (1904), *Following Darkness* (1912), *At the Door of the Gate* (1915), *Uncle Stephen* (1931), *The Retreat* (1936), *Young Man, or Very Mixed Company* (1944).

SAYERS, Peig (1873-1958) b. Kerry, skilled storywriter gifted with a wealth of folklore on the Great Blasket Island, off Kerry. Recordings of her folktales and stories was made by Irish Folklore Commission and later published as her autobiography *Peig* (1936).

SHERIDAN, Richard Brinsley (1715-1816) b. Dublin, playwright and politician. As a young man, eloped with a society beauty and married her. To support their lavish lifestyle, turned to writing for the stage. Bought a share in the Drury Lane Theatre from the actor Garrick. Found success in comic writing. Was elected to Parliament (1780-1812). A strong opponent of the Union and an advocate for free speech, noted as a brilliant orator. The theatre burnt down and Sheridan's extravagance led him into penury, in which he died. Works include *The Rivals* (1775), his most famous

and popular play *The School for Scandal* (1777), *The Critic* (1779)

STEPHENS, James (1880-1950) b. Dublin, writer. Best known works include *The Charwoman's Daughter* and *Crock of Gold*, which dealt with Irish folklore and fantasy, and *The Insurrection in Dublin* (1916) about the Easter Rising.

STOKER, Bram (1847-1912.) b. Dublin, best remembered for *Dracula* (1897), which took six years to create and inspired dozens of other works. Published a total of 18 books on mostly gothic themes. Manager of the Lyceum Theatre, London, for 27 years working with the actor Henry Irving. Final work was *Personal Reminiscences of Henry Irving* (1906).

SHAW, George Bernard (1856-1950) b. Dublin, playwright and Nobel laureate. Also noted essayist and music critic. Won Nobel Prize for Literature (1925). Was a heavily involved in the Fabian society and a passionate socialist and vegetarian. Initially successful in America, his works were recognised by English theatrical producer and writer, Granville-Barker, as masterpieces. Fell out of favour for his pacifist stance during WWI and for advocating the cause of his native country after the 1916 Rising. For many years refused to allow film versions of his work but was reconciled to the idea by Gabrial Pascal. Works include *Arms and the Man*, *Mrs Warren's Profession*, *Pygmalion*, *Major Barbara*, *Caesar & Cleopatra*, *Androcles and the Lion*, *Saint Joan*, *The Doctor's Dilemma*, *Heartbreak House*, *The Millionairess*.

SWIFT, Jonathan (1667-1745) b. Dublin, writer and dean of St Patrick's Cathedral. Took holy orders (1694) and was appointed to a Co. Antrim parish, returned to Surrey to act as a tutor to Hester Johnson 'Stella'. Given a vicarage near Trim, travelled between Ireland and London, and was noted as a wit and conversationalist. Was sought out and acted as an advocate of the Tories, attacking the Whigs. Given the deanery of St Patrick's and was followed by Esther Vanhomrigh - 'Vanessa' (controversy surrounds the roles played by Stella and Vanessa in his life). Works include *A Tale of a Tub*, *The Battle of the Books* (1704), *Drapier's Letters* (1724), the satirical *Gulliver's Travels* (1726).

SYNGE, John Millington (1871-1909) b. Co. Dublin, dramatist. Settled in Paris but returned to visit the Aran Islands. Met W.B. YEATS, who advised him to return to the islands. Did so (1899-1902) and started *The Aran Islands* (published 1907). Became involved with the Irish National Theatre and wrote the plays *The Shadow of the Glen* (1903), *Riders to the Sea* (1907) and *The Playboy of the Western World* (1907, causing a riot when first staged in the Abbey), *The Tinker's Wedding* (1908) and the unfinished *Deirdre of the Sorrows*.

WADDELL, Helen (1889-1965) renowned medieval Latin scholar with strong ties to Banbridge, Co. Down, where she is buried.

WALSH, Maurice (1879-1964) b. Kerry, novelist. Best known for *Blackrock's Feather* (1932) and *The Quiet Man*, a short story from his collection *Green Rushes* (1935), which was made into *The Quiet Man*, one of Ireland's most famous films with John Wayne and Maureen O'Hara (1952).

WILDE, Oscar Fingal O'Flahertie Wills (1854-1900) b. Dublin, noted wit and playwright. Educated at TCD and Oxford - won Newdigate Prize for poetry and graduated with double first. Founded aesthetic cult - 'art for art's sake', first published *Poems* (1898), *The Happy Prince and Other Tales* (1891),*The Picture of Dorian Gray* (1891), *A House of Pomegranates* (1891), the plays *Vera* (1883), *The Duchess of Padua* (1891) and *Salome* (1891, written in French and banned in England). Achieved overnight success with first comedy, *Lady Windermere's Fan* (1892) and continued with three more comedies *A Woman of No Importance* (1893 - 1st production), *An Ideal Husband* and*The Importance of Being Earnest* (both produced in 1895). Downfall came through his liaison with Lord Alfred Douglas, whose father, the Marquis of Queensberry, called Wilde a homosexual. Wilde sued and lost the libel action and was subsequently arrested and found guilty on charges of homosexuality, prosecuted by EDWARD CARSON. Served two years in Reading Jail, and afterwards went into exile in France. Wrote the moving *The Ballad of Reading Gaol* (1898) and *De Profundis* (1905). Died and was buried in Paris.

YEATS, William Butler (1865-1939) b. Dublin, playwright and one of Ireland's most celebrated poets. Family moved to London but spent childhood in Sligo with grandparents. Attended art school, became friendly with GEORGE RUSSELL - 'AE' - and other mystics. Began writing and was influenced by JOHN O'LEARY and others to include Irish themes in his work.Involved in Madame Blavatsky's Theosophism, helped found NATIONAL LITERARY SOCIETY to publicise the literature of Ireland. Published *The Wanderings of Oisin* (1889), *The Countess Cathleen* (1892) *The Celtic Twilight* (1893), and prose booksThe *Secret Rose, The Tables of Law* and *The Adoration of the Magi* (1897). Began his infatuation with MAUD GONNE MACBRIDE (1889) and met LADY AUGUSTA GREGORY with whom he founded the Irish Literary Theatre (1889). Wrote the play *On Baile's Strand* and *Cathleen Ni Houlihan* (1902) and founded ABBEY THEATRE (1904). Also met Ezra Pound who influenced his plays, married George Hyde-Lees (1917). Other plays include *Four Plays for Dancers - At the Hawk's Well, The only Jealousy of Emer, The Dreaming of the Bones* and *Calvary*. Published poetry books *The Green Helmet and Other Poems* (1910), *Responsibilities* (1914). *The Wild Swans at Coole* (1919), *Michael Robartes and the Dancer* (1921) *The Tower* (1928) and *The Winding Stair* (1933). Made member of Seanad Éireann (1922) and won Nobel Prize for Literature (1923). Most famous poems - *Lake Isle of Innisfree, September 1913, Easter 1916* and *The Circus Animal's Desertion.* Died in France (1939) but was re-interred in Ireland (1948).

MEDIA

ANDREWS, Eamon (1922-87) b. Dublin, broadcaster; newspaper columnist, amateur champion boxer, best-known for presenting *This is Your Life.* An astute analyser of the television business, set up his own production company and was served on the board that saw the launch of RTÉ.

BRACKEN, Brendan *1st Viscount* (1901-58) b. Kilmallock, journalist and Conservative politician. Was managing director of "The Economist" (1928-45).

BURKE, Sir John Bernard (1787-1848) b. Tipperary, genealogist and compiler of "Burke's Peerage" which he published annually from 1847 (the first dictionary of British peers).

CAMPBELL, Patrick (1913-80) b. Dublin, broadcaster and author. Wrote for the *Irish Times* and the *Sunday Times* and devised scripts for the BBC, taking up broadcasting for them. Most famous for the TV programme *Call My Bluff.*

COLLIER, Peter (1846-1909) b. Co. Carlow, pioneered the field of subscription publishing. Emigrated to the US and started printing books from a basement, which were then sold on an instalment plan. Established the national weekly *Collier's* (1895) which grew to have a subscription of over 3 million.

CRAWFORD, Emily (*c.* 1840-1915) b. Co. Longford, foreign correspondent. Lived in Paris and wrote articles on Paris's social and political life for English publications. Reported on the Franco-Prussian war, at considerable risk to herself, and became Paris correspondent of the *Daily News* and the *New York Tribune.*

GILL, Michael (1794-1879) b. Dublin, acknowledged as the father of printing in Dublin. Established a publishing house in Dublin (1856) M.H. Gill and Son which was later associated with Macmillan of London, becoming Gill and Macmillan (1968).

HARMSWORTH, Alfred Charles William *1st Viscount Northcliffe* (1865-1922) b. Dublin, journalist and newspaper magnate. Revolutionized Fleet Street with his *Daily Mail*, which had an American-style layout and news presentation. Launched a number of papers and bought many provincial papers with his brother Harold. Also launched the first newspaper for women, the *Daily Mirror*, and founded the Amalgamated Press for educational journals. In 1908, took over *The Times* and boosted its circulation.

HARRIS, Frank (1856-1931) b. Galway; journalist and writer. His autobiography (1923-7) was banned for pornography. Was the editor of the *Fortnightly Review, Saturday Review, Vanity Fair* and the *Evening News*, the latter being a pioneer in sensationalist journalism.

MORAN, D.P. (1871-1936) b. Waterford, founder and editor of the *Leader* renowned for its fierce nationalist tone.

MURPHY, William Martin (1844-1919) b. Cork, MP (1885-92); founder of the *Irish Independent* (1905), led the employers' federation during the 1913 Dublin Lock-out.

NEWMAN, Alec (1905-72) b. Waterford, editor of The *Irish Times* (1954-61).

O'HEHIR, Micheál (1920-1996) b. Dublin, legendary RTÉ commentator on Gaelic games and horse-racing, commentated on 99 All-Ireland finals between 1939 and 1984.

MUSIC

BALFE, Michael William (1808-70) b. Dublin, opera composer and violinist. Debuted as a violinist, aged 9 years. In 1823, went to London, then to Italy to study under Rossini. Returned to England in 1833 and wrote many operas for Drury Lane. The most enduring of his compositions is The Bohemian Girl (1843) and the music to La Scala's ballet, La Pérouse.

BAX, Sir Arnold (1883-1953) b. London, composer. Was inspired by YEATS'S The Wanderings of Oisín. Wrote poetry commemorating the Easter Rising and included among his friends PEARSE and other 1916 revolutionaries. His works include 7 symphonies, concertos and chamber music.

BECKETT, Walter (1914-96) musician and composer. Educated at Portora Royal School, Enniskillen and TCD. Lectured in TCD, was music critic for the Irish Times During the 1950s, wrote arrangements and original compositions for RTÉ. Professor of Harmony and composition at (and was elected as fellow) of the RIAM.

BOWLES, Michael (1909-98) composer.

CLANCY, Wilie (1918-75) b. Clare, instrumental musician. Noted as a master of several traditional instruments, but acclaimed as a piper. Now commemorated by international summer school Scoil Samhraidh Willie Clancy.

DOWLAND, John (1562-1626) b. Dublin, composer to Royal Courts at Copenhagen and London. Wrote three volumes of 'Books of Songs or Ayres'.

FIELD, John (1782-1837) b. Dublin, pianist, composer and pioneer of the nocturne. An infant prodigy, he studied under Clementi, who used him to show the capabilities of his pianos. In 1802, accompanied Clementi to Paris, Vienna and St Petersburg and stayed and worked as a music teacher. His 19 Nocturnes and other musical works were said to have influenced Chopin. Spent most of his life in Russia where he died.

FLEISCHMANN, Aloys (1910-92) b. Munich, composer. Made professor of music at UCC and stayed there until he retired (1934-1980). Regarded as one of the most influential figures in musical life in Ireland, founding the Cork Symphony Orchestra (1939) and the Cork International Choral and Folk Dance Festival (1954), as well as being an active member of numerous organisations - was a member of the RIAM and Aosdána. Compositions include 6 works for orchestra, 3 works for chamber orchestra and 15 works for vocal and choral performance.

FRENCH, Percy (1854-1920) b. Roscommon, singer/songwriter and artist. His most famous compositions are The Mountains of Mourne and Are ye Right there Michael.

GALLAGHER, Rory (1948-1995) b. Donegal. Internationally renowned rock/blues guitarist. Voted World's Top Guitarist. Formed Taste ('66) - Albums: Taste ('69); On The Boards (UK No 18 - '70). Went solo ('71) - Albums (1971-90): Rory Gallagher; Deuce; Blueprint; Tattoo; Against The Grain; Calling Card; Photo Finish; Top Priority; Jinx; Defender; Fresh Evidence. Live albums: Live! In Europe ('72); Irish Tour '74 ('74); Stage Struck. Compilations include: Rory Gallagher Boxed ('92).

GILMORE, Patrick Sarsfield (1829-92) b. Dublin, bandmaster. Emigrated to the US, formed a band and toured the country, served during the US Civil War. Composed military band pieces, dances and songs, including 'When Johnny Comes Marching Home'.

GROOCOCK, Joseph (1913-97) composer.

HARTY, Sir Hamilton (1880-1941) b. Hillsborough, Co. Down, composer and arranger. Conducted the Hallé Orchestra. Compositions include An Irish Symphony and many songs. Also made well-known arrangements of Handel's Fireworks and Watermusic suites.

HERBERT, Victor (1859-1924) b. Dublin, composer. A cellist, played in the orchestras of Johann Strauss and at the Stuttgart court. Moved to New York and became the leading cellist in the Metropolitan Opera Company's orchestra. Composed a popular comic opera - Prince Ananias - and serious operas Natoma (1911) and Madeleine (1914).

KELLY, Luke singer with the THE DUBLINERS, formed Dublin (1962), with himself, Ronnie Drew, Barney McKenna, Kieron Bourke and later John Sheehan Toured extensively and enjoyed much success all over Europe.

KENNEDY, Frankie (d. 1994) member of ALTAN, one of Ireland's top traditional music groups. Married to Band member Mairéad Ní Mhaonaigh.

KENNEDY, Jimmy (1902-84) b. Tyrone, wrote songs 'The Hokey Cokey', 'Red Sails in the Sunset', 'South of the Border, Down Mexico Way' and 'The Teddy Bear's Picnic'.

McCORMACK, Count John Francis (1884-1945) b. Athlone, tenor singer. After studying in Milan, was taken on by the Covent Garden Opera for the 1905-6 season. Due to his nationalist beliefs, did not appear in England during WWI and took US citizenship in 1919. For the rest of his career, sang popular sentimental songs, films include Song O' My Heart (1930) and Wings of the Morning (1937). Made a papal count in 1945.

NELSON, Havelock (1917-96) composer.

LYNOTT, Phil (1951-1986)formed THIN LIZZY Dublin (1969) after short spell with Brian Downey, Eric Bell, Eric Wrixon. Disbanded 1983. Lynott released two solo albums: Solo in Soho ('80); The Phil Lynott Album ('82). His heroin addiction ultimately led to his death

O'RIADA, Seán (1931-71) b. Cork, composer and musician who made a huge contribution to Irish musical culture. Studied music extensively in Ireland, Italy and France. Musical director to the ABBEY THEATRE, composed the score for Mise Éire (1959). Formed Ceoltóirí Cualann, a traditional ensemble much celebrated via a radio series. It included Paddy Maloney, Martin Fay and Sean Keane. Composed score to the film The Playboy of the Western World ('62).

POTTER, A.J. (1918-80) b. Belfast, composer, broadcaster and teacher. Studied composition under Vaughan Williams. Moved to Dublin and was Professor of Composition at the RIAM (1955-73). A prolific composer, his music incorporated a wide variety of techniques and his orchestration is recognised as being outstanding. Notable works include his Missa Brevis (1936 rev. 1940) which won the 1951 Festival of Britain Prize, Overture to a Kitchen Comedy (1950) and Sinfonia de Profundis (1969).

VICTORY, Gerard (1921-95) b. Dublin, composer and member of Aosdána. Director of Music at RTÉ (1967-82) and president of UNESCO's International Rostrum of Composers (1981-83). During a career as a composer spanning over 40 years, wrote around 200 works, including four symphonies, eight operas, a large-scale cantata, two piano concertos and scores for films, plays and celebratory events. The most notable of these being *Chatterton, An Evening for Three, The Rendezvous* and *Ultima Rerum*.

RELIGION

AIKENHEAD, Mary (1787-1858) b. Cork, founded the Irish Sisters of Charity. Born a Protestant, converted to Catholicism after the death of her father, founded ten houses and St. Vincent's Hospital - the first in Ireland administered by nuns.

ALEXANDER, Cecil Frances (1818-95) b. Dublin, hymn composer; most famous hymns are *All Things Bright and Beautiful* and *Once in Royal David's City*.

BEDELL, William (1571-1642) b. Essex, bishop and provost at Trinity College. Opposed the oppression of Catholics and ensured that students of divinity studied Irish. Had the Old Testament translated into Irish - later translated and printed as Bedell's Bible.

BERESFORD, John G. (1773-1862) b. Dublin, Church of Ireland Archbishop of Armagh and Primate of All Ireland (1822-62).

BERKELEY, George (1685-1753) b. Kilkenny, Church of Ireland Bishop of Cloyne (1734-52) and philosopher. His most important treatises were *Essay towards a New Theory of Vision* (1709), *A Treatise concerning the Principles of Human Knowledge* (1710) and *Three Dialogues between Hylas & Philonous* (1713), in which he developed the concept 'to be is to be perceived' - the contents of the material world are ideas that only exist when they are perceived by a mind. Obsessed with founding a college in America to propagate Christianity among the 'American savages' but was never to see this college founded in his lifetime.

BERNARD, John Henry (1860-1927) b. Wicklow, Church of Ireland Archbishop of Dublin (1915-27) and Provost of Trinity College (1919-27).

BRONTË, Rev. Patrick (1777-1861) b. Co. Down, his daughters were the famous writers Charlotte, Emily and Anne.

CONWAY, William (1913-1977) b. Belfast, Roman Catholic Archbishop of Armagh and Primate of All Ireland from 1963, created Cardinal 1965.

COOKE, Henry (1788-1868) b. Derry, moderator of Presbyterian General Assembly (1841 & 1862). Vociferous opponent of Repeal and the disestablishment of the Church of Ireland.

CULLEN, Paul (1803-78) b. Kildare, Ireland's first Cardinal. Archbishop of Armagh (1850-52), Archbishop of Dublin from 1852. Founded Catholic University (1854) and Clonliffe College (1859). Primate of All-Ireland from June 1866 until his death.

CUSACK, Margaret Anna *'the Nun of Kenmare'* (1829-1899) b. Dublin; social thinker and writer. An Anglican, converted to Catholicism (1858) and founded a convent in Kenmare. After coming into conflict with the church hierarchy, went to England and founded the Sisters of St Joseph of Peace. Honoured for setting up the Famine Relief Fund in 1879, but later fell out of favour for her work for women's suffrage - the Vatican

ordered her name be removed as founder of her order. Returned to her Anglican beliefs and spent her final years lecturing and writing. Published 100 books of biography, history, poetry, music and social reform.

D'ALTON, John (1883-1963) b. Mayo, Roman Catholic Archbishop of Armagh and Primate of All Ireland from 1946, created Cardinal 1953.

D'ARCY, Charles F. (1859-1938) born Dublin, Church of Ireland Archbishop of Armagh and Primate of All Ireland (1920-38).

DUNS SCOTTUS, Johannes (*c.* 1260-1308) medieval scholar. Held the Oxford chair of divinity. In the 16th century his teachings were ridiculed by humanists and others, and a derivation of his name - 'dunce' - referring to his adherents came to mean slow-witted.

ERIGENA, John Scotus (c. 810-c. 877) philosopher and theologian. A unique figure outside the mainstream of medieval thought, taught at the court of Charles I in France. Gave his support to the predestination controversy which was condemned as *sultes Scotorum* (Irishman's porridge) by the Council of Valence. His major work attempted to amalgamate Christianity and neo-Platonism but was condemned. According to legend, he was stabbed to death by his scholars with their pens 'for trying to make them think'.

FARLEY, John (1842-1918) b. Armagh, Archbishop of New York (1902-18), created Cardinal 1911.

HORAN, James (1912-86) b. Mayo, parish priest at Knock, Co. Mayo (1967-86). Built a new 10,000-capacity basilica, hosted Pope John Paul II on his trip to Ireland in 1979, driving force behind the building of Knock airport (completed 1986).

HUGHES, John (1797-1864) b. Tyrone, first Roman Catholic Archbishop of New York (1850-64).

KERNOHAN, Joseph (1869-1923) b. Derry, founded Presbyterian Historical Society (1906).

KILLEN, William (1806-1902) b. Antrim, President of the Presbyterian College Belfast in 1870s.

KING, William (1650-1729) b. Antrim, Church of Ireland Archbishop of Derry (1690-1703), Archbishop of Dublin (1703-1729).

LOGUE, Michael (1840-1924) b. Donegal, Archbishop of Armagh (1887-1924), created Cardinal 1893.

McAULEY, Catherine (1778-1841) b. Dublin, founded the Sisters of Mercy (1831). The Mercy order has been responsible for educating hundreds of thousands of Irish students (although controversy has grown around the treatment of orphans in their care). Her portrait is on the current Irish five-pound note.

McQUAID, John Charles (1895-1973) b. Cavan, archbishop, who had a strong influence on Irish social and political life. Ordained a priest in the Holy Ghost Fathers (1924), became the dean of studies and then president (1931) at Blackrock College, Dublin. Greatly influenced Éamon de Valera and was made archbishop of Dublin (1940) by Pius XII. Led opposition to Dr. Nöel Browne's Mother and Child scheme, a secular national health scheme (which ultimately led to the fall of the then government in 1951) and, being opposed to multi-denominational education, banned Catholics' attending at Trinity College. Retired in 1972.

MacHALE, John (1791-1881) b. Mayo, Archbishop of Tuam (1834-1881). An outspoken nationalist, he backed Catholic Emancipation, Repeal of the Union and Land Reform.

McKENZIE, John (1648-96) b. Tyrone, Presbyterian minister who survived the Siege of Derry and published his account of it in 1690, *'Narrative of the Siege of Londonderry'*.

McNAMARA, Kevin (1926) b. Clare, Roman Catholic Archbishop of Dublin (1985-87).

MacRORY, Joseph (1861-1945) b. Tyrone, Roman Catholic Archbishop of Armagh and Primate of All Ireland (1928-45), created Cardinal 1929.

MATTHEW, Fr Theobald (1790-1856) b. Tipperary, formed a temperance society in 1838, a forerunner of the current Pioneer Total Abstinence Association.

Ó FIAICH, Tomás (1923-90) b. Armagh, President of Maynooth College (1974-77). Roman Catholic Archbishop of Armagh and Primate of All Ireland (1977-90), created Cardinal 1979. Widely learned and popular, welcomed Pope John Paul II to Ireland during his visit (1979). Held strong nationalist views, but advocated a united Ireland through peaceful means. Was also active in promoting the ecumenical movement.

O'GROWNEY, Fr Eugene (1863-1899) b. Meath, a key figure in the revival of the Irish language in the last century, he was vice-president of the Gaelic League from 1893 and Professor of Irish at Maynooth College (1891-96).

RICE, Edmund (1762-1844) b. Kilkenny, founded his first school in 1803 in what was to be the beginning of the Christian Brothers. Pope Pius VII recognised the Brothers in 1820 and Brother Ignatius as he was then known became Superior-General. Beatified 1996.

SCRIVEN, Joseph (1819-86) b. Banbridge, Co. Down, wrote the hymn - 'What a Friend We have in Jesus' - which has been sung throughout the world and translated into many languages.

SHANAHAN, Joseph (1871-1943) b. Tipperary, Roman Catholic missionary priest to Nigeria from 1902, bishop in Nigeria (1920-31).

ST. BRENDAN (c.484-578) b. Kerry, 'Brendan the Navigator'. Believed to have discovered America between 535 and 553.

ST. BRIGID (d. 525) b. Louth, patron saint. Founded religious house in Kildare. Her miracles are said to have derived from legends about a Celtic goddess. Her feast day is February 1st, marked throughout Ireland, by the construction of crosses made from rushes.

ST. COLUMN CILLE (521-97) b. Donegal, patron saint. Founded monastic settlements at Derry and Kells, founded monastery at Iona in 563 from which missionaries brought Christianity to Scotland and northern England.

ST. PATRICK (d. 460) b. Wales, foremost of Ireland's three patron saints. A missionary bishop, he arrived in 432 bringing Christianity to Ireland. Established See at Armagh. His life was said to have been a confabulation to get the Primacy of the Irish church established at Armagh.

PLUNKETT, Saint Oliver (1625-81) b. Meath, Archbishop of Armagh from 1669. Hanged, drawn and quartered following spurious charges of involvement in a 'Popish Plot'. Canonised 1975.

TALBOT, Matthew (1856-1925) born Dublin, took a pledge of total abstinence in 1884 following an early life of heavy drinking. Devoted himself to religion and good deeds. Conferred with the title Venerable by the Catholic Church 1976.

WALKER, Rev George (1618) b. Tyrone, Protestant minister who was joint governor of Derry during the siege (1689). Appointed bishop of Derry following the siege, he was killed in battle in 1690.

SCIENCE / MEDICINE

ADAMS, Robert (1791-1875) b. Dublin, surgeon. Noted in his field in Ireland, he wrote *Treatise on Rheumatic Gout* (1857), which was a seminal work on the subject.

ALLMAN, George James (1812-98) b. Cork, noted pioneer in marine zoology. Best known for his work on hydroids.

ANDREWS, Thomas (1813-85) b. Belfast. Although a physician, most noted for his work as a physical chemist. Discovered the composition of ozone and the critical temperature of gases, above which they cannot be liquified, however great the pressure applied.

BALL, John (1818-89) b. Dublin; botanist, alpinist and author of the *Alpine Guide*. Wrote on the botany of Morocco and South America.

BARCROFT, Sir Joseph (1872-1947) b. Newry, Co. Down, physiologist who invented device for blood-gas analysis. Also studied the oxygen-carrying function of haemoglobin and led an expedition to the Andes to study acclimatization.

BATES *née O'Dwyer*, **Daisy May** (1863-1951) b. Tipperary, anthropologist. Emigrated to Australia in 1884. Renowned for investigating the condition of aborigines, became known as Kabbarli (grandmother) as she worked for aboriginal welfare and set up camps for the aged.

BEAUFORT, Francis (1774-1857) b. Meath, hydrographer. Served in the British navy as a hydrographer (1829-55). Devised the *Beaufort Scale* of wind measurement which is still in use today - it defines 12 wind conditions from dead calm to hurricane force.

BENNETT, Edward Hallaran (1837-1907) b. Cork, surgeon and authority on bone fractures. A professor of surgery, specialised in and made a collection of fractures and dislocations for the University of Dublin. Best known for his description of a fracture of the thumb now known as 'Bennett's fracture'.

BERNAL, John Desmond (1901-71) b. Nenagh, Co. Tipperary, regarded as the father of modern crystallography, founder of molecular biology and a pioneer worker on the structure of water. An ardent communist, actively supported international efforts for peace during the Cold War. Included among his major theses is "The Origin of Life" (1967) as well as the work *The Social Function of Science* (1939).

BLACK, Joseph (1728-99) b. Bordeaux of Belfast parents, established many of the basic principles of modern chemistry.

BOURKE, Austin (1913-95) b. Waterford, meteorologist. Director of Ireland Meteorological Service (1964), developed an interest in agricultural meteorology and devised a technique for predicting the occurrence of potato blight, still in use today.

BOYLE, Robert (1627-91) b. Waterford, pioneer of

modern chemistry. Son of the great earl of Cork, studied Galileo's works in Florence, took up residence in London and played a leading role in the college of contemporary philosophers, later the Royal Society. Performed experiments on the properties of air which led to his proposition that the volume of gas is inversely proportional to its pressure at a constant temperature (Boyle's Law). Investigated many other subjects in science - electricity, chemistry, specific gravity, refraction and crystallography.

BRENNAN, Louis (1852-1932) b. Castlebar, inventor. Emigrated to Australia, invented dirigible torpedo, gyrostat monorail and worked on the development of the helicopter.

BROUNCKER, William 2nd Viscount (1620-84) mathematician, who was the first to express π as a continuous fraction and found expressions for the logarithm as an infinite series.

BULL, Lucien (1876-1972) b. Dublin, invented electrocardiograph (1908) and pioneer in the development of rapid cinematography.

BURKITT, Denis (1911-93) b. Fermanagh, medical scientist. Served in Africa, diagnosed a form of cancer - now known as Burkitt's lymphoma, also was one of the first people to establish the link between fibre deficiency in the diet and many diseases of the Western World.

CALLAN, Fr. Nicholas (1799-1864) b. Louth, inventor of the induction coil (fore-runner of modern transformer) and pioneer in the field of electrical science.

COLLES, Abraham (1750-98) b. Kilkenny, surgeon. Professor of anatomy and surgery in the College of Surgeons, was the first to precisely diagnose 'Colles's fracture' - a fracture just above the wrist.

COOPER, Edward (1798-63) b. Dublin, astronomer. Built an observatory at Markree Castle, Co. Sligo. Systematically recorded stars and the minor planets and kept meteorological records (1833-63). His catalogue of stars contained the approximate location of 60,066 (of which only over 8,000 were already known).

DEASE, William (1750-98) b. Cavan, founded Royal College of Surgeons in Dublin 1784.

DUNLOP, John (1840-1921) b. Scotland, moved to Belfast in 1860s, produced the first pneumatic tyre.

EDGEWORTH, Richard Lovell (1744-1817) b. Bath, educationist and inventor, father of Maria Edgeworth. After time spent in England and France, returned to the family estate in Co. Longford. He came in contact with Erasmus Darwin and the Lichfield circle. He fathered 22 children and practised many of his educational theories on them. He also advocated parliamentary reform and Catholic emancipation.

FERGUSON, Harry George (1884-1960) b. Hillsborough, Co. Down, inventor and engineer. Built his own aeroplane - the first to fly from Irish soil in December 1909. Over many years he developed the renowned Ferguson farm tractor with a hydraulic linkage which controlled the depth of ploughing. These tractors went on to play a large role in the mechanization of agriculture during and after WWII.

FITZGERALD, George Francis (1851-1901) a professor of natural philosophy, made important discoveries in the fields of electrolysis and electromagnetic radiation. His name is linked with that of Hendrik Antoon Lorentz for the Fitzgerald-Lorentz contraction in the phenomenon of change in moving bodies as observed in the Michelson-Morley experiment.

GRAVES, Robert James (1796-1853) b. Dublin, physician. Studied medicine and after spending time on the continent, returned to Dublin and appointed to the Meath Hospital. Organized medical teaching there along the lines of the French system - with emphasis placed on notetaking, physical examination, and autopsies. Noted for his diagnosis of Graves' Disease, a form of hyperthyroidism.

GREATRAKES, Valentine (1629-83) b. Waterford, physician known as the touch doctor. He became famous for curing all types of illnesses by touching or stroking. Failed to demonstrate his powers before the king but his cures were attested by ROBERT BOYLE and others. His Brief Account (1666) was published as a rebuttal to his sceptics.

GREGG, John Robert (1867-1948) b. Monaghan, inventor of shorthand system and publisher. Working in Liverpool, he devised a new shorthand system and in 1888, published his system in the Gregg Shorthand Manual. Emigrated to the US in 1893 and set up a publishing company.

GRIFFITH, Sir Richard (1784-1878) b. Dublin, geologist and engineer. Surveyed Leinster and examined Irish bogs for a government commission. After the Irish Valuation Act, 1827, devised 'Griffith's Valuations' for country rate assessments and published his Geological Map of Ireland (1855). Consulted on all major building projects in Ireland, including the National Gallery and the Museum of Natural History.

HALPIN, Captain Robert Charles (1836-1894) b. Wicklow, laid first transatlantic cable (completed 1866) from Valentia to Newfoundland.

HAMILTON, Sir William Rowan (1805-65) b. Dublin, mathematician - inventor of quaternions. A child prodigy, knew 13 languages and at 15 had begun his own mathematical investigations, inspired by Newton's Principia. Appointed professor of astronomy at Dublin while an undergraduate and developed a new approach to dynamics which had a major bearing on the 20th-century development of quantum mechanics. Introduced quaternions as a new algebraic approach to three-dimensional geometry, since proved to be the foundation of much modern algebra.

HARVEY, William Henry (1811-66) b. Limerick, botanist. Colonial treasurer at Cape Town, created a large herbarium collection of South African plants. Published Genera of South African Plants (1838) and Manual of British Algae (1840). Appointed Keeper of the Herbarium at TCD (1840) and travelled extensively to collect seaweeds.

JOLY, John (1857-1933) inventor and physicist, developed first practical colour photography system and radioactivity treatment for cancer.

KELVIN, William Thomson 1st Baron (1824-1907) b. Belfast, physicist and mathematician. At 22, became professor of mathematics and natural philosophy. Proposed the absolute, or Kelvin, temperature scale in 1848 and, simultaneously with Rudolf Clausius, devised the second law of thermodynamics. His investigations covered geomagnetism and hydrodynamics, particularly wave and vortex motion. Oversaw the laying of the first Atlantic submarine cable and grew wealthy by patenting a mirror galvanometer for accelerating telegraphic transmission. Created 1st Baron Kelvin of Largs (1892) and is buried in Westminster Abbey beside Isaac Newton.

KENNELLY, Arthur Edwin (1861-1939) engineer. Emigrated to the US (1887) and assisted Edison, becoming a professor at Harvard (1902-1930). Proposed, simultaneously with Heaviside, the existence of an ionized layer in the atmosphere, termed the Kennelly-Heaviside layer.

KIRWAN, Richard (1733-1812) b. Galway, chemist. Published the first systematic English thesis on mineralogy (1784) and was one of the main proponents of the phlogiston theory - whereby a substance, supposed to exist in all combustible bodies, is released in combustion.

KYAN, John Howard (1774-1850) b. Dublin, inventor. Through his work in a brewery in England, he discovered a method of preserving wood - 'kyanizing' - which he subsequently patented in 1832.

LARDNER, Dionysius (1793-1859) b. Dublin, scientific writer. His works on algebraic geometry (1823) and calculus (1825) attracted much attention. Was made professor of natural philosophy and astronomy at London University. Remembered as creator and editor of Lardner's Cabinet Cyclopaedia (1829-49).

LONSDALE, née Yardley, **Dame Kathleen** (1903-71) b. Newbridge, Co. Kildare, eminent crystallographer. After studying physics at Bedford College, London, she joined William Bragg's research team. Using Bragg's X-ray diffraction method, she obtained the molecular structure of hexamethylbenzene (1929) and hexachlorobenzene (1931), using the Fourier analysis for the first time - a method which was later adopted as a common technique. Professor of chemistry at University College, London, and the first female fellow of the Royal Society (1945).

MALLET, Robert (1810-81) b. Dublin, pioneer of seismology (the study and measurement of earthquakes).

PARSONS, Charles (1854-1931) b. Offaly, invented turbine for use in ships and founded his own firm for its manufacture. Also produced optical glass and many noted astronomical instruments.

PARSONS, Lawrence (d. 1908) brother of Charles, determined the temperature of moon's surface.

PARSONS, William Third Earl of Rosse (1800-67) b. York, lived in Offaly, astronomer. Constructed the largest telescope of its time (mid-19th century), workmen from his Offaly estate helped to make its mirrors. This telescope was subsequently used by many prominent astronomers of the time who made important discoveries about star clusters. The earl himself discovered the spiral shape of galaxies.

STONEY, George Johnstone (d. 1911) first to propose existence of electrons.

WALTON, Ernest T.S. (1903-95) b. Waterford, awarded the Nobel Prize for Physics in 1951 with John Cockcroft for their work splitting the atom. Invented the Cockcroft-Walton accelerator used in this procedure.

ALLGOOD, Molly Máire O'Neill (1887-1952) b. Dublin, actress, sister of Sara Allgood. Played Pegeen Mike in the controversial 1907 production of Synge's The Playboy of the Western World. Was engaged to Synge and acted in his Deirdre of the Sorrows (1909). Films incl. Juno and the Paycock (1930), Someone at the Door (1950), Treasure Hunt (1952).

ALLGOOD, Sara (1883-1950) b. Dublin, actress. Film debut in Riders to the Sea (1904), repeated her greatest stage success in Hitchcock's Juno and the Paycock (1930). Emigrated to Hollywood (1940) and played motherly roles. Films include How Green was My Valley (1941), Jane Eyre (1944), Challenge to Lassie (1949).

BARRY, Spranger (1719-1777) b. Dublin, actor. Played Othello and was highly acclaimed. An intense rivalry grew between himself and Garrick. Opened up theatres in Dublin and Cork, but his extravagant lifestyle forced him to return to the stage in London.

BYRNE, Eddie (1911-81) character actor in British films which include The Gentle Gunman (1946), The Mummy (1959), Mutiny on the Bounty (1962), Star Wars (1977).

CAREY, Patrick (1916-94) born London, reared Ireland, documentary film-maker. Founded Aengus Films (1962). Films include Journey into Spring (1956), Waves, Wild Wings, Yeats Country, Oisín (1962-74), Flamingo - Variations on a theme, The Algonquin Trilogy (1975-83). Worked on A Man for All Seasons, Ryan's Daughter and Barry Lyndon.

CUSACK, Cyril (1910-93) b. South Africa, actor and star of over 57 films (1917-1990). Performed with Abbey, Gate and Old Vic theatres and the Royal Shakespeare Company. Film debut in Knockagow (1917). Major success with Carol Reed's Odd Man Out (1947). Acclaimed Broadway performance in Eugene O'Neill's A Moon for the Misbegotten (1957) opposite Wendy Hiller. Films include The Spy Who Came in from the Cold (1965), Fahrenheit 451 (1967), Little Dorrit (1988), Far and Away (1992) and As You Like it (1992). Father of actresses Sinéad, Niamh and Sorcha Cusack with whom he co-starred in the Gate Theatre's production of Chekhov's Three Sisters. (1990).

DEVLIN, J.G. (1907-91) b. Belfast, actor in theatre, TV and in films such The Rising of the Moon (1957), Darby O'Gill and the Little People (1959) and The Raggedy Rawney (1988).

DONLEVY, Brian (1899-1972) b. Portadown, actor, starred in 65 films over 40 years. Male model for shirts, made acting debut (1924), with a walk-on in a Broadway play and cameo role in a film. Played tough villain roles. Most notable in Beau Geste (1939), earning an Oscar nomination for Best Supporting Actor. Films include Jesse James (1939), Billy the Kid (1941), The Curse of the Fly (1969), Pit Stop (1969).

EDWARDS, Hilton (1903-82) b. London, actor and producer. Founded a new theatre company with MICHEÁL MACLIAMMÓIR at the Peacock (1928), subsequently moved to the Gate (1930). Directed over 400 productions and introduced systems of theatre production.

The company made successful tours abroad and introduced European classics, such as *Peer Gynt*, and new Irish works to Irish audiences. Directed a short film *Road to Glenascaul* (1951) nominated for an Academy Award. Also head of drama for RTÉ.

FITZGERALD, Barry William Shields (1888-1961) b. Dublin, actor. Film debut in *Land of Her Fathers* (1924) and Hitchcock's *Juno and the Paycock* (1930). Lured to Hollywood by John Ford, reprising his stage role in O'Casey's *The Plough and the Stars* (1937). Won an Oscar for Best Supporting Actor in *Going My Way (1944)*. Films include *Bringing up Baby* (1938), *How Green Was My Valley* (1941), *The Quiet Man* (1952), *Broth of a Boy* (1959).

GIBBONS, Cedric (1893-1960) b. Dublin, art director for over 76 films. MGM's Art Department Head, he was a key figure in creating MGM 'look,' designing the Oscar statuette, which he himself won 11 times for design and once for 'consistent excellence' (1950). Married actress Dolores del Rio (1930-1941). He worked on *Ben-Hur* (1926), *Tarzan and his Mate* (1934), *Treasure Island* (1934), *The Wizard of Oz* (1939), *Madame Curie* (1943), *National Velvet* (1944), *The Postman Always Rings Twice* (1946), *The Yearling* (1946), *Little Women* (1949), *Annie Get Your Gun* (1950), *An American in Paris* (1951), *Forbidden Planet* (1956).

HICKEY, Kieran (1936-93) b. Dublin, film director. One of the first film-makers to develop the Irish film industry. Produced films on Jonathan Swift and James Joyce in 1960s. Film/documentaries include *Stage Irishman* (1968), *Faithful Departed* (1969), *A Child's Voice* (1977), *Criminal Conversation* (1980), *Attracta* (1983), *Short Story - Irish Movies 1945-1958* (1986), *The Rockingham Shoot* (1987).

HUSTON, John Marcellus (1906-87) b. Missouri, film director. Started off as an actor and contributed to a number of screenplays, before making his directorial debut with *The Maltese Falcon* (1941). Proved to be adept in the action and film noir genres as displayed in *Key Largo* (1948), *The African Queen* (1951), *The Misfits* (1960), *The Man Who Would be King* (1975), but also made a haunting adaptation of James Joyce's *The Dead*, his last film. He became an Irish citizen in 1964 and lived periodically in Connemara. His daughter, Angelica, is the star of the film *The Mammy*, made in Ireland in 1998.

INGRAM, Rex (1893-1950) b. Dublin, film director, directed over 27 films. Emigrated to US and worked for Edison, Vitagraph, Fox (1913), Universal (1916) and Metro Film Studios (1920). Directed Rudolph Valentino in *The Four Horsemen of the Apocalypse* (1921) and *The Conquering Power* (1921). Set up film studio Victorine with aid of MGM after a row over direction of *Ben-Hur* but the advent of sound affected his future films. Made only one talking picture *Baroud* (1933). Worked as a sculptor, painter and novelist.

JORDAN, Dorothy (1761-1816) b. Waterford, a popular actress in Dublin, moved to London where she had great success at Drury Lane. Began a liaison with the Duke of Clarence (later William IV) in 1790, which lasted until 1811, bearing him ten children, the eldest of whom was made Earl of Munster by the king.

KERRIGAN, J.M. (1887-1964) b. Dublin, actor. Joined Abbey Players (1907), emigrated to US (1917) and played Irish characters on Broadway and in Hollywood. Films include *O'Neill of the Glen* (1916), *Song O' My Heart* (1930), *Werewolf of London* (1935), *The Plough and the Stars* (1936), *20,000 Leagues under the Sea* (1954), *The Fastest Gun Alive* (1956).

KNOWLES, James Sheridan (1784-1862) b. Cork, dramatist. Son of a schoolmaster and cousin to Richard Brinsley Sheridan, studied medicine but opted for a career on the stage. Did not succeed and opened a school in Belfast. His most famous works were *Love*, *The Hunchback* (1832), *The Wife* (1833), and *The Love Chase* (1837). He acted with much success in his own plays but changed career again to be a Baptist preacher and drew large crowds.

McCORMACK, F.J. Peter Judge (1891-1947) Irish character actor with Abbey Theatre. Films include *Odd Man Out* (1946), *The Plough and the Stars* (1937) and *Hungry Hill* (1946).

MCGINNIS, Niall (1913) film debut with *Turn of the Tide* (1935). Films include *Henry V* (1944), *The Nun's Story* (1958), *Becket* (1964), *Sinful Davy* (1969) and *The Mackintosh Man* (1973).

MacGOWRAN, Jack (1916-73) veteran character actor. Films: *The Quiet Man* (1952), *The Gentle Gunman* (1952), *The Rising of the Moon* (1957), *Darby O'Gill & the Little People* (1959), *Doctor Zhivago* (1965), *The Exorcist* (1973).

McKENNA, Siobhán (1923) b. Belfast, actress. Starred in both Irish and English language theatre/film. Films include *Daughter of Darkness* (1948), *The Playboy of the Western World* (1962), *The Lost People* (1949), *King of Kings* (1961), *Of Human Bondage* (1964), *Doctor Zhivago* (1965). Her last performance as Mommo in the Druid Theatre's production of *Tom Murphy's Bailegangaire* (1985) was highly acclaimed.

MacLIAMMÓIR, Mícheál (1899-1978) b. Cork, actor, writer, painter and theatre impressario. A child actor, became into a renowned painter and designer. Founded the Gate Theatre in Dublin with his lifelong friend Hilton Edwards. The theatre company capitalised on new Irish writing, drawing inspiration from and staging European drama, as well as the classics. Played Iago in Orson Welles' film of *Othello* (1949) and was the narrator in the film *Tom Jones* (1963). Also published fiction, plays and memoirs in both English and Irish. His one-man shows during the 1960s drew critical acclaim in Ireland and internationally. Works include *The Importance of Being Oscar* (1960), *I Must Be Talking to My Friends* (1963) and *Mostly About Yeats* (1970).

McNALLY, Ray (1925-89) b. Buncrana, versatile and prolific character actor on film, stage and TV. Screen debut (1930s). Best known for *The Mission* (1986) and *My Left Foot* (1989). Films include *Shake Hands with the Devil* (1959), *Billy Budd* (1962), *Angel* (1984), *Cal* (1984), *The Fourth Protocol* (1987), *The Sicilian* (1987), *White Mischief* (1988), *We're No Angels* (1989).

MACKLIN, Charles (c.1697-1797) b. Donegal, writer and actor. Acted in Drury Lane, but killed a fellow actor in an argument over a wig and was tried for murder. Wrote a tragedy and many farces and comedies, including *Love á la Mode* (1759) and *The Man of the*

World (1781).

MOORE, Owen (1886-1939) b. Meath, actor. Star of US silents and early talkies. Film debut in *Biograph* (1908) and appeared in many of D.W. Griffith's early productions, Mary Pickford's regular leading man in early stages of her career, married her secretly (1910) but they were later divorced (1920). Films include *The Honour of Thieves* (1909), *Women Love Diamonds* (1927), *Husbands for Rent* (1928), *She Done Him Wrong* (1933), *A Star is Born* (1937).

O'CONNOR, Una *Agnes Teresa McGlade* (1880-1959) actress born Belfast, portrayed maid, spinster and gossip characters. Her ear-piercing shriek was used to great effect in horror films. Films include *The Invisible Man* (1933), *The Bride of Frankenstein* (1935), *The Adventures of Robin Hood* (1938), *The Adventures of Don Juan* (1948), *Witness for the Prosecution* (1957).

O'DEA, Denis (1905-1978) actor. Films include *The Informer* (1935), *The Plough and the Stars* (1947), *Treasure Island* (1950), *The Rising of the Moon* (1957).

O'DEA, Jimmy (1899-1965) b. Dublin, comedian and actor. Well-known on the variety circuit in Dublin theatre, formed a successful comedy partnership with Maureen Potter in the early fifties, which lasted until his death. Starred in the film *Darby O'Gill and the Little People* (1959). Other films include *Casey's Millions* (1922), *Jimmy Boy* (1935), *Blarney* (1938), *The Rising of the Moon* (1957), *Johnny Nobody* (1960).

O'LEARY, Liam (1910-92) b. Cork, actor, director and archivist. Co-founded Irish Film Society (1936). Former Abbey Theatre Director. Made one of Ireland's most rousing propaganda films *Our Country* (1948). Starred in *Stranger at My Door/At a Dublin Inn* (1950). Published works include *Silent Cinema* (1965), *Invitation to the Film* (1945) and the first *Rex Ingram Biography* (1980).

O'NEILL, Eugene (1888-1953) Irish-American playwright with screen-play adaptations. Films include *Anna Christie* with Blanche Sweet (1923), and Greta Garbo (1930), *Strange Interlude* (1932), *The Emperor Jones* (1933), *The Long Voyage Home* (1940), *Summer Holiday* (1947), *Long Day's Journey into Night* (1960) and *The Iceman Cometh* (1973).

O'SULLIVAN, Maureen (1911-98) b. Roscommon, actress. Discovered at Dublin's International Horse Show (1930) by American Frank Borzage. Best remembered as Jane in the *Tarzan* jungle adventures. Married writer John Farrow and retired to raise their seven children, including actress Mia Farrow. Later hosted a syndicated TV series. Films include *Song O' My Heart* (1930), *David Copperfield* (1935), *Pride and Prejudice* (1940), *All I Desire* (1953), *Never too Late* (1965).

PURCELL, Noel (1900) actor and comedian. Films include *Captain Boycott* (1947), *Moby Dick* (1956), *Mutiny on the Bounty* (1962), *Lord Jim* (1965), *McKenzie Break* (1969), *Flight of the Doves* (1971), *The Mackintosh Man* (1973).

RYAN, Kathleen (1922-1985) actress. Films include *Odd Man Out* (1947), *Captain Boycott* (1947), *Esther Waters* (1948), *The Yellow Balloon* (1952), *Captain Lightfoot* (1953), *Jacqueline* (1956), *Sail into Danger* (1958).

SHIELDS, Arthur (d. 1970) born Dublin, actor. Brother of actor Barry Fitzgerald, player with Dublin's ABBEY, emigrated to US. Played priests, missionaries and fanatics. Films include *The Plough and the Stars* (1936), *How Green was My Valley* (1941), *National Velvet* (1944), *She Wore a Yellow Ribbon* (1949), *The Quiet Man* (1952), *The Pigeon that Took Rome* (1962).

TAYLOR, William Desmond *William Tanner* (1877-1922) film director of more than 39 films and former actor. Rose to fame as director of Mary Pickford films. Former president of the Screen Directors Guild. Films include *The Beggar Child* (1914), *Anne of Green Gables* (1919), *Huckleberry Finn* (1920), *The Green Temptation* (1922), *The Top of New York* (1922). Shot under suspicious circumstances in Hollywood.

INDEX

Abbreviations...vii
Accidents, Road..262
  by Road User Type...262-63
  Statistics..261-62
  at Work 1997, ROI...192
Acquisitions, Domestic Companies 169
  Foreign 169
  Irish..169-70
  Location...169
Advertising Rates, National Newspapers 360
  Provincial Papers...360
  Radio 364
  Television..353
Afforestation by County 1997, NI............................244
Agricultural, Imports and Exports 240-42
  Output..236-37
  Product Prices...237-38
  Trade 1997..242
  Wages 1994-97 236
  Associations 235
Agriculture...235-42
Agriculture & Labour Force Statistics 1994-97 236
AGRICULTURE, FORESTRY & FISHERIES.....233-94
Ambulance Station Statistics 265
Angling...408
Antrim, County Profile..135-36
Applications Summary...415-16
  Divorce 415
  Driving Licence..415-16
  Social Welfare Benefits....................................415
  Television Licence 415
Aquaculture Output Value 1986-96, ROI 246
Area by Province 1991 & 1996, ROI 119
Area Comparison Table 121
Armagh, County Profile..137-38
Art...313-16
ARTS...304-39
Arts Council, of Ireland......................................306-07
  Works of Art 317
  Northern Ireland 307
  Lottery Funding (NI) 307
  Sponsorship (ROI)..306
Assembly Members, NI...59
Athletics 395

Badminton..409
Balance of Payments, ROI 175-76
Banking Statistics 179
Banks and Post Offices 179-80
Basketball 401-02
Beaches, Blue Flag...255
Belfast City, Profile...136
Birds of Ireland...122
Blind Sports 411-12
Books, Best Selling 1997-98 308-09
Bord na Móna Statistics 1992-98, ROI....................196
Borough Councils NI, see Councils ....
Bowling 402
Boxing...396-97

Budget Highlights 171-72
BUPA Health Insurance Costs.................................264
BUSINESS, FINANCE & TRADE....................166-83

Camogie...403
Canoeing..411
Capital Account 1996-2000, ROI 176
Car Costs 1998..205
  Imports..205-06
  Maintenance Costs...206
  Registration Marks 202
Carlow, County Profile 138
Cars, 20 Most Popular Registered 1997 NI............203
  20 Most Popular Licensed 1997, ROI 203
  Used 1997 206
Casualties Classified by Age and Gender.............263
Catholic Bishops of Ireland....................................210
  Cardinals of Ireland 211
  Applicants and Entrants 215
  Nullity of Marriages..215
  Parishes, Churches and Schools 214
  Priests and Religious 214-15
Cavan, County Profile...138-39
Census Statistics 127-28
CHRONOLOGY OF THE YEAR.........................9-25
Church Membership 213
Church of Ireland Bishops 211
  Bishops, Former 212
  Statistics..213
Clare, County Profile 139-40
Classical Music/Opera..319-20
Coal Shipments, NI...196
Coillte Forestry Area..243
  Statistics by Species 245
Companies Overseas 191
Companies, Top 30...168-69
Competitive Countries, World's Top 20 192
Concert Venues..345
Concerts held in Ireland, 1998 346
Consumer Price Index 1990-98, ROI 183
Consumers' Expenditure 1990-95, NI......................183
Cork City, Profile..141-42
Cork, County Profile...140-41
Councils - City and County, NI 77-80
  City and County, ROI....................................73-77
COUNTIES OF IRELAND.................................135-65
Court System, NI 270
Court System, ROI 268
Courts, NI 270-71
Courts, ROI..269
Cricket...403-04
Crime Statistics...272-74
Crime, Domestic Violence, ROI 279
Crop Production 241
Croquet 411
Cross Border Passenger Movement, ROI 200
CULTURE..295-303
Currency Composition of Foreign Debt 1997, ROI..177
Current Account 1996-2000, ROI 177

Expenditure 1998, ROI......................................177
Revenue 1997-98, ROI.....................................176
Cycling 404

Dáil Éireann, Members of...............................43-46
Dance 318-19
Defence Headquarters, NI..............................276-77
Headquarters, ROI 276
Personnel, NI...277
Personnel, ROI 277
Staff, NI...276
Staff, ROI...276
Demographic Statistics 1991 & 1996 127
Derry City, Profile..142-43
Derry, County Profile...142
Diplomatic & Consular Missions, Abroad 419-20
Diplomatic Missions, Ireland...........................416-19
Divorce Applications 415
Statistics...133-34
Documents, Historical.....................................107-09
Recent...110-12
Donegal, County Profile..................................143-44
Down, County Profile......................................144-45
Drama...310-12
Amateur Competitions...................................312-13
Driving Licences 201-02
Licence Application 415-16
Minimum Age...205
Drug Offences by Region, ROI 278
Seizures 1997 278
Treatment Centres, ROI 264
Dublin City, Profile 146-47
Dublin, County Profile.....................................145-46

Earnings...188
Economic and Monetary Union 83-84
Economic Statistics 1992-96 178
EDUCATION...281-94
Education, Attendance 284-88
Expenditure...283
Graduate Destination 293-94
Numbers Employed at Third Level 287
Number of Schools/Colleges.........................285-86
Number of Teachers......................................286-87
Participation...284
Public Examinations & Qualifications.............291-92
Pupil-Teacher Ratios 283
School Leavers, Qualifications 285
School Leavers, Status of 285
Student Enrolment 283, 290, 292
Third Level Field of Study..................................290
Third Level Institutions NI..............................288-89
Third Level Institutions ROI 287-88
Third Level Points Requirements 289-90
University Degrees/Diplomas Awarded 292
Election Results, NI Assembly 1998 ....58-59, 61-63
Results, ROI by Elections 1998............................40
Results, ROI Presidential Election 1998 46
Elections, European Parliament 1994 17
NI Changing State of Parties 1977-98 65
NI Parliament 1921-73 63
NI to European Parliament 1979-94....................87

NI Westminster 1922-97......................................63
ROI to European Parliament 1979-94..................87
Electricity Statistics 1992-97, NI 195
Employment by Sector 1996-97 186
Statistics...187
Endangered Species 123
Energy...193-97
Consumption by Source, NI 195
Demands 1995-97, ROI 194
ENTERTAINMENT..340-47
Equestrian Sport...409
ESB Generation 1993-96, ROI 193-94
Statistics 1996-97, ROI 194
EU Countries, Agricultural Labour Force 1995........242
Life Expectancy...264
Road Death Comparisons...............................263-64
Forest Structures...243
European Commission, Members of 85-86
Commissioners, Former Irish 86
European Parliament, NI Members of 85
Parliament, ROI Members of..............................84
Eurovision Song Contest, Irish Entries 1965-98......345
Exchange Rate 1996-98, ROI................................175
Expenditure on Health Services, NI 261
on Medical Services, NI 261
Export Growth and Performance, ROI...............173-74
Markets Geographical Spread 1987-96, ROI......247
Markets, NI...174
Sales, NI...174
Exports and Imports......................................173-75
Volume and Price 174
Live Cattle 1994-96, ROI 240

Factfile of Ireland 118
Farming Employees 235
Farms by Size and Number 236
Fermanagh, County Profile.............................147-48
Film...321-39
Industry Expenditure and Funding................322-23
Filmography 1910-99, Irish and Irish Related 323-28
Films, Selected Profiles 328-39
Films, Top 1997...322
Finance...175-79
Houses 1992-96, NI 179
Fish Export Trends 1985-96, ROI 249
Exports by Production 1995-96, ROI 246
Exports by Value 1996, ROI..........................246-47
Fish Landings 247-49
Fishing..246-49
Associations 235
Personnel 1992-96, ROI...................................247
Forest and Area Resources 1992-97, NI...............243
Forestry..243-45
Area, NI 243
Associations 235
Employees 1996-97, NI 244
Statistics...243-45
Fuel Consumption by Source 1995-96, ROI...........195

GAA 381-87
Galleries/Art Centres 313-16
Galway City, profile 149

Galway, County Profile 148-49
Garda Strength, ROI..271-72
GEOGRAPHY & ENVIRONMENT 116-24
Golf 399-401
Government Departments, NI.............................71-72
  Departments, ROI 68-71
  System, EU Institutions....................................82-83
  System, NI...59-60
  System, ROI 40
  NI Ministers 60
  NI Secretaries of State 64
  ROI Ministers...42-43
Governors, Irish Free State 1922-37 112
  NI 1922-73..113
Greyhound Racing..403
Gross Domestic Product 1990-96, NI....................178
Gymnastics 402

HEALTH 256-65
Health Boards...258
  Personnel 1996-97, ROI.......................................258
  Personnel 1997, NI...259
Historical Anniversaries 112
  Movements and Organisations.....................99-106
HISTORY 88-115
History, Chronology of Irish history 2500 BC-......90-99
Hockey 405
Horse Racing..398-99
Hospital Statistics 1995, ROI 259
  Statistics, NI...260
House of Commons, NI Members.......................60-61
House Prices 1995-97, ROI...................................180
  Sales & Prices, NI 180-81
Houses Started and Completed 1995-97, ROI........181
Housing and Property....................................180-83
  Tenure...182

IDA Statistics 1993-97 190-91
IDB Statistics 1990-96 191
Imports & Exports, Composition ROI 173
Income and Expenditure on Health Services, ROI..261
Industrial Disputes ROI...190
  Production 1990-96...192
  Production Index 1990-96 191
  Stoppages, NI..190
Industry..186-93
INDUSTRY, ENERGY & TRANSPORT 184-206
Infant Mortality 1993-96, NI 261
  Rates 1993-96, ROI 260
Interest Rates 1990-98, ROI...................................182
Introduction, Dr Martin Mansergh..........................1-2
Irish Cultural Organisations 302-03
  Dancing...297-99
  First Names...299-301
  Folklore..301-02
  Language...295
  Language Phrases 296
  Speakers 297
  Traditional Music..299
Island of Ireland, Climate 119
  Geology 119
  Location 119

Judiciary, NI 270
Judiciary, ROI..268

Kerry, County Profile..149-50
Kildare, County Profile..150-51
Kilkenny, County Profile...151

Labour Force Statistics 1996-97...........................186
Land Sales 1994-97, ROI......................................235
  Use 238
Landings and Value of Seafish 1997, ROI..............246
Laois, County Profile...152
LAW AND DEFENCE...266-80
Leitrim, County Profile...152-53
Licensed Cars, 20 Most Popular 1997, ROI 203
Licensed Vehicles..200-01
Limerick City, Profile 154
Limerick, County Profile.......................................153-54
Livestock Figures 1994-97.................................239-40
Local Authority Expenditure 1994-97, NI................178
Longford, County Profile.....................................154-55
Lottery...347
Louth, County Profile..155-56

Magazines, Periodicals and Journals 355-60
Mammals of Ireland...123
Map of Important Sites..124
Marriages, Births & Deaths 1994-96 127
Mayo, County Profile 156-57
Meath, County Profile...157
MEDIA 348-67
Meteorological Stations 120
  Statistics, ROI...121
Methodist Church President and Chairmen 211
  Presidents, 1965-98.......................................212-13
  Statistics 213
Mileage and Kilometre Table..............................423-24
Mine and Quarry Production 1995-97, NI...............193
  Persons Employed, NI...193
Monaghan, County Profile...................................157-58
Mortgage Market 1993-97 182
Motor Rallying...406
Motorcycling...405-06
Music 342-46
  Charts 1997-98 342-44

National Borrowing Trend 1990-97, ROI..................178
  Debt 1977-97, ROI 177
  Debt Interest Cost 1990-97, ROI.........................177
Naval & Air Service, ROI 278
Netball..408-09
Newspapers, National...353
  Provincial..353-55
NI Assembly, Members...59
NI Prime Minister, Biographies...........................64-65
Non-National Road Grants 1993-97, NI 204
Notes & Coins 1997, ROI 175

OBITUARIES..29-33

Occupation Statistics 1991 131
  by Industrial Group 1991 131
Offaly, County Profile 158-59
Olympic Medallists 412
  Teams, 1924-98..412-14
OPENING PAGES..i-vii
Oscar Winners/Nominations 321-22

Parade Statistics, NI 275
Passports..415
Peace Process, History of 66-67
Peat and Briquette Statistics 1989-98, ROI.............196
Petrol Prices...195-96
Pitch and Putt 410
Police Strength, NI..271-72
  Strength, ROI...271-72
Political Leaders (past), ROI 40
  Leaders (past), NI..57
  Parties, NI...55-57
  Parties, ROI..37-39
POLITICS..34-87
Politics EU, History and Chronology of 81-82
POLITICS, EUROPEAN UNION......................81-87
POLITICS NI...54-67
  NI, introductory notes 54
POLITICS, PUBLIC ADMINISTRATION.............68-80
POLITICS ROI...34-53
  ROI, introductory notes 36-37
POPULATION 125-34
Population at each Census, 1901-96.....................132
  by Age-Group 1971-96....................................128
  by Council Area 1981-91, NI..........................128-29
  by Country of Birth 1996, NI 133
  by Country of Birth 1996, ROI......................132-33
  by Religious Denominations.........................129-30
  Density 1997 131
  of Main Cities 1991 & 1996 132
Position of Parties, NI 108
  of Parties, ROI..46
Post Office Statistics...179-80
Power Stations by Type and Capacity 1997, NI.......194
Presbyterian Church Statistics...............................214
  Moderators 211
  Moderators 1967-98 212
Presidential Speeches, Eamon deValera 114-15
  Speeches, Mary McAleese 26-28
Presidents of Ireland, Biographies......................47-48
Prime Minister, Biographies NI 64-65
Primary Education 284, 286
Primary Energy Supply 1992-96, NI.......................194
Print Media 353-60
Prison Statistics, NI..274
  Statistics, ROI..274
Psychiatric Patients 1990-95, ROI..........................265
Public Administration 68-80
  Capital Expenditure on Housing, ROI 182
  Expenditure 1994-2000, NI 178-79
  Roads, Length of..203-04
Publishing Houses...309-10

QUOTES OF THE YEAR...................................5-8

Radio 361-64
  Audience Share...363-64
  Stations, Local..361-63
  Stations, National 361
Referendum Results, NI..65
  Results, ROI 1937-98.......................................52-52
  Results, ROI 1997-98.......................................52
Registered Cars, 20 Most Popular 1997 NI............203
RELIGION 207-15
Religious Orders Contacts....................................209-10
River Water Quality, NI...121
Roscommon, County Profile...................................159-60
Rowing 407
Rugby 393-94

Sailing 407
Salaries, Political Representatives ROI 46
  Public Representatives EU...............................85
  Public Representatives NI 61
Sales by Sector, NI...175
Seanad Éireann, Members of..............................41
Secondary Education 284, 285, 287, 291
Sligo, County Profile 160
Soccer, Football Association of Ireland (ROI) 387-90
  Irish Football Association (NI) 390-92
Social Welfare Benefits Application 415
Special Sports..411
Species Planted 1992-97, NI 245
Speed Laws..203
SPORT 368-414
Sport Chronology of the Year 372-81
  Top Stories of the Year 370-71
Squash...410
Subsidies 239
Subsidies 239
Suicide Statistics 264-65
Summer Schools 320-21
Surfing 407-08
Swimming 397-98

Taekwondo..409
Taoisigh & Tánaistí 1922-98 48-49
  Biographies...49-51
Tax Tables 170-71
Taxation 170-72
  Yields, ROI 172
Taxes Collected, ROI 172
Telecommunications Statistics 1995-97, ROI 193
Telephone Codes..421-24
  International...425
Television 350-53
  Audience Share...350-51
  Licence Application 415
  Licences by County 350-51
  Most Popular Programmes..............................351-53
  Stations..350
Tennis...408
Third Level Education 284, 287-90, 291, 293-94
Tidy Towns/Best Kept Towns 254-55
Timber Production 1991-97, NI 244
Tipperary, County Profile 160-61
TOP NEWS STORIES......................................3-4
TOURISM 250-55

Trade Statistics...173
Transport...197-206
  Infrastructure, Roads 1997................................204
  Airline 199-200
  Bus 197
  Rail 197-98
  Sea...198-99
Trees of Ireland..122-23
Tug of War..410
Tyrone, County Profile 161-62

Unemployment by Area 1996-97 189
  Seasonally Adjusted 1992-97...............................189
  International Comparisons 190
Union Membership..192
Universities, see Education or Third Level Education ...
Used Cars 1997...206
USEFUL INFORMATION 415-25

Vehicles, Licensed...200-01
VHI Health Insurance Costs 264
Visitor Attractions, Most Popular.............................254

Visitor Statistics 251-54

Wage Costs Index 1987-97, ROI.............................189
Water Supply 1993-97, NI 197
Waterford City, Profile 163
Waterford, County Profile 162-63
Websites, Selected Addresses...........................364-65
Weights, Measures & Formulae 416
Westmeath, County Profile...................................163-64
Wexford, County Profile.......................................164-65
WHO IS WHO..426-64
WHO WAS WHO 465-
Wicklow, County Profile 165
World Time Differences..120
Wrestling...411

YEAR IN PICTURES......................................216-31

NOTES

NOTES

NOTES

NOTES

NOTES

NOTES

NOTES

NOTES

NOTES

NOTES

NOTES

YEAR PLANNER 1999

	JANUARY	FEBRUARY	MARCH	APRIL	MAY	JUNE
Mon		1	1			
Tue		2	2			1
Wed		3	3			2
Thur		4	4	1		3
Fri	1	5	5	2		4
Sat	2	6	6	3	1	5
Sun	3	7	7	4	2	6
Mon	4	8	8	5	3	7
Tue	5	9	9	6	4	8
Wed	6	10	10	7	5	9
Thur	7	11	11	8	6	10
Fri	8	12	12	9	7	11
Sat	9	13	13	10	8	12
Sun	10	14	14	11	9	13
Mon	11	15	15	12	10	14
Tue	12	16	16	13	11	15
Wed	13	17	17	14	12	16
Thur	14	18	18	15	13	17
Fri	15	19	19	16	14	18
Sat	16	20	20	17	15	19
Sun	17	21	21	18	16	20
Mon	18	22	22	19	17	21
Tue	19	23	23	20	18	22
Wed	20	24	24	21	19	23
Thur	21	25	25	22	20	24
Fri	22	26	26	23	21	25
Sat	23	27	27	24	22	26
Sun	24	28	28	25	23	27
Mon	25		29	26	24	28
Tue	26		30	27	25	29
Wed	27		31	28	26	30
Thur	28			29	27	
Fri	29			30	28	
Sat	30				29	
Sun	31				30	
Mon					31	
Tue						

JANUARY	FEBRUARY	MARCH	APRIL	MAY	JUNE